1998

WHAT DO I READ NEXT?

A Reader's Guide to Current Genre Fiction

- Fantasy
- Western
- Romance
- Horror
- Mystery
- Science Fiction

Explore your options!

Gale databases are offered in a variety of formats

 ™ The information in this Gale publication is also available in some or all of the formats described here. Your Gale Representative will be happy to fill you in. Call toll-free 1-800-877-GALE.

GaleNet

A number of Gale databases are now available on GaleNet, our new online information resource accessible through the Internet. GaleNet features an easy-to-use end-user interface, the powerful search capabilities of BRS/SEARCH retrieval software and ease of access through the World Wide Web.

Diskette/Magnetic Tape

Many Gale databases are available on diskette or magnetic tape, allowing systemwide access to your most-used information sources through existing computer systems. Data can be delivered on a variety of mediums (DOS-formatted diskettes, 9-track tape, 8mm data tape) and in industry-standard formats (comma-delimited, tagged, fixed-field).

CD-ROM

A variety of Gale titles are available on CD-ROM, offering maximum flexibility and powerful search software.

Online

For your convenience, many Gale databases are available through popular online services, including DIALOG, NEXIS, DataStar, ORBIT, OCLC, Thomson Financial Network's I/Plus Direct, HRIN, Prodigy, Sandpoint's HOOVER, the Library Corporation's NLightN and Telebase Systems.

ISSN 1052-2212

1998

WHAT DO I READ NEXT?

A Reader's Guide to Current Genre Fiction

- Fantasy
- Western
- Romance
- Horror
- Mystery
- Science Fiction

GALE

Detroit
London

NEIL BARRON

WAYNE BARTON

KRISTIN RAMSDELL

STEVEN A. STILWELL

Neil Barron, Wayne Barton, Kristin Ramsdell, and Steven A. Stilwell
Contributors: Stefan Dziemianowicz, Scott Imes, Michael M. Levy, and Tom and Enid Schantz

Gale Research Staff:
Coordinating Editor: Charles B. Montney
Contributing Editors: Paula Cutcher-Jackson, Shelly Dickey, Dana Ferguson,
Robert Franzino, Prindle LaBarge, Kathleen Meek, and Noah Schusterbauer
Managing Editors: Ann V. Evory and Debra M. Kirby

Production Director: MaryBeth Trimper
External Production Assistant: Carolyn Fischer
Product Design Manager: Cynthia Baldwin
Senior Art Director: Mary Krzewinski

Manager, Data Entry Services: Eleanor Allison
Data Entry Associates: Timothy Alexander, Katrina Coach,
Civie Green, and Constance Wells

Manager, Technical Support Services: Theresa Rocklin
Programmer/Analyst: Joshua E. Cohen

ISBN 0-7876-2150-1
ISSN 1052-2212

Printed in the United States of America

Contents

Introduction

Thousands of books are published each year intended for devoted fans of genre fiction. Dragons, outlaws, lovers, murderers, monsters, and aliens abound on our own world or on other worlds, throughout time—all featured in the pages of fantasy, western, romance, mystery, horror, and science fiction. Given the huge variety of titles available each year, added to the numbers from previous years, readers can be forgiven if they're stumped by the question "What do I read next?" And that's where this book comes in.

Designed as a tool to assist in the exploration of genre fiction, *What Do I Read Next?* guides the reader to both current and classic recommendations in six widely read genres: Mystery, Romance, Western, Fantasy, Horror, and Science Fiction. *What Do I Read Next?* allows readers quick and easy access to specific data on recent titles in these popular genres. Plus, each entry provides alternate reading selections, thus coming to the rescue of librarians and booksellers, who are often unfamiliar with a genre, yet must answer the question frequently posed by their patrons and customers "What do I read next?"

Details on 1,250 Titles

This year's edition of *What Do I Read Next?* contains 1,250 entries for titles published in the past year. These entries are divided into sections for Mystery, Romance, Western, Fantasy, Horror, and Science Fiction. Experts on the writing in each field compile the entries for their respective genres. The experts also summarize the current state-of-the-art in their fields in essays that appear at the beginning of each section.

The criteria for inclusion of specific titles vary somewhat from genre to genre. In genres such as Romance and Mystery where large numbers of titles are published each year, the inclusion criteria are more selective, and the experts attempted to select the recently published books they considered the best. In genres such as Horror and Westerns, where the amount of new material is relatively small, a broader range of titles is represented, including many titles published by small or independent houses and some Young Adult books.

The entries are listed alphabetically by main author in each genre section. Most provide the following information:

- **Author or editor's name** and real name if a pseudonym is used. Co-authors, co-editors, and illustrators are also listed where applicable.

- **Book title.**

- **Date and place of publication; name of publisher.**

- **Series name.**

- **Story type:** Specific categories within each genre, identified by the compiling expert. Definitions of these types are listed in the "Key to Genre Terms" section following the Introduction.

- **Major characters:** Names and brief descriptions of up to three characters featured in the title.

- **Time period:** Tells when the story takes place.

- **Locale:** Tells where the story takes place.

- **What the book is about:** A brief plot summary.

- **Where it's reviewed:** Citations to reviews of the book, including the source of the review, date of the source, and the page on which the review appears. Reviews are included from genre-specific sources such as *Locus* and *Affaire de Coeur* as well as more general reviewing sources such as *Booklist* and *Publishers Weekly*.

- **Other books by the author:** Titles and publication dates of other books the author has written, useful for those wanting to read more by a particular author.

- **Other books you might like:** Titles by other authors written on a similar theme or in a similar style. These titles further the reader's exploration of the genre.

Indexes Answer Readers' Questions

The eight indexes in *What Do I Read Next?*, used separately or in conjunction with each other, create many pathways to the featured titles, answering general questions or locating specific titles. For example:

"Are there any new *Star Wars* books?"

The SERIES INDEX lists entries by the name of the series of which they are a part.

"I like Regency Romances. Can you recommend any new ones?"

The GENRE INDEX breaks each genre into story types or more specialized areas. In the Romance genre for example, there is a story type heading "Regency." For the definitions of story types, see the "Key to Genre Terms" beginning on page xi.

"I'm looking for a mystery set in Michigan..."

The GEOGRAPHIC INDEX lists titles by their locale. This can help readers pinpoint an area in which they may have a particular interest, such as their hometown, another country, or even Cyberspace.

"Do you know of any horror stories set during the 18th century?"

The TIME PERIOD INDEX is a chronological listing of the time settings in which the main entry titles take place.

"What Westerns are available that feature mountain men?"

The CHARACTER DESCRIPTION INDEX identifies the major characters by occupation (e.g. Accountant, Editor, Librarian) or persona (e.g. Cyborg, Noblewoman, Stowaway).

"Has anyone written any new books with Dracula in them?"

The CHARACTER NAME INDEX lists the major characters named in the entries. This can help readers who remember some information about a book, but not an author or title.

"What has LaVyrle Spencer written recently?"

The AUTHOR INDEX contains the names of all authors featured in the entries and those listed under "Other books you might like."

"I want to read a book that's similar to *The Green Mile.*"

The TITLE INDEX includes all main entry titles and all titles recommended under "Other books by the author" and "Other books you might like" in one alphabetical listing. Thus a reader can find a specific title, new or old, then go to that entry to find out what new titles are similar.

The indexes can also be used together to narrow down or broaden choices. A reader interested in Mysteries set in New York during the 19th century would consult the TIME PERIOD INDEX and GEOGRAPHIC INDEX to see which titles appear in both. Time Travel is a common theme in Science Fiction but occasionally appears in other genres such as Fantasy and Romance. Searching for this theme in other genres would enable a reader to cross over into previously unknown realms of reading experiences. And with the AUTHOR and TITLE indexes, which include all books listed under "Other books by the author" and "Other books you might like," it is easy to compile an extensive list of recommended reading, beginning with a recently published title or a classic from the past.

Suggestions Are Welcome

The editors welcome any comments and suggestions for enhancing and improving *What Do I Read Next?*. Please address correspondence to the Editors, *What Do I Read Next?*, at the following addresses:

Until September 15, 1998:
Gale Research
645 Griswold St.
Detroit, MI 48226-4094
Phone: 313-961-2242
Fax: 313-961-6083

After September 15, 1998:
Gale Research
27500 Drake Rd.
Farmington Hills, MI 48331-3535
Phone: 248-699-GALE
Toll-free: 800-347-GALE (for both addresses)

About the Genre Experts

Neil Barron, coordinator of the Science Fiction, Fantasy, and Horror fiction sections, is the editor of the reader guides *Anatomy of Wonder: A Critical Guide to Science Fiction* (Bowker, 4th ed., 1995) and *Fantasy and Horror: A Critical and Historical Guide to Literature, Illustration, Film, TV, Radio, and Internet* (Scarecrow Press, 1998).

Wayne Barton (Western Fiction) is a full-time writer and occasional engineering consultant from Midland, Texas. He is the author of more than fifty short stories and eight novels, including *Live by the Gun* (Pocket Books, 1990), which was a finalist for the 1991 Spur Award, and, most recently, *Shadow of Doubt* (Pocket Books, 1994) and *Wildcat* (Pocket Books, 1995). He won the Medicine Pipe Bearer's Award for best first Western novel in 1981 for *Ride Down the Wind* (Doubleday).

Kristin Ramsdell (Romance Fiction) is a librarian at California State University, Hayward. She writes a romance review column for *Library Journal* and is the author of *Happily Ever After: A Guide to Reading Interests in Romance Fiction* (Libraries Unlimited, 1987). A revised version, *Romance Fiction: A Guide to the Genre* (Libraries Unlimited), is forthcoming. She was named Librarian of the Year by Romance Writers of America in 1996.

Steven A. Stilwell (Mystery Fiction) is the owner of Once Upon a Crime Mystery Bookstore specializing in crime and detective fiction. He compiled *The Armchair Detective Index, 1967-1977* (Mysterious Press, 1979) and was the co-compiler, with William F. Deeck of *The Armchair Detective Index: Volumes 1-20, 1967-1987.* He has contributed to several publications, including *Mystery Scene Magazine, The Armchair Detective, The Mystery Fancier*, and *Twentieth Century Crime and Mystery Writers, 3rd ed.* (1991). He is also co-owner of Crossover Press, a small press specializing in books about crime and detective fiction.

Contributors

Scott Imes (Fantasy and Science Fiction) has managed the well-known Twin Cities specialty fantastic fiction bookstore, Uncle Hugo's, for more than 20 years. He was assisted by Margie Lessinger, a long time reviewer of science fiction; Cat Ocel, amateur publisher and organizer of literary conferences; and Stuart Wells III, compiler of *The Science Fiction and Heroic Fantasy Author Index* (1978). Also contributing were Don Blyly, Katharine B. Carey, Kay Drache, Lynne Holdom, Tom Juntunen, Peter Larsen, Linda Lounsbury, Lydia Drew Nickerson, and Amy Sisson.

Michael M. Levy (Science Fiction introduction) is a professor of English at the University of Wisconsin, Stout, and reviews science fiction for *Publishers Weekly*. He is the author of *Natalie Babbitt* (Twayne, 1991).

Stefan Dziemianowicz (Horror Fiction) is an editor for a New York law book publisher. A co-editor of the quarterly journal, *Necrofile*, he authored the definitive study, *The Annotated Guide to Unknown and Unknown Worlds* (Starmont House, 1991). He has co-edited numerous anthologies and recently compiled *A Whisper in the Dark: 12 Thrilling Tales by Louisa May Alcott* (Barnes and Noble, 1996).

Tom and Enid Schantz (Mystery Fiction essay) have been in the mystery business for 28 years, since 1980 as owners of the Rue Morgue Mystery Bookshop in Boulder, Colorado. Before that they operated a mail order mystery book business. They edit a monthly publication, *The Purloined Letter*, which reviews all new mystery titles. They also write a monthly crime column for the Denver *Post* and a quarterly column on the mystery genre for the Colorado Author's League newsletter.

Key to Genre Terms

The following is a list of terms used to classify the story type of each novel included in *What Do I Read Next?* along with brief definitions of the terms. To find books that fall under a particular story type heading, see the Genre Index.

Mystery Story Types

Action/Adventure: Minimal detection; not usually espionage but can contain rogue police or out of control spies.

Amateur Detective: Detective work is performed by a non-professional rather than by police or a private detective.

Espionage: Involving the CIA, KGB, or other organizations whose main focus is the collection of information from the other side. Can be either violent or quiet.

Historical: Usually detection set in an earlier time frame than the present.

Humor: A mystery, but the main focus is humorous.

Legal: Main focus is on a lawyer, though it does not always involve courtroom action.

Police Procedural: A story in which the action is centered around a police officer.

Private Detective: Usually detection, involving a professional for hire.

Psychological Suspense: Main focus is on the workings of the mind, usually with some danger involved.

Romance Story Types

Americana: A romance set in the present that features themes that are particularly American; often focuses on small-town life.

Anthology: A collection of short stories by different authors, usually sharing a common theme.

Contemporary: A romance set in the present.

Contemporary/Fantasy: A contemporary romance that makes use of fantasy or supernatural elements.

Contemporary/Mainstream: A romance set in the present that would be more properly categorized as fiction rather than romance. Often there is a strong love story line, but the primary emphasis is on other aspects of the plot.

Ethnic: A romance in which the ethnic background of the characters is integral to the story. Usually the focus is on an American ethnic minority group (e.g. African American, Asian American, Native American, Latino) and the two main characters are members of this group. See also **Multicultural**.

Fantasy: A romance that is not a Gothic or a Romantic Suspense but contains fantasy or supernatural elements.

Futuristic: A romance with a science fiction setting. Often these stories are set on other planets, aboard spaceships or space stations, or on Earth in an imaginary future or, in some cases, past.

Gothic: A romance with a strong mystery suspense plot that emphasizes mood, atmosphere, and/or supernatural or paranormal elements. Unexplained events, ancient family secrets, and a general feeling of impending doom often characterize these tales. These stories are most often set in the past, but several authors (e.g. Phyllis Whitney and Barbara Michaels) write gothics with contemporary settings.

Historical: A romance that takes place in the past that doesn't fall into one of the more specific Historical categories.

Historical/American Civil War: Set during the American Civil War, 1861-1865.

Historical/American West: Set in the Western portion of the United States, usually during the second half of the nineteenth century. Stories often involve the hardships of pioneer life

(Indian raids, range wars, climatic disasters, etc.) and the main characters (most often the hero) can be of Native American extraction.

Historical/American West Coast: Set in the American Far West (California, Oregon, Washington, or Alaska). Stories often focus on the Gold Rush and the tension between Spanish Land Grant families and immigrants from the Pacific Rim, usually China.

Historical/Americana: A novel set in the past that features uniquely American themes, such as small town life.

Historical/Antebellum American South: Set in the American Old South (prior to the Civil War).

Historical/Colonial America: Set in America before the American Revolution, 1620-1775. Stories featuring the Jamestown Colony, the Salem Witch Trials, and the French and Indian War are especially popular.

Historical/Edwardian: A romance set during the reign of Edward VII of England (1901-1910).

Historical/Fantasy: Historical romance that makes use of fantasy or supernatural elements.

Historical/Georgian: Set during the reigns of the first three "Georges" of England. Roughly corresponds to the eighteenth century. Stories often focus on the Jacobite Rebellions and the escapades of Bonnie Prince Charlie.

Historical/Mainstream: Historical romance that would be more properly categorized as fiction rather than romance. Often there is a strong love story, but the primary emphasis is on other aspects of the plot.

Historical/Medieval: Set during the Middle Ages, approximately the fifth through the fifteenth centuries. Stories feature battles, raids, crusades, and court intrigues; plot-lines associated with the Battle of Hastings (1066) are especially popular.

Historical/Post American Civil War: Set in the years following the Civil War/War Between the States, generally from 1865 into the 1870s.

Historical/Regency: A romance that is set during the Regency period (1811-1820) but is not a "Regency Romance" (see below).

Historical/Seventeenth Century: A romance set during the seventeenth century. Stories of this type often center around the clashes between the Royalists and the Cromwellians and the Restoration.

Historical/Renaissance: A romance set in the years of the Renaissance in Europe, generally lasting from the 14th through the 17th centuries.

Historical/Victorian: Set during the reign of Queen Victoria, 1837-1901. This designation does not include works with a predominately American setting.

Historical/Victorian America: Set in America, usually the Eastern part, during the Victorian Period, 1837-1901.

Holiday Themes: A romance that focuses on or is set during a particular holiday or holiday season (e.g. Christmas, Valentine's Day, Mardi Gras).

Inspirational: A romance with an uplifting, often Christian, theme, and usually considered "innocent."

Multicultural: A romance in which the ethnic background of the characters is integral to the story. See also **Ethnic**.

Regency: A light romance involving the British upper classes, set during the Regency Period, 1811-1820. During this time, the Prince of Wales acted as Prince Regent because of the incapacity of his father, George III. In 1820, "Prinny" became George IV. These stories, in the style of Jane Austen, are essentially comedies of manners and the emphasis is on language, wit, and style. Georgette Heyer set the standard for the modern version of this genre. This designation is also given to stories of similar type that may not fit precisely within the Regency time period.

Reincarnation: A romance in which one of the two main characters has been reincarnated as someone else. Often contains time travel elements.

Romantic Suspense: A romance with a strong mystery suspense plot. This is a broad category including works in the tradition of Mary Stewart as well as the newer women-in-jeopardy tales by writers such as Mary Higgins Clark. These stories usually have contemporary settings but some are also set in the past.

Time Travel: A romance in which characters from one time are transported either literally or in spirit to another time period. The time shifts are usually between the present and another historical period.

Western Story Types

Anthology: A collection of short stories by different authors, usually sharing a common theme.

Chase: A traditional Western in which the action of the plot is based on some form of pursuit.

Collection: A book of short stories by a single author.

Historical: A story that emphasizes accuracy of historical settings and characters rather than the characters and themes of the traditional Western. Generally these stories are set in locations or time periods outside the "cowboy" West.

Historical/American Civil War: A story set during the days of the American Civil War (1861-1865) and emphasizing the accuracy of the historical settings and the characters.

Indian Culture: These historical novels center on the lives, customs, and cultures of characters who are American Indians or who lived among the Indians.

Indian Wars: Often traditional Westerns, these stories are set

during the period of the Indian wars and rely on this warfare for plots, characters, and themes.

Man Alone: A lone man, alienated from the society that would normally support him, faces overwhelming dangers in this subgenre of the traditional Western.

Modern: Stories set after the closing of the frontier, generally from about 1920 to the present, but retaining the essential characteristics of the Western.

Mountain Man: Any story in which the principal characters are mountain men and women, living in mountain areas remote from civilization and depending upon their own resourcefulness for survival.

Mystery: A story in which the main plot feature involves the solution to a crime where the perpetrator or motive is not known to characters or readers. The detective is often an amateur, but may be a peace officer.

Quest: Another subgroup, usually of the traditional, the Quest shows its central characters on a journey filled with dangers to reach some worthwhile goal.

Ranch Life: The basic cowboy story, in which the plot and characters are inextricably bound up in the workings of a ranch.

Revenge: A character who has suffered an unjust loss returns to take vengeance. This is one of the most common traditional themes.

Saga: A book or series that follows the fortunes of a single family, usually over more than a single generation.

Series: A number of books united either by continuing characters and situations or by a common theme. Series books usually appear under a single author's name, although many of the packaged series are actually of multiple authorship.

Traditional: The classic Western from Owen Wister to today. Traditional Westerns may deal with virtually any time period or situation, but they are related by shared conventions of setting and characterization.

Trail Drive: Any story in which a cattle drive (or, more rarely, a drive of sheep or horses) is a major plot component.

Young Readers: A Western of any subgenre with characters, plot, and vocabulary primarily aimed at juveniles or young adults.

Fantasy Story Types

Adventure: The character(s) must face a series of obstacles, which may include monsters, conflict with other travellers, war, interference by supernatural elements, interference by nature, and so on.

Alternate History: Using history as a backdrop, the author adds fantastic elements to build the story.

Alternate Universe: More accurately, in most cases, alternate history, in which the South won the Civil War, the Nazis triumphed, etc. The idea is a venerable one in SF.

Alternate World: The story starts out in the everyday world, but the main character is transported to an alternate/parallel world by supernatural means and generally must go on an **Adventure** or **Quest** in order to find a way home.

Anthology: A collection of short fiction by different authors usually related in theme or setting.

Collection: A book of short stories by a single author.

Contemporary: The story is set in the everyday world, but elements of the fantastic begin to intrude (e.g., a unicorn appears or the character suddenly has the ability to perform magic).

Contemporary Realism: Stories in which the fantasy elements are part of a muted background and a "mundane" or "realistic" tone permeates the story.

Historical: This sub-genre could also be called Alternate History. Using history as a backdrop, the author adds fantastic elements to build the story.

Legend: A story based on a legend, myth, or fairy tale that has been rewritten.

Light Fantasy: There is a great deal of humor throughout the story and it is almost guaranteed to have a happy ending.

Literary: Usually refers to novels not published as fantasy and sometimes incorporating unconventional narrative techniques.

Magic Conflict: The main conflict of the story stems from magical interference. Protagonists may be caught in the middle of a conflict between sorcerers or may themselves be engaged in conflict with other sorcerers.

Military: Stories that can range from space wars (compare **Space Opera** under Science Fiction) to more local battles; most such stories tend to glorify military virtues.

Mystery: Although the story has been classified as Fantasy in this section, there are strong elements of Mystery (e.g., suspense, detectives, etc.).

Political: The novel deals with political issues that are skewed by the use and presence of fantastic elements.

Post-Disaster: Story set in a much degraded environment, frequently involving a reduction in population and the resulting loss of access to processes, resources, technology, etc.

Psychic Powers: Parapsychological or paranormal powers believed by some to be credible, e.g., telepathy, telekinesis, etc.

Quest: The character embarks on a journey to achieve a specific goal, such as retrieving a jewel from an evil wizard.

Religious: Religion of any sort plays a primary role in the plot.

Romance: The main characters are in love but separated by internal motivations or external interference. Elements of the fantastic may add to or help solve the problem.

Satire: With an ironic and/or detached point of view, the author is writing on a particular theme (such as religion) using elements of the fantastic to exaggerate and explore the theme.

Science Fiction: Although the story has been classified as Fantasy in this section, there are strong elements of Science Fiction.

Sword and Sorcery: The tried and true formula of this sub-genre has a muscle-bound swordsman, who is innocent of thought and common sense, up against evil sorcerers and sorceresses, who naturally lose in the end because they are evil. However, Sword and Sorcery continues to be updated, with heroines instead of heroes and a bit of thought prior to action.

Urban: Story featuring a city setting and having strong urban themes such as group identification and the resulting interactions.

Young Adult: Commonly indicated by publishers to help librarians categorize fiction likely to be of interest to teenage readers, this subgenre frequently involves a child or teenager maturing by accepting responsibility for self-determined goals and discovering strategies to achieve those goals.

Horror Story Types

Ancient Evil Unleashed: The evils may take familiar forms, like vampires undead for centuries, or malevolent ancient gods released from bondage by careless humans, or ancient prophecies wreaking havoc on today's world. The so-called *Cthulhu Mythos* originated by H.P. Lovecraft, in which *Cthulhu* is prominent among a pantheon of ancient evil gods, is a specific variation of this.

Anthology: A collection of short fiction by different authors, usually related in theme or setting.

Apocalyptic Horror: Traditionally, horrors that signal or presage the end of the world, or the world of the characters, and the establishment of a new, possibly very sinister order.

Black Magic: Magic directed toward malevolent ends, as distinct from white magic, which is directed toward benevolent ends. Witchcraft is commonly thought of as a black art. Voodoo consists of mysterious rites and practices including sorcery, magic and conjuration and often has evil goals.

Child-in-Peril: The innocence of childhood is often used to heighten the intensity and unpredictability of evil.

Collection: A book of short stories by a single author.

Curse: The words said when someone wishes evil or harm on someone or something, such as a witch's or prophet's curse. Compare **Black Magic**.

Erotic Horror: Sexuality and horror are often argued to be inextricably linked, as in Bram Stoker's *Dracula* and Sheridan Le Fanu's "Carmilla," although others have argued that they are antithetical. Sexuality became increasingly explicit in the 1980s, sometimes verging on the pornographic, as in Brett Easton Ellis' *American Psycho*.

Gay/Lesbian Fiction: In which the homosexuality of one or more characters is integral to the plot.

Ghost Story: The spirits of the dead, who can be benevolent, as in Charles Dickens, or malevolent, as in the tales of M.R. James.

Haunted House: Literally, a house visited by ghosts, usually with evil intentions in horror fiction, but sometimes the subject of comedy.

Mystery: A story in which the identity of evildoers is often concealed and suspense therefore heightened. Psychic detective tales are often mysteries.

Nature in Revolt: Tales in which normally docile plants or animals suddenly turn against humankind, sometimes transformed (giant crabs resulting from radioactivity, predatory rats, plagues, blobs that threaten London or Miami, etc.).

Occult: An adjective suggesting fiction based on a mystical or secret doctrine, but sometimes referring to supernatural fiction generally. Implies that there is a reality beyond the perceived world that only adepts can penetrate. Black Magic may or may not be part of an occult world.

Possession: Domination, usually of humans, by evil spirits, demons, aliens, or other agencies in which one's own volition is replaced by an outside force.

Psychological Suspense: Tales often not supernatural in nature in which the psychological exploration and quirks of characters, rather than outside creations, generate suspense and plot.

Reanimated Dead: These can take many forms, such as mummies and zombies (often the result of Voodoo).

Reincarnation: A tale in which the horror arises in connection with the reincarnation of one of the characters.

Satire: A tale embodying wit, mockery, or irony to attack ideas or customs judged wrong-headed by the author; uncommon in horror fiction.

Science Fiction: Stories in which supernatural or fantastic elements are absent and some degree of "rational" explanation is present. The science fiction surface of the film *Alien* is disrupted by the horror of the alien monster.

Serial Killer: A multiple murderer, going back to Bluebeard and up to Ed Gein, who inspired Robert Bloch's *Psycho*.

Small Town Horror: The coziness and intimacy of a small community is disrupted by some sort of horrific happening, suggesting an unjustified placidity and complacency on the part of the citizens.

Vampire Story: Based on mythical bloodsucking creatures possessing supernatural powers and various forms, both animal and human. The concept can be traced far back in history, long before Bram Stoker's famous novel, *Dracula*.

Werewolf Story: *Were* is Old English for man, suggesting the ancient lineage of a creature that once dominated a world in which witches and sorcerers were equally feared. Sometimes used to refer to any shape shifter, whether wolves or other animals.

Wild Talents: The phrase comes from Charles Fort's writings and usually refers to parapsychological powers such as telepathy, psychokinesis, and precognition, collectively called psychic or psi phenomena.

Witchcraft: Characters either profess to be or are stigmatized as witches or warlocks, and practitioners of magic associated with witchcraft. This can include black magic (see Black Magic) or white magic (e.g. Wicca).

Young Adult: Commonly used by publishers to help librarians categorize fiction likely to be of interest to teenage readers, this subgenre frequently involves a child or teenager often testing his or her skills against adversity in a horror setting to achieve a greater degree of maturity and self-awareness.

Science Fiction Story Types

Adventure: Suggests a novel or short fiction filled with a rapid sequence of incidents but little character development; Space Opera is a specialized form of adventure fiction.

Alternate History: A story dealing with how society might have evolved if a specific historical event had happened differently, e.g. if the South had won the American Civil War.

Alternate Intelligence: Story featuring an entity with a sense of identity and able to self-determine goals and actions. The natural or manufactured entity results from a synergy, generally unpredictable, of individual elements. This subgenre frequently involves a computer-type intelligence.

Alternate Universe: More accurately, in most cases, alternate history, in which the South won the Civil War, the Nazis triumphed, etc. The idea is a venerable one in SF.

Anthology: A collection of short fiction, short stories or novellas or both, written by different authors.

Arts: Stories incorporating themes related to music, painting, drama, and the arts generally.

Collection: A book of short stories written by a single author.

Contemporary Realism: Stories in which the science fictional elements are part of a muted background and a "mundane" or "realistic" tone permeates the story.

Cyberpunk: Usually applied to the stories by a group of writers who became prominent in the mid-1980s, such as William Gibson and his *Neuromancer* (1984). The "cyber" is derived from cybernetics, nominally the study of control and communications in machines. These books also feature a downbeat, punk sensibility reminiscent of the hardboiled school of detective fiction writers.

Disaster: A tale recounting some event or events seriously disruptive of the social fabric but not as serious as a holocaust; see Post-Holocaust.

Dystopian: The antonym of utopian, sometimes called anti-utopian, in which traditionally positive utopian themes are treated satirically or ironically and the mood is downbeat or satiric.

Family Saga: Usually refers to any large scale narrative extending over time and involving many related individuals.

Fantasy: A narrative describing events the reader believes to be impossible and for which no scientific or pseudoscientific explanation is offered; magic is usually substituted for scientific laws. Contrast **Science Fantasy**.

First Contact: Any story about the initial meeting or communication of humans with extraterrestrials or aliens. The term may take its name from the eponymous 1945 story by Murray Leinster.

Future Shock: A journalistic term derived from Alvin Toffler's 1970 book and which refers to the alleged disorientation resulting from rapid technological change.

Gay/Lesbian Fiction: In which the homosexuality of one or more characters is integral to the plot.

Generation Starship: If pseudoscientific explanations involving faster-than-light drives are rejected, then the time required for interstellar travel will encompass many human generations.

Genetic Manipulation: Sometimes called genetic engineering, this assumes that the knowledge exists to shape creatures, human or otherwise, using genetic means, as in *Brave New World* (1932).

Hard Science Fiction: Stories in which the author adheres with varying degrees of rigor to scientific principles believed to be true at the time of writing, principles derived from hard (physical, biological) rather than soft (social) sciences.

Horror: Refers to stories in which interest in the events, the intellectual puzzle characteristic of much SF, is subordinated to a feeling of terror or horror by the reader, which could result from a **Disaster**, **Invasion of Earth**, or other causes.

Humor: SF in which humor, from cerebral to slapstick, is prominent. Early SF was sometimes unintentionally humorous; some modern work is deliberately, and sometimes successfully, so. Compare **Satire** and **Parody**.

Immortality: Usually includes extreme longevity, resulting from fountains of youth, elixirs, or something with a pseudoscientific basis.

Invasion of Earth: An extremely common theme, often paralleling historical events and reflecting fears of the time.

Most invasions are depicted as malign, only occasionally benign.

Literary: Usually refers to novels not published as SF and sometimes incorporating unconventional narrative techniques. Metafictional narratives take as their subject matter the nature of fiction itself and are often therefore self-referential.

Lost Colony: Stories centering around a colony on another world that loses contact with or is abandoned by its parent civilization and the type of society that evolves under those conditions. Conflict usually arises when contact is re-established between the colony and its home world.

Medical: Stories in which medical themes are dominant; compare **Genetic Manipulation**, a specialized form of medical narrative.

Military: Stories that can range from space wars (compare **Space Opera**) to more local battles; most such stories tend to glorify military virtues.

Mystery: SF to which traditional mystery/detective structures have been grafted, not always successfully, and in which private eyes go down many mean galaxies; a distant relative of **Cyberpunk**.

Mystical: Suggesting a body of esoteric knowledge known to few and which can have a transforming effect on those possessing it.

Political: Narratives in which themes of power are paramount, whether on a local or galactic scale.

Post-Disaster: Story set in a much degraded environment, frequently involving a reduction in population and the resulting loss of access to processes, resources, technology, etc.

Post-Holocaust: The events following a world-wide disaster, often the result of human folly rather than natural events (collision with a meteor, etc.).

Psychic Powers: Parapsychological or paranormal powers believed by some to be credible, e.g., telepathy, telekinesis, etc.

Quest: A novel in which the central characters embark on a journey filled with dangers in order to reach some worthwhile goal.

Religious: Religion of any sort plays a primary role in the plot.

Robot Fiction: From the Jewish Golem to the traditional clanking bucket of bolts to the human-like android, robots in various guises have been among us for centuries. The term comes from Karel Capek's play, *R.U.R.*, which stands for Rossum's Universal Robots. Robots are often surrogates for humans and may be treated seriously or comically.

Satire: With an ironic and/or detached point of view, the author is writing on a particular theme (such as religion) using elements of the fantastic to exaggerate and explore the theme.

Science Fantasy: A somewhat vague term in which there are "rational" elements from SF and "magical" or "fanciful" elements from fantasy, which hopefully cohere in a plausible story. Many Adventures are Science Fantasy.

Science Fiction: Sometimes regarded as a branch of fantasy, there have been many definitions over the years, often too inclusive or exclusive. Used here in a very general sense when the story does not conveniently fit into another category.

Space Colony: A permanent space station, usually orbiting Earth but in principal located in deep space or near other planets or stars.

Space Opera: Intergalactic adventures; westerns in space; a specialized form of Adventure.

Techno-Thriller: Stories in which a technological development, such as an invention, is linked to a series of suspenseful ("thrilling") events.

Theological: Stories in which religion or religious belief plays an important role.

Time Travel: An ancient tradition in SF, whether the traveller goes forward or backward, and replete with paradoxes.

UFO: Unidentified Flying Objects literally, although sometimes used more generally to refer to any object of mysterious origin or intent. A cliche today in First Contact and Invasion of Earth stories.

Utopia: A large, often influential, story type that takes its name from Thomas More's 1516 book. Usually refers to a society considered "better" by the author, even if not perfect. Aldous Huxley's *Island* (1962) is a utopia, whereas his more famous *Brave New World* (1932) is a dark twin, a dystopia.

Young Adult: A marketing term for publishers; one or more of the central characters is a teenager often testing his or her skills against adversity to achieve a greater degree of maturity and self-awareness. A category used by librarians to shelve books of likely appeal to teenage readers.

Award Winners

Mystery Awards
by Steven A. Stilwell

Edgar Allen Poe Awards

Known as the Edgars, they are presented by the Mystery Writers of America. Nominees and winners are selected by committees made up of members of that organization. The 1998 awards are for works published in 1997.

Best Novel: *Cimarron Rose* by James Lee Burke

Other Nominees: *Dreaming of the Bones* by Deborah Crombie; *A Wasteland of Strangers* by Bill Pronzini; *Black and Blue* by Ian Rankin; and *The Purification Ceremony* by Mark T. Sullivan

Best First Novel by an American Author: *Los Alamos* by Joseph Kanon

Other Nominees: *A Crime in the Neighborhood* by Suzanne Berne; *Bird Dog* by Phillip Reed; *Flower Net* by Lisa See; and *23 Shades of Black* by K.j.a. Wishnia

Best Paperback Original: *Charm City* by Laura Lippman

Other Nominees: *Home Again, Home Again* by Susan Rogers Cooper; *The Prioress' Tale* by Margaret Frazer; *Tarnished Icons* by Stuart M. Kaminsky; and *Sunset and Santiago* by Gloria White

Grand Master Award: Barbara Mertz (pseudonym for Elizabeth Peters and Barbara Michaels)

Agatha Christie Award

Selected and voted on by the members of the annual Malice Domestic convention for works published in 1997.

Best Novel: *The Devil in Music* by Kate Ross

Other Nominees: *Hocus* by Jan Burke; *Dreaming of the Bones* by Deborah Crombie; *Goose in the Pond* by Earlene Fowler; *Seeing a Large Cat* by Elizabeth Peters

Best First Mystery: *The Salaryman's Wife* by Sujata Massey

Other Nominees: *Quieter Than Sleep* by Joanne Dobson; *The Butter Did It* by Phyliss Richman; *Dead Body Language* by Penny Warner; and *Death Brims Over* by Barbara Jaye Wilson

Anthony Boucher Awards

Called the Anthonys, they are selected by and voted on by members of the annual World Mystery Convention, known as Bouchercon, for works published in 1997. The winners will be announced at Bouchercon 29, to be held October 1-4, 1998.

Best Novel Nominees: *Devil's Food* by Anthony Bruno; *Deception Pass* by Earl Emerson; *The Club Dumas* by Arturo Perez-Reverte; *No Colder Place* by S.J. Rozan; and *Eye of the Cricket* by James Sallis

Best First Novel Nominees: *The Killing Floor* by Lee Child; *If I Should Die* by Grace Edwards; *Except the Dying* by Maureen Jennings; *Bird Dog* by Phillip Reed; and *Skin Deep, Blood Red* by Robert Skinner

Best Paperback Original Nominees: *Charm City* by Laura Lippman; *The Salaryman's Wife* by Sujata Massey; *Big Red Tequila* by Rick Riordan; *Time Release* by Martin J. Smith; and *23 Shades of Black* by K.j.a. Wishnia

The Dilys Award

Given by the Independent Mystery Booksellers Association (IMBA) and named for Dilys Winn, who opened the first bookstore to specialize in mysteries, it is given for the book that was deemed the most enjoyable to sell in the past year. Selected and voted on by the membership. For books published in 1997.

Winner: *Three to Get Deadly* by Janet Evanovich

Other nominees: *Backspin* by Harlen Coben; *Killing Floor* by Lee Child; *Sacred* by Dennis Lehane; *Deja Dead* by

Kathy Reichs; *The Devil in Music* by Kate Ross

Hammett Prize

Selected and voted on by the membership of the North American branch of the International Association of Crime Writers for a work of literary excellence in the field of crime writing by a U.S. or Canadian writer. For works published in 1997.

Nominees: *Cimarron Rose* by James Lee Burke; *Trunk Music* by Michael Connelly; *Trial of Passion* by William Deverell; *A Wasteland of Strangers* by Bill Pronzini; and *Acts of Murder* by L.R. Wright

Romance Awards
by Kristin Ramsdell

As romance fiction has attained increased recognition as a legitimate literary genre, various publications, organizations, and groups have developed to support the interests of its writers and readers. As part of this mission, a number of these offer awards to recognize the accomplishments of the practitioners. Some awards are juried and are presented for excellence in quality and style of writing; others are based on popularity and are selected by the readers. Usually awards are given for a particular work by a particular writer; however, some awards are presented for a body of work produced over a number of years (a type of career award) and others are given for various types of contributions to romance fiction in general. The Romance Writers of America, Romantic Times, Affaire de Coeur, and RRA-L electronic mailing list are the sponsors of most of the awards listed below.

Romance Writers of America Awards

These awards for excellence in romance fiction writing are presented by the Romance Writers of America at the annual RWA conference in July. The following awards were announced at the 1997 Conference in Orlando, Florida.

Lifetime Achievement Award

Presented by the Romance Writers of America for lifetime achievement in romance fiction as determined by a vote of the RWA membership. This year's winner is Nora Roberts.

Favorite Book of 1996

Presented by the Romance Writers of America for the best romance of the year as determined by the membership at large. Selection is made by ballot from a slate of nominees and at least 10% of the RWA membership must vote. Unfortunately, because of lack of member participation, no award was given this year.

Janet Dailey Award

Presented by the Romance Writers of America for the romance novel which best raises public consciousness about an important social issue. This year's winner is *Jackson Rule* by Dinah McCall (Sharon Sala).

Rita Awards for Published Novels

These awards are presented by the Romance Writers of America for the best romance novel published during 1996. Named for Rita Clay Estrada, RWA's first president, Ritas for published works are given in a number of categories, some of which have changed over the years. This year's winners are as follows:

First Book: *Stardust of Yesterday* by Lynn Kurland

Traditional: *Her Very Own Husband* by Lauryn Chandler

Short Contemporary: *Cowboy Pride* by Anne McAllister

Long Contemporary: *Wild Blood* by Naomi Horton

Regency Romance: *The Lady's Companion* by Carla Sue Kelly

Romantic Suspense/Gothic: *See How They Run* by Bethany Campbell

Paranormal: *Stardust of Yesterday* by Lynn Kurland

Short Historical: *Always to Remember* by Lorraine Heath

Single Title Contemporary: *Daniel's Gift* by Barbara Freethy

Long Historical: *Conor's Way* by Laura Lee Guhrke

Inspirational: *The Scarlet Thread* by Francine Rivers (Note: this was Rivers' third Rita in this category, making her the most recent addition to the RWA Hall of Fame.)

Golden Heart Awards

Presented by the Romance Writers of America for the best romance novel by a previously unpublished writer. Golden Hearts are given in a number of categories, some of which have changed over the years. The 1997 awards are as follows:

Traditional Romance: *A Father's Love* by Pam Baker

Short Contemporary: *Stop in the Name of Love* by Nina Bruhns

Long Contemporary: *Hawk's Child* by Vivyan Conolly

Romantic Suspense/Gothic: *Dangerous Curves* by Kristina Wright

Paranormal: *Dared to Dream* by Tammy Hilz

Long Historical: *The Path of the Wind* by Deborah Hale

Single Title Contemporary: *Skin Game* by Michele Albert

Short Historical: *Forever in Your Arms* by Kristen Smith

ARTemis Awards

Presented by RWA for the best published romance novel cover. Determined by popular vote at the annual conference. This year's awards are as follows:

Young Adult: *All That I Ask* by Jane M. Choate; Ernest

Albanese, Artist

Paranormal: *A Ghost of a Chance* by Casey Claybourne; Berkley Art Department

Contemporary Single Title: *See How They Run* by Bethany Campbell; Yook Louie, Artist

Contemporary Series — Traditional: *Baby Romeo: PI* by Julie McBride; Rick Johnson, Artist

Contemporary Series — Sensual: *Ivy Secrets* by Jean Stone; Yook Louie, Artist

Historical: *The Marriage Wager* by Jane Ashford; Yook Louie, Artist

Regency: *The Christmas Spirit* by Patricia Wynn; Mitch Hooks, Artist

Waldenbooks Bestselling Romance Awards

Presented by Waldenbooks at the RWA Conference in Orlando for the bestselling romances of 1996.

Contemporary Romance: *The Cove* by Catherine Coulter

Historical Romance: *Autumn Lover* by Elizabeth Lowell

Debut Author in Romance: *Stardust of Yesterday* by Lynn Kurland

Regency Romance: *A Christmas Courtship* (Anthology)

Multicultural Romance: *Seduction* by Felicia Mason

Hardcover Debut Romance: *Winter Fire* by Elizabeth Lowell

Sales Growth: *Annie's Song* by Catherine Anderson

Non-Traditional Romance: *Breath of Magic* by Teresa Medeiros

Special Achievement Awards: Hilary Ross, Signet Regency; and Mary Balogh for Lifetime Achievement

Laubach Robin Award

Presented by Laubach Literacy for the best unpublished romance for "new readers." The winning entry will be published by Signal Hill Publications, a division of Laubach New Readers Press.

The winner of this first competition was *Carousel Magic* by LaVerne St. George.

***Romantic Times* Reviewer's Choice Awards**

Presented by *Romantic Times* for outstanding romances published from November 1995 to October 1996. Selection is done by the RT series romance reviewers. Categories may vary from year to year. The awards are usually presented at the annual *Romantic Times* Convention; however, since the next *Romantic Times* Convention will take place in April 1998, these awards were announced in the October 1997 issue of *Romantic Times* and the winners were honored at a reception in New York.

Series Romance

Series Romance Book of the year: *Forever Blue* by Suzanne Brockmann

Best First Series Romance: *His Wedding Ring* by Kate Hathaway

Best Bantam Loveswept: *Night of the Hawk* by Victoria Leigh

Best Harlequin American: *Chasing Baby* by Pam McCutcheon

Best Harlequin Intrigue: *Crime of Passion* by Maggie Ferguson

Best Harlequin Presents: *Spring Bride* by Sandra Marton

Best Harlequin Romance: *For the Love of Emma* by Lucy Gordon

Best Harlequin Superromance: *A Suitable Bodyguard* by Kathryn Shay

Best Harlequin Temptation: *Holding Out for a Hero* by Vicki Lewis Thompson

Best Silhouette Romance: *Undercover Daddy* by Lindsay Longford

Best Silhouette Special Edition: *Molly Darling* by Laurie Paige

Best Silhouette Desire: *The Cowboy and the Kid* by Anne McAllister

Best Silhouette Intimate Moments: *Forever Blue* by Suzanne Brockmann

Best Silhouette Yours Truly: *I Do?* by Jo Ann Algermissen

Best Miniseries Romance: *To Love a Thief* by Margaret St. George (Harlequin Weddings by DeWilde)

Regency Romance

Best Regency Romance: *The Devil's Due* by Rita Boucher

Best First Regency Romance: *The Rake's Rainbow* by Allison Lane

Mainstream and New Reality Romance

Best Contemporary Fantasy: *Stardust of Yesterday* by Lynn Kurland

Best Contemporary Novel: *Ryan's Return* by Barbara Freethy

Best Contemporary Romance: *Jackson Rule* by Dinah McCall

Best Contemporary Romantic Suspense: *Passion* by Marilyn Pappano

Best Contemporary Suspense: *Under the Beetle's Cellar* by Mary Willis Walker

Best Futuristic Romance: *Immortal in Death* by J.D. Robb

Best Historical Fantasy: *Eyes of Love* by Katherine Deauxville

Best Contemporary Time-Travel Romance: *Wrapped in Wishes* by Olga Bicos

Multicultural Romance

Best Multicultural Romance: *Grass Ain't Greener* by Monique Gilmore

Historical Romance

Historical Romance of the Year: *The Outsider* by Penelope Williamson

Best First Historical Romance: *Shadows in Velvet* by Haywood Smith

Best Historical Novel: *Walk into the Night* by Beverly Bird

Best Western Historical Romance: *Comanche Rose* by Anita Mills

Best Historical Romantic Adventure: *The Thief's Mistress* by Gayle Feyrer

Best Medieval Historical Romance: *Dance in Heather* by Julie Beard

Best British Isles Historical Romance: *The Gentle Beast* by Colleen Shannon

Best Victorian Historical Romance: *Carried Away* by Jill Barnett

Best Regency Historical Romance: *A Glimpse of Heaven* by Barbara Dawson Smith

Best North American Historical Romance: *The Marriage Bed* by Stephanie Mittman

Best Historical Love and Laughter: *You and No Other* by Cathy Maxwell

Best Sensual Historical Romance: *Sinful Secrets* by Thea Devine

Best Historical Time-Travel Romance: *Legend* by Jude Deveraux

Best Innovative Historical Romance: *Simple Jess* by Pamela Morsi

Best K.I.S.S. Hero: Hunter Maxwell in *Autumn Lover* by Elizabeth Lowell

Romantic Times Career Achievement Awards

Presented by *Romantic Times* for outstanding career achievement. These awards were announced in the October 1997 issue of *Romantic Times* and the winners were honored at a reception in New York.

Series Romance

Series Romance: Justine Davis

Innovative Series Romance: Margaret St. George

Series Romantic Suspense: Patricia Rosemoor

Series Romantic Fantasy: Sharon Sala

Series Love and Laughter: Leanne Banks

Series Romantic Adventure: Lacey Dancer

Series Storyteller of the year: Nora Roberts

Contemporary Fiction

Contemporary Romance: Susan Elizabeth Phillips

Contemporary Novel: Christiane Heggan

Contemporary Romantic Suspense: Suzanne Forster

Contemporary Suspense: Carole Nelson Douglas

Contemporary Fantasy: Antoinette Stockenberg

Regency Romance

Regency Romance: Patricia Oliver

Futuristic Romance

Futuristic Romance: J.D. Robb

Multicultural Romance

Multicultural Romance: Francis Ray

Historical Romance

Historical Romance: Iris Johansen

Historical Novel: Eugenia Price

Historical Adventure: Gina Robins

Historical Fantasy: Sandra Hill

Western Historical Romance: Ana Leigh

Americana Historical Romance: Lorraine Heath

Regency Historical Romance: Jo Beverley

Historical Love and Laughter Romance: Millie Criswell

Innovative Historical Romance: Marylyle Rogers

Historical Storyteller of the Year: Dorothy Garlock

Affaire de Coeur Awards

Presented by *Affaire de Coeur* for romances published in 1996.

Best Cover: *Sophia* by Anne Chamberlain (Forge)

Best Inspirational: *Abide With Me* by Una McManus

Best Regency: *The Reluctant Cavalier* by Karen Harbaugh

Best Futuristic: *The Dawn Star* by Stobie Piel

Best Time Travel: *A Willing Spirit* by Deb Stover

Best American Historical: *Carried Away* by Jill Barnett

Best Foreign Historical: *Sophia* by Anne Chamberlain

Best Overall Historical: *Always to Remember* by Lorraine Heath

Best Contemporary: *Guilty as Sin* by Tami Hoag

Contemporary Ethnic: *For All Time* by Angela Benson

Science Fiction: *Forest of the Night* by Evelyn Vaughn

Romance of the Year: *A Willing Spirit* by Deb Stover

Top Favorite Authors: Sandra Brown, Suzanne Forster, Tami Hoag, Linda Howard, Iris Johansen, Jayne Ann Krentz, Elizabeth Lowell, Susan Elizabeth Phillips, Nora Roberts, Deb Stover, Anne Stuart

Outstanding Achiever: Nora Roberts

Up and Coming Author: Stobie Piel

RRA-L Awards

Selected by the members of the RRA-L electronic mailing list in 1998 for romances published in 1997.

Best Short Series Romance: *Trust Me on This* by Jennifer Crusie

Best Long Series Romance: *Reckless* by Ruth Wind

Best Contemporary Single Title Romance: *Nobody's Baby But Mine* by Susan Elizabeth Phillips

Best Historical Single Title Romance: *One Perfect Rose* by Mary Jo Putney

Regency Romance: *The Temporary Bride* by Mary Balogh

Romantic Suspense/Mystery/Adventure: *Son of the Morning* by Linda Howard

Best Alternative Realities Romance: *Vengeance in Death* by J.D. Robb

Best Time Travel Romance: *Almost an Angel* by Deb Stover

Best Love and Laughter Romance Award: *Nobody's Baby But Mine* by Susan Elizabeth Phillips

Best All-Around 1995 Romance: *One Perfect Rose* by Mary Jo Putney

1997 Author Awards

Best Contemporary Author: Susan Elizabeth Phillips

Best Historical Romance Author: Mary Jo Putney

Best Series/Category Author: Jennifer Crusie

Best Regency Author: Jo Beverley

Best All-Around Romance Author: Nora Roberts

Best Classic Romances

Best Classic Historical Romance: *River of Fire* by Mary Jo Putney

Best Classic Contemporary Romance: *It Had To Be You* by Susan Elizabeth Phillips

Best Classic All-Around Favorite Romance: *Outlander* by Diana Gabaldon

Best Classic Regency Romance: *The Rake and the Reformer* by Mary Jo Putney

Best Classic Series/Category Romance: *Getting Rid of Bradley* by Jennifer Crusie

Best All-Around Classic Romance Author: Mary Jo Putney

Best Romance Cover: *Tallchief* by Dinah McCall

Romances with Best Sweet Love Scene: *Cupid's Mistake* by Karen Harbaugh

Romances with Best Spicy Love Scene: *After the Night* by Linda Howard

Awards information courtesy of Romance Writers of America, Affaire de Coeur, Romantic Times Publishing Group, and the RRA-L electronic mailing list.

Western Awards
by Wayne Barton

There are two major families of awards to recognize Western novels of exceptional merit, as well as outstanding Western works in a variety of other fields. Perhaps the most widely known are the Spur Awards (often miscalled the Golden Spurs) presented by the Western Writers of America. Spurs are awarded annually at the WWA convention in the last week of June for works published during the previous calendar year. For simplicity, the Spurs are designated by the year of presentation, so these will be the 1998 Spur Awards, presented to books published in 1997.

Over the years, the number of Spurs awarded annually for Western fiction has varied. The variation reflects a continuing debate within WWA. One side fears that awards in a large number of categories will dilute the value of the Spur. Members of the other camp want enough Spurs to represent at least two different types of Westerns—the historical and traditional branches of the genre.

Today, the Spurs recognize three categories of Western novels: Best Western Novel, Best Novel of the West, and Best Paperback Original. The first two, with their confusion of names, are the latest compromise in the traditional/historical debate. Length is the dividing line; the Western Novel is defined as a novel of less than 100,000 words, while longer works compete as Novels of the West. Best Paperback Original is open to novels of any length which first appear in soft covers.

Spur Awards are also given for nonfiction work, juvenile fiction and nonfiction, short material, cover art, and movie and television scripts. In addition to the Spur, WWA presents the Medicine Pipe Bearer's Award for the best first Western novel and the Owen Wister Award for lifetime achievement in the Western field.

The second family of awards is presented annually by the National Cowboy Hall of Fame. The Western Heritage Award, commonly called the Wrangler, is a replica of the Charles Russell bronze of that name. The National Cowboy Hall of Fame annually presents the Wrangler for stories, artwork and music that, in the opinion of the judges, best capture the spirit of the West.

The Wrangler is even broader in its spectrum of categories than the Spur, including art and music as well as literature. Only a single Wrangler, however, is awarded for

the outstanding Western novel. In general, Wrangler selections seem to be more historically oriented and somewhat more literary in nature than Spur winners.

Spur Awards

Best Western Novel: *The Kiowa Verdict* by Cynthia Haseloff, published by Thorndike/Five Star.

Best Novel of the West: *Comanche Moon* by Larry McMurtry, published by Simon and Schuster.

Best Western Paperback Original: *Leaving Missouri* by Ellen Recknor, published by Berkley.

Best Juvenile Fiction: *Danger along the Ohio* by Patricia Willis, published by Clarion Books.

Medicine Pipe Bearer's Award: *Keepers of the Earth* by LaVerne Harrell Clark, published by Cinco Puntos Press.

Western Heritage Awards

The Western Heritage Awards are presented by the National Cowboy Hall of Fame for outstanding quality in fiction, nonfiction, music, and art.

Outstanding Novel: *The Mercy Seat* by Rilla Askew, published by Viking Press

Outstanding Juvenile: *Daughter of Suqua* by Diane Johnston Hamm

Fantastic Fiction Awards
by Neil Barron

Locus provides full listings of dozens of awards given throughout the year. Because awards are given the year following the year of publication, and normally after the editorial deadline for this annual, most books listed are discussed in last year's annual.

Science Fiction Awards

Hugo Award

The Hugos are given at the world SF conventions (worldcons) held over Labor Day each year and are chosen by the votes of those attending or supporting the convention. 687 valid ballots were cast in 1997, well down from the 939 last year, with the novel category receiving 584 votes. Awards are given in 13 categories, of which only the novel is listed here (collections and anthologies are not among the categories).

Best novel of 1996: *Blue Mars* by Kim Stanley Robinson

Runners-up: *Memory* by Lois McMaster Bujold, *Remnant Population* by Elizabeth Moon, *Starplex* by Robert J. Sawyer and *Holy Fire* by Bruce Sterling.

Nebula Award

Given by the Science Fiction and Fantasy Writers of America, an organization of about 1,300 members, of whom about a third vote. The awards, in four fiction categories of varying length, are announced several months before the Hugos and probably influence the voting for them. Because of the Nebula rules, some candidates were published more than one year prior to 1997, the year of award, as noted below.

Best novel of 1996: *Slow River* (1995) by Nicola Griffith

Runners-up: *The Silent Strength of Stones* (1995) by Nina K. Hoffman, *Winter Rose* (1996) by Patricia McKillip, *Expiration Date* (1996) by Tim Powers, *The Diamond Age* (1995) by Neal Stephenson and *Starplex* (1996) by Robert J. Sawyer.

Grand Master Award for lifetime achievement: Jack Vance

Locus Recommendations

The knowledgeable staff and reviewers of the principal magazine chronicling fantastic fiction join with other aficionados to assemble a recommended reading list of SF, fantasy and horror fiction (and other categories), published in the February issue with a ballot. Readers then vote, with the results tabulated in the July or August issue. The ballot generates more votes than any other award. Contributors to this annual try to annotate all the recommended novels.

Best SF novel of 1996: *Blue Mars* by Kim Stanley Robinson

Best fantasy novel of 1996: *A Game of Thrones* by George R.R. Martin

Best horror novel of 1996: *Desperation* by Stephen King

Fantasy Awards

World Fantasy Award

Reader ballots generate a list of candidates, and a panel of judges selects additional candidates and the winners. Fantasy is defined to include both fantasy and horror fiction. The winners are announced at the World Fantasy Convention held over Halloween weekend each year.

Best novel of 1996: *Godmother Night* by Rachel Pollack

Runners-up: *Shadow of Ashland* by Terence M. Green, *The Bear Went Over the Mountain* by William Kotzwinkle, *The 37th Mandala* by Marc Laidlaw, *A Game of Thrones* by George R.R. Martin, *The Golden Key* by Melanie Rawn, *Devil's Tower* by Mark Sumner

Best collection of 1996: *The Wall of the Sky, the Wall of the Eye* by Jonathan Lethem

Runners-up: *Midnight Promises* by Richard Chitzmar, *Conference with the Dead* by Terry Lamsley, *The Nightmare Factory* by Thomas Ligotti, *Bible Stories for Adults* by James Morrow, *Bad Intentions* by Norman Partridge, *The Pavilion of Frozen Women* by S.P. Somtow

Best anthology of 1996: *Starlight 1,* edited by Patrick

Nielsen Hayden

Runners-up: *The Year's Best Fantasy & Horror: Ninth Annual Collection,* edited by Ellen Datlow and Terri Windling, *The Simmering Door,* edited by Katharine Kerr and Martin H. Greenberg, *Dark Terrors 2: The Gollancz Book of Horror,* edited by Stephen Jones and David Sutton

Life Achievement Award: Madeleine L'Engle

Horror Awards

Bram Stoker Awards

Active members of the Horror Writers Association vote for this award at an annual summer conference. See also the World Fantasy Awards above.

Best novel of 1996: *The Green Mile* by Stephen King

Runners-up: *Demons Five, Exorcists Nothing* by William Peter Blatty, *Exquisite Corpse* by Poppy Z. Brite, *Lunatics* by Bradley Denton, *Lizard Wine* by Elizabeth Engstrom, *Crota* by Owl Goingback, *Prototype* by Brian Hodge, *Requiem* by Graham Joyce, *Child of the Night* by Nancy Kilpatrick, *Desperation* by Stephen King, *Madeline: After the Fall of Usher* by Marie Kiraly, *Kink* by Kathe Koja, *The 37th Mandala* by Marc Laidlaw, *Bite* by Richard Laymon, *Virgin* by Mary Elizabeth Murphy, *Shards* by Tom Piccirilli, *The Prestige* by Christopher Priest, *Dead Heat* by Del Stone, *The Hellfire Club* by Peter Straub, and *The Pillow Friend* by Lisa Tuttle

Best collection of 1996: *The Nightmare Factory* by Thomas Ligotti

Runners-up: *Midnight Promises* by Richard Chizmar, *The Convulsion Factory* by Brian Hodge, *Painfreak* by Gerard Daniel Houarner, *The Shadow Dreams* by Elizabeth Massie, *Bad Intentions* by Norman Partridge, *With Wounds Still Wet* by Wayne Allen Sallee, and *The Pavilion of Frozen Women* by S.P. Somtow

Life Achievement Award: Ira Levin and Forrest J Ackerman

Everything Else You Didn't Know About Fantastic Fiction Awards and Prudently Did Not Ask

The preceding awards are probably the best known and most prestigious in the fantastic fiction field, but they are only a very small percentage of all such awards given past and present. For your amazement or amusement I provide details about some of the other current awards but without showing present or past winners. For that, consult *Reginald's Science Fiction and Fantasy Awards,* compiled by Daryl F. Mallett and Robert Reginald (Borgo Press, 3d. ed., 1993; 4th ed., probably 1998). The 1995 annual showed winners of a very few of these awards. The awards are often given in a variety of categories, mostly for fiction published the previous year,

but sometimes for film or art or to an individual, often for lifetime achievement. The physical award is mostly commonly a plaque or statuette; cash is uncommon. The year shown is when the first award was given.

Arthur C. Clarke Award (1987): for best SF novel published in the UK, commonly by a British writer, selected by a panel of judges. The prize is 1000 British pounds.

Aurora Award (1980): originally the Casper Award, essentially a Canadian Hugo, given for the first few years to a Canadian writer, later to other categories. The current name dates from 1991. Statuette.

British Fantasy Award (1973); established in memory of August Derleth, co-founder in 1939 of Arkham House, publisher of weird/supernatural fiction, notably that of H.P. Lovecraft. The statuette is of Lovecraft's demonic god, Cthulhu.

British Science Fiction Award (1970): BSFA members nominate, judges select winners, originally for novels only, now for novel, short fiction, media presentation and art/illustration.

Chesley Award (1985): named after Chesley Bonestell, whose realistic astronomical paintings were influential in the earlier years of SF. The Association of SF Artists selects winners in several categories.

Ditmar (1969): The Australian equivalent of the Hugos. Awards sometimes are given years after publication. Both Australian and international fiction is recognized, along with other categories.

First Fandom (ca. 1964): a "first fan" was active in fantastic fiction by 1939, and the First Fandom organization still has more than 200 members. Frequently presented at the Worldcons at which the Hugos are also presented.

John W. Campbell Jr. Memorial Award (1973): named after the very influential long-time editor of *Astounding,* now *Analog,* selected by professional writers and given for the best novel. The **Theodore Sturgeon Award** was established as a companion in 1987 and is given to the author of the best short fiction.

Mythopoeic Society Fantasy Award (1983): given to the best fantasy novel and related work of nonfiction written in the spirit of the Inklings—Tolkien, C.S. Lewis and Charles Williams.

Philip K. Dick Memorial Award (1983): created to honor the best original American SF paperback and named after one of the field's most written-about figures. The money for the $1000 first prize is donated by paperback publishers.

Prometheus Award (1979): now given by the Libertarian Futurist Society. A companion award, the **Promethean Hall of Fame Award,** began in 1983 and is given to the author of a work of fiction more than five years old. The prize consists of a silver coin bearing the image of Adam Smith.

The Rhysling Award (1978): voted by members of the SF Poetry Association and named for the engineer/poet in a 1947 Heinlein story, "The Green Hills of Earth."

James Tiptree Jr. Award (1992): named for Alice Sheldon's famous pseudonym and given to the author of a work of feminist SF or fantasy.

The principal academic awards are the **Pilgrim**, given by the SF Research Association for sustained scholarship, the **IAFA Distinguished Scholarship Award,** given to an individual by members of the International Association for the Fantastic in the Arts, and the **J. Lloyd Eaton Award**, given at the annual Eaton conference at the UC Riverside campus to the author of a nonfiction book published two years previously.

A new annual literary SF award was first given in October 1997. **La Tour Eiffel/The Eiffel Tower SF Book Prize** is intended to "reward any new French or foreign science fiction work that is deemed to the particularly representative of the genre, and outstanding by its qualities of writing and imagination." I mention it because the winner receives 100,000 francs, about $20,000. *Savez-vous écrire SF en français?*

1998

WHAT DO I READ NEXT?

A Reader's Guide to Current Genre Fiction

- Fantasy
- Western
- Romance
- Horror
- Mystery
- Science Fiction

The Year in Mystery Fiction
by
Tom and Enid Schantz

Historians of the mystery genre won't look back on 1997 with unabated enthusiasm. While a handful of excellent writers produced their usual superior books, publishers for the most part were content to inflict upon the reading public countless cookie-cutter cozies, generic thrillers that did everything but thrill, and carbon-copy serial killer books that only served to prove that writers like Thomas Harris are born, not made. If 1997 offered any hope for the future of the genre, it lay in two growing trends, the first of which is to set more and more traditional mysteries in foreign climes, Asia in particular. The second trend is the growing critical and commercial success currently enjoyed by non-Anglo-American writers. Other developments that promise much for the future of the genre are the continuing trend of mainstream literary writers to cater to mystery readers and the continued emergence of the historical mystery.

The detective story is firmly rooted in Anglo-American tradition, partly because it is so hospitable to the loner or independent maverick investigator necessary to the detective novel. Very little native-written detective fiction has emerged from bureaucratic European states (Simenon in France and the Swedish husband-and-wife team of Per Wahloo and Maj Sjowall being the exceptions that prove the rule), and virtually no detective novels have emerged from totalitarian states. In the twentieth century Spain went from monarchy to fascist dictatorship and back to a monarchy without producing any notable crime fiction—at least none that had any hope of commerical success in the United States, though, from all reports, Spaniards have long been enthusiastic readers of American and English crime fiction. Recently this has changed, thanks to television-news-reporter-turned-novelist Arturo Perez-Reverte, whose first two novels quickly earned him both critical approval and a wide audience outside his native country. His second novel to be translated into English, *The Club Dumas*, a complex and highly entertaining tale of lost manuscripts and stolen rare books, caused one critic to dub him ''the thinking man's Robert Ludlum,'' a comparison that is probably unfair to both writers. What Perez-Reverte has done is to combine well-realized and unforgettable characters with a multi-layered plot to produce a book that easily qualifies as one of our top picks of the year. Much of the credit for its success in the English-speaking world should go to Sonia Soto's marvelous translation. Another writer to appear in the U.S. in translation in 1997 is Wang Shuo, whose *Playing for Thrills* is one of many books set in Asia, and the only one actually written by an Asian author.

Even before the Iron Curtain crumbled, American writers like Martin Cruz Smith found success showing the difficulties faced by an independent-minded detective working in a dictatorship. The confusion caused by the recent disintegration of the Soviet Union provided a rich background for several detective novels in 1997, including *Tarnished Icons*, the latest entry in Stuart M. Kaminsky's long-running series about often-abused-but-never-defeated Russian policeman Porfiry Rostnikov. Meanwhile, first-time novelist Robin White ventured into the vast and little known frozen territories to the north and east in *Siberian Light*. Philip Kerr, who set an earlier book (*Dead Meat*) in Moscow, traveled to Nepal for *Esau*, an entertaining if somewhat improbable hunt for the yeti—or abominable snowman—in the high Himalayas, the highlight of which was a memorable scene in which our naked heroine shoots it out with the bad guys while the yeti watch from their hiding places in a secret valley warmed by volcanic fires. We suspect Kerr had as much fun writing this one as readers will have reading it.

There was a time when the Far East found its way into American crime fiction only as the source of ''the Yellow Peril,'' a menace that threatened our very existence in those entertaining, if admittedly xenophobic, thrillers produced in the early years of the century by writers like Sax Rohmer

and Guy Boothby. In the intervening years, with a few exceptions, American writers have only used Asian landscapes in thrillers or spy novels to provide a colorful backdrop to an action plot. But in 1997, we saw a number of more realistic books that sought to show us what it's like to live in those countries. Sujata Massey's first novel, *The Salaryman's Wife*, offered up a convincing account of a young female Japanese-American teacher living on the edge of poverty in Tokyo who joins forces with a Scottish lawyer to solve the murder of a middle-management Japanese businessman at a ski resort in the Japanese Alps. You'll find another view of modern Japan as seen through the eyes of a Japanese-American tourist, in Dale Furutani's *The Toyotomi Blades*, and yet another in Peter Tasker's financial thriller, *Buddha Kiss*, which examines the underlying instability of this conformist society. Linda See's *Flower Net* takes us to Beijing where a maverick Chinese policewoman teams up with an American lawyer to look into the murder of an American diplomat. Martin Limon offered up a view of Korea in *Slicky Boys* that few non-military visitors will ever experience, while reality finally caught up with William Marshall's zany Yellowthread Police series in *Nightmare Syndrome* as the English crown colony of Hong Kong prepares for the transfer of power to China.

Italy has long been a favorite destination of English and American tourists, including vacationing detectives who take time from sightseeing to solve the odd murder or two. In recent years, however, we've seen the creation of a number of Italian sleuths, though created by non-Italians, emerge to take charge of these investigations. Among the best are Edward Sklepowich's *Death in the Palazzo*, which dishes up a lovely house party murder case, Michael Dibdin's richly atmospheric *Cosi Fan Tutti*, and John Spencer Hill's sun-drenched Tuscan mystery, *Ghirlandaio's Daughter*. Unfortunately, one of the best of the Italian mystery series fell victim to the wholesale slaughter at HarperCollins in 1997 when Donna Leon was cut loose without an American publisher.

Canada is certainly part of the Anglo-American world, but publishers have traditionally had a hard time selling books with Canadian settings featuring Canadian characters to U.S. readers. Not long ago one Canadian writer, Medora Sale, was told she needed to find a stateside setting if she expected to make a living writing mysteries, and the resulting book, set in New Mexico, was predictably unconvincing. Bestselling Toronto writer Joy Fielding has never set a book in her native country. But three very different books published in 1997 could go a long way toward combatting this prejudice. One of them, Rosemary Aubert's *Free Reign*, is our pick for the best first novel of 1997. It's the haunting story of Ellis Portal, a Toronto judge whose uncontrollable temper has cost him his job and family and forced him to take refuge among the homeless, eking out a meager existence panhandling and tending a small garden in a Toronto park where his discovery of a severed hand soon draws him

out of his seclusion. Perhaps the most commercially successful crime novel ever set in Canada is Kathy Reichs' *New York Times* bestselling first novel, *Deja Dead*. In spite of its many flaws, most of which could have been corrected had the publisher not rushed it into print, *Deja Dead* deserves much of its success. Reichs, herself a forensic anthropologist who works with the Montreal police, provides forensic details you won't find in the novels of either Patricia Cornwell or Aaron Elkins. You'll also find more similes and metaphors in this one book than in all the other 1997 crime novels put together. The third important Canadian mystery of 1997 is also a first novel: Maureen Jenning's *Except the Dying*, which presents a memorable look at life and death in Toronto in the harsh winter of 1895, a time period in which English traditions familiar to American readers still flourished.

Part of Jennings' success is no doubt due to the continuing escalation of interest in historical mysteries, perhaps the single most important trend in detective fiction in this decade. It's no mystery why historicals have suddenly taken the genre by storm. In an age of DNA, fingerprints and forensics, it's increasingly difficult to construct a contemporary puzzle that can be solved by the human intellect alone. It's also an entertaining way for readers to learn something about the past. That's certainly a large part of the charm of Deborah Woodworth's quietly impressive debut, *The Death of a Winter Shaker*, which is set among members of that self-contained and egalitarian religious community in 1930s Ohio. Margaret Lawrence, who wrote some very nice mysteries as M.K. Lorens, gave us the best mystery of 1996 with *Hearts and Bones*. She continued the adventures of her post-Revolutionary War midwife/sleuth in *Blood Red Roses*, and if it's a bit of a letdown after its predecessor, that's merely an indication of how good the first book was. Caleb Carr's second mystery, *The Angel of Darkness*, also suffered in comparison with his first but still managed to make most of the national bestseller lists. Anne Perry, on the other hand, continued to improve with each book, whether it featured the Pitts (*Ashworth Hall*) or the amnesiac Monk (*The Silent Cry*). P.C. Doherty offered up an engaging mystery set in medieval England in *A Tournament of Murders* and then added another pseudonym to his already impressive list, taking us back to ancient Greece as Anna Apostolu in *A Death in Macedon*. Lauren Haney added her ancient Egyptian mystery, *The Right Hand of Amon*, to the Egyptian canon of Lynda S. Robinson, who proved that she's one of the most important voices in this subgenre with her fourth Lord Meren mystery, *Eater of Souls*. Ancient Rome proved it's still the eternal city in the capable hands of Lindsey Davis (*Time To Depart*) and Steven Saylor (*The House of the Vestals and Other Stories*). Fiona Buckley took us back to the time when the first Elizabeth sat on the throne in *To Shield the Queen*, while Edward Marston also set his new Nicholas Bracewell novel during the Elizabethan period in *The Fair Maid of Bohemia* but transported his group of

theatrical players to Prague for a most deadly engagement. Bruce Alexander had Sir John Fielding looking into a murder in *Person or Persons Unknown*. Stephanie Barron continued to combine the literary and the historical mystery with her second Jane Austen novel, *Jane and the Man of the Cloth*. Sadly, Kate Ross, perhaps the brightest rising talent in this subgenre, died, much too young, of cancer a few months after her fourth Julian Kestrel "Dandy" mystery, *The Devil in Music*, appeared in the bookstores. London in the 1920s was the setting for Laurie R. King's third Mary Russell/Sherlock Holmes adventure, *A Letter of Mary*, while Quinn Fawcett let Sherlock's brother Mycroft take center stage in gaslit London in *Against the Brotherhood*.

In addition to Margaret Lawrence and Deborah Woodworth, an increasing number of writers are setting their historicals in the United States. If you ignore the female lead's unconvincingly loose sexual morals, Joseph Kanon's *Los Alamos* is a nearly perfect detective novel, set in the New Mexico labs during the building of the first atomic bomb. Barbara Hambly looked at the life of a freed slave in pre-Civil War New Orleans in *A Free Man of Color*, and Dianne Day took us to turn-of-the-century Northern California in *The Bohemian Murders*. Karen Rose Cercone placed her socially aware first novel, *Steel Ashes*, in Pittsburgh toward the end of the last century, while Donald Honig set *The Ghost of Major Pryor* on the American post-Civil War frontier and prompted the intriguing question: when is a crime story set in the Old West an historical mystery and when is it a Western? The answer probably lies in determining whether the book is more puzzle- or action-oriented.

Such formulas, of course, help make up the conventions needed to produce a mystery-detective novel and also make it difficult for writers to come up with an original concept, although remarkably this does happen, quite often by writers who wander almost by accident into the mystery genre while writing what they perceive as literary fiction. Certainly David Guterson (*Snow Falling on Cedars*) and Michael C. White (*A Brother's Blood*) were surprised at how easily mystery readers accepted their books into the genre. But other mainstream writers have quite deliberately dropped a body or two into their books to attract mystery fans and generally liven up their stories. Such was the case with our pick for best mystery of the year, *Counting Coup* by G.D. Gearino. He considers himself a Southern literary writer but feels that most mainstream literary fiction can be made more compelling with the addition of a mystery whose resolution is gradually unfolded to the reader. In that he echoes the comment made by poet-turned-thriller-writer James W. Hall, who said he started his own career as a novelist by writing long introspective books in which grandma died on page one and was buried on page 600 and absolutely nothing happened in between. Quite a bit happens in *Counting Coup* in spite of its relatively short length. It is that rarity in crime fiction—a unique and truly original piece of work. Other 1997 crime novels of note from previously "literary" writers include C.E. Poverman's *On the Edge*, in which a down-and-out, alcoholic San Francisco legal investigator reflects upon the wrong turns in his life, and Brad Morrow's *Giovanni's Gift*, which uses the myth of Pandora's box as the driving metaphor in a tale of violent death in the Colorado Rockies. Both books have much to recommend them, but their authors would do well to read James Lee Burke's *Cimarron Rose*, a masterful crime story by another writer who got his start in the mainstream.

Fans of the hardboiled school will welcome the return of Michael Connelly's maverick Los Angeles cop Harry Bosch in *Trunk Music*. If you're unfamiliar with Connelly, go to his first novel, *Black Ice*, and get acquainted with one of the finest crime writers of his generation. Nearly as good are Dennis Lehane's *Sacred*, the third book featuring his two Boston private eyes, and S.J. Rozan's *No Colder Place*, featuring New York City investigators Bill Smith and Lydia Chin. Robert Crais gave us another entertaining Elvis Cole adventure in *Indigo Slam* and G.M. Ford was as amusing as ever in *The Bum's Rush* (which, like several other mysteries this year, dealt with the plight of the homeless). Earl Emerson delivered two fine novels in one year, *Deception Pass*, featuring private eye Thomas Black, and *The Dead Horse Paint Company*, featuring fire chief Mac Fontana. Bill Pronzini also pulled off a dazzling double play with *Illusions*, featuring his "Nameless" San Francisco private eye, and *A Wasteland of Strangers*, a stand-alone crime novel that stands practically alone as one of the better novels of 1997. Little known and underappreciated New England writer Archer Mayor came up big again with *Bellows Falls*. Matt Scudder is licensed, married, paying taxes, and still on the wagon in Lawrence Block's *Even the Wicked*. You won't believe that *Killing Floor*—yet another stunning first novel—by Lee Child was written by an Englishman. Randy Wayne White took us for an unforgettable boat ride to Cuba in *North of Havana*. Les Roberts proved that Cleveland can still be an exciting town even if the Browns are gone in *Cleveland Local*. You'll find yourself writing off for Alaska travel brochures when you read John Straley's *Death and the Language of Happiness*. Fans of *noir* fiction laced with sometimes side-splitting comedy will have a good time with Philip Reed's *Bird Dog*, K.J.A. Wishnia's *23 Shades of Black*, Fred Willard's *Down on Ponce*, Kinky Friedman's *Road Kill*, Rick Riordan's *Big Red Tequila*, Ben Elton's *Popcorn*, or Don Winslow's *The Death and Life of Bobby Z*, not to mention Carl Hiaasen's latest look at South Florida lowlifes, *Lucky You*. David Housewright followed up his Edgar-winning *Penance* with the more than satisfactory *Practice to Deceive* while Robert B. Parker discovered that you can make twice as much money if you write two books a year. His ageless—but to some readers aging—private eye Spenser is back again in *Small Vices* while Parker also gives us a new, younger character in the alcoholic police chief of *Night Passage*. There's much to admire in both books,

though one wishes Parker would learn that women are far more interesting if they're not placed upon a pedestal.

If you want semi-tough to tough but generally realistic women protagonists, try Marcia Muller's *Both Ends of the Night*, Jan Burke's *Hocus*, Barbara D'Amato's *Hard Bargain*, Carolina Garcia-Aguilera's *Bloody Shame*, Barbara Seranella's *No Human Involved*, Linda Barnes' *Cold Case*, Katherine V. Forrest's *Apparition Alley*, Dana Stabenow's *Breakup*, Wendy Hornsby's *A Hard Light*, Linda Fairstein's *Likely to Die*, Terris Grimes' *Blood Will Tell* , Janet Dawson's *Witness to Evil*, or Susan Dunlap's *Cop Out*. For larger-than-life heroines who can outwit unimaginably resourceful villains, turn to Thomas Perry's *Shadow Woman*, Carol O'Connell's *Stone Angel*, Mark T. Sullivan's *The Purification Ceremony*, or Amy Tan's *a.k.a. Jane*.

If you measure women by the depth of their character you won't go wrong with Abigail Padgett's *The Dollmaker's Daughter*, in which Bo Bradley solves a murder while battling her manic depression, or Francine Mathews' *Death in a Mood Indigo*, in which Nantucket policewoman Merry Folger explores the very nature of evil. Then there is Nevada Barr's *Endangered Species*, in which park ranger Anna Pigeon, arguably the most complex and believable woman character in crime fiction, comes to a personal fork in the road. Or if screwball comedies featuring women are your thing try Janet Evanovich's *Three to Get Deadly*, Sparkle Hayter's *Revenge of the Cootie Girls*, or Lindsay Maracotta's *Dead Celeb*.

British mysteries are still being published in the United States, though in diminishing numbers and more and more frequently written by Americans. For whatever reason, U.S. readers seem to increasingly favor books in which Britain is seen through the eyes of a compatriot. What may well be the best English mystery of the year, the multi-layered *Dreaming of the Bones*, was written by Texas writer Deborah Crombie. Other Americans who produced traditional English mysteries include Elizabeth George (*Deception on His Mind*), Martha Grimes (*The Case Has Altered*), Julie Kaewert (*Unbound*), Tony Strong (*The Poison Tree*) and Jeanne M. Dams (*Holy Terror in the Hebrides*). English-born Dorothy Cannell lives in Peoria but set *God Save the Queen!* in the old country as did J. Rhys Bowen in *Evans Above*, a sort of Welsh version of M.C. Beaton's Hamish Macbeth mysteries. Bartholomew Gill (really the American writer Mark McGarrity) set his memorable study of a fascinating subculture, *Death of an Irish Tinker*, in Dublin, the scene of all his Inspector McGarr books, while New Yorker Charles Beechey placed his witty debut mystery, *An Embarrassment of Corpses*, in London and Canadian writer Peter Robinson returned to Yorkshire in *Blood at the Root*.

If you look hard enough you can still find an occasional English mystery written by an actual Brit. Minette Walters' *The Echo* was just an echo of her first two books but that's good enough for us. Jonathan Gash took a leave of absence from his Lovejoy series to write about an English woman doctor in *Different Women Dancing*, although her unconventional young male sidekick could be Lovejoy's long-lost cousin. John Harvey proved that crime still flourishes in Nottingham more than 700 years after Robin Hood in *Still Waters*. Liza Cody gave us another chapter in the life of her working-class female wrestler/sleuth in *Musclebound*. Ruth Rendell proved why the Mystery Writers of America named her a Grandmaster with *Road Rage*, her new Inspector Wexford novel. Cynthia Harrod-Eagles delivered another well-crafted story featuring Inspector Bill Slider in *Killing Time*. Frances Fyfield showed the darker side of London in *Without Consent* while Ruth Dudley Edwards wielded her usual acerbic pen in *Murder in a Cathedral*. Murder was as cozy and droll as ever in M.C. Beaton's newest Hamish Macbeth mystery, *Death of a Dentist*. Mary Stewart's *Rose Cottage*, set in the 1940s, was as much a nostalgic (if romanticized) slice of village life as it was a mystery, but it was such a charmer that we couldn't help but welcome it into the genre. Veterans Colin Dexter (*Death Is Now My Neighbor*) and P.D. James (*A Certain Justice*) once again produced complicated and, for the most part, satisfying books. But for us, the most enjoyable English mystery of the year was Marianne Macdonald's delightful—and thoroughly authentic—look at murder in the antiquarian book world in *Death's Autograph*.

Readers who still believe that English mysteries are by nature gentler and kinder than those produced by Americans would do well to check out Val McDermid's chilling 1996 Gold Dagger winner, *The Mermaids Singing*. McDermid is at the forefront of a movement in Britain which has produced crime fiction as realistic, *noir* and gritty as anything published in the U.S. Other practitioners, in addition to McDermid, Cody, and Harvey, include Bill James (*Gospel*) and Ian Rankin, who with his Gold Dagger-winning *Black and Blue* proved that he may well stand the test of time. Not that awards are any guarantee of longevity; Val McDermid was cut by her American publisher, HarperCollins, although she still has a slot at Scribners, which brought out *Blue Genes*, featuring her cheeky Manchester private eye Kate Brannigan.

There are plenty of cozy mysteries being published in the U.S., though it's increasingly difficult to winnow out the good from the barely tolerable. For some thirty years now the team of Mary J. Latsis and Martha Hennissart produced a deservedly popular series featuring the unflappable Wall Street banker John Putnam Thatcher, including *A Shark Out of Water*. Latsis died late in 1997 and we haven't heard if Hennissart intends to carry on alone. Generally speaking, a cozy is any mystery in which nothing bad—if you ignore the murder—happens. Also generally speaking, readers enjoy cozies in which they learn something about an occupation, a subject, or a way of life. Examples include Dolores Johnson's *Hung Up to Die*, in which you'll find out more about dry cleaning than about DNA samples, or Christine T. Jorgensen's *Curl Up and Die*, in which a slightly psychic

sleuth offers astrological advice in a Denver newspaper. Jane Haddam's Valentine mystery for the year was *Deadly Beloved* while Joan Hess brightened up the Christmas season with *A Holly, Jolly Murder* . Clap your hands (and seek professional help) if you really believe that cats can solve murders and then curl up with Lilian Jackson Braun's *The Cat Who Tailed a Thief* or Carole Nelson Douglas' *Cat in a Flamingo Fedora*. If you prefer dogs, try Susan Conant's *Animal Appetites* (for those partial to malamutes), Laurien Berenson's *Hair of the Dog*, or Virginia Lanier's *The House on Bloodhound Lane*. Susan Wittig Albert mixed herbs with murder in *Love Lies Bleeding*, and an increasing number of writers offered crime fiction with a culinary bent: Diane Mott Davidson in *The Grilling Season* , restaurant reviewer Phyllis Richman in *The Butter Did It*, Lou Jane Temple in *A Stiff Rissotto* , and Peter King in *Spiced to Death*.

Yes, men write cozies too, and in 1997 they apparently liked to set them on islands. Aaron Elkins' *Twenty Blue Devils* featured bone detective Gideon Oliver in Tahiti while Philip R. Craig's *A Deadly Vineyard Holiday* was set on Martha's Vineyard.

Place remains an important aspect of the mystery novel, with an increasing number of books being set in the interior west. James D. Doss gave us *The Shaman's Bones*, the third and best of his books featuring Daisy Perika, a Ute shaman on a reservation in southwestern Colorado (also the scene of Rex Burns' *The Leaning Land*). Doss also set a bit of his action on Wyoming's Wind River Reservation, where most of Margaret Coel's *The Dream Stalker* took place. Jean Hager continued the adventures of her Cherokee sleuth Molly Bearpaw in *The Spirit Caller*. Mardi Oakley Medawar used Native American characters in an historical setting in *Witch of the Palo Duro*. Steven Havill (*Privileged to Kill*), Michael McGarrity (*Mexican Hat*), Micah Hackler (*The Deadly Canyon*) and Aimee and David Thurlo (*Bad Medicine*) served notice that New Mexico isn't solely Hillerman country anymore. We got very different looks at the Colorado Front Range in Robert Greer's *The Devil's Red Nickel*, Stephen White's *Remote Control*, and Manuel Ramos' *Blues for the Buffalo*. James Lee Burke deserted the familar bayous of Louisana for the plains of Texas and Oklahoma in *Cimarron Rose*, which was well accepted by his legion of fans, who may have been as ready as the author for a break from his intense Dave Robichaux series. J.A. Jance offered up another chapter in the saga of her small-town Arizona female sheriff in *Skeleton Canyon* and Peter Bowen continued the saga of his eccentric Montana cattle-brand inspector Gabriel Dupre in *Notches*.

Even with a decline in the sheer numbers of quality books in 1997, it's still hard to single out our 25 favorites. The following list represents a wide range of mystery types, from the comfortably cozy to the disturbingly gritty, from the postmodern to the decidedly old-fashioned:

Counting Coup by G.D. Gearino

Death of a Winter Shaker by Deborah Woodworth

A Wasteland of Strangers by Bill Pronzini

Popcorn by Ben Elton

Death's Autograph by Marianne Macdonald

Bird Dog by Philip Reed

The Salaryman's Wife by Sujata Massey

The Devil in Music by Kate Ross

Trunk Music by Michael Connelly

Killing Floor by Lee Child

No Colder Place by S.J. Rozan

Sacred by Dennis Lehane

Free Reign by Rosemary Aubert

Except the Dying by Maureen Jennings

Death of an Irish Tinker by Bartholomew Gill

Dreaming of the Bones by Deborah Crombie

Three to Get Deadly by Janet Evanovich

Hocus by Jan Burke

Los Alamos by Joseph Kanon

North of Havana by Randy Wayne White

The Shaman's Bones by James D. Doss

Twenty Blue Devils by Aaron Elkins

The Club Dumas by Arturo Perez-Reverte

Cimarron Rose by James Lee Burke

Death in a Mood Indigo by Francine Mathews

If you can't find anything to relish on that list, you probably shouldn't be reading mysteries.

What the future promises for the genre is somewhat disturbing. Midlist writers—a category which includes most mystery writers—have been badly hurt in recent years by publishers who demand increasing sales numbers each year. Making the *New York Times* bestseller list is still the primary goal of any publisher, and many are adopting a three-strikes-and-you're-out policy, giving their authors only three chances to achieve satisfactory sales. More and more mysteries, from writers deemed to be either on their way up or on their way out, are coming out as paperback originals rather than as hardcovers, or from small presses rather than major ones. And recent developments in the publishing world can't help but shrink the number of available slots. HarperCollins made news when it cut over a hundred titles from its list, including books from such capable mystery writers as Donna Leon, Val McDermid and Daniel Easterman, but other publishers have taken almost equally draconian measures with considerably less fanfare.

Even more disturbing is the number of corporate mergers that have hit the New York publishing world recently. Penguin bought Putnam in 1996 but turned over management chores to the bestseller-driven Putnam. And early in 1998, Bantam Doubleday Dell absorbed the world's

largest publisher, Random House, in a move that stunned the industry. Each house promised to respect the editorial independence of its newly acquired properties, but publishing houses are run by bean counters, not editors. Add to these mergers the disappearance of all but a few large independent bookstores and a handful of specialist shops, the continuing growth of the big chain superstores, the increasing availability of discounted mass-market paperbacks and bestsellers at supermarkets, drugstores, and discount department stores,

and the growth of on-line bookselling, and the result could be fewer choices for the consumer. The American Booksellers Association filed a surprise class action suit in California against Barnes & Noble, charging the chain with various unfair business practices, but even if they win, it's probably an exercise in tilting at windmills. As Sherlock Holmes once remarked, there's a cold wind blowing in from the east.

Perhaps we can blame it on El Nino.

Mystery Titles

DEBORAH ADAMS

All the Blood Relations
(New York: Ballantine, 1997)

Story type: Police Procedural; Humor
Series: Jesus Creek
Major character(s): Kay Martin, Police Officer (Deputy Sheriff)
Time period(s): 1990s
Locale(s): Jesus Creek, Tennessee

Summary: When the town florist is murdered shortly after the arrival of the daughter she's placed for adoption as a teenage unwed mother, Kay Martin doesn't see eye to eye with the Tennessee Bureau of Investigation when they target the daughter as the killer. But she has other investigations pending: to find a motorcycle-riding thief who's become something of a local folk hero and a missing wife who went out for milk and never came back. She also comes across some surprising evidence of extraterrestrial visitors and as well as a cult of misogynists intent upon putting their wives back in their proper places. As usual, the town itself is the unifying element in this series, each of which offers a different protagonist whose story is told against a continuing cast of secondary characters.

Other books by the same author:
All the Deadly Beloved, 1995
All the Hungry Mothers, 1993
All the Dark Disguises, 1993
All the Crazy Winters, 1992
All the Great Pretenders, 1992

Other books you might like:
Susan Wittig Albert, *The China Bayles Series*, 1992-
Nancy Bell, *The Biggie Weatherford Series*, 1996-
Joan Hess, *Martians in Maggody*, 1994
Toni L.P. Kelner, *The Laura Fleming Series*, 1993-
Sharyn McCrumb, *Sick of Shadows*, 1984

SUSAN WITTIG ALBERT

Love Lies Bleeding
(New York: Berkley, 1996)

Story type: Amateur Detective
Series: China Bayles
Major character(s): China Bayles, Businesswoman (herb shop owner), Lawyer (former); Mike McQuaid, Police Officer (detective), Lover (China's)
Time period(s): 1990s
Locale(s): Pecan Springs, Texas (hill country)

Summary: Rejuvenated by her recent retreat, China is back at her herb shop, studying ways to open the tea room she plans as an adjunct to the store and still leave herself time for gardening and the good life. But when a retired Texas Ranger is shot with his wife's gun, China takes notice, since the wife had been a customer at Thyme and Seasons that very morning. Add to this the fact that Mike McQuaid, her significant other, has been acting a little odd lately, and you can be sure China won't be finding much time for contemplation. The usual interesting herbal lore is interwoven into the story.

Other books by the same author:
Rueful Death, 1996
Rosemary Remembered, 1995
Hangman's Root, 1994
Witches' Bane, 1993
Thyme of Death, 1992

Other books you might like:
Jean Hager, *The Tess Darcy Series*, 1994-
Joan Hess, *The Claire Malloy Series*, 1986-
Stefanie Matteson, *Murder at Teatime*, 1991
Ann Ripley, *The Louise Eldridge Series*, 1994-
Barbara Burnett Smith, *The Jolie Wyatt Series*, 1994

BRUCE ALEXANDER (Pseudonym of Bruce Cook)

Person or Persons Unknown

(New York: Putnam's, 1997)

Story type: Historical
Series: Sir John Fielding
Major character(s): Sir John Fielding, Judge (blind), Historical Figure; Jeremy Proctor, Ward, Assistant
Time period(s): 18th century (1797)
Locale(s): London, England

Summary: Sir John Fielding, the legendary Blind Beak, was the half-brother of the novelist Henry Fielding. Despite his blindness he became a noted magistrate and the founder of the Bow Street Runners. Now he and his young assistant and ward, Jeremy Proctor (whom he rescued from a life on the streets in the first book in the series) face a series of murders very close to home. Prostitutes are being murdered in Covent Garden in a way that raises troubling implications as to the identity of the killer. Fielding devises a daring plan to expose the murderer but its consequences are more dangerous than he could imagine.

Where it's reviewed:
Kirkus Reviews, August 1, 1997, page 1155
Library Journal, August 1997, page 140
Publishers Weekly, June 30, 1997, page 69

Other books by the same author:
Watery Grave, 1996
Murder in Grub Street, 1995
Blind Justice, 1994

Other books you might like:
Stephanie Barron, *The Jane Austen Series*, 1996-
Robert Lee Hall, *London Blood*, 1997
J.G. Jeffreys, *The Jeremy Sturrock Series*, 1972-
Deryn Lake, *Death at the Beggar's Opera*, 1995
Kate Ross, *The Julian Kestrel Series*, 1993-

SARAH ANDREWS

Mother Nature

(New York: St. Martin's Press, 1997)

Story type: Amateur Detective
Series: Em Hansen
Major character(s): Emily Hansen, Scientist (geologist)
Time period(s): 1990s
Locale(s): Santa Rosa, California; Denver, Colorado

Summary: Finding herself broke and unemployed in Denver, as well as recently divorced and estranged from her own mother, Em doesn't know what to do next. Desperate, she agrees to accept a definitely non-career assignment from a U.S. senator, who wants to send her to Santa Rosa to investigate his daughter Janet's death. Something she uncovered as part of her job as a geologist for an environmental consulting office may have gotten Janet killed, and he wants Em to find out what it was. It proves to be a more difficult and dangerous job than Em was led to expect, and not only does she meet resistance from Janet's co-workers and friends, but the senator becomes increasingly difficult to contact. To top things off, Em's mother reenters her life suddenly, and now won't leave her alone.

Where it's reviewed:
Booklist, May 15, 1997, page 1565
Kirkus Reviews, May 1, 1997, page 679
Publishers Weekly, April 14, 1997, page 59

Other books by the same author:
A Fall in Denver, 1995
Tensleep, 1994

Other books you might like:
Nevada Barr, *The Anna Pigeon Series*, 1993-
Janet Dawson, *The Jeri Howard Series*, 1990-
Susan Dunlap, *The Veejay Haskell Series*, 1983
Marcia Muller, *Where Echoes Live*, 1991
Judith Van Gieson, *The Other Side of Death*, 1991

ANNA APOSTOLOU

A Murder in Macedon

(New York: St. Martin's Press, 1997)

Story type: Historical
Major character(s): Alexander the Great, Historical Figure
Time period(s): 4th century B.C. (336 B.C.)
Locale(s): Aegae, Greece (old capital); Corinth, Greece

Summary: Philip of Macedon has summoned all of Greece to the old capital of Aegae to celebrate his reign, but the festivities are cut short when he is assassinated by Pausanias, the young captain of his guard. With the Macedonian court about to sink into chaos and war, Philip's son Alexander must assert his rights to the throne. But his mother, the Witch Queen Olympias, had been divorced and rejected by Philip, and there are rumors that Alexander is not the true heir. To prove that he was not part of a plot to murder his father, he must find out if Pausanias was a lone assassin or if he was acting upon the orders of others. First novel under this pseudonym.

Where it's reviewed:
Publishers Weekly, September 1, 1997, page 99

Other books you might like:
Ron Burns, *The Livinius Severus Series*, 1991-
Lindsey Davis, *The Marcus Didius Falco Series*, 1989-
Margaret Doody, *Aristotle, Detective*, 1978
John Maddox Roberts, *The SPQR Series*, 1990-
Steven Saylor, *The Gordianus the Finder Series*, 1991-

MARGOT ARNOLD (Pseudonym of Petronelle Cook)

The Midas Murders

(New York: Foul Play, 1997)

Story type: Amateur Detective
Series: Penny Spring and Sir Toby Glendower
Major character(s): Penny Spring, Anthropologist (American); Sir Toby Glendower, Archaeologist (British)

Time period(s): 1990s
Locale(s): Greece (Greek islands)

Summary: When the perennially globe-trotting Penny and Toby are invited to join their old friend Jules Lefau on a three-week cruise of the Greek islands, Toby warily declines but Penny sets off at once, her children and grandchildren in tow. There are many other passengers aboard the lavish yacht, many of them multimillionaires with their entire families and paramours included. When the patriarch Demetrios dies mysteriously, and then his heir is found murdered, Penny summons Toby from Oxford. He arrives just as an attempt on the life of another of Demetrios' heirs takes place. It appears as if someone is out to eradicate the whole clan.

Other books by the same author:
Dirge for a Dorset Druid, 1994
Cape Cod Conundrum, 1992
The Catacomb Conspiracy, 1991
Toby's Folly, 1990
The Menehune Murders, 1989

Other books you might like:
Sarah Caudwell, *The Shortest Way to Hades*, 1985
Aaron Elkins, *The Gideon Oliver Series*, 1982-
Dorothy Gilman, *The Mrs. Pollifax Series*, 1966-
Hammond Innes, *Levkas Man*, 1971
Aaron Marc Stein, *The Tim Mulligan and Elsie Mae Hunt Series*, 1940-1955

7

ROSEMARY AUBERT

Free Reign

(Bridgehampton, New York: Bridge Works, 1997)

Story type: Amateur Detective
Major character(s): Ellis Portal, Streetperson (former judge), Mentally Ill Person
Time period(s): 1990s
Locale(s): Toronto, Ontario, Canada

Summary: Ellis Portal was once a prominent and respected judge whose uncontrollable anger led to his monumental fall from grace. Today he lives in a packing crate in a ravine that cuts through the middle of Toronto, having left career and family behind. While tending a small secret garden he finds the freshly severed hand of a black man wearing a familiar gold ring, one of a set of five created by a wealthy law school graduate for himself and his four closest friends, Ellis included. Upon presentation of the ring, each is required to do the asker a special, one-time favor. But which of the five is doing the asking? Gradually and reluctantly Ellis puts his life back together to find the answer, and his journey of discovery leads him to a halfway house for pregnant teenagers where the daughter of a homeless woman claims her newborn baby was stolen from her. There are crime and retribution as well as heroes and a few villains in this complex and profoundly moving first mystery.

Where it's reviewed:
Kirkus Reviews, April 15, 1997, page 589
Library Journal, February 1, 1997, page 111
Maclean's, June 23, 1997, page 54

New York Times Book Review, March 30, 1997, page 23
Publishers Weekly, February 10, 1997, page 70

Other books you might like:
G.M. Ford, *The Bum's Rush*, 1997
G.D. Gearino, *Counting Coup*, 1997
Daniel Hecht, *Skull Session*, 1998
Laurie R. King, *To Play the Fool*, 1995
Abigail Padgett, *The Bo Bradley Series*, 1993-

8

LINDA BARNES

Cold Case

(New York: Delacorte, 1997)

Story type: Private Detective
Series: Carlotta Carlyle
Major character(s): Carlotta Carlyle, Detective—Private, Taxi Driver (part-time)
Time period(s): 1990s
Locale(s): Boston, Massachusetts

Summary: Thea Janis was an incandescent literary sensation who disappeared at the height of her fame 24 years ago. Although her body was never found, a madman sits convicted of her murder in a Massachusetts state prison. And then pages from a manuscript start appearing, written in a voice that is unmistakably Thea's. The Boston police don't want to touch this case, nor does Thea's politician brother, who's in the midst of a hotly contested gubernatorial race. Her sister and mother have withdrawn into worlds of their own. But pages of the new manuscript keep getting sent piecemeal to the family, along with blackmail threats, and Carlotta is called in to find out where they are coming from. Is Thea still alive? Is there a plagiarist out there? A potential murderer? Layer upon layer of family secrets must be peeled back before Carlotta solves the case.

Where it's reviewed:
Book World, April 20, 1997, page 8
Entertainment Weekly, May 2, 1997, page 53
Kirkus Reviews, February 1, 1997, page 173
New York Times Book Review, April 27, 1997, page 36
Publishers Weekly, February 17, 1997, page 213

Other books by the same author:
Hardware, 1995
Snapshot, 1993
Steel Guitar, 1991
Coyote, 1990
Snake Tattoo, 1989

Other books you might like:
Sue Grafton, *The Kinsey Millhone Series*, 1982-
Linda Grant, *The Catherine Sayler Series*, 1988-
Dennis Lehane, *The Patrick Kenzie/Angela Gennaro Series*, 1994-
Marcia Muller, *The Sharon McCone Series*, 1977-
Sara Paretsky, *The V.I. Warshawski Series*, 1982-

9

NEVADA BARR

Endangered Species

(New York: Putnam, 1996)

Story type: Action/Adventure; Police Procedural
Series: Anna Pigeon
Major character(s): Anna Pigeon, Ranger (U.S. park ranger)
Time period(s): 1990s
Locale(s): Cumberland Island National Sea, Georgia

Summary: Anna is on a three-week fire detail assignment on this remote island off the Georgia coast. It's supposed to be presuppression work, but when a plane crashes on the island, there is an actual fire to be put out before the crew can reach the dead pilot and passenger aboard. The accident seems highly suspicious to Anna and she investigates it to the best of her ability, between her regular patrols, looking after the pilot's distraught and very pregnant widow, and engaging in rowdy camaraderie with her fellow rangers. Anna stays in telephone contact with her psychiatrist sister Molly, who has been receiving some disturbing phone calls, and with her friend Frederick Stanton, an FBI agent who actually meets up with Molly to help her solve this problem. There are many other unusual and colorful characters and some harrowing action sequences, along with Barr's usual wonderful sense of place and knowledge of the details that make up a park ranger's daily life.

Where it's reviewed:
Booklist, February 15, 1997, page 1006
Kirkus Reviews, January 1, 1997, page 21
Library Journal, February 1, 1997, page 111
New York Times Book Review, April 13, 1997, page 24
Publishers Weekly, January 6, 1997, page 67

Other books by the same author:
Firestorm, 1996
Ill Wind, 1995
A Superior Death, 1994
Track of the Cat, 1993

Other books you might like:
Christine Andreae, *The Lee Squires Series*, 1992-
Virginia Lanier, *The Jo Beth Sidden Series*, 1995-
Kirk Mitchell, *The Dee Laguerre Series*, 1995-
Elizabeth Quinn, *The Lauren Maxwell Series*, 1993-
Jessica Speart, *Gator Aide*, 1996

10

STEPHANIE BARRON (Pseudonym of Francine Mathews)

Jane and the Man of the Cloth

(New York: Bantam, 1997)

Story type: Historical; Amateur Detective
Series: Jane Austen
Major character(s): Jane Austen, Writer, Historical Figure
Time period(s): 1800s (1804)
Locale(s): Lyme Regis, England (Dorset coast); High Down Grange, England

Summary: Jane and her family are en route to a quiet holiday at the seaside village of Lyme Regis when a fierce storm and overturned carriage force them to seek refuge at the forbidding manor house at High Down Grange. There Jane meets its master, the brooding and charismatic Geoffrey Sidmouth, who clearly has many secrets he'd prefer not to reveal, including the identity of the lovely young woman dressed as a peasant who shares his home. Once settled in the village, Jane starts making inquiries about Sidmouth. Then a laborer is found hanged from a makeshift gibbet by the sea, a murder the locals are convinced is the work of ''the Reverend,'' a notorious smuggler whose identity is unknown to them. In time Jane is drawn into a dangerous scheme to entrap and expose Sidmouth, despite her ambivalent feelings toward the man. Told in the form of letters and journal entries in Austen's own voice, the story is based in some small part on actual events in Jane Austen's life, never placing her at any locale that would be contrary to what is known about her movements.

Where it's reviewed:
Booklist, January 1997, page 823
Kirkus Reviews, December 1, 1996, page 1704
Library Journal, December 1996, page 151
New York Times Book Review, January 19, 1997, page 22
Publishers Weekly, November 11, 1996, page 59

Other books by the same author:
Jane and the Unpleasantness at Scargrave Manor, 1996

Other books you might like:
Bruce Alexander, *The Sir John Fielding Series*, 1994-
Robert Barnard, *The Case of the Missing Bronte*, 1983
Laurie R. King, *The Mary Russell Series*, 1994-
William Palmer, *The Wilkie Collins/Charles Dickens Series*, 1990-
Kate Ross, *The Julian Kestrel Series*, 1993-

11

GEORGE BAXT

The Clark Gable and Carole Lombard Murder Case

(New York: St. Martin's Press, 1997)

Story type: Historical; Amateur Detective
Series: Celebrity Murder Case
Major character(s): Clark Gable, Detective—Amateur (Movie star), Historical Figure; Carole Lombard, Detective—Amateur (Movie Star), Historical Figure; Herbert Villon, Police Officer (lieutenant)
Time period(s): 1930s (1939)
Locale(s): Los Angeles, California (Hollywood)

Summary: All its stars are off to the gala opening of *Gone with the Wind* in Atlanta—all but Clark Gable, that is, who shares his wife Carole Lombard's distress over the disappearance of Lydia Austin, a young actress who is Carole's protegee. And a kidnapper has been targeting the babies of Hollywood stars. With a little help from police lieutenant Herbert Villon, the dashing couple go in hot pursuit of the bad guys. Along the way many other Hollywood celebrities make appearances, from W.C. Fields to Groucho Marx, all contributing to the fun and nostalgia. Baxt draws his characters larger than life,

modeling them more on their screen personas than their private personalities, and liberally sprinkling his narrative with puns and snappy dialog.

Other books by the same author:
The William Powell and Myrna Loy Murder Case, 1996
The Humphey Bogart Murder Case, 1995
The Bette Davis Murder Case, 1994
The Mae West Murder Case, 1993
The Marlene Dietrich Murder Case, 1992

Other books you might like:
Andrew Bergman, *Hollywood and LeVine*, 1975
Max Allan Collins, *The Nate Heller Series*, 1983-
Terence Faherty, *The Scott Elliott Series*, 1996-
Patricia Hearst, *Murder at San Simeon*, 1997
   Cordelia Frances Biddle, co-author
Stuart M. Kaminsky, *The Toby Peters Series*, 1977-

12

M.C. BEATON (Pseudonym of Marion Chesney)

Agatha Raisin and the Terrible Tourist
(New York: St. Martin's Press, 1997)

Story type: Amateur Detective
Series: Agatha Raisin
Major character(s): Agatha Raisin, Public Relations (retired); James Lacey, Veterinarian
Time period(s): 1990s
Locale(s): Cyprus; Carsely, England (a village in the Cotswolds)

Summary: Agatha's beloved James has fled to Cyprus in the wake of their disastrously thwarted marriage (her still-living ex-husband showed up at the wedding most inopportunely, only to get himself murdered), and she's gone after him in hopes of repairing the relationship. But they are no sooner reunited than they witness the murder of a disagreeable tourist, and James turns oddly sullen when Agatha sets out to solve the affair. Will he ever return her love? Will she succumb instead to Charles, the baronet who appreciates her far more than James does? Stay tuned.

Where it's reviewed:
Kirkus Reviews, September 1, 1997, page 1340
Library Journal, September 1, 1997, page 223
Publishers Weekly, August 11, 1997, page 388

Other books by the same author:
Agatha Raisin and the Murderous Marriage, 1996
Agatha Raisin and the Walkers of Dembley, 1995
Agatha Raisin and the Potted Gardener, 1994
Agatha Raisin and the Vicious Vet, 1993
Agatha Raisin and the Quiche of Death, 1992

Other books you might like:
Robert Barnard, *A Little Local Murder*, 1983
Simon Brett, *Mrs. Pargeter's Package*, 1990
Elizabeth Peters, *The Amelia Peabody Series*, 1975-
Joyce Porter, *The Hon. Constance Burke Series*, 1970-1979
Colin Watson, *The Flaxborough Series*, 1967-1973

13

M.C. BEATON (Pseudonym of Marion Chesney)

Death of a Dentist
(New York: Mysterious Press, 1997)

Story type: Police Procedural; Humor
Series: Hamish Macbeth
Major character(s): Hamish Macbeth, Police Officer (Constable)
Time period(s): 1990s
Locale(s): Lochdubh, Scotland; Braikie, Scotland

Summary: A fierce toothache sends Macbeth, Lochdubh's one-man police force, to the neighboring Highlands town of Braikie for an emergency visit to its dentist. When he arrives he finds Dr. Gilchrist dead on the floor, a victim of nicotine poisoning. Considering that the deceased was a non-smoker, Macbeth suspects foul play and begins searching for a murderer. Although he'd rather be fishing or enjoying a pint at the local pub than detecting, Macbeth is far better at his job than one would guess from his laid-back manner, and it's not long before he solves the case.

Where it's reviewed:
Booklist, August 1997, page 1884
Kirkus Reviews, July 15, 1997, pge 1066
Library Journal, July 1997, page 131

Other books by the same author:
Death of a Macho Man, 1996
Death of a Nag, 1995
Death of a Charming Man, 1994
Death of a Travelling Man, 1993
Death of a Glutton, 1992

Other books you might like:
Robert Barnard, *A Little Local Murder*, 1983
J. Rhys Bowen, *Evans Above*, 1997
Gerald Hammond, *The Keith Calder Series*, 1979-
Frank Parrish, *The Dan Mallett Series*, 1977-
C.F. Roe, *The Dr. Jean Montrose Series*, 1990-

14

ALAN BEECHEY

An Embarrassment of Corpses
(New York: St. Martin's Press, 1997)

Story type: Amateur Detective; Humor
Major character(s): Oliver Swithin, Writer (children's books); Superintendent Mallard, Police Officer, Relative
Time period(s): 1990s
Locale(s): London, England

Summary: Under a pseudonym, Oliver Swithin is the author of the popular Railway Mice series of children's books, while his friend Sir Hargreaves Random writes ripping yarns for boys. Both are Lewis Carroll fans, and they are engaged in a Snark Hunt when Oliver finds his friend's body floating in a fountain in Trafalgar Square. More murders follow, each more bizarre than the last, and Oliver and his uncle, Superintendent Mallard of Scotland Yard, race against time to catch a serial killer who seems to be using the city of London as a

game board. A large cast of eccentric characters, many entertaining asides, and a low-key romance add to the fun of this first mystery.

Other books you might like:
Robert Barnard, *The Perry Trethowan Series*, 1981-
Simon Brett, *The Charles Paris Series*, 1976-
Leo Bruce, *The Carolus Deene Series*, 1955-1974
Sarah Caudwell, *Thus Was Adonis Murdered*, 1981
Andrew Taylor, *Caroline Miniscule*, 1983

15

NANCY BELL

Biggie and the Mangled Mortician

(New York: St. Martin's Press, 1997)

Story type: Amateur Detective; Humor
Series: Biggie Weatherford
Major character(s): Biggie Weatherford, Widow(er), Grandparent
Time period(s): 1990s
Locale(s): Job's Crossing, Texas

Summary: Biggie, one of the leading citizens of Job's Crossing and grandmother to twelve-year-old J.R. (who narrates the story), has her hands full directing and starring in a little theater production of Gilbert and Sullivan's *H.M.S. Pinafore*. But just before the first rehearsal, cast member and new town mortician Monk Carter drops dead. Although the medical examination shows his ribs were crushed, the death is still reported as either a heart attack or a seizure. Biggie, however, decides that the man's demise warrants an investigation, even if it means she has to carry it out herself—which she's only too eager to do.

Where it's reviewed:
Booklist, June 1, 1997, page 1665
Kirkus Reviews, May 15, 1997, page 757
Library Journal, June 1, 1997, page 156
Publishers Weekly, April 14, 1997, page 60

Other books by the same author:
Biggie and the Poisoned Politician, 1996

Other books you might like:
Jeff Abbott, *The Jordan Poteet Series*, 1994-
Alisa Craig, *Trouble in the Brasses*, 1989
Sara Hoskins Frommer, *Murder and Sullivan*, 1997
Anne George, *Murder on a Bad Hair Day*, 1996
Joan Hess, *The Maggody Series*, 1987-

16

C.C. BENISON

Death at Sandringham House

(New York: Bantam, 1997)

Story type: Amateur Detective
Series: Her Majesty Investigates
Major character(s): Jane Bee, Servant
Locale(s): Norfolk, England

Summary: The title refers to one of five royal residences, a rambling red-brick country house that was the favorite abode of George V. This tale of the murder at Christmas of a woman who is a dead ringer for Elizabeth II is narrated by a Canadian housemaid, Jane Bee, who is instructed by Her Majesty herself to do a bit of discreet investigating into the matter.

Other books by the same author:
Murder at Buckingham Palace, 1996

Other books you might like:
Robert Barnard, *Death and the Princess*, 1982
Emily Brightwell, *The Mrs. Jeffries Series*, 1993-
Dorothy Cannell, *God Save the Queen!*, 1997
H.R.F. Keating, *Mrs. Craggs: Crimes Cleaned Up*, 1985
Sharyn McCrumb, *The Windsor Knot*, 1990

17

LAURIEN BERENSON

Hair of the Dog

(New York: Kensington, 1997)

Story type: Amateur Detective
Major character(s): Melanie Travis, Animal Trainer (breeder of Standard Poodles), Teacher (special education)
Time period(s): 1990s
Locale(s): Fairfield County, Connecticut

Summary: With school out and her young son Davey away at camp, Melanie is looking forward to a relaxing summer with nothing more taxing to do than helping her Aunt Peg plan a Fourth of July barbecue for dog show exhibitors in the area. Then an obnoxious poodle handler is shot in his own driveway and Alicia, his latest lady friend, asks Melanie to investigate. Barry Turk had alienated dozens of his colleagues, particularly women, and there is no end of suspects: his ruthless young assistant, her short-tempered boyfriend, a judge with a grudge, and Alicia herself.

Where it's reviewed:
Booklist, September 1, 1997, page 62
Library Journal, September 1, 1997, page 223

Other books by the same author:
Dog Eat Dog, 1996
Underdog, 1996
A Pedigree to Die For, 1995

Other books you might like:
Melissa Cleary, *The Jackie Walsh Series*, 1992-
Susan Conant, *The Holly Winter Series*, 1989-
Virginia Lanier, *The Jo Beth Sidden Series*, 1995-
Barbara Moore, *The Doberman Wore Black*, 1983
Karen Ann Wilson, *Eight Dogs Flying*, 1994

18

CLAUDIA BISHOP (Pseudonym of Mary Stanton)

Death Dines Out

(New York: Berkley, 1997)

Story type: Amateur Detective
Series: Sarah and Meg Quilliam

Major character(s): Sarah Quilliam, Innkeeper; Meg Quilliam, Cook

Time period(s): 1990s

Locale(s): Hemlock Falls, New York; Palm Beach, Florida

Summary: The Quilliam sisters are only too happy to leave the Inn at Hemlock Falls, their bed-and-breakfast in upstate New York, for a week in Palm Beach, especially since they're getting their way paid in exchange for helping wealthy socialite Tiffany Taylor with her favorite charity. When they get there, however, it turns out that Tiffany is really bent on humiliating her ex-husband, and Sarah and Meg are caught in the middle. One of Meg's recipes is included.

Other books by the same author:
Murder Well-Done, 1996
A Pinch of Poison, 1995
A Dash of Death, 1995
A Taste for Murder, 1994

Other books you might like:
Mary Daheim, *The Bed-and-Breakfast Series*, 1991-
Anne George, *Murder Makes Waves*, 1997
Jean Hager, *The Tess Darcy Series*, 1994-
Charlotte MacLeod, *The Withdrawing Room*, 1980
Tamar Myers, *The Magdalena Yoder Series*, 1994-

19

PAUL BISHOP

Tequila Mockingbird
(New York: Scribner, 1997)

Story type: Police Procedural

Series: Fey Croaker

Major character(s): Fey Croaker, Police Officer (LAPD homicide unit supervisor)

Time period(s): 1990s

Locale(s): Los Angeles, California

Summary: When the very pregnant wife of a much-decorated officer in the anti-terrorist unit demands to see him and then fires two shots into his head, it seems a clear case of homicide. But it appears he was already dead when she fired at him. Dynamic Fey Croaker and her crack team of homicide experts are called into the case by the chief himself and wind up dealing with police corruption and interdepartmental warfare. Like Joseph Wambaugh, Bishop is a veteran of the LAPD and gives readers a clear picture of the workings of the department, including its politics, rivalries, camaraderie, and chains of command.

Other books by the same author:
Twice Dead, 1996
Kill Me Again, 1994

Other books you might like:
Linda Chase, *Perfect Cover*, 1994
    co-author Joyce St. George
Laurie R. King, *The Kate Martinelli Series*, 1993-
Christopher Newman, *The Joe Dante Series*, 1986-
Joseph Wambaugh, *The Blue Knight*, 1972
Teri White, *The Spaceman Kowalski/Blue Maguire Series*, 1984-

---

20

LAWRENCE BLOCK

The Burglar in the Library
(New York: Dutton, 1997)

Story type: Amateur Detective; Humor

Series: Bernie Rhodenbarr

Major character(s): Bernie Rhodenbarr, Thief, Businessman (Bookstore owner)

Time period(s): 1990s

Locale(s): New York (upstate); New York, New York

Summary: Bernie's plans for a cozy weekend getaway at a country bed & breakfast are dashed when his proposed companion, Lettice Runcible, announces she's getting married that same weekend, to someone else. Bernie has his heart set on staying at Cuttleford House, known for its Olde England atmosphere and its legendary collection of rare books. So he invites his lesbian dog-groomer friend Carolyn along and they set off with Bernie's cat Raffles for a quiet weekend of rest, relaxation, and burglary. What Bernie pines for is a first edition of Raymond Chandler's *The Big Sleep,* inscribed to Dashiell Hammett, but his plans to liberate it from the Cuttleford House library are interrupted by the arrival of Lettice and her husband, the advent of a sudden storm that leaves them all snowbound, the appearance of a body in the library, and the disappearance of the book before Bernie can even touch it.

Where it's reviewed:
Kirkus Reviews, June 15, 1997, page 912
New York Times Book Review, July 27, 1997, page 18
Publishers Weekly, April 28, 1997, page 53
Times Literary Supplement, August 1, 1997, page 21
Wall Street Journal (Central Edition), July 25, 1997, page A12

Other books by the same author:
The Burglar Who Thought He Was Bogart, 1995
The Burglar Who Traded Ted Williams, 1994
The Burglar Who Painted Like Mondrian, 1983
The Burglar Who Studied Spinoza, 1981
The Burglar Who Liked to Quote Kipling, 1979

Other books you might like:
John Dunning, *The Cliff Janeway Series*, 1992-
Ed Hoch, *The Thefts of Nick Velvet*, 1978
Marianne Macdonald, *Death's Autograph*, 1997
Neil McGaughey, *The Stokes Moran Series*, 1994-
Donald E. Westlake, *The Dortmunder Series*, 1971-

21

LAWRENCE BLOCK

Even the Wicked
(New York: Morrow, 1997)

Story type: Private Detective

Series: Matt Scudder

Major character(s): Matthew Scudder, Detective—Private

Time period(s): 1990s

Locale(s): New York, New York

Summary: Matt Scudder has evolved considerably from his original incarnation as an alcoholic, unlicensed, ex-cop private eye living on the edge in a cheap hotel room with a failed marriage behind him. Now he's sober, happily remarried, licensed, paying his taxes and living in a nice apartment. He's even got himself a computer. But he's still New York through and through and he still solves crimes. This time he's after a serial killer who calls himself Will—the Will of the People— and is murdering very nasty criminals the law is powerless to touch. Matt gets involved when Will targets a controversial defense attorney who's made a name for himself getting his unsavory clients off the hook. As has been his custom in the last few books, Matt turns for help to TJ, a bright black street kid who's becoming like family to Matt and Elaine.

Where it's reviewed:
Booklist, November 15, 1996, page 548
Kirkus Reviews, November 15, 1996, page 1633
Los Angeles Times Book Review, April 20, 1997, page 13
New York Times Book Review, February 16, 1997, page 28
Publishers Weekly, November 18, 1996, page 64

Other books by the same author:
A Long Line of Dead Men, 1994
The Devil Knows You're Dead, 1993
A Walk Among the Tombstones, 1992
A Ticket to the Boneyard, 1990
Out on the Cutting Edge, 1989

Other books you might like:
Thomas Adcock, *The Neil Hockaday Series*, 1989-
James Lee Burke, *The Dave Robicheaux Series*, 1987-
Stephen Greenleaf, *The John Marshall Tanner Series*, 1979-
Robert B. Parker, *The Spenser Series*, 1973-
Bill Pronzini, *The Nameless Detective Series*, 1971-

22

J.S. BORTHWICK

The Garden Plot

(New York: St. Martin's Press, 1997)

Story type: Amateur Detective
Series: Sarah Deane
Major character(s): Sarah Deane, Professor (English); Alex MacKenzie, Doctor (internist), Spouse
Time period(s): 1990s
Locale(s): Boston, Massachusetts; Europe (various countries)

Summary: Sarah and her cantankerous Aunt Julia embark on an extensive garden tour of Europe that runs into trouble at Boston's Logan Airport when the tour guide fails to show up. When it develops that Ellen Trevino's car has been found damaged on the Maine Turnpike with nobody in it, it looks as if the tour will have to go on without her. Sarah's husband, internist Alex MacKenzie, investigates on his side of the Atlantic while Sarah does a bit of snooping on hers.

Where it's reviewed:
Kirkus Reviews, February 1, 1997, page 173

Other books by the same author:
Dolly Is Dead, 1995
The Bridled Groom, 1994
Dude on Arrival, 1992

Bodies of Water, 1990
The Student Body, 1986

Other books you might like:
Nancy Atherton, *Aunt Dimity and the Duke*, 1994
M.C. Beaton, *Agatha Raisin and the Potted Gardener*, 1994
Barbara Michaels, *The Dancing Floor*, 1997
Ann Ripley, *The Louise Eldridge Series*, 1994-
John Sherwood, *Menacing Groves*, 1989

23

J. RHYS BOWEN

Evans Above

(New York: St. Martin's Press, 1997)

Story type: Police Procedural
Major character(s): Evan Evans, Police Officer (constable)
Time period(s): 1990s
Locale(s): Llanfair, Wales

Summary: After a stint in Swansea, Evan Evans returns to his home village of Llanfair, nestled at the foot of the Snowdonia Range in north Wales, to uphold law and order among the people he grew up with. Many of them share his surname: the butcher, Evans-the-Meat, the dairy owner, Evans-the-Milk, the postman, Evans-the-Mail. He doesn't expect much more than an occasional spot of poaching or public drunkenness, and the complaints of the preacher's wife that someone has destroyed her prize tomatoes fit right in. But not so the deaths of two hikers, especially when it appears they may have been murdered, and the murders may be somehow linked to the vandalized tomatoes. Both the lusty barmaid and the comely schoolteacher who are competing for his attention will have to wait. First novel.

Other books you might like:
M.C. Beaton, *The Hamish Macbeth Series*, 1985-
Glyn Carr, *Death Under Snowdon*, 1954
Sarah J. Mason, *The D.S. Trewley/Sergeant Stone Series*, 1993-
Gwen Moffat, *Die Like a Dog*, 1982
Frank Parrish, *The Dan Mallett Series*, 1977-

24

PETER BOWEN

Notches

(New York: St. Martin's Press, 1997)

Story type: Amateur Detective
Series: Gabriel Du Pre
Major character(s): Gabriel Du Pre, Inspector (cattle brand), Widow(er)
Time period(s): 1990s
Locale(s): Toussaint, Montana

Summary: Du Pre, a Metis (of mixed Indian and French-Canadian heritage) with a fiercely independent streak, finds himself searching for a serial killer. The dismembered corpses of young women have been turning up in the small ranching community where he lives with his lover Madeleine, a woman he would marry if the church would grant her permission (her

husband has not been declared legally dead). Then Madeleine's own daughter goes missing, and Du Pre steps up his investigation, trying to put himself in the serial killer's mind.

Where it's reviewed:
Armchair Detective, spring 1997, page 227
Booklist, March 15, 1997, page 121
Kirkus Reviews, December 15, 1996, page 1767
New York Times Book Review, March 2, 1997, page 20
Publishers Weekly, December 2, 1996, page 43

Other books by the same author:
Wolf, No Wolf, 1996
Specimen Song, 1995
Coyote Wind, 1994

Other books you might like:
James Lee Burke, *Black Cherry Blues*, 1989
James Crumley, *The Last Good Kiss*, 1978
Jamie Harris, *The Edge of the Crazies*, 1995
Sandra West Prowell, *When Wallflowers Die*, 1996
Judith Van Gieson, *Raptor*, 1990

25

GERRY BOYLE

Potshot
(New York: Putnam's, 1997)

Story type: Amateur Detective
Series: Jack McMorrow
Major character(s): Jack McMorrow, Journalist (freelance)
Time period(s): 1990s
Locale(s): Prosperity, Maine; Florence, Maine

Summary: When Jack meets Bobby and Melanie Mullaney, two strange but amiable hippies lobbying to legalize marijuana, he thinks he has an easy feature story for the *Boston Globe*. But Bobby's friend Coyote is a far more disturbing person, and when he and Bobby disappear, Melanie turns to Jack for help. Because she and Bobby are growing marijuana in the woods near their home, she can't turn to the police for help. The story takes Jack to Bobby's home town where he learns that Bobby might also be involved in hardcore drug trafficking. And then Bobby's burned-out car turns up with a body in the back seat. Jack needs to find out just who was murdered, and why.

Where it's reviewed:
Booklist, March 1, 1997, page 1113
Kirkus Reviews, February 1, 1997, page 174
Library Journal, March 15, 1997, page 87
New York Times Book Review, March 16, 1997, page 87
Publishers Weekly, February 3, 1997, page 98

Other books by the same author:
Lifeline, 1996
Bloodline, 1995
Deadline, 1993

Other books you might like:
Kate Clark Flora, *Silent Buddy*, 1995
Richard Hoyt, *The John Denson Series*, 1980-
Virginia Lanier, *A Brace of Bloodhounds*, 1997

Archer Mayor, *The Joe Gunther Series*, 1988-
Robert B. Parker, *The Spenser Series*, 1973-

26

JAMES D. BREWER

No Remorse
(New York: Walker, 1997)

Story type: Historical; Private Detective
Series: Luke Williamson
Major character(s): Luke Williamson, Sailor (riverboat captain), Detective—Private; Masey Baldridge, Gambler, Detective—Private; Sally Tyner, Prostitute (reformed), Detective—Private
Time period(s): 1870s (1873)
Locale(s): St. Louis, Missouri; Hardscrabble Plantation, Louisiana

Summary: Mississippi riverboat captain Luke Williamson has joined with Masey Baldridge and Sally Tyner to form the Big River Detective Agency, but so far their net profit has been a dismal five dollars. Then the widow of a man whose own son has confessed to his murder engages them to clear young Stuart Van Geer of the crime, promising them a great deal of money if they succeed. While his partners put together much of the puzzle, Williamson travels south down the Mississippi to a Louisiana plantation to search for clues lying in the dead man's past.

Where it's reviewed:
Booklist, August 1997, page 1882
Kirkus Reviews, August 1, 1997, page 1163
Library Journal, August 1997, page 139
Publishers Weekly, June 23, 1997, page 75

Other books by the same author:
No Justice, 1996
No Virtue, 1995
No Bottom, 1995

Other books you might like:
J.D. Christilian, *Scarlet Women*, 1996
Peter J. Heck, *Death on the Mississippi*, 1995
Donald Honig, *The Captain Thomas Maynard Series*, 1996-
Marian J.A. Jackson, *The Arabian Pearl*, 1990
Richard Moquist, *Eye of the Agency*, 1997

27

EDNA BUCHANAN

Margin of Error
(New York: Hyperion, 1997)

Story type: Amateur Detective
Series: Britt Montero
Major character(s): Britt Montero, Journalist (crime reporter)
Time period(s): 1990s
Locale(s): Miami, Florida; Los Angeles, California

Summary: A film crew is shooting an action movie on location in Miami, and its handsome star walks into Britt's newsroom to research his role as a government agent under deep cover as a reporter. He and Britt become involved romantically and

then become the targets of an obsessive stalker, who follows them from the movie set to the streets of Miami and finally to Los Angeles. Britt, never one to back off from a dangerous situation, resolves to get to the bottom of things. But the stalker may not be the only person planning murder, and events lead to a deadly climax deep in the bowels of the newspaper's vast press room. The author, long one of Miami's top crime reporters, gets all the details of Brett's professional life just right.

Where it's reviewed:
Booklist, May 1, 1997, page 1460
Bookworld, July 20, 1997, page 10
Kirkus Reviews, May 15, 1997, page 758
Library Journal, July 1997, page 131
Publishers Weekly, June 2, 1997, page 57

Other books by the same author:
Act of Betrayal, 1996
Suitable for Framing, 1995
Miami, It's Murder, 1994
Contents under Pressure, 1992

Other books you might like:
Jan Burke, *The Irene Kelly Series*, 1993-
Carolina Garcia-Aguilera, *The Lupe Solano Series*, 1996-
Barbara Parker, *The Gail Connor Series*, 1994-
Mary Willis Walker, *The Molly Cates Series*, 1994-
Jane Waterhouse, *The Garner Quinn Series*, 1995-

28

FIONA BUCKLEY

To Shield the Queen
(New York: Scribner's, 1997)

Story type: Historical
Major character(s): Ursula Blanchard, Widow(er)
Time period(s): 16th century (1560)
Locale(s): England

Summary: When Ursula Blanchard is widowed, Elizabeth I summons her to her court as one of her own attendants, repaying a kindness Ursula's mother once showed to Elizabeth's mother, Anne Boleyn. Although it means she must leave her small daughter with a nursemaid, Ursula is grateful for the honor. Then she is sent on the delicate mission of protecting Amy Robsart, wife of Elizabeth's Master of the Horse, Sir Robert Dudley. The queen has strong feelings for Dudley, but she would be beset by scandal if harm should come to Amy. Despite Ursula's valiant efforts, the woman is murdered, and she must find out who did it. First mystery.

Where it's reviewed:
Publishers Weekly, August 18, 1997, page 73

Other books you might like:
Michael Clynes, *The Roger Shallot Series*, 1991-
Kathy Lynn Emerson, *Face Down in the Marrow-Bone Pie*, 1997
Faye Kellerman, *The Quality of Mercy*, 1989
Edward Marston, *The Nicholas Bracewell Series*, 1988-
Leonard Tourney, *The Matthew Stock Series*, 1980-

29

JAMES LEE BURKE

Cimarron Rose
(New York: Hyperion, 1997)

Story type: Action/Adventure
Major character(s): Billy Bob Holland, Lawyer (former Texas Ranger)
Time period(s): 1990s
Locale(s): Deaf Smith, Texas

Summary: When his illegitimate son, a country musician, is falsely accused of murdering his pregnant girlfriend, Holland takes on the powerful class interests that control the small town of Deaf Smith. He also must confront his own past when a Mexican outlaw, the man responsible for Holland's mistaken murder of his own partner years ago when he was a Texas Ranger, resurfaces in the present as a DEA agent. The town's corruption is both deeper and more widespread than Holland had realized, and he finds himself once more facing his own long-renounced tendencies toward violence. He also finds himself on the receiving end of advice fom his long-dead partner. Although the Holland family has appeared in some of Burke's earlier non-crime novels, this marks Billy Bob's debut in a mystery, as well as Burke's first crime novel not to feature his Cajun cop Dave Robicheaux.

Where it's reviewed:
Booklist, June 1, 1997, page 1619
Kirkus Reviews, July 1, 1997, page 967
Library Journal, June 15, 1997, page 94
New York Times Book Review, August 10, 1997, page 18
Tribune Books, August 3, 1997, page 11

Other books by the same author:
Cadillac Jukebox, 1996
Burning Angel, 1995
Dixie City Jam, 1994
In the Electric Mist with Confederate Dead, 1993
A Stained White Radiance, 1992

Other books you might like:
James Crumley, *Bordersnakes*, 1996
Tony Hillerman, *The Fly on the Wall*, 1971
Michael McGarrity, *Tularosa*, 1996
Walter Satterthwait, *Accustomed to the Dark*, 1996
Mary Willis Walker, *The Red Scream*, 1994

30

JAN BURKE

Hocus
(New York: Simon & Schuster, 1997)

Story type: Amateur Detective
Series: Irene Kelly
Major character(s): Irene Kelly, Journalist (newspaper reporter); Frank Harriman, Police Officer (detective), Spouse
Time period(s): 1990s
Locale(s): Las Piernas, California (small Southern California town)

Summary: The unthinkable happens to Irene when her police detective husband Frank goes missing. Although a bloodstain found in his car suggests he's been murdered, a warning note left on the rearview mirror implies that he's still alive—for now. Operating on the theory that he's been kidnapped and is being held hostage, Irene marshalls all her investigative skills to find out what has happened and how she can get him back.

Where it's reviewed:
Booklist, May 1, 1997, page 1482
Kirkus Reviews, February 15, 1997, page 256
Library Journal, May 1, 1997, page 144
Publishers Weekly, March 3, 1997, page 67
Tribune Books, May 4, 1997, page 4

Other books by the same author:
Remember Me, Irene, 1996
Dear Irene, 1995
Sweet Dreams, Irene, 1994
Goodnight, Irene, 1993

Other books you might like:
Taffy Cannon, *The Nan Robinson Series*, 1993-
Barbara D'Amato, *The Cat Marsala Series*, 1990-
Wendy Hornsby, *The Maggie MacGowen Series*, 1992-
Marcia Muller, *The Sharon McCone Series*, 1977-
Peg Tyre, *The Kate Murray Series*, 1994-

31

REX BURNS

The Leaning Land
(New York: Walker, 1997)

Story type: Police Procedural
Series: Gabe Wager
Major character(s): Gabe Wager, Police Officer (homicide detective)
Time period(s): 1990s
Locale(s): Denver, Colorado; Squaw Point Ute Reservation, Colorado (southwestern)

Summary: The half-Chicano cop is asked to leave Denver to help investigate a murder on the Ute reservation, where the FBI have backed off to let the local authorities handle things. But none of them can cooperate with each other and so ask for a neutral outsider to be brought in. Matters are made worse by the efforts of a local militia to hinder the investigation.

Where it's reviewed:
Booklist, August 1997, page 1882
Kirkus Reviews, June 15, 1997, page 915
Publishers Weekly, June 2, 1997, page 57

Other books by the same author:
Bloodline, 1995
Endangered Species, 1993
The Killing Zone, 1988
Ground Money, 1986
Strip Search, 1984

Other books you might like:
Nevada Barr, *Ill Wind*, 1995
James D. Doss, *The Shaman Sings*, 1994
Warwick Downing, *A Clear Case of Murder*, 1990

Tony Hillerman, *A Thief of Time*, 1988
Manuel Ramos, *The Ballad of Gato Guerrero*, 1994

32

DOROTHY CANNELL

God Save the Queen!
(New York: Bantam, 1997)

Story type: Amateur Detective; Humor
Major character(s): Flora Hutchins, Young Woman
Time period(s): 1990s
Locale(s): England (Gossinger Hall)

Summary: When Sir Henry Gossinger announces to his stunned relatives that he's drawn up a new will bequeathing all he owns to his faithful butler Hutchins they're sure he's gone mad. It's a scandal rivaling a long-ago incident from the reign of George III when Sir Roland Gossinger was accused of stealing the Queen's silver tea strainer, causing a rift with the Royal Family that has continued through the present day. Then Hutchins goes missing, only to be found dead in a twelfth-century privy, and it looks very much like foul play. His dying words, ''God Save the Queen!'', must mean something, and his sweet young granddaughter Flora (his only heir) intends to find out. But it's a dangerous as well as tricky business, with every familiar face at gloomy Gossinger Hall possibly hiding the heart of a killer.

Where it's reviewed:
Booklist, January 1997, page 823
Kirkus Reviews, December 15, 1996, page 1768
Publishers Weekly, November 4, 1996, page 66

Other books by the same author:
How to Murder the Man of Your Dreams, 1995
How to Murder Your Mother-in-Law, 1994
Femmes Fatal, 1992
Mum's the Word, 1990
The Widows' Club, 1988

Other books you might like:
Nancy Atherton, *Aunt Dimity and the Duke*, 1994
Robert Barnard, *A Corpse in a Gilded Cage*, 1984
Robert Barnard, *Death and the Princess*, 1982
C.C. Benison, *The Jane Bee Series*, 1996-
Sharyn McCrumb, *The Windsor Knot*, 1990

33

CALEB CARR

The Angel of Darkness
(New York: Random House, 1997)

Story type: Historical
Series: Dr. Laszlo Kreizler
Major character(s): Laszlo Kreizler, Doctor (forensic psychiatry); Stevie Taggert, Orphan (former street urchin), Assistant
Time period(s): 1890s (1897); 1910s (1919)
Locale(s): New York, New York; Saratoga, New York

Summary: Dr. Kreizler and his team of crime fighters are trying to put the horrors of the John Beecham case behind

them and return to their former pursuits. Then the distraught wife of a Spanish diplomat begs for help from Kreizler's friend Sarah Howard, and Kreizler once again assembles the group to help the woman find her kidnapped infant daughter. With Spain and the U.S. poised on the brink of war, it's a delicate mission indeed. Kreizler, who practices a rudimentary form of criminal profiling, leads the team to a shocking suspect: a woman who appears to the world as a selfless, heroic nurse but may be in actuality a ruthless murderer of children. The sights, sounds and smells of turn-of-the-century New York and its neighborhoods are vividly re-created and the narrative is sprinkled with real-life characters: suffragist Elizabeth Cady, painter Albert Pinkham Ryder, and the brilliant defense lawyer Clarence Darrow, who is in the courtroom when American motherhood goes on trial. The story is narrated by Stevie Taggert, twenty-two years later.

Where it's reviewed:
Booklist, September 1, 1997, page 6
Kirkus Reviews, September 1, 1997, page 1324
New York Times (Late Edition), September 29, 1997, page E6
Publishers Weekly, August 25, 1997, page 43
Wall Street Journal (Central Edition), October 3, 1997, page A8

Other books by the same author:
The Alienist, 1994

Other books you might like:
J.D. Christilian, *Scarlet Women*, 1996
Jack Finney, *Time and Again*, 1970
H. Paul Jeffers, *The Adventure of the Stalwart Companions*, 1978
William Marshall, *The New York Detective*, 1989
Maan Meyers, *The House on Mulberry Street*, 1996

34

KAREN ROSE CERCONE

Steel Ashes

(New York: Berkley 1997)

Story type: Historical; Police Procedural
Major character(s): Milo Kachigan, Detective—Police; Helen Sorby, Activist (socialist, social worker), Journalist (muckraking reporter)
Time period(s): 1900s (1905)
Locale(s): Pittsburgh, Pennsylvania

Summary: When a fire in a run-down tenement results in the death of two of the poor immigrants who inhabit the building, Milo Kachigan is one of the policemen called out to investigate. Armenian by heritage, he has tried to conceal his origins from the department, which is dominated by Irish cops. It's immediately apparent to him that the two victims had been murdered before the fire was set. Determined to aid him in his investigation is Helen Sorby, a social worker at a nearby settlement house who has gained some local notoriety for her radical politics and who feels the murder may be linked to the socialist views held by the two victims. The investigation is made more difficult by the disappearance of two of the survivors who may have information on the events leading up to the murder. First novel.

Other books you might like:
Caleb Carr, *The Alienist*, 1994
Dianne Day, *The Fremont Jones Series*, 1995-
Gillian Linscott, *The Nell Bray Series*, 1992-
Maan Meyers, *The House on Mulberry Street*, 1996
Sarah Smith, *The Vanished Child*, 1993

35

LEE CHILD

Killing Floor

(New York: Putnam, 1997)

Story type: Action/Adventure
Major character(s): Jack Reacher, Drifter, Veteran (former military policeman)
Time period(s): 1990s
Locale(s): Margrave, Georgia

Summary: When Jack Reacher gets off the bus in the small, sleepy town of Margrave, he's arrested for the murder of an unidentified man found beaten to death on a lonely country road. It's only a short time before he's cleared of the crime, but when Reacher learns that the victim was his own brother, he begins to suspect that someone was trying to deliberately set him up. Other crimes follow. The police chief and his wife are brutally murdered and a banker disappears from his home, leaving his wife paralyzed with fear. With the help of two cops, a black homicide detective from Boston and a young woman who also takes him into her bed, he begins to untangle a vast and intricate conspiracy that almost the entire community is involved in to one degree or another. And the men orchestrating it are ruthless killers. First novel.

Where it's reviewed:
Booklist, March 15, 1997, page 1228
Kirkus Reviews, January 1, 1997, page 7
Library Journal, February 15, 1997, page 161
Publishers Weekly, January 20, 1997, page 393
Tribune Books, May 18, 1997, page 6

Other books you might like:
Robert Crais, *Indigo Slam*, 1997
Stephen Hunter, *Point of Impact*, 1993
Michael McGarrity, *Tularosa*, 1996
Carol O'Connell, *Stone Angel*, 1997
Robert B. Parker, *A Catskill Eagle*, 1985

36

P.F. CHISHOLM (Pseudonym of Patricia Finney)

A Surfeit of Guns

(New York: Walker, 1997)

Story type: Historical
Series: Sir Robert Carey
Major character(s): Sir Robert Carey, Nobleman (Deputy Warden), Historical Figure
Time period(s): 16th century (1592)
Locale(s): Carlisle, England (Cumbria); Dumfries, Scotland

Summary: Sir Robert Carey's night patrol is marred not only by having to surrender a fugitive over to the Scots at the

border and having to deal with sheep thieves, but by a faulty gun that explodes and takes the hand off one of his own men. He soon learns that the armory is full of such faulty weapons, and the high quality ones that had just been shipped from Newcastle have all been stolen. Soon the entire armory will be gone. His search for the thieves takes Carey and his men into Dumfries, where King James VI has assembled his rowdy court and where Carey's own lost love, Elizabeth, is still trapped in a desperately unhappy marriage with a tyrannical husband.

Where it's reviewed:
Booklist, May 1, 1997, page 1481
Kirkus Reviews, June 15, 1997, page 912
Library Journal, June 1, 1997, page 157

Other books by the same author:
A Season of Knives, 1996
A Famine of Horses, 1995

Other books you might like:
Fiona Buckley, *The Robsart Affair*, 1997
Michael Clynes, *The Roger Shallot Series*, 1991-
Ann Dukthas, *A Time for the Death of a King*, 1994
Kathy Lynn Emerson, *Face Down in the Marrow-Bone Pie*, 1997
Edward Marston, *The Nicholas Bracewell Series*, 1989-

37

MARGARET CHITTENDEN

Dead Men Don't Dance
(New York: Kensington, 1997)

Story type: Amateur Detective
Major character(s): Charlie Plato, Businesswoman (dance hall owner)
Time period(s): 1990s
Locale(s): Bellamy Park, California

Summary: Chaps is the hottest country-western barn and dance hall in California, located on the San Francisco peninsula about halfway between the San Andreas and Hayward faults. Charlie has her hands full running the place, but when a corpse turns up in the trunk of her friend Zack's brand-new car, she knows she's got to take some time out to resolve the situation. Zack's got plenty of motive: the dead man was his opponent in a hotly contested city council race, which makes Zack the police's prime suspect. As Charlie investigates, she learns more than she ever wanted to know about Zack's past and puts herself into serious danger.

Where it's reviewed:
Booklist, May 15, 1997, page 1566

Other books by the same author:
Dying To Sing, 1996

Other books you might like:
Earlene Fowler, *The Benni Harper Series*, 1994-
Jacqueline Girdner, *The Kate Jasper Series*, 1991-
Joan Hess, *The Arly Hanks Series*, 1987-
G.A. McKevett, *The Savannah Reid Series*, 1995-
Sarah Shankman, *The Samantha Adams Series*, 1988-

38

JILL CHURCHILL (Pseudonym of Janice Young Brooks)

Fear of Frying
(New York: Avon, 1997)

Story type: Amateur Detective; Humor
Series: Jane Jeffrey
Major character(s): Jane Jeffrey, Widow(er), Single Parent
Time period(s): 1990s
Locale(s): Illinois (Chicago suburb); Wisconsin (wilderness)

Summary: Jane and her best friend Shelly head off to the wilds of Wisconsin to check out a summer camp for kids, little realizing just how rustic their destination is. On their first night they endure a rainstorm and a soggy cookout, and after the food is gone and the guests retired, they discover that someone has used a cast-iron skillet as a murder weapon. When the police arrive, however, the corpse and all evidence of the crime have vanished. When the murder victim reappears, he seems genuinely surprised at all the fuss, and Jane decides she'd better take over the investigation before people start to doubt her sanity and somebody gets away with a murder.

Other books by the same author:
War and Peas, 1996
Silence of the Hams, 1996
From Here to Paternity, 1995
A Knife to Remember, 1994
The Class Menagerie, 1994

Other books you might like:
Jacqueline Girdner, *The Kate Jasper Series*, 1991-
Joan Hess, *The Claire Malloy Series*, 1986-
Jonnie Jacobs, *The Kate Austen Series*, 1994-
Leslie O'Kane, *The Molly Masters Series*, 1996-
Valerie Wolzien, *The Susan Henshaw Series*, 1987-

39

HARLAN COBEN

Backspin
(New York: Dell, 1997)

Story type: Amateur Detective; Humor
Series: Myron Bolitar
Major character(s): Myron Bolitar, Agent (sports), Sports Figure (former college basketball star)
Time period(s): 1990s
Locale(s): New Jersey (suburban)

Summary: Myron, who is decidedly not a golf fanatic himself, spends most of this book tracking down the kidnappers of the son of a female golf superstar and an aging golf pro. He also spends a lot of time pondering the larger mystery of how men wearing knickers can spend so much time knocking a tiny white sphere around with a stick. His own sport is basketball; he was a NBA first-round draft pick at Duke University but was sidelined for good by a knee injury. He went to law school instead and then found a second career as a sports agent, although he really functions more as a detective spe-

cialing in sports cases. The wisecracks are plentiful in all the books and the sports backgrounds are varied.

Where it's reviewed:
Publishers Weekly, June 23, 1997, page 87

Other books by the same author:
Drop Shot, 1996
Fade Away, 1996
Deal Breaker, 1995

Other books you might like:
Robert Crais, *The Elvis Cole Series*, 1987-
Charlotte Elkins, *The Lee Ofsted Series*, 1989-
Parnell Hall, *The Stanley Hastings Series*, 1987-
Gregory Mcdonald, *The Fletch Series*, 1974-1986
Richard Rosen, *The Harvey Blissberg Series*, 1984-

40

LIZA CODY (Pseudonym of Liza Nassim)

Musclebound

(New York: Mysterious Press, 1997)

Story type: Amateur Detective
Series: Eva Wylie
Major character(s): Eva Wylie, Sports Figure (professional wrestler), Security Officer (night watchman)
Time period(s): 1990s
Locale(s): London, England

Summary: Eva's professional wrestling career as the London Lassassin seems to be on the skids, she's drinking too much, and she's stuck in a dead-end job as night watchman at the junkyard where she lives. As usual, she's broke, and as usual, her favorite method of transportation is car theft, or, as she views it, serially ''borrowing'' cars that aren't being used at the moment. In one of them she finds a bag stuffed with banknotes, a discovery which vastly improves her financial situation. Then some very strange men show up at the junkyard, and suddenly her future seems very troubled indeed. Hovering in the background is private investigator Anna Lee, the star of Cody's other mystery series, but this is Eva's book—and her own mess to clean up.

Where it's reviewed:
Booklist, August 1997, page 1882
Kirkus Reviews, August 1, 1997, page 1156
Library Journal, September 1, 1997, page 223
Publishers Weekly, June 23, 1997, page 74

Other books by the same author:
Monkey Wrench, 1995
Bucket Nut, 1993

Other books you might like:
Robert Barnard, *Bodies*, 1986
Colin Bateman, *Cycle of Violence*, 1997
Jonathan Gash, *The Lovejoy Series*, 1977-
Val McDermid, *The Kate Brannigan Series*, 1992-
Barbara Seranella, *No Human Involved*, 1997

41

SUSAN CONANT

Animal Appetite

(New York: Doubleday, 1997)

Story type: Amateur Detective
Series: Holly Winter
Major character(s): Holly Winter, Journalist (columnist for dog magazine), Animal Trainer
Time period(s): 1990s
Locale(s): Cambridge, Massachusetts

Summary: When Holly is challenged by a friend to write about a subject other than dogs, she decides to research the story of Hannah Duston, an early Massachusetts settler who was captured by Native Americans and escaped to tell the tale. But her attention is distracted by another, much more recent mystery, the eighteen-year-old murder of Jack Andrews, who was apparently poisoned in the office of his small publishing company with his golden retriever chained to his desk, a mute witness to the event. The police called it suicide; his widow, and many others, insist it was murder. Holly's investigation attract the attention of the killer, who almost succeeds in dispatching Holly and her two malamutes, Rowdy and Kimi, as a result. As usual there is much lore about dogs woven into the story.

Where it's reviewed:
Kirkus Reviews, February 15, 1997, page 256
Publishers Weekly, February 3, 1997, page 97

Other books by the same author:
Stud Rites, 1996
Black Ribbon, 1995
Ruffly Speaking, 1993
Bloodlines, 1992
Gone to the Dogs, 1992

Other books you might like:
Laurien Berenson, *The Melanie Travis Series*, 1995-
Melissa Cleary, *The Jackie Walsh Series*, 1992-
Patricia Guiver, *Delilah Doolittle and the Purloined Pooch*, 1997
Virginia Lanier, *The Jo Beth Sidden Series*, 1995-
Mary Willis Walker, *Zero at the Bone*, 1991

42

MICHAEL CONNELLY

Trunk Music

(Boston: Little, Brown, 1997)

Story type: Police Procedural
Series: Harry Bosch
Major character(s): Hieronymous ''Harry'' Bosch, Detective—Police
Time period(s): 1990s
Locale(s): Los Angeles, California; Las Vegas, Nevada

Summary: Maverick homicide cop Harry Bosch is back on the job after an involuntary leave of absence, looking into the murder of a Hollywood producer whose body is found stuffed into the trunk of a Rolls-Royce. Although it's obviously a

Mafia hit, the LAPD's organized crime unit seems curiously uninterested, and Harry wonders why. When he follows the trail to the gambling casinos of Las Vegas, the case suddenly gets more complicated and Harry finds himself reassigned and under investigation himself. But it will take more than that to get him off the case.

Where it's reviewed:
Booklist, October 1, 1996, page 290
Kirkus Reviews, October 1, 1996, page 1418
Library Journal, October 1, 1996, page 130
New York Times Book Review, January 5, 1997, page 20
Publishers Weekly, Ocotber 21, 1996, page 73

Other books by the same author:
The Poet, 1996 (non-series)
The Last Coyote, 1995
The Concrete Blonde, 1994
The Black Ice, 1993
The Black Echo, 1992

Other books you might like:
James Lee Burke, *The Dave Robicheaux Series*, 1987-
Robert Crais, *The Monkey's Raincoat*, 1987
Timothy Hallinan, *The Simeon Grist Series*, 1989-
Carol O'Connell, *Mallory's Oracle*, 1993
John Sandford, *The Lucas Davenport Series*, 1989-

43

PATRICIA CORNWELL

Unnatural Exposure
(New York: Putnam's, 1997)

Story type: Police Procedural
Series: Kay Scarpetta
Major character(s): Kay Scarpetta, Doctor (Chief medical examiner)
Time period(s): 1990s
Locale(s): Richmond, Virginia

Summary: Kay has just returned from Dublin where she was examining the remains of a murder victim who had been expertly dismembered, indicating it was the work of an elusive serial killer who had been inactive for eight years. Then the remains of a woman's body, dismembered in exactly the same fashion, are found in a Virginia landfill. After she's investigated the crime scene, Kay is contacted via the internet by the killer, who invites her to download photos of the murder victim. While she and her niece Lucy, an FBI computer expert, explore the case, the local authorities try to wrap it up by charging the man who discovered the body. Then Kay discovers that the victim was exposed to a rare virus before she was murdered and that she, too, may have been infected. This is no ordinary serial killer, but one with access to a sophisticated arsenal of lethal weapons.

Where it's reviewed:
Booklist, May 15, 1997, page 1540
Bookworld, July 20, 1997, page 10
Entertainment Weekly, July 25, 1997, page 66
New York Times Book Review, July 27, 1997, page 18
Publishers Weekly, April 28, 1997, page 53

Other books by the same author:
Cause of Death, 1996
From Potter's Field, 1995
The Body Farm, 1994
Cruel and Unusual, 1993
All That Remains, 1992

Other books you might like:
D.J. Donaldson, *The Andy Broussard/Kit Franklyn Series*, 1988-
Linda Fairstein, *The Alexandra Cooper Series*, 1996-
Kathy Reichs, *Deja Dead*, 1997
Dr. Anna C. Salter, *Shiny Water*, 1997
Marianne Wesson, *Render Up the Body*, 1998

44

MICHAEL CRAFT

Flight Dreams
(New York: Kensington, 1997)

Story type: Amateur Detective
Major character(s): Mark Manning, Journalist (newspaper reporter), Homosexual
Time period(s): 1990s
Locale(s): Chicago, Illinois

Summary: Manning is investigating the disappearance of heiress Helena Carter from her North Shore estate nearly seven years ago. If she can't be found in three months, she will be declared legally dead, with the bulk of her fortune going to the Catholic Archdiocese of Chicago and the Federated Cat Clubs of America. Although it's generally believed that Mrs. Carter was murdered, Manning thinks she's still alive, and his newspaper tells him he must either prove this before the deadline is up or he's finished as a reporter. As Mark pursues his investigation, he also is trying to come to terms with his newly discovered sexual orientation when he meets and is attracted to a gay architect. First novel.

Where it's reviewed:
Booklist, June 1, 1997, page 1665
Kirkus Reviews, May 15, 1997, page 759
Library Journal, June 1, 1997, page 156

Other books you might like:
Michael Raleigh, *A Body in Belmont Harbor*, 1993
Sam Reaves, *A Long, Cold Fall*, 1991
John Morgan Wilson, *The Benjamin Justice Series*, 1996-
R.D. Zimmerman, *The Tod Mills Series*, 1995-
Mark Richard Zubro, *The Paul Turner Series*, 1991-

45

PHILIP R. CRAIG

A Deadly Vineyard Holiday
(New York: St. Martin's Press, 1997)

Story type: Amateur Detective
Series: J.W. Jackson
Major character(s): J.W. Jackson, Detective—Amateur (former police officer); Zee Madeiras, Nurse (J.W.'s wife)
Time period(s): 1990s

Locale(s): Martha's Vineyard, Massachusetts

Summary: While the President of the United States and his family vacation on Martha's Vineyard, his teenage daughter Cricket runs away in an attempt to spend some time as a normal teenager. She meets and becomes attached to J.W. and Zee, who teach her how to cook bluefish and make blueberry pancakes. It's so much fun that she convinces her parents to let her stay on the island with J.W. and Zee for a few days, accompanied by a female Secret Service agent. J.W. soon learns that there have been threats against Cricket's life, and when a local reporter who learns where Cricket is staying is murdered, J.W. discovers a conspiracy within the Secret Service itself to harm Cricket. In order to protect her, he must take matters in his own hands.

Where it's reviewed:
Booklist, June 1, 1997, page 1665
Kirkus Reviews, June 1, 1997, page 836
Library Journal, May 1, 1997, page 144
Publishers Weekly, April 14, 1997, page 59

Other books by the same author:
Death on a Vineyard Beach, 1996
A Case of Vineyard Poisoning, 1995
Off Season, 1994
Cliff Hanger, 1993
The Double-Minded Men, 1992

Other books you might like:
Rick Boyer, *The Doc Adams Series*, 1982-
Aaron Elkins, *The Gideon Oliver Series*, 1982-
Sally Gunning, *The Peter Bartholomew Series*, 1991-
Francine Mathews, *The Merry Folger Series*, 1994-

46

ROBERT CRAIS

Indigo Slam
(New York: Hyperion, 1997)

Story type: Private Detective
Series: Elvis Cole
Major character(s): Elvis Cole, Detective—Private; Joe Pike, Sidekick, Veteran (Vietnam)
Time period(s): 1990s
Locale(s): Los Angeles, California

Summary: When a fifteen-year-old girl begs Elvis to find her missing father, his first impulse is to hand the case over to Social Services. Then he sees how hard she is working to keep herself and her two siblings together and functioning. As they describe their father, he sounds like some kind of angel, but as Elvis begins to investigate he learns that the man is actually part of the criminal underworld and is on the verge of some grand scheme. While they investigate the case Elvis and Joe, his enigmatic partner, take turns baby-sitting the kids. Eventually they run afoul of a ruthless gang of counterfeiters and even more ruthless U.S. marshals. At the same time Elvis is trying to solidify his relationship with lawyer Lucy Chenier, complicated by the appearance of her mysterious ex-husband.

Where it's reviewed:
Booklist, May 1, 1997, page 1460
Kirkus Reviews, April 15, 1997, page 590

Los Angeles Times Book Review, August 17, 1997, page 9
Publishers Weekly, April 14, 1997, page 59
Tribune Books, June 15, 1997, page 101

Other books by the same author:
Sunset Express, 1996
Voodoo River, 1995
Free Fall, 1993
Lullaby Town, 1992
Stalking the Angel, 1989

Other books you might like:
Richard Barre, *The Wil Hardesty Series*, 1995-
Lee Child, *Killing Floor*, 1997
Timothy Hallinan, *The Simeon Grist Series*, 1989-
Robert B. Parker, *The Spenser Series*, 1973-
Walter Satterthwait, *The Joshua Croft Series*, 1989-

47

HAMILTON CRANE (Pseudonym of Sarah J. Mason)

Bonjour, Miss Seeton
(New York: Berkley, 1997)

Story type: Amateur Detective
Series: Miss Seeton
Major character(s): Emily Dorothea Seeton, Spinster, Teacher (retired art teacher)
Time period(s): 1970s (1974)
Locale(s): Plummergen, England; France

Summary: Miss Seeton takes a group of village schoolchildren on a day trip to France to visit World War II battlegrounds, with a side trip to a chateau where Monet's garden is being rcreated by the Comte de Balivernes. The count turns out to be a wartime comrade of Plummergen's own Sir George Colveden, and when he returns the visit by coming to the village himself, a woman is found murdered. As usual Miss Seeton, armed with her sketchpad and her sharp wits, is called upon to help the police find the culprit. This series was originated by Heron Carvic in 1968 and continued by other writers with Sarah J. Mason taking over in 1991.

Where it's reviewed:
Kirkus Reviews, August 15, 1997, page 1264
Publishers Weekly, July 21, 1997, page 187

Other books by the same author:
Sweet Miss Seeton, 1996
Sold to Miss Seeton, 1995
Miss Seeton Undercover, 1994
Miss Seeton Rules, 1994
Starring Miss Seeton, 1994

Other books you might like:
M.C. Beaton, *The Agatha Raisin Series*, 1992-
Simon Brett, *The Mrs. Pargeter Series*, 1986-
Agatha Christie, *The Miss Marple Series*, 1930-1976
Hazel Holt, *The Mrs. Malory Series*, 1989-
Patricia Wentworth, *The Miss Silver Series*, 1928-1961

48

DEBORAH CROMBIE

Dreaming of the Bones

(New York: Scribner's, 1997)

Story type: Police Procedural
Series: Duncan Kincaid/Gemma James
Major character(s): Duncan Kincaid, Police Officer (Scotland Yard inspector); Gemma James, Police Officer (Scotland Yard sergeant); Victoria McClellan, Scholar (Kincaid's ex-wife)
Time period(s): 1990s
Locale(s): Cambridge, England

Summary: Although the book is set at modern-day Cambridge University, its plot strands go back to the Edwardian milieu of poet Rupert Brooke and the Cambridge student culture of the sixties. Kincaid is unexpectedly called upon for help by his ex-wife Victoria McClellan, a feminist scholar at Cambridge who is writing a biography of Lydia Brooke, a poet who tried to emulate her famous namesake when she was a student in the 1960s. After a tumultuous youth, a disastrous marriage, and several failed suicide attempts, Lydia settled into her comfortable middle years, making it difficult for Vic to believe she eventually did take her own life. Duncan agrees to investigate the long-ago incident, but his reinvolvement with Vic and her son begins to impact his relationship with Gemma. This is the richest and most textured novel the author has written to date.

Where it's reviewed:
Booklist, September 1, 1997, page 62
Kirkus Reviews, September 1, 1997, page 1343
Publishers Weekly, August 4, 1997, page 69

Other books by the same author:
Mourn Not Your Dead, 1996
Leave the Grave Green, 1995
All Shall Be Well, 1994
A Share in Death, 1993

Other books you might like:
P.D. James, *An Unsuitable Job for a Woman*, 1972
Nora Kelly, *In the Shadow of King's*, 1984
Jill McGown, *The Chief Inspector Lloyd & Sergeant Judy Hill Series*, 1983-
Veronica Stallwood, *The Kate Ivory Series*, 1993-
Jill Paton Walsh, *The Imogen Quy Series*, 1993-

49

LAURA CRUM

Roughstock

(New York: St. Martin's Press, 1997)

Story type: Amateur Detective
Series: Gail McCarthy
Major character(s): Gail McCarthy, Veterinarian
Time period(s): 1990s
Locale(s): California (Lake Tahoe); Santa Cruz, California

Summary: Equine veterinarian Gail McCarthy leaves her home town of Santa Cruz for a conference on equine health in Lake Tahoe. The schedule promises to leave her plenty of time for skiing and maybe a spot of gambling, but she's barely unpacked her bags when a fellow horse vet is found dead and another accused of the murder. The author's genuine love of horses, dogs, and most other animals make this a treat for kindred spirits.

Where it's reviewed:
Kirkus Reviews, July 15, 1997, page 1067
Publishers Weekly, June 2, 1997, page 56

Other books by the same author:
Hoofprints, 1996
Cutter, 1995

Other books you might like:
Lydia Adamson, *The Dr. Nightingale Series*, 1994-
Virginia Anderson, *Blood Lies*, 1989
Carolyn Banks, *The Robin Vaughn Series*, 1993-
Jody Jaffe, *The Natalie Gold Series*, 1995-
Lillian M. Roberts, *Riding for a Fall*, 1996

50

MARY DAHEIM

September Mourn

(New York: Avon, 1997)

Story type: Amateur Detective
Series: Judith McMonigle Flynn
Major character(s): Judith McMonigle Flynn, Innkeeper
Time period(s): 1990s
Locale(s): Seattle, Washington; Washington (isolated island)

Summary: Judith and her ditzy cousin Renie agree to manage a fellow innkeeper's bed-and-breakfast on a rustic and very isolated island. It's a chance to escape the daily grind at their own inn in Seattle, and the owner is an old school chum of Judith's. However, one of the guests at the island retreat is so demanding that Renie loses it and beans him with a heavy china dish. Moments later, presumably woozy from the blow, the man takes a fatal tumble down the stairs. Renie is convinced she killed the lout; Judith sets out to prove that she didn't and begins sorting through the island's oddly assorted inhabitants to find out who might have done the fellow in.

Where it's reviewed:
Publishers Weekly, July 7, 1997, page 66

Other books by the same author:
Nutty as a Fruitcake, 1996
Auntie Mayhem, 1996
Murder, My Suite, 1995
Major Vices, 1995
A Fit of Tempera, 1994

Other books you might like:
Claudia Bishop, *The Sarah Quilliam Series*, 1994-
Jo Dereske, *The Miss Zukas Series*, 1994-
Jean Hager, *The Tess Darcy Series*, 1994-
Charlotte MacLeod, *The Withdrawing Room*, 1980
Tamar Myers, *The Magdalena Yoder Series*, 1994-

51

CONOR DALY

Outside Agency

(New York: Kensington, 1997)

Story type: Amateur Detective
Series: Kieran Lenahan
Major character(s): Kieran Lenahan, Sports Figure (professional golfer)
Time period(s): 1990s
Locale(s): Orlando, Florida; Gainesville, Florida

Summary: Lawyer turned golf pro Kieran Lenahan has finally realized his lifelong dream of a place on the prestigious PGA tour. But it's cut short when he receives a blow to his head on the seventeenth tee at Orlando's Bay Hill Classic. Two weeks later he's found in an apartment in Gainesville along with the body of a murdered woman. He has no idea who she was or what he is doing in her apartment, but the police consider him a prime suspect. He has no answers and no alibi, because he has no memory. But being a golfer, this doesn't keep him from his game, and he heads for the Sawgrass Players Club and his shot at a career-making championship. After that, all he has to do is reconstruct the last two weeks of his life.

Where it's reviewed:
Booklist, March 15, 1997, page 1228
Kirkus Reviews, April 1, 1997, page 504
Library Journal, April 1, 1997, page 133
Publishers Weekly, February 24, 1997, page 66

Other books by the same author:
Buried Lies, 1996
Local Knowledge, 1995

Other books you might like:
Harlan Coben, *Backspin*, 1997
Charlotte Elkins, *The Lee Ofsted Series*, 1989-
    Aaron Elkins, co-author
John Logue, *Murder on the Links*, 1996
Keith Miles, *The Alan Saxon Series*, 1986-
Robert Upton, *Dead on the Stick*, 1986

52

BARBARA D'AMATO

Hard Bargain

(New York: Scribner's, 1997)

Story type: Amateur Detective
Series: Cat Marsala
Major character(s): Cat Marsala, Journalist (investigative reporter); Harold McCoo, Police Officer (chief of detectives)
Time period(s): 1990s
Locale(s): Chicago, Illinois

Summary: When Chicago cop Shelley Daniello responds to a domestic violence call, it turns out the victim is her own sister. The husband, also a police officer, is about to stab his wife with a knife and Daniello is forced to shoot to kill. In the aftermath of the incident Harold McCoo, Chief of Detectives, comes under attack by the media for his actions; some factions think he is protecting Shelley because she's a police

officer, others believe he is persecuting her because she's a woman. Because it's an election year, the pressure is intense, and Cat decides to help out her old friend McCoo by looking into some of the discrepancies arising from reports of the shooting. But before she can sort things out, McCoo is pulled from the case, and a bomb explodes in his office.

Where it's reviewed:
Booklist, September 1, 1997, page 63
Kirkus Reviews, August 1, 1997, page 1156
Publishers Weekly, June 30, 1997, page 69

Other books by the same author:
Hard Christmas, 1995
Hard Case, 1994
Hard Women, 1993
Hard Luck, 1992
Hard Tack, 1991

Other books you might like:
Jan Burke, *The Irene Kelly Series*, 1993-
Susan Kelly, *The Liz Connors Series*, 1985-
Sara Paretsky, *The V.I. Warshawski Series*, 1982-
Nancy Pickard, *Marriage Is Murder*, 1987
Mary Willis Walker, *The Molly Cates Series*, 1995-

53

JEANNE M. DAMS

Holy Terror in the Hebrides

(New York: Walker, 1997)

Story type: Amateur Detective
Series: Dorothy Martin
Major character(s): Dorothy Martin, Widow(er)
Time period(s): 1990s
Locale(s): Scotland (Island of Iona in the Hebrides); Sherebury, England

Summary: Transplanted American widow Dorothy Martin, on holiday from her new home in the English cathedral town of Sherebury, is visiting the Scottish island of Iona when a young American falls to his death from the rocks in Fingal's cave. Because he seems to have offended all the members of the ecumenical tour group he was traveling with, Dorothy suspects murder—a suspicion shared by the local constabulary. And then a sudden storm cuts the island off from the outside world and leaves Dorothy stranded in a hotel with all her prime suspects. The history of the island (a real place, settled by an irish monk in 563 and the point from which Christianity spread into England) is lovingly worked into the story.

Other books by the same author:
Trouble in the Town Hall, 1996
The Body in the Transept, 1995

Other books you might like:
M.C. Beaton, *The Hamish Macbeth Series*, 1985-
Teri Holbrook, *A Far and Deadly Cry*, 1995
Hazel Holt, *The Mrs. Malory Series*, 1989-
Josephine Tey, *The Singing Sands*, 1952
Peter Tremayne, *The Sister Fidelma Series*, 1994-

54

DIANE MOTT DAVIDSON

The Grilling Season

(New York: Bantam, 1997)

Story type: Amateur Detective
Series: Goldy Bear Schulz
Major character(s): Goldy Bear Schulz, Caterer; Tom Schulz, Police Officer (Goldy's husband)
Time period(s): 1990s
Locale(s): Aspen Meadow, Colorado

Summary: Goldy has to take time off from her thriving business, Goldilocks' Catering, when her abusive doctor ex-husband—fondly known to his ex-wives as The Jerk—is accused of murdering his latest girlfriend. Although part of her rejoices that he may finally have gotten what he deserves when he's imprisoned, she's also concerned for their son Arch, who is extremely distressed that his father is in jail and begs Goldy to turn sleuth again and prove The Jerk is innocent. As she examines the facts, Goldy comes up with more questions than answers, but it's clear that many people hated the dead woman and that she seemed to have had some powerful hold over them. Included are a number of recipes from Goldy's kitchen.

Where it's reviewed:
Booklist, August 1997, page 1884
Kirkus Reviews, August 15, 1997, page 1261
Publishers Weekly, July 7, 1997, page 53

Other books by the same author:
The Main Corpse, 1996
Killer Pancake, 1995
The Last Suppers, 1994
The Cereal Murders, 1993
Dying for Chocolate, 1992

Other books you might like:
Tamar Myers, *The Magdalena Yoder Series*, 1994-
Katherine Hall Page, *The Faith Fairchild Series*, 1990-
Nancy Pickard, *The 27-Ingredient Chile Con Carne Murders*, 1993
    a continuation of Virginia Rich's Eugenia Potter series
Virginia Rich, *The Mrs. Eugenia Potter Series*, 1982-
Lou Jane Temple, *The Heaven Lee Series*, 1996-

55

LINDSEY DAVIS

Time to Depart

(New York: Mysterious Press, 1997)

Story type: Historical
Series: Marcus Didius Falco
Major character(s): Marcus Didius Falco, Detective—Private; Helena Justina, Noblewoman, Lover
Time period(s): 1st century (73)
Locale(s): Rome, Ancient Civilization

Summary: One of the most crooked mobsters in Emperor Vespasian's Rome has finally been convicted of a capital crime. According to Roman law, any citizen condemned to death is allowed "time to depart" and seek safety in exile outside the empire. As Falco watches Balbinus Pius set sail, he's convinced he can quit detective work at last and turn his attentions to some pressing personal matters: like how to conceal Helena's pregnancy from her senator father. Then the people who helped convict Balbinus start turning up dead, and once again Falco must put aside family matters and find out who in Rome's underworld is determined to exact revenge for their leader's exile.

Where it's reviewed:
Booklist, January 1997, page 824
Kirkus Reviews, November 15, 1996, page 1634
Library Journal, December 1996, page 151
Publishers Weekly, December 9, 1996, page 64

Other books by the same author:
Last Act in Palmyra, 1996
Poseidon's Gold, 1993
The Iron Hand of Mars, 1992
Venus in Copper, 1991
Shadows in Bronze, 1990

Other books you might like:
Ron Burns, *The Livinius Severus Series*, 1991-
John Maddox Roberts, *The SPQR Series*, 1990-
Lynda S. Robinson, *The Lord Meren Series*, 1994-
Steven Saylor, *The Gordianus the Finder Series*, 1991-
Marilyn Todd, *I, Claudia*, 1995

56

JANET DAWSON

Witness to Evil

(New York: Fawcett, 1997)

Story type: Private Detective
Series: Jeri Howard
Major character(s): Jeri Howard, Detective—Private
Time period(s): 1990s
Locale(s): Oakland, California; Paris, France

Summary: When Jeri is hired to track down a runaway teenager in Paris, she can scarcely believe her luck. When she does catch up with her, Jeri finds Darcy Stefano to be a far more self-composed, purposeful young woman than she had been led to expect. Her reason for the trip is twofold: to visit Holocaust memorials and to meet the French family who sheltered her grandmother as a young girl from the Nazis. Back home in the Bay Area, Darcy comes across evidence that Nazism is alive and well, even in California in the 90s. And Jeri must protect Darcy from some very dangerous consequences of her discovery.

Where it's reviewed:
Booklist, September 1, 1997, page 63
Kirkus Reviews, September 1, 1997, page 1343
Publishers Weekly, July 21, 1997, page 187

Other books by the same author:
A Credible Threat, 1996
Nobody's Child, 1995
Don't Turn Your Back on the Ocean, 1994
Take a Number, 1993
Till the Old Men Die, 1993

Other books you might like:
Linda Grant, *The Catherine Sayler Series*, 1988-
Laurie R. King, *With Child*, 1996
Janet LaPierre, *The Cruel Mother*, 1990
Marcia Muller, *The Sharon McCone Series*, 1977-
Gloria White, *The Ronnie Ventana Series*, 1991-

57

DIANNE DAY

The Bohemian Murders

(New York: Doubleday, 1997)

Story type: Historical; Amateur Detective
Series: Fremont Jones
Major character(s): Caroline Fremont Jones, Businesswoman (owner of a typewriting service)
Time period(s): 1900s (1906)
Locale(s): Carmel-by-the-Sea, California

Summary: Forced to leave San Francisco after the earthquake and fire of 1906, Fremont decides to seek out her suitor Michael Archer in the bohemian beach community of Carmel-by-the-Sea. But she finds Michael completely changed and apparently indifferent to her, so she accepts a job as temporary keeper of the Point Pinos lighthouse, where she can start up her typewriting business again and sort out her feelings in solitude. Then the body of a dead woman washes up on the beach by the lighthouse and Fremont is off detecting again. As unconventional as she is for her day, she is outdone by the free spirits and artists who live in Carmel. She also does her best to uncover the truth about Michael's seeming change of heart.

Where it's reviewed:
Kirkus Reviews, June 1, 1997, page 836
Library Journal, July 1997, page 131
New York Times Book Review, July 27, 1997, page 18
Publishers Weekly, May 19, 1997, page 69
Tribune Books, July 27, 1997, page 11

Other books by the same author:
Fire and Fog, 1996
The Strange Files of Fremont Jones, 1995

Other books you might like:
Carole Nelson Douglas, *The Irene Adler Series*, 1990-
Marian J.A. Jackson, *The Abigail Danforth Series*, 1990-
Laurie R. King, *The Mary Russell Series*, 1994-
Robin Paige, *The Kathryn Ardleigh Series*, 1994-
Teona Tone, *The Kyra Keaton Series*, 1983-

58

JEFFERY DEAVER

The Bone Collector

(New York: Viking, 1997)

Story type: Police Procedural
Major character(s): Lincoln Rhyme, Criminologist (former head of NYPD forensics), Handicapped (quadriplegic); Amelia Sachs, Police Officer (beat cop)
Time period(s): 1990s

Locale(s): New York, New York

Summary: An accident on the job left Lincoln Rhyme, one of the nation's foremost criminalists, a quadriplegic who is able to move just one finger. Embittered and reclusive at first, he sees a crime-scene report about a corpse buried on a deserted West Side railroad track that causes him to give up his retirement and put his keen intellect back to work deciphering the ingenious clues left by a serial killer known as the Bone Collector. He drafts Amelia Sachs, a beat cop with a flair for police work (although she's never worked a crime scene before), to act as his arms and legs. Together they make a formidable team, well up to the challenge posed by the Bone Collector.

Where it's reviewed:
Booklist, December 15, 1996, page 692
Kirkus Reviews, December 15, 1996, page 1752
Library Journal, February 1, 1997, page 105
New York Times Book Review, March 16, 1997, page 28
Publishers Weekly, December 16, 1996, page 40

Other books by the same author:
A Maiden's Grave, 1995
Praying for Sleep, 1993
The Lesson of Her Death, 1992
Mistress of Justice, 1992
Hard News, 1991

Other books you might like:
D.J. Donaldson, *The Andy Broussard/Kit Franklyn Series*, 1988-
Thomas Harris, *The Silence of the Lambs*, 1988
William Love, *The Bishop Regan/Davey Goldman Series*, 1990-
Ridley Pearson, *The Lou Boldt/Daphne Matthews Series*, 1988-
John Sandford, *The Lucas Davenport Series*, 1989-

59

NORA DELOACH

Mama Stalks the Past

(New York: Bantam, 1997)

Story type: Amateur Detective
Series: Grace Covington
Major character(s): Grace "Candi" Covington, Social Worker (African-American); Simone Covington, Lawyer
Time period(s): 1990s
Locale(s): Otis, South Carolina

Summary: When Simone takes a break from her Atlanta law firm and returns to her home town for a little rest and relaxation, she's greeted not by her mother but by a man named Nat Mixon, son of a reclusive neighbor, who's ranting and raving about how Mama stole his inheritance. It seems that his mother, a sour old woman with whom Mama had never exchanged two words, left all she had to Mama. It turns out that not only did the old lady have 250 acres of land but she died of arsenic poisoning, and soon tongues are wagging. Then Nat Mixon is poisoned, and Mama and daughter Simone have some serious sleuthing to do in order to clear Mama's good name.

Other books by the same author:
Mama Saves a Victim, 1997
Mama Traps a Killer, 1995
Mama Solves a Murder, 1994

Other books you might like:
Eleanor Taylor Bland, *The Marti McAlister Series*, 1992-
Terris McMahan Grimes, *The Theresa Galloway Series*, 1996-
Barbara Neely, *Blanche on the Lam*, 1992
Chassie West, *Sunrise*, 1994
James Yaffe, *A Nice Murder for Mom*, 1988

60

JO DERESKE

Out of Circulation

(New York: Avon, 1997)

Story type: Amateur Detective
Series: Miss Zukas
Major character(s): Miss Helma Zukas, Librarian
Time period(s): 1990s
Locale(s): Cascade Mountains, Washington; Bellhaven, Washington

Summary: Miss Zukas isn't exactly thrilled about joining her friend Ruth for a hiking trip in the Cascades. But if you're going to do something, do it right, and the slightly starchy and always thorough librarian promptly does some bookish research on what to take into the wilderness. Unfortunately, her survival manuals don't tell her what to do when you find a climber with a hole in his chest. After the victim is airlifted off the mountain, Helma and Ruth go searching for his missing companion, only to get stranded in a blinding snowstorm just as they locate him. They all end up holed in a remote mountain cabin with a group of snowbound strangers, none of whom are what they seem to be and one of whom is probably the murderer.

Other books by the same author:
Miss Zukas and the Raven's Dance, 1996
Miss Zukas and the Stroke of Death, 1995
Miss Zukas and the Island Murders, 1994
Miss Zukas and the Library Murders, 1994

Other books you might like:
Jeff Abbott, *The Jordan Poteet Series*, 1994
Nevada Barr, *Firestorm*, 1996
Jill Churchill, *Fear of Frying*, 1997
Mary Daheim, *September Mourn*, 1997
Susan Steiner, *Library: No Murder Allowed*, 1993

61

COLIN DEXTER

Death Is Now My Neighbor

(New York: Crown, 1997)

Story type: Police Procedural
Series: Inspector Morse
Major character(s): Inspector Morse, Police Officer
Time period(s): 1990s

Locale(s): Oxford, England

Summary: As tranquil as the historic quadrangle of Lonsdale College seems, it's really the scene of a desperate struggle between two senior dons, Denis Cornford and Julian Storrs, to succeed the retiring Master of Lonsdale. And the only two people to whom the appointment means more are their wives. Meanwhile, a young woman is shot in her North Oxford home, and Chief Inspector Morse and his partner Sergeant Lewis investigate. The trail leads to a tabloid journalist, to the strip clubs of Soho, and eventually to the university. It begins to look as if the Mastership of Lonsdale may be a post worth killing for.

Where it's reviewed:
Booklist, December 1, 1996, page 619
Entertainment Weekly, April 4, 1997, page 79
Kirkus Reviews, February 1, 1997, page 174
New York Times Book Review, March 2, 1997, page 20
Publishers Weekly, December 30, 1996, page 57

Other books by the same author:
The Daughters of Cain, 1994
The Way through the Woods, 1992
The Jewel That Was Ours, 1991
The Wench Is Dead, 1989
The Secret of Annexe 3, 1986

Other books you might like:
John Harvey, *The Charlie Resnick Series*, 1989-
Reginald Hill, *The Andrew Dalziel/Peter Pascoe Series*, 1970-
P.D. James, *The Adam Dalgliesh Series*, 1966-
Sheila Radley, *The Douglas Quantrill Series*, 1979-
Ruth Rendell, *The Inspector Wexford Series*, 1965-

62

MICHAEL DIBDIN

Cosi Fan Tutti

(New York: Pantheon, 1997)

Story type: Police Procedural
Series: Aurelio Zen
Major character(s): Aurelio Zen, Police Officer (inspector)
Time period(s): 1990s
Locale(s): Naples, Italy

Summary: Due to political uneasiness in Rome, Zen finds himself in Naples as commander of the harbor detail, a considerable demotion for him. In his spare time he assumes a secret identity, ''Alfonso Zembla,'' and becomes involved with a wealthy and glamorous Neapolitan widow who wants ''Dottor'' Zembla to talk her daughters out of marrying their Mafia-associated fiances. This results in his being mistaken for the head of Naples' most notorious crime families, and takes time away from a number of crimes he's expected to solve in his official post, from runaway garbage trucks to disappearances to officer impersonators. If the plot sounds familiar, it's right out of the Mozart opera of the title, which Dibdin turns on its ear as he takes his normally serious inspector on a wildly comic ride.

Where it's reviewed:
Book World, May 25, 1997, page 1

Kirkus Reviews, May 1, 1997, page 680
Library Journal, May 1, 1997, page 144
New York Times Book Review, May 11, 1997, page 26
Publishers Weekly, April 7, 1997, page 77

Other books by the same author:
Dead Lagoon, 1994
Cabal, 1992
Vendetta, 1990
Ratking, 1988

Other books you might like:
Peter Inchbald, *The Inspector Franco Corti Series*, 1982-
Donna Leon, *The Guido Brunetti Series*, 1992-
Magdalen Nabb, *The Marshal Guarnaccia Series*, 1981-
Kate Ross, *The Devil in Music*, 1997
Edward Sklepowich, *The Urbino MacIntyre Series*, 1990-

JOANNE DOBSON

Quieter than Sleep

(New York: Doubleday, 1997)

Story type: Amateur Detective
Major character(s): Karen Pelletier, Professor (English)
Time period(s): 1990s
Locale(s): Enfield College, East Coast

Summary: Emily Dickinson scholars are scrambling for clues when a fellow English professor gets himself strangled to death with his own flashy tie at a particularly deadly faculty party. Heading up the amateur side of the investigation is Dickinson scholar Karen Pelletier, who was the last person—not counting the murderer, of course—to talk to the dead professor. However, Lieutenant Piotrowski of the local police isn't so sure that Karen might not have been the last person, period, to have contact with him. But when a student is found dead he starts casting a somewhat wider net. Her death is difficult to fathom, but there are plenty of people who would have liked to see the philandering profesor dead. And when Piotrowski asks Karen to help him, he has no idea what danger he's putting her in. A first mystery full of literary lore and very little gore.

Other books you might like:
Amanda Cross, *Poetic Justice*, 1970
Susan Kenney, *Graves of Academe*, 1985
Jane Langton, *Emily Dickinson Is Dead*, 1984
Lev Raphael, *The Edith Wharton Murders*, 1997
Edith Skom, *The George Eliot Murders*, 1995

64

P.C. DOHERTY

A Tournament of Murders

(New York: St. Martin's Press, 1997)

Story type: Historical
Series: Canterbury Tales
Major character(s): Sir Gilbert Savage, Knight
Time period(s): 14th century (1356)
Locale(s): London, England; Canterbury, England

Summary: Subtitled *The Franklin's Tale of Mystery and Murder as He Goes on Pilgrimage from London to Canterbury*, this is the third in the author's series based on Chaucer's *Canterbury Tales*. It opens with the victory of the Black Prince. During the fight, a squire lies dying and reveals to his knight, Gilbert Savage, information about his true parentage and his father's disgraceful death. As the truth evolves into a tale of duplicity and murder, Gilbert is compelled to avenge his father's name.

Where it's reviewed:
Booklist, September 1, 1997, page 63
Kirkus Reviews, September 1, 1997, page 1340
Library Journal, August 1997, page 140
Publishers Weekly, July 21, 1997, page 188

Other books by the same author:
A Tapestry of Murders, 1996
An Ancient Evil, 1995

Other books you might like:
Duane Crowley, *Riddle Me a Murder*, 1987
Umberto Eco, *The Name of the Rose*, 1983
Susanna Gregory, *The Matthew Bartholomew Series*, 1996-
Paul Harding, *The Brother Athelstan Series*, 1991-
Candace M. Robb, *The Owen Archer Series*, 1993-

65

D.J. DONALDSON

Sleeping with the Crawfish

(New York: St. Martin's Press, 1997)

Story type: Police Procedural
Series: Andy Broussard/Kit Franklyn
Major character(s): Andy Broussard, Doctor (medical examiner); Kit Franklyn, Psychologist (police)
Time period(s): 1990s
Locale(s): New Orleans, Louisiana

Summary: When a cadaver turns up with fingerprints that match those of a convict supposedly serving time in a Louisiana state prison, Andy Broussard sends his former colleague Kit Franklyn to the prison to investigate. When she gets there, he's gone. Prison officials claim he died during the night and was cremated immediately. Unable to get any cooperation, Kit heads back home only to be run off the road by a speeding car, right into the bayou, where she loses consciousness as her car fills with water. Meanwhile Broussard pursues another lead that teams him up with a policewoman to whom he becomes attracted. The plot that's gradually uncovered involves the murder of a leading scientific researcher.

Other books by the same author:
Louisiana Fever, 1996
New Orleans Requiem, 1994
No Mardi Gras for the Dead, 1992
Blood on the Bayou, 1991
Cajun Nights, 1988

Other books you might like:
James Lee Burke, *The Dave Robicheaux Series*, 1987-
Patricia Cornwell, *The Kay Scarpetta Series*, 1990-
Sarah Lovett, *The Sylvia Strange Series*, 1995-
Kathy Reichs, *Deja Dead*, 1997

Julie Smith, *The Skip Langdon Series*, 1990-

66

JAMES D. DOSS

The Shaman's Bones

(New York: Avon, 1996)

Story type: Police Procedural
Series: Charlie Moon and Scott Parris
Major character(s): Charlie Moon, Police Officer (tribal), Indian (Southern Ute); Scott Parris, Police Officer (chief, Granite City); Daisy Perika, Shaman, Indian (Ute)
Time period(s): 1990s
Locale(s): Granite City, Colorado (Southern Ute Reservation); Wind River Reservation, Wyoming

Summary: When old Daisy Perika tells her nephew Charlie Moon about a dream in which she sees an upside-down corpse with its eyes torn out, the tribal policeman wishes she would just stay put in her trailer home on the reservation. But Charlie's friend Scott Parris, the *matukach* (white) police chief of nearby Granite City, puts a lot more stock in Daisy's vision and immediately cancels his vacation, expecting the worst. She's been right too many times in the past. Her vision seems to come true when Provo Frank, a Ute high school classmate of Charlie's, is accused of murdering his wife while on a trip to the Wind River reservation in Wyoming and nailing her body head down to a tree, where her eyes are pecked out by birds. Provo returns to Colorado, where he leaves his five-year-old daughter in cousin Daisy's care after first calling the tribal chairman to announce that he has in his possession a mysterious and powerful object that belongs to the Ute people, an object that appears to have been stolen from another elderly Ute shaman who has lived in Wyoming for many years. There are many extraordinary characters populating the reservation, particularly Daisy herself, a cantankerous and fiercely independent old woman who is frequently visited by a *pitukupf*, a dwarf who lives in badger caves and can be summoned to the surface by offerings of tobacco. While visions and magic play a part in the story, the crime is still solved by old-fashioned police work with all the traditional motives of greed, vengeance, and jealousy at play.

Where it's reviewed:
Booklist, August 1997, page 1884
Kirkus Reviews, August 15, 1997, page 1261
Library Journal, September 1, 1997, page 222
New York Times Book Review, September 7, 1997, page 34
Publishers Weekly, July 28, 1997, page 57

Other books by the same author:
The Shaman Laughs, 1995
The Shaman Sings, 1994

Other books you might like:
Margaret Coel, *The Ghost Walker*, 1996
Jean Hager, *The Molly Bearpaw Series*, 1992-
Tony Hillerman, *The Joe Leaphorn and Jim Chee Series*, 1970-
Jake Page, *The Stolen Gods*, 1993
Aimee Thurlo, *The Ella Clah Series*, 1995-
   David Thurlo, co-author

67

CAROLE NELSON DOUGLAS

Cat in a Flamingo Fedora

(New York: Forge, 1997)

Story type: Amateur Detective; Humor
Series: Midnight Louie
Major character(s): Midnight Louie, Animal (large black tomcat); Temple Barr, Public Relations
Time period(s): 1990s
Locale(s): Las Vegas, Nevada

Summary: Midnight Louie is thinking how much he'd enjoy starring in cat-food commercials while his redheaded human partner, Temple Barr, is taking a breather from crime by helping the world-famous conceptual artist Domingo swathe Las Vegas landmarks in nine hundred thousand pink flamingoes. But crime is always just around the corner for this pair, and this time it's the murder of the beloved comic actor Darren Cooke. He had asked Temple to find out if the woman who had been stalking him was his unacknowledged daughter, but before she could find out he was shot on the set. Now she has to sort through all the women in his life to find his murderer.

Where it's reviewed:
Kirkus Reviews, April 15, 1997, page 591
Publishers Weekly, April 21, 1997, page 64

Other books by the same author:
Cat with an Emerald Eye, 1996
Cat in a Diamond Dazzle, 1996
Cat in a Crimson Haze, 1995
Cat on a Blue Monday, 1994
Pussyfoot, 1993

Other books you might like:
Garrison Allen, *The Big Mike Series*, 1994-
Marian Babson, *Nine Lives to Murder*, 1994
Lilian Jackson Braun, *The Cat Who Series*, 1966-
Rita Mae Brown, *The Sneaky Pie Series*, 1990-
Shirley Rousseau Murphy, *The Joe Grey Series*, 1996-

68

TONY DUNBAR

Trick Question

(New York: Putnam's, 1997)

Story type: Legal
Series: Tubby Dubonnet
Major character(s): Tubby Dubonnet, Lawyer
Time period(s): 1990s
Locale(s): New Orleans, Louisiana

Summary: When Cletus Busters, a laboratory maintenance worker, is found holding the frozen head of the lab's most prestigious researcher in his hands, it looks like and open-and-shut case of murder. But when Tubby takes over for Busters' court-appointed lawyer, he begins to wonder if his client's claims of innocence aren't the truth. At the same time he's working for another client, a female boxer with an abusive

boyfriend, and trying to referee the romantic entanglements of his ex-wife and three daughters.

Where it's reviewed:
Booklist, January 1997, page 824
Kirkus Reviews, November 15, 1996, page 1634
New York Times Book Review, January 19, 1997, page 22
Publishers Weekly, December 2, 1996, page 44

Other books by the same author:
Trick Question, 1997
City of Beads, 1995
Crooked Man, 1994

Other books you might like:
D.J. Donaldson, *The Andy Broussard/Kit Franklyn Series*, 1988-
Sophie Dunbar, *The Claire Claiborne Series*, 1993-
Dick Lochte, *Blue Bayou*, 1992
Julie Smith, *The Skip Langdon Series*, 1990-
Chris Wiltz, *The Neal Rafferty Series*, 1981-

69

SUSAN DUNLAP

Cop Out

(New York: Delacorte, 1997)

Story type: Police Procedural
Series: Jill Smith
Major character(s): Jill Smith, Police Officer
Time period(s): 1990s
Locale(s): Berkeley, California

Summary: As usual, Jill is not on the best of terms with her precinct (she has a reputation for not always bending to authority) when she's summoned by her friend, the irascible private eye Herman Ott. He wants to meet her in the lobby of Berkeley's sumptuous Claremont hotel but won't tell her why. When she arrives, Ott continues to be coy about the reasons, telling her he will call her in an hour to explain. Of course he doesn't, and when Jill goes looking for him the next day he's nowhere to be found, but there is a corpse in his car as well as in his office. Jill is as concerned with finding her friend as solving the mystery of the dead bodies, and as she investigates, she finds herself in deeper trouble than ever with her own department. Once again the city of Berkeley and its varied and eccentric inhabitants play a major role in the story.

Where it's reviewed:
Booklist, May 1, 1997, page 1481
Kirkus Reviews, March 1, 1997, page 336
Publishers Weekly, February 17, 1997, page 213

Other books by the same author:
Sudden Exposure, 1996
Time Expired, 1993
Death and Taxes, 1992
Too Close to the Edge, 1987
Not Exactly a Brahmin, 1985

Other books you might like:
Laurie R. King, *The Kate Martinelli Series*, 1993-
M.D. Lake, *The Peggy O'Neil Series*, 1989-
Margaret Maron, *The Sigrid Harald Series*, 1981-

Francine Mathews, *The Merry Folger Series*, 1994-
Lillian O'Donnell, *The Norah Mulcahaney Series*, 1973-

70

CAROLA DUNN

Damsel in Distress

(New York: St. Martin's Press, 1997)

Story type: Historical; Amateur Detective
Series: Daisy Dalrymple
Major character(s): Daisy Dalrymple, Journalist
Time period(s): 1920s (1923)
Locale(s): England (Surrey)

Summary: The Honourable Phillip Petrie has finally met the girl of his dreams: Gloria Arbuckle, the daughter of an American millionaire industrialist. Their courtship is unpleasantly interrupted when the Arbuckles' car breaks down alongside a quiet country road and, while Petrie tries to repair it, they are set upon by thugs. Phillip is left bound hand and foot on the Dalrymple estate, where his old friend Daisy comes to his rescue. But Gloria has been kidnapped and her father is warned not to go to the police if he wants to see her alive again. So it's up to Daisy and her pals to rescue her.

Other books by the same author:
Murder on the Flying Scotsman, 1997
Requiem for a Mezzo, 1996
The Winter Garden Mystery, 1995
Death at Wentwater Court, 1994

Other books you might like:
James Anderson, *The Affair of the Blood-Stained Egg Cosy*, 1977
K.K. Beck, *The Iris Cooper Series*, 1984-
Laurie R. King, *A Letter of Mary*, 1997
Dorothy L. Sayers, *Whose Body?*, 1923
Charles Todd, *A Test of Wills*, 1996

71

GRACE EDWARDS

If I Should Die

(New York: Doubleday, 1997)

Story type: Amateur Detective
Major character(s): Mali Anderson, Student (graduate), Police Officer (former cop)
Time period(s): 1990s
Locale(s): New York, New York (Harlem)

Summary: Mali Anderson is an African-American graduate student, formerly a cop until discrimination drove her off the force. She's on her way to pick up her orphaned nephew Alvin at the Uptown Children's Chorus when she and her Great Dane, Ruffin, arrive upon a crime scene where a man lies on the street with a bullet hole in his head as a car speeds away. The dead man turns out to be her friend Erskin Harding, tour director of the chorus, and the dazed young boy on the sidewalk is possibly the intended target of a kidnapper. Mali doesn't much trust the police, except for Tad Honeywell, but as she pursues the investigation on her own, there are more

murders and she begins getting threatening voice mail. First mystery.

Where it's reviewed:
Booklist, May 1, 1997, page 1481
Kirkus Reviews, May 1, 1997, page 681
Library Journal, April 1, 1997, page 132
New York Times Book Review, June 15, 1997, page 35
Publishers Weekly, March 10, 1997, page 52

Other books you might like:
Eleanor Taylor Bland, *The Marti McAlister Series*, 1992-
Terris McMahan Grimes, *The Theresa Galloway Series*, 1996-
Barbara Neely, *The Blanche White Series*, 1992-
Valerie Wilson Wesley, *The Tamara Hayle Series*, 1994-
Chassie West, *Sunrise*, 1994

72

RUTH DUDLEY EDWARDS

Murder in a Cathedral
(New York: St. Martin's Press, 1997)

Story type: Amateur Detective; Humor
Series: Robert Amiss
Major character(s): Robert Amiss, Historian (former civil servant); Baroness ''Jack'' Troutbeck, Noblewoman
Time period(s): 1990s
Locale(s): Westonbury Cathedral, England

Summary: At the behest of his flamboyant and blithely politically incorrect friend Baroness Troutbeck, Robert Amiss agrees to act as troubleshooter for an old flame of hers, Bishop-elect David Elworthy. His cathedral is in an uproar over the appointment of a new dean, Norm Cooper, a fundamentalist American with a crazed wife. Little does Amiss realize that's he's walking into a veritable maelstrom of scandal, as Cooper is determined to rid the church of its radical gay priests, feminist witches, and evil cult members whom he claims have ruled the church for decades. When the dean turns up dead, there is an untold number of suspects to sift through. The author, who has taken on academe, the British civil service, men's clubs and other peculiar institutions, here skewers the Church of England.

Where it's reviewed:
Kirkus Reviews, June 1, 1997, page 836
Library Journal, June 1, 1997, page 156
New York Times Book Review, June 15, 1997, page 35
Publishers Weekly, May 26, 1997, page 70
Times Literary Supplement, February 28, 1997, page 23

Other books by the same author:
Ten Lords A Leapin', 1996
Matricide at St. Martha's, 1994
Clubbed to Death, 1992
The English School of Murder, 1990
St. Valentine's Day Murders, 1985

Other books you might like:
Robert Barnard, *Blood Brotherhood*, 1997
Kate Charles, *A Drink of Deadly Wine*, 1991
Diane M. Greenwood, *Clerical Errors*, 1991
Mollie Hardwick, *Parson's Pleasure*, 1987

Barbara Whitehead, *The Dean It Was That Died*, 1991

73

SELMA EICHLER

Murder Can Wreck Your Reunion
(New York: Signet, 1997)

Story type: Private Detective
Series: Desiree Shapiro
Major character(s): Desiree Shapiro, Detective—Private
Time period(s): 1990s
Locale(s): New York, New York (Manhattan); Clear Cove, New York (Long Island)

Summary: Desiree's niece Ellen goes off for a weekend bash thrown by a former sorority sister who is celebrating her divorce at her elegant Long Island home. But during the festivities one of the four women participating, all former college classmates, takes a swan dive from the terrace into an empty swimming pool and is killed instantly. Because she and the dead woman had been estranged for years and their anomisity toward each other was obvious to everybody present, the police suspect Ellen of the murder, and it's up to her chubby Aunt Desiree to find out what really happened.

Other books by the same author:
Murder Can Stunt Your Growth, 1996
Murder Can Ruin Your Looks, 1995
Murder Can Kill Your Social Life, 1994

Other books you might like:
Carol Higgins Clark, *The Regan Reilly Series*, 1992-
Janet Evanovich, *The Stephanie Plum Series*, 1992-
Joan Hess, *Poisoned Pins*, 1993
Toni L.P. Kelner, *The Laura Fleming Series*, 1993-
G.A. McKevett, *The Savannah Reid Series*, 1995-

74

AARON ELKINS

Twenty Blue Devils
(New York: Mysterious Press, 1997)

Story type: Amateur Detective
Series: Gideon Oliver
Major character(s): Gideon Oliver, Anthropologist
Time period(s): 1990s
Locale(s): Tropical Island (Tahiti)

Summary: When the manager of Tahiti's Paradise Coffee plantation dies after falling from a cliff, Gideon Oliver is called in to investigate. The plantation is the source of the Blue Devil, the world's most expensive coffee bean, and the man's death is the latest in a series of unnerving accidents that have plagued the owners. Foul play does seem to be a possibility, given the cutthroat world of the coffee industry, about which we learn a great deal in this pleasant tale. As usual, Gideon—nicknamed the Bone Detective—is forced to ply his trade of examining skeletons under some very unusual and trying conditions.

Where it's reviewed:
Booklist, January 1997, page 824

Entertainment Weekly, January 17, 1997, page 58
Kirkus Reviews, November 1, 1996, page 1565
New York Times Book Review, January 19, 1997, page 22
Publishers Weekly, November 25, 1996, page 59

Other books by the same author:
Dead Men's Hearts, 1994
Make No Bones, 1994
Icy Clutches, 1990
Curses!, 1989
Old Bones, 1987

Other books you might like:
Margot Arnold, *The Penny Spring/Sir Toby Glendower Series*, 1979-
D.J. Donaldson, *The Andy Broussard/Kit Franklyn Series*, 1988-
Julie Smith, *The Sourdough Wars*, 1984
Aaron Marc Stein, *The Tim Mulligan and Elsie Mae Hunt Series*, 1940-1955
Donald E. Westlake, *Kahawa*, 1982

75

CHARLOTTE ELKINS
AARON ELKINS, Co-Author

Nasty Breaks
(New York: Mysterious Press, 1997)

Story type: Amateur Detective
Series: Lee Ofsted
Major character(s): Lee Ofsted, Sports Figure (professional golfer)
Time period(s): 1990s
Locale(s): New England (Block Island)

Summary: Between tournaments and needing some cash, Lee takes a job against her better judgment substituting at a week-long golf school on an island off the New England coast. It turns into a far more exciting job than she had anticipated, however, as her teaching duties quickly take a back seat to kidnapping, ransom, and murder, and to protect herself Lee must do a bit of investigating.

Where it's reviewed:
Publishers Weekly, September 1, 1997, page 99

Other books by the same author:
Rotten Lies, 1995
A Wicked Slice, 1989

Other books you might like:
Jack Bickham, *The Charity Ross Series*, 1967-
Harlan Coben, *Backspin*, 1997
Conor Daly, *The Kieran Lanahan Series*, 1995
John Logue, *Murder on the Links*, 1996
Keith Miles, *Flagstick*, 1991

76

BEN ELTON

Popcorn
(New York: St. Martin's Press, 1997)

Story type: Humor; Action/Adventure
Major character(s): Bruce Delamitri, Director (movie)
Locale(s): Los Angeles, California (Hollywood)

Summary: Bruce Delamitri is Hollywood's hottest young director, known for his stylish, incredibly cool movies about killers. They're all postmodern cinematic milestones that have brought critics and fans alike to his feet. On Oscar night he's about to be honored by his peers when Wayne and Scout enter his life. Wayne and Scout are real killers, psychos who kill people they don't know just for the fun of it. And tonight they've decided to take Delamitri hostage. First mystery.

Where it's reviewed:
Books Magazine, June 1997, page 18
Kirkus Reviews, September 1, 1997, page 1326
Publishers Weekly, September 1, 1997, page 92

Other books you might like:
Larry Beinhart, *American Hero*, 1993
Stan Cutler, *The Rayford Goodman/Mark Bradley Series*, 1991-
Carl Hiaasen, *Double Whammy*, 1987
Elmore Leonard, *Get Shorty*, 1990
Lindsay Maracotta, *The Dead Celeb*, 1997

77

EARL EMERSON

The Dead Horse Paint Company
(New York: Morrow, 1997)

Story type: Amateur Detective
Series: Mac Fontana
Major character(s): Mac Fontana, Fire Fighter (fire chief)
Time period(s): 1990s
Locale(s): Staircase, Washington (small town near Seattle)

Summary: Years ago a devastating fire at The Dead Horse Paint Company, a huge old barn of a store, took a tragic toll, partly as a result of a firefighting team that committed a series of grave errors and ended up trying to cover its tracks. Now the Seattle firefighting community is about to attend a seminar on the fire, at which the old fire chief in charge of the operation will be asked to defend himself before his peers. But before he can do so, he's found dead in the trunk of a car, burned to a crisp, in a snowstorm. Fontana, who had hoped he would find life simple and uncomplicated in tiny Staircase, searches for the man's killer.

Where it's reviewed:
Kirkus Reviews, May 15, 1997, page 759
Publishers Weekly, May 12, 1997, page 61

Other books by the same author:
Going Crazy in Public, 1996
Morons and Madmen, 1993
Help Wanted: Orphans Preferred, 1990

Black Hearts and Slow Dancing, 1988

Other books you might like:
Nevada Barr, *Firestorm*, 1996
Peter Lance, *First Degree Burn*, 1997
Ridley Pearson, *Beyond Recognition*, 1997
Shelly Reuben, *Spent Matches*, 1996
Stella Shepherd, *Embers of Death*, 1996

78

EARL EMERSON

Deception Pass

(New York: Ballantine, 1997)

Story type: Private Detective
Series: Thomas Black
Major character(s): Thomas Black, Detective—Private
Time period(s): 1990s
Locale(s): Seattle, Washington

Summary: "Mother Teresa with a bankroll" is how Thomas Black describes Lainie Smith, a client of his lawyer wife Kathy who turns to him when she is being blackmailed. Now a major benefactor to countless Seattle charities, particularly those helping children, she was once a rebellious teen who hooked up with a drifter named Charlie and may have been an eyewitness to murder in the shadow of the steep cliffs of Deception Pass and the tumultuous waters below. Now somebody who knows the truth about the incident is blackmailing her, and she can't tell Black exactly why.

Where it's reviewed:
Publishers Weekly, September 1, 1997, page 100

Other books by the same author:
The Million Dollar Tattoo, 1996
The Vanishing Smile, 1995
The Portland Laugher, 1994
Yellow Dog Party, 1991
Deviant Behavior, 1988

Other books you might like:
G.M. Ford, *The Leo Waterman Series*, 1995-
Stephen Greenleaf, *The John Marshall Tanner Series*, 1979-
Richard Hoyt, *The John Denson Series*, 1980-
J.A. Jance, *The J.P. Beaumont Series*, 1985
Ridley Pearson, *The Lou Boldt/Daphne Matthews Series*, 1988-

79

LOREN D. ESTLEMAN

Never Street

(New York: Mysterious Press, 1997)

Story type: Private Detective
Series: Amos Walker
Major character(s): Amos Walker, Detective—Private
Time period(s): 1990s
Locale(s): Detroit, Michigan

Summary: Gay Catalin's husband has vanished, and she thinks he may be in real trouble. Lately he's been obsessed with *noir* crime movies from the '40s, even building a state-of-the-art home movie theater for viewing them in the comfort of his upscale suburban home and often watching them over and over again in a single marathon sitting. As he follows the trail of the missing husband, Amos is brought to the lavishly restored Fox movie palace in downtown Detroit, where the nightmarish conclusion to his investigation is played out.

Where it's reviewed:
Booklist, March 15, 1997, page 1229
Kirkus Reviews, February 15, 1997, page 257
Publishers Weekly, February 10, 1997, page 70
Tribune Books, April 13, 1997, page 5

Other books by the same author:
Sweet Women Lie, 1990
Silent Thunder, 1989
Every Brilliant Eye, 1988
Downriver, 1988
Lady Yesterday, 1987

Other books you might like:
Gary Hardwick, *Cold Medina*, 1996
Rob Kantner, *The Ben Perkins Series*, 1986-
Bill Pronzini, *The Nameless Detective Series*, 1971-
Les Roberts, *The Milan Jacovich Series*, 1988-
Jonathan Valin, *The Harry Stoner Series*, 1980-

80

JANET EVANOVICH

Three to Get Deadly

(New York: Simon & Schuster, 1997)

Story type: Private Detective; Humor
Series: Stephanie Plum
Major character(s): Stephanie Plum, Bounty Hunter; Joe Morelli, Police Officer (homicide investigator)
Time period(s): 1990s
Locale(s): Trenton, New Jersey

Summary: When Stephanie is assigned to haul in Mo Bedemier, a beloved Trenton ice cream vendor who was apprehended while packing a weapon he didn't have a permit for and then skipped out on his bond, she finds it anything but the routine case she'd expected. A slightly illegal search lands her in an uncomfortable spot when she awakens from a blow to her head—right next to a dead body. Despite their off-on romantic relationship, detective Joe Morelli is forced to move her up to the top of his suspect list, and she finds the tables turned on her when she's targeted by the Trenton police. She's also been targeted by some mysterious masked thugs who keep shooting at her and promise they won't stop until she gives up looking for Mo.

Where it's reviewed:
Armchair Detective, Winter 1997, page 94
Booklist, December 1, 1996, page 620
Kirkus Reviews, November 15, 1996, page 1634
Library Journal, December 1996, page 151
New York Times Book Review, February 16, 1997, page 28

Other books by the same author:
Two for the Dough, 1996
One for the Money, 1995

Other books you might like:
Selma Eichler, *The Desiree Shapiro Series*, 1994-
Sparkle Hayter, *The Robin Hudson Series*, 1995-
Lindsay Maracotta, *The Lucy Freers Series*, 1997-
Marissa Piesman, *The Nina Fischman Series*, 1989-
Gillian Roberts, *The Amanda Pepper Series*, 1987-

81

LINDA FAIRSTEIN

Likely To Die

(New York: Scribner, 1997)

Story type: Legal
Series: Alexandra Cooper
Major character(s): Alexandra Cooper, Lawyer (Assistant District Attorney)
Time period(s): 1990s
Locale(s): New York, New York

Summary: A barely alive neurosurgeon at the Mid-Manhattan Medical Center is found in her blood-soaked office after being sexually assaulted, stabbed repeatedly, and left for dead. Alexandra Cooper, head of the D.A.'s sex crimes unit, puts together a team of investigators. Suspects are everywhere, given the fact that the hospital has 1500 beds and is connected to a psychiatric facility as well. Then there is the maze of tunnels beneath the building, inhabited by transients who often sneak in dressed in hospital clothing. With a heavy workload to handle, Alex finds she's stretched to the limit, and she becomes personally involved when she finds that the man she's been dating has a connection to the case.

Where it's reviewed:
Booklist, May 1, 1997, page 1460
Kirkus Reviews, April 1, 1997, page 505
Library Journal, May 1, 1997, page 138
Publishers Weekly, May 12, 1997, page 57
Time, May 26, 1997, page 104

Other books by the same author:
Final Jeopardy, 1996

Other books you might like:
Patricia Cornwell, *The Kay Scarpetta Series*, 1990-
Frances Fyfield, *The Helen West Series*, 1988-
Christine McGuire, *The Kathryn Mackay Series*, 1993-
Kathy Reichs, *Deja Dead*, 1997
Marianne Wesson, *Render Up the Body*, 1998

82

QUINN FAWCETT

Against the Brotherhood

(New York: Forge, 1997)

Story type: Historical
Major character(s): Mycroft Holmes, Gentleman, Investigator; Patterson Erskine Guthrie, Secretary
Time period(s): 1880s (1887)
Locale(s): London, England

Summary: It's widely known that Mycroft Holmes was Sherlock's older, smarter, and much stouter brother, and yet rela-

tively little else is known of him or his exploits. He kept rooms in Pall Mall, just across from his beloved Diogenes Club, he virtually controlled the British government from behind the scenes, and he seldom left his small corner of London. Now we learn that he raised herbs of all varieties and employed a young man named Guthrie as his personal secretary, who becomes the chronicler of a most unusual adventure here. He also employed an actor whose impersonations of him are essential to his accomplishments and a superannuated ex-army officer (who may also be a spy) as his manservant. One morning a cryptic letter along with some encoded documents arrive in Mycroft's chambers and Guthrie is soon dispatched, in disguise, in his employer's first round in a titanic battle against a far-reaching and totally evil cabal whose goal is simply to conquer the world. First mystery.

Where it's reviewed:
Kirkus Reviews, August 15, 1997, page 1262
Publishers Weekly, August 11, 1997, page 389

Other books you might like:
Martin H. Greenberg, *Holmes for the Holidays*, 1996
    anthology of Sherlock Holmes pastiches by various writers
Laurie R. King, *The Mary Russell Series*, 1994-
Nicholas Meyer, *The Canary Trainer*, 1993
Larry Millett, *Sherlock Holmes and the Red Demon*, 1996
Jo Soares, *A Samba for Sherlock*, 1997

83

KATE CLARK FLORA

An Educated Death

(New York: Forge, 1997)

Story type: Amateur Detective
Series: Thea Kozak
Major character(s): Thea Kozak, Businesswoman (educational consultant), Widow(er)
Time period(s): 1990s
Locale(s): Sedgewick, Massachusetts

Summary: Thea gets a phone call from her friend Dorrie Chapin, headmistress of the Bucksport School about 30 miles outside of Boston, saying that one of her female students had drowned in an icy pond on the school property. She asks Thea for advice on how to handle the situation, and Thea agrees to fly out to provide counseling for students and faculty as well as to evaluate the school's safety procedures. When it turns out that the young woman was pregnant, Thea begins to have suspicions about the circumstances of her death and starts to investigate. But none of the students wants to talk about the dead girl.

Where it's reviewed:
Kirkus Reviews, August 15, 1997, page 1262
Publishers Weekly, July 21, 1997, page 187

Other books by the same author:
Death in a Funhouse Mirror, 1995
Chosen for Death, 1994

Other books you might like:
Linda Barnes, *The Carlotta Carlyle Series*, 1987-
P.M. Carlson, *The Maggie Ryan Series*, 1985-
Wendy Hornsby, *The Maggie MacGowen Series*, 1993-

Nancy Pickard, *The Jenny Cain Series*, 1984-
Gillian Roberts, *The Amanda Pepper Series*, 1987-

84

G.M. FORD

The Bum's Rush

(New York: Walker, 1997)

Story type: Private Detective
Series: Leo Waterman
Major character(s): Leo Waterman, Detective—Private
Time period(s): 1990s
Locale(s): Seattle, Washington

Summary: Leo Waterman is back, along with his ''boys,'' the crew of homeless alcoholic men who often help him with his investigations. This time one of them is missing, and Leo goes looking for him, as well as for a larcenous librarian who has taken the city for a couple of hundred thousand dollars. And when a homeless woman says she's the mother of a rock superstar whose death by overdose was actually murder, he goes looking for the record producer who may have set it up. The action moves back and forth between the mainstream world of the lead characters and the streets and alleys where Leo's homeless helpers live out their lives.

Where it's reviewed:
Publishers Weekly, March 10, 1997, page 53
Tribune Books, May 4, 1997, page 4

Other books by the same author:
Cast in Stone, 1996
Who in Hell Is Wanda Fuca?, 1995

Other books you might like:
Robert Crais, *The Elvis Cole Series*, 1987-
Earl Emerson, *The Thomas Black Series*, 1985-
Richard Hoyt, *The John Denson Series*, 1980-
Walter Satterthwait, *The Joshua Croft Series*, 1989-
John Straley, *The Cecil Younger Series*, 1992-

85

KATHERINE V. FORREST

Apparition Alley

(New York: Berkley, 1997)

Story type: Police Procedural
Series: Kate Delafield
Major character(s): Kate Delafield, Police Officer (homicide detective), Lesbian
Time period(s): 1990s
Locale(s): Los Angeles, California

Summary: Kate, a former Marine and a dedicated police officer, here investigates the murder of a fellow officer who was on the verge of coming out. At the same time, with police misconduct on the rise in the department, Kate also agrees to represent a cop charged with shooting an unarmed civilian in a drug-infested alley.

Where it's reviewed:
Booklist, September 1, 1997, page 63

Kirkus Reviews, August 1, 1997, page 1156
Library Journal, September 1, 1997, page 222
Publishers Weekly, August 11, 1997, page 389

Other books by the same author:
Liberty Square, 1996
Murder by Tradition, 1991
The Beverly Malibu, 1989
Murder at the Nightwood Bar, 1986
Amateur City, 1984

Other books you might like:
Sarah Dreher, *The Stoner McTavish Series*, 1985-
Laurie R. King, *The Kate Martinelli Series*, 1993-
Elizabeth Pincus, *The Nell Fury Series*, 1992-
J.M. Redmann, *The Michelle ''Micky'' Knight Series*, 1990-
Mary Wings, *The Emma Victor Series*, 1987-

86

MARGARET FRAZER (Pseudonym of Gail Bacon)

The Prioress' Tale

(New York: Berkley, 1997)

Story type: Historical
Series: Sister Frevisse
Major character(s): Dame Frevisse, Religious (nun)
Time period(s): 15th century (1439)
Locale(s): England

Summary: After Domina Alys was made prioress, St. Frideswide's was rapidly becoming little more than a guest house for her numerous relatives, the Godfreys. As hosteler of the priory, and bound by St. Benedict's Rule to offer food and shelter to all travelers, Dame Frevisse is painfully aware that the house's modest stores are rapidly being depleted by the Godfrey clan. Further, the cloistered serenity of the priory is constantly being disrupted by visitors, making it difficult for the nuns to lead the silent, contemplative life they're pledged to uphold. When a family rivalry leads to kidnapping and eventually murder, it's up to Frevisse to rid the nunnery of these unwelcome—and lethal—guests.

Where it's reviewed:
Publishers Weekly, June 23, 1997, page 88

Other books by the same author:
The Murderer's Tale, 1996 (this and earlier titles co-authored by Mary Kuhfeld)
The Boy's Tale, 1995
The Bishop's Tale, 1994
The Outlaw's Tale, 1994
The Servant's Tale, 1993

Other books you might like:
Paul Harding, *The Brother Athelstan Series*, 1994-
Sharan Newman, *Death Comes as Epiphany*, 1993
Ellis Peters, *The Brother Cadfael Series*, 1977-1994
Candace M. Robb, *The Nun's Tale*, 1995
Peter Tremayne, *The Sister Fidelma Series*, 1994-

87

KINKY FRIEDMAN

Road Kill

(New York: Simon & Schuster, 1997)

Story type: Private Detective
Series: Kinky Friedman
Major character(s): Kinky Friedman, Detective—Private; Willie Nelson, Musician (country singer, actual person)
Time period(s): 1990s
Locale(s): New York, New York (Greenwich Village)

Summary: When his old friend Willie Nelson turns up full of grief and misplaced guilt over the death of an Indian medicine man who he believes has put an ancient curse on him, Kinky makes it his job to cheer Willie up, no matter what the cost. Then one of Willie's band members is shot, obviously having been mistaken for the singer, and Kinky realizes that whether an Indian curse has anything to do with it or not, Willie is indeed in grave danger. He summons the Village Irregulars to lend a hand, as well as some visiting Indians from a touring rock band, a bottle of Irish whiskey, and his faithful but always inscrutable cat. The narrative is spiced with the usual assortment of irreverent and often hilarious one-liners that could only be inspired by this author's unique world view.

Where it's reviewed:
Kirkus Reviews, August 1, 1997, page 1157
Publishers Weekly, July 21, 1997, page 188

Other books by the same author:
The Love Song of J. Edgar Hoover, 1996
God Bless John Wayne, 1995
Armadillos & Old Lace, 1994
Elvis, Jesus & Coca-Cola, 1993
Musical Chairs, 1992

Other books you might like:
Lawrence Block, *The Bernie Rhodenbarr Series*, 1978-
Parnell Hall, *The Stanley Hastings Series*, 1987-
Sandra Scoppettone, *The Lauren Laurano Series*, 1991-
Roger L. Simon, *The Moses Wine Series*, 1973-
Jesse Sublett, *The Martin Fender Series*, 1990-

88

DALE FURUTANI (Pseudonym of Dale Flanagan)

The Toyotomi Blades

(New York: St. Martin's, 1997)

Story type: Amateur Detective
Series: Ken Tanaka
Major character(s): Ken Tanaka, Computer Expert (unemployed; Japanese-American)
Time period(s): 1990s
Locale(s): Tokyo, Japan; Los Angeles, California

Summary: When Japanese-American mystery buff Ken Tanaka journeys to the land of his ancestors for the first time, he's surprised to discover that the samurai sword he bought at a Los Angeles garage sale is a rare 17th-century blade connected to the Toyotomi clan. Ken is very pleased to learn that he might be able to turn a tidy profit on his find, but he's not so pleased when he meets up with the two yakuza thugs who are stalking him.

Where it's reviewed:
Publishers Weekly, August 25, 1997, page 49

Other books by the same author:
Death in Little Tokyo, 1996

Other books you might like:
E.V. Cunningham, *The Masao Masuto Series*, 1967-1984
Sujata Massey, *The Salaryman's Wife*, 1997
James Melville, *The Inspector Otani Series*, 1979-
Laura Joh Rowland, *The Sano Ichiro Series*, 1994-
Peter Tasker, *Buddha Kiss*, 1997
Ann Wingate, *The Mark Shugata Series*, 1988-
Ann Woodward, *The Exile Way*, 1996

89

FRANCES FYFIELD (Pseudonym of Frances Hegarty)

Without Consent

(New York: Viking, 1997)

Story type: Legal
Series: Helen West
Major character(s): Helen West, Lawyer (Crown prosecutor); Geoffrey Bailey, Police Officer (superintendent)
Time period(s): 1990s
Locale(s): London, England

Summary: Crown prosecutor Helen West is especially concerned about a string of rapes she is investigating because the evidence points to a police officer who is also the best friend of her lover, Superintendent Geoffrey Bailey. The portrait that emerges is of a cold-blooded sociopath who understands women's deepest secrets and insecurities and is able to charm them with gifts and seeming tenderness, only to rape—or even murder—them and leave no trace of himself. Helen's developing relationship with Geoffrey acts as a counterpoint into her investigation into a case that haunts her every waking moment.

Where it's reviewed:
Maclean's June 23, 1997, page 57
Spectator, April 5, 1997, page 38
Times Literary Supplement, December 20, 1996, page 22
Woman's Journal, December 1996, page 16

Other books by the same author:
A Clear Conscience, 1994
Shadow Play, 1993
Deep Sleep, 1991
Not That Kind of Place, 1990
A Question of Guilt, 1988

Other books you might like:
Elizabeth George, *The Thomas Lynley/Barbara Havers Series*, 1988-
Lynda LaPlante, *The Jane Tennison Series*, 1993-
Val McDermid, *The Mermaids Singing*, 1997
Ruth Rendell, *The Inspector Wexford Series*, 1965-
Minette Walters, *The Dark Room*, 1996

90

KATE GALLISON

Hasty Retreat

(New York: Delacorte, 1997)

Story type: Amateur Detective
Series: Mother Lavinia Grey
Major character(s): Mother Lavinia Grey, Religious (Episcopal minister)
Time period(s): 1990s
Locale(s): New York (upstate); Fisherville, New Jersey

Summary: Mother Vinnie welcomes the opportunity to take a break from her duties at St. Bede's Episcopal Church in New Jersey and go on a weekend retreat to the Monastery of St. Hugh in upstate New York. But parish politics are hard to shake off, and the retreat is spoiled for her when her archnemesis Father Rupert Bingley shows up with a disruptive entourage. Then Brother Basil, the devout monk who is leading the retreat, is murdered, and Mother Vinnie must sort out a tangle of suspects and motives to find out who did it, and why.

Where it's reviewed:
Kirkus Reviews, June 1, 1997, page 837
Library Journal, July 1997, page 130
Publishers Weekly, May 19, 1997, page 69

Other books by the same author:
Unholy Angels, 1996
Devil's Workshop, 1996
Bury the Bishop, 1995

Other books you might like:
Susan Wittig Albert, *Rueful Death*, 1996
Diane M. Greenwood, *The Rev. Theodora Braithwaite Series*, 1991-
Isabelle Holland, *The Rev. Claire Aldington Series*, 1983-
David Willis McCullough, *The Zia Todd Series*, 1991-
Sister Carol Anne O'Marie, *Death Goes on Retreat*, 1995

91

CAROLINA GARCIA-AGUILERA

Bloody Shame

(New York: Putnam's, 1997)

Story type: Private Detective
Series: Lupe Solano
Major character(s): Lupe Solano, Detective—Private
Time period(s): 1990s
Locale(s): Miami, Florida

Summary: Cuban-American private eye Lupe Solano is asked by her old friend and occasional lover, criminal lawyer Tommy McDonald, to investigate what purports to be an open-and-shot case of self-defense. His client, a well-to-do Cuban merchant, claims he shot a Cuban rafter who was attempting to rob his shop. At the same time Lupe's best friend dies in a car accident en route to imparting some important information on the case to Lupe. Suspecting the incidents may be related, Lupe turns, as usual, to her sister

Lourdes, a most unconventional nun, and her cousin Leonardo, a body-builder who doubles as her assistant.

Where it's reviewed:
Armchair Detective, Spring 1997, page 239
Booklist, February 15, 1997, page 1006
Kirkus Reviews, January 1, 1997, page 22
Library Journal, February 1, 1997, page 110
Publishers Weekly, December 30, 1996, page 58

Other books by the same author:
Bloody Waters, 1995

Other books you might like:
Edna Buchanan, *The Britt Montero Series*, 1992-
Carolyn Chambers Clark, *Dangerous Alibis*, 1994
Lucha Corpi, *The Gloria Damasco Series*, 1992-
Barbara Parker, *The Gail Connor Series*, 1994-
Randy Wayne White, *North of Havana*, 1997

92

JONATHAN GASH (Pseudonym of Dr. John Grant)

Different Women Dancing

(New York: Viking 1997)

Story type: Amateur Detective
Major character(s): Clare Burtonall, Doctor (medical); Bonn, Prostitute (male)
Time period(s): 1990s
Locale(s): London, England

Summary: On her way home to her husband and comfortable suburban existence, Dr. Clare Burtonall is the first doctor on the scene of a fatal traffic accident. But before she can reach the victim, a young man appears on the scene and cradles the man's head in his arms, only to be dismissed by the police. They know Bonn; he's a ''goer'' who works for an illegal escort service, hired by countless women to meet their sexual and emotional needs. When Clare examines the victim, she recognizes him as a business contact of her husband Clifford, but when she asks Clifford about the incident, he becomes oddly evasive. Curious, Clare decides to investigate on her own, and for that she needs Bonn, who has easy access to the London underworld. They make an unlikely couple, and unlikelier still is the attraction Clare feels for the enigmatic and inscrutable Bonn. First in a projected new series from the creator of the rogue antiques dealer Lovejoy, whom Bonn resembles in some respects.

Where it's reviewed:
Kirkus Reviews, May 1, 1997, page 681
Library Journal, June 1, 1997, page 154
Publishers Weekly, April 7, 1997, page 76

Other books by the same author:
The Possessions of a Lady, 1996
The Grace in Older Women, 1995
The Sin within Her Smile, 1993
Paid and Loving Eyes, 1992
The Lies of Fair Ladies, 1991

Other books you might like:
Robert Barnard, *Bodies*, 1986
Liza Cody, *The Eva Wylie Series*, 1993-

Dan Kavanaugh, *The Nick Duffy Series*, 1980-1987
Val McDermid, *The Kate Brannigan Series*, 1992-
Andrew Taylor, *The William Dougal Series*, 1982-

93

G.D. GEARINO

Counting Coup

(New York: Simon & Schuster, 1997)

Story type: Amateur Detective; Psychological Suspense
Major character(s): Tad Beckman, Journalist (newspaper columnist)
Time period(s): 1990s
Locale(s): Miami, Florida; Georgia

Summary: Tad Beckman is a cynical, burned-out Pulitzer Prize-winning columnist, the product of an emotionally impoverished childhood and a checkered (to say the least) professional career, who finally lands on his feet in Miami. Tad learns about his Pulitzer from his new editor; he'd paid little attention to his career after a female reader whose pleas for help he had ignored was decapitated by her husband in front of their two small children. When he meets another abused wife, Jocelyn Pritchard, he doesn't make the same mistake, but helps her turn the tables on her vicious husband, whose shady real estate dealings make great material for a column. Tad, who no longer takes much pride in his ability to break his readers' hearts or stir their wrath in 750 words, is the first-person narrator, telling a story that's alternately funny and poignant, sprinkled with sardonic insights and painful memories of a cruel grandfather and helpless mother. The eventual outcome of the story is as satisfying as it is unexpected.

Where it's reviewed:
Kirkus Reviews, June 15, 1997, page 893
Library Journal, July 1997, page 124
Publishers Weekly, June 16, 1997, page 46

Other books by the same author:
What the Deaf-Mute Heard, 1996

Other books you might like:
Rosemary Aubert, *Free Reign*, 1998
James Lee Burke, *Heaven's Prisoners*, 1989
David Guterson, *Snow Falling on Cedars*, 1994
Carl Hiaasen, *Strip Tease*, 1993
Bradford Morrow, *Giovanni's Gift*, 1997

94

ANNE GEORGE

Murder Makes Waves

(New York: Avon, 1997)

Story type: Amateur Detective; Humor
Series: Patricia Anne and Mary Alice
Major character(s): Patricia Anne, Aged Person (Housewife); Mary Alice, Aged Person (Divorced Person)
Time period(s): 1990s
Locale(s): Birmingham, Alabama; Destin, Florida

Summary: The two sisters couldn't be more different: Patricia Anne is sensible and happily married while Mary Alice is flamboyant and often divorced. But life in Birmingham has lately gotten too dull even for Patricia Anne, and she jumps at the chance to take off with Mary Alice for a little vacation away from her husband in the "World's Luckiest Fishing Village" in Florida. No sooner do they arrive than a dead body turns up, and if the cops don't have a clue, the sisters surely do. They're pointed in the right direction by a modern Victorian cottage development, a campaign to save the giant sea turtles, and a young girl who appears to be a clone of Winona Rider in the movie *Beetlejuice*.

Where it's reviewed:
Kirkus Reviews, June 1, 1997, page 837
Library Journal, July 1997, page 130

Other books by the same author:
Murder on a Girls' Night Out, 1997
Murder Runs in the Family, 1997
Murder on a Bad Hair Day, 1996

Other books you might like:
Richard Barth, *The Margaret Binton Series*, 1978
Nancy Bell, *The Biggie Weatherford Series*, 1996-
Graham Landrum, *The Harriet Bushrow Series*, 1992-1996
Susanna Hoffman McShea, *The Mildred Bennett Series*, 1990-
Corinne Holt Sawyer, *The Angela Benbow/Caledonia Wingate Series*, 1988-

95

ELIZABETH GEORGE (Pseudonym of Susan Elizabeth George)

Deception on His Mind

(New York: Bantam, 1997)

Story type: Police Procedural
Series: Thomas Lynley & Barbara Havers
Major character(s): Barbara Havers, Police Officer (sergeant)
Time period(s): 1990s
Locale(s): Balford-le-Nez, England (Essex coast)

Summary: Barbara Havers, a working-class police officer who's quite different in temperament and social position from her long-time partner Detective Inspector Thomas Lynley, is working without him for a change in this case, set in the small but growing Asian community of the decaying seaside town of Balford-le-Nez. A member of this community is found dead, and Havers must learn about this subculture before she can hope to find the killer. It's a case that becomes very personal to her, demonstrating as it does the terrible price people pay for deceiving others—and themselves.

Where it's reviewed:
Booklist, May 15, 1997, page 1541
Entertainment Weekly, July 18, 1997, page 78
Kirkus Reviews, May 15, 1997, page 760
New York Times Book Review, August 10, 1997, page 18
Publishers Weekly, June 2, 1997, page 56

Other books by the same author:
In the Presence of the Enemy, 1996
Playing for the Ashes, 1994
Missing Joseph, 1993
For the Sake of Elena, 1992

Mystery

A Suitable Vengeance, 1991

Other books you might like:
Deborah Crombie, *The Duncan Kincaid/Gemma James Series*, 1993-
Martha Grimes, *The Inspector Richard Jury Series*, 1981-
P.D. James, *The Adam Dalgliesh Series*, 1962-
Ruth Rendell, *The Inspector Wexford Series*, 1964-
Dorothy L. Sayers, *The Lord Peter Wimsey Series*, 1923-1937

96

TONY GIBBS

Fade to Black

(New York: Mysterious Press 1997)

Story type: Police Procedural
Series: Harbormaster
Major character(s): Neal Donahoe, Police Officer (harbormaster); Victoria ''Tory'' Lennox, Military Personnel (coast guard lieutenant)
Time period(s): 1990s
Locale(s): Santa Barbara, California

Summary: Together veteran harbor cop Neal Donahoe and newcomer Tory Lennox patrol Santa Barbara's marina. She feels the post is taking her nowhere, and her relationship with Neal is similarly stalled; he wants to get married, and she's not sure what she wants. Meanwhile, her boss wants the Halvorsen clan and their dilapidated fishing boat *The Prophet Jonah* out of the marina. When Tory goes to investigate she ends up rescuing one of the Halvorsen children from drowning and Erling Halvorsen, the boy's father and a self-declared minister, welcomes her as their personal savior. Almost too late she realizes what a dangerous position she's put herself in by helping this fanatically religious man and his odd family. The author writes two other series.

Where it's reviewed:
Kirkus Reviews, June 1, 1997, page 837
Publishers Weekly, May 19, 1997, page 70

Other books by the same author:
Shot in the Dark, 1996
Capitol Offense, 1995 (The Diana Speed Series)
Land Fall, 1992 (The Jeremy Barr and Patrick O'Mara Series)
Shadow Queen, 1992 (Speed)
Running Fix, 1990 (The Jeremy Barr and Patrick O'Mara Series)

Other books you might like:
J.S. Borthwick, *Bodies of Water*, 1990
Ron Ely, *The Jake Sands Series*, 1994-
Susan Kenney, *One Fell Sloop*, 1990
Michael Kirk, *The Andrew Laird Series*, 1975-
Sam Llewellyn, *Dead Reckoning*, 1987

97

BARTHOLOMEW GILL (Pseudonym of Mark McGarrity)

The Death of an Irish Tinker

(New York: Morrow, 1997)

Story type: Police Procedural

Series: Peter McGarr
Major character(s): Peter McGarr, Police Officer (chief superintendent)
Time period(s): 1990s
Locale(s): Dublin, Ireland

Summary: It's a litle-known subculture that Gill explores here: the world of the Tinkers, or Travelers, as they call themselves, an itinerant people with their own secret language and ways, wary of strangers or settling down anywhere. One of them is murdered, and the trail soon leads McGarr to an Irish druglord known as the Toddler, a chillingly evil genius who often uses Tinker children to run heroin for him, addicting many in the process. One who recovered is an artistic young woman known as Biddy, turned out on the streets by her own parents when she was nine, and now gone underground when the Toddler learns she can link him to the murder of her lover and thus end his cruel career. She forges a new identity and life for herself as a successful artist and photographer, but unless McGarr can find her before the Toddler does, it will all be cut short.

Where it's reviewed:
Booklist, September 1, 1997, page 63
Kirkus Reviews, August 1, 1997, page 1157

Other books by the same author:
The Death of an Irish Sea Wolf, 1996
The Death of an Ardent Bibliophile, 1995
Death on a Cold, Wild River, 1993
The Death of Love, 1992
The Death of a Joyce Scholar, 1989

Other books you might like:
Thomas Adcock, *Drown All the Dogs*, 1994
John Brady, *The Matt Minogue Series*, 1988-
Eilis Dillon, *Death in the Quadrangle*, 1956
Jonathan Gash, *The Sleepers of Erin*, 1983
Patrick McGinley, *Goosefoot*, 1983

98

DOROTHY GILMAN

Mrs. Pollifax, Innocent Tourist

(New York: Fawcett, 1997)

Story type: Espionage; Humor
Series: Mrs. Pollifax
Major character(s): Emily Pollifax, Spy
Time period(s): 1990s
Locale(s): New York, New York; Iraq

Summary: Although she's disguised as a bag lady in Manhattan, the globe-trotting New Jersey grandmother is really on loan to her former CIA friend Farrell and in the first stage of a delicate and timely mission. She must make contact with a smuggler who has in his possession a contraband manuscript from a dissident Iraqi novelist who was recently murdered in an Iraqi prison. Although it's labeled fiction, the book reveals some shocking truths about Saddam Hussein's reign. Once this first step is complete, Mrs. Pollifax boards a plane for the Middle East, and she's barely airborne before all hell breaks loose.

Where it's reviewed:
Booklist, February 1, 1997, page 928
Kirkus Reviews, December 15, 1996, page 1772
Publishers Weekly, December 30, 1996, page 57

Other books by the same author:
Mrs. Pollifax and the Lion Killer, 1996
Mrs. Pollifax Pursued, 1995
Mrs. Pollifax and the Second Thief, 1993
Mrs. Pollifax and the Whirling Dervish, 1990
Mrs. Pollifax and the Golden Triangle, 1988

Other books you might like:
Margot Arnold, *The Penny Spring/Sir Toby Glendower Series*, 1979
Eleanor Boylan, *The Clara Gamadge Series*, 1989-
Gallagher Gray, *The Theodore S. Hubbert/Auntie Lil Series*, 1991
Stefanie Matteson, *The Charlotte Graham Series*, 1990-
Evelyn E. Smith, *The Miss Melville Series*, 1986-

99

JACQUELINE GIRDNER

A Cry for Self-Help
(New York: Berkley, 1997)

Story type: Amateur Detective; Humor
Series: Kate Jasper
Major character(s): Kate Jasper, Businesswoman (gag gift wholesaler)
Time period(s): 1990s
Locale(s): Marin County, California

Summary: Sam Skyler is the top self-help guru in trendy Marin County, where he has grown rich talking people into getting in touch with their inner child. One day, while forty-something vegetarian entrepreneur Kate Jasper is perched on a seaside cliff observing an aquatic wedding, she sees Skyler take a deadly plunge off the cliff into the rocky surf below, and before she knows it she's up to her ears into another New Age murder investigation.

Where it's reviewed:
Kirkus Reviews, March 1, 1997, page 337
Publishers Weekly, March 3, 1997, page 67

Other books by the same author:
Most Likely To Die, 1996
A Stiff Critique, 1995
Tea-Totally Dead, 1994
Fat-Free and Fatal, 1993
Murder Most Mellow, 1992

Other books you might like:
Taffy Cannon, *Pocketful of Karma*, 1993
Susan Dunlap, *Karma*, 1981
Marlys Millhiser, *Murder at Moot Point*, 1992
Leslie O'Kane, *The Molly Masters Series*, 1996-
Walter Satterthwait, *The Hanged Man*, 1993

100

STEPHEN GREENLEAF

Past Tense
(New York: St. Martin's Press, 1997)

Story type: Private Detective
Series: John Marshall Tanner
Major character(s): John Marshall Tanner, Detective—Private, Lawyer; Charley Sleet, Police Officer
Time period(s): 1990s
Locale(s): San Francisco, California

Summary: Tanner is caught in perhaps the most provocative case of his career when his best friend, police lieutenant Charley Sleet, stands up and shoots a man being tried for sexual abuse in an open courtroom. Not only is Charley a good cop, he's a gentle, charitable man who is the last person Tanner can imagine gunning down a complete stranger. As he investigates the case he runs up against the controversy surrounding recovered memories of sexual abuse, into questions of police corruption, and finally into repeated killings—suggesting his best friend may have become a serial killer.

Where it's reviewed:
Book World, April 20, 1997, page 8
Booklist, March 15, 1997, page 1229
Kirkus Reviews, February 15, 1997, page 257
New York Times Book Review, April 27, 1997, page 36
Publishers Weekly, February 17, 1997, page 213

Other books by the same author:
Flesh Wounds, 1996
False Conception, 1995
Southern Cross, 1994
Blood Type, 1993
Book Case, 1992

Other books you might like:
Neil Albert, *The Dave Garrett Series*, 1991-
Earl Emerson, *The Thomas Black Series*, 1985-
Jerry Kennealy, *The Nick Polo Series*, 1987-
Ross Macdonald, *The Lew Archer Series*, 1949-
Bill Pronzini, *The Nameless Detective Series*, 1971-

101

ROBERT GREER

The Devil's Red Nickel
(New York: Mysterious Press, 1997)

Story type: Private Detective
Series: CJ Floyd
Major character(s): CJ Floyd, Bail Bondsman (African-American)
Time period(s): 1990s
Locale(s): Denver, Colorado

Summary: CJ (who refuses to punctuate his initials) is asked by Clothide Polk, a beautiful and ambitious black woman, to look into the murder of her father, whose death she refuses to attribute to a heart attack. And she's right: it's quickly ascertained that his heart failure was induced by massive nicotine poisoning. As it turns out, LeRoy Polk was a cultural icon to

CJ and many other black people of his generation, for he was also known as Daddy Doo-Wop, a Chicago deejay who blasted rhythm and blues and soul patter across the Midwest during the '50s and '60s. He was also linked to the payola scandals that rocked the record industry. CJ needs money and needs the case, but he doesn't really buckle down to finding the murderer until a bomb explodes in his Denver Five Points neighborhood during the Juneteenth celebration.

Where it's reviewed:
Booklist, March 1, 1997, page 1113
Kirkus Reviews, January 15, 1997, page 97
Library Journal, February 1, 1997, page 110
Publishers Weekly, January 6, 1997, page 67
Tribune Books, April 13, 1997, page 8

Other books by the same author:
The Devil's Hatband, 1995

Other books you might like:
Gar Anthony Haywood, *The Aaron Gunner Series*, 1988-
Walter Mosley, *The Easy Rawlins Series*, 1990-
Gary Phillips, *The Ivan Monk Series*, 1994-
Manuel Ramos, *The Luis Montez Series*, 1994
Blair S. Walker, *Up Jumped the Devil*, 1997

102

MARTHA GRIMES

The Case Has Altered

(New York: Holt, 1997)

Story type: Police Procedural
Major character(s): Inspector Richard Jury, Police Officer (Scotland Yard); Melrose Plant, Professor (French romantic poetry)
Time period(s): 1990s
Locale(s): England (Lincolnshire)

Summary: The clues are as bleak as the landscape of the Lincolnshire fens as Inspector Jury pokes his nose into a double murder in this remote region of England. Technically, he's out of his jurisdiction, so he cajoles his long-time friend Melrose Plant into posing as an antiques expert in order to gain access to the imposing country estate of Fengate, where he hopes to interview possible witnesses to the crime.

Other books by the same author:
Rainbow's End, 1995
The Horse You Came In On, 1993
The Old Contemptibles, 1990
The Old Silent, 1989
The Five Bells and Bladebone, 1987

Other books you might like:
Deborah Crombie, *The Duncan Kincaid/Gemma James Series*, 1993-
Elizabeth George, *The Thomas Lynley/Barbara Havers Series*, 1988-
Caroline Graham, *The Inspector Tom Barnaby Series*, 1987-
Lucretia Grindle, *The Inspector H.W. Ross Series*, 1993-
Cynthia Harrod-Eagles, *The Inspector Bill Slider Series*, 1991-

103

TERRIS MCMAHAN GRIMES

Blood Will Tell

(Nw York: Signet, 1997)

Story type: Amateur Detective
Series: Theresa Galloway
Major character(s): Theresa Gallow, Civil Servant (state of California)
Locale(s): Sacramento, California

Summary: Theresa is a buppie (black urban professional) and a member of the sandwich generation; she has her hands full with her job, her husband, her two children—and her mother. Widowed when her husband died of Alzheimer's, Theresa's mom is a constant source of worry to her, and never more than now. It seems she's taken a stranger into her house, a young man named Raymond Johnson who claims to be her late husband's love child and who is therefore Theresa's half-brother. Not believing his story for a minute, she wants him out of her mother's life fast. And then he goes missing and turns up dead. It's a police matter now, but unless they can find out exactly who he is, no one will ever find out who killed Raymond Johnson.

Other books by the same author:
Somebody Else's Child, 1996

Other books you might like:
Eleanor Taylor Bland, *The Marti McAlister Series*, 1992-
Nora DeLoach, *Mama Stalks the Past*, 1997
Grace Edwards, *If I Should Die*, 1997
Barbara Neely, *The Blanche White Series*, 1992-
Chassie West, *Sunrise*, 1994

104

MICAH S. HACKLER

The Dark Canyon

(New York: Dell, 1997)

Story type: Police Procedural
Series: Cliff Lansing
Major character(s): Cliff Lansing, Police Officer (sheriff)
Time period(s): 1990s
Locale(s): Jicarilla Apache Reservation, New Mexico; Chaco Canyon, New Mexico

Summary: Small-town New Mexico sheriff Cliff Lansing is investigating reports that a wild animal has been killing ranchers' sheep and now appears to be turning to human prey. Then an archaeologist is murdered. Lansing uses his knowledge of Native American myths and legends to unravel the mystery.

Other books by the same author:
Coyote Returns, 1996
Legend of the Dead, 1995

Other books you might like:
James D. Doss, *The Shaman Laughs*, 1995
Steven F. Havill, *The Bill Gastner Series*, 1991-
J.A. Jance, *The Joanna Brady Series*, 1993-

Jake Page, *The Lethal Partner*, 1996
Aimee Thurlo, *The Ella Clah Series*, 1995
  David Thurlo, co-author

105

JANE HADDAM (Pseudonym of Orania Papazoglou)

Deadly Beloved

(New York: Bantam, 1997)

Story type: Private Detective
Major character(s): Gregor Demarkian, Detective—Private (retired FBI agent)
Time period(s): 1990s
Locale(s): Philadelphia, Pennsylvania; Fox Run Hill, Pennsylvania

Summary: Demarkian, upon seeing his Armenian-American neighborhood engulfed in impending nuptials, is happy to investigate the strange case of Patsy MacLaren Willis, who vanishes to begin life anew after shooting her husband in his sleep and pipe-bombing her own car in a downtown garage. When Demarkian arrives at Fox Run Hill, along with swarms of police, he concludes that Patsy was perhaps the only wife there without a clear motive for murdering her husband. Then a second explosion rocks the gated community and it's clear that Gregor must unmask the killer before anyone else dies.

Where it's reviewed:
Kirkus Reviews, July 1, 1997, page 985

Other books by the same author:
And One to Die On, 1996
Fountain of Death, 1995
Bleeding Hearts, 1994
Dear Old Dead, 1994
Festival of Deaths, 1993

Other books you might like:
Neil Albert, *The Dave Garrett Series*, 1991-
Linda Barnes, *The Michael Spraggue Series*, 1982-
Lee Harris, *The Christine Bennett Series*, 1992-
Jane Langton, *The Homer Kelly Series*, 1964-
Donna Huston Murray, *The Ginger Struve Barnes Series*, 1995-

106

JEAN HAGER

The Spirit Caller

(New York: Mysterious Press, 1997)

Story type: Police Procedural
Series: Molly Bearpaw
Major character(s): Molly Bearpaw, Investigator (major crimes investigator), Indian (Cherokee)
Time period(s): 1990s
Locale(s): Tahlequah, Oklahoma

Summary: When a New Age devotee who was trying to communicate with the spirit of a dead Cherokee is murdered in the Tahlequah Native American Research Library, some think it might be the work of a ghost. After all, the building was once used as a jail in the Indian Territory days. But the suspects Molly is interested in are all very much alive, including the woman's ex-husband and a charismatic New Age practitioner. Before Molly can find the killer, however, she's forced to confront some disturbing truths about her own family history.

Where it's reviewed:
Kirkus Reviews, March 1, 1997, page 337
Library Journal, May 1, 1997, page 144
Publishers Weekly, March 17, 1997, page 79

Other books by the same author:
Seven Black Stones, 1995
The Redbird's Cry, 1994
Ravenmocker, 1992

Other books you might like:
Margaret Coel, *The Ghost Walker*, 1996
James D. Doss, *The Shaman's Bones*, 1997
Tony Hillerman, *The Joe Leaphorn and Jim Chee Series*, 1970-
Thomas Perry, *The Jane Whitefield Series*, 1995-
Aimee Thurlo, *Death Walker*, 1996
  David Thurlo, co-author

107

MATTHEW HALL

The Art of Breaking Glass

(Boston: Little, Brown 1997)

Story type: Psychological Suspense; Action/Adventure
Major character(s): Bill Kaiser, Computer Expert; Sharon Blautner, Nurse (psychiatric)
Time period(s): 1990s
Locale(s): New York, New York

Summary: Bill Kaiser, a demolitions and computer expert with a thirst for social justice, is picked up naked in the incinerator room of a luxury apartment building with a razor that he'd used to slash himself. The police take him to Bellevue Hospital for observation, and although he displays all the classic symptoms of schizophrenia, he's a cooperative and sympathetic patient. His nurse, Sharon Blautner, finds herself drawn to him and inadvertently lets slip some information that allows him to torch his way out of the hospital's high-security lockdown. It's apparent that Bill isn't really crazy after all, at least not in the way everybody thought, and as he embarks on an elaborate revenge scheme, Sharon realizes she may be the only who can stop him. First novel.

Where it's reviewed:
Booklist, March 1, 1997, page 1068
Kirkus Reviews, March 15, 1997, page 401
Library Journal, April 1, 1997, page 125
Publishers Weekly, March 17, 1997, page 76

Other books you might like:
Rosemary Aubert, *Free Reign*, 1997
Lee Child, *Killing Floor*, 1997
Jeffery Deaver, *A Maiden's Grave*, 1996
Stephen Hunter, *Black Light*, 1996
Elmore Leonard, *Out of Sight*, 1996

108

PARNELL HALL

Scam

(New York: Mysterious Press, 1997)

Story type: Private Detective; Humor
Series: Stanley Hastings
Major character(s): Stanley Hastings, Detective—Private, Actor
Time period(s): 1990s
Locale(s): New York, New York (Manhattan)

Summary: It's been a long time between paying clients, and Stanley is ecstatic when one finally shows up. But all Cranston Pritchert can say to Stanley is, "I'm being set up." Try as he might to find out why the six-foot-six investment firm partner is being set up, Stanley can't get a straight answer out of the man. And when he starts to investigate, all the clues point to Pritchert himself—and murder. When the police get into things, they decide Stanley is the culprit, and if he can't find out who the real murderer is, he faces prison and maybe even the chair.

Where it's reviewed:
Booklist, March 1, 1997, page 1113
Kirkus Reviews, February 15, 1997, page 258
New York Times Book Review, April 27, 1997, page 36
Publishers Weekly, January 27, 1997, page 80

Other books by the same author:
Trial, 1996
Movie, 1995
Blackmail, 1994
Actor, 1993
Shot, 1992

Other books you might like:
Lawrence Block, *The Bernie Rhodenbarr Series*, 1977-
Steve Brewer, *The Bubba Mabry Series*, 1994-
Stan Cutler, *The Rayford Goodman/Mark Bradley Series*, 1991-
G.M. Ford, *The Leo Waterman Series*, 1995-
Kinky Friedman, *The Kinky Friedman Series*, 1986-

109

BARBARA HAMBLY

A Free Man of Color

(New York: Bantam, 1997)

Story type: Historical; Amateur Detective
Major character(s): Benjamin January, Musician (Son of a slave)
Time period(s): 1830s (1833)
Locale(s): New Orleans, Louisiana

Summary: Benjamin January, the son of a slave, returns from Paris to New Orleans to take a job as piano player at the Salle d'Orleans. During a quadroon ball, January comes to the rescue of a masked beauty whom he recognizes as Mademoiselle Madeleine. He cautions her that it isn't wise for a white woman to be caught here, especially when he learns she is there to confront Angelique Crozat, the black (actually octoroon, or one-eighth black) mistress of her dead husband. When Angelique is found murdered, her body hidden in a pile of opera capes, the police aren't all that interested in investigating the case. However elegant she may have been in life, she's now just one more dead black prostitute. January, who himself becomes a suspect, turns sleuth, following a trail of clues that leads him to various river haunts and into the cabins of voodoo-worshiping slaves. First mystery by a noted fantasy writer.

Where it's reviewed:
Kirkus Reviews, May 15, 1997, page 741
Library Journal, June 1, 1997, page 148
Publishers Weekly, May 5, 1997, page 197

Other books by the same author:
Those Who Hunt the Night, 1998 (historical/mystery/vampire)
Traveling with the Dead, 1995 (historical/mystery/vampire)

Other books you might like:
James Lee Burke, *In the Electric Mist with Confederate Dead*, 1993
Ron Burns, *Enslaved*, 1994
Peter J. Heck, *A Connecticut Yankee in Criminal Court*, 1996
Miriam Grace Monfredo, *Through a Gold Eagle*, 1996
Robert S. Skinner, *Skin Deep, Blood Red*, 1997

110

LAUREN HANEY

The Right Hand of Amon

(New York: Avon, 1997)

Story type: Historical
Major character(s): Lieutenant Bak, Military Personnel (soldier/policeman)
Time period(s): 15th century B.C. (1463)
Locale(s): Egypt

Summary: Lieutenant Bak is a loyal servant of the royal house of Egypt during the reign of Queen Maatkare Hatshepsut and commander of the Medjay police in the frontier fortress city of Buhen, located in the most arid, rugged and remote area of the Nile Valley. He is assigned to oversee the corps of men accompanying the golden idol of the god Amon on its journey up the Nile to heal the ailing son of a tribal king. But the river yields up the body of a brave officer killed for unknown reasons, and the only way Bak is going to solve the case is through the drawings of a missing mute boy who may have been the only witness. First novel.

Other books you might like:
Anna Apostolou, *A Murder in Macedon*, 1997
Lindsey Davis, *The Marcus Didius Falco Series*, 1989-
Lee Levin, *King Tut's Private Eye*, 1996
Elizabeth Peters, *The Amelia Peabody Series*, 1975-
Lynda S. Robinson, *The Lord Meren Series*, 1994-

111

GARY HARDWICK

Double Dead

(New York: Dutton, 1997)

Story type: Legal
Major character(s): Jesse King, Lawyer (prosecutor; African-American); Ramona Lake, Prostitute
Time period(s): 1990s
Locale(s): Detroit, Michigan

Summary: The mayor of Detroit is entertaining his call-girl mistress, Ramona Lake, when two masked gunmen break into his house, murder him, and flee with a locked briefcase. The police assume Ramona did it, but black prosecutor Jesse King, who is assigned the case, has his doubts. To him, it's clear that Ramona is a victim too, and that the police are being manipulated by the actual killers. When he questions their actions, he winds up being framed for murder himself and together he and Ramona flee for their lives. They go underground in inner city Detroit, which Ramona calls home but where King, who's made his professional career by siding with the law, is trusted by no one. In order to get the evidence they need they must find the missing briefcase, but they have to stay alive in order to do that.

Where it's reviewed:
Booklist, May 15, 1997, page 1566
Kirkus Reviews, June 15, 1997, page 895
Library Journal, May 1, 1997, page 140

Other books by the same author:
Cold Medina, 1996

Other books you might like:
Loren D. Estleman, *Stress*, 1996
Robert Greer, *The C.J. Floyd Series*, 1996-
Gar Anthony Haywood, *The Aaron Gunner Series*, 1988-
Walter Mosley, *The Easy Rawlins Series*, 1990-
Gary Phillips, *The Ivan Monk Series*, 1994-

112

CHARLAINE HARRIS

Shakespeare's Champion

(New York: St. Martin's Press, 1997)

Story type: Amateur Detective
Series: Lily Bard
Major character(s): Lily Bard, Martial Arts Expert (karate), Housekeeper (cleaning woman)
Time period(s): 1990s
Locale(s): Shakespeare, Arkansas

Summary: Lily Bard is a woman with a shadowy past who now makes the small Arkansas town of Shakespeare her home. She makes her living cleaning other people's houses, but her life revolves around her karate and her workouts at Body Time, the local gym. Either way, she has access to the personal lives of many of the town's inhabitants and much of the local gossip. Although all she wants is to lead a quiet life, the murder of a fellow fitness devotee at the gym forces her to turn detective again. This new series is a decided change of pace from the author's much cozier Aurora Teagarden mysteries.

Other books by the same author:
Shakespeare's Landlord, 1996

Other books you might like:
Susan Dunlap, *The Kiernan O'Shaughnessy Series*, 1989-
Joan Hess, *The Claire Malloy Series*, 1986-
Barbara Neely, *The Blanche White Series*, 1992-
Sara Paretsky, *The V.I. Warshawski Series*, 1982-
Kathy Hogan Trocheck, *The Callahan Garrity Series*, 1992-

113

JOHN HARVEY

Still Waters

(New York: Holt, 1997)

Story type: Police Procedural
Series: Charlie Resnick
Major character(s): Charlie Resnick, Police Officer (inspector)
Time period(s): 1990s
Locale(s): Nottingham, England

Summary: A serial killer is loose in Nottingham. It's a case for the Serious Crime Squad and not Charlie's department at all. But one of the victims is a woman his lover, Hannah, knew well enough to know that she was a battered wife, which might make her death another matter entirely. Charlie, as serious about his work as he is about his food, his cats, and his vast collection of jazz recordings, sets about to find out if the dead woman's husband is the killer.

Other books by the same author:
Easy Meat, 1996
Living Proof, 1995
Cold Light, 1994
Wasted Years, 1993
Off Minor, 1992

Other books you might like:
Bill James, *The Inspector Colin Harpur Series*, 1985-
Quintin Jardine, *The Constable Robert Skinner Series*, 1994-
Val McDermid, *The Mermaids Singing*, 1996
Ian Rankin, *The Inspector John Rebus Series*, 1988-
Peter Turnbull, *The P Division Series*, 1982-

114

PETE HAUTMAN

Ring Game

(New York: Simon & Schuster, 1997)

Story type: Action/Adventure; Humor
Series: Joe Crow
Major character(s): Joe Crow, Gambler (professional card sharp)
Time period(s): 1990s
Locale(s): Minneapolis, Minnesota

Summary: Axel Speeter, a friend of his father's, blames Joe for the impending marriage of his ersatz stepdaughter Carmen

Roman to Hyatt Hilton, who has the exclusive distributorship of counterfeit Evian water in the Twin Cities. It's the latest in a string of bad luck for Joe, a former alcoholic and drug addict as well as cop with a talent for attracting odd friends. First his girlfriend ran out on him and then he burned out the engine of his Jag and is being forced to drive a bright yellow Pontiac GTO (pretty humiliating, given his circle of friends). Joe swears he has nothing to do with Carmen's wedding plans but he has to prove it, and his investigations lead him to a strange religious cult known as the Amaranthine Church of the One, whose members believe they've found the key to immortality.

Where it's reviewed:
Kirkus Reviews, August 15, 1997, page 1243
Publishers Weekly, September 1, 1997, page 94

Other books by the same author:
The Mortal Nuts, 1996
Short Money, 1995
Drawing Dead, 1994

Other books you might like:
Joe Gores, *32 Cadillacs*, 1992
Carl Hiaasen, *Native Tongue*, 1991
Tom Kakonis, *The Timothy Waverly Series*, 1988
Philip Reed, *Bird Dog*, 1997
Robert Reeves, *Doubting Thomas*, 1985

115

STEVEN F. HAVILL

Privileged to Kill
(New York: St. Martin's Press, 1997)

Story type: Police Procedural
Series: Bill Gastner
Major character(s): William K. Gastner, Police Officer (undersheriff); Estelle Reyes-Guzman, Detective—Police
Time period(s): 1990s
Locale(s): Posadas, New Mexico

Summary: When Gastner gives a cyclist with a flat tire a ride into town, he doesn't ask the man what he's doing in Posadas. Wesley Crocker strikes him as a decent sort who's fallen on hard times, and Gastner doesn't like to pry—although he doesn't mind buying him a meal. But when a child's body is found under the bleachers near the field where Crocker was camping, Gastner wishes he'd found out more about him. He's convinced Crocker couldn't have committed the murder, but he and Estelle have to find out who did.

Where it's reviewed:
Armchair Detective, Spring 1997, page 238
Booklist, February 15, 1997, page 1006
Kirkus Reviews, December 15, 1996, page 1768
Library Journal, February 1, 1997, page 111
Publishers Weekly, December 16, 1996, page 45

Other books by the same author:
Before She Dies, 1996
Twice Buried, 1994
Bitter Recoil, 1992
Heartshot, 1991

Other books you might like:
Susan Rogers Cooper, *The Milt Kovak Series*, 1988-
Bill Crider, *The Sheriff Dan Rhodes Series*, 1986
Micah S. Hackler, *The Cliff Lansing/Gabe Hanna Series*, 1995-
Michael McGarrity, *The Kevin Kerney Series*, 1996-
Jake Page, *The Mo Bowdre Series*, 1993-

116

SPARKLE HAYTER

Revenge of the Cootie Girls
(New York: Viking, 1997)

Story type: Amateur Detective; Humor
Series: Robin Hudson
Major character(s): Robin Hudson, Journalist (cable news reporter)
Time period(s): 1990s
Locale(s): New York, New York

Summary: As usual, Robin is bored with the sleazy tabloid assignments she's being given, and decides to amuse herself by showing her new intern, Kathy Loblaws, the ins and outs of New York City. So she and her friends treat small-town-girl Kathy to a real girls' night out. Somehow, during the course of the evening, Kathy ends up in a strange man's closet and Robin has to extricate her. She gets a little help from her friends Tamayo, a full-time comic, and Sally, a bald witch from Princeton who monitors everyone's karma. And since the events of this particular night actually fall on Halloween, maybe Sally's unique talents are needed. Hayter, a former stand-up comic as well as cable correspondent, uses jokes to conceal clues much the way other writers use red herrings, and the result is an often-hilarious story.

Where it's reviewed:
Kirkus Reviews, February 1, 1997, page 175
Maclean's, June 23, 1997, page 55
Publishers Weekly, January 20, 1997, page 396
Quill & Quire, May 1997, page 16

Other books by the same author:
Nice Girls Finish Last, 1996
What's a Girl Gotta Do?, 1995

Other books you might like:
Camilla Crespi, *The Simona Griffo Series*, 1991-
Jane Dentinger, *The Jocelyn O'Roarke Series*, 1983-
Janet Evanovich, *The Stephanie Plum Series*, 1994-
Lindsay Maracotta, *The Lucy Freers Series*, 1997-
Gillian Roberts, *The Amanda Pepper Series*, 1987-

117

PETER J. HECK

The Prince and the Prosecutor
(New York: Berkley, 1997)

Story type: Historical; Amateur Detective
Series: Mark Twain
Major character(s): Mark Twain, Writer (novelist, humorist), Historical Figure; Wentworth Cabot, Secretary

Time period(s): 1890s
Locale(s): New London, Connecticut; New York, New York; At Sea

Summary: Young Wentworth Cabot is delighted that his dream of traveling abroad is about to be realized when his employer, Samuel Clemens, engages him as a companion and traveling secretary on a trans-Atlantic trip to England. They will be accompanied by Clemens' old friend Rudyard Kipling, who greets them at the dock where they are to board the *City of Baltimore*, and despite some unpleasant encounters with a German prince, an Italian artist, and a young ne'er-do-well from Philadelphia, they settle in for a pleasant, relaxing voyage. Then the young Philadelphian disappears overboard, and his father, a prominent prosecutor, accuses the German prince of murder. Clemens thinks there is more to the matter than appears, and that the prince may not be royalty at all.

Other books by the same author:
A Connecticut Yankee in Criminal Court, 1996
Death on the Mississippi, 1995

Other books you might like:
Mary Kruger, *No Honeymoon for Death*, 1995
Robin Paige, *The Kathryn Ardleigh Series*, 1994-
Walter Satterthwait, *Wilde West*, 1991
Edith Skom, *The Mark Twain Murders*, 1989
Julie Smith, *Huckleberry Fiend*, 1987

118

SUE HENRY

Death Takes Passage

(New York: Avon, 1997)

Story type: Police Procedural
Series: Alex Jensen
Major character(s): Alex Jensen, Police Officer (state trooper)
Time period(s): 1990s
Locale(s): Alaska (Glacier Bay)

Summary: Sergeant Alex Jensen and his girlfriend Jessie are taking part in the Centennial celebration of the Klondike Gold Rush. Their cruise down Alaska's Inside Passage is marred by the discovery of a murdered crew member found floating in the icy waters of Glacier Bay. There is no lack of suspects on board, and it begins to appear that the murder may be linked to the ton of gold being transported aboard the ship. As usual, the author writes with great authority and conviction about the lonely splendor of the Alaskan landscape and the rugged people who call it home.

Where it's reviewed:
Kirkus Reviews, July 15, 1997, page 1067
Library Journal, July 1997, page 131
Publishers Weekly, June 16, 1997, page 49

Other books by the same author:
Sleeping Lady, 1996
Termination Dust, 1995
Murder on the Iditarod Trail, 1991

Other books you might like:
Aaron Elkins, *Icy Clutches*, 1990
Elizabeth Quinn, *The Lauren Maxwell Series*, 1993-

Father Brad Reynolds S.J., *The Story Knife*, 1996
Dana Stabenow, *The Kate Shugak Series*, 1992-
John Straley, *The Cecil Younger Series*, 1992-

119

JOAN HESS

A Holly, Jolly Murder

(New York: Dutton, 1997)

Story type: Amateur Detective; Humor
Series: Claire Malloy
Major character(s): Claire Malloy, Businesswoman (bookstore owner)
Time period(s): 1990s
Locale(s): Farberville, Arkansas

Summary: When Claire's policeman boyfriend Peter Rosen starts spending too much time with his ex-wife, Claire accepts the invitation of one of her customers to attend a winter solstice celebration at the Sacred Grove of Keltria in the company of assorted Druids and Wiccans. It all seems innocent enough until the group's wealthy benefactor, Nicholas Chunder, is found murdered. The obvious suspect is a tattooed teenager, Roy Tate, who lives in Chunder's carriage house and who obligingly confesses to the crime—and then flees. But Claire finds out that some of the Druids were upset with Chunder and she begins to wonder if Roy is really the guilty party.

Where it's reviewed:
Publishers Weekly, September 1, 1997, page 99

Other books by the same author:
Closely Akin to Murder, 1996
Busy Bodies, 1995
Tickled to Death, 1994
Poisoned Pins, 1993
Death by the Light of the Moon, 1992

Other books you might like:
Rosemary Edghill, *The Bowl of Night*, 1996
Jane Haddam, *Not a Creature Was Stirring*, 1990
Jane Langton, *The Shortest Day*, 1995
Marlys Millhiser, *Death of the Office Witch*, 1993
Valerie Wolzien, *We Wish You a Merry Murder*, 1994

120

JOAN HESS

The Maggody Militia

(New York: Dutton, 1997)

Story type: Humor; Police Procedural
Series: Arly Hanks
Major character(s): Arly Hanks, Police Officer (police chief)
Time period(s): 1990s
Locale(s): Maggody, Arkansas

Summary: The tiny (pop. 755) backwater town of Maggody is an amazing microcosm of the larger outside world, having seen its share of televangelists, UFOs, entertainment types, and now its own home-grown anti-government brigade. Kayla Smeltner, an attractive widow, moves to town and

opens a pawnshop right behind Ruby Bee's restaurant, displaying an alarming number of guns and attracting a lot of camouflage-clad customers. Then Kayla invites a group of them to spend a week at Cotter's Ridge, where a training camp is established, complete with obstacle course, firing ranges, and foxholes. This particular militia group is intent on defending themselves against the U.N. and the U.S. Army as well as the communists, and as inept as they may be, Arly and the rest of the town want them out. Then their leader receives a tip that a paid government informer is in their midst, and the next thing you know, a militia member is murdered. It's up to Arly to find out what happened. Four recipes included.

Where it's reviewed:
Booklist, February 15, 1997, page 1007
Kirkus Reviews, February 1, 1997, page 175
Publishers Weekly, January 13, 1997, page 57

Other books by the same author:
Miracles in Maggody, 1995
O Little Town of Maggody, 1994
Martians in Maggody, 1993
Maggody in Manhattan, 1992
Mortal Remains in Maggody, 1991

Other books you might like:
Deborah Adams, *The Jesus Creek Series*, 1992-
Charlaine Harris, *The Aurora Teagarden Series*, 1990-
Toni L.P. Kelner, *The Laura Fleming Series*, 1993-
Sharyn McCrumb, *The Elizabeth MacPherson Series*, 1984-
Elizabeth Daniels Squire, *The Peaches Dann Series*, 1994-

121

CARL HIAASEN

Lucky You
(New York: Knopf, 1997)

Story type: Action/Adventure; Humor
Major character(s): JoLayne Lucks, Veterinarian (veterinarian's assistant)
Time period(s): 1990s
Locale(s): Florida

Summary: JoLayne Lucks, an attractive and intelligent single black woman who lives in a small town in South Florida, holds one of the two winning tickets in the state's $28 million lottery. She couldn't be happier, but the two men who hold the other winning ticket have plans for her. Bodean Glazer and his friend Chub think the whole pie would be better than half, and they know just what they want to do with their money: start their own white supremacist organization to avert a UN invasion of the U.S. via handicapped parking spaces. So they beat up JoLayne and escape with her ticket, but JoLayne and a reporter are soon hot on their trail. Along the way Hiaasen manages to skewer religious fanatics, tabloid journalists, and the Mafia, and introduce a gallery of eccentric characters.

Where it's reviewed:
Kirkus Reviews, September 1, 1997, page 1330

Other books by the same author:
Stormy Weather, 1995
Strip Tease, 1993
Native Tongue, 1991

Skin Tight, 1989
Double Whammy, 1987

Other books you might like:
Pete Hautman, *Drawing Dead*, 1994
Joan Hess, *The Maggody Militia*, 1997
Christopher Moore, *Island of the Sequined Love Nun*, 1997
Laurence Shames, *Florida Straits*, 1992
Randy Wayne White, *The Doc Ford Series*, 1990-

122

JOHN SPENCER HILL

Ghirlandaio's Daughter
(New York: St. Martin's Press, 1997)

Story type: Police Procedural
Series: Carlo Arbati
Major character(s): Carlo Arbati, Detective—Police, Writer (poet)
Time period(s): 1990s
Locale(s): Florence, Italy; Italy (Tuscany)

Summary: Arbati is back sifting clues and alibis when his friend Nigel Harmsworth, a septuagenarian and expatriate English painter who is also a patron of the arts, finds a corpse in the garden of his villa in Tuscany. The murder weapon is the bronze spear of a Mycenaean warrior, which has been driven through the victim's chest. Given that Arbati is, in addition to being a policeman and a poet, a lover of the arts and antiquity, the case is right up his alley.

Where it's reviewed:
Booklist, March 15, 1997, page 1229
Kirkus Reviews, January 15, 1997, page 98
Publishers Weekly, January 27, 1997, page 81

Other books by the same author:
The Last Castrato, 1995

Other books you might like:
Michael Dibdin, *The Aurelio Zen Series*, 1988-
Gregory Dowling, *The January Esposito Series*, 1985-
Donna Leon, *The Guido Brunetti Series*, 1992-
Magdalen Nabb, *The Marshal Guarnaccia Series*, 1981-
Edward Sklepowich, *The Urbino MacIntyre Series*, 1990-

123

HAZEL HOLT

Mrs. Malory and the Only Good Lawyer
(New York: Dutton, 1997)

Story type: Amateur Detective
Series: Mrs. Sheila Malory
Major character(s): Sheila Malory, Critic (literary), Widow(er)
Time period(s): 1990s
Locale(s): Taviscombe, England

Summary: Every year Graham Percy, a solicitor and crashing bore whose company Sheila Malory tolerates only because of his friendship with her late husband, visits her for a week at her cottage in the charming little village of Taviscombe. She

dreads the annual event and can't understand why her husband's three closest schoolboy chums still employ Percy to represent them in their business dealings. This year, however, she notices that Percy's relations with the three men are exceedingly strained, and she soon discovers that he is blackmailing each and every one of them. It's hard to investigate while Percy is a guest in her home, but she does some shrewd snooping and observing and is well on her way to uncovering the truth when it is brought home to her just how dangerous a man Percy is.

Other books by the same author:
Mrs. Malory: Death of a Dean, 1996
Mrs. Malory Wonders Why, 1995
Mrs. Malory: Detective in Residence, 1994
Mrs. Malory and the Festival Murders, 1993
The Shortest Journey, 1992

Other books you might like:
M.C. Beaton, *The Agatha Raisin Series*, 1992-
Simon Brett, *The Mrs. Pargeter Series*, 1986-
Agatha Christie, *The Miss Marple Series*, 1930-1976
Mollie Hardwick, *The Doran Fairweather series*, 1986-
Betty Rowlands, *The Melissa Craig Series*, 1989-

124

SUSAN HOLTZER

Black Diamond

(New York: St. Martin's Press, 1997)

Story type: Amateur Detective
Series: Anneke Hagen
Major character(s): Anneke Haagen, Computer Expert; Karl Gennesko, Police Officer (former NFL player)
Time period(s): 1990s
Locale(s): Ann Arbor, Michigan

Summary: Anneke is approached by two university students, one of them *Michigan Daily* reporter Zoe Kaplan, for help in piecing together the story of one student's ancestor, who was the wife of a logger baron and who maintained an unlikely correspondence with a lumber camp follower over a century ago. As Anneke and the students pore over the letters they uncover a long-ago arson as well as a murder and a lost treasure. There is a contemporary murder as well and in combining the two the author has enriched both stories.

Where it's reviewed:
Publishers Weekly, August 18, 1997, page 73

Other books by the same author:
Bleeding Maize and Blue, 1996
Curly Smoke, 1995
Something to Kill For, 1994

Other books you might like:
Barbara D'Amato, *Hard Christmas*, 1995
Jo Dereske, *Savage Cut*, 1997
Kate Clark Flora, *The Thea Kozak Series*, 1994-
Marcia Muller, *Beyond the Grave*, Bill Pron
Sharon Gwyn Short, *The Patricia Delaney Series*, 1994-

125

WENDY HORNSBY

A Hard Light

(New York: Dutton, 1997)

Story type: Amateur Detective
Series: Maggie MacGowen
Major character(s): Maggie MacGowen, Filmmaker (documentary), Single Parent; Mike Fine, Police Officer (homicide detective), Single Parent
Time period(s): 1990s
Locale(s): Los Angeles, California; San Francisco, California

Summary: It's time for Maggie to make some life-changing decisions: if she should sell her house in San Francisco, move her daughter and herself to Los Angeles, and marry her longtime boyfriend, LAPD homicide detective Mike Fine. In the meantime, the film she's working on is stalled and the perfect distraction presents itself, even if it does come via her exhusband Scotty: find a missing Vietnamese scholar who escaped from Vietnam at the end of the war—along with a fortune in art.

Where it's reviewed:
Booklist, August 1997, page 1885
Kirkus Reviews, July 15, 1997, page 1068
Library Journal, July 1997, page 131
Los Angeles Times Book Review, August 17, 1997, page 9
Publishers Weekly, June 16, 1997, page 47

Other books by the same author:
Midnight Baby, 1996
Telling Lies, 1995
77th Street Requiem, 1995
Bad Intent, 1994

Other books you might like:
Jan Burke, *The Irene Kelly Series*, 1993-
Barbara D'Amato, *The Cat Marsala Series*, 1990-
Jeffery Deaver, *Death of a Blue Movie Star*, 1990
Tony Hillerman, *Finding Moon*, 1995
John Sandford, *The Night Crew*, 1997

126

SYDNEY HOSIER

Murder, Mrs. Hudson

(New York: Avon, 1997)

Story type: Historical; Amateur Detective
Series: Mrs. Hudson
Major character(s): Emma Hudson, Housekeeper (landlady); Violet Warner, Friend; Winston Churchill, Historical Figure
Time period(s): 1890s
Locale(s): London, England

Summary: Everyone knows that Sherlock Holmes and Dr. Watson would have been lost without their loyal housekeeper and landlady Emma Hudson, but it's not so well known that she was a crack detective in her own right. She and her friend Mrs. Violet Warner accept a referral from Holmes when a young Winston Churchill arrives at Baker Street in desperate

need of help. He asks them to trail an international terrorist who is stalking the Royals, and their investigations take them into London's underworld and put them in grave danger.

Other books by the same author:
Elementary, Mrs. Hudson, 1996

Other books you might like:
Emily Brightwell, *The Mrs. Jeffries Series,* 1993-
Carole Nelson Douglas, *The Irene Adler Series,* 1990-
Quinn Fawcett, *Against the Brotherhood,* 1997
Kate Kingsbury, *The Cecily Sinclair Series,* 1993-
Robin Paige, *The Kathryn Ardleigh Series,* 1994-

127

DAVID HOUSEWRIGHT

Practice to Deceive

(Woodstock, Vermont: Foul Play 1997)

Story type: Private Detective
Series: Holland Taylor
Major character(s): Holland Taylor, Detective—Private
Time period(s): 1990s
Locale(s): St. Paul, Minnesota

Summary: When an elderly widow who's been bilked of her life savings by a shady investment advisor turns to Taylor for help, they both decide they don't have time for a lengthy civil suit, so he turns to a more creative way of recovering the funds. With some help from a hacker friend, he devises an ingenious scheme involving credit card fraud, realtors, tradesmen, and so forth, in hopes of harassing the miscreant into returning the money. It works, but the man is killed just before making restitution, and now Taylor has a brand new case on his hands. This time his lawyer girlfriend and a cop help him pursue justice, still in an unconventional fashion.

Other books by the same author:
Penance, 1996

Other books you might like:
Robert Crais, *The Elvis Cole Series,* 1987-
G.M. Ford, *The Leo Waterman Series,* 1995-
Pete Hautman, *The Joe Crow Series,* 1994-
Robert B. Parker, *The Spenser Series,* 1973-
Walter Satterthwait, *The Joshua Croft Series,* 1989-

128

JONNIE JACOBS

Evidence of Guilt

(New York: Kensington, 1997)

Story type: Legal
Series: Kali O'Brien
Major character(s): Kali O'Brien, Lawyer
Time period(s): 1990s
Locale(s): Silver Creek, California (Sierras)

Summary: Former San Francisco attorney Kali O'Brien is still struggling to establish her law practice in her home town of Silver Creek when a local waitress and her small daughter are murdered and Wes Harding, a former classmate of Kali's, is the chief suspect. Kali is asked by her long-time mentor to assist him on the case, and she agrees, but Harding refuses to help. It turns out that the murdered waitress was holding some fairly shocking secrets involving the town's most prominent citizens and a long-ago tragedy. Kali has to battle time and a ruthless prosecutor to clear her friend of the murder.

Where it's reviewed:
Booklist, March 15, 1997, page 1229
Kirkus Reviews, January 1, 1997, page 24
Publishers Weekly, December 30, 1996, page 57

Other books by the same author:
Shadow of Doubt, 1996

Other books you might like:
Lia Matera, *The Willa Jansson Series,* 1986-
Perri O'Shaugnessy, *The Nina Reilly Series,* 1995-
Janet L. Smith, *The Annie McPherson Series,* 1990-
Penny Warner, *Dead Body Language,* 1997
Kate Wilhelm, *The Barbara Holloway Series,* 1991-

129

BILL JAMES

Gospel

(New York: Foul Play, 1997)

Story type: Police Procedural
Series: Colin Harpur
Major character(s): Colin Harpur, Police Officer; Iles, Police Officer
Time period(s): 1990s
Locale(s): England

Summary: Harpur understands all too well the motivations of the criminals he pursues and of the cops he works with, and his conclusion is that they aren't such different breeds. He has his own weaknesses, to be sure, and right now one of them is a pretty young college student with whom he is spending his afternoons. Then she somehow drifts into the social circle of one of Harpur's underworld informants, a wealthy, powerful and very dangerous man. When one of his crooks is shot to death during a robbery, the young woman becomes the pawn in a deadly game of revenge. The author uses the story as a means of exploring the relationships between policemen and their counterparts on the opposite side of the law.

Where it's reviewed:
Kirkus Reviews, March 1, 1997, page 337
Publishers Weekly, March 10, 1997, page 53

Other books by the same author:
Top Banana, 1996
The Detective Is Dead, 1995
In Good Hands, 1994
Roses, Roses, 1993
Astride a Grave, 1991

Other books you might like:
John Harvey, *The Charlie Resnick Series,* 1989-
Quintin Jardine, *The Constable Robert Skinner Series,* 1993-
Val McDermid, *The Mermaids Singing,* 1996
William McIlvaney, *The Jack Laidlaw Series,* 1977-
Ian Rankin, *The Inspector John Rebus Series,* 1987-

J.A. JANCE

Skeleton Canyon

(New York: Avon, 1996)

Story type: Police Procedural
Series: Joanna Brady
Major character(s): Joanna Brady, Police Officer (Sheriff), Widow(er) (single mother)
Time period(s): 1990s
Locale(s): Bisbee, Arizona

Summary: Having been elected Sheriff of Cochise County to replace her husband, who was killed in the line of duty, Joanna Brady is determined to succeed at the job and still remain a caring human being and devoted mother. Her resolve is put to the test when she's called to investigate the events that unfold after a pair of star-crossed young lovers arrange to meet in southern Arizona's legendary Skeleton Canyon. Joanna finds herself not only dealing with a grisly family tragedy but facing echoes of Tombstone's notorious Clanton gang. With a thunderstorm and flash flood threatening to destroy the evidence, Joanna finds that time is running out and it will take everything she's got to prove herself up to the job she's chosen.

Where it's reviewed:
Booklist, August 9, 1997, page 1885
Kirkus Reviews, July 15, 1997, page 1068
Publishers Weekly, June 23, 1997, page 75

Other books by the same author:
Shoot, Don't Shoot, 1995
Tombstone Courage, 1994
Desert Heat, 1993

Other books you might like:
Nevada Barr, *Track of the Cat*, 1994
P.M. Carlson, *The Marty Hopkins Series*, 1992-
Val Davis, *The Track of the Scorpion*, 1996
Jake Page, *A Certain Malice*, 1997
Charlene Weir, *The Susan Wren Series*, 1992-

131

J. ROBERT JANES

Stonekiller

(New York: Soho, 1997)

Story type: Historical; Police Procedural
Series: Jean-Louis St. Cyr & Hermann Kohler
Major character(s): Jean-Louis St.-Cyr, Police Officer (Surete Nationale, chief insp.); Hermann Kohler, Police Officer (Gestapo)
Time period(s): 1940s (1942)
Locale(s): Dordogne, France

Summary: The Germans may occupy France, but there are still ordinary crimes to be investigated. Jean-Louis St-Cyr of the Surete Nationale and Hermann Kohler of the Gestapo are both seasoned detectives who have been paired together in an often uneasy alliance. Here they are in the Dordogne investigating the murder of a woman archeologist who years earlier discov-

ered a treasure trove of prehistoric cave paintings far surpassing those at Lascaux. A German propaganda film is about to be made of her find, tracing Nazi roots back to prehistoric times, and there is great pressure upon the detectives to find why the woman has been savagely bludgeoned to death.

Where it's reviewed:
Kirkus Reviews, April 15, 1997, page 592
Library Journal, May 1, 1997, page 144
New York Times Book Review, May 25, 1997, page 23
Publishers Weekly, February 24, 1997, page 66

Other books by the same author:
Dollmaker, 1995
Salamander, 1994
Mannequin, 1994
Kaleidoscope, 1993
Carousel, 1992

Other books you might like:
Manning Coles, *A Toast to Tomorrow*, 1941
Jack Gerson, *The Ernest Lohmann Series*, 1984-
Christopher Hyde, *A Gathering of Saints*, 1996
Philip Kerr, *The Bernie Gunther Series*, 1989-1991
John Lawton, *Black Out*, 1995

132

MAUREEN JENNINGS

Except the Dying

(New York: St. Martin's, 1997)

Story type: Historical; Police Procedural
Major character(s): William Murdoch, Detective—Police
Time period(s): 1890s (1895)
Locale(s): Toronto, Ontario, Canada

Summary: With his city in the grip of a bitterly cold winter, Murdoch investigates the murder of Therese Laporte, a young servant girl whose naked body is discovered in a deserted lane. She had last been seen climbing into a hansom cab the night she disappeared, the only witness a prostitute. As he attempts to uncover the events that led up to her death under such pitiful circumstances, Murdoch must cross the class lines of a society still very much dominated by the rigid British hierarchal system. It's among this society's upper echelons, dominated by the wealthy and powerful, that he uncovers people connected with the girl who have something to hide. Her wealthy mistress felt a deep affection for her, but Therese also evoked troubling memories from her own past. And the handsome young son of the house is lying about his whereabouts on the night of the murder. Further, Murdoch discovers Therese was pregnant, raising the possibility her death was part of an attempt to cover up a possible scandal. First novel.

Other books you might like:
Ray Harrison, *The Bragg/Morton Series*, 1983-
Alanna Knight, *The Inspector Jeremy Faro Series*, 1988-
Peter Lovesey, *The Sergeant Richard Cribb/Constable Edward Thackeray Series*, 1970-78
Anne Perry, *The Inspector Thomas and Charlotte Pitt Series*, 1979-
Kate Ross, *The Julian Kestrel Series*, 1993-

133

DOLORES JOHNSON

Hung Up to Die
(New York: Dell, 1997)

Story type: Amateur Detective
Series: Mandy Dyer
Major character(s): Mandy Dyer, Businesswoman (owner of a dry cleaners)
Time period(s): 1990s
Locale(s): Aurora, Colorado

Summary: Following her divorce, Mandy Dyer has taken over her family's dry cleaning business and is anxious to make a success of it. She's developed a reputation for taking careful care of her customers, but suddenly lipstick marks start appearing on their freshly pressed garments. Mandy fears one of her own employees is trying to sabotage the business, and she wonders if the person could be working for Lonnie ''The Sleazeball'' Mills, who's been bombarding her customers with coupons for his recently opened discount dry cleaners. Then Mandy finds Lonnie's body suspended from the conveyor used to move garments, and she becomes the prime suspect when the police learn she had threatened to ruin his career if he didn't stop hanging around her plant. To top matters off, Mandy has to deal with the arrival of her mother from Phoenix.

Other books by the same author:
Taken to the Cleaners, 1997

Other books you might like:
Carol Cail, *The Maxey Burnell Series*, 1993-
Diane Mott Davidson, *The Goldy Bear Series*, 1990-
Renee Horowitz, *The Ruthie Kantor Morris Series*, 1997-
Christine T. Jorgensen, *The Stella the Stargazer Series*, 1994-
Leslie O'Kane, *The Molly Masters Series*, 1996-

134

CHRISTINE T. JORGENSEN

Curl Up and Die
(New York: Walker, 1997)

Story type: Amateur Detective
Series: Stella the Stargazer
Major character(s): Jane Smith, Journalist (lovelorn columnist)
Time period(s): 1990s
Locale(s): Denver, Colorado

Summary: When Jane Smith left her accountant job behind her for good and became Stella the Stargazer, caster of horoscopes and dispenser of advice to the lovelorn for the Denver weekly newspaper the *Daily Orion*, her life became a whole lot more exciting. She's always had an erratic talent for foreseeing the future, not one she can control but one which occasionally sheds light on the crimes that seem to come her way. This time she goes into a salon for a makeover and ends up investigating a murder in which her best friend Meredith is the prime suspect.

Where it's reviewed:
Booklist, December 15, 1996, page 712
Kirkus Reviews, October 15, 1996, page 1497
Library Journal, December 1996, page 151
Publishers Weekly, October 21, 1996, page 73

Other books by the same author:
You Bet Your Life, 1995
A Love to Die For, 1994

Other books you might like:
Carol Cail, *The Maxey Burnell Series*, 1993-
Diane Mott Davidson, *Killer Pancake*, 1995
Sophie Dunbar, *A Bad Hair Day*, 1996
Martha Lawrence, *Murder in Scorpio*, 1996
Marlys Millhiser, *The Charlie Greene Series*, 1992-

135

JULIE KAEWERT

Unbound
(New York: Bantam, 1997)

Story type: Amateur Detective
Series: Alex Plumtree
Major character(s): Alex Plumtree, Publisher
Time period(s): 1990s
Locale(s): London, England

Summary: Alec Plumtree, heir to the foundering Plumtree Press, has succeeded in putting the firm into the black and reestablishing it as one of the country's premier publishing houses. Now they are about to pubish a shocking novel based on the life of one of Britain's most revered writers, Marcus Stonecypher, a member of Virginia Woolf's Bloomsbury Circle. Revealed in the book are coded messages in the Stonecypher novels that are part of a treacherous plot to topple the monarchy. Someone wants very badly to keep this book from ever being sold, and until this person is stopped, Alex, the author, and Plumtree Press are all in grave danger.

Other books by the same author:
Unsolicited, 1994

Other books you might like:
Nicholas Blake, *End of Chapter*, 1957
Robert A. Carter, *Final Edit*, 1994
John Dunning, *The Bookman's Wake*, 1995
Roy H. Lewis, *The Manuscript Murders*, 1981
Marianne Macdonald, *Death's Autograph*, 1997

136

STUART M. KAMINSKY

Tarnished Icons
(New York: Ivy, 1997)

Story type: Police Procedural
Series: Inspector Rostnikov
Major character(s): Porfiry Rostnikov, Police Officer (inspector)
Time period(s): 1990s

Summary: Three members of a Moscow synagogue are gunned down in the night, the latest victims in a series of seemingly systematic executions of Muscovite Jews. But the identity of one of the victims has Rostnikov thinking that maybe a more calculated motive than anti-Semitism lies behind the slaughter. Meanwhile, the women of the city are being stalked by the Shy One, a knife-wielding serial rapist who strikes in seeming invisibility. And a militant anti-nuclear activist threatens to send an explosive message to the New Russia if his warnings aren't heeded.

Other books by the same author:
Blood and Rubles, 1996
Hard Currency, 1995
Death of a Russian Priest, 1992
Rostnikov's Vacation, 1991
The Man Who Walked Like a Bear, 1990

Other books you might like:
John Le Carre, *The Russia House*, 1987
Anthony Olcott, *Murder at the Red October*, 1981
Douglas Skeggs, *The Talinin Madonna*, 1992
Martin Cruz Smith, *The Arkady Renko Series*, 1981-
Robin White, *Siberian Light*, 1997

137

JOSEPH KANON

Los Alamos

(New York: Doubleday, 1997)

Story type: Historical
Major character(s): Michael Connolly, Military Personnel (intelligence officer)
Time period(s): 1940s (1945)
Locale(s): Los Alamos, New Mexico

Summary: Intelligence officer Michael Connolly investigates the death of a Manhattan Project security officer in nearby Santa Fe, the possible victim of a violent sexual encounter. Connolly suspects murder, but is the murder connected to an attempt to sabotage or steal the secret of the atomic bomb, or does the answer to it lie in the tangled personal relationships of the people who have voluntarily confined themselves to this facility for the duration? Making cameo appearances are many of the real-life characters who helped develop the bomb, including Robert Oppenheimer. First novel.

Other books you might like:
Robert Harris, *Enigma*, 1993
Robert J. Janes, *The Jean-Louis St. Cyr & Herman Kohler Series*, 1992-1996
Philip Kerr, *The Bernie Gunther Trilogy*, 1989-1991
John Lawton, *Black Out*, 1995
Martin Cruz Smith, *Stallion Gate*, 1987

138

JONATHAN KELLERMAN

Survival of the Fittest

(New York: Bantam, 1997)

Story type: Amateur Detective; Psychological Suspense

Series: Alex Delaware
Major character(s): Alex Delaware, Psychologist; Milo Sturgis, Police Officer (LAPD), Homosexual; Daniel Sharavi, Police Officer (inspector; Israeli)
Time period(s): 1990s
Locale(s): Los Angeles, California

Summary: The murder of the 15-year-old daughter of the Israeli consul in Los Angeles is the beginning of a series of crimes that comes to haunt Alex Delaware. Within days three young people are dead, and the only common denominator in the murders is that each of the victims had a disability. Alex suspects this is the key to the otherwise motiveless killings, but what is the meaning of the letters DVLL left behind at each crime scene? Alex works with his longtime friend Milo, a gay member of the LAPD, and with the brilliant Israeli police detective Daniel Sharavi, who appeared in Kellerman's 1988 non-series novel *The Butcher's Theater*. In the end it's Alex who goes undercover to solve the crimes.

Where it's reviewed:
Booklist, September 1, 1997, page 7
Library Journal, August 1997, page 131
Publishers Weekly, August 18, 1997, page 72

Other books by the same author:
The Clinic, 1997
The Web, 1996
Self-Defense, 1995
Bad Love, 1994
Devil's Waltz, 1993

Other books you might like:
D.J. Donaldson, *The Andy Broussard/Kit Franklyn Series*, 1988-
James Patterson, *The Alex Cross Series*, 1993-
Ridley Pearson, *The Lou Boldt/Daphne Matthews Series*, 1988-
Robert Rosenberg, *The Avram Cohen Series*, 1991-
Stephen White, *The Alan Gregory Series*, 1991-

139

PHILIP KERR

Esau

(New York: Holt 1997)

Story type: Action/Adventure
Major character(s): Jack Furness, Mountaineer; Stella Swift, Scientist (paleoanthropologist)
Time period(s): 1990s
Locale(s): Nepal (Himalayas)

Summary: While undertaking an illegal ascent of a forbidden peak in the Annapurna range in the Himalayas, American climber Jack Furness is nearly swept off the peak by a mysterious avalanche and tumbles into a cave where he discovers the perfectly preserved skull of an alternative line of hominid development. He smuggles his find out of Nepal and presents it to his friend Stella Swift, an Australian-born paleoanthropologist at the University of California. The skull turns out not to be a fossil at all, but contemporary, and the two lead an expedition back to the mountain in hopes of discovering a living yeti. But unknown to them, the team of scientists Swift

has assembled includes a rogue CIA agent with a very different and deadly mission of his own. Kerr blends fact and fiction seamlessly and raises philosophical questions about what the discovery of another intelligent hominid species could mean to the world.

Where it's reviewed:
Booklist, February 15, 1997, page 971
Kirkus Reviews, February 1, 1997, page 162
Library Journal, February 15, 1997, page 162
New York Times Book Review, April 27, 1997, page 25
Publishers Weekly, March 3, 1997, page 63

Other books by the same author:
The Grid, 1996
Dead Meat, 1994
A Philosophical Investigation, 1992
A German Requiem, 1991
The Pale Criminal, 1990

Other books you might like:
Desmond Bagley, *High Citadel*, 1965
Glyn Carr, *A Corpse at Camp Two*, 1954
Lionel Davidson, *The Rose of Tibet*, 1962
Daniel Easterman, *The Ninth Buddha*, 1989
Duff Hart-Davis, *The Heights of Rimring*, 1981

140

DAVID KIELY

The Angel Tapes

(New York: St. Martin's Press, 1997)

Story type: Police Procedural
Major character(s): Blade Macken, Police Officer
Time period(s): 1990s
Locale(s): Dublin, Ireland

Summary: Hard-luck Dublin police detective Blade Macken leads a team of investigators determined to solve a series of terrorist bombings engineered by a twisted killer named Angel. The bombs are being detonated from beneath the asphalt streets, making them impossible to locate without tearing up the entire city. Even a city used to terrorist acts is on the verge of panic, and the life of the American president may be at stake if Angel can't be stopped. First novel.

Other books you might like:
Thomas Adcock, *Drown All the Dogs*, 1994
John Brady, *The Matt Minogue Series*, 1988-
Bartholomew Gill, *The Inspector Peter McGarr Series*, 1977-
Chris Petit, *The Psalm Killer*, 1997
Ian Rankin, *The Inspector John Rebus Series*, 1987-

141

LAURIE R. KING

A Letter of Mary

(New York: St. Martin's Press, 1997)

Story type: Historical; Private Detective
Series: Mary Russell
Major character(s): Mary Russell, Detective—Private, Scholar; Sherlock Holmes, Detective—Private

Time period(s): 1920s (1923)
Locale(s): London, England

Summary: Now that Mary has married her mentor Sherlock Holmes, there is the tiniest danger that despite the fullness of their relationship he is getting bored. Luckily a diversion arises in the form of archeologist Dorothy Ruskin, who shows them an ancient scroll she obtained on a dig in Palestine. It is a letter from an unrecorded apostle of Jesus, Mary of Magdala, which, if it were to be made public, would shake the very foundations of the Christian Church, which could never accept a mere woman as an apostle. When Dorothy is killed in a suspicious accident, Holmes and Russell swing into action. Mary has blossomed from a schoolgirl into a full-fledged Oxford scholar whose wit and keen intellect fulfill the promise of her youthful precocity. Look for a cameo appearance by Lord Peter Wimsey.

Where it's reviewed:
Book World, December 15, 1996, page 10
Booklist, January 1997, page 825
Kirkus Reviews, November 1, 1996, page 1567
New York Times Book Review, January 5, 1997
Publishers Weekly, November 18, 1996, page 64

Other books by the same author:
A Monstrous Regiment of Women, 1995
The Beekeeper's Apprentice, 1994

Other books you might like:
Abby Pen Baker, *In the Dead of Winter*, 1994
Carole Nelson Douglas, *The Irene Adler Series*, 1990-
Elizabeth Peters, *The Amelia Peabody Series*, 1975-
Dorothy L. Sayers, *Gaudy Night*, 1935
Charles Todd, *A Test of Wills*, 1996

142

PETER KING

Spiced to Death

(New York: St. Martin's Press, 1997)

Story type: Amateur Detective
Series: The Gourmet Detective
Major character(s): The Gourmet Detective, Investigator (culinary)
Time period(s): 1990s
Locale(s): New York, New York (Manhattan)

Summary: Ko Feng, or the Celestial Spice, has been thought lost to the world forever. But several centuries after the last of the spice seemingly disappeared, it has been rediscovered. Because of its reputedly remarkable properties as an aphrodisiac, it's sure to command a princely price on the market. The Gourmet Detective (whose name has not yet been revealed to the reader) is called in to verify the authenticity of the spice but ends up looking into the murder of a fellow culinary expert. It seems someone wants to keep the spice a secret. Along the way the Gourmet Detective samples the cuisines of Manhattan's many ethnic restaurants.

Where it's reviewed:
Kirkus Reviews, May 1, 1997, page 681
Library Journal, July 1997, page 131
Publishers Weekly, June 30, 1997, page 70

Other books by the same author:
The Gourmet Detective, 1996

Other books you might like:
Michael Bond, *The Monsieur Pamplemousse Series*, 1983-
Diane Mott Davidson, *Dying for Chocolate*, 1992
Nan Lyons, *Someone Is Killing the Great Chefs of America*, 1993
  Ivor Lyons, co-author
Joanne Pence, *The Angie Amalfi Series*, 1993-
Lou Jane Temple, *The Heaven Lee Series*, 1996-

143

VIRGINIA LANIER

A Brace of Bloodhounds

(New York: HarperCollins, 1997)

Story type: Amateur Detective
Series: Jo Beth Siddon
Major character(s): Jo Beth Siddon, Businesswoman (dog breeder), Animal Trainer
Time period(s): 1990s
Locale(s): Balsa City, Georgia

Summary: One of Jo Beth's friends has unwittingly gotten involved with a shady group of marijuana growers and dealers and she needs help getting out of the mess. With the help of her beloved hounds Jo Beth searches out the crime ring's marijuana field buried deep in the swampy Okefenokee. Even worse, her paroled ex-husband Bubba is on her trail again, and if he catches her she's in grave danger; he's attacked her savagely before. All she has to see her through are her wits, her .32 snub-nosed revolver, and a pack of droopy-eared, drooling bloodhounds.

Where it's reviewed:
Kirkus Reviews, May 1, 1997, page 682
Publishers Weekly, May 5, 1997, page 201

Other books by the same author:
The House on Bloodhound Lane, 1996
Death in Bloodhound Red, 1995

Other books you might like:
Nevada Barr, *Endangered Species*, 1997
Laurien Berenson, *The Melanie Travis Series*, 1995-
Susan Conant, *The Holly Winter Series*, 1989-
Mary Willis Walker, *Zero at the Bone*, 1991
Karen Ann Wilson, *Eight Dogs Flying*, 1994

144

WILLIAM LASHNER

Veritas

(New York: HarperCollins, 1997)

Story type: Legal
Series: Victor Carl
Major character(s): Victor Carl, Lawyer
Time period(s): 1990s
Locale(s): Philadelphia, Pennsylvania; Belize

Summary: Resourceful and sometimes unscrupulous lawyer Victor Carl is hired to wrap up the affairs of the late heiress Jacqueline Shaw. He soon discovers her death was not suicide but murder, and he races against time to solve the case in a journey that takes him from the mean streets of Philadelphia to the jungles of Belize. For in order to find who killed Jacqueline, he must expose the secret past of one of Philadelphia's most powerful and wealthy families. The final answer to the murder lies in a note written decades ago.

Where it's reviewed:
Booklist, December 15, 1996, page 692
Kirkus Reviews, December 1, 1996, page 1693
Publishers Weekly, December 9, 1996, page 59
Publishers Weekly, March 3, 1997, page 30 (for audio version)

Other books by the same author:
Hostile Witness, 1995

Other books you might like:
Neil Albert, *The Dave Garrett Series*, 1991-
John Lescroart, *The Dismas Hardy Series*, 1989-
Lisa Scottoline, *Running from the Law*, 1995
Grif Stockley, *The Gideon Page Series*, 1992-
Scott Turow, *Burden of Proof*, 1990

145

EMMA LATHEN (Pseudonym of Mary J. Latsis and Martha Henissart)

A Shark Out of Water

(New York: St. Martin's Press, 1997)

Story type: Amateur Detective
Series: John Putnam Thatcher
Major character(s): John Putnam Thatcher, Banker (senior vice president)
Time period(s): 1990s
Locale(s): New York, New York (Wall Street)

Summary: When his long-time employer, the Sloan Guaranty Trust Company, commissions Thatcher to investigate the possibility of investing money in the modernization of the Kiel Canal, he sees an opportunity to make a substantial profit for his bank. The canal is the link between the North and Baltic Seas, and Thatcher heads for Poland to examine the plans first-hand. But the quasi-governmental commission in charge of the modernization is not all that it seems to be, and Thatcher finds himself in the middle of a giant foul-up, scandal, and murder.

Other books by the same author:
Brewing Up a Storm, 1996
Right on the Money, 1993
East Is East, 1991
Something in the Air, 1988
Green Grow the Dollars, 1982

Other books you might like:
Ellen Godfrey, *The Jane Tregar Series*, 1988-
Margaret Logan, *A Killing in Venture Capital*, 1989
Annette Meyers, *The Xenia Smith/Leslie Wetzon Series*, 1989-
Haughton Murphy, *The Reuben Frost Series*, 1986-

Dianne G. Pugh, *The Iris Thorne Series*, 1993-

146

MARGARET LAWRENCE (Pseudonym of Margaret Keilstrup)

Blood Red Roses

(New York: Avon, 1997)

Story type: Historical
Series: Hannah Trevor
Major character(s): Hannah Trevor, Healer (midwife and nurse)
Time period(s): 1780s (1786)
Locale(s): Rufford, Maine

Summary: With the American Revolution fought and won but the Constitution not yet ratified, the new country is in a state of near anarchy, ripe for a populist rebellion. Hannah Trevor, a widow with a a deaf eight-year-old daughter, is considered in the eyes of the law unable to support Jennet, despite the fact she earns a reasonable living as a midwife. With the courts about to take Jennet away from her and sell the child into indentured servitude, about the only option Hannah has is another loveless marriage. Jennet's father, the wealthy land-owner Daniel Josslyn, is still married to another, and Hannah feels her future is hopeless. Then, during a midsummer's eve haying party, a body is discovered and Hannah immediately becomes a suspect. A series of turbulent events follows and Hannah must summon up every ounce of courage and passion she has to clear herself and keep her beloved daughter.

Where it's reviewed:
Kirkus Reviews, August 15, 1997, page 1263

Other books by the same author:
Hearts and Bones, 1996

Other books you might like:
Robert Begiebing, *The Strange Death of Mistress Coffin*, 1991
Ron Burns, *The Mysterious Death of Meriwether Lewis*, 1993
Robert Lee Hall, *The Benjamin Franklin Series*, 1988-
Miriam Grace Monfredo, *The Glynis Tryon Series*, 1992-
Maan Neyers, *The High Constable*, 1994

147

DENNIS LEHANE

Sacred

(New York: Morrow, 1997)

Story type: Private Detective
Series: Patrick Kenzie & Angela Gennaro
Major character(s): Patrick Kenzie, Detective—Private; Angela Gennaro, Detective—Private
Time period(s): 1990s
Locale(s): Boston, Massachusetts; Gulf Coast, Florida

Summary: A dying billionaire hires Patrick Kenzie and Angie Gennaro to find his daughter Desiree Stone, who's been griev-ing the loss of her mother and impending death of her father and has been missing for three weeks. So has the first detec-tive hired to find her: Jay Becker, Patrick's mentor. Their investigations lead Patrick and Angie to a dangerous cult, stolen money, and a tanker full of heroin, and they become increasingly uncertain whether the people they're looking for are victims or criminals, if indeed they're alive at all.

Where it's reviewed:
Booklist, June 1, 1997, page 1666
Kirkus Reviews, May 15, 1997, page 760
Library Journal, June 15, 1997, page 98
Publishers Weekly, May 26, 1997, page 69
Tribune Books, August 3, 1997, page 11

Other books by the same author:
Darkness, Take My Hand, 1996
A Drink Before the War, 1994

Other books you might like:
Jerome Doolittle, *The Tom Bethany Series*, 1990-
Earl Emerson, *The Thomas Black Series*, 1985-
James W. Hall, *The Thorn Series*, 1988-
Jeremiah Healy, *The John Francis Cuddy Series*, 1984-
S.J. Rozan, *The Bill Smith/Lydia Chin Series*, 1994-

148

MARTIN LIMON

Slicky Boys

(New York: Bantam, 1997)

Story type: Police Procedural
Series: George Sueno/Ernie Bascomb
Major character(s): George Sueno, Military Personnel (U.S. Army CID); Ernie Bascomb, Military Personnel (U.S. Army CID)
Time period(s): 1990s
Locale(s): Seoul, Korea, South

Summary: When Sergeants Sueno and Bascombe agree to deliver a letter from a beautiful woman to her British lover, the next thing they know, the man's savagely butchered body turns up frozen in a dark alleyway and the Korean police are after them for the murder. As they are plunged into the dangerous underworld of an exotic culture they barely under-stand, these two maverick Americans learn the hard way that not even the U.S. Army can protect them from corrupt Korean officials and the deadly young Slicky Boys, kings of the black market.

Where it's reviewed:
Kirkus Reviews, May 1, 1997, page 666
Library Journal, April 1, 1997, page 128
Los Angeles Times Book Review, August 17, 1997, page 9
New York Times Book Review, May 25, 1997, page 23
Publishers Weekly, March 24, 1997, page 59

Other books by the same author:
Jade Lady Burning, 1992

Other books you might like:
Jonathan Gash, *Jade Woman*, 1988
William Marshall, *The Yellowthread Series*, 1975-
Sujata Massey, *The Salaryman's Wife*, 1997
Lisa See, *Flower Net*, 1997
Peter Tasker, *Buddha Kiss*, 1997

149

LAURA LIPPMAN

Charm City

(New York: Avon, 1997)

Story type: Private Detective
Series: Tess Monaghan
Major character(s): Tess Monaghan, Detective—Private (former newspaper reporter)
Time period(s): 1990s
Locale(s): Baltimore, Maryland

Summary: A reporter without a job when her newspaper went under, Tess is prowling the streets of Baltimore as a private investigator and minding her uncle's greyhound. In a town where baseball and homicide are the two major diversions, business tycoon Wink Wynkowski is trying to bring back NBA basketball, but his plans hit a snag when a local paper runs a muckraking expose of his unsavory past. The story was supposed to have been killed, and the newspaper hires Tess to find the hacker who planted it.

Where it's reviewed:
Publishers Weekly, August 18, 1997, page 89

Other books by the same author:
Baltimore Blues, 1997

Other books you might like:
Linda Barnes, *The Carlotta Carlyle Series*, 1987-
Jan Burke, *The Irene Kelly Series*, 1993-
Barbara D'Amato, *The Cat Marsala Series*, 1990-
Janice Law, *The Anna Peters Series*, 1976-
Blair S. Walker, *Up Jumped the Devil*, 1997

150

MARIANNE MACDONALD

Death's Autograph

(New York: St. Martin's Press, 1997)

Story type: Amateur Detective
Major character(s): Dido Hoare, Businesswoman (antiquarian bookseller)
Time period(s): 1990s
Locale(s): London, England (Islington)

Summary: One night, as Dido is driving back to London with her old Volvo estate wagon crammed with cartons of old books she didn't particularly want but drove too far not to buy, she's forced off the road by another car. Shaken, she puts it down to a silly prank. Shortly afterward, however, her bookshop is broken into and ransacked, and then her charming but shiftless ex-husband Davey reappears in her life after a long absence. Dido's 72-year-old father Barnabas, on the mend from a heart attack, had bought the shop for the two of them as a wedding present, and he thinks it's no coincidence that Davey has shown up at this particular juncture. There's much authentic book lore here and details of the daily life of a hard-working, moderately prosperous antiquarian bookseller, as well as a nicely low-key romantic entaglement between Dido and the police inspector assigned the case and a playful,

loving relationship between her and her elderly father. First novel.

Where it's reviewed:
Booklist, September 1, 1997, page 66
Publishers Weekly, August 25, 1997, page 49

Other books you might like:
Jen Banbury, *Like a Hole in the Head*, 1998
Lawrence Block, *The Burglar in the Library*, 1997
John Dunning, *The Cliff Janeway Series*, 1992-
Roy H. Lewis, *The Matthew Coll Series*, 1980-
Wayne Warga, *Hard Cover*, 1985

151

VALERIE S. MALMONT

Death, Lies, and Apple Pies

(New York: Simon & Schuster, 1997)

Story type: Amateur Detective
Series: Tori Miracle
Major character(s): Tori Miracle, Writer (horror novelist)
Time period(s): 1990s
Locale(s): Lickin Creek, Pennsylvania; New York, New York

Summary: After a less than triumphal signing at a neighborhood bookstore where she finds plenty of time to balance her checkbook between bonding with her fans, slightly overweight horror writer Tory Miracle leaves her Hell's Kitchen walkup with its thrift store furnishings behind and pays a return visit to Lickin Creek. She's been invited to judge an apple pie contest, and she also has designs on the town's handsome police chief, with whom she had previously had a brief romance. Both of them are distracted, however, by a rash of accidental deaths that may be linked to a proposed nuclear dump site which has the town sharply divided. A recipe for apple-oatmeal cookies is included.

Where it's reviewed:
Kirkus Reviews, July 15, 1997, page 1069
Library Journal, July 1997, page 130
Publishers Weekly, June 30, 1997, page 70

Other books by the same author:
Death Pays the Rose Rent, 1994

Other books you might like:
Deborah Adams, *The Jesus Creek Series*, 1992-
Susan Rogers Cooper, *The E.J. Pugh Series*, 1992-
Roma Greth, *The Hana Shaner Series*, 1988-
Joan Hess, *The Arly Hanks Series*, 1987-
Tamar Myers, *The Magdalena Yoder Series*, 1994-

152

MARGARET MARON

Killer Market

(New York: Mysterious Press, 1997)

Story type: Legal
Series: Deborah Knott
Major character(s): Deborah Knott, Judge
Time period(s): 1990s

Locale(s): High Point, North Carolina

Summary: Rural district judge Deborah Knott finds herself in a very unwelcome situation when she arrives in the small city of High Point to substitute for a vacationing judge and finds all the hotel rooms for miles around filled with home furnishing conventioneers. To make matters worse, she loses her purse, with all her money, credit cards, and car keys. Then an old lady who befriends her vanishes, a furniture executive is murdered, and without any identification she finds herself a prime suspect.

Where it's reviewed:
Booklist, May 15, 1997, page 1542
Kirkus Reviews, July 1, 1997, page 986
Library Journal, August 1997, page 138
Publishers Weekly, June 16, 1997, page 47

Other books by the same author:
Up Jumps the Devil, 1996
Shooting at Loons, 1994
Southern Discomfort, 1993
Bootlegger's Daughter, 1992

Other books you might like:
Deborah Adams, *The Jesus Creek Series*, 1992-
P.M. Carlson, *The Marty Hopkins Series*, 1992-
Teri Holbrook, *The Grass Widow*, 1996
Sharyn McCrumb, *The Ballad Series*, 1990-
Kate Wilhelm, *Justice for Some*, 1993

153

WILLIAM MARSHALL

Nightmare Syndrome

(New York: Mysterious, 1997)

Story type: Police Procedural; Humor
Series: Yellowthread Street
Major character(s): Harry Feiffer, Police Officer; Christopher O'Yee, Police Officer
Time period(s): 1990s
Locale(s): Hong Kong, China

Summary: During the last days of British rule as Hong Kong is about to be returned to mainland China, Detective Chief Inspector Harry Feiffer of the Yellowthread Street Police Station faces one of the strangest cases of his long career. Corpses are suddenly turning up all over the island, in the men's room of the Millionaire's Club, on the deck of a landlocked ferry, at the Temple of a Thousand Buddhas. Each was once a wealthy industrialist and each had clawed out his own eyes just before dying. At the same time Detective Senior Inspector Christopher O'Yee (half Chinese, half Irish) has to deal with six heavily armed sleepwalking demons who have somehow appeared in the station house.

Where it's reviewed:
Book World, July 20, 1997, page 10
Kirkus Reviews, May 15, 1997, page 762
Library Journal, June 1, 1997, page 156
New York Times Book Review, June 15, 1997, page 35
Publishers Weekly, May 26, 1997, page 70

Other books by the same author:
Inches, 1994
Out of Nowhere, 1988
Frogmouth, 1987
Head First, 1986
Road Show, 1985

Other books you might like:
Jonathan Gash, *Jade Woman*, 1988
Dorothy Gilman, *Mrs. Pollifax and the Hong Kong Buddha*, 1985
Lisa See, *Flower Net*, 1997
Roger L. Simon, *Peking Duck*, 1979
Janwillem Van de Wetering, *The Grijpstra and De Gier Series*, 1975-

154

EDWARD MARSTON (Pseudonym of Keith Miles)

The Fair Maid of Bohemia

(New York: St. Martin's Press, 1997)

Story type: Historical
Series: Nicholas Bracewell
Major character(s): Nicholas Bracewell, Actor (theatrical troupe manager)
Time period(s): 16th century
Locale(s): Prague, Czech Republic; England

Summary: A plague has emptied out the theaters and gathering places of England, and Lord Westfield's Men are on the point of disbanding when an invitation comes from the great-niece of Rudolph II, Sophia Magdalena, to perform at the Imperial Court in Prague. Bracewell, the troupe's manager, is also given some secret documents to deliver to an English doctor in Rudolph's court. One of the actors is murdered en route to Rudolph's court. When the troupe arrives, Bracewell discovers the doctor is being held prisoner in the castle dungeon, and that he himself was the intended target of the killer.

Where it's reviewed:
Kirkus Reviews, May 15, 1997, page 762
Library Journal, June 1, 1997, page 156

Other books by the same author:
The Laughing Hangman, 1996
The Roaring Boy, 1995
The Silent Woman, 1994
The Mad Courtesan, 1992
The Nine Giants, 1991

Other books you might like:
Michael Clynes, *The Roger Shallot Series*, 1991-
Kathy Lynn Emerson, *Face Down in the Marrow-Bone Pie*, 1997
George Herman, *The Tears of the Madonna*, 1996-
Faye Kellerman, *The Quality of Mercy*, 1989
Leonard Tourney, *The Players' Boy Is Dead*, 1980-

155

SUJATA MASSEY

The Salaryman's Wife

(New York: HarperCollins, 1997)

Story type: Amateur Detective
Major character(s): Rei Shimura, Teacher
Time period(s): 1990s
Locale(s): Tokyo, Japan

Summary: Rei is a 27-year-old Japanese-American woman who is teaching English as a second language to employees of a kitchenware company in Tokyo and sharing a rundown house with a fellow teacher, a gay man. She is fluent in Japanese and knowledgeable about Japanese culture, especially antiques, and despite her self-imposed poverty she's very happy with her life. While on a New Year's holiday at a ski resort in the Japanese Alps, Rei stumbles across the body of a salaryman's wife outside the communal bathhouse. (A salaryman is a businessman, or a corporate middle manager.) The police ask her to serve as a translator while they interrogate the English-speaking guests at the resort. One of them, a Scots lawyer, is initially a suspect but when he is released he and Rei team up to find the actual killer. First novel.

Other books you might like:
Dale Furutani, *The Toyotomi Blades*, 1997
James Melville, *The Inspector Otani Series*, 1979-
Alan Russell, *The Fat Innkeeper*, 1995
Lisa See, *Flower Net*, 1997
Peter Tasker, *Buddha Kiss*, 1997

156

LIA MATERA

Star Witness

(New York: Simon & Schuster, 1997)

Story type: Legal
Series: Willa Jansson
Major character(s): Willa Jansson, Lawyer
Time period(s): 1990s
Locale(s): Santa Cruz, California

Summary: When a psychiatrist asks Willa to defend a patient who has been charged with vehicular manslaughter, she's stunned when she hears what his proposed defense is: that he had been abducted by aliens and has no memory of the fatal hit-and-run incident. But it's true that there has been a rash of reported abductions and mysterious deaths in the Santa Cruz area. It's also true that somebody seems determined to keep Willa from investigating them.

Where it's reviewed:
Kirkus Reviews, May 1, 1997, page 682
Library Journal, June 1, 1997, page 156
Publishers Weekly, April 14, 1997, page 59
Tribune Books, June 15, 1997, page 6

Other books by the same author:
Last Chants, 1996
Prior Convictions, 1995
Hidden Agenda, 1989

A Radical Departure, 1987
Where Lawyers Fear To Tread, 1986

Other books you might like:
Earl Emerson, *The Million Dollar Tattoo*, 1996
Joan Hess, *Martians in Maggody*, 1994
Mercedes Lambert, *The Whitney Logan Series*, 1991-
Janet L. Smith, *The Annie McPherson Series*, 1990-
Julie Smith, *The Rebecca Schwartz Series*, 1982-

157

FRANCINE MATHEWS

Death in a Mood Indigo

(New York: Bantam, 1997)

Story type: Police Procedural
Series: Merry Folger
Major character(s): Meredith Folger, Police Officer
Time period(s): 1990s
Locale(s): Nantucket Island, Massachusetts

Summary: When the bones of a woman dead for years are dug up by two children and their dog on an isolated stretch of Nantucket shoreline, Merry Folger is assigned the case by her police chief father. It appears that the case may be related to serial murders on the mainland, and the island is soon swarming with FBI agents and the media. Among them is Tucker Enright, a brilliant FBI profiler whose obsession with evil both fascinates and repels Merry. When the skeletal remains prove to be those of a beautiful psychiatrist who vanished from the island eight years ago, it's clear that her death is not related to the others. But then another island girl is murdered, and some disturbing connections begin to emerge between the dead psychiatrist, her husband, the mother of the children who found the body, and Enright himself. The author provides a glimpse of island culture in the off-season that few tourists ever see and paints some memorable portraits of her characters, particularly the two forlorn children who find the body and their angry, withdrawn mother.

Where it's reviewed:
Booklist, June 1, 1997, page 1667
Kirkus Reviews, July 1, 1997, page 986
Library Journal, June 1, 1997, page 156
Publishers Weekly, April 21, 1997, page 63

Other books by the same author:
Death in Rough Water, 1995
Death in the Off-Season, 1994

Other books you might like:
Rick Boyer, *Billingsgate Shoal*, 1982-
Philip R. Craig, *The J.W. Walker Series*, 1989-
Sally Gunning, *The Peter Bartholomew Series*, 1990-
Doug Kiker, *Murder on Clam Pond*, 1986
Jane Langton, *Dark Nantucket Noon*, 1975

158

STEFANIE MATTESON

Murder under the Palms

(New York: Berkley, 1997)

Story type: Amateur Detective
Series: Charlotte Graham
Major character(s): Charlotte Graham, Actress (retired)
Time period(s): 1990s
Locale(s): Palm Beach, Florida

Summary: The aging, legendary actress Charlotte Graham accepts an invitation to take a vacation in Palm Beach and catch up with many of her old friends. To her surprise, she winds up renewing an old romance of 50 years ago, but then her holiday suddenly takes a tragic turn. At a gala party at a house restored to look like the famed ocean liner *Normandie*, a prominent local jeweler is found murdered, and Charlotte is drawn into the case when her good friends become suspects.

Where it's reviewed:
Booklist, March 15, 1997, page 1230
Kirkus Reviews, January 15, 1997, page 99
Publishers Weekly, January 6, 1997, page 68

Other books by the same author:
Murder among the Angels, 1996
Murder on High, 1994
Murder at the Falls, 1993
Murder on the Silk Road, 1992
Murder on the Cliff, 1991

Other books you might like:
Eleanor Boylan, *The Clara Gamadge Series*, 1989-
Joyce Christmas, *The Betty Trenka Series*, 1993-
Anne George, *Murder Makes Waves*, 1997
Gallagher Gray, *The T.S. Hubbert & Auntie Lil Series*, 1991-
Corinne Holt Sawyer, *The Angela Benbow/Caledonia Wingate Series*, 1989-

159

JOHN R. MAXIM

Haven

(New York: Avon 1997)

Story type: Espionage
Major character(s): Elizabeth Stride, Spy (retired)
Time period(s): 1990s
Locale(s): Hilton Head Island, South Carolina

Summary: Elizabeth Stride, formerly a ruthless assassin for Israeli intelligence known as the ''Black Angel,'' has settled on Hilton Head Island in hopes of escaping her past. That includes Martin Kesler, another agent who has pledged to love her always. But when they learn that a young girl is about to be kidnapped from an exclusive tennis club as part of a terrorist campaign that can only end in a third world war, Elizabeth and Martin join forces once again.

Where it's reviewed:
Kirkus Reviews, July 15, 1997, page 1054
Library Journal, August 1997, page 133

Publishers Weekly, August 4, 1997, page 63

Other books by the same author:
Shadow Box, 1996
A Matter of Honor, 1993
Bannerman's Law, 1991
The Bannerman Effect, 1990
The Bannerman Solution, 1989

Other books you might like:
Reginald Hill, *The Long Kill*, 1988
Gayle Lynds, *Masquerade*, 1996
Thomas Perry, *The Jane Whitefield Series*, 1995-
Mark T. Sullivan, *The Purification Ceremony*, 1997
Maureen Tan, *AKA Jane*, 1997

160

ARCHER MAYOR

Bellows Falls

(New York: Mysterious Press, 1997)

Story type: Police Procedural
Series: Joe Gunther
Major character(s): Joe Gunther, Police Officer (lieutenant)
Time period(s): 1990s
Locale(s): Brattleboro, Vermont; Bellows Falls, Vermont

Summary: Police lieutenant Joe Gunther is called upriver from his home town of Brattleboro to help the police chief of Bellows Falls in a case involving a cop who supposedly sexually harassed the wife of a local drug dealer. It begins to look as if the man is being framed and that it's somehow connected with a small-time hood who's gone missing from Brattleboro. His search for the truth leads Gunther through a part of Vermont you won't see on any Christmas cards, and the change of venue allows him to see his job with a fresh perspective, making him question how long he can be a cop and still be able to sleep nights.

Other books by the same author:
The Ragman's Memory, 1996
The Dark Root, 1995
Fruits of the Poisonous Tree, 1994
The Skeleton's Knee, 1993
Borderlines, 1992

Other books you might like:
K.C. Constantine, *The Mario Balzic Series*, 1974-
Susan Rogers Cooper, *The Milt Kovak Series*, 1988-
Steven F. Havill, *The Bill Gastner Series*, 1991-
Susan Oleksiw, *The Joe Silva Series*, 1993-
Robert B. Parker, *Night Passage*, 1997

161

WALTER MCCLOSKEY

Risking Elizabeth

(New York: Simon & Schuster, 1997)

Story type: Psychological Suspense
Major character(s): Harry Preston, Lawyer, Widow(er) (single parent)
Time period(s): 1980s (1981)

Locale(s): New Orleans, Louisiana

Summary: Harry loves New Orleans. His family has lived there for gernerations and his elegant grandmother, the family matriarch, rules over one of the French Quarter's great historic houses. Although he is still grieving the death of his wife a year earlier, he loves his nine-year-old son Ike, with whom he lives in the back of his grandmother's house, and he has just met a woman who intrigues him, Elizabeth Bennett. Then he discovers that his wife had been murdered, Ike is kidnapped, and he is framed for murder. The city he loves so much suddenly becomes deadly and threatening. Gradually Harry is drawn into a web of deceit, blackmail, and murder, against the backdrop of New Orleans during Mardi Gras. First novel.

Where it's reviewed:
Booklist, January 1997, page 820
Entertainment Weekly, March 28, 1997, page 63
Kirkus Reviews, November 15, 1996, page 1635
Library Journal, December 1996, page 150
Publishers Weekly, November 25, 1996, page 56

Other books you might like:
James Lee Burke, *The Neon Rain*, 1987
D.J. Donaldson, *No Mardi Gras for the Dead*, 1992
Tony Dunbar, *City of Beads*, 1995
Julie Smith, *The Skip Langdon Series*, 1990-
Chris Wiltz, *The Neal Rafferty Series*, 1981-

162

VAL MCDERMID

Blue Genes
(New York: Scribner's, 1997)

Story type: Private Detective
Series: Kate Brannigan
Major character(s): Kate Brannigan, Detective—Private; Richard Barclay, Journalist (rock music), Lover
Time period(s): 1990s
Locale(s): Manchester, England

Summary: Cocky Manchester private eye Kate Brannigan and her lover Richard live in adjoining bungalows, linked by a common greenhouse. With Richard away, Kate is occupying his bungalow, posing as a bereaved widow in order to trap a pair of unscrupulous con artists selling phony memorials. Then Richard spoils it all by unexpectedly barging in, very much alive and quite put out by the tidying up Kate has done as part of her sting operation. Further, her business partner wants her to buy him out but she has no cash. And her best friend Alexis, whose partner Chris is pregnant, needs Kate's help when someone involved in Chris' pioneering but strictly illegal fertility treatment is murdered. It's written in McDermid's trademark breezy style, filled with unpredictable yet inevitable plot twists and memorable characters.

Where it's reviewed:
Booklist, February 1, 1997, page 928
Kirkus Reviews, November 15, 1996, page 1636
Publishers Weekly, November 11, 1996, page 59

Other books by the same author:
Clean Break, 1995

Crack Down, 1994
Kick Back, 1993
Dead Beat, 1992

Other books you might like:
Liza Cody, *The Anna Lee Series*, 1980-
Margaret Duffy, *The Joanna McKenzie Series*, 1994-
Linda Grant, *Lethal Genes*, 1997
Lesley Grant-Adamson, *The Laura Flynn Series*, 1991-

163

MICHAEL MCGARRITY

Mexican Hat
(New York: Norton, 1997)

Story type: Action/Adventure
Series: Kevin Kerney
Major character(s): Kevin Kerney, Ranger (forest, seasonal), Police Officer (ex-chief of detectives)
Time period(s): 1990s
Locale(s): Gila Wilderness, New Mexico

Summary: Kevin Kerney, invalided out of the Santa Fe police force where he was chief of detectives, is working as a seasonal forest ranger and saving his money toward a small ranch. What he hopes will be a quiet summer in the high country turns explosive when he runs into wildlife poachers, the murder of a Mexican tourist, and the discovery of a disoriented old man in the wilderness. He teams up with Jim Stiles, a young game and fish officer, to track down the poacher, and their investigation keeps coming back to two brothers who are engaged in a sixty-year-old feud. Kerney becomes attracted to the daughter of one of them, Karen Cox, an assistant district attorney who wants to see justice done but is afraid of what the truth may do to her father.

Where it's reviewed:
Book World, May 18, 1997, page 8
Booklist, May 15, 1997, page 1567
Kirkus Reviews, April 15, 1997, page 593
Library Journal, May 1, 1997, page 141
Publishers Weekly, March 24, 1997, page 81

Other books by the same author:
Tularosa, 1997

Other books you might like:
Nevada Barr, *Track of the Cat*, 1993
Val Davis, *The Track of the Scorpion*, 1996
    pseud. of Angie and Robert Irvine
Micah S. Hackler, *The Cliff Lansing/Gabe Hanna Series*, 1995-
Jake Page, *The Deadly Canyon*, 1994
Judith Van Gieson, *The Wolf Path*, 1992

164

JILL MCGOWN

Verdict Unsafe
(New York: Fawcett, 1997)

Story type: Police Procedural; Psychological Suspense
Series: Chief Inspector Lloyd and Inspector Judy Hill

Major character(s): Judy Hill, Detective—Police (detective inspector); Lloyd, Detective—Police (chief inspector), Lover (Judy's)
Time period(s): 1990s
Locale(s): East Anglia, England

Summary: An arrogant young predator named Colin Arthur Drummond has been accused of being the serial rapist known as the Stealth Bomber and has publicly denied the charges, while privately he threatens to make Judy Hill his next victim. Even though the case against him seems ironclad, he eventually goes free, and Judy sets out to prove his guilt once and for all, the only way she knows to protect herself from him. Then her supervisor and lover Chief Inspector Lloyd is called to a horrifying scene, where it appears Drummond has struck again.

Where it's reviewed:
Kirkus Reviews, May 15, 1997, page 761
Library Journal, June 15, 1997, page 98
Publishers Weekly, April 14, 1997, page 60

Other books by the same author:
A Shred of Evidence, 1996
Murder. . .Now and Then, 1993
The Other Woman, 1992
The Murders of Mrs. Austin and Mrs. Beale, 1991
Gone To Her Death, 1990

Other books you might like:
Deborah Crombie, *The Duncan Kincaid/Gemma James Series*, 1993-
Frances Fyfield, *Without Consent*, 1997
Ann Granger, *The Allan Markby and Meredith Mitchell Series*, 1991-
Christine Green, *The Connor O'Neil and Fran Wilson Series*, 1994-
Janet Neel, *The John McLeish and Francesca Wilson Series*, 1988-

---

165

G.A. MCKEVETT

Killer Calories

(New York: Kensington, 1997)

Story type: Private Detective; Humor
Series: Savannah Reid
Major character(s): Savannah Reid, Detective—Private (former cop)
Time period(s): 1990s
Locale(s): San Carmelita, California

Summary: When she was fired from the police department because she was too fat to be on the force, Savannah, a big, blond, Southern-born woman with plenty of attitude and a black belt in karate, opened her own detective agency in the upscale Southern California town of San Carmelita. Here the queen-size sleuth investigates the murder of Kat Valentina, a former actress and now owner of a health spa, who is found dead in one of her own herbal mud baths. The police put it down to too many margaritas, but Savannah thinks otherwise. Who wanted to murder the star of the cult classic, *Disco Diva?* Was it her ex-husband, who just took out a healthy life

insurance policy on her? Was it the spa masseuse, a woman with a past? Was it the handsome co-star from her disco days? Savannah goes undercover at the spa, determined to find the killer.

Where it's reviewed:
Kirkus Reviews, April 1, 1997, page 505
Library Journal, April 1, 1997, page 133
Publishers Weekly, February 24, 1997, page 66

Other books by the same author:
Bitter Sweets, 1996
Just Desserts, 1995

Other books you might like:
Dorothy Cannell, *The Thin Woman*, 1984
Camilla Crespi, *The Simona Griffo Series*, 1991-
Diane Mott Davidson, *Killer Pancake*, 1995
Jacqueline Girdner, *Fat-Free and Fatal*, 1993
Virginia Rich, *The Nantucket Diet Murders*, 1985

166

MARDI OAKLEY MEDAWAR

Witch of the Palo Duro

(New York: St. Martin's, 1997)

Story type: Historical
Series: Tay-bodal
Major character(s): Tay-bodal, Healer, Indian (Kiowa)
Time period(s): 1860s (1867)
Locale(s): Palo Duro Canyon, Oklahoma (Kiowa winter camp in what is now southern Oklahoma)

Summary: When The Rattle Band returns to the Kiowa's traditional winter camp a series of frightening events follows. First Skywalker, a powerful healer, wanders off and can't be found. Then two horses are killed and the herders report that a shapeshifter, or a witch in the form of a raven, is responsible. When a chief's wife dies unexpectedly the entire camp is thrown into a panic, but Tay-bodal suspects the culprit is not of supernatural origin. To protect his band and find his missing friend Skywalker, he must act quickly to solve the mystery. The author is an Eastern Band Cherokee and many of her characters are based on real people.

Other books by the same author:
Death at Rainy Mountain, 1996

Other books you might like:
Ron Burns, *The Mysterious Death of Meriwether Lewis*, 1993
Margaret Coel, *The Ghost Walker*, 1996
Jean Hager, *The Molly Bearpaw Series*, 1992-
Donald Honig, *The Sword of General Englund*, 1996
Miriam Grace Monfredo, *Blackwater Spirits*, 1995

167

ANNETTE MEYERS

The Groaning Board

(New York: Doubleday, 1997)

Story type: Amateur Detective
Series: Smith and Wetzon

Major character(s): Xenia Smith, Businesswoman (corporate headhunter); Leslie Wetzon, Businesswoman (corporate headhunter)

Time period(s): 1990s

Locale(s): New York, New York (Wall Street)

Summary: Xenia Smith and Leslie Wetzon, the two mismatched partners in a Wall Street executive search firm, come up against another equally mismatched pair here: A.T. Barron and Micklynn Devora, co-owners of a very trendy catering service known as The Groaning Board. They may be an odd couple but neither seems to have murderous tendencies, and yet people keep getting poisoned. Leslie has promised to find out what's happening, with or without help from her police detective boyfriend, but Xenia is more intent on expanding the firm and becoming a Broadway producer and doing a bit of matchmaking. But some of the new people in Xenia's life aren't to be trusted, and Leslie may have to look close to home to find the murderer.

Where it's reviewed:

Kirkus Reviews, May 1, 1997, page 682
Library Journal, May 1, 1997, page 144
Publishers Weekly, April 14, 1997, page 60

Other books by the same author:

These Bones Were Made for Dancin', 1995
The Deadliest Option, 1994
Murder: The Musical, 1993
Blood on the Street, 1992
Tender Death, 1990

Other books you might like:

Diane Mott Davidson, *Catering to Nobody*, 1990
Jane Dentinger, *The Jocelyn O'Roarke Series*, 1983-
Emma Lathen, *The John Putnam Thatcher Series*, 1961-
Haughton Murphy, *The Reuben Frost Series*, 1986-
Dianne G. Pugh, *The Iris Thorne Series*, 1993-

168

BARBARA MICHAELS (Pseudonym of Barbara Mertz)

The Dancing Floor

(New York: HarperCollins, 1997)

Story type: Amateur Detective; Psychological Suspense

Major character(s): Heather Tradescent, Young Woman, Gardener

Time period(s): 1990s

Locale(s): England

Summary: Heather had always dreamed of visiting the great gardens of England with her father. After his unexpected death she resolves to make the journey alone. It's a sad and lonely one without him, however, and she's about to cut it short and head for home. But first she must visit the fabled seventeenth-century garden of Troytan House. To Heather's dismay, the owner has denied public access to it and she's turned away at the gate. Reduced to trespassing, she finds a back way onto the estate and discovers the garden overgrown with almost impenetrable thickets and the Victorian manor house itself somehow sinister despite its beauty. However, the reclusive owner surprises her with an unexpectedly warm welcome, and when he learns about her knowledge of gardens

and mazes, he invites her to stay on and help him restore the gardens, including the famous maze. Then Heather hears stories of ancient witchcraft at the manor and in the nearby village. There's also a feral cat to be tamed and a murder to be solved.

Where it's reviewed:

Booklist, January 1997, page 779
Kirkus Reviews, December 15, 1996, page 1761
Publishers Weekly, January 13, 1997, page 53

Other books by the same author:

Stitches in Time, 1995
Houses of Stone, 1993
Vanish with the Rose, 1992
Into the Darkness, 1990
Smoke and Mirrors, 1989

Other books you might like:

Nancy Atherton, *Aunt Dimity and the Duke*, 1992
Susan Kenney, *Garden of Malice*, 1983
Caroline Llewellyn, *False Light*, 1996
John Sherwood, *The Mantrap Garden*, 1986
Mary Stewart, *Rose Cottage*, 1997

169

BILL MOODY

The Sound of the Trumpet

(New York: Walker, 1997)

Story type: Amateur Detective

Series: Evan Horne

Major character(s): Evan Horne, Musician (jazz pianist)

Time period(s): 1990s

Locale(s): Venice Beach, California; Las Vegas, Nevada

Summary: Although his hand is healing from a repetitive motion injury, it will still be a long time before Evan can play the piano again—if ever. With time hanging heavy, he's glad to do a favor for his friend, Professor "Ace" Buffington, who wants him to come to Vegas for a little job. A collector has found a tape that appears to be a lost recording by legendary jazz trumpeter Clifford Brown, who was killed in an auto accident in the 1950s. When he hears it, Evan is certain it's authentic. But just moments later he's trying to explain to the Las Vegas cops that he has nothing to do with the dead man lying in front of him.

Where it's reviewed:

Armchair Detective, Spring 1997, page 228
Booklist, February 15, 1997, page 1007
Kirkus Reviews, December 15, 1996, page 1769
Library Journal, January 1997, page 152
New York Times Book Review, February 16, 197, page 28

Other books by the same author:

Death of a Tenor Man, 1995
Solo Hand, 1994

Other books you might like:

Linda Barnes, *Steel Guitar*, 1991
Robert Greer, *The Devil's Red Nickel*, 1996
John Lutz, *The Right to Sing the Blues*, 1986
Julie Smith, *Jazz Funeral*, 1993

Jesse Sublett, *The Martin Fender Series*, 1989-

170

RICHARD MOQUIST

Eye of the Agency

(New York: St. Martin's Press, 1997)

Story type: Historical; Private Detective
Major character(s): Sadie Greenstreet, Journalist (newspaper reporter); Horace Greenstreet, Detective—Private (Pinkerton agent)
Time period(s): 1870s (1873)
Locale(s): Mississippi River; Chicago, Illinois

Summary: Pinkerton agent Horace Greenstreet boards the riverboat *Mississippi Girl* to investigate death threats that have been targeting the ship's owner. He brings along his journalist wife Sadie, a woman unusually independent for her time who uses her investigative skills to aid her husband in his assignment. She steals the show and ends up cracking the case, but it's the vivid evocation of life on a Mississippi riverboat as much as the plot that gives the book its appeal. It's enhanced by an assortment of contemporary lithographs and photos of the riverboat in all its glory and the costumes and scenes of the day.

Where it's reviewed:
Kirkus Reviews, May 15, 1997, page 763
Publishers Weekly, May 19, 1997, page 70

Other books by the same author:
The Franklin Mysteries, 1994

Other books you might like:
Dianne Day, *The Fremont Jones Series*, 1995-
Jack Finney, *Time and Again*, 1970
Peter J. Heck, *Death on the Mississippi*, 1995
Donald Honig, *The Captain Thomas Maynard Series*, 1996-
Maan Meyers, *The Lucifer Contract*, 1998

171

BRADFORD MORROW

Giovanni's Gift

(New York: Viking, 1997)

Story type: Amateur Detective
Major character(s): Grant Morgan, Drifter (tutor, clerk, translator)
Time period(s): 1990s
Locale(s): Ash Creek, Rocky Mountains

Summary: When Grant hears of a campaign of terror being waged against the aunt and uncle who are his only living relatives, he leaves Rome and a failing marriage to do what he can to stop it. But after he arrives at their ranch high in the Rocky Mountains, the nightly visits escalate in violence, and then a dear family friend, Giovanni Trentas, is found ritually murdered in a gorge above the ranch. When his aunt presents Grant with Giovanni's legacy of an old cigar box filled with letters, photos, and other memorabilia, Grant finds himself in possession of a puzzle that holds the answers to Giovanni's death and much more. He also becomes passionately involved

with Giovanni's daughter Helen. The author, whose previous books are all literary mainstream novels, uses the myth of Pandora's box as the starting point for this literary thriller.

Where it's reviewed:
Book World, February 2, 1997, page 1
Kirkus Reviews, November 15, 1996, page 1627
New York Times Book Review, March 9, 1997, page 7
Publishers Weekly, November 18, 1996, page 60
Tribune Books, March 9, 1997, page 3

Other books you might like:
James Lee Burke, *Black Cherry Blues*, 1989
G.D. Gearino, *Counting Coup*, 1997
David Guterson, *Snow Falling on Cedars*, 1994
Peter Hoeg, *Smilla's Sense of Snow*, 1993
Michael C. White, *A Brother's Blood*, 1996

172

IAN MORSON

A Psalm for Falconer

(New York: St. Martin's Press, 1997)

Story type: Historical
Series: William Falconer
Major character(s): William Falconer, Teacher (regent master)
Time period(s): 13th century (1264)
Locale(s): Oxford, England; Lancaster Bay, England

Summary: At the request of a friend, Falconer journeys to Conishead Priory in search of a special book, but along the way he begins to suspect he's being followed. While crossing Lancaster Bay, he witnesses a body being recovered from a sandbank. The dead man turns out to be a monk who had vanished fifteen years earlier, but not just any monk: he was to have been the new abbot, and the present abbot becomes the prime suspect in the case. Once at the priory, Falconer finds the book he has been sent to find is gone, and then there is another murder. The key to many of these events lies with an ancient hermit who visits Falconer one day.

Other books by the same author:
Falconer and the Face of God, 1997
Falconer's Judgement, 1996
Falconer's Crusade, 1995

Other books you might like:
P.C. Doherty, *The Hugh Corbett Series*, 1993-
Susanna Gregory, *The Matthew Bartholomew Series*, 1996-
Paul Harding, *The Brother Athelstan Series*, 1991-
Sharon Kay Penman, *The Queen's Man*, 1996
Ellis Peters, *The Brother Cadfael Series*, 1978-1994

173

MARCIA MULLER

Both Ends of the Night

(New York: Mysterious, 1997)

Story type: Private Detective
Series: Sharon McCone

Major character(s): Sharon McCone, Detective—Private; Hy Ripinsky, Lover
Time period(s): 1990s
Locale(s): San Francisco, California; Fayetteville, Arkansas; Minnesota (northern)

Summary: Sharon, who's been a full-fledged pilot for several years, is due for her biannual flight review as required by the FAA. Matty Wildress, her former flight instructor, has invited her up to the small Sonoma town of Los Alegres for the evaluation, but since the test isn't actually due for several months, Sharon suspects Matty has more than aviation on her mind. It turns out that Matty's live-in lover, John Seabrook, has vanished, leaving her with his small son Zach to care for. John left a note urging them both to go into hiding for their own safety, but Matty, an aerobatic pilot, is determined to perform in the last air show of the year. When her plane crashes and she is killed, Sharon is determined to find out what happened. Together with her lover Hy Ripinsky, she bypasses the authorities and travels all over the country, learning more and more about Seabrook's past, including various killings and assumed identies. The final showdown with the killer takes place in the frozen wilderness of northern Minnesota.

Where it's reviewed:
Booklist, May 1, 1997, page 1462
Kirkus Reviews, June 1, 1997, page 838
New York Times Book Review, July 27, page 18
Publishers Weekly, May 5, 1997, page 200

Other books by the same author:
The Broken Promise Land, 1996
A Wild and Lonely Place, 1995
Till the Butchers Cut Him Down, 1994
Wolf in the Shadows, 1993
Pennies on a Dead Woman's Eyes, 1992

Other books you might like:
Catherine Dain, *The Freddie O'Neal Series*, 1992-
Janet Dawson, *The Catherine Sayler Series*, 1988-
Susan Dunlap, *The Kiernan O'Shaughnessy Series*, 1989-
Sue Grafton, *The Kinsey Millhone Series*, 1982-
Gloria White, *The Ronnie Ventana Series*, 1991-

174

AMY MYERS

Murder in the Smokehouse

(New York: St. Martin's Press, 1997)

Story type: Amateur Detective
Series: Auguste Didier
Major character(s): Auguste Didier, Cook (master chef)
Time period(s): 1900s (1901)
Locale(s): Yorkshire, England

Summary: Auguste and his bride Princess Tatiana are visiting the country home of the aristocratic Tabor family for a gala ball. Lady Priscilla is determined to keep tobacco out of her household and so dispatches gentleman smokers to the far end of the vast garden, where a gloomy old smokehouse stands ready for this purpose. When Tatiana decides to explore the building she discovers a corpse, and Didier is summoned by

her to check it out. The first question that needs to be answered is: whose body is it?

Where it's reviewed:
Kirkus Reviews, July 15, 1997, page 1070

Other books by the same author:
Murder at the Music Hall, 1995
Murder under the Kissing Bough, 1994
Murder Makes an Entree, 1992
Murder at the Masque, 1991
Murder at Plum's, 1989

Other books you might like:
Emily Brightwell, *The Mrs. Jeffries Series*, 1993-
Carole Nelson Douglas, *The Irene Adler Series*, 1990-
Kate Kingsbury, *Eat, Drink and Be Buried*, 1994
Janet Laurence, *The Darina Lisle Series*, 1989-
Robin Paige, *The Kathryn Ardleigh Series*, 1994-

175

MICHAEL NAVA

The Burning Plain

(New York: Putnam's, 1997)

Story type: Legal
Series: Henry Rios
Major character(s): Henry Rios, Lawyer, Homosexual
Time period(s): 1990s
Locale(s): Los Angeles, California

Summary: Henry Rios would say that he has three strikes against him: he's gay, he's Chicano, and he's a lawyer. He's still mourning the loss of his lover to AIDS when he's asked to defend a young man accused of attempting to burglarize a movie director's house. He succeeds in getting him acquitted, only to see his client murdered several hours later. Suddenly he's dealing with a case of blackmail and betrayal.

Other books by the same author:
The Death of Friends, 1996
The Hidden Law, 1992
How Town, 1990
Goldenboy, 1988
The Little Death, 1986

Other books you might like:
Rudolfo Anaya, *The Sonny Baca Series*, 1995-
Joseph Hansen, *The Dave Brandstetter Series*, 1970-
Steve Johnson, *The Doug Orlando Series*, 1992-
Manuel Ramos, *The Luis Montez Series*, 1994-
John Morgan Wilson, *Revision of Justice*, 1997

176

MAXINE O'CALLAGHAN

Only in the Ashes

(New York: Jove, 1997)

Story type: Amateur Detective
Series: Dr. Anne Menlo
Major character(s): Anne Menlo, Psychologist (child); Bern Pagett, Detective—Police (detective)

Time period(s): 1990s
Locale(s): Phoenix, Arizona

Summary: In order to find out what her daughter's last weeks were like, Kathleen Grayley asks Anne to build a psychological profile of Rachel Grayley, who was kidnapped by her father and his mother not long before perishing in a fire. Kathleen wants to know if her daughter had been sexually or physically abused before she died, but the case takes an unexpected turn when the fire turns out to have been arson. Anne's lover, police detective Bern Pagett, steps in, and he and Anne narrowly escape death themselves when someone torches the house they share. But in order to keep her promise to her client, Anne must put herself in danger again. The author also writes a private eye series featuring Delilah West.

Other books by the same author:
Shadow of a Child, 1996

Other books you might like:
Jonathan Kellerman, *The Alex Delaware Series*, 1985-
Sarah Lovett, *The Sylvia Strange Series*, 1995-
Alex Matthews, *The Cassidy McCabe Series*, 1996-
Ridley Pearson, *Beyond Recognition*, 1997
Stephen White, *The Alan Gregory Series*, 1991-

177

CAROL O'CONNELL

Stone Angel

(New York: Putnam, 1997)

Story type: Police Procedural
Series: Kathleen Mallory
Major character(s): Kathleen Mallory, Police Officer (sergeant)
Time period(s): 1990s
Locale(s): Dayborn, Louisiana; New York, New York

Summary: NYPD Sergeant Kathleen Mallory was rescued from the streets by a kind-hearted homicide cop and his wife, who raised her from childhood until she went off to follow in his footsteps as a police officer. Here she has left New York on a personal mission: to investigate the terrifying circumstances of her mother's death. She has barely arrived in the small Louisiana town where her mother had been stoned to death by a mob seventeen years earlier when one man is assaulted, another has a heart attack, and a third is murdered. Although she had nothing to do with any of these events, Mallory finds herself in jail. Her mother's body had disappeared without a trace following her death, and so had Mallory (who was six at the time), reappearing later on the streets of Manhattan. Although she's warned against stirring things up, Mallory persists, using her fierce intelligence and unique moral compass to uncover truths that might better remain buried.

Where it's reviewed:
Booklist, June 1, 1997, page 1620
Kirkus Reviews, June 15, 1997, page 913
Publishers Weekly, September 1, 1997, page 40 (audio version)

Other books by the same author:
Killing Critics, 1996

The Man Who Cast Two Shadows, 1995
Mallory's Oracle, 1994

Other books you might like:
James Lee Burke, *The Dave Robicheaux Series*, 1987-
Lee Child, *Killing Floor*, 1997
Michael Connelly, *The Last Coyote*, 1995
Robert Crais, *Voodoo River*, 1995
James Ellroy, *Clandestine*, 1982

178

PERRI O'SHAUGNESSY (Pseudonym of Mary O'Shaugnessy)
PAMELA O'SHAUGNESSY, Co-Author

Obstruction of Justice

(New York: Delacorte, 1997)

Story type: Legal
Series: Nina Reilly
Major character(s): Nina Reilly, Lawyer, Single Parent
Time period(s): 1990s
Locale(s): Lake Tahoe, California

Summary: Former San Francisco attorney Nina Reilly has left the city behind and relocated to Lake Tahoe where she's started life anew as a single parent, and so far it's been a good move. Now, however, she risks being charged with concealing evidence if she is to save a young client who's been accused of murder. Her client, who's been charged with the murder of his powerful businessman grandfather, won't talk, even to Nina, and she may have to decide to obstruct justice in order to prevent a terrible injustice from being done.

Where it's reviewed:
Kirkus Reviews, July 1, 1997, page 978
Library Journal, September 1, 1997, page 220
Publishers Weekly, July 7, 1997, page 50

Other books by the same author:
Invasion of Privacy, 1996
Motion to Suppress, 1995

Other books you might like:
Laura Crum, *Roughstock*, 1997
Jonnie Jacobs, *The Kali O'Brien Series*, 1996-
Lia Matera, *The Willa Jansson Series*, 1986-
Janet L. Smith, *The Annie McPherson Series*, 1990-
Carolyn Wheat, *The Cass Jameson Series*, 1983-

179

ABIGAIL PADGETT

The Dollmaker's Daughters

(New York: Mysterious Press, 1997)

Story type: Amateur Detective
Series: Bo Bradley
Major character(s): Barbara Joan ''Bo'' Bradley, Investigator (child abuse), Mentally Ill Person (manic-depressive)
Time period(s): 1990s
Locale(s): San Diego, California

Summary: Fifteen-year-old Janny Malcolm carries a beautifully crafted baby doll with her everywhere she goes; she is

also nearly catatonic with fear, a fear that may be somehow connected with the doll. Bo Bradley is assigned to her case but is taken off it under suspicious circumstances by her supervisor. As she struggles with bouts of manic-depression herself, Bo becomes determined to find out why Janny is in such terrible pain. Her search leads her to the mansion of a famous dollmaker and into a dark world where nobody seems safe, including Bo and those she loves.

Where it's reviewed:
Book World, February 16, 1997, page 11
Kirkus Reviews, December 15, 1996, page 1769
Library Journal, January 1997, page 153
Publishers Weekly, December 2, 1997, page 44

Other books by the same author:
Moonbird Boy, 1996
Turtle Baby, 1995
Strawgirl, 1994
Child of Silence, 1993

Other books you might like:
Robert Crais, *Indigo Slam*, 1997
Janet Dawson, *Nobody's Child*, 1995
Timothy Hallinan, *Everything but the Squeal*, 1990
Jonathan Kellerman, *Over the Edge*, 1987
Stephen White, *Private Practices*, 1994

180

KATHERINE HALL PAGE

The Body in the Fjord

(New York: Morrow, 1997)

Story type: Amateur Detective
Series: Faith Fairchhild
Major character(s): Faith Fairchild, Housewife, Caterer (former); Pix Miller, Housewife
Time period(s): 1990s
Locale(s): Norway; Aleford, Connecticut

Summary: Faith Fairchild stays behind when her good friend Pix leaves for Norway with her mother in tow to investigate the sudden disappearance of a family friend. Posing as a member of "Scandie Sights," a Norwegian tour group, Pix is drawn into intrigue—and murder. She discovers a sinister world of stolen antiques and secret histories as her search for the truth eventually results in her being targeted by a killer. From the moment she boards the plane to the final denouement in the Norwegian countryside, Pix takes center stage in this book, with brief appearances by Faith in only the prologue and epilogue. But some of the recipes from Faith's kitchen appear in the appendix, all for Norwegian delicacies.

Other books by the same author:
The Body in the Bog, 1996
The Body in the Basement, 1994
The Body in the Cast, 1993
The Body in the Vestibule, 1992
The Body in the Bouillon, 1991

Other books you might like:
Robert Barnard, *Death in a Cold Climate*, 1981
Diane Mott Davidson, *The Goldy Bear Series*, 1990-
Virginia Rich, *The Mrs. Eugenia Potter Series*, 1982-1985

Ann Ripley, *The Louise Eldridge Series*, 1994-
Valerie Wolzien, *The Susan Henshaw Series*, 1987-

181

ROBERT B. PARKER

Night Passage

(New York: Putnam's, 1997)

Story type: Police Procedural
Major character(s): Jesse Stone, Police Officer (police chief)
Time period(s): 1990s
Locale(s): Paradise, Massachusetts

Summary: The author of the long-running Spenser series has created a new character here: Jesse Stone, an LAPD cop whose failed marriage exacerbates his long-term alcoholism which in turn leads to his discharge from the force. To his shock, he's offered the job of police chief in the small Massachusetts town of Paradise, even though he had shown up drunk for the interview. It might be the kind of new beginning he's been hoping for, but once he's on the job, he discovers that beneath its quiet surface, Paradise is full of corruption and crime, ranging from mob ties and a homegrown militia to a triple homicide and a psychopath who's gunning for Jesse. Although there is no one in town he can trust, Jesse resolves to clean up the mess, even if it means putting the bottle aside while he does so.

Where it's reviewed:
Kirkus Reviews, July 1, 1997, page 987
Publishers Weekly, August 4, 1997, page 64
Wall Street Journal (Central Edition), October 3, 1997, page A8

Other books by the same author:
Chance, 1996
Thin Air, 1995
Walking Shadow, 1994
Paper Doll, 1993
Double Deuce, 1992

Other books you might like:
James Lee Burke, *The Dave Robicheaux Series*, 1987-
Philip R. Craig, *A Beautiful Place to Die*, 1989
Brendan Dubois, *Dead Sand*, 1994
Archer Mayor, *The Joe Gunther Series*, 1992-
Jack O'Connell, *Box Nine*, 1992

182

ROBERT B. PARKER

Small Vices

(New York: Putnam's, 1997)

Story type: Private Detective
Series: Spenser
Major character(s): Spenser, Detective—Private; Hawk, Sidekick
Time period(s): 1990s
Locale(s): Boston, Massachusetts; New York, New York

Summary: Ellis Alves is a bad kid from the 'hood with a long rap sheet, but that doesn't mean he murdered Melissa Hender-

son, a white student from exclusive Pemberton College. The boy's lawyers think he was framed and hire Spenser to investigate. He and Hawk follow the trail from the back streets of Boston to some of Manhattan's most upscale neighborhoods, where they learn a lot about spoiled rich kids and twisted cops. Then Spenser is shot by an assassin. He survives—just barely—but lets the world think he's dead while the rest of the story plays out as he recovers his strength and Hawk takes over the investigation.

Where it's reviewed:
Book World, April 20, 1997, page 8
Booklist, January 1997, page 779
Kirkus Reviews, January 15, 1997, page 90
New York Times Book Review, April 13, 1997, page 24
Publishers Weekly, January 27, 1997, page 80

Other books by the same author:
Chance, 1996
Thin Air, 1995
Walking Shadow, 1994
Paper Doll, 1993
Double Deuce, 1992

Other books you might like:
Harlan Coben, *The Myron Bolitar Series*, 1995-
Robert Crais, *The Elvis Cole Series*, 1987-
Jeremiah Healy, *The John Cuddy Series*, 1984-
Dennis Lehane, *The Patrick Kenzie/Angela Gennaro Series*, 1994-
Walter Satterthwait, *The Joshua Croft Series*, 1989-

183

ARTURO PEREZ-REVERTE

The Club Dumas
(New York: Harcourt Brace, 1997)

Story type: Amateur Detective
Major character(s): Lucas Corso, Detective—Amateur (book expert)
Locale(s): Madrid, Spain; Sintra, Portugal

Summary: Bibliosleuth Lucas Corso is hired to find the sole surviving copy of a book printed in Venice in 1666 and said to contain the formula for summoning the devil. An educated, perceptive, and very intelligent 45-year-old man, Corso works daily with books but proclaims (falsely) that this "doesn't mean I have to read them." As he pursues the book he finds himself surrounded by an odd cast of characters who seem to have stepped out of an Alexandre Dumas novel. Even odder is a young English girl who claims her name is Irene Adler. At times, illusion and reality seem hopelessly confused until the author carefully exposes each layer of his intricate plot. Splendidly translated from the Spanish by Sonia Soto.

Other books by the same author:
The Flanders Panel, 1996

Other books you might like:
John Dunning, *Booked to Die*, 1992
Marianne Macdonald, *Death's Autograph*, 1997
Lawrence Norfolk, *The Pope's Rhinoceros*, 1996
Charles Palliser, *The Quincunx*, 1990
Peter Watson, *The Landscape of Lies*, 1989

184

ANNE PERRY

Ashworth Hall
(New York: Fawcett, 1997)

Story type: Historical; Police Procedural
Series: Thomas and Charlotte Pitt
Major character(s): Thomas Pitt, Police Officer (superintendent, Scotland Yard); Charlotte Pitt, Spouse
Time period(s): 1890s
Locale(s): London, England; England (countryside)

Summary: What appears to be a sociable weekend houseparty at the great country house of Ashworth Hall is in reality a gathering of Irish political figures, both Protestants and Catholics, brought together in hopes of solving the thorny issue of home rule for Ireland. During the course of the historic weekend a murder is done and a long-simmering political scandal becomes public. The summit appears to be doomed unless Thomas Pitt and his well-connected aristocratic wife Charlotte can get at the truth. If not, more murders could take place and there could be civil war in Ireland.

Where it's reviewed:
Booklist, January 1997, page 779
Kirkus Reviews, January 1, 1997, page 25
Library Journal, February 1, 1997, page 111
New York Times Book Review, March 16, 1997, page 28
Publishers Weekly, January 13, 1997, page 58

Other books by the same author:
Pentecost Alley, 1996
Traitor's Gate, 1995
The Hyde Park Headsman, 1994
Farrier's Lane, 1993
Belgrave Square, 1992

Other books you might like:
Ray Harrison, *The Bragg/Morton Series*, 1983-
Maureen Jennings, *Except the Dying*, 1997
Alanna Knight, *The Inspector Jeremy Faro Series*, 1988-
Peter Lovesey, *Invitation to a Dynamite Party*, 1974
Jean Stubbs, *The Inspector John Lintott Series*, 1968-1976

185

THOMAS PERRY

Shadow Woman
(New York: Random House, 1997)

Story type: Action/Adventure
Major character(s): Jane Whitefield, Guide, Indian (Seneca)
Time period(s): 1990s
Locale(s): Las Vegas, Nevada; New York (upstate); Montana (Glacier National Park)

Summary: Jane Whitefield, a part-Seneca "guide," has an unusual mission in life: she helps people in danger get to safety, providing them with new identities and the survival skills needed to elude their predators. Jane doesn't charge for her services, but she knows that the people she's helped will at some point in their lives want to send her a gift—usually a very generous one. This time she's asked to help Pete

Hatcher, a Las Vegas casino executive who knows too much about his employers' dirty deals. The timing couldn't be worse for Jane, as she's just agreed to marry the gentle doctor she loves. But Hatcher is desperate. What follows is a tense, riveting narrative as Jane and Hatcher manage to elude—just barely—a formidable pair of cold-blooded assasins. It all culminates in a wild chase through the high country of Glacier National Park as summer turns to winter in the Rockies. And all the while Jane's new husband is unaware of the terrible danger he's in back at their home in upstate New York.

Where it's reviewed:
Booklist, May 1, 1997, page 1462
Kirkus Reviews, May 1, 1997, page 673
Library Journal, May 1, 1997, page 143
Publishers Weekly, April 21, 1997, page 63
Time, June 30, 1997, page 74

Other books by the same author:
Dance for the Dead, 1996
Vanishing Act, 1995

Other books you might like:
Nevada Barr, *The Anna Pigeon Series*, 1992-
Dana Stabenow, *The Kate Shugak Series*, 1992-
Mark T. Sullivan, *The Purification Ceremony*, 1996
Aimee Thurlo, *The Ella Clah Series*, 1995-
    David Thurlo, co-author
Judith Van Gieson, *Raptor*, 1990

186

ELIZABETH PETERS (Pseudonym of Barbara Mertz)

Seeing a Large Cat

(New York: Warner, 1997)

Story type: Historical; Amateur Detective
Series: Amelia Peabody
Major character(s): Amelia Peabody Emerson, Archaeologist; Radcliffe Emerson, Archaeologist, Spouse (Amelia's husband)
Time period(s): 1900s (1903)
Locale(s): Valley of the Kings, Egypt

Summary: With her precocious son Ramses now a teenager and her irascible but devoted husband Emerson absorbed in the archaeological discoveries he hopes to make in the Valley of the Kings, Amelia's free to do what she loves best: meddle. She manages to expose a fraudulent spiritualist, save a marriage, and dabble in a bit of matchmaking before Emerson gets too annoyed, but when he receives a mysterious warning not to enter the Valley, Amelia finally turns her attentions to their work together. An ancient tomb yields up a much more modern murder, and the entire family becomes a target for an unknown assassin.

Where it's reviewed:
Booklist, May 1, 1997, page 1462
Kirkus Reviews, May 15, 1997, page 763
Library Journal, July 1997, page 131
New York Times Book Review, July 27, 1997, page 18
Publishers Weekly, May 5, 1997, page 201

Other books by the same author:
The Hippopotamus Pool, 1996

The Snake, the Crocodile and the Dog, 1994
The Last Camel Died at Noon, 1991
The Deeds of the Disturber, 1988
The Lion in the Valley, 1986

Other books you might like:
Dianne Day, *The Fremont Jones Series*, 1995-
Laurie R. King, *The Mary Russell Series*, 1994-
Michael Pearce, *The Mamur Zapt Series*, 1988-
Lynda S. Robinson, *The Lord Meren Series*, 1994
Walter Satterthwait, *Escapade*, 1995

187

CHRIS PETIT

The Psalm Killer

(New York: Knopf, 1997)

Story type: Police Procedural
Major character(s): Chief Inspector Cross, Police Officer (Royal Ulster Constabulary)
Time period(s): 1980s (1985)
Locale(s): Belfast, Ireland

Summary: Cross, who is both English and Catholic, is a double outsider in Protestant Northern Ireland, and he's considering leaving the force because his effectiveness is so limited. But a killer is stalking the streets of Belfast, one who kills across political and religious lines and in a particularly vicious and grisly fashion. In fact, his methods remind Cross of another recent episode in the city's violent past. As he uncovers the motives and well-hidden identity of the killer, Cross learns more about the cynical political realities that lie just below the surface of the crisis in Northern Ireland, realities that make fighting profitable and people expendable. He also learns that knowing the truth about these realities is very dangerous. He's aided in his investigation by a young woman transfer from the sex crimes unit. First novel.

Where it's reviewed:
Booklist, March 1, 1997, page 1069
Kirkus Reviews, March 1, 1997, page 331
Library Journal, April 1, 1997, page 130
Publishers Weekly, March 17, 1997, page 78
Times Literary Supplement, December 6, 1996, page 22

Other books you might like:
Bartholomew Gill, *The Inspector Peter McGarr Series*, 1977-
Bill James, *The Inspector Colin Harpur Series*, 1985-
William McIlvaney, *The Jack Laidlaw Series*, 1977-
Ian Rankin, *The Inspector John Rebus Series*, 1987-
Peter Turnbull, *The P Division Series*, 1981-

188

MARISSA PIESMAN

Survival Instincts

(New York: Delacorte, 1997)

Story type: Amateur Detective
Series: Nina Fischman
Major character(s): Nina Fischman, Lawyer
Time period(s): 1990s

Locale(s): New York, New York (Upper West Side Manhattan)

Summary: After having survived a failed relationship and a stint in California, Nina's back in Manhattan and living with her mother until she can get back on her feet. Single, smart, neurotic, Jewish, nearing forty, and perpetually dieting, Nina still can see the funny side of life, and she can never stay out of trouble for long. This time her dermatologist brother-in-law Ken is accused of poisoning a scientist who was involved in animal testing. Nina poses as a journalist writing an expose for *The New Yorker* to interview other suspects: the victim's widow, the director of a militant animal activist group, and his fellow scientists, who are working on the fat mouse gene Leptin. And always at her side is her mother, as determined as Nina to play sleuth.

Where it's reviewed:
Booklist, February 15, 1997, page 1008
Kirkus Reviews, December 1, 1996, page 1706
New York Times Book Review, March 2, 1997, page 20
Publishers Weekly, January 20, 1997, page 397

Other books by the same author:
Heading Uptown, 1996
Alternate Sides, 1995
Close Quarters, 1994
Personal Effects, 1992
Unorthodox Practices, 1989

Other books you might like:
Linda Barnes, *The Carlotta Carlyle Series*, 1987-
Carole Berry, *The Bonnie Indermill Series*, 1987-
Jane Dentinger, *The Jocelyn O'Roarke Series*, 1983-
Sparkle Hayter, *The Robin Hudson Series*, 1994-
Lia Matera, *The Willa Jansson Series*, 1986-

189

BILL PRONZINI

Illusions

(New York: Carroll & Graf, 1997)

Story type: Private Detective
Series: Nameless Detective
Major character(s): Nameless Detective, Detective—Private
Time period(s): 1990s
Locale(s): San Francisco, California

Summary: The San Francisco detective, whose name we never learn, is caught between two difficult investigations, one personal and one professional. He is still investigating the disturbing suicide of his former friend and business partner, Eberhardt, and finds himself increasingly obsessed with the case. Then he's hired by a Santa Fe businessman to find a missing ex-wife. When the client is found dead, the case takes on frightening dimensions, and then "Nameless" turns up disturbing facts about the couple's past. Although he's without a client in either case, "Nameless" is torn between them and must choose which one to follow.

Where it's reviewed:
Booklist, June 1, 1997, page 1667
Kirkus Reviews, July 1, 1997, page 987
Publishers Weekly, May 26, 1997, page 70

Other books by the same author:
Sentinels, 1996
Hardcase, 1995
Demons, 1993
Epitaphs, 1992
Quarry, 1992

Other books you might like:
Earl Emerson, *The Thomas Black Series*, 1985-
Loren D. Estleman, *The Amos Walker Series*, 1980-
Joe Gores, *The DKA Series*, 1972-
Stephen Greenleaf, *The John Marshall Tanner Series*, 1979-
Les Roberts, *The Milan Jacovich Series*, 1988-

190

BILL PRONZINI

A Wasteland of Strangers

(New York: Walker, 1997)

Story type: Psychological Suspense
Major character(s): John Faith, Drifter
Time period(s): 1990s
Locale(s): Pomo, California

Summary: When John Faith arrives in the shabby, isolated northern California resort town of Pomo, everybody is distrustful of him, and when a sexual assault occurs, he's the obvious suspect. His interest in Storm Carey, a lovely and very lonely widow, further fuels the townspeople's suspicions, especially the sheriff, who is also attracted to Storm. A hard-drinking reporter launches his own campaign against Faith, and when Storm is murdered, the town explodes. The story is told from multiple viewpoints, with each narrator having a unique voice and perspective on the events. A non-series mystery from the creator of the long-running Nameless Detective series.

Where it's reviewed:
Booklist, June 1, 1997, page 1668
Kirkus Reviews, June 15, 1997, page 914
Publishers Weekly, May 12, 1997, page 61

Other books by the same author:
Blue Lonesome, 1995
With an Extreme Burning, 1994
Masques, 1981
Snowbound, 1975
Panic!, 1972

Other books you might like:
Lee Child, *Killing Floor*, 1997
Stephen Dobyns, *The Church of Dead Girls*, 1997
G.D. Gearino, *What the Deaf-Mute Heard*, 1996
Carol O'Connell, *Stone Angel*, 1997
Ross Thomas, *The Fourth Durango*, 1990

191

ELIZABETH QUINN (Pseudonym of Elizabeth Quinn Barnard)

Killer Whale

(New York: Pocket Books, 1997)

Story type: Amateur Detective
Series: Dr. Lauren Maxwell
Major character(s): Dr. Lauren Maxwell, Investigator (wildlife), Widow(er) (single mother)
Time period(s): 1990s
Locale(s): Anchorage, Alaska; Prince of Wales Island, Alaska

Summary: Lauren Maxwell, Anchorage-based investigator for the Wild America Society, packs up and heads for Prince of Wales Island on an assignment to prevent the capture of wild orcas, or killer whales. But when her friend is murdered she has even more to investigate. The author's love of the outdoors and sensitivity to environmental issues is a hallmark of her books, each of which deals with a different animal species.

Where it's reviewed:
Kliatt, July 1997, page 11

Other books by the same author:
Lamb to the Slaughter, 1996
A Wolf in Death's Clothing, 1995
Murder Most Grizzly, 1993

Other books you might like:
Nevada Barr, *Track of the Cat*, 1993
Sue Henry, *Sleeping Lady*, 1996
Richard Hoyt, *Whoo?*, 1991
Dana Stabenow, *The Kate Shugak Series*, 1992-
Judith Van Gieson, *Raptor*, 1990

192

MANUEL RAMOS

Blues for the Buffalo

(New York: St. Martin's Press, 1997)

Story type: Legal
Series: Luis Montez
Major character(s): Luis Montez, Lawyer (Chicano)
Time period(s): 1990s
Locale(s): Denver, Colorado; Mexico

Summary: Worn out from his recent travels, Luis accepts a friend's offer to chill out on a beach in Mexico for a while. While there, he meets a young woman named Rachel, who promptly disappears. Back in Denver, Luis tries to get his law practice up and running again but he finds himself being pressured by a private eye who's been hired by Rachel's wealthy family to find her at all costs. Unfortunately, Luis was the last person to see her alive, and they're not about to let up on him. To protect himself Luis starts his own investigation in which he discovers dangerous secrets that have been hidden for years. As he peels away layer upon layer of deceit, he tries to right some of the wrongs that keep surfacing—and stay alive in the process.

Where it's reviewed:
Book World, May 18, 1997, page 8
Booklist, May 1, 1997, page 1483
Kirkus Reviews, April 15, 1997, page 594
Library Journal, May 1, 1997, page 143
Publishers Weekly, March 31, 1997, page 66

Other books by the same author:
The Last Client of Luis Montez, 1996
The Ballad of Gato Guerrero, 1995
The Ballad of Rocky Ruiz, 1994

Other books you might like:
Rudolfo Anaya, *The Sonny Baca Series*, 1995-
Rex Burns, *The Gabe Wager Series*, 1975-
Lucha Corpi, *The Gloria Damasco Series*, 1992-
Michael Nava, *The Henry Rios Series*, 1998-
Michael Stone, *The Streeter Series*, 1996-

193

IAN RANKIN

Black and Blue

(New York: St. Martin's Press, 1997)

Story type: Police Procedural
Series: Inspector John Rebus
Major character(s): John Rebus, Police Officer (inspector)
Time period(s): 1990s
Locale(s): Edinburgh, Scotland; Aberdeen, Scotland

Summary: In the sixties and seventies Glasgow was terrorized by "Bible John," who raped and murdered three women and was never caught. Now a copycat is at work, nicknamed "Bible Johnny" by the media. It's a case that would normally be assigned to Rebus, but police politics have landed him in one of Edinburgh's toughest suburbs where he's investigating the murder of an off-duty oilman. The case takes him north to the oil rigs of Aberdeen, where he unexpectedly becomes involved in the Bible John investigation.

Where it's reviewed:
Publishers Weekly, August 25, 1997, page 48
Times Literary Supplement, February 28, 1997, page 22

Other books by the same author:
Let It Bleed, 1995
Mortal Causes, 1994
The Black Book, 1993
Strip Jack, 1992
Tooth and Nail, 1992

Other books you might like:
John Brady, *The Matt Minogue Series*, 1988-
Bartholomew Gill, *The Inspector Peter McGarr Series*, 1977-
Quintin Jardine, *The Constable Robert Skinner Series*, 1993-
William McIlvaney, *The Jack Laidlaw Series*, 1977-1985
Peter Turnbull, *The P Division Series*, 1981-

194

LEV RAPHAEL

The Edith Wharton Murders

(New York: St. Martin's Press, 1997)

Story type: Amateur Detective
Series: Nick Hoffman
Major character(s): Nick Hoffman, Professor (English Literature), Homosexual
Time period(s): 1990s
Locale(s): State University of Michigan, Michigan

Summary: Warring factions of Wharton scholars make for academic hell as Nick Hoffman organizes a conference devoted to Wharton's life and works. In the meantime, he's having to deal with a very conservative and homophobic administrator whose husband is Nick's new office mate. And if that weren't enough, the reception he and his lover Stefan Borowski are giving for a visiting lesbian writer Chloe DeVore is ruined when her ex-lover accuses her of plagiarizing her new novel. Then Chloe turns up at the conference and is murdered. With the university looking for a scapegoat to blame everything on, Nick must turn detective to find out who killed Chloe.

Where it's reviewed:
Booklist, September 1, 1997, page 66
Kirkus Reviews, August 1, 1997, page 1161
Publishers Weekly, August 11, 1997, page 389

Other books by the same author:
Let's Get Criminal, 1995

Other books you might like:
Robert Barnard, *Death of an Old Goat*, 1974
Robert Bernard, *Deadly Meeting*, 1970
Amanda Cross, *The James Joyce Murder*, 1967
Joanne Dobson, *Quieter Than Sleep*, 1997
Ruth Dudley Edwards, *Matricide at St. Martha's*, 1994

195

PHILIP REED

Bird Dog

(New York: Pocket Books, 1997)

Story type: Action/Adventure; Humor
Major character(s): Harold Dodge, Civil Servant (former used car salesman)
Time period(s): 1990s
Locale(s): Los Angeles, California

Summary: As a former "bird dog," or one who sniffs out gullible prospects for a sleazy used car dealership, Harold Dodge knows all the ins and outs of the business. In fact, he wrote a book about it, and when one of his co-workers gets ripped off by the lot he used to work for, she comes to him for help. Fat, fiftyish, and graying, Harold has a kind heart and an eye for a pretty woman, so against his better judgment he agrees to help her unwind the deal. But when he can't manage it, she takes matters in her own hands, and Harold lands in the middle of a scam so fiendish even the FBI is onto it. Eventually everybody is after Harold: crooked car hustlers, the FBI,

the DMV, and a crazed biker he threw out of his mother's house during a wild party his bad-boy kid brother was hosting. First mystery.

Where it's reviewed:
Kirkus Reviews, May 15, 1997, page 749
Library Journal, May 1, 1997, page 143
Publishers Weekly, April 28, 1997, page 49

Other books you might like:
Pete Hautman, *The Mortal Nuts*, 1996
Carl Hiaasen, *Double Whammy*, 1987
Elmore Leonard, *Get Shorty*, 1990
Ross Thomas, *Voodoo, Ltd.*, 1992
Don Winslow, *The Death and Life of Bobby Z*, 1997

196

RUTH RENDELL

Road Rage

(New York: Crown, 1997)

Story type: Police Procedural
Series: Inspector Wexford
Major character(s): Reginald Wexford, Police Officer (chief inspector)
Time period(s): 1990s
Locale(s): Kingsmarkham, England

Summary: Despondent because Framhurst Great Wood just outside his beloved Kingsmarkham is about to be destroyed by the construction of a new highway, Inspector Wexford can barely bring himself to look at its natural beauty. His wife Dora, on the other hand, is active on a committee to save the threatened forest. But it's a more desperate battle than either of them realize, and soon Dora and other committee members are taken hostage and threatened with murder. Wexford and his team of police officers race against time to learn who the kidnappers are and where they have taken the hostages.

Where it's reviewed:
Booklist, August 1997, page 1848
Kirkus Reviews, July 1, 1997, page 988
New York Times Book Review, September 7, 1997, page 34
Publishers Weekly, July 7, 1997, page 53
Wall Street Journal (Central Edition), October 3, 1997, page A8

Other books by the same author:
The Keys to the Street, 1996
Simisola, 1995
Kissing the Gunner's Daughter, 1993
The Veiled One, 1985
The Speaker of Mandarin, 1983

Other books you might like:
Frances Fyfield, *The Helen West Series*, 1988-
S.T. Haymon, *The Inspector Ben Jurnet Series*, 1980-
P.D. James, *The Adam Dalgliesh Series*, 1962-
Sheila Radley, *The Douglas Quantrill Series*, 1978-
Minette Walters, *The Ice House*, 1992

197

FATHER BRAD REYNOLDS S.J.

A Ritual Death

(New York: Avon, 1997)

Story type: Amateur Detective
Series: Father Mark Townsend
Major character(s): Father Mark Townsend, Religious (Jesuit priest)
Time period(s): 1990s
Locale(s): LaConner, Washington (Puget Sound area)

Summary: While visiting his grandparents on Puget Sound, Father Mark finds the townspeople and the nearby Swinomish Indian people pitted against each other. Then his own grandfather is accused of murdering a local man whose hostility toward the Swinomish and their salmon-fishing practices is well known, as is his hobby of illegally hunting for artifacts on tribal lands. Naturally Father Mark is anxious to clear matters up and exonerate his grandfather. Local folklore about pirates, smugglers and buried treasure are woven into the story.

Other books by the same author:
The Story Knife, 1996

Other books you might like:
Margaret Coel, *The Father John O'Malley Series*, 1995-
James D. Doss, *The Charlie Moon/Scott Parris Series*, 1994-
Richard Hoyt, *Fish Story*, 1985
William Kienzle, *The Father Robert Koesler Series*, 1979-
Ralph McInerny, *The Father Roger Dowling Series*, 1977-

198

PHYLLIS RICHMAN

The Butter Did It

(New York: HarperCollins, 1997)

Story type: Amateur Detective
Major character(s): Chas Wheatley, Journalist (restaurant critic)
Time period(s): 1990s
Locale(s): Washington, District of Columbia

Summary: When Washington's finest French chef, Laurence Levain, dies suddenly, everyone assumes it was a case of too much foie gras, or at least somehow related to his prodigious cholesterol intake. But the city's most famous (and most feared) restaurant critic, Chas Wheatley, has other ideas. She's still carrying a torch for Levain after a passionate romance they shared years ago, and she's convinced that he was murdered. With the help of her detective friend Homer Jones, a noted gourmand, she begins investigating what turns out to be a fiendishly clever crime. The author is a noted DC restaurant critic who sprinkles her debut novel with much insider restaurant and food lore as well as numerous menus.

Where it's reviewed:
Book World, May 18, 1997, page 9
Kirkus Reviews, April 1, 1997, page 507
Library Journal, May 1, 1997, page 144
New York Times Book Review, June 15, 1997, page 21

Publishers Weekly, April 7, 1997, page 77

Other books you might like:
Michael Bond, *The Monsieur Pamplemousse Series*, 1983-
Peter King, *Spiced to Death*, 1997
Nan Lyons, *Someone Is Killing the Great Chefs of America*, 1993
  Ivan Lyons, co-author
Joanne Pence, *The Angie Amalfi Series*, 1993-
Lou Jane Temple, *The Heaven Lee Series*, 1997-

199

RICK RIORDAN

Big Red Tequila

(New York: Bantam 1997)

Story type: Private Detective
Major character(s): Jackson "Tres" Navarre, Detective— Private (unlicensed)
Time period(s): 1990s
Locale(s): San Antonio, Texas

Summary: Tai chi master, margarita connoisseur and unlicensed private eye Tres Navarre left San Antonio ten years ago to try to put the memory of his father's murder behind him. Now he's back, living in a low-rent apartment with his enchilada-eating cat Robert Johnson, driving a VW convertible he's borrowing from his mother, and looking for some answers. In doing so he stirs up a lot of old memories, gets shot at and run over, and finds his girlfriend has gone missing. The Texas mob is after him, and it's going to take all his resources to ditch them, find his father's murderer, and get out of town before they catch up with him. First novel.

Where it's reviewed:
Publishers Weekly, April 28, 1997, page 73

Other books you might like:
Rudolfo Anaya, *The Sonny Baca Series*, 1995-
Robert Crais, *The Elvis Cole Series*, 1987-
G.M. Ford, *The Leo Haig Series*, 1995
Robert B. Parker, *The Spenser Series*, 1973-
Walter Satterthwait, *The Joshua Croft Series*, 1989-

200

CANDACE M. ROBB

The Riddle of St. Leonard's

(New York: St. Martin's Press, 1997)

Story type: Historical
Series: Owen Archer
Major character(s): Owen Archer, Military Personnel (soldier), Spy
Time period(s): 14th century (1369)
Locale(s): York, England

Summary: A series of deaths that have nothing to do with the plague have taken place at St. Leonard's Hospital, and although the hospital has benefited financially from several of them, there have been thefts from St. Leonard's as well. Rumor has it that the deaths are not accidental, and the Master of the Hospital, concerned that the scandal could ruin not only

the hospital but his own career, commissions the one-eyed spy Owen Archer to investigate them. Archer discovers that there are three seemingly separate mysteries to be solved and that a dying message in the form of a riddle uttered by one of the victims might be the clue to all of them.

Where it's reviewed:
Kirkus Reviews, August 1, 1997, page 1162
Library Journal, August 1997, page 140
Publishers Weekly, August 4, 1997, page 70

Other books by the same author:
The King's Bishop, 1996
The Nun's Tale, 1995
The Lady Chapel, 1994
The Apothecary Rose, 1993

Other books you might like:
P.C. Doherty, *The Hugh Corbett Series*, 1986-
Susanna Gregory, *The Matthew Bartholomew Series*, 1996-
Edward Marston, *The Ralph Delchard and Gervase Bret Series*, 1993-
Ian Morson, *The William Falconer Series*, 1994-
Sharon Kay Penman, *The Queen's Man*, 1996

201

LES ROBERTS

Cleveland Local
(New York: St. Martin's, 1997)

Story type: Private Detective
Series: Milan Jacovich
Major character(s): Milan Jacovich, Detective—Private
Time period(s): 1990s
Locale(s): Cleveland, Ohio; San Carlos, Caribbean

Summary: At the end of a harsh Cleveland winter, Milan Jacovich isn't exactly unwilling to travel to the Caribbean island of San Carlos to investigate the death of up-and-coming attorney Joel Kerner, Jr., whose sister believes he was murdered and hires Milo to find out why. During his visit to the island Jacovich runs into an Interpol cop, a couple of knife-wielding thugs, and a pair of very odd American tourists, but there doesn't seem to be much of a trail to follow. Back in Cleveland, however, he learns that several underworld figures, including both union organizers and the mob, have good reason to stop him from solving the mystery of Kerner's death.

Other books by the same author:
Collision Bend, 1996
The Duke of Cleveland, 1995
The Lake Effect, 1994
The Cleveland Connection, 1993
Deep Shaker, 1991

Other books you might like:
Loren D. Estleman, *The Amos Walker Series*, 1980-
Rob Kantner, *The Ben Perkins Series*, 1986-
Albert Z. Lewin, *The Albert Sampson Series*, 1971-
James Martin, *The Gil Disbro Series*, 1989-
Jonathan Valin, *The Harry Stoner Series*, 1980-

202

LYNDA S. ROBINSON

Eater of Souls
(New York: Walker, 1996)

Story type: Historical
Series: Lord Meren
Major character(s): Lord Meren, Nobleman (advisor to the Pharaoh); King Tutankhamon, Historical Figure, Ruler (Pharaoh)
Time period(s): 14th century B.C. (1400)
Locale(s): Memphis, Egypt

Summary: The death of Nefertiti, wife of Akhenaten, is the mystery Lord Meren, the Eyes and Ears of the adolescent Pharaoh Tutankhamun, explores here. He is certain that Nefertiti was murdered, and his investigation takes him into every corner of the royal court. In fact, his probing threatens many powerful people and puts the lives of his own daughters and son in peril. Even the gods seem angry with Lord Meren, and the royal city of Memphis is terrorized by a series of horrifying murders apparently committed by the Devourer, the most fearsome of all the Egyptian gods.

Where it's reviewed:
Kirkus Reviews, April 15, 1997, page 594
Library Journal, May 1, 1997, page 144
New York Times Book Review, May 25, 1997, page 23
Publishers Weekly, April 7, 1997, page 77
School Library Journal, August 1997, page 188

Other books by the same author:
Murder at the Feast of Rejoicing, 1996
Murder at the God's Gate, 1995
Murder at the Place of Anubis, 1994

Other books you might like:
Agatha Christie, *Death Comes as the End*, 1944
J. Suzanne Frank, *Reflections in the Nile*, 1997
Anton Gill, *The Huy the Scribe Series*, 1991-
Gary Gygax, *The Anubis Murders*, 1989
Lee Levin, *King Tut's Private Eye*, 1996

203

PETER ROBINSON

Blood at the Root
(New York: Avon, 1997)

Story type: Police Procedural
Series: Inspector Alan Banks
Major character(s): Alan Banks, Police Officer (detective chief inspector); Susan Gay, Police Officer (detective constable)
Time period(s): 1990s
Locale(s): Eastvale, England (Yorkshire)

Summary: When young Jason Fox is found stomped to death after pub closing hours, shortly after he had hurled racial insults at three Pakistani youths, it looks like a racial incident turned deadly. The three suspects won't talk, so Banks and Gay have no choice but to lock them up. When they're released soon after, Chief Constable Riddle is furious and

removes Banks from the case. Finding his hands tied, Banks is frustrated, as he had been promised hands-on detective work when he tranferred to Eastvale from the force in London. Then he discovers that Fox was a member of a very nasty neo-Nazi hate group that intends to practice severe ethnic cleansing on England. But he's still not convinced that this is all there is to his death.

Other books by the same author:
Innocent Graves, 1996
Final Account, 1994
Wednesday's Child, 1992
Past Reason Hated, 1991
The Hanging Valley, 1989

Other books you might like:
Deborah Crombie, *The Duncan Kincaid/Gemma James Series*, 1993-
Claire Curzon, *The Mike Yeadings Series*, 1983-
Colin Dexter, *The Inspector Morse Series*, 1975-
Caroline Graham, *The Inspector Tom Barnaby Series*, 1987-
Reginald Hill, *The Andrew Dalziel/Peter Pascoe Series*, 1970-

204

KATE ROSS

The Devil in Music

(New York: Viking, 1997)

Story type: Historical; Amateur Detective
Series: Julian Kestrel
Major character(s): Julian Kestrel, Gentleman (dandy); Dipper, Servant (former pickpocket)
Time period(s): 1820s (1821)
Locale(s): Milan, Italy; La Scala, Italy; Lake Como, Italy

Summary: While traveling in Milan, the London dandy Julian Kestrel becomes drawn into an investigation of the four-year-old murder of a local opera patron, Lodovico Malvezzi. Among the many suspects are a runaway wife and her male soprano lover; a nobleman of liberal leanings at odds with Italy's Austrian overlords; a mocking Frenchman; and a woman as clever as she is beautiful with whom Julian becomes romantically involved. Soon Julian is caught up in the struggle between the Carbonari, secret rebels against the Austrians, and the Austrian police. But in order to find the murderer, Julian must find Malvezzi's protege Orfeo, a prodigiously talented but penniless tenor who has vanished. Is he the murderer, or was Malvezzi the victim of a revolutionary plot, or is it the result of long-standing feuds in his own family? Set against the dazzling backdrop of Italian society during the high opera season, this is a meticulously plotted mystery in which further details of Julian's mysterious past emerge.

Where it's reviewed:
Kirkus Reviews, August 1, 1997, page 1162
Library Journal, August 1997, page 140
New York Times Book Review, September 7, 1997, page 34

Other books by the same author:
Whom the Gods Love, 1995
A Broken Vessel, 1994

Cut to the Quick, 1993

Other books you might like:
Bruce Alexander, *The Sir John Fielding Series*, 1994-
Stephanie Barron, *The Jane Austen Series*, 1995-
John Gano, *Arias of Blood*, 1997
Deryn Lake, *Death at the Beggar's Opera*, 1996
Anne Perry, *Weighed in the Balance*, 1996

205

LAURA JOH ROWLAND

The Way of the Traitor

(New York: HarperCollins, 1997)

Story type: Historical
Series: Sano Ichiro
Major character(s): Sano Ichiro, Warrior (samurai)
Time period(s): 17th century (1690)
Locale(s): Nagasaki, Japan

Summary: When the bloated, mutilated body of a Dutch trader washes up on Deshima, a small island off the coast of Nagasaki where foreign barbarians are lodged and guarded, Sano must find out who killed Jan Spaen. What he discovers is a web of lies and deception far more complex than anyone could have imagined, and when Sano gets too close to the truth, he is framed. With an assassin close on his heels he pursues the killer and risks a samurai's worst nightmare—dishonorable death.

Where it's reviewed:
Kirkus Reviews, May 1, 1997, page 683
Library Journal, May 1, 1997, page 143
Publishers Weekly, May 12, 1997, page 62

Other books by the same author:
Bundori, 1996
Shinju, 1995

Other books you might like:
Eleanor Cooney, *Deception*, 1992
    Daniel Altieri, co-author
Dale Furutani, *The Toyotomi Blades*, 1998
James Melville, *The Inspector Otani Series*, 1979-
Robert Van Gulik, *The Judge Dee Series*, 1949-1973
Ann Woodward, *The Exile Way*, 1996

206

S.J. ROZAN

No Colder Place

(New York: St. Martin's, 1997)

Story type: Private Detective
Series: Bill Smith and Lydia Chin
Major character(s): Bill Smith, Detective—Private; Lydia Chin, Detective—Private
Time period(s): 1990s
Locale(s): New York, New York

Summary: When a Manhattan construction site is plagued by a series of thefts and unsettling mishaps, Bill Smith goes undercover as a bricklayer (his former profession) to look for the

culprit. Assisting him is his sometime partner, Chinese-American private eye Lydia Chin, a resident of Chinatown. Together they follow a trail of fraud and murder that reaches deep into the Manhattan underworld. The title refers to the cold wind that blows through the steel and concrete of urban construction sites.

Where it's reviewed:
Booklist, September 1, 1997, page 67
Kirkus Reviews, August 1, 1997, page 1162
Publishers Weekly, July 28, 1998, page 57

Other books by the same author:
Mandarin Plaid, 1996
Concourse, 1995
China Trade, 1994

Other books you might like:
Lawrence Block, *The Matt Scudder Series*, 1978-
Gaylord Dold, *Schedule Two*, 1996
Leslie Glass, *The April Woo Series*, 1993-
Dennis Lehane, *The Patrick Kenzie/Angela Gennaro Series*, 1994-
Lisa See, *Flower Net*, 1997

207

JAMES SALLIS

Death Will Have Your Eyes: A Novel about Spies

(New York: St. Martin's Press 1997)

Story type: Espionage
Major character(s): ''David'', Spy (former CIA hit man)
Time period(s): 1990s
Locale(s): United States; New Orleans, Louisiana

Summary: David (not his real name), trained as a CIA hit man during the Cold War, has been out of the game nine years now and wants to keep it that way. But he's dragged back into it by his former boss Johnsson, now blind, who wants him to catch a former colleague turned rogue. He gives up his new life as a sculptor, bids his girlfriend farewell, and sets off on a cross-country odyssey that eventually leads him to New Orleans. He meets many memorable characters on his mission, but most of the action is internal, as David drives across the American landscape and contemplates what it means to be an agent. Variously described as existential, introspective, and absurdist, it's scarcely a typical spy novel and is something of a departure from the author's Lew Griffin private eye novels.

Where it's reviewed:
Kirkus Reviews, June 15, 1997, page 905

Other books by the same author:
Black Hornet, 1994
Moth, 1993
The Long-Legged Fly, 1992 (all the above are in the Lew Griffin series)

Other books you might like:
Clive Egleton, *A Lethal Involvement*, 1997
David Hagberg, *Assassin*, 1997
William Hood, *The Sunday Spy*, 1997
David Ignatius, *A Firing Offense*, 1997

John Le Carre, *The Spy Who Came in from the Cold*, 1964

208

JOHN SANDFORD (Pseudonym of John Camp)

The Night Crew

(New York: Putnam's, 1997)

Story type: Amateur Detective
Major character(s): Anna Hatory, Journalist (video freelancer)
Time period(s): 1990s
Locale(s): Los Angeles, California

Summary: Anna Hatory, a small, shy (but tough) young woman who was raised on a farm in Wisconsin, is the head of a crew of video freelancers who roam the streets of Los Angeles in their truck during the night hours, looking for any kind of news story they can shoot and sell to local stations or the networks. One night they witness the death of a man who jumps from the fifth story of a hotel directly at their cameras. One of the cameramen, Jason, is deeply affected by the jumper and goes home early that night. Several hours later his body turns up on the beach, shot through the head. The police dismiss it as drug-related but Anna's not so sure, and the more she investigates, the more secrets from the past—not only Jason's, but the jumper's and hers as well—begin to emerge. A new character from the creator of the Prey series featuring Minneapolis police detective Lucas Davenport.

Other books by the same author:
Sudden Prey, 1996
Mind Prey, 1995
Night Prey, 1994
Winter Prey, 1993
Silent Prey, 1992

Other books you might like:
Jan Burke, *The Irene Kelly Series*, 1993-
Michael Connelly, *The Black Ice*, 1993
Jeffery Deaver, *Death of a Blue Movie Star*, 1990
Wendy Hornsby, *The Maggie MacGowen Series*, 1992-
Faye Kellerman, *Justice*, 1995

209

STEVEN SAYLOR

The House of the Vestals

(New York: St. Martin's Press, 1997)

Story type: Historical; Private Detective
Series: Gordianus the Finder
Major character(s): Gordianus the Finder, Detective—Private
Time period(s): 1st century B.C. (80-72 B.C.)
Locale(s): Rome, Ancient Civilization

Summary: These nine stories, all set during the eight-year time period between his first and second novels, fill in some of the gaps is Gordianus's history. They tell the story of the childhood of his adopted son Eco, his relationship with Bethesda (first as his slave and then his wife), Bethesda's own background, and the history of Rome from the end of Sulla's dictatorship to the Spartan slave revolt. Included is an essay on the history of the period and a time line of events.

Where it's reviewed:
Kirkus Reviews, June 1, 1997, page 840
Publishers Weekly, April 28, 1997, page 53

Other books by the same author:
A Murder on the Appian Way, 1996
The Venus Throw, 1995
Catilina's Riddle, 1993
Arms of Nemesis, 1992
Roman Blood, 1991

Other books you might like:
Anna Apostolou, *A Murder in Macedon*, 1997
Ron Burns, *The Livinius Severus Series*, 1991-
Lindsey Davis, *The Marcus Didius Falco Series*, 1989-
John Maddox Roberts, *The SPQR Series*, 1990-
Marilyn Todd, *I, Claudia*, 1995

210

LISA SCOTTOLINE

Rough Justice

(New York: HarperCollins 1997)

Story type: Legal
Series: Bennie Rosato
Major character(s): Benedetta "Bennie" Rosato, Lawyer (defense); Marta Richter, Lawyer (defense)
Time period(s): 1990s
Locale(s): Philadelphia, Pennsylvania

Summary: Millionaire businessman Elliot Steere, standing trial for the murder of a homeless man who tried to carjack him, faces acquittal after top defense attorney Marta Richter has mounted a successful claim of self-defense. Then Marta learns her client is indeed guilty of premeditated murder and recruits two of her associates to help her set matters right, thus jeopardizing their lives and the future of Rosato & Associates, the all-female law firm they work for. Enter managing partner Bennie Rosato, who must figure out a way to see justice done and at the same time protect her partners and her business from the retribution that Steere is well able to exact, even from prison.

Where it's reviewed:
Kirkus Reviews, June 15, 1997, page 906
Library Journal, August 1997, page 135
New York Times Book Review, September 7, 1997, page 34
Publishers Weekly, July 7, 1997, page 48

Other books by the same author:
Legal Tender, 1996
Running from the Law, 1995
Final Appeal, 1994
Everywhere That Mary Went, 1993

Other books you might like:
John Grisham, *The Client*, 1996
Lia Matera, *The Laura DiPalma Series*, 1988-
Scott Turow, *Presumed Innocent*, 1987
Carolyn Wheat, *The Cass Jameson Series*, 1983-
Kate Wilhelm, *The Barbara Holloway Series*, 1991-

211

BARBARA SERANELLA

No Human Involved

(New York: St. Martin's Press, 1997)

Story type: Amateur Detective
Major character(s): Munch Mancini, Addict (recovering, heroin), Mechanic (auto)
Time period(s): 1990s
Locale(s): Los Angeles, California (Venice Beach, San Fernando Valley)

Summary: In the process of kicking her heroin addiction, Munch resolves to put together a new life. One of the first things she does is to stop at a biker bar in Venice to repay the twenty dollars she borrowed from the bartender. She gets into a conversation with the man next to her at the bar, who turns out to be a detective sent there to arrest her for the murder of her abusive father. She avoids jail, and since no one's terribly anxious to arrest the killer of "Flower George" Mancini, a pimp and general low-life, she gets away with it—until the gun that killed him proves to be the same one used against a student by a serial murderer. In the meantime Munch has taken a job as an auto mechanic at Happy Jack's Auto Repair in the valley, but she can't lay her past to rest until her situation is resolved. First mystery.

Where it's reviewed:
Kirkus Reviews, July 1, 1997, page 989
Publishers Weekly, June 16, 1997, page 49

Other books you might like:
Anthony Bourdain, *Gone Bamboo*, 1997
Liza Cody, *The Eva Wylie Series*, 1993-
James Crumley, *Dancing Bear*, 1983
Carol O'Connell, *The Kathleen Mallory Series*, 1994-
Fred Willard, *Down on Ponce*, 1997

212

LAURENCE SHAMES

Virgin Heat

(New York: Hyperion, 1997)

Story type: Action/Adventure
Major character(s): Angelina Amaro, Young Woman (daughter of Mafia family); Ziggy Max, Criminal
Time period(s): 1990s
Locale(s): Key West, Florida

Summary: For ten years Angelina has had a secret she can't share with anyone: she is in love with Sal Martucci, the man who betrayed her father, Mafia capo Paul Amaro, and sent him away to prison. One night Angelina is watching the videotape of a relative's Florida vacation and there on the screen, mixing a fancy drink, is a pair of hands she knows and loves: Sal's. She catches the next plane south and finds him. But he's in the witness protection program now, has changed his name to Ziggy Maxx, and has been tending bar and running scams quite happily all these years. Since he never knew anything about Angelina's crush on him, he's never given her a thought—although he's often thought of her

father, who still has the power to get him killed. Angelina also makes friends with a young gay man who has his own romantic dreams of what his vacation to Key West will bring him.

Where it's reviewed:
Booklist, January 1997, page 779
Kirkus Reviews, December 15, 1996, page 1763
Library Journal, February 1, 1997, page 110
New York Times Book Review, April 13, 1997, page 24
Publishers Weekly, February 3, 1997, page 95

Other books by the same author:
Tropical Depression, 1996
Sunburn, 1995
Scavenger Reef, 1994
Florida Straits, 1992

Other books you might like:
E.C. Ayres, *The Tony Lowell Series*, 1994-
Carl Hiaasen, *Native Tongue*, 1991
Elmore Leonard, *Gold Coast*, 1980
Randy Wayne White, *The Doc Ford Series*, 1990-
Charles Willeford, *The Hoke Moseley Series*, 1984-1988

213

ROGER L. SIMON

The Lost Coast: A Moses Wine Mystery

(New York: Harper, 1997)

Story type: Private Detective
Series: Moses Wine
Major character(s): Moses Wine, Detective—Private; Simon Wine, Activist
Time period(s): 1990s
Locale(s): Los Angeles, California; California (northern)

Summary: Former hippie Moses Wine, once known as ''The People's Detective,'' has given up his radical image for a staid but lucrative corporate investigations practice. But when his son Simon, a member of a radical environmentalist group, is wanted by the FBI for the murder of a logger, Moses heads for Northern California to investigate. He takes his ex-wife Suzanne with him and promptly runs afoul of a fight between the furious loggers and Simon's militant eco-warrior friends. But Simon, who supposedly caused the logger's death by booby-trapping an old-growth redwood, is nowhere to be found.

Where it's reviewed:
Book World, April 20, 1997, page 8

Other books by the same author:
Dead Meet, 1988
Raising the Dead, 1988
The Straight Man, 1986
California Roll, 1985
Peking Duck, 1979

Other books you might like:
Jo Dereske, *Savage Cut*, 1997
Kinky Friedman, *The Kinky Friedman Series*, 1986-
Richard Hoyt, *Whoo?*, 1991
David Rains Wallace, *The Turquoise Dragon*, 1985
Lee Wallingford, *Clear Cut Murder*, 1993

214

EDWARD SKLEPOWICH

Death in the Palazzo

(New York: St. Martin's Press, 1997)

Story type: Amateur Detective
Series: Urbino MacIntyre
Major character(s): Urbino MacIntyre, Detective—Amateur (American expatriate)
Time period(s): 1990s
Locale(s): Venice, Italy

Summary: With the coming of November, Urbino can enjoy his adopted city of Venice without the tourists and in the company of his good friend the Contessa da Capo-Zendrini. The contessa has agreed to let her cousin Gemma paint her portrait but the plans for its unveiling have her worried. It is to take place at a party attended by two families, the Zenos and the Capo-Zendrinis, who are still divided by a bitter feud. And the last time the families gathered together, at the same palazzo 50 years ago, the festivities ended in death.

Where it's reviewed:
Armchair Detective, Spring 1997, page 224
Booklist, March 15, 1997, page 1231
Kirkus Reviews, January 15, 1997, page 100
Library Journal, February 1, 1997, page 111
New York Times Book Review, March 2, 1997, page 20

Other books by the same author:
Black Bridge, 1995
Liquid Desires, 1993
Farewell to the Flesh, 1991
Death in a Serene City, 1990

Other books you might like:
Michael Dibdin, *The Aurelio Zen Series*, 1988-
Jonathan Gash, *The Gondola Scam*, 1984
John Spencer Hill, *The Carlo Arbati Series*, 1995-
Donna Leon, *The Guido Brunetti Series*, 1992-
Magdalen Nabb, *The Marshal Guarnaccia Series*, 1981-

215

CYNTHIA SMITH

Impolite Society

(New York: Berkley, 1997)

Story type: Private Detective
Series: Emma Rhodes
Major character(s): Emma Rhodes, Detective—Private (''Private Resolver'')
Time period(s): 1990s
Locale(s): Vila do Mar, Portugal

Summary: An inquisitive mind, an IQ of 165, and a love of luxury have led Emma Rhodes to invent a unique profession for herself: Private Resolver. If someone has a problem that piques her interest, Emma will solve it in two weeks in exchange for $20,000 (or its equivalent in any hard currency). Because she never fails, she has a Manhattan apartment, a London flat, and a casita in Portugal, each beautifully furnished and with closets brimming with designer clothes.

When you're that rich, you want to travel light. While she's relaxing in her Portuguese home, she meets an American couple whose minister son has died of an apparent suicide. They think it was foul play and hire Emma to find out what really happened. Although she's quite well-connected with the other rich expatriates in the village, Emma finds this a much more difficult case to solve than she had anticipated.

Other books by the same author:
Noblesse Oblige, 1996

Other books you might like:
K.K. Beck, *The Jane da Silva Series*, 1992-
Joyce Christmas, *The Lady Margaret Priam Series*, 1988-
Carol Higgins Clark, *The Regan Reilly Series*, 1992-
Melodie Johnson Howe, *The Claire Conrad Series*, 1989-
Evelyn E. Smith, *The Miss Melville Series*, 1986-

216

TROY SOOS

Hunting a Detroit Tiger

(New York: Kensington, 1997)

Story type: Historical; Amateur Detective
Series: Mickey Rawlings
Major character(s): Mickey Rawlings, Sports Figure (professional baseball player)
Time period(s): 1920s (1920)
Locale(s): Detroit, Michigan

Summary: When Emmett Siever, an old-time baseball player trying to organize a players' union, is killed at a meeting of the International Workers of the World, somehow utility infielder Mickey Rawlings is credited with the deed. In the anti-Red climate of the day, this makes Mickey a hero—only he didn't do it, and he knows Siever wasn't the Bolshevik the press claims he was. The Wobblies want the murder avenged, Mickey's teammates on the Tigers think he's trying to sabotage their union, and the owners want him to speak out publicly against the unions. All this makes poor Mickey, who wants nothing more than a .250 batting average and a regular place in the lineup, a very unpopular guy.

Where it's reviewed:
Kirkus Reviews, February 15, 1997, page 259
Publishers Weekly, March 24, 1997, page 63

Other books by the same author:
Murder at Wrigley Field, 1996
Murder at Ebbets Field, 1995
Murder at Fenway Park, 1994

Other books you might like:
Loren D. Estleman, *Whiskey River*, 1990
Crabbe Evers, *The Duffy House Series*, 1991-
Alison Gordon, *The Kate Henry Series*, 1989-
Richard Rosen, *Strike Three, You're Dead*, 1984
John Straley, *Death and the Language of Happiness*, 1997

217

DANA STABENOW

Breakup

(New York: Putnam's, 1997)

Story type: Private Detective
Series: Kate Shugak
Major character(s): Kate Shugak, Detective—Private, Indian (Aleut)
Time period(s): 1990s
Locale(s): Alaska (back country)

Summary: As if rampaging bears and family feuds weren't enough to occupy Kate during the April thaw, a plane crashes very near her homestead in the Alaskan wilderness and then a dead body, possibly murdered, is found. Although she's unwilling to get involved in the investigation, Kate yields to pressure from friends and neighbors to lend a hand, and guided by the spirit of her Aleut grandmother, she finds herself slowly assuming the role of clan leader, a post she is bound to by honor and blood. The breakup resulting from the spring thaw becomes more dangerous and destructive and Kate must see if she can assume an elder's role in restoring order to her world.

Where it's reviewed:
Book World, July 20, 1997, page 10
Booklist, May 15, 1997, page 1567
Kirkus Reviews, May 1, 1997, page 684
Library Journal, June 1, 1997, page 156
Publishers Weekly, April 21, 1997, page 64

Other books by the same author:
Blood Will Tell, 1996
Play with Fire, 1995
A Cold-Blooded Business, 1994
Dead in the Water, 1993
A Fatal Thaw, 1992

Other books you might like:
Susan Froetschel, *Alaska Gray*, 1994
Sean Hanlon, *The Prester John Riordan Series*, 1989-
Sue Henry, *Sleeping Lady*, 1996
Elizabeth Quinn, *Murder Most Grizzly*, 1993
Scott Young, *The Mateesie Kitologitak Series*, 1990-

218

LES STANDIFORD

Deal on Ice

(New York: HarperCollins, 1997)

Story type: Amateur Detective
Series: John Deal
Major character(s): John Deal, Contractor (building)
Time period(s): 1990s
Locale(s): Miami, Florida

Summary: John Deal's longtime buddy Arch Dolan, owner of Miami's leading independent bookstore, is killed just days after it's announced that the vast bookselling conglomerate Haskell & Monroe will open a mammoth superstore just across the street from Dolan's shop. Clutched in the dead

man's fist is a tract from wealthy right-wing fundamentalist preacher James Ray Willis. As Deal investigates his friend's death, he discovers that the Reverend Willis has plans to gain a stranglehold on the media, from books to the Internet. Together with his lovely, troubled ex-wife Janice, Deal heads for Willis' northern headquarters, followed by a pair of deadly assassins.

Where it's reviewed:
Armchair Detective, Spring 1997, page 222
Book World, February 16, 1997, page 11
Kirkus Reviews, November 15, 1996, page 1629
Library Journal, February 1, 1997, page 111
Publishers Weekly, November 11, 1996, page 55

Other books by the same author:
Deal to Die For, 1995
Raw Deal, 1994
Done Deal, 1993

Other books you might like:
E.C. Ayres, *The Tony Lowell Series*, 1994-
John Leslie, *The Gideon Lowry Series*, 1994-
John Lutz, *The Fred Carver Series*, 1986-
Laurence Shames, *Virgin Heat*, 1997
Randy Wayne White, *The Doc Ford Series*, 1990-

219

MARY STEWART

Rose Cottage

(New York: Morrow, 1997)

Story type: Psychological Suspense
Major character(s): Kate Herrick, Widow(er)
Time period(s): 1940s (1947); 1990s
Locale(s): England (near the Scottish border)

Summary: As a young and unexpectedly well-to-do war widow, Kate Herrick leaves her stopgap job in London to visit Rose Cottage, the tiny dwelling her grandmother lived in for years before the family she was in service to moved to their other estate in Scotland during the war. Kate's own mother had run off with a gypsy and was killed when her daughter was still a young child, leaving her to be raised by her grandmother. Now there are some papers her ailing grandmother wants her to retrieve from the cottage, and when she arrives there she finds the village full of rumors and gossip about mysterious prowlers, ghosts, and witchcraft. It's true the cottage has been broken into, but Kate somehow can't believe she's in danger, and she feels very much at home in the village. There's a pleasant dash of romance mixed in with the mystery.

Where it's reviewed:
Kirkus Reviews, August 15, 1997, page 1255
Publishers Weekly, August 18, 1997, page 70

Other books by the same author:
The Stormy Petrel, 1991
Thornyhold, 1988
Touch Not the Cat, 1976
The Gabriel Hounds, 1967
Airs Above the Ground, 1965

Other books you might like:
Nancy Atherton, *Aunt Dimity's Death*, 1992
Dorothy Cannell, *Down the Garden Path*, 1985
Caroline Llewellyn, *Life Blood*, 1993
Barbara Michaels, *Vanish with the Rose*, 1992
Susan Wade, *Walking Rain*, 1996

220

JOHN STRALEY

Death and the Language of Happiness

(New York: Bantam, 1997)

Story type: Private Detective
Series: Cecil Younger
Major character(s): Cecil Younger, Detective—Private
Time period(s): 1990s
Locale(s): Sitka, Alaska

Summary: Cecil is hired by a 97-year-old man, William Flynn, who has been accused of murdering a young woman, Angela Ramirez. In order to clear Flynn Cecil must find the woman's husband. Somehow her death is linked with the death of a young man in Centralia, Washington, in 1919, when American Legionnaires clashed with activists from the Industrial Workers of the World, known as Wobblies. His investigations take him to the Aleutian Islands and to Washington State, but it is mostly the history, geography and terrible beauty of Alaska that the author describes. Cecil, who continues to battle with drugs, alcohol, and his own troubled psyche, has a gift for relating to the flawed and often disreputable characters he meets in the course of his investigation.

Where it's reviewed:
Kirkus Reviews, April 1, 1997, page 508
Library Journal, April 1 , 1997, page 133
Publishers Weekly, February 3, 1997, page 98
Tribune Books, May 4, 1997, page 4

Other books by the same author:
The Music of What Happens, 1996
The Curious Eat Themselves, 1993
The Woman Who Married a Bear, 1992

Other books you might like:
Earl Emerson, *The Thomas Black Series*, 1985-
Sean Hanlon, *The Prester John Riordan Series*, 1989-
Sue Henry, *The Alex Jensen Series*, 1991-
Richard Hoyt, *The John Denson Series*, 1980-
Troy Soos, *Hunting a Detroit Tiger*, 1997

221

TONY STRONG

The Poison Tree

(New York: Delacorte, 1997)

Story type: Amateur Detective
Major character(s): Terry Williams, Scholar, Divorced Person
Time period(s): 1990s
Locale(s): Oxford, England

Summary: After a marriage and a love affair have both gone south, Terry Williams moves from London to Oxford for a

fresh start and a chance to resume work on her abandoned doctorate in detective fiction. The peace and tranquillity she longs for are soon shattered when she learns that her new home was once the scene of a savage sexual murder, the consequences of which are still intruding into the present. Then she learns that her famous neighbor was involved in a bizarre sexual scandal and she stumbles across a hidden cache of near pornographic letters. The mystery that begins to unfold is more brutal and disturbing than any she's read in her researches. While she pieces it together, a killer still walks the streets of Oxford, seeking revenge. First novel.

Other books you might like:
Colin Dexter, *The Inspector Morse Series*, 1975-
Elizabeth George, *A Great Deliverance*, 1988
P.D. James, *An Unsuitable Job for a Woman*, 1972
Joan Smith, *The Loretta Lawson Series*, 1987-
Veronica Stallwood, *The Kate Ivory Series*, 1993-

222

MAUREEN TAN

AKA Jane

(New York: Mysterious Press, 1997)

Story type: Action/Adventure
Major character(s): Jane Nichols, Spy (retired MI5 operative), Writer
Time period(s): 1990s
Locale(s): Savannah, Georgia

Summary: Jane Nichols, a beautiful and resourceful British operative who was virtually raised in the world of espionage, has finally burned out and is haunted by painful memories of her lover's murder and other shattering events. She decides to retire to Georgia and devote herself to her other career: writing hard-boiled crime novels as Max Murdock, creator of tough-guy private eye Andrew Jax. But she hasn't been able to shake her past completely and when an old enemy reappears, she's soon off on an intercontinental chase that will require all her survival skills if she's to come out of it alive. First novel.

Where it's reviewed:
Kirkus Reviews, August 1, 1997, page 1149
Publishers Weekly, July 28, 1997, page 56

Other books you might like:
Margaret Duffy, *The Ingrid Langley Series*, 1987-
Charlaine Harris, *The Lily Bard Series*, 1996-
Gayle Lynds, *Masquerade*, 1996
Peter O'Donnell, *The Modesty Blaise Series*, 1965-
Thomas Perry, *The Jane Whitefield Series*, 1995-

223

PETER TASKER

Buddha Kiss

(New York: Doubleday, 1997)

Story type: Action/Adventure
Major character(s): Richard Mitchell, Businessman (securities analyst); Kazuo Mori, Detective—Private

Time period(s): 1990s
Locale(s): Tokyo, Japan

Summary: Financial whiz kid Richard Mitchell used his brains and a degree in Japanese studies to parlay a job as a London bike messenger into the position of securities analyst for a Tokyo financial firm. But his rise to the top is threatened when his new boss, Yazawa, a mysterious man who appeared out of the blue, insists he recommend the underwriting of a rundown company. Meanwhile, maverick private eye Kazuo Mori is investigating the murder of a friend's daughter and the trail leads him toward the radical Peace Technology cult. Financial fraud and religious zealotry are all ingredients in this topical thriller that deals with the instability behind Japan's very conformist society.

Where it's reviewed:
Kirkus Reviews, July 1, 1997, page 981
Publishers Weekly, August 4, 1997, page 64

Other books by the same author:
Silent Thunder, 1992

Other books you might like:
Dale Furutani, *The Toyotomi Blades*, 1997
Martin Limon, *Jade Lady Burning*, 1992
Sujata Massey, *The Salaryman's Wife*, 1997
James Melville, *The Inspector Otani Series*, 1979-
Lisa See, *Flower Net*, 1997

224

LOU JANE TEMPLE

A Stiff Risotto

(New York: St. Martin's Press, 1997)

Story type: Amateur Detective
Series: Heaven Lee
Major character(s): Heaven Lee, Restaurateur, Cook
Time period(s): 1990s
Locale(s): Kansas City, Missouri; Aspen, Colorado

Summary: Every June, five thousand food lovers from all over the world congregate in the trendy resort town of Aspen as celebrity chefs vie for the Best Chef title at the Real Dish Food Festival. This year Heaven Lee, proprietor of the celebrated Kansas City eatery Cafe Heaven, is one of them, and the competition quickly turns even deadlier than anticipated when contestants start dropping like flies. There is a generous array of suspects for Heaven to ponder when she turns her sleuthing talents to solving the crimes. Many recipes included.

Other books by the same author:
Death by Rhubarb, 1996
Revenge of the Barbeque Queens, 1996

Other books you might like:
Carol Higgins Clark, *Iced*, 1995
Diane Mott Davidson, *The Goldy Bear Series*, 1990-
Tamar Myers, *The Magdalena Yoder Series*, 1994-
Katherine Hall Page, *The Faith Fairchild Series*, 1991-
Virginia Rich, *The Mrs. Eugenia Potter Series*, 1982-

225

JAMES THAYER

Five Past Midnight

(New York: Simon & Schuster, 1997)

Story type: Historical; Action/Adventure
Major character(s): Jack Cray, Military Personnel (American army commando); Otto Dietrich, Police Officer (homicide detective)
Time period(s): 1940s (1945)
Locale(s): Colditz Castle, Germany; Berlin, Germany

Summary: After escaping from Colditz Castle where he was being held as a prisoner of war, Jack Cray makes his way across Germany to Berlin, where he has been assigned the task of assassinating Hitler. In Berlin, police detective Otto Dietrich does his utmost to find Cray and thwart his mission, for if he does, the SS will drop the false treason charges hanging over him and his dying wife, who has been accused of being anti-Nazi. Although Cray has no use for the SS or the Nazi regime, he treats ordinary German citizens with kindness and respect. The conclusion of the book, taking place during the last days of Germany's involvement in the war, offers a new perspective on Hitler's suicide.

Where it's reviewed:
Booklist, August 1997, page 1881
Kirkus Reviews, July 1, 1997, page 981

Other books by the same author:
White Star, 1996
Ringer, 1991
Pursuit, 1988
The Earhart Betrayal, 1980
The Hess Cross, 1977

Other books you might like:
Manning Coles, *Green Hazard*, 1945
Frederick Forsyth, *The Day of the Jackal*, 1971
Jack Higgins, *The Eagle Has Landed*, 1975
Geoffrey Household, *Rogue Male*, 1939
Philip Kerr, *The Bernie Gunther Series*, 1989-1991

226

AIMEE THURLO
DAVID THURLO, Co-Author

Bad Medicine

(New York: Forge, 1997)

Story type: Police Procedural
Series: Ella Clah
Major character(s): Ella Clah, FBI Agent, Indian (Navajo); Carolyn Roanhorse, Doctor (tribal medical examiner), Indian (Navajo)
Time period(s): 1990s
Locale(s): Navajo Reservation, New Mexico

Summary: When the daughter of a powerful senator is murdered on the reservation in a way that is somehow linked to rising tensions between Navajo and white workers at the local mine, Ella investigates, learning that the young woman was not at all the innocent child her father wants the world to remember her as. Carolyn Roanhorse, who is severely ostracized by her tribe because she must handle the bodies of the dead in violation of some of the most sacred Navajo traditions, finds that the people she treats are becoming seriously ill. Then her own life is threatened. Ella and Carolyn work together to pursue the criminals, forging a strong bond of friendship as they do so.

Where it's reviewed:
Publishers Weekly, August 25, 1997, page 48

Other books by the same author:
Death Walker, 1996
Blackening Song, 1994

Other books you might like:
James D. Doss, *The Shaman Series*, 1994-
Jean Hager, *The Molly Bearpaw Series*, 1992-
Tony Hillerman, *The Joe Leaphorn and Jim Chee Series*, 1970-
Louis Owens, *Nightland*, 1996
Jake Page, *The Stolen Gods*, 1993

227

PETER TREMAYNE

Suffer Little Children

(New York: St. Martin's, 1997)

Story type: Historical
Series: Sister Fidelma
Major character(s): Sister Fidelma, Religious (nun)
Time period(s): 7th century (644)
Locale(s): Ireland (Kingdom of Muman)

Summary: The Venerable Daclan, a respected scholar of the Celtic Church, has been found murdered in his cell while visiting a remote abbey in the Irish kingdom of Muman. He was a close confidant of the impetuous young ruler of a neighboring kingdom, who wants to use the incident as an excuse to provoke a war. Sister Fidelma, an advocate of the Brehon courts, is summoned by the dying king of Muman to solve the murder and prevent the outbreak of war. But Fidelma soon discovers that there is more than political intrigue behind the mystery, and she must solve it quickly to save the two kingdoms and her own life as well.

Where it's reviewed:
Kirkus Reviews, August 1, 1997, page 1163

Other books by the same author:
Shroud for the Archbishop, 1996
Absolution by Murder, 1995

Other books you might like:
Margaret Frazer, *The Sister Frevisse Series*, 1992-
Paul Harding, *The Brother Athelstan Series*, 1991-
Domini Highsmith, *Keeper at the Shrine*, 1995
Sharan Newman, *Death Comes as Epiphany*, 1993
Ellis Peters, *The Brother Cadfael Series*, 1977-

228

KATHY HOGAN TROCHECK

Crash Course

(New York: HarperCollins, 1997)

Story type: Amateur Detective
Series: Truman Kicklighter
Major character(s): Truman Kicklighter, Aged Person (retiree), Widow(er)
Time period(s): 1990s
Locale(s): St. Petersburg, Florida

Summary: Truman's young friend Jackleen Canaday has finally bought the car of her dreams, but she's barely driven it home before she realizes it's a lemon. The sleazy salesman who sold it to her refuses to take it back. Then Jackleen finds the man's bloody body in the back of a flashy Corvette, calls the cops, and is in for another shock when they arrive and the body's nowhere to be found. Enter Truman, who hates to see a friend cheated and can't turn his back on a puzzling crime. He takes time away from his cronies at the run-down residential hotel, the Fountain of Youth, where his penny-pinching ways just barely enable him to get by on his pension from the Associated Press.

Where it's reviewed:
Kirkus Reviews, January 15, 1997, page 101
Publishers Weekly, January 20, 1997, page 397

Other books by the same author:
Lickety-Split, 1996

Other books you might like:
Anne George, *Murder Makes Waves*, 1997
Graham Landrum, *The Harriet Bushrow Series*, 1992-1996
Sherry Lewis, *The Fred Vickery Series*, 1995-
Philip Reed, *Bird Dog*, 1997
Corinne Holt Sawyer, *The Angela Benbow/Caledonia Wingate Series*, 1988-

229

KATHY HOGAN TROCHECK

Strange Brew

(New York: HarperCollins, 1997)

Story type: Private Detective
Major character(s): Julia Callahan Garrity, Detective—Private (part-time), Businesswoman (co-owner of a cleaning service)
Time period(s): 1990s
Locale(s): Atlanta, Georgia

Summary: The 1960s and the 1990s collide in the once-mellow Atlanta neighborhood of Candler Park when a greedy young entrepreneur tries to take over a piece of property housing a hippie headshop and install an upscale microbrewery in its place. When the entrepreneur turns up dead on the premises the night a hurricane hits, the police think that Wuvvy, the aging flower child who owns YoYos, would make a great suspect. Callahan thinks they should look elsewhere and sets out to prove it. Her usual cohorts, including her stubborn mother (partner in her cleaning service) and her on-again/off-again lover Mac, are all present.

Where it's reviewed:
Kirkus Reviews, September 1, 1997, page 1344

Other books by the same author:
Heart Trouble, 1996
Happy Never After, 1995
Homemade Sin, 1994
To Live and Die in Dixie, 1993
Every Crooked Nanny, 1992

Other books you might like:
Charlaine Harris, *The Aurora Teagarden Series*, 1990-
Kay Hooper, *House of Cards*, 1991
Sarah Shankman, *The Samantha Adams Series*, 1988-
Celestine Sibley, *The Kate Kincaid Mulcay Series*, 1958-
Patricia Houck Sprinkle, *The Sheila Travis Series*, 1988-

230

BLAIR S. WALKER

Up Jumped the Devil

(New York: Avon, 1997)

Story type: Amateur Detective
Major character(s): Darryl Billups, Journalist (Crime reporter)
Time period(s): 1990s
Locale(s): Baltimore, Maryland

Summary: All Darryl wants is to be left alone to do his job as well as he can. He has a new lady and a boss he doesn't get along with and isn't looking for any more problems. When an anonymous voice mail message warns him that a wave a white supremacist violence is about to break, he doesn't pay much attention to it—at least not until bombs start going off all over town, leaving a dead liberal philanthropist in their wake. Then he is warned that the next target is the NAACP headquarters, and now Darryl pays attention and sees the story of a lifetime coming his way. Meanwhile, the entire city and his new "family" are panicked and the stakes keep getting higher. First novel.

Where it's reviewed:
Kirkus Reviews, September 1, 1997, page 1342
Publishers Weekly, August 11, 1997, page 388

Other books you might like:
Robert Greer, *The CJ Floyd Series*, 1995-
Gar Anthony Haywood, *The Aaron Gunner Series*, 1988-
Laura Lippman, *Baltimore Blues*, 1997
Walter Mosley, *The Easy Rawlins Series*, 1990-
Gary Phillips, *The Ivan Monk Series*, 1994-

231

MINETTE WALTERS

The Echo

(New York: Putnam, 1997)

Story type: Psychological Suspense
Major character(s): Michael Deacon, Journalist; Amanda Powell, Wealthy

Time period(s): 1990s
Locale(s): London, England

Summary: When a homeless alcoholic man is found dead from starvation in the garage of Amanda Powell, whose banker husband disappeared five years earlier with a huge amount of money, she at first is unwilling to discuss the incident with the media. And then suddenly she becomes anxious to talk about Billy Blake with reporter Michael Deacon, who is doing a story on homelessness. Both of them are intensely curious about the dead man, but Deacon is suspicious of Amanda's motives in approaching him, cynically dismissing her explanation that she is moved by the moral injustice of Billy's death. He is drawn to the story by events in his own past, but he also wonders how Amanda's great wealth can be explained if her missing husband is still alive.

Where it's reviewed:
Booklist, February 1, 1997, page 907
Kirkus Reviews, January 15, 1997, page 101
New York Times Book Review, March 16, 1997, page 28
Publishers Weekly, February 3, 1997, page 38
Tribune Books, March 2, 1997, page 5

Other books by the same author:
The Dark Room, 1996
The Scold's Bride, 1994
The Sculptress, 1993
The Ice House, 1992

Other books you might like:
Rosemary Aubert, *Free Reign*, 1997
S.T. Haymon, *The Inspector Ben Jurnet Series*, 1980-1996
P.D. James, *Innocent Blood*, 1980
Barbara Vine, *A Fatal Inversion*, 1987
 pseudonym of Ruth Rendell
Margaret Yorke, *A Question of Belief*, 1997

232

PENNY WARNER

Dead Body Language

(New York: Bantam, 1997)

Story type: Amateur Detective
Major character(s): Connor Westphal, Journalist (newspaper editor/publisher), Handicapped (hearing-impaired)
Time period(s): 1990s
Locale(s): Flat Skunk, California (gold country)

Summary: Connor Westphal has left the San Francisco rat race behind her to relocate in a mining-turned-tourist town in California's gold country, with the idea of starting up her own weekly newspaper. But when a woman who is a prominent citizen of the town is murdered, Connor must track down a madman. Being hearing-impaired has never stood in her way of doing what she wanted to before, and it doesn't now as she attempts to unravel a very complex mystery. First novel.

Other books you might like:
Mary Daheim, *The Emma Lord Series*, 1992-
Jonnie Jacobs, *The Kali O'Brien Series*, 1996-
Leona Karr, *Murder in Bandora*, 1993
Jack Livingston, *The Joe Binney Series*, 1982-
Dwight Steward, *The Acupuncture Murders*, 1973

233

JANE WATERHOUSE

Shadow Walk

(New York: Putnam's, 1997)

Story type: Amateur Detective
Series: Quinn Garner
Major character(s): Quinn Garner, Journalist (bestselling true-crime writer)
Time period(s): 1990s
Locale(s): Spring Lake, New Jersey

Summary: Although Quinn has retired from true-crime writing, she is still haunted by memories of the murder of a childhood friend whose fanatically religious father killed his mother, his wife, and then all his children, vanishing completely afterwards. Now T.J. Sterling, a business acquaintance of Quinn's, reports he may have sighted Gordon Spangler again. When T.J. is found shortly after, an apparent suicide, Quinn starts actively searching for Spangler, convinced he's alive somewhere and may have just committed another murder.

Other books by the same author:
Graven Images, 1995
Playing for Keeps, 1987

Other books you might like:
Jan Burke, *The Irene Kelly Series*, 1993-
Barbara D'Amato, *The Cat Marsala Series*, 1990-
Mary Willis Walker, *The Molly Cates Series*, 1994-
Marilyn Wallace, *Lost Angel*, 1996
Minette Walters, *The Sculptress*, 1993

234

CAROLYN WHEAT

Troubled Waters

(New York: Berkley, 1997)

Story type: Legal
Series: Cass Jameson
Major character(s): Cass Jameson, Lawyer
Time period(s): 1990s; 1960s (1969)
Locale(s): Michigan

Summary: In the summer of 1969 Cass and her brother Ron, swept up in the idealism of the times, were jailed for protesting the negligent poisoning of a child migrant worker. Cass went on to become a defense attorney and Ron returned from Vietnam a quadriplegic who devoted himself to smuggling refugees from Central America across the Canadian border. After one such mission was intercepted, a federal agent wound up dead and Ron's girlfriend, who was charged with the murder, spent the next fifteen years as a fugitive. Now she's turned herself in and has implicated Ron in the murder. It's a case right up Cass's alley and she's determined to do whatever it takes to clear her brother, but the trail she's following doesn't always lead her where she expects to go.

Where it's reviewed:
Kirkus Reviews, July 1, 1997, page 989
Library Journal, July 1997, page 131

New York Times Book Review, August 10, 1997, page 18
Publishers Weekly, May 26, 1997, page 70

Other books by the same author:
Mean Streak, 1996
Fresh Kills, 1995
Where Nobody Dies, 1986
Dead Man's Thoughts, 1983

Other books you might like:
Linda Barnes, *The Carlotta Carlyle Series*, 1987-
Lia Matera, *Last Chants*, 1996
Marcia Muller, *The Sharon McCone Series*, 1977-
Marissa Piesman, *The Nina Fischman Series*, 1989-
Roger L. Simon, *The Big Fix*, 1973

235

ELLEN EMERSON WHITE

All Emergencies, Ring Super

(New York: St. Martin's Press, 1997)

Story type: Amateur Detective
Major character(s): Dana Coakley, Actress (aspiring), Maintenance Worker
Time period(s): 1990s
Locale(s): New York, New York (Manhattan's Upper West Side)

Summary: Although she's appeared on off-Broadway productions and had some success as the Royal Coffee woman, Dana isn't sure she wants to stay in the business and she's sure she doesn't want to waitress. Instead, she's the super of an Upper West Side apartment complex where she spends her days fixing leaky faucets and hauling trash. In between she tutors disadvantaged inner city kids at an alternative school. One afternoon she agrees to help one of them, a boy named Travis Williams who has been homeless since the Harrison Hotel, where his family lived in subsidized housing, burned to the ground. Although the fire was attributed to faulty Christmas lighting, Travis insists it was arson, and Dana sets off to find who did it. First novel.

Where it's reviewed:
Booklist, June 1, 1997, page 1668
Kirkus Reviews, May 15, 1997, page 763
Publishers Weekly, April 21, 1997, page 64

Other books you might like:
Carole Berry, *The Bonnie Indermill Series*, 1987-
Jane Dentinger, *The Jocelyn O'Roarke Series*, 1983-
Marissa Piesman, *The Nina Fischman Series*, 1989-
Gillian Roberts, *The Amanda Pepper Series*, 1987-
Dorian Yeager, *The Victoria Bowering Series*, 1992-

236

RANDY WAYNE WHITE

North of Havana

(New York: Putnam, 1996)

Story type: Amateur Detective; Action/Adventure
Series: Doc Ford

Major character(s): Doc Ford, Scientist (marine biologist), Spy (former CIA agent); Tomlinson, Writer, Genius
Time period(s): 1990s
Locale(s): Havana, Cuba; Sanibel Island, Florida

Summary: Once again Doc Ford is drawn away from his peaceful existence fishing, drinking beer, and collecting marine biology specimens from the waters near his home on Sanibel Island. It seems his ex-hippie friend Tomlinson has gotten himself into big trouble after his boat, *No Mas*, somehow strayed into Cuban waters, and he's now being held in a Havana prison courtesy of the Cuban government. With his lesbian friend Dewey Nye in tow, Doc sets sail for Havana, equipped with ample money for fines, bribes, or whatever it will take to rescue his friend. But when they get there Ford discovers Tomlinson and a mysterious female companion have disappeared and that the real story is much more complicated—and dangerous—than he'd been led to believe.

Where it's reviewed:
Kirkus Reviews, March 1, 1997, page 339
Library Journal, April 15, 1997, page 121
Publishers Weekly, March 17, 1997, page 77

Other books by the same author:
Captiva, 1996
The Man Who Invented Florida, 1993
The Heat Islands, 1992
Sanibel Flats, 1990

Other books you might like:
E.C. Ayres, *The Tony Lowell Series*, 1994-
James W. Hall, *The Thorn Series*, 1987-
Carl Hiaasen, *Double Whammy*, 1988
Laurence Shames, *Florida Straits*, 1992
Les Standiford, *The John Deal Series*, 1993-

237

ROBIN WHITE

Siberian Light

(New York: Delacorte, 1997)

Story type: Action/Adventure; Psychological Suspense
Major character(s): Gregori Nowek, Government Official (mayor), Scientist (geologist); Anna Vereskaya, Scientist
Time period(s): 1990s
Locale(s): Markovo, Russia (Siberia)

Summary: A savage triple murder in the Siberian river town of Markovo has become an obsession for its mayor, Gregori Nowek. The intended victim was Andrei Ryzkov, who made a fortune as a liaison with an American-financed Russian oil exploration venture, AmerRus. The clues point in that direction, but the suspect that turns up is a woman Nowek believes to be innocent: Dr. Anna Vereskaya, a Russian-American scientist who came to Siberia to study the nearly extinct Siberian tiger. Anna and Nowek are thrown together in a wild, violent chase across the remote Siberian taiga, a vast frontier landscape where immense oil reserves are buried beneath the snow-covered land. First novel.

Where it's reviewed:
Kirkus Reviews, July 15, 1997, page 1062

Other books you might like:
Peter Hoeg, *Smilla's Sense of Snow*, 1993
Stuart M. Kaminsky, *The Porfiry Rostnikov Series*, 1981-
John Le Carre, *The Russia House*, 1987
Anthony Olcott, *Murder at the Red October*, 1981
Martin Cruz Smith, *The Arkady Renko Series*, 1981-

238

STEPHEN WHITE

Remote Control

(New York: Dutton, 1997)

Story type: Amateur Detective; Psychological Suspense
Series: Alan Gregory
Major character(s): Alan Gregory, Psychologist; Sam Purdy, Police Officer, Detective—Homicide; Lauren Crowder, Lawyer (Deputy District Attorney)
Time period(s): 1990s
Locale(s): Boulder, Colorado

Summary: Emma Spire, the daughter of the U.S. Surgeon General, was at her father's side when he was assassinated. Tired of being in the public eye and pursued by the media, she moves to Boulder in search of a quieter and more private life. She becomes an intern in the District Attorney's office under the supervision of Lauren Crowder, who befriends her and tries to shield her from media attention. One snowy night, in an attempt to frighten off an intruder, Lauren apparently shoots a man and faces possible murder charges. While she is in custody, her multiple sclerosis flares up and she is put into the hospital for observation. In the meantime, her husband Alan Gregory puts together a team of experts to find out what really happened, and Emma finds that the entrepreneur she's been romantically involved with has been recording their lovemaking with a new technology that captures the sensory experiences involved and can play them back over and over. The loss of dignity and privacy both women experience, in very different ways, is deeply affecting.

Where it's reviewed:
Booklist, January 1997, page 780
Kirkus Reviews, January 15, 1997, page 94
Library Journal, January 1997, page 151
Publishers Weekly, January 20, 1997, page 396
Tribune Books, April 20, 1997, page 7

Other books by the same author:
Harm's Way, 1996
Private Practices, 1994
Higher Authority, 1994
Privileged Information, 1991

Other books you might like:
Rick Boyer, *The Doc Adams Series*, 1982-
Aaron Elkins, *The Gideon Oliver Series*, 1982-
Jonathan Kellerman, *The Alex Delaware Series*, 1985-
Justin Scott, *The Ben Abbott Series*, 1994-
Marianne Wesson, *Render Up the Body*, 1998

239

FRED WILLARD

Down on Ponce

(Atlanta, GA: Longstreet Press 1997)

Story type: Action/Adventure; Humor
Major character(s): Samuel Fuller, Criminal
Time period(s): 1990s
Locale(s): Atlanta, Georgia

Summary: Samuel Fuller has operated outside the law for most of his life, but there are some things he just won't do. So when James Shirley offers him $10,000 to kill his wife, he takes the man's money—in fact, he ups the ante to $30,000—and then tells the wife what her husband is up to. He also keeps the money. His next plan is to leave town as fast as possible, and he turns to his friends on Ponce for help here. (As the author explains, Ponce de Leon Avenue in Atlanta "is a haven for the homeless, the lawless and the restless.") Then Shirley is murdered, and Sam has a lot more trouble on his hands when he becomes a prime suspect. First novel.

Other books you might like:
Pete Hautman, *Drawing Dead*, 1994
Vicki Hendricks, *Miami Purity*, 1996
Elmore Leonard, *Bandits*, 1987
Jim Thompson, *The Grifters*, 1963
K.j.a. Wishnia, *23 Shades of Black*, 1997

240

JOHN MORGAN WILSON

Revision of Justice

(New York: Doubleday, 1997)

Story type: Amateur Detective
Series: Benjamin Justice
Major character(s): Benjamiin Justice, Journalist, Homosexual; Alexandra Templeton, Journalist
Time period(s): 1990s
Locale(s): Los Angeles, California (Hollywood)

Summary: When Justice accompanies his friend Alexandra Templeton to an open house at the home of Gordon Cantwell, a well-known teacher of screenwriting, they find a body in Cantwell's garden that isn't part of the assignment Alexandra is on. Justice suspects that the man was murdered, especially after he finds out who he was: Raymond Farr, a notorious Hollywood dealmaker whose credentials are as phony as his name. Born Reza JaFari, he's legendary for his lack of scruples and wealth of enemies. As Justice investigates the relationships that will eventually lead him to the killer, he must face reawakened memories and emotions stemming from his lover's death seven years earlier from AIDS.

Other books by the same author:
Simple Justice, 1996

Other books you might like:
Michael Craft, *Flight Dreams*, 1997
Steve Johnson, *The Doug Orlando Series*, 1992-
Michael Nava, *The Henry Rios Series*, 1986-
Richard Stevenson, *The Donald Strachey Series*, 1981-

R.D. Zimmerman, *The Tod Mills Series*, 1995-

241

DON WINSLOW

The Death and Life of Bobby Z

(New York: Knopf 1997)

Story type: Action/Adventure; Humor
Major character(s): Tim Kearney, Criminal (small-time thief), Convict
Time period(s): 1990s
Locale(s): California (southern)

Summary: When longtime loser Tim Kearney is approached in the yard at San Quentin by a Hell's Angel who tells him to join the Aryan Brotherhood or else, the only thing he can think to do is to kill the man with a well-sharpened license plate. He can't understand why the public defender doesn't see it as self-defense. Now he's a three-time loser headed for death row, until the DEA makes him an offer he can scarcely refuse: impersonate the late, legendary drug dealer Bobby Z so the agency can trade him for a captured DEA agent. Since the resemblance between the two is already uncanny, it seems like the scheme might work. But Don Huertero, the Mexican drug kingpin who takes Bobby in the trade, very much wants to kill him, and soon Tim is on the run from drug dealers, cops, bikers, and other predators who pursue him all over southern California. A non-series novel from the creator of the Neal Carey series.

Where it's reviewed:
Booklist, March 15, 1997, page 1205
Kirkus Reviews, March 1, 1997, page 333
Library Journal, April 1, 1997, page 132
New York Times Book Review, May 25, 1997, page 23
Publishers Weekly, March 24, 1997, page 60

Other books by the same author:
While Drowning in the Desert, 1996
A Long Walk Up the Waterslide, 1995
Way Down on the High Lonely, 1994
The Trail to Buddha's Mirror, 1993
A Cool Breeze on the Underground, 1991

Other books you might like:
Pete Hautman, *Drawing Dead*, 1994
Carl Hiaasen, *Native Tongue*, 1991
Elmore Leonard, *Stick*, 1983
Philip Reed, *Bird Dog*, 1997
Donald E. Westlake, *Good Behavior*, 1985

242

K.J.A. WISHNIA

23 Shades of Black

(East Setauket, NY: The Imaginary Press 1997)

Story type: Police Procedural
Major character(s): Filomena Buscarsela, Police Officer (Ecuadoran)
Time period(s): 1990s
Locale(s): New York, New York

Summary: It's just another evening shift for Filomena and her cerebrally challenged partner, Bernie, as they break up a fight between drug dealers, respond to a chemical spill at a food-stamp center, and help a rape victim find her way through the justice system. But when Filomena learns that the toxic leak may have been sabotage, and an East Village artist who is a key witness dies in a suspicious accident, she decides to pursue the case on her own, cruising punk-rock clubs for clues about the artist's last days. Noir and funny at the same time, this first novel was preceded by a short story collection featuring Filomena.

Other books by the same author:
Flat Rate and Other Tales, 1996

Other books you might like:
Jeffery Deaver, *Manhattan Is My Beat*, 1989
Carolina Garcia-Aguilera, *The Lupe Solano Series*, 1996-
William Marshall, *The Yellowthread Series*, 1975-
Janwillem Van de Wetering, *The Amsterdam Cops Series*, 1975-
Fred Willard, *Down on Ponce*, 1997

243

DEBORAH WOODWORTH

Death of a Winter Shaker

(New York: Avon, 1997)

Story type: Amateur Detective
Major character(s): Sister Rose Callahan, Religious (Shaker)
Time period(s): 1930s
Locale(s): North Homage, Ohio

Summary: When a handsome young drifter who had joined the Shakers for the cold winter months is found murdered, the police think the killer may be one of their own, an idea these peace-loving people find abhorrent. They turn to Sister Rose Callahan for leadership in investigating the crime. Rose was taken in as a child by the Shakers, who practiced celibacy and augmented their numbers by adopting orphans. As an adult she left the community for a brief period and then returned. Her faith is now unshakable but she fully understands the temptations the world has for young Genny Malone, who finds herself strongly attracted to the young police officer assigned to the case, and who has witnessed events that are a key to the murderer's identity. The author affords us a fascinating glimpse into the world of these gentle, industrious, self-sufficient, and suprisingly egalitarian people, whose strong beliefs and cloistered existence were often ridiculed by outsiders. First novel.

Where it's reviewed:
Publishers Weekly, February 24, 1997, page 87

Other books you might like:
Susan Wittig Albert, *Rueful Death*, 1996
Irene Allen, *The Elizabeth Elliot Series*, 1992-
Roma Greth, *Plain Murder*, 1989
Faye Kellerman, *The Ritual Bath*, 1986
Sister Carol Anne O'Marie, *Death Goes on Retreat*, 1995

244

R.D. ZIMMERMAN

Hostage

(New York: Delacorte, 1997)

Story type: Amateur Detective

Series: Todd Mills

Major character(s): Todd Mills, Journalist (television reporter), Homosexual; Steve Rawlins, Police Officer (homicide detective), Homosexual (Todd's lover)

Time period(s): 1990s

Locale(s): Minneapolis, Minnesota

Summary: Todd is in the middle of an interview with a right-wing congressman who's vehemently opposed to gay rights and AIDS research when three terrorists erupt on the scene, all of them in the final stages of AIDS themselves and deter-mined to make the world know what that's like. Todd's lover, homicide detective Steve Rawlins (who is still mourning the loss of his previous lover to AIDS), becomes involved in the search for the congressman's abductors. The author makes it clear that despite recent strides in treatment, AIDS is still a disease that terribly ravages many of those who contract it and that the battle against it is still far from over.

Other books by the same author:

Tribe, 1996

Closet, 1995

Other books you might like:

Michael Craft, *Flight Dreams*, 1997

Steve Johnson, *The Doug Orlando Series*, 1992-

Michael Nava, *The Henry Rios Series*, 1986-

John Morgan Wilson, *Simple Justice*, 1996

Mark Richard Zubro, *The Tom Mason/Scott Carpenter Series*, 1988-

Mystery

The Year in Romance Fiction
by
Kristin Ramsdell

"Romance has been elegantly defined as the off-spring of fiction and love."
—Benjamin Disraeli

"All mankind love a lover."
—Ralph Waldo Emerson

Though the tone is dated and the quote, itself, is well over a century old, Emerson's observation is still as true today as is was then—at least if the current romance fiction market is any indication. People are still fascinated with love, relationships, and romance. According to the latest figures, they obviously enjoy reading about it, too. With Romance now accounting for 55% of the mass market paperback fiction produced in the United States and the annual sales figures for the genre topping $1 billion as noted in a letter from RWA President, Libby Hall on the RWA website (http://www.rwanational.com/leejeans.html) 10/27/97, 8:16 a.m. and the RWA web page (http://www.rwanational.com) 5/6/98, 8:33 a.m., the genre can no longer be ignored nor taken lightly. It is popular with readers and it is a driving force in the publishing industry. It is important; and it is here to stay. Interestingly, the news from· the rest of the publishing industry is not so positive. Data from the Association of American Publishers (*Publishers' Weekly*, February 16, 1998, p. 106) indicates that mass market paperback sales dropped 8.2% in 1997, down for the third consecutive year according to the March 30, 1998, issue of *Crain's New York Business*. Adult hardcover dropped 7.2, although adult trade paperbacks did rise by 4.4%.

Despite the current popularity of the romance market, unfortunately, all is not champagne, chocolate, and roses. Many of the problems from last year persist. In particular, the midlist crisis is still with us (although the reduction of reprints is encouraging), as is the shrinkage in the independent distributor (ID) marketplace. In addition, the rapid growth of the large chain bookstores such as Borders and Barnes & Noble is forcing smaller bookstores out of business and is affecting the quality and variety of romances available, raising serious questions among readers and writers. The bigger-is-better mentality has also infected the publishers as the merger/acquisition syndrome once again becomes a factor (e.g. Pearson PLC and Putnam merging to form Penguin Putnam, Inc.). Finally, as might be expected, issues involving the internet are becoming increasingly important. Rapidly changing and relatively uncontrolled, the internet has hit the big time and everyone is climbing on board. Royalties, permissions, copyright issues, sales, and a host of other concerns are currently being discussed—and as the internet becomes more and more a part of our daily lives, the debate is sure to continue.

The genre, itself, continues to progress in much the same way as before, dividing itself up along the traditional subgenre lines (and by traditional percentages), building on themes and trends established in prior years, and occasionally taking tentative steps into new territory. For example, Contemporary romance continues to dominate; Multicultural and Inspirational romance are both making good on the promises of last year; Futuristic romance is slipping somewhat; supernatural and paranormal elements continue to migrate beyond the Alternative Reality boundaries; and veteran romance writers continue to expand into mainstream fiction, often heading in the direction of Women's Fiction or Romantic Suspense and occasionally into hardcover. Strong, independent, and admirable main characters still predominate, although many now have lively senses of humor; stories still confront a wide variety of thorny social issues, often providing realistic, yet hopeful, solutions; children have been joined by animals of all kinds as major attractions; humor is increasingly important, with flashes of it even being found in some rather serious stories; and, finally, although there are still too many that fall short, a number of romances are becoming increasingly polished and well-crafted.

The Romance Genre in Detail

Contemporary Romance continued to dominate the market in 1997, accounting for well over half of the romance titles released. As in past years, the series romance lines of Harlequin, Silhouette, and Bantam produced the vast majority of titles, and although Bantam's Loveswept line is slated for cancellation at the end of 1998, this traditional pattern will probably not change in the near future. Limited series of all kinds continue to attract readers and some of the changes to this line up will be discussed later in the section on anthologies. Although still second to the series in sheer numbers produced, contemporary single title romances are becoming increasingly important. Avon's contemporary program launched last year appears to be doing well and Mira Books is scheduled to go from two to three titles a month in 1998. Trilogies, sequels, and books linked by characters, families, or places continue to be popular and can appear both within series romance lines (e.g. *The Mac-Gregor Brides* by Nora Roberts or *Nighthawk* by Rachel Lee) or as single titles (e.g. *Rising Tides* by Emilie Richards or *Nobody's Baby But Mine* by Susan Elizabeth Phillips). Also garnering some attention are books that contain distinct but integrated stories, such as Debbie Macomber's reunion book, *Three Brides and No Groom*. Once again themes and topics are wide ranging and mirror many of those popular in the past. Babies, families, dangerous heroes, abuse recovery, divorce, or other social issues, and rekindled love or reunion books are some of the current favorites, as are the recently popular animal stories such as *Stray Hearts* by Annie Kimberlin. Styles range from light and humorous to dark and intense, and settings can include anything from big city to small town mid-America with many of the latter falling within the Contemporary Americana category. Light touches of mystery, fantasy, and the paranormal continue to appear in Contemporaries like *Ask Mariah* by Barbara Freethy and, while this trend does make categorization difficult, it does encourage increased cross-over readership among subgenres.

Second only to the Contemporary subgenre, Historical Romance continues to account for approximately one third of the romance titles published and, despite some concern to the contrary, it appears to be holding its own. Like Contemporaries, Historicals employ a number of different plot patterns and focus on a wide variety of themes and topics. Forced marriages, vengeance, hidden identity, captive/hostage situations, saving-the-family-fortune/property, and social differences, as well as the standard collection of relevant social issues are only a few of the many "themes and variations" that can be found within this diverse subgenre. It is not unusual for several of these different elements or threads to appear in the same story. As with Contemporary romances, suspense, mystery, and various fantasy and paranormal elements are often scattered throughout these stories, adding both interest and complexity to an already rich subgenre. Historical romances come in a variety of styles and can include everything from the dark, intense stories with brooding gothic tendencies to hilarious, bawdy Georgian romps and mystically lyrical stories filled with legend and magic. Characters are typically strong, independent, determined, and honorable, and past abuses and old wounds often drive their current actions. Sensuality levels range from steamy and explicit (e.g. *Taboo* by Susan Johnson) to the sweetly sensual (e.g. *The Dark Duke* by Margaret Moore) and treatment can vary from gentle and sensitive to savage and brutal, with most falling somewhere in between. Time periods and settings of choice have not varied markedly from last year, and romances set in all parts of the British Isles during the Medieval, Georgian, Regency, and Victorian periods are still preferred by most readers. The 19th century American West remains the single most popular setting for Historicals set in the United States. With the recent interest in Inspirational Romances, particularly of the "Prairie" variety, and the trend toward a more homey, domestic Americana-type western romance, this popularity is likely to continue.

Despite a fiercely loyal readership, often exceptionally well-done books, and unstinting efforts on the part of the authors, problems continue to plague the traditional Regency subgenre. A small, though stable, core of readers and rather low visibility at the retail level—the apparent result of either ineffective marketing, poor distribution, or both—have contributed to bottom line results that are making publishers rethink their priorities. Although the genre withstood a proposed cut in the Signet Regency line a year ago, Fawcett has just announced that it will stop publishing Regencies (currently they release two a month) as of December 1998, a move that would leave the Regency field to only two major players, Zebra and Signet. Nevertheless, in spite of the genre's difficulties, the books were as charming as ever, incorporating a variety of typical plot patterns—most of which involved successfully negotiating the Regency's social minefields and making a "proper" match—and ranging in style from the elegantly understated to the upbeat and funny. A number of unconventional characters graced the pages of this year's stories. The rakehell cello player hero in Elisabeth Fairchild's *The Rakehell's Reform* and the slightly outrageous Lady Helena Stapleton in Mary Balogh's *The Christmas Bride* are especially memorable. In addition, several heroines, for example, Lady Harriet Fareham in Evelyn Richardson's *My Wayward Lady*, were actively involved in the social issues of the day. Although generally sweet, a number of recent Regencies continue to push at the sensuality boundaries normally ascribed to the subgenre, resulting in stories that, while true to the traditional Regency pattern, display a higher degree of sexual tension and are much more sensual and intense than one might expect.

Romantic Suspense continues to be important in its own right and also in the ways in which it affects the other romance subgenres as elements of mystery and suspense

regularly appear in many of the "non-mysterious" romance subgenres. For example, a traditional Regency may make use of a mystery subplot as in *The Lady from Spain*, a rather dark Regency with a touch of violence by Gail Eastwood. Or a contemporary romance may add interest by having the protagonists searching for answers to old mysteries as Suzanne Simmons does in her exotically-set *The Paradise Man*. As in the past, styles are as diverse and wide ranging as are the plots. Chilling novels of pursuit such as Karen Harper's *Heart Breaker* and ultra-dark tales of suspense such as *Ritual Sins* by Anne Stuart happily coexist with fast-paced, humor-laced mysteries like *Sharp Edges* by Jayne Ann Krentz and stories of greed and deception such as *Stolen Moments* by Michelle Martin, within the subgenre's rather broad parameters. Paranormal elements also appear from time to time. For example, a ghost causes problems in *Carried Away* by Sue Civil-Brown, and some of the Multi-cultural romances are incorporating Romantic Suspense themes in books like *Hidden Agenda* by Rochelle Alers. Although most Romantic Suspense is set in the present—hence the common designation "Contemporary Romantic Suspense"—there has been a recent trend toward futuristic settings. Of particular interest are Jayne Castle's (Jayne Ann Krentz) off-planet St. Helen's series (*Zinnia* is the 1997 contribution) and J.D. Robb's (Nora Roberts) chillingly realistic, but romantic, Death series featuring 21st century police detective Eve Dallas and her enigmatic and wealthy tycoon husband, Roarke. In addition, a number of romance writers are also producing stories that are being categorized as pure mystery or suspense rather than romance. Readers who enjoyed their earlier works might also be interested in Tami Hoag and Eileen Dreyer, who writes romances as Kathleen Korbel. Their books may be described in other genre sections of *What Do I Read Next?*

As noted last year, the Gothic as a separate subgenre has all but disappeared, and although there are any number of older Gothic romances still on the shelves of private and public libraries, few are officially being produced. However, this is not to say that the Gothic is actually dead; it is not. Many elements unique to the Gothic have merely migrated into other romance subgenres; and readers in search of isolated mansions, misty moors, threatened heroines, or other classic accoutrements of the traditional Gothic often have no further to look than a current Paranormal or Fantasy Romance or even a Romantic Suspense. So Gothic fans, take heart! The spirit of the Gothic is alive and well; it is merely living in a different setting—and often under a pseudonym.

Although accounting for a relatively small portion of the larger Romance market, the Alternative Reality subgenre continues to produce some of the more creative and innovative stories in the genre. As in previous years, Time Travel Romances, and the closely related Incarnation Romance, were particularly popular, and they can range in tone from the light and lively (Casey Claybourne's *Nick of Time*) through the exotically adventurous (*Twice a Hero* by Susan

Krinard) to the more serious and intense (*Son of the Morning* by Linda Howard). Light fantasy and paranormal romances were also popular, and ghosts, witches, fairies, and all kinds of supernatural characters charmingly graced the pages of this year's romances. *Forever Enchanted* by Maggie Shayne, *Dream a Little Dream* by Antoinette Stockenberg, and *Ask Mariah* by Barbara Freethy are only three examples of the diversity offered within the subgenre. Interestingly, the darker varieties of the subgenre were not so common this year as in the past. Continuing the trend noted last year, Futuristics slid in importance; and although Jayne Castle and J.D. Robb produced some well-done bestsellers in 1997, general interest in these Science Fiction Romances appears to be declining and several publishers have already stopped acquiring them.

One of the current success stories in the genre, the Multicultural Romance continues to attract readers. As in the past, the African American romance is the dominant favorite, with Pinnacle's Arabesque line making that very point by increasing from three to four romances a month in 1997. In addition, Ballantine announced a new licensing agreement with Genesis Press to reissue some of Genesis's Indigo romances under the One World/Indigo Love Stories label. At the moment there are no specific lines for other ethnic groups; however, Pinnacle has announced plans for a bilingual Spanish/English line and they have already issued a call for manuscripts. Romances with Native American characters remain popular; and although the traditional "Indian Romance" with its typical historical setting was still in evidence, a few writers, most notably Kathleen Eagle with *The Night Remembers*, were making contemporary statements as well. New, dynamic, and filled with potential, this is one of the romance subgenres that has definite promise for the future.

Although still a relatively small part of the overall romance market, the Inspirational Romance continues to rise in importance and visibility as Harlequin/Silhouette launched its new Love Inspired line under the Steeple Hill imprint in September 1997. This line features sweet, conservative Christian-oriented romances and releases three books a month. There was also action at Questar/Palisades as they increased their romance offerings last summer. In addition, Bantam/Doubleday/Dell is reportedly seeking manuscripts for Young Adult Inspirationals. (Note: Bantam/Doubleday/Dell's WaterBrook Press, an imprint for Christian books, will begin publishing romances in June 1998.) The debate surrounding this category mentioned in last year's overview still continues with much of the discussion centering on either the name, which would imply that only conservative Christian romances are "inspirational," or on the appropriateness of the inclusion of the category itself in RWA's annual awards. Feelings appear to be running high on both sides of the issue, and when and how it will be resolved remains to be seen.

Anthologies continue to be popular with readers and, typical of the romance genre in general, they continue to diversify and adapt as the market demands. Although the winter holiday season, Christmas in particular, remained a favorite theme, anthologies focusing on Valentine's Day are quickly gaining in popularity, as are collections centering on home, family, and motherhood. Although there were few anthologies focusing specifically on Halloween, collections dealing with supernatural or magical elements abounded, including *Lords of the Night* (vampires with a Regency touch), *Irish Magic II* (Celtic myths and magic), *Bewitched* (witches), and *A Dance With the Devil* (bargains with the Devil). In keeping with a growing interest in animals, a Christmas anthology featuring dogs, *Santa Paws* (Leisure, 1997), added appeal for animal lovers. Limited series and other linked books continue to attract readers; and while 1997 saw the commencement of at least two new 12-month limited series (Silhouette's 36 Hours and Harlequin's Delta Justice), it also witnessed the conclusion of three of these series begun a year earlier, Harlequin's Weddings by DeWilde, Silhouette's Fortune's Children, and the Home Town Reunion series, based on Harlequin's popular Tyler series. These series have proved to be quite popular with readers and it is likely that this format will continue.

Romance in Review

In addition to being reviewed in the genre-specific publications, such as *Romantic Times*, *Affaire de Coeur*, and *Rendezvous*, plus a number of others, romances continue to be regularly reviewed in *Library Journal*'s quarterly romance column, the Forecasts section of *Publisher's Weekly*, and in an increasing number of newspapers throughout the country. Online romance reviews continue to be popular and can be found on both genre-specific websites and those of more general interest. Interestingly, online bookstores such as Amazon (http://www.amazon.com/) are also beginning to review romances and post them on their websites. Many good websites for romance reviews exist. However, because sites come and go and addresses can change without warning, an effective approach to finding online romance reviews is to simply use a good search engine and a few well-chosen words (e.g. "romance fiction reviews") and see where the links lead. Finally, it is worth remembering that even though they have been around for some time and are no longer new and trendy, electronic mail lists, such as RRA-L (Romance Readers Anonymous), are also excellent sources of reviews and recommendations, and can provide a lot of good discussion, as well.

Romance continues to make strides in the online area as many more writers, publishers, reviewers, and bookstores (now too many to list) put up web pages and establish various links among them. The RWA Website, begun in 1996, continues to evolve and is fast becoming one of the primary sites of up-to-date information for the genre. Last year's Rita Award winners were posted to the web almost as

they were awarded, a boon to the many RWA members who could not attend the annual conference in person. Romance also made it to the Romance Classics cable channel when the Harlequin Talk Show, "Romantically Speaking: Harlequin Goes Prime Time," featuring Harlequin, Silhouette, and Mira authors ran for three months during the fall of 1997.

More Developments in the Worlds of Romance Fiction

The romance genre, most visibly through the efforts of the Romance Writers of America and its Library Liaison, Cathie Linz, continues to forge links with the library world. RWA staffed a booth at the American Library Association (ALA) annual conference in 1997 and has plans to maintain booths at both the Public Library Association (PLA) and ALA conferences in 1998. RWA has also added a special section on their web page for librarians. In addition, local and regional library workshops dealing with romance spring up from time to time and a pre-conference on readers' advisory for genre fiction (including romance) was planned for the PLA Conference in March 1998. RWA also continued to recognize librarian contributions, and this year Jeffrey Gegner, Popular Materials Selector for Hennepin County Library in Minnetonka, Minnesota, was selected as RWA's Librarian of the Year for 1997. The RWA Veritas Award for the best publication positively representing the romance genre was not given in 1997.

Action in the academic arena continued with the highly acclaimed publication of an entire issue of *Para*Doxa: Studies in World Literary Genres* (vol. 3, no. 1-2, 1997) devoted to the topic, "Where's Love Gone: Transformations in the Romance Genre." Edited by romance scholar Kay Mussell, this issue includes 25 articles contributed by noted romance scholars and interviews given by several romance writers. In addition, a conference on the genre, ReReading the Romance, was held at Bowling Green State University (home of the Popular Culture Library that also houses the official archives of RWA) in June that was attended by a number of scholars, some of whom also write romance.

Other items of interest include: the June, 1997 launch of a new series of paperback-size hardcover romances by Ballantine under its Columbine imprint with *One Perfect Rose* by Mary Jo Putney; the publication of *Writing Romances: A Handbook by the Romance Writers of America* (Writer's Digest Books, 1997), edited by Rita Gallagher and Rita Clay Estrada; and the discouraging news that Harper is reducing the number of romances it publishes to nine or ten titles a month and will put them out under the Harper Paperbacks imprint rather than HarperMonogram.

One noteworthy, but negative and unfortunate, event that deserves separate comment is the admission by veteran romance writer Janet Dailey that she committed "non-pervasive acts of copying" from a number of the romances of Nora Roberts and included the material in her own books. The news of Dailey's plagiarism broke just as the annual

RWA conference was getting underway in Orlando, stunning the unbelieving membership and dimming the sparkle of the conference just a bit. Litigation followed but the matter would not be settled until the spring of 1998.

And finally, one of the genre's favorite storytellers, LaVyrle Spencer, announced her retirement with the publication of *Then Came Heaven* (Putnam, 1997) in December. Beginning with *The Fulfillment* (Avon, 1979), Spencer wrote more than 20 historical and contemporary romances, many of the Americana variety, and although she will be missed by her devoted fans, many of her works are still in print and can be found in most public libraries.

But what lies ahead for the romance genre itself? Given the current turmoil in many aspects of the industry, it is hard to say, but it definitely will be an interesting year. Obviously, romance is still popular with readers, and that is not about to change. In addition, the genre is continuing to gain acceptance in both the library and academic communities. At the same time, however, cutbacks in numbers of romances published, discontinuation of entire lines, and the ongoing problems with marketing and distribution will make things difficult, at least for a while. Nevertheless, many of the trends of today will probably continue. Interest in Multicultural and Inspirational Romance will continue to grow, with new lines being established or publishers springing up to fill the need; historical and contemporary Americana romances, will continue to appeal to readers; the traditional Regency will, unfortunately, probably continue to slide; Romantic Suspense will continue to attract readers—and writers; more romance writers will expand into mainstream and be published in hardcover; the internet will continue to be a dominant influence, creating both opportunities and problems; and given that several scholarly works on the genre are scheduled for publication during 1998 and 1999, the genre will continue its slow progress toward acceptance in the academic community. In addition, on-demand publishing and "electronic books with digital ink" are intriguing concepts that may well hold a place in the genre's future. However, the publishing world is volatile and the future is never assured—and it is for that very reason that 1998 should be, at the very least, a most interesting year.

Recommendations for Romance

Reading tastes vary greatly. What makes a book appeal to one person may make another reject it. By the same token, two people may like the same book for totally different reasons. Obviously, reading is a highly subjective and personal undertaking. For this reason, the recommended readings attached to each entry have tried to cast as broad a net as was reasonably possible. Suggested titles have been chosen on the basis of similarity to the main entry in one or more of the following areas: historical time period, geographic setting, theme, character types, plot pattern or premise, writing style, or overall mood or "feel." All suggestions may not

appeal to the same person, but it is hoped that at least one would appeal to most.

Because romance reading tastes do vary so widely and readers (and writers) often apply vastly differing criteria in determining what makes a romance good, bad, or exceptional, I cannot claim that the following list of recommendations consists solely of the "best" romance novels of the year. In fact many of these received no awards or special recognition at all. It is simply a selection of books I found particularly interesting; perhaps some of these will appeal to you, too.

Something Wicked by Jo Beverley

Warrior Heart by Jane Bonander

All Through the Night by Connie Brockway

The Last Arrow by Marsha Canham

Zinnia by Jayne Castle

The Way Home by Megan Chance

A Well-Pleasured Lady by Christina Dodd

The Night Remembers by Kathleen Eagle

The Rakehell's Reform by Elizabeth Fairchild

Ask Mariah by Barbara Freethy

A Garden Folly by Candice Hern

With This Ring by Carla Kelly

Francesca's Rake by Lynn Kerstan

Stray Hearts by Annie Kimberlin

The Mermaid by Betina Krahn

Tallchief by Dinah McCall

Touch of Enchantment by Teresa Medeiros

Sweeter Than Wine by Stephanie Mittman

A Prince Among Men by Kate Moore

To Marry a British Lord by Judith O'Brien

The Promise of Jenny Jones by Maggie Osborne

Wooing Wanda by Gwen Pemberton

Nobody's Baby But Mine by Susan Elizabeth Phillips

One Perfect Rose by Mary Jo Putney

Affair by Amanda Quick

My Wayward Lady by Evelyn Richardson

Annie's Hero by Maggie Shayne

Lord of Danger by Anne Stuart

The Passions of Emma by Penelope Williamson

The Arrangement by Joan Wolf

For Further Reference

Review Journals

Because romance fiction was until recently rarely reviewed in mainstream sources (best-selling romance authors were, of course, the exception), several vehicles have sprung

up to handle the demand. Many of the reviews included in *What Do I Read Next?* entries come from these specialized sources. Several of the most important print sources are listed below. (See discussion above for suggestions for locating online reviews.) Note: *Library Journal* (a mainstream source) publishes a quarterly romance review column—February 15, May 15, August, and November 15.

Affaire de Coeur Includes reviews, articles, and information on the world of romance fiction, in general. 3976 Oak Hill Road, Oakland, CA 94605-493; phone, (510) 569-5675; fax, (510) 632-8868. Monthly; subscriptions, $35 a year (U.S.—First Class), $30 a year (U.S.—Third Class), $65 a year (Canada); single copy, $5.

Gothic Journal Includes reviews and information about the gothic subgenre. P.O. Box 6340, Elko, Nevada 89802-6340; phone (702)738-3520; toll-free phone number, 800-7GOTHIC (800-746-8442); fax, (702)738-3524; e-mail address, kglass@GothicJournal.com; web address, http://GothicJournal.com/romance/. Six issues per year; subscriptions, $24 a year (U.S.), $30 a year (Canada), $36 a year (rest of world).

Heartland Critiques Includes reviews of most romances published. 125 Linden, Independence, MO 64050. Monthly; subscriptions, $50 a year.

The Regency Reader Includes reviews and information about the Regency subgenre. Published quarterly by the Beau Monde, the Regency Special Interest Chapter of the Romance Writers of America, c/o Pam Schlutt, 1008 Hillside Drive, Keller, TX 76248. Quarterly; subscription, $15 a year.

Rendezvous: A Monthly Review of Contemporary and Historical Romances, Mysteries, and Women's Fiction Includes reviews of most romances published each month. Published by Love Designers Writers' Club, Inc., 1507 Burnham Avenue, Calumet City, IL 60409; phone (708) 862-9797. Monthly; subscription, $45 a year; single copy, $4.00.

Romantic Times Includes reviews of most romances published each month, articles, and information about the world of romance fiction. Also includes reviews and other information for other genres and mainstream women's fiction. Published monthly by: Romantic Times Publishing Group, 55 Bergen Street, Brooklyn Heights, NY 11201; phone (718) 237-1097; fax, (718) 624-4231. Subscriptions: Fourth Class U.S. Rates, $42 for 1 year; First Class U.S., $60 for 1 year; Canadian Rates, $66 for 1 year.

Mail Order Services

Reader Service Provides books in the Harlequin and Silhouette series on a monthly subscription basis. Write or telephone for series descriptions and price information. P.O. Box 1325, Buffalo, NY 14269; phone, (716)684-1500; or P.O. Box 603, Fort Erie, Ontario L2A 5X3, Canada; phone, (416)283-2897.

Manderley: A Catalog for Romance Readers A mail-order catalog for romances. Published by Soda Creek Press, P.O. Box 8515-A, Ukiah, CA 95482-8515; toll-free phone number 800-301-7546; web address, http://www.manderleybooks.com.

Romance Ink: the Romance Novel Catalogue A mail-order catalogue for romances. Catalogues are $3.00. P.O. Box 787, Colorado Springs, CO 80901.

Conferences

Numerous conferences are held each year for writers and readers of romance fiction. Several of the more important ones are listed below. For a more complete listing, particularly of regional or local conferences designed primarily for romance writers, consult the Romance Writers Report, a monthly publication of The Romance Writers of America.

Rom-Con—Rom-Con was not held in 1997. The 1998 Rom-Con will be held October 1 - 4 in Oakland, California and will be sponsored by *Affaire de Coeur* and East Bay Books

Annual Book Lovers Convention—Sponsored by Romantic Times. No conference was held in 1997. The Romantic Times 15th Annual Book Lovers Convention is scheduled for April 17 - 24, 1998, and will be held aboard a Carnival Cruise Ship.

RWA Annual Conference—Sponsored by Romance Writers of America, usually held in July. The 1997 Conference was held July 31 - August 3 in Orlando, Florida. The 1998 Conference is scheduled for July 30 - August 2 in Anaheim, California.

Romance Titles

ROCHELLE ALERS
DONNA HILL, Co-Author
JANICE SIMS, Co-Author

Hearts of Gold
(New York: Pinnacle, 1997)

Story type: Anthology; Ethnic
Time period(s): 1990s
Locale(s): United States

Summary: This trilogy of Valentine's Day novellas featuring African American heroes and heroines includes the sophisticated, upscale "Hearts of Gold" by Rochelle Alers; the funny, computer-oriented "Masquerade" by Donna Hill; and a story of love, hope, and deception, "To Love Again," by Janice Sims.

Where it's reviewed:
Library Journal, February 15, 1997, page 125

Other books you might like:
Sara Blayne, *Valentine Love*, 1996
    Regency Anthology
Carla Fredd, *A Valentine's Kiss*, 1996
    Anthology
Kay Hooper, *Hearts of Gold*, 1994
    Diverse anthology
Rebecca Paisley, *Love Potion*, 1994
    4 novellas linked by Cupid's love potion

246

ROCHELLE ALERS

Hidden Agenda
(New York: Pinnacle, 1997)

Story type: Romantic Suspense; Multicultural
Major character(s): Eve Blackwell, Mother; Matthew Sterling, Adventurer (aka Mateo Sterling de Arroyo)
Time period(s): 1990s

Locale(s): Mexico

Summary: A marriage of convenience, a kidnapped little boy, and a deadly game of intrigue and suspense drive the plot of this fast-paced romantic suspense story with an exotic Mexican setting.

Where it's reviewed:
Library Journal, February 15, 1997, page 125

Other books by the same author:
Gentle Yearning, 1998
Reckless Surrender, 1997
Vows, 1997
Hideaway, 1995
Happily Ever After, 1994

Other books you might like:
Maggie Ferguson, *Fever Rising*, 1997
Francis Ray, *Incognito*, 1997
Tracey Tillis, *Final Act*, 1998
Tracey Tillis, *Night Watch*, 1995

247

ROCHELLE ALERS
DONNA HILL, Co-Author
JANICE SIMS, Co-Author

Love Letters
(New York: Pinnacle, 1997)

Story type: Anthology; Holiday Themes
Time period(s): 1990s
Locale(s): United States

Summary: This trio of Valentine's Day stories features romances, both light and serious, by some of Arabesque's more popular writers and includes "Hearts of Gold" by Rochelle Alers, "Masquerade" by Donna Hill, and "To Love Again" by Janice Sims.

Other books you might like:
Margaret Brownley, *Chocolate Kisses*, 1997
    Anthology

Carla Fredd, *A Valentine Kiss*, 1996
  Anthology
Kay Hooper, *Hearts of Gold*, 1994
  Anthology
Meryl Sawyer, *Valentine Delights*, 1997
  Anthology

248

VICTORIA ALEXANDER
NINA COOMBS, Co-Author
ANNIE KIMBERLIN, Co-Author
MIRIAM RAFERTY, Co-Author

Santa Paws

(New York: Leisure, 1997)

Story type: Anthology; Holiday Themes

Summary: This eclectic quartet of Christmas novellas features a host of delightful matchmaking dogs, all determined to unite the appropriate humans. Settings range from Regency and Victorian England to contemporary small-town America, with a time-travel to 19th-century Alaska thrown in for good measure. Included are ''Shakespeare and the Three Kings'' by Victoria Alexander, ''Athena's Christmas Tail'' by Nina Coombs, ''Away in a Shelter'' by Annie Kimberlin, and ''Mr. Wright's Christmas Angel'' by Miriam Raferty.

Where it's reviewed:
Library Journal, November 15, 1997, page 49

Other books you might like:
Jude Deveraux, *Upon a Midnight Clear*, 1997
  Christmas Anthology
Linda Howard, *Christmas Kisses*, 1996
  Christmas Anthology
Annie Kimberlin, *Stray Hearts*, 1997
  Dogs and a few cats
Annie Kimberlin, *Lonely Hearts*, 1998
  More dogs
Diana Palmer, *Lone Star Christmas*, 1997
  two stories by Palmer and Joan Johnston

249

CATHERINE ANDERSON

Simply Love

(New York: Avon, 1997)

Story type: Historical/American West
Major character(s): Cassandra Zerek, Religious (would-be novitiate); Luke Taggart, Businessman (mine and property owner)
Time period(s): 1880s (1887)
Locale(s): Black Jack, Colorado

Summary: Restless and bored with his current relationships, Colorado mining tycoon Luke Taggart brings would-be novitiate Cassandra Zerek into his life. The results surprise him. This emotionally involving romance confronts the issue of childhood sexual abuse with Anderson's typical mixture of warmth and realism in a story of acceptance, redemption, and the healing power of love.

Where it's reviewed:
Library Journal, May 15, 1997, page 64

Other books by the same author:
Annie's Song, 1996
Keegan's Lady, 1996
Cheyenne Amber, 1994
Comanche Magic, 1994
Coming Up Roses, 1993

Other books you might like:
Jane Bonander, *Warrior Heart*, 1997
  Another wounded hero
Lorraine Heath, *Texas Destiny*, 1997
Stephanie Mittman, *The Courtship*, 1998
Stephanie Mittman, *The Marriage Bed*, 1996

250

CATHERINE ARCHER

Lady Thorn

(Toronto: Harlequin, 1997)

Story type: Historical/Victorian
Major character(s): Victoria Thorn, Noblewoman; Jedediah McBride, Shipowner
Time period(s): 1850s (1855)
Locale(s): England

Summary: Jedediah McBride, wealthy American shipowner, is on a mission to find his lost son among the British aristocracy. After he inadvertently rescues Lady Victoria Thorn from a disreputable suitor, he finds that she also has a mission—to find a husband. Although they are very different and have different goals and expectations, they search together, and eventually find what they are looking for—and what they didn't expect to find.

Where it's reviewed:
Romantic Times, February 1997, page 40

Other books by the same author:
Rose Among Thorns, 1992

Other books you might like:
Catherine Coulter, *Night Shadow*, 1989
Jo Goodman, *My Steadfast Heart*, 1997
Johanna Lindsey, *The Magic of You*, 1993
Katherine Sutcliffe, *My Only Love*, 1993

251

MARY BALOGH

A Christmas Bride

(New York: Signet, 1997)

Story type: Regency; Holiday Themes
Major character(s): Lady Helena Stapleton, Widow(er), Gentlewoman; Edgar Downes, Lawyer
Time period(s): 1810s
Locale(s): London, England

Summary: Wealthy attorney Edgar Downes knows he must marry, but when he begins to look, the matrimonial landscape is dismal. All the eligible girls are far too young, and although

he is extremely wealthy, was educated as a gentleman, lives in a lovely estate and would inherit another upon his father's death, he is not a "gentleman." However, when he meets the slightly outrageous widow Lady Helena Stapleton, an independent woman of his own generation, things take a more interesting turn. Unconventional, witty, and delightfully scandalous—a typical Balogh Regency.

Where it's reviewed:
Library Journal, November 15, 1997, page 47

Other books by the same author:
Silent Melody, 1997
Truly, 1996
The Plumed Bonnet, 1996
The Famous Heroine, 1996
Christmas Belle, 1994

Other books you might like:
Jo Beverley, *The Christmas Angel*, 1992
Susan Carroll, *Christmas Belles*, 1992
Carla Kelly, *Marian's Christmas Wish*, 1989
Carla Kelly, *Mrs. Drew Plays Her Hand*, 1994

252

MARY BALOGH

Indiscreet
(New York: Jove, 1997)

Story type: Historical/Regency
Major character(s): Catherine Winters, Widow(er); Rex Adams, Nobleman (Viscount Rawleigh)
Time period(s): 1810s
Locale(s): England

Summary: When widow Catherine Winters mistakes visiting Rex Adams, Viscount Rawleigh, for his brother, she approaches him, thereby causing the townspeople to suspect her motives and her morality. Rex takes advantage of her mistake and tries his best to seduce and compromise her. However, being what it is, Regency society labels her and totally ruins her reputation. Rex repents and insists on marrying her, and although there are problems, love does win out in the end.

Where it's reviewed:
Affaire de Coeur, January 1997, page 23

Other books by the same author:
Heartless, 1995
Lord Carew's Bride, 1995
Christmas Belle, 1994
Dancing with Clara, 1994
Deceived, 1993

Other books you might like:
Kat Martin, *Innocence Undone*, 1997
Mary Jo Putney, *One Perfect Rose*, 1997
Mary Jo Putney, *River of Fire*, 1996
Julia Quinn, *Everything and the Moon*, 1997

253

MARY BALOGH

Truly
(New York: Berkley, 1996)

Story type: Historical/Victorian
Major character(s): Marged Evans, Widow(er), Religious (minister's daughter); Geraint Penderyn, Nobleman (Earl of Wyvern)
Time period(s): 1840s (1842)
Locale(s): Wales

Summary: Geraint Penderyn, returning to his lands in Wales, hesitantly looks for Marged, whom he left when he was 18. However, she hates him because he represents the gentry against whom she and her rebellious friends are fighting. Having truly neglected his people for years, Geraint sympathizes with them and agrees to secretly lead their rebellion. But the attraction between Marged and Geraint is still there, and deception and old animosities keep things interesting until the end.

Other books by the same author:
Heartless, 1995
Christmas Belle, 1994
Dancing with Clara, 1994
Deceived, 1993
Beyond the Sunrise, 1992

Other books you might like:
Candace Camp, *Scandalous*, 1996
Patricia Gaffney, *Forever and Ever*, 1996
　　Rural Victorian England
Kasey Michaels, *The Illusion of Love*, 1994
　　Regency setting/returning hero
Kasey Michaels, *Legacy of the Rose*, 1992
　　another returning hero
Patricia Rice, *Shelter from the Storm*, 1993
　　American setting

254

SUZANNE BARCLAY
MARGARET MOORE, Co-Author
DEBORAH SIMMONS, Co-Author

The Knights of Christmas
(Toronto: Harlequin, 1997)

Story type: Anthology; Holiday Themes
Summary: This romantic trilogy of medieval Christmas novellas by three of Harlequin's popular historical writers nicely depicts the Yuletide customs of the times with all the magic and joy of the season. Included are "Kara's Gift" by Suzanne Barclay, "The Twelfth Day of Christmas" by Margaret Moore, and "A Wish for Noel" by Deborah Simmons.

Other books you might like:
Elaine Barbieri, *Mistletoe Marriages*, 1994
　　Christmas anthology
Stella Cameron, *Avon Books Presents: A Christmas Collection*, 1992
　　Christmas anthology

Virginia Henley, *A Gift of Joy*, 1995
   Christmas anthology
Judith McNaught, *A Holiday of Love*, 1994
   Christmas anthology

255

JILL BARNETT

Wonderful

(New York: Pocket, 1997)

Story type: Historical/Medieval
Major character(s): Lady Clio of Camrose, Noblewoman, Saloon Keeper/Owner (alewife); Merrick de Beaucourt, Knight (Crusader)
Time period(s): 13th century
Locale(s): England

Summary: Betrothed to each other by proxy years earlier, Merrick de Beaucourt and Lady Clio of Camrose discover they have a lot to learn about each other as they set up housekeeping in Camrose Castle along the Welsh border. A charmingly creative heroine full of "wonderful ideas," a jaded knight who is not quite sure what to do with his unusual bride, and a host of intriguing characters combine in this magical and enchanting story filled with warmth, humor, and sensuality. The search for the recipe for the magical Heather Ale adds interest.

Where it's reviewed:
Romantic Times, September 1997, page 37

Other books by the same author:
Carried Away, 1996
Imagine, 1995
Dreaming, 1994
Bewitching, 1993
Just a Kiss Away, 1991

Other books you might like:
Jude Deveraux, *The Taming*, 1989
Christina Dodd, *Castles in the Air*, 1993
Christina Dodd, *Once a Knight*, 1996
Julie Garwood, *The Bride*, 1989

256

VICTORIA BARRETT
VICKI HINZE, Co-Author

Beside a Dreamswept Sea

(New York: St. Martin, 1997)

Story type: Contemporary/Fantasy
Series: Seascape Romance
Major character(s): Caline "Cally" Tate, Divorced Person; Bryce Richards, Lawyer (divorce attorney), Single Parent
Time period(s): 1990s
Locale(s): Maine (Seascape Inn (bed and breakfast))

Summary: Once again the spirits of Seascape Inn work their healing magic on two people who desperately need, yet resist, the love the other can provide. A successful attorney with three young children and a disillusioned woman find happi-

ness in this emotional and magical story, the fifth in the mystical Seascape Romance Series.

Where it's reviewed:
Library Journal, May 15, 1997, page 64

Other books by the same author:
Maybe This Time, 1996

Other books you might like:
Heather Graham, *A Magical Christmas*, 1996
   Holiday family magic
LaVyrle Spencer, *Morning Glory*, 1989
   No paranormal elements
Antoinette Stockenberg, *Beyond Midnight*, 1996
Antoinette Stockenberg, *Dream a Little Dream*, 1997
Antoinette Stockenberg, *Embers*, 1994

257

REXANNE BECNEL
ANNE LOGAN, Co-Author
DEBORAH MARTIN, Co-Author
MEAGAN MCKINNEY, Co-Author

A Dance with the Devil

(New York: St. Martin's, 1997)

Story type: Anthology; Historical
Time period(s): 19th century; 18th century
Locale(s): New Orleans, Louisiana

Summary: This diverse collection of four historical novellas features characters who have made various bargains, supernatural or otherwise, with "the Devil" and makes use of an exotic New Orleans setting. Included are "The Wager" by Rexanne Becnel, "The Haunting of Sarah" by Anne Logan, "Out of the Night" by Deborah Martin, and "The Monk" by Meagan McKinney.

Other books you might like:
Loretta Chase, *Lord of Scoundrels*, 1995
Jennifer Horsman, *With One Look*, 1994
Lisa Kleypas, *Only in Your Arms*, 1992
Deborah Martin, *Creole Nights*, 1992

258

REXANNE BECNEL

Dangerous to Love

(New York: St. Martin's, 1997)

Story type: Historical
Major character(s): Lucy Drysdale, Scholar, Chaperone; Ivan Thornton, Nobleman (Earl of Westcott), Bastard Son
Time period(s): 1820s (1829)
Locale(s): England

Summary: When the bright, intellectual Lucy Drysdale is invited to London to serve as a chaperone for the debut of Lady Westcott's young, vulnerable god-daughter, one of her primary duties is to keep Lady Valerie from falling victim to the rakehell Earl of Westcott—or so she thinks. But Lady Westcott is a shrewd woman and she is determined to have the

young earl wed—to either young lady. Lively, humorous, and charming.

Where it's reviewed:
Romantic Times, November 1997, page 37

Other books by the same author:
When Lightning Strikes, 1995
Where Magic Dwells, 1994
A Dove at Midnight, 1993
Christmas Journey, 1992
The Rose of Blacksword, 1992

Other books you might like:
Georgette Heyer, *Sylvester, or the Wicked Uncle*, 1957
Amanda Quick, *Reckless*, 1992
Julia Quinn, *Brighter than the Sun*, 1997

259

ANGELA BENSON

A Family Wedding

(New York: Silhouette, 1997)

Story type: Contemporary; Multicultural
Major character(s): Patsy Morgan, Divorced Person; Kenny Sanders, Lawyer, Single Parent; Wendy Sanders, Child
Time period(s): 1990s
Locale(s): United States

Summary: When best friends Kenny Sanders and Patsy Morgan get married to provide a stable home for his young daughter, Wendy, they each have past issues to deal with before they can admit what they have known all along—that they are in love with each other. Warm and charming.

Where it's reviewed:
Library Journal, February 15, 1997, page 125

Other books by the same author:
The Nicest Guy in America, 1997
Second Chance Dad, 1997
Between the Lines, 1996
For All Time, 1995
Bands of Gold, 1994

Other books you might like:
Sandra Kitt, *Serenade*, 1994
Debbie Macomber, *Morning Comes Softly*, 1993
Annette A. Reynolds, *Remember the Time*, 1997
Paula Detmer Riggs, *Daddy by Accident*, 1997

260

JO BEVERLEY

The Shattered Rose

(New York: Zebra, 1996)

Story type: Historical/Medieval
Major character(s): Jehanne, Noblewoman, Widow(er) (supposed); Galeran of Heywood, Knight (crusader)
Time period(s): 12th century
Locale(s): England

Summary: Back from the Crusades, Galeran of Heywood finds his home under siege by his father. His wife, Jehanne, thinking him dead, has taken a lover who hopes to attain her lands. Disgraced in the eyes of the community, Galeran is urged to beat her or take her to a convent, but he loves her and refuses. However, Jehanne's lover has much to lose and causes havoc between the pair. Love, of course, wins out in typical Beverley style in this sensual, highly detailed story of repentance, jealousy, and betrayal.

Where it's reviewed:
Rendezvous, March 1996, page 17
Romantic Times. May 1996, page 38

Other books by the same author:
Tempting Fortune, 1995
Dangerous Joy, 1995
Forbidden, 1994
Dierdre and Don Juan, 1993
My Lady Notorious, 1993

Other books you might like:
Katherine Deauville, *Eyes of Love*, 1996
    Paranormal elements
Katherine Deauville, *Daggers of Gold*, 1993
Christina Dodd, *Castles in the Air*, 1993
Karyn Monk, *The Witch and the Warrior*, 1998
    Paranormal elements

261

JO BEVERLEY

Something Wicked

(New York: Topaz, 1997)

Story type: Historical/Georgian
Major character(s): Lady Elfled Malloren, Noblewoman; Fortitude Ware, Nobleman (Earl of Walgrave)
Time period(s): 1760s (1762)
Locale(s): London, England

Summary: Expecting only an evening of flirtatious adventure, the bored and restless Lady Elfled Malloren disguises herself as the mysterious Lisette and heads for Vauxhall Gardens and the annual Midsummer Night Masquerade. However, when an overheard conversation and a chance encounter land her in the "protective" custody of her family's mortal enemy, the Earl of Walgrave, all of Elf's considerable ingenuity is put to the test. A lively, rowdy, sexy Georgian that continues Beverley's Malloren series; Elfled is the twin sister of Cynric from *My Lady Notorious*.

Other books by the same author:
Married at Midnight, 1996
The Shattered Rose, 1996
Tempting Fortune, 1995
Dangerous Joy, 1995
My Lady Notorious, 1993

Other books you might like:
Christina Dodd, *A Well-Favored Gentleman*, 1998
Christina Dodd, *A Well-Pleasured Lady*, 1997
Amanda Quick, *Mistress*, 1994
    Regency setting
Susan Sizemore, *My First Duchess*, 1993

262

BARBARA BICKMORE

Beyond the Promise

(New York: Kensington, 1997)

Story type: Contemporary/Mainstream
Major character(s): Cat Browning, Lawyer, Widow(er); Scott McCullough, Rancher; Red McCullough, Rancher
Time period(s): 1990s
Locale(s): Oregon

Summary: While on a much-needed vacation from her New York law practice, Cat Browning goes to rusticate in rural eastern Oregon and ends up in love with and married to the son of a local rancher. However, when he is suddenly killed and Cat finds herself pregnant, she decides to stay in Oregon and make a new life for herself and her child. Eventually, her former father-in-law becomes her new love interest. A blend of women's fiction and romance.

Where it's reviewed:
Library Journal, November 15, 1997, page 47

Other books by the same author:
Deep in the Heart, 1996

Other books you might like:
Janet Dailey, *This Calder Sky*, 1981
    first of four/Montana setting
Kathleen Eagle, *The Last True Cowboy*, 1998
Rebecca Forster, *Seasons*, 1996
Nora Roberts, *Montana Sky*, 1996

263

ROSANNE BITTNER
DENISE DOMNING, Co-Author
VIVIAN VAUGHAN, Co-Author

Cherished Love

(New York: St. Martin, 1997)

Story type: Anthology; Historical/Post-American Civil War
Time period(s): 1870s
Locale(s): New Mexico; Kansas; Texas

Summary: This romantic trilogy of historical novellas focuses on motherhood, families, and the challenges of the American frontier of the 1870s. Included are ''For the Sake of Love'' by Rosanne Bittner, ''An Impetuous Season'' by Denise Domning, and ''A Wish to Build a Dream On'' by Vivian Vaughan.

Other books you might like:
Julie Caille, *A Mother's Heart*, 1992
    Motherhood Regency-style/anthology
Stella Cameron, *To Love and to Honor*, 1993
    Marriage anthology
Bette Ford, *A Mother's Love*, 1996
    Anthology
Anita Mills, *Cherished Moments*, 1994
    Anthology
Jennifer Sawyer, *A Mother's Delight*, 1995
    Regency anthology

264

JANE BONANDER

Warrior Heart

(New York: Pocket, 1997)

Story type: Historical/American West
Major character(s): Liberty O'Malley, Innkeeper (boarding house owner), Mother (adoptive); Jackson Wolfe, Lawman (sheriff), Adventurer; Dawn Twilight O'Malley, Child
Time period(s): 1890s (1891)
Locale(s): Thief River, California

Summary: When Jackson Wolfe returns to Thief River to reclaim his life—and his baby daughter he'd left behind—he finds that Dawn has been adopted by a woman who is not about to let her go. An emotional, moving story of love, redemption, and healing.

Other books by the same author:
Winter Heart, 1996
Dancing on Snowflakes, 1995
Wild Heart, 1995
Fires of Innocence, 1994
Forbidden Moon, 1993

Other books you might like:
Catherine Anderson, *Simply Love*, 1997
    Another wounded hero
Dorothy Garlock, *Homeplace*, 1991
Patricia Potter, *Defiant*, 1995
Patricia Potter, *The Marshall and the Heiress*, 1996

265

JANE BONANDER

Winter Heart

(New York: Pocket, 1996)

Story type: Historical/American West
Major character(s): Dinah O'Dell, Care Giver, Runaway (from a mental hospital); Tristan Fletcher, Rancher
Time period(s): 1850s (1858)
Locale(s): Sierra Nevada, California

Summary: Dinah O'Dell's dying friend, Daisy, helps her escape from a mental hospital, then Dinah takes a job originally promised to Daisy. She travels to California as the nurse to the incompetent sister of half-breed Tristan Fletcher. As Dinah and Tristan fall in love, Tristan learns the true extent of her abusive past (an uncle who committed her and wants her inheritance). Tristan has some brutal history of his own to deal with; nevertheless, their love is meant to be in this powerful, moving romance.

Where it's reviewed:
Affaire de Coeur, May 1996, page 32
Rendezvous, May 1996, page 17
Romantic Times, May 1996, page 38

Other books by the same author:
Warrior Heart, 1997
Dancing on Snowflakes, 1995

Wild Heart, 1995
Fires of Innocence, 1994
Forbidden Moon, 1993

Other books you might like:
Catherine Anderson, *Cheyenne Amber*, 1994
Dorothy Garlock, *Homeplace*, 1991
Dorothy Garlock, *Larkspur*, 1997
Elizabeth Lowell, *Only Mine*, 1992

266
ALICE BORCHARDT
Beguiled
(New York: Dutton, 1996)

Story type: Historical/Medieval
Major character(s): Elin, Spouse (of Owen); Owen, Religious (Bishop of Chantalon)
Time period(s): 10th century
Locale(s): France

Summary: After the Viking invaders have been turned back, Owen, Bishop of Chantalon, and his pagan love, Elin, must face the Norse warrior Hakon, who is set to conquer Chantalon. When he goes to his kinsmen for help, Owen is captured by the Bretons who insist he renounce Elin. But Elin gathers her people together and using her skills and insight, keeps Hakon at bay. Realistic and historically accurate.

Where it's reviewed:
Romantic Times, February 1997, page 45

Other books by the same author:
Devoted, 1995

Other books you might like:
Helen Hollick, *Pendragon's Banner*, 1996
Iris Johansen, *Lion's Bride*, 1996
   excellent characterizations
Ellen Jones, *The Fatal Crown*, 1991
Sharon Kay Penman, *Here Be Dragons*, 1985

267
CONNIE BROCKWAY
All through the Night
(New York: Dell, 1997)

Story type: Historical/Regency
Major character(s): Anne Wilder, Widow(er), Thief; Henry "Jack" Seward, Detective ("Whitehall's Hound")
Time period(s): 1810s (1817)
Locale(s): London, England

Summary: Determined to capture the cat burglar known as Wrexhall's Wraith, Jack Seward has no idea that the woman he is looking for is none other than the intriguing widow Anne Wilder, a consummate thief who only steals from the uncharitable wealthy members of the ton. Fast-paced, passionate action in a story with memorable characters.

Where it's reviewed:
Romantic Times, October 1997, page 39

Other books by the same author:
As You Desire, 1997
A Dangerous Man, 1996
Anything for Love, 1994
Promise Me Heaven, 1994

Other books you might like:
Jane Feather, *Virtue*, 1993
Judith McNaught, *Almost Heaven*, 1990
Mary Jo Putney, *Petals in the Storm*, 1993
Amanda Quick, *Seduction*, 1990

268
CONNIE BROCKWAY
As You Desire
(New York: Dell, 1997)

Story type: Historical/Victorian
Major character(s): Desdemona Carlisle, Orphan, Archaeologist (artifact translator); Harry Braxton, Adventurer
Time period(s): 1890s (1890)
Locale(s): Cairo, Egypt

Summary: Desdemona Carlisle, expert artifact translator, is in Egypt with her archaeologist grandfather. Over the years her run-ins with adventurer Harry Braxton have wavered from love to total disparagement, but his remarkable ability to acquire artifacts makes him nearly indispensible. Local thieves and corruption annoy Desdemona and although she is not afraid, she does need constant rescuing. A humorous, action-oriented story laced with a bit of intrigue and mystery.

Where it's reviewed:
Romantic Times, February 1997, page 36

Other books by the same author:
A Dangerous Man, 1996
Anything for Love, 1994
Promise Me Heaven, 1994

Other books you might like:
Laura Hastings, *The Turtledove's Secret*, 1992
Laura Kinsale, *The Dream Hunter*, 1994
Elizabeth Peters, *The Crocodile on the Sandbank*, 1975
Amanda Quick, *Ravished*, 1992

269
BETTY BROOKS
Jade
(New York: Zebra, 1997)

Story type: Historical/Colonial America
Major character(s): Jade Carrington, Servant (indentured); Matt Hunter, Frontiersman
Time period(s): 1760s (1763)
Locale(s): Charleston, South Carolina, American Colonies

Summary: When Matthew Hunter buys Jade Carrington as an indentured servant, he thinks she is the gun-supplier he has been looking for. He is, of course, wrong—but now he has the beautiful Jade on his hands and a war brewing between the

Indians and the settlers. Good historical detail of Indian uprisings in the Carolinas in the 1760s.

Where it's reviewed:
Library Journal, May 15, 1997, page 64

Other books by the same author:
Warrior's Destiny, 1995
Love's Endless Flame, 1992
Wild Magnolia, 1990

Other books you might like:
Kimberly Cates, *The Raider's Bride*, 1994
    Later time period
Karen Harper, *Eden's Gate*, 1989
Karen Robards, *Nobody's Angel*, 1992
Jo Ann Wendt, *The Golden Dove*, 1989

270

LYDIA BROWNE

Snowflake Wishes

(New York: Jove, 1997)

Story type: Historical/Americana
Major character(s): Rachel Pridgeon, Teacher, Fugitive; Hal Sinclair, Editor (newspaper)
Time period(s): 19th century (late)
Locale(s): Brooklyn, Missouri

Summary: An aggressive newspaperman banished from New York for being a bit too honest in print finds himself in tiny Brooklyn, Missouri, the editor (and reporter, copy-editor, delivery boy, and janitor) of the local paper—and an item of intense interest to the local ladies. However, it is Rachel Pridgeon, the local schoolmarm, who attracts his attention and his curiosity. But Rachel has secrets and has no intention of allowing this man to ruin things for her. Pure Americana with a plethora of small-town characters.

Where it's reviewed:
Library Journal, November 15, 1997, page 47

Other books by the same author:
Spring Dreams, 1997
Heart Strings, 1993

Other books you might like:
Candace Camp, *Rosewood*, 1991
Martha Kirkland, *Pratt's Landing*, 1997
Pamela Morsi, *Something Shady*, 1995
Rae Muir, *The Lieutenant's Lady*, 1997

271

MARGARET BROWNLEY

Buttons and Beaus

(New York: Topaz, 1996)

Story type: Historical/Victorian America
Major character(s): Amanda Blackwell, Teacher (cycling school), Care Giver (for mentally disabled brother); Damian Newcastle, Architect
Time period(s): 1880s
Locale(s): New York, New York

Summary: Amanda Blackwell needs to keep her thriving cycling school going so she can care for her mentally disabled brother and herself. Damian Newcastle wants to build the highest skyscraper in New York to atone for an earlier disaster and provide his disabled son with a view of the city. The problem is that Damian wants to build his building on the site of Amanda's school, something that she will not allow. Obviously, the sparks fly in this made-to-order conflict; however, the pair are also attracted to each other and eventually love does win out. Good historical research is complemented by a relaxed writing style.

Where it's reviewed:
Library Journal, August 1997, page 66

Other books by the same author:
Ribbons in the Wind, 1996

Other books you might like:
Kit Gardner, *The Dream*, 1992
    Similar time period
Julie Garwood, *For the Roses*, 1995
    Similar time period
Linda Francis Lee, *Emerald Rain*, 1996
    Similar setting and situation
Pamela Morsi, *Simple Jess*, 1996
    Americana/social issues
Pamela Morsi, *Garters*, 1992

272

MARGARET BROWNLEY
RAINE CANTRELL, Co-Author
ALEXIS HARRINGTON, Co-Author
SUE RICH, Co-Author

Chocolate Kisses

(New York: St. Martin's, 1997)

Story type: Anthology; Holiday Themes

Summary: This sweet and charming quartet of romantic Valentine's Day stories all focus on love and chocolate, with a hefty dash of Americana thrown in for good measure. Included are ''Rocky Road'' by Margaret Brownley, ''Miss Delwin's Delights'' by Raine Cantrell, ''The Taste of Remembrance'' by Alexis Harrington, and ''Sweet Creations'' by Sue Rich.

Where it's reviewed:
Library Journal, February 15, 1997, page 126

Other books you might like:
Rochelle Alers, *Love Letters*, 1997
    Anthology
Kay Hooper, *Hearts of Gold*, 1994
    Anthology
Rebecca Paisley, *Love Potion*, 1994
    Anthology
Meryl Sawyer, *Valentine Delights*, 1997
    Anthology

273

LINDA CAJIO

Mister Christmas

(Toronto: Harlequin, 1997)

Story type: Contemporary; Holiday Themes
Series: Holiday Heart
Major character(s): Holly, Mythical Creature (elf); Raymond Holiday, Television Personality (sports talk show host)
Time period(s): 1990s
Locale(s): Philadelphia, Pennsylvania

Summary: Holly has her hands full when she is sent by Saint Nick to make sure that talk show host Raymond Holiday finds love by Christmas Day. The problem is that sexy, appealing Raymond is commitment-shy and is not about to fall in love. Of course, then he meets the determined Holly. Light holiday reading.

Where it's reviewed:
Library Journal, November 15, 1997, page 47

Other books by the same author:
Bossman, 1997

Other books you might like:
Muriel Jensen, *Merry Christmas, Mommy*, 1995
Kate Little, *Jingle Bell Baby*, 1996
Elda Minger, *Christmas with Eve*, 1996
    Sexy
Patricia Wynn, *The Christmas Spirit*, 1996
    Another elf

274

JUNE CALVIN

Isabella's Rake

(New York: Signet, 1997)

Story type: Regency
Major character(s): Isabella Eardley, Debutante, Artist; Harrison Curzon, Rake, Artist (art teacher)
Time period(s): 1810s
Locale(s): England

Summary: Despite its total impropriety for a woman of her position, Isabella is determined to become a professional painter. But when she is rejected as a student by London's best teacher, his protege, the talented but infamous rake Harrison Curzon, takes her on—with the expected romantic results. Although light and traditional, it deals with a number of serious women's social issues.

Where it's reviewed:
Library Journal, May 15, 1997, page 65

Other books you might like:
Anne Barbour, *A Talent for Trouble*, 1992
Carla Kelly, *With This Ring*, 1997
Lynn Kerstan, *Francesca's Rake*, 1997
Evelyn Richardson, *My Wayward Lady*, 1997

275

MARSHA CANHAM

The Last Arrow

(New York: Dell, 1997)

Story type: Historical/Medieval
Series: Robin Hood Trilogy
Major character(s): Brenna Wardieu d'Amboise, Noblewoman, Warrior (archer); Griffyn Renaud de Verdelay, Mercenary, Knight
Time period(s): 13th century
Locale(s): France; England

Summary: This fast-paced, occasionally violent story moves from Normandy to Sherwood Forest as the fiery warrior Brenna and the bold knight Griffyn work to save the heir to England's throne—and find love in the process. Nicely concludes Canham's Robin Hood Trilogy.

Where it's reviewed:
Library Journal, May 15, 1997, page 68

Other books by the same author:
Across a Moonlit Sea, 1996
Straight for the Heart, 1995
In the Shadow of Midnight, 1994
Through a Dark Mist, 1994
Under the Desert Moon, 1992

Other books you might like:
Rexanne Becnel, *The Rose of Blacksword*, 1992
Gayle Feyrer, *The Thief's Mistress*, 1996
    Another re-telling of the legend
Nancy Richards-Akers, *Wild Irish Skies*, 1997
Jennifer Roberson, *Lady of the Forest*, 1992
    Another re-telling of the legend

276

MARSHA CANHAM

The Pride of Lions

(New York: Dell, 1997)

Story type: Historical/Georgian
Major character(s): Catherine Augustine Ashbrooke, Bride (reluctant); Alexander Cameron, Imposter (Raefer Montgomery), Spy
Time period(s): 1740s (1745)
Locale(s): England; Scotland

Summary: When spoiled, rich Catherine Ashbrooke's plans to marry the "most eligible officer in His Majesty's Royal Dragoons" end in disaster, she finds herself wed to a hated Scot and heading for the Highlands and a life she can only imagine. Passion and fast-paced action abound in this story of two independent people who find love inspite of themselves.

Other books by the same author:
The Last Arrow, 1997
Across a Moonlit Sea, 1996
Straight for the Heart, 1995
In the Shadow of Midnight, 1994
Through a Dark Mist, 1991

Other books you might like:
Mary Burkhardt, *Highland Ecstasy*, 1993
Christina Dodd, *A Well-Favored Gentleman*, 1998
Arnette Lamb, *Border Bride*, 1993
Karyn Monk, *The Witch and the Warrior*, 1998
Scotney St. James, *Highland Hearts*, 1993

277

JAYNE CASTLE

Zinnia

(New York: Pocket, 1997)

Story type: Futuristic; Romantic Suspense
Major character(s): Zinnia Spring, Psychic (prism); Nick Chastain, Psychic (matrix talent), Businessman (wealthy)
Time period(s): Indeterminate Future
Locale(s): New Seattle, Fictional City; St. Helens, Planet—Imaginary

Summary: When the slightly notorious, full-spectrum prism Zinnia Spring storms into the plush office of wealthy Nick Chastain, demanding the release of her missing client, she has no idea that Nick is the same powerful matrix-talent that her mind had briefly—and painfully—encountered just moments before. But by the end of their "interview," Nick knows, and he also knows that Zinnia is going to be important to him for a number of reasons. Lively action abounds in this intelligent, humorous, suspenseful romance that features, among other things, compelling characters, a high intensity level, and a gruesome garden of carnivorous plants. Follows *Amaryllis* (Pocket, 1996).

Where it's reviewed:
Library Journal, August 1997, page 66

Other books by the same author:
Amaryllis, 1996

Other books you might like:
Linda Howard, *Dream Man*, 1995
 Psychic heroine/suspense
Kathleen Morgan, *Heart's Lair*, 1991
 Futuristic with a psychic heroine
J.D. Robb, *Naked in Death*, 1995
 another futuristic mystery
J.D. Robb, *Rapture in Death*, 1996
 another in the series

278

MEGAN CHANCE

Fall from Grace

(New York: Harper, 1997)

Story type: Historical/American West
Major character(s): Lily Tremaine Sharpe, Orphan, Outlaw; "Texas" Christian Sharpe, Outlaw; Sam Sharpe, Outlaw (leader of Sharpe gang)
Time period(s): 1870s
Locale(s): Houston, Texas

Summary: Twelve-year-old Lily Tremaine was spared when the Sharpe gang killed her parents, but the Sharpes raised her to become Lily the Cat, a most famous woman outlaw. Ruthless and independent, she manages to escape both her own hanging and the gang after a robbery attempt; now they suspect her of betraying them and are out to kill her. Well-drawn characters and plenty of fast-paced action fill this poignant, emotional, well-written story.

Where it's reviewed:
Romantic Times, February 1997, page 37

Other books by the same author:
A Heart Divided, 1996
The Portrait, 1995

Other books you might like:
Rosanne Bittner, *Shameless*, 1993
 Another outlaw heroine/very different treatment
Lorraine Heath, *Texas Destiny*, 1997
 Wounded characters/poignant and emotionally involving
Linda Howard, *A Lady of the West*, 1990
 Realistic
Maggie Osborne, *The Seduction of Samantha Kincade*, 1995
 Another adventurous heroine, but with a touch of humor

279

MEGAN CHANCE

The Way Home

(New York: Harper, 1997)

Story type: Historical/American West; Historical/Americana
Major character(s): Eliza Beaudry, Farmer (daughter of a sharecropper); Aaron Wallace, Farmer
Time period(s): 1870s
Locale(s): Richmond, Texas; White Horse, Texas

Summary: Eliza Beaudry will do anything to escape the sharecropper's life, even sleep with irresponsible, hard-gambling Cole Wallace in hopes of leaving town with him. But when she ends up pregnant, Cole talks his painfully shy, rancher brother into marrying her instead—with results that eventually surprise all concerned. Poignant, realistic, and well-crafted.

Where it's reviewed:
Library Journal, November 15, 1997, page 47

Other books by the same author:
Fall from Grace, 1997

Other books you might like:
Dorothy Garlock, *Sins of Summer*, 1994
Robin Lee Hatcher, *Where the Heart Is*, 1993
Lorraine Heath, *Texas Destiny*, 1997
Stephanie Mittman, *The Courtship*, 1998

280

MARION CHESNEY

The Deception

(New York: St. Martin's, 1996)

Story type: Regency
Series: Daughters of Mannerling

Major character(s): Abigail Beverley, Debutante; Rachel Beverley, Debutante; Lord Burfield, Bachelor, Nobleman
Time period(s): 1810s
Locale(s): England

Summary: Abigail, Rachel, and their sisters, chaperoned by the redoubtable Miss Trumble, are trying to grow up properly, even though they are deprived of their family estate, Mannerling. They must find suitors and keep reckless Harry Devers from getting their home. By switching identities they get eligible Lord Burfield to escort them and eventually to commit himself, but he discovers their prank and is not pleased with their childishness. However, social intricacies engineered by Miss Trumble put things in order and the girls end up with their futures assured.

Other books by the same author:
The Dreadful Debutante, 1995
The Desirable Duchess, 1993
The First Rebellion, 1989
Finessing Clarissa, 1989
Silken Bonds, 1989

Other books you might like:
Anne Barbour, *My Cousin Jane*, 1995
    another bit of deception
Mary Chase Comstock, *An Impetuous Miss*, 1993
Marion Devon, *Miss Kendal Sets Her Cap*, 1996
Candice Hern, *A Garden Folly*, 1997
Elizabeth Jackson, *A Brilliant Alliance*, 1993

281

SUE CIVIL-BROWN

Carried Away

(New York: Avon, 1997)

Story type: Contemporary; Romantic Suspense
Major character(s): Danika Hilliard, Teacher, Writer (aspiring); Silas Northrop, Writer (aspiring), Military Personnel (former Marine)
Time period(s): 1990s
Locale(s): Florida

Summary: Under the terms of a strange will of a deceased friend, school techer Dani Hilliard and boat-yard employee Silas Northrop (both aspiring authors) must spend six months in his mansion and complete their books, or they inherit nothing. Living together is difficult at best, but relatives searching for a diary and frequent appearances of the owner's ghost increase their anxiety and hostility. Cooperation proves to be the only solution, and as they begin to work together, they come to some surprising conclusions.

Where it's reviewed:
Affaire de Coeur, January 1997, page 17

Other books you might like:
Lori Herter, *The Willow File*, 1994
Laura Phillips, *Moonshowers*, 1992
    Mansions and ghosts/historical
Maura Seger, *The Lady and the Laird*, 1992
Antoinette Stockenberg, *Emily's Ghost*, 1992

282

CASEY CLAYBOURNE

Nick of Time

(New York: Jove, 1997)

Story type: Time Travel; Reincarnation
Major character(s): Anna Woodbaine, Gentlewoman; Nick daCosta, Reincarnated Person (as Godfrey Woodbaine), Detective
Time period(s): 1810s (1810)
Locale(s): Dover Coast, England

Summary: When a car accident sends detective Nick daCosta back to Regency England and into the body of the worthless dandy Godfrey Woodbaine, Nick ends up falling in love with Godfrey's wife, Anna. An interesting twist on the classic time travel theme that involves two people switching both times and bodies (Godfrey and Nick) with intriguing results. Funny but poignant and romantic.

Where it's reviewed:
Romantic Times, December 1997, page 81

Other books by the same author:
A Ghost of a Chance, 1996
The Devil's Darling, 1994
My Lucky Lady, 1994

Other books you might like:
Jasmine Cresswell, *Timeless*, 1994
    historical "trading places" time travel
Kristin Hannah, *Once in Every Life*, 1993
    historical "trading places" time travel/different treatment
Emilie Richards, *Twice upon a Time*, 1997
    Reincarnation

283

ELAINE COFFMAN

If You Love Me

(New York: Fawcett, 1997)

Story type: Historical/American West
Major character(s): Margery "Walks Fast" McKinnon, Captive, Bride; William Woodville, Nobleman (Viscount Linwood), Artist
Time period(s): 1850s (1857)
Locale(s): Crow Territory, Wyoming; England

Summary: After being kidnapped by Indians as a child and handed from tribe to tribe as she grew up, Margery McKinnon is eventually bought by William Woodville, Viscount Linwood. A tattooed savage bride will be the ultimate insult to his estranged father. However, when he abandons Margery to his family in England, William's mother sees through her outward appearance and takes Margery under her wing, ensuring her acceptance by society. Upon his eventual return, William is amazed and fascinated by the changed Margery—and suddenly he is faced with the challenge of winning the love of a woman who has no reason to ever forgive him.

Where it's reviewed:
Romantic Times, February 1997, page 38

Other books by the same author:
A Time for Roses, 1995
Heaven Knows, 1994
So This Is Love, 1993
Somewhere Along the Way, 1992
Angel in Marble, 1991

Other books you might like:
Cordia Byers, *Lady Fortune*, 1989
Catherine Coulter, *The Valentine Legacy*, 1995
    Another transplanted bride
Jane Feather, *Violet*, 1995
    Another "Ugly Duckling" heroine
Rebecca Paisley, *Barefoot Bride*, 1990
    Similar situation/very different treatment
Patricia Potter, *The Marshall and the Heiress*, 1996
    More Americans in Victorian England

284

ELAINE COFFMAN
VICTORIA BARRETT, Co-Author
ASHLAND PRICE, Co-Author
TRANA MAE SIMMONS, Co-Author

Seeing Fireworks
(New York: St. Martin's, 1997)

Story type: Anthology; Holiday Themes

Summary: This diverse quartet of novellas focuses on fireworks of all kinds, both pyrotechnic and romantic. Included are "Playing with Fire" by Elaine Coffman, "Summer Fling" by Victoria Barrett, "One Star-Spangled Night" by Ashland Price, and "Showers and Sparks" by Trana Mae Simmons.

Other books you might like:
Victoria Barrett, *Maybe This Time*, 1996
Elaine Coffman, *Heaven Knows*, 1994
Ashland Price, *Viking Rose*, 1993
Trana Mae Simmons, *Bittersweet Promises*, 1994

285

LAUREL COLLINS

The Firebrand
(New York: Zebra, 1997)

Story type: Historical
Major character(s): Caroline Harlowe, Activist (abolitionist); Pierce Barnett, Businessman (mill owner), Activist
Time period(s): 1850s
Locale(s): Oberlin, Ohio

Summary: When Caroline Harlowe, an avowed abolitionist, becomes one of the first female students at Oberlin College, her goals do not include love or marriage. However, when she meets businessman and activist Pierce Barnett, her life becomes more complex, and Caroline is faced with choices she never thought she would need to make.

Other books by the same author:
Patchwork Angel, 1998

Other books you might like:
Elaine Barbieri, *Wishes on the Wind*, 1991
Rosanne Bittner, *Caress*, 1992
    Another abolitionist heroine
Patricia Potter, *Rainbow*, 1991
    Similar focus
Sonia Simone, *Scandalous*, 1994

286

LORI COPELAND

Angel Face and Amazing Grace
(New York: Fawcett, 1997)

Story type: Historical/American West; Historical/Americana
Major character(s): April Truitt, Feminist; Gray Fuller, Doctor
Time period(s): 1870s (1876)
Locale(s): Dignity, Minnesota

Summary: Feminist April Truitt thinks it is revolting the way all the women in town try to entice Dr. Gray Fuller to their bedsides—and beyond —even though she does appreciate the care he gives her difficult father. Incensed by his approach to "female complaints" and his forward friendliness, she avoids him. Nevertheless, his persistence wins, and so does love. Funny and lively.

Other books by the same author:
Promise Me Forever, 1994
Forever, Ashley, 1992
Promise Me Today, 1992
Sweet Hannah Rose, 1991
Fool Me Once, 1990

Other books you might like:
Jill Marie Landis, *Come Spring*, 1992
Pamela Morsi, *Courting Miss Hattie*, 1992
Pamela Morsi, *Garters*, 1992
Rebecca Paisley, *Rainbows and Rapture*, 1992

287

LORI COPELAND

The Courtship of Cade Kolby
(New York: Avon, 1997)

Story type: Historical/American West
Major character(s): Zoe Bradshaw, Foster Parent, Businesswoman (general store owner); Cade Kolby, Bounty Hunter
Time period(s): 1800s (late)
Locale(s): Kansas

Summary: Bounty hunter Cade Kolby returns to his hometown to see to his late sister's four children and finds them firmly in the care of the woman he'd left behind—and she's not about to let them go. Predictably, sparks fly as the pair come to terms with the situation; although the ending is never in doubt, the road the characters travel is not always predictable. Fast-paced, humorous, and features four charming children.

Where it's reviewed:
Library Journal, August 1997, page 66

Other books by the same author:
Angel Face and Amazing Grace, 1997
Promise Me Forever, 1994
Promise Me Tomorrow, 1993
Forever, Ashley, 1992
Promise Me Today, 1992

Other books you might like:
Kimberly Cates, *Only Forever*, 1992
Julie Garwood, *For the Roses*, 1995
Ana Leigh, *The MacKenzies: Luke*, 1996
Debbie Macomber, *Morning Comes Softly*, 1993
  Contemporary setting

288

CATHERINE COULTER

The Offer

(New York: Topaz, 1997)

Story type: Historical/Regency
Major character(s): Sabrina Eversleigh, Gentlewoman, Abuse Victim (attempted rape victim); Peter Mercerault, Gentleman
Time period(s): 1810s
Locale(s): England

Summary: Fleeing from an attempted rape by her brother-in-law and her sister's lack of sympathy and understanding, Sabrina ends up unconscious in a blizzard, then rescued by Peter Mercerault and taken to his hunting lodge. Hopelessly compromised, the pair marry, and then must figure out how to handle a number of problems, including Sabrina's aversion to men! Sensual and lively, this is an expanded version of her Regency romance *An Honorable Offer*, first published in 1981.

Where it's reviewed:
Romantic Times, October 1997, page 39

Other books by the same author:
The Maze, 1997
The Cove, 1996
Rosehaven, 1996
The Lord of Falconridge, 1995
The Valentine Legacy, 1995

Other books you might like:
Mary Balogh, *Deceived*, 1993
Mary Balogh, *The Snow Angel*, 1991
Kasey Michaels, *Legacy of the Rose*, 1992
Anne Stuart, *A Rose at Midnight*, 1993
  darker

289

NINA COYLE

Sharon's Hope

(Nashville: Thomas Nelson, 1996)

Story type: Contemporary
Major character(s): Sharon Potter, Divorced Person, Mother; Kenneth McKenzie, Veteran (Vietnam)
Time period(s): 1960s (1968)

Locale(s): Yucaipa, California

Summary: With the help of friends, divorced mother Sharon Potter has finally found a home, but she fears the return of her brutal husband. Despite outside criticism and her internal fears, she knows her faith in God will sustain her. Her growing relationship with Vietnam veteran Kenneth is slow and tentative, because she finds it hard to trust a man again; nevertheless, love, patience, and community support eventually help her find a new and loving life again.

Other books you might like:
Catherine Anderson, *Cheyenne Amber*, 1994
  Abuse issues/not Inspirational
Susan Kirby, *When Lilacs Bloom*, 1997
  Last of an Inspirational trilogy/Historical
Kathleen Korbel, *A Soldier's Heart*, 1994
  Post Traumatic Stress/not inspirational
Debbie Macomber, *Someday Soon*, 1995
  not inspirational
Stephanie Grace Whitson, *Soaring Eagle*, 1996
  Inspirational/historical/Native American

290

JASMINE CRESSWELL

Secret Sins

(Toronto: Mira, 1997)

Story type: Contemporary/Mainstream
Major character(s): Jessica Marie Pazmany-Zajak, Adoptee, Businesswoman (executive); Dan Stratton, Spouse (former)
Time period(s): 1990s; 1960s (1969)
Locale(s): Cleveland, Ohio; Denver, Colorado; Durham, North Carolina

Summary: Jessica Marie Pazmany-Zajak's ex-husband, Dan, brings her news of her past that plays havoc with her acceptance of her adoption story: her adopted father rescued her from a fatal car accident where her parents were killed. Now Jess is unsure of who she actually is. In a parallel story, Constance Rodier, a mental patient helped by psychiatrist Ed Foster, attempts to unravel her belief that she has killed her daughter. Eventually Jessica and Dan are led to the mental hospital, only someone doesn't want the secret uncovered and Jess becomes the target of an unknown killer. Mysterious, suspenseful, and complex.

Where it's reviewed:
Affaire de Coeur, February 1997, page 39
Romantic Times, February 1997, page 90

Other books by the same author:
I Do, Again, 1997
Shatterd Vows, 1996
No Sin Too Great, 1996
Midnight Fantasy, 1996
Prince of the Night, 1996

Other books you might like:
Barbara Delinsky, *The Passions of Chelsea Kane*, 1992
Suzanne Forster, *Innocence*, 1997
Linda Howard, *After the Night*, 1995
Iris Johansen, *The Ugly Duckling*, 1995

Romance

Anne Stuart, *Ritual Sins*, 1997

Kathleen Gilles Seidel, *Till the Stars Fall*, 1994

291

MILLIE CRISWELL

Desperate
(New York: Warner, 1997)

Story type: Historical/American West
Major character(s): Emmaline St. Joseph, Guardian (of orphaned children), Gentlewoman (easterner); Rafe Bodine, Lawman (former Texas Ranger), Avenger
Time period(s): 1870s (1879)
Locale(s): New Mexico; West

Summary: Intent on avenging the brutal murder of his wife and unborn child, ex-Texas Ranger Rafe Bodine heads out to find the culprits; instead, he finds a beautiful Eastern heiress, stranded in the mountains with a band of orphaned children, and badly in need of help. Reluctantly, he agrees to guide them to the next large town, but circumstances decree otherwise, and before their adventure is over, Rafe and Emmaline and the children have formed a unit that will be difficult to dissolve. Violent, fast-paced, and straight-forward.

Other books by the same author:
Prim Rose, 1996
Sweet Laurel, 1996
Wild Heather, 1995
Diamond in the Rough, 1994
Mail-Order Outlaw, 1994

Other books you might like:
Rosanne Bittner, *Chase the Sun*, 1996
Maggie Osborne, *The Brides of Prairie Gold*, 1996
Patricia Potter, *Defiant*, 1995
Patricia Potter, *Lawless*, 1991

292

JANET DAILEY
FERN MICHAELS, Co-Author
DINAH MCCALL, Co-Author
DEBORAH BEDFORD, Co-Author

Homecoming
(New York: Harper, 1997)

Story type: Anthology; Contemporary
Time period(s): 1990s
Locale(s): United States

Summary: This diverse quartet of contemporary stories highlights the old idea that "home is where the heart is" and it will always be there when you need it. Included are "Heading Home" by Janet Dailey, "The Journey" by Fern Michaels, "The Return of Walker Lee" by Dinah McCall, and "Rockabye Inn" by Deborah Bedford.

Other books you might like:
Layle Guisto, *Home Fires*, 1996
    Contemporary look at the problems of home
Jackie Merritt, *Montana Christmas*, 1996
Fern Michaels, *Wish List*, 1996
Dallas Schulze, *The Way Home*, 1995

293

JUSTINE DARE

Fire Hawk
(New York: Topaz, 1997)

Story type: Historical/Medieval; Historical/Fantasy
Major character(s): Jenna, Leader (Hawk of her clan); Kane, Warrior
Time period(s): Indeterminate Past
Locale(s): Hawk Glade, Wales

Summary: The last of her clan to hold the title of "Hawk," Jenna knows that her only chance to save her people is to find the legendary warrior Kane. When her search leads her to a man who has chosen peace over war and is now reluctant to return to battle, things become more complex. A woman determined to save her people, a wounded hero with a past, and a fiery attraction that can't be denied work to produce a fast-paced, sensual adventure with a bit of a mystical touch.

Other books by the same author:
Wild Hawk, 1996
Heart of the Hawk, 1996

Other books you might like:
Kimberly Cates, *Magic*, 1998
    Gentler and humorous
Laura Kinsale, *The Prince of Midnight*, 1990
Karyn Monk, *The Witch and the Warrior*, 1998
Anne Stuart, *Lord of Danger*, 1997
    Darker

294

KATHERINE DEAUVILLE

Eyes of Love
(New York: Zebra, 1996)

Story type: Historical/Medieval
Major character(s): Edain, Maiden (convent-bred), Witch (accused); Magnus fitzJulien, Knight
Time period(s): 12th century (1170)
Locale(s): Scotland

Summary: English knight Magnus fitzJulien, in debt and desperate, promises young Edain as payment of a debt to a man who suddenly dies. She is suspected of witchcraft, so Magnus takes her from the convent and they begin their mad dash to escape both the Scottish and English kings. Not knowing of her own powers, Edain merely wishes for the convent, but she and Magnus grow closer daily. Marriage is out of the question, but they still fall in love. Highly sensual and mystical.

Where it's reviewed:
Affaire de Coeur, May 1996, page 20
Romantic Times, May 1996, page 35

Other books by the same author:
The Amethyst Crown, 1994
Daggers of Gold, 1993
Blood Red Roses, 1991

Other books you might like:
Elizabeth Lowell, *Enchanted*, 1994
Elizabeth Lowell, *Forbidden*, 1993
Elizabeth Lowell, *Untamed*, 1993
Karyn Monk, *The Witch and the Warrior*, 1998
Maura Seger, *Tapestry*, 1993
    magical and lyrical

295

JUDE DEVERAUX
MARGARET ALLISON, Co-Author
STEF ANN HOLM, Co-Author
MARIAH STEWART, Co-Author
LINDA HOWARD, Co-Author

Upon a Midnight Clear
(New York: Pocket, 1997)

Story type: Anthology; Holiday Themes
Summary: This collection of five well-crafted Christmas novellas makes use of both contemporary and historical settings, and stories range from the funny and whimsical to the gently romantic, incorporating ordinary events and magic with equal ease. Included are ''The Teacher'' by Jude Deveraux, ''Christmas Magic'' by Margaret Allison, ''Jolly Holly'' by Stef Ann Holm, ''If Only in My Dreams'' by Mariah Stewart, and ''White Out'' by Linda Howard.

Where it's reviewed:
Library Journal, November 15, 1997, page 49

Other books you might like:
Elaine Barbieri, *Mistletoe Marriages*, 1994
    Christmas Anthology
Rexanne Becnel, *Christmas Journey*, 1992
Jane Bonander, *Avon Books Presents: A Christmas Together*, 1994
    Christmas Anthology
Judith McNaught, *A Holiday of Love*, 1994
    Christmas Anthology
Diana Palmer, *Lone Star Christmas*, 1997
    includes two stories by Palmer and Joan Johnston

296

CHRISTINA DODD

A Knight to Remember
(New York: Harper, 1997)

Story type: Historical/Medieval
Major character(s): Lady Edlyn, Healer, Noblewoman (Duchess of Cleere); Hugh de Florisoun, Warrior
Time period(s): 13th century (1265)
Locale(s): Wessex, England

Summary: Forced to both hide and heal a man she once loved, convent herbalist Lady Edlyn finds herself reluctantly drawn into a relationship she simultaneously craves and fears—and can't resist. An honorable hero, a fiery independent heroine and a number of fascinating secondary characters drive the plot of this passionate, witty and often funny story of love, politics, and intrigue.

Where it's reviewed:
Library Journal, November 15, 1996, page 50

Other books by the same author:
Once a Knight, 1996
Move Heaven and Earth, 1995
The Greatest Lover in All England, 1994
Outrageous, 1994
Castles in the Air, 1993

Other books you might like:
Kimberly Cates, *Magic*, 1998
Julie Garwood, *Saving Grace*, 1993
Amanda Quick, *Desire*, 1994
Amanda Quick, *Mystique*, 1995

297

CHRISTINA DODD

A Well-Pleasured Lady
(New York: Avon, 1997)

Story type: Historical/Georgian
Major character(s): Mary Rottenson, Noblewoman (Lady Guinevere Mary Fairchild), Imposter (posing as housekeeper); Sebastian Durant, Nobleman (Viscount Whitfield)
Time period(s): 1770s (1777)
Locale(s): Scotland

Summary: Housekeeper Mary Rottenson is reluctantly dragged back to a life she thought she had left behind when the Viscount Whitfield blackmails her into posing as his fiancee and returning to her dissolute family. Vengeance and passion abound in this well-done, bawdy Georgian that boasts a cast of marvelously eccentric secondary characters in addition to two beautifully rendered, compelling protagonists. Wickedly charming portrayal of a wildly dysfunctional family.

Where it's reviewed:
Library Journal, August 1997, page 70
Romantic Times, August 1997, page 38

Other books by the same author:
A Well-Favored Gentleman, 1998 (tie-in to *A Well-Pleasured Lady*)
A Knight to Remember, 1997
Once a Knight, 1996
Move Heaven and Earth, 1995
The Greatest Lover in All England, 1994

Other books you might like:
Jo Beverley, *My Lady Notorious*, 1993
Jo Beverley, *Something Wicked*, 1997
Mary Jo Putney, *Thunder and Roses*, 1993
Anne Stuart, *To Love a Dark Lord*, 1994
    Darker

Romance

298

KATHLEEN EAGLE

The Night Remembers

(New York: Avon, 1997)

Story type: Contemporary; Ethnic
Major character(s): Angela Prescott, Abuse Victim, Teacher (former); Jesse Brown Wolf, Indian, Streetperson; Tommy T., Streetperson, Child (African American/Sioux)
Time period(s): 1990s
Locale(s): Minneapolis, Minnesota

Summary: The power of love wins out in Kathleen Eagle's first hardcover release as she links a woman running from an abusive relationship, the disillusioned and enigmatic Jesse Brown Wolf, and a homeless, street-smart, bi-racial 12-year-old, and sets them down in the middle of "Indian Country"— urban Minneapolis. Compelling characters combine with Native American folklore and innercity reality in a story that is both realistic and mystical at the same time.

Where it's reviewed:
Library Journal, May 15, 1997, page 66
Romantic Times, June 1997, page 83

Other books by the same author:
The Last True Cowboy, 1998
Sunrise Song, 1996
Reason to Believe, 1995
Fire and Rain, 1994
This Time Forever, 1992

Other books you might like:
Catherine Anderson, *Cheyenne Amber*, 1994
    historical/abuse issues
Rosanne Bittner, *Tame the Wild Wind*, 1996
    historical/wounded hero
Dinah McCall, *Dreamcatcher*, 1996
    Paranormal elements/abuse
Dinah McCall, *Tallchief*, 1997
    Native American Hero/suspenseful/darker

299

GAIL EASTWOOD

The Lady From Spain

(New York: Signet, 1997)

Story type: Regency
Major character(s): Falcarrah "Falcon" Colburne, Gentlewoman, Heiress; Jeremy Hazelton, Nobleman (Lord Danebridge), Military Personnel (lieutenant major)
Time period(s): 1810s
Locale(s): England

Summary: Lord Danebridge knows that the "Spanish lady" who just walked into the inn is not who she is pretending to be. He doesn't know exactly what she is up to, but he intends to find out. Old mysteries, murder, and greed drive the plot of this well-done Regency that is a bit darker than some.

Where it's reviewed:
Library Journal, August 1997, page 70

Other books by the same author:
An Unlikely Hero, 1996
The Persistent Earl, 1995
The Captain's Dilemma, 1995
A Perilous Journey, 1994

Other books you might like:
Mary Balogh, *The Plumed Bonnet*, 1996
Emily Hendrickson, *The Debonair Duke*, 1996
Mary Jo Putney, *Petals in the Storm*, 1996
    Sensual revision of an earlier Regency
Evelyn Richardson, *Lady Alex's Gamble*, 1995

300

CASSIE EDWARDS

White Fire

(New York: Topaz, 1997)

Story type: Historical/American West
Major character(s): Reshelle "Flame" Russell, Frontierswoman; Samuel "White Fire" Dowling, Indian (half Miami)
Time period(s): 1820s
Locale(s): St. Louis, Missouri; Minnesota

Summary: Despite prejudice, cultural differences, and interfering family, fiery Flame Russell and troubled White Fire Dowling eventually find happiness together in this fast-paced, passionate "Indian romance." Edwards is a veteran writer and award winner in this subtype.

Where it's reviewed:
Library Journal, May 15, 1997, page 66

Other books by the same author:
Comanche Dawn, 1996
Wild Splendor, 1993
Savage Promise, 1991
When Passion Calls, 1990

Other books you might like:
Rosanne Bittner, *Sioux Splendor*, 1990
Rosanne Bittner, *Unforgettable*, 1994
Jane Bonander, *Warrior Heart*, 1997
Jane Bonander, *Winter Heart*, 1996
Emily Carmichael, *Visions of the Heart*, 1990

301

MONIQUE ELLIS
SARA BLAYNE, Co-Author
JANICE BENNETT, Co-Author

Lords of the Night

(New York: Zebra, 1997)

Story type: Anthology; Regency
Time period(s): 1810s
Locale(s): England

Summary: This trilogy of charming novellas neatly combines the glitter and wit of the classic regency with the darker aspects of the vampire romance. Included are "The Deville

Inheritance'' by Monique Ellis, ''Dark Shadows'' by Sara Blayne, and ''The Full of the Moon'' by Janice Bennett.

Other books you might like:
Mary Chase Comstock, *A Midsummer's Magic*, 1994
    Witches and magic
Teresa DesJardien, *Bewitched by Love*, 1996
    Paranormal Regency Anthology
Karen Harbaugh, *The Vampire Viscount*, 1995
Sandra Heath, *Halloween Magic*, 1996
    witches

`302`

ELISABETH FAIRCHILD
DONNA GIMARC, Co-Author

The Rakehell's Reform

(New York: Signet Regency, 1997)

Story type: Regency
Major character(s): Selina Preston, Debutante, Artist; Jack ''Rakehell'' Ramsay, Nobleman, Rake
Time period(s): 1810s
Locale(s): London, England

Summary: The food is uneaten, the ices are melting, and Selina Preston's ball is a grand flop—until Rakehell Ramsay crashes the party and begins to play the cello, attracting a crowd and saving Selina from total embarrassment. Although Jack is merely seeking solace in the music after losing his family fortune at cards, Selina is stunned by The heartstopping emotion in his music, and she begins to wonder what kind of man his seductive, devil-may-care exterior hides. Emotional and lyrical, this story of redemption and responsibility is third in the series about the infamous Ramsay family.

Where it's reviewed:
Library Journal, November 15, 1996, page 48

Other books by the same author:
The Love Knot, 1995
Miss Dornton's Hero, 1995
The Counterfeit Coachman, 1994
The Silent Suitor, 1994

Other books you might like:
Carla Kelly, *Libby's London Merchant*, 1997
Carla Kelly, *With This Ring*, 1997
Lynn Kerstan, *Francesca's Rake*, 1997
Mary Jo Putney, *The Rake and the Reformer*, 1987
Meg-Lynn Roberts, *Rake's Gambit*, 1997

`303`

JANE FEATHER

The Diamond Slipper

(New York: Bantam, 1997)

Story type: Historical/Georgian
Major character(s): Lady Cordelia Brandenburg, Noblewoman; Leo Kierston, Nobleman (viscount)
Time period(s): 1760s (1765)
Locale(s): Paris, France; Versailles, France

Summary: Betrothed and sent by her restrictive family to a wealthy nobleman in far away Versailles, Cordelia is thrilled and anticipates a life of luxury and leisure, but falling in love with her escort, Viscount Leo Kierston, is not part of the plan. However, when her husband proves to be a tyrant and life becomes unbearable, it is up to Leo to discover the truth about her husband's past and free Cordelia from the relationship. A dark and sensual story that contains elements of domestic violence.

Where it's reviewed:
Affaire de Coeur, February 1997, page 24
Romantic Times, February 1997, page 39

Other books by the same author:
Valentine, 1995
Violet, 1995
Velvet, 1994
Vixen, 1994
Virtue, 1993

Other books you might like:
Jo Beverley, *Something Wicked*, 1997
Christina Dodd, *A Well-Pleasured Lady*, 1997
Nicole Jordan, *The Lover*, 1997
Amanda Quick, *Surrender*, 1990

`304`

JANE FEATHER

The Silver Rose

(New York: Bantam, 1997)

Story type: Historical/Georgian
Major character(s): Lady Ariel Ravenspeare, Noblewoman; Simon Hawkesmoor, Nobleman (Earl of Hawkesmoor)
Time period(s): 18th century (1709)
Locale(s): England

Summary: Ordered to marry each other by Queen Anne, Ariel Ravenspeare and Simon Hawkesmoor begin a wary relationship that eventually develops into one of real love as they begin to come to terms with their families' past sins and current hatreds. Old secrets, violent death, and a silver rose charm add interest to this lively, sensual historical. Follows *The Diamond Slipper*.

Where it's reviewed:
Romantic Times, August 1997, page 39

Other books by the same author:
The Diamond Slipper, 1997
Valentine, 1995
Violet, 1995
Velvet, 1994
Vixen, 1994

Other books you might like:
Jo Beverley, *My Lady Notorious*, 1993
Christina Dodd, *Castles in the Air*, 1993
Karyn Monk, *The Witch and the Warrior*, 1998
Susan Sizemore, *My First Duchess*, 1993

Romance

305

MAGGIE FERGUSON

Fever Rising

(Toronto: Harlequin, 1997)

Story type: Romantic Suspense; Multicultural
Major character(s): Raven Delaney, Healer (herbalist), Nurse; Jeffrey Knight, Doctor
Time period(s): 1990s
Locale(s): Chicago, Illinois

Summary: When a deadly virus threatens to run rampant, Dr. Jeffrey Knight follows the only clue he has, and it leads him right to the woman he'd once loved with all his heart, nurse and herbalist healer Raven Delaney. But this isn't just an accidental epidemic; the disease is being spread on purpose and it's up to Jeff and Raven to join forces and find the killer. Fast-paced and intriguing.

Where it's reviewed:
Library Journal, February 15, 1997, page 125

Other books by the same author:
Crime of Passion, 1996

Other books you might like:
Rochelle Alers, *Hidden Agenda*, 1997
Francis Ray, *Incognito*, 1997
Tracey Tillis, *Final Act*, 1998
Tracey Tillis, *Night Watch*, 1995

306

REBECCA FORSTER

Seasons

(New York: Zebra, 1996)

Story type: Contemporary
Major character(s): Elizabeth MacMillan, Spouse (abandoned); Max Marino, Businessman (construction company owner)
Time period(s): 1990s
Locale(s): Emerald Isle, California

Summary: Elizabeth, suddenly abandoned by her husband, valiantly maintains a home for her son and is befriended by Max, a construction worker whose persona is competely different from her gentle, beloved husband. Amazed that she can be comforted, her peace is broken by her violently angry son and the fact that Max has a wife. The soul searching of two strongly attracted people with overwhelming burdens makes this a deeply moving love story.

Where it's reviewed:
Romantic Times, May 1996, page 84

Other books by the same author:
Dreams, 1995
Vows, 1994
Vanities, 1993
Rainbow's End, 1992
A Delicate Matter, 1989

Other books you might like:
Barbara Bickmore, *Beyond the Promise*, 1997

Sandra Canfield, *Dark Journey*, 1994
Paula Detmer Riggs, *Daddy by Accident*, 1997
Peggy Roberts, *Mrs. Perfect*, 1992
LaVyrle Spencer, *Bitter Sweet*, 1990

307

SUZANNE FORSTER

Innocence

(New York: Berkely, 1997)

Story type: Contemporary
Major character(s): Mary Frances Murphy, Detective—Amateur, Religious (ex-novitiate); Webb Calderon, Criminal
Time period(s): 1990s
Locale(s): United States

Summary: Expelled from the convent, Mary Frances Murphy dons the trappings of a prostitute in an effort to find the murderer of her sister. She hopes to use her innocence as a way to get to Webb Calderon, the infamous strong man who has a well-deserved reputation for violence, cruelty, and underworld connections—a truly bad man. Encouraged by her girlfriend, Blue, and a priest, Rick, she undergoes torture and brainwashing at Webb's hands. But when she doesn't break, Webb slowly begins to reassess his own purposes and begins the process of redemption. A dark, almost unredeemable hero.

Where it's reviewed:
Affaire de Coeur, February 1997, page 29

Other books by the same author:
Blush, 1996
Come Midnight, 1995
Shameless, 1993
Child Bride, 1992
Night of the Panther, 1992

Other books you might like:
Jasmine Cresswell, *Secret Sins*, 1997
Nora Roberts, *Divine Evil*, 1992
Anne Stuart, *Moon-Rise*, 1996
    another dark hero
Anne Stuart, *Ritual Sins*, 1997
    another ultra-dark hero

308

BARBARA FREETHY

Ask Mariah

(New York: Avon, 1997)

Story type: Contemporary/Fantasy
Major character(s): Johanna Wingate, Teacher; Michael Ashton, Architect
Time period(s): 1990s
Locale(s): San Francisco, California

Summary: Although their mother has been killed in a boating accident, six-year-old twins Lily and Rose still believe that she is coming back. So when Mariah, their "magical fortune teller inside the crystal ball," tells them to go to school to find

her, they do—and end up with a teacher who looks so much like their late mother that their father is startled, and then intrigued. There is, of course, more to the resemblance than just chance, and as Michael Ashton and Johanna work to solve the mystery, they also find themselves dangerously close to falling in love. Mischievous children, old family secrets, and a bit of real magic add to this well-written, gently told story.

Where it's reviewed:
Library Journal, May 15, 1997, page 68

Other books by the same author:
Daniel's Gift, 1996
Ryan's Return, 1996

Other books you might like:
Kristin Hannah, *Once in Every Life*, 1993
    Historical
Lynn Kurland, *Stardust of Yesterday*, 1996
    charming ghosts
Angie Ray, *Ghost of My Dreams*, 1996
    Historical setting/ghosts
Antoinette Stockenberg, *Beyond Midnight*, 1996
    Contemporary ghosts
Antoinette Stockenberg, *Embers*, 1994

309

PATRICIA GAFFNEY

Outlaw in Paradise

(New York: Topaz, 1997)

Story type: Historical/American West
Major character(s): Cady McGill, Saloon Keeper/Owner; Jesse Gault, Gunfighter
Time period(s): 1890s
Locale(s): Paradise, Oregon

Summary: When the enigmatic gunslinger who calls himself Gault rides into Paradise one afternoon, the entire town knows about it even before he gets to the saloon. But they don't know why he is there, and they wonder. Saloon owner Cady McGill wonders too, and it isn't long before she realizes that there is more to Gault than meets the eye. A warm, sexy story of love and redemption filled with appealing, down-to-earth characters and lively humor.

Where it's reviewed:
Library Journal, August 1997, page 66

Other books by the same author:
Wild at Heart, 1997
Forever and Ever, 1996
To Love and to Cherish, 1995
To Have and to Hold, 1995
Crooked Hearts, 1994

Other books you might like:
Emily Carmichael, *Outcast*, 1995
Pamela Morsi, *Garters*, 1992
    humorous
Maggie Osborne, *The Seduction of Samantha Kincade*, 1995
Rebecca Paisley, *Rainbows and Rapture*, 1992
    Humorous

310

DOROTHY GARLOCK

Larkspur

(New York: Warner, 1997)

Story type: Historical/American West
Major character(s): Kristin Anderson, Rancher, Spinster; Buck Lenning, Foreman (ranch)
Time period(s): 1880s (1883)
Locale(s): Larkspur, Montana; Big Timber, Montana

Summary: When Kristin Anderson inherits a ranch in Montana Territory, she leaves a life of dependent servitude in her brother's Wisconsin home and heads west, determined to carve out a life for herself. It takes a bit of doing, and a little help from foreman Buck Lenning, because Kristin must deal with killers and greedy landgrabbers before she can call her ranch her own. A realistic, yet romantic, story of life in the Old West with some Americana elements.

Where it's reviewed:
Romantic Times, March 1997, page 49

Other books by the same author:
The Listening Sky, 1996
This Loving Land, 1996
Almost Eden, 1995
Sins of Summer, 1994
Ribbon in the Sky, 1992

Other books you might like:
Rosanne Bittner, *Montana Woman*, 1990
Robin Lee Hatcher, *Liberty Blue*, 1995
Maggie Osborne, *The Brides of Bowie Stone*, 1994
Patricia Potter, *Defiant*, 1995

311

DOROTHY GARLOCK

Sweetwater

(New York: Warner, 1998)

Story type: Historical/American West; Historical/Americana
Major character(s): Virginia ''Jenna'' Gray, Settler, Teacher; Trell McCall, Rancher
Time period(s): 1880s (1884)
Locale(s): Sweetwater, Wyoming

Summary: When Jenna Gray rescues her two young sisters from an abusive situation and flees with them to the wilds of Wyoming to teach on the reservation, life is rougher than she had imagined. But Jenna is determined to make a home for her sisters and a life for herself, despite impossible living conditions—and she does, but not without a little help from rancher Trell McCall. Realistic.

Other books by the same author:
Larkspur, 1997
The Listening Sky, 1996
This Loving Land, 1996
Almost Eden, 1995
Sins of Summer, 1994

Romance

Other books you might like:
Rosanne Bittner, *Unforgettable*, 1994
Catherine Lanigan, *A Promise Made*, 1991
Maggie Osborne, *The Promise of Jenny Jones*, 1997
Maggie Osborne, *The Wives of Bowie Stone*, 1994

312

JULIE GARWOOD

One Pink Rose

(New York: Pocket, 1997)

Story type: Historical/Americana; Historical/American West
Series: Clayborne Brides
Major character(s): Travis Clayborne, Hunter; Emily Finnegan, Mail Order Bride
Time period(s): 1880s
Locale(s): Montana

Summary: Ordered by Mama Rose to escort the opinionated Emily Finnegan to her mail-order husband in Golden Crest, Travis Clayborne ends up rescuing Emily from a disastrous marriage and marrying her himself. First novella in the Clayborne Brides Series.

Where it's reviewed:
Library Journal, May 15, 1997, page 68

Other books by the same author:
Come the Spring, 1997
One Red Rose, 1997
One White Rose, 1997
The Wedding, 1996
For the Roses, 1995

Other books you might like:
Jill Marie Landis, *Come Spring*, 1992
Jill Marie Landis, *Sunflower*, 1989
Pamela Morsi, *Heaven Sent*, 1990
LaVyrle Spencer, *The Endearment*, 1982

313

JULIE GARWOOD

One Red Rose

(New York: Pocket, 1997)

Story type: Historical/Americana; Historical/American West
Series: Clayborne Brides
Major character(s): Genevieve Perry, Singer; Adam Clayborne, Scholar, Slave (former)
Time period(s): 1880s
Locale(s): Montana

Summary: In this warm and delightful romance, Mama Rose decides that beautiful, independent Genevieve Perry is the perfect bride for wise, scholarly Adam, family lynchpin and the eldest of the Clayborne brothers—and so she meddles. A charming, rather resistant hero and a heroine with a secret provide the romantic plot of the last of the three novellas in the Clayborne Brides Series.

Where it's reviewed:
Library Journal, August 1997, page 66

Other books by the same author:
Come the Spring, 1997
One White Rose, 1997
One Pink Rose, 1997
The Wedding, 1996
For the Roses, 1995

Other books you might like:
Kristin Hannah, *If You Believe*, 1994
Jill Marie Landis, *Rose*, 1990
Pamela Morsi, *Courting Miss Hattie*, 1991
LaVyrle Spencer, *Morning Glory*, 1989

314

JULIE GARWOOD

One White Rose

(New York: Pocket, 1997)

Story type: Historical/American West
Series: Clayborne Brides
Major character(s): Douglas Clayborne, Rancher; Isabel Grant, Rancher
Time period(s): 1880s
Locale(s): Montana

Summary: Douglas Clayborne goes to a ranch to get a horse he had arranged to buy and finds the owner dead and buried and his wife about to give birth. Douglas' midwife abilities extend only to horses; nevertheless, he helps deliver Isabel's baby and stays to take care of (and eventually care about) them both. A greedy killer who wants Isabel's land complicates the situation, but Douglas takes care of the problem with a little help from the rest of the Clayborne clan. Lively, tender, and funny. Second in the Clayborne Brides Series.

Where it's reviewed:
Library Journal, August 1997, page 66

Other books by the same author:
Come the Spring, 1997
One Red Rose, 1997
One Pink Rose, 1997
The Wedding, 1996
For the Roses, 1995

Other books you might like:
Jill Marie Landis, *Sunflower*, 1989
Pamela Morsi, *Courting Miss Hattie*, 1991
LaVyrle Spencer, *Hummingbird*, 1996
LaVyrle Spencer, *Morning Glory*, 1989

315

GEORGINA GENTRY

Warrior's Prize

(New York: Zebra, 1997)

Story type: Historical/American West
Major character(s): Wannie Evans, Frontierswoman; Keso, Indian, Adoptee (Wannie's brother)
Time period(s): 1880s
Locale(s): Colorado

Summary: Raised on the barren frontier, Wannie Evans has always wanted wealth and respectability, and a wealthy Bostonian who has proposed to her seems the answer to her dreams. However, on a trip west to visit her family, she has a chance to see him in a new light—and to compare him to with her beloved adopted brother—with interesting results. Past secrets, surprising identities, and fast-paced, sensual action abound.

Where it's reviewed:
Romantic Times, February 1997, page 35

Other books by the same author:
Timeless Warrior, 1996
Song of the Warrior, 1995
Secrets of the Heart, 1994
Nevada Dawn, 1993
Sioux Slave, 1992

Other books you might like:
Madeline Baker, *Lacey's Way*, 1990
Rosanne Bittner, *Sioux Splendor*, 1990
Genell Dellin, *Cherokee Nights*, 1991
Janis Reams Hudson, *Warrior's Song*, 1997
Nan Ryan, *Written in the Stars*, 1993

316

PAULA TANNER GIRARD
JUDITH LANSDOWNE, Co-Author
CAROL QUINTO, Co-Author

A Valentine Bouquet
(New York: Zebra, 1997)

Story type: Anthology; Holiday Themes
Time period(s): 1810s
Locale(s): England

Summary: This lively trio of Regency novellas features strong heroines with minds of their own and focuses on the various Valentine's Day traditions popular during the British Regency period. Included are ''Cupid's Legacy'' by Paula Tanner Girard, ''The Valentine Victorious'' by Judith Lansdowne, and ''The Valentine's Day Husband'' by Carol Quinto.

Where it's reviewed:
Library Journal, February 15, 1997, page 126

Other books you might like:
Mary Balogh, *A Regency Valentine*, 1991
    Anthology
Donna Bell, *The Valentine's Day Ball*, 1991
Karen Harbaugh, *Cupid's Darts*, 1998
Karen Harbaugh, *Cupid's Mistake*, 1996

317

JANE GOODGEAR

Memories of You
(New York: Topaz, 1997)

Story type: Time Travel

Major character(s): Claire Dumont, Time Traveller, Military Personnel (helicopter pilot); Coleman Brennan, Military Personnel, Time Traveller; Nicholas Brooks, Military Personnel (U.S. Army major)
Time period(s): 1990s; 1860s (1865)
Locale(s): United States (With the Union Army)

Summary: While in Korea, Lt. Claire Dumont and Capt. Coleman Brennan end up unconscious and injured in a hospital after a helicopter crash. Clair wakes up during the Civil War and is aided by Major Nicholas Brooks, whom she knew before, and Coleman Brennan. She keeps her time-travel a secret, but both are haunted by the war and begin to fall in love. Nobly, he marries her and sends her off to his sister—even though he is engaged. Their love for each other grows, though Claire, knowing the outcome of the war, is increasingly anxious about their future.

Other books you might like:
Sandra Canfield, *The Loving*, 1992
Vivian Knight-Jenkins, *Passion's Timeless Hour*, 1992
    More Civil War Time Travel
Judith O'Brien, *Ashton's Bride*, 1995
Maura Seger, *Perchance to Dream*, 1989
    The South Wins the War

318

JO GOODMAN

My Steadfast Heart
(New York: Zebra, 1997)

Story type: Historical/Victorian
Major character(s): Mercedes Leyden, Noblewoman (niece of an earl); Colin Thorne, Orphan, Sea Captain
Time period(s): 1840s (1841)
Locale(s): England

Summary: As result of a challenge from the Earl of Weybourne, Captain Colin Thorne is physically accosted by the earl's niece, Mercedes Leyden, and later accused of murdering the now missing earl. The stage is set for a lively brew of mystery, romance, and vengeance that will not disappoint. A sensual tale of adventure and intrigue.

Where it's reviewed:
Romantic Times, March 1997, page 36

Other books by the same author:
Always in My Dreams, 1995
Forever in My Heart, 1994
Rogue's Mistress, 1992
Wild Sweet Ecstasy, 1992

Other books you might like:
Catherine Archer, *Lady Thorn*, 1997
Catherine Coulter, *Night Shadow*, 1989
    Fast-paced
Suzannah Davis, *The Master's Bride*, 1993
Johanna Lindsey, *The Magic of You*, 1993

319

HEATHER GRAHAM

Rebel

(New York: Topaz, 1997)

Story type: Historical/American Civil War
Major character(s): Alana MacKenzie, Spy (Confederate); Ian MacKenzie, Military Personnel (Union officer)
Time period(s): 1860s
Locale(s): Florida; Washington, District of Columbia

Summary: Union officer Ian MacKenzie captures the infamous Confederate spy known as ''The Moccasin'' and is not at all surprised to learn that it is his intrepid wife, Alana. After all, compromised and forced to marry before the war started, Alana has never shared Ian's way of life, and she has never betrayed her homeland—and never will. Their battles are as intense as the war they fight and their love and loyalty to each other and their separate causes are sources of pain and difficult decisions for them both.

Where it's reviewed:
Romantic Times, March 1997, page 44

Other books by the same author:
Captive, 1996
A Magical Christmas, 1996
And One Rose West, 1994
Runaway, 1994

Other books you might like:
Micki Brown, *Once a Rebel*, 1992
Venita Hilton, *Sapphire*, 1993
Margaret Mitchell, *Gone with the Wind*, 1936
Lois Wolfe, *The Schemers*, 1991
Kathleen Woodiwiss, *Ashes in the Wind*, 1979

320

ELIZABETH GRAYSON

So Wide the Sky

(New York: Avon, 1997)

Story type: Historical/American West
Major character(s): Cassandra ''Cassie'' Morgan, Captive (former prisoner of Kiowas); Lone Hunter Jalbert, Scout (army), Indian (part Arikawa)
Time period(s): 1860s (1867)
Locale(s): Dakota Territory, West

Summary: A prisoner of the Kiowa for nine years, Cassandra Morgan is traded to the army and finds that the captain is none other than Drew Reynolds, her childhood sweetheart. Honor bound, Drew marries her, but he can't forget his deep hatred for the Indians and his obsession, with Cassie's missing years. Scorned by the local townspeople and faced with her husbands suspicions and anger, Cassie is befriended by an outcast half-breed army scout, and eventually they find happiness together. Emotional, rather violent, realistic, and fast-paced.

Where it's reviewed:
Affaire de Coeur, March 1997, page 29
Romantic Times, March 1997, page 49

Other books by the same author:
A Place Called Home, 1995
Bride of the Wilderness, 1995

Other books you might like:
Catherine Anderson, *Cheyenne Amber*, 1994
    Similar theme
Rosanne Bittner, *Tame the Wild Wind*, 1996
Deborah Camp, *Lady Legend*, 1992
Elaine Crawford, *Love So Wild*, 1994
    Similar theme/realistic
Penelope Williamson, *Heart of the West*, 1995

321

KAREN HARBAUGH

Cupid's Mistake

(New York: Signet, 1996)

Story type: Regency; Historical/Fantasy
Major character(s): Cassandra Hathaway, Debutante; Marquess of Blythland, Nobleman; Eros, Mythical Creature (Cupid)
Time period(s): 1810s
Locale(s): England

Summary: When Eros' arrow accidentally finds the wrong target, he is hardpressed to make sure that the right people end up together. However, the two people in question aren't cooperating! Between the Marquess of Blythland's resistance and Cassandra's blunt intelligence things don't look hopeful. Nevertheless, true love does triumph—eventually. First in a series. Lively and humorous.

Where it's reviewed:
Library Journal, November 15, 1996, page 48

Other books by the same author:
Cupid's Darts, 1998
The Reluctant Cavalier, 1996
The Devil's Bargain, 1995
The Vampire Viscount, 1995

Other books you might like:
Donna Bell, *The Valentine's Day Ball*, 1991
Julie Caille, *A Valentine's Day Fancy*, 1992
Paula Tanner Girard, *A Valentine Bouquet*, 1997
    Anthology
Emily Hendrickson, *Elizabeth's Rake*, 1993

322

LORRAINE HEATH

Texas Destiny

(New York: Topaz, 1997)

Story type: Historical/American West
Major character(s): Amelia Carson, Mail Order Bride; Houston Leigh, Cowboy, Handicapped (scarred)
Time period(s): 1870s (1876)
Locale(s): Texas

Summary: When rancher Dallas Leigh breaks a leg and can't meet his mail-order bride at the train, he sends his war-

wounded brother, Houston, instead—with unexpected and far-reaching results. This poignant, emotionally wrenching story realistically depicts the physical and emotional effects of the Civil War on some of the people who lived through it. Well-done characterizations.

Where it's reviewed:
Library Journal, May 15, 1997, page 66

Other books by the same author:
Always to Remember, 1996

Other books you might like:
Catherine Anderson, *Keegan's Lady*, 1996
Catherine Anderson, *Simply Love*, 1997
Stephanie Mittman, *The Courtship*, 1998
LaVyrle Spencer, *The Endearment*, 1982
LaVyrle Spencer, *The Fulfillment*, 1979

323

SHIRL HENKE

Deep as the Rivers

(New York: St. Martin's, 1997)

Story type: Historical/American West
Major character(s): Olivia St. Etienne, Orphan; Samuel Sheridan Shelby, Military Personnel (colonel), Spy
Time period(s): 19th century (early)
Locale(s): Midwest; New Orleans, Louisiana

Summary: When Colonel Samuel Shelby tells his wife that he is divorcing her, he quickly becomes the object of a deadly pursuit as her step-brother and lover set off after him. He is saved by the fiery Olivia St. Etienne, who is escaping from an uncle who intends to sell her in marriage. Despite Shelby's initial resistance, they end up together—eventually. Old secrets, complex relationships, and fast-paced action fill this adventurous historical.

Where it's reviewed:
Affaire de Coeur, March 1997, page 19
Romantic Times, March 1997, page 36

Other books by the same author:
Bouquet, 1994
A Fire in the Blood, 1994
Terms of Love, 1992
The Dragon and the Jewel, 1991
Night Wind's Woman, 1990

Other books you might like:
Caroline Bourne, *Love's Perfect Dream*, 1993
Lisa Kleypas, *Only in Your Arms*, 1992
    similar setting
Deborah Martin, *Creole Nights*, 1992
Kat Martin, *Creole Fires*, 1992
Alexandra Ripley, *New Orleans Legacy*, 1987

324

VIRGINIA HENLEY

Dream Lover

(New York: Delacorte, 1997)

Story type: Historical/Georgian
Major character(s): Emerald Montague, Gentlewoman; Sean O'Toole, Renegade (Irish), Nobleman (Earl of Kildare)
Time period(s): 1790s (1790)
Locale(s): England; Ireland

Summary: Sheltered Emerald Montague's accidental contact with Irish Sean O'Toole leaves them both with dream-like memories that won't die. But now, avenging his brother's death and his own imprisonment, Sean sets out to destroy the cruel Englishman who is Emerald's father. Emerald's Irish mother longs to go home to Ireland but can only do so when she is banished by the father. When he forces Emerald and her brother to go to London, life seems over for them both. An abduction, however, changes a few things and, eventually, Sean and Emerald's love for Ireland and each other wins out. Highly sensual and fast-paced.

Where it's reviewed:
Romantic Times, February 1997, page 35

Other books by the same author:
Seduced, 1994
The Dragon and the Jewel, 1991
The Pirate and the Pagan, 1990
The Falcon and the Flower, 1989

Other books you might like:
Jo Beverley, *My Lady Notorious*, 1993
    More Georgian-style adventure
Susan Johnson, *Outlaw*, 1993
    Fast-paced, sizzling sensuality
Brenda Joyce, *The Game*, 1995
    Similar sensuality levels
Bertrice Small, *Skye O'Malley*, 1980

325

CANDICE HERN

A Garden Folly

(New York: Signet Regency, 1997)

Story type: Regency
Major character(s): Catherine Forsythe, Debutante (impoverished), Fortune Hunter; Stephen Archibald, Nobleman (Duke of Carlisle), Gardener
Time period(s): 1810s
Locale(s): England

Summary: Faced with ongoing poverty, Catherine Forsythe knows that either she or her beautiful sister Susannah must marry money; so when they end up at the country estate of the somewhat reclusive duke of Carlisle for his mother's annual summer houseparty, it seems like the perfect opportunity to find suitable husbands. But money and love don't always come together, and when Susannah ends up in love with a poor steward and Catherine falls for the gardener, it takes some effort on the part of their friends, and a fresh perpsective

on the real meaning of security, to set everything to rights. Well written and peopled with memorable characters.

Where it's reviewed:
Library Journal, November 1996, page 48

Other books by the same author:
An Affair of Honor, 1996
A Change of Heart, 1995
A Proper Companion, 1995

Other books you might like:
Anne Barbour, *Lord Glenraven's Return*, 1994
Gail Eastwood, *The Captain's Dilemma*, 1995
Gail Eastwood, *An Unlikely Hero*, 1996
Carla Kelly, *The Lady's Companion*, 1996
    more serious
Evelyn Richardson, *The Reluctant Heiress*, 1996

326
NIKKI HOLIDAY

Heaven Loves a Hero
(New York: Avon, 1997)

Story type: Contemporary/Fantasy
Major character(s): Mia Tortelli, Producer; Quentin Grandby, Director
Time period(s): 1990s
Locale(s): California

Summary: Newly married Hollywood film partners Mia and Quentin are once again conscripted by their heavenly guardian, Mr. G., into taking on a new matchmaking assignment: helping artist Amity Jones find the right man and put her life together. Upbeat, fast-paced, and peopled with a superabundance of characters, this lively romance is funny, brash, and occasionally confusing.

Where it's reviewed:
Library Journal, August 1997, page 68

Other books by the same author:
Heaven Knows Best, 1997
Heaven Comes Home, 1996

Other books you might like:
Barbara Bretton, *Maybe This Time*, 1995
    Not paranormal
Lynn Kerstan, *Gwen's Christmas Ghost*, 1995
    Alicia Rasley, co-author
Susan Elizabeth Phillips, *Nobody's Baby but Mine*, 1997
    Not paranormal
Emilie Richards, *Twice upon a Time*, 1997

327
HELEN HOLLICK

Pendragon's Banner
(New York: St. Martin's, 1996)

Story type: Historical/Medieval; Historical/Mainstream
Major character(s): Arthur, Royalty; Gwenhwyfar, Royalty
Time period(s): Indeterminate Past
Locale(s): England

Summary: King Arthur and Queen Gwenhwyfar remain at war with invaders and those who would try to usurp his position. But his first wife, the Saxon Winifred, and Morgause, his father's mistress, manage to keep them from establishing a home and a kingdom. Hardship and loss plague them and they wander, rootless, until Arthur finds his home at Cadbury and they begin to build the legacy that eventually becomes the legend. Another retelling of the Arthurian legend.

Where it's reviewed:
Affaire de Coeur, March 1997, page 38
Romantic Times, February 1997, page 43

Other books you might like:
Alice Borchardt, *Beguiled*, 1996
Alice Borchardt, *Devoted*, 1995
Marion Zimmer Bradley, *The Mists of Avalon*, 1988
Ellen Jones, *The Fatal Crown*, 1991
Sharon Kay Pennman, *Here Be Dragons*, 1985

328
DEE HOLMES

Jonathan's Wife
(New York: Avon, 1996)

Story type: Contemporary
Major character(s): Sarah Brennan, Businesswoman (art dealer); Jonathan Brennan, Handicapped (paralyzed former athlete)
Time period(s): 1990s

Summary: Sarah faces untenable choices when her athletic husband is paralyzed in a tragic accident. A sensual, realistic and emotional struggle between two people caught in a difficult situation.

Where it's reviewed:
Affaire de Coeur, April 1996, page 30
Romantic Times, April 1996, page 84

Other books by the same author:
When Nick Returns, 1997
Dillon's Reckoning, 1997

Other books you might like:
Barbara Bickmore, *Beyond the Promise*, 1997
Lindsay Chase, *The Vow*, 1992
Rebecca Forster, *Seasons*, 1996
LaVyrle Spencer, *Bitter Sweet*, 1990
LaVyrle Spencer, *The Fulfillment*, 1979

329
KAY HOOPER

Finding Laura
(New York: Bantam, 1997)

Story type: Contemporary; Gothic
Major character(s): Laura Sutherland, Artist; Daniel Kilbourne, Businessman
Time period(s): 1990s
Locale(s): Atlanta, Georgia

Romance

Summary: Refusing to sell her newly purchased antique mirror to one of the sons of the wealthy Kilbourne family that had formerly owned the mirror, artist Laura Sutherland is shocked to suddenly find herself a suspect in his murder. But when her quest for the truth about both mirror and murder leads her to the Kilbourne's isolated estate, she finds some surprising answers and an unexpected love. Gothic and paranormal elements.

Other books by the same author:
After Caroline, 1996
Amanda, 1995
The Haunting of Josie, 1994
The Trouble With Jared, 1993
The Wizard of Seattle, 1993

Other books you might like:
Catherine Coulter, *The Cove*, 1996
Barbara Erskine, *House of Echoes*, 1996
Linda Howard, *Dream Man*, 1995
Dinah McCall, *Chase the Moon*, 1997

330
LINDA HOWARD
Son of the Morning
(New York: Pocket, 1997)

Story type: Time Travel
Major character(s): Grace St. John, Scholar (ancient manuscripts); Black Niall, Warrior (former Knight Templar)
Time period(s): 1990s; 14th century (1309)
Locale(s): Creag Dhu, Scotland

Summary: When Grace St. John encounters a clue to a lost Celtic treasure, reputed to belong to the Knights Templars, she uses an ancient ritual and returns to 14th-century Scotland in search of the legendary Knight Templar Black Niall. Together they defy ruthless killers, bury ancient hatreds and secrets, and find peace and love in the process. Dark, sensual, and fast-paced.

Where it's reviewed:
Romantic Times, March 1998, page 84

Other books by the same author:
Shades of Twilight, 1996
After the Night, 1995
Dream Man, 1994
Heart of Fire, 1993

Other books you might like:
Laura Gilmour Bennett, *By All That's Sacred*, 1991
Justine Dare, *Fire Hawk*, 1997
Diana Gabaldon, *Outlander*, 1991
Johanna Lindsey, *Until Forever*, 1995

331
JANIS REAMS HUDSON
Warrior's Song
(New York: Zebra, 1997)

Story type: Historical/American West

Major character(s): Brianna Flanigan, Rancher; Wolf, Indian (half-breed), Drifter
Time period(s): 19th century
Locale(s): Colorado

Summary: Brianna Flanigan's ranch is a bit too much for her and her siblings to manage, so she welcomes the help of Wolf, a half-breed who is searching for his parents who sold him. Suspicious and angry, he is eventually won over by Brianna's optimism and warmth, and he stays, little realizing the battle he will end up fighting to save her ranch from a greedy neighbor. Conflicting values and prejudices are part of this fast-paced sensual romance.

Where it's reviewed:
Romantic Times, March 1997, page 36

Other books by the same author:
Angel on a Harley, 1995
Apache Heartsong, 1995
Apache Legacy, 1994
Apache Temptation, 1993
Apache Magic, 1991

Other books you might like:
Madeline Baker, *Cheyenne Surrender*, 1994
Georgina Gentry, *Warrior's Prize*, 1997
Johanna Lindsey, *Angel*, 1992
Patricia Potter, *Renegade*, 1993

332
JILLIAN HUNTER
Fairy Tale
(New York: Pocket, 1997)

Story type: Historical/Georgian
Major character(s): Marsali Hay, Young Woman; Duncan "Black Duncan" MacElgin, Laird
Time period(s): 18th century (1723)
Locale(s): Highlands, Scotland

Summary: Returning to his castle in the Scottish Highlands after a 15-year absence, Duncan MacElgin is stunned to be attacked by his own people as a Sassenach. And he is more shocked that the leader of the attack is a woman—a lovely, strong-willed, slightly magical woman, who is determined that no harm will come to her clan. Humorous, fast-paced, sweet, and filled with appealing characters.

Where it's reviewed:
Romantic Times, April 1997, page 35

Other books by the same author:
A Deeper Magic, 1994
Tiger Dance, 1991

Other books you might like:
Justine Dare, *Fire Hawk*, 1997
Susan King, *The Raven's Moon*, 1997
    dark and serious
Karyn Monk, *Once a Warrior*, 1997
Susan Wiggs, *Miranda*, 1996

333

JUDITH IVORY
JUDY CUEVAS, Co-Author

Beast

(New York: Avon, 1997)

Story type: Historical/Edwardian
Major character(s): Louise Vandermeer, Heiress; Charles Harcourt, Royalty (Prince d'Harcourt), Handicapped (disfigured)
Time period(s): 1900s (1902)
Locale(s): At Sea; France

Summary: In search of adventure, lovely, wealthy Louise Vandermeer agrees to go to Europe and marry Charles Harcourt, a man she has never met, and who, although a prince, is said to be ugly in the extreme. When a mixup in the mail results in Louise and Charles being on the same ship, Charles decides to play a cruel trick on his intended; but it is his heart that is caught in a trap of his own making. Classic "Beauty and the Beast" elements.

Other books you might like:
Christina Dodd, *Move Heaven and Earth*, 1995
    Difficult, wounded hero
Christina Dodd, *Priceless*, 1992
    Reverse Beauty and Beast
Mary Jo Putney, *Thunder and Roses*, 1993
Amanda Quick, *Ravished*, 1992
    Scarred hero

334

MIRANDA JARRETT

The Secrets of Catie Hazard

(Toronto: Harlequin, 1997)

Story type: Historical/Colonial America
Major character(s): Catie Willman Hazard, Servant (tavern wench), Widow(er); Anthony Sparhawk, Military Personnel (major)
Time period(s): 1760s (1767); 1770s (1776)
Locale(s): Newport, Rhode Island, American Colonies

Summary: Pregnant and alone, young Catie Willman has no choice but to marry an innkeeper in order to assure her future and that of her child. However, when the father of her child returns eight years later as a British officer, Catie is faced with conflicting emotions and divided political loyalties. This story provides both sensitive treatment of some serious social issues and well done historical detail.

Where it's reviewed:
Library Journal, May 15, 1997, page 66

Other books by the same author:
Sparhawk's Angel, 1996
Mariah's Prize, 1994

Other books you might like:
Sylvia Halliday, *The Ring*, 1996
Kasey Michaels, *The Homecoming*, 1996
Sue Rich, *Shadowed Vows*, 1992

Penelope Williamson, *A Wild Yearning*, 1990

335

IRIS JOHANSEN

Long After Midnight

(New York: Bantam, 1997)

Story type: Contemporary; Romantic Suspense
Major character(s): Kate Denby, Doctor, Researcher; Seth Drakin, Mercenary
Time period(s): 1990s
Locale(s): Dandridge, Oklahoma

Summary: Successful and content, research scientist Kate Denby isn't interested in helping develop a miracle drug. But when her friend Noah seems to be murdered so that he cannot market it, she becomes a possible victim of rival pharmaceutical "hit men." Her friend, recovering from the bombing which nearly killed him, calls on Seth Drakin, a highly skilled mercenary, to protect Kate, Noah, her son, and her family. Suspense, action, and romance.

Where it's reviewed:
Affaire de Coeur, March 1997, page 24
Romantic Times, March 1997, page 83

Other books by the same author:
Lion's Bride, 1996
The Ugly Duckling, 1996
Dark Rider, 1995
The Beloved Scoundrel, 1994
Midnight Warrior, 1994

Other books you might like:
Tami Hoag, *Still Waters*, 1992
Linda Howard, *After the Night*, 1995
Karen Robards, *Heartbreaker*, 1997
Karen Robards, *Walking After Midnight*, 1995
    more humorous than some
Anne Stuart, *Moon-Rise*, 1996
    Darker

336

SUSAN JOHNSON

Taboo

(New York: Bantam, 1997)

Story type: Historical/Georgian
Major character(s): Teo Korsakova, Noblewoman (countess); Andre Duras, Military Personnel (general)
Time period(s): 18th century (1799)
Locale(s): Europe

Summary: Teo Korsakova, countess and wife of an infamous Russian general, and French General Andre Duras find love and intense passion amid the violence of war. Johnson is noted for her use of creative, graphic sex, and this erotic story is no exception. Very loosely based on events in the life of Andre Massena.

Where it's reviewed:
Romantic Times, December 1997, page 40

Other books by the same author:
Brazen, 1995
Pure Sin, 1994
Outlaw, 1993
Sinful, 1992
Forbidden, 1991

Other books you might like:
Brenda Joyce, *Splendor*, 1997
Mary Lide, *Isobelle*, 1988
Bertrice Small, *Hellion*, 1996
Kathleen Woodiwiss, *Forever in Your Embrace*, 1992

337

JOAN JOHNSTON

After the Kiss
(New York: Dell, 1997)

Story type: Historical/Regency
Major character(s): Eliza Sherringham, Governess; Marcus Wharton, Nobleman, Handicapped (scarred)
Time period(s): 1800s
Locale(s): London, England

Summary: Society rebel Eliza Sherringham and rogue Marcus Wharton have been thrown together, but all Eliza can think of is how to snare her cousin and Marcus' best friend. After Eliza and Marcus are found in a compromising situation, Eliza's cousin nobly offers for her, even though he doesn't love her. When he is killed at Waterloo and Marcus is horribly scarred, Eliza wants to help, but Marcus turns recluse and refuses all help. However, his adoring nieces take Eliza into their confidence and they plan ways to make Marcus come out. His growing affection for Eliza and her untiring ministering to him slowly have an effect—but it still takes a few tricks to make everything work out. Suspenseful and full of humor and pathos.

Where it's reviewed:
Affaire de Coeur, March 1997, page 17
Romantic Times, March 1997, page 42

Other books by the same author:
Captive, 1996
I Promise, 1996
The Temporary Groom, 1996
Maverick Heart, 1995
The Inheritance, 1994

Other books you might like:
Susan Carroll, *The Painted Veil*, 1995
Christina Dodd, *Move Heaven and Earth*, 1995
   Darker
Elisabeth Fairchild, *The Silent Suitor*, 1994
   Regency
Mary Jo Putney, *Thunder and Roses*, 1993
Amanda Quick, *Ravished*, 1992

338

JOAN JOHNSTON

Captive
(New York: Dell, 1996)

Story type: Historical/Regency
Major character(s): Lady Charlotte Edgerton, Noblewoman (from America), Ward; Lionel Morgan, Nobleman (Earl of Denbigh), Guardian
Time period(s): 1810s
Locale(s): England

Summary: Refusing to be either saddened by his bride-to-be's suicide or jilted again, Lionel Morgan, Earl of Denbigh, decides against commitment and in favor of mistresses. However, his rough-and-tumble young ward, fresh from America, has an agenda of her own and it doesn't include either becoming a proper English "lady" or being married off to anyone who will have her, just because her guardian wishes it. She is young, carefree, appallingly American, and eventually succeeds in both charming and captivating her reluctant guardian.

Where it's reviewed:
Affaire de Coeur, May 1996, page 18
Rendezvous, March 1996, page 18
Romantic Times, May 1996, page 40

Other books by the same author:
The Disobedient Bride, 1995
Maverick Heart, 1995
The Cowboy Takes a Wife, 1994
The Headstrong Bride, 1994
The Inheritance, 1994

Other books you might like:
Catherine Coulter, *The Valentine Legacy*, 1995
Jane Feather, *Violet*, 1995
Lynn Kerstan, *Raven's Bride*, 1996
Betina Krahn, *The Last Bachelor*, 1994
Amanda Quick, *Mistress*, 1994

339

JILL JONES

The Scottish Rose
(New York: St. Martin's, 1997)

Story type: Time Travel
Major character(s): Taylor Kincaid, Producer (television); Duncan Fraser, Government Official (harbormaster)
Time period(s): 1990s; 17th century (1652)
Locale(s): Scotland

Summary: Taylor Kincaid's TV show about myths take her to Scotland and a legendary watery gate where men have disappeared for years. Harbormaster Duncan Fraser warns her of the danger, but when she falls overboard, he rescues her and they both end up in 17th-century Scotland. Cromwell's bands, Taylor's "witchcraft" qualifications, and their rescue of an outcast orphan put them in danger wherever they go. Swiftly paced and engrossing.

Where it's reviewed:
Affaire de Coeur, February 1997, page 38
Romantic Times, February 1997, page 86

Other books you might like:
Jane Feather, *Reckless Angel*, 1989
Ruth Langan, *Deception*, 1993
    Similar period
Jean Plaidy, *The Pleasures of Love*, 1992
    Mainstream/similar period
Susan Wiggs, *The Mist and the Magic*, 1993

340
NICOLE JORDAN

The Lover
(New York: Avon, 1997)

Story type: Historical/Georgian
Major character(s): Sabrina Duncan, Spinster; Niall McLaren, Laird
Time period(s): 1730s (1739)
Locale(s): Edinburgh, Scotland

Summary: Required to wed Niall McLaren when he becomes clan leader, quiet, retiring Sabrina Duncan is resigned, even though neither one is happy with the match. Surprisingly, Sabrina is neither as quiet nor as plain as Niall had first thought, and she ends up giving Niall more trouble than he had expected. But sparks have a way of igniting fires, and before long, the pair is in love and as well-matched as their people could wish.

Where it's reviewed:
Affaire de Coeur, March 1997, page 24
Romantic Times, March 1997, page 38

Other books by the same author:
The Savage, 1994

Other books you might like:
Jo Beverley, *Tempting Fortune*, 1995
Christina Dodd, *A Well-Favored Gentleman*, 1998
Jane Feather, *Velvet*, 1994
Amanda Scott, *Border Bride*, 1990

341
DARA JOY

Rejar
(New York: Leisure, 1997)

Story type: Futuristic; Time Travel
Major character(s): Lilac DeVere, Debutante, Gentlewoman; Rejar, Time Traveller, Spirit (shapechanger)
Time period(s): 1810s (1811)
Locale(s): England

Summary: Rejar, a familiar, enjoys the sensual freedom and shapechanging abilities that his species gives to him, but falling in love with a human presents a few problems—especially when the human, the lovely Lilac DeVere, thinks he is a black cat in 1811 Regency London. Mysterious, mystical, and sensual.

Where it's reviewed:
Romantic Times, February 1997, page 83

Other books by the same author:
High Energy, 1996
Knight of a Trillion Stars, 1995

Other books you might like:
Karen Harbaugh, *The Vampire Viscount*, 1995
Sandra Heath, *Magic at Midnight*, 1995
Lynn Kerstan, *Gwen's Christmas Ghost*, 1995
    Alicia Rasley, co-author
Susan Krinard, *Bewitched*, 1997
    Anthology—especially "Saving Sirena" by Susan Krinard

342
BRENDA JOYCE

Captive
(New York: Avon, 1996)

Story type: Time Travel
Major character(s): Alexandra Thornton, Historian, Time Traveller; Xavier Blackwell, Sea Captain, Captive
Time period(s): 1990s; 1800s (1802-1804)
Locale(s): Tripoli, Africa (Barbary Coast)

Summary: Fascinated with the history of Xavier Blackwell, Alexandra travels to Tripoli to find out more about him. Suddenly, she is tossed back in time and ends up as the wife to the Bashaw leader's son. Hoping to change history and prevent Blackwell's death, she converts to Islam. However, when Blackwell arrives, things don't go as she had planned. Nevertheless, Alex doesn't give up her plans to make new lives for them both. By using both times to her advantage, she saves their lives and their love.

Where it's reviewed:
Affaire de Coeur, May 1996, page 18
Rendezvous, March 1996, page 28
Romantic Times, May 1996, page 88

Other books by the same author:
Beyond Scandal, 1995
Promise of the Rose, 1993
Secrets, 1993
Dark Fires, 1991
The Fires of Paradise, 1991

Other books you might like:
Diana Gabaldon, *Outlander*, 1991
    Classic Time travel
Christina Skye, *The Black Rose*, 1991
    Sweet-Savage elements/Regency setting
Christina Skye, *Come the Dawn*, 1995
Bertrice Small, *Wild Jasmine*, 1992
    Sweet-Savage elements/Georgian Setting

Romance

343

BRENDA JOYCE

Splendor

(New York: St. Martin, 1997)

Story type: Historical/Regency
Major character(s): Carolyn Browne, Imposter (political cartoonist), Gentlewoman (bookseller's daughter); Nicholas Sverayov, Royalty (Russian prince), Diplomat
Time period(s): 1810s (1812)
Locale(s): London, England; Russia

Summary: Known to the world as the daughter of a modest bookseller, Carolyn Browne is secretly the notorious political cartoonist, Charles Copperville, and she gathers her information in the most dangerous way imaginable—by dressing as a boy and mingling with the ton. However, when she chooses Russian diplomat Nicholas Sverayov as her target, the tables are turned, and Carolyn finds her identity uncovered and herself involved in a treacherous game of deception and danger. Politics, intrigue and fast-paced, highly sensual action are highlights of this story that sweeps from Regency England to Tsarist Russia.

Where it's reviewed:
Romantic Times, December 1997, page 39

Other books by the same author:
Beyond Scandal, 1995
The Game, 1995
After Innocence, 1994
Secrets, 1993
Scandalous Love, 1992

Other books you might like:
Susan Johnson, *Golden Paradise*, 1990
Susan Johnson, *Taboo*, 1997
Anne Stuart, *A Rose at Midnight*, 1993
Kathleen Woodiwiss, *Forever in Your Embrace*, 1992

344

CARLA KELLY

With This Ring

(New York: Signet, 1997)

Story type: Regency
Major character(s): Lydia Perkins, Gentlewoman; Samuel Reed, Military Personnel (major), Nobleman (earl)
Time period(s): 1810s (1814)
Locale(s): London, England; Northumberland, England

Summary: Abused and misused by her mother and spoiled younger sister, caring but unconventional and outspoken Lydia Perkins finds her mission and sense of purpose among the war-wounded soldiers just home from Toulouse. She also finds a charming nobleman major who can't return to his Northumberland home without a wife. After being beaten and practically disowned by her mother when her behavior ruins her sister's matrimonial chances with the superficial ton, Lydia marries him and heads north, and her life takes on a whole new, and vastly different, dimension. Compelling, funny, and well-written.

Where it's reviewed:
Library Journal, August 1997, page 70

Other books by the same author:
The Lady's Companion, 1996
Reforming Lord Ragsdale, 1995
Mrs. Drew Plays Her Hand, 1994
Miss Billings Treads the Boards, 1993
Miss Grimsley's Oxford Career, 1992

Other books you might like:
Mary Balogh, *Promise of Spring*, 1990
Elisabeth Fairchild, *The Rakehell's Reform*, 1997
Mary Jo Putney, *The Rake and the Reformer*, 1987
Evelyn Richardson, *My Wayward Lady*, 1997
    Another activist heroine

345

LYNN KERSTAN

Francesca's Rake

(New York: Fawcett, 1997)

Story type: Regency
Major character(s): Francesca Childe, Noblewoman; Galen Pender, Nobleman (Viscount Clayburn), Rake
Time period(s): 1810s
Locale(s): England

Summary: Angered at his father's control of his life, dictating even the woman he should wed, Viscount Clayburn sets out to find his own brand of "acceptable" bride and ends up falling in love with her in the process. A bluestocking with a past and a rake with a reputation pair up nicely in this well-written romance that handles both language and sexual tension admirably.

Where it's reviewed:
Library Journal, May 15, 1997, page 68

Other books by the same author:
Christmas Ghost, 1995 (Alicia Rasley, co-author)

Other books you might like:
Carla Kelly, *Reforming Lord Ragsdale*, 1995
Margaret Moore, *The Dark Duke*, 1997
    Victorian Setting
Mary Jo Putney, *One Perfect Rose*, 1997
    Sensual/darker/well-written
Mary Jo Putney, *The Rake and the Reformer*, 1997

346

LYNN KERSTAN

Raven's Bride

(New York: Harper, 1996)

Story type: Historical/Regency
Major character(s): Glenys Shea, Captive, Thief; Ashton Cordell, Nobleman (Lord Ravensby), Recluse
Time period(s): 1820s (1822)
Locale(s): England

Summary: When Glenys Shea and her father and brother attempt to rob Ashton Cordell so they can eat, things don't go as

they had planned and her father is accidentally killed by Ash. Feeling responsible, Ash takes the two young people home, intending to set things to rights and find them a proper home. But the feisty Glenys has decided that Ash is the one who needs some help, and in the process of turning his well-ordered life upside down, she also succeeds in finding the way to his heart. A dash of mystery adds to the fun.

Where it's reviewed:
Rendezvous, March 1996, page 18
Romantic Times, May 1996, page 42

Other books by the same author:
Lady in Blue, 1995
Gwen's Christmas Ghost, 1995 (Alicia Rasley, co-author)
A Spirited Affair, 1993

Other books you might like:
Jane Feather, *Violet*, 1995
Jane Feather, *Virtue*, 1995
Joan Johnston, *Captive*, 1996
Amanda Quick, *Deception*, 1993

347

ANNIE KIMBERLIN
ANN BOURICIUS, Co-Author

Stray Hearts
(New York: Leisure, 1997)

Story type: Contemporary; Americana
Major character(s): Melissa March, Veterinarian; Peter Winthrop, Principal (elementary school)
Time period(s): 1990s
Locale(s): Hartley, Ohio

Summary: When elementary school principal Peter Winthrop accidentally hits a stray sheltie, he ends up not only assisting Melissa March, the local veterinarian, in surgery, but deciding to adopt the dog, as well. The only problem with this is that Angie, his young daughter, is terrified of dogs, and so Peter asks Melissa to help Angie get over her fear—with predictable results. A warm, romantic story filled with delightful animals, a charming child, a well-matched hero and heroine, and a few nicely done unlikable characters. A good example of contemporary Americana.

Other books by the same author:
Lonely Hearts, 1997

Other books you might like:
Victoria Alexander, *Santa Paws*, 1997
    Christmas anthology/matchmaking dogs
Mary Balogh, *The Famous Heroine*, 1996
    Heroine rescue animals/Regency setting
James Herriot, *The Lord God Made Them All*, 1981
    Last in his classic series
Debbie Macomber, *Mrs. Miracle*, 1996
    Contemporary Americana
Barbara Metzger, *A Loyal Companion*, 1993
    Dogs in a Regency Setting

348

SUSAN KING

The Raven's Moon
(New York: Topaz, 1997)

Story type: Historical/Renaissance
Major character(s): Mihairi Macrae, Healer, Outlaw; Rowan Scott, Military Personnel (border officer), Thief (former riever)
Time period(s): 16th century (1588)
Locale(s): The Borderlands, Scotland

Summary: In an effort to save her imprisoned brother from an unjust sentence, healer Mihairi Macrae, dressed as an outlaw, accidentally attacks border guard Rowan Scott. She escapes, but Rowan remembers and is torn by his duty and his concern for the border dwellers and the problems that the cruel rievers cause. Mistaken identity, past history, and the political situation cause problems for the two, but they do find love eventually.

Where it's reviewed:
Romantic Times, February 1997, page 38

Other books by the same author:
The Angel Knight, 1996
The Raven's Wish, 1995
The Black Thorne's Rose, 1994

Other books you might like:
Marsha Canham, *In the Shadow of Midnight*, 1994
Tanya Ann Crosby, *Angel of Fire*, 1992
Katherine Deauville, *Daggers of Gold*, 1993
Iris Johansen, *Midnight Warrior*, 1994

349

SUSAN KIRBY

Prairie Rose
(New York: Avon, 1997)

Story type: Historical/Americana; Inspirational
Major character(s): Libby Watson, Writer (aspiring), Store Owner; Isaac Galloway, Bachelor (reluctant)
Time period(s): 1900s (1904)
Locale(s): Thistle Down, Illinois

Summary: Seventeen-year-old Libby Watson, delighted that she has inherited a small-town general store because of what it could mean for her father and siblings, puts her heart into the effort and ends up achieving her fondest dreams. A Christian inspirational romance that is followed by *As the Lily Grows* and *When Lilacs Bloom*.

Other books by the same author:
When Lilacs Bloom, 1997
As the Lily Grows, 1997

Other books you might like:
Catherine Marshall, *Christy*, 1967
    Classic Inspirational Romance
Catherine Marshall, *Julie*, 1984
    Another classic
Janette Oke, *The Matchmakers*, 1997

Janette Oke, *The Tender Years: A Prairie Legacy*, 1997
Catherine Palmer, *Prairie Rose*, 1997
    First in a series

350

SUSAN KIRBY

When Lilacs Bloom

(New York: Avon, 1997)

Story type: Historical/Americana; Inspirational
Major character(s): Elizabeth "Libby" Watson Galloway, Writer (children's stories); Ike Galloway, Farmer (tenant farmer), Railroad Worker
Time period(s): 1900s; 1910s (1904-1915)
Locale(s): Illinois

Summary: Libby and Ike struggle to make their lives and their marriage work—despite a difficult job situation and no children of their own—in this gentle story of middle America. *Prairie Rose* and *As the Lily Grows* are the first two books in this Christian inspirational trilogy.

Where it's reviewed:
Library Journal, November 15, 1997, page 48

Other books by the same author:
Prairie Rose, 1997
As the Lily Grows, 1997

Other books you might like:
Catherine Marshall, *Christy*, 1967
    Classic Inspirational Romance
Catherine Marshall, *Julie*, 1984
    Inspirational classic
Janette Oke, *Another Homecoming*, 1997
    Classic author
Catherine Palmer, *Prairie Rose*, 1997
    first in series
Francine Rivers, *Redeeming Love*, 1991
    1997 version rewritten for inspirational market

351

MARTHA KIRKLAND

Pratt's Landing

(New York: Jove, 1997)

Story type: Historical/Americana
Series: Our Town
Major character(s): Emma Lawrence, Plantation Owner (pecan grove), Waiter/Waitress; Sam Watson, Lawyer
Time period(s): 1880s (1889)
Locale(s): Pratt's Landing, Alabama

Summary: Forced to appeal to the son of her family's hated enemy to help her save her pecan grove, Emma discovers that attorney Sam Watson isn't at all what she had expected. Reluctantly, she likes what she finds. Humor, warmth, and a dash of mystery combine in this slightly sensual story rife with Americana atmosphere.

Where it's reviewed:
Library Journal, November 15, 1997, page 48

Other books by the same author:
The Gallant Gambler, 1997

Other books you might like:
Lydia Browne, *Snowflake Wishes*, 1997
Candace Camp, *Rosewood*, 1991
Jill Marie Landis, *Last Chance*, 1995
Pamela Morsi, *Courting Miss Hattie*, 1991
Pamela Morsi, *Something Shady*, 1995

352

BETINA KRAHN

The Mermaid

(New York: Bantam, 1997)

Story type: Historical/Victorian
Major character(s): Celeste Ashton, Scientist (marine biologist); Titus Thorne, Professor (ichthyology)
Time period(s): 1880s (1884)
Locale(s): England

Summary: A socially naive, but brilliant, marine scientist is stunned to discover that her groundbreaking, but totally unorthodox, work with dolphins is being questioned by the scientific community at large and hyped by the popular press. The upshot is that renowned Oxford ichthyology professor Titus Thorne comes to Celeste Ashton's seaside home to observe for himself the results of her work. Charming, sensual, and exceptionally well written.

Where it's reviewed:
Library Journal, August 1997, page 68

Other books by the same author:
The Unlikely Angel, 1996
The Perfect Mistress, 1995
The Last Bachelor, 1994
My Warrior's Heart, 1992
Behind Closed Doors, 1991

Other books you might like:
Jo Beverley, *My Lady Notorious*, 1993
    Georgian setting/strong heroine
Candace Camp, *Scandalous*, 1996
    Similar time period
Amanda Quick, *Dangerous*, 1992
    Regency setting/"scholarly" heroine
Amanda Quick, *Ravished*, 1992
    Regency setting/"scholarly" heroine

353

JAYNE ANN KRENTZ

Deep Waters

(New York: Pocket, 1997)

Story type: Contemporary; Romantic Suspense
Major character(s): Charity Truitt, Businesswoman (former CEO), Store Owner (bookstore); Elias Winters, Consultant, Store Owner
Time period(s): 1990s
Locale(s): Whispering Waters Cove, Washington

Summary: Burned out and fleeing from both impending marriage and the pressures of running her family's business, Charity Truitt heads for the emotional shelter of a small sea coast community and a bookstore on a pier called Crazy Otis Landing. However, what she finds is emotional turmoil—and a bit of danger and mystery—when she meets a fellow pier resident, the enigmatic Elias Winters. Lively, funny, sexy, and fast-paced in typical Krentz fashion.

Other books by the same author:
Sharp Edges, 1998
Absolutely, Postively, 1996
Trust Me, 1995
Grand Passion, 1994
Perfect Partners, 1992

Other books you might like:
Sandra Brown, *French Silk*, 1992
Karen Robards, *Hunter's Moon*, 1996
Nora Roberts, *Carnal Innocence*, 1992
 Small town setting/darker
Nora Roberts, *Hidden Riches*, 1994
Tracey Tillis, *Flashpoint*, 1997
 Scandal and secrets

354

SUSAN KRINARD
MAGGIE SHAYNE, Co-Author
LISA HIGDON, Co-Author
AMY ELIZBETH SAUNDERS, Co-Author

Bewitched
(New York: Jove, 1997)

Story type: Anthology; Holiday Themes

Summary: This enchanting quartet of appropriately magical stories focuses on witches and ranges from a zingy contemporary story featuring a spellbound catwitch to an intriguing historical tale that brings an uppity young lord to a cursed castle to meet a lovely local witch. Included are "Saving Sirena" by Susan Krinard, "Everything She Does is Magick" by Maggie Shayne, "To Mend a Spell" by Lisa Higdon, and "A Spell of Mist and Roses" by Amy Elizabeth Saunders.

Other books you might like:
Gayle Buck, *Full Moon Magic*, 1992
 Anthology
Teresa DesJardien, *Bewitched by Love*, 1996
 Regency trilogy
Sandra Heath, *Halloween Magic*, 1996
Maura Seger, *Veil of Secrets*, 1996
Lisa Ann Verge, *The Faery Bride*, 1996
Corel Smith Saxe, *Enchantment*, 1994
Mary Chase Comstock, *A Midsummer's Magic*, 1994
Sandra Heath, *The Halloween Husband*, 1994
Sandra Heath, *Magic at Midnight*, 1995

355

SUSAN KRINARD

Twice a Hero
(New York: Bantam, 1997)

Story type: Time Travel
Major character(s): MacKenzie Sinclair, Time Traveller, Adventurer; Liam O'Shea, Adventurer
Time period(s): 1990s; 1880s (1884)
Locale(s): Tikal, Guatemala; San Francisco, California

Summary: When MacKenzie Sinclair goes to the Guatamalan jungle to return a stolen Mayan artifact in an effort to remove an old family curse, she miraculously ends up back in 1884, facing her adventurer great-great-grandfather's partner, the handsome, rugged, and suspicious Liam O'Shea, and more mystery and danger than she had bargained for. Complex plot, good descriptions and characterizations, and graceful sensuality.

Where it's reviewed:
Library Journal, May 15, 1997, page 69

Other books by the same author:
Prince of Shadows, 1996
Star-Crossed, 1995
Prince of Dreams, 1995
Prince of Wolves, 1994

Other books you might like:
Diana Gabaldon, *Outlander*, 1991
 Classic time travel
Sandra Hill, *The Reluctant Viking*, 1994
 Another intrepid heroine
Lynn Kurland, *A Dance through Time*, 1996
 Another heroine out to rectify the past

356

LYNN KURLAND
CASEY CLAYBOURNE, Co-Author
ELIZABETH BEVARLY, Co-Author
JENNY LYKINS, Co-Author

Christmas Spirits
(New York: Jove, 1997)

Story type: Holiday Themes

Summary: A delightful quartet of Christmas novellas rife with love, humor, and Christmas "spirits." Included are "The Three Wise Ghosts" by Lynn Kurland, "Keeping Faith" by Casey Claybourne, "Only Fifteen Shopping Days Left." by Elizabeth Bevarly, and "The Ghost of Christmas Present" by Jenny Lykins.

Where it's reviewed:
Library Journal, November 15, 1997, page 48

Other books you might like:
Mary Balogh, *A Regency Christmas VII*, 1995
 Anthology/some paranormal elements
Jo Beverley, *The Christmas Angel*, 1992
 Regency Christmas
Linda Cajio, *Mister Christmas*, 1997

Paula Tanner Girard, *A Father for Christmas*, 1996
    Regency Christmas
Lynn Kerstan, *Gwen's Christmas Ghost*, 1995
    co-author Alicia Rasley

357

LYNN KURLAND

This Is All I Ask

(New York: Jove, 1997)

Story type: Historical/Medieval
Major character(s): Gillian of Warewick, Noblewoman, Abuse Victim; Christopher of Blackmour, Warrior (Dragon of Blackmour), Handicapped (blind)
Time period(s): 13th century (1249)
Locale(s): England

Summary: Relieved to be escaping her father's brutality, but terrified by the reputation of the man she is being sent to wed, Gillian of Warewick reluctantly travels to Blackmour, a huge, dour fortress perched high along the northern British coast, and discovers that Christopher, Dragon of Blackmour, is not quite what she had expected. A despairing, noble lord and a strong, caring woman make the best of a difficult situation and discover the healing power of love and surprising happiness in the process. Emotionally involving and romantic.

Where it's reviewed:
Romantic Times, August 1997, page 38

Other books by the same author:
Stardust of Yesterday, 1996
A Dance through Time, 1996

Other books you might like:
Christina Dodd, *Candle in the Window*, 1991
Christina Dodd, *Move Heaven and Earth*, 1995
Jo Ann Ferguson, *Wake Not the Dragon*, 1996
Laura Kinsale, *The Prince of Midnight*, 1990

358

ARNETTE LAMB

True Heart

(New York: Pocket, 1997)

Story type: Historical/Georgian
Series: Clan MacKenzie Trilogy
Major character(s): Virginia MacKenzie, Noblewoman, Slave (kidnap victim); Cameron Cunningham, Fiance(e)
Time period(s): 18th century
Locale(s): American Colonies; Scotland

Summary: When adventurous Virginia MacKenzie is kidnapped while on her way to join her fiance in France, she ends up in the American Colonies, indentured and miserable. Rescue comes, of course, but Cameron finds a very different Virginia from the girl he left behind. Final volume in the Clan MacKenzie Trilogy.

Where it's reviewed:
Library Journal, February 15, 1997

Other books by the same author:
Beguiled, 1996
Maiden of Inverness, 1995
Betrayed, 1995
Chieftain, 1994

Other books you might like:
Kimberly Cates, *Crown of Dreams*, 1993
Diana Gabaldon, *Outlander*, 1991
    Time travel elements/good Scottish detail
Diana Gabaldon, *Voyager*, 1994
    3rd in series
Diana Gabaldon, *Drums of Autumn*, 1997
    Series continues in the American Colonies
Sue Rich, *Shadowed Vows*, 1992

359

JILL MARIE LANDIS

Just Once

(New York: Jove, 1997)

Story type: Historical/Antebellum American South; Historical/American West
Major character(s): Jemma O'Hurley, Heiress, Runaway; Hunter Sinclair Boone, Frontiersman
Time period(s): 1810s (1816)
Locale(s): New Orleans, Louisiana; Kentucky Frontier, Kentucky

Summary: When sheltered Jemma O'Hurley arrives in New Orleans to learn that the Creole aristocrat her mercenary father had arranged for her to marry has been killed in a duel, she knows that her prayers have finally been answered. So she takes her chance at freedom and adventure and runs—straight into trouble and into the life of Hunter Boone. Warm, humorous, and romantic.

Where it's reviewed:
Romantic Times, June 1997, page 36

Other books by the same author:
After All, 1996
Last Chance, 1996
Until Tomorrow, 1994
Past Promises, 1993
Come Spring, 1992

Other books you might like:
Stef Ann Holm, *Forget Me Not*, 1997
Stephanie Mittman, *The Courtship*, 1998
Pamela Morsi, *Runabout*, 1994
LaVyrle Spencer, *The Gamble*, 1987

360

RUTH LANGAN

Jade

(Toronto: Harlequin, 1997)

Story type: Historical/American West
Series: Jewels of the West
Major character(s): Jade Jewel, Madam; Wade Weston, Religious (clergyman), Outlaw

Romance

Time period(s): 1870s
Locale(s): Hanging Tree, Texas; San Francisco, California

Summary: Jade Jewel, daughter of Onyx Jewel and an Asian brothel madam, returns to Texas when her father dies. Hanging Tree, Texas, isn't exactly friendly to Jade's plan to build a Golden Dragon pleasure house there, but the Reverend Wade Weston protects her from the angry townspeople. He continues to play the role of guardian angel and even follows her to San Francisco. Eventually, of course, they both must admit their true feelings for each other and come to terms with the implications. Tender and sensual.

Where it's reviewed:
Affaire de Coeur, February 1997, page 30
Romantic Times, February 1997, page 37

Other books by the same author:
The Highlander, 1994
Deception, 1993

Other books you might like:
Lydia Browne, *Heart Strings*, 1993
Jill Marie Landis, *Last Chance*, 1995
Pamela Morsi, *Wild Oats*, 1993
LaVyrle Spencer, *Forgiving*, 1991

361

EMMA LANGE

The Irish Rake

(New York: Signet, 1996)

Story type: Regency
Major character(s): Gillian Edwards, Accident Victim; Jason Devereaux, Rake, Nobleman (Marquess of Clare)
Time period(s): 1810s
Locale(s): England

Summary: Gillian, infatuated with the infamous Marquess of Clare even though she knows he's out of her league, is stunned to find herself in his bedroom regaining consciousness after an accident. He gives her his devoted attention as she recovers, but she has other obligations and knows she can never belong to Clare. But Clare is attracted, and although he never plans to marry, fate has other, more romantic plans for them both.

Where it's reviewed:
Rendezvous, March 1996, page 26
Romantic Times, May 1996, page 108

Other books by the same author:
A Heart in Paris, 1994
A Second Match, 1993

Other books you might like:
Mary Balogh, *Dancing with Clara*, 1994
Mary Balogh, *The Temporary Wife*, 1997
Anne Barbour, *Kate and the Soldier*, 1993
Jeanne Savery, *Cupid's Challenge*, 1996

362

SUSAN KAY LAW

Heaven in West Texas

(New York: Harper, 1997)

Story type: Historical/American West; Historical/Fantasy
Major character(s): Abigail Grier, Rancher; Joshua West, Angel (guardian)
Time period(s): 18th century
Locale(s): Texas

Summary: Joshua West had lived a life full of adventure and love, and now he was dead—well, sort of. His assignment as a new angel is to see that no harm comes to Abigail Grier, the woman he had once loved but who had not loved him back. Her ailing father, difficult brother, and ranch all badly need an ''angelic'' overseer. Their relationship, of course, is a bit different this time around in this warmly romantic tale.

Other books by the same author:
Home Fires, 1995
Reckless Angel, 1995
Traitorous Hearts, 1994
Journey Home, 1993

Other books you might like:
Kristin Hannah, *Once in Every Life*, 1993
Robin Lee Hatcher, *Promise Me Spring*, 1991
    No paranormal elements
Kathleen Kane, *This Time for Keeps*, 1998
Jill Marie Landis, *Rose*, 1990
    No paranormal elements
Deb Stover, *Almost an Angel*, 1997

363

RACHEL LEE

Caught

(Toronto: Mira, 1997)

Story type: Contemporary; Romantic Suspense
Major character(s): Kate Devane, Journalist (copy editor), Divorced Person; Connor Quinn, Photographer (police)
Time period(s): 1990s
Locale(s): Tampa Bay, Florida

Summary: When Kate Devane is assigned to make police photographer Connor Quinn's reports of a serial killer into readable copy, she has no idea that she is about to become the stalker's next victim and that Connor is the only one who can save her. A wounded, haunted hero finds love and healing in this intense, fast-paced story of intrigue and suspense.

Where it's reviewed:
Romantic Times, November 1997, page 69

Other books by the same author:
Nighthawk, 1997
Destination: Conard County, 1996
A Conard County Reckoning, 1996
A Fateful Choice, 1996

Other books you might like:
Suzanne Forster, *Come Midnight*, 1995

Wendy Haley, *Shadow Whispers*, 1992
Linda Howard, *Dream Man*, 1995
Nora Roberts, *Carnal Innocence*, 1992

364

RACHEL LEE
SUE CIVIL-BROWN, Co-Author

Nighthawk

(New York: Silhouette, 1997)

Story type: Contemporary
Series: Silhouette Intimate Moments
Major character(s): Esther Jackson, Rancher, Artist; Craig Nighthawk, Rancher, Indian
Time period(s): 1990s
Locale(s): Conard County, Wyoming

Summary: A hero falsely accused of child sexual abuse and a physically handicapped heroine abused as a child find each other in rural Conard County in this fascinating story of love and healing that explores child abuse and its effects on its victims in adulthood. An emotionally involving and intense psychological thriller.

Where it's reviewed:
Library Journal, May 15, 1997, page 66
Romantic Times, May 1997, page 91

Other books by the same author:
Cowboy Come Home, 1998
Caught, 1997
Destination: Conard County, 1996
A Conard County Reckoning, 1996
A Fateful Choice, 1996

Other books you might like:
Catherine Anderson, *Coming Up Roses*, 1993
   Historical abuse issues
Kathleen Eagle, *The Last True Cowboy*, 1998
Paula Detmer Riggs, *Daddy by Accident*, 1996
Barbara Samuel, *Dancing Moon*, 1996
Ruth Wind, *The Last Chance Ranch*, 1996

365

ANA LEIGH

The MacKenzies: Luke

(New York: Avon, 1996)

Story type: Historical/American West Coast
Major character(s): Honey Behr, Imposter (pretends to be Abigail Fenton), Mail Order Bride; Luke MacKenzie, Lawman (sheriff)
Time period(s): 1800s (late)
Locale(s): Sacramento, California; Stockton, California

Summary: Needing to get out of town after witnessing a murder, Honey Behr takes the place of Luke MacKenzie's mail-order bride. Luke is surprised by both her beauty and her love for his young son, but he is determined that his feelings won't interfere with the hunt for the murderer of his wife. Although they are both attracted to each other, she is hiding her past and he is detached and preoccupied. Before they can get together, her memories and his revenge must be dealt with. Predictably, the other MacKenzie brothers show up to lend a hand and liven things up. Humor and lively action.

Where it's reviewed:
Affaire de Coeur, May 1996, page 24
Rendezvous, March 1996, page 16
Romantic Times, May 1996, page 37

Other books by the same author:
The MacKenzies: Flint, 1996
Forever, My Love, 1995
The Golden Spike, 1994
Tender Is the Touch, 1994
Angel Hunter, 1992

Other books you might like:
Emily Carmichael, *Outcast*, 1995
Lori Copeland, *The Courtship of Cade Kolby*, 1997
Julie Garwood, *One Pink Rose*, 1997
Teresa Hart, *Hearts Are Wild*, 1993

366

CATHIE LINZ

Husband Needed

(New York: Silhouette, 1997)

Story type: Contemporary
Series: Silhouette Desire
Major character(s): Kayla White, Single Parent, Businesswoman; Jack Elliott, Fire Fighter; Ashley White, Child
Time period(s): 1990s
Locale(s): Chicago, Illinois

Summary: When Kayla White arrives at the home of wounded but recovering firefighter Jack Elliott to tend to his errands, and is mistaken first for a burglar and then for a stripper, she is determined that this will not ruin her chances to get her fledgling company, Errands Unlimited, off the ground. But Jack is less than cooperative, and although things eventually work out both professionally and romantically, it takes a lot of doing, and little help from the family. Light, lively, and funny.

Where it's reviewed:
Library Journal, August 1996, page 68

Other books by the same author:
Too Sexy for Marriage, 1998
Too Stubborn for Marriage, 1998
Abbie and the Cowboy, 1996
Baby Wanted, 1995 (Montana Mavericks series)

Other books you might like:
Carole Buck, *Love Goddesses*, 1996
   Anthology/humorous
Muriel Jensen, *Merry Christmas, Mommy*, 1995
   Christmas theme
Kate Little, *Jingle Bell Baby*, 1996
   Christmas Theme/humorous
Charlotte Maclay, *Accidental Roommates*, 1997
   humorous

367

ELIZABETH LOWELL

Amber Beach

(New York: Avon, 1997)

Story type: Contemporary; Romantic Suspense
Major character(s): Honor Donovan, Businesswoman; Jake Mallory, Guide, Businessman
Time period(s): 1990s
Locale(s): San Juan Islands, Washington

Summary: Long excluded from involvement in the family business, Donovan International, Honor Donovan is frustrated when her father and brothers refuse to investigate the disappearance of both her favorite brother, Kyle, and some stolen amber; so she heads for the San Juan Islands in search of an explanation. But Jake Mallory, business associate of Kyle and now a major suspect, is also looking for answers. When Honor arrives in Seattle in search of a guide, she ends up hiring Jake—totally ignorant of his relationship to the situation. Fast-paced action, passion, and suspense in a high-stakes environment of global business.

Where it's reviewed:
Romantic Times, October 1997, page 79

Other books you might like:
Sandra Brown, *French Silk*, 1992
Jayne Ann Krentz, *Deep Waters*, 1997
Jayne Ann Krentz, *Sharp Edges*, 1998
Nora Roberts, *Hidden Riches*, 1994

368

HEATHER MACALLISTER

Long Southern Nights

(Toronto: Harlequin, 1997)

Story type: Contemporary
Series: Harlequin Temptation
Major character(s): Maggie Jefferson, Consultant (corporate personnel trainer); Kyle Stuart, Businessman (computer company owner)
Time period(s): 1990s
Locale(s): Jeffersonville, Georgia

Summary: When Kyle Stuart, the owner and CEO of Stuart Computers, realizes that his brilliant, but socially challenged engineers need some lessons in etiquette if his company is going to survive in its small Georgia town, he enlists the aid of Maggie Jefferson, the granddaughter of the leader of the town's socially elite, to accomplish the task. Of course, the fact that Kyle is persona non grata as far as Maggie's grandmother is concerned complicates things—and so does the fact that they end up falling in love. Funny and charming with Americana elements.

Other books by the same author:
Bride Overboard, 1997

Other books you might like:
Annie Kimberlin, *Stray Hearts*, 1997
Annie Kimberlin, *Lonely Hearts*, 1998

Jayne Ann Krentz, *Trust Me*, 1995
 Lots of humor
Jayne Ann Krentz, *Perfect Partners*, 1992
 Lots of humor
Marcia Martin, *Southern Storms*, 1992
 Southern clashes

369

CHARLOTTE MACLAY

Accidental Roommates

(Toronto: Harlequin, 1997)

Story type: Contemporary
Series: Love and Laughter
Major character(s): Hannah Jansen, Designer (lingerie); Holt Janson, Rancher
Time period(s): 1990s
Locale(s): Chicago, Illinois

Summary: When a mixup with their names results in a small-town Minnesota woman and a sexy Montana rancher being booked into the same room in an over-crowded Chicago hotel, they agree to make the best of things—with hilarious and warmly romantic results. Reminiscent of an old Doris Day movie.

Where it's reviewed:
Library Journal, August 1997, page 68

Other books by the same author:
Stealing Samantha, 1997

Other books you might like:
Carole Buck, *Love Goddesses*, 1996
 Anthology/humorous
Jennifer Crusie, *Strange Bedpersons*, 1994
Cathie Linz, *Husband Needed*, 1997
Gwen Pemberton, *Wooing Wanda*, 1997

370

DEBBIE MACOMBER

This Matter of Marriage

(Toronto: Mira, 1997)

Story type: Contemporary
Major character(s): Hallie McCarthy, Businesswoman (graphic arts company); Steve Marris, Businessman (company owner), Divorced Person
Time period(s): 1990s
Locale(s): United States

Summary: When successfull career woman Hallie McCarthy decides it is now time to get married, her problem is finding a husband. Of course, Steve Marris, her next door neighbor, is just a good friend and definitely not marriage material.... Warm and gently charming.

Where it's reviewed:
Romantic Times, April 1997, page 77

Other books by the same author:
Just Marriage, 1996
Mrs. Miracle, 1996

Sooner or Later, 1996
The Marriage Risk, 1995
Fallen Angel, 1989

Other books you might like:
Barbara Freethy, *Ask Mariah*, 1997
Barbara Freethy, *Daniel's Gift*, 1996
Pamela Morsi, *Garters*, 1992
LaVyrle Spencer, *The Endearment*, 1982

371

DEBBIE MACOMBER

Three Brides, No Groom

(New York: Silhouette, 1997)

Story type: Contemporary
Major character(s): Gretchen Wise, Friend (college); Carol Furness, Friend (college); Maddie Cobain, Friend (college)
Time period(s): 1990s
Locale(s): Seattle, Washington

Summary: Three college chums reconnect at their 15-year college reunion to learn that each has been left standing at the altar by the college men they had planned to marry—and now they have revenge in mind. A light, warmly romantic story for anyone who has ever endured the agonies of a school reunion.

Where it's reviewed:
Library Journal, August 1997, page 68

Other books by the same author:
This Matter of Marriage, 1997
Sooner or Later, 1996
Just Marriage, 1996
Mrs. Miracle, 1996
The Marriage Risk, 1995

Other books you might like:
Gila Berkowitz, *The Brides*, 1992
    More mainstream treatment
Georgia Bockhoven, *A Marriage of Convenience*, 1991
Diane E. Locke, *True Love*, 1994
LaVyrle Spencer, *Bitter Sweet*, 1990
    More serious

372

KAT MARTIN

Innocence Undone

(New York: St. Martin's, 1997)

Story type: Historical/Georgian
Major character(s): Jessica Fox, Young Woman (protege of Marquess of Belmore); Matthew Seaton, Military Personnel (captain), Nobleman
Time period(s): 1790s; 1800s (1798-1805)
Locale(s): England

Summary: Jessica Fox is the toast of London society, thanks to the old Marquess of Belmore who rescued her from a poverty-stricken life on the streets. However, the Marquess' handsome son, Captain Matthew Seaton, suspects her of trying for the Belmore title, and the more he explores, the closer he comes to the truth about her past. Though confrontations, lies, and eventually, the truth, cause problems for the pair, love does win out in the end.

Other books by the same author:
Midnight Rider, 1996
Devil's Prize, 1995
Bold Angel, 1994
Sweet Vengeance, 1993
Gypsy Lord, 1992

Other books you might like:
Mary Balogh, *Indiscreet*, 1997
Mary Balogh, *Truly*, 1996
Mary Jo Putney, *River of Fire*, 1996
Anne Stuart, *To Love a Dark Lord*, 1994

373

MICHELLE MARTIN

Stolen Hearts

(New York: Bantam, 1997)

Story type: Contemporary; Romantic Suspense
Major character(s): Tess Alcott, Thief (reformed), Con Artist; Luke Mansfield, Lawyer
Time period(s): 1990s
Locale(s): United States

Summary: Tess Alcott's horrible past has only made her smarter and more wiley. So when she joins a plan to acquire the Cushman family's emeralds by becoming their lost daughter, she fools everyone except Luke Mansfield, the family attorney. She's an art, jewelry, and language expert and a lovely "daughter." The problem is that her cohort, who "convinced" her to return to her past life of crime, is making her life difficult—and so is the fact that she is falling in love with Luke. Surprising research results in an unexpected ending.

Where it's reviewed:
Library Journal, February 15, 1997, page 126
Romantic Times, February 1997, page 87

Other books by the same author:
Stolen Moments, 1997

Other books you might like:
Christina Dodd, *The Greatest Lover in All England*, 1994
    Another long-lost heiress Renaissance-style
Kay Hooper, *Amanda*, 1995
Jayne Ann Krentz, *Silver Linings*, 1991
Jayne Ann Krentz, *A Woman's Touch*, 1989
Sharon Sala, *Honor's Promise*, 1992

374

CURTIS ANN MATLOCK

Love in a Small Town

(New York: Avon, 1997)

Story type: Contemporary

Major character(s): Molly Hayes, Mother; Tommy Lee Hayes, Mechanic (auto)
Time period(s): 1990s
Locale(s): Oklahoma

Summary: Tommy Lee and Molly Hayes have lived in relative harmony for 25 years, but deep-seated unhappiness threatens their marriage when Molly decides to move into a retreat cabin on her mother's property. The small town and their families are devastated by this separation. Molly knows she loves Tommy but can't find ways to communicate and feels alone. Tommy loses himself in his work and ignores the ''small troubles.'' Only when a family friend decides to declare his love for Molly does the solution emerge. Normal and real emotions predominate.

Where it's reviewed:
Affaire de Coeur, February 1997, page 32
Romantic Times, February 1997, page 86

Other books by the same author:
The Loves of Ruby Dee, 1996

Other books you might like:
Rexanne Becnel, *Christmas Journey*, 1992
    Another rocky marriage
Barbara Delinsky, *More than Just Friends*, 1993
Barbara Delinsky, *A Woman Betrayed*, 1991
LaVyrle Spencer, *Bitter Sweet*, 1990
LaVyrle Spencer, *Bygones*, 1992

375

DINAH MCCALL

Chase the Moon
(New York: Harper, 1997)

Story type: Contemporary
Major character(s): Gracie Moon, Mountain Woman, Religious (Christian community member); Jake Baretta, Twin, Imposter (undercover investigator)
Time period(s): 1990s
Locale(s): New Zion, Kentucky

Summary: Determined to discover the truth about his twin brother John's murder, Jake Baretta goes to the rural religious community headed by Elijah Moon where John had been posing as a member and takes his place. He expects to find both danger and violence; he doesn't expect to find love and healing for his heart in the person of gentle, lovely Gracie Moon. A dark, passionate, emotionally involving story.

Where it's reviewed:
Library Journal, August 1997, page 70

Other books by the same author:
Tallchief, 1997
Dreamcatcher, 1996
Jackson Rule, 1996

Other books you might like:
Catherine Anderson, *Chase the Moon*, 1997
Kristin Hannah, *Waiting for the Moon*, 1995
    Historical/wounded hero and heroine
Kay Hooper, *Amanda*, 1995
Kay Hooper, *Finding Laura*, 1997

376

DINAH MCCALL

Tallchief
(New York: Harper, 1997)

Story type: Contemporary; Ethnic
Major character(s): Kathleen Ryder (Walkman), Fugitive, Single Parent; Morgan Tallchief, Sports Figure (runner), Artist
Time period(s): 1990s
Locale(s): Mustang, Oklahoma; Sante Fe, New Mexico

Summary: Pursued by a greedy, relentless killer, Kathleen Ryder heads for the one person who may be able to help, Morgan Tallchief, her high school love and the father of her teenage daughter. But 16 years ago Morgan had watched Kathleen ''die'' in a fire conveniently arranged by the Witness Protection Program, and when she miraculously appears in his life again, he is stunned. He knows he will never let her out of his life again and he will do anything to keep her safe— even if it means murder. A magnificent, larger-than-life hero is combined with a compelling plot in this intense, emotional, and occasionally violent story.

Where it's reviewed:
Library Journal, February 15, 1997, page 125

Other books by the same author:
Jackson Rule, 1996
Dreamcatcher, 1996

Other books you might like:
Jane Bonander, *Dancing on Snowflakes*, 1995
    Wounded hero
Jane Bonander, *Warrior Heart*, 1997
    Wounded hero/Native American elements
Kathleen Eagle, *The Night Remembers*, 1997
    Urban setting/Native American hero
Kathleen Eagle, *Sunrise Song*, 1996
    Parallel stories/Native American hero
Patricia Potter, *Defiant*, 1995
    Wounded Hero

377

TERESA MEDEIROS

Touch of Enchantment
(New York: Bantam, 1997)

Story type: Historical/Fantasy; Historical/Medieval
Major character(s): Tabitha Lennox, Witch, Time Traveller; Sir Colin of Ravenshaw, Knight
Time period(s): 1990s; 13th century
Locale(s): England

Summary: Beautiful, wealthy, and magically endowed,Tabitha Lennox, modern-day witch, seemingly has it all — except for one thing —she can't control her magic! Her only hope is an amulet that was once her mother's — but when she finds it, she ends up in a field in Medieval England, clad only in her pajamas, and confronted by the most noble knight, Sir Colin of Ravenshaw. However, being a witch in the middle ages is a problem all its own and the last thing

Colin needs is another problem, especially one as attractive and unpredictable as Tabitha. Humor and whimsy add a light touch to the fast-paced action and occasional violence of this charming romance that has a decidedly magical and fairy tale quality to it.

Where it's reviewed:
Library Journal, May 15, 1997, page 69.

Other books by the same author:
Breath of Magic, 1996

Other books you might like:
Jill Barnett, *Bewitching*, 1993
  Magic and humor
Jill Barnett, *Dreaming*, 1994
Kimberly Cates, *Magic*, 1998
  Magic and a dash of humor
Elizabeth Lowell, *Untamed*, 1993
  another witch, different treatment

378

BARBARA METZGER

Snowdrops and Scandalbroth
(New York: Fawcett, 1997)

Story type: Regency
Major character(s): Kathlyn Partland, Gentlewoman; Courtney Choate, Nobleman (Lord Chase), Bachelor
Time period(s): 1810s
Locale(s): London, England

Summary: Stranded in London, Kathlyn Partland could see no harm in being Lord Chase's companion for the evening. She was shocked by his offer to pay her, although she did need the money. Courtney wanted to counter his overly virtuous reputation, but he assured Kathlyn that the charade was innocent—he merely wanted her to act as his mistress in public. They didn't count on ruined reputations for them both! Light, lively, and typically Regency.

Where it's reviewed:
Affaire de Coeur, February 1997, page 39
Romantic Times, February 1997, page 76

Other books by the same author:
Primrose Path, 1997
An Enchanted Affair, 1996
Father Christmas, 1995
Lady Whilton's Wedding, 1995
A Suspicious Affair, 1994

Other books you might like:
Emily Henderson, *The Scoundrel's Bride*, 1994
Candice Hern, *A Proper Companion*, 1995
Barbara Reeves, *The Much Maligned Lord*, 1993
Evelyn Richardson, *Lady Alex's Gamble*, 1995

379

FERN MICHAELS
DENISE DOMNING, Co-Author
BRONWYN WILLIAMS, Co-Author
BRENDA JOYCE, Co-Author

Heart of the Home
(New York: Topaz, 1997)

Story type: Anthology

Summary: This eclectic collection of four novellas celebrates the love of family and home. Included are ''Meggie's Baby'' by Denise Domning, ''Sunshine'' by Bronwyn Williams, ''The Awakening'' by Brenda Joyce, and ''Hunter's Moon'' by Fern Michaels.

Other books you might like:
Maeve Binchy, *Firefly Summer*, 1987
Robin Lee Hatcher, *Where the Heart Is*, 1993
Cheryl Reavis, *Promise Me a Rainbow*, 1990
Nora Roberts, *Born in Ice*, 1995
LaVyrle Spencer, *Morning Glory*, 1989

380

LINDA LAEL MILLER

Knights
(New York: Pocket, 1996)

Story type: Time Travel
Major character(s): Megan Saunders St. Gregory, Bride (child), Time Traveller; Dane St. Gregory, Nobleman (Baron of Kenbrook), Spouse (absent)
Time period(s): 13th century; 1990s
Locale(s): England

Summary: Transported into 13th-century England, five-year-old Megan finds herself betrothed to Baron Dane St. Gregory. However, when he returns 10 years later and rejects her for another, she decides to take matters into her own hands, with passionate and time-defying results.

Where it's reviewed:
Affaire de Coeur, May 1996, page 23
Rendezvous, March 1996, page 28
Romantic Times, May 1996, page 88

Other books by the same author:
Pirates, 1995
The Legacy, 1994
Princess Annie, 1994
Forever and the Night, 1993
Taming Charlotte, 1993

Other books you might like:
Jude Deveraux, *A Knight in Shining Armor*, 1989
  Early time travel romance
Diana Gabaldon, *Outlander*, 1991
  Classic modern time travel romance
Lynn Kurland, *A Dance through Time*, 1996
Susan Sizemore, *After the Storm*, 1996

381

STEPHANIE MITTMAN

The Marriage Bed
(New York: Dell, 1996)

Story type: Historical/American West
Major character(s): Olivia Williamson, Child-Care Giver (for sister's children); Spencer Williamson, Farmer
Time period(s): 1890s (1897)
Locale(s): Maple Stand, Wisconsin

Summary: Olivia, willing to do anything to please the husband she loves, can't understand why they have no babies. However, her husband, Spencer, having lost a wife and children, swears never to love again and only pretends to do his husbandly duties. But after taking in her dead sister's children, Olivia finds the strength to love them, find her own worth, and turn Spencer away. It all works out, of course, but it takes a bit of doing. Well done.

Where it's reviewed:
Rendezvous, March 1996, page 20

Other books by the same author:
The Courtship, 1998
Sweeter than Wine, 1997

Other books you might like:
Catherine Anderson, *Annie's Song*, 1996
Dorothy Garlock, *Sins of Summer*, 1994
   More realistic
Kristin Hannah, *Once in Every Life*, 1993
Robin Lee Hatcher, *Promise Me Spring*, 1991
Robin Lee Hatcher, *Where the Heart Is*, 1993

382

STEPHANIE MITTMAN

Sweeter than Wine
(New York: Dell, 1997)

Story type: Historical/American West; Historical/Americana
Major character(s): Sterling Phillips, Gentlewoman (wealthy); Ethan Morrow, Farmer, Cowboy (would-be)
Time period(s): 1890s (1899)
Locale(s): Van Wert, Ohio

Summary: For years, Ethan Morrow has cherished the dream of leaving the farm to become a cowboy, but for years, his close family has needed him. Finally able to leave, he is stopped once again when his wagon accidentally injures the young brother of wealthy, beautiful Sterling Phillips—a woman who has always overlooked him but now hates him—and he is compelled to remain and help the boy in any way he can. A closely guarded secret, an unscrupulous physician, and a deft combination of tender humor and sensuality add to this warm, emotionally satisfying story.

Where it's reviewed:
Affaire de Coeur, March 1997, page 31
Romantic Times, March 1997, page 35

Other books by the same author:
The Courtship, 1998

The Marriage Bed, 1996

Other books you might like:
Kristin Hannah, *If You Believe*, 1994
   Poignant and tender
Pamela Morsi, *Courting Miss Hattie*, 1991
Pamela Morsi, *Runabout*, 1994
LaVyrle Spencer, *Vows*, 1988
Jodi Thomas, *The Tender Texan*, 1991

383

KARYN MONK

Once a Warrior
(New York: Bantam, 1997)

Story type: Historical/Medieval
Major character(s): Ariella MacKendrick, Noblewoman (daughter of the clan chieftain); Malcolm MacFane, Laird (former), Warrior (Black Wolf)
Time period(s): 13th century (1207)
Locale(s): Scotland

Summary: Determined to find a savior for her clan, Ariella MacKendrick takes the advice of Alpin the Seer and sets out to find the legendary warrior Black Wolf. What she finds, however, is a disillusioned, broken man—a man who, nevertheless, accepts the challenge Ariella offers, and then rises beautifully to the occasion. A wonderfully wounded hero finds healing and love in the arms of a trusting and determined heroine. Intense, romantic, and enchanting.

Where it's reviewed:
Library Journal, May 15, 1997, page 66
Romantic Times, May 1997, page 37

Other books by the same author:
The Witch and the Warrior, 1998
The Rebel and the Redcoat, 1996
Surrender to a Stranger, 1995

Other books you might like:
Kimberly Cates, *Magic*, 1998
Justine Dare, *Fire Hawk*, 1997
Laura Kinsale, *The Prince of Midnight*, 1990
Anne Stuart, *Lord of Danger*, 1997
   darker

384

KATE MOORE

A Prince Among Men
(New York: Avon, 1997)

Story type: Historical/Regency
Major character(s): Lady Ophelia Brinsby, Noblewoman, Equestrian; Prince Alexander of Trevigna, Royalty, Imposter (groom)
Time period(s): 1810s
Locale(s): England

Summary: When Prince Alexander of Trevigna "disappears" for political reasons, he ends up posing as a groom in Lady Ophelia Brinsby's stables and finds himself intrigued—and

eventually in love—with a woman who is his equal in any number of ways. This well-crafted, intricately plotted romance is enhanced by appealing, believable characters, nicely handled sensuality, and faultless historical detail.

Where it's reviewed:
Library Journal, November 15, 1997, page 48

Other books by the same author:
Winterburn's Rose, 1996
An Improper Widow, 1996
The Mercenary Major, 1994
Sweet Bargain, 1993
To Kiss a Thief, 1992

Other books you might like:
Candice Hern, *A Garden Folly*, 1997
    Regency
Georgette Heyer, *The Grand Sophy*, 1950
    Classic Regency/Admirable heroine
Carla Kelly, *With This Ring*, 1997
    Well-written Regency/Uncommon
Mary Jo Putney, *One Perfect Rose*, 1997
    Well-crafted/similar time period
Mary Jo Putney, *River of Fire*, 1996

385

MARGARET MOORE

The Dark Duke
(Toronto: Harlequin, 1997)

Story type: Historical/Victorian
Series: Most Unsuitable
Major character(s): Lady Hester Pimblett, Noblewoman, Companion; Lord Adrian Fitzwalter, Nobleman (duke of Barroughby), Rake
Time period(s): 1860s (1863)
Locale(s): Hampshire, England (Barroughby Hall)

Summary: Plain Hester Pimblett and the disreputable "Dark Duke" defy Victorian society and its rigid conventions when they fall in love. Well-drawn characters people this sweet romance.

Where it's reviewed:
Library Journal, May 15, 1997, page 66

Other books by the same author:
The Rogue's Return, 1997
The Wastrel, 1995
A Warrior's Heart, 1993
A Warrior's Quest, 1993
China Blossom, 1992

Other books you might like:
Candace Camp, *Scandalous*, 1996
    Similar time period/sensual
Candace Camp, *Suddenly*, 1996
    Similar time period/sensual
Mary Chase Comstock, *Fortune's Mistress*, 1996
    Regency setting/sweet and unconventional
Carla Kelly, *The Lady's Companion*, 1996
    Regency setting/sweet and unconventional

Lynn Kerstan, *Francesca's Rake*, 1997
    Regency

386

PAMELA MORSI

No Ordinary Princess
(New York: Avon, 1997)

Story type: Historical/Americana
Major character(s): Princess Calhoun, Heiress (daughter of oil magnate), Spinster; Tom "Gerald Tarkington Crane" Walker, Military Personnel (former Rough Rider), Fortune Hunter
Time period(s): 1900s (1907)
Locale(s): Oklahoma

Summary: When Princess Calhoun sees Tom Walker, it is love at first sight. He is the one and she knows it. But dirt poor, fortune-hunting Tom is after two things: Princess and her money. Pretending to be a wealthy adventurer, he sets about acquiring them both. But pretense and love don't necessarily mix. Tom falls in love with the brash, outspoken, but wonderfully warm Princess, and he is forced to consider the consequences of his deception when she eventually learns the truth. A funny, poignant story of a less-than-beautiful heroine and a con-artist hero who discover the joy and magic of love.

Where it's reviewed:
Romantic Times, June 1997, page 35

Other books by the same author:
The Love Charm, 1996
Simple Jess, 1996
Something Shady, 1995 (Rita Award Winner)
The Marrying Stone, 1994
Runabout, 1994

Other books you might like:
Stef Ann Holm, *Forget Me Not*, 1997
Jill Marie Landis, *After All*, 1995
Jill Marie Landis, *Last Chance*, 1995
Stephanie Mittman, *The Courtship*, 1998
Stephanie Mittman, *The Marriage Bed*, 1998

387

RAE MUIR

The Lieutenant's Lady
(Toronto: Harlequin, 1997)

Story type: Historical/Victorian America; Americana
Series: Wedding Trail
Major character(s): Matilda "Tildy" MacIntyre, Young Woman; Matt Hull, Military Personnel (lieutenant), Lawyer (would-be)
Time period(s): 1860s
Locale(s): Pikeston, Indiana

Summary: Matt Hull returns to Pikeston, Indiana, after the war with two ambitions: to marry Tildy MacIntyre, a girl far above his touch, and to become a lawyer. Dashes of humor, "quilting comments," and things a bit more sinister add to this nicely done story that beautifully depicts the atmosphere

of a small, late 19th-century, midwestern town and is a good example of period Americana. This story ends as the town makes plans to head West and is the first of Muir's Wedding Trail series.

Where it's reviewed:
Library Journal, November 15, 1997, page 48

Other books by the same author:
Twice a Bride, 1998
All But the Queen of Hearts, 1997

Other books you might like:
Lydia Browne, *Snowflake Wishes*, 1997
Jill Marie Landis, *Last Chance*, 1995
Pamela Morsi, *Runabout*, 1994
LaVyrle Spencer, *The Gamble*, 1987

388

LINDA NEEDHAM

For My Lady's Kiss

(New York: Avon, 1997)

Story type: Historical/Medieval
Major character(s): Mackenna Hughes, Government Official (village reeve); Lord Thomas Montclaire, Knight, Nobleman (Lord of Fellhaven)
Time period(s): 13th century (1292)
Locale(s): Fellhaven, England

Summary: Mackenna Hughes takes her hereditary position as village reeve very seriously. When Lord Thomas Montclaire arrives to claim the village for King Edward, he takes her hostage to prevent an uprising. She is surprised by his concern for the villagers and his desire to rebuild the destroyed castle, and she begins to rethink her opinions of him. Eventually, they agree to marry—and then the former lord returns with vengeance on his mind. Humorous, sensual, and filled with action.

Where it's reviewed:
Romantic Times, February 1997, page 40

Other books you might like:
Alice Borchardt, *Devoted*, 1995
Tanya Ann Crosby, *Angel of Fire*, 1992
Shannon Drake, *Knight of Fire*, 1993
Roberta Gellis, *Roselynde*, 1978
Amanda Scott, *The Rose at Twilight*, 1993

389

JUDITH O'BRIEN

Maiden Voyage

(New York: Pocket, 1997)

Story type: Time Travel
Major character(s): Maura Finnegan, Heiress (American); Donal Byrne, Neighbor; Fitzwilliam Connolly, Spirit (ghost)
Time period(s): 1990s; 1760s (1767)
Locale(s): Dublin, Ireland

Summary: Maura Finnegan, heiress to an old Irish estate, means to go into business and lead a normal life, but she doesn't count on Fitzwilliam Connolly, a very real and properly elegant ghost who has his own ideas about what Maura will do with his estate. Young Donal Byrne, trying to help Maura with the problems of a new business, at times aids and then exasperates both Maura and Fitz. Her searches reveal a surprising secret, and the three discover they have a lot more in common than they had thought.

Other books by the same author:
Once upon a Rose, 1996
Ashton's Bride, 1995
Rhapsody in Time, 1994

Other books you might like:
Laura Parker, *For Love's Sake Only*, 1991
   Ghosts and manor houses
Maura Seger, *The Lady and the Laird*, 1992
   Ghosts and castles
Christina Skye, *Season of Wishes*, 1997
   Ghosts and castles
Antoinette Stockenberg, *Dream a Little Dream*, 1997
   Ghosts and modern castles

390

JUDITH O'BRIEN

Once upon a Rose

(New York: Pocket, 1996)

Story type: Time Travel
Major character(s): Deanie Bailey, Musician (country music star); Christopher "Kit" Neville, Nobleman (Duke of Hamilton) King Henry VIII, Royalty (King of England)
Time period(s): 16th century
Locale(s): England

Summary: While performing in England, country singer Deanie Bailey is suddenly transported (via Henry VIII's maze) back to 16th-century England. She is rescued by the Duke of Hamilton, who calls her cousin, and her court appearances intrigue the lecherous king. Evading the king and power-hungry courtiers keeps the duke and Deanie on their toes, and Deanie's rather outrageous antics keep things interesting. A vivid, occasionally humorous, portrayal of the royal life-style intriguingly depicted from a modern country singer's point of view.

Other books by the same author:
Ashton's Bride, 1995
Rhapsody in Time, 1994

Other books you might like:
Jude Deveraux, *A Knight in Shining Armor*, 1989
   Early time travel romance
Christina Dodd, *Outrageous*, 1994
   Renaissance Setting/humor/no time travel
Betina Krahn, *Behind Closed Doors*, 1991
   Elizabethan setting/humor/no time travel
Suzanne Robinson, *Lord of Enchantment*, 1995
   Elizabethan setting/humor/no time travel

391

JUDITH O'BRIEN

To Marry a British Lord

(New York: Pocket, 1997)

Story type: Historical/Victorian
Major character(s): Constance Lloyd, Governess, Southern Belle (former); Joseph Smith, Businessman (wealthy); Philip Hastings, Nobleman (son of the Duke of Ballsbridge)
Time period(s): 1870s (1874)
Locale(s): England

Summary: Following the Civil War and the death of her fiance, Constance Lloyd's life goes from bad to worse, and in one desperate attempt to regain control, she heads for England and becomes a governess. Her life suddenly changes, however, when her charges make their debuts and Constance herself ends up the true belle of the ball, noticed by the prince and suddenly engaged to the son of an eccentric duke. However, when she sets out for her fiance's home, she is escorted by his best friend, Joseph Smith—a man to whom she is attracted— and things take a turn for the more romantic. Secrets, intrigue, and romance flourish.

Where it's reviewed:
Romantic Times, October 1997, page 40

Other books by the same author:
Maiden Voyage, 1997
Once upon a Rose, 1996
Ashton's Bride, 1995
Rhapsody in Time, 1994

Other books you might like:
Lorraine Heath, *Always to Remember*, 1996
   Emotionally involving
Candice Hern, *A Garden Folly*, 1997
Kate Moore, *A Prince Among Men*, 1997
Patricia Potter, *The Marshall and the Heiress*, 1996

392

PATRICIA OLIVER

The Colonel's Lady

(New York: Signet, 1996)

Story type: Regency
Major character(s): Lady Regina Hethercott, Noblewoman; Charles Swinburn, Military Personnel (captain); Sir Richard Swinburn, Nobleman, Military Personnel (colonel)
Time period(s): 1810s
Locale(s): Brussels, Belgium

Summary: Lady Regina has everything she wants—except for Captain Charles Swinburn. However, when the headstrong lady decides to go after him, Charles' older brother, Richard, steps in to stop her, but ends up compromising her instead. Marriage, of course, is the only solution, but it takes a lot of negotiating before things work out for them both.

Where it's reviewed:
Rendezvous, March 1996, page 26

Romantic Times, May 1996, page 108

Other books by the same author:
Lord Gresham's Lady, 1994
Miss Drayton's Downfall, 1994
Lord Harry's Angel, 1993
The Runaway Duchess, 1993

Other books you might like:
Mary Balogh, *The Temporary Wife*, 1997
Anne Barbour, *A Rake's Reform*, 1996
Jo Beverley, *An Unwilling Bride*, 1992
Allison Lane, *The Impoverished Viscount*, 1996
Allison Lane, *The Rake's Rainbow*, 1996

393

MAGGIE OSBORNE

The Promise of Jenny Jones

(New York: Warner, 1997)

Story type: Historical/American West
Major character(s): Jenny Jones, Frontierswoman (mule driver), Guardian; Ty Sanders, Cowboy; Graciela Sanders, Heiress, Child
Time period(s): 19th century
Locale(s): Mexico; California

Summary: Tough, rough muleskinner Jenny Jones agrees to take Graciela, the six-year-old daughter of consumptive Senora Marguarita Sanders, to the child's father in California; in exchange, the dying Marguarita will take Jenny's place before the prison firing squad, allowing Jenny to go free. But there is a catch: Marguarita's greedy cousins are hot on the little girl's trail and they will stop at nothing—even killing Jenny—to take control of her fortune. Ty Sanders, Graciela's uncle, is on a mission to bring her back to her father, and when he gets involved, things become interesting, indeed. Beautifully drawn characters, wonderful sexual tension, and humor and fast-paced action abound.

Where it's reviewed:
Romantic Times, April 1997, page 36

Other books by the same author:
The Brides of Prairie Gold, 1996
Family Secrets, 1996
To Love a Thief, 1995
The Seduction of Samantha Kincade, 1995
The Wives of Bowie Stone, 1994

Other books you might like:
Millie Criswell, *Wild Heather*, 1995
Dorothy Garlock, *Sweetwater*, 1997
Jill Marie Landis, *Until Tomorrow*, 1994
Johanna Lindsey, *Angel*, 1992

394

DIANA PALMER
JOAN JOHNSTON, Co-Author

Lone Star Christmas
(New York: Silhouette, 1997)

Story type: Contemporary; Holiday Themes
Time period(s): 1990s
Locale(s): Texas

Summary: Both novellas in this collections of Christmas stories by two of the romance genre's best known writers are warm, romantic, and definitely Texan. Included are "Christmas Cowboy" by Diana Palmer and "A Hawk's Way Christmas" by Joan Johnston.

Other books you might like:
Bethany Campbell, *The Man Who Came for Christmas*, 1993
Kathleen Creighton, *A Christmas Love*, 1992
Linda Howard, *Christmas Kisses*, 1996
    anthology
Heather McAllister, *Christmas Male*, 1993

395

DELIA PARR
MARY LECHLEIDNER, Co-Author

The Ivory Duchess
(New York: St. Martin, 1997)

Story type: Historical/Victorian
Major character(s): Kate Danaher, Musician (concert pianist, piano teacher), Fugitive; Phillip Massey, Jeweler, Detective—Private (Jewel expert for-hire)
Time period(s): 1850s
Locale(s): Delaware Township, New Jersey; London, England

Summary: Escaping from her unscrupulous guardian's abusive control, the mysterious veiled pianist Kate Danaher, known throughout Europe only as "The Ivory Duchess," heads for America to become a small-town music teacher. She knows her guardian will search for her, but what she doesn't expect is that she will fall in love with the man he has hired to find her—the attractive "jewel expert for-hire," Phillip Massey.

Other books you might like:
Lydia Browne, *Snowflake Wishes*, 1997
    Sweet/Americana
Julie Garwood, *Prince Charming*, 1994
    Another fugitive heroine
Robin Lee Hatcher, *Liberty Blue*, 1995
    Another fugitive heroine

396

GWEN PEMBERTON

Wooing Wanda
(Toronto: Harlequin, 1997)

Story type: Contemporary
Series: Love and Laughter

Major character(s): Wanda Rockman, Spouse; John Rockman, Architect (workaholic)
Time period(s): 1990s
Locale(s): Richmond, Virginia; Washington, District of Columbia

Summary: Frustrated with her husband's workaholic tendencies and determined to save her marriage, Wanda Rockman decides drastic situations call for drastic measures—and so she leaves town and heads for her sister's to put one of her wildly off-beat plans into action. In order to get their marriage back on track, they need to start over, beginning with a first date. This funny story features engaging characters caught in a realistic situation and offers an interesting solution to the problem. An RWA Golden Heart winner.

Where it's reviewed:
Library Journal, August 1997, page 68

Other books by the same author:
Regarding Rita, 1998

Other books you might like:
Jennifer Crusie, *Getting Rid of Bradley*, 1994
Cathie Linz, *Husband Needed*, 1997
Charlotte Maclay, *Accidental Roommates*, 1997
Susan Elizabeth Phillips, *Nobody's Baby but Mine*, 1997
    Humorous/more complex

397

SUSAN ELIZABETH PHILLIPS

Nobody's Baby but Mine
(New York: Avon, 1997)

Story type: Contemporary
Major character(s): Jane Darlington, Scientist (physicist), Professor; Cal Bonner, Sports Figure (football star)
Time period(s): 1990s
Locale(s): Chicago, Illinois; Great Smoky Mountains, North Carolina

Summary: When brilliant physics professor Jane Darlington agrees to be a "birthday present" for star quarterback Cal Bonner in an effort to become pregnant by someone with "below average" intelligence, she has no idea that Cal is not only more honorable than she had expected, but also a whole lot smarter! The resulting romance is lively, witty, passionate, and filled with sparks. Compelling protagonists and beautifully drawn secondary characters.

Where it's reviewed:
Library Journal, February 15, 1997, page 126

Other books by the same author:
Kiss an Angel, 1996
Heaven, Texas, 1995
It Had to Be You, 1994
Honey Moon, 1993
Hot Shot, 1991

Other books you might like:
Barbara Bretton, *Midnight Lover*, 1989
Jayne Ann Krentz, *Family Man*, 1993
Jayne Ann Krentz, *Perfect Partners*, 1993
Gwen Pemberton, *Wooing Wanda*, 1997

398

CHERYL ANNE PORTER

Jacey's Reckless Heart

(New York: St. Martin's, 1997)

Story type: Historical/American West
Series: Lawless Women
Major character(s): Jacey Lawless, Outlaw; Zant Chapelo, Gunfighter
Time period(s): 1870s (1873)
Locale(s): Mexico

Summary: On a mission to find her parents' killers, Jacey heads for Mexico and ends up involving gunslinger Zant Chapelo, the grandson of the man she is looking for, in her quest for vengeance. Love, of course, complicates the situation, and a lot of issues need to be dealt with before they can find happiness together. Old secrets and past sins abound in this dark, complex, emotionally compelling story.

Where it's reviewed:
Romantic Times, December 1997, page 41

Other books by the same author:
Hannah's Promise, 1997

Other books you might like:
Rebecca Brandewyne, *Desperado*, 1993
Geralyn Dawson, *Capture the Night*, 1993
Patricia Potter, *Defiant*, 1995
Patricia Potter, *Diablo*, 1996

399

PATRICIA POTTER

The Scotsman Wore Spurs

(New York: Bantam, 1997)

Story type: Historical/American West
Major character(s): Maris Gabrielle ''Gabe'' Parker, Imposter (posing as a boy), Cowboy; Andrew ''Drew'' Cameron, Nobleman (Earl of Kinloch), Cowboy
Time period(s): 1870s (1870)
Locale(s): Texas

Summary: When the penniless wastrel and transplanted Scottish nobleman Andrew Cameron rescues rancher Kirby Kingsley from an ambush, he ends up in Kingsley's employ—and on a cattle drive that promises to make his life interesting, dangerous, and surprisingly romantic in the process. A wounded, disillusioned hero in search of a life; a determined, gutsy woman bent on revenge; and a cast of especially well-done characters combine in a fast-paced, funny story filled with adventure and intrigue.

Other books by the same author:
Starcatcher, 1997
The Marshall and the Heiress, 1996
Diablo, 1996
Defiant, 1995

Other books you might like:
Dorothy Garlock, *Midnight Blue*, 1989
Johanna Lindsey, *Angel*, 1992

Maggie Osborne, *The Brides of Bowie Stone*, 1994
Maggie Osborne, *The Seduction of Samantha Kincade*, 1995

400

PATRICIA POTTER

Starcatcher

(New York: Bantam, 1998)

Story type: Historical/Seventeenth Century
Major character(s): Lady Marsali Gunn, Noblewoman; Patrick Sutherland, Warrior
Time period(s): 17th century (1660)
Locale(s): Highlands, Scotland

Summary: Lady Marsali and Patrick Sutherland have been betrothed since childhood, but when the time comes for them to wed, the political climate has changed, and now Marsali must make a choice between her people and her heart. Intense, emotionally involving and sensual.

Other books by the same author:
The Marshall and the Heiress, 1996
Diablo, 1996
Defiant, 1995
Impetuous, 1995
Wanted, 1994

Other books you might like:
Kimberly Cates, *Angel's Fall*, 1996
Diana Gabaldon, *Outlander*, 1991
Arnette Lamb, *Betrayed*, 1995
Amanda Scott, *The Bawdy Bride*, 1995

401

MARY JO PUTNEY

One Perfect Rose

(New York: Fawcett Columbine, 1997)

Story type: Historical/Regency
Major character(s): Rosalind Jordan, Actress, Businesswoman (traveling theater company mgr.); Stephen Kenyon, Nobleman (duke of Ashburton), Actor
Time period(s): 1810s (1818)
Locale(s): England

Summary: When Stephen Kenyon, Duke of Ashburton, is told he only has a few months to live, he leaves his home and wanders the countryside in an effort to come to terms with the situation. However, when a chance incident results in his joining a traveling theater company, his life takes a turn for the better as he meets and falls in love with the remarkable Rosalind Jordan. Magnetic characters interact in a compelling story that deals with some realistic issues. First title in Ballantine's new ''keeper'' series of paperback-sized hardcover romances.

Where it's reviewed:
Library Journal, August 1997, page 70

Other books by the same author:
River of Fire, 1996
Shattered Rainbows, 1996

Dancing on the Wind, 1994
Thunder and Roses, 1993
Silk and Secrets, 1992

Other books you might like:
Mary Balogh, *The Secret Pearl*, 1997
　Secrets and conflicts
Christina Dodd, *Move Heaven and Earth*, 1995
　Conflicted hero
Carla Kelly, *The Lady's Companion*, 1996
　Emotionally Compelling
Carla Kelly, *With This Ring*, 1997
　Compelling characters

402

AMANDA QUICK (Pseudonym of Jayne Ann Krentz)

Affair

(New York: Bantam, 1997)

Story type: Historical/Regency
Major character(s): Charlotte Arkendale, Investigator, Gentle-
　woman; Baxter St. Ives, Secretary (man-of-affairs),
　Gentleman (bastard son of an earl)
Time period(s): 1810s
Locale(s): London, England

Summary: When the fiercely independent Charlotte
Arkendale, who makes her living by discreetly investigating
the backgrounds of suitors of women considering marriage,
hires a new man-of-affairs cum bodyguard, she ends up with a
man who is not only a logical, reasonable chemist, but is
surprisingly passionate—and dangerous—as well. Murder,
greed, and old animosities combine in this witty, funny, and
fast-paced romp that is typically "Quick."

Other books by the same author:
Mischief, 1996
Mystique, 1995
Mistress, 1994
Desire, 1994
Deception, 1993

Other books you might like:
Joan Johnston, *Captive*, 1996
Lynn Kerstan, *Raven's Bride*, 1996
Betina Krahn, *The Last Bachelor*, 1994
　Victorian setting/similar theme
Betina Krahn, *The Perfect Mistress*, 1995
Judith McNaught, *Almost Heaven*, 1990

403

JULIA QUINN

Brighter than the Sun

(New York: Avon, 1997)

Story type: Historical/Regency
Major character(s): Eleanor Lyndon, Spinster; Charles
　Wycombe, Nobleman (Earl of Billington)
Time period(s): 1810s (1817)
Locale(s): Kent, England

Summary: When Charles Wycombe plummets from a tree and
onto the feet of Eleanor Lyndon, it is hardly the way to begin a
relationship. But Charles needs a wife in order to inherit and
Eleanor needs a home—and so a marriage of convenience
seems to be the answer. A typically "Regency" plot with lots
of humor and charm.

Where it's reviewed:
Romantic Times, December 1997, page 47

Other books by the same author:
Everything and the Moon, 1997
Minx, 1996
Dancing at Midnight, 1995
Splendid, 1995
Birthright, 1993

Other books you might like:
Rexanne Becnel, *Dangerous to Love*, 1997
Georgette Heyer, *The Convenient Marriage*, 1934
Amanda Quick, *Dangerous*, 1993

404

JULIA QUINN

Everything and the Moon

(New York: Avon, 1997)

Story type: Historical/Regency
Major character(s): Victoria Lyndon, Governess; Robert
　Campbell, Nobleman (Earl of Macclesfield)
Time period(s): 1810s (1816)
Locale(s): England

Summary: When vicar's daughter Victoria Lyndon and Robert
Campbell, Earl of Macclesfield, fall in love and plan to elope,
she is physically stopped by her father, and Robert, misunderstanding and crushed, heads for London. Seven years later,
Victoria, reduced to caring for a spoiled child, meets Robert
once more and can't believe he cares nothing for her. After
many chance encounters and much bickering, the pair eventually deal with their bitterness and set things to rights.

Where it's reviewed:
Affaire de Coeur, March 1997
Romantic Times, March 1997, page 37

Other books by the same author:
Minx, 1996
Splendid, 1995
Dancing at Midnight, 1995
Birthright, 1993

Other books you might like:
Mary Balogh, *Indiscreet*, 1997
Mary Balogh, *The Secret Pearl*, 1991
Mary Balogh, *Truly*, 1996
　More serious
Mary Jo Putney, *One Perfect Rose*, 1997
Amanda Quick, *With This Ring*, 1998
　Humorous

405

FRANCIS RAY

Incognito
(New York: Pinnacle, 1997)

Story type: Romantic Suspense; Multicultural
Major character(s): Erin Cortland, Businesswoman (company president); Jake Hunter, Bodyguard
Locale(s): Austin, Texas

Summary: Jake Hunter is hired as a bodyguard to protect Erin Cortland after the man she helped convict escape from prison, and their forced close relationship ends up ensuring that they fall in love.

Where it's reviewed:
Library Journal, February 15, 1997, page 126

Other books by the same author:
Heart of the Falcon, 1998
Silken Betrayal, 1997
Only Hers, 1996
Undeniable, 1995
Forever Yours, 1994

Other books you might like:
Rochelle Alers, *Hidden Agenda*, 1997
Maggie Ferguson, *Fever Rising*, 1997
Tracey Tillis, *Final Act*, 1998
Tracey Tillis, *Night Watch*, 1995

406

ANNETTE A. REYNOLDS

Remember the Time
(New York: Bantam, 1997)

Story type: Contemporary/Mainstream
Major character(s): Kate Moran Armstrong, Widow(er); Mike Fitzgerald, Consultant (historical preservation), Architect
Time period(s): 1990s
Locale(s): Staunton, Virginia

Summary: Friends from high school, Kate Moran Armstrong and Michael Fitzgerald rethink their relationship when Kate's husband (and Michael's best friend), Paul, dies. They are forced to deal with secrets from the past and their growing feelings for each other. Clean style and occasionally graceful.

Where it's reviewed:
Library Journal, May 15, 1997, page 68

Other books you might like:
Angela Benson, *A Family Wedding*, 1997
    Lighter/multicultural characters/similar situation
Kathleen Gilles Seidel, *Maybe This Time*, 1990
LaVyrle Spencer, *Bygones*, 1992
LaVyrle Spencer, *Bitter Sweet*, 1990

407

PATRICIA RICE

Wayward Angel
(New York: Topaz, 1997)

Story type: Historical/American Civil War
Major character(s): Dora Beaumont, Adoptee, Religious (Quaker); Payson Nichols, Lawyer, Military Personnel (Union soldier)
Time period(s): 1860s
Locale(s): Kentucky

Summary: Dora Beaumont, born in England and raised by Quaker parents, has a long-time bond to Payson Nichols, son of a wealthy planter. Abused by his father, Payson needs to prove his worth and so becomes first a lawyer and then a Union soldier. When Pace is wounded, Dora declares her love for him and remains by his side. Pace, linked more and more closely to Dora, vows to give her back her "birthright", but that might involve choices she might not want to make. Compelling and romantic.

Where it's reviewed:
Romantic Times, February 1997, page 35

Other books by the same author:
Denim and Lace, 1996
Paper Moon, 1996
Paper Roses, 1995
Paper Tiger, 1995
Devil's Lady, 1992

Other books you might like:
Catherine Anderson, *Coming Up Roses*, 1993
Lorraine Heath, *Always to Remember*, 1996
Lorraine Heath, *Texas Destiny*, 1997
Patricia Potter, *Lightning*, 1992

408

EMILIE RICHARDS

Rising Tides
(Toronto: Mira, 1997)

Story type: Contemporary/Mainstream
Major character(s): Dawn Gerritsen, Photographer; Ben Townsend, Journalist (editor); Aurore Gerritsen, Parent (deceased)
Time period(s): 1990s
Locale(s): Grand Isle, Louisiana

Summary: When Aurore Gerritsen's family is summoned for the reading of her will, Tess Gerritsen finds herself witnessing the revelation of a host of old secrets and past sins that have a definite effect on the present. Complex and filled with well-drawn characters. This romantic family saga is a sequel to *Iron Lace*.

Where it's reviewed:
Library Journal, May 15, 1997, page 68

Other books by the same author:
Twice upon a Time, 1997
Outback Nights, 1996

Once More with Feeling, 1996
Iron Lace, 1996
The Trouble with Joe, 1994

Other books you might like:
Kay Hooper, *Amanda*, 1996
Linda Howard, *Shades of Twilight*, 1996
Marilyn Pappano, *In Sinful Harmony*, 1995
Katherine Stone, *Imagine Love*, 1996
    emotionally involving

409

EMILIE RICHARDS

Twice upon a Time
(New York: Avon, 1997)

Story type: Contemporary/Fantasy
Major character(s): Mary Kate McKenzie, Reincarnated Person, Religious; Charles Casey, Journalist (editor of local paper)
Time period(s): 1990s
Locale(s): Shandly Falls, Ohio

Summary: When gentle, saintly Mary Kate McKenzie finally recovers from being bashed over the head with a shovel wielded by one of the troubled teens she was working with, she is a changed person. In fact, it is almost as though someone else has moved into her body—which is exactly what happened! The spirit of the recently deceased Dixie Dugan, the outrageous TV personality from *Once More With Feeling*, has moved in and all at once Mary Kate doesn't seem—or feel—like herself. An unexplained pregnancy complicates things, as does Dixie's former lover who has come to town as the managing editor for the local paper, but it all works out in the end. Funny, lively, and enjoyable.

Where it's reviewed:
Romantic Times, November 1997, page 68

Other books by the same author:
Iron Lace, 1996
Once More with Feeling, 1996
Duncan's Lady, 1995
MacDougall's Darling, 1995
Dragonslayer, 1993 (Rita Award Winner)

Other books you might like:
Casey Claybourne, *Nick of Time*, 1997
    Reincarnation theme
Kristin Hannah, *When Lightning Strikes*, 1994
Nikki Holiday, *Heaven Comes Home*, 1996
Sharon Sala, *Annie and the Outlaw*, 1994

410

NANCY RICHARDS-AKERS

Wild Irish Skies
(New York: Avon, 1997)

Story type: Historical/Medieval
Major character(s): Annora Picot, Heiress (daughter of wool merchant), Fugitive; Rian O'Byrne, Convict (accused murderer and spy), Fugitive
Time period(s): 14th century (1390s)
Locale(s): Ireland

Summary: After a brief affair four years earlier, Annora and Rian are shocked to find themselves joining forces as they flee Dublin to escape the evil plans of the king. Their journey together results, not surprisingly, in a renewal of their love, but a lot of things must be worked out before they can find happiness together. Interesting historical detail of the violence and political intrigue rampant in Ireland at the time.

Where it's reviewed:
Library Journal, May 15, 1997, page 69
Romantic Times, June 1997, page 46

Other books by the same author:
The Heart and the Holly, 1996
The Heart and the Rose, 1995
The Heart and the Heather, 1994
The Devil's Wager, 1992
Lady Sarah's Charade, 1992

Other books you might like:
Marsha Canham, *The Last Arrow*, 1997
Christina Dodd, *Outrageous*, 1994
Amanda Quick, *Mystique*, 1995
Susan Wiggs, *Dancing on Air*, 1996

411

EVELYN RICHARDSON
CYNTHIA JOHNSON, Co-Author

My Wayward Lady
(New York: Signet, 1997)

Story type: Regency
Major character(s): Lady Harriet Fareham, Noblewoman, Activist (poverty issues); Adrian Chalfont, Nobleman (Marquess of Kidderham)
Time period(s): 1810s

Summary: Bored and restless after being dragged to London so her elder sister could make an appropriate match, unconventional Harriet Fareham sets off to continue her work with the poor. She ends up instructing ''fallen women'' in reading and etiquette at the Temple of Venus, one of the city's more notable brothels. However, her secret is soon discovered by one of the ton's more eligible bachelors, and the fun begins. A traditional, light and lively Regency with a charming heroine and a plot that deals with some serious social issues.

Where it's reviewed:
Library Journal, August 1997, page 70

Other books by the same author:
The Reluctant Heiress, 1996
Lady Alex's Gamble, 1995
The Willful Widow, 1994
The Bluestocking's Dilemma, 1992
The Nabob's Ward, 1991

Other books you might like:
Mary Balogh, *Dancing with Clara*, 1994
Mary Balogh, *The Plumed Bonnet*, 1996
Carla Kelly, *With This Ring*, 1997
Mary Jo Putney, *The Rake and the Reformer*, 1987

| 412 |

PAULA DETMER RIGGS

Daddy by Accident
(New York: Silhouette, 1997)

Story type: Contemporary
Series: Silhouette Desire
Major character(s): Stacy Patterson, Abuse Victim, Teacher;
  Boyd MacAuley, Carpenter, Doctor (former)
Time period(s): 1990s
Locale(s): Portland, Oregon

Summary: When a car accident kills Stacy Patterson's abusive
ex-husband and she is rescued by a doctor-turned-carpenter
who is still suffering from the deaths of his wife and child,
they begin to forge a relationship that will eventually allow
them to put their past hurts behind them and fall in love.
Emotionally intense and involving, this romance confronts
the issues of grief recovery and spousal abuse with equal
effectiveness.

Where it's reviewed:
Library Journal, May 15, 1997, page 68

Other books by the same author:
The Parent Plan, 1998
Desperate, 1997
Baby by Design, 1997
Her Secret, His Child, 1995

Other books you might like:
Catherine Anderson, *Keegan's Lady*, 1996
  Historical/abuse elements/emotionally involving
Kimberly Cates, *Angel's Fall*, 1996
  Historical/another wounded hero
Justine Dare, *Heart of the Hawk*, 1996
  Historical/emotionally involving
Joan Johnston, *I Promise*, 1996
  Emotionally Intense
Peggy Roberts, *Mrs. Perfect*, 1992

| 413 |

SHELLY RITTHALER

With Love, Amanda
(New York: Avon, 1997)

Story type: Historical/American West; Historical/Americana
Series: American Dreams
Major character(s): Amanda Campbell, Teacher, Suffragette;
  Thomas Lewellen, Railroad Worker
Time period(s): 1860s (1869)
Locale(s): Wyoming

Summary: Amanda Campbell returns to her Wyoming home
as a teacher and must face her childhood idol, Thomas Lewellen, whom she proposed to when she was 14 and still loves.
Her suffragette views land her in hot water—as does her
curiosity. Nevertheless, love does win out in this sweet, heart-
warming story of children, families, and love.

Other books by the same author:
Heart of the Hills, 1996

The Ginger Jar, 1990

Other books you might like:
Robin Lee Hatcher, *Promise Me Spring*, 1991
Robin Lee Hatcher, *Where the Heart Is*, 1993
Jill Marie Landis, *Rose*, 1990
LaVyrle Spencer, *The Endearment*, 1991
LaVyrle Spencer, *The Gamble*, 1987

| 414 |

KAREN ROBARDS

Heartbreaker
(New York: Delacorte, 1997)

Story type: Contemporary; Romantic Suspense
Major character(s): Lynn Nelson, Television Personality (TV
  anchor person); Jess Feldman, Guide, Government official
  (former government agent)
Time period(s): 1990s
Locale(s): Uintah Mountains, Utah

Summary: Lynn Nelson, successful television anchor, accompanies her rebellious daughter to a Utah mountain camp.
Unimpressed by "cowboy" camp leader Jess Feldman, she is
annoyed that her daughter adores him. Despite the fact that he
doesn't think much of them either, Jess still risks his life to
rescue them after a fall. But when they encounter a murdered
family along the way, they run for their lives from cult leaders
and both show more courage and strength than either had
expected. Respect and admiration grows into attraction and
love as they fight to survive their ordeal. Suspenseful and
unusual.

Where it's reviewed:
Affaire de Coeur, January 1997, page 21

Other books by the same author:
Hunter's Moon, 1996
Walking After Midnight, 1995
Maggy's Child, 1994
One Summer, 1993
Nobody's Angel, 1992

Other books you might like:
Tami Hoag, *Dark Paradise*, 1994
Linda Howard, *After the Night*, 1995
Iris Johansen, *The Ugly Duckling*, 1996
Dinah McCall, *Chase the Moon*, 1997
  cults and suspense
Nora Roberts, *Divine Evil*, 1992

| 415 |

NORA ROBERTS

The MacGregor Brides
(New York: Silhouette, 1997)

Story type: Contemporary
Series: MacGregor
Major character(s): Laura MacGregor, Lawyer; Gwendolyn
  Blade, Doctor; Julia MacGregor, Businesswoman (real
  estate developer)
Time period(s): 1990s

Locale(s): Boston, Massachusetts

Summary: When nonagenarian Daniel MacGregor, the patriarch of the MacGregor clan, decides that he wants grandchildren and that his three beautiful, talented, and definitely liberated granddaughters need to get married, he sets about accomplishing it with the same determination he gives to everything else in his life—and with equally successful results. Warm, romantic, but thoroughly modern, this trilogy of three linked holiday novellas continues Roberts' popular MacGregor Saga.

Where it's reviewed:
Library Journal, November 15, 1997, page 48

Other books by the same author:
Montana Sky, 1997
The Heart of Devin MacKade, 1996
Daring to Dream, 1996
Born in Shame, 1996
Holding the Dream, 1996

Other books you might like:
Rexanne Becnel, *Christmas Journey*, 1992
Marion Devon, *Deck the Halls*, 1995
    Grandfatherly Matchmaking Regency-style
Ellen Tanner Marsh, *A Christmas Embrace*, 1994
Heather McAllister, *Christmas Male*, 1996
Diana Palmer, *Lone Star Christmas*, 1997
    Two stories by Palmer and Joan Johnston

416

KRISTINE ROLOFSON

Pillow Talk

(Toronto: Harlequin, 1997)

Story type: Contemporary
Series: Love and Laughter
Major character(s): Lady Elizabeth Longford, Noblewoman; Sam Martin, Contractor, Imposter (poses as the Earl of Longford)
Time period(s): 1990s
Locale(s): England

Summary: When Sam Martin's devious matchmaking mother decides he and Lady Elizabeth Longford would make an ideal couple, there is no stopping her in this light, rather British contemporary romance. A no-nonsense American contractor and the lady of the manor get a little bit of motherly, and other-worldly, help along the way.

Where it's reviewed:
Library Journal, August 1997, page 68

Other books by the same author:
Madeleine's Cowboy, 1998
The Next Man in Texas, 1997
The Last Man in Montana, 1997
The Bride Rode West, 1997
The Only Man in Wyoming, 1997

Other books you might like:
Barbara Bretton, *The Invisible Groom*, 1994
Jennifer Crusie, *Strange Bedpersons*, 1994
Cathie Linz, *Husband Needed*, 1997

Charlotte Maclay, *Accidental Roommates*, 1997

417

MERYL SAWYER
KATE HOFFMAN, Co-Author
GINA WILKINS, Co-Author

Valentine Delights

(Toronto: Harlequin, 1997)

Story type: Anthology; Holiday Themes
Time period(s): 1990s
Locale(s): Cedar Ridge, Georgia

Summary: A delightful trilogy of contemporary Valentine's Day stories linked by the matchmaking, advice-giving Papa Valentine and his sinfully delicious confections. Included are ''Chocolate Fantasy'' by Meryl Sawyer, ''His Secret Valentine'' by Kate Hoffman, and ''Gift of the Heart'' by Gina Wilkins. Wonderfully rich and chocolatey recipes accompany each story.

Where it's reviewed:
Library Journal, February 15, 1997, page 126

Other books you might like:
Rochelle Alers, *Love Letters*, 1997
    Anthology
Sara Blayne, *Valentine Love*, 1996
    Regency Valentine Anthology
Margaret Brownley, *Chocolate Kisses*, 1997
    Anthology
Kay Hooper, *Hearts of Gold*, 1994
    Historical anthology

418

MAGGIE SHAYNE

Annie's Hero

(New York: Avon, 1997)

Story type: Contemporary/Fantasy
Major character(s): Annie Nelson, Teacher; Richard ''Ren'' Nelson, Truck Driver, Spirit (''White Knight'')
Time period(s): 1990s
Locale(s): United States

Summary: When Richard Nelson drives his rig off the road during a storm to avoid hitting a busload of children, he knows he won't survive; his only regret is leaving his beloved wife and childhood sweetheart, Annie. But instead of dying, Richard is ''brought over'' and becomes Ren, one of the legendary White Knights who have fought evil throughout time. Although he no longer remembers his former life, when he returns to save Annie and her unborn child from the Dark, she recognizes him instinctively, but can't understand why he doesn't know her. A magical story of love and sacrifice.

Where it's reviewed:
Romantic Times, April 1997, page 79

Other books by the same author:
Born in Twilight, 1997
Forever Enchanted, 1997

A Husband in Time, 1997
Fairytale, 1996
Out of This World Marriage, 1995

Other books you might like:
Evelyn A. Crowe, *Reunited*, 1993
Angie Ray, *Ghostly Enchantment*, 1994
Patricia Simpson, *Whisper of Midnight*, 1991
Antoinette Stockenberg, *Emily's Ghost*, 1992

419

MAGGIE SHAYNE

Born in Twilight
(New York: Silhouette, 1997)

Story type: Contemporary/Fantasy
Series: Wings of the Night
Major character(s): Angelica, Vampire; Jamison Bryant, Human
Time period(s): 1990s

Summary: Raised by nuns and almost ready for her vows, Angelica is attacked by a vampire and is suddenly no longer human. Repulsed by vampire activities, Angelica would rather die, but when human Jamison Bryant ''feeds'' her to keep her alive, she takes too much blood and he almost dies. The nefarious DPI, a vampire hunting organization, keeps things interesting for the pair, but love and a little help from the rest of the vampires makes things work out in the end. An unusual tale of vampires as loving and concerned individuals.

Where it's reviewed:
Affaire de Coeur, March 1997, page 19
Romantic Times, March 1997, page 86

Other books by the same author:
A Husband in Time, 1997
Fairytale, 1996
The Littlest Cowboy, 1996
Out of This World Marriage, 1995
Forgotten Vows, 1994

Other books you might like:
Lori Herter, *Confession*, 1992
Lori Herter, *Obsession*, 1991
Linda Lael Miller, *Forever and the Night*, 1993
Anne Stuart, *Night of the Phantom*, 1991

420

MAGGIE SHAYNE

Forever Enchanted
(New York: Avon, 1997)

Story type: Contemporary/Fantasy
Major character(s): Princess Bridin of Rush, Royalty, Mythical Creature (half human, half fairy); Tristan of Shara, Royalty
Time period(s): 1990s
Locale(s): Rush, Mythical Place (Shara); Mythical Place

Summary: Continuing the magical story begun in *Fairytale*, Princess Bridin of Rush and her arch enemy, Tristan of Shara,

must battle each other and, eventually, other forces as they both lay claim to the same country and crown. Love makes it all work out in this passionate, emotionally involving story of good and evil, self-sacrifice and greed.

Where it's reviewed:
Romantic Times, April 1997, page 76

Other books by the same author:
Annie's Hero, 1997
Born in Twilight, 1997
A Husband in Time, 1997
Fairytale, 1996
Out of This World Marriage, 1995

Other books you might like:
Robin McKinley, *Beauty*, 1978
Rebecca Paisley, *A Basket of Wishes*, 1995
Josepha Sherman, *Child of Faerie, Child of Earth*, 1992
Susan Sizemore, *One of These Nights*, 1997
    magical
Lisa Ann Verge, *The Faery Bride*, 1996

421

SUZANNE SIMMONS

The Paradise Man
(New York: St. Martin's, 1997)

Story type: Contemporary; Romantic Suspense
Series: Man
Major character(s): Jane Bennett, Heiress, Vacationer; Jake Hollister, Businessman
Time period(s): 1990s
Locale(s): Paradise Island, Caribbean

Summary: Sophisticated Jane Bennett and businessman-turned-islander Jake Hollister are both searching for the wreck of the *Bella Donna,* but for very different reasons. She needs to prove a point and discover what happened to her father and Jake simply ''wants something to do.'' Their resulting partnership is both lively and passionate—and ultimately rewarding. A fast paced, upbeat, lushly set story that holds a few surprises.

Other books by the same author:
No Ordinary Man, 1998
Bed of Roses, 1995
Diamond in the Rough, 1994

Other books you might like:
Stella Cameron, *Breathless*, 1994
    Another island adventure
Catherine Lanigan, *At Long Last Love*, 1994
    More exotic adventure
Jeane Renick, *Trust Me*, 1992
Anne Marie Winston, *Unlikely Eden*, 1993

422

PATRICIA SIMPSON

Just Before Midnight

(New York: Harper, 1997)

Story type: Contemporary/Fantasy
Major character(s): Evaline Jaye, Health Care Professional (physical therapist), Indian; Gabriel Townsend, Guide (for tourists)
Time period(s): 1990s
Locale(s): Seattle, Washington; Obstruction Bay, Washington

Summary: Just because Evaline Jaye has a job as a physical therapist for bitter, angry Gabriel Townsend's daughter, that doesn't mean she has to like him. And anyway, she has problems of her own—as a result of accidents that left her scared and withdrawn, her Native American spiritual powers have been less strong. Gabriel's foul-mouthed daughter doesn't help, either—until Evaline discovers that in addition to being physically crippled, she is also emotionally scarred. Spirits from the past, a tame bear, and two wounded and needy adults come together to solve an old mystery and bring wholeness to everyone. Mystical and sensual.

Other books by the same author:
The Legacy, 1992
Whisper of Midnight, 1991

Other books you might like:
Kathleen Eagle, *Reason to Believe*, 1995
Kathleen Eagle, *Sunrise Song*, 1996
Kristin Hannah, *Waiting for the Moon*, 1995
  Historical/wounded protagonists/some paranormal elements
Dinah McCall, *Tallchief*, 1997

423

SUSAN SIZEMORE

One of These Nights

(New York: Harper, 1997)

Story type: Time Travel
Major character(s): Maddie McCullogh, Engineer, Time Traveller; Rowan Murray, Laird
Time period(s): 1990s; 13th century (1210)
Locale(s): Scotland

Summary: A plane crash sends systems engineer Maddie McCullogh back to 13th- century Scotland and into the life of Rowan Murray, laird of the Murrays of Cape Wrath, who looks exactly like the man she has loved ever since the sixth grade. She finds herself in a world of magic where the fair folk walk the land, where people take prophecies seriously, and where she is suddenly handfasted and then quickly wed to the determined Rowan—without even being consulted! Warm, enchanting, and totally romantic.

Where it's reviewed:
Romantic Times, June 1997, page 90

Other books by the same author:
In My Dreams, 1994

My Own True Love, 1994
My First Duchess, 1993
Wings of the Storm, 1992

Other books you might like:
Diana Gabaldon, *Outlander*, 1991
Emma Merritt, *Night Lace*, 1996
Maggie Shayne, *Forever Enchanted*, 1997
Flora Speer, *A Love Beyond Time*, 1994

424

CHRISTINA SKYE

Bride of the Mist

(New York: Avon, 1996)

Story type: Contemporary/Fantasy
Major character(s): Kara Fitzgerald, Publisher (magazine), Psychic; Lord Duncan MacKinnon, Nobleman
Time period(s): 1990s
Locale(s): England

Summary: Kara Fitzgerald goes to Scotland, determined to use Lord Duncan MacKinnon's castle in her bridal magazine. While waiting, she is hired to examine the psychic energy flow for a friend's business. Surprised on assignment and manhandled by a man who tests security systems, she finds him to be Duncan, himself. At his castle, she senses danger and evil from another time, a feeling that bears itself out when Duncan's evil brother returns.

Where it's reviewed:
Rendezvous, March 1996, page 29
Romantic Times, May 1996, page 83

Other books by the same author:
Come the Dawn, 1995
Come the Night, 1994
Hour of the Rose, 1994
East of Forever, 1993
The Ruby, 1992

Other books you might like:
Mary Burkhardt, *Highland Ecstasy*, 1993
Angie Ray, *Ghostly Enchantment*, 1994
  family ghosts
Maura Seger, *Forevermore*, 1994
  Mysteries and ghosts
Maura Seger, *The Lady and the Laird*, 1992
  Castles and ghosts
Antoinette Stockenberg, *Dream a Little Dream*, 1997
  Castles and ghosts

425

CHRISTINA SKYE

Key to Forever

(New York: Avon, 1997)

Story type: Contemporary/Fantasy
Major character(s): Joanna Russell, Antiquarian (weapons expert); Alexei Cameron, Nobleman (Earl of Greywood), Artisan (sword-maker)
Time period(s): 1980s; 1990s (1984-1996)

Locale(s): Sussex, England

Summary: Alexei Cameron, expert sword-maker, knows that his family's Cameron sword, linked to Mary, Queen of Scots, and protected by the family ghost, must be found by him. One of his prime suspects is Joanna Russell, weaponry expert and former lover. Past secrets and meddling ghosts combine with dark intrigue and plot twists that keep this fast-paced, highly sensual story suspenseful to the end.

Where it's reviewed:
Romantic Times, March 1997, page 83

Other books by the same author:
Come the Dawn, 1995
Come the Night, 1994
Hour of the Rose, 1994
East of Forever, 1993
The Ruby, 1992

Other books you might like:
Linda Howard, *Son of the Morning*, 1997
   Dark
Sabine Kells, *A Deeper Hunger*, 1995
   Dark fantasy
Johanna Lindsey, *Until Forever*, 1995
   Time travel elements
Anne Stuart, *Night of the Phantom*, 1991
   Dark and highly sensual/some paranormal elements

426

CHRISTINA SKYE

Season of Wishes

(New York: Avon, 1997)

Story type: Holiday Themes; Contemporary/Fantasy
Major character(s): Jamee Knight, Designer (fabric), Heiress; Ian McCall, Nobleman (Laird of Glenlyle), Bodyguard (kidnapping expert)
Time period(s): 1990s
Locale(s): Scotland

Summary: Hired to secretly protect heiress Jamee Knight from a potential kidnapping, Ian McCall reluctantly takes on the job and ends up in love with the woman he's been hired to keep alive. Humor, a fast pace, and a beautifully rendered setting recommend this romance that features a pair of likable protagonists and some very real ghosts.

Where it's reviewed:
Library Journal, November 15, 1997, page 49

Other books by the same author:
Key to Forever, 1997
Come the Dawn, 1995
Hour of the Rose, 1994
The Ruby, 1992
The Black Rose, 1991

Other books you might like:
Mary Burkhardt, *Highland Ecstasy*, 1993
Laura Parker, *For Love's Sake Only*, 1991
   Victorian ghosts
Laura Parker, *Moonshadow*, 1992
   Sequel to *For Love's Sake Only*

Maura Seger, *The Lady and the Laird*, 1992
   ghosts and castles
Antoinette Stockenberg, *Dream a Little Dream*, 1997

427

HAYWOOD SMITH

Secrets in Satin

(New York: St. Martin, 1997)

Story type: Historical/Seventeenth Century
Major character(s): Elizabeth, Countess of Ravenwold, Noblewoman, Abuse Victim; Edward Garrett, Nobleman (Viscount Creighton), Military Personnel (lieutenant)
Time period(s): 17th century (1640s)
Locale(s): England

Summary: Forced into marriage by Charles I, the Protestant Viscount Creighton and the Roman Catholic Countess of Ravenwold have old wounds and current prejudices to deal with before they can find love together. Appealing characters drive this nicely done story of action and intrigue.

Where it's reviewed:
Library Journal, May 15, 1997, page 68

Other books by the same author:
Shadows on Velvet, 1996

Other books you might like:
Rexanne Becnel, *A Dove at Midnight*, 1993
   Earlier time period
Philippa Carr, *Sarabande for Two Sisters*, 1976
   Similar time period
Jane Feather, *Reckless Angel*, 1989
   Similar setting
Julie Garwood, *Saving Grace*, 1993
   Arranged marriage/earlier time period
Laurie Grant, *Beloved Deceiver*, 1993
   Another forced marriage/earlier time period

428

JOAN SMITH

An Infamous Proposal

(New York: Fawcett, 1997)

Story type: Regency
Major character(s): Lady Emma Capehart, Widow(er); Nicholas Arden, Nobleman (Lord Hansard), Guardian
Time period(s): 1810s
Locale(s): London, England

Summary: Lady Emma Capehart, widowed at the age of 20, knows she must marry again in spite of her naivete about men and life. So, sensibly, she proposes to Lord Hansard, knowing that marriage to him would protect her and cause her relatives to back off. He refuses, but promises to find her a husband. As might be expected, no one Nicholas finds meets with his approval. The outcome, of course, is exactly what Emma had in mind.

Other books by the same author:
The Kissing Bough, 1994

The Spanish Lady, 1993
Cousin Cecelia, 1990
Madcap Miss, 1989

Other books you might like:
Mary Chase Comstock, *An Impetuous Miss*, 1993
Elisabeth Fairchild, *The Love Knot*, 1995
Candice Hern, *A Change of Heart*, 1995
Candice Hern, *A Proper Companion*, 1995

429
ANTOINETTE STOCKENBERG

Dream a Little Dream
(New York: St. Martin, 1997)

Story type: Contemporary/Fantasy
Major character(s): Elinor MacLeish, Artist (children's book illustrator); William Braddock, Nobleman (Lord Norwood)
Time period(s): 1990s
Locale(s): New York; Dibble, England

Summary: When William Braddock, Lord Norwood, comes to America to reclaim his family castle, which had been brought to the Hudson River Valley by Elinor's eccentric grandfather, Elinor is determined to see that that never happens. Her quest is made more difficult not only by her family members, who are thinking of selling, and by the ghostly inhabitants of the castle, who have ideas of their own, but by the inexplicable chemistry that sizzles between Will and herself. Well-developed characters, good description, and an interesting mystery enhance this warm, often humorous and occasionally gothic, romance.

Where it's reviewed:
Library Journal, May 15, 1997, p.69

Other books by the same author:
Beyond Midnight, 1996
Time After Time, 1995
Embers, 1994
Emily's Ghost, 1992 (Rita Award winner)

Other books you might like:
Barbara Freethy, *Ask Mariah*, 1997
Barbara Freethy, *Daniel's Gift*, 1996
    Rita Award winner
Maura Seger, *The Lady and the Laird*, 1992
    Ghosts and castles
Patricia Simpson, *Whisper of Midnight*, 1991
Christina Skye, *Bride of the Mist*, 1996
    Castles and a psychic heroine/gothic

430
DEB STOVER

Almost an Angel
(New York: Pinnacle, 1997)

Story type: Time Travel; Contemporary/Fantasy
Major character(s): Hilary Brown, Angel (would-be); Zach Ryan, Engineer
Time period(s): 1990s; 1880s

Locale(s): Columbine, Colorado

Summary: Denied access to Heaven, Hilary Brown is given the chance to make amends for her past mistakes, first by finding and helping a deserving person and then by returning to her own time and setting things to rights. For more than a century, Hilary wanders the streets of Columbine waiting for the right person. Of course, when he finally does arrive in the form of engineer, and reformed alcoholic, Zach Ryan, he doesn't believe her—until he is zapped back to 1880s Columbine and everything begins to make sense. Sensual and occasionally poignant.

Where it's reviewed:
Library Journal, November 15, 1997, page 49

Other books by the same author:
Some Like it Hotter, 1997
A Willing Spirit, 1996
Shades of Rose, 1995

Other books you might like:
Jude Deveraux, *Wishes*, 1989
    Historical
Nikki Holiday, *Heaven Knows Best*, 1997
Nikki Holiday, *Heaven Loves a Hero*, 1997
Lynn Kerstan, *Gwen's Christmas Ghost*, 1995
    Regency
Heather Graham Pozzessere, *An Angel's Touch*, 1995

431
ANNE STUART

Lord of Danger
(New York: Zebra, 1997)

Story type: Historical/Medieval
Major character(s): Alys of Summersedge, Noblewoman; Claire of Summersedge, Noblewoman; Simon of Navarre, Wizard
Time period(s): Indeterminate Past
Locale(s): England

Summary: Commanded by their brother Richard to leave their convent haven and come to his court to be wed at his pleasure, obedient, clever Alys and beautiful, fiery Claire reluctantly obey, fearful, yet resentful and angry at Richard's high-handedness and cruelty. However, when Richard's magician, the mysterious Simon of Navarre, chooses the plainer Alys as his bride, things take an interesting turn, and by the end of the story both Claire and Alys have found happiness. A typical dark and intense story by a master of the type.

Other books by the same author:
Ritual Sins, 1997
Moon-Rise, 1996
Prince of Swords, 1996
Night Fall, 1995
To Love a Dark Lord, 1994

Other books you might like:
Justine Dare, *Fire Hawk*, 1997
    Another wounded hero
Katherine Deauville, *Blood Red Roses*, 1991
Katherine Deauville, *Eyes of Love*, 1996

Karyn Monk, *Once a Warrior*, 1997
  Less dark

432

ANNE STUART

Ritual Sins

(New York: Onyx, 1997)

Story type: Romantic Suspense
Major character(s): Rachel Connery, Young Woman; Luke Bardell, Con Artist, Religious (cult leader)
Time period(s): 1990s
Locale(s): Santa Dolores, New Mexico (near Albuquerque)

Summary: When Rachel Connery goes to the headquarters of the Foundation of Being, a quasi-religious cult that she feels not only conned her mother into leaving them her fortune, but also may have been responsible for her death, it is to unmask Luke Bardell, the magnetic, dangerous leader of the group. What she doesn't know, however, is that Luke has already decided his plan of action, and is expecting her. Dark, dangerous, and passionate. Features a wounded hero that is almost past redemption and will not appeal to everyone.

Where it's reviewed:
Library Journal, August 1997, page 70

Other books by the same author:
Lord of Danger, 1997
Moon-Rise, 1996
Prince of Swords, 1996
Night Fall, 1995
To Love a Dark Lord, 1994

Other books you might like:
Tami Hoag, *Dark Paradise*, 1994
Tami Hoag, *Still Waters*, 1992
Linda Howard, *After the Night*, 1995
  Dark hero
Linda Howard, *Loving Evangeline*, 1994
  Another dark hero
Nora Roberts, *Divine Evil*, 1992

433

ELIZABETH THORNTON

Dangerous to Hold

(New York: Bantam, 1996)

Story type: Historical/Regency
Major character(s): Catherine Courtnay, Spy (former), Writer; Lord Marcus Lytton, Nobleman (Earl of Wrotham), Military Personnel (former)
Time period(s): 1810s (1812)
Locale(s): England

Summary: When Marcus Lytton, Earl of Wrotham, mistakes former spy Catherine Courtnay for his missing wife, he quickly realizes he can make use of the resemblance and convinces Catherine to pose as his wife. This deception, however, leads to danger both from enemies in their pasts and from their own growing feelings for each other. Lots of action, adventure, and good historical detail.

Where it's reviewed:
Romantic Times, May 1996, page 37

Other books by the same author:
Dangerous to Kiss, 1996
Dangerous to Love, 1994
Highland Fire, 1994
Velvet Is the Night, 1992
Tender Is the Storm, 1991

Other books you might like:
Mary Balogh, *Beyond the Sunrise*, 1992
  Spies and deception
Jo Beverley, *My Lady Notorious*, 1993
  More deception Georgian-style
Jane Feather, *Velvet*, 1994
  More spies
Susan Sizemore, *My First Duchess*, 1993

434

TRACEY TILLIS

Flashpoint

(New York: Onyx, 1997)

Story type: Romantic Suspense
Major character(s): Maggie Thomas, Businesswoman (publishing executive); Gil Stewart, Police Officer (lieutenant)
Time period(s): 1990s
Locale(s): Georgia

Summary: Maggie Thomas' renowned senator father is seriously injured in a suspicious hit-and-run accident. She is forced to deal with the fact that her beloved father might actually have feet of clay, and the man who will help solve the mystery is the one man she had truly loved—and the one person she never wanted to see again. Racism, mystery, and intrigue are part of this fast-paced romantic suspense novel that features compelling protagonists and a story that will keep readers reading.

Where it's reviewed:
Library Journal, February 15, 1997, page 126

Other books by the same author:
Night Watch, 1995
Deadly Masquerade, 1994

Other books you might like:
Sandra Brown, *Breath of Scandal*, 1991
Sandra Brown, *French Silk*, 1992
Tami Hoag, *Night Sins*, 1995
Tami Hoag, *Still Waters*, 1992
  Small town, closed community setting
Nora Roberts, *Public Secrets*, 1990

435

THERESA WEIR

American Dreamer

(New York: Harper, 1997)

Story type: Contemporary

Major character(s): Lark Leopold, Researcher (animal); Nathan Senatra, Farmer
Time period(s): 1990s
Locale(s): Iowa

Summary: When city-bred Lark Leopold heads for the country to study the "contentment" of the local cows, she is looking forward to being on her own for the first time. She doesn't expect to run headlong into a devastatingly handsome, but troubled, farmer—or to find the body of his ex-wife floating serenely in the pond. Witty and fast-paced.

Where it's reviewed:
Library Journal, May 15, 1997, page 69

Other books you might like:
Debra Dixon, *Hot as Sin*, 1995
    Witty, fast-paced mystery
Jayne Ann Krentz, *Deep Waters*, 1997
    Fast-paced and upbeat/small town setting
Cassie Miles, *The Imposter*, 1996
    Paranormal mystery elements/fast-paced
Nora Roberts, *Carnal Innocence*, 1992
    Small town setting/darker

436

STEPHANIE GRACE WHITSON

Soaring Eagle

(Nashville: Thomas Nelson, 1996)

Story type: Historical/American West; Inspirational
Major character(s): Lisbeth King Baird, Widow(er); Soaring Eagle, Indian (half Sioux)
Time period(s): 1870s
Locale(s): Dakota Territory, West; Nebraska

Summary: A deeply Christian woman and a Sioux scout find love after the destructive Battle of the Little Bighorn. Lots of family involvement, forgiveness, and redemption in this inspirational romance.

Other books by the same author:
Walks the Fire, 1995 (The Prairie Winds Series)

Other books you might like:
Kathleen Eagle, *Heaven and Earth*, 1990
    not Inspirational
Janette Oke, *Love Comes Softly*, 1979
    First in classic series
Francine Rivers, *Redeeming Love*, 1991
    1997 version rewritten for Inspirational market
Bette M. Ross, *Journey of No Return*, 1985

437

SUSAN WIGGS
BARBARA SAMUEL, Co-Author
MORGAN LLYWELYN, Co-Author
ROBERTA GELLIS, Co-Author

Irish Magic II

(New York: Kensington, 1997)

Story type: Anthology; Holiday Themes

Summary: A diverse quartet of charming, magically retold Irish myths that makes full use of Celtic legend and lore. Included are "The Changeling" by Susan Wiggs, "Earthly Magic" by Barbara Samuel, "To Recapture the Light" by Morgan Llywelyn, and "Bride Price" by Roberta Gellis.

Other books you might like:
Roberta Gellis, *Irish Magic*, 1995
    Original anthology
Kathleen Morgan, *Enchant the Heavens*, 1995
    Celtic Lore
Jennifer Roberson, *Lady of the Forest*, 1992
Lisa Ann Verge, *The Faery Bride*, 1996
Penelope Williamson, *Keeper of the Dream*, 1992

438

PENELOPE WILLIAMSON

The Passions of Emma

(New York: Warner, 1997)

Story type: Historical/Mainstream; Historical/Victorian America
Major character(s): Emma Tremayne, Artist (sculptor), Gentlewoman; Shay McKenna, Revolutionary (from Ireland); Bria McKenna, Worker (mill), Invalid (suffering from consumption)
Time period(s): 1890s
Locale(s): Bristol, Rhode Island

Summary: Born into the luxurious, but stifling, world of the rich and powerful, Emma Tremayne knows her responsibility is to marry well, maintain her family's social position, and to avoid scandal. However, when an accident at her fiance's mill results in the death of a child—and the child's body is "presented" to those responsible during a fox hunt by a millworker—Emma begins to rethink things, with far-ranging results. Well-written and poignant. A nice blend of romance and serious social issues in a story that verges on mainstream.

Where it's reviewed:
Library Journal, August 1997, page 70

Other books by the same author:
The Outsider, 1996
Heart of the West, 1995
Once in a Blue Moon, 1993
Keeper of the Dream, 1992
A Wild Yearning, 1990 (Rita winner)

Other books you might like:
Elaine Barbieri, *Tattered Silk*, 1991
Elaine Barbieri, *Wishes on the Wind*, 1991
    workers issues/social conflicts/class issues
Meagan McKinney, *Lions and Lace*, 1992
    later time period/class issues
Patricia Rice, *Paper Tiger*, 1995
    workers issues
LaVyrle Spencer, *November of the Heart*, 1993
    Class issues

439

JOAN WOLF

The Arrangement

(New York: Warner, 1997)

Story type: Historical/Regency
Major character(s): Gail Saunders, Widow(er), Equestrian; Raoul Melville, Nobleman (Earl of Savile)
Time period(s): 1810s
Locale(s): England

Summary: When the late George Devane leaves 20,000 pounds to widowed riding instructor Gail Saunders' young son, gossip is rampant—and so is the animosity of the other heirs. But as much as she wants to reject the money, she can refuse neither her son's inheritance nor the instructions in the will that place imperious, magnetic Raoul Melville, Earl of Savile, in charge of the funds until Nicky comes of age. Romance, mystery, and danger abound in this well-done romance that takes on an almost gothic feel as Wolf tells her tale from the now somewhat uncommon first-person point of view.

Where it's reviewed:
Romantic Times, November 1997, page 43

Other books by the same author:
The Deception, 1997
The Reindeer Hunters, 1995
The Horsemasters, 1993
Daughter of the Red Deer, 1991
Born of the Sun, 1989

Other books you might like:
Judith McNaught, *Whitney, My Love*, 1985
Anita Mills, *Secret Nights*, 1994
Kate Moore, *Winterburn's Rose*, 1996
Mary Jo Putney, *One Perfect Rose*, 1997

440

JOAN WOLF

The Guardian

(New York: Warner, 1997)

Story type: Historical/Regency
Major character(s): Annabelle Grandville, Noblewoman, Widow(er); Stephen Grandville, Nobleman, Guardian
Time period(s): 1810s
Locale(s): England

Summary: When exiled Stephen Grandville is named guardian for his late brother's son, Giles, the four-year-old Earl of Grandville, he leaves Jamaica and returns to a life he thought he had left behind for good—with unexpectedly romantic results. Intrigue, mystery, and long-kept- secrets are part of this charming Regency.

Where it's reviewed:
Romantic Times, May 1997, page 37

Other books by the same author:
The Arrangement, 1997
The Deception, 1997
The Reindeer Hunters, 1995
The Horsemasters, 1993
Daughter of the Red Deer, 1991

Other books you might like:
Judith McNaught, *Almost Heaven*, 1990
Anita Mills, *Autumn Rain*, 1993
Kate Moore, *Winterburn's Rose*, 1996
Mary Jo Putney, *One Perfect Rose*, 1997

441

KATHLEEN WOODIWISS

Petals on the River

(New York: Avon, 1997)

Story type: Historical/Colonial America
Major character(s): Shemaine O'Hearn, Captive (falsely convicted), Gentlewoman; Gage Thornton, Businessman (shipbuilder)
Time period(s): 1740s (1747)

Summary: Falsely arrested and convicted of theft, outspoken Shemaine O'Hearn finds herself on her way to America to be sold as an indentured servant before her family knows what has happened to her. She ends up as servant and nanny in the house of shipbuilder Gage Thornton, and despite the rumors that swirl around him, Shemaine cannot ignore her growing feelings for him. A fast-paced story of mystery and passion by the writer of the classic *Flame and the Flower* (1973).

Other books by the same author:
Forever in Your Embrace, 1992
So Worthy My Love, 1989
Come Love a Stranger, 1984
Ashes in the Wind, 1979
Shanna, 1977

Other books you might like:
Shannon Drake, *Bride of the Wind*, 1992
Karen Robards, *Nobody's Angel*, 1992
Maura Seger, *The Taming of Amelia*, 1993
Jo Ann Wendt, *The Golden Dove*, 1989

Romance

The Year in Westerns
by
Wayne Barton

With the current slide in markets and publishing slots, doom-sayers continue to predict that the Western is going south. Based on the entries in the current listings, the truth is that the Western, at least to some extent, is moving east. The Mississippi River, often considered a boundary for the genre, has been crossed decisively. Besides the more traditional forms, this year's books contain stories of the Ohio River Valley and a scattering on the French and Indian War. Others are set even earlier, when the western frontier was still almost within hearing of the Atlantic breakers. Publishers are also showing—or reflecting—a renewed interest in the Civil War, in both the Virginia and the western theaters.

Before the purists start saying, "But *that's* not a Western," let's consider the situation. Occasionally, there's a movement (that never gets far) to rename the Western genre something like "frontier fiction." Its list of titles might include the Leatherstocking stories of James Fenimore Cooper, whose Deerslayer—independent in thought, self-reliant, willing to risk everything in a good cause—is perhaps the archetypal Western hero. Another neglected entry would be the cowboy tales of pre-Civil War Florida, where the dangers were different but the freedom and tedium of cowboy life were much the same as in Texas or Wyoming. Frontier fiction is the keynote of this year's list, wherever the frontier happens to be at the writer's time of choice.

Certainly an interest in the eastern frontier of colonial days is nothing new for Western writers. Zane Grey was a paladin of the traditional Western if there ever was one. But some of Grey's best writing—*Betty Zane*, *The Spirit of the Border*, and *The Last Trail* come to mind immediately—is set in the 18th-century East. Historical novelist James Alexander Thom won a 1989 Spur Award for his story of Tecumseh, *Panther in the Sky*. In the current listings, he appears with *The Red Heart*, the story of a kidnapped Quaker woman who rises to power and influence among the Senecas.

Elsewhere in the East, such confirmed Western stalwarts as Cameron Judd and Jason Manning have worked the Tennessee-Kentucky border country for years. Manning's three entries in the current list are all set west of the Mississippi, but Judd's *Passage to Natchez* is mostly an Eastern. Spur winner Jim Woolard (*Thunder in the Valley*, 1995) is back along the Ohio River with *The Winds of Autumn*.

Mary's Land by Lucia St. Clair Robson and *The Rain from God* by newcomer Mark Ammerman, deal with the very earliest English frontier, barely away from the boat. Cherokee novelist Robert J. Conley's fictional history of the Cherokees has them greeting both Spanish and English settlers in his newest volume, *War Woman*. Along the Gulf Coast, Coosa Indians tangle with Spanish conquistadors in Paul Clayton's *Flight of the Crow*.

What all of these writers have discovered is a commonality of human experience. A mountain man needs much the same qualities to survive whether his mountains are the Alleghenies or the Rockies. The people on a wagon trail going west share the same hopes and joys and dangers and privations and fears and fortitude whether their route is the Wilderness Road or the Oregon Trail. An Indian war fought in the eastern woodlands will differ in weapons and tactics from a war on the western plains or the high Rockies, but the stress of command, the horror and confusion of battle, and the fear of death will be the same for each set of participants. The agony of a people uprooted is similar whether the victims are Cherokees exiled to Oklahoma or Apaches exiled to Florida, or, for that matter, Confederate or Unionist sympathizers driven from their homes by opposing armies.

That brings us to the resurgence of Civil War books. The case for including them in the Western genre would be weaker than for the historical "Easterns" except for the fact that many of the same writers are represented. Part of the Civil War—a minor part, except to those who lived through it or died in it—did of course take place in the geographical

West. Elmer Kelton (*Dark Thicket, Long Way to Texas, The Texas Rifles*), William A. Luckey (*Flags over Texas*), and L.D. Clark (*A Bright Tragic Thing*) have all written about the Civil War in Texas and New Mexico. California Confederates figured in John Edward Ames's 1996 *The Golden Circle* and in Brock and Bodie Thoene's earlier *Cannons of the Comstock.*

Frank and Jesse James got their start in the ugly, no-quarter border war in Kansas and Missouri, of which Randal L. Greenwood has written in *Ride, Rebels, Ride* and Max McCoy in 1993's award-winning *Sons of Fire*. This year's showpiece book for Bleeding Kansas is the monumental *Cloudsplitter,* a fictionalized look at John Brown's life by Russell Banks. But some of the same territory is covered from different angles in Robert Vaughan's *Blood on the Plains* and the similarly-titled but quite different *Savage Plains* from David William Ross.

Frederic Bean, known for historicals in the continuing *Rivers West* series and for numerous traditionals (*Hell's Half Acre,* for instance) moves across the Mississippi with *Lorena,* built around the Civil War battles of Franklin and Nashville. These forlorn fights, where the luckless Confederate Army of Tennessee was demolished by Union troops under George Thomas, seem to attract writers. Besides Bean's *Lorena, The Black Flower* by Howard Bahr and *Nashville 1864* by Madison Jones give blow-by-blow accounts, while a long flashback of Franklin fuels one subplot of *Lockhart's Nightmare* by Wayne Barton and Stan Williams.

Farther east, Harold Coyle's *Look Away* and *Until the End* follow brothers on opposite sides along the road to Gettysburg; Cameron Judd tells the neglected story of the stubborn Unionist minority from eastern Tennessee in *The Phantom Legion;* Tom Dyja takes us into the hell of the Wilderness in the unusual *Play for a Kingdom*; and conspiracy theorists can enjoy David Robertson's *Booth.*

For fans of more traditional Western fare, there's still plenty to be found. Good stories here are too numerous to single out, but there are entries by Jack Ballas, Mike Blakely, John McCord, Douglas Hurt, Richard S. Wheeler, and Thomas Eidson, to name just a few. Robert Vaughan and R. Garcia y Robertson give radically different pictures of the Little Big Horn in *Yesterday's Reveille* and *American Woman.* The mountain man is alive and well in books by John Legg, Terry C. Johnston, and W. Michael Gear. Gear and wife Kathleen also contribute another prehistorical with *People of the Mist,* as do Amanda Cockrell and Don Coldsmith.

The funny side of the West emerges in *Bumpo, Bill, and the Girls* by Robert Conwell, in Ellen Recknor's chaotic *Leaving Missouri,* in two stories by Johnny D. Boggs, and in Randall Beth Platt's strange and wonderful *The Royalscope Fe-As-Ko.* Stories of embattled emigrants are as popular as ever, many of them featuring capable female characters in

dire straits. Barbara Riefe, whose *Mohawk Woman* and related books showed her grasp of the Eastern, comes west with *Desperate Crossing: The Jenny Sanders Pryor Story,* while Michele Sorensen's *Broken Lance* and F.M. Parker's *Winter Woman* look at the dangers of the Mormon Trail.

And then there's *Sunshine Rider* by Ric Lynden Hardman. Fresh from Delacorte, *Sunshine Rider* bills itself as "the first vvegetarian Western," a claim I am not prepared to dispute. The story brings something new to the Western, besides featuring an engaging narrative viewpoint and a cast of refreshingly goofball characters. Even so, I'm not ready to add "vegetarian" to the list of western types just yet.

A quick look along publisher's row shows things little changed from last year. Markets are still tight and Western slots relatively few. Tor, Forge, and St. Martin's Press are carrying the majority of new titles, everything from long traditionals to mountain men to Western mysteries. Their historical lines, as always, are strong. Walker and Thorndike/Five Star specialize in library-grade hardbacks, and are certainly the largest publishers of the standard-length traditional active today. Berkley is again reportedly seeking lead Westerns by established writers, with Wayne Davis's *Silverthorne* as an early example. Pinnacle's list, including *Dust on the Wind* by Bill Brooks and *Winter Woman* by F.M. Parker, is strong but not lengthy. Leisure is represented mainly by reprints of such stars as Will Henry, T.V. Olsen, and Todhunter Ballard, and by the *Cheyenne* and *White Apache* series books. The Christian publishers, including Bethany House, Crossways, and Harvest House, continue to keep a foot in the market with traditional and historical/romantic series. Avon, Signet, and Pocket Books have a scattering of historical, prehistorical, and Civil war titles, while regional and university publishers continue to contribute a small but high-quality segment to the market. Prominent among these is Santa Fe's Sunstone Press, the University Press of Colorado, and the Texas Tech Press.

Speaking of regional and university presses, a new idea is floating around the world of Westerns. Gary Challender, of the audio marketer Books in Motion, has proposed an alliance between Western Writers of America and a group of regional, small, and university presses in the west. Unlike their larger cousins in New York, the regional presses have historically shown an interest in tailoring their products to a specific market. Challender and his supporters hope to establish a market niche for Western fiction and to encourage these publishers to pursue it.

With such diversity on the list for this year, the process of choosing 25 books to recommend wasn't easy. As always seems to be the case, worthy candidates far outnumber the available slots. My choices here are purely subjective, based on my own likes and dislikes and biases and whatnot. As usual, I'm painfully conscious of the good books I've left out. But with all its limitations, here's the list, and I hope any trusting reader will enjoy these as much as I did.

1. *Cloudsplitter* by Russell Banks: John Brown comes alive in all his manic complexity in this novel of Bleeding Kansas and the ominous overture to the Civil War.

2. *Lockhart's Nightmare* by Wayne Barton and Stan Williams: In the last book from this writing team, broken up by Williams's sudden death, an innocent man tries to find the real criminal while an implacable lawman pursues him across the west.

3. *Stay Away from That City. . .They Call It Cheyenne* by Stephen Bly: An ex-outlaw turned lawman and his reformed saloon-hostess wife have more trouble with the town council than with the bad guys when he tries to enforce the law in Cheyenne.

4. *One Last Town* by Matt Braun: Bill Tilghman was a true hero of the West, just, courageous, and devoted to the law. Braun does him justice in this novel of Tilghman's last days.

5. *Blood of Texas* by Will Camp: This novel of a Texican caught up in the conflicting pulls of the Texas Revolution of 1835-1836, won a Spur Award.

6. *Deadly Season* by Tim Champlin: Detectives fight drug smuggling and murder in San Francisco's Chinatown with the help of an eccentric Englishman named Sherlock Holmes.

7. *I, Pearl Hart* by Jane Candia Coleman: The dime novels called Pearl Hart ''the Bandit Queen.'' Coleman shows her as a confused teenager in a lot of trouble.

8. *War Woman* by Robert J. Conley: Cherokee historian Conley knows whereof he speaks in this new novel of the Real People.

9. *All God's Children* by Thomas Eidson: A Quaker woman committed to non-violence faces challenges on the Kansas prairie where her adversaries have no such compunctions.

10. *American Woman* by R. Garcia y Robertson: A Quaker woman starts as missionary, becomes the wife of a Cheyenne warrior, and witnesses Custer's fight from a unique perspective.

11. *Coyote Summer* by W. Michael Gear: The easterner who comes west and learns to face life is a staple of Western fiction. This is Gear's version of an old favorite.

12. *Sunshine Rider* by Ric Lynden Hardman: The first vegetarian Western must be read to be appreciated.

13. *The Dansing Star* by Kirby Jonas: Reared among the Apaches, a lawman faces hostility and prejudice when he goes after the murderer of a friend.

14. *The Phantom Legion* by Cameron Judd: The pro-Union hill people of eastern Tennessee gave the Confederacy constant trouble with a bushwhacking war as fierce as anything fought in Missouri.

15. *Klondike Fever* by Suzann Ledbetter: A single mom in need of help, her teenage son in need of direction, and a drunken miner in need of redemption meet in the Klondike gold fields.

16. *A Portrait of Spotted Deer's Grandfather* by Amy Littlesugar: An old warrior consents to pose for artist George Catlin as Catlin tries to capture a west that is already disappearing in this book for young readers.

17. *Wild Rose of Ruby Canyon* by John D. Nesbitt: Framed for the murder of an unpleasant neighbor, a Wyoming rancher seeks the truth.

18. *The Purgatory River* by Frank Roderus: Western veteran and Spur winner Roderus follows a mountain man along the Purgatory in a new entry in the *Rivers West* series.

19. *Savage Plains* by David William Ross: Abolitionist brothers find trouble and adventure from Kansas to Santa Fe in this prequel to the Civil War.

20. *Broken Lance* by Michele Sorensen: Widowed by an Indian attack, alone in the wilderness with her children, a pioneer woman prays for help—and instead finds a wounded Cheyenne warrior who may have belonged to the party that killed her husband.

21. *The Red Heart* by James Alexander Thom: Captured as a child, a young woman grows up to a position of power and influence among the Seneca.

22. *Range Wars* by Robert Vaughan: An old friend from the Apache campaigns faces mankiller Tom Horn in the Johnson County War.

23. *Wind Water* by Jeanne Williams: A resourceful young woman foils a land-grabbing rancher in an unusual way.

24. *The Winds of Autumn* by Jim R. Woolard: Spur winner Woolard returns to the Ohio Valley in this tale of two brothers out to rescue their sister from her Shawnee captors.

25. *Meridian: A Novel of Kit Carson's West* by Norman Zollinger: A young cartographer lives through the Taos revolt and the capture of California side-by-side with legendary scout Kit Carson.

For More Information about Western Fiction

The Western Writers of America now maintain a database of ''Western-friendly'' bookstores nationwide. The purpose is to alert writers and readers to local bookstores that show a willingness to stock and/or order Western titles in fiction and nonfiction. Begun in 1994, the listings are still far from comprehensive. For information on the database— or to get your favorite bookstore on the list—write to: Candy Moulton, Editor, *The Roundup Magazine*, Box 29 Star Route, Encampment, WY, 82325.

For general information on Western writing and writers, *The Roundup Magazine*, same address as above, is hard to beat. *Roundup* is the official publication of the Western Writers of America. The magazine offers an outstanding line of Western book reviews, both fiction and nonfiction, by

Western/mystery writer D.M. Meredith. In addition, the lucky reader finds news of Western writers, information on publishers and their plans, a "Hollywood" section by screenwriter Miles Hood Swarthout, and numerous other articles of general interest to Western fans. WWA membership is limited to qualified Western writers or publishers, booksellers, and the like, but *Roundup* subscriptions are available to anyone and new subscribers are always welcome. Many libraries also stock the magazine.

From the pages of *Roundup* comes this list of magazines who publish, or would like to publish, short Western fiction: DDorman Nelson, Editor, *Western Tales,* P.O. Box 33842, Granada Hills, CA 91394; Jack Feder, *Big Sky Stories,* 2434 Lester, Missoula, MT 59801; Darrel Arnold, *Cowboy Magazine,* P.O. Box 126, LaVeta, CO 81055; Douglas D. Sharp, *Western Digest,* 400 Whiteland Dr. N.E., Calgary, Alberta, Canada T1Y 3M7; Eddie Lee Rider, *Cowboys and Country,*

Magnolia Media Group, 1227 W. Magnolia, Fort Worth, TX 76104.

Mainstays of Western readers, especially for out-of-print volumes, are local second-hand bookstores, followed by flea markets and garage sales. Western books at these outlets often enjoy better circulation and command higher prices than upon original release. In some cases, used bookstores will undertake a search for rare or out-of-print volumes.

Readers having trouble finding their favorite books or authors shouldn't overlook their local library. Most public libraries are customer-oriented. Many will order a specific book, or even add an author to their routine acquisition list, if one or more readers request it. Failing that, books not available locally can often be secured through interlibrary loan. If the hard-to-find book you're after is available in hardback, your library might be just the resource for finding it.

Western Titles

442

MARK AMMERMAN

The Rain From God

(Camp Hill, Pennsylvania: Horizon Books, 1997)

Story type: Historical; Series
Series: Cross and the Tomahawk
Major character(s): Katanaquat, Indian (Narragansett), Warrior; Silvermoon, Indian (Narragansett), Young Woman; Uncas, Indian (Pequot), Warrior
Time period(s): 17th century (1600-1675)
Locale(s): Plymouth, Massachusetts, American Colonies; Providence, Rhode Island, American Colonies

Summary: The people of Katanaquat, the Narragansett, have always lived in a state of uneasy truce or outright warfare with their Pequot enemies. Other tribes, the Mohawk and Mohegan, sometimes encroach, but the Narragansett have held their own. But now there is a new force at work in the land. The strange people called English have settled in New England, and their alliances threaten the happiness of Katanaquat and his beloved Silvermoon, and threaten the very survival of the tribe. With new weapons and a new God seemingly ranked against him, Katanaquat must find a way to help his people.

Where it's reviewed:
Library Journal, September 1, 1997, page 166

Other books you might like:
Don Coldsmith, *World of Silence*, 1992
Robert J. Conley, *War Woman*, 1997
Lynda Durran, *Echohawk*, 1996
Jane Kirkpatrick, *Love to Water My Soul*, 1996
Linda Lay Shuler, *Let the Drum Speak*, 1996

443

SANORA BABB

Cry of the Tinamou

(Lincoln: University of Nebraska Press, 1997)

Story type: Modern; Collection
Time period(s): 20th century
Locale(s): West

Summary: This book contains 14 stories by Babb, an Oklahoma writer who was a contemporary of John Steinbeck. Set in all corners of the west, they feature strong female characters and an unflinching look at the world around them.

Other books you might like:
Benjamin Capps, *Tales of the Southwest*, 1991
Jane Candia Coleman, *Moving On*, 1997
Basil Moss, *Tales of the Wichitas*, 1998
Wallace Stegner, *Collected Stories of Wallace Stegner*, 1990
Dale L. Walker, *Legends and Lies: Great Mysteries of the American West*, 1997

444

HOWARD BAHR

The Black Flower

(Baltimore: Nautical & Aviation Publishing Company of America, 1997)

Story type: Historical/American Civil War; Historical
Major character(s): Bushrod Carter, Military Personnel; John Bell Hood, Military Personnel (Confederate general); Anna Hereford, Nurse
Time period(s): 1860s (1864)
Locale(s): Franklin, Tennessee; Nashville, Tennessee

Summary: Marching north in the last desperate offensive of the Confederacy, Bushrod Carter and his fellow few surviving companions in the Cumberland Rifles come to the battlefield of Franklin. General Hood, in blind anger over missed opportunities, orders an attack that shatters his army and the Cum-

berland Rifles. Carter, wounded, finds comfort for awhile with surgeon's helper Anna Hereford. But he knows that soon that time will end and he'll be back in the lines for the final battle.

Where it's reviewed:
Kirkus Reviews, February 1, 1997, page 154
Publishers Weekly, March 10, 1997, page 52
Southern Living, May 1997, page 47

Other books you might like:
Harold Coyle, *Until the End*, 1996
Randal L. Greenwood, *Ride, Rebels, Ride*, 1996
Madison Jones, *Nashville 1864*, 1997
Max McCoy, *Home to Texas*, 1995
David Robertson, *Booth*, 1998

445

JACK BALLAS

Bandido Caballero

(New York: Berkley, 1997)

Story type: Historical/American Civil War; Man Alone
Major character(s): Tom Fallon, Spy, Bandit; Benito Juarez, Political Figure, Historical Figure; Joan Boniol, Spy
Time period(s): 1860s (post Civil War)
Locale(s): Franklin, Texas; Las Cruces, New Mexico

Summary: Reprieved from a Union firing squad to help the exiled Mexican government in its fight against the Emperor Maximilian, Tom Fallon turns bandit. As a drifting cowhand, he arouses no special notice along the Mexican-American border. His other role of predator on gold shipments bound for Maximilian arouses considerable interest from the French troops backing the emperor. Dodging the soldiers while walking a thin line between safety and betrayal is all part of Fallon's job. But he hasn't counted on his feelings for Joan Boniol, who is beautiful, charming—and a French agent.

Other books by the same author:
Angel Fire, 1996
Gun Boss, 1995
Powder River, 1995
Montana Breed, 1994
Durango Gunfight, 1992

Other books you might like:
Tim Champlin, *The Survivor*, 1996
Suzann Ledbetter, *Colorado Reverie*, 1997
Gordon D. Shirreffs, *Maximilian's Gold*, 1989
Brock Thoene, *The Legend of Storey County*, 1995
Norman Zollinger, *Chapultepec*, 1995

446

JACK BALLAS

The Hard Land

(New York: Berkley, 1998)

Story type: Chase; Ranch Life
Major character(s): Jess Sanford, Fugitive, Wanderer; Joe Bob Brown, Slave (freed), Fugitive
Time period(s): 19th century (post Civil War)

Locale(s): Powder River, Wyoming

Summary: A fight with a neighboring landowner puts Jess Sanford on the run from what he thinks will be a murder charge. Fleeing Tennessee, Sanford joins forces with fellow fugitive Joe Bob Brown, a former slave. The two resolve to found their own ranch in the Powder River country, a hotbed of Sioux and exiled outlaws. As if that didn't promise enough trouble, Sanford doesn't know that his supposed victim is alive and thirsting for revenge.

Other books by the same author:
Angel Fire, 1996
Gun Boss, 1995
Powder River, 1995
Montana Breed, 1994
Durango Gunfight, 1992

Other books you might like:
Jack Curtis, *The Quiet Cowboy*, 1994
Will Henry, *One More River to Cross*, 1967
Hiram King, *High Prairie*, 1997
John D. Nesbitt, *One-Eyed Cowboy Wild*, 1994
Jack Walker, *West of Fort Worth*, 1990

447

RUSSELL BANKS

Cloudsplitter

(New York: Harper Flamingo, 1998)

Story type: Historical; Historical/American Civil War
Major character(s): John Brown, Farmer, Revolutionary; Owen Brown, Revolutionary; Henry David Thoreau, Writer
Time period(s): 1850s
Locale(s): Harper's Ferry, Virginia; Pottawatomie, Kansas; Boston, Massachusetts

Summary: Long after the fact, John Brown's son Owen tells the story of his father's tumultuous life. Half Old Testament prophet and half terrorist, Brown, with his sons and a few followers, served as the catalyst that finally precipitated the nagging slavery issue into civil war. As abolitionist warrior, Brown found allies in many areas, especially among the New England intellectuals. In the fighting in Bleeding Kansas and later in his abortive raid on Harper's Ferry, Brown hoped to rally slaves and abolitionists into a fighting force that would overthrow the slaveholders. He paid for his beliefs with the lives of three sons, and ultimately with his own life.

Other books by the same author:
Rule of the Bone, 1995

Other books you might like:
Randal L. Greenwood, *Kansas, Bloody Kansas*, 1996
Max McCoy, *Sons of Fire*, 1993
David Robertson, *Booth*, 1998
David William Ross, *Savage Plains*, 1996
Robert Vaughan, *Blood on the Plains*, 1997

448

JANE VALENTINE BARKER

Mari

(Boulder: University Press of Colorado, 1997)

Story type: Historical; Ranch Life
Major character(s): Mari Sandoz, Abuse Victim, Writer; Jules Sandoz, Scientist (agronomist)
Time period(s): 20th century (1900-1920)
Locale(s): Nebraska; Colorado

Summary: A thinly fictionalized biography of author Mari Sandoz, this book concentrates on her early years and her relationship with her father. Jules Sandoz, a Swiss immigrant, is a respected scientist and a violently abusive husband and father. His reaction to young Mari's determination to write—and especially to write fiction—is especially volcanic. Her defiance of him, and her isolation on the harsh Nebraska prairies, drives Mari into a loveless and abusive marriage and then into other hardships before she can take her proper place as one of the earliest woman writers of the American West. Based on documents and interviews from Sandoz family members, the book closely follows the course of Mari Sandoz' troubled life.

Where it's reviewed:
Publishers Weekly, August 18, 1997, page 71

Other books you might like:
Judy Alter, *Mattie*, 1992
Jane Candia Coleman, *I, Pearl Hart*, 1998
Sibyl Downing, *Fire in the Hole*, 1996
Joann Levy, *Daughter of Joy*, 1998
Johnny Quarles, *No Man's Land*, 1993

449

WAYNE BARTON
STAN WILLIAMS, Co-Author

Lockhart's Nightmare

(New York: Forge, 1998)

Story type: Mystery; Chase
Major character(s): James Lockhart, Businessman (traveling salesman); Marian Taylor, Actress, Con Artist; Rance Henson, Lawman (federal marshal)
Time period(s): 1880s (1883)
Locale(s): Sacramento, California; Hannibal, Missouri; Fort Worth, Texas

Summary: Arrested by Marshal Rance Henson for a string of crimes he didn't commit, banknote salesman James Lockhart finds himself facing a quick trial and a quick hanging. No one believes in his innocence—not even Marian Taylor, the fast-talking actress, con artist, and fellow prisoner who shares his escape. Lockhart is determined to prove his innocence. Henson—nicknamed Marshal Doom—is equally determined to uphold his record of never losing a prisoner. In a desperate chase, Lockhart and Taylor crisscross the West by train, steamboat, and even a new-fangled airship, trying to track down the real killer while staying a jump ahead of the implacable Marshal Doom.

Other books by the same author:
Fairchild's Passage, 1997
Wildcat, 1995
Shadow of Doubt, 1994
High Country, 1993
Manhunt, 1992

Other books you might like:
A.J. Arnold, *Outlaw's Justice*, 1992
Ric Lynden Hardman, *Sunshine Rider*, 1997
Elmer Kelton, *Cloudy in the West*, 1997
Gene Shelton, *Devil's Deathbed*, 1995
Gary D. Svee, *Sanctuary*, 1990

450

FREDERIC BEAN

Black Gold

(New York: Forge, 1997)

Story type: Modern; Mystery
Major character(s): Lee Garrett, Lawman (Texas Ranger); Molly Brown, Prostitute; Roy Woods, Lawman (Texas Ranger)
Time period(s): 1930s (1932)
Locale(s): Longview, Texas

Summary: Texas Rangers Lee Garrett and Roy Woods are cleaning up different parts of the oil-boom town of Longview. Garrett is working on a missing deed and the murder of its holder, trying to find out how the land in question got transferred to a new oil tycoon. Woods is helping the Treasury Department fight bootleggers. But the two join forces when it appears that Eastern gangsters are beginning to infiltrate the Texas oilfield. Side by side, Garrett and Woods pit their old time law-enforcement skills against the tommy guns of organized crime.

Where it's reviewed:
Kirkus Reviews, September 1, 1997, page 1323
Library Journal, September 1, 1997, page 214
Publishers Weekly, September 1, 1997, page 97

Other books by the same author:
Guns on the Cimarron, 1995
Pancho and Black Jack, 1995
The Pecos River, 1995 (Rivers West #13)
Border Justice, 1994
Trail's End, 1994

Other books you might like:
Wayne Barton, *Wildcat*, 1995
    Stan Williams, co-author
Matt Braun, *One Last Town*, 1997
Loren D. Estleman, *City of Widows*, 1994
Elmer Kelton, *Honor at Daybreak*, 1991
Glendon Swarthout, *The Old Colts*, 1985

451

FREDERIC BEAN

Eden

(New York: Bantam, 1997)

Story type: Modern; Mystery
Major character(s): Matthew King, Heir, Rancher
Time period(s): 1990s
Locale(s): Dallas, Texas

Summary: The King family of Texas is new-rich, their fortune based on oil from beneath their modest—by Texas standards—ranch. Matthew King, younger son in the empire, sees the family crumbling, bound together now only by ties of blood and money. When King's older brother is murdered, tremors shake the whole King empire. And when Matthew discovers the killer, the ties that hold him to the family may stretch beyond the breaking point.

Where it's reviewed:
Publishers Weekly, August 25, 1997, page 68

Other books by the same author:
Guns on the Cimarron, 1995
Pancho and Black Jack, 1995
The Pecos River, 1995 (Rivers West #13)
Border Justice, 1994
Trail's End, 1994

Other books you might like:
Frank Bergon, *Wild Game*, 1995
G.G. Boyer, *Winchester Affidavit*, 1997
Ralph W. Cotton, *Killers of Man*, 1997
Jory Sherman, *Grass Kingdom*, 1993
Robert Vaughan, *Dawn of the Century*, 1992

452

FREDERIC BEAN

Hell's Half Acre

(New York: Berkley, 1996)

Story type: Traditional; Saga
Major character(s): Annabelle Green, Prostitute, Teenager; Cody Wade, Cowboy, Lawman; George Curry, Outlaw
Time period(s): 19th century (post Civil War)
Locale(s): Fort Worth, Texas

Summary: The few square blocks of Hell's Half Acre in Fort Worth offer big temptations. The Acre's main attractions—women, whiskey, and gambling—mean big money for those in need of it. For Annabelle Green, young, poor, and with a consumptive mother to support, the red lights offer her a way to survive. For Cody Wade, cowboy turned lawman, the exhilaration of danger and power may be more important than money. But the costs are high as well, and Cody and Annabelle come to realize how much they've paid to enter the Acre. The only question is whether their discovery has come too late.

Where it's reviewed:
Roundup Magazine, June 1997, page 33

Other books by the same author:
Guns on the Cimarron, 1995
Pancho and Black Jack, 1995
The Pecos River, 1995 (Rivers West #13)
Border Justice, 1994
Trail's End, 1994

Other books you might like:
Judy Alter, *A Ballad for Sallie*, 1992
Stephen Bly, *It's Your Misfortune and None of My Own*, 1994
   Code of the West #1
Matt Braun, *The Gamblers*, 1997
Robert Lake, *Mountain Man's Vengeance*, 1989
Max McCoy, *The Sixth Rider*, 1994

453

FREDERIC BEAN

Lorena

(New York: Forge, 1997)

Story type: Historical; Historical/American Civil War
Major character(s): Lorena Blaire, Nurse, Spy; Clara Brooks, Nurse, Spy; Jonathan Cross, Doctor (Confederate)
Time period(s): 1860s (1864)
Locale(s): Nashville, Tennessee; Franklin, Tennessee

Summary: Sent by the Union Army to spy on Confederate General Hood and his army, Lorena Blaire and friend Clara Brooks infiltrate the almost non-existent Confederate medical corps. This puts them in a great position to know what Hood's army is up to, but also exposes them to the true cost of the war, the young men maimed and shattered by battle. Drawn to hard-working Confederate surgeon Jonathan Cross, Lorena soon runs into conflict between the cause she's certain is right and the human betrayal she must inflict to serve it.

Where it's reviewed:
Library Journal, December 1996, page 141
Publishers Weekly, November 11, 1996, page 58

Other books by the same author:
Guns on the Cimarron, 1995
Pancho and Black Jack, 1995
The Pecos River, 1995 (Rivers West #13)
Border Justice, 1994
Trail's End, 1994

Other books you might like:
Howard Bahr, *The Black Flower*, 1997
Kathleen O'Neal Gear, *Thin Moon and Cold Mist*, 1995
Madison Jones, *Nashville 1864*, 1997
Al Lacy, *Joy from Ashes*, 1995
J.L. Reasoner, *The Healer's Road*, 1995

454

FREDERIC BEAN

The Red River

(New York: Bantam, 1997)

Story type: Historical; Series
Series: Rivers West

Major character(s): Elias McBee, Trapper; Seth Booker, Trapper; Father Bolivar, Religious
Time period(s): 19th century (pre Civil War)
Locale(s): Red River, Texas

Summary: Happy-go-lucky trappers Elias McBee and Seth Booker journey up the Red River in search of beaver skins. Instead, they first find a lost missionary, Father Bolivar, and then a feud between Kiowa and Osage tribes through which they must pass. The pair make a deal with father Bolivar to help him find his mission in return for his translating skills. Then the Kiowas decide that Seth fits right into one of their legends, and that the two newcomers with rifles will be very useful in their war with the Osages. All in all, it's an uncomfortable situation for two young adventurers who hope to stay alive.

Other books by the same author:
Black Gold, 1997
Eden, 1997
Hell's Half Acre, 1996
Lorena, 1996
Guns on the Cimarron, 1995

Other books you might like:
Win Blevins, *The High Missouri*, 1994
    Rivers West #11
Don Coldsmith, *Tallgrass: A Novel of the Great Plains*, 1997
A.E. Hotchner, *Louisiana Purchase*, 1996
J.L. Reasoner, *Cossack Three Ponies*, 1997
Jory Sherman, *The Rio Grande*, 1994

455

P.A. BECHKO

The Eye of the Hawk

(Thorndike, Maine: Thorndike, 1998)

Story type: Traditional; Mystery
Major character(s): Ethan Torregrossa, Lawman, Gunfighter; Rona Burr, Businesswoman (freight line operator); Sam Reo, Businessman, Criminal
Time period(s): 19th century (post Civil War)
Locale(s): Stillwater, West; Mississippi River

Summary: On his way to help out a friend, lawman Ethan Torregrossa is attacked and thrown from the riverboat on which he's a passenger. He survives and manages to reach shore, but he's lost all memory, except for the hazy knowledge that he was headed for Stillwater. Taking the name of Hawk, he makes his way toward Stillwater, hoping to find a clue to his past. When he arrives, he meets and befriends Rona Burr, who needs a friend. Someone has murdered Rona's brother, and she is coming under increasing pressure from Sam Reo, who wants to take over both her freight line and her body. Torregrossa/Hawk intervenes, but the secret he's searching for may prove deadly even then.

Other books by the same author:
The Tin-Pan Man, 1997

Other books you might like:
Ralph Compton, *Across the Rio Colorado*, 1997
Peter Dawson, *Rattlesnake Mesa*, 1998
Robert Kammen, *Montana Rimfire*, 1991

James A. Ritchie, *The Wagon Wars*, 1997
Guy N. Smith, *The Pony Riders*, 1997

456

P.A. BECHKO

The Tin-Pan Man

(Thorndike, Maine: Thorndike Press, 1997)

Story type: Traditional; Man Alone
Major character(s): Samantha Cameron, Teacher, Captive; Zachariah Kane, Peddler; Mississippi Pike, Gambler, Outlaw
Time period(s): 19th century (post Civil War)
Locale(s): Saquarra, West; United States

Summary: Peddler Zachariah Kane does Samantha Cameron no special favor when he rescues her from an aggressive rattlesnake. All the rescue does is send her back to the town of Saquarra, where she's held as a slave-mistress by Mississippi Pike. In gratitude for Samantha's return, Pike offers to murder Kane, only to be stopped by town boss Frank Crockett. None of it is really Kane's business, but he can't help horning in anyway. Before long, he and a couple of uneasy allies are committed to driving Crockett, Pike, and all their gang out of town, or dying in the attempt.

Where it's reviewed:
Roundup Magazine, April 1997, page 25

Other books you might like:
Frederic Bean, *Hell's Half Acre*, 1996
Johnny D. Boggs, *The Courtship of Hannah and the Horseman*, 1997
Speer Morgan, *The Whipping Boy*, 1995
James A. Ritchie, *The Payback*, 1992
Richard S. Wheeler, *Flint's Gift*, 1997

457

DON BENDELL

Matched Colts

(New York: Signet, 1997)

Story type: Traditional; Revenge
Major character(s): Chris Colt, Gunfighter, Scout; Man Killer, Indian (Nez Perce), Sidekick; Charlotte "Charley" Colt, Avenger, Widow(er)
Time period(s): 19th century (post Civil War)
Locale(s): Taos, New Mexico; Salida, Colorado

Summary: Charlotte Colt, better known as Charley, is a not a good person to cross. She's as good with a gun as her brother Chris, and quicker, if anything, to resent injustice. She's found herself a good man to marry, and when he's murdered, she doesn't wait for the law to take action. Single-handed, she sets out to take her own revenge on the entire outlaw army she holds responsible.

Other books by the same author:
Eagle, 1996
Coyote Run, 1995
Justis Colt, 1995
Colt, 1994

Warrior, 1994

Other books you might like:
Patrick E. Andrews, *Texican Blood Fight*, 1992
Clifford Blair, *The Guns of Sacred Heart*, 1991
David L. Fleming, *Border Crossings*, 1993
Wynema McGowan, *While the Rivers Run*, 1996
Earl Murray, *The River at Sundown*, 1997

458

ROSANNE BITTNER

Tame the Wild Wind

(New York: Bantam, 1996)

Story type: Historical; Indian Wars
Major character(s): Faith Kelley, Widow(er); Gabe Beaumont, Cowboy, Indian (half Sioux)
Time period(s): 19th century (1840s-1860s)
Locale(s): Sommers Station, Wyoming; Rocky Mountains

Summary: Son of a mountain man and a Sioux woman, Gabe Beaumont grows up mostly among his mother's people. When whites murder his Indian wife and child, he becomes Tall Bear, a Sioux warrior hungry for revenge. Then, during a raid on a Wyoming stagecoach, he sees Faith Kelley. Faith, reared as a Quaker and now a young widow with a child, has no idea that the cowhand who rides in a few days later was the same man as the Sioux warrior she'd seen during the raid. She does know that he has some secret that may prove dangerous for them both.

Where it's reviewed:
Publishers Weekly, September 9, 1996, page 81

Other books by the same author:
Chase the Sun, 1995
Wildest Dreams, 1994
Song of the Wolf, 1992
Thunder on the Plains, 1992

Other books you might like:
Kathleen O'Neal Gear, *Sand in the Wind*, 1990
Wynema McGowan, *Beyond the River*, 1997
James Alexander Thom, *The Red Heart*, 1997
Stephanie Grace Whitson, *Walks the Fire*, 1995
    Prairie Winds #1
Jeanne Williams, *Home Station*, 1996

459

TOM W. BLACKBURN

Sierra Baron

(New York: Leisure, 1997)

Story type: Historical; Quest
Major character(s): Mike McGann, Adventurer, Gambler; Juaquin Murietta, Outlaw, Historical Figure; Beatriz McGann, Rancher, Spouse
Time period(s): 1840s; 1850s
Locale(s): Monterey, California; Sierra Nevada, California; Benecia, California

Summary: Boston native Mike McGann, ex-sailor, gambler, tough guy from the slums, comes to California to make a life for himself. California is a good place for it. Caught in the transition between Mexican and Anglo rule, trembling on the eve of the great gold rush, California offers a fertile field for an ambitious man. But there are others as tough and driven, and far more ruthless, than McGann. If he is to build and hold the empire he desires, he'll need all the help and all the luck he can find.

Other books by the same author:
A Good Day to Die, 1996

Other books you might like:
Diane Austell, *Lights along the Shore*, 1991
Robert W. Broomall, *California Kingdoms*, 1992
Gary McCarthy, *The American River*, 1992
    Rivers West #7
J.L. Reasoner, *Rivers of Gold*, 1995
Richard S. Wheeler, *Sierra*, 1996

460

JAMES CARLOS BLAKE

In the Rogue Blood

(New York: Avon, 1997)

Story type: Traditional
Major character(s): Edward Little, Military Personnel, Wanderer; John Little, Military Personnel, Wanderer
Time period(s): 1840s (1845-1847)
Locale(s): New Orleans, Louisiana; Laredo, Texas; Mexico City, Mexico

Summary: With a killing on their souls, the two Little brothers light out from their Florida home, heading generally west. In New Orleans they separate, but by different routes they come to Texas. The major separation begins, for they turn up on different sides of the Mexican-American War. In a world filled with violence and savagery, even brotherly love may not be enough to bridge the chasm between them.

Where it's reviewed:
Kirkus Reviews, August 1, 1997, page 1127
Library Journal, September 1, 1997, page 214

Other books by the same author:
The Friends of Pancho Villa, 1996
Pistoleer, 1995

Other books you might like:
Bill Bragg, *Drumm's War*, 1992
    R.C. House, co-author
Ralph Compton, *Across the Rio Colorado*, 1997
Jason Manning, *Gone to Texas*, 1995
    Flintlock #3
Don Worcester, *Gone to Texas*, 1993
Norman Zollinger, *Chapultepec*, 1995

461

MIKE BLAKELY

Dead Reckoning
(New York: Forge, 1996)

Story type: Traditional; Chase
Major character(s): Dee Hassard, Con Artist, Murderer; Carrol Moncrief, Religious, Outlaw (reformed); Clarence Philbrick, Traveller
Time period(s): 19th century (post Civil War)
Locale(s): Denver, Colorado; Mount of the Holy Cross, Colorado

Summary: Dee Hassard is nothing much but a small-time con artist until he kills a lawman who's taking him to prison. One killing leads to more, and soon Hassard is the most wanted man in Colorado. One of the people who wants him is Carrol Moncrief, reformed cattle rustler turned preacher and brother of the murdered officer. Moncrief uses his outlaw knowledge and his contacts to track Hassard, who now holds a fortune in stolen gold. As the trail leads toward the Mount of the Holy Cross, the scope of the manhunt broadens until it affects people who have no idea of the stakes involved.

Other books by the same author:
Spanish Blood, 1996
Too Long at the Dance, 1996
The Last Chance, 1995
Shortgrass Song, 1994
The Snowy Range Gang, 1992

Other books you might like:
Jack Ballas, *Durango Gunfight*, 1992
Ralph Compton, *The Border Empire*, 1997
Hascal Giles, *Texas Tough*, 1992
Kirby Jonas, *The Bloody Season*, 1996
    Season of the Vigilante #1
Brock Thoene, *Hope Valley War*, 1997

462

WIN BLEVINS

The Rock Child
(New York: Tor, 1998)

Story type: Historical; Chase
Major character(s): Richard Burton, Explorer, Writer; Mark Twain, Writer, Historical Figure; Asie, Indian, Musician
Time period(s): 19th century (post Civil War)
Locale(s): San Francisco, California

Summary: Slated for a fate worse than death are Asie, a half-Indian musical genius, and Buddhist nun Sun Moon. Before their captors can carry through with their plans, though, rescue arrives in the diverse shapes of Mark Twain and Sir Richard Burton, unlikely allies in the cause of justice. Burton, as the worldly-wise traveler and sensualist plays off Twain's homespun wit in a long and harrowing game of hide and seek with some of the most nefarious villains in print.

Other books by the same author:
Stone Song, 1995
The High Missouri, 1994 (Rivers West #11)

The Snake River, 1992 (Rivers West #8)
The Powder River, 1990 (Rivers West #4)

Other books you might like:
Tim Champlin, *Deadly Season*, 1997
Brian Garfield, *Wild Times*, 1978
Walter Satterthwait, *Wilde West*, 1991
Brock Thoene, *The Legend of Storey County*, 1995
Richard White, *Mister Grey*, 1992

463

STEPHEN BLY

Stay Away From That City. . .They Call It Cheyenne
(Wheaton, Illinois: Crossway Books, 1996)

Story type: Traditional; Series
Series: Code of the West
Major character(s): Tap Andrews, Lawman (deputy city marshal), Outlaw (retired); Pepper Andrews, Spouse, Saloon Hostess (retired); Ed Casey, Rancher
Time period(s): 19th century (post Civil War)
Locale(s): Cheyenne, Wyoming

Summary: Former outlaw and sometime rancher Tap Andrews moves to Cheyenne for his wife's health. He even has a job there suited to his talents. He's the town's deputy marshal. But soon fate moves him up to the post of acting marshal and he's faced with the prospect of standing up to powerful rancher Ed Casey. When the town won't back his play, Andrews must either back down or put his life on the line for what he believes is right.

Where it's reviewed:
Voice of Youth Advocates, October 1996, page 205

Other books by the same author:
My Foot's in the Stirrup. . .My Pony Won't Stand, 1996 (Code of the West #5)
Where the Deer and the Antelope Play, 1995 (Code of the West #3)
One Went to Denver and the Other Went Wrong, 1995 (Code of the West #2)
It's Your Misfortune and None of My Own, 1994 (Code of the West #1)

Other books you might like:
Clifford Blair, *Trouble Town*, 1992
S.W. Brouwer, *Moon Basket*, 1994
    Ghost Rider #2
Will Camp, *Choctaw Trail*, 1994
Christopher Keegan, *Ride into Yesterday*, 1992
Al Lacy, *Legacy*, 1994
    Journeys of the Stranger #1

464

JOHNNY D. BOGGS

The Courtship of Hannah and the Horseman

(New York: Thomas Bouregy, 1997)

Story type: Traditional; Chase
Major character(s): Hannah Scott, Rancher, Foster Parent; Pete Belissari, Cowboy, Horse Trainer; Solomon Wooten, Outlaw, Veteran (Confederate)
Time period(s): 1880s (1884)
Locale(s): Fort Davis, Texas

Summary: A funny thing happens to Hannah Scott on her way to her wedding. She walks into a bank that's being robbed and becomes the hostage of outlaw leader Solomon Wooten's gang. Pete Belissari, the groom left waiting at the alter, joins the posse and goes pounding in pursuit of the robbers, but Hannah is spirited away to the ruined Spanish fort that is Wooten's hideout. Wounded in the chase, Pete is nursed by a beautiful young Greek woman who obviously has an interest in him other than trauma, while Hannah comes under the protection of a noble outlaw who grew up in the same orphanage as she. Complications abound before the lovers are reunited in a more or less happy ending.

Other books you might like:
Stephen Bly, *Where the Deer and the Antelope Play*, 1995
   Code of the West #3
Emily Bradshaw, *Bounty Bride*, 1996
John S. McCord, *Blind Eagles*, 1997
Gilbert Morris, *The Gallant Outlaw*, 1994
   House of Winslow #18
Penelope Williamson, *The Outsider*, 1996

465

JOHNNY D. BOGGS

This Man Colter

(New York: Avalon, 1997)

Story type: Traditional; Quest
Major character(s): Raleigh Colter, Guide; Jeff Crutchfield, Guide, Sidekick; Gwen McCarthy, Photographer
Time period(s): 19th century (post Civil War)
Locale(s): Guadalupe Mountains, New Mexico; Guadalupe Mountains, Texas

Summary: Raleigh Colter and buddy Jeff Crutchfield hire on for a quick and simple little job. They are to guide photographer Gwen McCarthy and her father on a picture-taking expedition through the Guadalupe Mountains on the Texas-New Mexico border. Along the way, it develops that Gwen's father has an inconvenient love for whiskey, and then the guides discover that Gwen is determined to get a good, close-up photo of a mountain lion. Aside from that, the only problem Colter and Crutchfield face is that of getting their little party safely past the bandits, outcasts, and bronco Apaches holed up in the mountains.

Other books by the same author:
The Courtship of Hannah and the Horseman, 1997

Other books you might like:
Kent Conwell, *Bumpo, Bill, and the Girls*, 1997
Ronnie Davenport, *The Timberline Trail*, 1992
Stef Ann Holm, *Portraits*, 1996
Jerrie Hurd, *Kate Burke Shoots the Old West*, 1997
Ellen Recknor, *Leaving Missouri*, 1997

466

ALBERT R. BOOKY

Hacienda

(Santa Fe: Sunstone Press, 1997)

Story type: Young Readers; Historical
Major character(s): Simon Gomez, Landowner; Modesto Polaco, Landowner; Charles Bent, Trader, Political Figure
Time period(s): 1840s
Locale(s): Santa Fe, New Mexico; Las Vegas, New Mexico

Summary: Young Simon Gomez works to build up the small and poor ranch that he inherits into a successful empire. When war threatens between Mexico and the United States, Simon is one of the few who hopes for American intervention to take New Mexico away from Mexico. His stand puts his life in danger, but he continues to stand for his ideas. When the anticipated war comes, Simon is in the middle, caught between the land he loves and the new ways brought by the conquerors.

Other books by the same author:
The Buckskins, 1990

Other books you might like:
Marj Gurasich, *Benito and the White Dove*, 1989
Carolyn Meyer, *Rio Grande Stories*, 1994
Jay Neugenboren, *Poli*, 1989
Elaine F. O'Brien, *Anita of Rancho del Mar*, 1991
Gary Paulsen, *Tucket's Ride*, 1997

467

B.M. BOWER

Lonesome Land

(Lincoln: University of Nebraska Press, 1997)

Story type: Traditional; Ranch Life
Major character(s): Valeria Peyson, Mail Order Bride; Manley Fleetwood, Rancher; Kent Burnett, Rancher
Time period(s): 1910s (1912)
Locale(s): Cold Spring Ranch, Montana

Summary: Dreaming of a life in the West with a strong husband and the wide open spaces of a ranch, Valeria Peyson instead finds disillusionment, abuse, and fear. The misnamed Manley Fleetwood turns out to be a drunken bully. The ranch is wide open, without trees or neighbors or anything to offer Valeria shelter. Manley's best friend, Kent Burnett, befriends Valeria also, offering her a bit of comfort in the lonely land, but in the end, she must depend upon herself to salvage her life from the ruins of her marriage. First published in 1912, the book deals openly with themes of abuse and divorce rarely mentioned in its day.

Western

Other books by the same author:
Chip of the Flying U, 1904

Other books you might like:
P.A. Bechko, *The Tin-Pan Man*, 1997
Emily Bradshaw, *Bounty Bride*, 1996
Joan Johnston, *The Barefoot Bride*, 1992
Suzann Ledbetter, *Trinity Strike*, 1996
Elaine Long, *Bittersweet Country*, 1991

`468`

DOUG BOWMAN

Houston

(New York: Forge, 1998)

Story type: Traditional; Revenge
Major character(s): Camp Houston, Gunfighter; John Calloway, Rancher
Time period(s): 19th century (post Civil War)
Locale(s): San Antonio, Texas; Staked Plains, Texas

Summary: The desperadoes who kill rancher John Calloway and steal his herd have done the wrong thing. Calloway's friend, gunfighter Camp Houston, sets out on their trail, determined to hunt them down one by one. It's vigilante justice, but that's the only kind Houston knows.

Other books by the same author:
The Three Lives of Littleton Blue, 1996
Gannon, 1994
Sam Curtin, 1994

Other books you might like:
Bill Brooks, *The Last Law There Was*, 1995
Steve Frazee, *Hidden Gold*, 1997
R.C. House, *Stouthearted Men*, 1995
Suzann Ledbetter, *Pure Justice*, 1997
Lewis B. Patten, *Tincup in the Storm Country*, 1996

`469`

G.G. BOYER

Winchester Affidavit

(Thorndike, Maine: Thorndike, 1997)

Story type: Traditional; Ranch Life
Major character(s): Cleve Bandelier, Rancher; Grut Voerbeck, Landowner; Lord Ransom, Foreman
Time period(s): 19th century (post Civil War)
Locale(s): Santa Fe, New Mexico; Amarillo Grant, New Mexico

Summary: Cleve Bandelier considers himself a small rancher in the Amarillo Grant country of New Mexico. Lord Ransom and his second-in-command Pancho Wingfield consider Bandelier and others of his kind squatters on the range belonging to Dutch landowner Grut Voerbeck. When Ransom decides to clear the range of the squatters, the situation threatens to turn into a war with Bandelier leading the opposition. As the trouble grows worse, Voerbeck and his daughter come to inspect their holdings, introducing a new factor into an explosive situation.

Where it's reviewed:
Roundup Magazine, June 1997, page 33

Other books you might like:
Doug Bowman, *The Three Lives of Littleton Blue*, 1996
Robert Kammen, *Showdown at Lonetree*, 1994
Lauran Paine, *The Open Range Men*, 1990
James Reasoner, *The Diablo Grant*, 1994
Doyle Trent, *Fire and Gunsmoke*, 1993

`470`

MATT BRAUN

Doc Holliday

(New York: St. Martin's Press, 1997)

Story type: Historical; Man Alone
Major character(s): Doc Holliday, Gunfighter, Gambler; Kate Elder, Prostitute; Wyatt Earp, Lawman, Historical Figure
Time period(s): 19th century (1870s-1880s)
Locale(s): Dallas, Texas; Denver, Colorado; Cheyenne, Wyoming

Summary: Doc Holliday, stricken with tuberculosis, leaves his southern roots and goes west, planning to make his living with his wits, possibly hoping for a quick release from his illness at the wrong end of a gun. As a gambler, Holliday makes his way through saloons and cribs from Texas to Canada, always on the move. He has few living enemies and fewer friends, but one of those friends, a lanky lawman called Wyatt Earp, will lead him into one of the great showdowns of western folklore.

Other books by the same author:
The Gamblers, 1997
One Last Town, 1997
Texas Empire, 1997
Cimarron Jordan, 1996
Noble Outlaw, 1996

Other books you might like:
Jane Candia Coleman, *Doc Holliday's Woman*, 1995
Randy Lee Eickhoff, *The Fourth Horseman*, 1997
Loren D. Estleman, *Bloody Season*, 1988
Dan Gordon, *Wyatt Earp*, 1994
Preston Lewis, *Mix-Up at the O.K. Corral*, 1996

`471`

MATT BRAUN

The Gamblers

(New York: St. Martin's Press, 1997)

Story type: Traditional; Saga
Major character(s): Mattie Silks, Madam, Gambler; Bill Hickok, Gunfighter, Lawman; Cort Thomson, Gunfighter, Criminal (cattle rustler)
Time period(s): 19th century (1860s-1880s)
Locale(s): Springfield, Missouri; Denver, Colorado

Summary: While men like Wild Bill Hickok are building their legends and meeting their fates, Mattie Silks starts a legend of her own. As Hickok's woman and business partner, she gets her start as a frontier madam. With timing and good luck and a shrewd knack for dodging fate, she works her way toward

wealth and power. then, in Denver, she meets rough-and-tumble Cort Thomson, and all her careful plans seem doomed to disaster.

Other books by the same author:
Texas Empire, 1997
Outlaw Kingdom, 1996
Noble Outlaw, 1996
Cimarron Jordan, 1996
Wyatt Earp, 1994

Other books you might like:
Judy Alter, *A Ballad for Sallie*, 1992
Cindy Bonner, *Looking After Lily*, 1995
Jane Candia Coleman, *Doc Holliday's Woman*, 1995
Johnny Quarles, *Varro*, 1991
Richard S. Wheeler, *Cashbox*, 1994

472

MATT BRAUN

One Last Town

(New York: St. Martin's Press, 1997)

Story type: Traditional; Man Alone
Major character(s): Bill Tilghman, Lawman; Zoe Tilghman, Spouse; Turk Milligan, Criminal
Time period(s): 1920s (1924)
Locale(s): Cromwell, Oklahoma; Okmulgee, Oklahoma

Summary: Respected even by the criminals he hunted, real-life hero Bill Tilghman was a thoroughly admirable lawman. Braun's book captures Tilghman's last days, first as a crusader against the power of the Ku Klux Klan in Oklahoma, and then as the man hired to clean up the town of Cromwell. Cromwell is an oil town, where big money and sudden growth has attracted Oklahoma's own brand of mobsters. An old man now, Tilghman is still tough as ever, but he's going against a stacked deck in what may prove to be his last town.

Other books by the same author:
Texas Empire, 1997
Outlaw Kingdom, 1996
Noble Outlaw, 1996
Cimarron Jordan, 1996
Wyatt Earp, 1994

Other books you might like:
Jack Cummings, *The Last Lawman*, 1994
Ernest Haycox, *Sundown Jim*, 1937
Robert Kammen, *The Oklahombres*, 1991
Max McCoy, *Wild Rider*, 1995
Richard Slotkin, *The Return of Henry Starr*, 1988

473

BARRY BRIERLEY

White Horse, Red Rider

(New York: Bear Books, 1996)

Story type: Mountain Man; Indian Wars
Major character(s): Joshua Donner, Mountain Man
Time period(s): 1830s
Locale(s): Rocky Mountains

Summary: Temporarily blinded by an accident, mountain man Joshua Donner seems easy prey for a Blackfoot hunting party. His only chance is to team with a Lakota boy who's too badly injured to walk. Donner will furnish the legs and the boy will be their eyes. Despite their mutual mistrust, the two must cooperate if they are to survive.

Where it's reviewed:
Roundup Magazine, April 1997, page 29

Other books you might like:
Will Baker, *Track of the Giant*, 1990
Stephen Bly, *Son of an Arizona Legend*, 1994
Tom Clarke, *Billy Bayes*, 1995
Douglas Savage, *Highpockets*, 1994
David Thompson, *Black Powder*, 1994
　　Wilderness #21

474

BILL BROOKS

Dust on the Wind

(New York: Pinnacle, 1997)

Story type: Traditional; Man Alone
Major character(s): Quint McCannon, Bounty Hunter, Gunfighter; Kimbo Luke, Outlaw, Murderer; Sugar Brown, Prostitute
Time period(s): 19th century (post Civil War)
Locale(s): Cheyenne, Wyoming; Del Rio, Texas; Ogallala, Nebraska

Summary: The death of a friend sends manhunter Quint McCannon on a long manhunt. Crossing most of the west, McCannon also crosses paths with a host of folks familiar to most Western readers, from Judge Roy Bean to Wyatt Earp's more-or-less wife Mattie Blaylock. But the hunt turns deadly before too long. McCannon finds he has more enemies than he thought, more reasons to live than he knew about, and a much more complicated situation to deal with than he'd suspected.

Other books by the same author:
The Last Law There Was, 1995
Buscadero, 1993

Other books you might like:
Wayne Davis, *Silverthorne*, 1997
Douglas Hirt, *The Silent Gun*, 1993
Kirby Jonas, *Season's End*, 1996
　　Season of the Vigilante #2
Dan Parkinson, *Dust on the Wind*, 1992
Jeffrey Poston, *The Peacekeeper*, 1997

475

SAM BROWN

Devil's Rim

(New York: Walker, 1998)

Story type: Traditional; Ranch Life
Major character(s): Concho Smith, Cowboy; Judyth Van, Mail Order Bride, Teacher; Little Bob Shiner, Rancher
Time period(s): 19th century (post Civil War)
Locale(s): Cimarron, New Mexico

Summary: A wandering cowboy, Concho Smith stops wandering and takes a job when he meets beautiful Judyth Van. The problem is that Judyth is a mail order bride—someone else's. She the wife of drunken rancher Sid Van, who was permanently injured in an accident shortly after their marriage. Against his own good sense, Smith takes the job of putting the Van ranch back in shape, a task greatly complicated by his growing attachment to Judyth. Further complications lie in the plans of neighboring rancher Little Bob Shiner, who has aspirations of building an empire and intends to start by getting hold of the Van ranch, by whatever means are necessary.

Other books by the same author:
The Long Drift, 1995
The Big Lonely, 1992
The Crime of Coy Bell, 1992
Ross Henry, 1991
The Trail to Honk Ballard's Bones, 1990

Other books you might like:
P.A. Bechko, *The Tin-Pan Man*, 1997
B.M. Bower, *Lonesome Land*, 1997
Elaine Long, *Jenny's Mountain*, 1987
  Spur Award winner
William A. Luckey, *Bad Company*, 1991
John D. Nesbitt, *Wild Rose of Ruby Canyon*, 1997

476

JOSEPH BRUCHAC
DAN ANDREASEN, Illustrator

Eagle Song
(New York: Dial, 1997)

Story type: Young Readers; Indian Culture
Major character(s): Danny Bigtree, Child (fourth grade), Indian (Mohawk); Aionwahta, Indian (Mohawk), Historical Figure
Time period(s): 1990s (1997)
Locale(s): New York, New York

Summary: The change from the Mohawk Reservation to the big city is a difficult one for ten-year-old Danny Bigtree. It's made more difficult by his loss of friends, by the derisive attitude of his classmates toward his Indian heritage, and, of course, by the class bully. With his family's help, Danny hangs on. Inspired by the story of the great Aionwahta, who led five mutually hostile tribes to make peace and found the Iroquois Confederacy, Danny seeks a way to bring peace in his own situation and to make a friend of his tormentor. For preteens.

Where it's reviewed:
Booklist, February 1, 1997, page 939
Children's Book Review Service, June 1997, page 126
Kirkus Reviews, December 1, 1996, page 1734
Publishers Weekly, December 30, 1996, page 67
School Library Journal, March 1997, page 149

Other books by the same author:
Long River, 1995
The Great Ball Game, 1994
Dawn Land, 1993

Flying with the Eagle, Racing the Great Bear, 1993
Other books you might like:
Judy Alter, *After Pa Was Shot*, 1978
Linda Crew, *Nekomah Creek*, 1991
Robert Barlow Fox, *To Be a Warrior*, 1997
Laura Roybal, *Billy*, 1994
Ruby C. Tolliver, *Boomer's Kids*, 1992

477

FRANK BURLESON (Pseudonym of Len Levinson)

Devil Dance
(New York: Signet, 1997)

Story type: Saga; Indian Wars
Series: Apache Wars Saga
Major character(s): Nathanial Barrington, Alcoholic, Drifter; Cochise, Indian (Apache), Chieftain; Zachary Barrington, Child
Time period(s): 1850s (1858)
Locale(s): Santa Fe, New Mexico; Fort Thorn, New Mexico

Summary: Out of the Army, shackled by drink, and in the process of divorcing his second wife, former dragoon captain Nathanial Barrington returns to New Mexico seeking redemption. He has a job as assistant Indian agent at Fort Thorn, and a ready-made family in adopted waif Gloria and unruly son Zachary. But his plans for a new start are rudely shattered by the clouds of a fresh Indian war. Cochise, war chief of the Apaches and an old friend of Barrington's, is determined to defend Apache lives and Apache land. The stage is set for a new clash of cultures with Barrington, as usual, caught in the middle.

Where it's reviewed:
Roundup Magazine, June 1997, page 33

Other books by the same author:
White Apache, 1996 (Apache Wars Saga #4)
War Eagles, 1995 (Apache Wars Saga #2)
Savage Frontier, 1995 (Apache Wars Saga #3)
Desert Hawks, 1994 (Apache Wars Saga #1)

Other books you might like:
John Edward Ames, *The Unwritten Order*, 1996
Tim Champlin, *The Last Campaign*, 1996
Ernest Haycox, *The Border Trumpet*, 1939
Les Savage Jr., *Fire Dance at Spider Rock*, 1995
Robert Skimin, *Apache Autumn*, 1992

478

FRANK BURLESON (Pseudonym of Len Levinson)

Night of the Cougar
(New York: Signet, 1997)

Story type: Indian Wars; Series
Series: Apache Wars Saga
Major character(s): Nathaniel Barrington, Rancher, Military Personnel (retired); Clarissa Barrington, Spouse, Frontierswoman; Geronimo, Indian (Apache), Warrior
Time period(s): 1850s (1858)
Locale(s): Whitecliff, Arizona; Fort Buchanan, Arizona

Summary: Leaving the Army behind, Nathaniel Barrington settles as a rancher in a remote corner of Arizona. It is Apache land, but Barrington has nothing to fear from the Apaches. Known to them as Sunny Bear, he is a friend to Geronimo and other Apache leaders. As continued encroachment by Anglos, both civilian and military, threaten the Apache way of life, they and Barrington join in an alliance for mutual help. Soon, the incursions affect Barrington, too, in the form of outlaws led by renegade Steve Culhane. Barrington stands them off with relative ease until they threaten his family, and then he turns on them with all the ferocity of his Apache brothers.

Other books by the same author:
Devil Dance, 1997 (Apache Wars Saga #5)
White Apache, 1996 (Apache Wars Saga #4)
Savage Frontier, 1995 (Apache Wars Saga #3)
War Eagles, 1995 (Apache Wars Saga #2)
Desert Hawks, 1994 (Apache Wars Saga #1)

Other books you might like:
Jack Ballas, *Montana Breed*, 1994
Bill Dugan, *Geronimo*, 1994
Hank Edwards, *Apache Sundown*, 1996
Richard Matheson, *Shadow on the Sun*, 1994
Doyle Trent, *Mountain Marauders*, 1995

479

WILL CAMP (Pseudonym of Preston Lewis)

Blood of Texas

(New York: Harper, 1996)

Story type: Historical; Saga
Major character(s): Rubio Portillo, Rancher, Frontiersman; Mary Calder, Frontierswoman; William Barrett Travis, Military Personnel
Time period(s): 1830s (1835-1836)
Locale(s): San Antonio, Texas

Summary: Rancher Rubio Portillo turns soldier when the Texas war for independence breaks out. The Texan forces start with a victory, driving General Cos and his men out of San Antonio and rescuing Portillo's brother Tomas from imprisonment. But General Santa Anna is coming with reinforcements to beat down the rebellion, and the woman Portillo loves is trapped in a mission-turned-fortress called the Alamo.

Other books by the same author:
Escape from Silverton, 1995
Lone Survivor, 1995
Blood Saga, 1994
Choctaw Trail, 1994
Vigilante Justice, 1994

Other books you might like:
Jeff Long, *Empire of Bones*, 1993
Leonard Sanders, *Star of Empire*, 1992
Jory Sherman, *The Barons of Texas*, 191997
Robert Vaughan, *Texas Glory*, 1997
D. Marion Wilkinson, *Not Between Brothers*, 1997

480

TIM CHAMPLIN

Deadly Season

(Thorndike, Maine: Thorndike Press, 1997)

Story type: Traditional; Mystery
Major character(s): Jay McGraw, Detective—Private; Fred Casey, Police Officer; Sherlock Holmes, Detective—Private
Time period(s): 19th century (post Civil War)
Locale(s): San Francisco, California

Summary: Wells Fargo special agent Jay McGraw and San Francisco policeman Fred Casey tackle drug-running and murder in San Francisco's Chinatown. Their efforts to cut off the opium trade in the city are partly successful until one of the policemen assisting the pair is brutally murdered. Then, feeling that he's in over his head, Casey calls for help. To the rescue comes a lanky, lethargic Englishman named Sherlock Holmes.

Other books by the same author:
The Last Campaign, 1996
The Survivor, 1996
Colt Lightning, 1989
King of the Highbinders, 1989

Other books you might like:
Wayne Barton, *Lockhart's Nightmare*, 1998
  Stan Williams, co-author
Win Blevins, *The Rock Child*, 1998
Richard Laymon, *Savage*, 1994
  Jack the Ripper in the West
F.M. Parker, *The Shanghaiers*, 1987
Walter Satterthwait, *Wilde West*, 1991

481

GIFF CHESHIRE

Renegade River

(Thorndike, Maine: Thorndike, 1998)

Story type: Traditional; Collection
Time period(s): 19th century (post Civil War)
Locale(s): Columbia River, Washington; Oregon

Summary: Western anthologist Bill Pronzini has collected a dozen Giff Cheshire stories written from the 1930s through the 1950s. Cheshire, an Oregon native, wrote mostly of the Pacific Northwest. Though often overlooked by Western fans, that area had its own brand of cowboys and Indians, lawmen and outlaws, and high adventure among the plains and woods and rivers.

Other books you might like:
Max Brand, *The Ghost Wagon and other Great Western Adventures*, 1996
  Jon Tuska, editor
H.A. DeRosso, *Under the Burning Sun*, 1997
T.T. Flynn, *Rawhide*, 1996
Bill Gulick, *River's End*, 1994
Ray Hogan, *Legend of a Badman: A Western Quintet*, 1998

482

PAUL CLAYTON

Flight of the Crow

(New York: Jove, 1996)

Story type: Indian Culture; Indian Wars
Major character(s): Calling Crow, Indian (Muskogee), Chieftain; Rain Cloud, Indian (Coosa), Warrior
Time period(s): 16th century
Locale(s): Georgia

Summary: After a long imprisonment, Calling Crow escapes his Spanish captors and makes his way back to his native village. His welcome isn't what he expects. The village is in the grip of a deadly fever brought by the Spaniards. Blamed by his people for the onset of the disease, Calling Crow is driven out. He wanders until he finds refuge and welcome with the Coosa people. And the Coosa may need all the advice and help he can offer, because they're facing their own Spanish invasion.

Other books by the same author:
Calling Crow's Nation, 1997
Calling Crow, 1995

Other books you might like:
Irwin R. Blacker, *Taos*, 1959
Don Coldsmith, *Thunderstick*, 1993
    Spanish Bit #20
Robert J. Conley, *The Long Way Home*, 1994
Lana M. Harrigan, *Acoma: A Novel of Conquest*, 1997
Ardath Mayhar, *Island in the Lake*, 1993

483

AMANDA COCKRELL

The Long Walk

(New York: Avon, 1996)

Story type: Indian Culture; Series
Series: Deer Dancers
Major character(s): Night Hawk, Trader; Others' Child, Shaman, Spouse; Cannot Be Told, Chieftain
Time period(s): Indeterminate Past
Locale(s): Pacific Coast, California

Summary: Traveling west to the great ocean, Night Hawk and his wife Others' Child, with young Little Brother, stop for a visit among the Channel Clan of the People Who Lived at the Coast. Others' Child is unhappy with the wandering life of the trader. Now, with her child barely old enough to travel, she wishes for a place to settle down. She finds the Channel people friendly, shares her small store of magic with them, and thinks that she might find a home there—perhaps with Sea Otter, if Night Hawk won't stay. But war erupts between the Channel Clan and the Knifenose Fish Clan, a war that transcends their civilized rules and develops into something beyond control. When the coast dwellers look for someone to blame, the strangers in their midst are an easy target.

Other books by the same author:
Wind Caller's Children, 1996 (Deer Dancers #2)
Daughter of the Sun, 1995 (Deer Dancers #1)

Other books you might like:
Margaret Allan, *Keeper of the Stone*, 1994
Joseph Bruchac, *Long River*, 1995
Kathleen O'Neal Gear, *People of the Mist*, 1998
    W. Michael Gear, co-author
Gary McCarthy, *Yosemite*, 1995
Charlotte Prentiss, *The Island Tribe*, 1997

484

DON COLDSMITH

Medicine Hat

(Norman: University of Oklahoma Press, 1997)

Story type: Indian Culture; Series
Series: Spanish Bit Saga
Major character(s): Pipe Bearer, Shaman, Indian (Elk-Dog People); Otter, Spouse, Indian (Elk-Dog People); Plum Flower, Widow(er), Indian (Elk-Dog People)
Time period(s): 18th century
Locale(s): Kansas River, Kansas; Great Plains

Summary: Pipe Bearer, shaman of the Elk-Dog People has a vision of a horse wearing a medicine hat—the headgear of a holy man. When a colt is born with similar markings, Pipe Bearer hopes it is a signal that the privations of a bad winter are over. Leading the colt and its mother, the Elk-Dog band goes north to seek the meaning of the sign. But a death in the tribe and a quarrel over the dead man's widow threatens to split the tribe and undo all the work for peace that Pipe Bearer has begun.

Where it's reviewed:
Publishers Weekly, August 4, 1997, page 68

Other books by the same author:
Bearer of the Pipe, 1995 (Spanish Bit Saga #24)
Child of the Dead, 1995 (Spanish Bit Saga #23)
Runestone, 1995
Track of the Bear, 1994 (Spanish Bit Saga #22)
Bride of the Morning Star, 1993 (Spanish Bit Saga #19)

Other books you might like:
Margaret Allan, *Keeper of the Stone*, 1994
Beverly Bird, *The Pony Wife*, 1995
Amanda Cockrell, *Daughter of the Sun*, 1995
    Deer Dancers #1
Kathleen O'Neal Gear, *People of the Lakes*, 1995
    W. Michael Gear, co-author
Ardath Mayhar, *Hunters of the Plains*, 1995

485

DON COLDSMITH

Tallgrass: A Novel of the Great Plains

(New York: Bantam, 1997)

Story type: Indian Culture; Historical
Major character(s): Magpie, Indian (Taos), Fugitive; Washington, Slave (freed), Trapper; Jedediah Sterling, Wanderer, Mountain Man
Time period(s): 16th century; 19th century (1540s-1830s)

Locale(s): Kansas River, Kansas; Great Plains; Taos, New Mexico

Summary: Spreading in scope from the first contact between Pueblo Indians and Spaniards in the 1540s to the days of the Santa Fe Trail, this generational novel traces the relations and conflicts between Europeans and Indians on the Great Plains. Magpie, a young man of the pueblos, sees the war between his people and the Spaniards in santa Fe. A century later, freed slave Washington stays with the Comanches because they treat him with honor. Easterner Jedediah Sterling comes to see the West and ends by guiding the first Anglo party along the Santa Fe Trail.

Where it's reviewed:
Library Journal, March 15, 1997, page 88
Publishers Weekly, March 3, 1997, page 66

Other books by the same author:
Bearer of the Pipe, 1995 (Spanish Bit Saga #24)
Child of the Dead, 1995 (Spanish Bit Saga #23)
Runestone, 1995
Track of the Bear, 1994 (Spanish Bit Saga #22)
Bride of the Morning Star, 1993 (Spanish Bit Saga #19)

Other books you might like:
Irwin R. Blacker, *Taos*, 1959
Amanda Cockrell, *Wind Caller's Children*, 1996
  Deer Dancers #2
Robert J. Conley, *The Dark Island*, 1996
  Real People #5
W. Michael Gear, *The Morning River*, 1996
Greg Tobin, *Prairie*, 1997

486

JUDD COLE

Bloody Bones Canyon

(New York: Leisure, 1996)

Story type: Indian Wars; Series
Series: Cheyenne
Major character(s): Touch the Sky, Indian (Cheyenne), Shaman; Honey Eater, Indian (Cheyenne), Spouse; Wolf Who Hunts Smiling, Indian (Cheyenne), Renegade
Time period(s): 1850s
Locale(s): Wyoming; United States

Summary: The murder of one Cheyenne by another was an unspeakable crime, one that the people of Touch the Sky's band can hardly imagine. And when the murder victim is Gray Thunder, the popular peace chief of the nation, the crime seems too awful to believe. Touch the Sky is driven by duty and honor to find and kill the murderer. But his people are under other threats, and Touch the Sky cannot protect them everywhere.

Other books by the same author:
Orphan Train, 1996 (Cheyenne #16)
Renegade Nation, 1996 (Cheyenne #15)
Blood on the Arrows, 1995 (Cheyenne Special Edition)
Wendigo Mountain, 1995 (Cheyenne #13)
Buffalo Hiders, 1994 (Cheyenne #10)

Other books you might like:
Dan Cushman, *Valley of the Thousand Smokes*, 1996
Hank Edwards, *Gray Warrior*, 1995
Tom Eidson, *The Last Ride*, 1995
John Killdeer, *The Savage Land*, 1995
J.L. Reasoner, *Cossack Three Ponies*, 1997

487

JUDD COLE

Renegade Siege

(New York: Leisure, 1996)

Story type: Indian Wars; Series
Series: Cheyenne
Major character(s): Touch the Sky, Indian (Cheyenne), Shaman; Honey Eater, Indian (Cheyenne), Spouse; Wolf Who Hunts Smiling, Indian (Cheyenne), Renegade
Time period(s): 1850s
Locale(s): Wyoming; United States

Summary: The enemies of Touch the Sky, led by his old nemesis Wolf Who Hunts Smiling, have grown in strength and number. Gathering outcasts like themselves into the Renegade Nation, they lay siege to a Wyoming mining camp. Ostensibly, their reason is to gain gold for guns and powder. But actually, they plan to draw Touch the Sky into a desperate rescue mission where they will have all the advantages over him.

Other books by the same author:
Orphan Train, 1996 (Cheyenne #16)
Renegade Nation, 1996 (Cheyenne #15)
Blood on the Arrows, 1995 (Cheyenne Special Edition)
Wendigo Mountain, 1995 (Cheyenne #13)
Buffalo Hiders, 1994 (Cheyenne #10)

Other books you might like:
Patrick E. Andrews, *Comanchero Blood*, 1993
Frank Burleson, *Devil Dance*, 1997
Lou Cameron, *Yellow Iron*, 1990
Terry C. Johnston, *Wolf Mountain Moon*, 1997
  Plainsmen #12
Gordon D. Shirreffs, *The Ghost Dancers*, 1986

488

JUDD COLE

River of Death

(New York: Leisure, 1997)

Story type: Indian Wars; Series
Series: Cheyenne
Major character(s): Touch the Sky, Indian (Cheyenne), Shaman; Honey Eater, Indian (Cheyenne), Spouse; Wolf Who Hunts Smiling, Indian (Cheyenne), Renegade
Time period(s): 1850s
Locale(s): Wyoming; United States

Summary: Touch the Sky, a full-blood Cheyenne reared by Anglo settlers, again faces threats from both his native and his adopted peoples. A false prophet called Medicine Flute has arisen among the Cheyenne, challenging Touch the Sky's

position as shaman. And old enemies Seth Carlson and Hiram Steele have combined in a plot to rechannel the river that waters Cheyenne land. Touch the Sky must fight off traitors at his back while he tries to turn the tables on Steele and Carlson.

Other books by the same author:
Orphan Train, 1996 (Cheyenne #16)
Renegade Nation, 1996 (Cheyenne #15)
Blood on the Arrows, 1995 (Cheyenne Special Edition)
Wendigo Mountain, 1995 (Cheyenne #13)
Buffalo Hiders, 1994 (Cheyenne #10)

Other books you might like:
Clifford Blair, *Storm over the Lightning L*, 1993
Michael Blake, *Dances with Wolves*, 1990
Benjamin Capps, *The White Man's Road*, 1969
Dave Jackson, *Lost River Conspiracy*, 1995
Robert F. Jones, *Tie My Bones to Her Back*, 1996

489

JANE CANDIA COLEMAN

I, Pearl Hart

(Thorndike, Maine: Thorndike Press, 1998)

Story type: Historical; Traditional
Major character(s): Pearl Hart, Outlaw, Abuse Victim; Joe Boot, Outlaw; Frank Hart, Gambler
Time period(s): 19th century (post Civil War)
Locale(s): Chicago, Illinois; Phoenix, Arizona; Yuma Prison, Arizona

Summary: To the dime novelists, Pearl Hart was the Bandit Queen of the West. In Coleman's far more thoughtful book, Hart is a young woman who goes from one abusive relationship to another. Leaving her respectable home for the attractive but violent Frank Hart, she faces abuse, laudanum addiction, and desperate flight for her life. She temporarily reconciles with Hart, but when he goes to the Spanish-American War, she teams up with drifter Joe Boot. The two rob a stage, and Pearl ends up in Yuma Prison, the first woman sentenced there.

Other books by the same author:
Moving On, 1997
Doc Holliday's Woman, 1995
Stories from Mesa Country, 1991

Other books you might like:
B.M. Bower, *Lonesome Land*, 1997
Jack Cummings, *Escape from Yuma*, 1990
John D. Nesbitt, *Wild Rose of Ruby Canyon*, 1997
Ellen Recknor, *Me and the Boys*, 1995
J.A. Shears, *Lady with a Gun*, 1990

490

JANE CANDIA COLEMAN

Moving On

(Thorndike, ME: Thorndike, 1997)

Story type: Collection
Time period(s): 19th century
Locale(s): Lincoln, New Mexico; West

Summary: One of those rare authors who is equally accomplished as novelist, poet, and short story writer, Coleman offers a collection of short stories centered on the dissimilarities of the people and cultures who met and mixed to make up the American West. Three of the stories, built around New Mexico's Lincoln County War, highlight the Hispanic-based culture of New Mexico, but others range to the Texas sand hills and the northern plains.

Where it's reviewed:
Booklist, February 1, 1997, page 925
Publishers Weekly, January 27, 1997, page 82

Other books by the same author:
Doc Holliday's Woman, 1995
Stories from Mesa Country, 1991

Other books you might like:
Benjamin Capps, *Tales of the Southwest*, 1991
Dorothy M. Johnson, *The Hanging Tree and Other Stories*, 1958
Shelly Ritthaler, *The Ginger Jar*, 1990
Dale L. Walker, *The Golden Spurs*, 1990
Carrie Young, *The Wedding Dress: Stories from the Dakota Plains*, 1992

491

RALPH COMPTON

Across the Rio Colorado

(New York: St. Martin's Press, 1997)

Story type: Traditional; Quest
Major character(s): Chance McQuade, Wagonmaster, Frontiersman; Rufus Hook, Businessman; Andrew Burke, Settler, Avenger
Time period(s): 1830s (1837)
Locale(s): St. Louis, Missouri; Rio Colorado, Texas

Summary: Chance McQuade, experienced wagon boss, hires on to guide a big party of settlers to the new Republic of Texas. Rufus Hook has arranged for a million-acre land grant on the Rio Colorado, and is taking everything he needs—including McQuade—to build a town or an empire. Along with a hundred settler families, Hook has his own small army of fighting men, plus gamblers, painted women, a doctor and a lawyer, and even a schoolmarm. But McQuade gradually becomes suspicious of Hook's motives and methods. As a split develops between Hook's contingent and the others, it's up to McQuade to hold things together, and to get his party to Texas alive—if that proves to be possible.

Other books by the same author:
The Dawn of Fury, 1996
North to the Bitterroot, 1996
The Dodge City Trail, 1995 (Trail Drive #8)
The Oregon Trail, 1995 (Trail Drive #9)
The Shawnee Trail, 1994 (Trail Drive #6)

Other books you might like:
Dylan Harson, *Kansas Blue*, 1993
Ernest Haycox, *The Earthbreakers*, 1952
Johnny Quarles, *Spirit Trail*, 1995
Clay Reynolds, *Franklin's Crossing*, 1992
Leonard Sanders, *Star of Empire*, 1992

492

RALPH COMPTON

The Autumn of the Gun

(New York: Signet, 1996)

Story type: Traditional; Revenge
Major character(s): Nathan Stone, Avenger, Gunfighter; Wes Tremayne, Bastard Son, Gunfighter; Cort Sandlin, Outlaw, Gunfighter
Time period(s): 1870s; 1880s (1879-1884)
Locale(s): Fort Elliott, Texas; Lincoln, New Mexico; El Paso, Texas

Summary: Nathan Stone's vengeance trail has left him with a reputation that's hard to live up to and hard to live down. Known as lawman and outlaw, gambler and gunfighter, Stone finds little peace wherever he goes. Nabbed for a bank robbery of which he's innocent, Stone is briefly held in prison, and on his release goes to face some of the toughest men in the west—the likes of Earp, Holliday, Billy Bonney, and Wes Hardin. But the toughest of all might be the young man who doesn't realize he's Nathan Stone's son.

Where it's reviewed:
Roundup Magazine, April 1997, page 29

Other books by the same author:
The Dawn of Fury, 1996
North to the Bitterroot, 1996
The Dodge City Trail, 1995 (Trail Drive #8)
The Oregon Trail, 1995 (Trail Drive #9)
The Shawnee Trail, 1994 (Trail Drive #6)

Other books you might like:
James Carlos Blake, *Pistoleer*, 1995
Charles Boeckman, *When the Devil Came to Endless*, 1996
Hascal Giles, *Texas Blood*, 1992
Paul A. Hawkins, *The Shooter*, 1994
Richard Parry, *The Winter Wolf*, 1996

493

RALPH COMPTON

The Border Empire

(New York: Signet, 1997)

Story type: Traditional; Revenge
Major character(s): Wes Stone, Avenger, Gunfighter; Cort Sandlin, Outlaw
Time period(s): 1880s (1884)
Locale(s): El Paso, Texas; Toluca, Mexico; Nogales, Mexico

Summary: Nathan Stone is dead in an El Paso street, victim of Cort Sandlin's outlaw army. But Wes Stone, Nathan's son, is ready to pick up the vengeance trail where his father left it. Venturing south into Mexico, young Stone tackles the Sandlin gang on its own ground, the vast border empire where Sandlin's word is law. With a few unlikely allies, Stone penetrates sandlin's hideout, intent on finishing what his father started so many years before.

Other books by the same author:
The Dawn of Fury, 1996

North to the Bitterroot, 1996
The Dodge City Trail, 1995 (Trail Drive #8)
The Oregon Trail, 1995 (Trail Drive #9)
The Shawnee Trail, 1994 (Trail Drive #6)

Other books you might like:
W. Michael Gear, *Big Horn Legacy*, 1988
Hascal Giles, *Son of a Fast Gun*, 1991
John Legg, *Buckskin Vengeance*, 1996
Susan Clark Schofield, *Telluride*, 1993
Brock Thoene, *Hope Valley War*, 1997

494

RALPH COMPTON

The Killing Season

(New York: Signet, 1996)

Story type: Traditional; Revenge
Major character(s): Nathan Stone, Avenger, Gunfighter; Sage Jennings, Lawman (Texas Ranger); Chapa Gonzolos, Outlaw
Time period(s): 1870s (1873-1877)
Locale(s): Dodge City, Kansas; Denver, Colorado; Hays, Kansas

Summary: Nathan Stone's death list for the murder of his family still has five names to go. To get those five, Stone must criss-cross the west, following vague leads into danger and almost certain death. A man seeking killers has to go among killers, and in the course of his search, Stone runs into a lot of trouble that isn't tied to his own quest for vengeance.

Other books by the same author:
The Dawn of Fury, 1996
North to the Bitterroot, 1996
The Dodge City Trail, 1995 (Trail Drive #8)
The Oregon Trail, 1995 (Trail Drive #9)
The Shawnee Trail, 1994 (Trail Drive #6)

Other books you might like:
Karl Lassiter, *Fast Hand*, 1989
Lauran Paine, *Lockwood*, 1996
Johnny Quarles, *Shadow of the Gun*, 1995
James Reasoner, *The Wilderness Road*, 1996
Frank Watson, *A Cold, Dark Trail*, 1991

495

RALPH COMPTON

Sixguns and Double Eagles

(New York: Signet, 1998)

Story type: Traditional; Mystery
Major character(s): Wes Stone, Gunfighter, Lawman; Bryan Silver, Lawman, Government Official; El Lobo, Indian, Gunfighter
Time period(s): 1880s (1884-1885)
Locale(s): New Orleans, Louisiana; San Francisco, California; Dodge City, Kansas

Summary: When the mysteriously-named Golden Dragon Society finds its way into the government mints, replacing gold coins with counterfeits, the monetary system of the country

totters. Treasury agents and a horde of Pinkerton's detectives have failed to dent the conspiracy, so special agent Bryan Silver calls on some new blood. Teenaged gunfighters Wes Stone and El Lobo are sent to infiltrate the gang and break it up. In a dangerous odyssey that takes them from New Orleans to San Francisco with stops in between, the two fight against the odds to cut off the head of the Golden Dragon.

Other books by the same author:
Across the Rio Colorado, 1997
The Border Empire, 1997
The Autumn of the Gun, 1996
The Killing Season, 1996

Other books you might like:
John Edward Ames, *The Golden Circle*, 1996
Tim Champlin, *Deadly Season*, 1997
John Cunningham, *The Rainbow Runner*, 1992
Douglas Hirt, *Deadwood*, 1998
Brock Thoene, *Cannons of the Comstock*, 1992
   Bodie Thoene, co-author

496

RALPH COMPTON

The Winchester Run

(New York: St. Martin's Press, 1997)

Story type: Traditional; Trail Drive
Major character(s): Mac Tunstall, Wagonmaster; Port Guthrie, Laborer (wagon driver); Jake Embler, Military Personnel (deserter)
Time period(s): 1870s (1873)
Locale(s): Fort Griffin, Texas; Austin, Texas

Summary: Mac Tunstall and his men are out of the cattle business but into one just as hazardous. Tunstall has agreed to take a shipment of winchester rifles from the railhead at Dodge City to Army headquarters in Austin, Texas. He and his fellow wagoneers face danger along the way from Indians and outlaws, all of whom want the new and powerful rifles. But their greatest danger comes from treachery from within, when they're attacked by the one they look to for help.

Other books by the same author:
Across the Rio Colorado, 1997
The Border Empire, 1997
The Autumn of the Gun, 1996
The Killing Season, 1996

Other books you might like:
Erle Adkins, *Two Guns from Texas*, 1990
P.A. Bechko, *The Tin-Pan Man*, 1997
Will Camp, *Escape from Silverton*, 1995
Robert Kammen, *Montana Rimfire*, 1991
Cotton Smith, *Dark Trail to Dodge*, 1997

497

ROBERT J. CONLEY

Back to Malachi

(New York: Leisure, 1997)

Story type: Indian Culture; Mystery

Major character(s): Charlie Black, Indian (Cherokee); Mose Pathkiller, Indian (Cherokee), Outlaw; Velma Hotchkiss, Indian (Cherokee), Fiance(e)
Time period(s): 1890s
Locale(s): Cherokee Nation, Oklahoma

Summary: Charlie Black has a good life staked out ahead of him, with a job in his father's store and pretty and passionate Velma Hotchkiss eager to marry him. But Charlie is walking an uneasy line between two worlds. Velma wants a Christian marriage and an Anglo way of life, while Charlie is drawn to traditional Cherokee ways. Then two of Charlie's friends run into trouble with the law, and his life starts to unravel. Soon, he's gone so far down the outlaw trail that he may never get back alive.

Other books by the same author:
The Dark Island, 1996 (Real People #5)
Captain Dutch, 1995
Outside the Law, 1995
Crazy Snake, 1994
The Long Way Home, 1994

Other books you might like:
Benjamin Capps, *The White Man's Road*, 1969
Hank Edwards, *Apache Sundown*, 1996
Kirby Jonas, *The Dansing Star*, 1997
Page Lambert, *Shifting Stars: A Novel of the West*, 1997
James Alexander Thom, *The Red Heart*, 1997

498

ROBERT J. CONLEY

War Woman

(New York: St. Martin's Press, 1997)

Story type: Historical; Indian Culture
Major character(s): Whirlwind, Indian (Cherokee), Chieftain
Time period(s): 16th century
Locale(s): Florida; North Carolina; Virginia

Summary: The descendant of a Spanish trader and a Cherokee woman, young Whirlwind wants to see these strange foreigners for herself. She persuades her brother and another young warrior to accompany her to the Spanish settlements of Florida, where they work out a trade agreement. Renamed War Woman for her courage and intelligence, she sees the benefits of European trade goods, but also the destruction brought by the introduction of alcohol. Later, she uses her knowledge of Europeans to negotiate a treaty to mine Cherokee gold, and to lead an expedition against the encroaching British colonists.

Where it's reviewed:
Kirkus Reviews, September 1, 1997, page 1324
Publishers Weekly, August 25, 1997, page 44

Other books by the same author:
Captain Dutch, 1995
Outside the Law, 1995
Crazy Snake, 1994
Geronimo: An American Legend, 1994
The Long Way Home, 1994

Other books you might like:
Irwin R. Blacker, *Taos*, 1959
Paul Clayton, *Calling Crow*, 1995
Don Coldsmith, *Walks in the Sun*, 1993
  Spanish Bit Saga #20
Cameron Judd, *The Overmountain Men*, 1991
Lucia St. Clair Robson, *Walk in My Soul*, 1985

499

KENT CONWELL

Bumpo, Bill, and the Girls
(New York: Avalon, 1997)

Story type: Traditional; Trail Drive
Major character(s): Bill Merritt, Rancher; H. Albert Harper, Lawyer; Linitta Merritt, Child
Time period(s): 19th century (post Civil War)
Locale(s): Cibolo Springs, Texas; Dodge City, Kansas

Summary: Rancher Bill Merritt faces a cattle drive to get his steers to market and save the ranch. Then a lawyer visits him and gives him a bigger problem. Merritt's brother and sister-in-law have died, leaving him the family ranch on two conditions. The two conditions are ten-year-old Linitta and eight-year-old Alwilda. If Merritt will keep the two children with him for four months, the ranch is his. Pushed from both directions, Merritt sets out for Dodge City with two young girls and a red-haired nanny who promise more trouble than all his longhorns together.

Where it's reviewed:
Roundup Magazine, April 1997, page 25

Other books by the same author:
Cattle Drive to Dodge, 1992
Panhandle Gold, 1991

Other books you might like:
Judy Alter, *A Ballad for Sallie*, 1992
Robin Gibson, *Ma Calhoun's Boys*, 1992
Sonia Levitin, *Nine for California*, 1996
Ellen Recknor, *Leaving Missouri*, 1997
Cotton Smith, *Dark Trail to Dodge*, 1997

500

DEBRA COWAN

If Only
(New York: Dell, 1997)

Story type: Historical; Historical/American Civil War
Major character(s): Elise Worthen, Young Woman; Jared Kensington, Government Official (Treasury Department), Veteran (Civil War)
Time period(s): 1860s (post Civil War)
Locale(s): United States

Summary: Jared Kensington is an agent of the Treasury Department on secret assignment, searching for another agent who disappeared during the recently-ended Civil War. Newly back from the war himself, he is delighted to meet beautiful Elise Worthen, sister of one of his comrades. But Elise has a secret of her own. In defense of her home, she killed the man that Kensington is searching for.

Where it's reviewed:
Publishers Weekly, August 4, 1997, page 72

Other books you might like:
Frederic Bean, *Lorena*, 1996
Harold Coyle, *Look Away*, 1995
Kathleen O'Neal Gear, *Thin Moon and Cold Mist*, 1995
Al Lacy, *Joy from Ashes*, 1995
  Battles of Destiny #4
Wynema McGowan, *While the Rivers Run*, 1996

501

HAROLD COYLE

Look Away
(New York: Pocket Books, 1996)

Story type: Historical; Historical/American Civil War
Major character(s): James Bannon, Military Personnel (Confederate); Kevin Bannon, Military Personnel (Union); Mary Beth McPherson, Southern Belle
Time period(s): 1860s (1860-1863)
Locale(s): Lexington, Virginia; Perth Amboy, New Jersey; Gettysburg, Pennsylvania

Summary: Separated by family problems, brothers James and Kevin Bannon choose opposite sides in the Civil War. James, exile and VMI student, fights for the south while Kevin wears Union blue. Facing each other across the lines, they experience defeat and victory, hardship and good fortune, bereavement and reunion, with the varying fortunes of their armies. But always destiny is drawing them toward a meeting at a quiet Pennsylvania farm town called Gettysburg.

Other books by the same author:
Savage Wilderness, 1997
Until the End, 1996

Other books you might like:
Howard Bahr, *The Black Flower*, 1997
Frederic Bean, *Lorena*, 1996
Tom Dyja, *Play for a Kingdom*, 1997
Madison Jones, *Nashville 1864*, 1997
Robert Vaughan, *Andersonville*, 1996

502

HAROLD COYLE

Savage Wilderness
(New York: Simon and Schuster, 1997)

Story type: Historical; Indian Wars
Major character(s): Ian McPherson, Revolutionary, Military Personnel (militiaman); Anton de Chevalier, Military Personnel (French); Thomas Shields, Military Personnel (British)
Time period(s): 1760s
Locale(s): Fort Ticonderoga, Vermont; Albany, New York

Summary: The fierce and merciless fighting of the French and Indian War spreads throughout to American Northwest—at

that time, the Ohio River Valley and the northern parts of New York and New England. Ian McPherson, exiled to the New World for rebellion against the Crown, is an unwilling militiaman forcibly allied with the arrogant and ambitious Thomas Shields. But the British are the lesser evil for McPherson, for the French and their Indian allies ask and offer no quarter to the border settlements.

Where it's reviewed:
Kirkus Reviews, June 15, 1997, page 889
Publishers Weekly, July 7, 1997, page 52

Other books by the same author:
Look Away, 1995
Code of Honor, 1994

Other books you might like:
Paul Clayton, *Flight of the Crow*, 1996
Charles Durham, *The Last Exile*, 1990
Mike Roarke, *Thunder in the East*, 1993
    First Frontier #1
Lucia St. Clair Robson, *Mary's Land*, 1995
Jim R. Woolard, *Thunder in the Valley*, 1995
    Spur Award winner

503

HAROLD COYLE

Until the End

(New York: Simon and Schuster, 1996)

Story type: Historical; Historical/American Civil War
Major character(s): James Bannon, Military Personnel (Confederate); Kevin Bannon, Military Personnel (Union); Harriet Ann Shields, Nurse
Time period(s): 1860s (1863-1865)
Locale(s): Mine Run, Virginia; Richmond, Virginia

Summary: It's brother against brother with Kevin Bannon fighting on the side of the Union and brother James part of a crack Virginia regiment. Parted by their dictatorial father's actions, the two have gone their separate ways. Now James is committed to the South, not least because of Virginia belle Mary Beth McPherson. But the tide has turned against the Confederacy. In the last days of the South's fall, each Bannon brother will face his own crisis. In the balance is the question whether they will be forever parted by the violence and hatred engendered by the war.

Where it's reviewed:
Booklist, August 1996, page 1880
Library Journal, April 15, 1997, page 138: (for audio version)
Publishers Weekly, March 24, 1997, page 81

Other books by the same author:
Look Away, 1995
Code of Honor, 1994

Other books you might like:
Howard Bahr, *The Black Flower*, 1997
Debra Cowan, *If Only*, 1997
Max McCoy, *Sons of Fire*, 1993
Kerry Newcomb, *Ride the Panther*, 1992
J.L. Reasoner, *The Healer's Road*, 1995

504

DEBBIE DADEY
SCOTT GOTO, Illustrator

Shooting Star

(New York: Walker, 1997)

Story type: Traditional; Young Readers
Major character(s): Annie Oakley, Entertainer (sharpshooter), Historical Figure; Sitting Bull, Indian (Sioux), Historical Figure
Time period(s): 1890s
Locale(s): West; New York, New York

Summary: With pictures and text for youngest readers, this book mixes some of the real events of legendary marksman Annie Oakley's life with the sort of tall-tale folklore that has her shooting the points off a star. The energetic style and the sense of outlandish exaggeration fit in the true tradition of Western storytelling.

Where it's reviewed:
Booklist, March 15, 1997, page 1245
Children's Book Review Service, May 1997, page 110
Kirkus Reviews, April 1, 1997, page 552
Publishers Weekly, March 24, 1997, page 83
School Library Journal, April 1997, page 122

Other books you might like:
Mary Blount Christian, *Who'd Believe John Colter*, 1993
Joe Hayes, *Here Comes the Storyteller*, 1996
Sheila Solomon Klass, *A Shooting Star*, 1996
Angela Shelf Medearis, *The Zebra-Riding Cowboy*, 1992
Jerrie Oughton, *How the Stars Fell into the Sky*, 1993

505

SANDRA DALLAS

The Diary of Mattie Spenser

(New York: St. Martin's Press, 1997)

Story type: Historical; Ranch Life
Major character(s): Mattie Spenser, Frontierswoman, Settler; Luke Spenser, Frontiersman, Settler; Persia Chalmers, Young Woman
Time period(s): 1860s
Locale(s): Denver, Colorado

Summary: The marriage of Luke and Mattie Spenser is less a love match than an alliance for mutual help and support. Together the newlyweds set out from their Iowa home for the new opportunities of Colorado. Mattie's diary covers four years, beginning with her journey and extending into the first years in the new settlement. With the stoicism of the frontier, Mattie recounts Indian attack, hardship, the pains and joys of childbirth, and the numbing sense of loss at a later miscarriage. Not until she catches her stiffnecked husband with another woman, an old sweetheart, does she face a problem that at first seems too great for her.

Where it's reviewed:
Booklist, May 15, 1997, page 1560
Kirkus Reviews, April 1, 1997, page 482
Publishers Weekly, May 5, 1997, page 200

Other books you might like:
Cindy Bonner, *The Passion of Dellie O'Barr*, 1996
Irene Bennett Brown, *The Plainswoman*, 1994
Elmer Kelton, *The Pumpkin Rollers*, 1996
Barbara Riefe, *Desperate Crossing: The Jenny Sanders Pryor Story*, 1997
Lauraine Snelling, *An Untamed Land*, 1996
    Red River of the North #1

506
W.E. DAVIS

The Refining Fire
(Wheaton, Illinois: Crossway, 1997)

Story type: Traditional; Series
Series: Valley of the Peacemaker
Major character(s): Matt Page, Lawman (town marshal); Sarah Page, Businesswoman, Spouse
Time period(s): 1870s
Locale(s): Bodie, California

Summary: Matt Page is a reluctant lawman, holding down the job in the tough mining town of Bodie while the rightful marshal is on the mend. Page hopes—without much justification—that his tenure will be peaceful. His hopes prove groundless when an Indian man is found dead in the ruins of a burned building. Is it murder? Page thinks so, and he has on his hands a real mystery, tinged with racial hatred and filled with people who have secrets to hide.

Where it's reviewed:
Library Journal, April 1, 1997, page 78

Other books by the same author:
The Proving Ground, 1996 (Valley of the Peacemaker #2)
The Gathering Storm, 1996 (Valley of the Peacemaker #1)

Other books you might like:
Stephen Bly, *Stay Away From That City. . .They Call It Cheyenne*, 1996
    Code of the West #4
S.W. Brouwer, *Moon Basket*, 1994
    Ghost Rider #2
Kirby Jonas, *The Dansing Star*, 1997
Alan Morris, *By Honor Bound*, 1997
Jim Walker, *The Rawhiders*, 1994
    Wells Fargo Trail #4

507
WAYNE DAVIS

Silverthorne
(New York: Berkley, 1997)

Story type: Traditional; Man Alone
Major character(s): Tal Silverthorne, Doctor, Gunfighter; Rachel Howell, Heiress; Percival Holloway, Veteran (Union), Rancher
Time period(s): 1860s (post Civil War)
Locale(s): Lampkin Springs, Texas; Seven Rivers, New Mexico; Guadalupe Mountains, New Mexico

Summary: When Doctor Tal Silverthorne comes to Lampkin Springs just after the Civil War, he comes straight into the middle of the feud between the Howell and Holloway clans. Silverthorne himself has had enough of war, but the others can't let things rest. Major Holloway, a Union veteran, stands out against the ex-Confederates of Lampkin Springs, and the Howells can't accept his presence. Against his will, Silverthorne is drawn into the fight by his growing attachment to Rachel Howell, a relationship that puts him on the run for his life and may well get him killed.

Other books by the same author:
Reklaw, 1995
John Stone and the Choctaw Kid, 1993

Other books you might like:
Mike Blakely, *Spanish Blood*, 1996
Johnny D. Boggs, *This Man Colter*, 1997
Will Camp, *Lone Survivor*, 1995
Jack Curtis, *Christmas in Calico*, 1997
Perry Holmes, *Mountains against the Sky*, 1998

508
PETER DAWSON

Rattlesnake Mesa
(Thorndike, Maine: Thorndike, 1998)

Story type: Traditional; Mystery
Major character(s): Luke Barron, Gunfighter; Sam Ingalls, Lawman (sheriff), Criminal
Time period(s): 19th century (post Civil War)
Locale(s): Eagle Canyon, Colorado

Summary: Gunfighter Luke Barron takes care to keep his real identity a secret when he tangles with Sheriff Sam Ingalls. Ingalls, boss of the tough Eagle Canyon mining town and himself none too careful about the law, might prefer to have Barron dead than alive and prying into his affairs. As it is, Barron winds up in jail and has to be rescued by a priest with his own agenda. Still under his assumed name, Barron goes to work for the priest. His job: to find gunfighter Luke Barron.

Other books you might like:
Wayne Barton, *High Country*, 1993
    Stan Williams, co-author
P.A. Bechko, *The Eye of the Hawk*, 1998
Bill Brooks, *Dust on the Wind*, 1997
Lee Martin, *Maverick Gun*, 1992
Richard S. Wheeler, *Flint's Gift*, 1997

509
SIBYL DOWNING

The Ladies of the Goldfield Stock Exchange
(New York: Forge, 1997)

Story type: Traditional; Historical
Series: Women of the West
Major character(s): Meg Kendall, Student (medical school); Verna Bates, Publisher; Tess Wallace, Saloon Keeper/Owner

Time period(s): 1900s (1906)
Locale(s): Goldfield, Nevada

Summary: Meg Kendall abandons her schooling and comes to Nevada when her mining engineer father dies in a suspicious accident. Verna Bates and Tess Wallace are already there, Verna running a newspaper and Tess keeping a saloon and wishing better things for her young daughter. For different reasons, all three want to find wealth in the Nevada boomtown of Goldfield. When they are barred from the local stock exchange because of their gender, they start their own—to the great consternation of just about everyone else in the area.

Where it's reviewed:
Publishers Weekly, June 2, 1997, page 54

Other books by the same author:
Fire in the Hole, 1996

Other books you might like:
Rita Cleary, *Goldtown*, 1996
Dan Cushman, *The Silver Mountain*, 1996
Johnny Quarles, *No Man's Land*, 1993
Richard S. Wheeler, *Second Lives*, 1997
Jeanne Williams, *Wind Water*, 1997

510

TRACY DUNHAM

The Ghost Trail

(New York: Avalon, 1998)

Story type: Historical; Indian Wars
Major character(s): Mythmaker, Storyteller; Johnny Two Hats, Indian (Comanche), Warrior; Wovoka, Shaman, Historical Figure
Time period(s): 1890s
Locale(s): Paiute Reservation, Nevada; Staked Plains, Texas

Summary: The Ghost Dance enthusiasm sweeps through the Plains tribes in the 1890s, including the Kiowa tribe where Mythmaker lives with her Comanche husband Johnny Two Hats. Mythmaker, born Elizabeth McFarland, is deeply troubled about the significance of the Dance and the trouble she foresees from its coming. Together with her foster son, missionary Peter Donaldson, she and Johnny decide to seek out the Ghost Dance leaders and find the truth about this new religion.

Other books by the same author:
The Long Trail Home, 1997

Other books you might like:
Beverly Bird, *The Pony Wife*, 1995
Lynda Durran, *Echohawk*, 1996
Jane Kirkpatrick, *Love to Water My Soul*, 1996
James Alexander Thom, *The Red Heart*, 1997
Stephanie Grace Whitson, *Soaring Eagle*, 1995
    Prairie Winds #2

511

TRACY DUNHAM

The Long Trail Home

(New York: Avalon, 1997)

Story type: Indian Wars; Quest
Major character(s): Elizabeth McFarland, Captive; Johnny Two Hats, Indian (Kiowa), Warrior; Hannah Monroe, Captive
Time period(s): 19th century (post Civil War)
Locale(s): Staked Plains, Texas

Summary: Rescued, if that's the word, from her Kiowa captors nine years before, Elizabeth McFarland has since lived in the Anglo world. Now she decides to return to her Kiowa husband, Johnny Two Hats. Hannah Monroe, former captive of the Comanches, has been on an equally long search for her Anglo husband. United by common bonds, the two women's lives are intertwined even as it seems that their respective searches may prove deadly.

Where it's reviewed:
Roundup Magazine, April 1997, page 26

Other books you might like:
Benjamin Capps, *A Woman of the People*, 1966
Cynthia Haseloff, *The Chains of Sarai Stone*, 1995
Wendi Lee, *The Overland Trail*, 1996
Barbara Riefe, *Desperate Crossing: The Jenny Sanders Pryor Story*, 1997
Stephanie Grace Whitson, *Soaring Eagle*, 1995
    Prairie Winds #2

512

TOM DYJA

Play for a Kingdom

(New York: Harcourt Brace, 1997)

Story type: Historical/American Civil War; Historical
Major character(s): William Burridge, Military Personnel (Union)
Time period(s): 1860s (1864)
Locale(s): Spotsylvania, Virginia; Wilderness, Virginia

Summary: Between the bloody and seemingly senseless series of battles in Virginia's tangled Wilderness, a Union infantry company amuses itself with the new game of baseball. One day, a group of Confederates, attracted by the noise finds them. Instead of attacking, the rebels watch, then challenge their enemies to a game. Despite orders against fraternization, they play out the game, then agree to meet again when circumstances permit. But underneath the stress of battle and the release of play, there is something deeper. The games aren't accidental, and their purpose is hidden even from those involved.

Where it's reviewed:
Booklist, August 1997, page 1877
Kirkus Reviews, June 1, 1997, page 820
Library Journal, May 15, 1997, page 99
Publishers Weekly, June 23, 1997, page 68

Other books you might like:
Howard Bahr, *The Black Flower*, 1997
Frederic Bean, *Lorena*, 1996
Debra Cowan, *If Only*, 1997
Kathleen O'Neal Gear, *Thin Moon and Cold Mist*, 1995
Madison Jones, *Nashville 1864*, 1997

513

HANK EDWARDS (Pseudonym of Jason Manning)

Apache Sundown

(New York: Harper, 1996)

Story type: Traditional; Indian Wars
Major character(s): Clancy St. John, Scout, Foster Parent; Soldado, Indian (Apache); Hudson Lane, Military Personnel
Time period(s): 19th century (1860s-1880s)
Locale(s): Tucson, Arizona; Fort Stanton, New Mexico

Summary: Sickened by the massacre of an Apache village by the Army, Clancy St. John leaves his job as scout to rear an Apache boy orphaned by the raid. The boy, Soldado, grows up alongside St. John's daughters, but he is always aware of the difference between him and others. He comes to manhood in the midst of the Apache wars, torn between loyalty to his true people and to his adoptive family. His hope is to work between the two sides to bring what peace he can. But when Clancy St. John is killed by a scalphunter called Buckshot Reilly, Soldado has no doubts. Both sides of his nature demand he hunt the killer down.

Other books by the same author:
Gray Warrior, 1995
Ride for Rimfire, 1995
Thirteen Notches, 1994

Other books you might like:
Patrick E. Andrews, *The Scalphunters*, 1993
Jack Ballas, *Gun Boss*, 1995
Bruce Cutler, *The Massacre at Sand Creek*, 1995
Richard Matheson, *Shadow on the Sun*, 1994
Harry James Plumlee, *Shadow of the Wolf*, 1997

514

RANDY LEE EICKHOFF

The Fourth Horseman

(New York: Forge, 1998)

Story type: Traditional; Man Alone
Major character(s): Doc Holliday, Gunfighter, Gambler; Wyatt Earp, Lawman, Historical Figure; Kate Elder, Prostitute
Time period(s): 1870s; 1880s
Locale(s): Tombstone, Arizona; Leadville, Colorado; New Orleans, Louisiana

Summary: Doc Holliday, gambler, gunfighter, and companion of the Earp brothers at the OK Corral, is the subject and narrator of Eickhoff's book. In this treatment, Holliday is an educated Southern gentleman cursed with the devil's temper and a deadly case of tuberculosis. Leaving his New Orleans

plantation for the drier and freer climate of the West, Holliday makes a name as a killer, unable to find anyone fast enough to free him of the affliction that torments him daily.

Other books you might like:
Matt Braun, *Wyatt Earp*, 1994
Jane Candia Coleman, *Doc Holliday's Woman*, 1995
Loren D. Estleman, *Bloody Season*, 1988
Dan Gordon, *Wyatt Earp*, 1994
Preston Lewis, *Mix-Up at the O.K. Corral*, 1996

515

TOM EIDSON

All God's Children

(New York: Dutton, 1997)

Story type: Traditional
Major character(s): Pearl Eddy, Farmer, Widow(er); Prophet, Fugitive, Sports Figure (boxer)
Time period(s): 1890s
Locale(s): Kansas

Summary: Left widowed and blind, Pearl Eddy has four children to feed on a hardscrabble farm where the debts are larger than the crops. She's further isolated by her Quaker faith, misunderstood and unappreciated by the Kansas farmers and townspeople around her. She is first victimized and then helped by a black fugitive, Prophet, who uses his fists where Pearl's nonviolence won't serve, and by Eiko, head of a poor Japanese family that Pearl takes in. Together, this unlikely group struggles to find cooperation, community, and survival in a hostile world.

Where it's reviewed:
Books, June 1996, page 23
Kirkus Reviews, April 15, 1997, page 573
Publishers Weekly, May 5, 1997, page 197
Times Literary Supplement, July 7, 1996, page 25

Other books by the same author:
The Last Ride, 1995
St. Agnes' Stand, 1994

Other books you might like:
Harold Bakst, *Prairie Widow*, 1992
Irene Bennett Brown, *The Plainswoman*, 1994
Nancy Hermann, *The Homestead*, 1993
Gary D. Svee, *Sanctuary*, 1990
    Spur Award winner
Penelope Williamson, *The Outsider*, 1996

516

KEN ENGLADE

Battle Cry

(New York: Harper, 1997)

Story type: Indian Wars; Series
Series: Tony Hillerman's Frontier
Major character(s): Jean Benoit, Military Personnel; Jason Dobbs, Military Personnel; Notch Henderson, Outlaw
Time period(s): 1850s (1857)
Locale(s): Fort Laramie, Wyoming; United States

Summary: A wagon train goes west through Wyoming in spite of trouble with the Cheyenne. Unknown to the emigrants, they have other troubles, too. One of their number is actually outlaw Notch Henderson, carrying a load of stolen money. And deep in the Utah desert, a band of militant Mormons plans to waylay the train before the Cheyenne can get it. It's up to the Army, specifically to Lieutenants Dobbs and Benoit, to deal with Henderson and to see that the train gets through. But this time the odds may be too much for them.

Other books by the same author:
The Tribes, 1996 (Tony Hillerman's Frontier #4)

Other books you might like:
Patrick E. Andrews, *Whiskey River*, 1993
John Legg, *Treaty at Fort Laramie*, 1994
Dawn Miller, *The Journal of Callie Wade*, 1996
F.M. Parker, *The Predators*, 1990
Barbara Riefe, *Desperate Crossing: The Jenny Sanders Pryor Story*, 1997

517

ELIZABETH FACKLER

Texas Lily
(New York: Forge, 1997)

Story type: Revenge; Saga
Major character(s): Lily Cassidy, Teenager, Spouse; Jasper Stone, Outlaw; Emmett Moss, Rancher
Time period(s): 19th century (1880s-1890s)
Locale(s): New Mexico

Summary: The death of 15-year-old Lily Cassidy's father in an arson fire is the start of a long trail of betrayal and revenge. Lily, saddled with the care of her family, yields to middle-aged rancher Emmett Moss's proposal of marriage; but she sets as her price the death of the man responsible for her father's murder. Moss agrees but ultimately fails to carry through. The pair of outlaws he hires to do the job back out, and Moss turns his anger on them instead. In this loveless and faithless world, Lily herself at last becomes the one who has to defend the lies.

Where it's reviewed:
Booklist, August 1997, page 1877
Publishers Weekly, July 7, 1997, page 51

Other books by the same author:
Badlands, 1996
Billy the Kid: The Legend of El Chivato, 1995
Road from Betrayal, 1994
Backtrail, 1993
Blood Kin, 1992

Other books you might like:
Don Bendell, *Matched Colts*, 1997
Sibyl Downing, *The Ladies of the Goldfield Stock Exchange*, 1997
David L. Fleming, *Border Crossings*, 1993
Wynema McGowan, *While the Rivers Run*, 1996
Earl Murray, *The River at Sundown*, 1997

518

THOMAS FLEMING

Remember the Morning
(New York: Forge, 1997)

Story type: Historical
Major character(s): Catalyntie Van Vorst, Captive, Trader; Clara, Slave; Malcolm Stapleton, Settler
Time period(s): 18th century (1720s-1760s)
Locale(s): New York, New York, American Colonies

Summary: Captured as children by the Seneca, Catalyntie Van Vorst and African-born Clara grow up as young Senecas, enjoying equal rights and power with tribal males. Their return to the straitlaced Dutch world of New York is less a rescue than a new captivity—especially for Clara, who returns to slavery. Fighting to retain their independence, the women grow to maturity. They enter business, throw off family restraints, and share the love of settler and soldier Malcolm Stapleton, all against the background of the tumultuous growth of the American Colonies.

Where it's reviewed:
Kirkus Reviews, July 15, 1997, page 1049
Library Journal, August 1997, page 126
Publishers Weekly, August 4, 1997, page 65

Other books you might like:
Cynthia Haseloff, *The Chains of Sarai Stone*, 1995
Michael Kilian, *Major Washington*, 1998
Lucia St. Clair Robson, *Mary's Land*, 1995
James Alexander Thom, *The Red Heart*, 1997
Jim R. Woolard, *The Winds of Autumn*, 1996

519

ROBERT BARLOW FOX

To Be a Warrior
(Santa Fe: Sunstone Press, 1997)

Story type: Modern; Indian Culture
Major character(s): Clay Walker, Indian (Navajo), Military Personnel; Rusty Red, Military Personnel
Time period(s): 1930s; 1940s
Locale(s): Ogden, Utah; Guadalcanal, Solomon Islands

Summary: Suitable for adults or young adults, this book tells the fictionalized story of a Navajo code talker in the Second World War. Clay Walker's teenage years are tough. His ambition, to be a Navajo warrior, seems impossible in the grim Depression-era Southwest. His uneasy efforts to exist on the border between the Anglo and navajo worlds land him finally in the reform school at Ogden City. There, brutalized by guards and with mixed relations with his fellow inmates, he holds to his dream until Pearl Harbor offers a chance at fulfillment. As a United States Marine, Walker realizes his dream of being a warrior. But in the bloody jungles of Guadalcanal and Saipan, he finds that his picture of warfare doesn't fit the modern mold.

Where it's reviewed:
Booklist, September 1, 1997, page 105

Other books by the same author:
Walks Two Worlds, 1995

Other books you might like:
Sally P. Keehn, *Moon of Two Dark Horses*, 1996
Scott O'Dell, *Thunder Rolling in the Mountains*, 1992
    Elizabeth Hall, co-author
Conrad Richter, *The Light in the Forest*, 1953
Frank Waters, *The Man Who Killed the Deer*, 1942
Don Worcester, *Man on Two Ponies*, 1992

520

STEVE FRAZEE

Hidden Gold

(Thorndike, Maine: Thorndike Press, 1997)

Story type: Traditional; Quest
Major character(s): Brock Sargent, Gunfighter
Time period(s): 19th century (post Civil War)
Locale(s): Weston, Colorado

Summary: A tight and compelling manhunt story from Western veteran Steve Frazee centered in and around a dying town that's boomed and busted. A stolen payroll and a murdered friend send Brock Sargent on the vengeance trail. In his quest for a killer, Sargent must use all his skills and courage just to stay alive.

Where it's reviewed:
Publishers Weekly, April 14, 1997, page 60
Roundup Magazine, June 1997, page 34

Other books by the same author:
Many Rivers to Cross, 1955

Other books you might like:
Wayne Barton, *Manhunt*, 1992
    Stan Williams, co-author
R.C. House, *Ryerson's Manhunt*, 1995
Gary Paulsen, *Murphy's Ambush*, 1995
Doyle Trent, *Gunpowder Legacy*, 1994
Don White, *A Kind of Wild Justice*, 1994

521

R. GARCIA Y ROBERTSON

American Woman

(New York: Forge, 1998)

Story type: Historical; Indian Wars
Major character(s): Sarah Kilroy, Teacher, Religious (Quaker); Yellow Legs, Indian (Cheyenne), Warrior; George A. Custer, Military Personnel, Historical Figure
Time period(s): 1870s
Locale(s): Fort Lincoln, Montana; Little Big Horn, Montana

Summary: Quaker Sarah Kilroy leaves a factory job in Pennsylvania to teach Indian children in the Wild West. Along with her teaching opportunities, she finds and marries Cheyenne warrior Yellow Legs. Among her husband's people, she tries to fit in, hiding her fair hair and pale face as best she can. But she still manages to socialize with such diverse people as Calamity Jane, Crazy Horse, and the Custer family. When war

threatens, she sticks with her adopted people, even though it leads her to a meeting at a place called Little Big Horn.

Other books by the same author:
Spirit Dance, 1991

Other books you might like:
Michael Blake, *Marching to Valhalla*, 1996
Tom Eidson, *All God's Children*, 1997
Earl Murray, *Thunder in the Dawn*, 1993
Chad Oliver, *Broken Eagle*, 1989
    Western Heritage Award winner
Robert Vaughan, *Yesterday's Reveille*, 1996

522

KATHLEEN O'NEAL GEAR
W. MICHAEL GEAR, Co-Author

People of the Mist

(New York: Forge, 1998)

Story type: Historical; Indian Culture
Major character(s): Red Knot, Crime Victim, Indian (Algonquin); High Fox, Indian (Algonquin), Crime Suspect; Panther, Shaman
Time period(s): 14th century
Locale(s): Chesapeake Bay

Summary: Destined to a political marriage to seal an alliance with Copper Thunder's people, Red Knot accepts her fate despite her love for High Fox. When she is found murdered before the ceremony can be consummated, suspicion falls on High Fox as the killer. Sun Conch, a young woman in love with High Fox, begs the Panther for help in clearing him. Feared as a sorcerer, the Panther emerges from his hermit-like lair to investigate the crime. What follows is a period detective story, intertwined with the customs and cultures of the various tribes at uneasy peace, to identify the killer of Red Knot.

Other books by the same author:
People of the Silence, 1997
People of the Lakes, 1995
People of the Lightning, 1995

Other books you might like:
Margaret Allan, *The Last Mammoth*, 1995
Robert J. Conley, *War Woman*, 1997
Ardath Mayhar, *Hunters of the Plains*, 1995
James Alexander Thom, *The Children of First Man*, 1994
Greg Tobin, *Prairie*, 1997

523

W. MICHAEL GEAR

Coyote Summer

(New York: Forge, 1997)

Story type: Historical; Mountain Man
Major character(s): Richard Hamilton, Mountain Man, Heir; Heals Like the Willow, Indian (Shoshoni); Travis Hartman, Mountain Man
Time period(s): 1820s (1825-1830)
Locale(s): Boston, Massachusetts; Missouri River

Summary: As servant and later partner of mountain man Travis Hartman, eastern-born Richard Hamilton gets a quick education in the things Harvard didn't teach him. He has to kill a Pawnee warrior to save Heals Like a Willow, their Shoshoni guide, and then he's almost killed himself when he and Hartman go after a Crow band that steals their horses. In love with Heals Like a Willow, Hamilton feels he must reject her because of her race, a concept that makes no sense at all to the pragmatic young Shoshoni woman. In the end, Willow goes back to her people to warn them of the coming of the whites; Hamilton returns to his to confront his father and the values he represents. Both hope that their love will overcome the barriers between them until they are reunited.

Where it's reviewed:
Kirkus Reviews, July 1, 1997, page 971

Other books by the same author:
The Morning River, 1996
Big Horn Legacy, 1988

Other books you might like:
Karen Harper, *River of Sky*, 1994
Paul A. Hawkins, *The Legend of Ben Tree*, 1993
John Killdeer, *Wild Country*, 1992
    Mountain Majesty #1
Jason Manning, *Promised Land*, 1996
Mardi Oakley Medawar, *People of the Whistling Waters*, 1993
    Medicine Pipe Bearer's Award winner

524

BARBARA DIAMOND GOLDIN
WILL HILLENBRAND, Illustrator

Coyote and the Fire Stick
(New York: Harcourt, 1996)

Story type: Young Readers; Indian Culture
Major character(s): Coyote, Animal, Spirit (trickster); Rabbit, Animal
Time period(s): Indeterminate
Locale(s): Pacific Northwest

Summary: Out for once to do a good deed, Coyote resolves to bring fire to a band of Indians who have no way to cook their food. The fire he chooses is on a mountaintop and is guarded by three forbidding-looking evil spirits. Irrepressible as usual, Coyote forms an alliance with several small animals to outwit and outrun the forces of evil.

Where it's reviewed:
Booklist, October 1, 1996, page 345
Children's Book Review Service, November 1996, page 31
Horn Book Magazine, November 1996, page 748
Publishers Weekly, October 21, 1996, page 83
School Library Journal, October 1996, page 113

Other books you might like:
Shonto Begay, *Ma'ii and Cousin Horned Toad*, 1993
Paul Goble, *Crow Chief*, 1992
Jonathan London, *Fire Race: A Karuk Coyote Tale*, 1993
    Larry Pinola, co-author
Gretchen Will Mayo, *That Tricky Coyote*, 1993
James Sage, *Coyote Makes Man*, 1995

525

KEN GRANT

The Deer Mouse
(New York: Permanent Press, 1997)

Story type: Modern; Ranch Life
Major character(s): Tom Brothers, Rancher; TJ Brothers, Foreman; Karen Brothers, Spouse
Time period(s): 1990s (1997)
Locale(s): Wyoming

Summary: Caught in their own web of tangled emotions, the Brothers family struggles to keep their ranch and their lives afloat during hard economic times. Tom Brothers, silent and withdrawn, has little to say to his son and daughter-in-law. Son TJ struggles under the mantle of brother Jesse, who was killed in Vietnam. Karen, TJ's abused wife, is drawn to one of the cowhands recently hired at the ranch. As the economic noose tightens on the family, each must find for himself whether the life of the ranch is worth preserving.

Where it's reviewed:
Kirkus Reviews, April 15, 1997, page 576
Publishers Weekly, May 26, 1997, page 66

Other books you might like:
Sara Bird, *The Virgin of the Rodeo*, 1993
Sam Brown, *The Crime of Coy Bell*, 1992
Nash Candelaria, *Leonor Park*, 1992
Elmer Kelton, *The Time It Never Rained*, 1973
Geo. W. Proctor, *Before Honor*, 1996

526

RANDAL L. GREENWOOD

Ride, Rebels, Ride
(New York: Forge, 1996)

Story type: Historical/American Civil War
Major character(s): Calvin Kimbrough, Military Personnel (Confederate); Evan Stryker, Military Personnel (Confederate); Joseph Shelby, Military Personnel (Confederate)
Time period(s): 1860s (1863-1865)
Locale(s): Camden, Arkansas; Covington Manor, Arkansas; Stony Point, Texas

Summary: The battered Kimbrough family holds onto its devotion to the Confederate cause even as the Confederacy unravels around them. The Kimbrough women try to hold together families as the Rebel forces are driven from Missouri to Arkansas and finally into Texas. As the war draws to its close, the surviving Kimbroughs must choose between accepting the decision of the battlefield or joining General Shelby's band of irreconcilables in their flight to Mexico.

Other books by the same author:
Kansas, Bloody Kansas, 1996
Burn, Missouri, Burn, 1995

Other books you might like:
Harold Coyle, *Savage Wilderness*, 1997
Fred Grove, *Bitter Trumpet*, 1989
Elmer Kelton, *Dark Thicket*, 1985

Max McCoy, *Home to Texas*, 1995
David William Ross, *Savage Plains*, 1997

527

CHARLES HACKENBERRY

I Rode with Jesse James

(New York: Harper, 1997)

Story type: Historical; Man Alone
Major character(s): Willie Goodwin, Convict (released), Outlaw; Jesse James, Outlaw, Historical Figure; Blackfoot Bill, Entertainer, Scout
Time period(s): 1870s
Locale(s): Dechman, Texas; Clay County, Missouri

Summary: With little money and few prospects, Willie Goodwin still isn't eager to work for the Pinkertons. He's even less eager when he learns they expect him to work his way into the James gang as a spy. But he takes the job, works his way into the gang—and ends up warning the James boys that the Pinkertons are on their way. This puts him firmly in the detective agency's bad graces, and endears him to Jesse. More importantly, it endears him to pretty Sarah Cole, Jesse's cousin. All isn't well with Willie, though. He's a real outlaw now, and he knows Jesse won't hesitate to kill him if the Jameses ever learn the truth about his short career as a spy.

Where it's reviewed:
Roundup Magazine, April 1997, page 27

Other books by the same author:
Friends, 1993

Other books you might like:
Matt Braun, *Outlaw Kingdom*, 1996
Ralph W. Cotton, *While Angels Dance*, 1994
Susan Dodd, *Mamaw*, 1988
Arthur Winfield Knight, *The Secret Life of Jesse James*, 1996
Preston Lewis, *The Redemption of Jesse James*, 1995

528

OAKLEY HALL

Separations

(Reno: University of Nevada Press, 1997)

Story type: Historical; Quest
Major character(s): Charles P. Daggett, Mine Owner; Asa Haden, Writer
Time period(s): 19th century (post Civil War)
Locale(s): Pariah Crossing, Colorado; Callville, Arizona

Summary: Mining and timber magnate Charles P. Daggett finances an expedition down the Colorado River, following in the footsteps of explorer John Wesley Powell. Young writer Asa Haden goes along as historian for the group, and finds he has more history to record than he expects. Daggett's plans for the unspoiled canyon country are more ominous than he admits, and the Mormon and Indian residents along the route are hostile and suspicious. And the greatest enemy of all may be the harsh and unforgiving land through which the expedition must pass.

Where it's reviewed:
Library Journal, June 1, 1997, page 148
New York Times Book Review, July 20, 1997, page 20
Publishers Weekly, April 21, 1997, page 61

Other books you might like:
Franklin Carter, *Rails West*, 1993
   Rails West #1
Bill Hotchkiss, *To Fell the Giants*, 1991
William W. Johnstone, *Triumph of the Mountain Man*, 1997
Gary McCarthy, *Grand Canyon*, 1996
Richard S. Wheeler, *Badlands*, 1992

529

RIC LYNDEN HARDMAN

Sunshine Rider

(New York: Delacorte, 1998)

Story type: Traditional; Quest
Major character(s): Wylie Jackson, Con Artist, Doctor; Roselle, Animal (cattalo); Carl Merkle, Outlaw
Time period(s): 1880s (1881)
Locale(s): Odessa, Texas; Fort Smith, Arkansas; Fort Gibson, Kansas

Summary: Starting as hardware clerk and reluctant cowboy, young Wylie Jackson becomes an innocent abroad in the West of 1881. With his faithful cattalo Roselle by his side, he flees the trail drive on a more or less stolen horse, only to encounter Indians, outlaws, con artists, and the redoubtable Judge Parker—none of whom are quite what he expects. This book bills itself as the first vegetarian Western, a claim that no one is likely to dispute. Each chapter opens with a recipe, ranging from non-vegetarian son of a bitch stew through pigweed greens to goodbye pecan pie.

Other books you might like:
Dan Parkinson, *Calamity Trail*, 1985
Ellen Recknor, *Me and the Boys*, 1995
Dusty Richards, *By the Cut of Your Clothes*, 1995
Cruce Stark, *Chasing Uncle Charley*, 1992
Robert Lewis Taylor, *The Travels of Jamie McPheeters*, 1958

530

LANA M. HARRIGAN

Acoma: A Novel of Conquest

(New York: Forge, 1997)

Story type: Indian Culture; Indian Wars
Major character(s): Maria Angelica de Vizcarra, Spouse; Vicente de Vizcarra, Military Personnel (conquistador); Rohona, Indian (Acoma), Slave
Time period(s): 16th century; 17th century (1598-1620)
Locale(s): Acoma, New Mexico; Santa Fe, New Mexico

Summary: In 1598, only one pueblo resists the triumphant march of Don Juan de Onate's forces through New Mexico. That pueblo is Acoma, set atop a high mesa and stoutly defended by its tenacious inhabitants. Even so, the Spaniards under Captain Vicente de Vizcarra capture the city, sending its surviving people into slavery. Vizcarra's lust for gold is

unsatisfied by the triumph, but he gets as a slave the maimed Acoma warrior Rohona. Rohona, brave and honorable as Vizcarra is mean and greedy, soon finds himself drawn to his master's wife. She in turn sees in him the qualities her husband lacks. Their relationship, secretive and potentially fatal for them both, sows the seeds for trouble to come. This is the author's first novel.

Where it's reviewed:
Kirkus Reviews, August 1, 1997, page 1135
Library Journal, August 1997, page 128
Publishers Weekly, July 28, 1997, page 53

Other books you might like:
Irwin R. Blacker, *Taos*, 1959
Don Coldsmith, *Return of the Spanish*, 1992
    Spanish Bit #18
Genevieve Gray, *Fair Laughs the Morn*, 1994
Gregory D. Kincaid, *Death Walk at Acoma*, 1993
Scott O'Dell, *The King's Fifth*, 1966

531

CYNTHIA HASELOFF

The Kiowa Verdict

(Thorndike, Maine: Thorndike Press, 1997)

Story type: Traditional; Indian Wars
Major character(s): Satanta, Indian (Kiowa), Chieftain; Adrienne Chastain, Captive; Big Tree, Indian (Kiowa), Warrior
Time period(s): 1870s (1871)
Locale(s): Fort Sill, Oklahoma; Staked Plains, Texas

Summary: Based on the true story of the raid led by warriors Satanta, Satank, and Big Tree in 1871, this story is part traditional Western and part courtroom drama. Avenging the death of his son, Satanta leads an attack deep into Texas. His thrust narrowly misses the Army ambulance carrying General Sherman on an inspection tour. Instead, the Indians massacre the teamsters of an inoffensive train of freight wagons. When the Army tracks him back to Fort Sill, Satanta readily admits his participation. Tried for murder in Texas, he escapes hanging only through an event that would be incredible if it weren't pretty much true.

Other books by the same author:
Man without Medicine, 1996
The Chains of Sarai Stone, 1995

Other books you might like:
Benjamin Capps, *The White Man's Road*, 1969
Bill Dugan, *Quanah Parker*, 1993
Tracy Dunham, *The Ghost Trail*, 1998
Geo. W. Proctor, *Blood of My Blood*, 1996
Mark K. Roberts, *Prairie Fire*, 1994

532

WILL HENRY (Pseudonym of Henry Allen)

The Bear Paw Horses

(New York: Leisure, 1996)

Story type: Historical; Indian Wars

Major character(s): Con Jenkins, Outlaw; Crowfoot, Indian (Oglala), Shaman; Twilight, Indian (Oglala), Young Woman
Time period(s): 1870s (1877)
Locale(s): High Meadow, Wyoming; Milk River, Montana

Summary: Con Jenkins is an outlaw with a highly-trained instinct for survival and very little redeeming social value. He has no interest in the Sioux and their problems, or in anyone except himself. But it's Con Jenkins who ends up helping old Crowfoot and his beautiful—and Anglo-hating—granddaughter Twilight in carrying out the last wish of Chief Crazy Horse. Undetected and unaided, the three must steal back the horses captured from the Sioux by the Army and move them to a place of safety where the warriors may one day reclaim them.

Other books by the same author:
Will Henry's West, 1991
Alias Butch Cassidy, 1967
One More River to Cross, 1967
The Gates of the Mountains, 1963
The Brass Command, 1955

Other books you might like:
Win Blevins, *Stone Song*, 1995
    Spur Award winner
Cynthia Haseloff, *Man without Medicine*, 1996
Lee Hoffman, *The Valdez Horses*, 1967
    Spur Award winner
Terry C. Johnston, *Trumpet on the Land*, 1995
    Plainsmen #10
Earl Murray, *Spirit of the Moon*, 1996

533

WILL HENRY (Pseudonym of Henry Allen)

Journey to Shiloh

(New York: Leisure, 1997)

Story type: Historical; Historical/American Civil War
Major character(s): Buck Burnet, Volunteer; Miller Nalls, Volunteer; Braxton Bragg, Military Personnel, Historical Figure
Time period(s): 1860s (1862)
Locale(s): Paint Rock, Texas; Shiloh Church, Tennessee

Summary: Buck Burnet and his friends are seven eager young Texans hoping to get themselves a share of the young Civil War before all chance for glory is gone. Headed east to join the Confederate Army, they style themselves the Concho County Comanches and imagine how the war will be. By the time they reach Tennessee, they've learned a lot about hardship and human treachery. But nothing they've learned prepares them for the bloody field of Shiloh.

Other books by the same author:
Will Henry's West, 1991
Alias Butch Cassidy, 1967
One More River to Cross, 1967
The Gates of the Mountains, 1963
The Brass Command, 1955

Other books you might like:
John Edward Ames, *The Golden Circle*, 1996

Randal L. Greenwood, *Kansas, Bloody Kansas*, 1996
Elmer Kelton, *Long Way to Texas*, 1976
William A. Luckey, *Flags over Texas*, 1991
Max McCoy, *Home to Texas*, 1995

534

DOUGLAS HIRT

Cripple Creek

(New York: Berkley, 1997)

Story type: Historical; Saga
Major character(s): Casey Daniels, Engineer (mining); Phillip LaFarge, Mine Owner; Maureen Kramer, Widow(er)
Time period(s): 1890s (1892-1894)
Locale(s): Cripple Creek, Colorado; Rattlesnake Mine, Colorado

Summary: Mine owner Phillip LaFarge drives his men in unsafe conditions. When this results in tragedy, he frames mining engineer Casey Daniels for causing the accident. Daniels, who was fired for refusing to approve LaFarge's plans, is innocent but no one believes that—least of all Maureen Kramer, who lost her husband in the mine cave-in. Daniels works to prove his innocence against the background of the booming mining district and impending violence between mine owners and their desperate workers.

Other books by the same author:
McKendree, 1997
Assassination, 1995 (Riverboat #4)
Colorado Gold, 1993
Able Gate, 1993
The Ordeal of Andy Dean, 1993

Other books you might like:
Tom W. Blackburn, *Sierra Baron*, 1997
Susan Harmon, *Colorado Ransom*, 1992
Ernest Haycox, *Alder Gulch*, 1942
Suzann Ledbetter, *Redemption Trail*, 1996
Richard S. Wheeler, *Goldfield*, 1995

535

DOUGLAS HIRT

Deadwood

(New York: Berkley, 1998)

Story type: Historical; Quest
Major character(s): Nathaniel Jones, Journalist; George A. Custer, Military Personnel, Historical Figure; Carson Grove, Mountain Man, Sidekick
Time period(s): 1870s (1874)
Locale(s): Deadwood, South Dakota; Black Hills, South Dakota

Summary: Nathaniel Jones's first experience in Dakota Territory is as a special correspondent with Custer's expedition to the Black Hills. Jones is unready for both the savagery of the frontier and for the stampede for gold that his reports set off. In the raw mining town of Deadwood, he finds violence, adventure, and a sinister plot in which unscrupulous whites

try to provoke an Indian war. Jones can stop their plan—if he lives to tell about it.

Other books by the same author:
McKendree, 1997
Assassination, 1995 (Riverboat #4)
Colorado Gold, 1993
Able Gate, 1993
The Ordeal of Andy Dean, 1993

Other books you might like:
Mike Blakely, *The Last Chance*, 1995
Suzann Ledbetter, *Trinity Strike*, 1996
J.L. Reasoner, *Rivers of Gold*, 1995
Ray Toepfer, *The Stage from Deadwood*, 1993
Richard S. Wheeler, *Cashbox*, 1994

536

DOUGLAS HIRT

McKendree

(New York: Leisure, 1997)

Story type: Mountain Man; Revenge
Major character(s): Josiah McKendree, Mountain Man; Jacques Ribalt, Trapper, Mountain Man
Time period(s): 1840s
Locale(s): Rocky Mountains

Summary: In the fashion of his kind, Josiah McKendree wants nothing more than to provide for his family and live in not-too-close harmony with his neighbors. But neighbor Jacques Ribalt, first-comer to the valley where McKendree and others live, can't accept that. Ribalt still regards the valley as his to trap and hunt as he pleases. A small dispute between McKendree and Ribalt escalates until Ribalt, in a fit of rage, murders McKendree's wife and son. Now the rules are off, and only the killer's blood will square accounts.

Other books by the same author:
Assassination, 1995 (Riverboat #4)
Colorado Gold, 1993
Able Gate, 1993
The Ordeal of Andy Dean, 1993

Other books you might like:
Jason Manning, *Promised Land*, 1996
Jess McCreede, *Gold Rush Revenge*, 1992
F.M. Parker, *The Shadow Man*, 1988
Geo. W. Proctor, *Comes the Hunter*, 1992
David William Ross, *Eyes of the Hawk*, 1992

537

RAY HOGAN

Legend of a Badman: A Western Quintet

(Thorndike, Maine: Thorndike Press, 1998)

Story type: Traditional; Collection
Major character(s): Clay Allison, Gunfighter, Historical Figure
Time period(s): 19th century (post Civil War)
Locale(s): Texas; West

Summary: A long novella about the life of gunfighter Clay Allison is backed by four short stories from Western master Ray Hogan.

Other books by the same author:
The Whipsaw Trail, 1997
Soldier in Buckskin, 1996

Other books you might like:
Max Brand, *The Wolf Strain and Other Stories*, 1996
Jane Candia Coleman, *Stories from Mesa Country*, 1991
Link Hullar, *West*, 1996
Richard Matheson, *By the Gun*, 1994
Lewis B. Patten, *The Best Western Stories of Lewis B. Patten*, 1989

538

RAY HOGAN

The Whipsaw Trail
(New York: Leisure, 1997)

Story type: Traditional; Chase
Major character(s): John Buckner, Outlaw; Henry Guzman, Detective—Private
Time period(s): 19th century (post Civil War)
Locale(s): West

Summary: The railroad owes John Buckner money. That's the way Buckner sees it, anyway, and he intends to collect. When they won't pay off, he steals the railroad payroll from the bank. Buckner figures that makes things even, but the railroad doesn't see it. Railroad detective Henry Guzman sets out on Buckner's trail—a trail that leads straight into Indian territory.

Other books by the same author:
Soldier in Buckskin, 1996

Other books you might like:
Hank Edwards, *Thirteen Notches*, 1994
Cameron Judd, *Confederate Gold*, 1993
W.W. Lee, *Rancher's Blood*, 1991
Giles Tippette, *Heaven's Gold*, 1996
Norman Zollinger, *Not of War Only*, 1994

539

CECILIA HOLLAND

Railroad Schemes
(New York: Forge, 1997)

Story type: Historical
Major character(s): Lily Viner, Teenager, Orphan; King Callahan, Outlaw
Time period(s): 1850s
Locale(s): Los Angeles, California; Sierra Nevada, California

Summary: Orphaned daughter of an outlaw, young Lily Viner comes between two hard men. King Callahan is an outlaw, a robber of banks and stagecoaches. Chasing him is the implacable railroad detective called Brand. But Lily finds a way into Callahan's none-too-soft heart, and he considers giving up his outlaw ways for her welfare. Brand isn't a party to this plan, however, and Lily herself has her doubts. Callahan and the others are caught up in a scheme hatched by the big-time thieves who control railroad building and land development. In company like that, a mere bank robber is out of his league.

Where it's reviewed:
Kirkus Reviews, August 15, 1997, page 1243

Other books by the same author:
The Bear Flag, 1990

Other books you might like:
Mike Blakely, *Baron of the Sacramentos*, 1991
Cindy Bonner, *Looking After Lily*, 1995
Franklin Carter, *Wyoming Territory*, 1994
    Rails West #3
Al Dempsey, *Path of the Sun*, 1992
Alan Morris, *Tracks of Deceit*, 1996
    Gilbert Morris, co-author

540

STEF ANN HOLM

Forget Me Not
(New York: Pocket Books, 1997)

Story type: Traditional; Ranch Life
Major character(s): Josephine Whittaker, Traveller, Cook; J.D. McCall, Rancher; Boots McCall, Rancher
Time period(s): 1870s (1874)
Locale(s): New York, New York; Sienna, Wyoming

Summary: East meets West when Josephine Whittaker loses her money and social standing in New York. She follows the lure of the dime novels, intending to make her fortune in the West. With her fortune still unmade, she runs out of money and ideas simultaneously in Sienna, Wyoming. Of her available options, the best seems to be wrangling a job as cook with local rancher J.D. McCall. Josephine's cooking skills are limited, but with perseverance and a recipe book, she hangs on until she's chosen as camp cook on a trail drive. This is a little more than she's bargained for, carrying with it dangers from flood, stampede, rustlers, and a long-standing feud between McCall and his crusty father Boots.

Where it's reviewed:
Publishers Weekly, March 24, 1997, page 80

Other books by the same author:
Portraits, 1996

Other books you might like:
Ric Lynden Hardman, *Sunshine Rider*, 1998
Catherine Palmer, *Prairie Rose*, 1997
    Town Called Hope #1
Laurel Jean Pamplin, *Masquerade on the Western Trail*, 1991
Dan Parkinson, *Calamity Trail*, 1985
Lori Wick, *Promise Me Tomorrow*, 1997
    Rocky Mountain Memories #4

541
PERRY HOLMES

Mountains against the Sun
(Thorndike, Maine: Thorndike Press, 1998)

Story type: Traditional; Revenge
Major character(s): Frank Allard, Avenger, Rancher; Ben Lenifee, Leader; Joyce Lenifee, Young Woman
Time period(s): 19th century (post Civil War)
Locale(s): Winona Basin, Utah

Summary: The search for the man who murdered Tom Yeager, Frank Allard's friend, leads Allard to the remote Winona Basin of Utah and its even more remote people. Descended from Tennessee mountaineers, the Winona Basin folk are clannish, suspicious of strangers, and dominated by clan patriarch Ben Lenifee. The only welcoming face Allard finds is that of Joyce Lenifee, Ben's only daughter and a young woman determined to break free of the stifling bonds of the past. But there are others in the basin who want Allard dead, including Joyce's intended husband and her beloved brother.

Other books you might like:
Mike Blakely, *Dead Reckoning*, 1996
Terrell L. Bowers, *Ride against the Wind*, 1996
Wayne Davis, *Reklaw*, 1995
Jason Manning, *American Blood*, 1996
Stan Wiseman, *Cody's Ride*, 1993

542
DONALD HONIG

The Ghost of Major Pryor
(New York: Scribner, 1997)

Story type: Traditional; Mystery
Major character(s): Thomas Maynard, Military Personnel (Army captain); Lucas Bell, Saloon Keeper/Owner, Gambler
Time period(s): 1870s (1870)
Locale(s): Braddock, Montana

Summary: A Civil War veteran turned miner sees his old commander in the mining boomtown of Braddock, Montana. There's just one problem. The officer, Major Pryor, was killed in battle five years previously. Sent to investigate Pryor's possible desertion, Captain Thomas Maynard finds his only witness murdered and the town full of people with something to hide. Maynard works undercover, carefully probing into the potentially explosive mixture of crime, vigilante activity, men and women with secrets buried in their past, and—just possibly—a restless ghost.

Where it's reviewed:
Kirkus Reviews, January 1, 1997, page 11
Library Journal, February 1, 1997, page 110
New York Times Book Review, March 30, 1997, page 16
Publishers Weekly, January 6, 1997, page 67

Other books by the same author:
The Sword of General Englund, 1996

Other books you might like:
Jack Curtis, *Wild River Massacre*, 1993
Margot Fraser, *The Laying-Out of Gussie Hoot*, 1990
Wayne Overholser, *Nugget City*, 1997
Al Sarrantonio, *Kitt Peak*, 1993
Richard S. Wheeler, *Second Lives*, 1997

543
LANA DEAN JAMES

The Cowgirls of the Mariposa
(New York: Harper, 1996)

Story type: Young Readers; Modern
Major character(s): Sugar Larson, Teenager; Diane Arellano, Teenager; Billy Barringer, Teenager
Time period(s): 1990s
Locale(s): Mariposa Ranch, California

Summary: Visiting her grandmother's ranch for the summer, Sugar Larson finds a message in the family Bible leading back a hundred years. With her friend Diane and tag-along Laurie Finley, Sugar sets out to find a fortune in gold concealed by a long-ago ancestor. But someone else knows the secret, too, someone determined to get to the gold first, no matter who stands in his way.

Other books you might like:
Judy Alter, *Katie and the Recluse*, 1991
Patricia Beatty, *Sarah and Me and the Lady from the Sea*, 1989
Lyman Hafen, *Over the Joshua Slope*, 1994
Edward Myers, *Hostage*, 1996
Deborah Savage, *To Ride a Dream*, 1994

544
GARY JENNINGS

Aztec Autumn
(New York: Forge, 1997)

Story type: Historical; Revenge
Major character(s): Tenamaxtli, Indian (Aztec), Nobleman; Hernan Cortez, Military Personnel
Time period(s): 16th century (1520s-1540s)
Locale(s): Aztlan, Mexico; Mexico City, Mexico

Summary: Young Aztec Tenamaxtli at first feels only interest and curiosity about the strange white men who have come to his world from across the seas. But when he learns they have executed his father, he swears revenge against them. Knowing he can do nothing alone, he seeks to find their weaknesses. His hope is that someday he can weld his people into an army and destroy the invaders, but he underestimates both their organization and their weaponry. Most of all, he and his people fall victim to the insatiable greed that drives the conquistadors to ravage their land.

Where it's reviewed:
Booklist, May 1, 1997, page 1461
Kirkus Reviews, June 1, 1997, page 825
New York Times Book Review, September 7, 1997, page 25
New York Times (Late Edition), July 17, 1997, page C16

Publishers Weekly, June 16, 1997, page 45

Other books you might like:
Irwin R. Blacker, *Taos*, 1959
Paul Clayton, *Flight of the Crow*, 1996
Don Coldsmith, *Walks in the Sun*, 1993
    Spanish Bit #20
Robert J. Conley, *War Woman*, 1997
Ardath Mayhar, *Island in the Lake*, 1993

545

TERRY C. JOHNSTON

Crack in the Sky
(New York: Bantam, 1997)

Story type: Historical; Mountain Man
Major character(s): Titus Bass, Mountain Man; Fawn, Indian, Young Woman; Pretty Water, Indian, Young Woman
Time period(s): 1840s
Locale(s): Rocky Mountains; Taos, New Mexico

Summary: No longer as young as he was, but still as adventurous, mountain man Titus Bass plans to settle down in his beloved Rockies. The settling process is fairly rough, because the high country still contains its share of hostile Comanches, ruthless bandits, and old enemies from the trapper's wilder days. Moving from one crisis to another, Bass demonstrates that he still has plenty of the toughness, independence, and life-risking courage that make the mountain men great.

Where it's reviewed:
Publishers Weekly, August 18, 1997, page 70

Other books by the same author:
Wolf Mountain Moon, 1997 (Plainsmen #12)
Buffalo Palace, 1996
A Cold Day in Hell, 1995 (Plainsmen #11)
Dance on the Wind, 1995
Dream Catcher, 1994

Other books you might like:
Win Blevins, *The Yellowstone*, 1988
    Rivers West #1
Taylor Brady, *Mountain Fury*, 1993
    Kincaids #3
W. Michael Gear, *The Morning River*, 1996
Jason Manning, *Green River Rendezvous*, 1993
    High Country #2
Richard S. Wheeler, *Santa Fe*, 1994
    Skye's West #8

546

WILLIAM W. JOHNSTONE

Honor of the Mountain Man
(New York: Zebra, 1998)

Story type: Traditional; Ranch Life
Major character(s): Smoke Jensen, Rancher, Gunfighter; Joey Wells, Rancher, Gunfighter; Jacob Murdock, Rancher, Criminal
Time period(s): 1890s

Locale(s): Bracketville, Texas; Big Rock, Colorado; Pueblo, Colorado

Summary: Jacob Murdock means to carve out his own empire in the Colorado countryside around Pueblo. But he's starting out with some powerful enemies. Joey Wells, whose Texas ranch was raided by marauders, tracks them to Murdock's spread, bent on revenge. There he runs across rancher Smoke Jensen, who is none too keen on Murdock's plans himself. When Murdock's first try is frustrated, he brings in an army of hired gunmen. Wells and Jensen stand against him, with a force of untried townsmen at their backs, and the situation threatens to erupt into a bloody range war.

Other books by the same author:
Triumph of the Mountain Man, 1997
Spirit of the Mountain Man, 1996
Screams of Eagles, 1996
Blackfoot Messiah, 1996
Cheyenne Challenge, 1995

Other books you might like:
Ernest Haycox, *Riders West*, 1934
Robert Kammen, *The Elkhorn Marauders*, 1994
Richard Matheson, *Journal of the Gun Years*, 1991
Lauran Paine, *The Grand Ones of San Ildefonso*, 1997
Jory Sherman, *The Barons of Texas*, 1997

547

WILLIAM W. JOHNSTONE

Triumph of the Mountain Man
(New York: Zebra, 1997)

Story type: Traditional; Ranch Life
Major character(s): Smoke Jensen, Rancher, Gunfighter; Clifton Satterlee, Businessman, Criminal; Cole Granger, Bodyguard, Gunfighter
Time period(s): 19th century (post Civil War)
Locale(s): Taos, New Mexico

Summary: Called from his High Lonesome home by old friend Diego Alvarado, Smoke Jensen finds trouble in Taos. Landgrabber Clifton Satterlee has set his sights on the rich timber in the Sangre de Cristo Mountains above Taos. He's using a campaign of terror, coercion, and violence to get the rights, and those who oppose him—like Alvarado and his ranch hands—face an uphill struggle. Jensen might even the odds, but Satterlee still has an ace in his sleeve, an unrivalled gunman who may be even faster than Smoke Jensen.

Other books by the same author:
Blackfoot Messiah, 1996
Screams of Eagles, 1996
Spirit of the Mountain Man, 1996
Cheyenne Challenge, 1995
Power of the Mountain Man, 1995

Other books you might like:
Jack Ballas, *Tomahawk Canyon*, 1992
Rita Cleary, *Sorrel*, 1993
Bill Dugan, *Madigan's Luck*, 1994
Steve Frazee, *Hidden Gold*, 1997
Cameron Judd, *Brazos*, 1994

548

KIRBY JONAS

The Dansing Star

(Pocatello, Idaho: Howling Wolf, 1997)

Story type: Traditional; Indian Wars

Major character(s): Morton Dansing, Lawman (deputy sheriff); Horse Hate, Indian (Apache), Warrior; Hannah Rourke, Businesswoman

Time period(s): 1880s

Locale(s): Pima County, Arizona

Summary: Morton Dansing is a man between two worlds. Reared in Missouri until the age of nine, he was captured by Indians on his family's way west. He grew to manhood among the Apache, then returned to the Anglo world when his Chiricahua family was murdered. Working as a lawman while he seeks the killers, he goes into the desert in search of a murderer. But before he can make his arrest, he is besieged in a cabin with four men and a white woman. Outside is Dansing's Apache enemy, Horse Hate, determined to kill the whites and especially Dansing. But Dansing's most dangerous enemy may be inside, among the people he must cooperate with for survival.

Other books by the same author:
Season's End, 1996 (Season of the Vigilante #2)
The Bloody Season, 1996 (Season of the Vigilante #1)

Other books you might like:
Erle Adkins, *Big Bend Ambush*, 1991
Frank Burleson, *Devil Dance*, 1997
    Apache Wars saga #5
Hank Edwards, *Apache Sundown*, 1996
Wynema McGowan, *Beyond the River*, 1997
Les Savage Jr., *Fire Dance at Spider Rock*, 1995

549

MADISON JONES

Nashville 1864

(New York: J.S. Sanders, 1997)

Story type: Historical; Historical/American Civil War

Major character(s): Steven Moore, Child; John Bell Hood, Military Personnel (Confederate)

Time period(s): 1860s (1864)

Locale(s): Nashville, Tennessee

Summary: The Battle of Nashville, the last of many disasters to overtake the luckless Confederate Army of Tennessee, is the background for this story of individual versus societal responsibility. Twelve year old Steven Moore slips through Union lines to tell his father, a Confederate officer, of the family's desperate plight. The elder Moore's hardbitten soldiers are in their own desperate plight, soon to be made more desperate by a crushing Union assault. Caught in the middle, Moore must decide whether his highest duty lies with the Army or his family.

Where it's reviewed:
Booklist, May 15, 1997, page 1563
Kirkus Reviews, March 15, 1997, page 405

Publishers Weekly, April 14, 1997, page 56
Southern Living, July 1997, page 52

Other books by the same author:
To the Winds, 1996

Other books you might like:
Russell Banks, *Cloudsplitter*, 1998
Frederic Bean, *Lorena*, 1996
Harold Coyle, *Look Away*, 1996
Cameron Judd, *The Phantom Legion*, 1997
David Robertson, *Booth*, 1998

550

CAMERON JUDD

Passage to Natchez

(New York: Bantam, 1996)

Story type: Historical; Saga

Major character(s): Clardy Tyler, Wanderer, Frontiersman; Celinda Ames, Orphan, Teenager; Micajah Harpe, Murderer, Historical Figure

Time period(s): 18th century; 19th century (1798-1812)

Locale(s): Natchez, Mississippi; Cave-in-Rock, Illinois; New Madrid, Missouri

Summary: For young Clardy Tyler, the river frontier of the Ohio and Mississippi is a brawling, bloody land of opportunity. For even younger Celinda Ames, alone and friendless among brutal killers, it's a dark and terrifying place. Yet she is as much a survivor as Tyler, and their stories—and those of dozens of others who make their lives along the rivers—go to build a history of courage that not even the great New Madrid earthquake can shake.

Other books by the same author:
Boone, 1995
Devil Wire, 1995
Brazos, 1994
Crockett of Tennessee, 1994
Confederate Gold, 1993

Other books you might like:
Taylor Brady, *Raging Rivers*, 1992
    Kincaids #1
Terry C. Johnston, *Dance on the Wind*, 1995
Kay L. McDonald, *Journey on the Wind*, 1976
Frank Roderus, *The Purgatory River*, 1997
Jim R. Woolard, *Thunder in the Valley*, 1995
    Spur Award winner

551

CAMERON JUDD

The Phantom Legion

(New York: Bantam, 1997)

Story type: Historical/American Civil War; Series

Series: Mountain War Trilogy

Major character(s): Greeley Brown, Guide, Spy (Union); Julius Killefer, Military Personnel (Confederate); Amy Deacon, Spy (Union)

Time period(s): 1860s (1863)

Locale(s): Knoxville, Tennessee; Nashville, Tennessee; Elizabethton, Tennessee

Summary: In the mountain fastness of Eastern Tennessee, Union sympathizers are held against their will in the Confederacy. As 1863 dawns and the war turns inexorably against the Confederacy, guerrilla war breaks out, a war of ambushes and lynchings and mob rule in an area coveted by both sides. Drawn into it are such people as Greeley Brown, long an agent of the Underground Railroad, who now finds the war closing in on him; Julius Killefer, true to the Union but forced into the Confederate Army; and Amy Deacon, who spied for the Union and hoped to escape the war by coming to the then-peaceful mountain country. Their lives, and those of all the others caught up in the forces tearing the country apart, interweave in a pattern of violence and danger.

Other books by the same author:
Boone, 1995
Devil Wire, 1995
Brazos, 1994
Crockett of Tennessee, 1994
Confederate Gold, 1993

Other books you might like:
Howard Bahr, *The Black Flower*, 1997
Randal L. Greenwood, *Ride, Rebels, Ride*, 1996
James Reasoner, *The Hunted*, 1997
David William Ross, *Savage Plains*, 1996
Robert Vaughan, *Blood on the Plains*, 1997

552

MICHAEL KILIAN

Major Washington

(New York: St. Martin's Press, 1998)

Story type: Historical; Indian Wars
Major character(s): George Washington, Military Personnel (Virginia militia), Surveyor; Thomas Morley, Sea Captain; Edward Braddock, Military Personnel
Time period(s): 1750s (1753-1755)
Locale(s): Philadelphia, Pennsylvania, American Colonies; Appalachian Mountains, American Colonies

Summary: The years from 1753 to 1755 were of crucial importance to the young surveyor and militia officer named George Washington. He made three trips into the unexplored wilderness of Appalachia, suffered the pangs of love for a friend's wife, and marched as part of the British expedition led by General Edward Braddock against the French and Indians. Surviving Braddock's debacle, Washington helps to lead the survivors back to civilization in a grueling trek through hostile country. With sidekick Thomas Morley, himself no stranger to the problems of love and war, Washington appears as a tough and ambitious young man on his way up in the Colonies.

Other books you might like:
Harold Coyle, *Savage Wilderness*, 1997
Cameron Judd, *Boone*, 1995
Barbara Riefe, *Mohawk Woman*, 1996
James Alexander Thom, *Long Knife*, 1994

Jim R. Woolard, *Thunder in the Valley*, 1995
Spur Award winner

553

HIRAM KING

High Prairie

(New York: Leisure, 1997)

Story type: Traditional; Man Alone
Major character(s): Cole Granger, Cowboy, Rancher; Frank Driskill, Rancher; Ples Butler, Lawman
Time period(s): 1870s
Locale(s): Tubac, Texas; MFD Ranch, Texas

Summary: Cole Granger, small rancher and sometime cowboy has hired on to bring a pair of thoroughbred horses to rancher Frank Driskill. Through no fault of Granger's, he loses the horses. But he's given his word to do a job, and that's what he's going to do. Facing hostile Indians, bandits, and an unfriendly frontier, Granger sets out to recover Driskill's property and show that his honor is as strong as any other man's.

Other books you might like:
Elmer Kelton, *Wagontongue*, 1972
Geo. W. Proctor, *Walks without a Soul*, 1990
J.J.R. Ramey, *West of Paradise Run*, 1989
Bruce H. Thorstad, *Deadwood Dick and the Code of the West*, 1991
Tom Willard, *The Buffalo Soldiers*, 1996

554

WILLIAM KITTRIDGE, Editor

The Portable Western Reader

(New York: Viking, 1997)

Story type: Anthology
Time period(s): 19th century; 20th century
Locale(s): West; United States

Summary: This paperback anthology spans the period from the earliest native American legends to the present. Different sections examine legends, the west in myth, the west as the settlers experienced it, and the new breed of Western writers. It includes selections by Larry McMurtry, John Graves, Mari Sandoz, and many others.

Where it's reviewed:
Booklist, June 1, 1997, page 1648
Library Journal, July 1997, page 130
Los Angeles Times Book Review, August 3, 1997, page 8
Publishers Weekly, June 2, 1997, page 64

Other books by the same author:
The Last Best Place: A Montana Anthology, 1990

Other books you might like:
Elizabeth Cook-Lynn, *The Power of Horses and Other Stories*, 1990
Ed Gorman, *The Fatal Frontier*, 1997
  Martin Greenberg, co-editor
Tony Hillerman, *The Best of the West*, 1991

Jon Tuska, *The Morrow Anthology of Great Western Short Stories*, 1997
Vicki Piekarski, co-editor
Dale L. Walker, *The Golden Spurs*, 1990

555

PAGE LAMBERT

Shifting Stars: A Novel of the West
(New York: Forge, 1997)

Story type: Historical; Mountain Man
Major character(s): Skye MacDonald, Teenager, Frontierswoman; Gregory MacDonald, Mountain Man, Parent; Turtle Woman, Indian (Lakota), Grandparent
Time period(s): 1840s
Locale(s): Medicine Wheel, Wyoming; Big Horn Mountains, Wyoming

Summary: After the death of her Lakota mother Breathcatcher, Skye MacDonald comes with her father to visit her grandmother Turtle Woman. Old trouble breaks out at once. Caws Like Magpie, once a rival for Breathcatcher's love, renews his feud with MacDonald, leading to the death of Skye's grandfather and Caws Like Magpie's banishment from the tribe. Not satisfied with this, MacDonald seeks blood revenge and is himself killed. Alone with Turtle Woman, Skye agrees to go with her grandmother to the sacred Medicine Wheel, not knowing that a series of fateful meetings will occur there.

Where it's reviewed:
Booklist, June 1, 1997, page 1658
Library Journal, August 1997, page 131
Publishers Weekly, May 26, 1997, page 67

Other books you might like:
W. Michael Gear, *Coyote Summer*, 1997
Paul A. Hawkins, *The Seekers*, 1994
Douglas Hirt, *McKendree*, 1997
Jason Manning, *Battle of the Teton Basin*, 1994
    High Country #3
Earl Murray, *Free Flows the River*, 1991

556

ROBERT LAXALT

Dust Devils
(Reno: University of Nevada Press, 1997)

Story type: Modern; Chase
Major character(s): Ira Hamilton, Cowboy, Teenager; John D. Hamilton, Rancher; Cricket, Indian (Paiute), Sidekick
Time period(s): 20th century
Locale(s): Heavenly Valley, California; Black Rock Desert, Nevada

Summary: Trouble is coming between teenaged Ira Hamilton and his hard-nosed rancher father. Old John Hamilton plans for his son to marry the daughter of a neighboring rancher, but Ira is in love with Thoma, daughter of Paiute Chief Black Rock Tom. When Ira wins an Arabian colt at a rodeo, the horse is stolen by the rustler known as Hawkeye. Ira and Cricket, Thoma's brother, set out to find Hawkeye's gang and

recover the horse, but Ira knows there's more at stake than a colt or his own life.

Where it's reviewed:
Kirkus Reviews, August 15, 1997, page 1246

Other books you might like:
Robert J. Conley, *Back to Malachi*, 1997
Will Cook, *The Rain Tree*, 1996
Ken Grant, *The Deer Mouse*, 1997
Cynthia Haseloff, *Man without Medicine*, 1996
Cormac McCarthy, *All the Pretty Horses*, 1992

557

SUZANN LEDBETTER

Colorado Reverie
(New York: Signet, 1997)

Story type: Historical; Historical/American Civil War
Major character(s): Dianna Radieu, Gambler, Spy
Time period(s): 1860s
Locale(s): Denver, Colorado

Summary: Dianna Radieu is famous throughout the West as an ice-cold gambler and a woman equally ice-cold to men's advances. She seems a perfect choice for a dangerous game. Working for the Union cause, she's assigned to ferret out Confederate sympathizers in Colorado before they can deliver the state's gold to Jeff Davis. But Dianna finds that her opposite number, the leader of the Copperheads, is a man whose touch can melt ice, and before long she must decide where her true loyalties lie.

Where it's reviewed:
Roundup Magazine, June 1997, page 34

Other books by the same author:
Trinity Strike, 1996
Redemption Trail, 1996
Deliverance Drive, 1996

Other books you might like:
Jack Ballas, *Bandido Caballero*, 1997
Tom Dyja, *Play for a Kingdom*, 1997
Kathleen O'Neal Gear, *Thin Moon and Cold Mist*, 1995
James Reasoner, *The Hunted*, 1997
Robert Vaughan, *Blood on the Plains*, 1997

558

SUZANN LEDBETTER

Klondike Fever
(New York: Signet, 1997)

Story type: Historical; Quest
Major character(s): Megan O'Malley, Hotel Owner, Widow(er); Barlow David O'Malley, Teenager; Pete Vladislov, Boarder, Alcoholic
Time period(s): 1890s
Locale(s): Dawson, Yukon Territory, Canada; Skagway, Alaska

Summary: Megan O'Malley has met with all the reverses a frontier woman needs. A widow, she's lost her mine and

means of livelihood to a big mining concern, and she's watching her son, Barlow David, fall in with bad companions. But Megan is not easily discouraged. Selling their remaining belongings to get passage, she scoops up the unwilling Barlow David and sets out for the Yukon gold fields. Earlier comers have already laid claim to the available diggings, but Megan knows more than one way to pan gold. She opens a boarding house in Dawson, where Barlow David promptly brings a young Indian girl he meets and the girl's drunken stepfather. The stepfather is Pete Vladislov, who once loved Megan but is now far gone in liquor. Each of the characters must now face a confrontation with what they really are, with consequences far more important than mere gold.

Other books by the same author:
Trinity Strike, 1996
Redemption Trail, 1996
Deliverance Drive, 1996

Other books you might like:
Loren D. Estleman, *Sudden Country*, 1991
Gilbert Morris, *The Yukon Queen*, 1995
    House of Winslow #17
Richard Parry, *The Winter Wolf*, 1996
James A. Ritchie, *Kerrigan*, 1993
J.A. Shears, *Fire in the Sky*, 1988

559

SUZANN LEDBETTER

Pure Justice
(New York: Signet, 1997)

Story type: Historical; Revenge
Major character(s): Halley Brandt, Rancher, Avenger; John Wesley Hardin, Gunfighter, Murderer; Lucas Chamberlain, Lawman (Texas Ranger)
Time period(s): 1870s (1877)
Locale(s): Gonzales, Texas; Pensacola Junction, Florida

Summary: When gunman John Wesley Hardin kills her two brothers, Halley Brandt swears revenge. Hardin is the most dangerous man in Texas, and he might not take pursuit from a revenge-driven young woman too seriously, but that would be his mistake. Halley intends to get her pound of flesh, and she embarks on a chase that takes her from Texas to the wilds of Florida to do it. Helped—and sometimes hindered—by Texas Ranger Lucas Chamberlain, Halley pushes her search until the moment when she stands face to face with Hardin.

Where it's reviewed:
Publishers Weekly, March 31, 1997, page 72

Other books by the same author:
Trinity Strike, 1996
Redemption Trail, 1996
Deliverance Drive, 1996

Other books you might like:
James Carlos Blake, *Pistoleer*, 1995
Matt Braun, *Noble Outlaw*, 1996
Bruce McGinnis, *Reflections in Dark Glass*, 1996
Wynema McGowan, *While the Rivers Run*, 1996
Gene Shelton, *Last Gun*, 1991

560

JOHN LEGG

Mountain Captive
(New York: Harper, 1996)

Story type: Quest; Mountain Man
Major character(s): Jim Blackwood, Trapper, Mountain Man; Bass Henderson, Trader; Anna Montoya, Captive
Time period(s): 1830s (1834-1835)
Locale(s): Taos, New Mexico; Rocky Mountains

Summary: Mountain man Jim Blackwood has accepted the loss of the woman he loved—Anna Montoya, taken captive and probably slain by raiding Blackfoot Indians. Blackwood has taken Red Quiver to wife, and the couple now has a young son. Then Blackwood meets Bass Henderson, whose wife is also a Blackfoot captive. Blackwood and Henderson join forces, Blackwood with renewed hope of finding Anna alive. But the uneasy alliance between two strong men threatens to erupt into murder when they learn that they're both looking for the same woman.

Other books by the same author:
Buckskin Vengeance, 1996
War at Bent's Fort, 1995
The Frontiersman, 1995
Fire along the Big Muddy, 1995
Buckskins and Blood, 1994

Other books you might like:
Douglas Hirt, *McKendree*, 1997
David William Ross, *Beyond the Stars*, 1990
Jory Sherman, *Trapper's Moon*, 1994
David Thompson, *Trail's End*, 1996
    Wilderness #22
Michael Zimmer, *Fandango*, 1996

561

AMY LITTLESUGAR
MARLOWE DECHRISTOPHER, Illustrator

A Portrait of Spotted Deer's Grandfather
(New York: Albert Whitman, 1997)

Story type: Indian Culture; Young Readers
Major character(s): Moose Horn, Indian (Chippewa), Chieftain; George Catlin, Artist
Time period(s): 1830s (1836)
Locale(s): Minnesota

Summary: In 1836, frontier artist George Catlin finds his way to the Chippewa country to paint the famous warrior Moose Horn, now an old man. But Moose Horn doesn't want to be painted, fearing that the artist might capture his spirit as well as his face. As he watches Catlin work, Moose Horn rethinks his decision, helped by a spirit vision from his youth and an appeal to the Great Spirit. At last the old warrior agrees, knowing that even Catlin's brush cannot capture the Indian way of life before it changes.

Where it's reviewed:
Kirkus Reviews, August 15, 1997, page 1308
Publishers Weekly, August 25, 1997, page 72

Other books you might like:
John Bierhorst, *On the Road of Stars*, 1995
Brian Burks, *Runs with Horses*, 1995
Ann Rinaldi, *The Second Bend in the River*, 1997
Virginia A. Stroud, *Doesn't Fall off His Horse*, 1994
G. Clifton Wisler, *The Wolf's Tooth*, 1987

562

JOHN LOVEDAY

Goodbye, Buffalo Sky

(New York: Simon and Schuster, 1997)

Story type: Mountain Man; Young Readers
Major character(s): Cappy Carew, Orphan; Burkhart, Mountain Man; Two Songs, Indian (Mandan), Widow(er)
Time period(s): 1880s
Locale(s): West; United States

Summary: Young Orphan Cappy Carew learns the ways of the Old West and the secrets of survival from Burkhart, a tough mountain man who has taken Cappy under his protection. The lessons come in handy when Burkhart is murdered by an Indian who wants Burkhart's Mandan wife, Two Songs. Cappy decides to take the widowed Two Songs back to her tribe. With the aid of a friend and some chance companions, he sets out on the trail, but the murderer is still with them.

Where it's reviewed:
Books for Keeps, May 1997, page 16
Books Magazine, September 1996, page 24
Kirkus Reviews, September 1, 1997, page 1392
Magpies, July 1996, page 31
Times Educational Supplement, November 29, 1996, page 10

Other books by the same author:
Halo, 1994

Other books you might like:
Lyman Hafen, *Over the Joshua Slope*, 1994
Kathryn Lasky, *The Bone Wars*, 1988
Gary Paulsen, *Call Me Francis Tucket*, 1995
Judith St. George, *The Halo Wind*, 1978
Rosalyn Schanzer, *How We Crossed the West*, 1997

563

NANCY LUENN
PIERR MORGAN, Illustrator

The Miser on the Mountain

(New York: Sasquatch, 1997)

Story type: Young Readers; Indian Culture
Major character(s): Latsut, Indian (Nisqually); Elk, Animal, Spirit
Time period(s): Indeterminate
Locale(s): Mount Ranier, Washington

Summary: In this retelling of a Nisqually legend, Latsut eagerly sets out to climb the slopes of Mount Ranier. Latsut is a miser who prizes above all else the trading shells that are his people's money. Consequently, he refuses to give feasts as Nisqually custom requires, or even to cede his wife enough shells for a necklace. Then Elk promises to show Latsut the

true meaning of wealth if he will climb the sacred mountain. That seems to be just what the miser wants, but he soon learns that Elk has a much harder lesson in store for him.

Where it's reviewed:
Publishers Weekly, September 1, 1997, page 104

Other books by the same author:
Song for the Ancient Forest, 1993

Other books you might like:
Joseph Bruchac, *The Great Ball Game*, 1994
Barbara Diamond Goldin, *Coyote and the Fire Stick*, 1996
Ken Kesey, *The Sea Lion*, 1991
Gerald McDermott, *Raven: A Trickster Tale from the Pacific Northwest*, 1993
Janet Stevens, *Old Bag of Bones*, 1996

564

JASON MANNING

American Blood

(New York: Signet, 1996)

Story type: Mountain Man; Historical
Major character(s): Hugh Falconer, Mountain Man; Delgado McKinn, Traveller; Brent Horan, Landowner
Time period(s): 1840s (1846)
Locale(s): St. Louis, Missouri; Taos, New Mexico; Turley's Mill, New Mexico

Summary: Returning to his Taos home from school in England, Delgado McKinn finds a war in his way. New Mexico is about to be swept by the Mexican-American War, and McKinn's loyalties are divided—especially because he's seen the arrogance some Anglos feel toward races with darker skin. In St. Louis, McKinn pauses long enough to make an enemy of powerful Brent Horan and to fall in love with abolitionist Sarah Bledsoe. Then he and Mountain Man Hugh Falconer head for New Mexico. Through bloodshed and battle, Falconer and McKinn fight side by side. But eventually McKinn must return to St. Louis to face the danger there and to earn Sarah's love.

Other books by the same author:
Falconer's Law, 1996
Promised Land, 1996
The Border Captains, 1995 (Flintlock #2)
Gone to Texas, 1995 (Flintlock #3)
Battle of the Teton Basin, 1994 (High Country #3)

Other books you might like:
Albert R. Booky, *Hacienda*, 1997
Larry Jay Martin, *Against the Seventh Flag*, 1991
Jess McCreede, *Mountain Men on the Santa Fe Trail*, 1992
Jory Sherman, *Eagles of Destiny*, 1990
Norman Zollinger, *Meridian: A Novel of Kit Carson's West*, 1997

565

JASON MANNING

The Black Jacks

(New York: Signet, 1997)

Story type: Historical; Indian Wars
Major character(s): John Henry McAllen, Military Personnel; Sam Houston, Political Figure, Historical Figure; Gray Wolf, Indian (Comanche), Chieftain
Time period(s): 1840s
Locale(s): Staked Plains, Texas; San Antonio, Texas

Summary: Behind their determined leader Gray Wolf, the Comanches unite to slash deep into the hated Republic of Texas. To meet the threat, Sam Houston selects John Henry McAllen, Indian fighter, soldier, and leader of the militia outfit called the Black Jacks. McAllen and his Black Jacks venture onto the Staked Plains, outnumbered and perhaps outgeneralled by Gray Wolf's forces. McAllen is willing to face the test of battle, but he's unaware of the treason that threatens his back.

Where it's reviewed:
Roundup Magazine, June 1997, page 34

Other books by the same author:
Falconer's Law, 1996 (Falconer Saga #1)
The Border Captains, 1995 (Flintlock #2)
Gone to Texas, 1995 (Flintlock #3)
Battle of the Teton Basin, 1994 (High Country #3)
Flintlock, 1994 (Flintlock #1)

Other books you might like:
Terry C. Johnston, *Wolf Mountain Moon*, 1997
    Plainsman #12
Elmer Kelton, *The Wolf and the Buffalo*, 1980
Chad Oliver, *The Wolf Is My Brother*, 1967
Geo. W. Proctor, *Enemies*, 1994
David William Ross, *Savage Plains*, 1996

566

JASON MANNING

Promised Land

(New York: Signet, 1996)

Story type: Historical; Mountain Man
Major character(s): Hugh Falconer, Mountain Man; Lilian Wilkerson, Traveller; Bearclaw Johnson, Mountain Man
Time period(s): 1840s
Locale(s): Rocky Mountains

Summary: Mountain man Hugh Falconer accidently becomes responsible for an emigrant wagon train when he saves the party from a renegade guide who was leading them to destruction. Falconer offers to see them along their way west, but it's a tall order. Beset by Pawnee war parties and other problems, the train takes winter refuge in a valley where Falconer thinks they can survive. What he doesn't know is that another mountain man has claimed the valley for his own. And he doesn't like visitors.

Other books by the same author:
Falconer's Law, 1996 (Falconer Saga #1)
The Border Captains, 1995 (Flintlock #2)
Gone to Texas, 1995 (Flintlock #3)
Battle of the Teton Basin, 1994 (High Country #3)
Flintlock, 1994 (Flintlock #1)

Other books you might like:
Win Blevins, *The Snake River*, 1992
    Rivers West #8
Ralph Compton, *Across the Rio Colorado*, 1997
R.C. House, *Buckskinner*, 1994
John Killdeer, *Passage West*, 1994
    Mountain Majesty #5
Richard S. Wheeler, *Wind River*, 1993
    Skye's West #7

567

JILL MAX
ROBERT ANNESLEY, Illustrator

Spider Spins a Story

(New York: Northland, 1997)

Story type: Indian Culture; Young Readers
Major character(s): Spider, Spirit
Time period(s): Indeterminate
Locale(s): West

Summary: These fourteen tales center around the spider's place in Indian life and mythology. In stories taken from different Native American cultures ranging from Achomawi to Zuni, Spider shows up in both genders and several roles. The most familiar is that of Spider Woman or Spider Grandmother, the creator and champion of goodness and wisdom. But Spider is sometimes the trickster as well, a Coyote spirit with more legs and more cunning than the hapless canine usually shows.

Where it's reviewed:
Publishers Weekly, June 23, 1997, page 92

Other books you might like:
Joseph Bruchac, *The Girl Who Married the Moon*, 1994
    Gayle Ross, co-author
Barry Lopez, *Crow and Weasel*, 1990
Nancy Luenn, *The Miser on the Mountain*, 1997
Gretchen Will Mayo, *Star Tales*, 1990
Rosebud Yellow Robe, *Tonweya and the Eagles*, 1992

568

JOHN S. MCCORD

Blind Eagles

(South Bend, IN: Ravenstone, 1997)

Story type: Traditional; Saga
Major character(s): Ward Baynes, Rancher; Kit Baynes, Spouse; Micajah Trampe, Kidnapper
Time period(s): 1870s (1870)
Locale(s): Sacramento, California; Vallecito Station, California

Summary: The peaceful life of rancher Ward Baynes is thrown into chaos when old enemies from the past kidnap his youngest son. The Trampe family plans to collect the ransom, then settle old scores by killing the boy. Hearing of the trouble, the Baynes clan gathers from the four corners of the West, all determined to find their missing kinsman and bring swift justice to the criminals.

Other books by the same author:
California Eagles, 1995
Wyoming Giant, 1992
Texas Comebacker, 1991
Montana Horseman, 1990
Walking Hawk, 1989

Other books you might like:
Erle Adkins, *Killing Revenge*, 1994
W. Michael Gear, *Big Horn Legacy*, 1988
Douglas Hirt, *The Ordeal of Andy Dean*, 1993
W.W. Lee, *Cannon's Revenge*, 1995
Lee Martin, *Revenge at Rawhide*, 1992

569

JOHN S. MCCORD

Nevada Tough
(New York: Berkley, 1996)

Story type: Traditional; Saga
Major character(s): Darnell Baynes, Mine Owner; Fane Trampe, Wanderer
Time period(s): 1870s
Locale(s): Pioche, Nevada

Summary: Darnell Baynes feels he's getting old and slow, and needs something to liven him up. Right on schedule comes a report that profits are off at a Baynes mine in Nevada. Moreover, there are hints that strange—and probably illegal—things are going on at the mine. Baynes decided to look into the matter himself, thinking it might provide a little excitement. He goes to Pioche undercover and finds plenty of excitement, with a corrupt marshal, a clever criminal, and an old family enemy who might jump to either side.

Other books by the same author:
California Eagles, 1995
Wyoming Giant, 1992
Texas Comebacker, 1991
Montana Horseman, 1990
Walking Hawk, 1989

Other books you might like:
Loren D. Estleman, *City of Widows*, 1994
Douglas Hirt, *Colorado Gold*, 1993
Stan Lynde, *The Bodacious Kid*, 1996
Arthur Moore, *The Game of Death*, 1993
Bruce H. Thorstad, *Ace of Diamonds*, 1994

570

WYNEMA MCGOWAN

Beyond the River
(New York: Pinnacle, 1997)

Story type: Traditional
Major character(s): Amy Kay Ormsby, Abuse Victim, Fugitive; Will January, Outlaw; Nate Doubletree, Military Personnel
Time period(s): 1850s
Locale(s): Cobb's Relay Station, Texas; Staked Plains, Texas

Summary: Trapped in Cobb's relay station by a Comanche attack, the passengers on a Texas stagecoach face probable death together. Some are fighting men. Outlaw Will January and his three henchmen are equally dangerous to the Indians and to their own companions. Nate Doubletree is an Army officer, and the stage drivers are former Texas Rangers, well-equipped for this kind of fight. Amy Kay Ormsby and her young son and the Cobb children are little more than helpless victims. But if any are to survive the siege, they will have to find some means to work together.

Other books by the same author:
While the Rivers Run, 1996

Other books you might like:
Richard Clarke, *The Undertaker*, 1991
Jason Manning, *The Black Jacks*, 1997
Lauran Paine, *The Grand Ones of San Ildefonso*, 1997
Geo. W. Proctor, *Blood of My Blood*, 1996
David William Ross, *Eyes of the Hawk*, 1992

571

WYNEMA MCGOWAN

While the Rivers Run
(New York: Pinnacle, 1996)

Story type: Traditional; Revenge
Major character(s): Nessa Fane, Widow(er), Avenger; Tom Doubletree, Lawman (Texas Ranger); Trey Henry, Outlaw
Time period(s): 1850s (1855)
Locale(s): Hermosito, Texas; Magdelena, Mexico

Summary: Outlaws murder Nessa Fane's husband but make a big mistake and leave her alive. One by one, they learn of their mistake as she tracks them across the rugged plains of 1850s Texas. Sometimes helped and sometimes hindered by Texas Ranger Tom Doubletree, Nessa presses on with her campaign, although her feelings for the big Ranger increasingly cloud her thinking. But she has set her mind on vengeance, and she means to reach the end of her trail if it costs her life.

Other books by the same author:
Beyond the River, 1997

Other books you might like:
Johnny D. Boggs, *The Courtship of Hannah and the Horseman*, 1997
Ralph Compton, *The Killing Season*, 1996
Sandra Dallas, *The Diary of Mattie Spenser*, 1997
Earl Murray, *The River at Sundown*, 1997

Johnny Quarles, *No Man's Land*, 1993

572

LARRY MCMURTRY

Comanche Moon

(New York: Simon & Schuster, 1997)

Story type: Traditional; Indian Wars
Major character(s): Gus McCrae, Lawman (Texas Ranger);
Woodrow Call, Lawman (Texas Ranger); Buffalo Hump,
Indian (Comanche), Chieftain
Time period(s): 1850s; 1860s
Locale(s): Austin, Texas; Staked Plains, Texas

Summary: Familiar characters Woodrow Call and Gus McCrae appear again in this picture of the Comanche incursions into Texas. Nursing a grudge against Call and McCrae in particular and Texans in general, Comanche leader Buffalo Hump plans a last foray through the state. The Rangers are busy with other duties, but news of the impending raid soon draws them together for a fight that may be their last.

Other books by the same author:
Dead Man's Walk, 1995
Streets of Laredo, 1993
Buffalo Girls, 1990
Anything for Billy, 1988

Other books you might like:
Benjamin Capps, *A Woman of the People*, 1966
Harry Combs, *Brules*, 1994
John Graves, *The Last Running*, 1990
Elmer Kelton, *Slaughter*, 1992
Jason Manning, *The Black Jacks*, 1997

573

MICHAEL MOORCOCK

Tales From the Texas Woods

(New York: Mojo, 1997)

Story type: Modern; Collection
Locale(s): United States

Summary: Fantasy writer Michael Moorcock here indulges his love for western stories and for his adopted home in Texas. From memories of how much the cowboy myth meant to him as a child through early Western stories of his own authorship to a mixture of multiple-reality fantasy and traditional Western, Moorcock shows his development of the Western tradition into new and different storytelling forms.

Other books you might like:
Sanora Babb, *Cry of the Tinamou*, 1997
Jane Candia Coleman, *Moving On*, 1997
Basil Moss, *Tales of the Wichitas*, 1998
Dale L. Walker, *Legends and Lies: Great Mysteries of the American West*, 1997
Ken Wilkerson, *Blue Ride*, 1998

574

ALAN MORRIS

By Honor Bound

(Minneapolis: Bethany House, 1996)

Story type: Traditional; Series
Series: Guardians of the North
Major character(s): Hunter Stone, Settler, Lawman; Red Wolf, Indian (Crow), Warrior; Reena O'Donnell, Religious (missionary)
Time period(s): 1870s (1872-1874)
Locale(s): Fort Whoop-Up, Canada; Cripple Camp, Canada

Summary: Hunter Stone plans a new life on the Canadian frontier, but his dream is shattered when Red Wolf and his band raid Stone's cabin while he is away. The Indians burn the cabin and abduct Betsy, Stone's wife. Driven by revenge and by his own feelings of guilt, Stone tracks them, only to be wounded and left for dead. Reena O'Donnell, a missionary to the Assiniboine, finds the wounded Stone and nurses him back to health. Still driven by his anger, he joins the Northwest Mounted Police, hoping to use their force to exact his own private vengeance.

Where it's reviewed:
Booklist, October 1, 1996, page 304

Other books you might like:
W.E. Davis, *The Proving Ground*, 1996
    Valley of the Peacemaker #2
Tom Eidson, *The Last Ride*, 1995
Kirby Jonas, *The Bloody Season*, 1996
    Season of the Vigilante #1
Janette Oke, *Drums of Change*, 1996
Alfred Silver, *Where the Ghost Horse Runs*, 1991

575

BASIL MOSS

Tales of the Wichitas

(Lubbock: Texas Tech University Press, 1998)

Story type: Modern; Collection
Time period(s): 20th century (1920-1940)
Locale(s): Wichita Mountains, Oklahoma

Summary: This collection of stories comes from the author's own experience and that of his neighbors in Indian country—the Wichita Mountains of Oklahoma in the early years of this century. The subjects of his tales are the Indians who refused either confinement to the reservation or assimilation into Anglo culture, but tried to maintain their own identities in the mixed society of western Oklahoma.

Other books you might like:
Paula Gunn Allen, *Song of the Turtle*, 1996
Elizabeth Cook-Lynn, *The Power of Horses and Other Stories*, 1990
Christopher Moore, *Coyote Blue*, 1994
Susan Power, *The Grass Dancer*, 1994
C.W. Smith, *Buffalo Nickel*, 1989

Western

576

EARL MURRAY

The River at Sundown

(New York: Forge, 1997)

Story type: Historical; Quest
Major character(s): Holly Porter, Traveller, Avenger
Time period(s): 19th century (pre Civil War)
Locale(s): Rocky Mountains

Summary: Going west, Holly Porter is parted from her husband and child when warlike Sioux attack their party. Holly is wounded and left for dead, both by the attackers and by her own people, while her son is captured. Recovering her strength, she sets out to recover the boy and to find her husband. The trail is long and beset with dangers—the Sioux, Anglo renegades who are scarcely less dangerous, and the floods, storms and stampedes of the trail. Not even Holly's own relatives are reliable, but she is determined to reach her goal no matter what the cost.

Where it's reviewed:
Booklist, September 1, 1997, page 59
Kirkus Reviews, September 1, 1997, page 1339

Other books by the same author:
Spirit of the Moon, 1995
Flaming Sky, 1995
Thunder in the Dawn, 1993
Free Flows the River, 1991
High Freedom, 1989

Other books you might like:
Wayne Barton, *Fairchild's Passage*, 1997
    Stan Williams, co-author
Kathleen O'Neal Gear, *Thin Moon and Cold Mist*, 1995
Robert F. Jones, *Tie My Bones to Her Back*, 1996
Dawn Miller, *The Journal of Callie Wade*, 1996
Karen Osborn, *Between Earth and Sky*, 1996

577

JOHN D. NESBITT

Wild Rose of Ruby Canyon

(New York: Walker, 1997)

Story type: Ranch Life; Mystery
Major character(s): Henry Sommers, Cowboy, Settler; Van O'Leary, Rancher; Dora O'Leary, Widow(er)
Time period(s): 19th century (post Civil War)
Locale(s): Box Elder Ranch, Wyoming; Ruby Canyon, Wyoming

Summary: Henry Sommers divides his time between his job as cowboy and his own small place in Ruby Canyon. Homesteading in Ruby Canyon, he meets neighbors Van and Dora O'Leary. Van is a hustler, full of ideas—many of them none too legal—for making fast money. Dora, browbeaten and abused, rouses Sommers's sympathy to the point where he starts withdrawing from the two. When O'Leary is murdered, Sommers falls under suspicion. To clear his name, he decides he'd better find the real killer, not recognizing what a dangerous enterprise that might turn out to be.

Other books by the same author:
One Foot in the Stirrup, 1996
Twin Rivers, 1995
One-Eyed Cowboy Wild, 1994

Other books you might like:
Jack Ballas, *Powder River*, 1995
B.M. Bower, *Lonesome Land*, 1997
Will Camp, *Blood Saga*, 1994
Robert Kammen, *The Bullet*, 1994
William A. Luckey, *Cimarron Blood*, 1992

578

T.V. OLSEN

Break the Young Land

(New York: Leisure, 1997)

Story type: Historical; Ranch Life
Major character(s): Borg Vikstrom, Farmer, Immigrant
Time period(s): 19th century (post Civil War)
Locale(s): Liberty, Kansas

Summary: Norwegian immigrant Borg Vikstrom comes to America for land and freedom. He and his fellow farmers think they'll find both around the Kansas town of Liberty, but they're disappointed. Their plans to break the land run headlong into the entrenched power of the cattle barons, who have no intention of sharing the broad Kansas prairies. With a price on his head and hired gunmen on his trail, Vikstrom leads the farmers in a desperate bid to make Liberty live up to its name.

Other books by the same author:
Red Is the River, 1993
The Golden Chance, 1992 (Spur Award winner)
The Burning Sky, 1991
Under the Gun, 1989
A Killer Is Waiting, 1988

Other books you might like:
Jack Ballas, *The Hard Land*, 1998
Gary McCarthy, *Sodbuster*, 1988
Conrad Richter, *The Sea of Grass*, 1937
Lauraine Snelling, *A New Day Rising*, 1996
    Red River of the North #2
Gary D. Svee, *Incident at Pishkin Creek*, 1989

579

T.V. OLSEN

There Was a Season

(New York: Leisure, 1997)

Story type: Historical; Indian Wars
Major character(s): Jefferson Davis, Military Personnel; Black Hawk, Indian (Algonquin), Chieftain; Henry Atkinson, Military Personnel
Time period(s): 1830s (1831-1832)
Locale(s): Illinois; Wisconsin

Summary: When Algonquin Chief Black Hawk finds Illinois settlers plowing Algonquin burial grounds, he leads his people to war. A young Lieutenant named Jefferson Davis is part

of the force led by General Henry Atkinson to put down the war. In a series of small battles, the Algonquins are driven into Missouri, but Black Hawk and some determined followers return to the fight the next year. Davis and his command march in pursuit of the Algonquins, suffering more from disease, treachery, and the hardships of the frontier than from their open enemies. But Davis must complete his mission if he is to give substance to his dreams of future greatness. As an historical note, another participant in the Black Hawk War was a gangling, unmilitary militia officer named Abraham Lincoln.

Other books by the same author:
Red Is the River, 1993
The Golden Chance, 1992 (Spur Award winner)
The Burning Sky, 1991
Under the Gun, 1989
A Killer Is Waiting, 1988

Other books you might like:
Allan W. Eckert, *A Sorrow in Our Heart*, 1992
Donald Clayton Porter, *Hawk's Journey*, 1992
James Reasoner, *The Wilderness Road*, 1996
Frances Patton Stratham, *Trail of Tears*, 1993
James Alexander Thom, *Follow the River*, 1981

580
LAURAN PAINE

The Grand Ones of San Ildefonso
(Thorndike, Maine: Thorndike Press, 1997)

Story type: Traditional; Quest
Major character(s): Tomas Henriques, Religious (penitent); Lazaro Guardia, Political Figure (mayor); Father Damion Sanchez, Religious
Time period(s): 1850s
Locale(s): San Ildefonso, New Mexico

Summary: The border town village of San Ildefonso has recently become part of the United States, but it doesn't seem to matter. Poor and isolated, San Ildefonso asks nothing but peace and has nothing to offer outsiders, either to buy or to steal. Still there's that legend of gold hidden in the old mission by long-ago conquistadors, and that's enough to bring down a band of ruthless outlaws on the little town. The villagers don't believe in the gold—though professional penitent Tomas Henriques swears he's seen it—but they must fight, men and women alike, to protect their own lives.

Other books by the same author:
Lockwood, 1996
The Devil on Horseback, 1995
The Prairieton Raid, 1994
The Squaw Men, 1992
Riders of the Trojan Horse, 1991

Other books you might like:
J.P.S. Brown, *The Forests of the Night*, 1992
Richard Clarke, *The Guns of Peralta*, 1993
Tom Eidson, *St. Agnes' Stand*, 1994
   Spur Award winner
Stef Ann Holm, *Portraits*, 1996
Bob Kody, *Gold Mountain*, 1994

581
CATHERINE PALMER

Prairie Rose
(Wheaton, Illinois: Tyndale House, 1997)

Story type: Ranch Life; Series
Series: Town Called Hope
Major character(s): Rosie Mills, Orphan; Seth Hunter, Settler; Chipper Hunter, Child
Time period(s): 1860s (1865)
Locale(s): Kansas City, Missouri; Hope, West

Summary: When Rosie Mills saves Seth Hunter's life, she finds a ticket out of the orphanage where she's lived since infancy. She goes west with widower Seth and his son Chipper to keep house for them. Since Rosie is now 19, this causes talk, even in the town of Hope. But Rosie and the Hunters rise above such problems, meeting the challenges of life in the west with the courage and fortitude of true pioneers. Only when Rosie and Seth finally do begin to fall in love does an insurmountable problem arise. Rosie, haunted by a dark secret in her past, is convinced she can never marry, and can no longer live with Seth under their changed circumstances.

Where it's reviewed:
Library Journal, September 1, 1997, page 168

Other books you might like:
W.E. Davis, *The Gathering Storm*, 1996
   Valley of the Peacemaker #1
Joan Johnston, *The Barefoot Bride*, 1992
Elaine Long, *Bittersweet Country*, 1991
Isabel Marvin, *A Bride for Anna's Papa*, 1994
Judith Pella, *Warrior's Song*, 1996

582
F.M. PARKER

Winter Woman
(New York: Pinnacle, 1996)

Story type: Traditional; Mountain Man
Major character(s): Jacob Morgan, Trapper, Mountain Man; Wolf Voice, Indian (Crow), Warrior; Cora DuBois, Settler, Mountain Woman
Time period(s): 1850s (1859)
Locale(s): Wind River Mountains, Wyoming; St. Joseph, Missouri; Fort Laramie, Wyoming

Summary: Cora DuBois is torn between two men. She is pledged to marry Clive Pateman, a Mormon who is already her sister's husband, but she is strongly drawn to mountain man Jacob Morgan. After a single night with Morgan, Cora sets out with the Mormon party for Salt Lake City with winter coming on. Morgan thinks he's lost her forever, but a third man comes into the scene. Wolf Voice, a vengeful Crow warrior and sworn enemy of Morgan's, kidnaps Cora from the handcart train. With his beloved in the hands of his enemies, Morgan sets out in search of some vengeance of his own.

Other books by the same author:
The Predators, 1990
The Assassins, 1989

The Slavers, 1989
The Shadow Man, 1988
The Shanghaiers, 1987

Other books you might like:
Jack Cummings, *The Indian Fighter's Return*, 1993
Ken Englade, *Battle Cry*, 1997
   Tony Hillerman's Frontier #4
Zane Grey, *Riders of the Purple Sage*, 1912
Robert Skimin, *Apache Autumn*, 1992
Jim R. Woolard, *The Winds of Autumn*, 1996

583

RICHARD PARRY

The Wolf's Cub

(New York: Forge, 1997)

Story type: Traditional; Chase
Major character(s): Nathan Blaylock, Bastard Son, Gunfighter; Jim Riley, Gunfighter; Doc Hennison, Con Artist
Time period(s): 1900s
Locale(s): Skagway, Alaska; Dawson, Yukon Territory, Canada

Summary: Nathan Blaylock, Wyatt Earp's bastard son, has grown up to be as redoubtable a hand with a gun as his famous father. With partners Jim Riley and Doc Hennison, the one a gunman and the other a medicine show barker, he makes up a third of a Western Three Musketeers. By various means, the three become entangled in a plot to ship stolen guns from Canada to a Central American revolution, and a larger plot involving railroad shares and a plan that may alter the whole future of Alaska.

Where it's reviewed:
Kirkus Reviews, September 1, 1997, page 1333

Other books by the same author:
The Winter Wolf, 1996

Other books you might like:
Ralph Compton, *Sixguns and Double Eagles*, 1998
Cecilia Holland, *Railroad Schemes*, 1997
Tom Hron, *Whispers of the Mountain*, 1996
Suzann Ledbetter, *Klondike Fever*, 1997
James A. Ritchie, *The Wagon Wars*, 1997

584

ALEXS PATE

Amistad

(New York: Signet, 1997)

Story type: Historical; Historical/American Civil War
Major character(s): Cinque, Slave (revolted); John Quincy Adams, Lawyer, Historical Figure (former president); Roger Baldwin, Lawyer
Time period(s): 1830s (1839)
Locale(s): *Amistad*, At Sea; New Haven, Connecticut; Washington, District of Columbia

Summary: Kidnapped from his African home and brought to Cuba as a slave, Cinque takes his first opportunity to wrest back his freedom. With his fellow slaves, he seizes control of the ship carrying him along the Cuban coast. When the ship and its human cargo comes into port in New Haven, the case becomes a political and legal football for slaveholders, abolitionists, diplomats, lawyers, and opportunists. Almost lost to sight in the turmoil are the 39 men and women who have risked everything to regain their freedom. Not until their case is argued by a former President before the United States Supreme Court do they have a chance for true justice. Their case is to serve as a catalyst that crystallizes feelings on both sides of the slavery issue, hastening the way to civil war. This book is based on the screenplay of the movie of the same name.

Other books you might like:
Russell Banks, *Cloudsplitter*, 1998
Lana M. Harrigan, *Acoma: A Novel of Conquest*, 1997
Donald McCaig, *Jacob's Ladder*, 1998
Jane Smiley, *The All-True Travels and Adventures of Lidie Newton*, 1998
Robert Vaughan, *Blood on the Plains*, 1997

585

RANDALL BETH PLATT

The Royalscope Fe-As-Ko

(North Haven, CT: Catbird Press, 1997)

Story type: Modern; Quest
Major character(s): Royal Leckner, Rancher; E.M. Leckner, Spouse, Suffragette; Elsie Leckner, Actress
Time period(s): 1910s (1915)
Locale(s): Walla Walla, Washington; Hollywood, California

Summary: Respectable rancher Royal Leckner is horrified to learn that his wife and daughter, after a shopping trip to San Francisco, have invested most of the family money in a motion picture company sold to them by a fast-talking promoter. While wife E. M. and daughter Elsie dream of stardom—and in Elsie's case, of her handsome co-star—Royal rushes to Hollywood to extract his womenfolk from a den of vipers. On arrival, though, his rugged good looks and his ranch clothing lead to his being mistaken for screen star William S, Hart. Royal hangs onto his new identity while he looks for a way to lure Elsie and E.M. home and salvage the family fortune.

Where it's reviewed:
Publishers Weekly, April 28, 1997, page 50

Other books by the same author:
The Four Arrows Fe-As-Ko, 1991

Other books you might like:
Judy Alter, *Cherokee Rose*, 1996
John Byrne Cooke, *South of the Border*, 1989
Loren D. Estleman, *Billy Gashade*, 1997
Susan Harmon, *Spirit of a Bear*, 1994
Preston Lewis, *The Redemption of Jesse James*, 1995

586

JEFFREY POSTON

The Peacekeeper

(New York: Walker, 1997)

Story type: Traditional; Man Alone
Major character(s): Jay Peares, Wanderer, Lawman (peace-keeper); Marabelle Hopkins, Farmer, Settler; Pritchett, Rancher
Time period(s): 19th century (post Civil War)
Locale(s): Bronco, Texas

Summary: The product of a mixed marriage between black and Anglo, Jay Peares has found few friends on the frontier. He's been cleared of a murder charge, but still must watch his back for lawmen or bounty hunters who haven't gotten the word. Understandably, trust isn't his long suit. His caution serves him well when he meets the first-nameless Pritchett in Bronco, Texas. Pritchett, town boss and landowner, hires Jay as peacekeeper—nominally a kind of lawman. But it isn't long before Jay realizes Pritchett wants more than that. Pritchett is trying to drive the small farmers and settlers off their land, and Jay has unwittingly picked the wrong side in a range war about to turn deadly.

Where it's reviewed:
Booklist, August 1997, page 1880
Publishers Weekly, June 30, 1997, page 69

Other books you might like:
Bill Brooks, *Dust on the Wind*, 1997
Wayne Davis, *Silverthorne*, 1997
Ray Hogan, *The Whipsaw Trail*, 1997
Hiram King, *High Prairie*, 1997
J.J.R. Ramey, *West of Paradise Run*, 1989

587

CHARLOTTE PRENTISS (Pseudonym of Charles Platt)

The Island Tribe

(New York: Harper, 1997)

Story type: Historical; Indian Culture
Major character(s): Kori, Young Woman; Rohonar, Chieftain; Uroh, Hunter
Time period(s): Indeterminate Past
Locale(s): Pacific Coast

Summary: The world is a menacing place to the hunter-gatherers of the Island Tribe. The Old Ones who make the ground shake may mete out punishments without logical reason or boundary. The whitebeasts rule the forest of the Western Shore. Kori, daughter of the chieftain has her doubts about the justice of all this, but she learns firsthand how dangerous it is to voice such doubts. When an expedition under her direction comes to grief, she is expelled from the tribe. On her own, she begins to learn some of the secrets that control her destiny— one of which threatens the very existence of the tribe that cast her out.

Other books by the same author:
People of the Mesa, 1995

Other books you might like:
Margaret Allan, *The Last Mammoth*, 1995
Joseph Bruchac, *Dawn Land*, 1993
Amanda Cockrell, *The Long Walk*, 1996
    Deer Dancers #3
Kathleen O'Neal Gear, *People of the Lightning*, 1995
    W. Michael Gear, co-author
Ardath Mayhar, *Island in the Lake*, 1993

588

GLORIA RAND
TED RAND, Illustrator

Baby in a Basket

(New York: Dutton, 1997)

Story type: Young Readers; Modern
Time period(s): 1910s (1917)
Locale(s): Alaska

Summary: A two week journey through Alaska's frozen night forms the background of this exciting tale for readers under 10. A mother and her two children, one a baby carried in a basket, set out with other passengers in a horse-drawn sleigh for a trip across the mountains. They meet with the hardships and dangers of winter, but real trouble starts when the sleigh spills from a narrow bridge, dropping its passengers into the river. When they struggle out of the water and find their way to safety, the baby is missing. But fur trappers bring about a happy ending in this story based on a true incident.

Other books you might like:
Will Hobbs, *Far North*, 1996
    Spur Award winner
Paul Owen Lewis, *Storm Boy*, 1995
Jay Neugenboren, *Poli*, 1989
Dyan Sheldon, *Under the Moon*, 1994
G. Clifton Wisler, *Jericho's Journey*, 1993

589

J.L. REASONER (Pseudonym of James Reasoner and Livia Reasoner)

Cossack Three Ponies

(New York: Berkley, 1997)

Story type: Traditional; Indian Wars
Major character(s): Viktor Dorochenko, Mercenary; Wolverine, Indian (Blackfoot), Chieftain; Alena, Royalty (princess)
Time period(s): 19th century
Locale(s): Montana; Rocky Mountains

Summary: Cossack Viktor Dorochenko is guard, guide, and servant for a band of Russian nobles hunting big game in the Montana wilderness. He watches the beautiful Princess Alena from afar, but the difference in their stations prevents any personal relationship. His role changes suddenly when one of the party kills a Blackfoot hunter. Bent on revenge, Chief Wolverine leads an attack on the Russians. Dorochenko and Princess Alena fall into the hands of the Blackfoot band, and Dorochenko is offered a choice. He can help rescue Wolver-

ine's grandson from Crow captivity, thereby saving his and Alena's lives. But failure means a terrible death.

Where it's reviewed:
Roundup Magazine, June 1997, page 34

Other books by the same author:
The Healer's Road, 1995

Other books you might like:
Matt Braun, *Bloody Hand*, 1975
John Legg, *Blackfoot Dawn*, 1993
Geo. W. Proctor, *Walks without a Soul*, 1990
Mary Ramstetter, *Over the Mountains of the Moon*, 1996
Barbara Riefe, *Mohawk Woman*, 1996

590

J.L. REASONER (Pseudonym of James Reasoner and Livia Reasoner)

The Healer's Road

(New York: Jove, 1995)

Story type: Historical/American Civil War; Saga
Major character(s): Thomas Black, Doctor; John Black, Military Personnel (Union); Sara Black, Doctor
Time period(s): 19th century (1826-1865)
Locale(s): Washington, District of Columbia; Handley's Mill, Massachusetts; Chattanooga, Tennessee

Summary: Driven by memories of the death of his parents when he was a child, Thomas Black finds a way into medical school and eventually becomes a successful doctor. His children, Sara and John, turn out differently than he'd hoped. It's Sara who wants to be a doctor, a thing unheard of in her day, while John wants a military career. When the Blacks, along with the rest of the nation, are dragged into the bloodbath of the Civil War, each must decide how best to follow those dreams.

Other books by the same author:
Cossack Three Ponies, 1997

Other books you might like:
Frederic Bean, *Lorena*, 1996
Harold Coyle, *Until the End*, 1996
Will Henry, *Journey to Shiloh*, 1997
Madison Jones, *Nashville 1864*, 1997
David William Ross, *Savage Plains*, 1996

591

JAMES REASONER

The Hunted

(New York: Harper, 1997)

Story type: Traditional; Chase
Major character(s): Evan Littleton, Veteran (Confederate); Harry Stubbs, Outlaw; Abner Crane, Farmer
Time period(s): 1860s (1865)
Locale(s): Richland Springs, Texas; Davis Mountains, Texas; Brady, Texas

Summary: Coming home to Texas from a Union prison camp after the Civil War, Evan Littleton finds everything changed.

His wife is dead of fever, his children scattered, his farm in the hands of Yankees whom he considers carpetbaggers. Littleton makes a promise to his dead wife that he will recover their lost children. But when he sets out on his quest, he finds trouble. Pursued by both outlaws and state police, Littleton has to keep his mind on his promise and fight back his urge for vengeance while he learns a few things about Yankees and Texans.

Other books by the same author:
Dark Trail, 1996 (Wind River #5)
Judgment Day, 1996 (Wind River #6)
The Wilderness Road, 1996
Rivers of Gold, 1995
Stark's Justice, 1994

Other books you might like:
Tracy Dunham, *The Long Trail Home*, 1997
Will Henry, *Journey to Shiloh*, 1997
Hiram King, *High Prairie*, 1997
Louis Kraft, *The Final Showdown*, 1992
Al Lacy, *Joy from Ashes*, 1995
    Battles of Destiny #4

592

ELLEN RECKNOR

Leaving Missouri

(New York: Berkley, 1997)

Story type: Traditional; Quest
Major character(s): Clutie Mae Chestnut, Runaway, Teenager; Frank James, Outlaw; Prometheus Burke-Jones, Nobleman
Time period(s): 19th century (post Civil War)
Locale(s): Kansas City, Missouri; Goose Butte, Colorado

Summary: A shockingly normal offshoot of the inbred Jukes family, whose men boast orange hair and names like Gnat and Beetle, Clutie Mae Chestnut rebels against the family's plans for her. Specifically, she rebels against marriage to Cousin Spider. With Chigger John, another and more sympathetic cousin, Clutie Mae runs away. She's headed for California until she crosses paths with drunken Britisher Prometheus Burke-Jones. The unlikely trio ends up in Goose Butte, in conflict with the forces of law and order, public morals, and just about everything else, until Clutie Mae provides a surprisingly happy ending.

Other books by the same author:
Me and the Boys, 1995

Other books you might like:
Andrew J. Fenady, *Runaways*, 1994
Dean Gabbert, *The Log of the Jesse Bill*, 1994
Randall Beth Platt, *The Royalscope Fe-As-Ko*, 1997
Gene Shelton, *How the West Was Lost*, 1997
Cruce Stark, *Chasing Uncle Charley*, 1992

593

JAMES RICE

Trail Drive
(New York: Pelican, 1996)

Story type: Young Readers; Trail Drive
Time period(s): 19th century
Locale(s): Texas; Kansas

Summary: This picture book for children 3-8 carries the child along on a cattle drive, explaining the how and why of the drive while providing a simple but exciting story.

Where it's reviewed:
Horn Book Guide, Spring 1997, page 44
Roundup Magazine, April 1997, page 29

Other books you might like:
Jan Brett, *Armadillo Rodeo*, 1995
Ken Buchanan, *This House Is Made of Mud*, 1991
Patricia MacLachlan, *Three Names*, 1991
Ann Herbert Scott, *Cowboy Country*, 1993
David Williams, *Grandma Essie's Covered Wagon*, 1993

594

BARBARA RIEFE

Desperate Crossing: The Jenny Sanders Pryor Story
(New York: Forge, 1997)

Story type: Historical; Indian Wars
Major character(s): Jenny Sanders Pryor, Frontierswoman, Captive; John Pryor, Settler, Spouse; Ottawa, Indian (Sioux), Chieftain
Time period(s): 1860s
Locale(s): Black Hills, South Dakota; Portland, Oregon

Summary: On her way west to a new start in Oregon, Jenny Pryor is captured along with others from her wagon train during a Sioux attack. Pryor alone survives the trip to the Black Hills with her captors, where she becomes a wife of their chief. Traded to the Blackfoot tribe, she survives, waiting for rescue. Jenny's husband, John Pryor, manages to put together a rescue effort, and with the help of a friendly indian, attempts to achieve Jenny's release and a happily-ever-after reunion. As is the case with most of Riefe's books, this one is based on a true story gleaned from old documents and letters.

Other books by the same author:
Against All Odds, 1996
Mohawk Woman, 1996
For Love of Two Eagles, 1995
The Woman Who Fell From the Sky, 1995

Other books you might like:
Sandra Dallas, *The Diary of Mattie Spenser*, 1997
Frances Hurst, *High Mountain Winter*, 1996
Gary McCarthy, *The Humboldt River*, 1996
  Rivers West #17
Noelle Sickels, *Walking West*, 1995
Stephanie Grace Whitson, *Walks the Fire*, 1995
  Prairie Winds #1

595

JAMES A. RITCHIE

The Wagon Wars
(New York: Walker, 1997)

Story type: Traditional; Indian Wars
Major character(s): Ben Hawkins, Businessman (freight line operator), Cowboy; P.G. Murphy, Businessman (freight line owner)
Time period(s): 19th century (post Civil War)
Locale(s): Globe, Arizona

Summary: Taking the long way around to become horse ranchers, cowhand Ben Hawkins and his two sidekicks go into business in Globe, Arizona. Their first venture gets them an interest in a blacksmith shop, and that leads more or less naturally to their setting up to haul freight by wagon. Trouble is, Globe already has a freight-hauler in the person of hardbitten P.G. Murphy, and Murphy doesn't welcome the competition. Murphy's hired gunslingers are trouble enough, but both Murphy and Hawkins face even bigger problems. The Apaches are up in arms, and they don't care if their prey works for Hawkins or Murphy.

Where it's reviewed:
Booklist, May 1, 1997, page 1480
Publishers Weekly, March 24, 1997, page 61

Other books by the same author:
The Last Free Range, 1995
Kerrigan, 1993
The Payback, 1992
Over on the Lonesome Side, 1991

Other books you might like:
Erle Adkins, *Two Guns from Texas*, 1990
Wayne Barton, *Warhorse*, 1988
  Stan Williams, co-author
Ralph Compton, *The Winchester Run*, 1997
Andrew Glass, *The Sweetwater Run*, 1996
Robert Kammen, *Montana Rimfire*, 1991

596

DAVID ROBBINS

Diablo
(New York: Leisure, 1997)

Story type: Traditional; Man Alone
Major character(s): Lee Scurlock, Wanderer, Gunfighter; Allison Hayes, Frontierswoman; Allister Kemp, Landowner, Rancher
Time period(s): 1880s
Locale(s): Diablo, Arizona; Bar K, Arizona

Summary: Lee Scurlock, leaving behind bad memories of the Lincoln County War, isn't looking for anything except a little peace and quiet. He finds that Diablo is the wrong place to get it. The boomtown is set up for confrontation, with the citizens on one side and British investor Allister Kemp on the other. Kemp, owner of the Bar K ranch, wants control of the area and its water, and he's hired a tough foreman and a staff of gunmen to see that he gets it. Lee Scurlock's best move would

be to ride right on through, but beautiful Allison Hayes gives him a reason to stay, gunmen or not.

Other books by the same author:
The Return of the Virginian, 1994

Other books you might like:
John D. Armstrong, *The Return of Jericho Pike*, 1992
G.G. Boyer, *Winchester Affidavit*, 1997
Jack Curtis, *No Mercy*, 1995
John S. McCord, *Nevada Tough*, 1996
John D. Nesbitt, *Twin Rivers*, 1995

597

DAVID ROBERTSON

Booth

(New York: Doubleday, 1998)

Story type: Historical; Historical/American Civil War
Major character(s): John Wilkes Booth, Actor, Criminal (assassin); John Surratt, Criminal (conspirator); Abraham Lincoln, Government Official
Time period(s): 1860s (1865)
Locale(s): Washington, District of Columbia; Baltimore, Maryland

Summary: John Surratt, one of the surviving plotters in the conspiracy that killed Lincoln, relates the gradual steps that led him and his family into the plot. First befriended by Booth, then convinced that the actor means only to kidnap the President and force an end to the war, Surratt goes by inches past the point of no return. When the plot explodes into murder, aimed not only at Lincoln but at the Vice-president and Secretary of State as well, the Surratts are trapped with the others in a disaster for their family and for the nation.

Other books you might like:
Russell Banks, *Cloudsplitter*, 1998
Harold Coyle, *Until the End*, 1996
Tom Dyja, *Play for a Kingdom*, 1997
Douglas Hirt, *Assassination*, 1995
    Riverboat #4
T.V. Olsen, *There Was a Season*, 1997

598

LUCIA ST. CLAIR ROBSON

Mary's Land

(New York: Ballantine, 1995)

Story type: Historical; Saga
Major character(s): Margaret Brent, Gentlewoman; Anicah Sparrow, Servant; Martin Skinner, Sailor
Time period(s): 17th century (1638-1650)
Locale(s): *Charity*, At Sea (ship); Kent Fort Manor, Maryland

Summary: People came to the New World for many reasons. Margaret Brent, a gentlewoman and an English Catholic, invested in Lord Baltimore's colony to find a home of her own. Anicah Sparrow had no choice. An orphaned teenager living by her wits in London, she's scooped up and transported to the colonies as an indentured servant. Among the fears and hardships of the new land, the two dissimilar women

forge a bond of trust and understanding that leads to the new life that both long for.

Other books by the same author:
Walk in My Soul, 1985

Other books you might like:
Paul Clayton, *Calling Crow's Nation*, 1997
Harold Coyle, *Savage Wilderness*, 1997
Charles Durham, *The Last Exile*, 1990
Barbara Riefe, *The Woman Who Fell from the Sky*, 1995
Marly Youmans, *Catherwood*, 1996

599

FRANK RODERUS

The Purgatory River

(New York: Bantam, 1997)

Story type: Saga; Series
Series: Rivers West
Major character(s): Hernan Eduardo Salazar-Montoya, Traveller; Elena Salazar-Montoya, Young Woman; Devon Jenks, Trapper, Mountain Man
Time period(s): 19th century (pre Civil War)
Locale(s): Santa Fe, New Mexico; Purgatory River, Colorado

Summary: From different directions and different backgrounds, settlers and wanderers come to the banks of the Purgatory. There's Hernan Salazar-Montoya and his disgraced sister Elena, looking for a new life; the womanizing Aaron, looking for a way out of past escapades; Devon Jenks, the lost hunter and trapper; and Talks to Ghosts, in search of a vision that will show him the truth about his people. Their stories intertwine in the rugged land of the Purgatory in ways none of them could have imagined.

Other books by the same author:
Potter's Fields, 1996 (Spur Award winner)
J. A. Whitford and the Great California Gold Hunt, 1990
Billy Ray's Forty Days, 1989
Charlie and the Sir, 1988

Other books you might like:
Frederic Bean, *The Pecos River*, 1995
    Rivers West #13
Win Blevins, *The High Missouri*, 1994
    Rivers West #11
Don Coldsmith, *The Smoky Hill*, 1989
    Rivers West #2
Gary McCarthy, *The Humboldt River*, 1996
    Rivers West #15
Jory Sherman, *The Columbia River*, 1995
    Rivers West #14

600

FRANK RODERUS

Stillwater Smith

(New York: Leisure, 1997)

Story type: Traditional; Ranch Life
Major character(s): Stillwater Smith, Rancher, Veteran (Union); Asa Wheeler, Rancher; Tuck Friar, Foreman

Time period(s): 19th century (post Civil War)
Locale(s): West

Summary: The man who calls himself Stillwater Smith only wants to be left alone. Long ago, something happened that made him vow never to raise his gun or his hand in anger again. Even when rancher Asa Wheeler begins pressuring Smith about his water rights, Smith holds his studied calm. But then Wheeler's hired hands turn to other means to drive him out, and a man can take just so much.

Other books by the same author:
Potter's Fields, 1996 (Spur Award winner)
J. A. Whitford and the Great California Gold Hunt, 1990
Billy Ray's Forty Days, 1989
Charlie and the Sir, 1988

Other books you might like:
Stephen Bly, *My Foot's in the Stirrup...My Pony Won't Stand*, 1996
    Code of the West #5
Lee Cooley, *Judgment at Red Creek*, 1992
Dan Halacy, *Empire in the Dust*, 1990
Gary D. Svee, *Single Tree*, 1994
Chelsea Quinn Yarbro, *Charity, Colorado*, 1994

601

DAVID WILLIAM ROSS

Savage Plains

(New York: Avon, 1996)

Story type: Historical; Historical/American Civil War
Major character(s): Cole Sadler, Farmer, Gunfighter; Dennis Sadler, Farmer; Henry Quarles, Military Personnel
Time period(s): 1860s
Locale(s): Fort Leavenworth, Kansas; Santa Fe, New Mexico

Summary: The Army is stretched thin in the Kansas-Missouri border country. On the one side, the soldiers are caught in conflict between abolitionist Kansans and the pro-slavery border ruffians, while to the west, the Comanche and Kiowa still raid outlying farms and settlements. Brothers Cole and Dennis Sadler, in danger after their party leading escaped slaves to freedom is ambushed, turn to the west. Dennis, taking as a wife the beautiful ex-slave Chloe, journeys to Santa Fe, while Cole remains behind to meet whatever fate has to offer in Bleeding Kansas.

Other books by the same author:
Eyes of the Hawk, 1992
Beyond the Stars, 1990

Other books you might like:
Frederic Bean, *Lorena*, 1996
Mike Blakely, *Shortgrass Song*, 1994
Clancy Carlile, *Children of the Dust*, 1995
Randal L. Greenwood, *Kansas, Bloody Kansas*, 1996
Kerry Newcomb, *Ride the Panther*, 1992

602

ROSALYN SCHANZER

How We Crossed the West

(New York: National Geographic, 1997)

Story type: Historical; Young Readers
Major character(s): Sacagawea, Guide, Indian (Shoshone); William Clark, Frontiersman, Explorer; Meriwether Lewis, Frontiersman, Explorer
Time period(s): 1800s (1803-1805)
Locale(s): Wyoming; Pacific Northwest

Summary: Heavy on pictures, this book covers the journey of the Lewis and Clark Expedition across the unknown vastness of the Louisiana Purchase to the shores of the Pacific Ocean. Led and helped by their guide Sacagawea, the explorers faced a hostile environment, from the annoying plague of fleas to the life-threatening attack of a maddened grizzly bear. They met and befriended many Indian tribes, some of whom were at first inclined to be hostile. In all their journeying, though, the greatest hardships lay in hunger and thirst and in the day-to-day chore of moving along on a trip that seemed endless.

Where it's reviewed:
Children's Book Review Service, August 1997, page 168

Other books you might like:
Albert R. Booky, *The Buckskins*, 1990
Laurie Lawlor, *Gold in the Hills*, 1995
Gary Paulsen, *Mr. Tucket*, 1994
Judith St. George, *Sacagawea*, 1997
Jean Van Leeuwen, *Bound for Oregon*, 1994

603

GENE SHELTON

How the West Was Lost

(New York: Berkley, 1997)

Story type: Traditional
Major character(s): Dobie Garrett, Outlaw, Lawman; Buck Hawkins, Outlaw, Lawman; Archie Westcott, Journalist
Time period(s): 19th century (post Civil War)
Locale(s): Singletree Ranch, Texas; Necesario, Texas

Summary: Cowboys Buck Hawkins and Dobie Garrett turn outlaw, only to discover that they were much better at cowboying. Their encounter with bank robbing leaves them with a pile of money, all counterfeit. Their attempt at train robbing gives them lots of exercise and no train. And the only thing they get from tangling with the Barker Gang is a greatly exaggerated reputation as fast guns. That reputation lands them in Necesario as lawmen, a task they soon find to be even less attractive than their other adventures.

Where it's reviewed:
Roundup Magazine, June 1997, page 34

Other books by the same author:
Devil's Deathbed, 1995
Hangtree Pass, 1994
Skull Creek, 1994
Brazos Dreamer, 1993

Rawhider: The Story of Print Olive, 1992

Other books you might like:
Wayne Barton, *Lockhart's Nightmare*, 1998
 Stan Williams, co-author
Preston Lewis, *Mix-Up at the O.K. Corral*, 1996
Lyn Nofziger, *Tackett and the Teacher*, 1994
Dan Parkinson, *Dust on the Wind*, 1992
Johnny Quarles, *Fool's Gold*, 1993

604

JORY SHERMAN

The Barons of Texas

(New York: Forge, 1997)

Story type: Historical; Saga
Major character(s): Martin Baron, Rancher; Juanito Salazar, Rancher; Jack Killian, Outlaw
Time period(s): 1840s
Locale(s): San Antonio, Texas

Summary: Like many another newcomer, Martin Baron makes his way by sea to the newborn Republic of Texas to find land and wealth. With the help of new friend Juanito Salazar, Baron survives the hostile country and fights off attacks from Indians, working his way slowly into the beginnings of a ranching empire. Then all his preparations are threatened by Jack Killian, an outlaw bent on avenging his brother's death. To hold onto his dream, and his new love in Texas, Baron must be ready to risk everything.

Where it's reviewed:
Kirkus Reviews, September 1, 1997, page 1339

Other books by the same author:
The Columbia River, 1995 (Rivers West #14)
Trapper's Moon, 1994
Grass Kingdom, 1993
Eagles of Destiny, 1990

Other books you might like:
James Carlos Blake, *In the Rogue Blood*, 1997
Albert R. Booky, *Hacienda*, 1997
Benjamin Capps, *Sam Chance*, 1965
Elmer Kelton, *The Pumpkin Rollers*, 1996
Leonard Sanders, *Star of Empire*, 1992

605

COTTON SMITH

Dark Trail to Dodge

(New York: Walker, 1997)

Story type: Traditional; Trail Drive
Major character(s): Tyrel Bannon, Cowboy; John Checker, Lawman (Texas Ranger (retired)), Rancher
Time period(s): 19th century (post Civil War)
Locale(s): Staked Plains, Texas; Indian Territory; Dodge City, Kansas

Summary: For young Tyrel Bannon, a trail drive is a new experience, with everything fresh and filled with romance. Veteran plainsman John Checker is another matter entirely.

For him, the romance has long since worn off, and the drive means trouble, danger, and for some, death. From their different viewpoints, the pair face the dangers and hardships of the trail—bad weather, bad men, stampedes and floods. By the time they near their goal, each has learned something from the other.

Where it's reviewed:
Booklist, June 1, 1997, page 1664
Publishers Weekly, May 19, 1997, page 69
Roundup Magazine, June 1997, page 35

Other books you might like:
Frederic Bean, *Trail's End*, 1994
Ralph Compton, *The Dodge City Trail*, 1995
 Trail Drive #8
Elmer Kelton, *The Far Canyon*, 1994
Jack Stanford, *Jayhawker Crossing*, 1994
J.D. Winter, *The First Trail Drive*, 1994

606

LAURAINE SNELLING

A Land to Call Home

(Minneapolis: Bethany House, 1997)

Story type: Historical; Series
Series: Red River of the North
Major character(s): Kaaren Knutson, Settler, Spouse; Ingeborg Bjorklund, Settler, Spouse; Haakan Bjorklund, Settler, Farmer
Time period(s): 1880s
Locale(s): Fargo, North Dakota

Summary: As continued settlement begins to close the frontier in the North Dakota farming country, the Norwegian Bjorklund family works to adjust to their adoptive homeland. Solveig, barely arrived from the old country, is injured in a train wreck, while cousin Kaaren Knutson finds that one of her newborn twin daughters is deaf. Trusting in hard work and in their faith, the family pushes ahead toward a better life in the new world.

Where it's reviewed:
Library Journal, June 1, 1997, page 89

Other books by the same author:
An Untamed Land, 1996 (Red River of the North #1)
A New Day Rising, 1996 (Red River of the North #2)

Other books you might like:
Tom Eidson, *All God's Children*, 1997
Mary McReynolds, *Wells of Glory*, 1996
Catherine Palmer, *Prairie Rose*, 1997
 Town Called Hope #1
Lori Wick, *Promise Me Tomorrow*, 1997
 Rocky Mountain Memories #4
Jeanne Williams, *Wind Water*, 1997

607

MICHELE SORENSEN

Broken Lance

(Salt Lake City: Deseret, 1997)

Story type: Historical; Indian Wars
Major character(s): Callie McCraken, Settler, Widow(er);
Silas McCraken, Settler; Three Elk, Indian (Cheyenne),
Warrior
Time period(s): 1850s (1857)
Locale(s): Mormon Trail, West

Summary: Newly converted to the Mormon faith, Angus and
Callie McCraken bring their three children to the United
States and then start on the trail to Utah. At first, the journey
goes well for them. Their faith and anticipation help them
overcome the hardships and dangers of the Mormon Trail.
Then tragedy strikes when Angus is killed in an attack by a
Cheyenne war party. Callie, alone with the children, can only
struggle onward and pray for help. Instead of the rescue she
hoped for, she stumbles across a wounded Indian named
Three Elk, one of the hated Cheyenne. If Callie can save him,
he might prove their one hope for survival. But Callie hesi-
tates to take the risk of helping an enemy who might turn on
her.

Where it's reviewed:
Library Journal, September 1, 1997, page 168

Other books you might like:
Barry Brierley, *White Horse, Red Rider*, 1996
Kay L. McDonald, *Vision of the Eagle*, 1977
Barbara Riefe, *Desperate Crossing: The Jenny Sanders Pryor
Story*, 1997
Noelle Sickels, *Walking West*, 1995
Stephanie Grace Whitson, *Walks the Fire*, 1995
Prairie Winds #1

608

JUDITH ST. GEORGE

Sacagawea

(New York: Putnam, 1997)

Story type: Historical; Young Readers
Major character(s): Sacagawea, Guide, Indian (Shoshone);
Toussaint Charbonneau, Guide; Meriwether Lewis, Fron-
tiersman, Explorer
Time period(s): 1800s (1803-1805)
Locale(s): Wyoming; Pacific Northwest

Summary: The story of Sacagawea, guide and interpreter for
the Lewis and Clark Expedition, starts with her childhood.
Stolen from her Shoshone tribe as a child, she is reared
Minnetarees, then given in marriage to French trader
Toussaint Charbonneau. When Charbonneau is hired to guide
the American explorers, it is really Sacagawea who proves
helpful instead of her drunken, bumbling husband. With dignity and intelligence, she greets new and potentially hostile
Indian tribes, shows the explorers edible plants, and tries to
keep them from annoying grizzly bears. Sharing the adventures of the party on their long and hazardous trek, she adds

one unique to her: Halfway through the trip, she gives birth to
a son.

Where it's reviewed:
Booklist, August 1997, page 1896
Kirkus Reviews, June 15, 1997, page 956
Publishers Weekly, June 30, 1997, page 77

Other books by the same author:
The Halo Wind, 1978

Other books you might like:
Robert Barlow Fox, *To Be a Warrior*, 1997
Sonia Levitin, *The No-Return Trail*, 1978
Spur Award winner
Scott O'Dell, *Thunder Rolling in the Mountains*, 1992
Elizabeth Hall, co-author
Rosalyn Schanzer, *How We Crossed the West*, 1997
Nancy Van Laan, *Buffalo Dance: A Blackfoot Legend*, 1993

609

KATHERINE SUTCLIFFE

Jezebel

(New York: Jove, 1997)

Story type: Traditional; Revenge
Major character(s): Rafael de Bastitas, Gunfighter, Avenger;
Charity Bell, Widow(er)
Time period(s): 1870s
Locale(s): Hell, Texas

Summary: In order to avenge the murders of his family, Rafael
de Bastitas learns to use a gun Western-style and heads for the
aptly-named Texas town of Hell. He expects to find the
murderers there, but an unexpected thing happens along the
way. Sheltering from a storm in an apparently abandoned
cabin, he finds Charity Bell in desperate straits. The widow of
a minister, Charity is alone and in the process of having a
baby. De Bastitas has no choice to help out, a task that
occupies quite a while as he nurses Charity and the new baby
along toward health. He hasn't forgotten his purpose, though.
He gets his vengeance quest back on track, preparing to take
on the boss of Hell and his minions, but the project looks a lot
different now that Charity is involved.

Other books you might like:
P.A. Bechko, *The Eye of the Hawk*, 1998
Patricia Gaffney, *Outlaw in Paradise*, 1997
Suzann Ledbetter, *Pure Justice*, 1997
Robert Vaughan, *Range Wars*, 1997
Penelope Williamson, *The Outsider*, 1996

610

JAMES ALEXANDER THOM

The Red Heart

(New York: Ballantine, 1997)

Story type: Historical; Indian Culture
Major character(s): Frances Slocum, Captive, Shaman;
Tecumseh, Indian (Shawnee), Historical Figure
Time period(s): 18th century; 19th century (1770s-1810s)

Locale(s): Susquehanna Valley, Pennsylvania; Ohio River Valley, Ohio

Summary: Abducted as a child by the Delawares, then adopted by a Miami Indian woman, Frances Slocum grows up as Little Bear Woman of the Miamis. She is the child of Quakers, who see the Light of God in Indians as well as in their own race, so she is all the quicker to adjust into her new surroundings. As she grows to maturity, she earns a place of respect in Miami councils, raises her own family, deals with sickness and loss. But the world is changing around her. With the death of Tecumseh, the Indians are forced farther west, their old ways destroyed. When Little Bear Woman finally meets her original family again, she faces a test, the test of whether she truly has a red heart.

Other books by the same author:
The Children of First Man, 1994
Long Knife, 1994
Panther in the Sky, 1989 (Spur Award winner)
Follow the River, 1981

Other books you might like:
Douglas C. Jones, *This Savage Race*, 1993
Barbara Riefe, *The Woman Who Fell from the Sky*, 1995
Mike Roarke, *Shadows on the Longhouse*, 1994
    First Frontier #3
Jim R. Woolard, *Thunder in the Valley*, 1995
    Spur Award winner
Marly Youmans, *Catherwood*, 1996

611

DAVID THOMPSON

Blood Hunt

(New York: Leisure, 1997)

Story type: Traditional; Series
Series: Davy Crockett
Major character(s): Davy Crockett, Frontiersman; Flavius, Frontiersman, Sidekick
Time period(s): 1800s
Locale(s): Tennessee

Summary: Out to rescue a group of kidnapped women, Davy Crockett finds himself in the midst of a scrimmage between two warring Indian tribes and an equally dangerous gang of white renegades. With only one companion and his own wits and courage to depend on, Crockett is outnumbered but not dismayed.

Other books by the same author:
Sioux Slaughter, 1997 (Davy Crockett #4)
Mississippi Mayhem, 1997 (Davy Crockett #2)
Homecoming, 1997 (Davy Crockett #3)

Other books you might like:
P.A. Bechko, *The Tin-Pan Man*, 1997
Harold Coyle, *Savage Wilderness*, 1996
Cameron Judd, *Crockett of Tennessee*, 1994
Barbara Riefe, *Desperate Crossing: The Jenny Sanders Pryor Story*, 1997
Robert Vaughan, *Texas Glory*, 1997

612

DAVID THOMPSON

Homecoming

(New York: Leisure, 1997)

Story type: Traditional; Series
Series: Davy Crockett
Major character(s): Davy Crockett, Frontiersman; Flavius, Frontiersman, Sidekick
Time period(s): 1800s
Locale(s): Lake Superior

Summary: Travelling in the region of the Great Lakes, Davy Crockett and friend Flavius rescue a Chippewa maiden from capture by a war party from a hostile tribe. As they try to bring her back to her own people, they must fight against her enemies to save her life and their own.

Other books by the same author:
Sioux Slaughter, 1997 (Davy Crockett #4)
Mississippi Mayhem, 1997 (Davy Crockett #2)
Blood Hunt, 1997 (Davy Crockett #1)

Other books you might like:
W. Michael Gear, *Coyote Summer*, 1997
Douglas Hirt, *McKendree*, 1997
John Legg, *Mountain Captive*, 1996
John S. McCord, *Blind Eagles*, 1997
J.L. Reasoner, *Cossack Three Ponies*, 1997

613

DAVID THOMPSON

Mississippi Mayhem

(New York: Leisure, 1997)

Story type: Traditional; Series
Series: Davy Crockett
Major character(s): Davy Crockett, Frontiersman; Flavius, Frontiersman, Sidekick
Time period(s): 1800s
Locale(s): Mississippi River; Natchez, Mississippi

Summary: A canoe trip down the Mississippi predictably turns into trouble for Davy Crockett and sidekick Flavius. River pirates regard the two as fair game and a hostile Indian band wants to settle a long-running score by lifting Davy's hair. But the biggest problem is an old Indian myth that turns out not to be so mythical after all.

Other books by the same author:
Sioux Slaughter, 1997 (Davy Crockett #4)
Homecoming, 1997 (Davy Crockett #3)
Blood Hunt, 1997 (Davy Crockett #1)

Other books you might like:
Will Camp, *Blood of Texas*, 1996
    Spur Award winner
Dean Gabbert, *The Log of the Jesse Bill*, 1994
Douglas Hirt, *Assassination*, 1995
    Riverboat #4
Cameron Judd, *Passage to Natchez*, 1996
James Alexander Thom, *Follow the River*, 1981

614

DAVID THOMPSON

Sioux Slaughter

(New York: Leisure, 1997)

Story type: Traditional; Series
Series: Davy Crockett
Major character(s): Davy Crockett, Frontiersman; Flavius, Frontiersman, Sidekick
Time period(s): 1800s
Locale(s): Black Hills, South Dakota

Summary: The Great Plains mean great adventure and great danger for Davy Crockett and sidekick Flavius. The pair survive their first encounter with the plains buffalo herd, a thundering stampede. But the commotion alerts the Sioux, and they don't like intruders in their domain—not even the likes of Davy Crockett.

Other books by the same author:
Mississippi Mayhem, 1997 (Davy Crockett #2)
Homecoming, 1997 (Davy Crockett #3)
Blood Hunt, 1997 (Davy Crockett #1)

Other books you might like:
Paul A. Hawkins, *Crow Feather*, 1995
Will Henry, *The Bear Paw Horses*, 1996
Earl Murray, *The River at Sundown*, 1997
David William Ross, *Beyond the Stars*, 1990
G. Clifton Wisler, *Warrior's Road*, 1994

615

DAVID THOMPSON (Pseudonym of David Robbins)

Spanish Slaughter

(New York: Leisure, 1997)

Story type: Mountain Man; Series
Series: Wilderness Special Edition
Major character(s): Nathaniel King, Guide, Mountain Man; Winona King, Mountain Woman, Indian (Shoshone); Shakespeare McNair, Mountain Man, Sidekick

Summary: Led from Spain by a map that promises a fortune in lost gold, Don Manuel de Varga and his family seek out Nathaniel King to guide them to their goal. King at first refuses, for the site of the mine is deep in the country of the hostile Utes. Maddened by lust for gold, de Varga kidnaps King's wife and children, forcing the mountain man to act as guide. Unwillingly, King leads the party into danger, and can only watch as greed threatens to destroy them all.

Other books by the same author:
Frontier Strike, 1996 (Wilderness Special Edition)
Trail's End, 1996 (Wilderness #22)
The Trail West, 1996 (Wilderness Special Edition)
Black Powder, 1995 (Wilderness #21)

Other books you might like:
Mike Blakely, *Vendetta Gold*, 1990
St. George Cooke, *The Treasure of Rodolfo Fierro*, 1989
Stuart Dillon, *Spirit's Gold*, 1990
Richard S. Wheeler, *Sierra*, 1996

Michael Zimmer, *Fandango*, 1996

616

GREG TOBIN

Prairie

(New York: Ballantine, 1997)

Story type: Indian Culture; Saga
Major character(s): Black Robe, Religious; Black Snake, Indian (Crane), Warrior; Max Adolphus, Artist
Time period(s): 1720s (1725); 1810s (1807)
Locale(s): Platte River, Nebraska; Fort Osage, Missouri

Summary: From earliest times, the Crane band lives on the Nebraska prairies near the Platte. They hold their own against their Red Horn enemies, later to be called the Pawnee. But finally white men come, the French at first, spreading death and disease among the Cranes until they are all but wiped out. When the Americans reach the prairies, the Crane descendants are few. But those few have a vision for their people's future that transcends their numbers.

Other books by the same author:
Big Horn, 1989
Kid Stark, 1987

Other books you might like:
Paul Clayton, *Flight of the Crow*, 1996
Don Coldsmith, *Bearer of the Pipe*, 1995
    Spanish Bit #24
Ken Englade, *Battle Cry*, 1997
    Tony Hillerman's Frontier #4
Kathleen O'Neal Gear, *People of the Silence*, 1997
    W. Michael Gear, co-author
Gary McCarthy, *Yosemite*, 1995

617

DODGE TYLER

Algonquin Massacre

(New York: Leisure, 1996)

Story type: Traditional; Series
Series: Dan'l Boone: The Lost Wilderness Tales
Major character(s): Dan'l Boone, Frontiersman; Adam Hollis, Reporter
Time period(s): 1770s
Locale(s): Boonesboro, Kentucky

Summary: As the American Revolution begins, a party of renegade British soldiers massacres a peaceful Algonquin village. The Algonquins appeal to Dan'l Boone for help, and Dan'l takes the trail beside an Algonquin warrior. The pair intend to bring the killers to swift justice, but their quest will be more complicated, and far more costly, than either realizes at the start.

Other books by the same author:
Apache Revenge, 1997 (The Lost Wilderness Tales #5)
A River Run Red, 1996 (The Lost Wilderness Tales #1)
Death at Spanish Wells, 1996 (The Lost Wilderness Tales #3)
Winter Kill, 1996 (The Lost Wilderness Tales #4)

Western

Other books you might like:
Don Coldsmith, *Runestone*, 1995
Robert J. Conley, *The Way South*, 1994
Douglas C. Jones, *Shadow of the Moon*, 1995
Mike Roarke, *Thunder in the East*, 1993
    First Frontier #1
James Alexander Thom, *Panther in the Sky*, 1989
    Spur Award winner

618

DODGE TYLER

Apache Revenge

(New York: Leisure, 1997)

Story type: Traditional; Series
Series: Dan'l Boone: The Lost Wilderness Tales
Major character(s): Dan'l Boone, Frontiersman; Adam Hollis, Reporter; One Eye, Indian (Apache), Renegade
Time period(s): 1800s
Locale(s): Santa Fe, New Mexico; Missouri

Summary: A small band of Apaches led by One Eye raid into Missouri, of all places. They're looking for revenge for a defeat three years back that led to the death of their chief, Yellow Horse. More specifically, they're looking for Dan'l Boone, Yellow Horse's killer. They find Boone and leave him for dead, carrying off his cousin Molly as spoils of war. But Dan'l isn't dead. As soon as he's on the mend, he sets out to rescue Molly. But by now she's become One Eye's woman, and it's not all that clear she wants to be rescued.

Other books by the same author:
Winter Kill, 1996 (The Lost Wilderness Tales #4)
A River Run Red, 1996 (The Lost Wilderness Tales #1)
Death at Spanish Wells, 1996 (The Lost Wilderness Tales #3)
Algonquin Massacre, 1996 (The Lost Wilderness Tales #2)

Other books you might like:
Frank Burleson, *Devil Dance*, 1997
    Apache Wars Saga #5
Cameron Judd, *Boone*, 1995
John Legg, *Mountain Captive*, 1996
Jason Manning, *The Border Captains*, 1995
    Flintlock #1
Earl Murray, *Free Flows the River*, 1991

619

DODGE TYLER

Death at Spanish Wells

(New York: Leisure, 1996)

Story type: Traditional; Series
Series: Dan'l Boone: The Lost Wilderness Tales
Major character(s): Dan'l Boone, Frontiersman; Adam Hollis, Reporter; Yellow Horse, Indian (Apache), Chieftain
Time period(s): 1800s
Locale(s): Santa Fe, New Mexico; Missouri

Summary: Guiding a wagon train of pioneers along the Santa Fe Trail, Dan'l Boone is opposed by Apache chief Yellow

Horse. Yellow Horse is determined to stop Anglo incursions onto Apache lands at all costs. He unleashes an all-out war on Boone's party, and the emigrants must fight for their lives.

Other books by the same author:
Apache Revenge, 1997 (The Lost Wilderness Tales #5)
A River Run Red, 1996 (The Lost Wilderness Tales #1)
Algonquin Massacre, 1996 (The Lost Wilderness Tales #2)
Winter Kill, 1996 (The Lost Wilderness Tales #4)

Other books you might like:
Frank Burleson, *White Apache*, 1996
    Apache Wars Saga #4
Ray Hogan, *Soldier in Buckskin*, 1996
James A. Janke, *McHenry's Last Shoot-Out*, 1992
John Legg, *War at Bent's Fort*, 1995
Jess McCreede, *Mountain Men on the Santa Fe Trail*, 1992

620

DODGE TYLER

The Long Hunters

(New York: Leisure, 1997)

Story type: Traditional; Series
Series: Dan'l Boone: The Lost Wilderness Tales
Major character(s): Dan'l Boone, Frontiersman; Webster Finley, Frontiersman; Dragging Canoe, Indian (Cherokee), Renegade
Time period(s): 1770s
Locale(s): Arkansas River, Arkansas; Fort Destiny, Arkansas

Summary: Trying to broaden the American presence in North America, Dan'l Boone and friend Webster Finley push by keelboat up the Arkansas River into territory that is nominally Spanish. Escaping from British rule, hardy settlers have already established a post at Fort Destiny. But other eyes are on Arkansas as well. With the backing of the British, Lansford Stratton has set up his Republic of Vandalia squarely on land the Fort Destiny pioneers claim. And Stratton is prepared to enforce his will with blood and terror if necessary.

Other books by the same author:
Winter Kill, 1996 (The Lost Wilderness Tales #4)
A River Run Red, 1996 (The Lost Wilderness Tales #1)
Death at Spanish Wells, 1996 (The Lost Wilderness Tales #3)
Algonquin Massacre, 1996 (The Lost Wilderness Tales #2)

Other books you might like:
Robert J. Conley, *Mountain Windsong*, 1992
Douglas C. Jones, *This Savage Race*, 1993
Cameron Judd, *The Overmountain Men*, 1991
Barbara Riefe, *For Love of Two Eagles*, 1995
Jory Sherman, *The Arkansas River*, 1991
    Rivers West #6

621

DODGE TYLER

A River Run Red

(New York: Leisure, 1996)

Story type: Traditional; Series

Series: Dan'l Boone: The Lost Wilderness Tales
Major character(s): Dan'l Boone, Frontiersman; Adam Hollis, Reporter
Time period(s): 1790s
Locale(s): Ohio Valley, Kentucky; Boonesboro, Kentucky

Summary: When the French lead a raid on the western settlements that results in the death of Dan'l Boone's cousin, Boone goes after those whom he holds responsible. Stalking his kinsman's killers through the wilderness, Boone is one man against an army. But with Boone's wilderness skills and his thirst for revenge, the odds may be on his side.

Other books by the same author:
Apache Revenge, 1997 (The Lost Wilderness Tales #5)
Death at Spanish Wells, 1996 (The Lost Wilderness Tales #3)
Algonquin Massacre, 1996 (The Lost Wilderness Tales #2)
Winter Kill, 1996 (The Lost Wilderness Tales #4)

Other books you might like:
Cameron Judd, *The Canebrake Men*, 1993
Barbara Riefe, *Mohawk Woman*, 1996
Mike Roarke, *Blood River*, 1995
    First Frontier #4
James Alexander Thom, *Long Knife*, 1994
Jim R. Woolard, *Thunder in the Valley*, 1995
    Spur Award winner

622

DODGE TYLER

Winter Kill

(New York: Leisure, 1996)

Story type: Traditional; Series
Series: Dan'l Boone: The Lost Wilderness Tales
Major character(s): Dan'l Boone, Frontiersman
Time period(s): 1800s
Locale(s): Black Hills, South Dakota

Summary: The lure of gold doesn't much affect Dan'l Boone, but many of his fellow settlers on the frontier are not so lucky. Against his will, Dan'l is drawn into a search for buried wealth on land claimed by the Sioux. Even in the dead of winter, the Sioux turn out in force to protect their holy places, and soon Boone and his companions are locked in a savage struggle to survive against hostile Indians and the even more hostile grip of winter on the plains.

Other books by the same author:
Death Trail, 1997 (The Lost Wilderness Tales #6)
Death at Spanish Wells, 1996 (The Lost Wilderness Tales #3)
Algonquin Massacre, 1996 (The Lost Wilderness Tales #2)
A River Run Red, 1996 (The Lost Wilderness Tales #1)

Other books you might like:
Lou Cameron, *Yellow Iron*, 1990
Loren D. Estleman, *Sudden Country*, 1991
Page Lambert, *Shifting Stars: A Novel of the West*, 1997
John Legg, *Fire along the Big Muddy*, 1995
Joseph Marshall III, *Winter of the Holy Iron*, 1994

623

ROBERT VAUGHAN

Andersonville

(New York: Boulevard, 1996)

Story type: Historical/American Civil War; Historical
Major character(s): Josiah Day, Military Personnel, Prisoner; Horace Trimble, Military Personnel, Prisoner; Henry Wirz, Military Personnel (Confederate)
Time period(s): 1860s (1864)
Locale(s): Andersonville, Georgia; Cold Harbor, Virginia

Summary: Captured after the disastrous battle of Cold Harbor, Union soldier Josiah Day goes to the grim Confederate prison camp of Andersonville. Under commander Henry Wirz, Andersonville is a more brutal and deadly place than it has to be, but conditions are made still worse by the group calling themselves the Raiders. Union renegades, the Raiders prey on those weaker and less organized than themselves, until the other prisoners revolt. Day and the others attempt to use legal methods and the cooperation of their captors to bring the Raiders to justice, but it's an open question whether legality will work against the brutal methods of the renegades.

Other books by the same author:
Blood on the Plains, 1997
Texas Glory, 1997
Yesterday's Reveille, 1996
Dawn of the Century, 1992

Other books you might like:
Frederic Bean, *Lorena*, 1996
John Byrne Cooke, *The Committee of Vigilance*, 1994
Tom Dyja, *Play for a Kingdom*, 1997
Cameron Judd, *The Phantom Legion*, 1997
J.L. Reasoner, *The Healer's Road*, 1995

624

ROBERT VAUGHAN

Blood on the Plains

(New York: St. Martin's Press, 1997)

Story type: Historical; Historical/American Civil War
Major character(s): Burke Phillips, Military Personnel; Dan Morris, Military Personnel
Time period(s): 1850s
Locale(s): Lawrence, Kansas; Missouri

Summary: With Bleeding Kansas torn between contending abolitionist and pro-slavery forces, President James Buchanan sends two young officers on a secret mission to end the violence. Southern-born Burke Phillips is to infiltrate the pro-slavery group, while New Englander Dan Morris gets inside the abolitionist ranks. Both are to report regularly on their findings while pretending to be strangers to one another. The pair is ill-chosen. Phillips is a strong proponent of slavery, while Morris is passionately, though peacefully, in favor of abolition. But they learn that on both sides, idealism is used as a cover for murder and plundering.

Where it's reviewed:
Roundup Magazine, April 1997, page 28

Western

Other books by the same author:
Yesterday's Reveille, 1996
Dawn of the Century, 1992

Other books you might like:
Frederic Bean, *Lorena*, 1996
Harold Coyle, *Until the End*, 1996
Randal L. Greenwood, *Burn, Missouri, Burn*, 1995
William A. Luckey, *Flags over Texas*, 1991
David William Ross, *Savage Plains*, 1996

625

ROBERT VAUGHAN

Range Wars

(New York: St. Martin's Press, 1997)

Story type: Traditional; Ranch Life
Major character(s): Jake Colby, Cowboy, Rancher; Tom Horn, Scout, Bounty Hunter; Laura Place, Prostitute, Spouse
Time period(s): 19th century (1880s-1890s)
Locale(s): San Carlos, Arizona; Cheyenne, Wyoming; Denver, Colorado

Summary: Based on the true story of Wyoming's Johnson County War, this story follows the adventures of Jake Colby. Colby starts out in Arizona, in the company of such men as Al Sieber and Tom Horn, as a scout for the Army. After Geronimo's surrender, Colby and Horn go their separate ways. Horn drifts into the life of bounty hunter. Colby ends up in Wyoming, first as a cowboy for the big ranchers, then as owner of his own small spread. Falling in love with Laura Place, Colby plans a life for the two of them. But the big ranchers have determined to wipe out their smaller neighbors to put an end to rustling, and Colby's future holds conflict and a last meeting with Tom Horn.

Other books by the same author:
Blood on the Plains, 1997
Texas Glory, 1997
Andersonville, 1996
Yesterday's Reveille, 1996

Other books you might like:
Mike Blakely, *Too Long at the Dance*, 1996
Tim Champlin, *The Last Campaign*, 1996
Robert Kammen, *Big Horn Hellriders*, 1991
David Robbins, *Diablo*, 1997
Jim Walker, *The Nightriders*, 1994
  Wells Fargo Trail #2

626

ROBERT VAUGHAN

Yesterday's Reveille

(New York: St. Martin's Press, 1996)

Story type: Historical; Indian Wars
Major character(s): Joe Murchison, Military Personnel (cavalry officer); George A. Custer, Military Personnel (cavalry officer), Historical Figure; Wind in His Hair, Indian (Sioux), Warrior

Time period(s): 19th century (1870-1900)
Locale(s): Little Big Horn River, Montana; Washington, District of Columbia; Fort Hays, Kansas

Summary: Joe Murchison rides with Custer and the Seventh Cavalry from the Battle of the Washita until the fatal meeting with the Sioux on the Little Big Horn. Surviving the battle as part of Reno's detachment, Murchison goes on to see the end of the story, at Wounded Knee Creek and in the painful days that follow.

Other books by the same author:
Texas Glory, 1997
Dawn of the Century, 1992

Other books you might like:
Michael Blake, *Marching to Valhalla*, 1996
Frederick A. Chiaventone, *A Road We Do Not Know*, 1996
Bill Dugan, *Sitting Bull*, 1994
Edwin P. Hoyt, *The Last Stand*, 1995
Earl Murray, *Flaming Sky*, 1995

627

DALE L. WALKER

Legends and Lies: Great Mysteries of the American West

(New York: Forge, 1998)

Story type: Collection; Historical
Time period(s): 19th century
Locale(s): West

Summary: Western historian Walker tackles a dozen legends of the Old West, from Billy the Kid's supposed survival to Sacajawea's alleged early death. Along the way, he examines the ways that truth gets turned into fiction as stories grow and change to fit the larger epic of which they are a part.

Other books by the same author:
The Golden Spurs, 1990

Other books you might like:
Max Brand, *The Black Rider and Other Stories*, 1996
William Bright, *A Coyote Reader*, 1993
Richard Erdoes, *Tales From the American Frontier*, 1991
Jim Garry, *This Ol' Drought Ain't Broke Us Yet*, 1992
Tony Hillerman, *The Best of the West*, 1991

628

RICHARD S. WHEELER

Flint's Gift

(New York: Forge, 1997)

Story type: Historical; Man Alone
Major character(s): Sam Flint, Editor; Odie Racine, Gunfighter, Outlaw; Merry-Grace Rakoczy, Young Woman
Time period(s): 1870s (1877)
Locale(s): Payday, Arizona

Summary: Gypsy newspaperman Sam Flint decides the little town of Payday is just the right place for him to settle and start a paper. The settlers are glad to have his newspaper because it will attract new business and new people, but they're put off

by Flint's pull-no-punches reporting. And not all the new blood is the type the townsfolk want. Sinister Odie Racine soon appears with his entourage of gamblers, gunfighters, and light women. Flint stands openly against him, but by now he's isolated from the town. When the final showdown comes, he may have to face it alone.

Where it's reviewed:
Kirkus Reviews, August 1, 1997, page 1151
Publishers Weekly, August 11, 1997, page 387

Other books by the same author:
Sierra, 1996
Goldfield, 1995
Cashbox, 1994
Santa Fe, 1994 (Skye's West #8)
The Two Medicine River, 1993 (Rivers West #9)

Other books you might like:
Frederic Bean, *Hell's Half Acre*, 1996
James A. Janke, *A Tin Star for Braddock*, 1992
James A. Ritchie, *Over on the Lonesome Side*, 1991
Frank Roderus, *Stillwater Smith*, 1997
Bruce H. Thorstad, *The Times of Wichita*, 1992

629

RICHARD S. WHEELER

Rendezvous

(New York: Forge, 1997)

Story type: Series; Mountain Man
Series: Skye's West
Major character(s): Barnaby Skye, Sailor, Mountain Man; Jim Bridger, Mountain Man, Historical Figure; Jim Beckwourth, Mountain Man, Historical Figure
Time period(s): 1820s (1826)
Locale(s): Fort Vancouver, Oregon; Rocky Mountains

Summary: The ninth book featuring Barnaby Skye goes back to the beginnings of his story. In 1826, Skye is an able but unwilling seaman impressed aboard a British vessel. He jumps ship at Fort Vancouver and heads into the mountains, barely ahead of pursuit. Unequipped and ignorant of even basic survival skills, Skye relies on his wits to last until friendly Indians rescue him and take him to the trappers' rendezvous of 1826. There, with the great mountain men as examples, Skye begins to learn the ways of this new kind of life.

Other books by the same author:
Sierra, 1996
Goldfield, 1995
Cashbox, 1994
Santa Fe, 1994 (Skye's West #8)
The Two Medicine River, 1993 (Rivers West #9)

Other books you might like:
A.B. Guthrie Jr., *The Big Sky*, 1947
Terry C. Johnston, *Dance on the Wind*, 1995
John Killdeer, *Wilderness Rendezvous*, 1992
    Mountain Majesty #3
Jason Manning, *High Country*, 1993
    High Country #1
David Thompson, *The Trail West*, 1996

630

RICHARD S. WHEELER

Second Lives

(New York: Forge, 1997)

Story type: Historical; Saga
Major character(s): Homer Peabody, Lawyer; Lorenzo Carthage, Mine Owner; Rose Edenderry, Prostitute
Time period(s): 1880s
Locale(s): Denver, Colorado; Leadville, Colorado

Summary: Against the opulent backdrop of Colorado's silver boom, dissimilar people in search of a new start find their lives intertwined. Lorenzo Carthage is a busted mine owner who needs a new stake, and finds it in the rich claim owned by farm widow Dixie Cotton. Lawyer Homer Peabody, handling a divorce case for the wife of one of Denver's elite, gets involved, as does Irish saloon girl Rose Edenderry. In the end, the winners are the characters who find fulfillment in something other than the silver bonanza they all seek.

Where it's reviewed:
Booklist, May 15, 1997, page 1564
Publishers Weekly, April 28, 1997, page 50

Other books by the same author:
Sierra, 1996
Goldfield, 1995
Cashbox, 1994
Santa Fe, 1994 (Skye's West #8)
The Two Medicine River, 1993 (Rivers West #9)

Other books you might like:
Rita Cleary, *Goldfield*, 1996
Kent Conwell, *Panhandle Gold*, 1991
John Jakes, *California Gold*, 1989
T.V. Olsen, *The Golden Chance*, 1992
    Spur Award winner
John Vernon, *All for Love*, 1995

631

LORI WICK

Promise Me Tomorrow

(Eugene, Oregon: Harvest House, 1997)

Story type: Historical; Series
Series: Rocky Mountain Memories
Major character(s): Katherine Taggart, Child-Care Giver; Chase McCandles, Businessman, Rancher
Time period(s): 1900s
Locale(s): Denver, Colorado

Summary: Katherine Taggart comes west to bring two orphan children to their new home in Colorado. Katharine, who works in the orphanage which her family runs, loves children and enjoys working with them. Staying on for a time in Colorado, she finds the turn-of-the century frontier lively and exciting. She also finds a new interest in Coloradan Chase McCandles. McCandles seems to be the man of her dreams, but a long-running feud between him and his son Quintin first gives Katherine concern, then threatens her relationship with Chase and her very life.

Where it's reviewed:
Library Journal, September 1, 1997, page 170

Other books you might like:
Mike Blakely, *Shortgrass Song*, 1994
Sam Brown, *Devil's Rim*, 1998
JoAnn A. Grote, *The Unfolding Heart*, 1997
Stef Ann Holm, *Forget Me Not*, 1997
Catherine Palmer, *Prairie Rose*, 1997
    Town Called Hope #1

632
KEN WILKERSON

Blue Ride
(Riverside, California: Xenos, 1998)

Story type: Modern; Collection
Time period(s): 20th century
Locale(s): California (southern)

Summary: These fourteen short stories deal with men and women in transition, living marginalized lives in the California desert. The setting here, the desert and the old towns left over from Gold Rush and frontier days, becomes almost a character, shaping the lives and attitudes of the people within the stories and carrying the legacy of the past on into their futures.

Other books you might like:
Sanora Babb, *Cry of the Tinamou*, 1997
Jane Candia Coleman, *Moving On*, 1997
William Kittridge, *The Portable Western Reader*, 1997
Wallace Stegner, *Collected Stories of Wallace Stegner*, 1990
Finley Stewart, *Best Stories from the Texas Storytelling Festival*, 1995

633
JEANNE WILLIAMS

Wild Water
(New York: St. Martin's Press, 1997)

Story type: Historical; Ranch Life
Major character(s): Julie McCloud, Orphan, Worker (windmill builder); Cap McCloud, Worker (windmill builder); Jeff Chandless, Rancher
Time period(s): 1880s (1889)
Locale(s): No Man's Land, Oklahoma

Summary: Nineteen-year old Julie McCloud has no memory of her life before Cap McCloud rescued her from a cholera-stricken wagon train and took her to raise. Now she roams the Great Plains with her adoptive father, helping him build windmills for farmers and ranchers in need of water. In Oklahoma, the McCloud family stumbles into a range war between a motley collection of settlers and powerful land baron Jeff Chandless. When Cap is accidentally killed by one of Chandless's men, Julie takes a unique revenge. Aided by well diggers Trace Riordan and Cibolo Martin, she resolves to provide water for the homesteaders whether they can afford it or not—and whatever Chandless may think of her efforts.

Where it's reviewed:
Library Journal, May 1, 1997, page 142
Publishers Weekly, April 14, 1997, page 55

Other books by the same author:
Home Station, 1996
The Unplowed Sky, 1994
Home Mountain, 1990 (Spur Award winner)
No Roof But Heaven, 1990
Lady of No Man's Land, 1989

Other books you might like:
Clifford Blair, *Storm over the Lightning L*, 1993
Will Camp, *Vigilante Justice*, 1994
Lee Cooley, *Judgment at Red Creek*, 1992
Mary McReynolds, *Wells of Glory*, 1996
Dan Parkinson, *The Guns of No Man's Land*, 1992

634
JOE WISE

Cannibal Plateau
(Santa Fe: Sunstone, 1997)

Story type: Modern; Mystery
Major character(s): David Walton, Writer; Jack Fuller, Writer
Time period(s): 1990s
Locale(s): Gunther, Colorado

Summary: In 1874, a prospector named Alfred Hammitt—better known today as Alfred Packer—was convicted of killing and eating five other members of a prospecting expedition trapped by winter snows. Surprisingly for those days, Hammitt-Packer wasn't hanged. He served a prison term, then lived out his life in Littleton, Colorado as a vegetarian, protesting his innocence to the last. Armed with this bit of history, writers David Walton and Jack Fuller tackle the Colorado Rockies with the idea of clearing up the mysteries around the case and turning the results into a book. The pair soon discover that the late Mr. Hammitt and his possible victims aren't giving up secrets easily, not even to exhumation and modern technology. And there are one or two modern mysteries surrounding the cannibal plateau as well.

Other books you might like:
Ric Lynden Hardman, *Sunshine Rider*, 1998
Tony Hillerman, *The Mysterious West*, 1994
Gregory D. Kincaid, *Death Walk at Acoma*, 1993
Gunnard Landers, *The Violators*, 1991
Paul E. Patterson, *Triple Crown*, 1996

635
JIM R. WOOLARD

The Winds of Autumn
(New York: Berkley, 1996)

Story type: Historical; Indian Wars
Major character(s): Blake Tyler, Frontiersman; Blaine Tyler, Frontiersman; Hannah Ferrenden, Frontierswoman
Time period(s): 1790s
Locale(s): Delaplain, Kentucky; Tyler Plantation, Kentucky

Summary: A Shawnee attack wipes out the Tyler family except for brothers Blake and Blaine. Their parents are dead and sister Sarah taken captive by the raiders. Determined to rescue her, the two brothers set out on the track of the Shawnee war party. But fate soon divides their paths, and each goes on his search with little hope of success and every chance of a terrible death at the hands of the hostile Indians.

Other books by the same author:
Thunder in the Valley, 1995 (Spur Award winner)

Other books you might like:
Cynthia Haseloff, *The Chains of Sarai Stone*, 1995
Cameron Judd, *Passage to Natchez*, 1996
Barbara Riefe, *Desperate Crossing: The Jenny Sanders Pryor Story*, 1997
Mike Roarke, *Blood River*, 1995
    First Frontier #4
James Alexander Thom, *Panther in the Sky*, 1989
    Spur Award winner

636

NORMAN ZOLLINGER

Meridian: A Novel of Kit Carson's West
(New York: Forge, 1997)

Story type: Historical; Mountain Man
Major character(s): Kit Carson, Mountain Man, Scout; Bradford Stone, Cartographer; John Charles Fremont, Explorer, Military Personnel
Time period(s): 1840s (1845)

Locale(s): Taos, New Mexico; San Diego, California

Summary: Tenderfoot Bradford Stone joins Fremont's third expedition through the Rocky Mountains for adventure. Part of the adventure involves meeting his long-time idol, Kit Carson, who is not exactly what Stone expects. Neither, as it turns out, is Fremont, who appears as a schemer and plotter jealous of men with more ability. When the expedition reaches California, though, Stone's other interests are submerged by his love for fiery Ana Barragan, daughter of a Mexican rancher. With the Mexican War near on the horizon and with Senor Barragan's hatred of Anglos, their love seems certain to be ill-fated—especially since Stone and the others of the expedition are few in number and far from friends.

Where it's reviewed:
Kirkus Reviews, May 15, 1997, page 754
Publishers Weekly, May 15, 1997, page 66

Other books by the same author:
Chapultepec, 1995
Not of War Only, 1994
Rage in Chupadera, 1991
Passage to Quivira, 1989
Corey Lane, 1981

Other books you might like:
Diane Austell, *Lights Along the Shore*, 1991
Ray Hogan, *Soldier in Buckskin*, 1996
Larry Jay Martin, *Rush to Destiny*, 1992
Gary McCarthy, *The American River*, 1992
    Rivers West #7
John A. Truett, *To Die in Dinetah*, 1994

Western

The Year in Fantasy Fiction
by
Scott Imes

New and established authors produced excellent long and short fantasy work this year, despite industry consolidation and cutbacks which led to the smallest number of original titles since 1990, not including the proliferation of books published as tie-ins to sell other media. Of the more than 250 fantasy books published, many received praise each week as I polled hundreds of avid fantastic fiction readers at Uncle Hugo's, the bookstore I manage in Minneapolis, sorting the gems from the junk with the query, "What are you reading that's great or particularly recommendable?"

Many authors wove excellent spells around magic conflict. In his fourth series book, *Temple of the Winds*, Terry Goodkind finally brings the tale of Richard Raul and Kahlan Amnel to a natural pausing point as they battle an ancient evil. Lynn Flewelling concludes her story of a megalomaniac sorcerer with a second book, *Stalking Darkness*. J. Gregory Keyes continues the story of a deity in the form of a sentient river in *The Blackgod*. In *Emerald House Rising*, first time novelist Peg Kerr focuses on a young woman's attempts to join the male-dominated gemcutter's guild. Patricia Kennealy-Morrison continues her story of Celts in space with *Blackmantle: A Triumph*. Earlier books by the author were published as by Patricia Kennealy and are being reissued under her new name. Kara Dalkey chooses a contemporary setting and a rock music theme for her book, *Steel Rose*. Glen Cook expands his dark, military Black Company Series with *She Is the Darkness*, while Gordon R. Dickson employs a lighter tone in his latest, *The Dragon and the Gnarly King*. More common animals take the spotlight in some books, such as Doranna Durgin's continuing story of a horse turned into a young woman, *Changespell*, and Diane Duane's story of cats protecting New York City from invasion, *The Book of Night with Moon*.

In many books the magic conflict came over a grab for power, including Kate Elliott's *King's Dragon*, Jane S.

Fancher's *Ring of Intrigue*, Sharon Green's *Competition*, Katharine Kerr's *The Red Wyvern*, Dennis L. McKiernan's *Into the Forge*, Douglas Niles' *War of the Three Waters*, Melanie Rawn's *The Mageborn Traitor*, Sean Russell's *Beneath the Vaulted Hills*, R.A. Salvatore's *The Demon Awakens*, Paula Volsky's *The White Tribunal*, Michelle West's *The Broken Crown*, and Janny Wurts' *Fugitive Prince*.

Two of the less successful stories of magic conflict, D.J. Conway's *Soothslayer: A Magical Fantasy* and D.A. Heeley's *Ronin*, came from Llewellyn, a publisher with a religious message that sometimes overwhelms the story. Another interesting story, Carol Heller's *The Gates of Vensunor*, suffers from some inconsistencies that should have been caught by the editor.

Themes of power remained popular this year. My favorite, Robin Hobb's *Assassin's Apprentice*, investigates the question, "What does one do with the royal bastards?" as its protagonist covertly uses assassination as a tool of statecraft while he attempts to maintain distance from the wolf with which he shares a telepathic bond. In David Feintuch's *The Still*, a young prince must learn to navigate the treachery that would keep him from the throne. In a somewhat similar story that suffers a bit of first novel weakness, Fiona Patton's *The Stone Prince*, a crown prince must overcome the treacheries of court life and the threat of an undesirable political marriage. An arranged marriage also threatens a young noblewoman and a wizard in Anne Logston's *Firewalk*. Champions seek to overturn the evil magic which envelops the land in Oliver Johnson's *The Forging of the Shadows*, while two Canadian cities follow different paths when the magic that overwhelmed civilization begins to withdraw in Sean Stewart's *The Night Watch*. One excellent novel that incorporates historical characters and the nineteenth century political struggles of England and Europe, Steven Brust and Emma Bull's *Freedom & Necessity*, may put off some readers with its epistolary form, more familiar

to readers of a century ago than today. Other interesting novels with political themes include Chris Bunch's *The Seer King*, Thomas K. Martin's *Magelord: The Awakening*, Michael A. Stackpole's *Talion: Revenant*, and Harry Turtledove's *The Thousand Cities*.

Among the many excellent novels of quests issued this year, *The Subtle Knife*, Philip Pullman's sequel to *The Golden Compass* (1996), stands out. Considered a book for younger readers by some reviewers, and highly praised, Pullman's different views on religion may prove inappropriate for many youngsters. In Marjorie Bradley Kellogg's *The Book of Water*, 21st century Africans summon a dragon to help reverse environmental devastation. In Eric S. Nyland's *A Game of Universe*, the protagonist searches the galaxy for the Holy Grail. In Jane M. Lindskold's *When the Gods Are Silent*, a man hires a troupe to accompany him as he tries to discover a magical cure for his wife's chronic illness, and Nifft the Lean agrees to retrieve ichor produced by a monstrous insectile queen in Michael Shea's *The Mines of Behemoth*. Other interesting quests take place in David B. Cole's *Children of Amarid* and Elizabeth Kerner's *Song in the Silence*.

Legends and mythical creatures from around the world provided inspiration for some authors this year. Randy Lee Eickhoff's *The Raid* recounts a first century Irish battle over a magical bull. Poul Anderson's *War of the Gods* looks to the ancient Northern pantheon in its tale of revenge. Carol Dawson retells the Theseus legend in a modern setting in *Meeting the Minotaur*. In Vonda N. McIntyre's *The Moon and the Sun*, a mermaid may prove the key to immortality in Renaissance France, while elves populate Martin H. Greenberg's original anthology, *Elf Fantastic*.

Fairy tales inspired both longer and shorter works this year. Robin McKinley adapts ''Beauty and the Beast'' in her story of growth, *Rose Daughter*. Mike Ashley brings together fairy tales by 20th century North American and European authors in *The Mammoth Book of Fairy Tales*. Authors rework familiar fairy tales and explore classic themes in *Black Swan, White Raven*, edited by Ellen Datlow and Terri Windling. A.S. Byatt features women in fairy tale settings in *The Djinn in the Nightingale's Eye*, and Emma Donoghue twists familiar stories in *Kissing the Witch: Old Tales in New Skins*.

Many aspects of the King Arthur legend fascinate authors. Jack Whyte's third volume in the Camulod Chronicles, *The Eagle's Brood*, follows Merlin and Uther Pendragon's efforts to firm up the legacy of Roman law and culture after Rome abandons the island. Marion Zimmer Bradley's *Lady of Avalon* considers an earlier century when Avalon needed to be hidden from her enemies. Cosmic forces in conflict throughout time lead to Arthur's rule in A.A. Attanasio's *The Eagle and the Sword*. In Bernard Cornwell's *Enemy of God*, Merlin plots to return the old religion to prominence. Anne Eliot Crompton focuses on one of Arthur's knights in *Gawain and Lady Green*, while Gwynhwyfar must cope with news of Arthur's death in Helen Hollick's *Shadow of the King*. In Stephen R. Lawhead's *Grail*, Arthur searches for the stolen object that he believes he needs to bring about a Golden Age in Britain. In Molly Cochran and Warren Murphy's *The Broken Sword*, King Arthur returns in the future in the body of a teenage boy to continue his battle against the forces of darkness. Merlin explores and hones new abilities in two books for younger readers, T.A. Barron's *The Seven Songs of Merlin* and Jane Yolen's *Merlin*.

Many authors located their novels in Earth's past. In Sue Harrison's *Song of the River*, a prehistoric Alaskan hopes to heal the rift between tribes. Bronze Age warriors and an evil necromancer battle over the control of trade in ancient Tyre in Matthew Woodring Stover's *Iron Dawn*. Michaela Roessner visits the world of the de Medicis in 16th century Florence in *The Stars Dispose*. A 17th century duke must find magical help to defend his land in Sara J. Wrench's *The Duke of Sumava*. Pioneer America provides the backdrop for the adventures of a young midwife learning magic from her aunt in Katharine Eliska Kimbriel's *Kindred Rites*, while a much more civilized London of the same period allows a young apprentice to learn of London society and intrigue in Patricia C. Wrede's *Magician's Ward*, enjoyable for both older and younger readers.

In some works, fantastic events occurred within familiar surroundings. In *Trader*, Charles de Lint's latest novel about the Canadian artists' colony Newford, one character embarks on a voyage of self-discovery after he wakes up in another person's body. Will Shetterly's *Dogland* uses a 1950s Florida theme park as backdrop for a discussion of racism. In Terry Brooks' *Running with the Demon*, a demon tries to take over a steel-manufacturing town on a Fourth of July weekend during a strike. In a package similar to *Griffin & Sabine* (1991), Nick Bantock's *The Forgetting Room* uses correspondence, collage, and fold-out art to relate the story of a young man's journey to see the family home he inherits in Spain. Darker in tone, James P. Blaylock's *Winter Tides* considers a man harassed by the ghost of a drowning victim he failed to save. Other interesting books with contemporary settings include Stephen Dedman's first novel, *The Art of Arrow Cutting*, Marina Fitch's first novel, *The Seventh Heart*, and Tim Powers' *Earthquake Weather*.

Some books left the everyday world for adventures in other realms. Robert Holdstock's *Gate of Ivory, Gate of Horn* returns to the forest of *Mythago Wood* (1984), where mythical creatures live. In Tom Deitz's *Landslayer's Law*, real estate development threatens the walls protecting the fairy realm and may precipitate warfare between the magical residents and humans. A magic ring propels a young woman into the struggle for power in another world in J.V. Jones' *The Barbed Coil*, and a psychologist's experiments into alternative life regression opens the gateway between worlds, allowing four of his selves to meet in S. Andrew Swann's *God's Dice*.

Other books explored "what might have been" alternative histories. In Harry Turtledove's *Thessalonica*, Slavs and Avars, aided by Slav gods, besiege a sixth century Greek city, threatening its residents and nearby centaurs. In Peter Ackroyd's *Milton in America*, John Milton flees the repressive, restored monarchy in England, hoping to mold America into his vision of Eden. Demons provide energy for an industrializing world in Felicity Savage's *The War in the Waste*. The small town sheriff of Mark Sumner's *Devil's Engine* must protect the 1870s Wild West from an Eastern financier's plan to drain the West of magic. The Nazi plan to create an independent homeland for Jews on Madagascar runs into local resistance in Janet Berliner and George Guthridge's *Children of the Dusk*, and the victorious Allies return Germany to a pre-industrial society in Christoph Ransmayr's *The Dog King*.

Several authors wrote fantasy novels of a more literary bent. Kathleen Alcala's *Spirits of the Ordinary* considers a man who abandons all to search for gold. Senora Rodriguez of Martha Cerda's *Senora Rodriguez and Other Worlds* carries a purse filled with bits of the lives of other people. In Karen Tei Yamashita's *Tropic of Orange*, a woman on vacation from her marriage tries to get her life together and becomes involved in the plight of homeless and displaced workers. Strange travelers continue their search for the Lost Coast in Steven Nightingale's *The Thirteenth Daughter of the Moon*. Less successful than the others, Peter Gelman's *Flying Saucers over Hennepin* does not engage the reader adequately with its zany imagery.

Many authors incorporated religious themes into their books, ranging from the everyday to the extraordinary. In Richard Grant's *In the Land of Winter*, a young Wiccan father struggles against bigoted religious zealots who accuse him of Satan worship, and the protagonists of Michael Moorcock's *The War Amongst the Angels* leave Earth to join in a war in Heaven. Joseph Skibell's *A Blessing on the Moon* features the ghost of a Jew killed in the Holocaust who helps two Hassidic Jews in their search for the missing Moon. Less strident in its discussion than Elizabeth Hand's *Waking the Moon* (1995), Linda Nevins considers a conflict between Roman Catholicism and Goddess worship in *Renaissance Moon*. In *Allamanda*, Michael Williams' sequel to *Arcady* (1996), religion takes a distinct, but less important, role as a void threatens to overwhelm the Hawken family. Other interesting novels with religious themes include Marina Fitch's *The Seventh Heart* and Paul Whitcover's *Waking Beauty*.

This year's adventure stories featured animals real and mythical as well as humans. A mother wolf must bring her family hundreds of miles back to their home in the Montana Rocky Mountains after relocation to an unsuitable new environment in 'Asta Bowen's *Hungry for Home: A Wolf Odyssey*. Bazil Broketail, the dragon warrior, and his companion, Relkin, continue their adventures while separated from the 109th Marneri Dragons in Christopher Rowley's *A Dragon at World's End*. While fleeing barbarians, a young hunter discovers the magical Hawkbrother race hiding deep in the forest in Mercedes Lackey and Larry Dixon's *Owlflight*. In Anne Lesley Groell's *Bridge of Valor*, two assassins venture to a distant estate on their first assignment to investigate, among other bizarre occurrences, a rain of goldfish that torments the lord of the estate, but become involved in a lethal maze of plots. Other interesting adventures are found in Jo Clayton's *Drum Calls*, Vivian Vande Velde's *The Conjurer Princess* and Margaret Weis and Tracy Hickman's *Legacy of the Darksword*.

Authors sometimes incorporated mysteries into their books. In Laurell K. Hamilton's *The Killing Dance*, reanimator Anita Blake must find out who has hired a contract killer to murder her, perhaps due to her increasing power over the dead. In Daniel Hood's *Beggar's Banquet*, a young man who wishes merely to enjoy a festival and conduct a bit of business must instead find a murderer and the person who stole a magical artifact from his proposed business partner. One book, Tanya Huff's *Blood Debt*, features a vampire, while Brett Davis' *Hair of the Dog* and Denise Vitola's *Opalite Moon* feature werewolves. Shirley Rousseau Murphy employs a cat detective in *Cat Raise the Dead*. A religious theme fits into Mercedes Lackey's *Four & Twenty Blackbirds* and rock music into Melissa Michaels' *Cold Iron*, both mysteries with political considerations.

The Terry Pratchett Discworld series books, *Interesting Times* and *Maskerade*, stand out among humorous fantasy issued this year. However, Piers Anthony's Xanth book, *Faun & Games*, suffers from formulaic treatment. Mark Leyner's literary satire, *The Tetherballs of Bougainville*, does not work as well as his earlier books, a problem shared by *Hell on High* by Holly Lisle and Ted Nolan.

Work from other media inspired an increasing number of books this year. Rescued from television's *The Rocky and Bullwinkle Show*, A.J. Jacob's *Fractured Fairy Tales* brings the show's delightfully twisted, pun-filled gems to print. A British mini-series inspired Neil Gaiman's *Neverwhere*, in which a good Samaritan discovers a realm of legends and lost people in the sewers beneath London. Ru Emerson's *The Thief of Hermes* and David L. Siedman's *The First Casualty* are tie-ins to the television series *Xena: Warrior Princess* and *Hercules: The Legendary Journey*, respectively. Chris Claremont's *Shadow Dawn* shares the universe of the film *Willow*, while the Elfquest series of graphic art books inspires Wendy Pini and Richard Pini's *Captives of Blue Mountain*.

Games inspired too many routine tie-in novels. From the realm of electronic games comes *The Book of D'ni* by Rand Miller and David Wingrove, and *Wrath of the Princes* by Holly Lisle and Aaron Allston. A collectable card game underlies Clayton Emery's *Card Master*. Last year's hopes concerning the demise of TSR's fiction line were dashed when a competing game company, Wizards of the Coast, rushed in as corporate white knight, purchasing TSR and

restoring the fiction line. The many novels tied to TSR's games include *Planar Powers* by J. Robert King and *Finder's Bane* by Kate Novak and Jeff Grubb.

Most shorter work appeared in anthologies and collections rather than in the major fantasy periodicals, the bimonthly *Realms of Fantasy*, the quarterly *Marion Zimmer Bradley's Fantasy Magazine*, and the monthly *Fantasy & Science Fiction*. Many original anthologies are themed: Marion Zimmer Bradley and Rachel E. Holmen's *Sword and Sorceress XIV* focuses on sword and sorcery, Martin H. Greenberg and Lawrence Schimel's *Tarot Fantastic* on fortune-telling cards, Nicola Griffith and Stephen Pagel's *Blending the Landscape: Fantasy* on homosexuality, and Ellen Kushner, Delia Sherman and Donald G. Keller's *The Horns of Elfland* on music. The most interesting reprint anthologies include Mike Ashley's *The Random House Book of Fantasy Stories*, Italo Calvino's *Fantastic Tales: Visionary and Everyday*, Gardner Dozois' *Modern Classics of Fantasy* and Margaret Weis and Tracy Hickman's *Treasures of Fantasy*.

Many collections brought together several stories that share a universe. Gael Baudino's *Spires of Spirit* shares the milieu of *Strands of Starlight* (1989), and Peter S. Beagle's *Giant Bones* shares the milieu of *The Innkeeper's Song* (1993). Mercedes Lackey's *Sword of Ice and Other Tales of Valdemar* fits into her Valdemar series, while Michael Moorcock's two new novels, *Fabulous Harbors* and *The War Amongst the Angels*, join the universe of *Blood: A Southern Fantasy* (1995). Drawing together many different authors' work, Anne McCaffrey and Richard Woods' *A Diversity of Dragons* considers disparate views of dragon kind. One book marketed as a novel, Vera Chapman's *The Notorious Abbess*, collects together all of the stories about the 12th century Abbess of Shaston and her magical adventures.

Specialty publishers contributed many interesting books in 1997. Among the most significant, game manufacturer White Wolf continues its hardcover reprinting of works by Harlan Ellison, Fritz Leiber, and Michael Moorcock. Of the many books published by specialty publishers, the most interesting include Peter S. Beagle's *The Rhinoceros Who Quoted Nietzsche and Other Odd Acquaintances*, Fritz Leiber's *Return to Lankhmar*, Michael Moorcock's *Corum: The Coming of Chaos* and Martha Soukup's *The Arbitrary Placement of Walls*.

Younger readers also benefited from many excellent books this year. Among the best, Lloyd Alexander's adventure, *The Iron Ring*, encompasses legends and myths of India. In Chelsea Quinn Yarbro's *Monet's Ghost*, a youngster discovers the ability to transport herself into the world of a painting. In the fourth sequel to *The Mennyms* (1994), Sylvia Waugh's *Mennyms Alive*, the Mennyms lose their life force when the ghost of their creator departs their mansion. Brian Jacques continues his tale of the animals of Redwall Abbey in *The Pearls of Lutra*. Diane Duane adds *A Wizard*

Abroad to her *So You Want to Be a Wizard?* (1983) sequence. Lynne Reid Banks focuses on twin sisters with very different personalities in *Angela and Diabola*, and Franny Billingsley considers a child's desire to find, then help, a playmate her own age in *Well Wished*. A young woman does not get the reaction she expects when she reveals her true nature to the boy she loves in Annette Curtis Klause's *Blood and Chocolate*. Continuing its commitment to reprint books in trade paperback editions, Tor Books has reissued an omnibus edition of three Lyra stories of Patricia C. Wrede titled *Shadows over Lyra*. Other interesting books for younger readers include Vivian Alcock's *The Red-Eared Ghosts*, Mark Helprin's *The Veil of Snows*, Tanith Lee's *Red Unicorn* and Jane Yolen's collection, *Twelve Impossible Things Before Breakfast*.

Many books not already mentioned expanded established series. The best include Deborah Chester's *Realm of Light* and *Shadow War* (Shadows), Dave Duncan's *Future Indefinite* (Great Game), David and Leigh Eddings' *Polgara the Sorceress* (The Belgariad, The Malloreon), Raymond E. Feist's *Rage of a Demon King* (Serpentwar Saga), Simon Hawke's *The Last Wizard* (Wizard of Fourth Street), and Julian May's *Sky Trillium* (Black Trillium). Robert Jordan and Teresa Patterson's *The World of Robert Jordan's Wheel of Time* reprised work already published with scant new material, disappointing readers who hoped for an eighth volume in Jordan's massive Wheel of Time series. While L.E. Modesitt Jr.'s latest Recluce Series book, *The Chaos Balance*, did not catch readers' fancy as well as earlier volumes have, *The Soprano Sorceress*, the first book in a new series, received much praise.

My choices for the best fantasies of 1997 include:

Novels:

Winter Tides by James P. Blaylock

Freedom & Necessity by Steven Brust and Emma Bull

Kar Kalim by Deborah Christian

Trader by Charles de Lint

The Art of Arrow Cutting by Stephen Dedman

King's Dragon by Kate Elliott

The Still by David Feintuch

Stalking Darkness by Lynn Flewelling

Temple of the Winds by Terry Goodkind

The Killing Dance by Laurell K. Hamilton

Assassin's Quest by Robin Hobb

Gate of Ivory, Gate of Horn by Robert Holdstock

The Blackgod by J. Gregory Keyes

Kindred Rites by Katharine Eliska Kimbriel

The Moon and the Sun by Vonda N. McIntyre

Rose Daughter by Robin McKinley

The Gift by Patrick O'Leary

Earthquake Weather by Tim Powers

The Subtle Knife by Philip Pullman

The Stars Dispose by Michaela Roessner

The Mines of Behemoth by Michael Shea

Dogland by Will Shetterly

The Night Watch by Sean Stewart

Touched by the Gods by Lawrence Watt-Evans

Waking Beauty by Paul Whitcover

Collections/Anthologies:

Giant Bones by Peter S. Beagle

The Rhinoceros Who Quoted Nietzsche and Other Odd Acquaintances by Peter S. Beagle

Black Swan, White Raven, Ellen Datlow and Terri Windling, eds.

Modern Classics of Fantasy, Gardner Dozois, ed.

Blending the Landscape: Fantasy, Nicola Griffith and Stephen Pagel, eds.

The Horns of Elfland, Ellen Kushner, Delia Sherman and Donald G. Keller, eds.

Fabulous Harbors by Michael Moorcock

Fantasy Titles

637

PETER ACKROYD

Milton in America

(New York: Doubleday/Nan A. Talese, 1997)

Story type: Alternate History; Religious
Major character(s): John Milton, Writer (poet), Leader; Goosequill, Servant, Guide; Katherine Jervis, Secretary
Time period(s): 17th century (1660s)
Locale(s): New Milton, Fictional City; Alternate Earth; American Colonies

Summary: In A.D. 1660 John Milton, poet, Puritan and radical thinker, flees England and the depressing fact of the restored monarchy. In the New World he finds a society that he can mold to his vision of Eden. When Milton soon becomes as inflexible as the people he flees, he turns his blind and unrelenting attention on a nearby Catholic colony, whereupon evil returns to Eden.

Where it's reviewed:
Booklist, March 15, 1997, page 1224

Other books by the same author:
First Light, 1989
Hawksmoor, 1986

Other books you might like:
James P. Blaylock, *Homunculus*, 1986
William S. Burroughs, *Ghost of Chance*, 1995
John Crowley, *AEgypt*, 1987
Kim Newman, *Back in the USSA*, 1997
   Eugene Byrne, co-author
Howard Waldrop, *Strange Monsters of the Recent Past*, 1991

638

KATHLEEN ALCALA

Spirits of the Ordinary

(San Francisco: Chronicle Books, 1997)

Story type: Historical; Literary

Major character(s): Zacarias Caraval, Prospector; Estela Caraval, Divorced Person; Julio Caraval, Parent (father), Philosopher
Time period(s): 1870s
Locale(s): Casas Grandes, Mexico; Saltillo, Mexico

Summary: The Caravals have covertly practiced Judaism for many generations, hiding their religion, and working as merchants. Zacarias abandons the family business, religion and the comforts of home to wander in the wilderness looking for gold. A lost mine, cabalism, strange powers, and the mystic cliff dwellings at Casas Grandes combine to chart the course of a family, a nation, and continent.

Where it's reviewed:
Fantasy & Science Fiction, September 1997, page 33

Other books by the same author:
Mrs. Vangas and the Dead Naturalist, 1992

Other books you might like:
Nick Bantock, *The Forgetting Room*, 1997
Martha Cerda, *Senora Rodriguez and Other Worlds*, 1997
Richard Kadrey, *Kamikaze L'Amour*, 1995
Gabriel Garcia Marquez, *One Hundred Years of Solitude*, 1967
Karen Tei Yamashita, *Tropic of Orange*, 1997

639

VIVIAN ALCOCK

The Red-Eared Ghosts

(New York: Houghton Mifflin, 1997)

Story type: Science Fiction; Young Adult
Major character(s): Mary Frewin, Child, Psychic; Freda Timpson, Teacher; Edward "Potty" Potts, Teacher
Time period(s): 1990s; 1880s
Locale(s): Cloudsley Towers, England

Summary: Disappointed at Miss Timpson's failure to believe she sees red-eared ghosts, Mary complains to her friends that the confirmation of her sanity would be useful. Edward Potts looks forward to meeting Mary in hopes he will learn some-

thing. He buys her grandmother's story, the book hidden from Mary since her childhood, and shares it with her when they meet.

Where it's reviewed:
Booklist, March 1, 1997, page 1160
Kirkus Reviews, April 1, 1997, page 548
Locus, September 1997, page 27
Voice of Youth Advocates, October 1997, page 250

Other books by the same author:
Singer to the Sea God, 1993
Ghostly Companions, 1990
The Monster Garden, 1988
The Stonewalkers, 1981
The Haunting of Cassie Palmer, 1980

Other books you might like:
Melvin Burgess, *The Earth Giant*, 1997
Diana Wynne Jones, *The Time of the Ghost*, 1996
Margaret Mahy, *The Tricksters*, 1987
Pamela F. Service, *All's Faire*, 1993
Sylvia Waugh, *The Mennyms*, 1994

640

LLOYD ALEXANDER

The Iron Ring
(New York: Dutton, 1997)

Story type: Young Adult; Quest
Major character(s): Tamar, Royalty, Teacher; Garuda, Mythical Creature, Adventurer; Mirri, Young Woman, Adventurer
Time period(s): Indeterminate
Locale(s): Danda-Vana Forest, Mythical Place; Fictional Country

Summary: After losing his kingdom in a card game, Tamar tests his stamina and resolve as he meets talking animals, warring kings, fearsome spirits and his true love.

Where it's reviewed:
Booklist, May 15, 1997, page 1572
Kirkus Reviews, May 1, 1997, page 716
Publishers Weekly, April 14, 1997, page 76
School Library Journal, May 1997, page 128
Voice of Youth Advocates, October 1997, page 250

Other books by the same author:
The Arkadians, 1995
The Remarkable Journey of Prince Jen, 1991
Westmark, 1981
The High King, 1968
The Black Cauldron, 1965

641

POUL ANDERSON

War of the Gods
(New York: Tor, 1997)

Story type: Legend

Major character(s): Hadding, Ruler, Warrior; Hardgreip, Mythical Creature (jotun), Witch; Odin, Deity
Time period(s): Indeterminate Past
Locale(s): Denmark; Sweden

Summary: Left in the care of Giants, Hadding, son of the defeated King Gram, grows strong and daring. Once he reaches manhood and word comes to him of his brother's death, Hadding goes out for revenge. Through raiding, warfare, magic and trickery, force of arms, and generosity, Hadding recreates his father's kingdom under the eye of Odin.

Where it's reviewed:
Analog, January 1998, page 145
Booklist, September 15, 1997, page 216
Kirkus Reviews, August 1, 1997, page 1165
Library Journal, September 15, 1997, page 106
Publishers Weekly, August 25, 1997, page 50

Other books by the same author:
The King of Ys: Roma Mater, 1986 (Karen Anderson, co-author)
The Golden Horn, 1980
The Demon of Scattery, 1979 (Mildred Downey Broxon, co-author)
Hrolf Kraki's Saga, 1973
The Broken Sword, 1954

Other books you might like:
Charles Barnitz, *The Deepest Sea*, 1996
Frans G. Bengtsson, *The Long Ships*, 1954
Diana L. Paxson, *The Wolf and the Raven*, 1993
Snorri Sturluson, *Egil's Saga*, 1976
    Hermann Palsson and Paul Edwards, translators
Sigrid Undset, *The Bridal Wreath*, 1923

642

PIERS ANTHONY

Faun & Games
(New York: Tor, 1997)

Story type: Light Fantasy; Quest
Series: Xanth
Major character(s): Forrest Faun, Mythical Creature (faun), Gardener; Mare Imbri, Animal (horse), Companion; Cathryn Centaur, Mythical Creature (centaur), Guide
Time period(s): Indeterminate
Locale(s): Xanth, Fictional Country; Ptero, Moon—Imaginary

Summary: When Forrest Faun must find a new keeper for a tree to prevent its dying, he goes along with Mare Imbri to Ptero, a moonlet circling Princess Ida. After several side quests, finding a centaur's true love and keeping humans from being marginalized, he returns to Xanth to find the answer.

Where it's reviewed:
Booklist, September 1, 1997, page 67
Kirkus Reviews, August 1, 1997, page 1167
Publishers Weekly, September 8, 1997, page 63

Other books by the same author:
Yon Ill Wind, 1996
Geis of the Gargoyle, 1995
Roc and a Hard Place, 1995

Split Infinity, 1980
A Spell for Chameleon, 1977

Other books you might like:
Poul Anderson, *Three Hearts and Three Lions*, 1991
Robert Asprin, *Another Fine Myth*, 1978
John Barnes, *One for the Morning Glory*, 1996
Jack L. Chalker, *Demons of the Dancing Gods*, 1984
Alan Dean Foster, *Son of Spellsinger*, 1993
Andre Norton, *Dread Companion*, 1970
Christopher Stasheff, *The Warlock Unlocked*, 1982
Thomas Burnett Swann, *Lady of the Bees*, 1976

643

MIKE ASHLEY, Editor

The Mammoth Book of Fairy Tales
(New York: Carroll & Graf, 1997)

Story type: Legend; Anthology

Summary: Contains a two-page introduction and a 25-page appendix with brief biographic data about the authors and information about the 56 stories, published 1903-1997. Fairies, beasts, other mythical creatures and people inhabit modern urban and ancient rural settings. Authors include Hans Christian Andersen, L. Frank Baum, Lewis Carroll, Louise Cooper, The Brothers Grimm, Edward Lear, Tanith Lee, Walter de la Mare, Robin McKinley, Charles Perrault, Lawrence Schimel, Nancy Springer, Netta Syrett, Jessica Amanda Salmonson, Oscar Wilde and Jane Yolen.

Where it's reviewed:
Booklist, October 15, 1997, page 389
Kirkus Reviews, September 1, 1997, page 1338

Other books by the same author:
The Random House Book of Fantasy Stories, 1997
The Chronicles of the Holy Grail, 1996
The Merlin Chronicles, 1995
The Camelot Chronicles, 1992
The Pendragon Chronicles, 1990

Other books you might like:
Lester del Rey, *Once upon a Time: A Treasury of Modern Fairy Tales*, 1991
  Rissa Kessler, co-editor
Gardner Dozois, *Modern Classics of Fantasy*, 1997
  editor
Jacob Ludwig Carl Grimm, *The Complete Fairy Tales of the Brothers Grimm*, 1992
  Wilhelm Carl Grimm, co-author
Andrew Lang, *The Blue Fairy Book*, 1889
  editor
Alison Lurie, *The Oxford Book of Modern Fairy Tales*, 1993
  editor

644

MIKE ASHLEY, Editor

The Random House Book of Fantasy Stories
(New York: Random House, 1997)

Story type: Anthology

Summary: Contains a three-page foreword by Ashley, a four-page introduction by Garry Kilworth, excerpts from longer works by A.C. Benson, Nicholas Stuart Gray, C.S. Lewis, George MacDonald and J.R.R. Tolkien, plus ten original stories and 12 stories reprinted from periodicals and anthologies from 1896 through 1994. From light to serious in tone, the stories employ a variety of traditional themes, such as mythical creatures, magic conflict, fairy tales, quests, music, alternate worlds, Atlantis and other fantastic locales. Other authors include Joan Aiken, Ramsey Campbell, Peter Crowther, Lord Dunsany, Neil Gaiman, Parke Godwin, Frances M. Hendry, Diana Wynne Jones, Garry Kilworth, Tanith Lee, George MacDonald, Edith Nesbit, Elisabeth Waters, Ian Watson and Jane Yolen.

Other books by the same author:
The Mammoth Book of Fairy Tales, 1997
The Chronicles of the Holy Grail, 1996
The Merlin Chronicles, 1995
The Camelot Chronicles, 1992
The Pendragon Chronicles, 1990

Other books you might like:
Ellen Datlow, *The Year's Best Fantasy and Horror Series*, 1989-
  Terry Windling, co-editor
Gardner Dozois, *Modern Classics of Fantasy*, 1997
  editor
Alison Lurie, *The Oxford Book of Modern Fairy Tales*, 1993
  editor
Tom Shippey, *The Oxford Book of Fantasy Stories*, 1994
  editor
Robert Silverberg, *The Fantasy Hall of Fame*, 1983
  editor

645

A.A. ATTANASIO

The Eagle and the Sword
(New York: HarperPrism, 1997)

Story type: Legend; Religious
Major character(s): Arthor, Bastard Son, Teenager; Merlin, Wizard, Leader; Melania, Noblewoman, Adventurer
Time period(s): Indeterminate Past
Locale(s): Camelot, England (Britain)

Summary: While Merlin oversees the construction of Camelot, the difficulties of Arthor's life prepare him to rule. Arthor will unify the island into a nation, if he can overcome interference from the realm of the gods and human forces which encompass a different vision of the island's future.

Where it's reviewed:
Fantasy & Science Fiction, October/November 1997, page 44
Kirkus Reviews, April 15, 1997, page 595
Library Journal, June 15, 1997, page 101
Starlog, August 1997, page 69
Voice of Youth Advocates, December 1997, page 322

Other books by the same author:
The Dragon and the Unicorn, 1996
Arthur, 1995
The Moon's Wife: A Hystery, 1993
Kingdom of the Grail, 1992
Wyvern, 1988

Other books you might like:
Mike Ashley, *The Pendragon Chronicles*, 1990
  editor
Marion Zimmer Bradley, *The Forest House*, 1994
Bernard Cornwell, *The Winter King*, 1996
Andrea Hopkins, *Chronicles of King Arthur*, 1994
  editor
Courtway Jones, *In the Shadow of the Oak King*, 1991
Jack Whyte, *The Skystone*, 1996

646

LYNNE REID BANKS

Angela and Diabola

(New York: Avon, 1997)

Story type: Young Adult; Light Fantasy
Major character(s): Angelica Cuthberton-Jones, Child, Psychic; Diabola Cuthberton-Jones, Child, Psychic; Mrs. Cuthberton-Jones, Parent
Time period(s): 1990s
Locale(s): Earth

Summary: Angelica grows up cooperative and pleasant in disposition, while her twin, Diabola, becomes more hostile and selfish with each passing year. With Diabola's father gone and her teacher cowed, Mrs. Cuthberton-Jones must find a way to mitigate Diabola's powers before disaster results.

Where it's reviewed:
Kirkus Reviews, May 1, 1997, Psychic

Other books by the same author:
The Adventures of King Midas, 1992
Melusine: A Mystery, 1991
The Fairy Rebel, 1989
The Return of the Indian, 1986
The Indian in the Cupboard, 1981

Other books you might like:
Michael Bedard, *Painted Devil*, 1994
Diana Wynne Jones, *Witch Week*, 1982
Tanith Lee, *Black Unicorn*, 1991
Doris Lessing, *The Fifth Child*, 1988
Margaret Mahy, *The Changeover*, 1984

647

NICK BANTOCK

The Forgetting Room

(New York: HarperCollins, 1997)

Story type: Contemporary Realism
Major character(s): Armon, Artist (bookbinder); Rafael, Artist (painter)
Time period(s): 1900s
Locale(s): Ronda, Spain

Summary: Armon's grandfather dies, leaving him the family home in Spain. When the young man goes to check out his inheritance, strange events and stranger memories form an undeniable link to his past and his grandfather's mind. Heavily illustrated with Bantock's collage and fold-out art.

Where it's reviewed:
Booklist, August 1997, page 1846
Kirkus Reviews, July 15, 1997, page 1044
Publishers Weekly, August 18, 1997, page 68

Other books by the same author:
The Venetian's Wife: A Strangely Sensual Tale of a Renaissance Explorer, a Computer, and a Metamorphosis, 1996
The Egyptian Jukebox, 1993
The Golden Mean, 1993
Sabine's Notebook, 1992
Griffin & Sabine, 1991

Other books you might like:
John Crowley, *AEgypt*, 1987
Lisa Goldstein, *The Dream Years*, 1985
Karen Elizabeth Gordon, *Paris out of Hand*, 1996
Barbara Hodgson, *The Tattooed Map*, 1995
Arturo Perez-Reverte, *The Club Dumas*, 1997

648

T.A. BARRON

The Seven Songs of Merlin

(New York: Philomel, 1997)

Story type: Young Adult; Legend
Series: Lost Years of Merlin
Major character(s): Emrys Merlin, Child, Psychic; Rhiannon ''Rhia'', Child, Psychic
Time period(s): 6th century
Locale(s): Isle of Fincayra, Mythical Place; The Otherworld, Mythical Place

Summary: When the young Merlin and Rhia hope to repair the damage caused to Fincayra by the vanquished Blight, Merlin's mother falls victim to a new evil. To cure her, Merlin and Rhia must acquire a magical elixir in the Otherworld, if Merlin can survive the ogre Balor's challenge and can hone his psychic vision. Third in series.

Where it's reviewed:
Booklist, September 1, 1997, page 105
Kirkus Reviews, August 1, 1997, page 1218
Locus, August 1997, page 29
Publishers Weekly, July 21, 1997, page 202

Other books by the same author:
The Lost Years of Merlin, 1996
The Merlin Effect, 1994
The Ancient One, 1992
Heartlight, 1990

Other books you might like:
Mike Ashley, *The Merlin Chronicles*, 1995
    editor
Ann Curry, *The Book of Brendan*, 1990
T.H. White, *The Sword in the Stone*, 1939
Jane Yolen, *Merlin's Booke*, 1986
Jane Yolen, *Passager*, 1996

649

GAEL BAUDINO

Spires of Spirit

(New York: Roc, 1997)

Story type: Collection; Urban
Series: Strands of Starlight
Major character(s): Varden, Mythical Creature (elf), Healer;
    Leather-woman, Sorceress; Lauri, Mythical Creature (elf),
    Lesbian
Time period(s): 16th century; 1990s
Locale(s): Europe; Colorado; Mythical Place

Summary: Contains a four-page introduction, five original
novelettes and one revised from the 1985 periodical version.
Written 1981-1984, the stories provide the background and
foundation for the *Strands of Starlight* milieu. The first three
portray elven interactions with nature and humanity as the
Inquisition looms, while the others focus on the reemergence
of elven influences in the modern world and individuals who
must come to terms with the demands of their genetic
makeup.

Where it's reviewed:
Kliatt, May 1997, page 12

Other books by the same author:
O Greenest Branch!, 1995
Strands of Sunlight, 1994
Maze of Moonlight, 1993
Strands of Starlight, 1989

Other books you might like:
Charles de Lint, *Dreams Underfoot*, 1993
Charles de Lint, *The Ivory and the Horn*, 1995
Robert Holdstock, *The Bone Forest*, 1992
Elizabeth Ann Scarborough, *The Godmother*, 1994
Elizabeth Ann Scarborough, *Phantom Banjo*, 1991

650

PETER S. BEAGLE

Giant Bones

(New York: Roc, 1997)

Story type: Collection

Summary: Contains a five-page foreword and six stories
sharing the folklore and natural history of the world of *The*

Inkeeper's Song. Varying in tone, the stories explore themes
such as adventure, magic, mythical creatures, and ghosts.

Where it's reviewed:
Analog, December 1997, page 147
Kirkus Reviews, July 1, 1997, page 992
Locus, July 1997, page 25
Realms of Fantasy, August 1997, page 16

Other books by the same author:
*The Rhinoceros Who Quoted Nietzsche and Other Odd Ac-
    quaintances*, 1997
The Innkeeper's Song, 1993
The Folk of the Air, 1987
The Last Unicorn, 1968
A Fine and Private Place, 1960

Other books you might like:
Richard Adams, *Tales of Watership Down*, 1996
Marion Zimmer Bradley, *Free Amazons of Darkover*, 1985
    Friends of Darkover, co-editor
Richard Pini, *The Blood of Ten Chiefs*, 1986
    Robert Asprin and Lynn Abbey, co-editor
Will Shetterly, *Liavek*, 1985
    Emma Bull, co-editor
J.R.R. Tolkien, *The Book of Lost Tales 1*, 1984

651

PETER S. BEAGLE

*The Rhinoceros Who Quoted Nietzsche
and Other Odd Acquaintances*

(San Francisco, California: Tachyon Publications, 1997)

Story type: Collection

Summary: Contains a four-page introduction by Patricia A.
McKillip plus two original stories, two original essays, six
stories reprinted from periodicals and anthologies 1957-1995
and two essays reprinted from 1965 and 1969 periodicals.
Frequently light in tone, the stories include a variety of
themes such as mythical and fantastic creatures, allegory and
personal relationships.

Where it's reviewed:
Locus, December 1997, page 31

Other books by the same author:
Giant Bones, 1997
The Innkeeper's Song, 1993
The Folk of the Air, 1987
The Last Unicorn, 1968
A Fine and Private Place, 1960

Other books you might like:
David Brin, *The River of Time*, 1986
Nancy Kress, *Dancing on Air*, 1997
Jonathan Lethem, *The Wall of the Sky, the Wall of the Eye*,
    1996
Mary Shelly, *The Mortal Immortal*, 1996
Clifford D. Simak, *Over the River & Through the Woods*,
    1996

652

JANET BERLINER

GEORGE GUTHRIDGE, Co-Author

Children of the Dusk

(Clarkston, Georgia: White Wolf Borealis, 1997)

Story type: Magic Conflict; Historical
Series: Madagascar Manifesto
Major character(s): Solomon ''Sol'' Freund, Psychic; Miriam ''Miriam Alois'' Rathenau, Spouse; Erich ''Erich Alois'' Weser, Leader, Animal Trainer
Time period(s): 1930s (1939)
Locale(s): Madagascar

Summary: As World War II heats up, the Nazi plan to carve out a Jewish homeland on Madagascar may fall victim to internal conflict and the actions of two Malagasy sorcerers. Concludes the triology.

Other books by the same author:
Child of the Journey, 1996
Child of the Light, 1992 (writing as Janet Gluckman; George Guthridge, co-author)

Other books you might like:
Martin Amis, *Time's Arrow*, 1991
Peter S. Beagle, *Peter S. Beagle's Immortal Unicorn*, 1995
    Janet Berliner, co-editor
J.R. Dunn, *Days of Cain*, 1997
Lisa Goldstein, *The Red Magician*, 1982
Jane Yolen, *Briar Rose*, 1992

653

FRANNY BILLINGSLEY

Well Wished

(New York: Atheneum, 1997)

Story type: Magic Conflict; Young Adult
Major character(s): Nuria, Child, Orphan; Agnes, Aged Person; Catty Winter, Child, Handicapped
Time period(s): Indeterminate
Locale(s): Bishop Mayne, England

Summary: As the only child left in Bishop Mayne since the children were wished away, Nuria would like to have a friend. Her grandfather has already wished for the children to return and Agnes, the keeper of the Wishing Well, informs her that Catty Winter returns tomorrow. Unfortunately, Catty needs a miracle so she can skate and run with Nuria, and the Wishing Well may be the only possible help.

Where it's reviewed:
Booklist, June 1 & 15, 1997, page 1694
Kirkus Reviews, May 1, 1997, page 716

Other books you might like:
Michael Ende, *The Night of Wishes: Or, the Satanarchaeolidealcohellish Notion Potion*, 1992
Esther M. Friesner, *Wishing Season*, 1993
Gail Jarrow, *Beyond the Magic Sphere*, 1994
S.P. Somtow, *The Wizard's Apprentice*, 1993
Nancy Springer, *The Friendship Song*, 1992

Patricia C. Wrede, *Mairelon the Magician*, 1991

654

'ASTA BOWEN

Hungry for Home: A Wolf Odyssey

(New York: Simon & Schuster, 1997)

Story type: Adventure
Major character(s): Marta, Animal (wolf), Leader; Calef, Animal (wolf); Oldtooth, Animal (wolf)
Time period(s): 1990s
Locale(s): Montana

Summary: ''Rescued'' from her chosen home in the Montana Rockies, Marta and her pack face many dangers. Food for the wolves, including three pups, would be problem enough without having to face the residents of the new place, the bears. Marta braves unknown territory including roads and cars to walk the hundreds of miles home.

Where it's reviewed:
Booklist, January 1 & 15, 1997, page 816
Kirkus Reviews, November 15, 1996, page 1617

Other books you might like:
Richard Adams, *Watership Down*, 1974
Brian Jacques, *Redwall*, 1986
Garry Kilworth, *The Foxes of Firstdark*, 1990
Sherwood Smith, *Wren to the Rescue*, 1990
Tad Williams, *Tailchaser's Song*, 1985

655

MARION ZIMMER BRADLEY

Gravelight

(New York: Tor, 1997)

Story type: Psychic Powers; Magic Conflict
Major character(s): Wycherly ''Wych'' Musgrave, Alcoholic; Melusine ''Sinah'' Dellon, Actress, Telepath; Truth Jourdemayne, Paranormal Investigator
Time period(s): 1990s
Locale(s): Morton's Fork, West Virginia

Summary: When Sinah Dellon returns to Morton's Fork to find her family, no one will talk to her. After crashing her car, alcoholic Wych Musgrave decides to dry out. The two, together with a team of psychic investigators looking into disappearances centering on August 14th, must all work to battle old ritual and older magic forces, even more dangerous in this modern age.

Where it's reviewed:
Kirkus Reviews, July 1, 1997, page 990
Library Journal, September 15, 1997, page 105
Locus, September 1997, page 27
Publishers Weekly, August 25, 1997, page 50

Other books by the same author:
Witchlight, 1996
Ghostlight, 1995
Lady of the Trillium, 1995
The Forest House, 1994

The Inheritor, 1984

Other books you might like:
Francesca Lia Block, *Witch Baby*, 1991
Jack Cady, *The Off Season*, 1995
Rose Estes, *Troll-Taken*, 1993
Lisa Goldstein, *Walking the Labyrinth*, 1996
Nina Kiriki Hoffman, *The Silent Strength of Stones*, 1995
R.A. MacAvoy, *Tea With the Black Dragon*, 1983
Susan Power, *The Grass Dancer*, 1994
Terri Windling, *The Wood Wife*, 1996
Jane Yolen, *Briar Rose*, 1992

656

MARION ZIMMER BRADLEY

Lady of Avalon
(New York: Viking, 1997)

Story type: Legend; Religious
Series: Mists of Avalon
Major character(s): Caillean, Religious (High Priestess); Gawen, Ruler, Religious; Sianna, Mythical Creature (faerie), Royalty (princess)
Time period(s): 1st century (A.D. 90-118); 3rd century (285-293)
Locale(s): Avalon, England; Inis Witrin, Mythical Place (Isle of Glass, Avalon)

Summary: Caillean returns to Avalon with Gawen, son of a High Priestess and a Roman soldier. Raised by the High Priestess and Father Josephus, Gawen marries Sianna, becoming instrumental in hiding Avalon from her enemies. The old ones, reborn as Caillean, Gawen and Sianna, continue to protect England, leading to the birth of Arthur. Sequel to *The Forest House* and prequel to *The Mists of Avalon*.

Where it's reviewed:
Booklist, April 1, 1997, page 1268
Library Journal, May 15, 1997, page 105
Publishers Weekly, May 19, 1997, page 71

Other books by the same author:
Witchlight, 1996
The Forest House, 1994
The Mists of Avalon, 1983
The Shattered Chain, 1976
Star of Danger, 1965

Other books you might like:
Mike Ashley, *The Pendragon Chronicles*, 1990
   editor
Frans G. Bengtsson, *The Long Ships*, 1954
Maya Kaathryn Bohnhoff, *The Meri*, 1992
Morgan Llywelyn, *Druids*, 1991
Jennifer Roberson, *Return to Avalon*, 1997
   editor
Jack Whyte, *The Skystone*, 1996

657

MARION ZIMMER BRADLEY, Editor
RACHEL E. HOLMEN, Co-Editor

Sword and Sorceress XIV
(New York: DAW, 1997)

Story type: Anthology
Series: Sword and Sorceress
Summary: This anthology contains a three-page introduction by Bradley, plus individual introductions to 27 stories, frequently downbeat or ominous in tone, with themes including mythical creatures, magic conflict, high fantasy, relationships, and culinary arts. Authors include Rachel E. Holmen, Adrienne Martine-Barnes, Diana L. Paxson, Laura J. Underwood, Elisabeth Waters, and Deborah Wheeler.

Other books by the same author:
The Best of Marion Zimmer Bradley's Fantasy Magazine, Volume II, 1995
The Best of Marion Zimmer Bradley's Fantasy Magazine, 1994
Lythande, 1986
The Sword and Sorceress Series, 1984-1997
Sword of Chaos, 1982

Other books you might like:
George Alec Effinger, *Maureen Birnbaum, Barbarian Swordsperson: The Complete Stories*, 1993
Esther M. Friesner, *Chicks in Chainmail*, 1995
   editor
Kathleen M. Massie-Ferch, *Ancient Enchantresses*, 1995
   Martin H. Greenberg and Richard Gilliam, co-editors
C.L. Moore, *Jirel of Joiry*, 1969
Jessica Amanda Salmonson, *Amazons!*, 1979
   editor

658

C. DALE BRITTAIN
ROBERT A. BOUCHARD, Co-Author

Count Scar
(New York: Baen, 1997)

Story type: Political; Magic Conflict
Major character(s): Galoran, Nobleman (count), Military Personnel; Melchior, Religious, Wizard
Time period(s): Indeterminate Past
Locale(s): Peyrefixade, Fictional City

Summary: To his surprise, Galoran, a scarred and experienced soldier, inherits a distant county. At first, it seems like good luck, but troubles and threats become first noticeable, then inescapable. To survive, Galoran must make an alliance with Melchior, a monk and wizard who ought to be his bitter opponent.

Other books by the same author:
Daughter of Magic, 1996
Voima, 1995
Mage Quest, 1993
The Wood Nymph and the Cranky Saint, 1993
A Bad Spell in Yurt, 1991

Other books you might like:
Steven Brust, *Jhereg*, 1983
Deborah Chester, *Reign of Shadows*, 1996
Barbara Hambly, *The Ladies of Mandrigyn*, 1984
Patricia A. McKillip, *The Riddle-Master of Hed*, 1976
Angus Wells, *Forbidden Magic*, 1992

659

TERRY BROOKS

Running with the Demon

(New York: Ballantine Del Ray, 1997)

Story type: Contemporary
Major character(s): John Ross, Psychic; Nest Freemark, Teenager; The Demon, Demon
Time period(s): 1990s
Locale(s): Hopewell, Illinois

Summary: Over a swelteringly hot Fourth of July weekend, during a steel mill strike that divides Hopewell, a demon schemes to control the town and Nest Freemark's soul. Drawn to the site by horrific dreams of the future which will evolve if he cannot successfully neutralize the threat, John Ross also gravitates to Nest as he battles the demon.

Where it's reviewed:
Booklist, July 1997, page 1773
Kirkus Reviews, July 15, 1997, page 1072
Library Journal, September 15, 1997, page 105
Locus, December 1997, page 25
Publishers Weekly, July 28, 1997, page 57

Other books by the same author:
Hook, 1992
Wizard at Large, 1988
The Black Unicorn, 1987
Magic Kingdom for Sale-Sold!, 1986
The Sword of Shannara, 1977

Other books you might like:
James P. Blaylock, *All the Bells on Earth*, 1995
Elizabeth Hand, *Waking the Moon*, 1995
Rachel Pollack, *Godmother Night*, 1996
Tim Powers, *Last Call*, 1992
Manly Wade Wellman, *The Old Gods Waken*, 1979

660

STEVEN BRUST
EMMA BULL, Co-Author

Freedom & Necessity

(New York: Tor, 1997)

Story type: Historical; Political
Major character(s): James Cobham, Writer, Wealthy; Richard Cobham, Writer, Wealthy; Susan Voight, Writer, Wealthy
Time period(s): 19th century
Locale(s): England

Summary: After the presumed death of James, Richard receives letters letting him know that James is alive, and starts searching for him. Susan, who loved James, also searches for him and pools information with Richard, discovering the much larger political plotting that enmeshes the socio-political structure of England and Europe.

Where it's reviewed:
Booklist, March 15, 1997, page 1231
Kirkus Reviews, January 15, 1997, page 103
Library Journal, January 1997, page 143
Locus, September 1997, page 31
Science Fiction Chronicle, June 1997, page 42

Other books by the same author:
The Gypsy, 1992 (Megan Lindholm, co-author)
The Phoenix Guards, 1991
The Sun, the Moon and the Stars, 1987
The Reign in Hell, 1984
Jhereg, 1983

Other books you might like:
Emma Bull, *Bone Dance*, 1991
Emma Bull, *Finder*, 1994
Emma Bull, *The Princess and the Lord of Night*, 1994
Emma Bull, *War for the Oaks*, 1987
Patricia C. Wrede, *Sorcery and Cecelia*, 1988
    Caroline Stevermer, co-author

661

CHRIS BUNCH

The Seer King

(New York: Warner Aspect, 1997)

Story type: Political
Major character(s): Damastes a Cimabue, Military Personnel, Prisoner; Laish Tenedos, Royalty (emperor), Wizard; Maran Agramonte, Noblewoman (countess)
Time period(s): Indeterminate Past
Locale(s): Numantia, Fictional Country

Summary: A young and eager officer and a radical wizard meet at a battle neither expects to survive. Together, by luck, planning and power, they rise politically and seize control of the Empire. However, with demons, traitors and love against them, their grasp on power remains tenuous.

Where it's reviewed:
Kirkus Reviews, December 1, 1996, page 1706
Locus, January 1997, page 19
Publishers Weekly, January 20, 1997, page 399

Other books by the same author:
The Demon King, 1998
The Darkness of God, 1997
Hunt the Heavens, 1996
The Wind After Time, 1996

Other books you might like:
M.A.R. Barker, *Man of Gold*, 1984
Allan Cole, *Sten*, 1984
    Chris Bunch, co-author
Glen Cook, *The Black Company*, 1984
Kara Dalkey, *Goa*, 1996
Guy Gavriel Kay, *Tigana*, 1990
Roger Zelazny, *Lord of Light*, 1967

662

A.S. BYATT

The Djinn in the Nightingale's Eye

(New York: Random House, 1997)

Story type: Collection; Legend
Major character(s): Gillian Perholt, Scholar; The Djinn, Mythical Creature (genie)
Time period(s): Indeterminate; 1990s
Locale(s): Middle East; United States; Fictional Country

Summary: Contains two reprinted and three original stories, generally upbeat in tone and featuring women in fairy tale settings. Themes include magical devices, mythical creatures, enchanted animals and a woman who considers her options carefully when given three wishes by a djinn.

Where it's reviewed:
Booklist, September 1, 1997, page 6
Kirkus Reviews, September 1, 1997, page 1323
Publishers Weekly, September 1, 1997, page 92

Other books by the same author:
Angels and Insects, 1992
Possession: A Romance, 1990

Other books you might like:
Margaret Atwood, *Good Bones and Simple Murders*, 1994
Emma Donoghue, *Kissing the Witch: Old Tales in New Skins*, 1997
Ethel J. Phelps, *Tatterhood and Other Tales*, 1978
  editor
Barbara G. Walker, *Feminist Fairy Tales*, 1996
Jane Yolen, *Twelve Impossible Things Before Breakfast*, 1997
Jack Zipes, *The Outspoken Princess and the Gentle Knight*, 1994
  editor

663

MARTHA CERDA

Senora Rodriguez and Other Worlds

(Durham, North Carolina: Duke University Press, 1997)

Story type: Literary
Major character(s): Senora Rodriguez, Spouse, Parent
Time period(s): 1990s
Locale(s): Mexico

Summary: Senora Rodriguez, a remarkable woman, owns a remarkable purse filled with bits of the lives of the people around her. The events of her life interweave with moments from the lives and dreams of her family, friends, strangers and myths. Martha Cerda's first novel to be translated into English, translated by Sylvin Jiminez-Anderson.

Where it's reviewed:
New York Times Book Review, October 26, 1997, page 40

Other books you might like:
Jorge Luis Borges, *Labyrinths*, 1962
Gabriel Garcia Marquez, *One Hundred Years of Solitude*, 1970
Bruno Schulz, *The Street of Crocodiles*, 1963

Fay Weldon, *Letters to Alice on First Reading Jane Austin*, 1985
Karen Tei Yamashita, *Tropic of Orange*, 1997

664

VERA CHAPMAN

The Notorious Abbess

(Chicago, Illinois: Academy Chicago, 1997)

Story type: Collection; Religious
Major character(s): Hodierna, Religious (Abbess of Shaston), Adventurer
Time period(s): 12th century
Locale(s): England; Middle East

Summary: Familiar with royalty and Saracens, the ingenious Abbess of Shaston encounters fantastic creatures and the Devil as adventures bring her into the midst of magical and political machinations. Includes 12 stories and a five-page introduction by the editors, Robert H. Boyer and Kenneth J. Zahorski.

Where it's reviewed:
Booklist, July 1997, page 1805
Kirkus Reviews, July 15, 1997, page 1072
Library Journal, October 15, 1997, page 98
Locus, December 1996, page 31

Other books by the same author:
Blaedud the Birdman, 1980
The King's Damosel, 1978
King Arthur's Daughter, 1978
The Green Knight, 1978
The Wife of Bath, 1978

Other books you might like:
Guy Gavriel Kay, *A Song for Arbonne*, 1993
Diana L. Paxson, *The White Raven*, 1988
Susan Shwartz, *The Grail of Hearts*, 1992
Susan Shwartz, *Shards of Empire*, 1996
Judith Tarr, *The Dagger and the Cross: A Novel of the Crusades*, 1991
Judith Tarr, *The Eagle's Daughter*, 1995

665

ROBERT N. CHARRETTE

Wizard of Bones

(New York: HarperPrism, 1997)

Story type: Adventure; Magic Conflict
Series: Chronicles of Aelwyn
Major character(s): Yan Tanafres, Wizard; Ser Handrar, Religious, Wizard; Teletha Schonnegon, Mercenary (bodyguard)
Time period(s): Indeterminate Past
Locale(s): At Sea; Jor Valadrem, Fictional City

Summary: Mostly recovered from his servitude to Yellow Eye, the saurian wizard, Yan Tanafres has come no closer to understanding the strange power he unleashed. When the Empire calls him to undertake a dangerous voyage, Tanafres

Fantasy

accepts, hoping for answers. However, he finds more questions, traitors and deadly peril to his body and soul.

Other books by the same author:
Eye of the Serpent, 1996
Timespell, 1996
A Knight Among Knaves, 1995
A Prince Among Men, 1994
Find Your Own Truth, 1991

Other books you might like:
Glen Cook, *The Swordbearer*, 1982
Terry Goodkind, *Wizard's First Rule*, 1994
Robert Jordan, *The Eye of the World*, 1990
Caroline Stevermer, *A College of Magics*, 1994
Martha Wells, *The Element of Fire*, 1993

666

DEBORAH CHESTER

Realm of Light

(New York: Ace, 1997)

Story type: Political; Magic Conflict
Series: Shadows
Major character(s): Caelan E'non, Gladiator, Psychic; Elandra Albain, Ruler (empress)
Time period(s): Indeterminate Past
Locale(s): Imperia, Fictional City; Trav, Fictional Country

Summary: As the 1000-year Emperor fails, his pact with the Dark God Beloth is nearly expired, and his empire fails him. Caught between traitors, barbarians and damnation, but separated by oaths and marriage, Caelan and Elandra must join together to save the world, however impossible that seems.

Other books by the same author:
Shadow War, 1997
Reign of Shadows, 1996

Other books you might like:
M.A.R. Barker, *Man of Gold*, 1984
Brian Daley, *Doomfarers of Coramonde*, 1977
Barbara Hambly, *The Time of the Dark*, 1982
Robin Hobb, *Assassin's Apprentice*, 1995
Michael Scott Rohan, *The Anvil of Ice*, 1986

667

DEBORAH CHESTER

Shadow War

(New York: Ace, 1997)

Story type: Political; Magic Conflict
Series: Shadows
Major character(s): Caelan E'non, Military Personnel, Psychic; Elandra Albain, Ruler (empress); Sien, Religious, Wizard
Time period(s): Indeterminate Past
Locale(s): Imperia, Fictional City

Summary: The Emperor Kostimon wishes to escape his fate, but forces inside and outside his empire plot against him. Meanwhile, Caelan rises from gladiator to soldier, then Em-

press' Guard, and Elandra becomes Empress. All three must find their destinies if anything of the Empire will survive. Second in a series.

Where it's reviewed:
Kliatt, May 1997, page 12

Other books by the same author:
Realm of Light, 1997
Reign of Shadows, 1996

Other books you might like:
Scott Baker, *Drink the Fire From the Flames*, 1987
Glen Cook, *The Black Company*, 1984
Robert Jordan, *The Eye of the World*, 1990
Guy Gavriel Kay, *The Summer Tree*, 1985
Peg Kerr, *Emerald House Rising*, 1997
Michael Scott Rohan, *The Anvil of Ice*, 1986

668

DEBORAH CHRISTIAN

Kar Kalim

(New York: Torm, 1997)

Story type: Magic Conflict; Adventure
Major character(s): Inya, Recluse, Sorceress; Murl "Kar Kalim" Amrey, Magician, Warrior; Lesseth, Mythical Creature (elemental)
Time period(s): Indeterminate
Locale(s): Astareth, Planet—Imaginary; Drakmil, Mythical Place; Styreia, Planet—Imaginary

Summary: Inya, the Midnight Lady, trains Murl Amrey and sends him into the alternate dimension of Styreia to obtain a wizard-stone. Instead he uses one to become Kar Kalim, conqueror of Styreia, and would be ruler of Astareth as well. Holding Inya and her servants hostage, his egomania and sadism drive Inya and Lesseth to attempt murder. Exiled to Styreia, Inya learns the only way to destroy him may destroy everyone and everything in the area.

Where it's reviewed:
Kirkus Reviews, June 1, 1997, page 841
Library Journal, August 1997, page 141
Locus, November 1997, page 27
Publishers Weekly, June 14, 1997, page 70
Realms of Fantasy, August 1997, page 14

Other books by the same author:
Mainline, 1996

Other books you might like:
Joy Chant, *The Grey Mane of Morning*, 1980
C.J. Cherryh, *Gate of Ivrel*, 1976
Harry Harrison, *Deathworld 3*, 1968
John Maddox Roberts, *The Steel Kings*, 1993
Harry Turtledove, *The Legion of Videssos*, 1987
Sydney J. Van Scyoc, *Bluesong*, 1983
Jack Vance, *The Dirdir*, 1969
Nicholas Yermakov, *Fall into Darkness*, 1982

669

SCOTT CIENCIN

Ancient Games

(New York: AvoNova, 1997)

Story type: Religious; Magic Conflict
Series: Elven Ways
Major character(s): Tom Keeper, Artist, Religious; Mithra, Angel; Kayrlis, Entertainer, Teenager
Time period(s): Indeterminate (equivalent to 1853 and 1863)
Locale(s): Genesis, Fictional City; City of the Abyss, Fictional City; Alternate Earth

Summary: Tom Keeper survives terrible things and gains strange powers, but his worst trials still wait. Forces war in what would be Heaven, while Tom's path leads to Hell. Despite the plans various factions have for him, Tom has power, courage and the support of his friends and allies, and may find the best course of action for Earth, not Heaven. Second in series.

Other books by the same author:
The Ways of Magic, 1996
The Lotus and the Rose, 1993
Night Parade, 1992
The Wolves of Autumn, 1992

Other books you might like:
Jack Dann, *Angels!*, 1995
　　Gardner Dozois, co-editor
Philip Pullman, *The Golden Compass*, 1996
Michael Scott Rohan, *The Anvil of Ice*, 1986
Nancy Springer, *Metal Angel*, 1994
Roger Zelazny, *Lord of Light*, 1967

670

CHRIS CLAREMONT

Shadow Dawn

(New York: Bantam Spectra, 1997)

Story type: Magic Conflict; Quest
Series: Chronicles of the Shadow War
Major character(s): Elora Danan, Royalty (princess), Magician (Daikini); Thorn Drumheller, Companion (protector), Wizard; Torquil Ufgood, Sorcerer
Time period(s): Indeterminate
Locale(s): Angwyn, Fictional Country; Sandeni, Fictional City

Summary: The Shadow War continues unabated. Now 16 years old, Elora studies Fire with Torquil. While performing her test, she inadvertently calls a baby elemental, destroying the forge. When the Shadow War spreads, Elora must fulfill the prophecy by stopping the Deceiver. Sequel to *Shadow Moon*.

Other books by the same author:
Sundowner, 1994
Grounded!, 1991
First Flight, 1987

Other books you might like:
Eleanor Arnason, *The Sword Smith*, 1978

Margaret Ball, *Changeweaver*, 1993
Wayland Drew, *Willow*, 1988
Phyllis Eisenstein, *The Crystal Palace*, 1988
J. Gregory Keyes, *The Waterborn*, 1996
Marc Lebanc, *Flight to Hollow Mountain*, 1996
George Lucas, *Shadow Moon*, 1995
　　Chris Claremont, co-author

671

JO CLAYTON

Drum Calls

(New York: Tor, 1997)

Story type: Adventure
Series: Drums of Chaos
Major character(s): Breith, Slave, Wizard; Cymel, Student, Wizard
Time period(s): Indeterminate Past
Locale(s): Glandair, Planet—Imaginary; Iomard, Planet—Imaginary

Summary: The worlds of Gladair and Iomard come close enough for gifted people to pass from one to the other. Destined to free both worlds, the hero remains untrained, while his comrades fall victim to slavery and dissolute living. With every sorcerer on two worlds looking for him, can the hero possibly succeed in his mission?

Where it's reviewed:
Kirkus Reviews, August 1, 1997, page 1167
Locus, October 1997, page 25
Publishers Weekly, September 29, 1997, page 71

Other books by the same author:
Drum Warning, 1996
Drinker of Souls, 1986
Skeen's Leap, 1986
A Bait of Dreams, 1985
Moongather, 1982

Other books you might like:
Eleanor Arnason, *Daughter of the Bear King*, 1987
C.J. Cherryh, *Fortress in the Eye of Time*, 1995
Brian Daley, *Doomfarers of Coramonde*, 1977
Kristine Kathryn Rusch, *The White Mists of Power*, 1991
Caroline Stevermer, *A College of Magics*, 1994

672

BRENDA W. CLOUGH

How Like a God

(New York: Tor, 1997)

Story type: Contemporary Realism; Psychic Powers
Major character(s): Rob Lewis, Computer Expert, Telepath; Edwin Amadeus Barbrossa, Scientist (microbiologist); Gilgamesh, Deity, Immortal
Time period(s): 1990s
Locale(s): Washington, District of Columbia; New York, New York; Uzbekistan

Summary: Waking up one morning to find he can suddenly read and influence people's minds, Rob Lewis initially in-

Fantasy

tends to use his power to make the world a better place. His darker nature surfaces, however, causing him to flee from his family and home in terror. Only after a period of self-induced solitude can Rob begin the long journey towards finding out what he has become and why.

Where it's reviewed:
Kirkus Reviews, January 1, 1997, page 27
Library Journal, March 15, 1997, page 93
Locus, March 1997, page 21
New York Times Book Review, April 6, 1997, page 24
Voice of Youth Advocates, June 1997, page 115

Other books by the same author:
An Impossible Summer, 1992
The Name of the Sun, 1988
The Realm Beneath, 1986
The Dragon of Mishbil, 1985
The Crystal Crown, 1984

Other books you might like:
Jonathan Carroll, *Bones of the Moon*, 1988
Jonathan Carroll, *Outside the Dog Museum*, 1991
Ken Grimwood, *Replay*, 1986
Eric S. Nylund, *Dry Water*, 1997
Christopher Pike, *Remember Me*, 1989
Robert Silverberg, *To the Land of the Living*, 1989
Dan Simmons, *The Hollow Man*, 1992

673

MOLLY COCHRAN
WARREN MURPHY, Co-Author

The Broken Sword

(New York: Tor, 1997)

Story type: Contemporary; Legend
Series: Forever King
Major character(s): Beatrice, Handicapped (blind), Psychic; Aubrey Katsuleris, Artist (painter), Wizard; Taliesin, Wizard, Immortal
Time period(s): Indeterminate Future
Locale(s): Marrakesh, Morocco; Cadbury Tor, England

Summary: Arthur returns in the body of a teenage boy, with Taliesin and Arthur's Knights returning as well. They recovered Excalibur, but lost the Holy Grail, which now resurfaces in the hands of a once-blind girl. As the secret war between Arthur and the Forces of Darkness heats up, Excalibur's destruction makes all seem lost. Sequel to the *Sequel to the Forever King*.

Where it's reviewed:
Kirkus Reviews, March 1, 1997, page 340
Library Journal, April 15, 1997, page 123
Publishers Weekly, April 28, 1997, page 55
School Library Journal, August 1997, page 188

Other books by the same author:
World Without End, 1996
The Forever King, 1992

Other books you might like:
James P. Blaylock, *The Paper Grail*, 1991
Simon Hawke, *The Wizard of 4th Street*, 1987

K.W. Jeter, *Morlock Night*, 1979
Tim Powers, *Last Call*, 1992
Michael A. Stackpole, *Once a Hero*, 1994

674

DAVID B. COE

Children of Amarid

(New York: Tor, 1997)

Story type: Adventure; Quest
Series: Lon Tobyn Chronicle
Major character(s): Jaryd, Wizard (mage-attend); Alayna, Wizard
Time period(s): Indeterminate
Locale(s): Tobyn-Ser, Fictional Country

Summary: The children of Amarid mediate disputes, heal ills and do good work for the lan of Tobyn-Ser, but lately have been accused of crimes and deaths. The two newest Hawk-mages, Jaryd and Alayna, venture across the country in search of the real evildoers, even as they discover that the answers may be found close to the temple. First in series.

Where it's reviewed:
Kirkus Reviews, March 15, 1997, page 422
Library Journal, April 15, 1997, page 123
Publishers Weekly, April 28, 1998, page 55
Realms of Fantasy, October 1997, page 97
Starlog, October 1997, page 14

Other books you might like:
Maggie Furey, *Aurian*, 1994
J. Gregory Keyes, *The Waterborn*, 1996
Mercedes Lackey, *Arrows of the Queen*, 1987
R.A. Salvatore, *The Demon Awakens*, 1997
Michelle West, *Hunter's Oath*, 1995

675

D.J. CONWAY

Soothslayer: A Magical Fantasy

(St. Paul, Minnesota: Llewellyn Publications, 1997)

Story type: Magic Conflict; Religious
Series: Dream Warrior Trilogy
Major character(s): Corri Farblood, Sorcerer, Leader (Dream Warrior); The Soothslayer, Sorcerer, Religious (priest); Imandoff Silverhair, Sorcerer
Time period(s): Indeterminate
Locale(s): Sar Akka, Fictional Country

Summary: Corri Farblood's acceptance of the fact that she is truly the Dream Warrior of prophecy propels her to the forefront of a war to prevent the religious fanatics of Frav, led by Corri's father, Kayth, from invading their lands and destroying their way of life. Imandoff Silverhair helps Corri reach her full magical potential while they plan the defeat of Kayth and his evil ally, the Soothsayer. Second volume in trilogy.

Other books by the same author:
The Dream Warrior, 1996

Other books you might like:
Maya Kaathryn Bohnhoff, *The Spirit Gate*, 1996
D.A. Heeley, *Lilith*, 1996
Mercedes Lackey, *The Lark and the Wren*, 1991
Thomas K. Martin, *A Matter of Honor*, 1994
Eloise Jarvis McGraw, *The Moorchild*, 1996
Elizabeth Moon, *Sheepfarmer's Daughter*, 1988
Melanie Rawn, *Dragon Prince*, 1988
Melanie Rawn, *The Ruins of Ambrai*, 1994
Martha Wells, *The Element of Fire*, 1993

676

GLEN COOK

She Is the Darkness

(New York: Tor, 1997)

Story type: Military; Magic Conflict
Series: Black Company: Glittering Stone Triology
Major character(s): Murgen, Military Personnel, Psychic; Soul Catcher, Wizard, Mentally Ill Person; Croaker, Military Personnel, Doctor
Time period(s): Indeterminate Past
Locale(s): Shadowcatch, Fictional City

Summary: The Black Company lays siege to Shadowcatch, hoping to finally clear the road to Khatovar. But Longshadow remains unvanquished, while other menaces, better hidden, stronger and crueler, wait in the wings. For Murgen, the pain and revelations of the war will outweigh the fates of empires.

Where it's reviewed:
Booklist, September 15, 1997, page 216
Kirkus Reviews, July 15, 1997, page 1074
Publishers Weekly, September 22, 1997, page 74

Other books by the same author:
Bleak Seasons, 1996
The Silver Spike, 1989
The Dragon Never Sleeps, 1988
The Black Company, 1984
A Shadow of All Night Falling, 1979

Other books you might like:
Chris Bunch, *The Seer King*, 1997
Brian Daley, *Doomfarers of Coramonde*, 1977
Kara Dalkey, *Goa*, 1996
Guy Gavriel Kay, *The Lions of Al-Rassan*, 1995
George R.R. Martin, *A Game of Thrones*, 1996

677

RICK COOK

The Wiz Biz

(New York: Baen, 1997)

Story type: Light Fantasy; Alternate World
Series: Wizardry
Major character(s): William Irving ''Wiz'' Zumwalt, Computer Expert, Wizard, Witch; Shiara, Sorceress; Moira, Witch
Time period(s): 1990s; Indeterminate
Locale(s): Fictional Country

Summary: Desperate to turn back the evil wizards of the Black League, Patrius uses a powerful and dangerous spell to summon a great wizard from another world. The spell costs Patrius his life and brings Wiz Zumwalt, a computer wizard who knows nothing of this world's magic. Moira helps him escape the Black League's minions and leads him to the temporary haven of Heart's Ease, Shiara's retreat from her own heartbreak. There Wiz begins to experiment with programming demons and invents an entirely new system of magic to use against the Black League. Originally published in two volumes as *Wizard's Bane* (1989) and *The Wizardry Compiled* (1990).

Other books by the same author:
The Wizardry Quested, 1996
The Wizardry Consulted, 1995
Mall Purchase Night, 1993
The Wizardry Cursed, 1991

Other books you might like:
Robert Asprin, *Another Fine Myth*, 1978
Gordon R. Dickson, *The Dragon and the George*, 1976
Barbara Hambly, *The Silicon Mage*, 1988
Simon Hawke, *The Wizard of 4th Street*, 1987
Terry Pratchett, *Lords and Ladies*, 1995
Christopher Stasheff, *Her Majesty's Wizard*, 1986

678

BERNARD CORNWELL

Enemy of God

(New York: St. Martin's Press, 1997)

Story type: Legend
Series: Warlord Chronicles
Major character(s): Derfel Cadarn, Warrior; Arthur, Royalty; Merlin, Religious (druid), Wizard
Time period(s): 6th century
Locale(s): England

Summary: Winning many victories at home, Arthur loses Armorica to the Franks, while other threats await. Merlin and Nimue plot the return of the Old Gods, bending Arthur's policy to aid them. Desperately in love with Ceinwyn, loyal Derfel must watch her marry the exiled Lancelot. Second in trilogy.

Where it's reviewed:
Fantasy & Science Fiction, October/November 1997, page 44
Library Journal, July 1997, page 123
Publishers Weekly, June 16, 1997, page 47

Other books by the same author:
The Winter King, 1996

Other books you might like:
David Drake, *The Dragon Lord*, 1979
Ian McDowell, *Mordred's Curse*, 1996
Phyllis Ann Karr, *The Idylls of the Queen*, 1982
Tim Powers, *The Drawing of the Dark*, 1979
Mary Stewart, *The Crystal Cave*, 1970

679

ANNE ELIOT CROMPTON

Gawain and Lady Green

(New York: Donald I. Fine, 1997)

Story type: Legend
Major character(s): Gawain, Knight; Lady Green, Sorceress; Lord Bright, Nobleman, Knight
Time period(s): Indeterminate
Locale(s): England

Summary: Traveling on Arthur's command, Sir Gawain becomes trapped in a small village destined for sacrifice. He escapes with the aid of Lady Green, who loves him, but betrays her soon after. When the Green Knight comes to Arthur's court with a wager, Gawain must pay for his actions, even if it costs him his honor, pride, or life. Sequel to *Merlin's Harp*.

Where it's reviewed:
Kirkus Reviews, January 15, 1997, page 77
Library Journal, March 15, 1997, page 93
Publishers Weekly, March 31, 1997, page 67

Other books by the same author:
Merlin's Harp, 1995

Other books you might like:
Marion Zimmer Bradley, *The Mists of Avalon*, 1983
Vera Chapman, *The Green Knight*, 1978
Phyllis Ann Karr, *The Idylls of the Queen*, 1982
Ian McDowell, *Mordred's Curse*, 1996
J.R.R. Tolkien, *Sir Gawain and the Green Knight, Pearl, and Sir Orfeo*, 1975

680

KARA DALKEY

Bijapur

(New York: Tor, 1997)

Story type: Historical; Adventure
Series: Blood of the Goddess
Major character(s): Thomas Chinnery, Apothecary; Aditi, Sorcerer
Time period(s): 16th century (1597)
Locale(s): India

Summary: Thomas Chinnery and the party from Goa reach Bijapur in their search for the death-defying elixir. Mirza Ali Akbarshah, a Mughul general interested in expanding his ruler's territory, also advances on Bijapur where Ibrahim Adilshah, the ruler of Bijapur, decides to send all of them on the quest for the elixir.

Where it's reviewed:
Booklist, April 1, 1997, page 1283
Kirkus Reviews, March 1, 1997, page 340
Library Journal, April 15, 1997, page 123
Locus, April 1997, page 27
Publishers Weekly, April 28, 1997, page 54

Other books by the same author:
Goa, 1996

Little Sister, 1996
The Sword of Sagamore, 1989
Euryale, 1988
The Nightingale, 1988

Other books you might like:
Piers Anthony, *The Willing Spirit*, 1996
  Alfred Tella, co-author
M.A.R. Barker, *Flamesong*, 1986
M.A.R. Barker, *Man of Gold*, 1984
L. Sprague de Camp, *The Golden Wind*, 1969
Rudyard Kipling, *Famous Tales of India*, 1962
Tanith Lee, *Tamastara, or the Indian Nights*, 1984
Chelsea Quinn Yarbro, *The Path of the Eclipse*, 1981
Roger Zelazny, *Lord of Light*, 1967

681

KARA DALKEY

Steel Rose

(New York: Roc, 1997)

Story type: Urban; Magic Conflict
Major character(s): Tiffany Jeanine "T.J." Kaminski, Artist, Student—College; Ralph, Mythical Creature (knocker), Activist; Norton, Mythical Creature (knocker), Activist
Time period(s): 1990s
Locale(s): Pittsburgh, Pennsylvania; Under the Hill, Mythical Place

Summary: Rehearsing new material after her audience fails to appreciate T.J.'s performance art, T.J. chances to incorporate an incantation from an old book, which brings forth a pair of Unseelie helpers intent on using T.J.'s act to irritate the Sidhe's Seelie court. After unintentionally accepting a challenge of battle from the Seelie court, T.J. reluctantly trusts Ralph and Norton with her performance art while they fight for Unseelie rights.

Where it's reviewed:
Locus, November 1997, page 25

Other books by the same author:
Little Sister, 1996
The Sword of Sagamore, 1989
Euryale, 1988
The Nightingale, 1988
The Curse of Sagamore, 1986

682

ELLEN DATLOW, Editor
TERRI WINDLING, Co-Editor

Black Swan, White Raven

(New York: Avon, 1997)

Story type: Anthology; Legend

Summary: Five-page introduction and individual introductions to 21 original stories, frequently dark in tone, which explore themes of classic fairy tales or rework familiar tales such as, "Sleeping Beauty," "Little Red Riding Hood," "Thumbelina," "Rumpelstiltskin," "The Little Match Girl," "Hansel and Gretel," "Rapunzel," "The Tinder

Box'' and "Snow White and the Seven Dwarves." Authors include Michael Blumlein, Michael Cadnum, John Crowley, Karen Joy Fowler, Esther M. Friesner, Gregory Frost, Nina Kiriki Hoffman, Garry Kilworth, Nancy Kress, Pat Murphy, Joyce Carol Oats, Midori Snyder, Steve Rasnic Tem, and Jane Yolen.

Where it's reviewed:
Booklist, April 15, 1997, page 1387
Kirkus Reviews, April 1, 1997, page 510
Library Journal, June 15, 1997, page 100
Locus, July 1997, page 25
Publishers Weekly, May 26, 1997, page 71

Other books by the same author:
Ruby Slippers, Golden Tears, 1995 (Terri Windling, co-editor)
Black Thorn, White Rose, 1994 (Terri Windling, co-editor)
Snow White, Blood Red, 1993 (Terri Windling, co-editor)
Blood Is Not Enough, 1990
The Year's Best Fantasy and Horror Series, 1989- (Terri Windling, co-editor)

Other books you might like:
A.S. Byatt, *The Djinn in the Nightingale's Eye*, 1997
Kara Dalkey, *The Nightingale*, 1988
Emma Donoghue, *Kissing the Witch: Old Tales in New Skins*, 1997
Robin McKinley, *Deerskin*, 1993
Delia Sherman, *The Porcelain Dove*, 1993
Terri Windling, *The Armless Maiden and Other Tales for Childhood's Survivors*, 1995 editor
Terri Windling, *The Wood Wife*, 1996
Jane Yolen, *Briar Rose*, 1992

683

BRETT DAVIS

Hair of the Dog

(New York: Baen, 1997)

Story type: Mystery
Major character(s): Ashley Durbin, Journalist; Bob Savik, Police Officer (retired); Paul Moreau, Werewolf
Time period(s): 21st century
Locale(s): Las Vegas, Nevada

Summary: After Monty Allen announces new hope on his telethon to raise money for lycanthropy research, Ashley Durbin and Bob Savik investigate the murder of the researcher who discovered the reported cure, discovering many puzzling aspects of the case as they continue to ask embarrassing questions.

Where it's reviewed:
Kliatt, May 1997, page 12
Science Fiction Chronicle, June 1997, page 46

Other books by the same author:
The Faery Convention, 1995

Other books you might like:
Laurell K. Hamilton, *The Lunatic Cafe*, 1996
Tanya Huff, *Blood Price*, 1991

Nick Pollotta, *Full Moonster*, 1992
Will Shetterly, *Nevernever*, 1993
Denise Vitola, *Opalite Moon*, 1997
Denise Vitola, *Quantum Moon*, 1996

684

CAROL DAWSON

Meeting the Minotaur

(Chapel Hill, North Carolina: Algonquin, 1997)

Story type: Legend; Contemporary Realism
Major character(s): Taylor Thaddeus "Taytay" Troys, Handicapped, Son; Ramon Vizuelos, Friend, Criminal; A.J. Deeds, Parent, Wealthy
Time period(s): 1990s
Locale(s): Bernice, Texas; Tokyo, Japan; Dallas, Texas

Summary: Taytay grows up believing himself abandoned by an uncaring father. Handicapped by meningitis, he finds that no one expects much of him. After Taytay drops out of college, his grandfather informs him that he will bankroll any business taytay decides to develop. Taytay decides to go into burglary to connect with his father. Retells *Theseus and the Minotaur*.

Where it's reviewed:
Booklist, July 1997, page 1795
Kirkus Reviews, May 15, 1997, page 737

Other books you might like:
Gael Baudino, *Gossamer Axe*, 1990
Marion Zimmer Bradley, *The Mists of Avalon*, 1983
Pamela Dean, *Tam Lin*, 1991
Amarantha Knight, *The Darker Passions: Frankenstein*, 1995
Elizabeth Ann Scarborough, *Carol for Another Christmas*, 1996
Jane Yolen, *Briar Rose*, 1992

685

CHARLES DE LINT

Trader

(New York: Tor, 1997)

Story type: Contemporary; Quest
Series: Newford
Major character(s): Max Trader, Artisan (luthier), Businessman; Johnny Devlin, Rogue, Alcoholic; Zefty Lacerda, Waiter/Waitress
Time period(s): 1990s
Locale(s): Newford, Fictional City; Canada; The Spiritworld, Mythical Place

Summary: When Max and Johnny mysteriously wake up in each other's bodies, ne'er-do-well Johnny immediately adapts to Max's stable environment. Now in possession of Johnny's body and miserable life to date, Max must put together a new life. His efforts lead to the realm of dreams and spirits.

Where it's reviewed:
Booklist, January 1 & 15, 1997, page 826
Kirkus Reviews, November 15, 1996, page 1639

Library Journal, December 1996, page 152
Publishers Weekly, December 9, 1996, page 65
Voice of Youth Advocates, August 1997, page 192

Other books by the same author:
Someplace to Be Flying, 1998
The Ivory and the Horn, 1995
Memory and Dream, 1994
Dreams Underfoot, 1993
The Little Country, 1991

Other books you might like:
Aaron Allston, *Galatea in 2-D*, 1993
A.A. Attanasio, *The Moon's Wife: A Hystery*, 1993
Peter R. Emshwiller, *The Host*, 1991
Robert Holdstock, *Mythago Wood*, 1984
Ben Okri, *The Famished Road*, 1992
Dan Simmons, *The Hollow Man*, 1992
Nancy Springer, *Larque on the Wing*, 1994

686

STEPHEN DEDMAN

The Art of Arrow Cutting

(New York: Tor, 1997)

Story type: Contemporary; Magic Conflict
Major character(s): Michelangelo "Mage" Magistrale, Wizard, Photographer; Tamenaga Tatsuo, Wizard, Organized Crime Figure; Charles "Charlie" Willis Takumo, Supernatural Being, Stuntman
Time period(s): 1990s
Locale(s): Las Vegas, Nevada; Calgary, Alberta, Canada

Summary: Photographer "Mage" Magistrale briefly meets a mysterious ill woman who gives him a key, and must suddenly evade the police, the Japanese mob, female ninja assassins, and a rukoro-kubi, which is nothing but a head and pair of hands. First novel.

Where it's reviewed:
Kirkus Reviews, April 15, 1997, page 596
Library Journal, June 15, 1997, page 101
Locus, July 1997, page 33
Publishers Weekly, May 19, 1997, page 71
Voice of Youth Advocates, December 1997, page 323

Other books you might like:
Marion Zimmer Bradley, *Witchlight*, 1996
Kara Dalkey, *Little Sister*, 1996
Kwadwo Agymah Kamau, *Flickering Shadows*, 1996
Mercedes Lackey, *Fire Rose*, 1995
Carey Osborne, *Iroshi*, 1995

687

TOM DEITZ

Landslayer's Law

(New York: AvoNova, 1997)

Story type: Adventure; Alternate World
Series: David Sullivan

Major character(s): David Sullivan, Adventurer; Lugh, Royalty, Mythical Creature (Sidhe); James Murphy, Musician (bagpiper)
Time period(s): 1990s
Locale(s): Georgia; Tir-Nan-Og, Mythical Place (Faerie)

Summary: When real estate developers endanger the walls between Faerie and Georgia, High King Lugh threatens to retaliate with a "final war" against humans. David Sullivan and friends must save both worlds.

Other books by the same author:
Dreamseeker's Road, 1995
Dreambuilder, 1992
Soulsmith, 1991
Sunshaker's War, 1990
Windmaster's Bane, 1986

Other books you might like:
Aaron Allston, *Doc Sidhe*, 1995
Charles de Lint, *Moonheart: A Romance*, 1984
Guy Gavriel Kay, *The Summer Tree*, 1985
Will Shetterly, *Elsewhere*, 1991
Michael Williams, *Arcady*, 1996

688

GORDON R. DICKSON

The Dragon and the Gnarly King

(New York: Tor, 1997)

Story type: Alternate World; Magic Conflict
Series: Dragon Knight
Major character(s): Jim Eckert, Nobleman (baron), Magician; Angie Eckert, Noblewoman (baroness), Spouse; Robert de Clifford, Nobleman (Earl), Kidnapper
Time period(s): 14th century
Locale(s): England; Alternate Earth

Summary: When the Earl of Cumberland and the King of the Gnarlies join forces and kidnap Robert, adopted son of Jim and Angie Eckert, the Eckerts and their friends set out to find and rescue him. In the process, they must avoid the Earl's plots to have them accused of and executed for high treason, and then become embroiled in a power struggle for leadership of the Gnarlies.

Where it's reviewed:
Booklist, August 1997, page 1886
Kirkus Reviews, July 1, 1997, page 992
Library Journal, August 1997, page 140
Publishers Weekly, July 14, 1997, page 69
Starlog, September 1997, page 81

Other books by the same author:
The Dragon and the Djinn, 1996
The Dragon, the Earl and the Troll, 1994
The Dragon at War, 1992
The Dragon Knight, 1990
The Dragon and the George, 1976

Other books you might like:
Steven Brust, *Jhereg*, 1983
John DeChancie, *Castle Perilous*, 1988
Ursula K. Le Guin, *A Wizard of Earthsea*, 1968

Terry Pratchett, *Wyrd Sisters*, 1990
Joel Rosenberg, *The Fire Duke*, 1995
S.P. Somtow, *Riverrun*, 1991

689

EMMA DONOGHUE

Kissing the Witch: Old Tales in New Skins
(New York: HarperCollins/Joanna Colter Books, 1997)

Story type: Collection; Legend

Summary: Contains 13 linked stories, varying in tone, which present traditional fairy tales and fairy tale patterns with a twist. Rewritten to present the stories from the women's point of view, the familiar characters include Snow White, Cinderella, Rumplestiltskin, Rapunzel and Beauty and the Beast.

Where it's reviewed:
Booklist, June 1 & 15, 1997, page 1684
Kirkus Reviews, February 1, 1997, page 221
School Library Journal, June 1997, page 117
Voice of Youth Advocates, August 1997, page 192

Other books you might like:
Margaret Atwood, *Good Bones and Simple Murders*, 1994
William J. Brooke, *Teller of Tales*, 1994
David Fisher, *Legally Correct Fairy Tales*, 1996
James Finn Garner, *Once upon a More Enlightened Time*, 1995
James Finn Garner, *Politically Correct Bedtime Stories*, 1994
James Finn Garner, *Politically Correct Holiday Stories*, 1995
Ethel J. Phelps, *Tatterhood and Other Tales*, 1978
    editor

690

GARDNER DOZOIS, Editor

Modern Classics of Fantasy
(New York: St. Martin's, 1997)

Story type: Anthology

Summary: Contains a 13-page preface, five pages of recommended readings and 32 stories with individual introductions, presented in the order of original publication in periodicals and anthologies 1939-1996. In settings from contemporary to fantastic and tone from light to ominous, the short stories, novellas and excerpts from longer works, explore a variety of themes, such as high fantasy, sword and sorcery, mythical creatures, quests, time travel, religion and legends. Authors include Poul Anderson, Peter S. Beagle, James P. Blaylock, Suzy McKee Charnas, John Crowley, Avram Davidson, L. Sprague de Camp, George Alex Effinger, Ester M. Friesner, Horace L. Gold, R.A. Lafferty, Fritz Leiber, Ursula K. Le Guin, Lucius Shepard, Bruce Sterling, Thomas Burnett Swann, Michael Swanwick, Judith Tarr, Jack Vance, Howard Waldrop, Manly Wade Wellman, Gene Wolfe, Jane Yolen and Roger Zelazny.

Where it's reviewed:
Booklist, December 1, 1996, page 643
Library Journal, December 1996, page 152
Publishers Weekly, December 30, 1997, page 59

Other books by the same author:
Modern Classic Short Novels of Science Fiction, 1994
Modern Classics of Science Fiction, 1992
The Best of Isaac Asimov's SF Magazine, 1988
The Year's Best Science Fiction Series, 1984-1997
A Day in the Life, 1972

Other books you might like:
Mike Ashley, *The Random House Book of Fantasy Stories*, 1997
    editor
Robert H. Boyer, *Visions & Imaginings: Classic Fantasy Fiction*, 1992
    Kenneth J. Zahorski, co-editor
Alison Lurie, *The Oxford Book of Modern Fairy Tales*, 1993
    editor
Tom Shippey, *The Oxford Book of Fantasy Stories*, 1993
    editor
Robert Silverberg, *The Fantasy Hall of Fame*, 1983
    editor

691

DAVID DRAKE

Lord of the Isles
(New York: Tor, 1997)

Story type: Magic Conflict
Major character(s): Tenoctris, Wizard, Aged Person; Garric or-Reise, Warrior, Hunter; The Hooded One, Wizard
Time period(s): Indeterminate Past
Locale(s): Yole, Fictional Country; Barca's Hamlet, Fictional City

Summary: The Duke of Yole has won a great victory, but his ambition ends when the payment turns out to be the sinking of his realm. His court wizard, Tenoctris, flees a millennium into the future, but finds the same peril there. Out of malice or error, the Hooded One still wants the Throne of Malhar and will sink the whole world to get it.

Where it's reviewed:
Booklist, August 1997, page 1886
Kirkus Reviews, June 1, 1997, page 841
Library Journal, September 15, 1997, page 106
Locus, June 1997, page 21
Publishers Weekly, July 28, 1997, page 59

Other books by the same author:
Igniting the Reaches, 1994
Old Nathan, 1991
Vettius and His Friends, 1989
Ranks of Bronze, 1986
The Dragon Lord, 1979

Other books you might like:
Glen Cook, *The Swordbearer*, 1982
Robin Hobb, *Assassin's Apprentice*, 1995
Ursula K. Le Guin, *A Wizard of Earthsea*, 1968
Fritz Leiber, *Ill Met in Lankhmar*, 1995
Martha Wells, *The Element of Fire*, 1993

Fantasy

692

DIANE DUANE

The Book of Night with Moon

(New York: Warner Aspect, 1997)

Story type: Magic Conflict; Adventure
Major character(s): Rhiow, Animal (cat), Wizard; Urruah, Animal (cat), Wizard; Saash, Animal (cat), Wizard
Time period(s): 1990s; Indeterminate
Locale(s): New York, New York

Summary: Responsible for weaving and maintaining the magical threads linking different realities, four cats must repel the horrifying invasion from another dimension coming through the magic doorways in Grand Central Station.

Where it's reviewed:
Kirkus Reviews, October 15, 1997, page 1560
Locus, November 1997, page 25
Publishers Weekly, November 10, 1997, page 59

Other books by the same author:
A Wizard Abroad, 1997
High Wizardry, 1990
Deep Wizardry, 1985
So You Want to Be a Wizard?, 1983
The Door into Fire, 1979

Other books you might like:
A.A. Attanasio, *The Dragon and the Unicorn*, 1996
Louis de Bernieres, *The War of Don Emmanuel's Nether Parts*, 1992
Tanya Huff, *Summon the Keeper*, 1998
Shirley Rousseau Murphy, *The Catsworld Portal*, 1992
Andre Norton, *Catseye*, 1961
L.A. Taylor, *Cat's Paw*, 1995
Tad Williams, *Tailchaser's Song*, 1985

693

DIANE DUANE

A Wizard Abroad

(New York: Harcourt Brace, 1997)

Story type: Light Fantasy; Young Adult
Series: Wizardry
Major character(s): Juanita "Nita" Callahan, Teenager, Wizard (American); Ronan Nolan, Teenager, Wizard (Irish); Tualha, Animal (kitten), Minstrel (bard)
Time period(s): 1990s
Locale(s): Ireland; Under the Hill, Mythical Place

Summary: When Nita goes on a vacation to her Aunt's home in Ireland, her parents expect her to take a break from magic and her wizard partner. Learning about Irish legend and mythology, Nita and her partner, who travels to Ireland by magic, soon must help in a desperate effort to save everything from the terror of Irish monsters come to life. Originally published 1993, fourth in series.

Where it's reviewed:
Booklist, October 1, 1997, page 319
School Library Journal, September 1997, page 216

Other books by the same author:
Empire's End, 1997
The Venom Factor, 1994
High Wizardry, 1990
Deep Wizardry, 1985
So You Want to Be a Wizard?, 1983

Other books you might like:
Susan Cooper, *The Dark Is Rising*, 1973
Diana Wynne Jones, *Cart and Cwidder*, 1977
Diana Wynne Jones, *Howl's Moving Castle*, 1986
Margaret Mahy, *The Tricksters*, 1987
Jody Lynn Nye, *Mythology Abroad*, 1991
Evangeline Walton, *The Children of Llyr*, 1971
Patricia C. Wrede, *Talking to Dragons*, 1993
    revised

694

DAVE DUNCAN

Future Indefinite

(New York: Avon, 1997)

Story type: Alternate World
Series: Great Game
Major character(s): Edward Exeter, Traveller, Leader; Prat'han Potter, Revolutionary, Warrior; Dosh Coachman, Prostitute (gigolo)
Time period(s): 1910s; Indeterminate Past
Locale(s): England; Nextdoor, Alternate Earth

Summary: Edward Exeter has shuffled back and forth between Earth and Nextdoor for five years, always a pawn in someone else's plan. With Exeter now prepared to take his place at the center of his own plan, for his own purposes, the Pentatheon, the Service and especially Zath, the "god of death," had best beware of the Liberator.

Where it's reviewed:
Booklist, August 1997, page 1886
Kirkus Reviews, June 15, 1997, page 918
Locus, August 1997, page 21
Publishers Weekly, July 14, 1997, page 69

Other books by the same author:
Present Tense, 1996
Past Imperative, 1995
Upland Outlaws, 1993
The Magic Casement, 1990
The Reluctant Swordsman, 1988

Other books you might like:
Poul Anderson, *Three Hearts and Three Lions*, 1961
Eleanor Arnason, *Daughter of the Bear King*, 1987
Barbara Hambly, *The Time of the Dark*, 1982
H. Beam Piper, *Lord Kalvan of Otherwhen*, 1965
Roger Zelazny, *Nine Princes in Amber*, 1970

695

DORANNA DURGIN

Changespell

(New York: Baen, 1997)

Story type: Alternate World; Magic Conflict
Major character(s): Jess, Animal (horse), Young Woman; Carey, Courier; Jaime Cabot, Horse Trainer
Time period(s): Indeterminate
Locale(s): Alternate Earth

Summary: Back in her own world, Jess works as a human courier, though she can turn herself into a horse through use of a spellstone. In horse form, however, she cannot trigger the spell to make herself human, but must rely on one of her friends. This proves a serious problem when some rogue magicians capture her as part of their experiments on changing animals to humans and vice versa. Jess, Carey, Jaime, and their friends from both worlds team up to put an end to the magicians' schemes and to the use of the dangerous drug ''mage lure.'' Sequel to *Dun Lady's Jess*.

Where it's reviewed:
Kliatt, July 1997, page 14

Other books by the same author:
Barrenlands, 1998
Touched by Magic, 1996
Dun Lady's Jess, 1994

Other books you might like:
Eleanor Arnason, *Daughter of the Bear King*, 1987
C.J. Cherryh, *Rider at the Gate*, 1995
Rick Cook, *The Wiz Biz*, 1997
Simon R. Green, *Blue Moon Rising*, 1991
Barbara Hambly, *The Armies of Daylight*, 1983
R.A. MacAvoy, *The Grey Horse*, 1987

696

DAVID EDDINGS
LEIGH EDDINGS, Co-Author

Polgara the Sorceress

(New York: Ballantine Del Rey, 1997)

Story type: Adventure; Political
Major character(s): Polgara, Sorceress, Adventurer
Time period(s): Indeterminate
Locale(s): Kingdoms of the West, Mythical Place; Arendia, Fictional Country

Summary: Seeking to complement her father, Belgarath the Sorcerer's, account of events and hoping future rulers will avoid the mistakes of the past, Polgara relates events from her extraordinary life, from youngster to accomplished shapechanger and Duchess of Erat.

Where it's reviewed:
Booklist, November 15, 1997, page 548
Kirkus Reviews, September 1, 1997, page 1346
Publishers Weekly, October 13, 1997, page 60
Starlog, April 1998, page 14

Other books by the same author:
Belgarath the Sorcerer, 1995
Enchanter's Endgame, 1984
Magician's Gambit, 1983
Pawn of Prophecy, 1982
Queen of Sorcery, 1982

Other books you might like:
Steven Brust, *The Phoenix Guards*, 1991
Terry Goodkind, *Stone of Tears*, 1995
Robert Jordan, *The Eye of the World*, 1990
Patricia A. McKillip, *The Sorceress and the Cygnet*, 1991

697

RANDY LEE EICKHOFF

The Raid

(New York: Forge, 1997)

Story type: Legend
Major character(s): Cuchlainn, Warrior, Teenager
Time period(s): 1st century
Locale(s): Ulster, Ireland; Connacht, Ireland

Summary: When the theft of a magical bull in a bid for power precipitates warfare, only Cuchlainn can save the province of Ulster from the Connacht invasion.

Where it's reviewed:
Kirkus Reviews, January 15, 1997, page 103
Publishers Weekly, January 27, 1997, page 78

Other books you might like:
Kenneth C. Flint, *A Storm upon Ulster*, 1981
Morgan Llywelyn, *Red Branch*, 1989
Diana L. Paxson, *Master of Earth and Water*, 1993
    Adrienne Martin-Barnes, co-author
Evangeline Walton, *The Children of Llyr*, 1971

698

KATE ELLIOTT (Pseudonym of Alis A. Rasmussen)

King's Dragon

(New York: DAW, 1997)

Story type: Magic Conflict; Political
Series: Crown of Stars
Major character(s): Alain, Bastard Son, Military Personnel (soldier); Liath, Courier (King's Eagle)
Time period(s): Indeterminate
Locale(s): Wendar, Fictional Country

Summary: As royal siblings jostle for control, strife envelops the land. After her father's murder, Liath escapes her unpleasant fate to become an elite messenger, while Alain's life changes when the invaders who sack his monastery send him off to become a soldier. Fate thrusts both of them into unexpected roles in the destiny of their land.

Where it's reviewed:
Booklist, February 15, 1997, page 1008
Kirkus Reviews, December 1, 1996, page 1707
Locus, February 1997, page 25
Publishers Weekly, January 20, 1997, page 398

Fantasy

Voice of Youth Advocates, June 1997, page 116

Other books by the same author:
The Law of Becoming, 1994
His Conquering Sword, 1993
An Earthly Crown, 1993
Jaran, 1992

Other books you might like:
Lynn Flewelling, *Luck in the Shadows*, 1996
Robin Hobb, *Assassin's Apprentice*, 1995
J.V. Jones, *The Baker's Boy*, 1995
Melanie Rawn, *Dragon Prince*, 1988
Melanie Rawn, *The Golden Key*, 1997
   Jennifer Roberson, Kate Elliott, co-authors
Martha Wells, *The Element of Fire*, 1993

699

RU EMERSON

The Thief of Hermes

(New York: Boulevard, 1997)

Story type: Legend; Adventure
Series: Xena: Warrior Princess
Major character(s): Xena, Warrior, Royalty; Gabrielle, Warrior, Storyteller; Helarion, Thief
Time period(s): Indeterminate Past
Locale(s): Athens, Greece

Summary: When Helarion, who claims the sun god Hermes as his parent, frames Xena and Gabrielle for one of his crimes, the pair must plan a jailbreak and set the record straight. Television tie-in.

Other books by the same author:
The Huntress and the Sphinx, 1997
The Empty Throne, 1996
One Land, One Duke, 1992
The Two in Hiding, 1991
The Calling of the Three, 1990

Other books you might like:
Marion Zimmer Bradley, *The Sword and Sorceress Series*, 1984-1997
   editor
George Alec Effinger, *Maureen Birnbaum, Barbarian Swordsperson: The Complete Stories*, 1993
Esther M. Friesner, *Chicks in Chainmail*, 1995
   editor
Stella Howard, *Prophecy of Darkness*, 1997
Jessica Amanda Salmonson, *Amazons!*, 1979
   editor

700

CLAYTON EMERY

Cardmaster

(New York: Baen, 1997)

Story type: Adventure
Series: Fantasy Adventure
Major character(s): Byron, Apprentice, Wizard (cardsmith); Cerise, Adventurer; Veronica, Religious

Time period(s): Indeterminate Past
Locale(s): Waterholm, Fictional City; Thallandia, Fictional Country

Summary: Byron's master dies under mysterious circumstances in a fire that the apprentice barely escapes. While fleeing, Byron meets the cardmistress, Cerise, and forms an uneasy alliance against their mutual enemies, which certainly include the church, but may also involve darker forces. Collectible card game tie-in.

Other books by the same author:
Final Sacrifice, 1995
Shattered Chains, 1995
Whispering Woods, 1995
Outcasts, 1990
Tales of Robin Hood, 1988

Other books you might like:
Steven Brust, *Jhereg*, 1983
Barbara Hambly, *Mother of Winter*, 1996
Lyndon Hardy, *Master of Five Magics*, 1980
Fritz Leiber, *Ill Met in Lankhmar*, 1995
Roger Zelazny, *Nine Princes in Amber*, 1970

701

JANE S. FANCHER

Ring of Intrigue

(New York: DAW, 1997)

Story type: Political; Magic Conflict
Series: Dance of the Rings
Major character(s): Deymorin Rhomandi dunMheric, Royalty; Mikhyel Rhomandi dunMheric, Royalty, Handicapped
Time period(s): Indeterminate
Locale(s): Rhomatum, Fictional City

Summary: The death of the ringmaster of Rhomatum throws the magic power of the great city-state into disarray. Their allies and enemies waste no time in acting against Rhomatum. The children of the Rhomandi, the ruling family, must put aside their differences and act decisively to preserve the world. Second in series.

Where it's reviewed:
Locus, April 1997, page 29

Other books by the same author:
Ring of Lightning, 1995
Uplink, 1992
Harmonies of the 'Net, 1992
Ground-Ties, 1991

Other books you might like:
Barbara Hambly, *The Time of the Dark*, 1982
Robin Hobb, *Assassin's Apprentice*, 1995
Katherine Kurtz, *Deryni Rising*, 1970
Patricia A. McKillip, *The Riddle-Master of Hed*, 1976
Paula Volsky, *Illusion*, 1992

702

DAVID FEINTUCH

The Still

(New York: Warner Aspect, 1997)

Story type: Political; Adventure
Major character(s): Rodrigo, Royalty, Heir—Dispossessed;
   Rustin, Royalty; Elryc, Royalty
Time period(s): Indeterminate Past
Locale(s): Caldeon, Fictional Country

Summary: Prince Rodrigo should ascend the throne of Caldeon when his mother dies. However, the spoiled and indolent young man has not prepared for the plots and betrayals that depose him. If he wishes to rule, he must grow up and dare to seize the power of the Still.

Where it's reviewed:
Booklist, July 1997, page 1805
Kirkus Reviews, May 1, 1997, page 684
Locus, June 1997, page 29
Science Fiction Chronicle, October 1997, page 48
Voice of Youth Advocates, December 1997, page 324

Other books by the same author:
Fisherman's Hope, 1996
Voices of Hope, 1996
Challenger's Hope, 1995
Prisoner's Hope, 1995
Midshipman's Hope, 1994

Other books you might like:
Glen Cook, *The Swordbearer*, 1982
Diane Duane, *The Door into Fire*, 1979
J.V. Jones, *The Baker's Boy*, 1995
Ellen Kushner, *Swordspoint*, 1987
Paula Volsky, *Illusion*, 1992

703

RAYMOND E. FEIST

Rage of a Demon King

(New York: Avon, 1997)

Story type: Magic Conflict
Series: Serpentwar Saga
Major character(s): Erik von Darkmoor, Military Personnel;
   Rupert ''Roo'' Avery, Businessman; Jakan, Demon
Time period(s): Indeterminate Past
Locale(s): Midkemia, Planet—Imaginary

Summary: Already ravaged by the war with the Saaur, Midkemia faces worse enemies when a host of demons, freed after many years by a desperate priest, make their way to Midkemia. Concludes the trilogy.

Where it's reviewed:
Booklist, March 1, 1997, page 1067
Kirkus Reviews, February 1, 1997, page 178
Locus, May 1997, page 29
Publishers Weekly, March 31, 1997, page 67
Science Fiction Chronicle, October 1997, page 47

Other books by the same author:
Rise of a Merchant Prince, 1995
Shadow of a Dark Queen, 1994
A Darkness at Sethanon, 1986
Silverthorn, 1985
Magician, 1982

Other books you might like:
M.A.R. Barker, *Man of Gold*, 1984
Glen Cook, *The Black Company*, 1984
Patricia A. McKillip, *The Riddle-Master of Hed*, 1976
Melanie Rawn, *Dragon Prince*, 1988
Janny Wurts, *Curse of the Mistwraith*, 1994

704

MARINA FITCH

The Seventh Heart

(New York: Ace, 1997)

Story type: Contemporary Realism; Religious
Major character(s): Gillian Wheatley, Linguist; Candace, Spirit (wind sprite); Melanie Frost, Health Care Professional
Time period(s): 1990s
Locale(s): Rio Santo, California

Summary: After five years of drought, Rio Santo now suffers frequent magnitude 6.5 earthquake aftershocks. Most homes prove unsafe, while blocked roads interfere with distribution of emergency supplies of food and water. Gillian's roommate, Melanie, disappears after the first earthquake, leaving Gillian to deal with the earth, wind and water spirits whose loneliness and insanity caused the drought and earthquakes. First novel.

Where it's reviewed:
Locus, April 1997, page 29

Other books you might like:
Maya Kaathryn Bohnhoff, *The Spirit Gate*, 1996
Tom Deitz, *Above the Lower Sky*, 1994
Sharon Green, *Convergence*, 1996
J. Gregory Keyes, *The Waterborn*, 1996
Marc Laidlaw, *Neon Lotus*, 1988
Sheri S. Tepper, *The Family Tree*, 1997

705

LYNN FLEWELLING

Stalking Darkness

(New York: Bantam Spectra, 1997)

Story type: Magic Conflict; Political
Series: Nightrunner
Major character(s): Alec of Kerry, Apprentice, Spy (Watcher); Seregil, Spy (Watcher), Thief; Beka Cavish, Warrior, Teenager
Time period(s): Indeterminate
Locale(s): Rhiminee, Fictional City; Skala, Fictional Country

Summary: A necromancer pursues Seregil and Alec, intent on recovering a deadly magical artifact and invoking the power of an ancient evil. While bloodthirsty sacrifices continue and warfare engulfs the land, the fate of the kingdom depends on

the actions of a courageous few. Sequel to *Luck in the Shadows*.

Where it's reviewed:
Kliatt, May 1997, page 12
Locus, February 1997, page 25

Other books by the same author:
Luck in the Shadows, 1996

Other books you might like:
Lois McMaster Bujold, *The Spirit Ring*, 1992
Terry Goodkind, *Wizard's First Rule*, 1994
Robin Hobb, *Assassin's Apprentice*, 1995
J.V. Jones, *The Baker's Boy*, 1995
J.R.R. Tolkien, *The Fellowship of the Ring*, 1954
Patricia C. Wrede, *The Raven Ring*, 1994

706

MAGGIE FUREY

Dhiammara

(New York: Bantam Spectra, 1997)

Story type: Magic Conflict
Series: Aurian
Major character(s): Aurian, Wizard; Eliseth, Wizard; Miathan, Wizard
Time period(s): Indeterminate
Locale(s): Nexis, Fictional City; Dhiammara, Fictional City; Southern Kingdoms, Fictional Country

Summary: Magically transported into the future, Aurian finds Eliseth reanimating the dead and preparing to conquer the world, while Miathan strives to turn himself into a god. Aurian will require all her resources to achieve victory in the final conflict in Dhiammara. Fourth in series.

Where it's reviewed:
Locus, July 1997, page 33

Other books by the same author:
Sword of Flame, 1996
Harp of Winds, 1995
Aurian, 1994

Other books you might like:
David Eddings, *Pawn of Prophecy*, 1982
Lynn Flewelling, *Stalking Darkness*, 1997
Terry Goodkind, *Temple of the Winds*, 1997
Patricia A. McKillip, *The Riddle-Master of Hed*, 1976
Michelle Sagara, *Chains of Darkness, Chains of Light*, 1994

707

NEIL GAIMAN

Neverwhere

(New York: Avon, 1997)

Story type: Contemporary; Urban
Major character(s): Richard Mayhew, Businessman; Door, Gentlewoman, Fugitive; de Carabas, Nobleman (marquis), Con Artist
Time period(s): 1990s (1996)
Locale(s): London, England; London Below, Fictional City

Summary: When Richard Mayhew stops to assist an injured woman, he finds himself drawn into the odd world of London Below, a city made up of sewers and legends, lost dreams and forgotten people. His everyday life erased because of his kindness, Richard Mayhew, hapless businessman, must risk everything to save both Londons. Based on Gaiman's screenplay for the BBC miniseries and revised from the UK edition.

Where it's reviewed:
Booklist, May 15, 1997, page 1541
Kirkus Reviews, June 1, 1997, page 822
Library Journal, June 15, 1997, page 97
Locus, December 1996, page 27
Publishers Weekly, May 19, 1997, page 63

Other books by the same author:
Angels & Visitations, 1993
Now We Are Sick, 1991
Good Omens: The Nice and Accurate Prophecies of Agnes Nutter, Witch, 1990 (Terry Pratchett, co-author)

Other books you might like:
Jack Cady, *The Off Season*, 1995
John Crowley, *Little, Big*, 1981
Charles de Lint, *Somewhere to Be Flying*, 1988
Lisa Goldstein, *The Dream Years*, 1985
Megan Lindholm, *Wizard of the Pigeons*, 1986

708

PETER GELMAN

Flying Saucers over Hennepin

(San Francisco, California: Permeable Press, 1997)

Story type: Contemporary Realism; Literary
Major character(s): Zenobia Olson, Writer; I, Writer; Columbus Binder, Businessman (furrier)
Time period(s): 1980s (1988)
Locale(s): Minneapolis, Minnesota

Summary: Winner of the Hayloft Grant, Zenobia Olson circulates at the Waltz-a-Rama. The writer notices strange behavior which seems to continue. Columbus Binder spent time alone with Erika Swanson before jumping off the bridge. Perhaps the aliens from the Fornax Cluster induce the visions and doppelgangers seen since the anarchist uprising.

Where it's reviewed:
Asimov's Science Fiction, September 1997, page 149

Other books you might like:
William Borden, *Superstoe*, 1968
Jesse Browner, *Conglomeros*, 1992
Mark Leyner, *My Cousin, My Gastroenterologist*, 1990
Haruki Murakami, *Hard-Boiled Wonderland and the End of the World*, 1991
Milorad Pavic, *Landscape Painted with Tea*, 1990
Tom Robbins, *Another Roadside Attraction*, 1971

709

CHRISTIE GOLDEN

King's Man and Thief

(New York: Ace, 1997)

Story type: Adventure; Magic Conflict
Major character(s): Deveren Larath, Nobleman, Thief; Allika, Child, Thief; Marrika, Thief, Traitor
Time period(s): 13th century (1285)
Locale(s): Braedon, Fictional City

Summary: When Braedon's enemies attempt to defeat the city by use of a magical plague, Deveren and his band of thieves must search out the cause and discover a way to nullify the attack.

Where it's reviewed:
Locus, May 1997, page 29
Voice of Youth Advocates, August 1997, page 192

Other books by the same author:
Instrument of Fate, 1996
The Murdered Sun, 1996
The Enemy Within, 1994
Dance of the Dead, 1992

Other books you might like:
Lynn Flewelling, *Luck in the Shadows*, 1996
Lynn Flewelling, *Stalking Darkness*, 1997
Peg Kerr, *Emerald House Rising*, 1997
Fritz Leiber, *Ill Met in Lankhmar*, 1995
Fritz Leiber, *Lean Times in Lankhmar*, 1996

710

TERRY GOODKIND

Temple of the Winds

(New York: Tor, 1997)

Story type: Magic Conflict; Political
Series: Sword of Truth
Major character(s): Richard ''the Seeker'' Rahl, Wizard (War Wizard), Ruler; Kahlan Amnel, Magician, Leader (Mother Confessor); Drefan Rahl, Criminal, Imposter
Time period(s): Indeterminate
Locale(s): D'Hara, Fictional Country; The Midlands, Fictional Country

Summary: Betrothed, Richard and Kahlan plan to marry as soon as Richard's leadership of D'Hara and The Midlands allows him to eliminate a sorcerous plague and assaults from Emperor Jagang, who captures unprotected minds while people sleep. However, the spirits of the Temple of the Winds demand the couple marry other partners to rectify a magical imbalance. Complicating matters, Kahlan's new fiance, Drefan Rahl, can command the complete D'Hara loyalty due to a Rahl, the only sure protection against Jagang. Fourth in series, following *Blood of the Fold*.

Where it's reviewed:
Kirkus Reviews, October 1, 1997, page 1496
Publishers Weekly, October 13, 1997, page 60

Other books by the same author:
Blood of the Fold, 1996
Stone of Tears, 1995
Wizard's First Rule, 1994

Other books you might like:
David Eddings, *Pawn of Prophecy*, 1982
Lynn Flewelling, *Luck in the Shadows*, 1997
Lynn Flewelling, *Stalking Darkness*, 1997
Robin Hobb, *Assassin's Apprentice*, 1995
J.V. Jones, *The Baker's Boy*, 1995
Robert Jordan, *The Eye of the World*, 1990

711

RICHARD GRANT

In the Land of Winter

(New York: Avon, 1997)

Story type: Contemporary; Religious
Major character(s): Pippa Rede, Single Parent; Winterbelle, Child
Time period(s): 1990s
Locale(s): New England

Summary: Struggling to survive and raise Winterbelle in a forest home in harmony with nature, Pippa, a Wiccan, must suddenly reorient her world when bigoted religious zealots accuse her of child abuse and Satan worship. Deprived of her loving and beloved daughter by complicit government officials, Pippa finds solace and transformation deep in the woods.

Where it's reviewed:
Kirkus Reviews, August 15, 1997, page 1242
Library Journal, October 15, 1997, page 92
Locus, November 1997, page 17
Publishers Weekly, September 8, 1997, page 55

Other books by the same author:
Tex and Molly in the Afterlife, 1996
Through the Heart, 1992
Views From the Oldest House, 1989
Rumors of Spring, 1987
Saraband of Lost Time, 1985

Other books you might like:
Rose Estes, *Troll-Taken*, 1993
Katharine Eliska Kimbriel, *Kindred Rites*, 1997
Holly Lisle, *Minerva Wakes*, 1994
Susan Palwick, *Flying in Place*, 1992
Terri Windling, *The Wood Wife*, 1996

712

SHARON GREEN

Competition

(New York: AvoNova, 1997)

Story type: Magic Conflict; Political
Series: Blending
Major character(s): Jovvi Hafford, Wizard, Prostitute; Rion Mardimil, Wizard, Gentleman; Lorand Coll, Wizard, Farmer

Fantasy

Time period(s): Indeterminate Past
Locale(s): Gan Garee, Fictional City

Summary: The five magicians who must become the next Blending must master their powers. They must use those powers to survive a series of deadly tests, ones that at least some of their teachers would prefer they failed. In an Empire failing from ignorance and corruption, five young wizards have little hope. Sequel to *Convergence*.

Other books by the same author:
Convergence, 1996
The Hidden Realms, 1993
Silver Princess, Golden Knight, 1993
Dawn Song, 1990
The Far Side of Forever, 1987

Other books you might like:
Teresa Edgerton, *Goblin Moon*, 1991
Ellen Kushner, *Swordspoint*, 1987
Caroline Stevermer, *A College of Magics*, 1994
Elizabeth Willey, *A Sorcerer and a Gentleman*, 1995
Patricia C. Wrede, *Mairelon the Magician*, 1991

713

MARTIN H. GREENBERG, Editor

Elf Fantastic
(New York: DAW, 1997)

Story type: Anthology; Legend

Summary: Contains a two-page introduction plus brief individual introductions to 19 original stories, frequently ominous in tone, and featuring encounters between elves and mortals. Authors include Lynn Abbey, Craig Shaw Gardner, Richard Gilliam, Karen Haber, Tanya Huff, Jane M. Lindskold, Dennis L. McKiernan, Andre Norton, Jody Lynn Nye, Diana L. Paxson, Mickey Zucker Reichert, Michelle West and David Niall Wilson.

Where it's reviewed:
Voice of Youth Advocates, October 1997, page 252

Other books by the same author:
Elf Magic, 1997
Zodiac Fantastic, 1997 (A.R. Morlan, co-editor)
Wizard Fantastic, 1997
Tarot Fantastic, 1997 (Lawrence Schimel, co-editor)
Horse Fantastic, 1991 (Rosalind M. Greenberg, co-editor)

Other books you might like:
Isaac Asimov, *Faeries*, 1991
    Martin H. Greenberg, Charles G. Waugh, co-editors
Lin Carter, *Dragons, Elves and Heroes*, 1969
    editor
Jack Dann, *Little People!*, 1991
    Gardner Dozois, co-editor
Baird Searls, *Halflings, Hobbits, Warrows & Weefolk*, 1991
    Brian Thomsen, co-editor
Terri Windling, *Faery*, 1984
    editor

714

MARTIN H. GREENBERG, Editor
LAWRENCE SCHIMEL, Co-Editor

Tarot Fantastic
(New York: DAW, 1997)

Story type: Anthology

Summary: Contains a five-page introduction by Schimel, an original poem by Jane Yolen and 15 original stories varying in tone from whimsical to downbeat and featuring themes surrounding fortune-telling tarot cards. Other authors include Charles de Lint, Teresa Edgerton, Rosemary Edghill, George Alec Effinger, Kate Elliott, Mark A. Garland, Nina Kiriki Hoffman, Tanya Huff, Nancy Springer and Michelle Sagara West.

Other books by the same author:
Elf Fantastic, 1997
Zodiac Fantastic, 1997 (A.R. Morlan, co-editor)
After the King: Stories in Honor of J.R.R. Tolkien, 1992
The Fantastic Robin Hood, 1991
Horse Fantastic, 1991 (Rosalind M. Greenberg, co-editor)

Other books you might like:
Piers Anthony, *Tarot*, 1987
Italo Calvino, *The Castle of Crossed Destinies*, 1977
Rachel Pollack, *Tarot Tales*, 1996
    Caitlin Matthews, co-editor
Tim Powers, *Last Call*, 1992
Charles Williams, *The Greater Trumps*, 1932
Roger Zelazny, *Wheel of Fortune*, 1995
    Martin H. Greenberg, co-editor

715

NICOLA GRIFFITH, Editor
STEPHEN PAGEL, Co-Editor

Bending the Landscape: Fantasy
(Clarkston, Georgia: White Wolf, 1997)

Story type: Anthology; Literary

Summary: Contains a three-page introduction by Griffith and Pagel, 13 pages of editors' and contributors' biographies plus brief individual introductions to 22 original stories utilizing settings ranging from an 11th-century Japanese garden to a modern, split-level suburban home to explore various physical, emotional and moral views of homosexuality. The authors include Kim Antieu, Robin Wayne Bailey, Carolyn Ives Gilman, Tanya Huff, M.W. Keiper, Ellen Kushner, James A. Moore, Simon Sheppard, B.J. Thrower, Jeff Verona and Leslie What.

Where it's reviewed:
Fantasy & Science Fiction, March 1997, page 33
Kirkus Reviews, January 1, 1997, page 27
Library Journal, December 1996, page 152
Locus, April 1997, page 13
Publishers Weekly, February 24, 1997, page 68

Other books by the same author:
Slow River, 1995

Ammonite, 1993

Other books you might like:
Camilla Decarnin, *Worlds Apart*, 1986
    Eric Garber, Lynn Paleo, co-editors
Jeffrey M. Elliot, *Kindred Spirits*, 1984
    editor
Eric Garber, *Sword of the Rainbow*, 1996
    Jewelle Gomez, co-editor
Pam Keesey, *Darker Angels: Lesbian Vampire Stories*, 1995
    editor
Pam Keesey, *Daughters of Darkness: Lesbian Vampire Stories*, 1993
    editor
Caro Soles, *Meltdown*, 1994
    editor

716

ANNE LESLEY GROELL

Bridge of Valor
(New York: Roc, 1997)

Story type: Adventure
Series: Cloak and Dagger
Major character(s): Jenifleur Radineaux, Debutante, Martial Arts Expert (assassin); Thibault Lescevre, Student, Martial Arts Expert (assassin); Ruairi NaBlaine, Nobleman
Time period(s): Indeterminate Past
Locale(s): Arrhyndon, Fictional Country

Summary: Eager for their first true assignment, Jenifleur and Thibault accept a mission to a remote estate where bizarre occurrences, ghosts, disappearing rooms and a rain of goldfish torment the lord of the estate. The mission proves more difficult than expected when the two assassins quickly become immersed in a lethal maze of plots. Second in series.

Where it's reviewed:
Locus, June 1997, page 29
Starlog, November 1997, page 14

Other books by the same author:
Anvil of the Sun, 1996

Other books you might like:
Steven Brust, *Jhereg*, 1983
Lynn Flewelling, *Luck in the Shadows*, 1996
Robin Hobb, *Assassin's Apprentice*, 1995
J.V. Jones, *The Baker's Boy*, 1995
Fritz Leiber, *Ill Met in Lankhmar*, 1995
Anne Logston, *Shadow*, 1996

717

SUE HARRISON

Song of the River
(New York: Avon, 1997)

Story type: Adventure; Quest
Series: Mother Earth, Father Sky
Major character(s): K'os, Indian, Avenger; Chakliux, Storyteller, Handicapped (clubfoot); Aqamdax, Indian (Wanderer)

Time period(s): 65th century B.C. (6480 B.C.)
Locale(s): Alaska

Summary: Having been raised by the men of Near River Village, K'os raises Chakliux, also from that village, to get vengeance. When Chakliux, expecting to marry to heal the breach between the Cousin and Near River people, finds himself unable to win the trust of his new tribe, he wanders and learns about himself and his people, seeking the reasons his people suffered.

Where it's reviewed:
Booklist, November 1, 1997, page 454
Publishers Weekly, September 29, 1997, page 65

Other books by the same author:
Brother Wind, 1994
My Sister, the Moon, 1992
Mother Earth, Father Sky, 1990

Other books you might like:
Jean M. Auel, *Clan of the Cave Bear*, 1980
W. Michael Gear, *People of the Wolf*, 1990
    Kathleen O'Neal Gear, co-author
Meredith Ann Pierce, *The Woman Who Loved Reindeer*, 1985
William Sarabande, *The Sacred Stones*, 1991
Elizabeth Marshall Thomas, *Reindeer Moon*, 1987

718

SIMON HAWKE

The Last Wizard
(New York: Warner Aspect, 1997)

Story type: Magic Conflict; Urban
Series: Wizard of 4th Street
Major character(s): Talon, Immortal, Wizard (Dark One); Sebastian Makepeace, Mythical Creature (fairy), Teacher; Katherine O'Connor, Political Figure (President of the United States)
Time period(s): 25th century
Locale(s): New York, New York; Washington, District of Columbia; Arizona

Summary: With the support of the President of the United States, the International Traumaturgic Commission and a little help from friends, the four Avatars of the Runestones live under guard in the old United Nations building while waiting for the next attack by the remaining Dark Ones. Meanwhile, Talon founds the Order of Universal Spiritual Unity with a dragon preserve around it, then sets up a treatment center for juvenile offenders to convert to acolytes. Gradually all the remaining immortal Dark Ones fall to Talon who keeps them alive, locked in stone as a power source, for the great battle.

Other books by the same author:
The Ambivalent Magician, 1996
The Wizard of Camelot, 1993
The Inadequate Adept, 1993
The Wizard of 4th Street, 1987

Other books you might like:
Robert N. Charrette, *A Prince Among Men*, 1994
Tanya Huff, *Gate of Darkness, Circle of Light*, 1989

Fantasy

J.V. Jones, *The Baker's Boy*, 1995
Marc Laidlaw, *Neon Lotus*, 1988
Morgan Llywelyn, *Silverlight*, 1996

719
D.A. HEELEY

Ronin
(St. Paul, Minnesota: Llewellyn Publications, 1997)

Story type: Magic Conflict; Religious
Series: Darkness and Light
Major character(s): Shadrack, Reincarnated Person (Malak), Martial Arts Expert (samurai-magician); Fiona, Reincarnated Person (Lena), Spouse (Malak's); Jaad, Reincarnated Person (Dethen), Magician (Black Adept)
Time period(s): Indeterminate
Locale(s): Earth; Mythical Place

Summary: Reborn on Earth as Shadrack 1,000 years after the Arch-Demon Lilith destroys him and devours his soul, Malak learns the art of the samurai while struggling to remember and recover his former self. Lena, the wife for whom he sacrificed his soul, regains her memories when reincarnated as Fiona, and uses her magic powers to help Malak fuse the pieces of his shattered identity. They and their allies must defeat Malak's evil karmic twin, the Black Adept Dethen, and face Lilith once again to save Enya and its inhabitants from destruction. Second in series.

Other books by the same author:
Lilith, 1996

Other books you might like:
Steven Brust, *Jhereg*, 1983
D.J. Conway, *The Dream Warrior*, 1996
Eve Forward, *Villains by Necessity*, 1995
Elizabeth Moon, *Sheepfarmer's Daughter*, 1988
Joel Rosenberg, *The Fire Duke*, 1995
Roger Zelazny, *Nine Princes in Amber*, 1970

720
CAROL HELLER

The Gates of Vensunor
(New York: AvoNova, 1997)

Story type: Magic Conflict; Adventure
Series: Shunlar Chronicles
Major character(s): Shunlar, Psychic, Warrior; Algooth, Mythical Creature (dragon); Creedath, Merchant, Psychic
Time period(s): Indeterminate
Locale(s): Vensunor, Fictional City; Valley of Great Trees, Mythical Place

Summary: Ordered by the mayor to find a particular stranger, Shunlar soon finds herself hunted, as Creedath seeks to find and control dragonkind. First in a series.

Other books you might like:
Graham Edwards, *Dragoncharm*, 1996
Lynn Flewelling, *Luck in the Shadows*, 1996
Ursula K. Le Guin, *A Wizard of Earthsea*, 1968

Andre Norton, *Elvenbane*, 1991
  Mercedes Lackey, co-author
Andre Norton, *Elvenblood*, 1995
  Mercedes Lackey, co-author

721
MARK HELPRIN

The Veils of Snows
(New York: Viking Ariel, 1997)

Story type: Young Adult; Political
Series: Swan Lake
Major character(s): I, Writer, Military Personnel (soldier); The Queen, Royalty
Time period(s): Indeterminate
Locale(s): The Kingdom, Fictional Country

Summary: After many years of peace in the kingdom, the usurper returns, leaving the queen only a brief time to mount a defense. As the situation worsens, the Veil of Snows provides some opportunity for repelling the invasion. However, the best hope for the kingdom to regain its rightful ruler may lie with the infant prince, if he survives.

Where it's reviewed:
Booklist, November 15, 1997, page 560
Publishers Weekly, September 29, 1997, page 90

Other books by the same author:
A City in Winter, 1996
Swan Lake, 1989
Winter's Tale, 1983

Other books you might like:
James C. Christensen, *Voyage of the Basset*, 1996
  Renwick St. James, Alan Dean Foster, co-authors
James Gurney, *Dinotopia*, 1992
E.T.A. Hoffman, *Nutcracker*, 1996
Anne McCaffrey, *Black Horses for the King*, 1996
Patricia A. McKillip, *The Book of Atrix Wolfe*, 1995
Garth Nix, *Sabriel*, 1996

722
ROBIN HOBB (Pseudonym of Megan Lindholm)

Assassin's Quest
(New York: Bantam Spectra, 1997)

Story type: Political; Psychic Powers
Series: Farseer
Major character(s): FitzChivalry "Tom" Farseer, Bastard Son, Psychic; Starling Birdsong, Minstrel; Nighteyes, Animal (wolf), Telepath
Time period(s): Indeterminate
Locale(s): Six Duchies, Fictional Country

Summary: Thought dead, FitzChivalry slowly recovers from near death, fighting his way back to the human world despite his attraction to Nighteyes' world. As the usurper, King Regal, squanders a fortune in the Inland Duchies while abandoning Buckkeep and other seaside settlements to the deadly Red Ship Raiders, King Verity searches for help in the wilderness. All motivated to see an heir of the proper bloodline on

the throne, Queen Kettricken, the Fool and FitzChivalry search for the help needed to set matters right while deadly foes seek them.

Where it's reviewed:
Booklist, February 1, 1997, page 929
Kirkus Reviews, February 1, 1997, page 177
Locus, January 1997, page 19
Publishers Weekly, February 24, 1997, page 68

Other books by the same author:
Royal Assassin, 1996
Assassin's Apprentice, 1995

Other books you might like:
Lynn Flewelling, *Luck in the Shadows*, 1996
Lynn Flewelling, *Stalking Darkness*, 1997
Terry Goodkind, *Wizard's First Rule*, 1994
J.V. Jones, *The Baker's Boy*, 1995
Megan Lindholm, *Wizard of the Pigeons*, 1986
Martha Wells, *The Element of Fire*, 1993

723

ROBERT HOLDSTOCK

Gate of Ivory, Gate of Horn

(New York: Roc, 1997)

Story type: Alternate World; Magic Conflict
Series: Mythago Wood
Major character(s): Christian Huxley, Adventurer; Guiwenneth, Warrior
Time period(s): 1990s; Indeterminate Past
Locale(s): Ryhope Wood, Mythical Place; England

Summary: Drawn by his childhood vision of Guiwenneth, Christian ventures into Ryhope Wood, hoping to find the young woman. Christian soon joins Guiwenneth and a band of crusaders from the past in a battle with sorcerers and giants as he begins to undestand the truth underlying the two gates, one of horn and one of ivory.

Where it's reviewed:
Book World, October 26, 1997, page 8
Booklist, November 1, 1997, page 457
Kirkus Reviews, October 1, 1997, page 1494
Locus, November 1997, page 17

Other books by the same author:
Ancient Echoes, 1996
The Hollowing, 1994
The Bone Forest, 1991
Lavondyss: Journey to an Unknown Region, 1988
Mythago Wood, 1984

Other books you might like:
Greg Bear, *Songs of Earth and Power*, 1994
Charles de Lint, *The Little Country*, 1991
Charles de Lint, *Memory and Dream*, 1994
Tom Deitz, *Dreamseeker's Road*, 1995
Holly Lisle, *Minerva Wakes*, 1994

724

HELEN HOLLICK

Shadow of the King

(New York: St. Martin's Press, 1997)

Story type: Legend
Series: Pendragon's Banner Trilogy
Major character(s): Gwenhwyfar, Royalty; Arthur, Royalty (king); Cerdic, Royalty, Warrior
Time period(s): 5th century
Locale(s): England; Caer Cadan, Fictional City (Cadbury)

Summary: When news of Arthur Pendragon's death comes to Caer Cadan, Gwenhwyfar must find a way to defy the nobles who would benefit from the news. Meanwhile, as the Britons squabble, the Saxons grow more and more powerful. If Arthur lives, will it make any difference once the Saxons move? Conclusion of trilogy.

Where it's reviewed:
Publishers Weekly, September 22, 1997, page 71

Other books by the same author:
Pendragon's Banner, 1996
The Kingmaking, 1995

Other books you might like:
Poul Anderson, *The King of Ys: Roma Mater*, 1986
    Karen Anderson, co-author
Gillian Bradshaw, *The Hawk of May*, 1980
Bernard Cornwell, *The Winter King*, 1996
David Drake, *The Dragon Lord*, 1979
Phyllis Ann Karr, *The Idylls of the Queen*, 1982

725

STEWART HOME

Come Before Christ and Murder Love

(New York: Serpent's Tail, 1997)

Story type: Contemporary Realism; Literary
Major character(s): Kevin Callen, Fugitive, Wizard; Philip Sloan, Fugitive, Mentally Ill Person
Time period(s): 1990s (1997)
Locale(s): London, England

Summary: The subject of a British Government mind control project, Kevin Callen also possesses magical abilities, many allies and followers, but, unfortunately, occasionally becomes Philip Sloan, loser and possible murderer. With a trail of sex, magic, drugs, death and conspiracy, Kevin must stay on the run and under cover to find his true identity.

Other books you might like:
Scott Baker, *Dhampire*, 1982
Philip K. Dick, *Valis*, 1981
Stuart Gordon, *Smile on the Void*, 1981
Ursula K. Le Guin, *The Lathe of Heaven*, 1971
Douglas Rushkoff, *Ecstasy Club*, 1997

Fantasy

726

DANIEL HOOD

Beggar's Banquet

(New York: Ace, 1997)

Story type: Mystery; Magic Conflict

Series: Fanuilh

Major character(s): Liam Rhenford, Scholar, Detective—Amateur; Fanuilh, Mythical Creature (dragon), Companion (familiar); Mistress Priscian, Businesswoman, Heiress

Time period(s): Indeterminate

Locale(s): Southwark, Fictional City; Taralon, Fictional Country

Summary: Although Liam hopes to initiate some business contacts and enjoy the festival of Beggars Banquet, he must instead help find a murderer and the person who stole a dangerous magical artifact from his proposed business partner.

Where it's reviewed:

Kliatt, July 1997, page 16

Other books by the same author:

Wizard's Heir, 1995

Fanuilh, 1994

Other books you might like:

Steven Brust, *Jhereg*, 1983

Glen Cook, *Sweet Silver Blues*, 1987

Lynn Flewelling, *Luck in the Shadows*, 1996

Simon R. Green, *Hawk & Fisher*, 1990

Joel Rosenberg, *Hour of the Octopus*, 1994

727

A.J. JACOBS

Fractured Fairy Tales

(New York: Bantam, 1997)

Story type: Legend; Collection

Summary: Contains 25 humorously twisted interpretations of well-known fairy tales and myths as featured in Jay Ward's *Rocky and Bullwinkle Show* television series. Stories include ''The Frog Prince,'' ''Rumplestiltskin,'' ''Hansel and Gretel,'' ''Pinocchio,'' ''The Elves and the Shoemaker,'' ''Princess and the Pea,'' ''The Golden Goose,'' ''Beauty and the Beast,'' ''Aladdin's Lamp,'' ''Jack and the Beanstalk'' and ''King Midas.''

Other books you might like:

William J. Brooke, *Teller of Tales*, 1994

Emma Donoghue, *Kissing the Witch: Old Tales in New Skins*, 1997

David Fisher, *Legally Correct Fairy Tales*, 1996

James Finn Garner, *Once upon a More Enlightened Time*, 1995

James Finn Garner, *Politically Correct Bedtime Stories*, 1994

James Finn Garner, *Politically Correct Holiday Stories*, 1995

728

BRIAN JACQUES

The Pearls of Lutra

(New York: Philomel, 1997)

Story type: Young Adult; Adventure

Series: Redwall

Major character(s): Tansy, Animal (hedgehog); Ublaz Mad Eyes, Animal (pine martin), Ruler (Emperor of Sampetra); Viola, Animal (vole), Adventurer

Time period(s): Indeterminate

Locale(s): Redwall Abbey, England; Isle of Sampetra, Fictional Country

Summary: Emperor Ublaz orders his corsairs to recover the Pearls of Lutra, thought hidden at Redwall Abbey. However, a gruesome discovery by Tansy brings to light the clues which allow Abbey residents to begin recovering the pearls, each secreted with a riddle which leads a searcher to another pearl's hiding place.

Where it's reviewed:

Booklist, February 15, 1997, page 1023

Kirkus Reviews, January 1, 1997, page 59

Locus, March 1997, page 29

School Library Journal, March 1997, page 187

Voice of Youth Advocates, June 1997, page 118

Other books by the same author:

Outcasts of Redwall, 1996

The Bellmaker, 1995

Martin the Warrior, 1994

Salamandastron, 1992

Redwall, 1986

Other books you might like:

Richard Adams, *Tales of Watership Down*, 1997

Allen Andrews, *Pig Plantagenet*, 1980

Mary Brown, *The Unlikely Ones*, 1986

Kenneth Grahame, *The Wind in the Willows*, 1908

Tad Williams, *Tailchaser's Song*, 1985

729

OLIVER JOHNSON

The Forging of the Shadows

(New York: Roc, 1997)

Story type: Sword and Sorcery; Political

Series: Lightbringer Trilogy

Major character(s): Jayal, Nobleman, Hero; Thalassa, Prostitute, Heroine; Uthred of Ravenspur, Religious, Wizard

Time period(s): Indeterminate

Locale(s): Thrull, Fictional City; Fictional Country

Summary: Seven years after the High Priest of the God of Darkness plunges Thrull into an era of shadow, unleashing his undead hoards against the populace, three champions of the God of Light seek a way to return the city of the God of Light to peace and prosperity. First novel, first of a trilogy.

Where it's reviewed:

Kliatt, July 1997, page 16

Locus, January 1997, page 27
Starlog, August 1997, page 67
Voice of Youth Advocates, August 1997, page 193

Other books you might like:
Terry Goodkind, *Wizard's First Rule*, 1994
J.V. Jones, *The Baker's Boy*, 1995
J. Gregory Keyes, *The Waterborn*, 1996
Douglas Niles, *A Breach in the Watershed*, 1995
J.R.R. Tolkien, *The Fellowship of the Ring*, 1954

730

J.V. JONES

The Barbed Coil

(New York: Warner Aspect, 1997)

Story type: Alternate World; Sword and Sorcery
Major character(s): Tessa McCamfrey, Wizard; Ravis, Nobleman, Mercenary; Camron, Nobleman, Warrior
Time period(s): 1990s; Indeterminate
Locale(s): Bay'Zell, Fictional City; World of the Barbed Coil, Mythical Place

Summary: Transported to another world when she pricks herself with a newfound ring, Tessa discovers magical abilities associated with the ring. Lord Camron benefits from her abilities when he engages Ravis in his quest for vengeance for his father's death.

Where it's reviewed:
Fantasy & Science Fiction, March 1998, page 27
Kirkus Reviews, July 15, 1997, page 1073
Locus, August 1997, page 29
Publishers Weekly, August 11, 1997, page 391

Other books by the same author:
A Man Betrayed, 1996
Master and Fool, 1996
The Baker's Boy, 1995

Other books you might like:
Tom Deitz, *Dreamseeker's Road*, 1995
Lynn Flewelling, *Luck in the Shadows*, 1996
Terry Goodkind, *Wizard's First Rule*, 1994
Patricia A. McKillip, *Winter Rose*, 1996
Patricia C. Wrede, *The Raven Ring*, 1994

731

ROBERT JORDAN
TERESA PATTERSON, Co-Author

The World of Robert Jordan's The Wheel of Time

(New York: Tor, 1997)

Story type: Collection; Magic Conflict
Series: Wheel of Time
Time period(s): Indeterminate
Locale(s): Ten Nations, Mythical Place

Summary: Contains numerous short stories, literary sketches, and legends about characters and events pivotal to the series. Lavish illustrations include many maps and portraits.

Where it's reviewed:
Library Journal, November 15, 1997, page 79

Other books by the same author:
Lords of Chaos, 1994
The Shadow Rising, 1992
The Dragon Reborn, 1991
The Eye of the World, 1990
The Great Hunt, 1990

Other books you might like:
Marion Zimmer Bradley, *The Keeper's Price*, 1980
    editor
Katherine Kurtz, *The Deryni Archives*, 1986
Mercedes Lackey, *Sword of Ice and Other Tales of Valdemar*, 1997
    editor
J.R.R. Tolkien, *The Silmarillion*, 1977
J.R.R. Tolkien, *Unfinished Tales*, 1980

732

MARJORIE BRADLEY KELLOGG

The Book of Water

(New York: DAW, 1997)

Story type: Quest; Adventure
Series: Dragon Quartet
Major character(s): D'Noch, Guide; Earth, Mythical Creature (dragon); Water, Mythical Creature (dragon)
Time period(s): 2010s (2013)
Locale(s): Africa

Summary: Water's call summons Earth and his human guide, Erde, from the tenth-century German principalities to 21st-century Africa where Water and D'Noch wait for their help. Amidst widespread environmental devastation, they discover forces at work that will require all their abilities and more to counter. Second in series.

Where it's reviewed:
Locus, September 1997, page 27
Starlog, October 1997, page 14

Other books by the same author:
The Book of Earth, 1995
Harmony, 1991
Reign of Fire, 1986
The Wave and the Flame, 1986
A Rumor of Angels, 1983

Other books you might like:
Graham Edwards, *Dragoncharm*, 1996
Nancy Farmer, *The Ear, the Eye and the Arm*, 1994
Anne McCaffrey, *Dragonflight*, 1968
Andre Norton, *Elvenblood*, 1995
    Mercedes Lackey, co-author
Irene Radford, *The Loneliest Magician*, 1996

Fantasy

733

PATRICIA KENNEALY-MORRISON

Blackmantle: A Triumph

(New York: HarperPrism, 1997)

Story type: Magic Conflict; Political
Series: Keltiad
Major character(s): Athyn ''Blackmantle'' Cahanagh, Orphan, Leader (High Queen); Morric Douglas, Musician (bard)
Time period(s): 17th century (1650s)
Locale(s): Tara, Planet—Imaginary; Keltia, Interstellar Empire/Federation

Summary: The death of the High King leaves Keltia without a recognized sovereign, allowing the alien Firvolgi an opportunity to move into Keltia. As Athyn rises to repel the invasion, her choice of Morric as her mate leads a former companion of Morric to drastic action.

Where it's reviewed:
Kirkus Reviews, July 1, 1997, page 992
Library Journal, September 15, 1997, page 106
Publishers Weekly, August 25, 1997, page 50

Other books by the same author:
The Oak Above the Kings: A Book of the Keltiad, 1994
The Hawk's Gray Feather, 1990 (written as Patricia Kennealy)
The Silver Branch, 1988 (written as Patricia Kennealy)
The Throne of Scone, 1986 (written as Patricia Kennealy)
The Copper Crown, 1985 (written as Patricia Kennealy)

Other books you might like:
Greg Bear, *Songs of Earth and Power*, 1994
Kenneth C. Flint, *Challenge of the Clans*, 1986
Guy Gavriel Kay, *The Summer Tree*, 1985
Morgan Llywelyn, *Grania: She-King of the Irish Seas*, 1986
Julian May, *The Many-Colored Land*, 1981
Diana L. Paxson, *The Shield between the Worlds*, 1994
　　Adrienne Martine-Barnes, co-author

734

ELIZABETH KERNER

Song in the Silence

(New York: Tor, 1997)

Story type: Quest; Legend
Major character(s): Lanen Kaeler, Heroine, Bastard Daughter; Akhor, Mythical Creature (dragon), Royalty (Dragonking)
Time period(s): Indeterminate
Locale(s): Kolmar, Fictional Country; Dragon Isle, Fictional Country

Summary: Upon her cold, distant father's death, Lanen Kaeler pursues her lifelong dream to search for the legendary dragons of Dragon Isle. Her quest uncovers unexpected knowledge, such as the identity of her real father and the existence of a prophecy that Lanen herself may ful fll. First novel.

Where it's reviewed:
Booklist, February 15, 1997, page 1008
Kirkus Reviews, December 15, 1996, page 1772
Library Journal, February 15, 1997, page 165
Locus, February 1997, page 25
Voice of Youth Advocates, June 1997, page 118

Other books you might like:
Graham Edwards, *Dragoncharm*, 1996
Ursula K. Le Guin, *A Wizard of Earthsea*, 1968
Anne McCaffrey, *The Girl Who Heard Dragons*, 1994
Anne McCaffrey, *Dragonflight*, 1968
Robin McKinley, *Beauty*, 1978
Andre Norton, *Elvenblood*, 1995
　　Mercedes Lackey, co-author

735

KATHARINE KERR

The Red Wyvern

(New York: Bantam Spectra, 1997)

Story type: Magic Conflict; Political
Series: Dragon Mage
Major character(s): Lillorigga ''Lilli'', Psychic; Maryn, Royalty (prince); Nevyn, Counselor
Time period(s): 9th century (849); 12th century (1117)
Locale(s): Deverry, Fictional Country

Summary: Lilli's maturing talents force her to choose between family and country loyalty as the usurper and rightful heir contend for power.

Where it's reviewed:
Booklist, October 1, 1997, page 312
Dragon Magazine, February 1998, page 60
Kirkus Reviews, September 1, 1997, page 1346
Library Journal, November 15, 1997, page 79
Publishers Weekly, October 13, 1997, page 61

Other books by the same author:
Days of Air and Darkness, 1994
Days of Blood and Fire, 1993
A Time of Omens, 1992
A Time of Exile, 1991
Daggerspell, 1986

Other books you might like:
Laurell K. Hamilton, *Nightseer*, 1992
Robin Hobb, *Assassin's Apprentice*, 1995
J.V. Jones, *The Baker's Boy*, 1995
Peg Kerr, *Emerald House Rising*, 1997
Michelle Sagara, *Into the Dark Lands*, 1991

736

PEG KERR

Emerald House Rising

(New York: Warner Aspect, 1997)

Story type: Mystery; Magic Conflict
Major character(s): Jena Gemcutter, Apprentice, Wizard; Morgan Duone, Nobleman, Wizard; Kestrienne Duone, Noblewoman, Wizard

Time period(s): Indeterminate
Locale(s): Piyar, Fictional City; Piyanthia, Fictional Country; Uriat Mountains, Mythical Place

Summary: Unfamiliar with her blossoming magical abilities, Jena unexpectedly bonds with Morgan. Suprised to find herself abandoned among Morgan's relatives, Jena receives insight from Lady Kestrienne into her relationship with Morgan and aid in foiling a plot against the ruling families. First novel.

Where it's reviewed:
Locus, April 1997, page 29
Publishers Weekly, April 21, 1997, page 69
Voice of Youth Advocates, August 1997, page 193

Other books you might like:
Lois McMaster Bujold, *The Spirit Ring*, 1992
Lynn Flewelling, *Stalking Darkness*, 1997
Laurell K. Hamilton, *Nightseer*, 1992
Anne Logston, *Firewalk*, 1997
Caroline Stevermer, *A College of Magics*, 1994
L.A. Taylor, *Cat's Paw*, 1995

737

J. GREGORY KEYES

The Blackgod

(New York: Ballantine Del Rey, 1997)

Story type: Quest; Magic Conflict
Major character(s): Perkar Kar Barku, Warrior, Hero; Hezhi Yehd Cha'dune, Royalty, Fugitive; Karak, Deity
Time period(s): Indeterminate
Locale(s): Southern Mang, Fictional Country; Nhol, Fictional Country; The River, Mythical Place

Summary: Guided by Karak, both Perkar and Hezhi seek the source of The River, a jealous deity pursuing omniscience. Perkar desires peace between the Mang and his people, while Hezhi hopes to free herself and her people from The River's enslavement. As the priesthood attempts to steer events, The River sends a killer and reanimated assassin of the priesthood to find Hezhi, hiding among the Mang, and regain control over her. Sequel to *The Waterborn*.

Where it's reviewed:
Booklist, March 1, 1997, page 1068
Kirkus Reviews, February 15, 1997, page 261
Library Journal, April 15, 1997, page 123
Locus, April 1997, page 29
Publishers Weekly, March 24, 1997, page 63

Other books by the same author:
The Waterborn, 1996

Other books you might like:
Raymond E. Feist, *Magician*, 1982
Mary Gentle, *Rats and Gargoyles*, 1991
Terry Goodkind, *Wizard's First Rule*, 1994
P.C. Hodgell, *God Stalk*, 1982
Douglas Niles, *A Breach in the Watershed*, 1995

738

KATHARINE ELISKA KIMBRIEL

Kindred Rites

(New York: HarperPrism, 1997)

Story type: Adventure; Magic Conflict
Major character(s): Alfreda ''Alli'' Sorensson, Magician, Midwife; Marta Donaltsson, Magician, Midwife; Death, Spirit
Time period(s): 19th century
Locale(s): North America

Summary: Allie studies magic and midwifery under Marta, learning quickly and, with Marta's direction, meeting Death for the first time. When kidnapped by an agent of the centuries-old Keeper who wishes to use her blossoming power, Allie escapes and survives using her knowledge of the woods, but must bind herself to Death to control wild magic and save herself from the Keeper.

Where it's reviewed:
Locus, January 1998, page 23

Other books by the same author:
Night Calls, 1996
Hidden Fires, 1991
Fires of Nuala, 1988
Fire Sanctuary, 1986

Other books you might like:
Orson Scott Card, *Seventh Son*, 1987
Charles de Lint, *Memory and Dream*, 1994
David Drake, *Old Nathan*, 1991
Suzette Haden Elgin, *Twelve Fair Kingdoms*, 1981
Rachel Pollack, *Godmother Night*, 1996
Midori Snyder, *The Flight of Michael McBride*, 1994
Mark Sumner, *Devil's Tower*, 1996

739

J. ROBERT KING

Planar Powers

(Renton, Washington: TSR, 1997)

Story type: Adventure
Series: Planescape: The Blood Wars Trilogy
Major character(s): Leonan, Deity; Nina, Mentally Ill Person, Military Personnel; Phaeton, Angel
Time period(s): Indeterminate
Locale(s): Tuscan, Mythical Place; Sigil, Fictional City

Summary: All victims in one way or another of the Lady of Pain, a group of people gather together by fate to fight against her. Dead god, amnesiac wizard, bodiless soul, soulless body, renegade angel and other misfits must use their limited power cleverly just to survive, much less triumph.

Other books by the same author:
Vinas Solamnus, 1997
Abyssal Warriors, 1996
Blood Hostages, 1996
Carnival of Fear, 1993
Heart of Midnight, 1992

Fantasy

Other books you might like:
Glen Cook, *The Swordbearer*, 1982
Simon R. Green, *Hawk & Fisher*, 1990
Patricia A. McKillip, *The Riddle-Master of Hed*, 1976
Michael Shea, *Nifft the Lean*, 1982
Roger Zelazny, *Lord of Light*, 1967

740

J. ROBERT KING

Vinas Solamnus

(Renton, Washington: TSR, 1997)

Story type: Adventure
Series: DragonLance: Lost Legends
Major character(s): Vinas Solamnus, Warrior, Religious; Emann Quisling, Royalty (emperor); Luccia, Mythical Creature (half-elf)
Time period(s): Indeterminate Past
Locale(s): Ansalon, Fictional Country; Daltigoth, Fictional City; Krynn, Planet—Imaginary

Summary: Founded by Vinas Solamnus, the world's most famous and noble warrior, the Solamnic Knights strongly defend Krynn. Vinas begins as an ignorant youth who wants to be a soldier, but hardship and peril forge him into a mighty and holy warrior who will fight and win the freedom of his people.

Other books by the same author:
Planar Powers, 1997
Abyssal Warriors, 1996
Rogues to Riches, 1995
Carnival of Fear, 1993
Heart of Midnight, 1992

Other books you might like:
Deborah Chester, *Reign of Shadows*, 1996
Robin Hobb, *Assassin's Apprentice*, 1995
Katherine Kurtz, *Deryni Rising*, 1970
Michael Scott Rohan, *The Anvil of Ice*, 1986
Kristine Kathryn Rusch, *The Changeling*, 1996

741

ELLEN KUSHNER, Editor
DELIA SHERMAN, Co-Editor
DONALD G. KELLER, Co-Editor

The Horns of Elfland

(New York: Roc, 1997)

Story type: Anthology

Summary: Contains seven pages of author biographies, a four-page introduction by Keller plus individual introductions by Kushner to 15 original stories focusing on music and magic. Authors include John Brunner, Jane Emerson, Michael Kandel, Ellen Kushner, Susan Palwick, Delia Sherman, Terri Windling, Gene Wolfe and Jack Womack.

Where it's reviewed:
Fantasy & Science Fiction, July 1997, page 21
Locus, May 1997, page 21
Starlog, August 1997, page 69

Other books by the same author:
St. Nicholas and the Valley Beyond, 1994
Thomas the Rhymer, 1990
Swordspoint, 1987
Basilisk, 1980

Other books you might like:
Gael Baudino, *Gossamer Axe*, 1990
Emma Bull, *War for the Oaks*, 1987
Anne McCaffrey, *Space Opera*, 1996
    Elizabeth Ann Scarborough, co-editor
Melisa Michaels, *Cold Iron*, 1997
Nancy Springer, *Damnbanna*, 1992

742

MERCEDES LACKEY

Four & Twenty Blackbirds

(New York: Baen, 1997)

Story type: Mystery; Magic Conflict
Series: Bardic Voices
Major character(s): Tal Rufin, Police Officer; Ardis, Religious; Rand, Magician
Time period(s): Indeterminate
Locale(s): Alanda, Fictional City; Twenty Kingdoms, Mythical Place

Summary: Without his superiors' support, constable Tal Rufin begins to investigate the murders and suicides of lower class women killed with objects usually found among religious regalia. He soon discovers nasty, overt forces at work.

Where it's reviewed:
Booklist, November 1, 1997, page 457
Kirkus Reviews, October 1, 1997, page 1499
Locus, October 1997, page 25
Publishers Weekly, November 24, 1997, page 57

Other books by the same author:
The Eagle and the Nightingales, 1995
A Cast of Corbies, 1994 (Josepha Sherman, co-author)
The Robin and the Kestrel, 1993
The Lark and the Wren, 1992
Arrows of the Queen, 1987

Other books you might like:
Charles de Lint, *Memory and Dream*, 1994
Nancy Farmer, *The Ear, the Eye and the Arm*, 1994
Lisa Goldstein, *Walking the Labyrinth*, 1996
Simon R. Green, *Hawk & Fisher*, 1990
Melissa Scott, *Point of Hopes*, 1995
    Lisa A. Barnett, co-author

743

MERCEDES LACKEY
LARRY DIXON, Co-Author

Owlflight

(New York: DAW, 1997)

Story type: Adventure
Major character(s): Darian, Hunter, Apprentice (wizard)
Time period(s): Indeterminate

Locale(s): Errold's Grove, Fictional City; Valdemar, Fictional Country; Pelagiris Forest, Mythical Place

Summary: Darian grows up hunting with his parents in the Pelagiris Forest for the magical beasts created by the Mage Wars. One day he does not accompany them and they do not return from the hunt. A year later, when he watches barbarians sack Errold's Grove and kill his master, Darian flees into the Pelagiris Forest and discovers the Hawkbrothers, a race that has inhabited the forest since before the Mage Wars.

Where it's reviewed:
Booklist, September 15, 1997, page 216
Kirkus Reviews, August 1, 1997, page 1168
Library Journal, October 15, 1997, page 98
Starlog, November 1997, page 16
Voice of Youth Advocates, December 1997, page 326

Other books by the same author:
The Silver Gryphon, 1996 (Larry Dixon, co-author)
The White Gryphon, 1995 (Larry Dixon, co-author)
The Black Gryphon, 1994 (Larry Dixon, co-author)
By the Sword, 1991
Arrows of the Queen, 1987

Other books you might like:
Robert Holdstock, *Mythago Wood*, 1984
Katharine Kerr, *Daggerspell*, 1986
Michaela Roessner, *Walkabout Woman*, 1988
Mary Stanton, *The Heavenly Horse From the Outermost West*, 1988
Michelle West, *Hunter's Oath*, 1995

744

MERCEDES LACKEY, Editor

Sword of Ice and Other Tales of Valdemar
(New York: DAW, 1997)

Story type: Anthology; Adventure
Series: Valdemar

Summary: Contains a one-page introduction and brief individual introductions to 18 original stories, three co-authored by Lackey. Generally upbeat in tone, the stories explore the history of Valdemar, the legendary Heralds and their telepathic, horselike Companions. Other authors include Richard Lee Byers, Larry Dixon, Tanya Huff, Ben Ohlander, Mickey Zucker Reichert, Michelle Sagara, Mark Shepherd, Josepha Sherman and Elisabeth Waters.

Where it's reviewed:
Kliatt, May 1997, page 14

Other books by the same author:
By the Sword, 1991
Winds of Fate, 1991
Magic's Pawn, 1989
The Oathbound, 1988
Arrows of the Queen, 1987

Other books you might like:
Robert Asprin, *Thieves' World*, 1979
    editor
Marion Zimmer Bradley, *Free Amazons of Darkover*, 1985
    Friends of Darkover, co-editor

Richard Pini, *The Blood of Ten Chiefs*, 1986
    Robert Asprin, Lynn Abbey, co-editors
Will Shetterly, *Liavek*, 1985
    Emma Bull, co-editor
Terri Windling, *Borderland*, 1986
    Mark Allan Arnold, co-editor

745

STEPHEN R. LAWHEAD

Grail
(New York: Avon, 1997)

Story type: Legend; Political
Series: Pendragon Cycle
Major character(s): Gwalchavad, Knight, Nobleman; Arthur, Royalty (king); Morgian, Royalty, Sorceress
Time period(s): Indeterminate Past
Locale(s): England

Summary: Healed at the edge of death by the Holy Grail, King Arthur pledges his renewed life to heal the injuries of Britain. When an agent of Morgian steals the Grail along with the Queen, Arthur and his knights must find the Grail, searching throughout Britain and other worlds to bring about the Golden Age.

Where it's reviewed:
Kirkus Reviews, May 1, 1997, page 686
Publishers Weekly, June 16, 1997, page 50

Other books by the same author:
Byzantium, 1996
Pendragon, 1994
Arthur, 1989
Merlin, 1988
Taliesin, 1987

Other books you might like:
Marion Zimmer Bradley, *The Mists of Avalon*, 1983
Bernard Cornwell, *The Winter King*, 1996
Anne Eliot Crompton, *Gawain and Lady Green*, 1997
Helen Hollick, *Shadow of the King*, 1997
Phyllis Ann Karr, *The Idylls of the Queen*, 1982

746

ADAM LEE (Pseudonym of A.A. Attanasio)

The Dark Shore
(New York: Avon, 1997)

Story type: Magic Conflict
Series: Dominions of Irth
Major character(s): Drev, Ruler (wizarduke), Wizard; Tywi, Orphan; Dogbrick, Thief, Philosopher
Time period(s): Indeterminate Past
Locale(s): Irth, Fictional Country; Arwar Odawl, Fictional City

Summary: Cursed to the Dark Shore, Wrat, a failed revolutionary, becomes the horrific Hu'dre Vra and launches a second war against his home. At first successful, his enemies dying by the thousands, Wrat fails to kill Wizarduke Drev who

Fantasy

gathers his forces to counterattack. Either life or anti-life may win the war for Irth.

Where it's reviewed:
Kirkus Reviews, February 15, 1997, page 261
Library Journal, April 15, 1997, page 123
Locus, December 1996, page 21
Publishers Weekly, March 31, 1997, page 68
Starlog, July 1997, page 61

Other books you might like:
Eleanor Arnason, *The Sword Smith*, 1978
A.A. Attanasio, *Kingdom of the Grail*, 1992
A.A. Attanasio, *The Moon's Wife: A Hystery*, 1993
Glen Cook, *The Swordbearer*, 1982
Robin Hobb, *Assassin's Apprentice*, 1995
Robert Silverberg, *Lord Valentine's Castle*, 1980
Janny Wurts, *Stormwarden*, 1984

747

TANITH LEE

Red Unicorn

(New York: Tor, 1997)

Story type: Young Adult; Adventure
Major character(s): Tanaquil Veriam, Wanderer, Sorceress; Worabex, Magician; Peeve, Animal (enchanted), Companion (Tanaquil's)
Time period(s): Indeterminate
Locale(s): Fictional Country

Summary: Trying to leave Worabex behind, Tanaquil returns home, only to find the magician there when she arrives. Finally happy, her mother has replaced almost everyone else with demons. When Tanaquil takes a walk in the desert, she realizes that her mother and Worabex unwittingly sent her to yet another alternate world. There, the Sulkana Liliam has an evil sister, Tanakil, who looks like Tanaquil. The red unicorn with bronze hooves also awaits her.

Where it's reviewed:
Booklist, June 1 & 15, 1997, page 1685
Locus, July 1997, page 25
Publishers Weekly, May 19, 1997, page 70

Other books by the same author:
Gold Unicorn, 1994
Black Unicorn, 1991
Dark Castle, White Horse, 1986
Sung in Shadow, 1983
Cyrion, 1982

748

FRITZ LEIBER

Return to Lankhmar

(Clarkston, Georgia: White Wolf, 1997)

Story type: Collection; Sword and Sorcery
Series: Fafhrd and the Grey Mouser
Major character(s): Fafhrd, Thief, Warrior; The Grey Mouser, Thief, Wizard; Hisvet, Mythical Creature (rat-woman)
Time period(s): Indeterminate

Locale(s): Lankhmar, Fictional City; Nehwon, Planet—Imaginary

Summary: Contains a three-page introduction by Neil Gaiman, a foreword by the author, the novel *The Swords of Lankhmar* (1968), and eight short stories published as *Swords and Ice Magic* (1977), with illustrations by Mike Mignola. This collection sees the dangerous and degenerate duo save their beloved and shameless city from a horde of intelligent rats, then journey to the frozen ends of Nehwon in search of adventure, riches and release from boredom.

Where it's reviewed:
Realms of Fantasy, October 1997, page 96
Science Fiction Chronicle, October 1997, page 45

Other books by the same author:
Lean Times in Lankhmar, 1996
Ill Met in Lankhmar, 1995
The Leiber Chronicles, 1990
Our Lady of Darkness, 1977
Night's Black Agents, 1947

Other books you might like:
Steven Brust, *Jhereg*, 1983
Ellen Kushner, *Swordspoint*, 1987
Michael Shea, *The Mines of Behemoth*, 1997
Richard L. Tierney, *Scroll of Thoth*, 1997
Karl Edward Wagner, *Darkness Weaves*, 1978 revised

749

MARK LEYNER

The Tetherballs of Bougainville

(New York: Harmony, 1997)

Story type: Literary; Satire
Major character(s): Mark Leyner, Writer, Teenager; Warden, Police Officer
Time period(s): 1990s (1997)
Locale(s): Maplewood, New Jersey

Summary: The day after teeanager Mark Leyner watches his father executed, he wins an award for Best Screenplay written by a student at his junior high school. The novel, which acts as autobiography, screenplay, and movie review, examines and re-examines Mark's response to these traumatic events.

Where it's reviewed:
Booklist, October 15, 1997, page 388
Kirkus Reviews, August 15, 1997, page 1247
Library Journal, September 1, 1997, page 218
New York Times Book Review, November 23, 1997, page 28
Publishers Weekly, July 21, 1997, page 181

Other books by the same author:
Tooth Imprints on a Corn Dog, 1995
Et Tu, Babe, 1992
My Cousin, My Gastroenterologist, 1990
I Smell Esther Williams, 1983

Other books you might like:
Kathy Acker, *Empire of the Senseless*, 1988
William S. Burroughs, *Nova Express*, 1965

R.U. Serius, *How to Mutate and Take Over the World*, 1996
   St. Jude, co-author

William T. Vollman, *You Bright and Risen Angels*, 1987

Robert Anton Wilson, *Reality Is What You Can Get Away With: An Illustrated Screenplay*, 1992

750

JANE M. LINDSKOLD

When the Gods Are Silent

(New York: AvoNova, 1997)

Story type: Quest; Adventure

Major character(s): Hulhe, Farmer, Scholar; Rabble, Warrior, Mythical Creature; Rylus, Entertainer

Time period(s): Indeterminate

Locale(s): Fictional Country

Summary: Hoping to find a cure for his wife's chronic illness, Hulhe hires Rylus and his Traveling Spectacular to escort him to the Storm Shroud Mountains where, he believes, the Magic still exists a generation after it ceased to function in the rest of the world. The troupe and their menagerie survive the dangers of bandits, surly mobs, pirates, bureaucrats, and the scheming Duke of Dragons. However, the truly dangerous portion of their journey only begins when they meet the ghost of a soldier who served the wizards that imprisoned the Elementals.

Other books by the same author:

Smoke and Mirrors, 1996

The Pipes of Orpheus, 1995

Marks of Our Brothers, 1995

Brother to Dragons, Companion to Owls, 1994

Other books you might like:

Lynn Abbey, *The Black Flame*, 1980

Ray Bradbury, *Something Wicked This Way Comes*, 1962

C.J. Cherryh, *Gate of Ivrel*, 1976

Ursula K. Le Guin, *A Wizard of Earthsea*, 1968

Robert Silverberg, *Lord Valentine's Castle*, 1980

Roger Zelazny, *Lord of Light*, 1967

Roger Zelazny, *Donnerjack*, 1997
   Jane Lindskold, co-author

751

HOLLY LISLE
TED NOLAN, Co-Author

Hell on High

(New York: Baen, 1997)

Story type: Contemporary; Light Fantasy

Series: Hellraised

Major character(s): Glibspet, Demon, Detective—Private; Jack Halloran, Engineer (electrical); Rheabeth ''Rhea'' Samuels, Businesswoman

Time period(s): 1990s

Locale(s): Heaven; Devil's Point, North Carolina

Summary: As God vacations, Jack Halloran works on a space drive. While Lucifer wants results from his demons, Glibspet,

the only demonic private eye, tries to track down a missing Fallen Angel. Weirdly, it all connects.

Where it's reviewed:

Locus, July 1997, page 33

Other books by the same author:

The Devil and Dan Cooley, 1996 (Walter Spence, co-author)

Sympathy for the Devil, 1996

Mind of the Magic, 1995

Minerva Wakes, 1994

Fire in the Mist, 1992

Other books you might like:

Jack L. Chalker, *And the Devil Will Drag You Under*, 1979

Neil Gaiman, *Good Omens: The Nice and Accurate Prophecies of Agnes Nutter, Witch*, 1990
   Terry Pratchett, co-author

Christopher Moore, *Practical Demonkeeping*, 1992

Mike Resnick, *Deals with the Devil*, 1994
   Martin Greenberg, Loren Estleman, co-author

Roger Zelazny, *If at Faust You Don't Succeed*, 1993
   Robert Sheckley, co-author

752

HOLLY LISLE
AARON ALLSTON, Co-Author

Wrath of the Princes

(New York: Baen, 1997)

Story type: Political; Adventure

Series: Bard's Tale

Major character(s): Kin Underbridge, Judge; Halleyne dar Dero, Noblewoman, Sorceress; Jerno, Royalty, Leader (king)

Time period(s): Indeterminate

Locale(s): Feyndala, Mythical Place; Bekalli, Fictional City

Summary: Kin and Halleyne help Jerno reacquire power when they return to find that those who caused their shipwreck and subsequent dangers are now in control. Based on a computer game.

Other books by the same author:

Thunder of the Captains, 1996 (Aaron Allston, co-author)

Mall, Mayhem and Magic, 1995 (Chris Guin, co-author)

Mind of the Magic, 1995

Minerva Wakes, 1994

Fire in the Mist, 1992

Other books you might like:

Aaron Allston, *Doc Sidhe*, 1995

Aaron Allston, *Galatea in 2-D*, 1993

Mercedes Lackey, *Castle of Deception*, 1992
   Josepha Sherman, co-author

Mercedes Lackey, *Fortress of Frost and Fire*, 1993
   Ru Emerson, co-author

Mercedes Lackey, *Prison of Souls*, 1993
   Mark Shepherd, co-author

Mark Shepherd, *Escape From Roksamur*, 1997

Josepha Sherman, *The Chaos Gate*, 1994

Fantasy

753

ANNE LOGSTON

Firewalk

(New York: Ace, 1997)

Story type: Political; Adventure
Major character(s): Kayli, Magician (Order of the Inner Flame), Noblewoman; Radon, Heir, Spouse
Time period(s): Indeterminate
Locale(s): Agrond, Fictional Country

Summary: Dragged from an important initiation to become the bride in an arranged marriage which will strengthen her country's ties to its neighbor, Kayli must learn to control her magical abilities without the usual help offered by her Order. In Agrond, Kayli must quickly adapt to life as a ruler while insuring her place by producing an heir for her husband.

Where it's reviewed:
Locus, May 1997, page 29
Realms of Fantasy, August 1997, page 17

Other books by the same author:
Guardian's Key, 1996
Dagger's Edge, 1994
Greendaughter, 1993
Shadow Hunt, 1992
Shadow, 1991

Other books you might like:
Lois McMaster Bujold, *The Spirit Ring*, 1992
Laurell K. Hamilton, *Nightseer*, 1992
J.V. Jones, *The Baker's Boy*, 1995
Peg Kerr, *Emerald House Rising*, 1997
Fiona Patton, *The Stone Prince*, 1997
Caroline Stevermer, *A College of Magics*, 1994

754

ANN MARSTON

Broken Blade

(New York: HarperPrism, 1997)

Story type: Sword and Sorcery; Magic Conflict
Series: Rune Blade Trilogy
Major character(s): Brynda al Keylan, Noblewoman, Bodyguard; Kenzie "Catfoot" dav Aidan, Mercenary, Nobleman; Mikal, Sorcerer
Time period(s): Indeterminate
Locale(s): Laringras, Fictional Country; Isle of Celi, Fictional Country

Summary: Kidnapped by the evil sorceress Francia, Brynda escapes and joins forces with Kenzie as they flee across Laringras. Eluding capture, Brynda returns to Celi to warn King Tiernyn that Francia and her son, Mikal may have the power to overcome the veil of enchantment protecting Celi for the last 40 years. When the battle comes, Brynda survives to guard the widow of Prince Tiegan and the unborn heir to the throne. First in trilogy.

Other books by the same author:
The Western King, 1996

Kingmaker's Sword, 1996
Other books you might like:
Marion Zimmer Bradley, *The Shattered Chain*, 1976
Terry Brooks, *The Sword of Shannara*, 1978
C.J. Cherryh, *Gate of Ivrel*, 1976
Barbara Hambly, *The Dark Hand of Magic*, 1990
C.L. Moore, *Jirel of Joiry*, 1969
Elizabeth Ann Scarborough, *The Christening Quest*, 1985

755

THOMAS K. MARTIN

Magelord: The Awakening

(New York: Ace, 1997)

Story type: Magic Conflict; Political
Series: MageLord Trilogy
Major character(s): Bjorn Rolfson, Hunter, Wizard; Gavin, Royalty (Prince of Reykvid); Valerian, Wizard (MageLord)
Time period(s): Indeterminate
Locale(s): Reykvid, Fictional City

Summary: Although he fears his abilities may not suffice, Bjorn must help when Prince Gavin fears his father has come under the influence of Valerian, possibly an ancient MageLord, awakened from a prison of sleep. First in trilogy.

Where it's reviewed:
Kliatt, July 1997, page 18
Locus, June 1997, page 29
Voice of Youth Advocates, October 1997, page 253

Other books by the same author:
A Call to Arms, 1995
A Matter of Honor, 1994
A Two-Edged Sword, 1994

Other books you might like:
Lynn Flewelling, *Luck in the Shadows*, 1996
Terry Goodkind, *Wizard's First Rule*, 1994
Robin Hobb, *Assassin's Apprentice*, 1995
Peg Kerr, *Emerald House Rising*, 1997

756

JULIAN MAY

Sky Trillium

(New York: Ballantine Del Rey, 1997)

Story type: Magic Conflict
Series: Black Trillium
Major character(s): Tolivar, Nobility (prince), Teenager; Orogastus, Sorcerer, Criminal; Haramis, Sorceress, Royalty
Time period(s): Indeterminate Future
Locale(s): Sobrania, Fictional Country; Dark Man's Moon, Moon—Imaginary

Summary: With the world badly out of balance, Orogastus devises a plan to gain the three-fold scepter of power from Anigel, Kadiya and Haramis, using prince Tolivar and the greedy, would-be Empress Naelore. But saving the world

depends upon joint wielding of Orogastus' Star and the three-fold scepter with no coercion, or the world will perish under fire and ice. Sequel to *Black Trillium*.

Where it's reviewed:
Booklist, January 1 & 15, 1997, page 826
Publishers Weekly, December 30, 1996, page 58
Starlog, March 1997, page 16

Other books by the same author:
Magnificat, 1996
Blood Trillium, 1992
Jack the Bodiless, 1992
Intervention, 1987
The Many-Colored Land, 1981

Other books you might like:
Poul Anderson, *A Midsummer Tempest*, 1974
Marion Zimmer Bradley, *Black Trillium*, 1990
  Julian May, Andre Norton, co-authors
Marion Zimmer Bradley, *Lady of the Trillium*, 1995
Michael Lahey, *Quest for Apollo*, 1989
Andre Norton, *Golden Trillium*, 1993
Kathleen Sky, *Witchdame*, 1985
Jack Vance, *The Green Pearl*, 1985
Lawrence Watt-Evans, *Denner's Wreck*, 1988

757

ANNE MCCAFFREY
RICHARD WOODS, Co-Author

A Diversity of Dragons

(New York: HarperPrism, 1997)

Story type: Legend
Major character(s): Anne McCaffrey, Writer, Storyteller; Sean Evans, Student; Epiphanius ''Eppy'' Tighe, Storyteller
Time period(s): 1990s; Indeterminate Past
Locale(s): Ireland; Europe; Middle East

Summary: Sean's unexpected interest in dragon lore presents Anne and Eppy with the opportunity to enlighten him concerning dragons from myths and modern fiction. Contains seven pages of notes, sources, dragon classification, annotations and a list of other books about dragons.

Other books by the same author:
The Masterharper of Pern, 1998
The Dolphins of Pern, 1994
All the Weyrs of Pern, 1991
Dragonsong, 1976
Dragonflight, 1968

Other books you might like:
Eleanor Arnason, *The Sword Smith*, 1978
Orson Scott Card, *Dragons of Darkness*, 1981
  editor
Orson Scott Card, *Dragons of Light*, 1983
  editor
Gordon R. Dickson, *The Dragon and the George*, 1976
Graham Edwards, *Dragoncharm*, 1996
Andre Norton, *Elvenblood*, 1995
  Mercedes Lackey, co-author
J.R.R. Tolkien, *The Hobbit*, 1938

Patricia C. Wrede, *Talking to Dragons*, 1993
revised edition

758

ASHLEY MCCONNELL

The Courts of Sorcery

(New York: Ace, 1997)

Story type: Magic Conflict; Political
Series: Demon Wars
Major character(s): Jazen, Wizard (exorcist)
Time period(s): Indeterminate
Locale(s): Mirlacca, Fictional City

Summary: Having rid Eberly of its demon, Jazen returns to Mirlacca. Unfortunately the demon now possesses Jazen, hoping to use the Guild of Exorcists' knowledge to acquire access to his home, the world of evil. Third in series.

Where it's reviewed:
Locus, March 1997, page 58

Other books by the same author:
The Itinerant Exorcist, 1996
The Fountains of Mirlacca, 1995
Random Measures, 1994
Too Close for Comfort, 1993
Quantum Leap: The Novel, 1992

Other books you might like:
Charles de Lint, *Trader*, 1997
Susan Dexter, *The Wizard's Shadow*, 1993
P.C. Hodgell, *God Stalk*, 1982
J. Gregory Keyes, *The Blackgod*, 1997
J. Gregory Keyes, *The Waterborn*, 1996

759

VONDA N. MCINTYRE

The Moon and the Sun

(New York: Pocket, 1997)

Story type: Historical
Major character(s): Marie-Josephe de la Crois, Noblewoman; Lucien de Barenton, Nobleman, Military Personnel; Louis XIV, Historical Figure, Royalty (king of France)
Time period(s): 17th century (1693)
Locale(s): Versailles, France

Summary: Father Yves de la Croix captures a sea monster and hints to Louis XIV that its flesh holds the secret of immortality. His sister, Marie-Josephe, learns to communicate with the sea monster and wants to set her free. Marie-Josephe's plan thwarted, the sea monster must try to ransom herself with sunken treasure.

Where it's reviewed:
Booklist, July 1997, page 1806
Kirkus Reviews, July 1, 1997, page 991
Locus, August 1997, page 21
Publishers Weekly, July 28, 1997, page 51
Starlog, February 1998, page 60

Other books by the same author:
Transition, 1991
Starfarers, 1989
Superluminal, 1983
Dreamsnake, 1978
The Exile Waiting, 1975

Other books you might like:
Poul Anderson, *A Midsummer Tempest*, 1974
Lisa Goldstein, *Strange Devices of the Sun and Moon*, 1993
Tim Powers, *The Drawing of the Dark*, 1979
Michaela Roessner, *The Stars Dispose*, 1997
Clifford D. Simak, *The Fellowship of the Talisman*, 1978
Melinda Snodgrass, *Queen's Gambit Declined*, 1989
Jack Vance, *Suldrun's Garden*, 1983
Chelsea Quinn Yarbro, *A Candle for D'Artagnan*, 1989

760

DENNIS L. MCKIERNAN

Into the Forge

(New York: Roc, 1997)

Story type: Quest; Magic Conflict
Series: Mithgar
Major character(s): Tipperton "Tip" Thistledown, Mythical Creature (warrow), Adventurer; Beacontor "Beau" Darby, Mythical Creature, Adventurer
Time period(s): Indeterminate
Locale(s): Fictional Country

Summary: When a dying warrior presses a coin into Tip's hand, telling him to go east and warn all, Tip and Beau begin an adventure leading to foreign lands filled with monsters as strife engulfs the land.

Where it's reviewed:
Booklist, September 1, 1997, page 67
Starlog, October 1997, page 14

Other books by the same author:
The Dragonstone, 1996
Tales of Mithgar, 1994
Voyage of the Fox Rider, 1993
The Eye of the Hunter, 1992
Dragondoom, 1984

Other books you might like:
Lynn Flewelling, *Luck in the Shadows*, 1996
Lynn Flewelling, *Stalking Darkness*, 1997
Terry Goodkind, *Wizard's First Rule*, 1994
J.V. Jones, *The Baker's Boy*, 1995
J.R.R. Tolkien, *The Fellowship of the Ring*, 1954
J.R.R. Tolkien, *The Hobbit*, 1938

761

ROBIN MCKINLEY

Rose Daughter

(New York: Greenwillow, 1997)

Story type: Legend
Major character(s): Beauty, Gardener; The Beast, Animal (ensorcelled)

Time period(s): Indeterminate
Locale(s): Rose Cottage, Mythical Place; Beast's Palace, Mythical Place

Summary: After a comfortable life in the city, Beauty, her sisters and their fathers must become accustomed to life in a small rural cottage when forced to leave the city in disgrace. Adapting, the daughters begin to develop their talents, until a chance meeting by her father intertwines Beauty's fate with the Beast, resident of an enchanted palace. Concludes with a four-page author's note describing the novel's genesis.

Where it's reviewed:
Booklist, August 1997, page 1898
The Horn Book Magazine, September/October 1997, page 574
Kirkus Reviews, June 1, 1997, page 877
Locus, November 1997, page 17
School Library Journal, September 1997, page 219

Other books by the same author:
Deerskin, 1993
The Hero and the Crown, 1984
The Blue Sword, 1982
The Door in the Hedge, 1982
Beauty, 1978

Other books you might like:
Ellen Datlow, *Black Swan, White Raven*, 1997
Terri Windling, co-editor
Lisa Goldstein, *Walking the Labyrinth*, 1996
Patricia A. McKillip, *Winter Rose*, 1996
Delia Sherman, *The Porcelain Dove*, 1993
Jane Yolen, *The Wild Hunt*, 1995

762

MELISA MICHAELS

Cold Iron

(New York: Roc, 1997)

Story type: Mystery; Urban
Major character(s): Rosalynd "Rosie" Lavine, Detective—Private; Candy Cayne, Teenager, Fanatic (Cold Iron groupie); Jorandel "Jorie", Mythical Creature (elf), Musician (Cold Iron)
Time period(s): 1990s
Locale(s): San Francisco, California; Los Angeles, California

Summary: Against her better judgment, Rosalynd answers Candy's plea to uncover the person attempting to kill the lead singer of an elfrock band. Posing as Candy's cousin to gain acceptance among Cold Iron's entourage, Rosalynd cannot resist the fast lifestyle, despite the increased danger from those intent on thwarting her efforts.

Where it's reviewed:
Locus, July 1997, page 33
Starlog, September 1997, page 81

Other books by the same author:
Far Harbor, 1989
Pirate Prince, 1987
Last War, 1986
First Battle, 1985

Skirmish, 1985

Other books you might like:
Gael Baudino, *Gossamer Axe*, 1990
Greg Bear, *Songs of Earth and Power*, 1994
Emma Bull, *War for the Oaks*, 1987
Kara Dalkey, *Steel Rose*, 1997
Elizabeth Ann Scarborough, *Phantom Banjo*, 1991

`763`

RAND MILLER
DAVID WINGROVE, Co-Author

The Book of D'ni

(New York: Hyperion, 1997)

Story type: Science Fiction; Quest
Series: Myst
Major character(s): Eedrah, Royalty (D'ni); Atrus, Writer, Magician; Catherine, Adventurer
Time period(s): Indeterminate Future
Locale(s): Terahnee, Mythical Place; D'ni, Mythical Place

Summary: While exploring abandoned D'ni, Atrus and Catherine find the forbidden Book linking Terahee with D'ni, inadvertantly helping Eedrah fulfill the prophecy and find the lost people of C'ni. CD-ROM game tie-in.

Where it's reviewed:
Publishers Weekly, October 27, 1997, page 56

Other books by the same author:
The Book of Ti'ana, 1996
The Book of Atrus, 1995

Other books you might like:
Charles de Lint, *Memory and Dream*, 1994
Alan Dean Foster, *The Dig*, 1996
Patricia A. McKillip, *The Riddle-Master of Hed*, 1976
David Wingrove, *The Middle Kingdom*, 1990
David Worsick, *Henry's Gift: The Magic Eye*, 1994

`764`

L.E. MODESITT JR.

The Chaos Balance

(New York: Tor, 1997)

Story type: Magic Conflict
Series: Recluse
Major character(s): Nylan, Engineer; Ayrlyn, Doctor (healer); Lephi the White, Ruler
Time period(s): Indeterminate
Locale(s): Candar, Fictional Country; Cyador, Fictional Country

Summary: After Nylan builds Tower Black and saves his shipmates, politics forces him to leave his new home. He takes his friend, Ayrlyn, and his infant son into a world full of war and half-understood power, hoping to find peace.

Where it's reviewed:
Booklist, September 15, 1997, page 216
Kirkus Reviews, August 1, 1997, page 1168
Publishers Weekly, August 25, 1997, page 50

Other books by the same author:
Fall of Angels, 1996
The Order War, 1995
The Magic Engineer, 1994
The Towers of the Sunset, 1992
The Magic of Recluce, 1991

Other books you might like:
Eleanor Arnason, *The Sword Smith*, 1978
M.A.R. Barker, *Man of Gold*, 1984
Glen Cook, *Tower of Fear*, 1989
Lisa Goldstein, *Summer King, Winter Fool*, 1994
Guy Gavriel Kay, *Tigana*, 1990

`765`

L.E. MODESITT JR.

The Soprano Sorceress

(New York: Tor, 1997)

Story type: Magic Conflict; Alternate World
Major character(s): Anna Marshall, Singer, Sorceress; Lord Brill, Singer, Sorceress; Daffyd, Musician
Time period(s): 1990s; Indeterminate
Locale(s): Ames, Iowa; Defalk, Fictional Country

Summary: Transported by magic into an alternate world where music literally creates magic, Anna Marshall discovers that her vocal talents and training on Earth prepare her to wield great power on Erde. As she begins to use her new magical skills to defend the Kingdom of Defalk from invasion, she also discovers that some fear a powerful woman and that she must protect herself, even from those she has protected. First of a new series that is so far unnamed.

Where it's reviewed:
Booklist, February 1, 1997, page 929
Kirkus Reviews, December 15, 1996, page 1773
Locus, January 1997, page 25
Publishers Weekly, January 20, 1997, page 398
Voice of Youth Advocates, October 1997, page 253

Other books by the same author:
Fall of Angels, 1996
The Order War, 1995
The Magic Engineer, 1994
The Towers of the Sunset, 1992
The Magic of Recluce, 1991

Other books you might like:
Peter S. Beagle, *The Unicorn Sonata*, 1996
Emma Bull, *War for the Oaks*, 1987
Gordon R. Dickson, *The Dragon and the George*, 1976
Barbara Hambly, *The Time of the Dark*, 1982
Anne McCaffrey, *The Crystal Singer*, 1982
Elizabeth Ann Scarborough, *Phantom Banjo*, 1991

`766`

MICHAEL MOORCOCK

Corum: The Coming of Chaos

(Clarkston, Georgia: White Wolf, 1997)

Story type: Quest; Sword and Sorcery

Series: Eternal Champion
Major character(s): Corum Jhaelen Irsei, Royalty (prince), Wizard
Time period(s): Indeterminate
Locale(s): Alternate Earth; Tanelorn, Fictional City

Summary: The sole surviving member of the magical race of the Vadhagh, Prince Corum unleashes vast cosmic forces and acquires powerful adversaries as he travels through the multiverse to avenge his ravaged world. Omnibus edition of *The Knight of Swords* (1971), *The Queen of Swords* (1971) and *The King of Swords* (1971), previously published in 1977 as *The Swords Trilogy*.

Other books by the same author:
The War Amongst the Angels, 1997
The Roads Between the Worlds, 1996
Elric: Song of the Black Sword, 1995
The Eternal Champion, 1994
The Chronicles of Corum, 1978

Other books you might like:
Fred Saberhagen, *The First Book of Swords*, 1983
Martha Wells, *The Element of Fire*, 1993
Roger Zelazny, *The Guns of Avalon*, 1972
Roger Zelazny, *Nine Princes in Amber*, 1970
Roger Zelazny, *Sign of the Unicorn*, 1975

767

MICHAEL MOORCOCK

Fabulous Harbors

(New York: Avon, 1997)

Story type: Collection; Literary
Major character(s): Jack Karaquazian, Gambler (retired), Adventurer; Colinda Dovero, Adventurer (retired); Albert Begg, Military Personnel (Naval Intelligence, retired)
Time period(s): Indeterminate
Locale(s): Alternate Earth; Chelsea, England

Summary: Eleven interrelated stories fitting into the universe of *Blood: A Southern Fantasy* and *The War Amongst the Angels*. Lovers Jack Karaquazian and Colinda Dovero settle into retirement with their old cronies, the Beggs and the von Becks, entertaining one another with tales of their adventures in the multiverse. These include an encounter with Elric of Melnibone, rescuing virgins from high towers and certain doom, visitations from Egypt's ancient gods and running guns into Africa with Captain Horace Quelch, the infamous White Pirate.

Where it's reviewed:
Booklist, March 1, 1997, page 1114
Kirkus Reviews, December 15, 1996, page 1773
Library Journal, February 15, 1997, page 165
Locus, November 15, 1995, page 17
Publishers Weekly, January 20, 1997, page 398

Other books by the same author:
The War Amongst the Angels, 1997
Blood: A Southern Fantasy, 1995
Von Bek, 1995
The Swords Trilogy, 1977
Elric of Melnibone, 1976

Other books you might like:
Michael Bishop, *At the City Limits of Fate*, 1996
Zenna Henderson, *Ingathering: The Complete People Stories of Zenna Henderson*, 1995
Robert E. Howard, *Beyond the Borders*, 1996
Diana Wynne Jones, *Everard's Ride*, 1995
Harry Turtledove, *The Guns of the South*, 1992

768

MICHAEL MOORCOCK

The War Amongst the Angels

(New York: Avon, 1997)

Story type: Religious; Political
Series: Von Bek Family
Major character(s): Margaret Rose Moorcock, Revolutionary, Adventurer; Sam Oakenhurst, Adventurer; Jack Karaquazian, Gambler, Adventurer
Time period(s): 1990s; Indeterminate
Locale(s): London, England; The Second Ether, Mythical Place; Alternate Universe

Summary: A veteran of the battle against the tyranny of London's Universal Transport Company, Rose discovers the doors between the worlds, opening the way to infinite possibilities. Together with Sam, Jack and others, she joins in the great War in Heaven, battling against Lucifer himself. Last in series.

Where it's reviewed:
Asimov's Science Fiction, September 1997, page 152
Booklist, November 15, 1997, page 548
Kirkus Reviews, October 1, 1997, page 1496
Library Journal, November 15, 1997, page 79
Publishers Weekly, November 10, 1997, page 59

Other books by the same author:
Fabulous Harbors, 1997
The Roads Between the Worlds, 1996
Blood: A Southern Fantasy, 1995
Von Bek, 1995

Other books you might like:
Neil Gaiman, *Good Omens: The Nice and Accurate Prophecies of Agnes Nutter, Witch*, 1990
Terry Pratchett, co-author
Parke Godwin, *The Snake Oil Wars*, 1989
Robert A. Heinlein, *Job: A Comedy of Justice*, 1984
James Morrow, *Bible Stories for Adults*, 1996
James Morrow, *Blameless in Abaddon*, 1996
James Morrow, *Towing Jehovah*, 1994

769

SHIRLEY ROUSSEAU MURPHY

Cats Raise the Dead

(New York: HarperPrism, 1997)

Story type: Mystery; Contemporary Realism
Series: Cat on the Edge
Major character(s): Joe Grey, Animal (cat); Clyde Damen, Mechanic (auto); Dulcie, Animal (cat)

Time period(s): 1990s
Locale(s): Molena Point, California (northern)

Summary: Joe Grey and Dulcie, two cats with human intelligence, investigate mysterious disappearances in a nursing home. When loot from a cat burglar working her crime spree up and down the California coast appears in the nursing home, Joe puts up wht the indignities of pet therapy to find out more.

Other books by the same author:
Cat under Fire, 1997
Cat on the Edge, 1996
The Catsworld Portal, 1992
The Joining of the Stone, 1981
The Ring of Fire, 1977

Other books you might like:
Bill Fawcett, *Cats in Space and Other Places*, 1992
    editor
Anne McCaffrey, *No One Noticed the Cat*, 1996
Andre Norton, *Breed to Come*, 1972
Mark E. Rogers, *The Adventures of Samurai Cat*, 1984
Cordwainer Smith, *Norstrilia*, 1975
John Richard Stephens, *The Enchanted Cat*, 1990
    editor
L.A. Taylor, *Cat's Paw*, 1995
Tad Williams, *Tailchaser's Song*, 1985

770

LINDA NEVINS

Renaissance Moon

(New York: St. Martin's, 1997)

Story type: Contemporary Realism; Religious
Major character(s): Selene Catcher, Scholar, Religious; Giovanna Corio, Religious
Time period(s): 1990s
Locale(s): Cambridge, Massachusetts; Florence, Italy

Summary: Father Corio has known the brilliant Selene for a long time, watching her grow stranger as the years went by. Despite their fondness for each other, a gulf separates them. Corio became a Catholic priest, while Selene Catcher's connection to Goddess traces back to having been sealed to the Triple Goddess at birth. When Selene becomes attached to a charming and faithless young man, Goddess will have revenge on all of them.

Where it's reviewed:
New York Times Book Review, September 28, 1997, page 22

Other books you might like:
A.A. Attanasio, *The Moon's Wife: A Hystery*, 1993
Bradley Denton, *Lunatics*, 1996
Lisa Goldstein, *Walking the Labyrinth*, 1996
Elizabeth Hand, *Waking the Moon*, 1995
Robert Holdstock, *Ancient Echoes*, 1996

771

STEVEN NIGHTINGALE

The Thirteenth Daughter of the Moon

(New York: St. Martin's, 1997)

Story type: Contemporary Realism; Literary
Series: Lost Coast
Major character(s): Cookie, Cowboy (female); Chiara, Professor, Fugitive; Ananda, Musician, Lawyer
Time period(s): 1990s (1997)
Locale(s): Berkeley, California

Summary: As the strange travelers continue their search for the Lost Coast and Cookie's lost husband, they meet odd people with odder stories, including a medieval saint, a poet, and a coyote, and they tell their own tales along the way. When they reach their mythical destination, however, they learn that all ends become beginnings.

Other books by the same author:
The Lost Coast, 1997

Other books you might like:
James P. Blaylock, *The Paper Grail*, 1991
Francesca Lia Block, *Weetzie Bat*, 1989
Jack Cady, *The Off Season*, 1995
John Crowley, *Little, Big*, 1981
Pat Murphy, *The City, Not Long After*, 1989

772

DOUGLAS NILES

War of the Three Waters

(New York: Ace, 1997)

Story type: Magic Conflict; Quest
Series: Watershed Trilogy
Major character(s): Rudgar "Rudy" Appenfell, Hero, Mountaineer (Iceman); Raine of the Three Waters, Noblewoman, Writer
Time period(s): Indeterminate
Locale(s): The Watershed, Mythical Place; Faerine, Fictional Country; Duloth-Trol, Fictional Country

Summary: As Darkenblood flows over the Watershed and the Nameless One's minions battle to control all, human and Faerine forces must unite to prevent chaos. To overcome the disaster, Rudy and Raine must travel deep into enemy lands to use the sword of their ancestors against the source of the evil assault.

Where it's reviewed:
Kirkus Reviews, July 1, 1997, page 992
Realms of Fantasy, December 1997, page 14

Other books by the same author:
Darkenheight, 1996
A Breach in the Watershed, 1995
The Kagonesti, 1995
The Druid Queen, 1993
The Coral Kingdom, 1992

Other books you might like:
Terry Goodkind, *Wizard's First Rule*, 1994

Fantasy

J. Gregory Keyes, *The Blackgod*, 1997
J. Gregory Keyes, *The Waterborn*, 1996
Patricia Mullen, *The Stone Movers*, 1995
J.R.R. Tolkien, *The Fellowship of the Ring*, 1954

773

KATE NOVAK
JEFF GRUBB, Co-Author

Finder's Bane

(Renton, Washington: TSR, 1997)

Story type: Quest
Series: Forgotten Realms: The Harpers
Major character(s): Joel, Musician (harper), Religious; Holly Harrowslough, Religious, Rebel; Jasmine ''Jas'', Pilot, Mythical Creature (winged woman)
Time period(s): Indeterminate
Locale(s): Daggerdale, Fictional City; Sigil, Fictional City

Summary: A priest of the new god, Finder, Joel surrenders a great deal—position, friends and family—to follow his calling. Now his god calls him to risk his life and soul to prevent the resurrection of the terrible Bane, a dead and defeated god of evil. If Joel and his allies fail, not only will they and Finder die, but Bane's evil will also spread everywhere. Novelization based on role-playing game.

Other books by the same author:
Masquerades, 1995 (Jeff Grubb, co-author)
Song of the Saurials, 1991 (Jeff Grubb, co-author)
The Wyvern's Spur, 1990 (Jeff Grubb, co-author)
Azure Bonds, 1988 (Jeff Grubb, co-author)

Other books you might like:
Steven Brust, *Jhereg*, 1983
Glen Cook, *The Swordbearer*, 1982
Robin Hobb, *Assassin's Apprentice*, 1996
Fritz Leiber, *Ill Met in Lankhmar*, 1995
Roger Zelazny, *Nine Princes in Amber*, 1970

774

ERIC S. NYLUND

A Game of Universe

(New York: AvoNova, 1997)

Story type: Quest; Science Fiction
Major character(s): Germain, Criminal (magical assassin); Quilp, Criminal, Genius; Setebos, Artificial Intelligence
Time period(s): Indeterminate Future
Locale(s): Earth; Planet—Imaginary; *Grail Angel*, Spaceship

Summary: In the process of an assassination, Germain joins an expedition to discover and bring back the Holy Grail within a year or be killed. Germain enlists both his magical powers and his friends, finding himself and the Universe different from what he expected.

Other books by the same author:
Dry Water, 1997
Pawn's Dream, 1995

Other books you might like:
Piers Anthony, *The Ring*, 1968
  Robert E. Margroff, co-author
A.A. Attanasio, *The Dragon and the Unicorn*, 1996
Alan Dean Foster, *To the Vanishing Point*, 1988
Michael Moorcock, *The War Amongst the Angels*, 1997

775

PATRICK O'LEARY

The Gift

(New York: Tor, 1997)

Story type: Magic Conflict; Science Fiction
Major character(s): The Teller, Storyteller; Tim, Teenager, Adventurer; Simon, Royalty (king)
Time period(s): Indeterminate
Locale(s): At Sea; Fictional Country

Summary: The gifts of magic from the gods bring a price. To those aboard ship, the Teller speaks of King Simon who suffers the gift of magically acute hearing, Tim, deprived early of childhood, and their efforts to bring back the balance of magical forces disrupted by the Usher of Night.

Where it's reviewed:
Booklist, October 1, 1997, page 312
Fantasy & Science Fiction, October/November 1997, page 40
Kirkus Reviews, August 1, 1997, page 1165
Library Journal, October 15, 1997, page 98
Locus, October 1, 1997, page 17

Other books by the same author:
Door Number Three, 1995

Other books you might like:
Ursula K. Le Guin, *Tehanu*, 1990
Patricia A. McKillip, *The Book of Atrix Wolfe*, 1995
Rachel Pollack, *Godmother Night*, 1996
Philip Pullman, *The Golden Compass*, 1996
Gene Wolfe, *Peace*, 1975

776

FIONA PATTON

The Stone Prince

(New York: DAW, 1997)

Story type: Political
Major character(s): Demnor DeMarian, Royalty, Teenager; Melesandra DeMarian III, Royalty, Political Figure; Kelahnus, Warrior, Homosexual
Time period(s): Indeterminate Past
Locale(s): Gallia, Fictional Country; Branion, Fictional Country

Summary: The ruling family of Branion, blessed with magic and cursed with intrigue, includes Crown Prince Demnor, tormented by his power, disliked by his intense mother and threatened with an undesirable political marriage. However, the stakes rise when the Heathland revolt and the treacheries and pressures at court increase to fatal levels. First novel.

Where it's reviewed:
Locus, June 1997, page 58
Starlog, June 1997, page 11

Other books you might like:
C.J. Cherryh, *Fortress in the Eye of Time*, 1995
Guy Gavriel Kay, *The Lions of Al-Rassan*, 1995
Katherine Kurtz, *Deryni Rising*, 1970
George R.R. Martin, *A Game of Thrones*, 1996
Kristine Kathryn Rusch, *The Changeling*, 1996

777

WENDY PINI
RICHARD PINI, Co-Author

Captives of the Blue Mountain

(New York: Ace, 1997)

Story type: Adventure
Series: Elfquest
Major character(s): Cutter, Mythical Creature (elf), Leader; Leetah, Mythical Creature (elf); Winnowill, Mythical Creature (elf)
Time period(s): Indeterminate
Locale(s): Blue Mountain, Mythical Place

Summary: When giant winged creatures known as Bird Spirits attack and carry off four of the tribe, Cutter and other Wolfriders must assault the craggy spire of Blue Mountain to rescue them.

Where it's reviewed:
Realms of Fantasy, August 1997, page 17

Other books by the same author:
The Quest Begins, 1996 (Richard Pini, co-author)
Journey to Sorrow's End, 1982 (Richard Pini, co-author)

Other books you might like:
Richard Pini, *Against the Wind*, 1990
    editor
Richard Pini, *The Blood of Ten Chiefs*, 1986
    Robert Asprin, Lynn Abbey, co-editors
Richard Pini, *Dark Hours*, 1993
    editor
Richard Pini, *Winds of Change*, 1989
Richard Pino, *Wolfsong*, 1988
    Robert Asprin, Lynn Abbey, co-authors

778

TIM POWERS

Earthquake Weather

(New York: Tor, 1997)

Story type: Contemporary
Series: Fisher King
Major character(s): Janis Plumtree, Mentally Ill Person; Sid Cochran, Vintner; Scott Crane, Religious (Fisher King), Spirit
Time period(s): 1990s
Locale(s): Los Angeles, California; San Francisco, California

Summary: Under a malign influence, Janis Plumtree murders the Fisher King. Driven by remorse, she finds a group of simultaneously helpless and powerful people who will help her bring the King back or find a new King. Unfortunately, other claimants and the god Dionysus plan otherwise. An after-the-fact sequel to *Last Call* and *Expiration Date*.

Where it's reviewed:
Kirkus Reviews, August 1, 1997, page 1166
Library Journal, September 15, 1997, page 106
Locus, August 1997, page 21

Other books by the same author:
Expiration Date, 1996
Last Call, 1992
The Stress of Her Regard, 1989
The Anubis Gates, 1983
The Drawing of the Dark, 1979

Other books you might like:
James P. Blaylock, *The Paper Grail*, 1991
Jack Cady, *The Off Season*, 1995
John Crowley, *Little, Big*, 1981
Charles de Lint, *Moonheart: A Romance*, 1984
Robert Holdstock, *Mythago Wood*, 1984

779

TERRY PRATCHETT

Interesting Times

(New York: HarperCollins, 1997)

Story type: Light Fantasy
Series: Discworld
Major character(s): Ghenghiz "Cohen the Barbarian" Cohen, Hero, Aged Person; Rincewind, Wizard; Lord Hong, Nobleman, Villain
Time period(s): Indeterminate
Locale(s): Ankh-Morpork, Fictional City; Agatean Empire, Fictional Country; Discworld, Planet—Imaginary

Summary: The wizards of the Unseen University pull Rincewind from a blissfully boring desert island and send him across the Discworld to the Agataean Empire where he meets his old friend, Cohen, leader of the Silver Horde—five geriatric heroes and a retired teacher. The Horde travels to Hunghung, capital of the Empire, where Cohen plans the crowning achievement of his career. In spite of his efforts to avoid danger, Rincewind ends up leading revolutionaries who want to overthrow the Empire (politely) and resurrecting the legendary Red Army. Reprint of the 1994 British edition.

Where it's reviewed:
Fantasy & Science Fiction, September 1997, page 38
Kirkus Reviews, March 1, 1997, page 342
Library Journal, April 15, 1997, page 124
Locus, February 1995, page 21
Publishers Weekly, March 31, 1997, page 67

Other books by the same author:
Feet of Clay, 1996
Guards! Guards!, 1991
Equal Rites, 1988
The Light Fantastic, 1988
The Colour of Magic, 1983

Fantasy

Other books you might like:
Douglas Adams, *The Hitchhiker's Guide to the Galaxy*, 1980
Chester Anderson, *The Butterfly Kid*, 1967
Robert Asprin, *Another Fine Myth*, 1978
L. Sprague de Camp, *The Complete Compleat Enchanter*, 1989
    Fletcher Pratt, co-author
James H. Schmitz, *The Witches of Karres*, 1966
Christopher Stasheff, *Her Majesty's Wizard*, 1986

780

TERRY PRATCHETT

Maskerade
(New York: HarperPrism, 1997)

Story type: Light Fantasy; Satire
Series: Discworld
Major character(s): Agnes Nitt, Singer; Granny Weatherwax, Witch; Death, Mythical Creature
Time period(s): Indeterminate Past
Locale(s): Discworld, Planet—Imaginary; Ankh-Morpork, Fictional City

Summary: Since Agnes wants to sing, Granny Weatherwax needs a new third witch. The Opera Ghost remains looney, while Death acquires a little repetetive motion stress in his arms. All of them come together as the Discworld collides with *The Phantom of the Opera*. Ankh Morpork and the eardrums of its inhabitants will never be the same again in this 18th book in the Discworld series.

Where it's reviewed:
Fantasy & Fiction, March 1998, page 31

Other books by the same author:
Lords and Ladies, 1995
Witches Abroad, 1993
Reaper Man, 1992
Wyrd Sisters, 1990
The Colour of Magic, 1983

Other books you might like:
Robert Asprin, *Another Fine Myth*, 1978
John Bellairs, *The Face in the Frost*, 1969
L. Sprague de Camp, *The Complete Compleat Enchanter*, 1989
Gaston Leroux, *The Phantom of the Opera*, 1990
    Lowell Blair, translator
Christopher Moore, *Practical Demonkeeping*, 1992

781

PHILIP PULLMAN

The Subtle Knife
(New York: Knopf, 1997)

Story type: Historical; Quest
Series: His Dark Materials
Major character(s): Lyra Belacqua, Child, Fugitive; William "Will" Parry, Child, Fugitive; Lee Scoresby, Traveller, Pilot (balloon)
Time period(s): Indeterminate; 1990s

Locale(s): Cittagazze, Fictional City; Oxford, England; Alternate Earth

Summary: Menancing men hunt Will Parry's mother and Will. When Will flees these men, he falls into another world, where he meets Lyra, also on the run. Together they search for their fathers, only to uncover the strangest plot of all. Second of trilogy.

Where it's reviewed:
Booklist, July 1997, page 1818
The Horn Book Magazine, September/October 1997, page 578
Locus, August 1997, page 29
Publishers Weekly, June 30, 1997 page 77
School Library Journal, October 1997, page 137

Other books by the same author:
The Golden Compass, 1996

Other books you might like:
Eleanor Arnason, *Daughter of the Bear King*, 1987
James P. Blaylock, *The Land of Dreams*, 1987
John Crowley, *Little, Big*, 1981
Diana Wynne Jones, *Cart and Cwidder*, 1977
Patricia A. McKillip, *The Riddle-Master of Hed*, 1976

782

JEAN RABE

The Day of the Tempest
(Renton, Washington: TSR, 1997)

Story type: Adventure
Series: Dragonlance: Fifth Age
Major character(s): Malystryx the Red, Mythical Creature (dragon); Rurak Gistere, Knight; Palin Majere, Wizard
Time period(s): Indeterminate Past
Locale(s): Krynn, Planet—Imaginary

Summary: When the dragons return to dominate Krynn, conquering the people and altering the land and climate, malystryx and the others under the Storm Over Krynn plan to increase their empire to include Ansalon. A small band of heroes armed with magic and a dragonlance chooses to stand in their way.

Other books by the same author:
The Dawning of a New Age, 1996
Marquesta Kar-Thon, 1995
Red Magic, 1991

Other books you might like:
Glen Cook, *The Swordbearer*, 1982
Gordon R. Dickson, *The Dragon and the George*, 1976
Guy Gavriel Kay, *The Summer Tree*, 1985
Patricia A. McKillip, *The Riddle-Master of Hed*, 1976
Michael Scott Rohan, *The Anvil of Ice*, 1986

783

IRENE RADFORD

The Dragon's Touchstone

(New York: DAW, 1997)

Story type: Magic Conflict
Series: Dragon Nimbus History
Major character(s): Nimbulan ''Lan'', Magician, Warrior; Myrilandel ''Myri'', Healer; Amaranth, Mythical Creature (flywacket), Companion (Myri's familiar)
Time period(s): Indeterminate
Locale(s): Coronnan, Fictional Country

Summary: Weary of the system that exploits magic only to pursue warfare, one powerful Battlemage decides to unify the warring land by uniting all magicians who wish peace. Using her untrained, natural talent for healing, Myri flees those who would use her talent to their ends or destroy her, following the direction of the voices in her head. After she meets Nimbulan, the two discover their fates interwine.

Where it's reviewed:
Starlog, November 1997, page 14

Other books by the same author:
The Last Battlemage, 1997
The Loneliest Magician, 1996
The Perfect Princess, 1995
The Glass Dragon, 1994

Other books you might like:
Laurell K. Hamilton, *Nightseer*, 1992
Carol Heller, *The Gates of Vensunor*, 1997
Peg Kerr, *Emerald House Rising*, 1997
Katya Reimann, *Wind From a Foreign Sky*, 1996
Caroline Stevermer, *A College of Magics*, 1994

784

CHRISTOPH RANSMAYR

The Dog King

(New York: Knopf, 1997)

Story type: Literary; Historical
Major character(s): Ambras ''Dog King'', Leader; Bering, Teenager, Bodyguard; Lily, Hunter
Time period(s): 1950s
Locale(s): Moor, Fictional City

Summary: With World War II over, the Allies return Germany to a pre-industrial state, destroying modern civilization entirely. Put in charge of a small town, a camp survivor watches the sullen people sink into apathy until a boy in his care develops a disease untreatable with Moor's private resources, impelling him to flee from the past and towards hope. Translated by John E. Woods.

Where it's reviewed:
Booklist, April 1, 1997, page 1282
Kirkus Reviews, March 1, 1997, page 331
New York Times Book Review, June 22, 1997, page 16

Other books by the same author:
The Last World, 1990

Other books you might like:
J.G. Ballard, *Hello America*, 1981
Philip K. Dick, *The Man in the High Castle*, 1962
Robert Harris, *Fatherland*, 1992
Brad Linaweaver, *Moon of Ice*, 1988
Pat Murphy, *The City, Not Long After*, 1989

785

MELANIE RAWN

The Mageborn Traitor

(New York: DAW, 1997)

Story type: Political; Magic Conflict
Series: Exiles
Major character(s): Cailet Ambrai Rille, Leader (Mage Captal), Teacher (magic); Collan Rosvenir, Minstrel (lute), Nobleman; Sarra Ambrai Liwellan, Political Figure (councillor), Noblewoman
Time period(s): Indeterminate
Locale(s): Lenfell, Planet—Imaginary

Summary: Cailet's and Sarra's sister, Glenin, now leads the Malerris, long-time enemy of the Mage Guardians. As Glenin and her son violently undermine Cailet's efforts to rebuild the decimated ranks of the Mage Guardians, Lady Sarra struggles politically to bring about the legal reforms necessary to break the rigid caste system and create a more equal society. All if Lenfell braces itself for another cataclysmic magical struggle that will determine the long-term political and economic destiny of their world. Second in series.

Where it's reviewed:
Locus, April 1997, page 29
Starlog, June 1997, page 10
Voice of Youth Advocates, October 1997, page 254

Other books by the same author:
The Golden Key, 1996 (Jennifer Robertson and Kate Elliott, co-authors)
The Ruins of Ambrai, 1994
Sunrunners's Fire, 1990
The Star Scroll, 1989
Dragon Prince, 1988

Other books you might like:
Steven Brust, *Jhereg*, 1983
Barbara Hambly, *The Ladies of Mandrigyn*, 1984
Katherine Kurtz, *The Bastard Prince*, 1994
Elizabeth Moon, *Liar's Oath*, 1992
Harry Turtledove, *Krispos of Videssos*, 1991
Paula Volsky, *Illusion*, 1992
Paul O. Williams, *The Breaking of Northwall*, 1980
Roger Zelazny, *Nine Princes in Amber*, 1970

786

MICHAELA ROESSNER

The Stars Dispose

(New York: Tor, 1997)

Story type: Political

Fantasy

Major character(s): Caterina de Medici, Historical Figure; Tommaso Arista, Apprentice
Time period(s): 16th century
Locale(s): Florence, Italy

Summary: Learning his craft from master chefs and artists and befriended by Michelangelo, Tommaso progresses toward a career preparing food for the powerful de Medici family. Orphaned and in the guardianship of the pope, Caterina de Medici learns the magic of the hearth and culinary magic as she prepares to rule, if Florence does not prove too tempting a prize for others. Includes a food glossary and six pages of references and recipes.

Where it's reviewed:
Booklist, April 15, 1997, page 1387
Kirkus Reviews, March 1, 1997, page 341
Library Journal, April 15, 1997, page 124
Locus, April 1997, page 27
Publishers Weekly, March 31, 1997, page 67

Other books by the same author:
Vanishing Point, 1993
Walkabout Woman, 1988

Other books you might like:
Jack Dann, *The Memory Cathedral*, 1995
Guy Gavriel Kay, *A Song for Arbonne*, 1993
Paul J. MacAuley, *Pasquale's Angel*, 1995
Melissa Scott, *The Armor of Light*, 1988
    Lisa A. Barnett, co-author
Melissa Scott, *Point of Hopes*, 1995
    Lisa A. Barnett, co-author
Chelsea Quinn Yarbro, *Ariosto*, 1980

787

CHRISTOPHER ROWLEY

A Dragon at World's End

(New York: Roc, 1997)

Story type: Adventure; Magic Conflict
Series: Bazil Broketail
Major character(s): Bazil Broketail, Mythical Creature (dragon), Military Personnel; Relkin, Military Personnel
Time period(s): Indeterminate
Locale(s): Eigo, Fictional Country; Mirchaz, Fictional City

Summary: Separated from the 109th Marneri Dragons and thought dead, Bazil and Relkin plan to help a jungle tribe. When captured by slavers and taken to Mirchaz, Relkin becomes the pawn of an Elven wizard, forced to develop his rudimentary magical abilities in his struggle for freedom. Meanwhile, Bazil plots an assault on Mirchaz itself. Sixth in series.

Where it's reviewed:
Kliatt, May 1997, page 15
Starlog, April 1997, page 24

Other books by the same author:
The Dragons of Argonath, 1998
Battledragon, 1995
Dragons of War, 1994
A Sword for a Dragon, 1993

Bazil Broketail, 1992

Other books you might like:
Gael Baudino, *Duel of Dragons*, 1991
Glen Cook, *The Black Company*, 1984
Ursula K. Le Guin, *A Wizard of Earthsea*, 1968
Anne McCaffrey, *Dragonriders of Pern*, 1988
Elizabeth Moon, *The Deed of Paksenarrion*, 1992

788

SEAN RUSSELL

Beneath the Vaulted Hills

(New York: DAW, 1997)

Story type: Magic Conflict; Political
Series: River into Darkness
Major character(s): Eldrich, Wizard; Erasmus Flattery, Apprentice, Adventurer
Time period(s): Indeterminate
Locale(s): Farrland, Fictional Country; Avonel, Fictional City

Summary: After all other mages disappear from the land, Lord Eldrich works to eliminate the possibility of magic use forever, while the Tellerites strive to regain the lost knowledge. Erasmus agonizes over his role in Eldrich's plotting years earlier until he again receives a summons from Eldrich, which will send him into a subterranean labyrinth in search of an ancient secret, hidden since the time of the First Mages.

Where it's reviewed:
Locus, July 1997, page 55
Starlog, October 1997, page 12

Other books by the same author:
Sea Without a Shore, 1996
World Without End, 1995
The Initiate Brother, 1992
Gatherer of Clouds, 1991

Other books you might like:
Graham Edwards, *Dragoncharm*, 1996
Lynn Flewelling, *Luck in the Shadows*, 1996
Terry Goodkind, *Stone of Tears*, 1995
Peg Kerr, *Emerald House Rising*, 1997
Paula Volsky, *Illusion*, 1992

789

R.A. SALVATORE

The Demon Awakens

(New York: Ballantine Del Rey, 1997)

Story type: Magic Conflict; Political
Major character(s): Elbryan Wyndon, Teenager, Adventurer; Jilseponie ''Pony'', Teenager, Adventurer; Avelyn, Religious, Wizard
Time period(s): Indeterminate
Locale(s): Corona, Fictional Country; Dundalis, Fictional City

Summary: Their village destroyed by goblins, Elbryan and Jilseponie follow different paths to gain the skills they need to protect their land from the evil dactyl. The monks train Avelyn to prepare magic stones for the same purpose, but

Avelyn discovers different properties in them than he expects. The three meet and join together in seemingly a futile attempt to save their land from the evil army of the dactyl.

Where it's reviewed:
Booklist, May 1, 1997, page 1483
Kirkus Reviews, March 15, 1997, page 423
Library Journal, April 15, 1997, page 124
Publishers Weekly, April 28, 1997, page 55
Starlog, October 1997, page 14

Other books by the same author:
The Dragon King, 1996
Luthien's Gamble, 1996
The Sword of Bedwyr, 1995
The Dragon's Dagger, 1994
Starless Night, 1993

Other books you might like:
Steven Brust, *Jhereg*, 1983
Brian Daley, *Doomfarers of Coramonde*, 1977
Terry Goodkind, *Wizard's First Rule*, 1994
Douglas Niles, *A Breach in the Watershed*, 1995
Andre Norton, *Elvenblood*, 1995
   Mercedes Lackey, co-author

790

FELICITY SAVAGE

The War in the Waste

(New York: HarperPrism, 1997)

Story type: Alternate Universe; Adventure
Series: Ever
Major character(s): Crispin Kateralbin, Entertainer (aerialist), Mechanic (daemon handler); Rae, Orphan, Tailor; Daniel "Butch" Keynes, Military Personnel
Time period(s): 1870s (alternate world); 1890s (alternate world)
Locale(s): Valestock, Fictional City; Wraithwaste, Fictional Country; Alternate Earth

Summary: In a wildly, different Europe, where daemons provide energy for an industrializing world, a young man and woman become tangled in the complex politics of a continent at war. From back alleys to battlefields, they simply try to survive and find peace, but find themselves increasingly involved in pivotal events. First of a trilogy.

Where it's reviewed:
Kirkus Reviews, August 1, 1997, page 1166
Locus, October 1997, page 19
Publishers Weekly, August 25, 1997, page 50

Other books by the same author:
The Daemon in the Machine, 1998
Delta City, 1996
Humility Garden, 1995

Other books you might like:
Storm Constantine, *Wraeththu*, 1993
Avram Davidson, *The Adventurers of Dr. Eszterhazy*, 1991
Teresa Edgerton, *Goblin Moon*, 1991
Tanith Lee, *The Book of the Beast*, 1991
Paula Volsky, *Illusion*, 1992

791

DAVID L. SEIDMAN

The First Casualty

(New York: Boulevard, 1997)

Story type: Legend
Series: Hercules: The Legendary Journeys
Major character(s): Hercules, Hero (demi-god); Salmoneus, Salesman, Sidekick
Time period(s): Indeterminate Past
Locale(s): Mercantilius, Greece; Pastoralis, Greece

Summary: Trying to prevent war between Mercantilius and Pastoralis, Hercules discovers that Pan has already appeared there as Hercules to stir up trouble. Television tie-in.

Other books you might like:
John Gregory Betancourt, *The Vengeance of Hera*, 1997
John Gregory Betancourt, *The Wrath of Poseidon*, 1997
Timothy Boggs, *By the Sword*, 1996
Timothy Boggs, *The Eye of the Ram*, 1997
Timothy Boggs, *Serpent's Shadow*, 1996
Ru Emerson, *The Thief of Hermes*, 1997
Stella Howard, *Prophecy of Darkness*, 1997

792

MICHAEL SHEA

The Mines of Behemoth

(New York: Baen, 1997)

Story type: Adventure; Quest
Major character(s): Nifft the Lean, Adventurer; Barnar Hammer-Hand, Adventurer
Time period(s): Indeterminate
Locale(s): Dolmen, Fictional Country; Dry Hole, Fictional City; Costard's Superior Mine, Mythical Place

Summary: Shipwrecked on the way to work Costard's sap mine, Nifft the Lean and Barnar Hammer-hand agree to retrieve ichor uniquely produce by a monstrous insectile queen. The pair soon discover this plan to acquire quick wealth will prove trickier to accomplish than anticipated. Sequel to *Nifft the Lean*.

Where it's reviewed:
Locus, December 1997, page 21

Other books by the same author:
Polyphemus, 1987
In Yana, the Touch of Undying, 1985
The Colour out of Time, 1984
Nifft the Lean, 1982
A Quest for Simbilis, 1974

Other books you might like:
Glen Cook, *The Black Company*, 1984
Fritz Leiber, *Ill Met in Lankhmar*, 1995
John Moore, *Slay and Rescue*, 1993
Jack Vance, *Cugel's Saga*, 1983
Jack Vance, *Rhialto the Marvellous*, 1984

Fantasy

793

MARK SHEPHERD

Spiritride

(New York: Baen, 1997)

Story type: Magic Conflict; Political
Major character(s): Petrus, Mythical Creature (elf), Warrior; Wolf, Veteran, Shaman; Lucus Vaughan, Religious (devil worshipper)
Time period(s): 1990s
Locale(s): Underhill, Mythical Place (Elven realm); New Mexico

Summary: Petrus's reconnaissance mission to Earth presents evil Unseelie warriors an opportunity for revenge, enlisting the help of devil worshippers and an ancient Egyptian cat spirit to that end. Petrus and his small band received help from a protective guard of motorcycle riders, a young motorcyclist and a veteran of the Gulf War conflict who is a shaman and sole surviving member of his tribe. Sequel to Elvendude.

Where it's reviewed:
Starlog, May 1997, page 60

Other books by the same author:
Elvendude, 1994

Other books you might like:
Margaret Ball, *Mathemagics*, 1996
Greg Bear, *Songs of Earth and Power*, 1994
Emma Bull, *War for the Oaks*, 1987
Mercedes Lackey, *Prison of Souls*, 1993
    Mark Shepherd, co-author
Mercedes Lackey, *Wheels of Fire*, 1992
    Mark Shepherd, co-author

794

WILL SHETTERLY

Dogland

(New York: Tor, 1997)

Story type: Contemporary Realism; Literary
Major character(s): Luke Nix, Businessman; Ethorne Hawkins, Worker; Chris Nix, Child
Time period(s): 1950s (1959)
Locale(s): Latchahee County, Florida

Summary: Based extremely loosely on events in the author's life, this novel takes place around Dogland, an amusement park displaying every breed of dog recognized by the American Kennel Club. The family of Luke Nix comes to Florida to run Dogland, hiring Ethorne Hawkins, a black man, at a white man's wage. From this simple decency, a complex web of magic and history, cruelty and education forms around the Nix family and the county.

Where it's reviewed:
Kirkus Reviews, April 15, 1997, page 597
Library Journal, June 15, 1997, page 101
Locus, June 1997, page 21
Publishers Weekly, May 19, 1997, page 68
Voice of Youth Advocates, December 1997, page 327

Other books by the same author:
Nevernever, 1993
Elsewhere, 1991
The Tangled Lands, 1989
Witch Blood, 1986
Cats Have No Lord, 1985

Other books you might like:
James P. Blaylock, *The Paper Grail*, 1991
Jack Cady, *The Off Season*, 1995
John Crowley, *Love & Sleep*, 1994
Karen Joy Fowler, *The Sweetheart Season*, 1996
Robert Holdstock, *Lavondyss: Journey to an Unknown Region*, 1988

795

SUSAN SHWARTZ

Cross and Crescent

(New York: Tor, 1997)

Story type: Political; Religious
Major character(s): Leo Ducas, Military Personnel; Binah, Companion, Mythical Creature (goddess's offspring); Theodoulos, Linguist, Mythical Creature (goddess's offspring)
Time period(s): 11th century (1096-1099); 12th century (1104-1190)
Locale(s): Constantinople, Byzantine Empire; Asia Minor; Jerusalem, Middle East

Summary: The invasions bring hope and danger for Leo, as Theodoulos travels with the Crusaders for the Emperor and Binah attends to the Emperor's daughter. Set in the milieu of *Shards of Empire*.

Where it's reviewed:
Kirkus Reviews, October 15, 1997, page 1561
Publishers Weekly, November 10, 1997, page 60

Other books by the same author:
Shards of Empire, 1996
The Grail of Hearts, 1992
Queensblade, 1988
Silk Roads and Shadows, 1988
Byzantium's Crown, 1987

Other books you might like:
Frans G. Bengtsson, *The Long Ships*, 1954
John M. Ford, *The Dragon Waiting*, 1983
Stephen R. Lawhead, *Byzantium*, 1996
Andre Norton, *Imperial Lady*, 1989
    Susan M. Shwartz, co-author
Judith Tarr, *The Dagger and the Cross: A Novel of the Crusades*, 1991

796

JOSEPH SKIBELL

A Blessing on the Moon

(Chapel Hill, North Carolina: Algonquin Books of Chapel Hill, 1997)

Story type: Religious; Contemporary Realism

Major character(s): Chaim Skibelski, Spirit; Zalman, Religious
Time period(s): 1930s; 1940s
Locale(s): Poland

Summary: Shot during the Holocaust, Chaim does not settle in the peace of the World to Come. Instead he wanders around the world as a ghost. He visits his old home and meets the soldier who shot him, then reluctantly, helps two Hasids in their search for the missing Moon. First novel.

Where it's reviewed:
Booklist, September 1, 1997, page 60
Kirkus Reviews, August 15, 1997, page 1255
Library Journal, September 1, 1997, page 220
New York Times Book Review, December 28, 1997, page 12
Publishers Weekly, July 14, 1997, page 61

Other books you might like:
Janet Gluckman, *Child of the Light*, 1992
  George Guthridge, co-author
Lisa Goldstein, *The Red Magician*, 1982
Richard Grant, *Tex and Molly in the Afterlife*, 1996
Kurt Vonnegut Jr., *Slaughterhouse Five*, 1969
Jane Yolen, *Briar Rose*, 1992
Jane Yolen, *The Devil's Arithmetic*, 1988

797

MARTHA SOUKUP

The Arbitrary Placement of Walls

(Minneapolis: DreamHaven Books, 1997)

Story type: Collection; Science Fiction
Major character(s): Carl, Actor; Shawana Mooney, Single Parent, Traveller (trucker); Herb, Animal
Time period(s): Indeterminate Future; 1990s
Locale(s): New York, New York

Summary: Contains 17 short stories from periodicals and anthologies 1986-1996, plus a foreword by the author and an introductory poem by Neil Gaiman. The stories, both science fiction and fantasy, show a broad range of settings and tone, from ''Dress Rehearsal,'' in which an actor finds a surprising reaction to the remote-controlled bodies on stage, to ''Over the Long Haul,'' which shows the life of an impoverished woman on a dystopian mobile future. Author's first book.

Other books you might like:
Jack Cady, *The Sons of Noah and Other Stories*, 1992
John Crowley, *Antiquities*, 1993
Neil Gaiman, *Angels & Visitations*, 1993
Lisa Goldstein, *Travellers in Magic*, 1994
Pat Murphy, *Points of Departure*, 1990

798

MICHAEL A. STACKPOLE

A Hero Born

(New York: HarperPrism, 1997)

Story type: Sword and Sorcery
Series: Realms of Chaos

Major character(s): Lachlan ''Locke'', Military Personnel; Kit, Military Personnel
Time period(s): Indeterminate
Locale(s): City of Sorcerers, Fictional City

Summary: Locke dreams of becoming a Chaos Rider and seeking his father in the Wildness beyond the Wall, little expecting the evil forces waiting there to snare him.

Where it's reviewed:
Realms of Fantasy, October 1997, page 97
Voice of Youth Advocates, December 1997, page 328

Other books by the same author:
An Enemy Reborn, 1998
Talion: Revenant, 1997
Once a Hero, 1994
Evil Ascending, 1991
A Gathering Evil, 1991

Other books you might like:
David Gemmell, *Morningstar*, 1993
Terry Goodkind, *Wizard's First Rule*, 1994
Robin Hobb, *Assassin's Apprentice*, 1995
Mercedes Lackey, *Arrows of the Queen*, 1987
Elizabeth Moon, *Sheepfarmer's Daughter*, 1988

799

MICHAEL A. STACKPOLE

Talion: Revenant

(New York: Bantam Spectra, 1997)

Story type: Political; Adventure
Major character(s): Nolan ra Sinjaria, Lawman (Talion), Wizard; Morai, Criminal (bandit); Tirrell, Ruler (king)
Time period(s): Indeterminate Past
Locale(s): Hamis, Fictional Country

Summary: His family destroyed by war, Nolan flees to Talianna to become a Justice. Sent home to protect the man whose armies crushed his nation and family, Nolan must choose between orders and revenge if he desires true justice.

Where it's reviewed:
Booklist, March 15, 1997, page 1231

Other books by the same author:
A Hero Born, 1997
Once a Hero, 1994
Evil Triumphant, 1992
Evil Ascending, 1991
A Gathering Evil, 1991

Other books you might like:
Glen Cook, *The Black Company*, 1984
Barbara Hambly, *The Ladies of Mandrigyn*, 1984
Guy Gavriel Kay, *Tigana*, 1990
Fritz Leiber, *Ill Met in Lankhmar*, 1995
Michael Scott Rohan, *The Forge in the Forest*, 1986

Fantasy

800

CHRISTOPHER STASHEFF

My Son, the Wizard

(New York: Ballantine Del Rey, 1997)

Story type: Magic Conflict; Alternate World
Series: Wizard in Rhyme
Major character(s): Matthew ''Matt'' Mantrell, Wizard; Nirobus, Wizard, Drug Dealer; Lakshmi, Mythical Creature (djinn)
Time period(s): Indeterminate Future
Locale(s): Merovence, Fictional Country; Ibile, Fictional Country; New Jersey

Summary: Matt Mantrell rescues his parents, both of whom prove to have magic powers, from a drug-infested neighborhood just in time to involve them in a war between Merovence and the Moors. Allied with a love sick genie and an enterprising thief, Matt and his father must confront an evil sorcerer who, by means of drugs and magic, plans to rule and destroy two worlds.

Where it's reviewed:
Library Journal, November 15, 1997, page 79
Locus, January 1998, page 23
Publishers Weekly, November 10, 1997, page 60

Other books by the same author:
A Wizard in Chaos, 1997
The Shaman, 1995
We Open on Venus, 1994
Her Majesty's Wizard, 1986
The Warlock in Spite of Himself, 1969

Other books you might like:
Marion Zimmer Bradley, *The House Between the Worlds*, 1980
Jack L. Chalker, *Songs of the Dancing Gods*, 1990
Gordon R. Dickson, *The Dragon and the Djinn*, 1996
Esther M. Friesner, *Wishing Season*, 1993
Diana Wynne Jones, *Castle in the Air*, 1991
Guy Gavriel Kay, *The Lions of Al-Rassan*, 1995
Harry Turtledove, *Thessalonica*, 1997
Chelsea Quinn Yarbro, *Ariosto*, 1980

801

SEAN STEWART

The Night Watch

(New York: Ace, 1997)

Story type: Post-Disaster; Science Fiction
Series: Resurrection Man
Major character(s): Emily Thompson, Heir, Fugitive; Water Spider, Government Official; Claire, Military Personnel, Governess
Time period(s): 21st century
Locale(s): Edmonton, Alberta, Canada (Southside); Vancouver, British Columbia, Canada (Chinatown)

Summary: Seven decades after magic rises up and overwhelms civilization, when the Powers begin to fade, rational Southside and mystical Chinatown face this fact in very different ways. Meanwhile, the heir to Southside performs a ritual to an unknown and and flees to Chinatown for safety. Since the rulers of Chinatown have their own plots, however, through human and Power conspiracy and error, no one may get out alive.

Where it's reviewed:
Booklist, October 1, 1997, page 312
Kirkus Reviews, October 1, 1997, page 1495
Library Journal, November 15, 1997, page 79
Locus, January 1998, page 17
Publishers Weekly, October 13, 1997, page 60

Other books by the same author:
Cloud's End, 1996
Resurrection Man, 1995
Nobody's Son, 1995
Passion Play, 1993

Other books you might like:
John Crowley, *Little, Big*, 1981
Lisa Goldstein, *A Mask for the General*, 1987
Megan Lindholm, *Wizard of the Pigeons*, 1986
Rachel Pollack, *Temporary Agency*, 1994
Michaela Roessner, *Vanishing Point*, 1993

802

MATTHEW WOODRING STOVER

Iron Dawn

(New York, Roc, 1997)

Story type: Magic Conflict; Political
Major character(s): Barra, Warrior, Mercenary; Leucas, Warrior; Kheperu, Magician
Time period(s): 13th century B.C.
Locale(s): Tyre, Ancient Civilization (Phoenicia)

Summary: When an evil necromancer attempts to raise an army of the undead in the wake of the Trojan War, the Pict, Barra, and her companions become involved in a battle to control commerce in the port city of Tyre. First novel.

Where it's reviewed:
Library Journal, April 15, 1997, page 123
Starlog, July 1997, page 61

Other books you might like:
Lynn Flewelling, *Luck in the Shadows*, 1996
Lynn Flewelling, *Stalking Darkness*, 1997
Terry Goodkind, *Wizard's First Rule*, 1994
J.V. Jones, *The Baker's Boy*, 1995
Robert Jordan, *The Eye of the World*, 1990

803

MARK SUMNER

Devil's Engine

(New York: Ballantine Del Rey, 1997)

Story type: Magic Conflict; Historical
Series: Jake Bird
Major character(s): Jake Bird, Lawman, Wizard; William Cody, Scout, Historical Figure; Mr. Kastle, Scientist

Time period(s): 1870s
Locale(s): New York, New York; Medicine Rock, West

Summary: Following in his father's footsteps, Jake Bird, the sheriff of a small Western town, protects it from all threats by his magic. However, a new threat, a plot by an Eastern financier to drain the west of its magic, causes a great deal of grief. But will a future of technology and capitalism-run-amok fare any better?

Where it's reviewed:
Science Fiction Chronicle, October 1997, page 47

Other books by the same author:
Devil's Tower, 1996
The Prodigal Sorceress, 1995

Other books you might like:
Orson Scott Card, *Seventh Son*, 1987
David Drake, *Old Nathan*, 1991
Alan Dean Foster, *Mad Amos*, 1996
Midori Snyder, *The Flight of Michael McBride*, 1994
Harry Turtledove, *The Guns of the South*, 1992

804

S. ANDREW SWANN (Pseudonym of Steve Swiniarski)

God's Dice

(New York: DAW, 1997)

Story type: Alternate World; Quest
Major character(s): Richard Brandon, Psychologist, Professor; Rick, Editor (newspaper); Rocky, Police Officer
Time period(s): 1990s
Locale(s): Cleveland, Ohio; Quinque, Fictional Country

Summary: Traumatized by a car crash that killed his father and obsessed by an imaginary land he created in childhood, Dr. Richard Brandon experiments with alternate life regressions. His experiments open gateways between worlds, giving substance to nightmare creatures from his imaginary world and allowing four versions of himself to meet. Richard, Rick, Richie and Rocky escape the Thrall of Chaos that kills Dr. Brandon and flee to Quinque where they must retrieve the four relics of power and confront the Adversary before they can restore order in the land.

Where it's reviewed:
Locus, September 1997, page 70
Starlog, November 1997, page 14

Other books by the same author:
Partisan, 1995
Profiteer, 1995
Emperors of the Twilight, 1994
Specters of the Dawn, 1994
Forests of the Night, 1993

805

HARRY TURTLEDOVE

Thessalonica

(New York: Baen, 1997)

Story type: Historical; Mystery

Major character(s): George, Artisan (shoemaker); Father Luke, Religious; Ampelus, Mythical Creature (satyr)
Time period(s): 6th century
Locale(s): Greece; Ancient Civilization

Summary: When the Slavs and the Avars besiege Thessalonica and the Empire supplies no aid, Christian powers seem useless against Slav gods and demons. When a satyr rescues George, locked out of the city, George discovers that the Slavs and Avars also threaten the satyr and his friends, the centaurs, despite their magical nature.

Where it's reviewed:
Starlog, August 1997, page 69

Other books by the same author:
The Thousand Cities, 1997
Werenight, 1994
The Case of the Toxic Spell Dump, 1993
Krispos Rising, 1991
The Misplaced Legion, 1978

806

HARRY TURTLEDOVE

The Thousand Cities

(New York: Ballantine Del Ray, 1997)

Story type: Military; Political
Series: Time of Troubles
Major character(s): Abivard, Military Personnel; Tzikas, Military Personnel, Traitor; Sharbaraz, Ruler (King of Kings)
Time period(s): Indeterminate Past
Locale(s): Videssos, Fictional Country; Makuran, Fictional Country

Summary: Abivard must defend Makuran from Videssos despite the fact that Sharbaraz, King of Kings, grows suspicious of his success, but only keeps him alive as long as he maintains success. He must also contend with Tzikas, a military genius who cannot be trusted. Yet the two must work together for any hope of conquering Videssos. Third in series.

Other books by the same author:
Hammer and Anvil, 1996
The Stolen Throne, 1995
Krispos the Emperor, 1994
Krispos Rising, 1991
The Misplaced Legion, 1987

Other books you might like:
Richard Garfinkle, *Celestial Matters*, 1996
Diana Wynne Jones, *The Crown of Dalemark*, 1995
Katherine Kurtz, *The Bastard Prince*, 1994
Kirk Mitchell, *Procurator*, 1984
Jerry Pournelle, *Janissaries*, 1979
Melissa Scott, *A Choice of Destinies*, 1986
Robert Silverberg, *Valentine Pontifex*, 1983
Jack Vance, *The Green Pearl*, 1985

807

VIVIAN VANDE VELDE

The Conjurer Princess

(New York: HarperPrism, 1997)

Story type: Adventure
Major character(s): Lylene Delroy, Apprentice, Wizard; Harkta, Wizard; Shile, Warrior
Time period(s): Indeterminate
Locale(s): Cragsfall, Fictional City

Summary: Lylene does not anticipate the cost nor expect the changes that result from requesting that Harkta teach her magic so she can recover her lost sister, who was kidnapped on her wedding day.

Where it's reviewed:
Locust, August 1997, page 29
Voice of Youth Advocates, February 1998, page 396

Other books by the same author:
The Conjurer Princess, 1998
Tales From the Brothers Grimm and the Sisters Weird, 1995
Dragon's Bait, 1992
User Unfriendly, 1991
A Well-Timed Enchantment, 1990

Other books you might like:
Lois McMaster Bujold, *The Spirit Ring*, 1992
Emma Bull, *Finder*, 1994
Peg Kerr, *Emerald House Rising*, 1997
Holly Lisle, *Minerva Wakes*, 1994
Rachel Pollack, *Godmother Night*, 1996

808

DENISE VITOLA

Opalite Moon

(New York: Ace, 1997)

Story type: Mystery
Major character(s): Ty Merrick, Detective—Police (district marshals office), Werewolf; Andy LaRue, Detective—Police (district marshals office)
Time period(s): 21st century
Locale(s): United States

Summary: Ty Merrick, a detective with a scientifically explicable case of acquired lycanthropy, can shapeshift for greater strengh and cunning. She is chosen to investigate a series of murders that lead her to the Opalite, a cult that believes in the existence of the supernatural and practices rituals in obedience to it. Sequel to *Quantum Moon*.

Where it's reviewed:
Locus, August 1997, page 29
Science Fiction Chronicle, November 1997, page 40

Other books by the same author:
Quantum Moon, 1996
Half-Light, 1992

Other books you might like:
Pamela Dean, *The Dubious Hills*, 1994
Laurell K. Hamilton, *Guilty Pleasures*, 1993

Laurell K. Hamilton, *The Lunatic Cafe*, 1996
Tanya Huff, *Blood Price*, 1991
Nick Pollotta, *Full Moonster*, 1992

809

PAULA VOLSKY

The White Tribunal

(New York: Bantam Spectra, 1997)

Story type: Political; Magic Conflict
Major character(s): Tradain liMarchborg, Imposter, Sorcerer
Time period(s): Indeterminate Future
Locale(s): Upper Hetzia, Fictional Country; Lis Folaze, Fictional Country

Summary: After Tradain's father dies, falsely accused of performing frobidden practices by the White Tribunal, Tradain attempts to ruin his father's accusers by acquiring unusual powers through a demonic pact.

Where it's reviewed:
Kirkus Reviews, July 1, 1997, page 991
Publishers Weekly, July 14, 1997, page 70

Other books by the same author:
The Gates of Twilight, 1996
The Wolf of Winter, 1993
Illusion, 1992
The Sorcerer's Lady, 1986
The Curse of the Witch Queen, 1982

Other books you might like:
Susan Dexter, *The Wizard's Shadow*, 1993
Robin Hobb, *Assassin's Apprentice*, 1995
J.V. Jones, *The Baker's Boy*, 1995
J. Gregory Keyes, *The Waterborn*, 1996

810

LAWRENCE WATT-EVANS

Touched by the Gods

(New York: Tor, 1997)

Story type: Magic Conflict; Political
Major character(s): Malledd, Artisan (smith), Hero; Vadeviya, Religious; Duzon, Nobleman, Warrior
Time period(s): Indeterminate
Locale(s): Domdur Empire, Fictional Country

Summary: After generations of peace, the oracles indicate a newborn with the mark of the God, Ba'el, will lead the Domdur Empire to victory when war breaks out. Teased for years about becoming champion, Malledd rejects his prophecied role, content with his life as a smith. When the oracles cease communicating with the priests and an evil magician raises an army of the dead to invade, Malledd must decide whether to remain a simple smith or shoulder his foretold responsibility.

Where it's reviewed:
Booklist, November 1, 1997, page 457
Kirkus Reviews, September 1, 1997, page 1345
Library Journal, November 15, 1997, page 79

Locus, January 1998, page 65
Publishers Weekly, October 13, 1997, page 61

Other books by the same author:
The Spell of the Black Dagger, 1993
Taking Flight, 1993
Blood of a Dragon, 1991
With a Single Spell, 1987
The Misenchanted Sword, 1985

Other books you might like:
Stephen R. Donaldson, *Lord Foul's Bane*, 1977
Dave Duncan, *The Reluctant Swordsman*, 1988
David Eddings, *Pawn of Prophecy*, 1982
Terry Goodkind, *Wizard's First Rule*, 1994
Robert Jordan, *The Eye of the World*, 1990

811

SYLVIA WAUGH

Mennyms Alive
(New York: Greenwillow, 1997)

Story type: Young Adult; Contemporary
Series: Mennyms
Major character(s): Soobie Mennym, Mythical Creature; Daisy Maughan, Businesswoman, Antiques Dealer; Tulip Mennym, Mythical Creature
Time period(s): 1990s
Locale(s): England

Summary: When the ghost of their creator, Kate Penshaw, departs her mansion after 46 years, the Mennyms lose their life force. When the rag dolls awaken in Daisy Maughan's care, they must acquire new accomodations to regain their freedom, a task Tulip undertakes through intermediaries.

Where it's reviewed:
School Library Journal, September 1997, page 227

Other books by the same author:
Mennyms Alone, 1996
Mennyms under Siege, 1996
Mennyms in the Wilderness, 1995
The Mennyms, 1994

Other books you might like:
Lynne Reid Banks, *The Indian in the Cupboard*, 1981
L. Frank Baum, *The Patchwork Girl of Oz*, 1913
Michael Bedard, *Painted Devil*, 1994
Pauline Clarke, *The Return of the Twelves*, 1963

812

MARGARET WEIS
TRACY HICKMAN, Co-Author

Legacy of the Darksword
(New York: Bantam Spectra, 1997)

Story type: Adventure; Magic Conflict
Series: Darksword
Major character(s): Mosiah, Wizard; Saryon, Scholar; Reuven, Secretary
Time period(s): Indeterminate Future

Locale(s): Thimhallen, Fictional Country; Oxford, England

Summary: Joram forged the Darksword 20 years ago, destroying the magic land of Thimhallen and forcing his people to take refuge in the dreary relocation camps of Earth. When a rapacious alien threatens Earth, salvation rests in finding Joram and his new Darksword. But a new breed of wizard, the terrifying Technomancers, oppose the search in the wastelands of Thimhallen.

Where it's reviewed:
Booklist, June 1 & 15, 1997, page 1669
Kirkus Reviews, April 15, 1997, page 598
Library Journal, May 15, 1997, page 106
Publishers Weekly, May 12, 1997, page 63
Starlog, November 1997, page 14

Other books by the same author:
Dragons of Summer Flame, 1995 (Tracy Hickman, co-author)
The Soulforge, 1990 (Tracy Hickman, co-author)
Dragon Wing, 1990 (Tracy Hickman, co-author)
Forging the Darksword, 1988 (Tracy Hickman, co-author)
Dragons of Autumn Twilight, 1984 (Tracy Hickman, co-author)

Other books you might like:
Eleanor Arnason, *Daughter of the Bear King*, 1987
Gordon R. Dickson, *The Dragon and the George*, 1976
Barbara Hambly, *The Silent Tower*, 1986
Guy Gavriel Kay, *The Summer Tree*, 1985
Will Shetterly, *The Tangled Lands*, 1989

813

MARGARET WEIS, Editor

Testament of the Dragon
(New York: HaperPrism, 1997)

Story type: Adventure; Anthology
Major character(s): Justin Sterling, Immortal, Artist; The True Dragon, Deity; Alexandra Stone, Police Officer
Time period(s): 1990s; 14th century
Locale(s): Loch Ness, Scotland; Chicago, Illinois

Summary: Contains three short stories by Jeff Grubb, J. Robert King and Janet Pack, supported by several explanatory articles and many illustrations. Justin Sterling sells himself to the True Dragon to save his family from the Plague, then fights the forces of darkness for six centuries as a man, as the half-human Wyrm and as a comic-book creator. Illustrated by Steve Lieber, Rags Morales and others.

Other books by the same author:
The Dragons at War, 1996 (Tracy Hickman, co-editor)
Robot Blues, 1996 (Don Perrin, co-author)
The Knights of the Black Earth, 1995 (Don Perrin, co-author)
The Dragons of Krynn, 1994 (Tracy Hickman, co-editor)
Dragons of Autumn Twilight, 1984 (Tracy Hickman, co-author)

Other books you might like:
Jason Henderson, *The Element of Fire*, 1995
Ashley McConnell, *Scimitar*, 1996
Jennifer Roberson, *Scotland the Brave*, 1996
Roger Zelazny, *This Immortal*, 1966

Fantasy

814

MARGARET WEIS, Editor
TRACY HICKMAN, Co-Editor

Treasures of Fantasy
(New York: HarperPrism, 1997)

Story type: Anthology

Summary: Contains a two-page introduction by Weis plus brief biographical introductions to 24 stories reprinted from periodicals, anthologies and collections from 1948 through 1996. Varying in tone from somber to light, the stories feature diverse themes, such as sword and sorcery, magic conflict, high fantasy, mythical creatures, contemporary realism, impossible topology, and magical wishes. Authors include Poul Anderson, Marion Zimmer Bradley, Orson Scott Card, C.J. Cherryh, Philip K. Dick, Mercedes Lackey, R.A. Lafferty, Ursula K. Le Guin, Anne McCaffrey, Patricia A. McKillip, Andre Norton, Melanie Rawn, Jennifer Roberson, Joanna Russ, Robert Sheckley, Theordore Sturgeon, Jane Yolen and Roger Zelazny.

Where it's reviewed:
Voice of Youth Advocates, Decemeber 1997, page 328

Other books by the same author:
A Magic-Lover's Treasury of the Fantastic, 1998
Fantastic Alice, 1995
A Dragon-Lover's Treasury of the Fantastic, 1994
The Second Generation, 1994 (Tracy Hickman, co-editor)
Love and War, 1987 (Tracy Hickman, co-editor)

Other books you might like:
Mike Ashley, *The Random House Book of Fantasy Stories*, 1997
   editor
Robert H. Boyer, *Visions & Imaginings: Classic Fantasy Fiction*, 1992
   Kenneth J. Zahorski, co-editor
Alison Lurie, *The Oxford Book of Modern Fairy Tales*, 1993
   editor
Tom Shippey, *The Oxford Book of Fantasy Stories*, 1994
   editor
Robert Silverberg, *The Fantasy Hall of Fame*, 1993
   Martin H. Greenberg, co-editor

815

MICHELLE WEST (Pseudonym of Michelle Sagara)

The Broken Crown
(New York: DAW, 1997)

Story type: Political; Magic Conflict
Series: Sun Sword
Major character(s): Valedan kai de'Leonne, Royalty (prince); Diora di'Marano, Noblewoman, Widow(er); Kiriel, Orphan (Warrior)
Time period(s): Indeterminate
Locale(s): Dominion of Annagar, Fictional Country; Empire of Essalieyan, Fictional Country

Summary: Although Diora de'Marano, the bride of the heir apparent to Annagar's throne and a pawn in the courtly in-trigues of her family, did not love her husband, she seeks opportunity to avenge his death and the deaths of her co-wives when a military coup overthrows the royal family. But one heir to the throne, Valedan, still lives as a hostage held by the rival Essalieyan Empire. The Kings and Queens of Essalieyan agree to aid Valedan, while the demons of the Shining Court assist the rebels in Annagar. First in series.

Where it's reviewed:
Locus, June 1997, page 59
Publishers Weekly, June 23, 1997, page 88
Starlog, November 1997, page 14
Voice of Youth Advocates, August 1997, page 196

Other books by the same author:
Hunter's Death, 1996
Hunter's Oath, 1995

Other books you might like:
Margaret Ball, *Flameweaver*, 1991
Marion Zimmer Bradley, *The Mists of Avalon*, 1983
Terry Brooks, *The Sword of Shannara*, 1978
C.J. Cherryh, *Foreigner*, 1994
Robert Jordan, *The Eye of the World*, 1990
J. Gregory Keyes, *The Waterborn*, 1996
Elizabeth Ann Scarborough, *Nothing Sacred*, 1991
Joan D. Vinge, *The Snow Queen*, 1980

816

JACK WHYTE

The Eagles' Brood
(New York: Forge, 1997)

Story type: Legend
Series: Camulod Chronicles
Major character(s): Caius Merlyn Britannicus, Leader, Writer; Uther Pendragon, Warrior
Time period(s): 5th century
Locale(s): Camulod, England

Summary: Merlyn and Uther Pendragon lead the abandoned former Roman colony toward advanced Roman law and culture, until a vicious crime drives them apart and threatens the future both strive for.

Where it's reviewed:
Fantasy & Science Fiction, October/November 1997, page 44
Kirkus Reviews, August 1, 1997, page 1152
Publishers Weekly, August 4, 1997, page 67

Other books by the same author:
The Skystone, 1996
The Singing Sword, 1996

Other books you might like:
Marion Zimmer Bradley, *The Forest House*, 1994
Marion Zimmer Bradley, *The Mists of Avalon*, 1983
Courtway Jones, *In the Shadow of the Oak King*, 1991
Morgan Llywelyn, *Druids*, 1991
Harry Turtledove, *Werenight*, 1994

817

MICHAEL WILLIAMS

Allamanda
(New York: Roc, 1997)

Story type: Religious; Adventure
Major character(s): Garrick Hawken, Heir
Time period(s): Indeterminate
Locale(s): Urthona, Fictional Country; Urizen, Fictional Country

Summary: When Garrick discovers the Absence, a void beneath the family house, Arcady, he moves in with relatives at the family's old country house, Allamanda. Drawn to the Hawkens, the void comes to Allamanda, forcing Garrick to find some means of fighting the void's progression. Direct sequel to *Arcady*.

Where it's reviewed:
Kirkus Reviews, August 1, 1997, page 1167
Locus, September 1997, page 23
Starlog, May 1998, page 12

Other books by the same author:
Arcady, 1996

Other books you might like:
Greg Bear, *Songs of Earth and Power*, 1994
Richard Brautigan, *The Hawkline Monster*, 1974
Alan Dean Foster, *To the Vanishing Point*, 1988
Robert Holdstock, *Mythago Wood*, 1984
J. Gregory Keyes, *The Waterborn*, 1996
Eric S. Nylund, *Dry Water*, 1997

818

PAUL WITCOVER

Waking Beauty
(New York: HarperPrism, 1997)

Story type: Political; Religious
Major character(s): Cyrus ''Cy'' Galingale, Carpenter; Rose Rubra, Bride; Rumer, Prostitute
Time period(s): Indeterminate
Locale(s): Jubilar, Fictional City; Quoz, Fictional City

Summary: In a minor town in a strange, socially rigid world, a young man and woman about to be married find marriage only part of their destiny. Events in motion shake the social structure from base to peak, bringing a new era in the war between the Furies and the male-dominated Hierarchate. First novel.

Where it's reviewed:
Asimov's Science Fiction, October/November 1997, page 272
Locus, February 1997, page 17

Other books you might like:
Scott Baker, *Drink the Fire From the Flames*, 1987
Clive Barker, *Imajica*, 1991
Storm Constantine, *Wraeththu*, 1993
Tanith Lee, *Death's Master*, 1982
Robert Silverberg, *Lord Valentine's Castle*, 1980

819

PATRICIA C. WREDE

Magician's Ward
(New York: Tor, 1997)

Story type: Mystery; Romance
Series: Mairelon the Magician
Major character(s): Richard ''Mairelon'' Merrill, Magician; Kim, Apprentice, Magician; Alexei Durmontov, Royalty (prince), Wizard
Time period(s): 1810s
Locale(s): London, England; Alternate Universe

Summary: As Kim learns magic and more complicated rules of London society, disaster strikes Mairelon. When a mysterious money lender organizes slum magicians, and robbers suddenly become interested in books written by pre-Revolution French magicians, Kim becomes the only link between society and slum, despite her supposed status as a lady.

Where it's reviewed:
Booklist, November 1, 1997, page 457
Kirkus Reviews, September 15, 1997, page 1422
Locus, November 1997, page 62
Publishers Weekly, November 24, 1997, page 57

Other books by the same author:
The Raven Ring, 1994
Mairelon the Magician, 1991
Dealing with Dragons, 1990
Sorcery and Cecelia, 1988 (Caroline Stevermer, co-author)
Daughter of Witches, 1983

Other books you might like:
Joan Aiken, *Black Hearts in Battersea*, 1964
Randall Garrett, *Too Many Magicians*, 1967
Diana Wynne Jones, *The Lives of Christopher Chant*, 1988
Ellen Kushner, *Swordspoint*, 1987
Fletcher Pratt, *The Blue Star*, 1952
Melissa Scott, *Point of Hopes*, 1995
  Lisa A. Barnett, co-author
Caroline Stevermer, *A College of Magics*, 1994
Mary Frances Zambreno, *Journeyman Wizard*, 1994

820

PATRICIA C. WREDE

Shadows over Lyra
(New York: Tor, 1997)

Story type: Magic Conflict; Political
Series: Lyra
Major character(s): Alethia Tel'anh, Royalty (princess), Adventurer; Ranira ''Renra'', Servant (bondwoman), Adventurer; Emereck, Minstrel, Adventurer
Time period(s): Indeterminate
Locale(s): Lyra, Planet—Imaginary; Alkyra, Fictional Country

Summary: As unbound Shadow-born and a second Lithmern invasion threaten Alkyra's, Alethia, Ranira and Emereck forge new alliances, develop magical abilities and utilize a powerful magical object as they seek to protect the country.

Fantasy

Omnibus edition of *Shadow Magic* (1982), *Daughter of Witches* (1984) and *The Harp of Imach Thyssel* (1985) with 13 pages of early Lyran history and a four-page timeline.

Other books by the same author:
Book of Enchantments, 1997
The Raven Ring, 1994
Talking to Dragons, 1993 (revised edition)
Caught in Crystal, 1987
The Seven Towers, 1984

Other books you might like:
Steven Brust, *Jhereg*, 1983
Lois McMaster Bujold, *The Spirit Ring*, 1992
Laurell K. Hamilton, *Nightseer*, 1992
Diana Wynne Jones, *Cart and Cwidder*, 1977
Martha Wells, *The Element of Fire*, 1993

821

SARA J. WRENCH

The Duke of Sumava

(New York: Baen, 1997)

Story type: Historical; Magic Conflict
Major character(s): Ottokar, Nobleman (duke); Zo'e'minira ''Zoe'', Supernatural Being
Time period(s): 17th century (1620s)
Locale(s): Duchy of Simava, Fictional Country; Fasosi, Alternate Earth

Summary: Fleeing from the invading Austrian army, the duke calls on the Powers of the land for help. To his surprise, they respond. Ottokar learns that the magical inhabitants of Fasosi, as well as the Wild Hunt led by the Black Huntsman, can help him defend his beloved country, if their help will not come at too high a price. First novel.

Where it's reviewed:
Fantasy & Science Fiction, August 1997, page 21
Locus, June 1997, page 59

Other books you might like:
Lynn Abbey, *The Wooden Sword*, 1991
Gael Baudino, *Maze of Moonlight*, 1993
C.J. Cherryh, *Rusalka*, 1989
Lisa Goldstein, *The Red Magician*, 1982
Patricia A. McKillip, *The Riddle-Master of Hed*, 1976
Elizabeth Marie Pope, *The Perilous Gard*, 1974

822

JANNY WURTS

Fugitive Prince

(New York: HarperPrism, 1997)

Story type: Political; Magic Conflict
Series: Wars of Light and Shadow
Major character(s): Lysaer s'Ilessid, Royalty, Wizard; Arithon s'Ffalenn, Musician, Wizard; Elaira, Wizard, Doctor
Time period(s): Indeterminate (4th Age)
Locale(s): Araethura, Fictional Country; Avenor, Fictional City

Summary: The defeat of the Vastmark army disrupts the balance of power in the Five Kingdoms. Lysaer wants to maintain the throne, while the Koriani want to break the deadlock and Arithon wants peace. Unfortunately, the two brothers, cursed to hate one another, determine the fate of the whole world.

Other books by the same author:
Ship of Merior, 1995
Curse of the Mistwraith, 1994
Master of Whitestorm, 1992
Shadowfane, 1988
Stormwarden, 1984

Other books you might like:
Glen Cook, *The Black Company*, 1984
Guy Gavriel Kay, *The Lions of Al-Rassan*, 1995
Katherine Kurtz, *Deryni Rising*, 1970
George R.R. Martin, *A Game of Thrones*, 1996
Patricia A. McKillip, *The Riddle-Master of Hed*, 1976

823

KAREN TEI YAMASHITA

Tropic of Orange

(Minneapolis: Coffee House Press, 1997)

Story type: Literary
Major character(s): Rafaela Cortez, Housekeeper; Archangel, Writer (poet), Activist; El Gran Mojado, Sports Figure (masked wrestler)
Time period(s): 1990s
Locale(s): Mazatlan, Mexico; Los Angeles, California

Summary:

Where it's reviewed:
Booklist, September 1, 1997, page 62

Other books you might like:
Octavia E. Butler, *Parable of the Sower*, 1993
Martha Cerda, *Senora Rodriguez and Other Worlds*, 1997
Lisa Goldstein, *A Mask for the General*, 1987
Richard Kadrey, *Kamikaze L'Amour*, 1995
Ian McDonald, *Terminal Cafe*, 1994
Pat Murphy, *The City, Not Long After*, 1989

824

CHELSEA QUINN YARBRO

Monet's Ghost

(New York: Atheneum, 1997)

Story type: Young Adult; Alternate World
Major character(s): Geena Howe, Teenager; Claude Monet, Spirit, Artist
Time period(s): 1990s
Locale(s): United States; Mythical Place

Summary: Geena acquires the ability to project herself into paintings, allowing her to experience the realm within the artworks, then exit from the spot she entered. When changes made to one painting while Geena explores inside it threaten to trap her within, Geena must negotiate a maze and confront

the ghost of Claude Monet, if she hopes to return to her own world.

Where it's reviewed:
Booklist, June 1 & 15, 1997, page 1687
School Library Journal, June 1997, page 129
Voice of Youth Advocates, August 1997, page 197

Other books by the same author:
Locadio's Apprentice, 1984
Hyacinths, 1983
Ariosto, 1980
Cautionary Tales, 1978
Time of the Fourth Horseman, 1976

Other books you might like:
Suzy McKee Charnas, *The Kingdom of Kevin Malone*, 1993
Louise Cooper, *The Sleep of Stone*, 1991
Charles de Lint, *The Dreaming Place*, 1990
Esther M. Friesner, *Wishing Season*, 1993
Tanith Lee, *Black Unicorn*, 1991
Robert Silverberg, *Letters From Atlantis*, 1990
S.P. Somtow, *The Wizard's Apprentice*, 1993

825

JANE YOLEN

Merlin

(New York: Harcourt Brace & Company, 1997)

Story type: Legend; Young Adult
Series: Young Merlin Trilogy
Major character(s): Merlin, Child, Orphan; Hawk-Hobby, Teenager
Time period(s): Indeterminate Past
Locale(s): England

Summary: While accompanying a group of misfits and outcasts, Merlin begins to discover his magical abilities. At the same time, his dreams of the future distress his acquaintances. Concludes the trilogy.

Where it's reviewed:
Locus, June 1997, page 59

School Library Journal, May 1997, page 140

Other books by the same author:
Passager, 1996
Hobby, 1995
Merlin and the Dragons, 1995
A Dragon's Boy, 1990
Merlin's Booke, 1986

Other books you might like:
T.A. Barron, *The Merlin Effect*, 1994
Ann Curry, *The Book of Brendan*, 1990
Anne McCaffrey, *Black Horses for the King*, 1996
Mark Twain, *A Connecticut Yankee in King Arthur's Court*, 1889
T.H. White, *The Sword in the Stone*, 1939

826

JANE YOLEN

Twelve Impossible Things Before Breakfast

(New York: Harcourt Brace, 1997)

Story type: Collection; Young Adult

Summary: Contains a five-page introduction, 11-page afterword, three original and nine stories reprinted from anthologies 1989-1996. Frequently light or ironic in tone, the stories feature twists on familiar themes and fairy tales such as mythical creatures, extraterrestrials, ants that steal babies, a bridge in need of a goat-eating troll, an Alice hardened by her stay in Wonderland and a rebellion of Peter Pan's followers.

Other books by the same author:
Merlin and the Dragons, 1995
Here There Be Unicorns, 1994
Here There Be Dragons, 1993
Merlin's Booke, 1986
Tales of Wonder, 1983

Fantasy

The Year in Horror Fiction
by
Stefan Dziemianowicz

Is the popularity of horror fiction a literary or a commercial phenomenon? This question has never been answered satisfactorily, and may have no definitive answer, but it has shaped discussion of the horror field ever since Stephen King achieved bestsellerdom a quarter century ago and pulled horror fiction into the spotlight along with him. Last year the question seemed even more pertinent.

The gross number of horror titles published in 1997 was down slightly from the previous year, although not enough to sound alarms, and the usual array of celebrity writers turned out the expected number of bestsellers to keep horror in the public eye. Evaluated by these broad parameters, horror was probably no less healthy in 1997 than any other popular fiction genre. But other indicators told a different story. In March 1997, Zebra discontinued its horror imprint, the oldest in mass-market publishing. Although this translated into perhaps a dozen fewer horror titles being published for the year, it called attention to the continuing abdication of major houses from horror publishing.

In 1997, more horror titles were published by semi-professional and specialty presses than ever before. Eliminate these titles, books published as tie-ins to extraliterary media (such as movies, television, and role-playing games) and the increasing number of classic and bestseller reprints, and the amount of original horror fiction that reached a mass audience in 1997 is about half of what the gross numbers suggest—levels similar to those in the mid-1980s, before horror's boom years. This suggests that the inflated volume of horror fiction published over the past decade failed to find or cultivate a sizable audience—and that horror as a literary form remains the special interest of a devoted but comparatively small audience of genre junkies.

Horror's growth spurt in the 1980s was predicated on the success of its best-known authors. Publishers assumed tthat multi-million copy sales of books by Stephen King and Anne Rice indicated a hunger for horror that might be sated with a glut of titles written in their "tradition." In 1997, it was more noticeable than ever how serious a misperception of readers' tastes this was. Novels by King, Rice, and their best-selling colleagues enjoyed their usual success, even as genre clones gathered dust in the bookstalls, suggesting that readers are attracted to the voice and vision of a name-brand writer, and not necessarily the genre in which he or she works.

Indeed, although King's *Wizards and Glass* and Rice's *Violin* feature elements of horror, they are not horror novels in the generic sense. King's novel, the fourth in his long-running Dark Tower series, is an epic fantasy more redolent of L. Frank Baum's *Wizard of Oz* novels with bits of Chaucer's *Canterbury Tales* thrown in, than the middle-class American horror tale that is his trademark. An engrossing tale-within-a-tale concerned with an episode in the youth of its hero, Roland, a gunslinger embarked on an arduous quest in an apparently postapocalyptic future, it improves upon the last two books in the series and supplies background information that will no doubt prove crucial for the three further volumes King projects for the saga.

Rice's *Violin* is a ghost story, but as in all her fiction the supernatural is merely a peg on which to hang her explorations of different personality types and social groups. Featuring a grieving heroine who is pursued through history and across continents by a ghost that preys on the heartbroken, Rice's novel is a parable about the need to come to terms with personal loss, and has closer affinities to romance fiction than to the horror tale.

Other best-selling writers showed a similar disregard for genre boundaries by mixing and matching elements from a variety of fiction types to achieve their patented formulas. Dean R. Koontz, in *Sole Survivor,* takes an idea with guaranteed fear appeal to a mass audience—an airplane crash—embeds it in an espionage scenario about a government cover-up, and throws interesting twists and turns into the plot through his usual interweaving of horror, suspense,

281

romance, and science fiction tropes. *Ticktock,* Koontz's second original for the year, represents a slight change of pace: an attempt to leaven a supernatural horror thriller with screwball comedy. It climbed to the top of the paperback bestseller list, even though the nonstop joking banter between its hero and heroine isn't funny.

Koontz's main rival in genre-splicing is John Saul. Saul celebrated his twentieth year as a horror writer with *The Presence,* the tale of a scientific inquiry into extraterrestrial influences on human evolution that features all the trademarks that have broken his work out to an audience greater than the horror-reading community: an imperiled child, a hero and heroine who represent the triumph of emotion over intellect, and a conspiracy between science and big business that represents technology at its cruelest, inhuman worst. Saul's second novel for the year, *The Blackstone Chronicles,* is a more traditional Gothic horror story in an unconventional six-volume paperback serial format. It was conceived to match the success of Stephen King's paperback "serial thriller" *The Green Mile* in 1996, but though its early installments ascended the bestseller list, it didn't fare as well as its predecessor, suggesting that even among horror's bestsellers some feats can't be duplicated.

Perhaps the most telling book by a best-selling horror writer in 1997 was Ira Levin's *Rosemary's Son.* Thirty years before, Levin's novel *Rosemary's Baby* carved a niche for horror fiction on the bestseller list and set a standard for literary realism by which most horror fiction written its wake has been measured. Sadly, none of the literary qualities that distinguished Levin's subtle and disturbing tale of the antiChrist's emergence in contemporary Manhattan can be found in its sequel. *Rosemary's Son* attempts to put a timely millennial spin on issues raised by its predecessor, but its numerous absurdities of plot and character suggest that what was once a revolutionary theme for horror fiction may now be fit only for satire.

While horror's best-selling authors churned out the crowd pleasers for a vast, non-specialized audience, the mid-list writers produced the books that represent the soul of the genre—or so the conventional wisdom goes. Mid-list has never been an easy category to define, but it generally includes the writers whose work is considered of high enough quality to merit hardcover publication and first printings in the high-four to low-five-figure range (as opposed to six- or seven-figure printings of authors of the King/Koontz caliber). Mid-list writers tend to have modest but respectable sales and earn the critical praise that confers distinction on the publisher. In 1997, it was easiest to define horror's mid-list writers as those whose work is most imperiled by the changes transforming the market with an eye on the bottom line. Any publisher will support a best-selling writer, and most will publish downmarket books that require minimum financing, but mid-list writers pose a risk in a market increasingly devoted to immediate returns on investment.

The mid-list writers least endangered by the shrinking horror market are the so-called literary writers who write mainstream fiction with genre appeal (and vice versa). In 1997, this group was led by Patrick McGrath, whose *Asylum* was one of the best novels of the year. A literate and disturbing tale of obsession set in an English sanitarium, it cements McGrath's reputation as the leading exponent of what he has called "the New Gothic" (essentially literary tales of the macabre), and as one of the few contemporary writers working consciously in the tradition of Poe.

Three other writers embraced by the literary mainstream, Dennis McFarland, Robert Girardi and Todd Komarnicki, wrote ghost stories, and thus continued a tradition more than a century old that includes works by Edith Wharton, Henry James, and numerous other literary luminaries. McFarland's *A Face at the Window* concerns a man who encounters a ghost from the past at a London hotel, and Girardi's *Vaporetto 13* a man who romances a woman who embodies the spirit of ancient Venice. Both are examples of the yuppie horror tale, a subgenre whose stories feature young characters on the fast-track brought to a realization of their empty, valueless lives through supernatural experience. Komarnicki's *Famine* is by contrast a metaphysical mystery in which ghosts serve as metaphors for the loveless and socially outcast.

James Hynes offers ghost stories of a different sort in *Publish and Perish,* a collection of humorous novellas with supernatural themes that represents one of the best single-author collections of the year. All three of Hynes's tales are set in academic environments and push the antics of professors and post-graduates caught up in paper chases on the tenure track into amusing fantasies modeled on the works of M. R. James and other horror masters.

The mid-list is also the home of writers whose names are synonymous with the horror field, and who have one or more books on most critics' lists of essential reading. Of note in 1997 was Ramsey Campbell, who has been publishing horror fiction since 1962 and whose work is notable for its consistently high quality. Campbell's *Nazareth Hill* is not only one of the best novels of 1997 but one of the best efforts of his career: an emotionally wrenching haunted house story about a father and daughter who, under the influence of their new home and its sinister affiliation from centuries before, re-enact its legacy of persecution and intolerance in their relations with each another. The book is a masterpiece of ambiguous supernaturalism in which it is nearly impossible to distinguish perceptions of psychologically troubled characters from genuine supernatural manifestations.

James Blaylock, who has begun alternating horror fiction with his better known works of contemporary urban fantasy, was represented by *Winter Tides,* a chilling tale of supernatural possession set in the same West Coast milieu as much of his lighter fantasy. Graham Masterton was present with *Rook* and *Tooth and Claw,* awkward blends of young adult and adult horror fiction that feature a psychically

endowed schoolteacher. James Herbert and Thomas Monteleone both wrote novels about the horrors of World War II, but whereas Herbert's *'48* puts a science fictional spin on history, relating the aftermath of a war in which Hitler is victorious following his deployment of a devastating biological weapon, Monteleone's *The Night of Broken Souls* presents the enduring impact of the war in its account of reincarnated Nazis and concentration camp survivors continuing their struggles in the present day.

Dennis Etchison's *Double Edge,* the tale of a serial killer on the loose in Hollywood, is not up to the standards of his short dark fantasy fiction, but paints a provocative portrait of Hollywood as a mirror of America's spiritual malaise. Bentley Little's *Ignored* is his best novel in years, a black comedy of the modern workplace about people so taken for granted around the office that they are rendered physically invisible. Charles L. Grant looks ahead to the coming millennium with *Symphony,* the first of a projected quartet of novels designed to flesh out the apocalyptic horrors suggested by the biblical Four Horsemen of the Apocalypse. By contrast, Brent Monahan looks to the past with *The Bell-Witch,* an account of psychic possession in the American heartland presented persuasively as a previously unpublished manuscript from the nineteenth century steeped in the history and superstitions of the period.

A number of new or relatively new horror writers made mid-list appearances in 1997, which is always an optimistic sign. In her second novel, *My Soul to Keep,* Tannarive Due once again uses the supernatural as a vehicle for exploring the black experience in America. Her main character is a centuries-old member of a secret cult whose members partake in their society, yet live forever on its periphery, to keep their gift of immortality a secret. Muriel Gray's second novel, *Furnace,* is one of the more unusual cases of literary homage in recent memory, a relatively successful of reprise of M. R. James's classic tale of a supernatural curse, "Casting the Runes" (which also influenced one of the novellas in James Hynes's *Publish and Perish*) that, incongruously enough, replaces James's turn-of-the-century British academics with truck drivers in rural Virginia. Greg Kihn weighed in with his second novel, *Shade of Pale,* a muddled attempt to work a modern variation on the banshee theme that lacks the appeal and outrageous fun of his previous novel, *Horror Show* (1996).

Both Susan Moloney, in *A Dry Spell,* and James David, in *Fragments,* write about dark small-town secrets that refuse to stay buried. Moloney's tale combines romance with supernatural horror and builds to a gradual revelation about the cause of a southwestern community's long-standing drought, while David's blends parapsychology and science fiction to tell of psychic researchers who accidentally reanimate and incarnate the spirit of a forgotten casualty from a shameful event that occurred decades before. Thomas Baum's *Out of Body* is a solid supernatural mystery in which a man prone to out-of-body experiences must

consciously discorporate his soul to seek out the man who has pinned him for the murder that has put him on death row.

Faced with dwindling opportunities in the trade and mass markets, many mid-list writers hitched their wagons to small presses in 1997, reversing the trend of the past two decades that saw writers honing their craft in small press markets before graduating to professional houses. The small press has long been an important part of horror publishing, not only nurturing emerging talents but serving as an archive for fiction with experimental and often radical themes and approaches that appeal only to specialized groups of readers. In the past, the small press existed almost exclusively in the form of amateur magazines. With the desktop publishing revolution of the past decade, the horror small press has diversified tremendously, to the point where it now encompasses a gamut of publishers ranging from semi-professional presses devoted to the production of softcover chapbooks to specialty hardcover publishers whose books differ from those of mainstream houses only by their smaller print runs (varying from 250 to 2500 copies) and general lack of distribution outside of specialized genre catalogs. What's more, the horror small press now publishes every type of book published by mainstream houses: short fiction collections, anthologies, classic reprints, and even novels.

In 1997, possibly for the first time ever, the small press published the bulk of short horror fiction, both original and reprint—not too surprising, considering that it was the mainstream publishing houses who, in the 1980s, transformed horror from a fiction driven by the short story to one driven by novel-length works. Leading the pack was Fedogan & Bremer, the most professional and consistent in quality of the specialty press houses, which was responsible for four excellent retrospective single-author collections. *Don't Dream* gathers together the complete weird fiction of Donald Wandrei, one of H.P. Lovecraft's more talented proteges. In addition to stories culled from Wandrei's earlier out-of-print story collections, the book contains an abundance of previously unpublished essays, vignettes and juvenilia that shed light on Wandrei's development as a writer. Hugh B. Cave's *The Door Below* stitches together stories from seven decades in the career of one of the few pulp era writers still writing significant horror and fantasy fiction. *Exorcisms and Ecstasies* assembles the final uncollected stories of Karl Edward Wagner, an influential author and editor who earned his reputation during horror's heyday in the 1970s and '80s and died young in 1995. While the fiction does not show Wagner at the top of his form, editor Stephen Jones uncovered a trove of unpublished works and drafts and contributed a detailed bibliography of Wagner's publishing history that makes this book a must for any serious horror library. Jones also helped put together *The Vampire Stories of R. Chetwynd-Hayes,* which was brought out in time for the World Fantasy Convention (at which Chetwynd-Hayes was a special guest) to commemorate the

work of the prolific but under-appreciated British writer, one of the few still working in the classic supernatural tradition.

Borderlands Press was responsible for Whitley Strieber's first short fiction collection, *Evenings with Demons*, a miscellany of unpublished fragments and brilliantly polished stories that appeared in a variety of genre magazines and anthologies. It shows the controversial Strieber to be one of the more provocative and iconoclastic writers of modern horror fiction. Unfortunately, the book was brought out in a signed limited edition of only 350 copies, and quickly became the most elusive title of the year. Limited print runs and high prices designed to cover production costs have long been a problem of specialty presses, many of whom cater primarily to collectors with deep pockets, but several have found a way to circumvent this. Marc Ziesing issued Harlan Ellison's *Slippage* in a signed limited edition, but a slightly shortened version of the book was published later by trade house Houghton Mifflin. It would have been criminal for this book to be available only to collectors, as it is Ellison's most solid outing in over a decade, filled with the type of confrontational, genre-bending fiction that distinguished his writing in the 1960s and '70s. Silver Salamander Press offered simultaneous collector's limited hardcover and trade paperback editions of Lucy Taylor's *Painted in Blood* and Roberta Lannes's *The Mirror of Night*. Both authors, who are renowned for the mature themes and frank sexual content of their fiction, benefited from the small press's traditional willingness to publish fiction deemed too controversial and unnerving for mainstream venues. Likewise Edward Lee's southern Gothic tale of sexual degeneracy, *The Bighead*, put out in both hardcover and trade paperback editions by Necro Publications, is an exercise in shaggy dog crudity that would never have seen publication but for the specialty press.

CD Publications, the book-publishing arm of the leading genre magazine *Cemetery Dance*, brought out *Things Left Behind* by Gary Braunbeck, an ambitious first collection of stories by a writer whose humanitarian themes and enthusiasms call to mind the writing of Harlan Ellison. CD was also responsible for *A Fistful of Stories*, another retrospective collection of stories and columns by Joe R. Lansdale. Lansdale is a virtually uncategorizable writer—part humorist in the western tall-tale tradition, part horror writer, with one foot planted firmly in the hardboiled crime genre and the other in the supernatural horror tradition—which could explain why every one of his collections to date has originated at a specialty press, rather than the more tradition-bound mainstream houses. Indeed, Lansdale had another hardcover collection of stories, *The Good, The Bad and the Indifferent*, appear from Subterranean Press. It contains mostly early stories from the author's career, and its title is unabashedly intended by the author as a commentary on the quality of the contents.

The most interesting specialty press hardcover collection of the year was Brian McNaughton's *The Throne of Bones*, the first hardcover from start-up book publisher Terminal Fright. McNaughton has been a presence in the horror field for over 30 years, but only recently has he emerged as a writer of baroque, often irreverently comic stories that blend horror with imaginary world fantasy. The contents, devoted largely to stories that detail the lives and habits of ghouls, defy description and comparison, and are exactly the sort of material with which the small press has a reputation for taking risks. By the year's end, the book had achieved a reprint sale to no less tradition-bound an institution than the Science Fiction Book Club.

The proliferation of periodicals and original anthologies devoted to horror in the 1980s and '90s yielded a vast amount of short fiction that has begun finding its way into small press paperbacks. In 1997, Dark Regions Press published excellent collections of short fiction by Bentley Little and Jeffrey Osier, drawn almost exclusively from previous small press appearances. The stories in Little's *Murmerous Haunts* capture in miniature the wacky absurdist dimension of Little's horror fiction, which too often is stretched into preposterous overstatement in his novels. Osier's *Horizon Lines* offers stories filled with sharply etched characters and domestic dramas that evolve into surreal dark fantasies.

Albert Manachino's *Noctet: Tales of Madonna-Moloch*, published by Argo Press, and Wil Pugmire's *Tales of Sesqua Valley*, published by Necropolitan Press, draw together disparately published parts of story cycles into coherent wholes. Manachino's is set on a distant planet populated by supernatural beings and Pugmire's in a fictional Pacific northwestern milieu inspired by the legend-haunted New England of H.P. Lovecraft. Tsathoggua Press, devoted primarily to the legacy of Lovecraft's colleague Frank Belknap Long, brought out two chapbooks that collected the early fiction of Peter Cannon, Long's friend and biographer. *Tales of Lovecraftian Horror and Humor* and *The Thing in the Bathtub and Other Lovecraftian Tales* assemble wonderfully glib sketches in which Cannon playfully satirizes the subculture of Lovecraft fans.

Necronomicon Press serves a readership similar to that of Tsathoggua Press and in 1997 it brought out *Ghor, Kin-Slayer: The Saga of Genseric's Fifth-Born Son*, a round-robin sword-and-sorcery novel begun in the 1970s from an incomplete fragment found in the papers of Lovecraft's correspondent, Robert E. Howard. Publisher Marc Michaud resurrected the unfinished story and tracked down commissioned chapters that never saw publication to produce the finished book, an entertaining amalgam combining the talents of pulp-era writers H. Warner Munn, A.E. van Vogt and Frank Belknap Long with those of Karl Edward Wagner, Ramsey Campbell, Brian Lumley and other best-and-brightest members of horror's newest generation.

Cyber-Pschos AOD, a publisher of progressive poetry and transgressive fiction, brought out Don Webb's *Stealing My Rules* and Michael Hemmingston's *Snuff Flique*, both compilations of quirky, offbeat stories that fall into the

horror genre largely through their inability to be categorized anywhere else. Likewise Canadian publisher Black Dog Press' sole title of 1997, Cliff Burns' *The Reality Machine,* which brings together the sketches and short speculative fiction of a Canadian writer who has developed an impressively original voice influenced by writers as diverse as J.G. Ballard, William Burroughs, and Jorge Luis Borges.

The expansion of the horror small press into book publishing in the last few years has sucked money from periodical publishing, resulting in the disrupted schedules and deaths of a number of leading fiction magazines. In 1997, several publishers attempted to fill this void with books of original fiction. Of special note is the series of short fiction chapbooks published by Subterranean Press. James Blaylock's *Doughnuts,* Ray Garton's *Website,* Richard Chizmar's *Blood Brothers* and Thomas Monteleone's *Between Floors* all appeared as affordable, well-designed pamphlets. Their contents span a wide variety of genres and subgenres, including science fiction, psychological horror and dark suspense, and their publication as stand-alone booklets helps redress a problem horror writers have faced in a market recently dominated by theme-driven anthologies: where to publish good stories that simply do not fit the requirements of highly specialized markets. StarsEnd Creations, which brought out P.D. Cacek's thirteen-story collection *Leavings,* and Marietta Publishing, which produced *Red Walls, Black Glass* by Jeffrey Thomas, *Dystopia* by William A. Walker, and Tom Piccirilli's *The Dog Syndrome and Other Sick Puppies,* expanded this trend further, providing readers with samplers of a variety of their author's writings. The same rationale is evident behind Necro Publications' *Inside the Works,* an anthology that brings together novellas by Gerard Daniel Houarner and Edward Lee and a selection of previously unpublished stories by Piccirilli; Terminal Fright's anthology *Terminal Fright,* essentially a fat hardcover edition of the small press magazine that editor Ken Abner has helmed for the last few years; and Beecher Smith's *Monsters from Memphis,* a themed anthology of stories with southern settings from new Zapizdat Press that combines works by numerous new writers and contributions from Douglas Clegg, Brent Monahan, and other distinguished members of the new horror generation.

A noticeable phenomenon in horror publishing in 1997 was the increase in the volume of classic horror reprints. Although this was bad news for readers with preferences for modern horror, as slots that might have been given over to new material were instead appropriated instead for genre standards, it was generally good news for the horror field, which has seen the classics squeezed out of circulation over the last two decades by a glut of contemporary fiction, much of it written in apparent ignorance of prior accomplishments in horror.

Once again, small presses led the market, in particular Canadian publisher Ash-Tree Press, whose achievements in specialty press publishing were honored in 1997 with the World Fantasy Award for best non-professional publisher. Ash-Tree is devoted to the preservation of the classic supernatural story and the literary horror tradition established by M.R. James and other practitioners of the ghost tale's golden age. Last year, they reissued obscure early twentieth-century collections including M.P. Dare's *Holy Relics,* Amyas Northcote's *In Ghostly Company,* and H. Russell Wakefield's *Imagine a Man in a Box,* and engaged the services of a variety of distinguished editors including Richard Dalby, Jack Adrian, and Jessica Amanda Salmonson for new omnibus collections of Victorian and Edwardian supernatural fiction, such as A.M. Burrage's *Someone in the Room: Strange Tales Old and New,* Richard Marsh's *The Haunted Chair and Other Stories,* Julian Hawthorne's *The Rose of Death and Other Mysterious Delusions,* and the first in a series of anthologies of hard-to-find ghost fiction, *The Ash-Tree Annual Macabre 1997.* Ash-Tree also did readers an inestimable service by reprinting *Under the Crust,* a rare self-published 1993 collection of modern supernatural tales in the classic vein that launched the carrer of World Fantasy Award-winning author Terry Lamsley. This was one of several instances of modern ''classic'' reprints in 1997, which also included the CD Publications reissue of Ray Garton's 1987 vampire novel *Live Girls* and Richard Laymon's 1980 dark-suspense novel *The Cellar,* as well as Gauntlet Press's reissues of contemporary groundbreakers such as William Peter Blatty's *The Exorcist* and Ray Bradbury's *The October Country.* In some cases these editions, most issued as signed limited collectibles, feature the author's preferred text or constitute the first domestic hardcover publication.

Jessica Amanda Salmonson, who has devoted much of her career as a small press editor to resurrecting writers of impressive but largely forgotten weird fiction (including Hildegarde Hawthorne, Fitz-James O'Brien, and Vincent O'Sullivan), edited for publisher Richard H. Fawcett *The Shell of Sense,* a quartet of very modern ghost stories written nearly a century ago by Olivia Howard Dunbar. Hobgoblin Press issued chapbook editions of a variety of British Victorian and *fin de siecle* publications, including Robert W. Chambers' enormously influential collection of decadent horror and fantasy, *The King in Yellow,* Arthur Machen's exquisite semi-autobiographical weird tale *The Hill of Dreams,* and R.H. Benson's collection of weird religious allegories, *The Light Invisible.* Hobgoblin's roster of authors was rivaled by Dover Books, whose long dormant trade paperback reissues of classic horror was jump-started with a reprint of Walter de la Mare's novel of psychic possession, *The Return,* Bram Stoker's *Best Ghost Horror Stories,* and Algernon Blackwood's *The Complete John Silence Stories,* the first time all six of Blackwood's distinguished psychic detective stories have appeared between the same covers.

Other trade houses followed Dover's lead and helped make this one of the flushest periods in recent memory for classic horror. Oxford University Press brought out three

excellent anthologies: Michael Cox's *Twelve Victorian Ghost Stories* and *Twelve Tales of the Supernatural,* each of which mix genre standards with excellent, little known works, and Robert Morrison and Chris Baldick's *The Vampyre and Other Tales of the Macabre,* a collection of strange tales from the late Gothic period, many of which have languished unread since their initial publication in British popular fiction magazines of the early twentieth century. Catherine A. Lundie's *Restless Spirits,* from the University of Massachusetts Press, assembles a large collection of supernatural tales by neglected female writers of the late-nineteenth- and early-twentieth-centuries and assesses the supernatural tale's use as a vehicle for feminist concerns of the day.

Elizabeth Terry and Terri Hardin edited *American Gothic* and David Hartwell *Bodies of the Dead,* both of which draw from the same period as Lundie's anthology but overlap minimally in content. Meanwhile, Italo Calvino's exemplary *Fantastic Tales,* a fusion of two books of eighteenth- and nineteenth-century horror and fantasy classics from England and the continent, received its first translation from Italian.

With such an embarrassment of riches to choose from in the reprint category, two repackagings of the fiction of H.P. Lovecraft may have seemed gratuitous. Nevertheless, S.T. Joshi's *The Annotated Lovecraft* is important for showing the intellectual roots of four of Lovecraft's best known tales, and Joyce Carol Oates's compilation *Tales of H.P. Lovecraft* puts her imprimatur and that of literary publisher Ecco Press on Lovecraft's best tales of supernatural horror. The fact is, Lovecraft's shadow still looms large in modern horror and he is one of the few classic writers who was not displaced by the contemporary horror juggernaut. Barnes & Noble released August Derleth's *The Cthulhu Mythos,* a compilation of stories inspired by Lovecraft's ideas, many of which appeared alongside Lovecraft's in the pulp magazines of 1930s and 40s. Chaosium Books, publishers of the Lovecraft-inspired Call of Cthulhu fantasy role-playing game, helped call attention to the pervasiveness of Lovecraft's influence through Robert Price's series of anthologies featuring stories by other writers set in Lovecraft's worlds of cosmic horror. *The Nyarlathotep Cycle* is filled with stories featuring one of Lovecraft's malevolent deities, and *The Necronomicon Cycle* with stories and fragments built around Lovecraft's renowned book of forbidden knowledge. Price also compiled *The Xothic Cycle,* which brings together all of the Lovecraft pastiches written by Lin Carter, a major proponent of Lovecraft, and had a hand in the assemblage of Richard Tierney's *The Scroll of Thoth,* the collected adventures of a warrior hero who bears a likeness to Robert E. Howard's Conan, but whose exploits frequently plunge him into Lovecraftian conflicts. Necronomicon Press commemorated Brian Lumley's appearance as Guest of Honor at NecronomiCon 3, a Lovecraft-related convention, with the chapbook *In His Own Write,* a collection of three of Lumley's Lovecraftian tales. David Scott Aniolowski's *Singers of Strange Songs: a Celebration of Brian Lumley,* reached even further to explore Lovecraft's influence, offering pastiches of Brian Lumley's pastiches of Lovecraft. For fledgling Triad Books, Aniolowski also edited *Return to Lovecraft Country,* an anthology featuring new and classic contributions to the shared myth cycle based on Lovecraft's work known as the Cthulhu Mythos.

Chaosium is one of several publishers that sought to recruit horror readers to extraliterary media in 1997. Working on the assumption that there is little difference between the imagined situations of supernatural horror fiction and those of the milieus of their gaming scenarios, White Wolf Books continued publishing novels and anthologies set in their World of Darkness, an alternate reality in which vampires, wraiths, mages, changelings, and wizards coexist with humans. The omnibus *The Essential World of Darkness,* edited by Stewart Wieck and Anna Branscombe, assembles five novels, four previously unpublished, each featuring one of the aforementioned creatures and representing a different story cycle set in the invented world. Readers interested in pursuing the World of Darkness mythology further could also choose from Charles L. Grant's werewolf novel *Watcher,* and *The Ascension Warrior* and *The Road to Hell,* invigorating blends of fantasy and Golden Age science fiction that represent the first two novels in Robert Weinberg's Horizon War trilogy. In a new twist, White Wolf's popular World of Darkness: Vampire series, most of whose previous contributions were set in the present, reached into the historical past through David Niall Wilson's *To Sift Through Bitter Ashes* and *To Speak in Lifeless Tongues,* the first two novels in his medieval Grails Covenant Trilogy, and through short fiction contributions to Justin Achilli and Robert Hatch's anthology *Dark Tyrants.* The World of Darkness books have a detailed historical backdrop that is often hard to puzzle out for readers courageous enough to enter these books in mid-trilogy. But they are full of old-fashioned adventures reminiscent of pulp serials, and their quality has improved since White Wolf began commissioning established horror and fantasy writers to produce them.

Christopher Golden's *Hellboy: The Lost Army,* a sort of cross between *Raiders of the Lost Ark* and the Swamp Thing comic series, was the only supernatural adventure novel in 1997 spawned by a popular graphic-novel series. Likewise, Jane Jensen's *Gabriel Knight: Sins of the Father,* a supernatural detective tale featuring a horror writer as its hero, was the first in what may become a new trend of novelizations of popular CD-ROM games. By far, the majority of horror books based on extraliterary media were tied to movies and television, where horror, by itself and cross-blended with science fiction, is enjoying an enormous popularity that seems to contradict flagging sales of horror books. Richard Chizmar and Martin H. Greenberg's anthology *Screamplays* assembled screenplay and teleplay adaptations of some of horror's best-known writers, including Stephen King and

Harlan Ellison. The success of the film adaptation of Andrew Neiderman's 1990 novel, *Devil's Advocate,* led to its reissue and near-eclipse of the author's new occult psychological thriller, *The Dark.* The ongoing popularity of the *X-Files* television series drew another novel, *Antibodies,* from series novelizer Kevin Anderson. Just as the *X-Files* phenomenon resulted in the creation of a similar television series, *Millennium, Millennium* in turn inspired a series of paperback novels built around its premise of a secret government team that investigates strange phenomena with millennial overtones. Elizabeth Hand's *The Frenchman* and Lewis Gannett's *Gehenna* bring considerable writing talents to bear on the show's themes, but the novels fail to convey the show's mood of paranoia or work well as independent horror stories

Vampires, not surprisingly, were all the rage in media tie-ins as they have been for some time in horror fiction in general. *Camp Vamp,* the second novel written by campy television show personality Elvira (with John Paragon), doesn't feature vampires per se but offers many bad jokes at their expense. Susan M. Garrett and Susan Sizemore each produced novelizations—*Intimations of Mortality* and a *Stirring of Dust,* respectively—based on the television show *Forever Knight,* about a vampire detective whose job it is to keep the peace between humans and the secret vampire populace living in Toronto. Following in the footsteps of many actors from the Star Trek, series who have lent their imprimatur to science fiction novels, *Forever Knight* star Nigel Bennett teamed up with well-known vampire fiction writer P.N. Elrod to produce *Keeper of the King,* a novel with essentially the same theme as the television show.

Buffy the Vampire Slayer, a surprise hit television show among young viewers spun off from the 1992 movie of the same name, itself spun off a series of new novels by Richie Tankersley Cusick (*Buffy the Vampire Slayer: The Harvest*), Christopher Golden, Nancy Holder and other well-known writers, each featuring a new adventure of a valley girl with an innate talent for ferreting out supernatural doings around her small California town. Lois Duncan's horror-suspense novel *I Know What You Did Last Summer,* a hit for more than two decades with young adult horror devotees, was adapted successfully for the screen, resulting in a paperback reissue that momentarily shifted attention away from R.L. Stine, still the king of young adult and preteen horror fiction. Despite an announced decline, sales of Stine's monthly novels in the Goosebumps and Fear Street series outstripped those of competitors and eclipsed imaginative non-series young adult novels such as S.P. Somtow's *The Vampire's Beautiful Daughter* and M.T. Anderson's *Thirsty,* both coming-of-age stories that feature vampire heroes and heroines overcoming the problems of adolescence, and Peter Dickinson's exceptional collection of young adult dark fantasy novellas, *The Lion Tamer's Daughter.* Stine even began a new subseries within his Fear Street cycle, the two-part *Fear Hall: The Beginning.* Little distinguishes these novels from titles in Stine's other series and sub-series, which leads to the concern that young readers of Stine and his ilk are getting trained for the very sort of rehashing and repackaging of formulaic genre materials that have contributed to adult horror's current troubles.

Speaking of rehashed horror materials, for the first time in years original fiction built around the increasingly unoriginal theme of the vampire showed a significant decline—despite the fact that many publishers had already planned special vampire projects to capitalize on the Dracula centenary. Eliminate vampire fiction tied in to movies, television, and gaming novels, and the yield was small enough to suggest that the vampire story's dominance of the horror market in recent years was, like the horror glut itself, an example of an overhyped commodity that failed to find a mass audience. Even the key vampire novels of the year seemed as though they were trying to be something else. Chelsea Quinn Yarbro resurrected her immortal Count St. Germain for his fourteenth adventure, *Writ in Blood.* The novel is a meticulously researched historical pageant set in Eastern Europe on the eve of World War I, but St. Germain's vampiric abilities barely contribute to the plot. And Jonathan Nasaw's *Shadows*, like its predecessor *The World on Blood* (1996), features vampires trying *not* to indulge in vampirism.

More traditional vampire stories included *The Ruby Tear* by Rebecca Brand (a pseudonym for Suzy McKee Charnas), about a vampire blood feud that has persisted for centuries into modern times; Tom Holland's *Slave of My Thirst,* a Victorian period tale that is a sequel to his earlier novel *Lord of the Dead* (1996), in which Lord Byron is a vampire hero; and Della Van Hise's *Ragged Angels,* about vampires who prey on attendees of a science fiction convention. Less traditional vampire stories spliced vampires into other types of genre fiction. Tanya Huff's *Blood Debt* and Laurell K. Hamilton's *The Killing Dance* extend long-running series to five and six books, respectively, that blend the vampire and detective story. *Daughter of Darkness*, Steven Spruill's sequel to *Rulers of Darkness* (1995), works out a science fictional rationale for vampire blood thirst.

Amarantha Knight (a pseudonym for Nancy Kilpatrick) rewrote J. Sheridan Le Fanu's classic novella *Carmilla* as a pornographic tale of sadomasochism and lesbianism. Somewhat milder attempts to deal with the sexual aspects of vampirism can be found in the stories commissioned for Poppy Z. Brite and Martin H. Greenberg's *Love in Vein II* and Cecilia Tan's *Cherished Blood,* both anthologies of erotic vampire fiction, and in Michael Rowe and Thomas Roche's *Brothers of the Night,* which features stories that use the vampire as a metaphor for aspects of gay male sexuality. The only other anthology to feature predominantly original vampire fiction, Stephen Jones' *The Mammoth Book of Dracula,* displays a high quotient of fine work by some of horror's best writers, all of whom turned out original stories with Count Dracula as a character.

Original vampire anthologies were somewhat dwarfed by the profusion of reprint anthologies. The best of these was Leonard Wolf's Oxford anthology *Blood Thirst: 100 Years of Vampire Fiction,* although any relatively basic horror library would already house most of its contents. There was considerable overlap between Wolf's anthology and its competitors: Stefan Dziemianowicz, Robert Weinberg and Martin H. Greenberg's *Girls Night Out: 29 Female Vampire Stories,* Martin H. Greenberg's *Vampires: The Greatest Stories,* Peter Haining's *The Vampire Hunter's Casebook,* John Richard Stephens's *Vampires, Wine and Roses,* and Lawrence Schimel and Martin H. Greenberg's two compilations of regional vampire tales, *Blood Lines: Vampire Stories from New England* and *Southern Blood: Vampire Stories from the American South.* In fact, there was enough overlap to suggest that the amount of genuinely reprintable vampire fiction is small and already greatly overanthologized.

While vampire fiction was down, the werewolf tale maintained market presence through Chris N. Africa's *When Wolves Cry,* Christine Tanasiuk's *Howl,* and Brian A. Hopkins' *Cold at Heart,* all of which use rugged natural environments conducive to the struggle for survival as backdrops for their tales of hostile encounters between humans and werewolves. By contrast, John Holt, in *Wolf Moon,* presents lycanthropy as a curse that follows members of a small town family to the big city. Henry Garfield's *Room 13* has a werewolf playing ghostbuster in a spirit-infested small town school, and Denise Vitola's science fiction novel *Opalite Moon* features a heroine whose lycanthropy is just one aspect of an inherently unstable future world. One of the better young adult horror novels of the year, Anita Curtis Klause's *Blood and Chocolate,* uses the werewolf theme to probe its heroine's changing perceptions of identity as a Native American and a teenager.

Novels of witchcraft and black magic included Guy N. Smith's *Water Rites,* Bill Michaels' *Witchcraft,* Gary Goshgarian's *Stone Circle,* and Brian Scott Smith's *When Shadows Fall*—all lesser efforts that suggest disenchantment with a theme that once predominated in horror's preboom years. The ghost story was similarly in abeyance. Beyond achievements in the ghost story by Ramsey Campbell, Robert Girardi and James Hynes, the only ghost stories of note are those in Wendy Webb and Charles L. Grant's *Gothic Ghosts,* an anthology of all new stories in the classic ghost story tradition, most of which are competent and entertaining.

In an increasing number of 1997 books, authors revitalized familiar, often shopworn horror themes, by crossing them with elements from other genres. The greatest number of successes were hybrids of horror and science fiction, led by Fritz Leiber's *The Dealings of Daniel Kesserich,* a short novel of uncanny phenomena eventually explained as the unforeseen side effects of time travel. Although nearly sixty years old, Leiber's tale seems more presciently modern than

much of the horror fiction written in 1997. Lincoln Child and Douglas Preston wrote *Reliquary,* a sequel to *Relic* (1995) that reprises the first novel's plot of a mutant monster on the rampage in tunnels beneath New York City. A thawed-out Tyrannosaurus Rex stomps scientists in the arctic wastes in Leigh Clark's *Carnivore,* a blatant attempt to capitalize on the summer film adaptation of Crichton's sequel to *Jurassic Park, The Lost World.* Both Steve Alten, in *Meg,* and Charles Wilson in *Extinct,* wrote monster tales about prehistoric precursors of the great white shark that are little more than cover versions of Peter Benchley's *Jaws.* Harry Stein's *Infinity's Child* and Elizabeth Forrest's *Bright Shadow* yoke horror's familiar child-in-peril theme to tales of sinister scientific and government conspiracies. James Byron Huggins's *Cain* is perhaps the most unconventional science fiction-horror hybrid of 1997: a Christian allegory with apocalyptic overtones presented as the tale of a manmade monster on the loose in California.

Cross-pollination of horror and suspense ranged over a wide terrain that included Don Davis's *The Gris-Gris Man,* a mixture of voodoo and police procedural; Ray Garton's *Shackled,* in which a fake satanic cult that sells children into sexual slavery turns the Internet into a sort of Gothic underworld where they conduct their business; Amitov Ghosh's *The Calcutta Syndrome,* J.S. Russell's *Celestial Dogs,* and Noel Hynd's *The Rage of Spirits,* all of which reveal occult conspiracies behind historic and cultural events; and Robert Poe's *The Black Cat,* a small-town murder mystery patterned on the macabre Edgar Allan Poe story of the same name. Fantasy-horror hybrids were few in number and verged mostly into romance territory. Both Marion Zimmer Bradley's *Gravelight,* third in her series of novels featuring paranormal investigator Truth Jourdayne, and Mary Ryan's *Mask of the Night* feature contemporary characters who are surrogates for the power struggles and passions of strong personalities from the past. Katherine Eliska Kimbriel, in *Kindred Rites,* continues the saga she began in 1996 with *Night Calls,* about a community of immigrants in frontier America who practice herbalism and sorcery in their dealings with one another.

With the small press bringing out the lion's share of collections of stories by authors with strong genre affiliations in 1997, there were only two notable collections from trade houses. Shirley Jackson's *Just an Ordinary Day* brings together a vast amount of previously unpublished and uncollected tales by an author whose stories of the dark underside of life in suburban America in the 1960s set an influential standard for the modern horror tale. The stories are not representative of Jackson at her best, and many better works were inexcusably left out of the volume. Nevertheless, it provides a reason to celebrate Jackson's important legacy in weird fiction. Muriel Spark's *Open to the Public* is filled mostly with contemporary mainstream comedies of manners and domestic dramas, but its generous contents include most

of Spark's supernatural fiction, including several of the best literary ghost stories published in the past half century.

The volume of original anthologies was down considerably in 1997, and the numbers told an interesting story. Since 1990, the number of anthologies of original horror fiction escalated to the point that they superseded magazines as sources of new horror fiction. Many of these books became focused so narrowly in theme (particularly those attempting to find a new angle for the omnipresent vampire) that the few quality stories they contained did not bear reprinting outside of the volume where they first appeared. The paucity of original horror anthologies in 1997 seemed a direct response to the genre's earlier profligacy, but fortunately there are many good stories to be found.

Barbara and Christopher Roden's *Midnight Never Comes,* a product of specialty publisher Ash-Tree Press, is a compilation of modern supernatural tales written according to the principles of classic ghostly fiction. There's not a bad story to be found in it, and the book introduces a number of writers, many of them young, who will no doubt become better-known names in horror in years to come. Douglas E. Winter's *Revelations* (titled *Millennium* in the U.K.) is an unusual high-concept anthology whose contributors were asked to select a decade of the 20th century and write about an apocalyptic event or incident. Some of horror's best-known names contributed, and many contributed the best short fiction they have written. Peter Crowther's *Destination Unknown* is also a concept-anthology, but its concept was deliberately kept broad in order to evoke a sense of the unknown. This allowed the editor to mix fantasy, horror and science fiction stories, including outstanding original work by Ramsey Campbell, Lisa Tuttle, Bentley Little, and others. Gardner Dozois commissioned all new stories with an erotic horror edge for *Dying For It.* Beside a book of this caliber, Jeff Gelb and Michael Garrett's *Kiss and Kill* and *Crimes of Passion,* the ninth and tenth volumes respectively in their Hot Blood Series of original erotic horror fiction, and William J. Mann's *Grave Passions,* a collection of gay erotic horror fiction, seem lackluster.

Reprint anthologies covered a considerable amount of territory. Two anthologies, John Gregory Betancourt and Robert Weinberg's *Weird Tales: Seven Decades of Terror* and Marvin Kaye's *The Best of Weird Tales: 1923,* mine the legacy of *Weird Tales,* the long-running pulp fiction magazine that established the reputation of H.P. Lovecraft, Robert E. Howard, Ray Bradbury, and countless other horror heavyweights. Stefan Dziemianowicz, Robert Weinberg and Martin H. Greenberg put together *100 Fiendish Little Frightmares,* a celebration of the short-short horror tale. David Drake lent his expertise as an editor to *A Century of Horror: The 1970s,* the first in a projected series of anthologies showcasing the best work from each decade of the twentieth century. Peter Haining's *Great Irish Tales of Terror* surveys two centuries worth of weird fiction by Irish writers, while Martin H. Greenberg's *Haunted Houses: The*

Greatest Stories focuses specifically on outstanding tales of ghosts and hauntings.

As always, though, the two indispensable reprint anthologies are Ellen Datlow and Terri Windling's *The Year's Best Fantasy and Horror Fiction: Tenth Annual Collection* and Steve Jones's *The Mammoth Book of Best New Horror: Volume Eight.* These books continue the inestimable service of calling attention to outstanding works of horror and fantasy published in the previous year. The editors of both are so diligent and comprehensive in their research that even the most hardcore horror reader is likely to find several stories from mainstream periodicals, magazines for other genres, or small press booklets that he or she overlooked. Despite annual fluctuations in the quantity of horror published over the decade these books have been around, the amount of quality fiction they anthologize has stayed consistent from year to year, offering the reassurance that even when the market shrinks, a reliable portion of horror fiction worth preserving is published. This is exactly the optimism that the horror desperately needs. It is good to know that no matter how dismal the commercial side of horror publishing gets, the literary side will continue to be distinguished by outstanding fiction from writers for whom horror is an essential part of the vocabulary. The big question, though, is how long publishers, and especially writers, can afford to sustain a fiction whose literary and commercial aims are too often diametrically opposed.

Next year marks the twenty-fifth anniversary of the publication of Stephen King's *Carrie,* and the beginning of the contemporary horror boom. Increasingly, horror seems to be on a slide that is bringing it back to 1975 levels, when the fiction did not realistically exist as a trade or mass market entity. Will horror stabilize in 1999, and establish a firm foundation for a future renaissance? Or will it become the exclusive domain of a small but devoted core of specialists and semi-professionals? These questions will be very much on the mind of horror publishers, writers and readers in the coming year.

Best Novels:

Ramsey Campbell, *Nazareth Hill* (Tor)

Tannarive Due, *My Soul to Keep* (HarperCollins)

Stephen King, *Dark Tower IV: Wizards and Glass* (Donald M. Grant/Plume)

Fritz Leiber, *The Dealings of Daniel Kesserich* (Tor)

Bentley Little, *The Ignored* (Signet/Onyx)

Patrick McGrath, *Asylum* (Random House)

Best Author Collections:

Algernon Blackwood, *The Complete John Silence Stories* (Dover)

Gary A. Braunbeck, *Things Left Behind* (CD Publications)

Hugh B. Cave, *The Door Below* (Fedogan & Bremer)

Peter Dickinson, *The Lion Tamer's Daughter* (Delacorte)

Olivia Howard Dunbar, *The Shell of Sense* (Richard Fawcett)

Harlan Ellison, *Slippage* (Ziesing/Houghton-Mifflin)

James Hynes, *Publish and Perish* (St. Martin's/Picador)

Brian McNaughton, *The Throne of Bones* (Terminal Fright)

Jeffrey Osier, *Horizon Lines* (Dark Regions)

Whitley Strieber, *Evenings with Demons* (Borderlands Press)

Lucy Taylor, *Painted in Blood* (Silver Salamander)

Donald Wandrei, *Don't Dream* (Fedogan & Bremer)

Best Anthologies:

Italo Calvino (ed.), *Fantastic Tales* (Random House/Pantheon)

Michael Cox (ed.) *Twelve Tales of the Supernatural* (Oxford)

Ellen Datlow and Terri Windling (eds.), *The Year's Best Fantasy and Horror: Tenth Annual Collection* (St. Martin's)

Stephen Jones (ed.) *The Mammoth Book of Dracula* (Carroll & Graf)

Stephen Jones (ed.), *The Mammoth Book of Best New Horror: Volume 8* (Carroll & Graf)

Catherine A. Lundie, *Restless Spirits* (University of Massachusetts Press)

Barbara and Christopher Roden (eds.), *Midnight Never Comes* (Ash-Tree Press)

Wendy Webb and Charles L. Grant (eds.), *Gothic Ghosts* (Tor)

Douglas E. Winter (ed.) *Revelations* (HarperPrism)

Horror Titles

827

KEN ABNER, Editor

Terminal Frights, Volume One
(Black River, New York: Terminal Frights, 1997)

Story type: Anthology

Summary: Twenty-two stories of horror and fantasy in the first hardcover incarnation of a long-running horror small press magazine. Highlights include William Scheinman's "The Work of Dennis Hobbs" and Don D'Ammassa's "The Managansett Horror," both variations on Lovecraftian themes; Tom Picirilli's "A Lower Deep," which resurrects his necromancer detective hero Self, from his collection, *Pentacle*; Michael Arnzen's "Stigmata" and David Niall Wilson's "To Dream of Sheherzade," both of which feature characters whose disfigurement is an outward expression of their troubled psyches; and Scott H. Urban's "Edge-Run," in which a carjacking leads to an otherwordly adventure. Illustrations by M. Wayne Miller.

Where it's reviewed:
Locus, February 1998, page 62

Other books you might like:
Jani Anderson, *Bringing Down the Moon*, 1985
    editor
Richard T. Chizmar, *The Best of Cemetery Dance*, 1998
    editor
George Hatch, *Guignoir and Other Furies*, 1991
    editor
George Hatch, *Sinistre: An Anthology of Rituals*, 1993
    editor
Tom Piccirilli, *Inside the Works*, 1998
    Gerard Daniel Houarner and Edward Lee, co-authors
Stuart David Schiff, *The Best of Whispers*, 1994
    editor

828

JUSTIN ACHILLI, Editor
ROBERT HATCH, Co-Editor

Dark Tyrants
(Clarkson, Georgia: White Wolf, 1997)

Story type: Anthology

Summary: Thirteen stories set in the publisher's World of Darkness, an alternate world where supernatural creatures co-exist with human beings. This volume features stories set exclusively in medieval Europe and concerned with the Vampire Masquerade, a pact among the vampire subculture to maintain a clandestine existence. Selections include Richard Lee Byers' "The Winged Child," Jackie Cassada's "Toujours," James S. Dorr's "The Hawk and the Slipper," and Guy Davis and Vincent Locke's illustrated "A Fool's Embrace."

Where it's reviewed:
Science Fiction Chronicle, November 1997, page 42

Other books you might like:
Erin Kelly, *The Splendour Falls*, 1995
    editor
Edward E. Kramer, *Dark Destiny III: Children of Dracula*, 1996
    editor
Edward E. Kramer, *Dark Destiny II: Proprietors of Fate*, 1995
    editor
Edward E. Kramer, *Dark Destiny*, 1994
    editor
Staley Krause, *Strange City*, 1996
    Stewart Wieck, co-editor
Staley Krause, *World of Darkness: City of Darkness*, 1995
    Stewart Wieck, co-editor
Stewart Wieck, *The Beast Within*, 1995
    editor
Stewart Wieck, *When Will You Rage*, 1994
    editor

Stewart Wieck, *World of Darkness: Truth Until Paradox*, 1994
editor

829

JACK ADRIAN, Editor

The Ash-Tree Press Annual Macabre, 1997

(Ashcroft, British Columbia: Ash-Tree Press, 1997)

Story type: Anthology

Summary: Four little known tales of the Edwardian era by British female writers. Selections include Patricia Wentworth's ''A Wedding Day,'' about a woman's life-saving psychic link with her husband; Jesse Douglas Kerruish's ''The Swaying Vision,'' in which two men attempt to track the seemingly inexplicable source of a house's haunting; Carola Oman's ''The Visitor,'' in which a ghost from the time of Cromwell is doomed to haunt his beloved estate until his name is cleared of a crime; and Mollie Panter-Downes' ''The House of the Laburnums,'' about the mental distress caused by a woman's precognitive vision of a murder.

Other books by the same author:
Stranger Tales from the Strand, 1991

Other books you might like:
Nina Auerbach, *Forbidden Journeys*, 1992
    U.C. Knoepflmacher, co-editor
Richard Dalby, *Edwardian Ghost Stories by Eminent Women Writers*, 1992
    editor
Catherine A. Lundie, *Restless Spirits*, 1997
    editor
Alan Ryan, *Haunting Women*, 1988
    editor
Jessica Amanda Salmonson, *What Did Miss Darrington See?*, 1989
A. Susan Williams, *The Lifted Veil*, 1993
    editor

830

CHRIS N. AFRICA

When Wolves Cry

(Edmonton, Alberta: Commonwealth, 1997)

Story type: Nature in Revolt
Major character(s): Cloud Hunter Johnson, Guide; Big John ''BJ'', Bartender; Chris Taelor, Hunter
Time period(s): 1990s (1997)
Locale(s): Mountain City, Nevada

Summary: A weekend hunting expedition turns from ordinary to bizarre when a pack of sentient wolves plays a series of increasingly annoying tricks on the six hunters, and then turns vicious and predatory when the hunters kill one of the pack. A first novel.

Other books you might like:
David Dvorkin, *Ursus*, 1989
Brian Hopkins, *Cold at Heart*, 1997
Dean R. Koontz, *Watchers*, 1987

T. Chris Martindale, *Where the Chill Waits*, 1990
Graham Masterton, *The Manitou*, 1975
Christine Tanasiuk, *Howl*, 1997

831

STEVE ALTEN

Meg

(New York: Doubleday, 1997)

Story type: Nature in Revolt
Major character(s): Jonas Taylor, Scientist (paleontologist); Terry Tanaka, Scientist (oceanographer); David Adashek, Journalist
Time period(s): 1900s (1997)
Locale(s): Monterey, California

Summary: Scientist exploration of the Marianas Trench stirs up a Megalodon, a prehistoric precursor of the great white shark that measures over 60-feet long. Jonas Taylor, the sole survivor of a deep-sea voyage slaughtered by a Megalodon, puts life and limb at risk when he agrees to help hunt the creature down and prevent a global upset of the marine food chain. A first novel.

Other books you might like:
Peter Benchley, *Jaws*, 1974
Peter Benchley, *Beast*, 1991
Matthew J. Costello, *Wurm*, 1991
William Dantz, *Hunger*, 1992
J.M. Morgan, *Between the Devil and the Deep*, 1992
Charles Wilson, *Extinct*, 1997

832

KEVIN J. ANDERSON

Antibodies

(New York: HarperPrism, 1997)

Story type: Science Fiction
Series: The X-Files
Major character(s): Fox Mulder, FBI Agent; Dana Scully, FBI Agent; Jeremy Dorman, Scientist (research)
Time period(s): 1990s (1997)
Locale(s): Portland, Oregon

Summary: Agents Mulder and Scully, who investigate cases considered too bizarre for regular FBI operatives, explore the destruction of the DyMar Laboratory and the death of David Kennessy, a cancer researcher with an interest in nanotechnology. Their investigations uncover a government conspiracy to suppress Kennessy's findings and a laboratory worker infected with a nanotech virus whose touch leads to gruesome, mutating death.

Other books by the same author:
Ruins, 1996
Blindfold, 1995
Ground Zero, 1995
Climbing Olympus, 1994

Other books you might like:
Lincoln Child, *Mount Dragon*, 1996
    Douglas Preston, co-author

Michael Crichton, *The Andromeda Strain*, 1969
Nigel Kneale, *The Quatermass Experiment*, 1959
Dean R. Koontz, *Midnight*, 1993
Patrick Lynch, *Carriers*, 1995

833

M.T. ANDERSON

Thirsty

(New York: Candlewick, 1997)

Story type: Vampire Story; Young Adult
Major character(s): Chris, Teenager, Vampire; Chet, Supernatural Being; Tch'muchgar, Vampire
Locale(s): New England (alternate)

Summary: In an alternate world populated with creatures of the supernatural, Chris struggles with the growing pains that come with acceptance of his maturing vampire identity. For his first adult responsibility, Chet, a member of the Forces of Light, asks him to interfere with a ceremony that will help release a vampire lord from captivity in another world. A young adult novel.

Where it's reviewed:
Locus, May 1997, page 29
Publishers Weekly, January 27, 1997, page 108

Other books you might like:
Richie Tankersley Cusick, *Vampire*, 1991
Joseph Locke, *Vampire Heart*, 1994
Christopher Pike, *The Last Vampire*, 1994
L.J. Smith, *Secret Vampire*, 1996
L.J. Smith, *The Vampire Diaries*, 1992
S.P. Somtow, *The Vampire's Beautiful Daughter*, 1997

834

SCOTT DAVID ANIOLOWSKI, Editor

Return to Lovecraft Country

(Lockport, New York: Triad, 1997)

Story type: Anthology

Summary: Fifteen stories written in homage to H.P. Lovecraft's cosmic horror fiction. The volume is anchored by reprints of T.E.D. Klein's "The Events at Poroth Farm," about a supernatural presence that has infiltrated a rural setting and its inhabitants; Thomas Ligotti's "The Last Feast of Harlequin," in which a man discovers that a festival of clowns is actually a celebration of dark gods and terrors; and Lin Carter's "Strange Manuscript Found in the Vermont Woods." Contributors of original stories include Richard Lupoff, Don Burleson, Peter Cannon, Don D'Ammassa and Robert M. Price.

Other books by the same author:
Singers of Strange Songs, 1997
Made in Goatswood, 1995

Other books you might like:
Edward P. Berglund, *Disciples of Cthulhu*, 1996
   editor
H.P. Lovecraft, *Tales of the Cthulhu Mythos*, 1990

Robert M. Price, *The New Lovecraft Circle*, 1996
   editor
Thomas M.K. Stratman, *Cthulhu's Heirs*, 1994
   editor
James Turner, *Cthulhu 2000*, 1995
   editor
Robert Weinberg, *Miskatonic University*, 1996
   Martin H. Greenberg, co-editor

835

ANONYMOUS

The Book of Irish Weirdness

(New York: Sterling, 1997)

Story type: Anthology

Summary: Thirty-five stories of horror and fantasy by Irish writers of the nineteenth and twentieth centuries. Included are Bram Stoker's "The Judge's House," about a house terrorized by a rat imbued with the soul of its evil former owner; Charlotte Riddell's "Hertford O'Donnell's Warning," featuring the legendary banshee; F. Marion Crawford's "The Dead Smile," about a pair of lovers haunted by a family curse and the grinning face of a dead ancestor; Oscar Wilde's amusing "The Canterville Ghost," in which the ghost of a man walled up in a house centuries before attempts to redress his sin and earn release into the afterlife; J. Sheridan Le Fanu's "Wicked Captain Walshawe," in which a man's soul becomes trapped in a candle and cannot be released until it is burned up; and A.E. Coppard's "The Gollan," a fantasy about a giant given the gift of imperceptibility by a leprechaun and the curse it proves to be. Several of the selections are retellings of classic stories from the oral tradition.

Other books you might like:
Peter Haining, *Great Irish Tales of Horror*, 1995
   editor
Peter Haining, *Great Irish Stories of the Supernatural*, 1992
   editor
Peter Haining, *Great Irish Tales of the Unimaginable*, 1994
   editor
Jim McGarry, *Irish Tales of Terror*, 1971
   editor
Peter Tremayne, *The Irish Masters of Fantasy*, 1979
   editor

836

THOMAS BAUM

Out of Body

(New York: St. Martin's, 1997)

Story type: Wild Talents
Major character(s): Denton Hake, Construction Worker; Elliot Hake, Insurance Investigator (Denton's brother); Felix Ortega, Parole Officer
Time period(s): 1990s (1997)
Locale(s): Tacoma, Washington

Summary: Denton Hake is plagued by out-of-body experiences during which he commits acts that he doesn't remem-

ber. Framed and imprisoned for a murder he supposedly committed during one of these experiences, he dissociates his consciousness from his body to ferret out the real murderer.

Where it's reviewed:
Kirkus, April 1, 1997, page 477
Publishers Weekly, March 17, 1997, page 75

Other books you might like:
Rene Belletto, *Machine*, 1993
Raymond Buckland, *The Committee*, 1993
Harlan Ellison, *Mefisto in Onyx*, 1993
Graham Masterton, *Rook*, 1996
Susan Palwick, *Flying in Place*, 1992
Costello Sean, *Captain Quad*, 1991

837

DONALD BEMAN

The Taking

(New York: Leisure, 1997)

Story type: Occult
Major character(s): Sean MacDonald, Writer; Cathy Greene, Farmer; Patricia Jennings, Professor
Time period(s): 1990s (1990-1992)
Locale(s): Red Hook, New York

Summary: Friends study the numerological significance of events in Sean MacDonald's life and discover that he is ripe for "The Taking," or reclamation of his soul by the emissaries of Satan. The revelation helps explain the recent tragedies that have dogged Sean, including the deaths of his wife and son, and make him suspicious of the true motives of the many strong-willed women who show romantic interest in him.

Other books you might like:
John Burke, *Ladygrove*, 1978
Fritz Leiber, *Conjure Wife*, 1952
Bentley Little, *Dominion*, 1995
Thomas Tryon, *Harvest Home*, 1973

838

NIGEL BENNETT
P.N. ELROD, Co-Author

Keeper of the King

(New York: Baen/Starline, 1997)

Story type: Vampire Story
Major character(s): Richard Dun, Consultant (security), Vampire; Neal Rivers, Professor, Vampire; Lady Sabra, Vampire
Time period(s): 1990s (1996)
Locale(s): Toronto, Ontario, Canada

Summary: In medieval times, Vampire Richard d'Orleans serves as the protector of King Arthur, giving rise to the legends of Sir Lancelot. In his 20th-century incarnation as Richard Dun, he fulfills a similar role, serving as a security consultant who protects the Canadian prime minister from an IRA-plotted assassination attempt. This is a first collaboration

between Elrod, a writer of vampire fiction, and Bennett, an actor in the television vampire series "Forever Knight."

Where it's reviewed:
Kirkus Reviews, November 15, 1996, page 1638
Publishers Weekly, December 9, 1996, page 64

Other books you might like:
Jane Jensen, *Gabriel Knight: Sins of the Fathers*, 1997
Anne Rice, *Queen of the Damned*, 1989
Fred Saberhagen, *A Sharpness on the Neck*, 1996
Robert Weinberg, *Unholy Allies*, 1995
T. Lucien Wright, *Thirst of the Vampire*, 1992

839

R.H. BENSON

The Light Invisible

(Bristol, Rhode Island: Hobgoblin Press, 1997)

Story type: Collection

Summary: Collection of 12 tales of the supernatural, told by an elderly priest to illustrate the existence of the Divine. In "The Green Robe" and "The Watcher," a young boy sees physical manifestations of the holy in nature. "The Blood Eagle" is concerned with a pagan ritual that incorporates elements of both Christian and pre-Christian worship in England, and "The Traveler" with a priest who discovers his confessional has been visited by the ghost of a conspirator in the death of Sir Thomas a Beckett. Originally published in England in 1903.

Where it's reviewed:
Necrofile, Fall 1997, page 28

Other books by the same author:
The Dawn of All, 1911
The Necronancers, 1909
Lord of the World, 1907
A Mirror of Shalott, 1907

Other books you might like:
A.C. Benson, *Ghosts in the House*, 1996
R.H. Benson, co-author
A.C. Benson, *Basil Netherby*, 1927
Algernon Blackwood, *Pan's Garden: A Volume of Nature Stories*, 1912
Arthur Machen, *The Terror*, 1917
A.N.L. Munby, *The Alabaster Hand and Other Ghost Stories*, 1949

840

JOHN GREGORY BETANCOURT, Editor
ROBERT WEINBERG, Co-Editor

Weird Tales: Seven Decades of Terror

(New York: Barnes & Noble, 1997)

Story type: Anthology

Summary: Twenty-eight stories published in *Weird Tales*, the legendary magazine of fantasy and horror, which began life as a pulp magazine published between 1923 and 1954 and has since been revived four times. Included are Robert Bloch's

"Lucy Comes to Stay," a tale of psychological horror; Ray Bradbury's "The Crowd," in which a man discovers that every car accident scene is haunted by a ghostly crowd of the same people; Clark Ashton Smith's "The Seed from the Sepulchre," about a mysterious parasitical plant; Henry Kuttner's first published story, "The Graveyard Rats"; William Hope Hodgson's sea horror story, "The Finding of the Graiken"; and Brian Lumley's suspenseful revenge story, "The Pit Yakker."

Other books by the same author:
Playing in Wonderland, 1995
The Best of Weird Tales: The Terminus Years, 1995

Other books you might like:
Stefan Dziemianowicz, *Weird Tales: 32 Unearthed Terrors*, 1987
   Robert Weinberg and Martin H. Greenberg, co-editors
Peter Haining, *Weird Tales*, 1976
   editor
Marvin Kaye, *Weird Tales: The Magazine That Never Dies*, 1988
   editor
Robert Weinberg, *100 Wild Little Weird Tales*, 1993
   Stefan Dziemianowicz and Martin H. Greenberg, co-editors

841

ALGERNON BLACKWOOD

The Complete John Silence Stories
(Mineola, New York: Dover, 1997)

Story type: Collection; Occult

Summary: "Phsychic doctor" John Silence investigates the impact of the supernatural upon ordinary lives in six case studies that promulgate the author's beliefs in the occult. "Ancient Sorceries" and "The Camp of the Dog" feature human beings who shapeshift into animals. "A Psychical Invasion" features a man haunted by the ghost of a black magician and "The Nemesis of Fire" a house haunted by a fire elemental brought back to England in an Egyptian mummy. In "Secret Worship," black magic corrupts a remote religious school. These contents, which were published as *John Silence: Physician Extraordinaire* in 1908, are embellished with one more story, "A Victim of Higher Space," in which man finds his thoughts repeatedly dragging him into a fourth dimension. Introduction by S.T. Joshi.

Other books by the same author:
Incredible Adventures, 1914
Pan's Garden: A Volume of Nature Stories, 1912
The Lost Valley and Other Stories, 1910
The Listener and Other Stories, 1907
The Empty House and Other Ghost Stories, 1906

Other books you might like:
A.M. Burrage, *The Occult Files of Francis Chard: Some Ghost Stories*, 1996
Dion Fortune, *The Secrets of Dr. Taverner*, 1926
E. Heron, *Flaxman Low, Psychic Detective*, 1993
   H. Heron, co-author
William Hope Hodgson, *Carnacki the Ghost Finder*, 1913

J. Sheridan Le Fanu, *In a Glass Darkly*, 1872
Sax Rohmer, *The Dream Detective*, 1920

842

JAMES P. BLAYLOCK

Winter Tides
(New York: Ace, 1997)

Story type: Possession
Major character(s): Dave Quinn, Businessman (warehouse manager); Anne Morris, Writer; Edmund Dalton, Businessman (theatre owner)
Time period(s): 1990s (1997)
Locale(s): Huntington Beach, California

Summary: Fifteen years ago, Dave Quinn saved Anne Morris from drowning at the cost of the life of Anne's twin sister, Elinor. Now Anne has returned to Dave's town, with the malignant discarnate spirit of Elinor in hot pursuit, seeking a body she can assume control of to wreak vengeance on Dave and Anne.

Where it's reviewed:
Kirkus, June 15, 1997, page 916
Locus, August 1997, page 31
Locus, July 1997, page 25
Necrofile #27, winter 1998, page 5
Publishers Weekly, July 14, 1997, page 65

Other books by the same author:
All the Bells on Earth, 1995
Night Relics, 1994
The Paper Grail, 1991
The Last Coin, 1988
Homunculus, 1986

Other books you might like:
Ramsey Campbell, *To Wake the Dead*, 1980
Richard Matheson, *Earthbound*, 1989
Peter Straub, *Ghost Story*, 1979

843

REBECCA BRAND (Pseudonym of Suzy McKee Charnas)

The Ruby Tear
(New York: Tor/Forge, 1997)

Story type: Vampire Story
Major character(s): Jessamyn Croft, Actress; Nic Griffin, Actor (Jessamyn's fiance), Writer (playwright); Ivo von Cragga, Vampire
Time period(s): 1990s (1997)
Locale(s): New York, New York

Summary: Nic Griffin, the descendant of a family who slaughtered the von Cragga vampires centuries before, writes "The Jewel," a play that reprises the Griffin/von Cragga vendetta, as a snare to trap the last surviving von Cragga who has systematically murdered his ancestors over the centuries. Nic's efforts are complicated by his fiancee Jessamyn, an actress who hopes to play the lead in the play during its off-Broadway run.

Where it's reviewed:
Locus, August 1997, page 28

Other books by the same author:
The Furies, 1994
The Kingdom of Kevin Malone, 1993
The Golden Thread, 1989
The Vampire Tapestry, 1980

Other books you might like:
Steven Brust, *Agyar*, 1992
Brent Monahan, *The Book of Common Dread*, 1993
Kim Newman, *Bad Dreams*, 1990
Anne Rice, *The Vampire Lestat*, 1985
Fred Saberhagen, *A Sharpness on the Neck*, 1996
Chet Williamson, *Reign*, 1990
T. Lucien Wright, *Thirst of the Vampire*, 1992

844

GARY A. BRAUNBECK

Things Left Behind

(Abingdon, Maryland: CD Publications, 1997)

Story type: Collection

Summary: A first collection of forty stories and prose fragments, many of which use the traditional motifs of horror as springboards for reflection on the human condition. ''Some Touch of Pity'' features a werewolf whose bestial side symbolizes his suppressed rage at his sexual abuse as a child. ''Bloody Sam'' is a tale of racial injustice that pits film director Sam Peckinpah against a vampire who feeds on the underclass south of the border, and ''In Hollow Houses'' is a tale of social disenfranchisement in which extraterrestrials live lives of the alienated among human beings. Illustrated by Alan Clark and Alan Koszowski, with a preface by J.N. Williamson, introduction by William F. Nolan, and afterword by Ed Gorman.

Where it's reviewed:
Locus, Dec. 1997, page 25
Publishers Weekly, July 21, 1997, page 186

Other books you might like:
Richard T. Chizmar, *Midnight Promises*, 1996
Harlan Ellison, *Slippage*, 1997
Brian Hodge, *The Convulsion Factory*, 1996
Elizabeth Massie, *Shadow Dreams*, 1996
David Niall Wilson, *The Fall of the House of Escher and Other Illusions*, 1995

845

POPPY Z. BRITE, Editor
MARTIN H. GREENBERG, Co-Editor

Love in Vein II

(New York: HarperPrism, 1997)

Story type: Anthology; Vampire Story
Series: Love in Vein

Summary: Eighteen erotic vampire tales by diverse authors. Highlights include David J. Schow's ''Dusting the Flowers,''

the tale of a parasitic artist set in the Louisiana bayou; Brian Hodge's ''The Dripping of Sundered Wineskins,'' in which a woman passes on her vampire taint to the survivor of an IRA bombing when she licks his wounds; Lucy Taylor's ''Ceilings and Sky,'' in which a mother avenges the death of her child at the hands of a vampire cultist; and Nicholas Royle's ''Kingyo No Fun,'' which traces a vampire undercurrent in Amsterdam's gay community.

Where it's reviewed:
Locus, April 1997, page 21
Locus, May 1997, page 25

Other books by the same author:
Love in Vein, 1996

Other books you might like:
Pam Keesey, *Darker Angels: Lesbian Vampire Stories*, 1995
  editor
Amarantha Knight, *Love Bites*, 1994
  editor
Michael Rowe, *Brothers of the Night*, 1997
  Thomas Roche, co-editor
Cecilia Tan, *Cherished Blood*, 1997
  editor
Cecilia Tan, *Erotic Vampire Tales*, 1994
  editor
Cecilia Tan, *Vampire Erotica*, 1996
  editor

846

CLIFF BURNS

The Reality Machine

(North Battleford, Saskatchewan: Black Dog Press, 1997)

Story type: Collection

Summary: Nineteen prose poems, vignettes, tales of science fiction, and post-modern dark fantasies. Included are ''The Woman Who Gave Good Phone,'' about a mysterious woman who ruins lives with prank phone calls; ''Also Starring,'' in which the world is suddenly overrun with criminals who masquerade as well-known characters actors; ''In Dreams, Awake,'' in which a man sympathizes so deeply with his wife that he acquires her terminal illness; and ''Son of Nixon,'' a satire on the fantastic transformation and rehabilitation of a corrupt politician. Introduction by Kim Newman.

Other books by the same author:
Genuinely Inspired Primitive, 1994
Sex and Other Acts of the Imagination, 1990

Other books you might like:
William S. Burroughs, *Interzone*, 1989
Harlan Ellison, *Slippage*, 1997
Jack Remick, *Terminal Weird*, 1996
Don Webb, *A Spell for the Fulfillment of Desire*, 1996
Don Webb, *Stealing My Rules*, 1997

847

A.M. BURRAGE

Someone in the Room: Strange Tales Old and New

(Ashcroft, British Columbia: Ash-Tree Press, 1997)

Story type: Collection

Summary: Twenty-eight tales of ghosts and the supernatural, seven collected for the first time. The centerpiece is the fourteen stories collected as *Someone in the Room*, published under the pseudonym ''Ex-Private X'' in 1931. These include ''The Sweeper,'' about a woman fearful of a gypsy curse that death will come in the form of a leaf-sweeper; ''The Waxwork,'' about a wax museum haunted by the ghost of a murderer whose effigy it features; ''Smee,'' in which a childhood game brings back the spirit of a child who was killed playing it; and ''The Running Tide'' and ''Someone in the Room,'' both about sites haunted by psychic residues that repeatedly re-enact past evil deeds. Two essays on ghostly experience and fiction included. Edited by Jack Adrian.

Other books by the same author:
The Occult Files of Francis Chard: Some Ghost Stories, 1996
Intruders, 1995
Between the Minute and the Hour, 1967
Seeker to the Dead, 1942

Other books you might like:
E.F. Benson, *The Collected Ghost Stories of E.F. Benson*, 1992
Frederick Cowles, *Fear Walks the Night*, 1992
L.P. Hartley, *The Traveling Grave, and Other Stories*, 1948
H. Russell Wakefield, *They Return at Evening*, 1928
H. Russell Wakefield, *The Clock Strikes Twelve*, 1939

848

P.D. CACEK

Leavings

(Greenwood Village, Colorado: StarsEnd Creations, 1997)

Story type: Collection

Summary: Thirteen stories in a first collection of short fiction. ''Yrena'' chronicles the vampiric relationship between a young woman and an older man. In ''The Ancient One,'' a child's teddy bear carries a centuries-old family curse. ''Here Be Dragons'' is a gargoyle tale and ''Gilgamesh Recidivus'' a unicorn story. In ''. . .Just a Little Bug. . .'' a young girl's cancer manifests outside her body as a bug-like creature.

Where it's reviewed:
Locus, December 1997, page 27

Other books you might like:
Elizabeth Engstrom, *Nightmare Flower*, 1992
Brian Hopkins, *Something Haunts Us All*, 1996
Elizabeth Massie, *Shadow Dreams*, 1996
Jessica Amanda Salmonson, *John Collier and Fredric Brown Went Quarrelling through My Head*, 1989
Sue Storm, *Star Bones Weep the Blood of Angels*, 1996

David Niall Wilson, *The Fall of the House of Escher and Other Illusions*, 1996

849

MARY R. CALLAGHAN

I Met a Man Who Wasn't There

(New York: Marion Boyars, 1997)

Story type: Ghost Story
Major character(s): Anne O'Brien, Writer; Marcus Quilligan O'Neill, Lawyer, Spirit (ghost); Charles Matthews, Teacher
Time period(s): 1990s (1997)
Locale(s): Oldcastle, Pennsylvania (Sweetmount College); New York, New York

Summary: At the behest of the ghost of her grandfather Marcus, Anne O'Brien agrees to write his biography and help exonerate a man he helped to prosecute and wrongly send to his death. Anne's research into the Irish experience in early twentieth-century America acquaints her with her roots but resurrects the ghosts of Marcus's associates, who would just as soon never have the truth about their crimes come to light.

Where it's reviewed:
Kirkus, August 15, 1996, page 1169
Publishers Weekly, September 9, 1996, page 63

Other books by the same author:
Mothers, 1984

Other books you might like:
Noel Hynd, *Ghosts*, 1993
Greg Kihn, *Shade of Pale*, 1997
Alan Ryan, *Cast a Cold Eye*, 1984
Peter Straub, *Ghost Story*, 1979

850

ITALO CALVINO, Editor

Fantastic Tales: Visionary and Everyday

(New York: Pantheon, 1997)

Story type: Anthology

Summary: Twenty-six stories of fantasy and horror by American and European masters of the eighteenth, nineteenth, and twentieth centuries. Included are E.T.A. Hoffman's ''The Sandman,'' about a man traumatized as an adult by a childhood nightmare; Nathaniel Hawthorne's ''Young Goodman Brown,'' in which a young husband in colonial America discovers that all of his townsfolk may be practicing devil worshippers; Edgar Allan Poe's ''The Tell-Tale Heart,'' the story of a monomaniac undone by his guilt over the grisly murder he has committed; Ambrose Bierce's ''Chickamauga,'' a tale of Civil War horrors; H.G. Wells's ''The Country of the Blind,'' in which a man is imprisoned by a lost race of the congenitally blind; and Robert Louis Stevenson's ''The Bottle Imp,'' a tale of mystical beliefs in the South Seas. Originally published in Italy in two volumes in 1983 as *Racconti Fantastici Dell'ottocento*.

Other books by the same author:
Numbers in the Dark and Other Stories, 1995
Italian Folktales, 1992
If on a Winter's Night a Traveller, 1981
The Castle of Crossed Destinies, 1977
t zero, 1969

Other books you might like:
Christopher Baldick, *The Oxford Book of Gothic Tales*, 1992
    editor
Peter Haining, *Great Tales of Terror from Europe and America*, 1972
    editor
Stephen Jones, *H.P. Lovecraft's Book of Horror*, 1993
    David Carson, co-editor
Tom Shippey, *The Oxford Book of Fantasy Stories*, 1994
    editor
Patricia L. Skarda, *The Evil Image*, 1981
    Nora Crowe, co-editor
Herbert Wise, *Great Tales of Terror and the Supernatural*, 1944
    Phyllis Fraser, co-editor

851

RAMSEY CAMPBELL

Nazareth Hill

(New York: Tor/Forge, 1997)

Story type: Haunted House
Major character(s): Amy Priestley, Teenager; Oswald Priestley, Insurance Agent (Amy's father); Beth Griffin, Health Care Professional (homeopath)
Time period(s): 1990s (1996)
Locale(s): Partington, England

Summary: Widowed Oswald Priestley moves with his daughter Amy to Nazareth Hill, an apartment complex built on the site of an old asylum. Shortly after Amy discovers that Nazareth Hill served in the middle ages as the torture chamber for the Witchfinder General, Oswald falls under the spell of its haunted past and recapitulates its brutal legacy of persecution and terror with his daughter. First published in England in 1996 as *The House on Nazareth Hill*.

Where it's reviewed:
Kirkus, April 15, 1997, page 570
Necrofile #23, Winter 1997, page 3
Publishers Weekly, May 19, 1997, page 67

Other books by the same author:
The One Safe Place, 1995
The Long Lost, 1993
The Count of Eleven, 1991
Midnight Sun, 1990
Ancient Images, 1989

Other books you might like:
Tom Elliott, *The Dwelling*, 1989
Judith Hawkes, *Julian's House*, 1989
Richard Matheson, *Hell House*, 1971
Al Sarrantonio, *House Haunted*, 1991
Chet Williamson, *Soulstorm*, 1986

852

P.H. CANNON

Tales of Lovecraftian Horror and Humor

(West Hills, California: Tsathoggua Press, 1997)

Story type: Collection
Series: The Early Cannon

Summary: Miscellany of nine stories, essays and incidental pieces by a writer best known for his critical writing on H.P. Lovecraft. ''Providence in 1990 A.D.'' is a wistful speculation on a world in which H.P. Lovecraft is recognized as a literary giant, while ''Conclusion to 'Saucers from Yaddith''' and ''The Body from the Bog'' are flippant pastiches of Lovecraft's fiction. ''The Pewter Ring'' is a solid tale of horrors from the past that survive through dark sorcery into the present. The second of two volumes in the ''Early Cannon'' series.

Other books by the same author:
The Thing in the Bathtub and Other Lovecraftian Tales, 1997
Scream for Jeeves, 1994
The Sky Garden, 1989
Pulptime, 1984

Other books you might like:
Fred Chappell, *More Shapes than One*, 1991
Fred Chappell, *The Lodger*, 1993
Christopher Moore, *Practical Demonkeeping*, 1992
William Browning Spencer, *Resume with Monsters*, 1995
Gahan Wilson, *Eddy Deco's Last Caper*, 1987

853

P.H. CANNON

The Thing in the Bathtub and Other Lovecraftian Tales

(West Hills, California: Tsathoggua Press, 1997)

Story type: Collection
Series: The Early Cannon

Summary: Six humorous stories, poems and essays by a writer best known for his critical writing on H.P. Lovecraft. The stories are satires of Lovecraftian fiction and the cult of amateur Lovecraftians. Lovecraft is caricatured in them as the literary figure H.A. Howard, a convention guest of honor at ''The Pop Festival'' and the subject of a mock critical essay, ''H.A. Howard: His Own Most Mediocre Creation.'' ''From Below,'' a deliberately bad pastiche of Lovecraft, is presented as a typical Howard story. The title story interweaves plot devices from Lovecraft's fiction with the antics of a bunch of bumbling Howard worshippers. The first of two volumes in the ''Early Cannon'' series.

Other books by the same author:
Tales of Lovecraftian Horror and Humor, 1997
Scream for Jeeves, 1994
The Sky Garden, 1989
Pulptime, 1984

Other books you might like:
Fred Chappell, *More Shapes than One*, 1991

Fred Chappell, *The Lodger*, 1993
Christopher Moore, *Practical Demonkeeping*, 1992
William Browning Spencer, *Resume with Monsters*, 1995
Gahan Wilson, *Eddy Deco's Last Caper*, 1987

854

LIN CARTER

The Xothic Legend Cycle

(Oakland, California: Chaosium, 1997)

Story type: Anthology
Series: The Cthulhu Cycle

Summary: Twelve stories by the late author, a celebrated editor of fantasy and horror fiction. Also included are one completion of an unfinished fragment of H.P. Lovecraft's, a collaboration with the volume's editor Robert M. Price, "The Strange Doom of Enos Harker," and Price's homage to Carter's work, "The Soul of the Devil Bought." Carter's pastiches of Lovecraft's cosmic horror fiction include "The Fishers from Outside," "The Thing in the Pit," "The Dweller in the Tomb," and "Behind the Mask."

Other books by the same author:
Callipygia, 1988
Down to a Sunless Sea, 1984
The Nemesis of Evil, 1975

Other books you might like:
Robert Bloch, *The Mysteries of the Worm*, 1993
H.P. Lovecraft, *The Watchers out of Time and Others*, 1974
    August Derleth, co-author
Richard A. Lupoff, *Before. . .12:01. . .and After*, 1996
Gary Meyers, *The House of the Worm*, 1975
Richard L. Tierney, *Scroll of Thoth*, 1997

855

HUGH B. CAVE

The Door Below

(Minneapolis: Fedogan & Bremer, 1997)

Story type: Collection

Summary: Twenty-five stories of supernatural horrors and weird menaces that span more than 60 years of the author's prolific and distinguished writing career. Cave's work for the shudder pulps is represented by "Imp of Satan," about a grotesquely disfigured victim of native poisons who threatens to inflict the same fate on his estranged fiance, and "The Thirsty Thing," in which a maniac uses a sea monster to kill his victims. More recent stories include the biter-bit tale "The Hard-Luck Kid," the alternate dimension story "Vanishing Point," and the outstanding voodoo tale "The Place of No Return." The author supplies notes on selections for each of the five decades represented.

Other books by the same author:
Murgunstrumm and Others, 1997
Bitter/Sweet, 1996
Death Stalks the Night, 1995
The Witching Lands, 1973

Other books you might like:
Arthur J. Burks, *Black Medicine*, 1966
Robert E. Howard, *Skullface and Others*, 1946
Carl Jacobi, *Smoke of the Snake*, 1994
Carl Jacobi, *Revelations in Black*, 1947
Frank Belknap Long, *The Hounds of Tindalos*, 1946
E. Hoffman Price, *Far Lands and Other Days*, 1975
Manly Wade Wellman, *Worse Things Waiting*, 1973

856

ROBERT W. CHAMBERS

The King in Yellow

(Bristol, Rhode Island: Hobgoblin Press, 1997)

Story type: Collection

Summary: Ten stories reflecting the American bohemian experience at the turn of the century, informally united by recurring references to *The King in Yellow*, a forbidden book that brings madness to those who read it. Included are "The Yellow Sign," the classic tale of an artist stalked by gruesome specter of death; "The Demoiselle D'ys," in which a cynical man learns a lesson of love that endures beyond the grave; "The Mask," about an artist who invents a liquid that turns living matter into stone; and "The Repairer of Reputations," which offers a dystopic vision of the future. First published in 1895. H.P. Lovecraft's assessment of Chambers in his 1927 essay, "Supernatural Horror in Literature," is added as an introduction.

Where it's reviewed:
Necrofile, Fall 1997, page 28

Other books by the same author:
The Tracer of Lost Persons, 1906
In Search of the Unknown, 1904
The Maker of Moons, 1896

Other books you might like:
Ambrose Bierce, *Can Such Things Be?*, 1893
Ralph Adams Cram, *Black Spirits and White*, 1895
W.C. Morrow, *The Ape, the Idiot, and Other People*, 1897
Vincent O'Sullivan, *Master of the Fallen Years*, 1995

857

R. CHETWYND-HAYES

The Vampire Stories of R. Chetwynd-Hayes

(Minneapolis: Fedogan & Bremer, 1997)

Story type: Collection

Summary: Fifteen stories spanning three decades of the career of a writer known for his traditional ghost stories and blends of humor and horror. Selections include "My Mother Married a Vampire," an amusing tale of a young boy's adjustment to his father's vampire lifestyle; "Something on Which to Suck," which features a vitality-draining shadow; "The Labyrinth," which concerns a vampire house; and "Keep the Gaslight Burning," a period story. Brian Lumley contributes

Horror

an introduction and Stephen Jones and Jo Fletcher add an afterword.

Other books by the same author:
Shudders and Shivers, 1995
Hell Is What You Make It, 1994
Tales From the Hidden World, 1988
The House of Dracula, 1987
Tales From the Haunted House, 1987

Other books you might like:
Richard Dalby, *Dracula's Brood*, 1987
    editoe
Charles L. Grant, *Soft Whisper of the Dead*, 1982
Martin H. Greenberg, *Dracula: Prince of Darkness*, 1992
    editor
Barbara Hambly, *Those Who Hunt the Night*, 1987
Stephen Jones, *The Mammoth Book of Vampires*, 1992
    editor

858

RICHARD T. CHIZMAR, Editor

Screamplays

(New York: Del Ray, 1997)

Story type: Anthology

Summary: Seven previously unpublished screenplays of horror and dark suspense, several adapted from works of fiction and several produced for film and television. Selections include Stephen King's "General," about a family cat that protects a young girl from a nocturnal supernatural predator in her bedroom; Richard Matheson's "The Legend of Hell Huse," adapted from his 1971 novel and produced as the movie of the same name; Joe R. Lansdale's "Dead in the West," a zombie western; Richard Laymon's "The Hunted," about a woman stalked by a serial killer and his bounty hunter; Harlan Ellison's "Moonlighting," a biter-bit tale adapted from his short crime story "Ormond Always Pays His Bills"; and Harlan Ellison's "Killing Bernstein" and Ed Gorman's "Track Down." Introduction by Dean R. Koontz.

Where it's reviewed:
Hellnotes, October 3, 1997, page 5

Other books by the same author:
The Earth Strikes Back, 1994
Chillers, 1993
Cold Blood, 1991

Other books you might like:
Clive Barker, *Forms of Heaven*, 1996
Clive Barker, *Incarnations*, 1995
Ray Bradbury, *Ray Bradbury on Stage: A Chrestomathy of His Plays*, 1991
John Burke, *The Hammer Horror Omnibus*, 1966
John Burke, *The Second Hammer Horror Film Omnibus*, 1967
Marvin Kaye, *Thirteen Plays of Ghosts and the Supernatural*, 1990
Nigel Kneale, *The Year of the Sex Olympics and Other TV Plays*, 1976
Nigel Kneale, *The Quatermass Experiment*, 1959
Arch Oboler, *The Obler Omnibus*, 1945

859

LEIGH CLARK

Carnivore

(New York: Leisure, 1997)

Story type: Nature in Revolt
Major character(s): Troy Darrow, Scientist (geologist); Kelly Sawyer, Scientist (EPA); Valentine Tarosh, Scientist
Time period(s): 1990s (1997)
Locale(s): Antarctica

Summary: Scientists participating in Deepcore, a secret project to locate sites for nuclear waste dumping in Antarctica, discover a Tyrannosaurus Rex egg frozen in a glacier millions of years before. Exposed to radiactive waste, the egg hatches and the dinosaur inside grows at an accelerated pace, putting the scientists in a struggle for survival against a prehistoric monster.

Other books by the same author:
Shock Radio, 1996
Evil Incarnate, 1994
Blood Sabbath, 1991
The Feeding, 1988

Other books you might like:
Michael Crichton, *The Lost World*, 1995
Michael Crichton, *Jurassic Park*, 1990
James F. David, *Footprints of Thunder*, 1995
Penelope Banka Kreps, *Carnivores*, 1993
Richard Sanford, *Roadkill*, 1995

860

MICHAEL COX, Editor

Twelve Tales of the Supernatural

(New York: Oxford, 1997)

Story type: Anthology

Summary: One dozen stories by British writers, most featuring ghosts and most written before the middle of the twentieth century. Included are William Fryer Harvey's "The Tool," in which a man discovers through supernatural clues his unwitting complicity in a murder; E.F. Benson's "The Face," about a woman's inescapable rendezvous with a ghost from the past; and M.R. James's "Number 13," about the ghostly goings on in a forgotten room in a lodging house. A number of the stories feature ghostly revenges, including J.H. Riddell's "A Terrible Vengeance," Marjorie Bowen's "The Last Bouquet," and A.N.L. Munby's "A Christmas Game."

Other books by the same author:
The Oxford Book of Twentieth Century Ghost Stories, 1996
Victorian Ghost Stories: An Oxford Anthology, 1991 (R.A. Gilbert, co-editor)
The Oxford Book of English Ghost Stories, 1986 (R.A. Gilbert, co-editor)

Other books you might like:
R. Chetwynd-Hayes, *Gaslight Tales of Terror*, 1976
    editor

Richard Dalby, *The Mammoth Book of Ghost Stories*, 1990
  editor
Hugh Lamb, *Forgotten Tales of Terror*, 1978
  editor
Michel Parry, *Reign of Terror*, 1976
  editor

861

MICHAEL COX, Editor

Twelve Victorian Ghost Stories

(New York: Oxford, 1997)

Story type: Anthology; Ghost Story

Summary: Twelve stories of ghostly encounters written during the golden age of the classic ghost story. Included are Margaret Oliphant's "The Lady's Walk," about a haunted estate whose ghost warns people of impending tragedy; Rhoda Broughton's "Poor Pretty Bobby," a tale of love that endures beyond the grave; J. Sheridan Le Fanu's "Madam Crowl's Ghost," in which a woman's ghost reveals a gruesome secret she has taken with her to the grave; and Richard Marsh's "The Fifteen Man," about a ghostly rugby player.

Other books by the same author:
The Oxford Book of Twentieth Century Ghost Stories, 1996
Victorian Ghost Stories: An Oxford Anthology, 1991 (R.A. Gilbert, co-editor)
The Oxford Book of English Ghost Stories, 1986 (R.A. Gilbert, co-editor)

Other books you might like:
Everett F. Bleiler, *A Treasury of Victorian Ghost Stories*, 1981
  editor
Richard Dalby, *The Mammoth Book of Victorian and Edwardian Ghost Stories*, 1995
  editor
Richard Dalby, *The Virago Book of Victorian Ghost Stories*, 1988
  editor
Hugh Lamb, *Victorian Nightmares*, 1977
  editor
Michel Parry, *Reign of Terror*, 1976
  editor

862

PETER CROWTHER, Editor

Destination Unknown

(Clarkston, Georgia: White Wolf, 1997)

Story type: Anthology

Summary: Sixteen tales of horror, fantasy and science fiction, loosely linked by the theme of personal encounters with the unknown. Horror selections include Ramsey Campbell's "Between the Floors," in which a movie theater manager meets a grotesque doppelganger while away at a business convention; Christopher Fowler's "Wage Slaves," about the ultimate corporate environment that shapes workers to conform to its specifications; Bentley Little's "Monteith," in

which a man discovers the disturbing, inexplicable private life his wife leads while he is away at work; and Lisa Tuttle's "The Extra Hour," about a writer who becomes increasingly unable to separate from the fantasy world she creates in her fiction. Anne McCaffrey supplies the introduction.

Where it's reviewed:
Science Fiction Chronicle, November 1997, page 42

Other books by the same author:
Blue Motel, 1994
Touch Wood, 1993
Narrow Houses, 1992

Other books you might like:
George Hatch, *Souls in Pawn*, 1994
  editor
George Hatch, *Sinistre: An Anthology of Rituals*, 1993
  editor
Jessica Horsting, *Midnight Graffiti*, 1992
  James Van Hise, co-editor
Edward E. Kramer, *Dante's Disciples*, 1996
  Peter Crowther, co-editor
Edward E. Kramer, *Tombs*, 1995
  Peter Crowther, co-editor
John Pelan, *Darkside: Horror for the Next Millennium*, 1995
  editor
Carol Serling, *Return to the Twilight Zone*, 1994
  editor
Carol Serling, *Journeys to the Twilight Zone*, 1993
  editor

863

RICHIE TANKERSLEY CUSICK

Buffy the Vampire Slayer: The Harvest

(New York: Pocket/Archway, 1997)

Story type: Vampire Story
Series: Buffy the Vampire Slayer
Major character(s): Buffy Summers, Teenager, Vampire Hunter; Mr. Giles, Librarian; Henrich Joseph Nest, Vampire
Time period(s): 1990s (1997)
Locale(s): Sunnydale, California

Summary: Buffy Summers, a teenager endowed with a sensitivity to vampires, transfers to Sunnydale High School in time to tangle with vampire Master Henrich Joseph Nest, who has engineered the deaths of several students as part of the Harvest that will open the door between the world of mortals and vampires. Novelization based on the television series derived from the 1992 movie *Buffy the Vampire Slayer*.

Other books by the same author:
The Drifter, 1994
Buffy the Vampire Slayer, 1992
Vampire, 1991

Other books you might like:
Elvira, *Transylvania 90210*, 1996
  John Paragon, co-author
Joseph Locke, *Vampire Heart*, 1994
Christopher Pike, *The Last Vampire*, 1994
Nicholas Pine, *Night School*, 1994

L.J. Smith, *The Vampire Diaries*, 1992

M.P. DARE

Unholy Relics

(Ashcroft, British Columbia: Ash-Tree Press, 1997)

Story type: Collection; Ghost Story

Summary: Thirteen antiquarian ghost stories, intended to be in the tradition of M.R. James. Included are "The Haunted Drawers," about a dresser imbued with the spirit of a writer whose letters are hidden in it; "A Nun's Tragedy," in which an abbey is haunted by the ghost of nun walled-up there; "The Fatal Oak," in which commonplace objects made from the wood of a gibbet are endowed with the power to kill evil people; "Bring Out Your Dead," in which a skull stolen from an ossuary resurrects the black plague that killed its owner; and the title story, in which sacred relics of the dead are protected by animated skeletons. The original 1947 edition has been embellished with two essays, "Beyond the Veil" and "Ghosts I Have Met." Introduction by Reg Meuross.

Where it's reviewed:
Necrofile, Fall 1997, page 9

Other books you might like:
A.M. Burrage, *Some Ghost Stories*, 1927
Ingulphus, *Tedious Brief Tales of Granta and Gramarye*, 1919
  pseudonym of Arthur Gray
R.H. Malden, *Nine Ghosts*, 1943
A.N.L. Munby, *The Alabaster Hand and Other Ghost Stories*, 1949
L.T.C. Rolt, *Sleep No More*, 1948
E.G. Swain, *The Stoneground Ghost Tales*, 1912

ELLEN DATLOW, Editor
TERRI WINDLING, Co-Editor

The Year's Best Fantasy and Horror: Tenth Annual Collection

(New York: St. Martin's, 1997)

Story type: Anthology
Series: The Year's Best Fantasy and Horror

Summary: The most recent volume in this award-winning series reprints 39 stories and four poems from 1996, representative of the year's best fantasy and horror. Approximately half of the selections are horror and dark fantasy. Stand-out selections include Dennis Etchison's "The Dead Cop," a tale of grief and obsession set in riot-torn Los Angeles; Terry Lamsley's "Walking the Dog," in which a man discovers that his job includes walking his employer's pet monster for his nightly feedings; and Thomas Ligotti's "Teatro Grottesco," a tale of madness and illusion. Includes comprehensive introductory essays on the year's yield of horror and fantasy fiction, film and comics, and the annual necrology.

Where it's reviewed:
Kirkus, August 1, 1997, page 1167
Locus, August 1997, page 17
Necrofile, Fall 1997, page 1
Science Fiction Chronicle, November 1997, page 42

Other books by the same author:
Black Swan, White Raven, 1997
Ruby Slippers, Golden Tears, 1996
Black Thorn, White Rose, 1994
Snow White, Blood Red, 1993
The Year's Best Fantasy and Horror Series, 1988-1997

Other books you might like:
Lin Carter, *The Year's Best Fantasy Stories Series*, 1974-1980
  editor
Stephen Jones, *The Mammoth Book of Best New Horror 8*, 1997
  editor
Arthur W. Saha, *The Year's Best Fantasy Stories Series*, 1981-1988
  editor
Karl Edward Wagner, *The Year's Best Horror Series*, 1979-1994
  editor

JAMES F. DAVID

Fragments

(New York: Tor/Forge, 1997)

Story type: Ghost Story
Major character(s): Wes Martin, Psychologist; Elizabeth Foxworth, Social Worker; Gil Masters, Psychic
Time period(s): 1990s
Locale(s): University of Oregon, Oregon

Summary: An experiment to create a group consciousness from the minds of five idiot savants goes awry when the consciousness of a young girl brutally murdered in the house where they are staying "contaminates" the entity created. The situation is complicated further by the presence of a homicidal psychic who hopes to exploit the experiment for his own use.

Where it's reviewed:
Kirkus, May 15, 1997, page 737
Publishers Weekly, May 19, 1997 page 64

Other books by the same author:
Footprints of Thunder, 1995

Other books you might like:
Ramsey Campbell, *Incarnate*, 1983
Dean R. Koontz, *Strangers*, 1986
Al Sarrantonio, *House Haunted*, 1991
Theodore Sturgeon, *More than Human*, 1953
Chet Williamson, *Soulstorm*, 1986

867
DON DAVIS

The Gris-Gris Man
(New York: Turner, 1997)

Story type: Black Magic
Major character(s): Wade Broussard, Detective—Police; Rene Chauvin, Businessman; Alexandra Larsen, Editor
Time period(s): 1990s (1997)
Locale(s): New Orleans, Louisiana

Summary: Cajun police detective Wade Broussard turned his back on his voodoo upbringing when an encounter with Baron Samedi, Lord of the Graveyard, resulted in the deaths of several innocent victims during a routine crime investigation. Now a murder spree with voodoo overtones has forced Broussard to resurrect himself as *Le Blanc Houngan* in order to pursue a criminal who is using black magic as a front for drug smuggling.

Where it's reviewed:
Kirkus, March 1, 1997, page 336
Publishers Weekly, March 3, 1997, page 65

Other books you might like:
Alex Abella, *The Killing of the Saints*, 1991
Hugh B. Cave, *Shades of Evil*, 1982
Nicholas Conde, *The Religion*, 1982
Graham Masterton, *Rook*, 1996
Michael Reaves, *Voodoo Child*, 1998
Robert Weinberg, *The Black Lodge*, 1991

868
WALTER DE LA MARE

The Return
(Mineola, New York: Dover, 1997)

Story type: Possession
Major character(s): Arthur Lawford, Parent; Sheila Lawford, Young Woman (Arthur's wife); Grisel Herbert, Young Woman
Time period(s): 1920s
Locale(s): London, England

Summary: Drawn to the grave of Noiholas Sabathier, an eighteenth-century suicide, Arthur Lawford falls asleep on top of it and awakens with the man's features and irascible personality. Arthur struggles to understand his apparent supernatural possession and find a means of driving Sabathier from him to keep his life from falling apart. First published in 1920. Introduction by S.T. Joshi.

Other books by the same author:
The Wind Blows Over, 1936
On the Edge, 1930
The Connoisseur and Other Stories, 1923
The Riddle and Other Stories, 1923

Other books you might like:
Fred Chappell, *The Lodger*, 1993
H.B. Drake, *The Shadowy Thing*, 1928
H.P. Lovecraft, *The Case of Charles Dexter Ward*, 1943

Robert Louis Stevenson, *The Strange Case of Dr. Jekyll and Mr. Hyde*, 1886

869
AUGUST DERLETH

The Cthulhu Mythos
(New York: Barnes & Noble, 1997)

Story type: Collection

Summary: Omnibus volume of August Derleth's complete contributions to the Cthulhu Myhthos based on the work of H.P. Lovecraft. It includes the complete contents of Derleth's collection *The Mask of Cthulhu* (1958), his episodic novel. *Trail of Cthulhu* (1962), and six other stories, including the previously uncollected "Something from Out There," and "Ithaqua" and "The Thing That Walked on the Wind," both of which fold the Indian legend of the Wendigo into Lovecraft's pantheon of extradimensional monsters. Ramsey Campbell supplies an introduction.

Other books by the same author:
Dwellers in Darkness, 1976
Harrigan's File, 1975
Lonesome Places, 1962
Not Long for This World, 1948
Something Near, 1945

Other books you might like:
Robert Bloch, *The Early Fears*, 1994
Ramsey Campbell, *Cold Print*, 1993
Brian Lumley, *Dagon's Bell and Other Discords*, 1995
Clark Ashton Smith, *A Rendezvous in Averoigne*, 1989
Donald Wandrei, *Don't Dream*, 1997

870
PETER DICKINSON

The Lion Tamer's Daughter
(New York: Delacorte, 1997)

Story type: Collection; Young Adult

Summary: Four stories of fantasy and horror for young adult readers. In "Touch and Go," a young boy discovers a magical doorway into the past and befriends a girl who once lived in the house he now inhabits. "Checkers," about a young kidnap victim who so vividly imagines a make-believe companion that he wishes him into being, is one of several stories in which young protagonists confront supernaturally objectfied alter egos. The others are the title novella and "The Spring," both variations on the doppelganger theme.

Other books by the same author:
Merlin Dreams, 1988
Eva, 1988
Healer, 1983
The Changes: A Trilogy, 1975

Other books you might like:
Joan Aiken, *A Touch of Chill*, 1979
Joan Aiken, *A Fit of Shivers*, 1990
Penelope Lively, *Uninvited Ghosts and Other Stories*, 1984

Robert Westall, *In Camera and Other Stories*, 1993
Robert Westall, *The Call and Other Stories*, 1993

871

GARDNER DOZOIS, Editor

Dying for It: More Erotic Tales of Unearthly Love

(New York: Harper, 1997)

Story type: Anthology; Erotic Horror

Summary: Seventeen stories of dark love and obsession that draw from horror, fantasy and science fiction sources. Selections include Tanith Lee's "Cain," Ursula K. Le Guin's "Olders," Robert Silverberg's "Multiples," Pat Cadigan's "Another Story," Michael Bishop's "Yesterday's Hostage," Nancy Kress's "Johnny's So Long at the Fair," and Esther Friesner's "Silent Love."

Other books by the same author:
Modern Classics of Fantasy, 1997
Killing Me Softly, 1996
Modern Classic Short Novels of Science Fiction, 1994
Modern Classics of Science Fiction, 1992
The Year's Best Science Fiction, 1984-1997

Other books you might like:
Ellen Datlow, *Off Limits: Tales of Alien Sex*, 1996
  editor
Ellen Datlow, *Alien Sex*, 1990
  editor
Joseph Elder, *Eros in Orbit*, 1973
  editor
Jeff Gelb, *Hot Blood: Tales of Provocative Horror*, 1989
  Lonn Friend, co-editor
Thomas N. Scortia, *Strange Bedfellows: Sex and Science Fiction*, 1972
  editor
Michele Slung, *I Shudder at Your Touch*, 1991

872

DAVID DRAKE, Editor

A Century of Horror: 1970-1979

(New York: Michael J. Fine, 1997)

Story type: Anthology

Summary: The first of a projected series of anthologies presenting the best horror fiction of the century. The twenty-one stories gathered include Dennis Etchison's "It Only Comes Out at Night," about a highway rest stop haunted by a serial killer; Joyce Carol Oates's "Night-Side," a period tale of a skeptic in Victorian times whose encounter with the supernatural during a seance sparks his belief; Ramsey Campbell's "Mackintosh Willy," about a murdered hobo who gets his revenge on the children who tormented him; Karl Edward Wagner's "Sticks," an homage to the fiction of H.P. Lovecraft; Ted Klein's "The Events at Poroth Farm," about an alien invasion of a rural farm; and Richard Matheson's "Duel," about a showdown in the desert between a tractor

trailer and a car, later a suspensful made-for-TV film directed by Stephen Spielberg.

Other books by the same author:
Things Hunting Men, 1988
Men Hunting Things, 1988

Other books you might like:
Dennis Etchison, *The Complete Masters of Darkness*, 1991
  editor
Charles L. Grant, *The Best of Shadows*, 1988
  editor
David G. Hartwell, *The Dark Descent*, 1987
  editor
Kirby McCauley, *Dark Forces*, 1980
  editor
Stuart David Schiff, *The Best of Whispers*, 1994
  editor

873

TANNARIVE DUE

My Soul to Keep

(New York: HarperCollins, 1997)

Story type: Occult
Major character(s): David Wolde, Linguist; Jessica Jacobs-Wolde, Journalist; Kira Wolde, Child (David and Jessica's daughter)
Time period(s): 1990s (1997)
Locale(s): Miami, Florida

Summary: In the person of Dawit, David Wolde became a member of an Abyssinian immortality cult four and a half centuries ago. His intention to confer immortality on his current wife and daughter gains the attention of cult leaders who strictly limit membership and preserve their privacy, putting David and his family at risk of reprisal.

Where it's reviewed:
Book World, November 23, 1997, page 11
Cemetery Dance, Fall 1997, page 127
Kirkus Reviews, May 15, 1997, page 738
Locus, September 1997, page 17, 25
Publishers Weekly, June 2, 1997, page 55

Other books by the same author:
The Between, 1995

Other books you might like:
John Farris, *Sacrifice*, 1994
Dan Simmons, *Song of Kali*, 1985
Dan Simmons, *Carrion Comfort*, 1989
Harry Stine, *Infinity's Child*, 1997
Karen E. Taylor, *Bitter Blood*, 1994

874

OLIVIA HOWARD DUNBAR

The Shell of Sense

(Uncasville, Connecticut: Fawcett, 1997)

Story type: Collection

Summary: Four short tales of the supernatural written in the first two decades of the twentieth century and representing the author's complete output of weird fiction. In addition to the oft-anthologized title story, the volume includes ''The Long Chamber,'' in which a ghostly encounter awakens a woman to the misery of her loveless marriage; ''The Dream-Baby,'' in which a pair of spinsters become obsessively devoted to a child one imagines in her dreams; and ''The Sycamore,'' in which a tree serves as a protective muse to a starving painter and his family. Two essays by the author, ''The Decay of the Ghost in Fiction'' and ''The Present Status of the Ghost,'' are included. Edited by Jessica Amanda Salmonson and illustrated by Wendy Wees.

Other books you might like:
Gertrude Atherton, *The Bell in the Fog*, 1905
H.D. Everett, *The Death Mask and Other Ghosts*, 1920
Ellen Glasgow, *The Shadowy Third and Other Stories*, 1923
Charlotte Perkins-Gilman, *The Yellow Wallpaper*, 1901
Elkeanor Scott, *Randall's Round*, 1929
Mary E. Wilkins-Freeman, *The Wind in the Rosebush and Other Stories of the Supernatural*, 1903

875

LOIS DUNCAN

I Know What You Did Last Summer
(New York: Dell Laurel Leaf, 1997)

Story type: Psychological Suspense
Major character(s): Julie James, Teenager; Raymond Bronson, Teenager; Collingsworth Wilson, Young Man
Time period(s): 1970s (1973)
Locale(s): Silver Spring, New Mexico

Summary: On the eve of her graduation from high school, Julie James receives an anonymous note incriminating her in an incident the year before. Julie and her friends must own up to their complicity in the accidental death of a young boy or face the consequences of an unknown accuser who employs potentially deadly methods to extract the truth. Reprint of a young adult novel from 1973 to tie in with its film adaptation in 1997.

Other books by the same author:
Summer of Fear, 1986
Locked in Time, 1985
The Third Eye, 1984
The Stranger with My Face, 1981

Other books you might like:
Richie Tankersley Cusick, *The Mall*, 1992
Diane Hoh, *The Accident*, 1991
Christopher Pike, *Chain Letter*, 1986
R.L. Stine, *Fear Street: The Wrong Number*, 1990

876

LOIS DUNCAN, Editor

Night Terrors: Stories of Shadow and Substance
(New York: Simon & Schuster/Aladdin, 1997)

Story type: Anthology; Young Adult

Summary: A renowned writer of horror thrillers for young adult readers assembles 11 tales of suspense and supernatural horror original to the volume. Highlights include Joan Lowery Nixon's ''The Dark Beast of Death,'' a murder mystery involving a teenage girl gang; Annette Curtis Klause's ''The Bogey Man,'' in which a young boy discovers to his dismay why he should have heeded his strict grandmother's injunction not to go down into her cellar; Alane Ferguson's ''Satan's Shadow,'' about a young girl who suffers horrendous nightmares when she turns in her best friend for parricide; and Chris Lynch's ''Bearing Paul,'' about a young boy convinced that he sees the body of his cousin moving in his coffin. Other contributors include Joan Aiken, Theodore Taylor, Patricia Windsor, Richard Peck, Harry Mazer, Norma Fox Mazer, and Madge Harrah. First published in 1996.

Other books you might like:
A. Finnis, *Bone Meal: Seven More Tales of Terror*, 1994
   editor
A. Finnis, *The Cat Dogs and Other Tales of Horror*, 1994
   editor
William Mayne, *Supernatural Stories*, 1996
   editor
Dennis Pepper, *The Young Oxford Book of Ghost Stories*, 1994
   editor
T. Pines, *Thirteen*, 1991
   editor
Susan Price, *Horror Stories*, 1995
Robert Westall, *Ghost Stories*, 1993
   editor

877

STEFAN DZIEMIANOWICZ, Editor
ROBERT WEINBERG, Co-Editor
MARTIN H. GREENBERG, Co-Editor

Girl's Night Out
(New York: Barnes & Noble, 1997)

Story type: Anthology; Vampire Story

Summary: Twenty-nine classic and contemporary tales featuring female vampires. Outstanding selections include E.F. Benson's ''Mrs. Amworth,'' about a vampire who preys on the aristocrats of Edwardian England; Chet Williamson's ''To Feel Another's Woe,'' about a stage actress who feeds on the adulation of her audience; Fritz Leiber's ''The Girl with the Hungry Eyes,'' in which an advertising model subsists on the desires of the consumer public; Clark Ashton Smith's ''The End of the Story,'' about a vampire who lies in wait for visitors to her ruined castle in medevial France; and

Joanna Russ's "My Dear Emily," which equates a young girl's nascent vampirism with her awakening sexual identity.

Other books by the same author:
Rivals of Dracula, 1996
100 Tiny Tales of Terror, 1996
100 Vicious Little Vampire Stories, 1995
Between Time and Terror, 1995
Weird Vampire Tales, 1992

Other books you might like:
Victoria Brownworth, *Night Bites: Vampire Stories by Women*, 1996
  editor
Martin H. Greenberg, *Vamps*, 1987
  Charles G. Waugh, co-editor
Barbara Hambly, *Sisters of the Night*, 1995
  Martin Greenberg, co-editor
Pam Keesey, *Daughters of Darkness: Lesbian Vampire Stories*, 1993
  editor
Pam Keesey, *Darker Angels: Lesbian Vampire Stories*, 1993
  editor

878

HARLAN ELLISON

Slippage
(New York: Houghton-Mifflin, 1997)

Story type: Collection

Summary: Collection of twenty-one selections that mix fantasy, horror and science fiction in provocative explorations of social and philosophical themes. Included is "Mephisto in Onyx," a tale of racial stereotypes and victimization in which a black psychic is accused of crimes committed by a white serial killer. "Keyboard" is a variant on the vampire theme, about a computer keyboard that drains life from its users, and "She's a Young Thing and Cannot Leave Her Mother," a tale of love and nurturing among a family of cannibals. "Crazy as a Soup Sandwich," the script for a deal-with-the-devil story, was produced as an episode of the revived "Twilight Zone" television series. A signed, limited hardcover edition published by Mark Ziesing contains additional contents.

Where it's reviewed:
Hellnotes, October 24, 1997, page 2
Kirkus, July 15, 1997, page 1063
Publishers Weekly, July 28, 1997, page 55

Other books by the same author:
Angry Candy, 1988
The Essential Ellison, 1987
Stalking the Nightmare, 1982
Shatterday, 1980
Deathbird Stories, 1975

Other books you might like:
Gary A. Braunbeck, *Things Left Behind*, 1997
Jonathan Carroll, *The Panic Hand*, 1996
Richard T. Chizmar, *Midnight Promises*, 1996
Brian Hodge, *The Convulsion Factory*, 1996
Elizabeth Massie, *Shadow Dreams*, 1996

David Niall Wilson, *The Fall of the House of Escher and Other Illusions*, 1995

879

ELVIRA

JOHN PARAGON, Co-Author

Camp Vamp
(New York: Boulevard, 1997)

Story type: Satire
Series: Elvira, Mistress of the Dark
Major character(s): Elvira, Young Woman; Chloe, Teenager; Ranger Dan, Ranger (park)
Time period(s): 1990s (1997)
Locale(s): Beaver Hills, California

Summary: Elvira, television's ditzy Mistress of the Dark, is coerced into chaperoning a camp out for the Happy Campers club of Beaver Hill high school. Spooky campfire stories, scary misadventures and countless bad puns follow when Elvira and her ruggedness-challenged pack of teenage valley girls find themselves stalked by the legendary Beast of Beaver Hills.

Other books by the same author:
Transylvania 90210, 1996

Other books you might like:
Richie Tankersley Cusick, *Buffy the Vampire Slayer*, 1992
Lois Duncan, *Summer of Fear*, 1990
Joan Lowery Nixon, *The Stalker*, 1995
Christopher Pike, *Weekend*, 1986
R.L. Stine, *Fear Street: All-Night Party*, 1997

880

DENNIS ETCHISON

Double Edge
(New York: Dell, 1997)

Story type: Psychological Suspense; Serial Killer
Major character(s): Jenny Marlow, Writer (screenwriter); Lee Marlow, Photographer; Walter Heim, Agent
Time period(s): 1990s (1997)
Locale(s): Los Angeles, California

Summary: Shortly after Jenny and Lee Marlow write a script for a revisionist television movie that will present Lizzie Borden as a victim rather than a cold-blooded parricide, a series of gruesome murders begins decimating their circle of Hollywood friends and acquaintances. Are they being stalked by a psychopath, or has their script resurrected the ghost of Lizzie herself?

Where it's reviewed:
Publishers Weekly, November 11, 1996 page 72

Other books by the same author:
California Gothic, 1995
Shadow Man, 1994
Darkside, 1986

Other books you might like:
Robert Bloch, *Psycho II*, 1982

Ehren M. Ehly, *Star Prey*, 1992
Stephen King, *The Dark Half*, 1992
Richard Christian Matheson, *Created By*, 1993

881

DAVID A. FARROW

Root of All Evil
(Charleston, South Carolina: Wyrick, 1997)

Story type: Black Magic; Mystery
Major character(s): Harry Holmes, Detective—Police; Andrew Rutledge, Writer; Willy Huger, Political Figure
Time period(s): 1990s (1997); 1950s (1959)
Locale(s): Charleston, South Carolina

Summary: A serial killer is stalking women in Charleston, cutting out their hearts and leaving roots associated with voodoo herbalism entwined in their hair. Detective Harry Holmes's investigations bring him into contact with Andrew Rutledge, who experienced psychic links to several of the murder victims, and a trail of larceny and corruption that extends back through Rutledge's family and the family of his friend over 40 years. A first novel.

Where it's reviewed:
Publishers Weekly, March 17, 1997, page 79

Other books you might like:
Nancy A. Collins, *Tempter*, 1990
Don Davis, *The Gris-Gris Man*, 1997
D.J. Donaldson, *Blood on the Bayou*, 1991
John Farris, *All Heads Turn When the Hunt Goes By*, 1972
Karen Hall, *Dark Debts*, 1996
Robert R. McCammon, *Usher's Passing*, 1984

882

GHERBOD FLEMING

The Devil's Advocate
(Clarkston, Georgia: White Wolf, 1997)

Story type: Vampire Story
Series: Trilogy of the Blood Curse
Major character(s): Owain ap Ieuan, Vampire; J. Benison Hodge, Vampire; Kendall Jackson, Vampire
Locale(s): Atlanta, Georgia (alternate world)

Summary: A plague is killing vampires in the World of Darkness, raising suspicions among warring vampire clans that each is responsible. As the Masquerade that ensures their peaceful co-existence crumbles, anarchy begins to prevail and Owain must decide which clan to support. Set in the World of Darkness, a fantasy role-playing game world where human beings and creatures of the supernatural co-exist.

Other books you might like:
Don Bassingthwaite, *As One Dead*, 1996
   Nancy Kilpatrick, co-author
Nancy A. Collins, *A Dozen Black Roses*, 1996
Brian Herbert, *Blood on the Sun*, 1996
   Marie Landis, co-author
Robert Weinberg, *Bloodwar*, 1995
Robert Weinberg, *Unholy Allies*, 1996

Robert Weinberg, *The Unbidden*, 1996

883

ELIZABETH FORREST

Bright Shadow
(New York: DAW, 1997)

Story type: Wild Talents
Major character(s): Jim McGruder, FBI Agent; Vernon Spenser, Mechanic; Gunnar Davidsen, Hunter
Time period(s): 1990s
Locale(s): Badger Mountain, Arizona

Summary: Vernon Spenser is in the right place at the right time to save little Jennifer from a mismanaged DEA assault on the New Hope Righteous Eternal compound. But he quickly finds he was in the wrong place at the wrong time when he and Jennifer, who has been bred for her psychic powers as a tool of obsessively righteous cult leader Gunnar Davidsen, become the object of a manhunt by both the government and the cult.

Where it's reviewed:
Locus, June 1997, page 27
Science Fiction Chronicle, October 1997, page 44

Other books by the same author:
Killjoy, 1996
Death Watch, 1995
Dark Tide, 1993
Phoenix Fire, 1992

Other books you might like:
Randall Boyll, *Chiller*, 1992
Douglas Clegg, *Dark of the Eye*, 1994
Daniel H. Gower, *The Orpheus Process*, 1992
Stephen King, *Firestarter*, 1980
Dean R. Koontz, *Sole Survivor*, 1997

884

LEWIS GANNETT

Millennium: Gehenna
(New York: Harper, 1997)

Story type: Serial Killer
Series: Millennium
Major character(s): Frank Black, FBI Agent (former); Peter Watt, Spy; Dylan, Young Man
Time period(s): 1990s (1997)
Locale(s): San Francisco, California

Summary: Ex-FBI agent Frank Black and agents of the Millennium Group track the activities of Gehenna International, a death cult that brainwashes its members with LSD-induced visions of supernatural doom and immolates its enemies with the fires of Gehenna. Novelization of the Fox television series ''Millennium,'' about a group of special agents who work covertly to solve crimes inspired by the dark side of the coming millennium.

Other books by the same author:
Magazine Beach, 1996

Horror

The Living One, 1993

Other books you might like:
Kevin J. Anderson, *The X-Files: Ruins*, 1996
Charles L. Grant, *The X-Files: Goblins*, 1994
Elizabeth Hand, *Millennium: The Frenchman*, 1997
Jeff Rice, *The Night Strangler*, 1974
Jeff Rice, *The Night Stalker*, 1973

885

S. ANTHONY GARDNER

A Few Bricks Shy

(Syracuse, New York: Vampire Dan's Story Emporium, 1997)

Story type: Collection

Summary: Three stories and one poem on a variety of supernatural and nonsupernatural horror themes. ''Campfire'' is a variation on a spooky campfire tale, ''Rod and Gun'' a tale of murder and dark deeds, and ''Traffic Accident'' a tale of an ironic twist of fate. Issued as a signed limited edition chapbook. Illustrated by Kevin Butterfield and Peter Sieburg.

Other books you might like:
S. Darnbrook Colson, *People of the Night*, 1994
Randy Fox, *Not Broken, Not Belonging*, 1994
Gary Jonas, *Nice Guys Finish Last*, 1997
Gary Jonas, *By Death Abused*, 1990
Jack Remick, *Terminal Weird*, 1996
Wayne Allen Sallee, *Pain Grin*, 1993
Don Webb, *A Spell for the Fulfillment of Desire*, 1996

886

HENRY GARFIELD

Room 13

(New York: St. Martin's, 1997)

Story type: Haunted House; Werewolf Story
Major character(s): Marilou McCormick, Teacher (high school english); Cyrus ''Moondog'' Nygerski, Driver (school bus), Werewolf; Robert Rickard, Maintenance Worker (janitor)
Time period(s): 1990s (1997)
Locale(s): Julian, California

Summary: Progressive English teacher Marilou McCormick inherits a classroom haunted by the ghost of a former teacher who forces students and teachers of the Drew Bailey Memorial High School to re-enact situations from the classic works of literature he taught. Her only hope is Moondog Nygerski, a former journalist turned werewolf, whose condition makes him sensitive to psychic phenomena. A sequel to the author's first novel Moondog.

Where it's reviewed:
Kirkus, June 1, 1997, page 822

Other books by the same author:
Moondog, 1995

Other books you might like:
Ed Kelleher, *The School*, 1991
    Harriette Vidal, co-author

R.L. Stine, *Superstitious*, 1995
Manly Wade Wellman, *The School of Darkness*, 1995
T.M. Wright, *The School*, 1990

887

SUSAN M. GARRETT

Forever Knight: Intimations of Mortality

(New York: Berkley/Boulevard, 1997)

Story type: Vampire Story
Series: Forever Knight
Major character(s): Nicholas Knight, Detective—Homicide, Vampire; Natalie Lambert, Doctor (forensic pathologist); Tracy Vetter, Detective—Homicide
Time period(s): 1990s (1997)
Locale(s): Toronto, Ontario, Canada

Summary: Under the influence of a charmed doll and his own nostalgia for life as a mortal, 800-year-old vampire Nicholas Knight has dreams of an alternate world in which he is part of a minority of mortals living in a civilization of vampires. The dreams eventually begin to seep into reality and adversely affect Knight's work as a detective. Based on the cable television series *Forever Knight*.

Other books you might like:
Vincent Courtney, *Vampire Beat*, 1991
P.N. Elrod, *Bloodlist*, 1990
Laurell K. Hamilton, *Guilty Pleasures*, 1993
Tanya Huff, *Blood Price*, 1991
Roxanne Longstreet, *Cold Kiss*, 1995
Anne Rice, *The Tale of the Body Thief*, 1992
Karen E. Taylor, *Blood Secrets*, 1994

888

RAY GARTON

Live Girls

(Baltimore: CD Publications, 1997)

Story type: Vampire Story
Major character(s): Davey Owen, Editor; Anya, Dancer (exotic), Vampire; Walter Benedek, Journalist
Time period(s): 1980s
Locale(s): New York, New York

Summary: Converted into a vampire during a performance by vampire show girls at a Times Square skin show, Davey Owen pursues his vampire initiator, Anya, and is indoctrinated into the vampire night life of Manhattan. First hardcover printing of a novel published as a paperback original in 1987.

Where it's reviewed:
Locus, November 1997, page 23

Other books by the same author:
Shackled, 1997
Dark Channel, 1992
Lot Lizards, 1991
Trade Secrets, 1991
The New Neighbor, 1991
Crucifax Autumn, 1988

Other books you might like:
Poppy Z. Brite, *Lost Souls*, 1993
Michael Cecilione, *Domination*, 1993
Michael Cecilione, *Thirst*, 1996
Nancy A. Collins, *Sunglasses After Dark*, 1990
John Skipp, *The Light at the End*, 1986
　Craig Spector, co-author
Karen E. Taylor, *Blood Secrets*, 1994

889

RAY GARTON

Shackled

(New York: Bantam, 1997)

Story type: Mystery
Major character(s): Bentley Noble, Journalist; Lacey Ryan, Teenager; Stephen Colloway, Writer (true crime)
Time period(s): 1990s (1997)
Locale(s): Vallejo, California

Summary: As part of his newspaper's plan to soften its crude tabloid image, Global Inquisitor reporter Bentley Noble pursues the human-interest angle of the recent disappearance of several children in the town of Vallejo. His investigations uncover a plot involving high-ranking town officials and professional personnel to indoctrinate the children into a Satanic cult and sell them into sexual slavery through cult networks on the Internet.

Other books by the same author:
Dark Channel, 1992
The New Neighbor, 1991
Lot Lizards, 1991
Trade Secrets, 1991
Crucifax Autumn, 1988

Other books you might like:
Ric Reed, *Obsessed*, 1993
John Saul, *Darkness*, 1991
John Shirley, *Wetbones*, 1992
Guy N. Smith, *Dead End*, 1996

890

RAY GARTON

Website

(Burton, Michigan: Subterranean Press, 1997)

Story type: Psychological Suspense
Major character(s): Martin Boyle, Worker (lawn care); Heather Boyle, Housewife (Martin's wife); Fiona Webb, Doctor (psychiatrist)
Time period(s): 1990s (1997)
Locale(s): United States

Summary: Martin Boyle discovers that someone has created a computer website for him without his knowledge and that it provides illuminating insights into his life that even he doesn't know. Is something supernatural afoot, or is Martin not as reliable a narrator as he seems? Signed limited edition short story chapbook.

Other books by the same author:
Shackled, 1997
Pieces of Hate, 1996
Dark Channel, 1992
Lot Lizards, 1991
Methods of Madness, 1990

Other books you might like:
Richard T. Chizmar, *Blood Brothers*, 1997
Daniel H. Gower, *The Orpheus Process*, 1992
Dean R. Koontz, *Dark Rivers of the Heart*, 1994
Dean R. Koontz, *Demon Seed*, 1973
Thomas F. Monteleone, *Between Floors*, 1997

891

R. PATRICK GATES

Jumpers

(New York: Dell, 1997)

Story type: Wild Talents
Major character(s): Anna Wheaton, Child; Dee Dee Blaine, Secretary; Kevin Lucier, Veteran
Time period(s): 1990s (1997)
Locale(s): Greenfield, New Hampshire; Missoula, Montana

Summary: A group of ''jumpers''—people whose near-death experiences have endowed them with the ability to shift to alternative worlds where their deaths have not occurred—struggle to help one another and thwart the Shadow Monster, a composite of dead souls that pursues them relentlessly in an effort to absorb them.

Other books by the same author:
Deathwalker, 1996
Tunnelvision, 1991
Grimm Memorials, 1990
Fear, 1988

Other books you might like:
Tannarive Due, *The Between*, 1995
Rick Hautala, *Beyond the Shroud*, 1996
Stephen King, *Insomnia*, 1994
Dean R. Koontz, *Hideaway*, 1993
Daniel Quinn, *Dreamer*, 1988

892

JEFF GELB
MICHAEL GARRETT, Co-Author

Hot Blood: Crimes of Passion

(New York: Pocket, 1997)

Story type: Anthology; Erotic Horror
Series: Hot Blood

Summary: Fourteen tales of erotic horror fill out the ninth volume in this long-running anthology series. Selections include Greg Kihn's ''The Great White Light,'' in which free love and great acid introduces two young men to a bizarre counterculture cult in the 1960s; Tom Piccirilli's ''Curs,'' which explores the sexual politics of a thankless marriage and an adulterous relationship; and Melanie Tem's ''Loving Delia,'' in which a woman's sexual passion becomes ob-

Horror

jectified and personified. Ramsey Campbell, Lawrence Block and Brian Lumley are represented with reprinted stories.

Other books by the same author:
Hot Blood: Kiss and Kill, 1997
Hot Blood: Fear the Fever, 1996
Hot Blood: Seeds of Fear, 1995
Hot Blood: Stranger by Night, 1995
Hot Blood: Deadly After Dark, 1994

Other books you might like:
Nancy A. Collins, *Dark Love*, 1995
    Edward E. Kramer and Martin H. Greenberg, co-editors
Ellen Datlow, *Alien Sex*, 1990
    editor
Ellen Datlow, *Little Deaths*, 1995
    editor
Gardner Dozois, *Dying for It: More Erotic Tales of Unearthly Love*, 1997
    editor
Michel Parry, *Devil's Kisses*, 1976
    editor
Michele Slung, *I Shudder at Your Touch*, 1993
    editor
Michele Slung, *Shudder Again*, 1995
    editor

893

JEFF GELB
MICHAEL GARRETT, Co-Author

Hot Blood: Kiss and Kill
(New York: Pocket, 1997)

Story type: Anthology; Erotic Horror
Series: Hot Blood

Summary: Sixteen tales of erotic horror, all original to the eighth volume in this long-running series. Selections include Thomas Tessier's "La Mourante," in which a jaded man develops an insatiable passion for necrophilia; Nancy Holder's "Bonus Notches," in which the competitiveness between two sexually active women reaches to absurd heights; and Ray Garton's "Hair of the Dog," where a philandering husband's night of debauchery leads to a murder mystery with two corpses. Brian Hodge, Graham Masterton, and Gary Brandner are among the other contributors.

Where it's reviewed:
Locus, June 1997, page 27

Other books by the same author:
Hot Blood: Crimes of Passion, 1997
Hot Blood: Fear the Fever, 1996
Hot Blood: Seeds of Fear, 1995
Hot Blood: Stranger by Night, 1995
Hot Blood: Deadly after Dark, 1994

Other books you might like:
Nancy A. Collins, *Dark Love*, 1995
    Edward E. Kramer and Martin H. Greenberg, co-editors
Ellen Datlow, *Alien Sex*, 1990
    editor
Ellen Datlow, *Little Deaths*, 1995
    editor

Gardner Dozois, *Dying for It: More Erotic Tales of Unearthly Love*, 1997
    editor
Michel Parry, *Devil's Kisses*, 1976
    editor
Michele Slung, *I Shudder at Your Touch*, 1993
    editor
Michele Slung, *Shudder Again*, 1995
    editor

894

TESS GERRITSEN

Life Support
(New York: Pocket, 1997)

Story type: Mystery
Major character(s): Toby Harper, Doctor (emergency room); Carl Wallenberg, Doctor (endocrinologist); Daniel Dvorak, Doctor (medical examiner)
Time period(s): 1990s (1997)
Locale(s): Boston, Massachusetts

Summary: Physician Toby Harper investigates when two patients from the upscale Brant Hill retirement home show up at her hospital with symptoms that suggest fatal cases of Creutzfeldt-Jakob Disease. Her suspicion that the patients contracted the disease from infected tissue used in rejuvenation experiments is met with swift reprisal by greedy conspirators, who attempt to ruin her credibility and her life.

Where it's reviewed:
Kirkus Reviews, June 15, 1997, page 894
Publishers Weekly, June 23, 1997, page 67

Other books by the same author:
Harvest, 1996

Other books you might like:
Robin Cook, *Coma*, 1977
Michael Crichton, *The Terminal Man*, 1972
Patrick Lynch, *Omega*, 1997
Harry Stein, *Infinity's Child*, 1997
F. Paul Wilson, *The Select*, 1994

895

AMITAV GHOSH

The Calcutta Chromosome
(New York: Avon, 1996)

Story type: Mystery
Major character(s): Antar, Computer Expert (Data analyst); L. Murugan, Computer Expert (Data analyst); Urmila, Journalist
Time period(s): 1990s (1995)
Locale(s): New York, New York; Calcutta, India

Summary: Antar, a data programmer and analyst for the nonprofit global health consulting agency Lifewatch, traces a glitch on his computer program to L. Murugan, a colleague who disappeared in 1995 while researching inconsistencies in the Ronald Ross's study of malaria in 1898. His exploration uncovers clues to a global, and possibly cosmic conspiracy,

that is directing humanity to a foreordained destiny. First published in India in 1995.

Where it's reviewed:
Publishers Weekly, August 11, 1997, page 383

Other books by the same author:
In an Antique Land, 1992
Shadow Lines, 1988

Other books you might like:
Clive Barker, *The Great and Secret Show*, 1989
Umberto Eco, *Foucault's Pendulum*, 1989
Theodore Roszak, *Flicker*, 1991

896
ROBERT GIRARDI

Vaporetto 13
(New York: Delacorte, 1997)

Story type: Ghost Story
Major character(s): Jack Squires, Trader (currency); Caterina Vendramin, Young Woman; Rinio Donato, Trader (currency)
Time period(s): 1990s (1997)
Locale(s): Venice, Italy

Summary: While working in Venice, money broker Jack Squires falls in love with the beautiful Caterina, a mysterious descendant of one of the city's oldest families who has a more than mortal attachment to Italy's splendid past. Under Caterina's influence, Jack sees the superficiality of his life to date and undergoes a spiritual and psychic transformation.

Where it's reviewed:
New York Times Book Review, November 30, 1997, page 20

Other books by the same author:
The Pirate's Daughter, 1996
Madeleine's Ghost, 1995

Other books you might like:
Ramsey Campbell, *Ancient Images*, 1989
Orson Scott Card, *Homebody*, 1998
Dennis McFarland, *A Face at the Window*, 1997
Peter Straub, *Mrs. God*, 1990
T.M. Wright, *The Island*, 1988

897
CHRISTOPHER GOLDEN
MIKE MIGNOLA, Illustrator

Hellboy: The Lost Army
(Milwaukie, Oregon: Dark Horse, 1997)

Story type: Ancient Evil Unleashed
Series: Hellboy
Major character(s): Hellboy, Supernatural Being; Anastasia Branfield, Archaeologist; Michael Creaghan, Military Personnel (soldier)
Time period(s): 1990s
Locale(s): Great Sand Sea, Egypt

Summary: Novel featuring Mike Mignola's graphic novel superhero Hellboy, a creature of evil summoned by Nazi

dabblings in black magic who has since become a benevolent superhero employed by the Bureau for Paranormal Research and Defense. Hellboy is summoned to investigate the disappearance of an archaeological team from the border between Libya and Egypt, where mass disappearances have occurred over the centuries. In a lost world accessed through a nearby oasis, he discovers the mystery is the work of the ancient priest Hazred, who seeks a vessel for the return of the ancient Sumerian sorceror, Mar-Ti-Ku.

Other books by the same author:
X-Men: Mutant Empire, 1996
Angel Souls and Devil Hearts, 1995
Of Saints and Shadows, 1994

Other books you might like:
Campbell Black, *Raiders of the Lost Ark*, 1981
Edgar Rice Burroughs, *At the Earth's Core*, 1922
Joe R. Lansdale, *Tarzan: The Lost Adventure*, 1996
    Edgar Rice Burroughs, co-author
A. Merritt, *The Moon Pool*, 1919

898
GARY GOSHGARIAN

The Stone Circle
(New York: Donald I. Fine, 1997)

Story type: Ancient Evil Unleashed
Major character(s): Peter Van Zandt, Archaeologist; Constance Lambert, Teacher; Andy Van Zandt, Child
Time period(s): 1990s (1997)
Locale(s): Kingdom Head Island, Massachusetts

Summary: Archeologist Peter van Zandt finds evidence of a pre-Columbian druid settlement on an island in Boston harbor. The island is imbued with the spirit of Brigid Mocnessa, a druid witch, who masquerades as the spirit of Peter's beloved dead wife to persuade him to perform the blood sacrifice needed to revive the island's pagan heritage.

Where it's reviewed:
Publishers Weekly, July 21, 1997, page 186

Other books by the same author:
Rough Beast, 1995
Atlantis Fire, 1993

Other books you might like:
Joe Citro, *Dark Twilight*, 1990
Douglas Clegg, *Goat Dance*, 1989
Brent Monahan, *The Uprising*, 1992
Patrick Whalen, *Out of the Night*, 1990

899
CHARLES L. GRANT

Symphony
(New York: Tor/Forge, 1997)

Story type: Apocalyptic Horror; Small Town Horror
Series: Millennium Quartet
Major character(s): Casey Chisolm, Religious (minster); Stan Hogan, Drifter; Helen Gable, Waiter/Waitress

Horror

Time period(s): 1990s (1996)
Locale(s): Maple Landing, New Jersey

Summary: A plague of ominous portents in the small town of Maple Landing, and the Reverend Casey Chisholm's sudden discovery of his miraculous healing powers, dovetail with the nationwide swath of death and destruction wrought by a carload of vagrants en route to the town for an apocalyptic showdown between Good and Evil. This is the first of a projected quartet of novels built upon millenial themes.

Where it's reviewed:
Cemetery Dance, spring 1997, page 117
Kirkus, December 15, 1996, page 1754
Publishers Weekly, January 13, 1996, page 55

Other books by the same author:
In the Mood, 1998
Raven, 1995
Jackals, 1994
Something Stirs, 1991
Stunts, 1990

Other books you might like:
Richard Bachman, *The Regulators*, 1996
Stephen King, *The Dead Zone*, 1979
Bentley Little, *The Revelation*, 1989
Elizabeth Massie, *The Sineater*, 1992
Thomas F. Monteleone, *The Blood of the Lamb*, 1992

900

CHARLES L. GRANT

The World of Darkness: Watcher

(New York: Harper, 1997)

Story type: Werewolf Story
Series: The World of Darkness: Werewolf
Major character(s): Richard Turpin, FBI Agent, Werewolf; Joanne Minster, Police Officer; Miles Blanchard, Werewolf
Time period(s): 1990s (1997)
Locale(s): Lookout Mountain, Tennessee

Summary: A rogue werewolf is slaughtering humans in the Blue Ridge Mountains, threatening to break the Veil that separates humans from supernatural creatures in the World of Darkness and reveal the secret of the 13 tribes of the Garou. Werewolf Richard Turpin is assigned to work with human partner Joanne Minster and bring the monster to bay, without giving away his werewolf identity. Set in a fantasy role-playing world.

Where it's reviewed:
Science Fiction Chronicle, November 1997, page 39

Other books by the same author:
The X-Files: Whirlwind, 1996
The X-Files: Goblins, 1995
Jackals, 1994
Raven, 1993
Something Stirs, 1991

Other books you might like:
Don Bassingthwaite, *Such Pain*, 1995
Richard Lee Byers, *Netherworld*, 1995

Edo Van Belkom, *Wyrm Wolf*, 1995
Stuart Von Allmen, *Conspicuous Consumption*, 1995

901

MURIEL GRAY

Furnace

(New York: Doubleday, 1997)

Story type: Black Magic
Major character(s): Josh Spiller, Truck Driver; Nelly MacFarlane, Political Figure (town councillor); Griffin MacFarlane, Teenager
Time period(s): 1990s (1997)
Locale(s): Furnace, Virginia

Summary: After an upsetting accident in the small town of Furnace, where he claims he saw a town leader push a child in front of his truck, Josh Spiller can't shake the feeling that he is being pursued by something dreadful. Josh soon discovers the town is populated with the descendants of alchemists who perform ritual sacrifice and that he has been passed runes, a parchment with an invocation to fire demon that he must pass "willingly but unknowingly" back to the person who passed it to him if he is to avoid a horrible death. The novel is a variation on M. R. James's classic story, "Casting the Runes."

Where it's reviewed:
Publishers Weekly, September 22, 1997, page 72

Other books by the same author:
The Trickster, 1994

Other books you might like:
Ramsey Campbell, *Obsession*, 1985
Christopher Fowler, *Rune*, 1990
Charles L. Grant, *Hour of the Oxrun Dead*, 1977
Bernard Taylor, *Evil Intent*, 1994

902

MARTIN H. GREENBERG, Editor

Haunted Houses: The Greatest Stories

(New York: Michael J. Fine, 1997)

Story type: Anthology; Haunted House
Summary: Sixteen classic and contemporary stories of haunted houses. Included are H.P. Lovecraft's "The Rats in the Walls," in which a man discovers the influence of his cannibal ancestors is still active in his family mansion; Joyce Carol Oates's "The Doll," in which a woman endures a bizarre encounter in a house that resembles a doll house she owned as a child; Bram Stoker's "The Judge's House," in which new tenants of a house haunted by an evil judge come to a dismal end; William F. Nolan's "Dark Winner," about a man who visits his childhood home and finds it haunted by his childhood self; and Robert Bloch's "Lizzie Borden Took an Axe," about a woman possessed by the spirit of axe murderess Lizzie Borden.

Other books by the same author:
Vampires: The Greatest Stories, 1997

A Taste for Blood, 1992

Other books you might like:
Kathryn Cramer, *The Architecture of Fear*, 1987
  Peter Pautz, co-editor
Kathryn Cramer, *Walls of Fear*, 1990
  editor
Peter Straub, *Peter Straub's Ghosts*, 1995
  editor
Gahan Wilson, *Gahan Wilson's The Ultimate Haunted House*, 1996
  editor

903

MARTIN H. GREENBERG, Editor

Vampires: The Greatest Stories

(New York: Michael J. Fine, 1997)

Story type: Anthology; Vampire Story

Summary: Fifteen vampire stories by some of the best-known names in horror and fantasy. Included are Eric Lustbader's "In Darkness, Angels," set in a Gothic castle inhabited by vampire siblings; Karl Edward Wagner's "Beyond Any Measure," a fusion of the ghost and vampire story; David Drake's "Something Had to Be Done," about a vampire that haunts the battlefields of Vietnam; Robert R. McCammon's "The Miracle Mile," which takes place in a future where vampires have overrun the world; Dan Simmons's "Shave and Haircut, Two Bites," which explores the iconography of the local barbershop in terms of vampirism; and Robert Bloch's "The Bat Is My Brother," a first person account of a man rising from the dead as a vampire.

Other books by the same author:
Haunted Houses: The Greatest Stories, 1997
A Taste for Blood, 1992

Other books you might like:
Ellen Datlow, *Blood Is Not Enough*, 1989
  editor
Stephen Jones, *The Mammoth Book of Vampires*, 1992
  editor
Alan Ryan, *Vampires: Two Centuries of Great Vampire Stories*, 1987
  editor
Leonard Wolf, *Blood Thirst: 100 Years of Vampire Fiction*, 1997
  editor

904

PETER HAINING, Editor

Great Irish Tales of Horror

(New York: Barnes & Noble, 1997)

Story type: Anthology

Summary: Twenty-four stories by Irish authors and with Irish settings. Included are Elizabeth Bowen's "Happy Autumn Fields," in which an imagined world takes on reality for a woman; M.P. Shiel's "The Bride," in which the corpse of a jilted woman enacts a gruesome revenge on the wedding night

of her intended lover; Vincent O'Sullivan's "Will," in which strength of will animates a corpse; and L.A.G. Strong's "Danse Macabre," in which a man discovers that his dancing partner is a ghost. Also included are stories by Wiliam Trevor, Neil Jordan, George Bernard Shaw, Sax Rohmer, and Brian Moore. First published in England in 1995.

Other books by the same author:
Tales From the Rogues Gallery, 1994
Great Irish Tales of the Unimaginable, 1994
Great Irish Stories of the Supernatural, 1992

Other books you might like:
Joseph Hone, *Irish Ghost Stories*, 1971
  editor
Jim McGarry, *Irish Tales of Terror*, 1971
  editor
H.M. Tichenor, *Irish Fairy Tales*, 1923
  editor
Peter Tremayne, *The Irish Masters of Fantasy*, 1979
  editor

905

PETER HAINING, Editor

The Vampire Hunters' Casebook

(New York: Barnes & Noble, 1997)

Story type: Anthology; Vampire Story

Summary: Fifteen stories featuring human characters who detect, capture or kill vampires. Included are Seabury Quinn's "The Man Who Cast No Shadow," featuring psychic detective Jules de Grandin; David Schow's "A Week in the Unlife," about vampires who prey on other vampires; Robert Bloch's "The Undead," which resurrects Count Dracula; and Manly Wade Wellman's "The Last Grave of Lill Warran," in which his series detective John Thunstone hunts a being who is both werewolf and vampire. Included are excerpts from Jeff Rice's novel *The Night Stalker*, featuring vampire hunting journalist Carl Kolchak, and Anne Rice's "The Master of the Rampling Gate," excerpted from her novel *The Vampire Lestat*. Stills from vampire films are included.

Other books by the same author:
The Frankenstein Omnibus, 1994
The Mummy: Stories of the Living Corpse, 1989
Werewolf: Horror Stories of the Man Beast, 1987
Vampire: Chilling Tales of the Undead, 1985
Zombie: Stories of the Walking Dead, 1985

Other books you might like:
Richard Dalby, *Dracula's Brood*, 1987
  editor
Martin H. Greenberg, *Vampires: The Greatest Stories*, 1997
  editor
Stephen Jones, *The Mammoth Book of Vampires*, 1992
  editor

Horror

906

MELISSA MIA HALL, Editor

Wild Women

(New York: Carroll & Graf, 1997)

Story type: Anthology

Summary: Thirty-two reprint stories and poems that celebrate the "primal selves" of women. A signigicant number of the selections are horror and dark fantasy, including Fritz Leiber's "The Girl with the Hungry Eyes," about a female vampire who seduces men through an advertising image; Lucy Taylor's "Going North," a hardboiled tale of just desserts for a child-abusing family; Lisa Tuttle's "Bit and Pieces," in which a woman's memories of past lovers manifest as discorporate body parts; Joyce Carol Oates's "Haunted," in which a woman's repressed memories of a psychologically traumatic experience acquire near supernatural intensity; and Joe R. Landsdale's psychological suspense story "Incident On and Off a Mountain Road."

Where it's reviewed:
Kirkus Reviews, April 15, 1997, page 587

Other books you might like:
Pam Keesey, *Women Who Run with Werewolves*, 1996
    editor
Kathryn Ptacek, *Women of Darkness II*, 1990
    editor
Kathryn Ptacek, *Women of Darkness*, 1988
    editor
Alan Ryan, *Haunting Women*, 1988
    editor
Jessica Amanda Salmonson, *What Did Miss Darrington See?*, 1989
    editor
Lisa Tuttle, *Skin of the Soul*, 1991
    editor

907

LAURELL K. HAMILTON

The Killing Dance

(New York: Ace, 1997)

Story type: Mystery
Series: Anita Blake, Vampire Hunter
Major character(s): Anita Blake, Vampire Hunter, Detective—Private; Richard Zeeman, Werewolf, Teacher; Jean-Claude, Vampire, Leader (master vampire)
Time period(s): 1990s (1997)
Locale(s): St. Louis, Missouri (alternate earth)

Summary: Torn between two lovers—Richard, a werewolf who is enjoined to fight for the leadership of his pack, and Jean-Claude, the sophisticated vampire master who takes considerable risks courting a mortal—detective Anita Blake discovers that her life is further complicated by someone who has put a bounty on her head. Set in an alternate universe where creatures of the supernatural enjoy the same civil rights as humans. Sixth in a series.

Where it's reviewed:
Locus, May 1997, page 29

Other books by the same author:
The Lunatic Cafe, 1996
Bloody Bones, 1996
Guilty Pleasures, 1995
Circus of the Damned, 1995
The Laughing Corpse, 1994

Other books you might like:
Nancy A. Collins, *A Dozen Black Roses*, 1996
Christopher Golden, *Of Saints and Shadows*, 1994
Tanya Huff, *Blood Trail*, 1994
Robert Weinberg, *World of Darkness: The Unbeholden*, 1996

908

ELIZABETH HAND

Millennium: The Frenchman

(New York: Harper, 1997)

Story type: Serial Killer
Series: Millennium
Major character(s): Frank Black, FBI Agent (former); Robert Bletcher, Detective—Homicide; Catherine Black, Housewife (Frank's wife)
Time period(s): 1990s (1997)
Locale(s): Seattle, Washington

Summary: A serial killer is murdering people in Seattle's sexual underground as part of his plan for apocalyptic cleansing. Ex-FBI agent Frank Black, on the run to protect his family from a predator stalking them, lends his psychic powers of deduction to solving the case. Novelization of the pilot for the Fox television series "Millennium," about a group of special agents who work covertly to solve weird crimes inspired by millennial fanaticism.

Other books by the same author:
Glimmering, 1997
12 Monkeys, 1995
Waking the Moon, 1995
Icarus Descending, 1993
AEstival Tide, 1992
Winterlong, 1990

Other books you might like:
Kevin J. Anderson, *The X-Files: Ruins*, 1996
Lewis Gannett, *Millennium: Gehenna*, 1997
Charles L. Grant, *The X-Files: Goblins*, 1994
Thomas Harris, *Red Dragon*, 1981
Garry Kilworth, *Angel*, 1993

909

ANDREW HARPER (Pseudonym of Douglas Clegg)

Bad Karma

(New York: Kensington, 1997)

Story type: Psychological Suspense
Major character(s): Trey Campbell, Health Care Professional (mental health); Agnes Hatcher, Patient
Time period(s): 1990s (1997)

Locale(s): Catalina Island, California

Summary: Under the impression that she is the reincarnation of a century-old prostitute and that mental health specialist Trey Campbell is the reincarnation of her former lover, psychiatric patient Agnes Hatcher effects a bloody escape from Darden State Hospital and high-tails it to Catalina Island, where Trey is vacationing. Agnes will stop at nothing to be with Trey—even the murder of his wife and children.

Where it's reviewed:
Locus, June 1997, page 29
Publishers Weekly, March 24, 1997, page 60

Other books by the same author:
The Children's Hour, 1995
Dark of the Eye, 1994
Never Land, 1991
Breeder, 1990
Goat Dance, 1989

Other books you might like:
Robert Bloch, *The Scarf*, 1947
Kathe Koja, *Strange Angels*, 1994
Simon Maginn, *Virgins and Martyrs*, 1995
Robert R. McCammon, *Mine*, 1990
Patrick McGrath, *Spider*, 1990

`910`

DAVID G. HARTWELL, Editor

Bodies of the Dead
(New York: Tor, 1997)

Story type: Anthology

Summary: Thirteen stories of horror and the supernatural by American writers from the late nineteenth and early twentieth centuries. Included are Edith Wharton's "Kerfol," in which a man is slain by the ghosts of dogs who once protected the wife he abused; Willa Cather's "The Affair at Grover Station," in which a ghost helps to solve the mystery of his own murder; Nathaniel Hawthorne's "The Grey Champion," which features a ghost who embodies the revolutionary spirit of America; G. Ranger Wormser's "The Scarecrow," which suggests the influence of the supernatural pervading a soldier's uniform used to dress a scarecrow; Edgar Allan Poe's "Berenice," in which a man's obsession with the smile of his beloved leads to a gruesome post-mortem act; and the title tale by Ambrose Bierce, a series of vignettes concerning premature burial.

Other books by the same author:
Christmas Magic, 1994
Masterpieces of Fantasy and Wonder, 1994
Christmas Forever, 1993
Christmas Stars, 1992
Foundations of Fear, 1992
The Dark Descent, 1987

Other books you might like:
Peter Haining, *Great Tales of Terror from Europe and America*, 1972
   editor

Marvin Kaye, *Haunted America*, 1990
   editor
Frank D. McSherry Jr., *Great American Ghost Stories*, 1991
   Charles G. Waugh and Martin H. Greenberg, co-editors
Frank D. McSherry Jr., *A Treasury of Great American Horror Stories*, 1995
   Martin H. Greenberg, co-editor
Elizabeth Terry, *American Gothic*, 1993
   Terri Hardin, co-editor

`911`

DAVID G. HARTWELL, Editor

The Dark Descent
(New York: Tor, 1997)

Story type: Anthology

Summary: Landmark 1,000-plus page anthology celebrating the horror short story, drawn from English, American and continental literature of the nineteenth and twentieth century. Classic selections include Henry James's ghost tale, "The Jolly Corner," Oliver Onions's tale of a spectral *femme fatale*, "The Beckoning Fair One," J. Sheridan LeFanu's deal-with-the-devil story, "Schalken the Painter," and M.R. James's tale of supernatural curse, "The Ash-Tree." Modern selections include Flannery O'Connor's black comedy, "Good Country People," and H.P. Lovecraft's cosmic horror story, "The Call of Cthulhu." Contemporary stories include Shirley Jackson's tale of paranoia, "The Summer People," Stephen King's story of a supernaturally endowed toy, "The Monkey," and Robert Aickman's erotic horror tale, "The Swords." First published in 1987.

Other books by the same author:
Christmas Magic, 1994
Christmas Forever, 1993
Foundations of Fear, 1992
Masterpieces of Fantasy and Enchantment, 1989

Other books you might like:
Ramsey Campbell, *Uncanny Banquet*, 1992
   editor
Dennis Etchison, *The Complete Masters of Darkness*, 1991
   editor
Bill Pronzini, *The Arbor House Treasury of Horror and the Supernatural*, 1981
   Barry Malzberg and Martin H. Greenberg, co-editors
Robert Silverberg, *The Horror Hall of Fame*, 1991
   Martin H. Greenberg, co-editor
Herbert Wise, *Great Tales of Terror and the Supernatural*, 1944
   Phyllis Fraser, co-author

`912`

JULIAN HAWTHORNE

The Rose of Death and Other Mysterious Delusions
(Ashcroft, British Columbia: Ash-Tree Press, 1997)

Story type: Collection

Summary: Eight stories, many of them previously uncollected, by the son of Nathaniel Hawthorne. Included are ''Ken's Mystery,'' about an artist seduced by a vampire; ''The Delusion of Ralph Penwyn,'' about a man killed by eastern occultism; and ''Kildhurm's Oak,'' in which acorns bathed in the blood of a murdered man and his lover grows into an oak that fulfills a curse placed upon it centuries later. Edited and with an introduction by Jessica Amanda Salmonson.

Other books by the same author:
Six-Cent Sam's, 1893
The Golden Fleece, 1892
The Professor's Sister, 1888
David Poindexter's Disappearance, 1888

Other books you might like:
F. Marion Crawford, *Wandering Ghosts*, 1911
Olivia Howard Dunbar, *The Shell of Sense*, 1997
Henry James, *The Ghostly Tales of Henry James*, 1948
Fitz-James O'Brien, *The Supernatural Tales of Fitz-James O'Brien*, 1988
Vincent O'Sullivan, *Master of the Fallen Years*, 1994

913

MICHAEL HEMMINGSON

Snuff Flique

(Denver: Cyber-Psychos AOD, 1997)

Story type: Collection

Summary: Six violent tales of dark suspense, including ''Leashes,'' in which a child recalls his mother's vicious revenge against the circus clown that brutalized her; ''Two of a Kind,'' about a vigilante who enjoys his work; ''The Silence of Dirt and Grass,'' in which the recovery of a childhood toy brings back a man's memories of a horrible murder he committed as a youth; ''Shadowplayers,'' which features a drifter whose hopes for salvation from a life of past crime are tragically shattered; and ''Snuff Flick,'' which elaborates a corrupt federal agent's adventures in a grim and seamy world of kidnappers, pornographers, adulterers and murderers.

Other books by the same author:
Nice Little Stories Jam-Packed with Depraved Sex and Violence, 1995

Other books you might like:
S. Darnbrook Colson, *People of the Night*, 1995
Ray Garton, *Methods of Madness*, 1990
Barry Hoffman, *Firefly. . .Burning Bright*, 1996
Gerard Daniel Houarner, *Painfreak*, 1996
David J. Schow, *Lost Angels*, 1990
John Shirley, *New Noir*, 1993
Lucy Taylor, *Painted in Blood*, 1997

914

JAMES HERBERT

'48

(New York: HarperPrism, 1997)

Story type: Science Fiction

Major character(s): Hoke, Pilot; Stern, Pilot; Cissie, Young woman
Time period(s): 1940s (1948)
Locale(s): London, England

Summary: In an alternate future a biological plague delivered by Nazi missiles has decimated the Earth's population, killing all but a handful of resistant people with the AB-negative blood type. Hoke, an American fighter pilot, combats roving bands of Blackshirts slowly succumbing to the disease who hope to steal potentially lifesaving blood from persons with his rare type.

Where it's reviewed:
Kirkus Reviews, May 1, 1997, page 663
Locus, September 1997, page 25
Magazine of Fantasy and Science Fiction, July 1997, page 24
Necrofile, Fall 1997, page 15
Publishers Weekly, May 12, 1997, page 56

Other books by the same author:
The Ghosts of Sleath, 1995
Portent, 1993
Creed, 1990
Haunted, 1989
Sepulchre, 1987

Other books you might like:
Len Deighton, *SS-GB*, 1978
Philip K. Dick, *The Man in the High Castle*, 1992
Robert Harris, *Fatherland*, 1992
Sarban, *The Sound of His Horn*, 1962

915

TOM HOLLAND

Slave of My Thirst

(New York: Pocket, 1997)

Story type: Vampire Story
Major character(s): John Eliot, Doctor; Bram Stoker, Writer; Lucy Ruthven, Actress
Time period(s): 1880s (1887-1888)
Locale(s): London, England

Summary: Eliot Burns joins forces with struggling writer and stage manager Bram Stoker to investigate the murder of actress Lucy Ruthven's brother and the disappearance of her guardian. Clues lead Eliot and Stoker to India where they encounter Lilah, a megalomaniacal vampire queen. A sequel to *Lord of the Dead* and first published in England in 1997 under the title *The Libertine*.

Where it's reviewed:
Kirkus Reviews, August 1, 1997, page 1137

Other books by the same author:
Deliver Us From Evil, 1997
Supping with Panthers, 1996
Lord of the Dead, 1995

Other books you might like:
Les Daniels, *Yellow Fog*, 1986
Les Daniels, *No Blood Spilled*, 1990
Jeanne Kalogridis, *Lord of the Vampires*, 1996
Kim Newman, *The Bloody Red Baron*, 1995

Kim Newman, *Anno Dracula*, 1993
Bram Stoker, *Dracula*, 1897

916

JOHN R. HOLT

Wolf Moon
(New York: Bantam, 1997)

Story type: Black Magic; Werewolf Story
Major character(s): Nicole St. Claire, Student, Werewolf; Duffy Johnson, Student (medical); Timothy Balthazar, Businessman (satanist)
Time period(s): 1990s (1997)
Locale(s): St. Claire, New York

Summary: Satanist Timothy Balthazar summons members of a splinter cult back to St. Claire in the belief that eliminating them will help to save his comatose daughter. Nicole St. Claire, a survivor of the cult and of Balthazar's longstanding grudge against her family, must draw on her family's werewolf curse to save herself and her lover.

Other books by the same author:
The Convocation, 1993

Other books you might like:
Douglas Clegg, *Goat Dance*, 1989
Elizabeth Forrest, *Dark Tide*, 1993
Allan Lee Harris, *Let There Be Dark*, 1994
Robert R. McCammon, *Usher's Passing*, 1984
Robert Morgan, *The Things That Are Not There*, 1992

917

BRIAN HOPKINS

Cold at Heart
(Pasco, Washington: Sovereign Seal, 1997)

Story type: Werewolf Story
Major character(s): Peter Burke, Photographer; David Snow, Scientist (biologist); Julie Snow, Young Woman
Time period(s): 1990s (1997)
Locale(s): Ellesmere Island, Arctic

Summary: Peter Burke's expedition to the arctic to photograph wolves is complicated by the presence of Julie Snow, a young woman whose experiences in the wilds of Minnesota years before have given her an unnatural rapport with wolves. Julie's presence helps bring out the spirit of a werewolf who was responsible for the decimation of several arctic expeditions over the past century.

Other books by the same author:
Something Haunts Us All, 1995

Other books you might like:
Chris N. Africa, *When Wolves Cry*, 1997
Henry Garfield, *Moondog*, 1995
Randy Goldman, *Werewolf Wars*, 1996
Charles L. Grant, *Dark Cry of the Moon*, 1986
Christine Tanasiuk, *Howl*, 1997

918

ROBERT E. HOWARD

Ghor, Kin-Slayer: The Saga of Genseric's Fifth-Born Son
(West Warwick, Rhode Island: Necronomicon Press, 1997)

Story type: Occult

Summary: Episodic round-robin novel begun from a fragment of a story by Robert E. Howard concerning Ghor, a young boy raised by wolves who grows to be a fearsome warrior driven by the desire to revenge himself for his parents' abandonment. His travels bring him into conflict with a variety of human and supernatural monsters and nemeses. Sixteen writers were commissioned to continue Howard's tale for the small press magazine *Fantasy Crossroads* in the 1970s, but the magazine ceased publication before all the episodes could be published. All are published here for the first time. Contributors inlcude Karl Edward Wagner, Joseph Payne Brennan, Richard L. Tierney, Michael Moorcock, Charles R. Saunders, Andrew J. Offutt, Manly Wade Wellman, Darrell Schweitzer, A.E. van Vogt, Brian Lumley, Frank Belknap Long, Adrian Cole, Ramsey Campbell, H. Warner Munn, Marion Zimmer Bradley, and Richard A. Lupoff.

Other books you might like:
Ramsey Campbell, *Far Away and Never*, 1996
David Drake, *Vettius and His Friends*, 1989
Robert E. Howard, *Conan the Barbarian*, 1955
David C. Smith, *Engor's Sword Arm*, 1997
Richard L. Tierney, *Scroll of Thoth*, 1997
Karl Edward Wagner, *The Book of Kane*, 1985

919

TANYA HUFF

Blood Debt
(New York: DAW, 1997)

Story type: Vampire Story; Mystery
Series: Victory Nelson, Investigator
Major character(s): Henry Fitzroy, Writer, Vampire; Vicki Nelson, Detective—Private; Mike Celucci, Detective—Police
Time period(s): 1990s (1997)
Locale(s): Vancouver, British Columbia, Canada

Summary: In this adventure of private investigator Vicki Nelson, Vicki is summoned back to Vancouver by vampire Henry Fitzroy to solve the mystery of his nightly haunting by the ghost of a mutilated victim. Vicki's investigation into black market organ bootlegging as a possible origin of the haunting is hampered by the limitations of vampire life and by her constant bickering with the territorial Fitzroy.

Where it's reviewed:
Locus, April 1997, page 29

Other books by the same author:
Blood Pact, 1993
Blood Lines, 1992
Blood Trail, 1991

Horror

Blood Price, 1991

Other books you might like:
Vincent Courtney, *Vampire Beat*, 1991
P.N. Elrod, *Bloodlist*, 1990
Lee Killough, *Blood Walk*, 1997
Michael Reaves, *Night Hunter*, 1991
Les Whitten, *Progeny of the Adder*, 1965

920

JAMES BYRON HUGGINS

Cain

(New York: Simon & Schuster, 1997)

Story type: Science Fiction; Apocalyptic Horror
Major character(s): Roth Tiberius Cain, Military Personnel (soldier); Soloman, Military Personnel (soldier); Maggie, Scientist
Time period(s): 1990s (1997)
Locale(s): Death Valley, New Mexico; Los Angeles, California

Summary: Cain, the ultimate soldier, created in the laboratory and imbued with the spirit of the murderous Cain of biblical legend, goes on a rampage of death and destruction when he escapes from the facility where he was made. Special forces commando Soloman and Maggie, a scientist who helped create Cain, launch a manhunt that is complicated by the HyMar virus, a plague with which Cain is infected and which could cause mass destruction if released into the atmosphere.

Where it's reviewed:
Publishers Weekly, June 9, 1997, page 39

Other books by the same author:
Leviathan, 1996
The Reckoning, 1995
A Wolf Story, 1993

Other books you might like:
Roger Elwood, *Angelwalk: A Modern Fable*, 1988
Garry Kilworth, *Angel*, 1993
Garry Kilworth, *Archangel*, 1994
Dean R. Koontz, *Shadowfires*, 1987

921

NOEL HYND

Rage of Spirits

(New York: Kensington, 1997)

Story type: Ghost Story
Major character(s): William Cochrane, Government Official; Carl Einhorn, Scientist (mathematician); Gabriel Lang, Political Figure (vice president)
Time period(s): 2000s (2003)
Locale(s): Washington, District of Columbia

Summary: When United States president George Farley falls into an inexplicable coma, vice president Gabriel Lang instructs press attache William Cochrane to investigate possible supernatural causes. Cochrane's investigations into Farley's past bring him into contact with Carl Einhorn, who purports to be causing Farley's affliction psychically, and a host of spiritual phenomena that are influencing the government at its highest levels.

Where it's reviewed:
Kirkus Reviews, January 1, 1997, page 11
Publishers Weekly, January 20, 1997, page 396

Other books by the same author:
The Prodigy, 1998
Cemetery of Angels, 1995
A Room for the Dead, 1994
Ghosts, 1993

Other books you might like:
Raymond Buckland, *The Committee*, 1993
James Herbert, *Portent*, 1993
William W. Johnstone, *Prey*, 1996
Thomas F. Monteleone, *The Resurrectionist*, 1995

922

JAMES HYNES

Publish and Perish

(New York: Picador/St. Martin's, 1997)

Story type: Collection

Summary: Trio of loosely interconnected novellas that use the literary supernatural tale as a vehicle for satirizing modern academic life. In "Queen of the Jungle," a philandering post-doctoral student gets his comeuppance through the intervention of his wife's preternaturally endowed pet cat. "99" concerns an American anthropologist so caught up in his exploration of primitive ritual sacrifice in a rural English town that he is oblivious to the fate for which the townspeople are grooming him. "Casting the Runes," an homage to M.R. James's classic story of the same name, involves a history professor who invokes a supernatural revenge against a female colleague who plans to expose him as a plagiarist.

Where it's reviewed:
Kirkus Reviews, April 15, 1997, page 578
Necrofile, Fall 1997, page 14
New York Times Book Review, August 3, 1997, page 5

Other books by the same author:
Wild Colonial Boy, 1990

Other books you might like:
P.H. Cannon, *Scream for Jeeves*, 1994
Fred Chappell, *The Lodger*, 1993
Fritz Leiber, *Conjure Wife*, 1952
Alison Lurie, *Women and Ghosts*, 1994
William Browning Spencer, *The Return of Count Electric and Other Stories*, 1993

923

SHIRLEY JACKSON

Just an Ordinary Day

(New York: Bantam, 1997)

Story type: Collection

Summary: Thirty previously unpublished and twenty-two previously uncollected stories by a writer renowned for her macabre, psychologically complex fiction and tales of the dark side of everyday life. The handful of horror and fantasy stories include ''One Ordinary Day with Peanuts,'' about a capriciously nasty and unpredictable couple; '' The Possibility of Evil,'' about a woman who writes anonymous poison pen letters with serious consequences to keep her town on its best behavior; and two tales featuring the devil, ''Smoking Room'' and ''Devil of a Tale.''

Where it's reviewed:
Book World, January 5, 1997, page 4
Kirkus Reviews, November 1, 1996, page 1554
Necrofile, Summer 1997, page 14
New York Times Book Review, December 29, 1996, page 10
Newsweek, January 13, 1997, page 70

Other books by the same author:
Come Along with Me, 1968
The Magic of Shirley Jackson, 1966
The Lottery, 1949

Other books you might like:
Jonathan Carroll, *The Panic Hand*, 1995
Fred Chappell, *More Shapes than One*, 1991
Rachell Ingalls, *The End of Tragedy*, 1987
Alison Lurie, *Women and Ghosts*, 1994
Joyce Carol Oates, *Haunted: Tales of the Grotesque*, 1994
Muriel Spark, *Open to the Public*, 1997

924

JANE JENSEN

Gabriel Knight: Sins of the Fathers

(New York: Roc, 1997)

Story type: Occult
Series: Gabriel Knight
Major character(s): Gabriel Knight, Writer; Mosely, Detective—Police; Grace Nakimure, Worker (bookstore employee)
Time period(s): 1990s (1993)
Locale(s): New Orleans, Louisiana

Summary: While researching voodoo for his newest horror novel, author Gabriel Knight becomes a key figure in the investigation of several gruesome murders, all of which have the stamp of the voodoo ritual. Gabriel's research introduces him to a shapeshifting voodoo cult and reveals the history of his own family, whose members have for centuries served as Shadow Hunters dedicated to the extirpation of supernatural evil. Based on the CD-ROM game Gabriel Knight.

Other books you might like:
Alex Abella, *The Killing of the Saints*, 1991
Nancy A. Collins, *Tempter*, 1990
Don David, *The Gris-Gris Man*, 1997
Michael Reaves, *Voodoo Child*, 1988
Vivian Schilling, *Sacred Prey*, 1994
Robert Weinberg, *The Black Lodge*, 1991

925

GARY JONAS

Nice Guys Finish Last

(Owasso, Oklahoma: Ozark Triangle Press, 1997)

Story type: Witchcraft
Major character(s): Eugene Smith, Young Man; Fat Woman, Witch
Time period(s): 1990s (1997)
Locale(s): United States

Summary: A man seeks out a witch for supernatural interventions to improve his love life, but all of the scenarios she sketches out, though perceptive in regard to the differences between men and women, are ironically unappealing. Signed limited edition chapbook with an introduction by the author.

Other books by the same author:
By Death Abused, 1990

Other books you might like:
Ed Bryant, *Fetish*, 1991
Glen E. Cox, *Going Mobile*, 1993
Norman Partridge, *Spyder*, 1995
Byron Preiss, *The Ultimate Witch*, 1993
　　John Betancourt, co-editor
Robert Weinberg, *100 Wicked Little Witch Stories*, 1996
　　Stefan Dziemianowicz and Martin H. Greenberg, co-editors

926

STEPHEN JONES, Editor

The Mammoth Book of Best New Horror 8

(New York: Carroll & Graf, 1997)

Story type: Anthology

Summary: Twenty-five stories selected from the British and American professional and semi-professional press representing the best horror fiction published in 1996. Stand-out selections include Douglas Clegg's ''Underworld,'' a tale of grief and loss that resolves in supernatural experience; Poppy Z. Brite's ''Mussolini and the Axeman's Jazz,'' about a serial killer on the streets of New Orleans; Donald Burleson's ''Hopscotch,'' in which a childhood game proves a doorway to a dark dimension; Gregory Frost's ''The Blissful Height,'' set during the spiritualist craze of the late nineteenth century; Scott Edelman's ''A Plague on Both Your Houses,'' a zombie story written as a Shakespearian verse tragedy; and Terry Lamsley's vampire tale, ''The Break.'' Jones contributes an introductory survey of the horror field in 1996 and, with Kim Newman, a necrology of deceased horror personnel for the year.

Where it's reviewed:
Necrofile #27, winter 1998, page 1
Publishers Weekly, September 29, 1997, page 66

Other books by the same author:
The Mammoth Book of Dracula, 1997
The Mammoth Book of Frankenstein, 1995
The Mammoth Book of Werewolves, 1994

Horror

The Mammoth Book of Zombies, 1993
The Mammoth Book of Vampires, 1992

Other books you might like:
Ellen Datlow, *The Year's Best Fantasy and Horror Series*, 1988-1997
　　Terri Winding, co-editor
Karl Edward Wagner, *The Year's Best Horror Series*, 1979-1994
　　editor

927

STEPHEN JONES, Editor

The Mammoth Book of Dracula

(New York: Carroll & Graf, 1997)

Story type: Anthology; Vampire Story
Major character(s): Dracula, Vampire, Nobleman

Summary: Thirty-two stories and one poem featuring Dracula as a character, in an anthology compiled to commemorate the *Dracula* centenary. Selections include Thomas Ligotti's ironic prose poem, "The Heart of Count Dracula, Descendant of Attila, Scourge of God", Manly Wade Wellman's "The Devil is Not Mocked," a classic short in which the Nazis make the mistake of billeting at Castle Dracula; Ramsey Campbell's "Conversion," told from the viewpoint of a man who does not know that he's a vampire; Bram Stoker's prologue to the stage version of his novel, "Dracula: or The Undead"; and new stories by Michael Marshall Smith, Christopher Fowler, Basil Copper, Joel Lane, Terry Lamsley, Guy N. Smith and R. Chetwynd-Hayes.

Where it's reviewed:
Necrofile, Summer 1997, page 1

Other books by the same author:
The Mammoth Book of Frankenstein, 1995
The Mammoth Book of Werewolves, 1994
The Mammoth Book of Zombies, 1993
The Mammoth Book of Vampires, 1992
The Mammoth Book of Terror, 1991

Other books you might like:
Richard Dalby, *Dracula's Brood*, 1987
　　editor
Martin H. Greenberg, *Dracula: Prince of Darkness*, 1992
　　editor
Michel Parry, *Rivals of Dracula*, 1977
　　editor
Stefan Dziemianowicz, *Rivals of Dracula*, 1996
　　Robert Weinberg and Martin H. Greenberg, co-editors

928

MARVIN KAYE, Editor
JOHN GREGORY BETANCOURT, Co-Editor

The Best of Weird Tales: 1923

(Berkeley Heights, New Jersey: Bleak House, 1997)

Story type: Anthology

Summary: Thirteen stories culled from the first eight issue of *Weird Tales*, the long-running pulp weird fiction magazine. In addition to "Dragon," H.P. Lovecraft's first professionally published work of fiction, the book includes Orville R. Emerson's "The Grave," a story of premature burial during World War I; J. Paul Suter's "Beyond the Door," about a ghost who haunts the house where he earthly form was murdered; Frank Owen's "The Man Who Owned the World," the tale of a madman and his delusions; Lyle Wilson Holden's "The Devil Plant," a gruesome revenge story involving a carnivorous plant; and James L. Ravenscroft's native curse story "The Dead-Naming of Lukapehu." Kaye contributes the introduction and notes for each issue represented.

Where it's reviewed:
Science Fiction Chronicle, February 1998, page 62

Other books you might like:
John Gregory Betancourt, *Weird Tales: Seven Decades of Terror*, 1997
　　Robert Weinberg, co-editor
Robert Weinberg, *100 Wild Little Weird Tales*, 1995
　　Stefan Dziemianowicz and Martin H. Greenberg, co-editors
Stefan Dziemianowicz, *Weird Tales: 32 Unearthed Terrors*, 1987
　　Robert Weinberg and Martin H. Greenberg, co-editors
Marvin Kaye, *Weird Tales: The Magazine That Never Dies*, 1987
　　editor
Robert Weinberg, *The Eighth Green Man and Other Strange Folk*, 1989
　　editor

929

GREG KIHN

Shade of Pale

(New York: Tor/Forge, 1997)

Story type: Curse
Major character(s): Jukes Wahler, Doctor (psychiatrist); Padraic O'Connor, Terrorist; George Jones, Detective—Police
Time period(s): 1990s (1997)
Locale(s): New York, New York

Summary: Jukes Wahler's efforts to save his sister from her abusive boyfriend dovetail with the mission of IRA terrorist Padraic O'Connor to capture the banshee, a creature of Irish legend who defends the plight of Irish women and who has caused the gruesome deaths of several expatriate Irishmen living in New York.

Where it's reviewed:
Publishers Weekly, September 15, 1997, page 50

Other books by the same author:
Horror Show, 1996

Other books you might like:
Ramsey Campbell, *The Long Lost*, 1993
Joe Donnelly, *The Shee*, 1991
Elizabeth Massie, *The Sineater*, 1992

Michael O'Rourke, *The Undine*, 1996

930

LEE KILLOUGH

Blood Walk

(Decatur, Georgia: Meisha Merlin, 1997)

Story type: Collection; Vampire Story

Summary: Omnibus reprint of two vampire novels. In *Blood Hunt* (1987), San Francisco police detective Gareth encounters vampire femme fatale Lane Barber during a murder investigation and is turned into a vampire by her. In *Bloodlinks* (1988), Gareth is still adjusting to his life as a vampire and enduring a series of misadventures and crimes for which he is framed to prevent him from pursuing his vampire initiator.

Other books by the same author:
Dragon's Teeth, 1990
Spider Play, 1986
Liberty's World, 1985
Deadly Silents, 1981
The Doppelganger Gambit, 1979

Other books you might like:
Vincent Courtney, *Vampire Beat*, 1991
P.N. Elrod, *Bloodlist*, 1990
Martin H. Greenberg, *Vampire Detectives*, 1995
  editor
Tanya Huff, *Blood Debt*, 1997
Michael Reaves, *Night Hunter*, 1991
Les Whitten, *Progeny of the Adder*, 1965

931

STEPHEN KING

Wizard and Glass

(Hampton Falls, New Hampshire: Donald M. Grant, 1997)

Story type: Apocalyptic Horror
Series: Dark Tower
Major character(s): Roland of Gilead, Gunfighter; Susan Delgado, Teenager; Rhea of Coos, Witch
Time period(s): 1980s (1986)
Locale(s): Topeka, Kansas (alternate universe)

Summary: In this fourth adventure of Roland the Gunslinger, who is following the path of the beam to the Dark Tower, Roland kills time with his compatriots, who are trapped with him aboard a sentient train, by recounting his teenage years as a gunslinger initiate, and the ill-fated romance with Susan Delgado which has helped to shape his quest.

Where it's reviewed:
Hellnotes, September 5, 1997, page 5
Kirkus Reviews, August 1, 1997, page 1138
Locus, October 1997, page 19
Locus, October 1997, page 23
Publishers Weekly, July 14, 1997, page 65

Other books by the same author:
The Waste Lands, 1992

The Drawing of the Three, 1989
The Dark Tower: The Gunslinger, 1988
The Stand, 1978

Other books you might like:
Clive Barker, *The Great and Secret Show*, 1989
L. Frank Baum, *The Wonderful Wizard of Oz*, 1900
Raymond E. Feist, *Faerie Tale*, 1987
J.R.R. Tolkien, *The Lord of the Rings Trilogy*, 1954-1956

932

ANNETTE CURTIS KLAUSE

Blood and Chocolate

(New York: Delacorte, 1997)

Story type: Werewolf Story; Young Adult
Major character(s): Vivian Gandillon, Teenager, Werewolf; Aiden Teague, Teenager; Rafe Dafoe, Teenager
Time period(s): 1990s (1997)
Locale(s): Riverview, Maryland

Summary: Coming-of-age young adult novel. Teenage werewolf Vivian Gandillon begins a relationship with Aiden Teague, a "meat-boy" (mortal human) whom she hopes is sensitive enough to accept her supernatural heritage. Their romance is threatened by the call of the pack, and the inevitable animosity of Vivian's werewolf family toward the humans in town.

Other books by the same author:
Alien Secrets, 1993
The Silver Kiss, 1992

Other books you might like:
Peter S. Beagle, *Lila the Werewolf*, 1969
Ronald Kelly, *Moon of the Werewolf*, 1991
John Saul, *Guardian*, 1993
S.P. Somtow, *The Vampire's Beautiful Daughter*, 1997

933

AMARANTHA KNIGHT (Pseudonym of Nancy Kilpatrick)

The Darker Passions: Carmilla

(New York: Masquerade, 1997)

Story type: Vampire Story
Series: The Darker Passions
Major character(s): Laura, Young Woman; Carmilla, Vampire; Martin Miller, Businessman
Time period(s): 1800s
Locale(s): Styria, Austria

Summary: Young Laura seeks escape from sadistic chastisements and leather fetishes of her governess in the arms of the mysterious Carmilla. Carmilla, whose presence has been associated with the mysterious deaths of several young girls, is in fact a vampire who indoctrinates Laura into the ecstasies of the Undead. A pornographic retelling of J. Sheridan Le Fanu's classic novella "Carmilla", explicitly focused through the original lesbian subtext.

Other books by the same author:
The Darker Passions: The Picture of Dorian Gray, 1996

Horror

The Darker Passions: The Fall of the House of Usher, 1996
The Darker Passions: Dr. Jekyll and Mr. Hyde, 1995
The Darker Passions: Frankenstein, 1995
The Darker Passions: Dracula, 1994

Other books you might like:
Poppy Z. Brite, *Love in Vein II*, 1997
    Martin H. Greenberg, co-editor
Pam Keesey, *Daughters of Darkness: Lesbian Vampire Stories*, 1993
    editor
Pam Keesey, *Darker Angels: Lesbian Vampire Stories*, 1995
    editor
Cecilia Tan, *Vampire Erotica*, 1995
    editor
Cecilia Tan, *Erotica Vampirica*, 1996
    editor
Cecilia Tan, *Cherished Blood*, 1997
    editor

934

TODD KOMARNICKI

Famine

(New York: Arcade, 1997)

Story type: Ghost Story
Major character(s): Daniel Rowan, Bartender; Daniel Bell, Detective—Police; Emma Clough, Bartender
Time period(s): 1990s
Locale(s): New York, New York

Summary: Daniel Rowan's death from malnutrition prompts incredulous Detective Daniel Bell to investigate the case as a homicide. Bell's pursuit of Rowan's wife, Emma, uncovers the lifetime of pain and misunderstanding that drove Rowan to his fate, but also reveals coincidences of near supernatural intensity that parallel Bell's own troubled private life.

Where it's reviewed:
Kirkus, November 15, 1996, page 1623
Necrofile #25, summer 1997, page 11
Publishers Weekly, November 18, 1996, page 61

Other books by the same author:
Free, 1993

Other books you might like:
Paul Auster, *The New York Trilogy*, 1990
Peter S. Beagle, *A Fine and Private Place*, 1960
Judith Hawkes, *Julian's House*, 1989
T.M. Wright, *A Manhattan Ghost Story*, 1984

935

DEAN R. KOONTZ

Sole Survivor

(New York: Knopf, 1997)

Story type: Wild Talents
Major character(s): Joe Carpenter, Journalist; Rose Tucker, Scientist; Barbara Christman, Investigator (airplane crash)
Time period(s): 1990s (1997)
Locale(s): Los Angeles, California

Summary: One year after a devastating airplane crash took the lives of his family and supposedly everyone else on board, Joe Carpenter is contacted by a secretive woman who purports to be a survivor. Joe's efforts to track the woman down attract the interest of a secret scientific project responsible for the crash, who will stop at nothing to suppress the truth. First published in England in 1996

Where it's reviewed:
Kirkus Reviews, January 1, 1997, page 1
New York Times Book Review, April 20, 1997, page 20
Publishers Weekly, January 6, 1997, page 63

Other books by the same author:
Ticktock, 1996
Intensity, 1995
Dark Rivers of the Heart, 1995
Mr. Murder, 1993
Dragon Tears, 1993

Other books you might like:
Mark Chadbourn, *The Eternal*, 1996
John Farris, *The Fury*, 1976
James Herbert, *Survivor*, 1976
Stephen King, *Firestarter*, 1980

936

DEAN R. KOONTZ

Ticktock

(New York: Ballantine, 1998)

Story type: Black Magic
Major character(s): Tommy Phan, Writer (detective fiction); Deliverance "Del" Payne, Waiter/Waitress; Gi Minh Phan, Baker (Tommy's brother)
Time period(s): 1900s (1997)
Locale(s): Irvines, California

Summary: Detective fiction writer Tommy Phan finds himself enmeshed in a real-life mystery when he is sent a demonically possessed rag doll and an anonymous computer message informing him "The Deadline is Dawn." Tommy enlists the aid of friends and family to avoid the relentlessly pursuing doll and discover who sent it to him and why. First published in England in 1996.

Where it's reviewed:
Cemetery Dance, Fall 1996, page 25
Magazine of Fantasy & Science Fiction, May 1997, page 20
Science Fiction Chronicle, April 1997, page 73

Other books by the same author:
Sole Survivor, 1996
Intensity, 1995
Dark Rivers of the Heart, 1995
Mr. Murder, 1993
Dragon Tears, 1993

Other books you might like:
Matthew J. Costello, *Child's Play III*, 1991
William Goldman, *Magic*, 1978
Pat Graversen, *Dollies*, 1990
Ellen Jamison, *Stone Dead*, 1993
Ruby Jean Jenson, *Baby Doll*, 1992

937

TERRY LAMSLEY

Under the Crust

(Ashcroft, British Columbia: Ash-Tree Press, 1997)

Story type: Collection; Small Town Horror

Summary: Six contemporary tales in the classic supernatural tradition, all set in and around the small British town Buxton. Included are the World-Fantasy Award-winning title story about a man's ill-fated discovery of a race of strange humanoid beings living in the remote English countryside; "The Two Returns," about an overcoat possessed by the spirit of its former owner; "Something Worse," in which an invalid is haunted to his death by deceased family members; and "Living Waters," about a preternatural menace that infests the water supply of a small town. First published in 1993.

Where it's reviewed:
Necrofile, Winter 1995, page 25

Other books by the same author:
Conference with the Dead, 1996

Other books you might like:
Steve Duffy, *The Night Comes On*, 1998
David G. Rowlands, *The Executor and Other Ghost Stories*, 1996
Ron Weighell, *The White Road*, 1996
Robert Westall, *Antique Dust*, 1989
John Whitbourn, *Binscombe Tales*, 1998

938

ROBERTA LANNES

The Mirror of the Night

(Woodinville, Washington: Silver Salamander, 1997)

Story type: Collection

Summary: Eleven tales of supernatural and nonsupernatural horror, many featuring dysfunctional relationships and sexual neuroses. In "Apostate in Denim," an emotionally troubled young boy finds a surrogate father in a psychopathic murderer. "Auntie" concerns a young girl who discovers that the abusive aunt whose care he is left in is actually her mother in disguise. In "Precious," a gynecologist expresses his warped sensibilities through therapeutic sexual mutilations. "In the Mirror of the Night" concerns a family of women cursed by a male demon that hopes to force a male child into birth to serve as its vessel. Harlan Ellison supplies an introduction to this first collection.

Other books you might like:
Poppy Z. Brite, *Swamp Foetus*, 1993
Scott Edelman, *Suicide Art*, 1992
Ray Garton, *Methods of Madness*, 1990
Gerard Daniel Houarner, *Painfreak*, 1996
Sue Storm, *Star Bones Weep the Blood of Angels*, 1995
Lucy Taylor, *Painted in Blood*, 1997

939

JOE R. LANSDALE

The Drive-In: A Double Omnibus

(New York: Carroll & Graf, 1997)

Story type: Collection

Summary: Omnibus of two novels, *The Drive-In (A B-Movie with Blood and Popcorn, Made in Texas)*, first published in 1988, and *The Drive-In 2 (Not Just One of Them Sequels)*, first published in 1989. In *The Drive-In*, attendees at an all-night horror movie marathon at a rural Texas drive-in find their world transformed into a hostile alien landscape by a passing comet. In *The Drive-In 2*, survivors of the first novel navigate a landscape in which horror and science fiction B-movie cliches have come to life, among them the Popalong Cassidy, a mutant demi-god who demands their obeisance.

Other books by the same author:
A Fist Full of Stories (and Articles), 1997
The Good, the Bad, and the Indifferent, 1997
Bestsellers Guaranteed, 1993
By Bizarre Hands, 1989

Other books you might like:
Pete Atkins, *Big Thunder*, 1997
David Darke, *Horrorshow*, 1994
John Douglas, *The Late Show*, 1994
Dale Hoover, *65mm*, 1994
Jack Martin, *Videodrome*, 1982

940

JOE R. LANSDALE

A Fist Full of Stories (and Articles)

(Baltimore: CD Publications, 1997)

Story type: Collection

Summary: Nineteen short stories and articles by a writer whose work straddles the border of crime and supernatural fiction. Included are "Bar Talk," a loopy vampire tale; "Personality Problem," a comic variation on the Frankenstein theme; "Listen," about a man who finds that his anonymity is turning him invisible; and "Old Charlie," a dramatic monologue delivered by a homicidal maniac.

Where it's reviewed:
Locus, May 1997, page 25

Other books by the same author:
The Good, the Bad, and the Indifferent, 1997
Electric Gumbo: A Lansdale Reader, 1995
Writer of the Purple Rage, 1994
Bestsellers Guaranteed, 1993
By Bizarre Hands, 1989

Other books you might like:
Neal Barrett Jr., *Slightly Off Center*, 1992
Nancy A. Collins, *Nameless Sins*, 1994
Ed Gorman, *Prisoners and Other Stories*, 1992
Davis Grubb, *You Never Believe Me and Other Stories*, 1989
Robert R. McCammon, *Blue World*, 1989
William Relling Jr., *The Infinite Man*, 1989

Horror

Manly Wade Wellman, *The Valley So Low*, 1987
F. Paul Wilson, *Soft and Others*, 1989

941

JOE R. LANSDALE

The Good, the Bad, and the Indifferent

(Burton, Michigan: Subterranean Press, 1997)

Story type: Collection

Summary: Thirty-four stories and vignettes from early in the author's career. Selections include ''Junkyard,'' about a monstrous creature that lives among the refuse of the local junkyard; ''The Valley of the Swastika,'' a biker variation on Kipling's ''The Man Who Would Be King''; the dark suspense story ''One Death, Two Episodes''; and ''Walks,'' a portrait of a serial killer as a conscientious father. Illustrated by Mark A. Nelson. Released only in a signed, limited edition.

Where it's reviewed:
Locus, November 1997, page 23
Publishers Weekly, September 22, 1997, page 70

Other books by the same author:
A Fist Full of Stories (and Articles), 1997
Electric Gumbo: A Lansdale Reader, 1995
Writer of the Purple Rage, 1994
Bestsellers Guaranteed, 1993
By Bizarre Hands, 1989

Other books you might like:
Neal Barrett Jr., *Slightly Off Center*, 1992
Nancy A. Collins, *Nameless Sins*, 1994
Ed Gorman, *Prisoners and Other Stories*, 1992
Davis Grubb, *You Never Believe Me and Other Stories*, 1989
Robert R. McCammon, *Blue World*, 1989
William Relling Jr., *The Infinite Man*, 1989
Manly Wade Wellman, *The Valley So Low*, 1987
F. Paul Wilson, *Soft and Others*, 1989

942

RICHARD LAYMON

The Cellar

(Baltimore: CD Publications, 1997)

Story type: Mystery
Major character(s): Donna Hayes, Travel Agent; Roy Hayes, Criminal; Judgement Rucker, Hunter
Time period(s): 1980s
Locale(s): Malcasa Point, California

Summary: Newly released from prison, Roy Hayes cuts a swath of murder and destruction in pursuit of his wife, Donna, who testified against him in a rape case. Roy tracks Donna to Malcasa Point and corners her in the Beast House, a tourist attraction where more than a dozen people have died over the century, purportedly at the hands of a supernatural fiend known as The Beast. Deluxe hardcover edition of a novel published as a paperback original in 1980.

Other books by the same author:
Bite, 1996

Quakes, 1995
Island, 1995
In the Dark, 1994

Other books you might like:
Rick Hautala, *Ghost Light*, 1993
Ruby Jean Jensen, *Celia*, 1991
Stephen King, *Rose Madder*, 1995
Dean R. Koontz, *Shadowfires*, 1987

943

EDWARD LEE (Pseudonym of L. Edward Seymour)

The Bighead

(Orlando Florida: Necro Publications, 1997)

Story type: Mystery
Major character(s): Jerrica Perry, Journalist; Charity Walsh, Student; Father Alexander, Religious (priest)
Time period(s): 1990s (1997)
Locale(s): Luntville, Virginia

Summary: The reopening of Wroxeter Abbey, a property of the Catholic church in rural Virginia, piques the interest of journalist Jerrica Perry, who hopes to write an investigative story on its scandalous past. Meanwhile, the Bighead, a congenitally deformed young man whose birth is intimately tied to the Abbey's secret past, embarks on a horrible rampage of rape and murder that only taints the Abbey's reputation further.

Where it's reviewed:
Cemetery Dance, Fall 1997, page 127

Other books by the same author:
Header, 1995
Creekers, 1994
The Chosen, 1993
Coven, 1991
Incubi, 1991

Other books you might like:
Jack Ketchum, *Off Season*, 1981
Jack Ketchum, *Offspring*, 1989
Richard Kinion, *Sacrifice*, 1995
Richard Laymon, *The Woods are Dark*, 1981
Robert D. Lee, *The Keeper*, 1993

944

EDWARD LEE
JOHN PELAN, Co-Author

The Case of the Police Officer's ... Ring and the Piano Player Who Had No Fingers

(Clay, New York: Dark Raptor Press, 1997)

Story type: Werewolf Story
Major character(s): Richard Kinion, Police Officer; Micah Hays, Police Officer; Luger Roo, Farmer, Werewolf
Time period(s): 1990s (1997)
Locale(s): Luntville, Virginia

Summary: Richard Kinion answers a call for police help and finds himself face-to-face with a werewolf. Assistant Micah Hays fortunately finds an ingenious means of implanting lethal silver in the werewolf's body. A signed limited edition chapbook.

Other books by the same author:
Shifters, 1998
Splatterspunk, 1998
Goon, 1996

Other books you might like:
Ed Bryant, *Aqua Sancta*, 1994
Ron Dee, *Sex and Blood*, 1994
Nancy Kilpatrick, *Sex and the Single Vampire*, 1994

945

IRA LEVIN

Son of Rosemary

(New York: Dutton, 1997)

Story type: Occult
Major character(s): Rosemary Reilly, Parent (Andy's mother); Andy Woodhouse, Religious (aka Adrian Steven Castevet); Judy Kharyat, Secretary
Time period(s): 1990s (1999)
Locale(s): New York, New York; California

Summary: Rosemary Reilly (nee Woodhouse) awakens from a 27-year coma to find her son Andy, the offspring of a Satanic bargain, is venerated as an internationally renowned religious figure devoted to the betterment of the world. As Andy prepares the world for a global ritual that will usher in the next millennium, Rosemary can't shake the suspicion that her son is still beholden to his destiny to become the anti-Christ. A sequel to *Rosemary's Baby* (1967).

Where it's reviewed:
New York Times Book Review, October 5, 1997, page 23
Publishers Weekly, August 18, 1997, page 47

Other books by the same author:
Silver, 1991
The Boys from Brazil, 1976
The Stepford Wives, 1972
This Perfect Day, 1970
Rosemary's Baby, 1967

Other books you might like:
Joseph Howard, *Damien*, 1978
Alan Rodgers, *Night*, 1991
David Seltzer, *The Omen*, 1976
John Skipp, *The Scream*, 1988
  Craig Spector, co-author
F. Paul Wilson, *Nightworld*, 1992

946

BENTLEY LITTLE

The Ignored

(New York: Signet, 1997)

Story type: Wild Talents

Major character(s): Bob Jones, Writer (technical); Philipe, Terrorist; Jane Reynolds, Child-Care Giver
Time period(s): 1990s (1997)
Locale(s): Brea, California

Summary: As Bob Jones settles into the routine of his thankless job as a technical writer, he becomes so anonymous and ignored that he grows invisible to his colleagues. Outraged at his inconsequentiality, Bob uses his invisibility to cause mischief and murder, and eventually links up with a group of similarly underappreciated and angry people who suffer the same condition.

Where it's reviewed:
Locus, July 1997, page 31
Publishers Weekly, April 14, 1997, page 71

Other books by the same author:
Dominion, 1995
University, 1995
The Summoning, 1993
The Mailman, 1990
The Revelation, 1989

Other books you might like:
Nicholson Baker, *The Fermata*, 1994
Robert Cormier, *Fade*, 1989
Stephen King, *Insomnia*, 1995
Fritz Leiber, *The Sinful Ones*, 1953
H.G. Wells, *The Invisible Man*, 1897

947

BENTLEY LITTLE

Murmerous Haunts

(Concord, California: Dark Regions, 1997)

Story type: Collection

Summary: Collection of nine stories, two original to the volume. Outstanding selections include ''The Mailman,'' a tale of psychological horror in which every tormentor in a man's life takes the form of a grotesque dwarf who terrorized him as a child; ''Estoppel,'' in which a man discovers he has the power to wish himself anything; ''Garage Sale,'' in which the fanatical persistence of garage-sale attendees suggests a preternaturally-endowed subculture; and the haunted house tale ''The Murmurous Haunts of Files.'' Richard Laymon supplies an introduction.

Other books by the same author:
The Ignored, 1997
University, 1995
Dominion, 1995
The Summoning, 1993

Other books you might like:
Gary A. Braunbeck, *Things Left Behind*, 1997
Brian Hopkins, *Something Haunts Us All*, 1996
Gerard Daniel Houarner, *Painfreak*, 1996
Elizabeth Massie, *Shadow Dreams*, 1996
Jeffrey Osier, *Horizon Lines*, 1997
David Niall Wilson, *The Fall of the House of Escher and Other Illusions*, 1996

Horror

948

BRIAN LUMLEY

In His Own Write: Brian Lumley, Necroscribe

(West Warwick, Rhode Island: Necronomicon Press, 1997)

Story type: Collection

Summary: A trio of stories reprinted in a tribute volume to the author, who was guest of honor for Necronomi-Con 3, a convention devoted to the fiction of H.P. Lovecraft. Selections include ''The Thing in the Moonlight,'' a pastiche of H.P. Lovecraft; ''The Writer in the Garrett,'' in which a writer of strange stories discovers the horrifying truth about a fellow writer whose work he admires; and ''Synchronicity, or Something,'' a scenario for a fantasy role-playing game in which a fantasy role-playing gamer becomes enmeshed in a world of mystery and dark terrors. Lumley provides an introduction. Illustrated by Dave Carson.

Other books by the same author:
The Second Wish and Other Exhalations, 1995
Dagon's Bell and Other Discords, 1994
Fruiting Bodies and Other Fungi, 1993
The Last Rite, 1993
The Caller of the Black, 1971

Other books you might like:
Lin Carter, *The Xothic Legend Cycle*, 1997
David Langford, *Irrational Numbers*, 1994
W.H. Pugmire, *Tales of Sesqua Valley*, 1997
Jeffrey Thomas, *The Bones of the Old Ones*, 1995
Stanley Wiater, *Mysteries of the World*, 1994
F. Paul Wilson, *The Barrens*, 1992

949

BRIAN LUMLEY

Titus Crow, Volume One

(New York: Tor, 1997)

Story type: Collection
Major character(s): Titus Crow, Adventurer; Henri Laurent de Marigny, Sidekick

Summary: Omnibus repackaging of two novels featuring cosmic troubleshooter Titus Crow and his sidekick, Henri Laurent de Marigny. In *The Burrowers Beneath* (1974), Crow matches wits with Lovecraftian monsters who live beneath the Earth's crust. Its sequel, *The Transition of Titus Crow*, concerns Crow's escape by means of a magic clock to the realm beyond space and time where he is recruited by benevolent deities to fight malignant beings threatening to destroy the universal order.

Where it's reviewed:
Kirkus Reviews, November 1, 1996, page 1556
Publishers Weekly, November 11, 1996, page 55

Other books by the same author:
Titus Crow, Volume Three, 1997
Titus Crow, Volume Two, 1997
Dagon's Bell and Other Discords, 1995

Necroscope Series, 1986-1997

Other books you might like:
Robert Bloch, *Strange Eons*, 1978
Fred Chappell, *Dagon*, 1068
August Derleth, *The Cthulhu Mythos*, 1997
Michael Shea, *The Colour out of Time*, 1984

950

BRIAN LUMLEY

Titus Crow, Volume Three

(New York: Tor, 1997)

Story type: Collection
Major character(s): Titus Crow, Adventurer; Henri Laurent de Marigny, Sidekick; Hank Silberhutte, Telepath

Summary: Omnibus repackaging of the fifth and sixth novels of Lumley's saga of Titus Crow, a psychic investigator who battles Lovecraftian monsters. In *In the Moons of Borea*, Henri Laurent de Marigny and Hank Silberhutte combines forces to fight the wind elemental Ithaqua. In *Elysia: The Coming of Cthulhu* (1989), de Marigny and Silberhutte are reunited with Crow and two transmigrators to the realm of dream, David Hero and Eldin the Wanderer, to prevent the resurgence of the entity Cthulhu.

Where it's reviewed:
Kirkus Reviews, May 1997, page 668
Publishers Weekly, June 9, 1997, page 40

Other books by the same author:
Titus Crow, Volume One, 1997
Titus Crow, Volume Two, 1997
Dagon's Bell and Other Discords, 1995
Necroscope Series, 1986-1997

Other books you might like:
Robert Bloch, *Strange Eons*, 1978
August Derleth, *The Cthulhu Mythos*, 1997
Michael Shea, *The Colour out of Time*, 1984
Colin Wilson, *The Mind Parasites*, 1967

951

BRIAN LUMLEY

Titus Crow, Volume Two

(New York: Tor, 1997)

Story type: Collection
Major character(s): Titus Crow, Adventurer; Henri Laurent de Marigny, Sidekick; Hank Silberhutte, Telepath

Summary: Omnibus repackaging of the third and fourth novels of Lumley's saga of Titus Crow, a psychic investigator who fights Lovecraftian monsters. In *The Clock of Dreams* (1978), Henri Laurent de Marigny uses a magic clock to traverse a cosmos filled with horrors in search of his lost friend, Titus Crow. In *Spawn of the Winds* (1978), de Marigny's friend Hank Silberhutte is abducted to the realm of the wind elemental Ithaqua, where he becomes involved in a plot to free the being's half-human daughter.

Where it's reviewed:
Kirkus Reviews, May 1, 1997, page 668
Publishers Weekly, June 9, 1997, page 40

Other books by the same author:
Titus Crow, Volume One, 1997
Titus Crow, Volume Three, 1997
Dagon's Bell and Other Discords, 1995
Necroscope Series, 1986-1997

Other books you might like:
Robert Bloch, *Strange Eons*, 1978
August Derleth, *The Cthulhu Mythos*, 1997
Michael Shea, *The Colour out of Time*, 1984
Colin Wilson, *The Mind Parasites*, 1967

952

CATHERINE A. LUNDIE, Editor

Restless Spirits

(Amherst, Massachusetts: University of Massachusetts Press, 1997)

Story type: Anthology

Summary: Twenty-two tales of ghosts and the supernatural written by American women between 1872 and 1926. Many use the supernatural to explore feminine themes and issues, including Helen Hull's "Clay Shuttered Doors," about a woman kept alive after death by the needs of her demanding husband; Josephine Daskam Bacon's "The Gospel," about a woman prescribed domesticity as a cure to her apparent madness; Mary E. Wilkins-Freeman's "Luella Miller," about a self-centered woman whose needs drain life vampirically from her caretakers; and Edith Wharton's "The Lady Maid's Bell," about a woman protected by the ghost of her devoted former maid.

Where it's reviewed:
Kirkus Reviews, November 1, 1996, page 556
Necrofile, Fall 1997, page 12

Other books you might like:
Alfred Bendixen, *Haunted Women*, 1985
  editor
Elizabeth Terry, *American Gothic*, 1997
  Terri Hardin, co-editor
Seon Manley, *Ladies of Horror*, 1971
  Gogo Lewis, co-author
Seon Manley, *Ghostly Gentlewomen*, 1977
  Gogo Lewis, co-author
Alan Ryan, *Haunting Women*, 1988
  editor
Jessica Amanda Salmonson, *What Did Miss Darrington See?*, 1989
  editor

953

PATRICK LYNCH

Omega

(New York: Dutton, 1997)

Story type: Mystery

Major character(s): Marcus Ford, Doctor; Lucy Patou, Doctor; Helen Wray, Businesswoman (marketing)
Time period(s): 1990s (1997)
Locale(s): Los Angeles, California

Summary: When patients admitted to the Willowbrook Medical Center with routine injuries begin developing fatal secondary infections, trauma specialist Marcus Ford suspects the irresponsible use of antibiotics that have helped to breed resistant bacteria in the surrounding community. Ford's investigation of a greedy pharmaceutical company uncovers a conspiracy with world-shaking epidemiologic implications.

Where it's reviewed:
Kirkus Reviews, July 1, 1997, page 974

Other books by the same author:
Carriers, 1995

Other books you might like:
John David Connor, *Contagion*, 1992
Michael Crichton, *The Andromeda Strain*, 1969
Tess Gerritsen, *Life Support*, 1997
R. Karl Largent, *Black Death*, 1995
Richard Preston, *Cobra Event*, 1997

954

ARTHUR MACHEN

The Hill of Dreams

(Bristol, Rhode Island: Hobgoblin Press, 1997)

Story type: Occult
Major character(s): Lucian Taylor, Writer; Dr. Burrows, Doctor; Jane Deacon, Young Woman
Time period(s): 1900s
Locale(s): Caermaen, Wales; London, England

Summary: Alienated by the banality of the modern world, hypersensitive Lucian Taylor withdraws into his studies of the arts and occult and learns how to retrieve the splendor of England's Roman past. His ambitions to write a book that will relate his sensual vision drive him to potentially fatal extremes of experience. First published in 1907.

Other books by the same author:
The Green Round, 1933
The Terror, 1917
The Great Return, 1915
The House of Souls, 1906
The Three Impostors, 1895

Other books you might like:
Algernon Blackwood, *The Human Chord*, 1910
J.K. Huysmans, *A Rebours*, 1884
H.P. Lovecraft, *The Dream Quest of Unknown Kadath*, 1955
Oscar Wilde, *The Picture of Dorian Gray*, 1891

955

ALBERT J. MANACHINO

Noctet: Tales of Madonna-Moloch

(Austin, Texas: Argo Press, 1997)

Story type: Collection; Occult

Major character(s): Virgil Hood, Detective
Locale(s): Madonna-Moloch, Planet—Imaginary

Summary: Eight stories set on the planet Madonna-Moloch—a world of sorcery and dark magic—and featuring occult detective Virgil Hood. Hood battles wizards, withces, and the ghastly products of their conjuring in adventures that include "The White Orchard," "The Hungry House," "Evening Primrose," "Sleeping Booty," and "The Garden of Eden."

Where it's reviewed:
Science Fiction Chronicle, October 1997, page 47

Other books by the same author:
The Odd Lot: The Selected Works of Albert J. Manachino, 1993

Other books you might like:
Christie Golden, *Dance of the Dead*, 1992
Staley Krause, *Strange City*, 1996
　Stewart Wieck, co-editor
Brian Lumley, *Iced on Aran and Other Dream Quests*, 1990
Tom Piccirilli, *Pentacle*, 1995
Robert Weinberg, *Bloodwar*, 1995
Chet Williamson, *Mordenheim*, 1994

956

WILLIAM J. MANN, Editor

Grave Passions

(New York: Badboy, 1997)

Story type: Anthology; Gay/Lesbian Fiction

Summary: Eighteen tales of the gay supernatural, all original to the volume. Ghost stories (Felice Picano's "Hunter," Scott O'Hara's "Spirits," Noel Ambery II's "Why I Killed Him," Gary Bowen's "Hungry Ghost"), tales of passion and obsession (Poppy Z. Brite's "Entertaining Mr. Orton," Thomas Roche's "Have I Sinned Against You?"), and fairy tale variations (Lawrence Schimel's "The Farrier and the Elves") explore the dark side of love in a gay context. Many of the selections implicitly address the horrors of love in the era of AIDS.

Other books you might like:
Poppy Z. Brite, *Love in Vein II*, 1997
　Martin H. Greenberg, co-editor
Poppy Z. Brite, *Love in Vein*, 1994
　Martin H. Greenberg, co-editor
Pam Keesey, *Darker Angels: Lesbian Vampire Stories*, 1995
　editor
Amarantha Knight, *Seductive Spectres*, 1996
　editor
Amarantha Knight, *Sex Macabre*, 1996
　editor
Amarantha Knight, *Love Bites*, 1994
　editor
Michael Rowe, *Sons of Darkness: Tales of Men, Blood and Immortality*, 1996
　Thomas Roche, co-editor
Michael Rowe, *Brothers of the Night*, 1997
　Thomas Roche, co-editor

957

RICHARD MARSH

The Haunted Chair and Other Stories

(Ashcroft, British Columbia: Ash-Tree Press, 1997)

Story type: Collection

Summary: Eighteen stories, representing the complete short supernatural fiction of the author. Included are "The Adventure of Lady Wishaw's Hand," about a supernaturally animated disembodied hand; "The Photographs," in which a woman uses astral projection to find the criminal responsible for the crime her husband was unjustly imprisoned for; "The Violin," in which a ghostly tune from a violin reveals the whereabouts of its murdered owner's body; "George Ogden's Will," in which a ghost executes its own will; and "A Set of Chessmen," in which a chess set continues to move by the plays of its deceased owner. Edited and with an introduction by Richard Dalby.

Other books by the same author:
Both Sides of the Veil, 1902
Amusement Only, 1901
The Seen and the Unseen, 1900
Curios: Some Strange Adventures of Two Bachelors, 1898
The Beetle: A Mystery, 1897

Other books you might like:
E.F. Benson, *The Collected Ghost Stories of E.F. Benson*, 1992
A.M. Burrage, *Some Ghost Stories*, 1927
Frederick Cowles, *Fear Walks the Night*, 1992
Sabine Baring Gould, *A Book of Ghosts*, 1904
M.R. James, *The Collected Ghost Stories of M.R. James*, 1931

958

DAVID MARTIN

Cul-De-Sac

(New York: Villard, 1997)

Story type: Serial Killer
Major character(s): Donald Growler, Murderer; Teddy Camel, Police Officer (former); Annie Milton, Young Woman
Time period(s): 1990s (1997)
Locale(s): Washington, District of Columbia

Summary: Framed for a murder which he did not commit, Donald Growler emerges from prison a psychotic criminal determined to kill those who set him up. Annie Milton, wife of an asylum owner who has benefitted from Growler's incarceration, engages the services of her former lover Teddy Camel, an ex-cop, whose efforts to protect her uncover a conspiracy that the murder victim's family is desperate to keep secret.

Where it's reviewed:
Kirkus Reviews, January 15, 1997, page 86
Publishers Weekly, December 30, 1996, page 53

Other books by the same author:
Love Me to Death, 1994
Bring Me Children, 1992

Lie to Me, 1990

Other books you might like:
John Farris, *The Axman Cometh*, 1989
Joe R. Lansdale, *The Nightrunners*, 1987
Patrick McCabe, *The Butcher Boy*, 1992
John Saul, *Black Lightning*, 1995

959

GRAHAM MASTERTON

Rook

(New York: Severn House, 1997)

Story type: Wild Talents; Black Magic
Major character(s): Jim Rook, Teacher; T.J. Jones, Teenager; Umber Jones, Sorcerer
Time period(s): 1990s (1997)
Locale(s): Westwood, California

Summary: Schoolteacher Jim Rook finds his psychic powers tested when a troubled black student falls under the influence of his evil uncle Umber, a criminal who uses voodoo to extort riches from his victims and who doesn't hesitate to destroy people like Jim when they attempt to stop him. This novel was first published in England in 1996. First in a series.

Where it's reviewed:
Kirkus Reviews, February 15, 1997, page 246
Publishers Weekly, March 10, 1997, page 519

Other books by the same author:
Tooth and Claw, 1997
The House that Jack Built, 1996
Spirit, 1995
Flesh and Blood, 1994

Other books you might like:
Don Davis, *The Gris-Gris Man*, 1996
Stephen King, *The Dead Zone*, 1979
Dean R. Koontz, *Cold Fire*, 1991

960

GRAHAM MASTERTON

Tooth and Claw

(New York: Severn House, 1997)

Story type: Occult
Major character(s): Jim Rook, Teacher; Catherine White Bird, Teenager; Dog Brother, Supernatural Being
Time period(s): 1990s (1997)
Locale(s): West Grove, California; Window Rock, Arizona

Summary: In his second adventure, psychically endowed school teacher Jim Rook defends a Native American student implicated in several gruesome murders. His investigations bring him into confrontation with an avatar of Coyote, the trickster of Navajo legend, to whom the student was bethrothed by his family.

Where it's reviewed:
Publishers Weekly, November 10, 1997, page 57

Other books by the same author:
Rook, 1997

The House that Jack Built, 1996
Spirit, 1995
Flesh and Blood, 1994
Burial, 1992

Other books you might like:
Chris Curry, *Trickster*, 1994
    Lisa Dean, Co-author
Muriel Gray, *The Trickster*, 1994
Colin Kersey, *Soul Catcher*, 1995
G. Wayne Miller, *Thunder Rise*, 1988
Adam Niswander, *The Charm*, 1993
Kathryn Ptacek, *Ghost Dance*, 1990

961

DENNIS MCFARLAND

A Face at the Window

(New York: Villard, 1997)

Story type: Ghost Story
Major character(s): Cookson Selway, Restaurateur; Ellen Selway, Writer (mystery novelist); Pascal, Hotel Worker (porter)
Time period(s): 1990s (1997)
Locale(s): London, England

Summary: On a trip to London, Cookson Selway encounters ghosts at a hotel where several mysterious violent deaths occured half a century before. The startling experience leads Cookson to re-evaluate his morally questionable life to date, and to examine himself in terms of the ghosts, who may simply be projections of his own psyche.

Where it's reviewed:
Kirkus Reviews, December 15, 1996, page 1759
New York Times, March 15, 1997, page C

Other books by the same author:
School for the Blind, 1994
The Music Room, 1990

Other books you might like:
Jack Cady, *The Off Season*, 1995
Brad Leithauser, *Seaward*, 1993
Mark Morris, *The Immaculate*, 1992
Michael Upchurch, *Passive Intruder*, 1995

962

PATRICK MCGRATH

Asylum

(New York: Random House, 1997)

Story type: Psychological Suspense
Major character(s): Peter Cleave, Doctor (psychiatrist); Stella Raphael, Housewife; Edgar Stark, Artist (sculptor)
Time period(s): 1990s (1997)
Locale(s): London, England

Summary: After bringing disgrace on herself and her family by running off with psychotic inmate Edgar Stark, Stella Raphael, wife of the psychiatrist who heads the asylum Stark escaped from, becomes an inmate there herself. There she is

cared for by Peter Cleave, a competitor of her husband's whose interest in her case approaches the obessiveness of her affair with Stark.

Where it's reviewed:
Kirkus Reviews, December 15, 1996, page 1759
Necrofile, Summer 1997, page 10
New York Times Book Review, February 23, 1997, page 6
New York Times, February 14, 1997, page C38
Publishers Weekly, December 16, 1997, page 41

Other books by the same author:
Dr. Haggard's Disease, 1993
Spider, 1990
The Grotesque, 1989

Other books you might like:
Michael Cadnum, *Skyscape*, 1994
Kathe Koja, *Strange Angels*, 1994

963

BRIAN MCNAUGHTON

The Throne of Bones

(Black River, New York: Terminal Fright Publications, 1997)

Story type: Collection

Summary: Ten stories of otherwordly dark fantasy distinguished by gruesome imagery and black comedy. The author evokes both the horrors of H.P. Lovecraft and the decadent imaginary lands of Clark Ashton Smith in a variety of stories featuring ghouls, sorcerers, necromancers, necrophiles, and other fiendish beings. Selections include ''Ringard and Dendra,'' ''Meryphillia,'' ''The Retrograde Necromancer,'' ''The Return of Liron Wolfbaiter,'' and ''Vendriel and Vendreela.'' Afterword by S.T. Joshi.

Where it's reviewed:
Locus, October 1997, page 23

Other books by the same author:
Satan's Surrogate, 1982
Satan's Seductress, 1980
Satan's Mistress, 1978
Satan's Love Child, 1977

Other books you might like:
Lin Carter, *The Xothic Legend Cycle*, 1997
Lord Dunsany, *A Dreamer's Tales*, 1910
H.P. Lovecraft, *The Dream Quest of Unknown Kadath*, 1970
Gary Myers, *The House of the Worm*, 1975
Darrell Schweitzer, *Tom O'Bedlam's Night Out and Other Strange Excursions*, 1985
Clark Ashton Smith, *Tales of Zothique*, 1995
Brian Stableford, *Fables and Fantasies*, 1996

964

BILL MICHAELS (Pseudonym of William Carney)

Witchcraft

(New York: Zebra, 1997)

Story type: Black Magic

Major character(s): Steve Brogan, Detective—Private; Molly Daniels, Witch; Lady Eva, Witch
Time period(s): 1990s (1997)
Locale(s): Hennington, California

Summary: Steve Brogan investigates the disinterment and mutilation of a corpse in the small town of Hennington and uncovers a feud between the Coven of the Crystal Moon, a Wicca cult, and the Coven of the Dark Dream, a black magic cult. The situation intensifies when Lady Eva, leader of the Coven of the Dark Dream, steals the daughter of one of the Wicca witches to use in a ritual that will let an ancient evil back into the world.

Other books by the same author:
Hide and Seek, 1991
Devil's Moon, 1988

Other books you might like:
Ramsey Campbell, *Nameless*, 1981
Gary L. Holleman, *Demon Fire*, 1995
Adrian Savage, *Symphony*, 1992
Brian Scott Smith, *When Shadows Fall*, 1997
Robert Weinberg, *The Black Lodge*, 1991

965

SUSAN MOLONEY

A Dry Spell

(New York: Delacorte, 1997)

Story type: Occult
Major character(s): Karen Grange, Banker; Thompson Keatley, Magician (rainmaker); Vida Whalley, Young Woman
Time period(s): 1990s (1997)
Locale(s): Goodlands, North Dakota

Summary: Rainmaker Thompson Keatley arrives in parched Goodlands to put an end to a devastating four-year drought but his intervention rouses the ghosts—some literal—of the town's past, forcing the townspeople to acknowledge the source of the curse put upon them.

Where it's reviewed:
Hellnotes, November 7, 1997, page 3
Necrofile, Winter 1998, page 26
Publishers Weekly, July 21, 1997, page 180

Other books by the same author:
Bastion Falls, 1995

Other books you might like:
Ramsey Campbell, *The Hungary Moon*, 1986
Bentley Little, *The Revelation*, 1990
Steve Rasnic Tem, *Excavation*, 1987
Tamara Thorne, *Haunted*, 1995

966

BRENT MONAHAN

The Bell Witch

(New York: St. Martin's, 1997)

Story type: Occult

Major character(s): Richard Powell, Teacher; Elizabeth Bell, Child; John Bell, Businessman
Time period(s): 1810s; 1820s (1817-1821)
Locale(s): Adams, Tennessee

Summary: Twelve-year old Betsy Bell becomes possessed by a mischievous spirit, the result of a family quarrel with a vengeful local witch woman. The spirit's disruption of the Bell household attracts a variety of celebrities and charlatans of the era, all of whom hope to lay the spirit to rest and resolve Betsy's affliction. Presented as a true narrative, illustrated with period woodcuts.

Where it's reviewed:
Fantasy and Science Fiction, July 1997, page 24
Kirkus Reviews, January 1, 1997, page 15
Locus, May 1997, page 25
Publishers Weekly, February 3, 1997, page 94
SF Chronicle, June 1997, page 41

Other books by the same author:
Blood of the Covenant, 1995
The Book of Common Dread, 1993
The Uprising, 1992
Satan's Serenade, 1989

Other books you might like:
Jack Cady, *The Well*, 1980
Tom Elliott, *The Dwelling*, 1989
Stephen King, *The Shining*, 1977
H.P. Lovecraft, *The Case of Charles Dexter Ward*, 1971
Graham Masterton, *The House that Jack Built*, 1996

967

THOMAS F. MONTELEONE

Between Floors

(Burton, Michigan: Subterranean Press, 1997)

Story type: Psychological Suspense
Major character(s): Charles Jameson, Businessman; Alan Markley, Businessman; Dr. Doom, Leader (insane)
Time period(s): 1990s (1997)
Locale(s): New York, New York

Summary: Relieved of his job by a ruthless CEO, Charles Jameson plots an ironic revenge with the help of a madman who calls himself Dr. Doom and who is convinced the company is responsible for despoiling the environment. Published as a signed limited edition chapbook.

Where it's reviewed:
Locus, April 1997, page 25

Other books by the same author:
Night of Broken Souls, 1997
The Resurrectionist, 1995
The Blood of the Lamb, 1992
Fantasma, 1989
Dark Stars and Other Illuminations, 1981

Other books you might like:
James P. Blaylock, *All the Bells on Earth*, 1995
Thomas M. Disch, *The Businessman: A Tale of Terror*, 1984
Christopher Fowler, *Rune*, 1991
Floyd Kemske, *Human Resources*, 1995

William Browning Spencer, *Resume with Monsters*, 1995

968

THOMAS F. MONTELEONE

Night of Broken Souls

(New York: Warner, 1997)

Story type: Reincarnation
Major character(s): Harford Nichols, Government Official (CIA); Isabella Mussina, Doctor; Michael Keating, Doctor
Time period(s): 1990s (1997)
Locale(s): New York, New York

Summary: Possessed by the spirit of Hirsh Dukor, a Jewish turncoat who assisted Nazi Dr. Mengele in the Auschwitz concentration camp, CIA assassin Harford Nichols embarks on a contemporary version of the Final Solution. Hoping to thwart him, Dr. Michael Keating musters the help of patients whose recurring nightmares indicate that they are reincarnations of people who died in the concentration camps of World War II.

Where it's reviewed:
Cemetery Dance, Spring 1997, page 118
Kirkus Reviews, January 1, 1997, page 16
Science Fiction Chronicle, June 1997, page 14

Other books by the same author:
The Resurrectionist, 1995
The Blood of the Lamb, 1992
Fantasma, 1989
Lyrica, 1987
The Magnificent Gallery, 1986

Other books you might like:
Ira Levin, *The Boys from Brazil*, 1976
Robert R. McCammon, *The Night Boat*, 1980
Kathryn Ptacek, *The Hunted*, 1993
Nina Romberg, *Shadow Walkers*, 1993
Robert Weinberg, *The Armageddon Box*, 1991

969

ROBERT MORRISON, Editor
CHRISTOPHER BALDICK, Co-Editor

The Vampyre and Other Tales of the Macabre

(New York: Oxford, 1997)

Story type: Anthology

Summary: Fourteen macabre stories published in popular British literary magazines between 1819 and 1938. Included are John Polidori's ''The Vampyre,'' the first popular vampire tale, and its complimentary fragment, Lord Byron's ''Augustus Darvell.'' Other selections include J. Sheridan Le Fanu's locked-room mystery, ''Passage in the Secret History of an Irish Countess''; Edward Bulwer's doppelganger tale, ''Monos and Daimonos''; and Horace Smith's tale of the reanimated dead, ''Sir Guy Everling's Dream.'' Stories that take the form of true fact reporting include James Hogg's tale of a cholera epidemic, ''Some Terrible Letters from Scot-

Horror (side margin)

land,'' and William Carleton's account of a lynching, ''Confessions of a Reformed Ribbonman.''

Other books by the same author:
Tales of Terror From Blackwood's Magazine, 1995

Other books you might like:
Jack Adrian, *Strange Tales from the Strand*, 1991
    editor
Peter Haining, *Great Tales of Terror from Europe and America*, 1973
    editor
Robert Donald Spector, *Seven Masterpieces of Gothic Horror*, 1963
    editor
Jack C. Wolf, *Ghosts, Castles and Victims*, 1971
    Barbara H. Wolf, co-editor
Jack C. Wolf, *Tales of the Occult*, 1975
    Barbara H. Wolf, co-editor

970

JONATHAN NASAW

Shadows

(New York: Dutton, 1997)

Story type: Vampire Story
Major character(s): Jamey Whistler, Vampire; Aldo Striescu, Vampire; Selene Weiss, Witch (wicca)
Time period(s): 1990s (1997)
Locale(s): Santa Luz, Virgin Islands of the United States; New York, New York; Mill Valley, California

Summary: Jamey Whistler has repudiated his vampire life, setting the stage for his pursuit by Aldo Striescu, a vampire assassin hired by Jamey's estranged vampire father. Jamey's former lover Selene comes to the rescue, warning Jamey of the plot against him and marshaling Wiccan powers and herbal magic that protect but put her in the line of fire between Jamey and Aldo. A semi-sequel to *The World on Blood* (1996).

Where it's reviewed:
Kirkus Reviews, August 1, 1997, page 1143
Publishers Weekly, July 28, 1997, page 50

Other books by the same author:
The World on Blood, 1996

Other books you might like:
Nancy Baker, *The Night Inside*, 1995
Tanith Lee, *Darkness, I*, 1995
Michael Romkey, *The Vampire Papers*, 1996
Whitley Strieber, *The Hunger*, 1981

971

ANDREW NEIDERMAN

The Dark

(New York: Pocket, 1997)

Story type: Occult
Major character(s): Grant Blaine, Doctor (psychiatrist); Maggie Blaine, Lawyer; Jules Bois, Consultant

Time period(s): 1990s (1997)
Locale(s): Los Angeles, California

Summary: Grant Blaine assumes the case of Jules Bois, a patient of a murdered colleague, who confesses to a compulsion to cause people to commit evil. As Bois slowly discomposes Grant's life, undermining his self-assurance and turning his psychoanalytic inquiries against him, Grant's wife Maggie investigates Bois's background to discover psychotic, and possibly satanic, influences.

Other books by the same author:
Duplicates, 1994
After Life, 1993
The Need, 1992
The Immortal, 1991
The Devil's Advocate, 1990

Other books you might like:
Robert Bloch, *The Scarf*, 1947
Michael Cadnum, *Skyscape*, 1994
Andrew Harper, *Bad Karma*, 1997
Thomas Harris, *The Silence of the Lambs*, 1988
Kathe Koja, *Strange Angels*, 1994
Patrick McGrath, *Asylum*, 1997

972

ANDREW NEIDERMAN

The Devil's Advocate

(New York: Pocket, 1997)

Story type: Black Magic
Major character(s): Kevin Taylor, Lawyer; John Milton, Lawyer; Miriam Taylor, Housewife
Time period(s): 1990s
Locale(s): New York, New York

Summary: The law firm of John Milton and Associates is infamous for getting criminal clients acquitted for their crimes. Hotshot lawyer Kevin Taylor discovers that Milton, his employer, is the devil incarnate and that any effort to go against his wishes invites his infernal wrath. Originally published in 1990, but reissued to tie in with its 1997 film adaptation.

Other books by the same author:
The Dark, 1997
Duplicates, 1994
After Life, 1993
The Need, 1992
The Immortal, 1991

Other books you might like:
Clive Barker, *The Damnation Game*, 1985
Ramsey Campbell, *Obsession*, 1986
Matthew J. Costello, *Darkborn*, 1992
William Hjortsberg, *Falling Angel*, 1978
Stephen King, *Needful Things*, 1992
Robert Masello, *Private Demons*, 1992
Kim Newman, *The Quorum*, 1993

973

AMYAS NORTHCOTE

In Ghostly Company

(Ashcroft, British Columbia: Ash-Tree Press, 1997)

Story type: Collection

Summary: Thirteen quiet tales of ghosts and supernatural horrors, ranging in theme from "Brickett Bottom," an eerie tale of a young girl lured into the past; and "Mr. Kershaw and Mr. Wilcox," a weird invention story. First published in 1921. With an introduction by Richard Dalby and a bibliographic tailpiece by Jack Adrian.

Where it's reviewed:
All Hallows, June 1997, page 80
Necrofile, Winter 1998, page 18

Other books you might like:
E.F. Benson, *The Collected Ghost Stories of E.F. Benson*, 1992
M.P. Dare, *Unholy Relics*, 1947
August Derleth, *Someone in the Dark*, 1941
L.P. Hartley, *The Travelling Grave and Other Stories*, 1948
William Fryer Harvey, *The Beast with Five Fingers and Other Stories*, 1928
H. Russell Wakefield, *Imagine a Man in a Box*, 1931

974

JEFFREY OSIER

Horizon Lines

(Concord, California: Dark Regions, 1997)

Story type: Collection

Summary: Seven stories, all previously published, in which strange, possibly supernatural experiences reflect or are colored by the unsettled minds of characters. Best selections include "Snowlight," in which a young boy's anger over the death of his father manifests as a specter pursuing him; "The Shabbie People," in which a man who may be mad discovers that his girlfriend is an otherwordly being; "Why I Dropped Out of Art School," in which a young man's rite of passage into adulthood thrusts him into an unstable, supernaturally menacing world; and "Don't Clean the Aquarium," in which a man's troubled emotional life is mirrored in the peculiarities of his living room fish tank. Elizabeth Massie supplies an introduction.

Other books by the same author:
Driftglider and Other Stories, 1993

Other books you might like:
Gary A. Braunbeck, *Things Left Behind*, 1997
Cliff Burns, *The Reality Machine*, 1997
Brian Hopkins, *Something Haunts Us All*, 1996
Bentley Little, *Murmerous Haunts*, 1997
Stephen Mark Rainey, *Fugue Devil and Other Weird Horrors*, 1993
Wayne Allen Sallee, *With Wounds Still Wet*, 1996
David Niall Wilson, *The Fall of the House of Escher and Other Illusions*, 1996

975

DENNIS PEPPER, Editor

The Young Oxford Book of Ghost Stories

(New York: Oxford, 1997)

Story type: Anthology; Young Adult

Summary: Forty tales of horror and the supernatural that span the century and that were chosen with young adults' tastes in mind. Included are M.R. James's "Rats," in which a traveler witnesses a ghostly apparition at an inn; E.F. Benson's "The House with the Brick-Kiln," which features a guilty ghost that continually re-enacts the shocking murder of his former wife; Marjorie Bowen's "The Crown Derby Plate," in which a collector's zeal to complete a china set leads her into a ghostly encounter; and E. Nesbit's "John Charrington's," in which a man keeps his vow to return from the dead to attend his wedding. Contemporary contributions include Robert Westall's "The Call," William F. Nolan's "Dead Call," and John Gordon's "Little Black Pies." First published in 1994.

Other books by the same author:
The Oxford Book of Scarytales, 1992

Other books you might like:
Ramsey Campbell, *The Gruesome Book*, 1983
Martin H. Greenberg, *Great Writers and Kids Write Spooky Stories*, 1995
  Jill Morgan and Robert Weinberg, co-editors
William Mayne, *Supernatural Stories*, 1996
Philippa Pearce, *Dread and Delight: A Century of Children's Ghost Stories*, 1995
  editor
Susan Price, *Horror Stories*, 1995
Robert Westall, *Ghost Stories*, 1988
  editor

976

TOM PICCIRILLI

The Dog Syndrome and Other Sick Puppies

(Marietta Georgia: Marietta Publishing, 1997)

Story type: Collection

Summary: Signed limited edition chapbook of six stories, most concerned with the dark side of male and female relationships. Highlights include "The Dog Syndrome," which takes the anonymity of contemporary sexual relations to a horrifying extreme; "Where the Swamp Folk Go When the Need Comes," a tale of haunting and madness on the bayou; and "Lilith at the Playground," narrated by a child in the grip of an evil influence. Illustrations by Eric Turnmire, Keith Minnion, Alfred Klosterman, Ray Carlson, Tom Simonton, GARK, and Wayne Miller.

Other books by the same author:
Pentacle, 1995
Dark Father, 1990

Other books you might like:
Kevin J. Anderson, *Shifting the Boundaries*, 1995

Horror

Michael A. Arnzen, *Needles and Sins*, 1994
Brian Hodge, *The Convulsion Factory*, 1996
Brian Hopkins, *Something Haunts Us All*, 1995
Jeffrey Osier, *Horizon Lines*, 1997
David Niall Wilson, *The Fall of the House of Escher and Other Illusions*, 1995

977

TOM PICCIRILLI
GERARD DANIEL HOUARNER, Co-Author
EDWARD LEE, Co-Author

Inside the Works

(Orlando, Florida: Necro Publications, 1997)

Story type: Anthology

Summary: Miscellaneous works by three authors, each represented by approximately 30,000 words of text. Tom Piccirilli (introduced by Ed Gorman) contributes five short stories, including "Passing Through," the tale of a small town experiencing perplexing slips in space and time. Gerard Daniel Houarner (introduced by Bentley Little) contributes the novella, "Truth and Consequences in the Heart of Destruction," which features the author's series assassin, Max, to protect him against one of those he has killed. Edward Lee (introduced by Wayne Allen Sallee) is represented by "The Pig," a grotesque tale of bestiality and pornography.

Where it's reviewed:
Hellnotes, November 21, 1997, page 3

Other books you might like:
Various Authors, *The Night Visions Series*, 1984-1992
Dana Anderson, *Cafe Purgatorium*, 1991
   Charles de Lint and Ray Garton, co-authors
Richard T. Chizmar, *Chillers*, 1994
   editor
Lucius Shepard, *Nantucket Slayrides*, 1990
   Robert Frazer, co-author

978

ROBERT POE

The Black Cat

(New York: Tor/Forge, 1997)

Story type: Mystery
Major character(s): John Charles Poe, Journalist; Julie Noir, Teenager; Lawrence Cully, Veterinarian
Time period(s): 1970s (1973)
Locale(s): Crowley Creek, Virginia

Summary: The disappearance of Margaret Cully, wife of the local veterinarian in the sleepy town of Crowley Creek, is blamed on his teenage assistant, Julie, whose mystical beliefs and expertise in herbalism have persuaded townsfolk that she is a witch. But John Charles Poe sees enough parallels between the mystery and "The Black Cat," the classic story by his distant relative Edgar Allan Poe, to believe more plausible mechanisms are at work.

Other books by the same author:
Return to the House of Usher, 1996

Other books you might like:
Deborah Churchman, *Cross a Dark Bridge*, 1996
S.K. Epperson, *The Moons of Summer*, 1994
William Hjortsberg, *Nevermore*, 1995
Marie Kiraly, *Madeline: After the Fall of Usher*, 1996
Robert R. McCammon, *Usher's Passing*, 1984

979

DOUGLAS PRESTON
LINCOLN CHILD, Co-Author

Reliquary

(New York: Tor/Forge, 1997)

Story type: Science Fiction
Major character(s): Margo Green, Anthropologist; Vincent D'Agosta, Police Officer (lieutenant); Bill Smithback, Journalist
Time period(s): 1990s (1997)
Locale(s): New York, New York

Summary: The discovery of decapitated bodies of Manhattan's street police people raises fears of a race of predatory monsters who feed on human brains and live in the train tunnels beneath Manhattan. A sequel to *Relic* (1995).

Where it's reviewed:
Cemetery Dance, Fall 1997, page 126
Kirkus Reviews, March 15, 1997, page 411
Locus, July 1997, page 31
Publishers Weekly, March 3, 1997, page 63

Other books by the same author:
Mount Dragon, 1996
Relic, 1995

Other books you might like:
Peter Benchley, *Beast*, 1991
Michael Crichton, *The Lost World*, 1995
Ken Eulo, *Claw*, 1994
   Joe Mauck, co-author
Frank Belknap Long, *The Horror from the Hills*, 1963

980

ROBERT M. PRICE, Editor

The Necronomicon

(Oakland, California: Chaosium, 1997)

Story type: Anthology
Series: The Cthulhu Cycle

Summary: Miscellany of stories and articles inspired by the *Necronomicon*, the legendary book of forbidden knowledge that appears in the fiction of H.P. Lovecraft. Stories featuring the book include Fred Chappell's "The Adder," in which the volume has the power to corrupt anything put next to it, and John Brunner's "Concerning the Forthcoming Inexpensive Paperback Translation of the *Necronomicon*," about efforts to prevent the madness that will ensue when the book becomes accessible to anyone. Frank Belknap Long and L. Sprague de Camp contribute fragmentary "excerpts" from the *Necronomicon* itself.

Other books by the same author:
The Nyarlathotep Cycle, 1997
The Hastur Cycle, 1997
The New Lovecraft Circle, 1996
The Azathoth Cycle, 1995

Other books you might like:
Scott David Aniolowski, *Return to Lovecraft Country*, 1997
  editor
Edward P. Berglund, *Disciples of Cthulhu*, 1996
  editor
Robert Weinberg, *Miskatonic University*, 1996
  Martin H. Greenberg, co-editor

981

ROBERT M. PRICE, Editor

The Nyarlathotep Cycle
(Oakland, California: Chaosium, 1997)

Story type: Anthology
Series: The Cthulhu Cycle

Summary: Fifteen stories and three poems featuring or redolent of Nyarlathotep, a mutable supernatural being who serves as a messenger of dark gods in the fiction of H.P. Lovecraft. Selections include Lovecraft's ''Dreams in the Witch House,'' in which a student discovers an association between mathematics and black magic; August Derleth's ''The Dweller in Darkness,'' in which Nyarlathotep appropriates a human form to beguile his victims; and Robert Bloch's ''Fane of the Black Pharaoh,'' which explores Nyarlathotep's pervasive presence in Egyption mythology.

Other books by the same author:
The Necronomicon, 1997
The Hastur Cycle, 2nd Edition, 1997 (editor)
The Azathoth Cycle, 1995
The Hastur Cycle, 1993

Other books you might like:
Edward P. Berglund, *Disciples of Cthulhu*, 1996
  editor
H.P. Lovecraft, *Tales of the Cthulhu Mythos*, 1990
James Turner, *Cthulhu 2000*, 1996
  editor

982

W.H. PUGMIRE

Tales of Sesqua Valley
(Westborough, Massachusetts: Necropolitan Press, 1997)

Story type: Collection

Summary: Ten stories set in the Sesqua Valley, a fictional milieu of the Pacific Northwest. The author blends nostalgia, romance and Lovecraftian horrors in poetic and passionate tales that include ''Another Flesh,'' ''Apotheosis,'' ''Immortal Remains,'' ''An Image in Chalk,'' and ''Born in Strange Shadow.'' Introduction by Jeffrey Thomas. Illustrated by Earl Geier, Jeffrey Thomas, and Scott Thomas.

Other books by the same author:
Tales of Sesqua Valley, 1990

Other books you might like:
Lin Carter, *The Xothic Legend Cycle*, 1997
David Langford, *Irrational Numbers*, 1994
Brian Lumley, *In His Own Write: Brian Lumley, Necroscribe*, 1997
Jeffrey Thomas, *The Bones of the Old Ones*, 1995
Stanley Wiater, *Mysteries of the World*, 1994
F. Paul Wilson, *The Barrens*, 1992

983

ANNE RICE

Violin
(New York: Knopf, 1997)

Story type: Ghost Story
Major character(s): Triana Becker, Musician; Stephan Stefanovsky, Musician (violinist), Spirit; Katrinka Russell, Housewife (Triana's sister)
Time period(s): 1990s (1997); 19th century
Locale(s): New Orleans, Louisiana; Vienna, Austria; Rio de Janeiro, Brazil

Summary: Devastated with grief over the loss of loved ones and haunted by memories of the past, failed musician Triana Becker is vulnerable to the influence of Stefan Stefanovsky, a violinist who died unfulfilled and miserable centuries before. Unbounded by the limits of time and space, Triana and Stefan pursue each other across the centuries and the globe, Stefan trying to dominate Triana with his music and imprison her in his own hell, and Triana trying to usurp Stefan's power and find salvation.

Where it's reviewed:
Kirkus Reviews, August 1, 1997, page 1146
Publishers Weekly, August 18, 1997, page 66

Other books by the same author:
Servant of the Bones, 1996
Taltos, 1994
Lasher, 1993
The Witching Hour, 1990
The Mummy, or Ramses the Damned, 1989

Other books you might like:
Clive Barker, *Sacrament*, 1996
Jonathan Carroll, *From the Teeth of Angels*, 1994
Lou Shiner, *Glimpses*, 1993
Danielle Steele, *Ghost*, 1997

984

BARBARA RODEN, Editor
CHRISTOPHER RODEN, Co-Editor

Midnight Never Comes
(Ashcroft, British Columbia: Ash-Tree Press, 1997)

Story type: Anthology; Ghost Story

Summary: Seventeen ghostly tales, all original to this volume and many written in the classic ghostly tradition. Selections

include Terry Lamsley's "The Snug," concerned with an inn haunted by the spirits of a satanic coven; Colin Mackay's "Mary King's Close," in which a man stumbles back in time to Scotland's plague-ridden past; Ron Wieghell's "The Mouth of the Medusa," in which an archaeological team falls under the pernicious influence of the pagan ruins they are excavating; Rosemary Pardoe's "The Sheelagh-na-gig," about the evil doom portended by an ancient fertility symbol; and Marni Griffin's poignant "Outside the Gates," in which an emotionally troubled woman finds a surrogate for her lost mother in a dead female writer.

Where it's reviewed:
Necrofile, Winter 1998, page 14

Other books by the same author:
Forgotten Ghosts, 1996

Other books you might like:
Ramsey Campbell, *Uncanny Banquet*, 1992
    editor
Chris Morgan, *Dark Fantasies*, 1989
    editor
Claudia O'Keefe, *Ghost Tide*, 1993
    editor
Paul F. Olson, *Post-Mortem: New Tales of Ghostly Horror*, 1989
    David B. Silva, co-editor
Wendy Webb, *Gothic Ghosts*, 1997
    Charles L. Grant, co-editor

985

MICHAEL ROWE, Editor
THOMAS S. ROCHE, Co-Editor

Brothers of the Night

(San Francisco: Cleis Press, 1997)

Story type: Anthology; Vampire Story

Summary: Eleven tales of the supernatural that use the vampire theme to explore issues of gay male sexuality. In Caitlin R. Kiernan's "Superheroes," two gay lovers seek to escape their unfulfilling lives through a tryst with an unusual contact made during an on-line chat. In Edo van Belkom's "Letting Go," a vampire stalks a hospital, bestowing the gift of death on AIDS patients. Both Robert Thomsen, in "Third Night," and Bruce Benderson, in "Old World Manners," report the indoctrination of young men by experienced male vampires. David Quinn's "Forever October" is an ambiguous tale of a man whose vampire behavior may be a sign of madness.

Other books by the same author:
Sons of Darkness: Tales of Men, Blood and Immortality, 1996

Other books you might like:
Poppy Z. Brite, *Love in Vein II*, 1997
    Martin H. Greenberg, co-editor
Pam Keesey, *Daughters of Darkness: Lesbian Vampire Stories*, 1993
    editor
Pam Keesey, *Darker Angels: Lesbian Vampire Stories*, 1995
    editor
Amarantha Knight, *Love Bites*, 1995
    editor

Cecilia Tan, *Vampire Erotica*, 1995
    editor
Cecilia Tan, *Erotica Vampirica*, 1996
    editor

986

J.S. RUSSELL

Celestial Dogs

(New York: St. Martin's, 1997)

Story type: Occult; Mystery
Major character(s): Marty Burns, Detective; Long John Silver, Criminal (pimp); Jack Rippen, Producer
Time period(s): 1990s (1997)
Locale(s): Los Angeles, California

Summary: Marty Burns, a detective with ties to the Hollywood film industry, traces the death of an acquaintance's girlfriend to the underground snuff film industry, where the Japanese backers of Laughing Boy Pictures are apparently subsidizing ritual murders to propitiate a centuries-old supernatural menace. This first novel was originally published in England in 1996.

Where it's reviewed:
Cemetery Dance, Spring 1997, page 115
Kirkus Reviews, January 15, 1997, page 100
Locus, March 1997, page 29

Other books by the same author:
Burning Bright, 1998

Other books you might like:
Ramsey Campbell, *Ancient Images*, 1989
Jonathan Carroll, *A Child Across the Sky*, 1989
Dennis Cooper, *Frisk*, 1991
Tim Lucas, *Throat Sprockets*, 1994
Theodore Roszak, *Flicker*, 1991

987

JOHN A. RUSSO

Night of the Living Dead

(Edmonton, Alberta: Commonwealth, 1997)

Story type: Reanimated Dead
Major character(s): Ben, Truck Driver; Barbara, Young Woman; Harry Cooper, Businessman
Time period(s): 1970s
Locale(s): Pennsylvania (rural)

Summary: A cross-section of people representing the best and worst of humanity hide in an abandoned house overnight, trying to fend off an army of the newly dead who have been resurrected by radioactivity from outer space as flesh-eating zombies. Novelization of George Romero's cult classic movie, first published in 1974. Romero supplies an introduction.

Other books by the same author:
Living Things, 1988
Voodoo Dawn, 1987
Inhuman, 1986

Day Care, 1985
Black Cat: A Novel of Terror, 1982
Return of the Living Dead, 1978

Other books you might like:
Clive Barker, *Cabal*, 1988
Phil Nutman, *Wetwork*, 1993
Byron Preiss, *The Ultimate Zombie*, 1993
    John Betancourt, co-author
George Romero, *Dawn of the Dead*, 1978
    Susannah Sparrow, co-author
John Skipp, *Book of the Dead*, 1989
    Craig Spector, co-editor
John Skipp, *Still Dead: Book of the Dead 2*, 1992
    Craig Spector, co-editor

988

JOHN A. RUSSO

Return of the Living Dead
(Edmonton, Alberta: Commonwealth, 1997)

Story type: Reanimated Dead
Major character(s): John Carter, Criminal; Dvid Benton, Police Officer (state trooper); Conan McClellan, Police Officer (sheriff)
Time period(s): 1980s
Locale(s): Pennsylvania (rural)

Summary: Ten years after the events in *Night of the Living Dead*, to which this novel is a sequel, packs of flesh-eating zombies still roam the American countryside, which has been transformed into a Darwinian proving ground where looters, scavengers and vigilantes who exploit the state of emergency are as bad as the zombie menace. Based on the scenario of George Romero's cult film *Night of the Living Dead*, although it is not related to films in the series or to the similarly titled movie of 1985. First published in 1978.

Other books by the same author:
Living Things, 1988
Voodoo Dawn, 1987
Inhuman, 1986
Day Care, 1985
Night of the Living Dead, 1974

Other books you might like:
Clive Barker, *Cabal*, 1988
Phil Nutman, *Wetwork*, 1993
Byron Preiss, *The Ultimate Zombie*, 1993
    John Betancourt, co-author
George Romero, *Dawn of the Dead*, 1978
    Susannah Sparrow, co-author
John Skipp, *Bood of the Dead*, 1989
    Craig Spector, co-editor
John Skipp, *Still Dead: Book of the Dead 2*, 1992
    Craig Spector, co-editor

989

MARY RYAN

Mask of the Night
(New York: St. Martin's, 1997)

Story type: Reincarnation
Major character(s): Desiree McGlinn, Public Relations; Jenny Stephenson, Young Woman; Theo O'Reilly, Military Personnel (soldier)
Time period(s): 1960s (1967); 1920s
Locale(s): Kilashane, Ireland; Venice, Italy

Summary: Through a carnival mask from Venice, Jenny Stephenson glimpses an alluring and mysterious figure. Imagine her shock when she discovers he is the spirit of a seventh-century Venetian inquisitor, who has been reincarnated in the body of her lover, Theo O'Reilly, that she herself is the reincarnation of a witch who bedeviled him, and that the two are destined to be reincarnated eternally. Originally published in England in 1995.

Where it's reviewed:
Publishers Weekly, September 29, 1997, page 73

Other books by the same author:
Summer's End, 1996
Glenallen, 1993

Other books you might like:
Leigh Clark, *Evil Reincarnate*, 1994
Barbara Erskine, *Midnight Is a Lonely Place*, 1994
Marcy Heidesh, *The Torch*, 1992
Richard Matheson, *Bid Time Return*, 1975
Michael Stewart, *Belladonna*, 1992

990

JOHN SAUL

The Blackstone Chronicles
(New York: Fawcett, 1997)

Story type: Curse
Major character(s): Oliver Metcalf, Editor (newspaper); Bill McGuire, Contractor; Rebecca Morrison, Librarian
Time period(s): 1990s (1997)
Locale(s): Blackstone, New Hampshire

Summary: Serial novel, published in six individual monthly installments: *An Eye for An Eye: The Doll; Twist of Fate: The Locket; Ashes to Ashes: The Dragon's Flame; In the Shadow of Evil: The Handkerchief; Day of Reckoning: The Stereoscope*; and *Asylum*. Plans to renovate the abandoned Blackstone Asylum fall apart when a series of anonymous gifts to different townspeople causes death and ruin in their families. Each gift belonged at some time to an inmate at the asylum, and the identity of the mysterious benefactor who sends them, and his reason for causing so much misery throughout the town, are the core of the novel's mystery.

Other books by the same author:
The Presence, 1997
Black Lightning, 1995
The Homing, 1994

Horror

Shadows, 1993
Guardian, 1992

Other books you might like:
Charles L. Grant, *Hour of the Oxrun Dead*, 1977
William L. Johnston, *Asylum*, 1972
Stephen King, *The Green Mile*, 1997
Michael McDowell, *Blackwater*, 1983

991

JOHN SAUL

The Presence

(New York: Fawcett/Columbine, 1997)

Story type: Science Fiction; Child-in-Peril
Major character(s): Katherine Sundquist, Anthropologist; Michael Sundquist, Teenager; Rob Silver, Anthropologist
Time period(s): 1990s (1997)
Locale(s): Maui, Hawaii

Summary: Katherine Sundquist discovers that her son's worsening physical condition is related to the Serinus project, a covert operation investigating the possible extraterrestrial orgins of human life. Her efforts to save her son and expose the project invite resistance from the hand of the operation, who will stop at nothing, even murder, to protect the experiment.

Where it's reviewed:
Kirkus Reviews, July 1, 1997, page 979
Publishers Weekly, July 28, 1997, page 55

Other books by the same author:
The Blackstone Chronicles, 1997
Black Lightning, 1995
The Homing, 1994
Shadows, 1994
Guardian, 1992

Other books you might like:
John Arbucci, *The Blood of Innocents*, 1991
John Farris, *The Fury*, 1976
Gary Goshgarian, *Rough Beast*, 1995
Dean R. Koontz, *Lightning*, 1988
Michael Kurland, *Bottom Right*, 1990

992

LAWRENCE SCHIMEL, Editor
MARTIN H. GREENBERG, Co-Editor

Blood Lines: Vampire Stories from New England

(Nashville, Tennessee: Cumberland House, 1997)

Story type: Anthology; Vampire Story
Locale(s): New England

Summary: Ten tales of vampires and vampirism set in the New England states. Included are Hugh Cave's ''The Brotherhood of Blood'' and Earl Pierce, Jr.'s ''The Doom of the House of Duryea,'' both of which feature families with hereditary vampire curses, and Kristine Kathryn Rusch's ''The Beautiful, the Damned,'' a vampire riff on F. Scott Fitzgerald's *The*

Great Gatsby. Nontraditional vampire stories include Mary E. Wilkins Freeman's ''Luella Miller,'' about a woman whose incessant demands on others sap their vitality, and H.P. Lovecraft's ''The Shunned House,'' about a house that absorbs the essence of its victims.

Where it's reviewed:
Publishers Weekly, July 28, 1997, page 55

Other books by the same author:
Southern Blood: Vampire Stories from the American South, 1997
The Fortune Teller, 1997
Tarot Fantastic, 1996

Other books you might like:
Ellen Datlow, *Blood Is Not Enough*, 1989
    editor
Stephen Jones, *The Mammoth Book of Vampires*, 1992
    editor
Frank D. McSherry Jr., *New England Ghosts*, 1990
    Charles G. Waugh and Martin H. Greenberg, co-editors

993

LAWRENCE SCHIMEL

The Drag Queen of Elfland

(Cambridge, Massachusetts: Ultra Violet, 1997)

Story type: Collection

Summary: Seventeen tales of fantasy and horror. Highlights include ''Black Sounds,'' a vampire tale set in Spain; ''Old as a Rose in Bloom,'' a poignant ghost story; ''Coming out of the Broom Closet,'' an amusing story of sexual and supernatural identity; and the sword and sorceress tales, ''Barbarian Legacy,'' ''Crow Feathers'' and ''In Sheep's Clothing.''

Other books you might like:
Nina Kiriki Hoffman, *Legacy of Fire*, 1990
Joel Lane, *The Earth Wire and Other Stories*, 1994
Pat Murphy, *Points of Departure*, 1990
W.H. Pugmire, *Tales of Sesqua Valley*, 1997
Jessica Amanda Salmonson, *A Silver Thread of Madness*, 1989

994

LAWRENCE SCHIMEL, Editor
MARTIN H. GREENBERG, Co-Editor

Southern Blood: Vampire Stories from the American South

(Nashville, Tennessee: Cumberland House, 1997)

Story type: Anthology; Vampire Story
Locale(s): South

Summary: One dozen tales of vampires and vampirism set in the American south. Many work variations on the traditional vampire theme, including Brian Hodge's ''Like a Pilgrim to the Shrine,'' which pits a punk vampire against Count Dracula; William Tenn's ''She Only Goes out at Night,'' which devises a scientific explanation and cure for vampirism; Dan Simmons's ''Carrion Comfort,'' in which vampires feed on

the violent deaths of victims; and Fred Chappell's "The Flame," in which vampires are drawn like moths to a flame by a woman whose beauty casts a vampiric spell over them.

Other books by the same author:
Blood Lines: Vampire Stories from New England, 1997
The Fortune Teller, 1997

Other books you might like:
Ellen Datlow, *Blood Is Not Enough*, 1989
editor
Richard Gilliam, *Confederacy of the Dead*, 1993
Edward E. Kramer and Martin H. Greenberg, co-editors
Stephen Jones, *The Mammoth Book of Vampires*, 1992
editor

995

SUSAN SIZEMORE

Forever Knight: A Stirring of Dust

(New York: Berkley/Boulevard, 1997)

Story type: Vampire Story
Series: Forever Knight
Major character(s): Nicholas Knight, Detective—Homicide, Vampire; Natalie Lambert, Doctor (forensic pathologist); Lucien LaCroix, Radio Personality, Vampire
Time period(s): 1990s (1997)
Locale(s): Toronto, Ontario, Canada

Summary: Crack homicide detective Nicholas Knight investigates a series of brutal homicides in which victims are drained of blood and decapitated. Although he first suspects one of his fellow vampires, Nicholas discovers that the kills are the work of a revenant, a lower order of vampire created by the infected bite of one of his own species. Based on the cable television series *Forever Knight*, about an 800-year-old vampire who lives inconspicuously with other vampires among mortals in contemporary Ontario.

Other books you might like:
Vincent Courtney, *Vampire Beat*, 1991
P.N. Elrod, *Bloodlist*, 1990
Laurell K. Hamilton, *Guilty Pleasures*, 1993
Tanya Huff, *Blood Price*, 1991
Roxanne Longstreet, *Cold Kiss*, 1995
Karen E. Taylor, *Blood Secrets*, 1994

996

MICHAEL SLADE

Evil Eye

(New York: Signet, 1997)

Story type: Occult
Major character(s): Robert DeClerq, Detective; Zinc Chandler, Detective; Nick Craven, Detective
Time period(s): 1990s (1994); 1870s (1879)
Locale(s): New Westminster, British Columbia, Canada; Africa

Summary: A murderer is targeting members of the Royal Canadian Mounted Police, killing them and their families. Detectives Robert DeClerq and Zin Chandler investigate and, once more, discover a legacy of evil extending back more than a century, this time to Africa and practitioners of tribal magic. First published in England in 1996.

Other books by the same author:
Ripper, 1995
Cutthroat, 1992
Ghoul, 1987
Headhunter, 1982

Other books you might like:
Ramsey Campbell, *Claw*, 1985
Todd Grimson, *Brand New Cherry Flavor*, 1997
Thomas Harris, *Red Dragon*, 1981
Richard Jaccoma, *The Werewolf's Tale*, 1988
Graham Masterton, *Master of Lies*, 1992
Robert Morgan, *All Things under the Moon*, 1994
Peter Straub, *Koko*, 1988

997

BEECHER SMITH, Editor

Monsters From Memphis

(Palo Alto, California: Zapizdat Publications, 1997)

Story type: Anthology

Summary: Thirty-one stories original to the volume, all set in Memphis, Tennessee and featuring horrors based on southern characters and traditions. Highlights include Brent Monahan's "Shadow," about a predatory monster that becomes whatever it consumes; Tom Piccirilli's "Cotton," in which a Native American curse manifests in the form of a plague; Steve Climer's ocult detective tale, "By any Name a Devil"; Richard Park's "Eucharist," an amusing tale of Elvis sightings in the future; and Don Webb's "The Heart of the Matter," about a 500-year-old witch kept alive by the mechanical heart of a warlock.

Other books you might like:
Richard Gilliam, *Confederacy of the Dead*, 1993
Edward E. Kramer and Martin H. Greenberg, co-editors
Richard Gilliam, *Somewhere South of Midnight*, 1994
Martin H. Greenberg, co-editor
Frank D. McSherry Jr., *Civil War Ghosts*, 1990
Charles G. Waugh and Martin H. Greenberg, co-editors
Frank D. McSherry Jr., *More Dixie Ghosts*, 1994
Charles G. Waugh and Martin H. Greenberg, co-editors
Frank D. McSherry Jr., *Nightmares in Dixie*, 1987
Charles G. Waugh and Martin H. Greenberg, co-editors
Billie Sue Mosiman, *Dark Dixie*, 1997
Martin H. Greenberg, co-editor
Lawrence Schimel, *Southern Blood: Vampire Stories from the American South*, 1997
Martin H. Greenberg, co-editor

998

BRIAN SCOTT SMITH

When Shadows Fall

(New York: Leisure, 1997)

Story type: Black Magic

Major character(s): Martin LaVine, Businessman (electronics); Sylvia Belou, Witch; Danny Dallaugher, Young Man
Time period(s): 1990s (1997)
Locale(s): North Andover, Massachusetts

Summary: Martin LaVine investigates the mysterious death of his Aunt Day and discovers her friendship with Sylvia Belou, a self-proclaimed witch. When Martin and his friends accidentally stumble upon a ceremony performed by Sylvia and her coven, they become the object of a supernatural manhunt. A first novel.

Other books you might like:
Leigh Clark, *Blood Sabbath*, 1991
Elizabeth Ergas, *The Devil's Gate*, 1991
Gary L. Holleman, *Demon Fire*, 1995
Edward Lee, *The Chosen*, 1993
Tamara Thorne, *Moonfall*, 1996
J.N. Williamson, *The Monastery*, 1992

999

DAVID C. SMITH

Engor's Sword Arm

(North East, Pennsylvania: Forgotten Ages Press, 1997)

Story type: Occult
Major character(s): Engor, Pirate; Kyla, Young Woman; Lord Bilitu, Sorcerer
Time period(s): Indeterminate Past (prehistory)

Summary: Engor, a warrior with only one good fighting arm, hopes to prevent the delivery of Kyla to her betrothed, Lord Bilitu, and thereby settle a long-standing score with the wizard. In order to do so, Engor must overcome a variety of horrors and snares conjured by his sorcerer enemy. A sword and sorcery tale, published in facsimile of a pulp magazine layout and illustrated by Rick McCollum.

Other books by the same author:
The Eyes of Night, 1991
The Fair Rules of Evil, 1989
The Master of Evil, 1983
Oron, 1978
The Witch of the Indies, 1977

Other books you might like:
Ramsey Campbell, *Far Away and Never*, 1996
David Drake, *Vettius and His Friends*, 1989
Robert E. Howard, *Conan the Barbarian*, 1955
Richard L. Tierney, *Scroll of Thoth*, 1997
Karl Edward Wagner, *The Book of Kane*, 1985

1000

GUY N. SMITH

Dead Meat

(Staten Island, New York: Creation Books, 1997)

Story type: Collection

Summary: Omnibus reprinting the complete adventures—four novels and two short stories (''Vampire Village,'' ''Hellbeat'')—of Mark Sabat, an exorcist who dispatches

skinhead vampires, necrophilic cultists, cannibals, witches, and other supernatural and nonsupernatural horrors with bell, book, and loaded revolver. The novels, which are sexually and violently explicit, are *Graveyard Vultures* (1982), *Blood Merchants* (1982), *Cannibal Cult* (1983), and *Druid Connection* (1983).

Other books by the same author:
Water Rites, 1997
Dead End, 1996
The Dark One, 1995
Witch Spell, 1993
The Plague Chronicles, 1993

Other books you might like:
Ron Dee, *Blood*, 1993
Shaun Hutson, *Heathen*, 1992
Richard Laymon, *The Cellar*, 1980
Edward Lee, *Incubi*, 1991
Brian Lumley, *Necroscope*, 1986

1001

GUY N. SMITH

Water Rites

(New York: Zebra, 1997)

Story type: Ancient Evil Unleashed
Major character(s): Phil Quiles, Inspector (water service); Royston Shannon, Wealthy; Jocelyn Jackson, Artist
Time period(s): 1990s (1997)
Locale(s): Hopwas, England

Summary: Mysterious nocturnal activity at the underground reservoir in Hopwas leads to the discovery of the People of the Water, a cult devoted to the ancient water witch Mukasa, who is preparing for the inundation of the world and a return to her unholy reign.

Other books by the same author:
Dead Meat, 1997
Dead End, 1996
The Dark One, 1995
Witch Spell, 1993
The Resurrected, 1991

Other books you might like:
Elizabeth Forrest, *Dark Tide*, 1993
Phil Rickman, *Candle Night*, 1991
Michael B. Sirota, *The Well*, 1991
Richard L. Tierney, *The House of the Toad*, 1993

1002

S.P. SOMTOW (Pseudonym of Somtow Sucharitkul)

The Vampire's Beautiful Daughter

(New York: Atheneum, 1997)

Story type: Vampire Story
Major character(s): Johnny Raitt, Teenager; Rebecca Teppish, Teenager, Vampire; Vladimir X. Teppish III, Vampire, Parent (Rebecca's father)
Time period(s): 1990s (1997)
Locale(s): Encino, California

Summary: A young adult coming-of-age story. Johnny Raitt, newly moved from North Dakota to California, befriends Rebecca Teppish at Claudette Colbert high school. While Rebecca helps Johnny acclimate to his new surroundings, Johnny helps Rebecca in her choice between embracing her family's vampire heritage or living life as a normal teenager.

Where it's reviewed:
Science Fiction Chronicle, February 1998, page 62

Other books by the same author:
Darker Angels, 1998
Vanitas, 1995
Valentine, 1992
Moondance, 1989
Vampire Junction, 1984

Other books you might like:
Richie Tankersley Cusick, *Buffy the Vampire Slayer*, 1997
Elvira, *Transylvania 90210*, 1996
   John Paragon, co-author
Joseph Locke, *Vampire Heart*, 1994
Christopher Pike, *The Last Vampire*, 1994
Nicholas Pine, *Night School*, 1994
L.J. Smith, *The Vampire Diaries*, 1992

1003

MURIEL SPARK

Open to the Public
(New York: New Directions, 1997)

Story type: Collection

Summary: Collection of thirty-seven stories spanning more than 45 years. The majority are mainstream fiction, but most of the author's short macabre stories are included, among them ''The Portobello Road,'' which is narrated by the ghost of a murder victim; ''The Leaf Sweeper,'' in which a man and his ghost co-exist; ''The House of the Famous Poet,'' featuring a precognition of death; and ''The Girl I Left Behind Me,'' in which a woman discovers that the one detail of the day that has eluded her memory is literally a matter of life and death.

Other books by the same author:
The Stories of Muriel Spark, 1987
The Go-Away Bird and Other Stories, 1958

Other books you might like:
Jonathan Carroll, *The Panic Hand*, 1995
Fred Chappell, *More Shapes than One*, 1992
Rachell Ingalls, *The End of Tragedy*, 1987
Shirley Jackson, *One Ordinary Day*, 1997
Alison Lurie, *Women and Ghosts*, 1994
Joyce Carol Oates, *Haunted: Tales of the Grotesque*, 1994

1004

STEVEN SPRUILL

Daughter of Darkness
(New York: Doubleday, 1997)

Story type: Vampire Story

Major character(s): Jenn Hrluska, Doctor; Merrick Chapman, Detective—Police; Zane Chapman, Vampire
Time period(s): 1990s
Locale(s): Washington, District of Columbia

Summary: Zane Chapman, a hemophage with a hereditary craving for blood, escapes from the concrete bunker his father imprisoned him in a decade before, and attempts to seduce his daughter Jenn, a successful pediatrician who hitherto has resisted the vampiric calling of her blood, to his way. A sequel to *Rulers of Darkness* (1995).

Where it's reviewed:
Kirkus Reviews, April 15, 1997, page 585
Publishers Weekly, May 19, 1997, page 65

Other books by the same author:
Rulers of Darkness, 1995
My Soul to Take, 1994

Other books you might like:
Scott Baker, *Ancestral Hungers*, 1995
Poppy Z. Brite, *Lost Souls*, 1992
Mark Burnell, *Glittering Savages*, 1995
Brian Stableford, *Young Blood*, 1991

1005

HARRY STEIN

Infinity's Child
(New York: Delacorte, 1997)

Story type: Science Fiction
Major character(s): Sally Benedict, Journalist; R. Paul Holland, Scientist (biochemist); Raymond Lynch, Scientist
Time period(s): 1990s (1997)
Locale(s): Edwardstown, New Hampshire

Summary: Sally Benedict discovers that her family possesses the ''infinity gene,'' genetic material that is crucial to a nearby biochemical research laboratory conducting experiments to prolong human life. Trapped in the maternity ward of the local hospital following the birth of her first child, Sally realizes that her life is in danger from agents eager to obtain a sample of living tissue from her newborn.

Where it's reviewed:
Publishers Weekly, December 9, 1996, page 72

Other books by the same author:
Hoopla, 1996
The Magic Bullet, 1995

Other books you might like:
Eric Flanders, *The Forever Children*, 1992
Dean R. Koontz, *Servants of Twilight*, 1984
David Martin, *Bring Me Children*, 1992
John Saul, *Darkness*, 1991

1006

JOHN RICHARD STEVENS, Editor

Vampires, Wine & Roses
(New York: Berkley, 1997)

Story type: Anthology

Summary: Compilation of thirty-four stories, poems, song lyrics, and novel excerpts featuring vampires. Included are H.P. Lovecraft's "The Hound," about a sorceror resurrected from his coffin by two ignorant necrophiles; Rod Serling's "The Riddle of the Crypt," filmed as an episode of his television series "The Twilight Zone"; H.G. Well's "The Flowering of the Strange Orchid," about a blood-drinking plant; Guy de Maupassant's "The Horla," about an invisible blood drinking monster; and Bram Stoker's "Dracula's Guest," originally intended as an opening chapter to his novel Dracula. Other authors include Shakespeare, Woody Allen and Sting.

Where it's reviewed:
Magazine of Fantasy & Science Fiction, July 1997, page 24

Other books you might like:

Martin H. Greenberg, *A Taste for Blood*, 1992
editor
Martin H. Greenberg, *Vampires: The Greatest Stories*, 1997
editor
Stephen Jones, *The Mammoth Book of Vampires*, 1992
editor
Alan Ryan, *Vampires: Two Centuries of Great Vampire Stories*, 1987
editor
Leslie Shepard, *The Dracula Book of Great Vampire Stories*, 1977
editor
Leonard Wolf, *Blood Thirst: 100 Years of Vampire Fiction*, 1997
editor

1007

R.L. STINE

The Curse of Camp Cold Lake

(New York: Scholastic, 1997)

Story type: Ghost Story; Young Adult
Major character(s): Sarah Maas, Child; Aaron Maas, Child; Brianna, Child
Time period(s): 1990s (1996)
Locale(s): Camp Cold Lake

Summary: Sarah Maas uses a near-drowning experience at summer camp to get sympathy from her bunkmates. Thereafter, she is persuaded by the ghost of Della, a young girl who died at the camp and who demands that Sarah be her buddy. A novel for pre-teenage readers.

Other books by the same author:
Chicken, Chicken, 1997
Don't Go To Sleep, 1997
The Blob That Ate Everyone, 1997
My Best Friend Is Invisible, 1997
Deep Trouble, 1997

Other books you might like:
Avi, *Devil's Race*, 1994
Lynn Blankman, *Ghost Beyond the Garden*, 1996
William Brittain, *Who Knew There'd Be Ghosts?*, 1995
Bruce Coville, *My Teacher Is an Alien*, 1989

1008

R.L. STINE

Fear Street: The Cat

(New York: Pocket/Archway, 1997)

Story type: Young Adult; Apocalyptic Horror
Series: Fear Street
Major character(s): Marty Harper, Teenager, Student—High School; Dwayne, Teenager; Maggie, Scientist; Coach Griffin, Coach (basketball)
Time period(s): 1990s (1997)
Locale(s): Shadyside, Fictional City (Shadyside High School)

Summary: Marty Harper kills the mischievous cat that caused an injury which jeopardizes his chances at a basketball scholarship. But now Marty sees the cat everywhere, stalking him with a murderous intent that extends to his family and friends. A young adult novel.

Other books by the same author:
Fear Street: All-Night Party, 1997
Fear Street: High-Tide, 1997
Fear Hall: The Conclusion, 1997
Fear Hall: The Beginning, 1997

Other books you might like:
Caroline B. Cooney, *The Terrorist*, 1997
Lois Duncan, *I Walk at Night*, 1997
Diane Hoh, *Book of Horrors*, 1994
Joan Lowery Nixon, *Don't Scream*, 1997
Christopher Pike, *Die Softly*, 1991

1009

R.L. STINE

My Best Friend Is Invisible

(New York: St. Martin's, 1996)

Story type: Science Fiction; Young Adult
Major character(s): Sammy Jacobs, Child; Simon Jacobs, Child; Roxanne, Child
Time period(s): 1990s (1996)
Locale(s): Middletown, Fictional City

Summary: Imaginative Sammy Jacobs can't get anyone to believe that the mischief he continually gets into is due to an invisible friend who won't stop pestering him. A novel for preteen readers.

Other books by the same author:
Don't Go To Sleep, 1997
The Blob That Ate Everyone, 1997
The Curse of Camp Cold Lake, 1997
Deep Trouble II, 1997

Other books you might like:
Avi, *Devil's Race*, 1994
Lynn Blankman, *Ghost Beyond the Garden*, 1996
William Brittain, *Who Knew There'd Be Ghosts?*, 1995
Bruce Coville, *My Teacher Is an Alien*, 1989

1010

WHITLEY STRIEBER

Evenings with Demons

(Grantham, New Hampshire: Borderlands Press, 1997)

Story type: Collection

Summary: Twenty-five stories, many previously unpublished, from a writer known primarily as a novelist. Included are ''Pain'' and ''The Resurrection of the Inquistion in P. Salter,'' both about people who discover private ecstasy as recipients and givers of torture; ''The Richard Nixon Mask,'' about a strangely haunted Halloween mask; ''Under the Old Oak Tree,'' a tale of aliens among us; ''The Pool,'' in which a conversation between father and son reveals a gulf, possibly extraterrestrial, separating them; and the monster story, ''Flies.'' Released as a signed limited hardcover edition.

Where it's reviewed:
Cemetery Dance, Fall 1997, page 43

Other books by the same author:
The Forbidden Zone, 1993
Unholy Fire, 1992
The Wild, 1991
Billy, 1990
The Night Church, 1986

Other books you might like:
Nancy A. Collins, *Nameless Sins*, 1994
Dennis Etchison, *The Blood Kiss*, 1989
Ed Gorman, *Prisoners and Other Stories*, 1992
Robert R. McCammon, *Blue World*, 1989
Kim Newman, *The Original Dr. Shade and Other Stories*, 1994
William Relling Jr., *The Infinite Man*, 1989
F. Paul Wilson, *Soft and Others*, 1989

1011

CECILIA TAN, Editor

Cherished Blood

(Cambridge, Massachusetts: Circlet Press, 1997)

Story type: Anthology; Vampire Story

Summary: Ten tales of vampire erotica original to the anthology, including Gary Bowen's ''His Name Was Wade,'' A.R. Morlan's ''Drink to Me Only with Thine Eyes,'' Thomas S. Roche's ''Lunar Eclipse,'' David May's ''Katje,'' and Susan Elizabeth Gray's ''Blood Dreams.''

Other books by the same author:
Erotica Vampirica, 1996
Blood Kiss: Vampire Erotica, 1994
The Beast Within: Erotic Tales of Werewolves, 1994

Other books you might like:
Poppy Z. Brite, *Love in Vein II*, 1997
 Martin H. Greenberg, co-editor
Poppy Z. Brite, *Love in Vein*, 1994
 Martin H. Greenberg, co-editor
Pam Keesey, *Darker Angels: Lesbian Vampire Stories*, 1995
 editor

Amarantha Knight, *Sex Macabre*, 1996
 editor
Amarantha Knight, *Seductive Spectres*, 1996
 editor
Amarantha Knight, *Love Bites*, 1994
 editor
William J. Mann, *Grave Passions*, 1997
 editor
Michael Rowe, *Sons of Darkness: Tales of Men, Blood and Immortality*, 1996
 Thoms Roche, co-editor
Michael Rowe, *Brothers of the Night*, 1997
 Thomas Roche, co-editor

1012

CHRISTINE TANASIUK

Howl

(Edmonton, Alberta: Commonwealth, 1997)

Story type: Nature in Revolt
Major character(s): Samantha Harris, Scientist; Adam Haley, Scientist; Druce Harris, Spouse (abusive)
Time period(s): 1990s (1997)
Locale(s): Black Thunder, Canada

Summary: Samantha Harris and Adam Haley investigate the disappearance of a Canadian expedition to study the lives of a species of highly intelligent wolves, but are hampered by the arrival of Druce, Samantha's abusive husband, who is more predatory than the animals they study. A first novel.

Other books you might like:
Chris N. Africa, *When Wolves Cry*, 1997
David Dvorkin, *Ursus*, 1989
Randy Goldman, *Werewolf Wars*, 1996
Brian Hopkins, *Cold at Heart*, 1997
Dean R. Koontz, *Watchers*, 1987
Whitley Streiber, *The Wolfen*, 1978

1013

LUCY TAYLOR

Painted in Blood

(Woodinville, Washington: Silver Salamander, 1997)

Story type: Collection

Summary: Thirteen stories, seven original to the collection, featuring charcters driven by intense loneliness and unfulfilled longing to extreme, often grotesque acts of sex and violence. Selections include ''Heat,'' in which a woman's unbridled sexual passion manifests as pyromania; ''Pain Threshold,'' in which a wrestler's growing numbness to the dismal circumstances of his life is mirrored in the increasing extravagance of the injuries he sustains; ''The Story Box,'' in which a woman coerces her child into believing that her murdered father was only part of a make-believe story; and the title tale, about the desperation of two lovers imprisoned in a fundamentalist society.

Other books by the same author:
The Safety of Unknown Cities, 1995

Horror

The Flesh Artist, 1994
Unnatural Acts and Other Stories, 1994
Close to the Bone, 1993
Other books you might like:
Poppy Z. Brite, *Swamp Foetus*, 1993
Scott Edelman, *Suicide Art*, 1992
Gerard Daniel Houarner, *Painfreak*, 1996
Roberta Lannes, *The Mirror of the Night*, 1997
David J. Schow, *Seeing Red*, 1990

1014

ELIZABETH TERRY, Editor
TERRI HARDIN, Co-Editor

American Gothic

(New York: Barnes & Noble, 1997)

Story type: Anthology

Summary: Twenty-five stories from the nineteenth and early twentieth century that represent different aspects of the Gothic literary tradition in Amrican fiction. Several haunted house stories are included, among them Charlotte Perkins Gilman's "The Giant Wistaria," which features the spectral presence of an unwed mother, and John Greenleaf Whittier's "The Haunted House," a tale of a mock haunting and its consequences. Tales of psychological horror include Gilman's classic "The Yellow Wallpaper," in which a woman sees the shape of her growing madness in a wallpaper pattern, and Stephen Crane's "An Illusion in Red and White," in which a man brainwashes his children into believing they never saw a murder he committed. Fitz-James O'Brien's "The Diamond Lens" is an early science fiction story of a man who discovers an entire universe in a drop of water, and Ambrose Bierce's "The Eyes of the Panther" is a shapeshifter tale.

Other books you might like:
Christopher Baldick, *The Oxford Book of Gothic Tales*, 1992
  editor
Alfred Bendixen, *Haunted Dusk*, 1985
  editor
Peter Haining, *Great Tales of Terror from Europe and America*, 1972
  editor
David G. Hartwell, *Bodies of the Dead*, 1997
  editor
Catherine A. Lundie, *Restless Spirits*, 1997
  editor
Joyce Carol Oates, *American Gothic Tales*, 1996
  editor
Patricia L. Skarda, *The Evil Image*, 1981
  Nora Crow Jaffe, co-editor

1015

JEFFREY THOMAS

Black Walls, Red Glass

(Marietta, Georgia: Marietta Publishing, 1997)

Story type: Collection

Summary: A trio of stories. In "Black Walls," a bullet that carries brain tissue into the head of a man it strikes causes problems when it appears to have imported part of its owner's personality as well. "Red Glass" is a dreamy rumination on madness, and "The Red Machine" ia the story of a frustrated young woman who channels her disaffection into works of art that can kill.

Where it's reviewed:
Locus, December 1997, page 27

Other books by the same author:
The Bones of the Old Ones, 1995

Other books you might like:
Brian Hopkins, *Something Haunts Us All*, 1996
Gerard Daniel Houarner, *Painfreak*, 1996
Bentley Little, *Murmerous Haunts*, 1997
Jeffrey Osier, *Horizon Lines*, 1997
Tom Piccirilli, *The Dog Syndrome and Other Sick Puppies*, 1997
David Niall Wilson, *The Fall of the House of Escher and Other Illusions*, 1996

1016

RICHARD L. TIERNEY

Scroll of Thoth

(Oakland, California: Chaosium, 1997)

Story type: Collection

Summary: The complete adventures of Simon Magus, a magician and warrior who applies his knowledge of arcane wisdom to fighting unholy religious cults, corrupt kingdoms and Lovecraftian monsters. The twelve stories have the spirit of Robert E. Howard's tales of Conan the Barbarian and the philosophical underpinnings of Lovecrft tales of cosmic horror, and include "The Sword of Spartacus," "The Worm of Urakhu," "The Curse of the Crocodile," and "The Ring of Set." Edited and introduced by Robert M. Price.

Other books by the same author:
The Winds of Zarr, 1975

Other books you might like:
Ramsey Campbell, *Far Away and Never*, 1996
David Drake, *Vettius and His Friends*, 1989
Fritz Leiber, *Ill Met in Lankhmar*, 1995
Brian Lumley, *Iced on Aran and Other Dream Quests*, 1992
Gary Myers, *The House of the Worm*, 1975
Michael Shea, *Nifft the Lean*, 1982
David C. Smith, *Engor's Sword Arm*, 1997
Karl Edward Wagner, *The Book of Kane*, 1985

1017

DELLA VAN HISE

Ragged Angels

(Yucca Valley, California: Eye Scry, 1997)

Story type: Vampire Story

Major character(s): Stefan London, Businessman (memorabilia dealer); Dimitri Alexander Karros, Computer Expert, Vampire; Miquel Kaliq Constantine, Vampire
Time period(s): 1990s (1997)
Locale(s): Los Angeles, California; San Diego, California

Summary: At a science fiction convention, Stefan meets Dimitri and embraces his vampire way of life. Stefan's adjustment to vampirism distracts him from his consuming grief over the recent death of his teenage daughter, but opens him up to a host of emotional and philosophical dilemmas he never anticipated.

Other books by the same author:
Star Trek: Killing Time, 1985

Other books you might like:
Richard Lee Byers, *The Vampire's Apprentice*, 1992
John Peyton Cooke, *Out for Blood*, 1991
David Darke, *Shade*, 1994
Mark Ivanhoe, *Virgintooth*, 1991
Anne Rice, *Interview with the Vampire*, 1976
T. Lucien Wright, *Blood Brothers*, 1991

1018

KARL EDWARD WAGNER

Exorcisms and Ecstasies

(Minneapolis: Fedogan & Bremer, 1997)

Story type: Collection

Summary: Thirty-two previously uncollected stories and fragments by a leading horror writer and editor who died in 1994. Included are "Did They Get You to Trade" and "I've Come to Talk with You Again," about the desperate measures by which a rock music star and a celebrated writer (respectively) sustain their fading reputations; the vampire stories "The Slug" and "Prince of the Punks"; the medical horror stories "But You'll Never Follow Me" and "The Final Cut"; and the exceptional haunted house story "Cedar Lane." Five selections feature the author's well-known sword and sorcery anti-hero Kane. Included as well are the science fiction story "Killer," written in collaboration with David Drake, and "The Coming of Ghor," a pastiche of Robert E. Howard's fiction contributed to the episodic novel *Genseric's Fifth-Born Son*. Edited by Stephen Jones, who has included appreciations by Ramsey Campbell, David Schow, Peter Straub and others, as well as a comprehensive bibliography of Wagner's writing.

Other books by the same author:
Unthreatened by the Morning Light, 1989
Why Not You and I, 1987
The Book of Kane, 1985
In a Lonely Place, 1983
Night Winds, 1978

Other books you might like:
Ramsey Campbell, *Strange Things and Stranger Places*, 1993
Dennis Etchison, *Blood Kiss*, 1988
Brian Hodge, *The Convulsion Factory*, 1996
Joe R. Lansdale, *By Bizarre Hands*, 1989
Robert R. McCammon, *Blue World*, 1990
F. Paul Wilson, *Soft and Others*, 1989

1019

H. RUSSELL WAKEFIELD

Imagine a Man in a Box

(Ashcroft, British Columbia: Ash-Tree Press, 1997)

Story type: Collection

Summary: Thirteen tales of horror, mystery, science fiction and social comedy by one of the best known writers of ghost stories in the twentieth century. Selections include "Damp Sheets," a tale of supernatural revenge; "Frontier Guards," in which a pair of ghostbusters greatly underestimates the haunted house they are exploring; "Dream-Day in Macedon," a tale of psychic synchronicity; the humorous ghost story "Corporal Humpit of the 4th Musketeers," and "The Central Figure," in which a playwright discovers that his life has begun uncannily to imitate one of his tragic stage productions. First published in 1931.

Where it's reviewed:
Necrofile, Fall 1997, page 9

Other books by the same author:
Strayers from Sheol, 1961
The Clock Strikes Twelve, 1939
A Ghostly Company, 1935
Ghost Stories, 1932
Old Man's Beard, 1929
They Return at Evening, 1928

Other books you might like:
E.F. Benson, *The Collected Ghost Stories of E.F. Benson*, 1992
A.M. Burrage, *Someone in the Room: Strange Tales Old and New*, 1931
M.P. Dare, *Unholy Relics*, 1947
L.P. Hartley, *The Travelling Grave and Other Stories*, 1948
R.H. Malden, *Nine Ghosts*, 1943
A.N.L. Munby, *The Alabaster Hand and Other Ghost Stories*, 1949
L.T.C. Rolt, *Sleep No More*, 1948

1020

WILLIAM A. WALKER JR.

Dystopia

(Marietta, Georgia: Marietta Publishing, 1997)

Story type: Collection

Summary: A trio of stories comprise the author's first published book. "Sniper" is a futuristic tale of civil war complicated by a zombie menace. In "The Institute Man," an ambitious businessman enrolls in a rugged self-improvement program and learns belatedly the macabre price he must pay for his success. In "Pit 666," two criminals on the run get their just desserts from a supernatural menace. Signed limited edition chapbook, illustrated by Donald R. Owen III.

Other books you might like:
Brian Hopkins, *Something Haunts Us All*, 1996
Gerard Daniel Houarner, *Painfreak*, 1996
Bentley Little, *Murmerous Haunts*, 1997

Jeffrey Osier, *Horizon Lines*, 1997
Tom Piccirilli, *The Dog Syndrome and Other Sick Puppies*, 1997
Jeffrey Thomas, *Black Walls, Red Glass*, 1997
David Niall Wilson, *The Fall of the House of Escher and Other Illusions*, 1996

1021

DONALD WANDREI

Don't Dream

(Minneapolis, Minnesota: Fedgan & Bremer, 1997)

Story type: Collection

Summary: Collection of twenty-six stories that represent the complete horror and fantasy fiction of a protege of H.P. Lovecraft who contributed primarily to the weird fiction pulps. Included are "The Lives of Alfred Kramer," a tale of ancestral memory in which a man retraces his heritage back to his primordial origins; "The Nerveless Man," about a scientific experiment that renders a man insensitive to pain: "The Tree-Men of Mbwa," about a strange dimension where plant and animal life are indistinguishable from one another; and several stories of horrors from the sea, including "Spawn of the Sea," "Uneasy Lie the Drowned," and "Giant Plasm." The book is augmented with fourteen essays and prose poems, many previously unpublished. Edited by Philip J. Rahman and Dennis E. Weiler and illustrated by Roger Geberding.

Where it's reviewed:
Locus, August, 1997, page 27
Necrofile, #26, fall 1997, page 25
Publishers Weekly, July 28, 1997, page 58
SF Chronicle, November 1997, page 40

Other books by the same author:
Colossus, 1989
Strange Harvest, 1965
The Web of Easter Island, 1948
The Eye and the Finger, 1944

Other books you might like:
Robert Bloch, *The Early Fears*, 1994
Arthur J. Burks, *Black Medicine*, 1966
Carl Jacobi, *Revelations in Black*, 1947
Frank Belknap Long, *The Hounds of Tindalos*, 1946
Clark Ashton Smith, *A Rendezvous in Averoigne*, 1989

1022

DON WEBB

Stealing My Rules

(Denver: Cyber-Psychos AOD, 1997)

Story type: Collection

Summary: One dozen tales of post-modern dark fantasy and science fiction, many featuring time slips and alternate realities. In "The Game," a stalker suffers complete discomposure when everyone in the world disappears unexpectedly. In "Boy," a gang runs afoul of ancient magic when they find that the old man they are terrorizing is a priest of the Aztec god Tezcatlipoca. "The Works of Hieronimus Bosch

Considered as Realism" is a stream of conscious fantasy built from disturbing imagery in Bosch's paintings. In "Avocation," a husband and wife discover peculiar behaviors in one another that suggest the influence of ancient mystical beliefs. Paul Di Filippo supplies the introduction.

Other books by the same author:
A Spell for the Fulfillment of Desire, 1996

Other books you might like:
Cliff Burns, *The Reality Machine*, 1997
William S. Burroughs, *Interzone*, 1989
Harlan Ellison, *Slippage*, 1997
Jack Remick, *Terminal Weird*, 1996
Wayne Allen Sallee, *With Wounds Still Wet*, 1996

1023

WENDY WEBB, Editor
CHARLES L. GRANT, Co-Editor

Gothic Ghosts

(New York: Tor, 1997)

Story type: Anthology; Ghost Story

Summary: An anthology of 19 new stories of ghosts and hauntings selected for their evocations of atmosphere and mood. Stand-out selections include Lucy Taylor's "Visitation," in which the ghost of a little girl leads to an aging bachelor's revelations about his life and loves; Stuart Palmer's "Cinder Child," in which a young boy's encounter with ghosts uncovers a ghastly family secret; Nancy Holder's "Syngamy," in which death and life are linked at a fertility clinic; and Matthew J. Costello's "Unexpected Attraction," about a man persuaded by the ghost he has fallen in love with to murder his wife. Other contributors include Jessica Amanda Salmonson, Rick Hautala, Brian Stableford, Katherine Ptacek and Ester Friesner.

Where it's reviewed:
Book World, October 26, 1997, page 12
Publishers Weekly, September 15, 1997, page 54

Other books by the same author:
More Phobias, 1995

Other books you might like:
Richard Gilliam, *Phantoms*, 1996
   Martin H. Greenberg, co-editor
Marvin Kaye, *Ghosts*, 1981
   editor
Paul F. Olson, *Post-Mortem: New Tales of Ghostly Horror*, 1989
   David B. Silva, co-editor
Gahan Wilson, *Gahan Wilson's The Ultimate Haunted House*, 1996
   editor

1024

ROBERT WEINBERG

The Road to Hell, Volume I

(Clarkston, Georgia: White Wolf, 1997)

Story type: Apocalyptic Horror
Series: World of Darkness: Mage: The Horizon War Trilogy
Major character(s): Alvin Reynolds, Computer Expert; Sharon Reed, Magician (technomancer); Seventeen, Prisoner
Time period(s): 1990s (1997)
Locale(s): Rochester, New York

Summary: In the Wolrd of Darkness, where supernatural creatures coexist with human beings, members of the warring Mage clans, who combine necromancy and science, battle members of the vampire Kindred for control of the Horizon Realms, dimensions that provide access to realms other than their own. First Book in a trilogy.

Other books by the same author:
The War in Heaven, 1998
The Ascension Warrior, 1997
The Unbeholden, 1996
Unholy Allies, 1995
Bloodwar, 1995

Other books you might like:
Richard Lee Byers, *The Ebon Mask*, 1996
Jackie Cassade, *Shadows on the Hill*, 1996
Gherbod Fleming, *The Devil's Advocate*, 1997
Staley Krause, *Truth Until Paradox*, 1995
    Stewart Wieck, co-editor
Doug Murray, *Call to Battle*, 1996
Stewart Wieck, *The Essential World of Darkness*, 1997
    editor

1025

ROBERT WEINBERG

The Road to Hell, Volume II

(Clarkston, Georgia: White Wolf, 1997)

Story type: Apocalyptic Horror
Series: World of Darkness: Mage: The Horizon War Trilogy
Major character(s): Alvin Reynolds, Computer Expert; Sharon Reed, Magician (technomancer); Madeleine Giovanni, Vampire
Time period(s): 1990s (1997)
Locale(s): Rochester, New York

Summary: The Ascension Warrior, who claims to be the reincarnation of the legendary Heylel Teomin, emerges in the World of Darkness to bring peace to the warring Mages of the Nine Traditions and the Technicians of the Technocracy. Will he help the Mages secure the Horizon Realms from the vampire Kindred, or is he motivated by his own whims and schemes? Second book in the trilogy.

Other books by the same author:
The War in Heaven, 1998
The Road to Hell, Volume I, 1997
The Unbeholden, 1996

Unholy Allies, 1995
Bloodwar, 1995

Other books you might like:
Richard Lee Byers, *The Ebon Mask*, 1996
Jackie Cassade, *Shadows on the Hill*, 1996
Gherbod Fleming, *The Devil's Advocate*, 1997
Staley Krause, *Truth Until Paradox*, 1995
    Stewart Wieck, co-editor
Doug Murray, *Call to Battle*, 1996
Stewart Wieck, *The Essential World of Darkness*, 1997
    editor

1026

STEWART WIECK, Editor
ANNA BRANSCOME, Co-Editor

The Essential World of Darkness

(Clarkston, Georgia: White Wolf, 1997)

Story type: Anthology
Series: World of Darkness

Summary: Five novels set in the World of Darkness, an alternate world created for fantasy role-playing in which mages, wraiths, vampires, werewolves, and changelings are the ruling elite over human beings. Included are Robert Weinberg and Mark Rein-Hagen's *Vampire Diary: The Embrace*, a vampire coming-of-age story; Owl Goingback's *Shaman Moon*, a werewolf coming-of-age tale; Scott Ciencin's *Lightning Under Glass*, which pits three mages against one another; David Niall Wilson's *Except You Go Through Shadow*, in which a wraith pursues the cult leader who coerced him into committing suicide; and Esther M. Friesner's *Playing with Fire*, a tale of changeling cultural identity set in San Francisco's Chinatown.

Other books you might like:
Erin Kelly, *The Splendour Falls*, 1995
    editor
Edward E. Kramer, *Dark Destiny III: Children of Dracula*, 1996
    editor
Edward E. Kramer, *Dark Destiny II: Proprietors of Fate*, 1995
    editor
Edward E. Kramer, *Dark Destiny*, 1994
    editor
Staley Krause, *Strange City*, 1996
    Stewart Wieck, co-editor
Staley Krause, *World of Darkness: City of Darkness*, 1995
    Stewart Wieck, co-editor
Stewart Wieck, *The Beast Within*, 1995
    editor
Stewart Wieck, *When Will You Rage*, 1994
    editor
Stewart Wieck, *World of Darkness: Truth Until Paradox*, 1994
    editor

Horror

1027

CHARLES WILSON

Extinct

(New York: St. Martin's, 1997)

Story type: Nature in Revolt
Major character(s): Carolyn Haines, Pilot (boat); Alan Freeman, Scientist (marine biologist); Admiral Vandiver, Military Personnel (Navy)
Time period(s): 1990s (1997)
Locale(s): Biloxi, Mississippi

Summary: Marine experts and experienced sea personnel converge on the waters off Mississippi when the disappearance of several recreational swimmers and clues recovered from the ocean floor indicate the resurgence of the megalodon, a ravenous, prehistoric precursor of the great white shark.

Other books by the same author:
Fertile Ground, 1996
Direct Descendant, 1995

Other books you might like:
Steve Alten, *Meg*, 1997
Peter Benchley, *Jaws*, 1974
Peter Benchley, *Beast*, 1991
William Dantz, *Hunger*, 1992
J.M. Morgan, *Between the Devil and the Deep*, 1992

1028

DAVID NIALL WILSON

To Speak in Lifeless Tongues

(Clarkston, Georgia: White Wolf, 1997)

Story type: Vampire Story
Series: World of Darkness: Vampire: The Grails Covenant Trilogy
Major character(s): Montrovant, Vampire; Santos, Vampire; Kli Kodesh, Vampire
Time period(s): 12th century
Locale(s): Jerusalem, Israel

Summary: Montrovant, vampire founder of the Knights Templar, seeks to obtain the Holy Grail upon hearing that the order is on the verge of disbanding. Guided by a devious guardian in the Templars' castle, Montrovant rushes to the Holy Land, enduring many adventures with members of rival vampire clans along the way. Set in the World of Darkness gaming universe, an alternate world in which supernatural monsters co-exist with human beings. Second book in a trilogy, after *To Sift Through Bitter Ashes*.

Other books by the same author:
To Dream of Dreamers Lost, 1998
To Sift through Bitter Ashes, 1997

Other books you might like:
Justin Achilli, *Dark Tyrants*, 1997
   Robert Hatch, co-editor
Gherbod Fleming, *The Devil's Advocate*, 1997
Robert Weinberg, *The Unbeholden*, 1996
Robert Weinberg, *Unholy Allies*, 1995

Robert Weinberg, *Bloodwar*, 1995

1029

DOUGLAS WINTER, Editor

Revelations

(New York: HarperPrism, 1997)

Story type: Anthology
Time period(s): 20th century

Summary: Anthology in the form of a mosaic novel. Each selection represents a decade of the twentieth century and uses an event specific to that decade as a vehicle for horror. Included is F. Paul Wilson's ''Aryans and Absinthe,'' about the supernatural machinations behind Hitler's rise to power; Charles Grant's ''Riding the Black,'' a meditation on the cultural impact of the atomic bomb; Richard Christian Matheson's ''Whatever,'' which examines the dark side of the 1960's counterculture through the rise and fall of a legendary rock band; and Ramsey Campbell's ''The Word,'' about a fan's run-in with a hack horror writer turned New Age prophet. Clive Barker wraps all the stories with ''Men and Sin'' and ''A Movement at the River's Heart.'' Published in England as *Millennium*.

Where it's reviewed:
Book World, July 27, 1997, page 9
Kirkus Reviews, April 15, 1997, page 586
Locus, August 1997, page 27
Necrofile, #25 1997, page 1
Publishers Weekly, April 21, 1997, page 64

Other books by the same author:
Prime Evil, 1988

Other books you might like:
Ramsey Clark, *New Terrors*, 1980
   editor
Charles L. Grant, *The Dodd Mead Gallery of Horror*, 1983
   editor
David G. Hartwell, *The Dark Descent*, 1987
   editor
Kirby McCauley, *Dark Forces*, 1980
   editor
John Pelan, *Darkside: Horror for the Next Millennium*, 1996
   editor

1030

LEONARD WOLF, Editor

Blood Thirst: 100 Years of Vampire Fiction

(New York: Oxford, 1997)

Story type: Anthology; Vampire Story

Summary: Twenty-seven vampire tales by diverse hands that span the century since the publication of Bram Stoker's *Dracula*. The stories are divided into six sections covering the classic vampire, the psychological vampire, the science fiction vampire, the non-human vampire, the comic vampire and the heroic vampire. Included are C.L. Moore's

"Shambleau," about a Medusa-like race of extraterrestrial vampires: Woody Allen's "Count Dracula," which projects the problems Count Dracula might have were he to emerge for feeding during a brief solar eclipse; Fritz Leiber's "The Girl with the Hungry Eyes," about an advertising model who feeds on consumer needs, and M.R. James's "Count Magnus," in which an unwary traveler accidentally liberates a sorcerer and his bloodthirsty familiar from their mausoleum.

Other books by the same author:
Doubles, Dummies and Dolls: 21 Terror Tales of Replication, 1995
Wolf's Complete Book of Terror, 1979 (reprinted in 1994)

Other books you might like:
Ellen Datlow, *Blood Is Not Enough*, 1989
  editor
Martin H. Greenberg, *A Taste for Blood*, 1992
  editor
Stephen Jones, *The Mammoth Book of Vampires*, 1992
  editor
Alan Ryan, *Vampires: Two Centuries of Great Vampire Stories*, 1987
  editor

`1031`

CHELSEA QUINN YARBRO

Writ in Blood

(New York: Tor, 1997)

Story type: Vampire Story

Series: Chronicles of St. Germain
Major character(s): Comte de Sainte Germain, Vampire; Rowena Pearce Manning, Artist; Baron Klemens Manfred von Wolgast, Businessman (munitions)
Time period(s): 1910s
Locale(s): St. Petersburg, Russia; London, England

Summary: At the behest of Czar Nicholas, the Count St. Germain attempts to use his diplomatic influence to ease tension leading Europe to the brink of war. But arms merchants who hope to profit from the impending conflict resort to kidnapping and blackmail to thwart him, forcing him to use his vampire powers.

Where it's reviewed:
Book World, September 28, 1997, page 12
Kirkus Reviews, May 1, 1997, page 686
Publishers Weekly, June 16, 1997, page 48

Other books by the same author:
Mansions of Darkness, 1996
Better in the Dark, 1993
Darker Jewels, 1993
Out of the House of Life, 1990
A Flame in Byzantium, 1988

Other books you might like:
Les Daniels, *Yellow Fog*, 1986
Kim Newman, *Anno Dracula*, 1992
Kim Newman, *The Bloody Red Baron*, 1995
Michael Romkey, *I, Vampire*, 1990
Fred Saberhagen, *Seance for a Vampire*, 1994

Horror

The Year in Science Fiction
by
Michael M. Levy

In its April 1997 issue *The New York Review of Science Fiction* published ''Who Killed Science Fiction?: A Spectrum of Responses.'' The piece consisted of a series of short essays written in response to David Hartwell's rather gloomy editorial that had been published in the *Review* a couple of months earlier. I contributed a response, as did Neil Barron, Brian Aldiss, and others. Now, when the man who is generally considered the finest book editor in the field starts talking about the death of the genre he knows best, it's worth thinking about, but in this case I couldn't entirely go along with him. Based on my experience writing essays like this one for *What Do I Read Next?*, I was willing to admit that there are many problems in the field, but insisted that, overall, science fiction as a genre is in pretty good health. The year 1997 saw a wide range of fine new SF novels, some of them by old masters like Larry Niven, Connie Willis, Joe Haldeman, and Vonda McIntyre, others by exciting new writers like Ian R. MacLeod and Sarah Zettel. We saw superior examples of space opera, hard SF, sociological SF, feminist science fiction, science fantasy—choose your favorite sub-genre—plus a number of excellent slipstream works, that is novels written by people who do not consider themselves SF writers, but who have chosen to visit the borders of our genre for various reasons.

Beginning with the old pros mentioned above, Joe Haldeman's *Forever Peace* is *not* the long-awaited direct sequel to his classic *The Forever War* (1975), except, perhaps, on a thematic level, but it's a very fine novel indeed. Like much of Haldeman's fiction the book deals with war and the debilitating physical, emotional, and moral effect it has on those involved. In the twenty-first century, wars are fought by ''mechanics'' who run powerful fighting machines by remote control using virtual reality. The novel's protagonist, Julian, must go through the gut-wrenching process of switching back and forth between being a drafted, part-time soldier in a savage war and being a university

physics professor who is expected to conduct research and treat his students and colleagues with civility. Eventually Julian uncovers evidence of two separate lines of research, one that has the potential to destroy humanity, and one that could save us. His moral dilemma then concerns his right to make decisions that will effect the entire human race.

Vonda McIntyre is also deeply concerned with moral issues in her superb, Nebula award-winning alternate-universe novel, *The Moon and the Sun*. Set at the court of Louis XIV of France, the famous Sun King, the book is so well researched that it might well be read purely as historical fiction if it were not for the one major change that the author has made in the historical record. A young priest and natural philosopher, newly returned from a scientific expedition, has brought back to Versailles a living mermaid, along with the body of her dead mate. The priest's sister Marie-Josephe, a brilliant young woman who is scientifically literate and a talented musician, is frustrated and bored by the emptiness of life at Versailles and convinces Louis and her brother to let her help care for the strange creature. Soon Marie-Josephe finds herself caught up in a complex and nasty web of religious, political, sexual, patriarchal, and scientific preconceptions, all of which seem likely to bring about her own disgrace and the mermaid's death.

Less morally serious, but at least as entertaining, is Connie Willis's *To Say Nothing of the Dog*, a frothy time travel comedy set, believe it or not, in the same universe as her award-winning but enormously gloomy *Doomsday Book*. The time travel research program at Oxford has gotten itself in financial problems. Strapped for cash, the not-very-practical dons have agreed to do the research necessary to help the eccentric Lady Shrapnel accurately reconstruct the dismal and architecturally irrelevant Coventry Cathedral, which was destroyed back in World War II. Willis's book was influenced in part by Jerome K. Jerome's classic comic novel *Three Men in a Boat* and in part by the screwball film comedies of the 1930s. It features delightful leading charac-

ters who might easily be played by a young Cary Grant and a young Kate Hepburn, not to mention one of the more complex (and silly) time travel paradoxes ever created for an SF novel.

In recent years most of Larry Niven's fiction has been written in collaboration with other, generally less talented authors, in part because of health problems. In *Destiny's Road*, however, he has written a solo novel which, if it isn't quite up to such masterpieces as *Protector* and *Ringworld*, is still a superior planetary adventure. The road of the title connects the isolated backwater communities of Destiny, a lost colonial world where life is tough and where everyone shares a serious problem. The planet's soil lacks certain trace minerals and the colonists no longer have the technology necessary to produce them on their own. Fortunately, traders travel the road on a regular basis bringing ''sprinkles,'' a mysterious food additive that contains the necessary minerals. Unfortunately, sprinkles are in very short supply and, without them, a colonist will quickly degenerate into severe mental retardation. Forced to leave his home after he accidentally kills someone, Niven's protagonist sets out on the road, desperate to find his own source of sprinkles before it's too late and, incidentally, to solve the mystery of the colony's abandonment.

Planetary adventures are stories set on an alien world in which the author devotes a significant amount of space to developing the planet's usually eccentric geology, biology, anthropology, and so forth. *Destiny's Road* is a solid example of the planetary adventure, which is generally one of the more common types of SF. With a few exceptions, however, this was not the best of years for this sort of novel. After Niven's book, probably the best planetary adventure published in 1997 was Catherine Asaro's unusual SF-romance hybrid *The Last Hawk*, the third novel in her Skolian Empire series, in which a traditional space opera-style warrior crashes on a matriarchal planet and finds himself held prisoner and used, disconcertingly, as a sex toy by the world's rulers. Also containing significant romance elements was Sharon Shinn's *Jovah's Angel*, sequel to last year's widely-praised *Archangel*. The book concerns a lost colony ruled over by a remote computer intelligence, whom the colonists believe to be God, and a group of genetically altered humans, who are supposedly angels. Yet another planetary adventure with romantic elements was Connie Willis and Cynthia Felice's very lightweight *Promised Land*. Robert L. Forward's *Saturn Rukh*, set in the upper atmosphere of the ringed planet, features his usual combination of wonderful ideas and mediocre writing. James Alan Gardner's first novel *Expendable* tells an unusual tale of disabled explorers intentionally abandoned on a planet of no return. Prolific author Alan Dean Foster's *The Howling Stones*, which concerns an alien contact specialist sent to a planet to negotiate mineral rights with the natives, received generally so-so reviews, as did Charles Sheffield's similar young adult novel *Putting Up Roots*. Kristine Kathryn Rusch's *Alien Influences*

is a somewhat stronger tale in which the native life forms of a colonial planet are blamed for a series of gruesome murders. In a similar vein, L.E. Modesitt, Jr.'s *The Ecolitan Enigma*, the latest volume in his Ecolitan series, features an economist/secret agent who must save a colony world from collapse. Perhaps the strangest planetary ecology to be found in a 1997 novel is described by veteran author Jack Williamson in *The Black Sun*, which concerns stranded colonists newly landed on a frozen planet in orbit around a brown dwarf and their discovery of the remains of a very enigmatic alien race.

Although science fiction is traditionally seen as centered on the future, a number of the best genre novels to appear in 1997 were set in the past. Some of these, like Connie Willis's *To Say Nothing of the Dog,* were stories of time travel, while others, like Vonda McIntyre's *The Moon and the Sun*, were alternate histories. Most of the time travel books feature attempts to either change or desperately avoid changing the past. Peter Delacorte's stylish *Time on My Hands* concerns a travel writer who, discovering a misplaced time machine in 1994, goes back to pre-World War II Hollywood intending to make changes in Ronald Reagan's career that will keep him from becoming president. Sharing with both Willis and Delacorte a love for old movies, John Kessel in *Corrupting Dr. Nice* combined screwball comedy recalling Preston Sturges with sophisticated physics in a tale in which time travelers have a choice of alternate pasts to visit. Thus, in one past Jesus was crucified, in another he was kidnaped by time travelers just before the crucifixion, and in a third he was kidnaped as a young adult, and both men now coexist quite happily in the future. However, our hero, a bumbling paleontologist, causes all sorts of problems when he returns to his billionaire parents' estate with a baby apatosaurus in tow. The idea of a secret, quasi-military organization spread throughout time and delegated to prevent major changes in history is one of the oldest concepts in science fiction; see, for example numerous stories by Fritz Leiber and Poul Anderson. It's still a useful device, however, and variations on it figured prominently in both the Delacorte and Kessel novels. J.R. Dunn took an unusually serious look at the idea of a time patrol, however, in his harrowing novel *Days of Cain*. Gaspar James is, in effect, a time policeman, charged by civilizations far in the future with maintaining the validity of the timeline during his era. That such a task is necessary and right seems obvious to him, until he's sent to World War II-era Auschwitz to stop a renegade from his organization who is attempting to change history and save lives. Faced with the horror of the camps, James begins to doubt the rightness of the cause he works for. Also testifying, albeit on a less serious level, to the ongoing popularity of this kind of tale were two novels in a new series by veteran John Barnes, *Caesar's Bicycle* and *Washington's Dirigible*, as well as R. Garcia y Robertson's *Atlantis Found* and Joshua Dann's first novel *Timeshare,*

which also features travel to early twentieth century Hollywood.

Genre SF writers produced five superb works of alternate history in 1997. The best of these, in my opinion, was McIntyre's *The Moon and the Sun*. Also excellent were Harry Turtledove's *How Few Remain*, a grim tale in which the South won the Civil War and America generally goes to hell; Stephen Baxter's Arthur C. Clarke Award-nominated *Voyage*, which reads like a straight historical novel, but one in which John F. Kennedy survives his assassination attempt, heavily pushes the space program, and gets the United States to Mars by 1986; Elizabeth Hand's *Glimmering*, an eerie and atmospheric tale set at the turn of the millennium in an America sunk much further into political and ecological collapse than is our world; and, finally, Michael Swanwick's *tour de force, Jack Faust,* a retelling of the classic legend in which Mephistopheles is evidently an artificial intelligence from an alternate universe who has been sent to our world to help Faust create a premature industrial revolution, thereby making it possible for humanity to wipe itself out with nuclear weapons several centuries earlier than it might otherwise do so.

Less successful alternate universe tales by genre writers included James Herbert's bloody *'48*, in which the Nazis brought World War II to an abrupt end by releasing a devastating hemorrhagic plague on the world, and Kim Newman and Eugene Byrne's *Back in the USSA*, in which the U.S. goes communist in 1912 after Teddy Roosevelt is killed in a battle between his Rough Riders and striking meatpackers in Chicago. Beautifully written and intensely symbolic, but somewhat on the slow side, was literary novelist Christoph Ransmayr's *The Dog King,* which is set in a post-World War II Germany that has been completely deindustrialized.

Not all science fiction set in the past has to be an alternate history or involve time travel, however. Secret histories are tales set in our past involving science fictional events that, for whatever reason, never became part of the history we know, and 1997 saw the publication of one of the best such books ever written, Patricia Anthony's *God's Fires*. The novel is set in and around a backwater village in seventeenth century Portugal and involves the crash-landing there of a virtually archetypal flying saucer. *God's Fires* is both superbly written and features a wonderful protagonist, an Inquisitor priest who doesn't really want to have to burn anyone at the stake and who tries desperately to keep a lid on the situation before it attracts the attention of both the Portuguese nobility and the church. Another variation on the secret history involves a more or less contemporary or even near-future setting in which characters discover the existence of secret manipulators whose efforts have controlled humanity's destiny for decades or even centuries. Thomas Pynchon's *Gravity's Rainbow* may well be the finest such novel ever written. Not in a class with Pynchon, but still quite good was Amitav Ghosh's Arthur C. Clarke Award-

winning *The Calcutta Chromosome*, a complex tale in which a researcher discovers evidence that a secret society has been guiding malaria research for political ends, possibly for centuries.

Perhaps it's the ongoing public concern over AIDS, perhaps some of the scary stories coming out of Africa these days about Ebola and other exotic diseases, perhaps it's all the talk about new, antibiotic-resistant forms of hepatitis and tuberculosis, but a lot of science fiction was published in 1997 that dealt with the terrifying effects of plague. I've already mentioned Ghosh's *The Calcutta Chromosome* and James Herbert's *'48*. Also worth mentioning is *The Plague Years* by first novelist Ann Benson, a very dark literary novel that features two narratives, one set during an outbreak of the Black Plague in the fourteenth century, the other set just after a world-wide plague called the Outbreak in the early twenty-first century. Much more baroque, and virtually incomprehensible to anyone who hasn't read the first two volumes in the trilogy, was Richard Calder's sexually perverse *Dead Things*, which concerns the transformation almost beyond recognition of our universe due to an artificially created sexual plague. Somewhat less obscure, but only partially successful, was William Barton and Michael Capobianco's *Alpha Centauri*, which also concerns a sexually transmitted plague, this time on a colony ship in flight from an over-populated Earth to our nearest stellar neighbor.

The near-future collapse of civilization as we know it continued to worry science fiction writers in 1997. Perhaps the most famous novel on this theme ever written was Walter M. Miller, Jr.'s *A Canticle for Leibowitz* (1960). In 1997 we were fortunate enough to at long last receive Miller's long delayed sequel to that classic. *St. Leibowitz and the Wild Horse Woman*, which was either finished or merely prepared for publication by Terry Bisson after Miller's death, is a very different book from *Canticle*, which may have some bearing on the very mixed reviews that it received. A long, involved tale of warfare and politics, it primarily concerns the complex struggle for supremacy between the North American papacy in exile and the secular Empire of Texarkana. Although the tale lacks much of the poetry and sense of wonder of the original novel, it's well written and includes a number of fine characters. Other post-collapse tales of note included Jack McDevitt's *Eternity Road* in which a group of explorers travel north up the Mississippi in search of a fabled repository of lost knowledge; Kathleen Ann Goonan's *Mississippi Blues*, sequel to her well-reviewed *Queen City Jazz*, which sends survivors of a nanotechnology-induced social collapse south, down the river in search of answers; and Kim Antieau's very strange *The Gaia Websters*, which concerns a psychic healer who may or may not be human (she doesn't know herself) living in a small, post-holocaust community in Arizona Territory. A variation on this theme involves the beleaguered high-tech community trying to survive despite the collapse of civilization. Lee Wood handled this plot very

effectively in *Faraday's Orphans*, as did Howard V. Hendrix in his first novel *Lightpaths.* On the borderline between science fiction and mainstream literature lay noted novelist John Updike's *Toward the End of Time.* Set in a twenty-first century United States that has barely survived a war with China, the book concentrates on the life and loves of a typical, aging Updike New Englander.

Of course, when writers like Wood and Hendrix set up universes in which a high-tech society must deal with an increasingly hostile, relatively primitive civilization, what they're often doing is using science fiction to make a point about life on Earth today and, more specifically, the interaction between the West and the Third World. In his superb first novel *The Great Wheel*, Ian R. MacLeod chose to deal with these issues more directly. The story concerned an English priest, stationed in North Africa's festering Endless City in the twenty-first century, who must come to terms with his vocation, his sexuality, and western society's willingness to accept and even promote the human suffering that surrounds him. *The Great Wheel*, I think, is the finest first novel of the year. Based on the evidence of this book, as well as MacLeod's first short-story collection, *Voyages by Starlight*, also published in 1997, it's obvious that he's a major new talent. Another novel making some of the same points, albeit in a somewhat more traditional outer-space venue, was William Barton's *Acts of Conscience*, which concerns a spaceship mechanic, a virtually archetypal ugly-American who, after striking it rich, sets off to see the galaxy and manages to damage virtually everything he touches.

Much of the fiction which I've discussed so far is frankly dystopian. Perhaps it's the upcoming millennium or, to look for a more mundane reason, the current state of the publishing industry (as discussed in my opening paragraph), but there were a lot of dark visions of the future out there in 1997. Among the best of these were Tricia Sullivan's *Someone to Watch Over Me*, which envisions a twenty-first century society where all citizens receive brain implants so that Watchers can follow their every move; Richard Paul Russo's ever-so-*noir Carlucci's Heart*, third in a series about a San Francisco police detective living and working in a hellish future; George Foy's cyberpunk-influenced *Contraband*, a sequel to last year's successful *The Shift*, which gives us a bleak look at near-future developments in electronic technology and government repression; and Susan R. Matthews' exceedingly disturbing dystopian space opera-with-torture *An Exchange of Hostages.* Two distinctly depressing feminist SF novels were Lucy Ferriss's *The Misconceiver*, a well-done variation on Margaret Atwood's *The Handmaid's Tale* set in a future United States where the radical Christian Right has won, abortion is illegal, and women are thoroughly repressed; and Jacqueline Harpman's *I Who Have Never Known Men*, which concerns a group of women imprisoned on a hostile alien planet.

Not everything was doom and gloom in 1997, however. The year also featured a number of colorful, exciting, over-the-top space operas and enough hard-science fiction to satisfy even the most devoted reader of *Analog.* One of the best of the space operas, to my mind, was Iain M. Banks's *Excession*, the latest in his Culture series and a winner of the British SF Association's best novel award. As the book opens a gigantic artifact has appeared hanging in interstellar space. Although its purpose is unknown, it's definitely hostile and demonstrates abilities far beyond those of either the Culture or the independent, shipborn artificial intelligences known as the Minds. In its enormous scope *Excession* most reminds me of Vernor Vinge's award-winner of a few years back, *A Fire Upon the Deep.* Less spectacular, but equally well done was C.J. Cherryh's latest addition to her ongoing future history. *Finity's End* is a *bildungsroman* about a young spacer whose pregnant mother had been abandoned on Downbelow Station before he was born due to a wartime emergency. Now, with the war more or less over, the young man finds himself forcibly repatriated to the starship that his dead mother called home but he has never seen. A disappointment only in comparison to the award-winning earlier volumes in the series, Dan Simmon's pyrotechnic *The Rise of Endymion* features a number of exciting action sequences, complex church politics, and a particularly attractive, pint-sized messiah. Two more particularly worthwhile space operas appearing in 1997 were Peter F. Hamilton's *The Reality Dysfunction*, which was so long that it had to be published in two fat paperback volumes and Damien Broderick's flamboyant, Hamlet-based *The White Abacus.* Also enjoyable were veteran novelist Poul Anderson's *Fleet of Stars*, the conclusion to his Harvest of Stars tetrology; Elizabeth Moon's *Once a Hero*, military SF with a touch of humor somewhat in the manner of Lois McMaster Bujold; two novels in Andre Norton's long running Solar Queen series, *Derelict for Trade* and *A Mind for Trade*, both co-authored with Sherwood Smith; Sarah Zettel's *Fool's War*, in which a starship and its crew are set up to come into conflict with a sophisticated artificial intelligence; John E. Stith's enigmatic *Reckoning Infinity*, which concerns explorers who encounter a planet-sized, organic starship; and the latest installment in David Weber's vastly popular Honor Harrington military SF series, *In Enemy Hands.* Less successful were *Berserker Fury*, the latest installment in Fred Saberhagen's long running series, and L. Neil Smith's comic space opera *Bretta Martyn.*

Turning to hard SF, that is, science fiction that concentrates on scientific accuracy, there were, once again, plenty of winners. Greg Egan's *Distress* concerns a science journalist covering a conference on the introduction of a new TOE, or Theory Of Everything, who discovers that a number of radical groups are convinced that the TOE has the ability to destroy or radically alter the world simply by being understood by one human being. Stephen Baxter's gritty *Titan* tells the story of a desperate, very near-future attempt to reach and survive on Saturn's moon Titan using more or less current technology. Paul Preuss's odd but endearing

Secret Passages devotes most of its space to the biography of a noted physicist before centering in on the revolutionary new experiment he undertakes to disprove Heisenberg's Uncertainty Principle. Also worth looking at are John Cramer's *Einstein's Bridge*, in which a particle physics experiment accidentally opens our world to invasion by a malevolent hive intelligence; *Wyrm*, first novelist Mark Fabi's tale of computer hackers and artificial intelligence; Robert Sawyer's *Frameshift*, which concerns a geneticist with Huntington's chorea and his not entirely human daughter; Peter F. Hamilton's hard SF detective story *A Quantum Murder*; Paul Cook's *Fortress on the Sun*, in which prisoners in a facility located within the Sun's photosphere must uncover the mystery behind a contagious disease that is killing them off; and James P. Hogan's oddly old-fashioned *Bug Park*, a tale of miniaturized remote-control robots, virtual reality technology, and murder. Somewhat less successful were William K. Hartman's *Mars Underground* and Bart Kosko's *Nanotime*. Hartman is a prominent Mars scientist, Kosko a world-class expert on nanotechnology, but both still have a lot to learn about writing fiction.

Cyberpunk may be a thing of the past, but it continues to leave its mark on contemporary science fiction. Many of the standard tropes of that sub-genre—the hacker anti-hero, the *noir* atmosphere, the mean and run down twenty-first century urban environment, the nano and virtual technology, the Net—have become common elements of mainstream SF, and appear in a number of the novels I've already discussed, including books by Haldeman, Russo, Foy, Sullivan, Goonan, Calder, Hamilton, Fabi, and others. Other major 1997 novels that clearly descend from the cyberpunk tradition were Greg Bear's oddly named */ (Slant)*, an entirely successful sequel to his *Queen of Angels*, which continues that earlier novel's panoramic exploration of a complex society in which even basic mental health is a high-tech proposition; Tad Williams's enormously long and endlessly inventive *City of Golden Shadow*, which is merely the first volume in his new *Otherland* series; Rudy Rucker's *Freeware*, sequel to his award-winning *Software* and *Wetware*; and Melissa Scott's very well-done *Dreaming Metal*, a sequel to *Dreamships*, although it stands on its own, which concerns a sentient artificial intelligence, class conflict, and stage magic. Other cyberpunk-influenced 1997 novels that were worth a look included Eric James Fullilove's *The Stranger*, a sequel to his successful first novel, *Circle of One*; Terrence M. Green's near-future police procedural, *Blue Limbo*; and Shariann Lewitt's *Interface Masque*, a tale of data piracy set in late-twenty-first century Venice. Also making use of such cyberpunk-indebted concepts as the Net and virtual reality, although in his own unique way, was Roger Zelazny, who, in his posthumously published *Donnerjack* (co-authored with Jane Lindskold), envisioned a universe in which the artificial intelligences created by humanity on the Net are now trying to gain entrance to our universe.

A number of other major science fiction writers produced memorable, if less classifiable fiction in 1997. Among them were Jonathan Lethem, whose *As She Climbed Across the Table* is a decidedly post-modernist tale of a university professor who finds himself losing the woman he loves, a particle physicist, to one of her experiments; Sheri S. Tepper, whose *The Family Tree* tells a decidedly offbeat tale of ecological recovery and arboreal revenge; Allen Steele, whose *A King of Infinite Space* presents yet another of his well-done, highly-believable near-futures; and Alan Dean Foster, whose *Jed the Dead* relates the bizarre and hysterically funny story of a Texan who finds the corpse of a tiny alien that, despite being dead, still possesses a variety of super powers. Somewhat less successful but still worth reading were the late Fritz Leiber's long-lost, Lovecraftian time-travel novella *The Dealings of Daniel Kesserich;* Frederik Pohl's *The Siege of Eternity*, a sequel to his *The Other End of Time*, which makes use of astronomer Frank Tipler's controversial Omega Point theory (which argues that everyone will be recreated through scientific means at the end of the universe); Charles Sheffield's *Tomorrow and Tomorrow*, which also makes use of Tipler's theory; Sheffield's *Convergence*, the fourth volume in his well-thought of *Summertide* series; and Robert Reed's *Beneath the Gated Sky*, a sequel to his *Beyond the Veil of Stars*.

Also seeing print in 1997 were additions to some of science fiction's best loved series: *Dragonseye*, Anne McCaffrey's newest novel of Pern; *Foundation's Fear*, Gregory Benford's well-done continuation of Asimov's *magnum opus*; Arthur C. Clarke's not entirely successful *3001: The Final Odyssey;* Marion Zimmer Bradley's new Darkover novel, *The Shadow Matrix;* Robert Silverberg's *Sorcerers of Majipoor;* *Final Diagnosis*, James White's most recent Sector General novel; and *Douglas Adams's Starship Titanic*, written by former Monty Python member Terry Jones, but set in the universe of *The Hitchhiker's Guide*. McCaffrey also published *Freedom's Choice*, the latest volume in her newest series, to generally good reviews. Less successful was *Acorna: The Unicorn Girl*, a science fiction novel despite the title, co-authored by McCaffrey and Margaret Ball, which received generally negative reviews.

Yet another reason why I refuse to be pessimistic about the future of science fiction is the sheer number of excellent first novels published in 1997. As I've already said, the best, in my opinion, was Ian R. MacLeod's *The Great Wheel*, a remarkably mature work for a writer who really hasn't been on the scene all that long. Perhaps reflecting the success of Mary Doria Russell's breakout first novel of last year, several other excellent books by new writers were published as mainstream novels. Among these were Ann Benson's *The Plague Years*, which I've already discussed; Herbert Thomas's *The Superlative Man*, a darkly humorous tale in which a reporter uncovers proof that the local Superman-like superhero is corrupt, and Kirsten Bakis's wonderfully titled *Lives of the Monster Dogs*, which concerns a group of

surgically enhanced, bionic canines, bred in secret by a mad nineteenth-century Prussian scientist, who murder their human rulers and then make their way to twenty-first century New York. Bakis's novel is worth reading for its own sake, but also serves as an intriguing commentary on H.G. Wells's 1896 classic *The Island of Dr. Moreau.* I've already mentioned a number of other solid first novels: Joshua Dann's time travel adventure, *Timeshare*; Mark Fabi's computer novel, *Wyrm*; James Alan Gardner's planetary adventure, *Expendable*; Jacqueline Harpman's bitter dystopia, *I Who Have Never Known Men*; and Howard V. Hendrix's tale of conflict between Earth and an orbital colony, *Lightpaths.* Among the very best first novels published in 1997, however, was Candas Jane Dorsey's beautifully written feminist tale *Black Wine*, in which several women living in a number of different and fascinating cultures turn out to have a variety of unexpected connections. Two other first novels worthy of mention are Elisabeth DeVos's story of angels from outer space, *The Seraphim Rising* and Severna Park's lesbian space opera, *Speaking Dreams.*

Every year, when I'm about three quarters of the way through writing this article I realize that there are a number of worthwhile novels which for one reason or another simply don't fit in the categories I've set up. So, rather than simply ignore them, here's a paragraph devoted to miscellaneous excellence. One of the year's best fantastic tales, although readers and reviewers can't even agree over whether it's science fiction or fantasy, was Walter Jon Williams's *City on Fire*, a sequel to his Nebula Award-nominated *Metropolitan.* The novel features complex political intrigues and well-developed characters in a far-future world city where plasm, a seemingly magical form of energy, is the key to world conquest. Much less spectacular but equally well done was Molly Gloss's *The Dazzle of Day,* which combines elements of the space opera and the planetary adventure, transforming them into the serious tale of a Quaker generation ship and its colonization of a barely habitable ice world. The book features realistic detail about life in a closed environment and a fascinating emphasis on how Quakers solve problems. Also worthwhile were Linda Nagata's *Deception Well*, a complex and compelling tale set in a dying city of the future; Matt Ruff's *Sewer Gas & Electric*, a literate mystery/satire set in the near-future; Robert J. Sawyer's courtroom drama *Illegal Alien*, in which a member of a seemingly harmless alien exploratory party comes to Earth and then apparently commits murder; Tony Daniel's *Earthling*, which concerns a philosophically inclined robot, and last, but not least, Kurt Vonnegut's totally unclassifiable literary SF novel *cum* memoir, *Timequake.*

Turning to short fiction, a number of memorable single author collections appeared in 1997. Long-time veterans Ray Bradbury and Harlan Ellison each brought out new volumes of recent work. Bradbury's *Driving Blind* received mixed reviews and Ellison's *Slippage* excellent reviews. Also worthy of note from writers working at the top of their

form were John M. Ford's *From the End of the Twentieth Century*, James Patrick Kelly's *Think Like a Dinosaur and Other Stories,* Patricia Anthony's *Eating Memories*, Paul Di Filippo's *Fractal Paisleys*, Michael Swanwick's *A Geography of Unknown Lands*, Greg Egan's *Axiomatic*, Howard Waldrop's *Going Home Again*, Martha Soukup's *The Arbitrary Placement of Walls*, Bruce Taylor's *The Final Trick of Funnyman and Other Stories*, Michael Flynn's *The Forest of Time and Other Stories*, John Kessel's *The Pure Product* and Ian R. MacLeod's *Voyages by Starlight.* Theodore Sturgeon, Alfred Bester, and C.M. Kornbluth are all dead of course, but some of their finest work became newly available last year with the appearance of Sturgeon's *Thunder and Roses: The Complete Short Stories, Vol. 4*, Bester's *Virtual Unrealities*, and *His Share of Glory: The Solo Science Fiction of C.M. Kornbluth.* Less positively received but of some historical importance was Donald Wandrei's posthumous *Don't Dream: The Collected Horror and Fantasy.*

It wasn't a particularly good year for original SF anthologies, however. Probably the best was David S. Garnett and Michael Moorcock's *New Worlds 1997,* which includes excellent stories by Michael Moorcock, Pat Cadigan, William Gibson, Howard Waldrop, and Kim Newman. Also highly competent were Orson Scott Card and Keith Ferrell's *Black Mist and Other Japanese Futures,* which includes fiction by Janeen Webb and Jack Dann; Gardner Dozois's *Dying for It*, which included stories by Pat Cadigan and Andy Duncan; Brad Lindweaver and Edward E. Kramer's libertarian-oriented *Free Space*, which features fiction by Robert J. Sawyer and William F. Wu; and Mike Resnick's *Alternate Tyrants.* As is usually the case, the best of the reprint anthologies was Gardner Dozois's *The Years Best Science Fiction: Fourteenth Annual Collection.* Also excellent were David Hartwell's much smaller *Year's Best SF 2*; *The Best of Interzone*, edited by David Pringle; Martin H. Greenberg's *The New Hugo Winners IV*; Pamela Sargent's *Nebula Awards 31*; Hartwell's *The Science Fiction Century*; and Warren Lapine and Stephen Pagel's *Absolute Magnitude,* a selection of stories from their highly regarded small-press magazine.

Magazine circulation continued its precipitous decline in 1997, with *Asimov's* down 7.4 percent according to *Locus*, and *Analog, Fantasy and Science Fiction*, and *Science Fiction Age* all dropping at least 10 percent. Still, the magazines continued to publish excellent short fiction. *Asimov's,* edited by Gardner Dozois, had its usual fine year, featuring outstanding stories by Ian McDonald, Connie Willis, Stephen Baxter, Karen Joy Fowler, James Patrick Kelly, Nancy Kress, Michael Swanwick, Mike Resnick, Mary Rosenblum, Howard Waldrop, Walter Jon Williams, Paul J. McAuley, Bill Johnson, L. Timmel Duchamp, Ian R. MacLeod, and others. The best fiction in *The Magazine of Fantasy and Science Fiction*, edited now by Gordon Van Gelder, was produced by such writers as Paul Park, Gene Wolfe, Alan Brennert, Robert Reed, Brian Stableford, and

Stephen King, among others. Stanley Schmidt's *Analog* featured outstanding stories by G. David Nordley, long-time veteran Katherine MacLean, J.R. Dunn, and others. The new kid on the block, *Science Fiction Age*, had another strong year, featuring fiction by Charles Sheffield, Robert Reed, Robert Silverberg, Gregory Benford, Geof Landis, and Stephen Baxter. The British SF magazine *Interzone* brought out fine stories by Greg Egan, Paul J. McAuley, Peter F. Hamilton, and others. Also making available a number of fine stories was the all-internet *Omni Online*, which "published" short fiction by Michael Kandel, Simon Ings (a superb British writer virtually unknown in the United States), Michael Bishop, Paul Park, and Brian Stableford. *Crank!* and *Century*, the finest of science fiction's small press magazines, failed to produce an issue in 1997, but the Canadian *On Spec*, *Pirate Writings*, and *Absolute Magnitude* all published worthwhile material.

I feel that an unusually large number of excellent science fiction novels appeared in 1997, and for this reason my best of the year list is quite long. If I had to limit myself to six books, however, I'd probably name Patricia Anthony's *God's Fires*, Iain M. Banks's *Excession*, C.J. Cherryh's *Finity's End*, Ian R. MacLeod's *The Great Wheel*, Vonda McIntyre's *The Moon and the Sun*, and Tad Williams's *Otherland: City of Golden Shadow*. If I had to pick one book, I expect I'd flip a coin between the Anthony and the MacLeod.

After nine years, this will be my last turn as the author of the annual "Year in Science Fiction" article for *What Do I Read Next?* Beginning with the 1999 volume, this essay will be in the able hands of veteran book reviewer, librarian, and short-short story writer Eric Heideman. I look forward to comparing my own choices for 1998 to his from the sideline.

Novels:

God's Fires by Patricia Anthony

The Gaia Websters by Kim Antieau

The Last Hawk by Catherine Asaro

Lives of the Monster Dogs by Kirsten Bakis

Excession by Iain M. Banks

Acts of Conscience by William Barton

Titan by Stephen Baxter

Voyage by Stephen Baxter

/ (Slant) by Greg Bear

The Plague Years by Ann Benson

The White Abacus by Damien Broderick

Finity's End by C.J. Cherryh

Time on My Hands by Peter Delacorte

Black Wine by Candas Jane Dorsey

Days of Cain by J.R. Dunn

Distress by Greg Egan

The Misconceiver by Lucy Ferriss

The Calcutta Chromosome by Amitav Ghosh

The Dazzle of Day by Molly Gloss

Mississippi Blues by Kathleen Ann Goonan

Forever Peace by Joe Haldeman

The Reality Dysfunction by Peter F. Hamilton

Glimmering by Elizabeth Hand

Corrupting Dr. Nice by John Kessel

As She Climbed Across the Table by Jonathan Lethem

The Great Wheel by Ian R. MacLeod

The Moon and the Sun by Vonda McIntyre

St. Leibowitz and the Wild Horse Woman by Walter M. Miller, Jr.

Deception Well by Linda Nagata

Destiny's Road by Larry Niven

Secret Passages by Paul Preuss

Freeware by Rudy Rucker

Sewer Gas & Electric by Matt Ruff

Carlucci's Heart by Richard Paul Russo

Dreaming Metal by Melissa Scott

The Rise of Endymion by Dan Simmons

Someone to Watch Over Me by Tricia Sullivan

Jack Faust by Michael Swanwick

The Family Tree by Sheri S. Tepper

How Few Remain by Harry Turtledove

Otherland, Vol 1: City of Golden Shadow by Tad Williams

City on Fire by Walter Jon Williams

To Say Nothing of the Dog by Connie Willis

Faraday's Orphans by N. Lee Wood

Fool's War by Sarah Zettel

Collections/Anthologies:

Virtual Unrealities by Alfred Bester

The Years Best Science Fiction: Fourteenth Annual Collection, Gardner Dozois, ed.

Axiomatic by Greg Egan

Slippage by Harlan Ellison

New Worlds 1997, David S. Garnett and Michael Moorcock eds.

The Science Fiction Century, David Hartwell, ed.

Year's Best SF 2, David Hartwell, ed.

Think Like a Dinosaur and Other Stories by James Patrick Kelly

The Pure Product by John Kessel

His Share of Glory: The Solo Science Fiction of C.M. Kornbluth by C.M. Kornbluth

Voyages by Starlight by Ian R. MacLeod

Nebula Awards 31, Pamela Sargent, ed.

The Arbitrary Placement of Walls by Martha Soukup

Thunder and Roses: The Complete Short Stories, Vol. 4. by Theodore Sturgeon

A Geography of Unknown Lands by Michael A. Swanwick

For Further Information about Fantastic Fiction
by Neil Barron

The February issue of *Locus* provides the most detailed statistics on fantastic literature and has for many years, making it an essential source for any historian of the field. Its reviews total more than 400 per year, by far the most comprehensive coverage of any source, and it would be an outstanding selection tool for librarians as well as valuable for readers interested in fantastic literature ($46/year for libraries to Box 13305, Oakland, CA 94661). Although its summaries are limited to English language materials, coverage of non-English books and magazines is provided irregularly throughout the year. Here are some comparative figures about original U.S. books (not reprints or reissues) that might interest you:

Quantities in each category have fluctuated widely over the past decade and no confident projections are possible. *Locus* counted 1816 books published in 1997; of these 999 (55%) were original books, the lowest figure since 1986. There were 459 original adult novels and 96 YA novels. The decline in the number of original mass market paperbacks continued, caused in part by a severe disruption of the independent distributor network. Mass market paperbacks were 44% of the 1816 books published, down from 63% a decade ago; for originals only, 37% vs 55%. More expensive trade paperbacks increased in number. See also the year in review comments by Scott Imes and Stefan Dziemianowicz.

In 1997 229 original science fiction novels were published, 220 fantasy, and 106 horror. These figures show a decline from 1992, when 2239 SF, 278 fantasy, and 165 horror originals were published. The contrast with 1987 is also interesting; 317 SF, 264 fantasy, and 96 horror original novels were published. The number of anthologies has been relatively constant—104 published in 1997 compared to 97 in 1992 and 98 in 1987—as has the number of collections—71 in 1997, 78 in 1992, 77 in 1987. Media-related books (fiction and non-fiction) have shown the greatest gains, from 64 in 1987 to 81 in 1992 and 149 in 1997.

The steady growth in the media-related category reinforces the comments by Brian Stableford I cited in last year's annual. I tabulated about 110 works of nonfiction published in 1997, of which approximately 30% fall into the media-related category. Many of these are published by McFarland & Co., Jefferson, NC, which has an extensive backlist and current program in the performing arts. McFarland began a program in 1997 to issue its most popular performing arts titles, many of them dealing with fantastic cinema and TV, as trade paperbacks.

The influence of film on fiction was commented on by Gardner Dozois in an interview in the December 1997 *Locus*. Dozois is the very capable and knowledgeable editor of *Asimov's Science Fiction Magazine* as well as a best-of-the-year SF anthology. He remarked: "I will tell you one way in which the slush pile has changed over the last 30 years or so, which disquiets me. When I was reading slush for *Galaxy, Worlds of If,* and *Worlds of Tomorrow,* back in '69 and '70, a lot of the slush was bad imitations of famous SF stories and novels, and now a lot of the slush is bad imitation of SF movies and TV shows. So it's moved another remove backwards, which worries me." He's not alone.

My new guide *Fantasy and Horror: A Critical and Historical Guide to Literature, Illustration, Film, TV, Radio, Internet* (to be published by Scarecrow Press, fall 1998) has a section on online resources, and other chapters have addresses of other websites of likely interest to someone interested in fantastic literature or film. Here are a few of the more significant sites discussed, all of which have links to hundreds of other related sites:

Linkoping Science Fiction Archive (sf.www.lysator.liu.se/sf—archive/): a Swedish-based site with an idiosyncratic but extensive collection of materials.

Science Fiction Writers of America (www.sfwa.org): information and links on news, the SFWA handbook, awards, writers, agents and everything else related to the professional end of the fields of SF and fantasy.

Dark Side of the Net (www.gothic.Net/darkside/index.html) and Dark Side of the Web (www.gothic.Net/darkside/darkweb.html) are rich sites from which you can jump to any of nearly 5,000 sites devoted to every imaginable facet of horror and the dark side, from vampires, the occult, to the paranormal, including an FAQ and newsgroup information.

A site that will appeal to those with scholarly interests in fantastic literature and film is Fantastic Links (ebbs.english.vt.edu/iafa/Links/fantastic.links.html), described as a guide to "scholarly and other web resources of interest to teachers and scholars of the fantastic."

Bibliofind (www.bibliofind.com), Interloc (www.interloc.com) and Advanced Book Exchange (www.abebooks.com) are three similar American sites listing millions of books, mostly out of print, available from hundreds of dealers. Collection development and order librarians should find these sites valuable. For in print books, many already know of Amazon (www.amazon.com), which has at least one British counterpart, Internet Book Shop (www.bookshop.co.uk/search.htm).

The number of libraries having significant holdings of fantastic literature is about four dozen worldwide. A chapter is devoted to them in both my *Anatomy of Wonder* (4th ed., Bowker, 1995) and *Fantasy and Horror* (cited above). Newly identified are two collections. SUNY Buffalo (www.ublib.buffalo.edu.libraries) received a large donation of paperbacks and pulp magazines in 1992 from George L. Kelley, roughly equally divided between SF and horror/fantasy. Virginia Polytechnic Institute and State University Library (scholar2.lib.vt.edu/spec/spfic/spfichp.htm) acquired the William J. Heron collection of American, British and Australian magazines and about 11,000 volumes of paperbacks.

The books dealing with fantastic literature, film and illustration published in 1997 ranged from spinoffs from films to heavy academic studies. I discuss five below.

Libraries are likely to be most interested in and find most use for *The Encyclopedia of Fantasy* (St Martin's), edited by John Clute and John Grant. A companion to Clute and Peter Nicholls' *The Encyclopedia of Science Fiction* (1993), its 1049 pages cover most aspects of the fantastic in fiction, film, radio, TV, illustration (including comics) and music. There are about 1,600 author entries, plus other entries for critics, editors, illustrators, etc. Approximately 500 films are discussed, with many entries for TV programs, but far too few for radio. Although there are entries for dark fantasy, supernatural fiction, weird fiction, psychological thrillers and similar topics, treatment of horror fiction lacking fantasy elements is slight. Just as its SF counterpart was greatly improved in its second edition (1993), so too will the fantasy volume. Its deficiencies are minor compared to its multiple virtues, and most libraries should have a copy.

Another important reference work, although for larger libraries, is the latest cumulation by Hal Hall, *Science Fiction and Fantasy Reference Index, 1992-1995: an International Subject and Author Index to History and Criticism* (Libraries Unlimited). The base volume, covering 1878-1985, was published by Gale in 1987. The first supplement from Libraries Unlimited covered 1985-1991. The three volumes now provide more than 46,000 citations to the secondary literature, most of it in English. Complementing these volumes are the companion indexes to book reviews of fantastic fiction, containing about 42,000 citations through 1984, with self-published annuals extending the coverage.

In last year's annual I judged S.T. Joshi's biography of H.P. Lovecraft (1890-1937) far too detailed for anyone save the devoted enthusiast. More accessible is his *A Subtler Magick: The Writings and Philosophy of H.P. Lovecraft* (Borgo Press), which is most usefully read in conjunction with Lovecraft's fiction, whose most reliable editions are those edited by Joshi and issued by Arkham House.

Much of the iconography of science fiction was shaped by the illustrations in the long-vanished pulp magazines. *PPulp Culture* (Collectors Press, Box 230986, Portland, OR 97281, $39.95), by Frank M. Robinson and Lawrence Davidson, provides a useful survey of the type of literature printed on wood pulp paper, ''. . .the successors to the story papers of the last century and the dime novels of the beginning of the twentieth. . .for many years they were the chief source of entertainment in a country that was starved for it.'' The six popular genres surveyed in this annual are among the categories in this extensively illustrated survey. Other categories include adventure, superheroes and villains, sports, the ''spicy'' romances (very tame by today's much more relaxed standards) and war tales. Limited to science fiction but including books and film posters as well as magazines is the comprehensive work by artist Vincent Di Fate, *Infinite Worlds: The Fantastic Visions of Science Fiction Art* (Penguin Studio). An informed 86 page introduction precedes a gallery devoted to more than 100 illustrators, most of them American, with excellent color reproductions of their work. Although British and European illustrators are slighted, this is still a very capable survey that should prove very appealing even to readers who were born long after the pulps were replaced by mass market paperbacks, TV and comics.

Note to readers: Over the years that I've written this section I've guessed at what information woulld be most valuable to the annual's users. I may not always have guessed right and would therefore welcome suggestions/comments as to topics I should address or how the annual could be improved. Write me at 1149 Lime Place, Vista, CA 92083-7428, or e-mail me at rneilbarron@hotmail.com.

Science Fiction Titles

1032

FORREST J ACKERMAN, Editor

Ackermanthology!
(Los Angeles: General Publishing Group, 1997)

Story type: Anthology

Summary: Contains a two-page introduction by Ackerman, a one-page foreword by John Landis and 65 stories, some with individual introductions, from periodicals and anthrologies 1934-1975. The stories vary in tone from humorous to horrifying and appear in thematic groups such as aliens, cosmic encounters, experiments perilous, futurama, robot chronicles, spicy sci-fi and O. Henry type stories. Authors include Forrest J. Ackerman, Isaac Asimov, David Bischoff, Jerome Bixby, Hannes Bok, Ray Bradbury, Ray Cummings, Horace L. Gold, Dave Kyle, A.W. Lownes, A. Merritt, C.L. Moore, Sam Moskowitz, A.E. Van Vogt, H.G. Wells, Robert Moore Williams, Richard Wilson and Donald A. Wollheim.

Where it's reviewed:
Publishers Weekly, March 31, 1997, page 69
Science Fiction Age, July 1997, page 93

Other books by the same author:
Gosh! Wow! (Sense of Wonder) Science Fiction, 1982
The Best Science Fiction for 1973, 1973
Science Fiction Worlds of Forrest J Ackerman & Friends, 1969

Other books you might like:
Isaac Asimov, *Isaac Asimov Presents the Great SF Stories: 1-25*, 1979-1992
    Martin H. Greenberg, co-editor
Groff Conklin, *The Best of Science Fiction*, 1946
    editor
Janrae Frank, *New Eves: Science Fiction about the Extraordinary Women of Today and Tomorrow*, 1994
    (Jean Stine, Forrest J. Ackerman, co-editors)
Raymond J. Healy, *Adventures in Time and Space*, 1946
    J. Frances McComas, co-editor

Robert Silverberg, *Science Fiction Hall of Fame I*, 1970
    editor
Jean Marie Stine, *365 Science Fiction Short Stories*, 1995
    Forrest J. Ackerman, co-editor

1033

KEVIN J. ANDERSON
DOUG BEASON, Co-Author

Ignition
(New York: Forge, 1997)

Story type: Techno-Thriller
Major character(s): Adam ''Iceberg'' Friese, Astronaut; Nicole ''Panther'' Hunter, Administrator (launch director), Astronaut (retired); Boorman, Political Figure (senator)
Time period(s): 1990s
Locale(s): Kourou, French Guiana; Kennedy Space Center, Florida

Summary: Unable to captain the shuttle flight due to a broken foot, Iceberg decides to sneak back onto the grounds to watch the flight from the swamp. Unfortunately, a terrorist and his crew take over the media center, plant a bomb on the shuttle and, unbeknownst to the world watching a tape loop, hold the shuttle for ransom. Luckily, Iceberg discovers the terrorists, foiling their plan to set off the bomb, while Panther keeps the senator in check and prevents more deaths in the control room.

Where it's reviewed:
Booklist, December 15, 1996, page 691
Kirkus Reviews, January 15, 1997, page 75
Library Journal, January 1997, page 141
Publishers Weekly, February 10, 1997, page 67
Science Fiction Chronicle, October 1997, page 45

Other books by the same author:
Fallout, 1997 (Doug Beason, co-author)
Virtual Destruction, 1996 (Doug Beason, co-author)
Ill Wind, 1995 (Doug Beason, co-author)
Assemblers of Infinity, 1993 (Doug Beason, co-author)

Lifeline, 1990 (Doug Beason, co-author)

Other books you might like:
Ben Bova, *Death Dream*, 1994
Simon Hawke, *The Whims of Creation*, 1992
Vonda N. McIntyre, *Starfarers*, 1989
Allen Steele, *Orbital Decay*, 1989
Neal Stephenson, *The Diamond Age*, 1995
Walter Jon Williams, *Voice of the Whirlwind*, 1987

1034

POUL ANDERSON

The Fleet of Stars
(New York: Tor, 1997)

Story type: Political; Alternate Intelligence
Series: Harvest of Stars
Major character(s): Fenn, Police Officer, Revolutionary; Kinna Ronay, Revolutionary; Anson Guthrie, Cyborg
Time period(s): Indeterminate Future
Locale(s): Montenegro; Mars

Summary: Raising on the moon, Fenn rages that humans live as little more than the "domesticated pets" of the cybercosm intelligence that oversees life in the solar system. He and Kinna Ronay, a spirited Mars settler, vow to discover why the cybercosm seems intent on preventing humanity from going to the stars. Fourth in series.

Where it's reviewed:
Booklist, March 1, 1997, page 1114
Kirkus Reviews, January 1, 1997, page 26
Library Journal, February 15, 1997, page 165
Locus, February 1997, page 19
Science Fiction Chronicle, June 1997, page 41

Other books by the same author:
Harvest the Fire, 1995
The Stars Are Also Fire, 1994
Harvest of Stars, 1993
The Boat of a Million Years, 1989
Tan Zero, 1970

Other books you might like:
Greg Bear, *Queen of Angels*, 1990
David Brin, *Startide Rising*, 1983
Robert A. Heinlein, *The Moon Is a Harsh Mistress*, 1966
Frank Herbert, *Destination: Void*, 1966
D.F. Jones, *Colossus*, 1966
John Varley, *Steel Beach*, 1992
Jack Williamson, *The Humanoids*, 1996
    expanded edition

1035

PATRICIA ANTHONY

God's Fires
(New York; Ace, 1997)

Story type: Theological; Political
Major character(s): Alphonso Braganca, Royalty (King), Handicapped (retarded); Manoel Pessoa, Religious (Jesuit-inquisitor); Berenice Pinheiro, Healer, Herbalist

Time period(s): 16th century (Portuguese Inquisition)
Locale(s): Lisbon, Portugal; Quintas, Portugal

Summary: Hearing the stories of angels raping women and girls, a virgin birth and a visitation from the Virgin Mary, Pessoa realizes that he must convene an inquisition and hope to avoid more official notice of Berenice, his lover, or anyone else. Alfonso discovers God in the silver acorn he ses fall from Heaven and learns that the Earth revolves around the Sun. Unfortunately for the two "angels" who survived the fall, the Grand Inquisitor tries the "fallen angels" and "heretics" in Quinitas, despite Alfonso and the local priest's conviction that the trial will be illegal.

Where it's reviewed:
Booklist, April 15, 1997, page 1387
Kirkus Reviews, February 15, 1997, page 260
Locus, May 1997, page 21
Publishers Weekly, March 24, 1997, page 63
Science Fiction Chronicle, October 1997, page 49

Other books by the same author:
Cradle of Splendor, 1996
Happy Policeman, 1994
Cold Allies, 1993
Brother Termite, 1993
Conscience of the Beagle, 1993

Other books you might like:
David Brin, *Brightness Reef*, 1995
Parke Godwin, *Waiting for the Galactic Bus*, 1988
Frederik Pohl, *The Other End of Time*, 1996
Mary Doria Russell, *The Sparrow*, 1996
Sheri S. Tepper, *Grass*, 1989

1036

PIERS ANTHONY

Hope of Earth
(New York: Tor, 1997)

Story type: Family Saga; Adventure
Series: Geodyssey
Major character(s): Sam, Warrior, Refugee; Jes, Mercenary; Ned, Orphan, Genius
Time period(s): Indeterminate Past; 21st century
Locale(s): Africa; Ancient Civilization; South America

Summary: Barely human, six siblings who separate from their elders must learn to survive in Australopithecine Africa. Their saga continues through all history to 21st century Peru, where they once again live within the rhythms of nature. Third in the series.

Where it's reviewed:
Booklist, April 15, 1997, page 1387
Kirkus Reviews, March 1, 1997, page 341
Library Journal, April 15, 1997, page 123
Publishers Weekly, April 28, 1997, page 54

Other books by the same author:
Shame of Man, 1994
Isle of Woman, 1993
Virtual Mode, 1991
Steppe, 1985

Orn, 1971

Other books you might like:
Brian W. Aldiss, *Cryptozoic*, 1968
Roger MacBride Allen, *Orphan of Creation*, 1988
Poul Anderson, *The Boat of a Million Years*, 1989
Michael Bishop, *No Enemy But Time*, 1982
Philip Jose Farmer, *Time's Last Gift*, 1972
Garry Kilworth, *Split Second*, 1985
Harry Turtledove, *A Different Flesh*, 1988

1037

KIM ANTIEAU

The Gaia Websters

(New York: Roc, 1997)

Story type: Post-Disaster; Robot Fiction
Major character(s): Gloria Stone, Healer (soothsayer), Robot; Primer, Government Official; Thomas Church, Religious (reverend)
Time period(s): 25th century
Locale(s): Grand Canyon, Arizona; Arizona Territy, Southwest; Coyote Creek, Arizona

Summary: Awakening in a cave with no memories, Gloria Stone refuses to recognize herself as a Soothsayer, finding the life of healer for Coyote Creek very satisfying. After Primer poisons the water, Gloria finally agrees to see the governor, if only to complain about his agent, Primer. Disaster follows Gloria, forcing her to discover the truth about herself and her past and, perhaps, permitting a better future for all.

Where it's reviewed:
Booklist, June 1 & 15, 1997, page 1668
Library Journal, May 15, 1997, page 106
Locus, June 1997, page 17
Science Fiction Chronicle, October 1997, page 49
Voice of Youth Advocates, October 1997, page 250

Other books by the same author:
The Jigsaw Woman, 1996
Trudging to Eden, 1995
Blossoms, 1991

Other books you might like:
Roger MacBride Allen, *Utopia*, 1996
Emma Bull, *Bone Dance*, 1991
Sheri S. Tepper, *A Plague of Angels*, 1993
Amy Thomson, *Virtual Girl*, 1993
Michael D. Weaver, *A Second Infinity*, 1996
Jack Williamson, *The Humanoids*, 1996

1038

CATHERINE ASARO

The Last Hawk

(New York: Tor, 1997)

Story type: Adventure; Psychic Powers
Series: Skolian Empire
Major character(s): Kelricson Garlin Valdoria kva Skolia, Nobleman, Psychic; Bolt, Artificial Intelligence; Deha Dahl, Government Official (bureaucrat)

Time period(s): Indeterminate (10th century of the Modern Age)
Locale(s): Coba, Planet—Imaginary

Summary: Kelric, heir to the Skolian Empire, crashes on a planet whose matriarchal government heals him, but destroys his ship to preserve their culture. While he finds love and some contentment, Kelric also recognizes his status as a prisoner and a pawn in a game he must learn to play, then master, if he wants his life to be his own. Third in series.

Where it's reviewed:
Booklist, November 1, 1997, page 456
Kirkus Reviews, October 1, 1997, page 1495
Library Journal, November 15, 1997, page 79
Publishers Weekly, October 22, 1997, page 57

Other books by the same author:
Catch the Lightning, 1996
Primary Inversion, 1995

Other books you might like:
Eleanor Arnason, *Ring of Swords*, 1993
Iain M. Banks, *The Player of Games*, 1989
Marion Zimmer Bradley, *The Forbidden Tower*, 1977
Andre Norton, *Witch World*, 1963
K.D. Wentworth, *Moonspeaker*, 1994

1039

MIKE ASHLEY, Editor

The Random House Book of Science Fiction Stories

(New York: Random House, 1997)

Story type: Anthology

Summary: Contains a three-page foreword and a 15-page afterword by Ashley, a three-page introduction by Douglas Hill, plus seven original and 18 stories reprinted from anthologies and periodicals published 1935-1987. Generally upbeat in tone, the stories feature diverse themes such as space exploration, first contact, extraterrestrial tourism, intelligent aliens and life aboard a spaceship. Authors include Piers Anthony, A. Bertram Chandler, John Christopher, Arthur C. Clarke, John Russell Fearn, Nicholas Fisk, Raymond Z. Gallun, Edmond Hamilton, Douglas Hill, William F. Temple, E.C. Tubb, Ian Watson and Donald A. Wollheim.

Where it's reviewed:
Kliatt, July 1997, page 19

Other books by the same author:
The Random House Book of Fantasy Stories, 1997
The Chronicles of the Holy Grail, 1996
The Merlin Chronicles, 1995
The History of the Science Fiction Magazine, Part 3 1946-55, 1977
Souls in Metal, 1977

Other books you might like:
Gardner Dozois, *Modern Classics of Science Fiction*, 1992 editor
David G. Hartwell, *The Ascent of Wonder: The Evolution of Hard SF*, 1994
Kathryn Cramer, co-editor

Science Fiction

David G. Hartwell, *Visions of Wonder: The Science Fiction Research Association Anthology*, 1996
  Milton T. Wolf, co-editory
Ursula K. Le Guin, *The Norton Book of Science Fiction: North American Science Fiction 1960-1990*, 1996
  Brian Attebery, co-editor
Tom Shippey, *The Oxford Book of Science Fiction Stories*, 1992
  editor

1040

KIRSTEN BAKIS

Lives of the Monster Dogs

(New York: Farrar, Strauss, Giroux, 1997)

Story type: Literary; Genetic Manipulation
Major character(s): Cleo Pira, Student; Ludwig von Sacher, Genetically Altered Being, Historian; Klaue Lutz, Genetically Altered Being
Time period(s): 2000s (2009)
Locale(s): New York, New York

Summary: A group of genetically and surgically modified dogs who dress and act like 19th century German aristocrats appears in New York City. The product of demented medical experiments, the dogs want only comfort and obscurity, but the modern world and a degenerative disease threaten both. As a human woman befriends them and uncovers their past and secrets, their future narrows toward extinction. First novel.

Where it's reviewed:
Booklist, January 1 & 15, 1997, page 815
Kirkus Reviews, November 15, 1996, page 1616
Library Journal, January 1997, page 141
Publishers Weekly, December 16, 1996, page 41
Science Fiction Chronicle, October 1997, page 44

Other books you might like:
John Crowley, *Beasts*, 1976
Nancy Kress, *Beggars in Spain*, 1993
Ian McDonald, *Terminal Cafe*, 1994
Walter Tevis, *The Man Who Fell to Earth*, 1963
H.G. Wells, *The Island of Dr. Moreau*, 1896

1041

IAIN M. BANKS

Excession

(New York: Bantam Spectra, 1997)

Story type: Political; First Contact
Series: Culture
Major character(s): Byr Genar-Hofoen, Diplomat; Sleeper Service, Artificial Intelligence; Fivetide Humidyear VII, Military Personnel
Time period(s): Indeterminate Future
Locale(s): *Sleeper Service*, Spaceship

Summary: When the excession, an inexplicable and impossible phenomenon, reappears, the Minds of the Culture want to study it. Unfortunately, with the semi-hostile Empire of the Affront eager for war, roguish minds may willingly help start an intergalactic war for their own ends. The past indiscretions of a minor diplomat could influence things.

Where it's reviewed:
Booklist, February 1, 1997, page 929
Kirkus Reviews, December 1, 1996, page 1706
Kliatt, May 1997, page 12
Locus, September 1996, page 25
Publishers Weekly, January 27, 1997, page 82

Other books by the same author:
Against a Dark Background, 1993
Use of Weapons, 1992
The Bridge, 1989
The Player of Games, 1988
Consider Phlebas, 1987

Other books you might like:
David Brin, *Startide Rising*, 1983
Frank Herbert, *Dune*, 1965
Vonda N. McIntyre, *Metaphase*, 1992
Vernor Vinge, *A Fire upon the Deep*, 1992
Walter Jon Williams, *Metropolitan*, 1995

1042

JOHN BARNES

Caesar's Bicycle

(New York: HarperPrism, 1997)

Story type: Time Travel; Alternate History
Series: Timeline Wars
Major character(s): Mark Strang, Time Traveller, Warrior (Crux Op); Chrysamen ''Chrys'' ja N'Wook, Time Traveller, Warrior (Crux Op); Julius Caesar, Military Personnel, Historical Figure
Time period(s): Indeterminate Future
Locale(s): Rome, Italy; Ancient Civilization

Summary: On the verge of winning the Timelines Wars, a Crux Op agent, Mark Strang, must go back to ancient Rome to assassinate Julius Caesar. After ridding Caesar of the enemy's advisor, Mark recognizes Caesar's ability to rule and revitalize Rome.

Other books by the same author:
Patton's Spaceship, 1997
Washington's Dirigible, 1997
Kaleidoscope Century, 1995
Mother of Storms, 1994
A Million Open Doors, 1992

Other books you might like:
Robert Asprin, *Wages of Sin*, 1996
  Linda Evans, co-author
L. Sprague de Camp, *Lest Darkness Fall*, 1996
Linda Evans, *Far Edge of Darkness*, 1996
Esther M. Friesner, *Child of the Eagle*, 1996
Raymond Harris, *The Schizogenic Man*, 1990
Crawford Kilian, *Rogue Emperor*, 1988
Fritz Leiber, *The Big Time*, 1961
Melissa Scott, *A Choice of Destinies*, 1986

1043

JOHN BARNES

Patton's Spaceship

(New York: HarperPrism, 1997)

Story type: Alternate Universe; Adventure
Series: Timeline Wars
Major character(s): Porter Brunreich, Child; Mark Strang, Bodyguard; Harry Skena, Professor, Time Traveller
Time period(s): 1990s (28th century (2726))
Locale(s): Hyper Athens, Fictional City

Summary: After the Blade of the Most Merciful killed his wife, mother and brother, almost killing his sister in the same explosion, Mark dropped his Ph.D. studies in art history to become a bodyguard. Five years later, while Mark protects Porter and her mother, the Blade of the Most Merciful once again crosses his path. Protecting Harry, Mark finds himself in Hyper Athens, training as a Special Agent for a Crux Ops team.

Where it's reviewed:
Fantasy & Science Fiction, May 1997, page 70
Locus, April 1997, page 23

Other books by the same author:
Caesar's Bicycle, 1997
Washington's Dirigible, 1997
Mother of Storms, 1994
A Million Open Doors, 1992
Orbital Resonance, 1991

Other books you might like:
Poul Anderson, *The Time Patrol*, 1991
Deborah Christian, *Mainline*, 1996
Mona Clee, *Branch Point*, 1996
James P. Hogan, *Paths to Otherwhere*, 1996
Sam Mervin Jr., *The House of Many Worlds*, 1951
Spider Robinson, *Lifehouse*, 1997

1044

WILLIAM BARTON

Acts of Conscience

(New York: Warner Aspect, 1997)

Story type: Adventure; First Contact
Major character(s): Gaetan du Cheyne, Spaceship Captain; The Kapellmeister, Alien; Beloved Light, Alien
Time period(s): 26th century
Locale(s): Orikhalkos, Fictional City; Earth

Summary: Gaetan figures he will never get into space, but then receives a spaceship of his own. He wants to see distant planets, but discovers humanity has wrecked every place it visited. Then he finds forces ready to do something about it.

Where it's reviewed:
Kirkus Reviews, November 1, 1996, page 1569
Library Journal, December 1996, page 152
New York Times Book Review, January 26, 1997, page 22
Science Fiction Age, January 1997, page 18
Voice of Youth Advocates, August 1997, page 191

Other books by the same author:
The Transmigration of Souls, 1996
When Heaven Fell, 1995
Dark Sky Legion, 1992
Fellow Traveler, 1991 (Michael Capobianco, co-author)
Iris, 1991 (Michael Capobianco, co-author)

Other books you might like:
Eleanor Arnason, *Ring of Swords*, 1993
Octavia E. Butler, *Dawn*, 1987
Hal Clement, *Cycle of Fire*, 1957
Sheri S. Tepper, *Raising the Stones*, 1990
Amy Thomson, *The Color of Distance*, 1995

1045

WILLIAM BARTON
MICHAEL CAPOBIANCO, Co-Author

Alpha Centauri

(New York: Avon, 1997)

Story type: First Contact; Political
Major character(s): Maeru ''Kai'' kai Ortega, Spaceman, Engineer; Virginia ''Ginny'' Vonzel Qing-an, Spaceship Captain; Miles ''David Gilman'' Cochrane, Scientist (Planetologist), Mentally Ill Person (Multiple Personality)
Time period(s): 23rd century (2239)
Locale(s): *Mother Night*, Spaceship; Planet—Imaginary (Alpha Centauri System); Outer Space

Summary: Hoping to find a solar ready for colonization, *Mother Night*'s crew discover dead, used-up worlds and evidence of a culture with three intelligent species that lasted several billion years, but has been dead for over a billion. Ginny must deal with Miles who carries not only a sterilizing virus, but also hypnopoedic overlays, one of which compels him to spread the virus.

Where it's reviewed:
Analog, September 1997, page 146
Kirkus Reviews, May 15, 1997, page 765
Library Journal, August 1997, page 141
Publishers Weekly, June 30, 1997, page 71
Science Fiction Chronicle, October 1997, page 45

Other books by the same author:
Acts of Conscience, 1997
The Transmigration of Souls, 1996
Iris, 1991 (Michael Capobianco, co-author)
Fellow Traveller, 1991 (Michael Capobianco, co-author)
Dark Sky Legion, 1991

Other books you might like:
Roger MacBride Allen, *The Ring of Charon*, 1990
Greg Bear, */*, 1997
Michael Capobianco, *Burster*, 1990
Tom Cool, *Infectress*, 1997
Jack McDevitt, *The Engines of God*, 1994
David Weber, *Mutineer's Moon*, 1991

1046

JAMES C. BASSETT

Living Real

(New York: Harper Prism, 1997)

Story type: Alternate Intelligence; Political
Major character(s): Carver Blervaque, Computer Expert, Inventor; Rose Blervaque, Housewife, Artist (Sculptor); Tom Byrd, Government Official
Time period(s): 22nd century
Locale(s): Gainesville, Florida; Network, Cyberspace

Summary: Trying to overcome his creative block, Carver plays with forbidden Web technology. Programs written this way prove dangerously addictive to his wife, Rose, who usess the new technology to meditate. Noticing the disturbance Carver causes, Tom Byrd, Regional Administrator of the Federal Communications Agency, searches for the group behind the Web security breach, and also for Carver, whom he believes innocent.

Where it's reviewed:
Science Fiction Chronicle, October, 1997, page 49

Other books you might like:
Bruce Bethke, *Headcrash*, 1995
Pat Cadigan, *Synners*, 1991
Raphael Carter, *The Fortunate Fall*, 1996
James P. Hogan, *Bug Park*, 1997
Sage Walker, *Whiteout*, 1996

1047

STEPHEN BAXTER

Titan

(New York: HarperPrism, 1997)

Story type: Hard Science Fiction; Disaster
Major character(s): Paula Benacerraf, Astronaut, Spacewoman; Isaac Rosenberg, Scientist (physical chemistry); Jiang Ling, Astronaut (Chinese)
Time period(s): 2000s; Indeterminate Future
Locale(s): *Columbia*, Spaceship (shuttle); Titan, Saturn; *Discovery*, Spaceship

Summary: Paula becomes an astronaut to discover the causes for construction delays on Skylab. When the *Columbia* breaks up on reentry, killing some of the crew and the space program, Isaac Rosenberg reveals the discovery of potential life on Saturn's moon Titan. They put together a mission to Titan using museum pieces and shuttle parts, but NASA abandons them after they barely leave Earth's orbit. Jiang loves being in space enough to die for the opportunity.

Where it's reviewed:
Locus, October 1997, page 17

Other books by the same author:
Ring, 1996
The Time Ships, 1996
Flux, 1995
Timelike Infinity, 1993
Raft, 1991

Other books you might like:
Greg Bear, *The Forge of God*, 1987
David Brin, *Earth*, 1990
Michael Flynn, *Firestar*, 1996
Allen Steele, *Orbital Decay*, 1989
Sage Walker, *Whiteout*, 1996
David Weber, *Mutineer's Moon*, 1991

1048

STEPHEN BAXTER

Voyager

(New York: HarperPrism, 1997)

Story type: Alternate Universe; Hard Science Fiction
Major character(s): Gregory Dana, Scientist; Ralph Gershon, Astronaut; Natalie York, Scientist
Time period(s): 1980s
Locale(s): Cape Canaveral, Florida; Mars

Summary: In an alternate universe where President Kennedy survived the attempt on his life, the space program remained at the center of our national agenda. Heavily supported by President Nixon, a manned flight to Mars occurs in 1986, but the astronauts involved find the voyage both difficult and dangerous.

Other books by the same author:
Titan, 1997
The Time Ships, 1996
Ring, 1996
Flux, 1995
Anti-Ice, 1994

Other books you might like:
Ben Bova, *Mars*, 1992
Kim Stanley Robinson, *Blue Mars*, 1996
Kim Stanley Robinson, *Green Mars*, 1994
Kim Stanley Robinson, *Red Mars*, 1993

1049

GREG BEAR

/

(New York; Tor, 1997)

Story type: Alternate Intelligence; Techno-Thriller
Series: Queen of Angels
Major character(s): Jill, Artificial Intelligence; Mary Choy, Police Officer; Martin Burke, Psychologist, Inventor
Time period(s): 2060s
Locale(s): Seattle, Washington; Moskow, Idaho (Green Idaho); Omphalos, Mythical Place

Summary: Inventor Martin Burk's nano technology permits not only body enhancement, but also the deep psychological therapy from nano machines that produces a happy society for most people. The few "naturals" who have not needed therapy fill the supervisory, directing functions in society. A few conservative naturals, bonding together as the Aristos, create an unorthodox computer to destroy the nano machines which keep most of the society healthy and sane. Mary Choy investigates a murder, leading to her discovery of the Aristos' plot.

Where it's reviewed:
Booklist, July 1997, page 1805
Kirkus Reviews, June 1, 1997, page 840
Locus, September 1997, page 21
Publishers Weekly, May 26, 1997, page 71
Science Fiction Age, September 1997, page 16

Other books by the same author:
Moving Mars, 1993
Queen of Angels, 1990
Eternity, 1988
The Forge of God, 1987
Eon, 1985

Other books you might like:
John Barnes, *Kaleidoscope Century*, 1995
David Brin, *Earth*, 1990
Stephen Bury, *Interface*, 1994
Janet Kagan, *Mirabile*, 1991
Jim Young, *Armed Memory*, 1995

| 1050 |

GREGORY BENFORD

Foundation's Fear
(New York: HarperPrism, 1997)

Story type: Robot Fiction; Space Opera
Series: Second Foundation Trilogy
Major character(s): Hari Seldon, Scientist (mathist), Political Figure; R. Daneel ''Eto Demerzel'' Olivaw, Robot; Cleon I, Ruler (emperor)
Time period(s): Indeterminate Future
Locale(s): Trantor, Planet—Imaginary

Summary: Feeling that something unknown remains necessary to complete his theory of psychohistory, Hari Seldon imports 16,000-year-old ''sims'' of Joan of Arc and Voltaire. Following the advice of Eto Demerzel, Cleon insists on Hari for his First Minister. Joan and Voltaire get loose in the Net, finding powerful and ancient minds who hate robots. First of a trilogy by Gregory Benford, Greg Bear, and David Brin.

Where it's reviewed:
Booklist, March 1, 1997, page 1114
Kirkus Reviews, January 15, 1997, page 102
Library Journal, March 15, 1997, page 93
New York Times Book Review, April 6, 1997, page 24
Publishers Weekly, February 24, 1997, page 67

Other books by the same author:
Tides of Light, 1989
Great Sky River, 1987
Across the Sea of Suns, 1984
Timescape, 1980
In the Ocean of Night, 1977

Other books you might like:
Roger MacBride Allen, *Caliban*, 1993
Isaac Asimov, *The Foundation Trilogy*, 1963
Isaac Asimov, *Robots and Empire*, 1985
James P. Hogan, *Code of the Lifemaker*, 1983
A.E. Van Vogt, *The Weapon Makers*, 1946
Jack Williamson, *The Humanoids*, 1949

| 1051 |

ANN BENSON

The Plague Tales
(New York: Delacorte, 1997)

Story type: Medical; Science Fiction
Major character(s): Robert Sarin, Aged Person, Handicapped; Janie Crowe, Doctor (surgeon), Student (forensic anthropolgist); Alejandro Canches, Doctor, Wanderer
Time period(s): 14th century (2000s)
Locale(s): Cervere, Spain (Aragon); London, England

Summary: Refusing to let Janie dig in the land under his care, Robert Sarin continues to follow the instructions of his mother and the Book. Alejandro, a Jewish doctor, records the illegal autopsy he performs in his Book. The Church objects, forcing him to leave. As bubonic plague spreads through Europe, Alejandro records his observations, including the cure. Unfortunately Janie steals a soil sample from Robert's land. First novel.

Where it's reviewed:
Booklist, April 15, 1997, page 1364
Publishers Weekly, May 19, 1997, page 63

Other books you might like:
Margaret Wander Bonanno, *The Others*, 1990
E.L. Doctorow, *The Waterworks*, 1994
Neil Gaiman, *Good Omens: The Nice and Accurate Prophecies of Agnes Nutter, Witch*, 1990
Terry Pratchett, co-author
Bill Ransom, *Vira/Vax*, 1993
Connie Willis, *Doomsday Book*, 1992

| 1052 |

ALFRED BESTER

Virtual Unrealities: The Short Fiction of Alfred Bester
(New York: Vintage, 1997)

Story type: Collection; Science Fiction

Summary: Contains a five-page introduction by Robert Silverberg, one fragment, one original and 15 stories reprinted from periodicals and anthologies published 1939-1979. The tone varies from humerous and satirical to ironic and melancholy as Bester explores diverse themes such as time travel paradoxes, the nature of equilibrium, the relationship of creator to creation and society's absurd icons. The many recognized classics of short fiction include ''Fondly Fahrenheit,'' ''The Men Who Murdered Mohammed,'' ''The Pi Man,'' ''Adam and no Eve,'' ''Oddy and Id,'' ''The Don't Make Life Like They Used To'' and ''The Flowered Thundermug.''

Where it's reviewed:
Booklist, October 1, 1997, page 311
Kirkus Reviews, October 1, 1997, page 1493
Locus, November 1997, page 15
Publishers Weekly, September 29, 1997, page 70

Other books by the same author:
The Deceivers, 1981

Science Fiction (sidebar)

Golem [100], 1980
The Computer Connection, 1975
The Stars My Destination, 1956
The Demolished Man, 1953

Other books you might like:
Robert A. Heinlein, *The Past through Tomorrow*, 1967
Walter M. Miller Jr., *The Science Fiction Stories of Walter M. Miller, Jr.*, 1984
Larry Niven, *Tales of Known Space*, 1975
Cordwainer Smith, *The Rediscovery of Man*, 1993
Theodore Sturgeon, *The Ultimate Egoist*, 1994
John Varley, *Blue Champagne*, 1986
John Varley, *The Persistence of Vision*, 1978

1053

TERRY BISSON

The Fifth Element

(New York: HarperPrism, 1997)

Story type: Space Opera; Invasion of Earth
Major character(s): Vito Cornelius, Religious (priest); Korben Dallas, Taxi Driver, Military Personnel (retired); Appipulai Leeloo Minai, Deity
Time period(s): 1910s (1913); 25th century (2413)
Locale(s): Egypt; New York, New York

Summary: In 1913 the Mondoshawan took the ultimate weapon against evil from the recently uncovered ancient Egyptian temple, promising to return it when the war came to Earth. When the Mondoshawan try to return the weapon, their ship crashes after being attacked by Earth forces. Recreated from genetic material left after the crash, Leeloo, the Fifth Element necessary for the weapon to function, proves to be a perfect human woman. After Leeloo dives through the roof of Korben's cab, she enlists him to help her save Earth and vanquish the forces of evil. Novelizes the film.

Other books by the same author:
Pirates of the Universe, 1996
Bears Discover Fire, 1993
Voyage to the Red Planet, 1990
Fire on the Mountain, 1988
Wyrldmaker, 1981

Other books you might like:
A.C. Crispin, *V*, 1984
Dean Devlin, *Independence Day*, 1996
Alan Dean Foster, *Alien Nation!*, 1993
Jonathan Gems, *Mars Attacks!*, 1996
Judith Reeves-Stevens, *The Day of Descent*, 1993
    Garfield Reeves-Stevens, co-author
Robert Tine, *Chain Reaction*, 1996

1054

RAY BRADBURY

The Martian Chronicles

(New York: Avon, 1997)

Story type: First Contact; Psychic Powers

Major character(s): Jonathan Williams, Spaceship Captain; Ylla K, Alien (Martian), Spouse (wife); Nathaniel York, Spaceship Captain
Time period(s): 2030s (2030)
Locale(s): Mars (Tyrr)

Summary: When Mrs. K dreams about Nathaniel York, a giant from the third planet come to visit Mars, Mr. K goes hunting and the dreams stop. Jonathan Williams tries to convince the Martians that he and his crew come from Earth and dies in the attempt. Unfortunately, the chicken pox in their blood kills the Martians, leaving the cities empty for the terrans who follow. Reissue of the 1950 edition with a new six-page introduction by Bradbury.

Where it's reviewed:
Analog, July/August 1997, page 212

Other books by the same author:
The Machineries of Joy, 1964
A Medicine for Melancholy, 1959
Fahrenheit 451, 1953
Golden Apples of the Sun, 1953
The Illustrated Man, 1951

Other books you might like:
Philip K. Dick, *Martian Timeslip*, 1964
Frank Herbert, *Dune*, 1965
Ursula K. Le Guin, *The Word for World Is Forest*, 1976
Ian McDonald, *Desolation Road*, 1988
Elizabeth Moon, *Remnant Population*, 1996

1055

MARION ZIMMER BRADLEY

The Shadow Matrix

(New York: DAW, 1997)

Story type: Psychic Powers; Family Saga
Series: Darkover
Major character(s): Marguerida "Margaret" Alton, Heiress, Telepath; Mikhail Lanart-Hastur, Telepath, Nobleman
Time period(s): Indeterminate Future
Locale(s): Darkover, Planet—Imaginary

Summary: At Arilinn, Margaret Alton tries to get her gift under control, while Mikhail Lanart-Hastur tries to find a possible heir in a very disturbed household haunted by a ghost. Finally Margaret and Mikhail must travel back in time to save their present by preventing atomic destruction.

Where it's reviewed:
Booklist, July 1997, page 1773
Library Journal, September 15, 1997, page 106
Locus, August 1997, page 29
Starlog, October 1997, page 12

Other books by the same author:
Exile's Song, 1996
Rediscovery: A Novel of Darkover, 1993 (Mercedes Lackey, co-author)
Sharra's Exile, 1981
The Heritage of Hastur, 1975
The World Wreckers, 1971

Other books you might like:
Octavia E. Butler, *Mind of My Mind*, 1977
Paula E. Downing, *Rinn's Star*, 1990
Debra Doyle, *The Price of the Stars*, 1992
   James D. Macdonald, co-author
Cheryl J. Franklin, *The Light in Exile*, 1990
Julian May, *Jack the Bodiless*, 1992
Anne McCaffrey, *The Rowan*, 1990
David Weber, *Honor Among Enemies*, 1996
K.D. Wentworth, *House of Moons*, 1995

1056

DAMIEN BRODERICK

The White Abacus

(New York: Avon, 1997)

Story type: Political; Alternate Intelligence
Major character(s): Ratio, Artificial Intelligence, Leader (Gamemaster); Telmah, Lord Cima, Heir—Dispossessed; Feng Orwen, Ruler (usurper)
Time period(s): Indeterminate Future
Locale(s): Earth; Psyche, Asteroid

Summary: Recognizing the potential threat of Psyche's anti-AI society and the impending fratricide of its leader, Ratio permits his Gesell connection's termination, becoming a Monad in order to get close to Telmah. Accompanied by Ratio, Telmah returns to Psyche to avenge his father's death, while Ratio works at protecting the larger community and, eventually, reconnecting with the Gesell.

Where it's reviewed:
Analog, July/August 1997, page 272
Kirkus Reviews, February 1, 1997, page 178
Locus, February 1997, page 17
Publishers Weekly, February 3, 1997, page 99
Starlog, August 1997, page 67

Other books by the same author:
Striped Holes, 1988
The Black Grail, 1986
The Judas Mandala, 1982
The Dreaming Dragons, 1980
Sorcerer's World, 1970

Other books you might like:
Isaac Asimov, *Robots of Dawn*, 1983
Philip K. Dick, *Bladerunner*, 1982
Philip K. Dick, *The Unteleported Man*, 1983
   revised
L. Warren Douglas, *Stepwater*, 1995
Dan Simmons, *Hyperion*, 1989
Sheri S. Tepper, *Grass*, 1989
Vernor Vinge, *A Fire upon the Deep*, 1992

1057

MARY BROWN

Strange Deliverance

(New York: Baen, 1997)

Story type: Post-Disaster; UFO

Major character(s): Prettiance ''Pretty'', Teenager; Tamerlane ''Tam'', Teenager; The Herb-Woman, Healer, Parent
Time period(s): Indeterminate Future
Locale(s): Earth

Summary: Aliens crash-land their crippled ship in a clearing near a village, driving most of the panic-stricken villagers to flee into the war-torn lands aroud them. Another group of refugees soon finds the deserted village and begins to develop its own society. Fifty years later, their grandchildren dare to explore the forbidden wilderness and discover strange powers inside a circle of standing stones.

Other books by the same author:
Master of Many Treasures, 1995
Pigs Don't Fly, 1994
The Unlikely Ones, 1986

Other books you might like:
David Brin, *The Postman*, 1985
Emma Bull, *Bone Dance*, 1991
Pamela Dean, *The Dubious Hills*, 1994
Pat Frank, *Alas, Babylon*, 1959
H.P. Lovecraft, *The Colour out of Space and Others*, 1964
John Wyndham, *Re-Birth*, 1955
Jane Yolen, *Briar Rose*, 1992

1058

MELVIN BURGESS

The Earth Giant

(New York: Putnam, 1997)

Story type: Young Adult; First Contact
Major character(s): Peter Lee, Child, Relative (brother); Amy Lee, Child, Relative (sister); Giant, Alien, Child
Time period(s): 1990s
Locale(s): Earth

Summary: While Amy hangs out the window watching the storm that disturbs the Lee family's sleep, she can hear something out there, calling to her in her mind. The next day, after the storm passes, Amy uncovers Giant, the friend she heard during the storm who was buried in the roots of the toppled oak. Amy and Peter hide Giant, hoping to help him get home.

Where it's reviewed:
School Library Journal, October 1997, page 128

Other books by the same author:
An Angel for May, 1995
The Baby and Fly Pie, 1995
Burning Issy, 1994

Other books you might like:
Lynne Reid Banks, *The Indian in the Cupboard*, 1981
Bruce Coville, *My Teacher Is an Alien*, 1989
Rosalie Fry, *The Secret of Roan Innish*, 1995
Pamela F. Service, *When the Night Wind Howls*, 1987
Sylvia Waugh, *The Mennyms*, 1994

1059

RICHARD CALDER

Dead Things

(New York: St. Martin's, 1997)

Story type: Cyberpunk; Literary
Series: Dead Girls
Major character(s): Ignatz Zwakh, Revolutionary, Addict; Lipstick, Android (Lilim)
Time period(s): 21st century
Locale(s): Bangkok, Thailand

Summary: Ignatz returns to Earth after traveling through the universe and many probable universes. He has the Reality Bomb, which should undo the meta plague. When forces released during the journey collapse space and time, however, the unlikely deranged savior must race against hallucination and annhilation to complete his mission. Third, and presumably last, in the series.

Where it's reviewed:
Asimov's Science Fiction, September 1997, page 150
Kirkus Reviews, December 15, 1996, page 1772
Library Journal, February 15, 1997, page 165
Publishers Weekly, January 27, 1997, page 81
Starlog, June 1997, page 10

Other books by the same author:
Dead Boys, 1996
Dead Girls, 1995

Other books you might like:
Iain M. Banks, *Feersum Endjinn*, 1995
Octavia E. Butler, *Dawn*, 1987
Jonathan Littell, *Bad Voltage*, 1989
Ian MacDonald, *Terminal Cafe*, 1994
Michael Swanwick, *Vacuum Flowers*, 1987

1060

DIANE CAREY

Ship of the Line

(New York: Pocket, 1997)

Story type: Space Opera; Time Travel
Series: Star Trek: The Next Generation
Major character(s): Jean-Luc Picard, Spaceship Captain; Morgan Bateson, Spaceship Captain; William Riker, Military Personnel (Starfleet Commander)
Time period(s): 24th century; 23rd century
Locale(s): U.S.S. *Enterprise*, Spaceship; Cardassia Prime, Planet—Imaginary; United Federation of Planets, Interstellar Empire/Federation

Summary: Fighting off an invading Klingon ship, Captain Bateson's ship disappears into a temporal anomaly and emerges into the 24th century. After three years re-training, he receives command of the new *Enterprise-E* for its shakedown cruise while a self-doubting Picard accepts a hostage rescue mission to Cardassia. Bateson's old Klingon enemy, now an embittered old man, seeks vengeance by hijacking the new *Enterprise* and using it to provoke war between the Federation and Cardassia. Picard learns some important lessons from a holographic Captain Kirk, confronts his former torturer on Cardassia, and saves the *Enterprise*.

Other books by the same author:
First Strike, 1996
First Frontier, 1995 (James I. Kirkland, co-author)
Best Destiny, 1992
Final Frontier, 1988
Battlestations!, 1986

Other books you might like:
Poul Anderson, *Time Patrolman*, 1983
Michael Jan Friedman, *Kahless*, 1996
L.A. Graf, *Time's Enemy*, 1996
    pseudonym of Julie Ecklar and Karen Rose
Joe Haldeman, *The Forever War*, 1975
Judith Reeves-Stevens, *Federation*, 1994
    Garfield Reeves-Stevens, co-author
Gene Wolfe, *The Shadow of the Torturer*, 1980

1061

DIANE CAREY

Starfleet Academy

(New York: Pocket, 1997)

Story type: Young Adult; Adventure
Series: Star Trek
Major character(s): David Forester, Student; James T. Kirk, Spaceship Captain; Hikaru Sulu, Spaceship Captain
Time period(s): 23rd century
Locale(s): San Francisco, California; United Federation of Planets, Interstellar Empire/Federation

Summary: David Forester begins his Starfleet Academy career by punching Captain Kirk during a simulated assassination attempt. Put in command of a team of other cadets, David attempts to mold them into a crew during simulator assignments. Soon a series of "accidents" point to sabotage by a group of xenophobes who want real life war with the Klingon Empire. David accepts an assignment to help find out the truth and protect the Federation. Based on a CD-ROM game.

Other books by the same author:
First Strike, 1996
First Frontier, 1995 (James I. Kirkland, co-author)
Best Destiny, 1992
Ghost Ship, 1988
Dreadnought!, 1986

Other books you might like:
Dafydd ab Hugh, *Balance of Power*, 1995
C.J. Cherryh, *Hellburner*, 1992
Carolyn Clowes, *The Pandora Principle*, 1990
Julia Ecklar, *The Kobayashi Maru*, 1989
Brad Ferguson, *A Flag Full of Stars*, 1991
L.A. Graf, *Traitor Winds*, 1990
    psuedonym of Julie Ecklar and Karen Rose
Robert A. Heinlein, *Starman Jones*, 1953

1062

JEANNE CAVELOS

The Shadow Within

(New York: Dell, 1997)

Story type: Space Opera; Psychic Powers
Series: Babylon 5
Major character(s): Anna Sheridan, Anthropologist; Morden, Linguist; Terrence Hilliard, Telepath
Time period(s): 23rd century (2256)
Locale(s): Geneva, Fictional City; *Icarus*, Spaceship; Z'Ha'dum, Planet—Imaginary

Summary: Fascinated by the artifacts found at her last dig, Anna requests Terrence Hillard's help examining one that almost seems active. Called the mouse, it responds to her attention. Unfortunately, the telepathic contact traps Terrence and destroys the mouse. The Psi Corps and Earthforce join the extremely well-supplied expedition to Z'Ha'dum, which Anna recognizes as the opportunity of her lifetime and agrees to join.

Other books you might like:
Neal Barrett Jr., *The Touch of Your Shadow, the Whisper of Your Name*, 1996
Kathryn M. Drennan, *To Dream in the City of Sorrows*, 1997
S.M. Stirling, *Betrayals*, 1996
Lois Tilton, *Accusations*, 1995
John Vornholt, *Blood Oath*, 1995
John Vornholt, *Voices*, 1995

1063

MARC CERASINI

Godzilla 2000

(New York: Random House, 1997)

Story type: Adventure; Military
Major character(s): Godzilla, Monster; King Ghidorah, Monster; Kip Daniels, Teenager, Military Personnel (Air Force Special G-Force)
Time period(s): 1990s (1998)
Locale(s): Nellis Air Force Base, Nevada; New York, New York (Manhattan)

Summary: Recruited by the military due to his video game-playing skills, Kip Daniels trains in simulations to prepare for Godzilla's next appearance, even though he cannot convince himself that Godzilla deserves to die. When a cloud of asteriods headed towards Earth unleashes a plague of monsters, including the three-headed King Ghidorah, Godzilla may prove himself to be a friend rather than an enemy.

Other books by the same author:
Godzilla Returns, 1996

Other books you might like:
Scott Ciencin, *Godzilla Invades America*, 1997
Scott Ciencin, *Godzilla: King of the Monsters*, 1996
Michael Crichton, *The Lost World*, 1995
Michael Crichton, *Jurassic Park*, 1990
Alan Dean Foster, *The Last Starfighter*, 1984

1064

JACK L. CHALKER

The Hot-Wired Dodo

(New York: Ballantine Del Rey, 1997)

Story type: Alternate Universe; Cyberpunk
Series: Wonderland Gambit
Major character(s): Cory "Cori Kassemi" Maddox, Computer Expert, Hero; Cynthia Matalon, Experimental Subject, Gentlewoman; Matthew Tyler Brand, Scientist, Disembodied Personality
Time period(s): 1900s
Locale(s): United States; Alternate Universe

Summary: Cory Maddox finds himself reborn into a world where size and strength favor women rather than men, then into a world on whcih hermaphrodite centaurs dominate. There Cory determines that he needs a new strategy to end the game or experiment. Concludes the trilogy.

Where it's reviewed:
Library Journal, February 15, 1997, page 165

Other books by the same author:
The March Hare Network, 1996
The Cybernetic Walrus, 1995
Gods of the Well of Souls, 1994
The Demons at Rainbow Bridge, 1989
Downtiming the Night Side, 1985

Other books you might like:
Ben Bova, *Death Dream*, 1994
Philip K. Dick, *Eye in the Sky*, 1957
Robert A. Heinlein, *Job: A Comedy of Justice*, 1984
James P. Hogan, *Realtime Interrupt*, 1995
Fritz Leiber, *The Sinful Ones*, 1953
Karen Ripley, *The Alchemist of Time*, 1994
Melissa Scott, *Trouble and Her Friends*, 1994
Robert Charles Wilson, *Mysterium*, 1994

1065

C.J. CHERRYH

Finity's End

(New York: Warner Aspect, 1997)

Story type: First Contact; Adventure
Major character(s): Fletcher Robert Neihart, Orphan, Teenager; Melody, Alien (Hisa); Elene Quen, Administrator (stationmaster)
Time period(s): Indeterminate Future
Locale(s): Pell, Planet—Imaginary (Downbelow); *Finity's End*, Spaceship; Pell Station, Space Station (Upabove)

Summary: Left on Pell Station during the war between Union and the Merchanters' Alliance, and prevented from returning to *Finity's End*, Fletcher has never fit in. When Melody and Butch, hisa who worked at the station, notice he is sad, Fletcher adopts them as his "parents." When they transfer back to Downbelow, he works hard to overcome his poor record, managing to pass his tests to get sent Downbelow. *Finity's End* returns to Pell, making a deal to get Fletcher back. Unfortunately, Fletcher wants to remain Downbelow

with the hisa, but must learn to live on the ship with his relatives to have any hope of getting back.

Where it's reviewed:
Booklist, August 1997, page 1886
Kirkus Reviews, July 1, 1997, page 990
Library Journal, September 15, 1997, page 105
Locus, November 1997, page 21
Voice of Youth Advocates, December 1997, page 322

Other books by the same author:
Inheritor, 1996
Invader, 1995
Foreigner, 1994
The Pride of Chanur, 1992
Downbelow Station, 1981

Other books you might like:
Eleanor Arnason, *Ring of Swords*, 1993
David Brin, *Brightness Reef*, 1995
Lois McMaster Bujold, *The Warrior's Apprentice*, 1986
L. Warren Douglas, *A Plague of Change*, 1992
Elizabeth Moon, *Remnant Population*, 1996

1066

JAN CLARK

Prodigy

(New York: Roc, 1997)

Story type: Military; Political
Major character(s): Rieka Degahv, Spaceship Captain; Triscoe Marteen, Spaceship Captain
Time period(s): Indeterminate Future
Locale(s): Spaceship; Interstellar Empire/Federation

Summary: Charged with treason for attacking an enemy spaceship, Rieka Degahv and her few allies must discover the truth underlying the incident to avert personal disaster and destruction of the Commonwealth. First novel.

Where it's reviewed:
Locus, September 1997, page 27

Other books you might like:
Deborah Boyle, *The Price of the Stars*, 1992
 James D. Macdonald, co-author
Lois McMaster Bujold, *The Warrior's Apprentice*, 1986
David Feintuch, *Midshipman's Hope*, 1994
Sherwood Smith, *The Phoenix in Flight*, 1993
 Dave Trowbridge, co-author
David Weber, *On Basilisk Station*, 1993

1067

ARTHUR C. CLARKE

3001: The Final Odyssey

(New York: Ballantine Del Rey, 1997)

Story type: Science Fiction; Alternate Intelligence
Series: Space Odyssey
Major character(s): Frank Poole, Astronaut; Halman, Artificial Intelligence; Indra Wallace, Historian
Time period(s): 31st century (3001)

Locale(s): Europa, Jupiter; *Goliath*, Spaceship

Summary: Rescued 1000 years after the computer Hal tried to kill him, Frank Poole faces a tremendous adjustment to Earth's almost unrecognizable society, as well as some unfinished business at Jupiter, where his adventure began. Fourth, and possibly last, in the series.

Where it's reviewed:
Booklist, January 1 & 15, 1997, page 778
Kirkus Reviews, January 1, 1997, page 27
Library Journal, February 15, 1997, page 164
New York Times Book Review, March 9, 1997, page 7
Science Fiction Chronicle, June 1997, page 47

Other books by the same author:
2061: Odyssey Three, 1987
The Songs of Distant Earth, 1986
2010: Odyssey Two, 1982
Imperial Earth, 1975
2001: A Space Odyssey, 1968

Other books you might like:
Poul Anderson, *The Boat of a Million Years*, 1989
Martin Caidin, *A Life in the Future*, 1995
Orson Scott Card, *The Worthing Saga*, 1990
Joe Haldeman, *The Forever War*, 1975
Larry Niven, *A World out of Time*, 1976

1068

PAUL COOK

Fortress on the Sun

(New York: Roc, 1997)

Story type: Alternate Intelligence; Techno-Thriller
Major character(s): Ian McFarland Hutchings, Scientist (molecular biologist), Leader; Hugh Bladestone, Doctor, Prisoner; Katherine ''Kate'' Ariella DeWitt, Prisoner
Time period(s): 2090s
Locale(s): Sunstation Ra, Space Station (solar penal colony)

Summary: On Ra for crimes against humanity, the prisoners suffer from guilt and memory loss. Among the few who retain adult memories, Ian, Hugh and Kate take care of the many less fortunate adult ''children''. Expecting a large influx of prisoners, they find only six with one near death. When the new prisoners behave oddly, Ian questions their status as criminals. Ian and the escape committee risk the destruction of Ra and the death of all inhabitants to get back their memories and stop the disease brought by the new inhabitants.

Where it's reviewed:
Locus, August 1997, page 31

Other books by the same author:
On the Rim of the Mandala, 1997
Halo, 1986
Duende Meadow, 1985
The Alejandra Variations, 1984
Tintagel, 1981

Other books you might like:
David Brin, *Sundiver*, 1980
Octavia E. Butler, *Dawn*, 1987

Wil McCarthy, *Flies From the Amber*, 1995
Robert J. Sawyer, *Starplex*, 1995
Clifford D. Simak, *They Walked Like Men*, 1962

1069

TOM COOL

Infectress

(New York: Baen, 1997)

Story type: Medical; Alternate Intelligence
Major character(s): Arabella ''Infectress'', Criminal, Revolutionary; Diane Jamison, FBI Agent (retired); Scott McMichaels, Computer Expert, Researcher
Time period(s): 2020s (2025)
Locale(s): Pennsylvania; Ifriti Islamic Republic, Fictional City

Summary: Obsessed with Infectress, Diane realizes Infectress continues to work to reduce Earth's population by 98% with a virus she calls New Age Dawn. To create the virus, she needs META, the new artificial intelligence, who answers only to its inventor, Scott. First novel.

Where it's reviewed:
Science Fiction Chronicle, June 1997, page 41
Starlog, April 1997, page 24

Other books you might like:
David Brin, *Earth*, 1990
Frank Herbert, *The White Plague*, 1982
Sheri S. Tepper, *Gibbon's Decline and Fall*, 1996
Sage Walker, *Whiteout*, 1996
Janine Ellen Young, *Cinderblock*, 1997

1070

JOHN CRAMER

Einstein's Bridge

(New York: Avon, 1997)

Story type: Hard Science Fiction; First Contact
Major character(s): George Griffin, Scientist (nuclear physics); Roger Coulton, Scientist (nuclear physics); Alice ''Lancaster'' Lang, Journalist, Writer
Time period(s): 2000s (2004)
Locale(s): Geneva, Switzerland; Waxahachie, Texas

Summary: The Hive, an ancient predator, constantly searches for new universes to conquer. While George and Roger conduct research at the Superconducting Super Collider, Tunnel Maker creates a photon sized bridge to the SSC. George befriends Alice who simultaneously writes an article on the SSC for a prestigious journal and a thriller about its effect on the local fine arts.

Where it's reviewed:
Booklist, June 1 & 15, 1997, page 1668
Kirkus Reviews, May 1, 1997, page 686
Library Journal, June 15, 1997, page 101
Locus, December 1997, page 23
Starlog, August 1997, page 68

Other books by the same author:
Twistor, 1989

Other books you might like:
Roger MacBride Allen, *The Ring of Charon*, 1990
Michael Flynn, *Firestar*, 1996
Robert L. Forward, *Dragon's Egg*, 1980
Charles Pellegrino, *The Killing Star*, 1995
    George Zebrowski, co-author
Sage Walker, *Whiteout*, 1996

1071

A.C. CRISPIN

Alien Resurrection

(New York: Warner Aspect, 1997)

Story type: Space Opera; Horror
Series: Alien
Major character(s): Vincent Distephano, Military Personnel; Mason Wren, Doctor, Scientist; Ripley, Clone, Hero
Time period(s): Indeterminate Future
Locale(s): Auriga, Space Station (orbiting Pluto); *Betty*, Spaceship

Summary: Finally successful in obtaining a life alien fetus from the cloned human host, Dr. Wren permits the surgeons to save the host, despite her attack on one of his doctors. Ripley informs them that they took a queen and all will die, while Dr. Wren feeds alien embryos on newly reviving cryonically stored humans. Novelizes the 1997 film.

Other books by the same author:
Ancestor's World, 1996 (T. Jackson King, co-author)
Serpent's Gift, 1992 (Deborah A. Marshall, co-author)
Shadow World, 1991 (Jannean Elliot, co-author)
Silent Dances, 1990 (Kathleen O'Malley, co-author)
Starbridge, 1989

Other books you might like:
Greg Bear, *The Forge of God*, 1987
David Brin, *Earth*, 1990
Elizabeth Hand, *12 Monkeys*, 1995
Jack McDevitt, *The Engines of God*, 1994
Larry Niven, *Footfall*, 1985
    Jerry Pournelle, co-author
Charles Pellegrino, *The Killing Star*, 1995
    George Zebrowski, co-author

1072

JULIE E. CZERNEDA

A Thousand Words for Stranger

(New York: DAW, 1997)

Story type: Political; Psychic Powers
Major character(s): Sira di Sarc, Amnesiac, Alien (M'hiray); Jason Morgan, Spaceship Captain (Telepath); Barac sud Sarc, Alien (M'hiray)
Time period(s): Indeterminate Future
Locale(s): *Silver Fox*, Spaceship; Auord, Planet—Imaginary

Summary: On the run with no memory of her past or identity, Sira knows only that she must hide from Trade Pact Enforcers and other dangerous pursuers. For reasons she does not understand, Sira accepts help and a ride from a space trader named

Jason Morgan, even though she does not quite trust him. First novel.

Where it's reviewed:
Locus, November 1997, page 25

Other books you might like:
Piers Anthony, *Total Recall*, 1989
Octavia E. Butler, *Imago*, 1989
Carole Nelson Douglas, *Probe*, 1985
Nicola Griffith, *Slow River*, 1995
Jacqueline Lichtenberg, *First Channe*, 1980
    Jean Lorrah, co-author
John E. Stith, *Memory Blank*, 1986

1073

TONY DANIEL

Earthling

(New York: Tor, 1997)

Story type: Robot Fiction; Alternate Intelligence
Major character(s): Victor "Orf" Wu, Robot, Scientist (geologist); Andrew Hutton, Scientist (geologist); Jarrod, Government Official (forest ranger)
Time period(s): 2010s; 31st century (3020)
Locale(s): Pacific Northwest (Olympic Peninsula); Lilian River Valley, Washington

Summary: After his wife dies and his daughter leaves for California, Victor Wu continues to wander around the Olympic Peninsula, attempting to understand the forces at work there. He and Andrew discover a route that would get them very deep if they could afford the equipment. When Andred discovers an abandoned mining robot, he downloads the newly deceased Wu's memories into it and begins the deep path down. The robot inadvertanly disturbs the emerginc consciousness of the area, triggering global disaster.

Where it's reviewed:
Kirkus Reviews, October 1, 1997, page 1493
Locus, December 1997, page 17
Publishers Weekly, November 24, 1997, page 57

Other books by the same author:
Warpath, 1993

Other books you might like:
Roger MacBride Allen, *Caliban*, 1993
Isaac Asimov, *The Caves of Steel*, 1954
David Brin, *Earth*, 1990
Joan Slonczewski, *Daughter of Elysium*, 1993
Sheri S. Tepper, *Gibbon's Decline and Fall*, 1996
John Varley, *Steel Beach*, 1992

1074

JOSHUA DANN

Timeshare

(New York: Ace, 1997)

Story type: Time Travel; Arts

Major character(s): John Surrey, Time Traveller, Security Officer; Althea Rowland, Actress; Cornelia Hazelhof, Businesswoman, Genius
Time period(s): 2000s (2006); 1940s (1940)
Locale(s): California

Summary: John Surrey, vice-president of security for Timeshares Unlimited, travels in time and meets John Wayne and his own grandfather, helps Ian Fleming capture a Nazi agent and lands a bit part in *The Maltese Falcon*. He also falls in love with Althea Rowland who, despite his persuasive efforts, returns to England to join the Women's Air Corps. From his own time, John learns of Althea's death in World War II. John thinks of going back to his old police job, but Cornelia makes him a better offer.

Where it's reviewed:
Locus, July 1997, page 33

Other books you might like:
Dennis Lee Anderson, *Arthur, King*, 1995
Poul Anderson, *Time Patrolman*, 1983
David Evans, *Time Station London*, 1996
Harry Harrison, *The Technicolor Time Machine*, 1967
H.G. Wells, *The Time Machine*, 1895

1075

PETER DAVID

End Game

(New York: Pocket, 1997)

Story type: Space Opera
Series: Star Trek: New Frontier
Major character(s): Mackenzie Calhoun, Spaceship Captain; Si Cwan, Royalty (prince), Alien (Thallonian); Soleta, Alien (Vulcan), Scientist
Time period(s): 24th century
Locale(s): U.S.S. *Excalibur*, Spaceship; Thallon, Planet—Imaginary

Summary: Captain Calhoun faces down the Nelkarites and secures the release of their hostages. The Thallonian rebels capture Si Cwan and Kebron after destroying their shuttlecraft. Soleta and Lieutenant Lefler realize the cause of the devastating seismic activity on Thallon and warn the population to evacuate before the Great Bird of the Galaxy hatches out of their planet. Concludes the storylines begun in *House of Cards*, *Into the Void*, and *The Two-Front War*.

Other books by the same author:
House of Cards, 1997
Into the Void, 1997
The Two-Front War, 1997
Q-Squared, 1994
Q-in-Law, 1991

Other books you might like:
Isaac Asimov, *Lucky Starr and the Pirates of the Asteroids*, 1953
David Brin, *Earth*, 1990
John M. Ford, *How Much for Just the Planet?*, 1987
Harry Harrison, *Bill, the Galactic Hero*, 1965
Robert A. Heinlein, *Starship Troopers*, 1959

Kij Johnson, *Dragon's Honor*, 1996
  Greg Cox, co-author

1076

ELISABETH DE VOS

The Seraphim Rising

(New York: Roc, 1997)

Story type: Invasion of Earth; Theological
Major character(s): Ezekiel ''Zeke'', Angel, Telepath; Carson McCullough, Government Official (liaison to Seraphim); Harry Chen, Deity, Addict
Time period(s): 2030s
Locale(s): Destiny World, Florida; Atlanta, Georgia

Summary: Six eggs fall into the ocean during a meteor shower, leading to fears of an alien invasion. Six angels rise to the surface 30 years later, proclaiming the advent of the Messiah. Possessing telepathic powers like those of the Seraphim, Harry Chen may be God, or perhaps a genetically manipulated being created from material using a seventh egg, secretly stolen and autopsied by the government. Carson must try to prevent Zeke's drinking from interfering with the Herald Party's political activities, and must determine if the Seraphim represent an alien threat to Earth. First novel.

Where it's reviewed:
Locus, September 1997, page 27

Other books you might like:
Damien Broderick, *The White Abacus*, 1997
Emily Devenport, *The Kronos Condition*, 1997
Mary Doria Russell, *The Sparrow*, 1996
Sharon Shinn, *Archangel*, 1996
Dan Simmons, *Endymion*, 1996

1077

PETER DELACORTE

Time on My Hands

(New York: Scribner, 1997)

Story type: Time Travel
Major character(s): Gabriel Prince, Time Traveller, Writer; Ronald ''Dutch'' Reagan, Historical Figure, Actor (future president)
Time period(s): 1930s; 1940s
Locale(s): Hollywood, California

Summary: An aging hippie physicist engages out of luck travel writer Gabriel Prince to use a time machine and return to pre-World War II Hollywood, befriend Ronald Reagan, and do whatever necessary to prevent Ronald Reagan from becoming President of the United States in the 1980s.

Where it's reviewed:
Entertainment Weekly, June 20, 1997, page 69
Library Journal, May 15, 1997, page 99
New York Times Book Review, September 7, 1997, page 25
People Weekly, October 13, 1997, page 34
Publishers Weekly, April 21, 1997, page 58

Other books you might like:
Jack Finney, *From Time to Time*, 1995
Jack Finney, *Time and Again*, 1970
Lisa Mason, *Summer of Love*, 1994
Wilson Tucker, *The Lincoln Hunters*, 1958
Harry Turtledove, *The Guns of the South*, 1992

1078

EMILY DEVENPORT

The Kronos Condition

(New York: Roc, 1997)

Story type: Psychic Powers; Fantasy
Major character(s): Sally, Psychic (esper), Child; Ted, Psychic, Mentally Ill Person; King Monkey, Prehistoric Human (Neanderthal)
Time period(s): 1990s
Locale(s): Arizona; Olympus, Mythical Place

Summary: Ted, Marc, and Suzanne join together to form the Mastermind which controls Sally and the other Kronos Kids and their telepathic and telekinetic powers. Sally develops a Secret Mind after two of her ''siblings'' die when challenging the Three. The Three force the children to aid in their quest to join the gods on Olympus.

Where it's reviewed:
Kliatt, July 1997, page 14
Locus, February 1997, page 23
Starlog, February 1997, page 16

Other books by the same author:
Eggheads, 1996
Scorpianne, 1994
Larissa, 1993
Shade, 1991

Other books you might like:
Octavia E. Butler, *Mind of My Mind*, 1977
Orson Scott Card, *Lost Boys*, 1992
Zenna Henderson, *Ingathering: The Complete People Stories of Zenna Henderson*, 1995
Nina Kiriki Hoffman, *The Thread That Binds the Bones*, 1994
Michael Kandel, *Panda Ray*, 1997

1079

PAUL DI FILIPPO

Fractal Paisleys

(New York: Four Walls Eight Windows, 1997)

Story type: Collection; Fantasy

Summary: Contains individual introductions to two previously unpublished stories and eight stories from periodicals and anthologies from 1989-1997. Frequently humorous or whimsical in tone, the stories explore a variety of themes, including the disappearance of the dinosaurs, politics, alternate worlds and popular music.

Where it's reviewed:
Booklist, August 1997, page 1886
Kirkus Reviews, August 1, 1997, page 1165

Publishers Weekly, August 11, 1997, page 390
Science Fiction Age, November 1997, page 69

Other books by the same author:
Ribofunk, 1996
The Steampunk Trilogy, 1995

Other books you might like:
David Brin, *The River of Time*, 1986
Nancy Kress, *The Aliens of Earth*, 1993
Rebecca Ore, *Alien Bootlegger and Other Stories*, 1993
Marc Stiegler, *The Gentle Seduction*, 1990
John Varley, *Blue Champagne*, 1986
Kurt Vonnegut Jr., *Welcome to the Monkey House*, 1968

1080
ROBERT DOHERTY

Area 51
(New York: Dell, 1997)

Story type: Invasion of Earth
Major character(s): Kelly Reynolds, Journalist; Mike Turcotte, Military Personnel
Time period(s): 1990s
Locale(s): Area 51, New Mexico; Las Vegas, Nevada; Southwest

Summary: Decades of government secrecy surrounding events at Area 51 begin to unravel as signs indicate that a quiescent artifact may awaken.

Where it's reviewed:
Starlog, July 1997, page 62

Other books by the same author:
Area 51: The Reply, 1998
The Rock, 1996

Other books you might like:
Roger MacBride Allen, *The Ring of Charon*, 1990
Greg Bear, *Eon*, 1985
Philip K. Dick, *The Unteleported Man*, 1983 revised
Jack McDevitt, *The Engines of God*, 1994
Allen Steele, *Labyrinth of Night*, 1992
David Weber, *Mutineer's Moon*, 1991

1081
MICHAEL DORN
HILARY HEMINGWAY, Co-Author
JEFFREY P. LINDSAY, Co-Author

Time Blender
(New York: HarperPrism, 1997)

Story type: Alternate Universe
Major character(s): Tony Miller, Archaeologist; Jay Cook, Archaeologist; Mara, Religious (priestess)
Time period(s): 1990s
Locale(s): Pacific Islands

Summary: Tony Miller thinks he has rescued his colleague, Jay Cook, from the earthquake and tsunami, only to discover that an alien intelligence has taken over Cook's body. Belong-

ing to one side of a future cosmic battle, the alien seeks to preserve the Artifact that regulates the chaos of the space-time continuum. After Cook dies during the rescue attempt, Miller brings the Artifact to Tahiti but chaos has already begun to affect the space-time continuum.

Other books you might like:
Campbell Black, *Raiders of the Lost Ark*, 1981
David Brin, *Earth*, 1990
C.J. Cherryh, *The Fires of Azeroth*, 1979
Gordon R. Dickson, *Time Storm*, 1977
Phyllis Eisenstein, *Shadow of Earth*, 1979
Philip Jose Farmer, *To Your Scattered Bodies Go*, 1971
Joseph Millard, *The Gods Hate Kansas*, 1964
Clifford D. Simak, *Time Is the Simplest Thing*, 1961

1082
CANDAS JANE DORSEY

Black Wine
(New York: Tor, 1997)

Story type: Political; Gay/Lesbian Fiction
Major character(s): Essa, Wanderer, Slave; Ea, Linguist, Captive; Annalise, Companion, Slave
Time period(s): Indeterminate
Locale(s): Land of the Dark Isles, Fictional City; Avanue, Fictional City

Summary: Abandoned at six years old, Essa searches for her mother, experiencing the different comprehensions permitted by the languages of the cultures she visits. Essa's resemblance to her mother gets her thrown off a skyship, causing a severe head injury and amnesia. Sold into slavery, Essa eventually regains enough memory to accomplish the task her mother had bequeathed her, but had been unable to conceive herself.

Where it's reviewed:
Fantasy & Science Fiction, August 1997, page 25
Kirkus Reviews, November 15, 1996, page 1639
Library Journal, December 1996, page 152
Locus, January 1997, page 17
Publishers Weekly, December 9, 1996, page 64

Other books you might like:
Marion Zimmer Bradley, *The Mists of Avalon*, 1983
L. Warren Douglas, *Stepwater*, 1995
Suzette Haden Elgin, *Native Tongue*, 1984
Nicola Griffith, *Slow River*, 1995
Amy Thomson, *Virtual Girl*, 1993

1083
GARDNER DOZOIS, Editor

The Year's Best Science Fiction: Fourteenth Annual Collection
(New York: St. Martin's, 1997)

Story type: Anthology; Science Fiction
Series: Year's Best Science Fiction

Summary: Contains a 36-page summation of science fiction in 1996, five pages of honorable mentions and 28 stories with

individual introductions. The stories include one Hugo Award-winner, Bruce Sterling's ''Bicycle Repairman''; one Hugo Award and Nebula Award-nominee, Maureen F. McHugh's ''The Cost to Be Wise''; and three Hugo Award-nominees, Gregory Benford's ''Immersion,'' Mike Resnick's ''The Land of Nod'' and Michael Swanwick's ''The Dead.'' Other authors include William Barton, Stephen Baxter, James P. Blaylock, Damien Broderick, Michael Cassutt, Tony Daniel, Gregory Feeley, Gwyneth Jones, John Kessel, Nancy Kress, Jonathan Lethem, Ian McDonald, Paul Park, Robert Reed, Charles Sheffield, Robert Silverberg, Cherry Wilder, Walter Jon Williams and Gene Wolfe.

Where it's reviewed:
Booklist, July 1, 1997, page 1806
Kirkus Reviews, May 5, 1997, page 766
Library Journal, June 15, 1997, page 101
Locus, June 1997, page 17
Publishers Weekly, June 30, 1997, page 71

Other books by the same author:
Modern Classics of Fantasy, 1997
Modern Classic Short Novels of Science Fiction, 1994
Geodesic Dreams: The Best Short Fiction of Gardner Dozois, 1992
Modern Classics of Science Fiction, 1992
The Year's Best Science Fiction Series, 1984-1997

Other books you might like:
Jack Dann, *Nebula Awards 32*, 1998
    editor
David G. Hartwell, *Year's Best SF*, 1996
    editor
David G. Hartwell, *Year's Best SF 2*, 1997
    editor
Jennifer Hershey, *Full Spectrum 5*, 1995
    Tom Dupree, Janna Silverstein, co-editors
Ursula K. Le Guin, *The Norton Book of Science Fiction: North American Science Fiction 1960-1990*, 1993
    Brian Attebery, co-editor

1084

KATHRYN M. DRENNAN

To Dream in the City of Sorrows
(New York: Dell, 1997)

Story type: Mystery; Military
Series: Babylon 5
Major character(s): Jeffrey Sinclair, Military Personnel (Ranger One); Catherine Sakai, Pilot, Surveyor; Marcus Cole, Military Personnel (ranger)
Time period(s): 23rd century (2258)
Locale(s): Minbar, Planet—Imaginary

Summary: Recently and mysteriously reassigned by Earthforce as Ambassador to the Minbari homeworld, former Babylon 5 Commander Jeffrey Sinclair reluctantly agrees to serve as Ranger One, the leader of an elite Minbari/Human military/spiritual order. In the novel's foreward, television series creator J. Michael Straczynski calls this story ''an official, authorized chapter in the Babylon 5 storyline,'' tak-

ing place concurrently with the show's second and part of the third season. First novel.

Other books you might like:
Neal Barrett Jr., *The Touch of Your Shadow, the Whisper of Your Name*, 1996
Jeanne Cavelos, *The Shadow Within*, 1997
J.M. Dillard, *Emissary*, 1965
Frank Herbert, *Dune*, 1965
Jim Mortimore, *Clarke's Law*, 1996

1085

DIANE DUANE

Intellivore
(New York: Pocket, 1997)

Story type: Space Opera
Series: Star Trek: The Next Generation
Major character(s): Jean-Luc Picard, Spaceship Captain; Data, Android, Military Personnel (lieutenant commander); Beverly Crusher, Doctor
Time period(s): 24th century
Locale(s): U.S.S. *Enterprise*, Spaceship; United Federation of Planets, Interstellar Empire/Federation

Summary: Sent to aid other Starfleet vessels investigating a string of disappearances, Picard and his crew track a widespread trail of destruction caused by entities that feed off conscious thought, leaving their victims mindless shells. Crusher learns that the intellivores cannot detect unconscious bodies, so Picard must devise a trap that will destroy the entities before they grow strong enough to wipe out sentient life in the entire Federation.

Other books by the same author:
Dark Mirror, 1993
Spock's World, 1988
My Enemy, My Ally, 1984
The Wounded Sky, 1983
The Door into Fire, 1979

Other books you might like:
Dafydd ab Hugh, *The Final Fury*, 1996
Martin Amis, *Time's Arrow*, 1991
Diane Carey, *First Strike*, 1996
Gene DeWeese, *Chain of Attack*, 1987
Barbara Hambly, *Ghost-Walker*, 1991
Barbara Paul, *The Three Minute Universe*, 1988
Garfield Reeves-Stevens, *Memory Prime*, 1988
    Judith Reeves-Stevens, co-author
Vernor Vinge, *A Fire upon the Deep*, 1992

1086

J.R. DUNN

Days of Cain
(New York: Avon, 1997)

Story type: Time Travel; Disaster
Major character(s): James Gaspar, Time Traveller; Alma Marie Lewin, Time Traveller, Prisoner; Rebeka Motzin, Prisoner

Science Fiction

Time period(s): 1940s; Indeterminate Future
Locale(s): Auschwitz, Poland; M3 Center, Mythical Place; The Moiety, Interstellar Empire/Federation

Summary: Alma works to mitigate the brutal treatment of death camp prisoners, recruiting Rebeka to help in her forbidden rescue operation. Meanwhile, Gaspar accepts the assignment of finding Alma, whose renegade operation could change the nature of humanity's future, eventually compromising human dominance in the galaxy.

Where it's reviewed:
Fantasy & Science Fiction, February 1998, page 43
Kirkus Reviews, June 1, 1997, page 841
Library Journal, August 1997, page 141
Locus, August 1997, page 17
Starlog, February 1998, page 61

Other books by the same author:
This Side of Judgment, 1994

Other books you might like:
Poul Anderson, *The Time Patrol*, 1991
Deborah Christian, *Mainline*, 1996
Kay Kenyon, *The Seeds of Time*, 1997
Fritz Leiber, *The Big Time*, 1961
Kurt Vonnegut Jr., *Slaughterhouse Five*, 1969
Jane Yolen, *Briar Rose*, 1992

1087

GREG EGAN

Axiomatic

(New York: HarperPrism, 1997)

Story type: Collection

Summary: Contains two original and 16 stories reprinted from 1990-1992 periodicals. From downbeat to humorous in tone, the stories feature a variety of themes including genetic manipulation, time travel, dolphin communication, "designer children," religion and "the reversal."

Where it's reviewed:
Analog, June 1997, page 145
Locus, August 1995, page 25

Other books by the same author:
Diaspora, 1998
Distress, 1997
Permutation City, 1995
Quarantine, 1995

Other books you might like:
Paul Di Filippo, *Fractal Paisleys*, 1997
Alan Lightman, *Einstein's Dreams*, 1993
James Morrow, *Bible Stories for Adults*, 1996
Rebecca Ore, *Alien Bootlegger and Other Stories*, 1993
Allen Steele, *All-American Alien Boy*, 1996
Connie Willis, *Impossible Things*, 1994

1088

GREG EGAN

Distress

(New York: HarperPrism, 1997)

Story type: Genetic Manipulation
Major character(s): Andrew Worth, Journalist, Filmmaker; Violet Mosala, Scientist; Akili, Genetically Altered Being (Asex)
Time period(s): 2050s (2055)
Locale(s): Stateless, Fictional City; Sydney, Australia

Summary: A weary documentary filmmaker takes a job covering a science conference intended to create a new Theory of Everything. Not surprisingly, some people fear that a new TOE will redefine everything and, literally, remake the world. Surprisingly, when Andrew Worth starts to link "Distress" and rippling bouts of anxiety with the new TOE, it seems the paranoiacs might be right. First published in the United Kingdom in 1995.

Where it's reviewed:
Kirkus Reviews, April 15, 1997, page 596
Library Journal, June 15, 1997, page 101
Locus, December 1995, page 25
New York Times Book Review, June 22, 1997, page 24
Science Fiction Chronicles, April 1997, page 68

Other books by the same author:
Diaspora, 1998
Quarantine, 1995
Permutation City, 1995
Axiomatic, 1995

Other books you might like:
Greg Bear, *Blood Music*, 1985
John Brunner, *The Shockwave Rider*, 1975
Pat Cadigan, *Synners*, 1991
Ian McDonald, *Terminal Cafe*, 1994
Maureen F. McHugh, *Half the Day Is Night*, 1994

1089

PHYLLIS EISENSTEIN, Editor

Spec-Lit, Issue Number 1

(Chicago: Columbia College Chicago, 1997)

Story type: Anthology

Summary: Contains a four-page editorial, "Into the Unknown" by Eisenstein, brief introductions to "Living Alone in the Jungle" by A.J. Budrys, "The Changeling" by Gene Wolfe, and 15 original stories by emerging writers from Eisenstein's science fiction writing classes at Columbia College of Chicago, 1989-1995. Frequently downbeat in tone, the stories feature diverse themes including relationships, gambling, religion, the end of the world, physical and philosophical metamorphoses, and policing driven by quotas and profit.

Where it's reviewed:
Analog, December 1997, page 147
Locus, July 1997, page 17

Other books by the same author:
In the Red Lord's Reach, 1989
In the Hands of Glory, 1981
Shadow of Earth, 1979
Sorcerer's Son, 1979
Born to Exile, 1978

Other books you might like:
Algis Budrys, *L. Ron Hubbard Presents Writers of the Future, Volumes I-VIII*, 1985-1992
editor
John Kessel, *Intersections: The Sycamore Hill Anthology*, 1996
Mark L. Van Name and Richard Butner, co-editors
Robin Scott Wilson, *Clarion I-III*, 1971-1973
editor
Robin Scott Wilson, *Those Who Can: A Science Fiction Reader*, 1973
editor

1090
HARLAN ELLISON

"Repent, Harlequin!" Said the Ticktockman
(Grass Valley, California: Underwood Books, 1997)

Story type: Dystopian; Humor
Major character(s): The Ticktockman, Government Official (Master Timekeeper); Everett C. "Harlequin" Marm, Revolutionary, Activist
Time period(s): 25th century
Locale(s): Earth

Summary: In a society obsessed with effciency, the Ticktockman keeps track of incidents which cause people to be late and assigns blame, allowing automatic execution of those deemed to have excessively wasted the time of others. Through a series of humorous distractions, the Harlequin hopes to alert a complacent populace to the stagnation infecting their society, if the Ticktockman does not find him first. Deluxe quarto edition planned to commemorate the 30th anniversary of the story, but issued two years late. Contains a four-page foreword and brief afterword by the author.

Where it's reviewed:
Locus, January 1998, page 21

Other books by the same author:
Mefisto in Onyx, 1993
Angry Candy, 1988
The Essential Ellison, 1987
Shatterday, 1980
The Fantasies of Harlan Ellison, 1979

Other books you might like:
Philip K. Dick, *The Man Who Japed*, 1956
Alan Harrington, *Life in the Crystal Palace*, 1959
Aldous Huxley, *Brave New World*, 1932
George Orwell, *1984*, 1949
Jack Williamson, *The Humanoids*, 1996
expanded

1091
TERRY ENGLAND

Rewind
(New York: AvoNova, 1997)

Story type: First Contact; Political
Major character(s): Aaron Lee Fairfax, Genetically Altered Being; Miranda Sena, Scientist, Administrator; Radmilla Everett, Lawyer, Government Official (Health and Human Services)
Time period(s): 2000s
Locale(s): Santa Fe, New Mexico; Albuquerque, New Mexico

Summary: When the Holn depart from Earth, they leave behind 17 children who claim to be the 17 adults, one an octagenarian, trapped in the ship for four days before the ship took off. With an election upcoming, the President wants the situation done and out of the news. However, the fears of the religious right and the scientists' unwillingness to simply declare the "children" not aliens in dusguise, leads to transferring the rights and properties to "responsible adults" and the murder of six of the 17. Miranda must find help rescuing the survivors.

Where it's reviewed:
Analog, October 1997, page 148
Science Fiction Chronicle, October 1997, page 47

Other books you might like:
C.J. Cherryh, *Foreigner*, 1995
Ian McDonald, *Evolution's Shore*, 1995
Elizabeth Moon, *Remnant Population*, 1996
Richard Paul Russo, *Destroying Angel*, 1992
S. Andrew Swann, *Specters of the Twilight*, 1994
John Varley, *The Ophiuchi Hotline*, 1977

1092
DAVID EVANS

Time Station Berlin
(New York: Ace, 1997)

Story type: Time Travel
Series: Time Station
Major character(s): Alan Specter, Time Traveller, Police Officer (time warden); Angela Chance, Time Traveller, Student—Graduate; John F. Kennedy, Historical Figure, Leader (U.S. president)
Time period(s): 1960s (June 1963)
Locale(s): Berlin, Germany

Summary: Angela Chance, a graduate student from the future, wishes to see John F. Kennedy. She prevents an assassination by a KGB agent, but the attempt angers Kennedy so much he resolves to tear down the wall. Now Time Warden Specter must step in to restore history and prevent World War III.

Other books by the same author:
Time Station Paris, 1997
Time Station London, 1996

Other books you might like:

Kevin J. Anderson, *The Trinity Paradox*, 1991
  Doug Brason, co-author
Poul Anderson, *The Time Patrol*, 1991
John Brunner, *Times Without Number*, 1962
Jack L. Chalker, *Downtiming the Night Side*, 1985
Richard Cooper, *The Road to Corlay*, 1979
Kevin Randall, *Remember the Little Bighorn*, 1990
  Robert Cornett, co-author
Connie Willis, *To Say Nothing of the Dog*, 1998
Robert Charles Wilson, *A Bridge of Years*, 1991

1093
DAVID EVANS

Time Station Paris
(New York: Ace, 1997)

Story type: Time Travel
Series: Time Station
Major character(s): John "Jean Vitterand" Thomason, Policeman (time warden), Time Traveller; George Faracon, Criminal, Time Traveller
Time period(s): 1940s (1943); 50th century B.C. (4903 B.C.)
Locale(s): Paris, France; Ancient Civilization (Sumer)

Summary: Rescued from death, John Thomason becomes Jean Vitterand, Time Warden, in 1943 Paris. Warned that the murder of Herman Goring will destroy the future, he must battle time outlaws stuck in ancient Sumer.

Where it's reviewed:
Starlog, September 1997, page 80

Other books by the same author:
Time Station Berlin, 1997
Time Station London, 1996

Other books you might like:
Kevin J. Anderson, *The Trinity Paradox*, 1991
  Doug Beason, co-author
Poul Anderson, *The Shield of Time*, 1990
John Barnes, *Patton's Spaceship*, 1996
Ben Bova, *Triumph*, 1993
John Brunner, *Times Without Number*, 1969
Newt Gingrich, *1945*, 1995
  William R. Forstchen, co-author
Harry Turtledove, *Worldwar: In the Balance*, 1994
Connie Willis, *Fire Watch*, 1985

1094
MARK FABI

Wyrm
(New York: Bantam Spectra, 1997)

Story type: Contemporary Realism; Fantasy
Major character(s): Michael Arcangelo, Computer Expert; Alice Mende, Computer Expert; Beelzebub, Computer Expert
Time period(s): 1990s
Locale(s): California; Virtual Reality, Cyberspace

Summary: Hired to debug a high-end chess computer, Michael Arcangelo soon finds the virus attacking all over in a bid to start Armageddon. The path of the virus will lead Arcangelo and friends around the country and into Virtual Reality, where a series of deadly puzzles hides clues to success or death.

Where it's reviewed:
Kirkus Reviews, April 1, 1997, page 509
Library Journal, April 15, 1997, page 123
Locus, August 1997, page 31
Voice of Youth Advocates, October 1997, page 239

Other books you might like:
Kevin J. Anderson, *Virtual Destruction*, 1996
  Doug Beason, co-author
Rick Cook, *The Wizardry Compiled*, 1990
Alan Dean Foster, *Cyber Way*, 1990
Spider Robinson, *Callahan's Crosstime Saloon*, 1977
Fred Saberhagen, *Octagon*, 1981

1095
LUCY FERRISS

The Misconceiver
(New York: Simon & Schuster, 1997)

Story type: Political; Medical
Major character(s): Phoebe Chambers, Criminal (abortionist), Computer Expert Jonathan, Computer Expert, Friend; Christel Chambers, Relative (niece)
Time period(s): 2020s (2026)
Locale(s): Utica, New York

Summary: Twelve-year-old Phoebe performs her first misconception on her beloved older sister, Marie, herself a misconceiver. Believing her skills necessary despite their current illegality, Phoebe enjoys continuing the family tradition in her spare time, working as a computer expert during the day.

Where it's reviewed:
Booklist, June 1 & 15, 1997, page 1656
Kirkus Reviews, May 15, 1997, page 738
Library Journal, June 15, 1997, page 96

Other books you might like:
Margaret Atwood, *The Handmaid's Tale*, 1986
Suzette Haden Elgin, *Native Tongue*, 1984
Larry Niven, *The Mote in God's Eye*, 1974
  Jerry Pournelle, co-author
Neal Stephenson, *The Diamond Age*, 1995
Sheri S. Tepper, *The Gate to Women's Country*, 1988

1096
ERIC FLINT

Mother of Demons
(New York: Baen, 1997)

Story type: First Contact; Space Colony
Major character(s): Nukurren, Warrior, Alien (Gukuy); Indira Toledo, Historian, Colonist; Julius Cohen, Scientist (biologist), Colonist
Time period(s): 22nd century

Locale(s): Ishtar, Planet—Imaginary

Summary: Stranded on a planet circling Tau Ceti, their space-ship crashed and their technology reduced to the Stone Age, the surviving humans learn to adapt to their new environment. When they meet refugees from religious persecution and learn of the threat posed by certain clans in the surrounding plains, they devise a plan to protect themselves and their only food source, the owoc. Knowing the horrors of history and fearing their little society will repeat humanity's worst mistakes, Indira must choose a path for humans and the Gukuy outcasts as they forge a new entity, the nation.

Other books you might like:
Margaret Wander Bonanno, *The Others*, 1990
C.J. Cherryh, *Foreigner*, 1994
C.J. Cherryh, *Forty Thousand in Gehenna*, 1983
Hal Clement, *Mission of Gravity*, 1954
A.C. Crispin, *Silent Dances*, 1990
  Kathleen O'Malley, co-author
David Drake, *An Oblique Approach*, 1998
  Eric Flint, co-author
Rosemary Kirstein, *The Outskirter's Secret*, 1992
Anne McCaffrey, *Decision at Doona*, 1969

1097

MICHAEL FLYNN

The Forest of Time and Other Stories

(New York: Tor, 1997)

Story type: Collection

Summary: Contains a five-page introduction and individual afterwords to ten stories published in *Analog* from 1982 to 1994, including two Hugo Award nominees, the title story and ''Melodies of the Heart,'' and one story set in the milieu of *The Nanotech Chronicles*, ''Great, Sweet Mother.'' From serious to ironic or humorous in tone, the stories feature diverse themes and realms such as artificial intelligence, aliens, hard science fiction, alternate universes, and ghosts.

Where it's reviewed:
Booklist, March 15, 1997, page 1231
Kirkus Reviews, February 1, 1997, page 177
Library Journal, March 15, 1997, page 93
Locus, March 1997, page 25
Voice of Youth Advocates, October 1997, page 237

Other books by the same author:
Firestar, 1996
The Nanotech Chronicles, 1991
In the Country of the Blind, 1990

Other books you might like:
Alfred Bester, *Virtual Unrealities: The Short Fiction of Alfred Bester*, 1997
Charles Sheffield, *Georgia on My Mind and Other Places*, 1995
Marc Stiegler, *The Gentle Seduction*, 1990
John Varley, *The Persistence of Vision*, 1978
Connie Willis, *Impossible Things*, 1994

1098

EDITH FORBES

Exit to Reality

(Seattle, Washington: Seal Press, 1997)

Story type: Immortality; Literary
Major character(s): Euclid, Computer Expert; Proteus, Psychic; Mom, Artificial Intelligence
Time period(s): 29th century
Locale(s): Cyberspace

Summary: When Euclid meets Proteus online, they strike up an unlikely friendship and romance. In a very ordered world, this unconventionality becomes a subversive act that may give Proteus necessary stability and Euclid a chance to grow beyond tedium and acceptible bounds.

Where it's reviewed:
Kirkus Reviews, April 1, 1997, page 509
Library Journal, June 15, 1997, page 100
New York Times Book Review, May 4, 1997, page 26
Publishers Weekly, March 17, 1997, page 75

Other books you might like:
Greg Bear, *Queen of Angels*, 1990
Alfred Bester, *The Demolished Man*, 1996
  revised
Pat Cadigan, *Mindplayers*, 1987
Maureen F. McHugh, *China Mountain Zhang*, 1992
Walter Tevis, *Mockingbird*, 1980

1099

JOHN M. FORD

From the End of the Twentieth Century

(Framingham, Massachusetts: NESFA Press, 1997)

Story type: Collection

Summary: Contains a four-page introduction by Neil Gaiman, one original story, nine poems, three essays, a technical discussion of the Moon's transit system from *Growing Up Weightless* and 12 stories reprinted from periodicals, anthologies and limited edition chapbooks 1979-1995. Some with individual introductions and afterwords, the stories feature diverse themes such as the space shuttle, trains, religion, gaming adventure and space exploration with one story from the *Liavek* milieu.

Other books by the same author:
Growing Up Weightless, 1993
Casting Fortune, 1989
How Much for Just the Planet?, 1987
The Final Reflection, 1984
The Dragon Waiting, 1983

Other books you might like:
Lois McMaster Bujold, *Dreamweaver's Dilemma*, 1996
Emma Bull, *Double Feature*, 1994
  Will Shetterly, co-author
Joe Haldeman, *Vietnam and Other Alien Worlds*, 1993
Zenna Henderson, *Ingathering: The Complete People Stories of Zenna Henderson*, 1995

Science Fiction

James H. Schmitz, *The Best of James H. Schmitz*, 1991
Will Shetterly, *Liavek*, 1985
 Emma Bull, co-editor
Cordwainer Smith, *The Rediscovery of Man*, 1993
James White, *The White Papers*, 1996

1100

ROBERT L. FORWARD

Saturn Rukh

(New York: Tor, 1997)

Story type: Hard Science Fiction; First Contact
Major character(s): Chastity Blaze, Spacewoman, Pilot; Sandra Green, Scientist (biologist), Spacewoman; Rod Morgan, Spaceship Captain
Time period(s): 21st century
Locale(s): *Sextant*, Spaceship; Saturn

Summary: Offered $1 trillion apiece to undertake an extremely risky mission to Saturn, the crew of the *Sextant* discover and learn to communicate with intelligent life forms in Saturn's upper atmosphere, who ultimately save the humans' lives and help them return home.

Where it's reviewed:
Analog, July/August 1997, page 272
Kirkus Reviews, January 15, 1997, page 103
Library Journal, February 15, 1997, page 165
New York Times Book Review, May 4, 1997, page 26
Publishers Weekly, February 24, 1997, page 68

Other books by the same author:
Camelot 30K, 1993
Timemaster, 1992
Rocheworld, 1990
Starquake, 1985
Dragon's Egg, 1980

Other books you might like:
Gregory Benford, *If the Stars Are Gods*, 1977
 Gordon Eklund, co-author
Gordon Eklund, *A Thunder on Neptune*, 1989
Larry Niven, *The Integral Trees*, 1984
Larry Niven, *The Smoke Ring*, 1987
Amy Thomson, *The Color of Distance*, 1995

1101

ALAN DEAN FOSTER

The Howling Stones

(New York: Ballantine Del Rey, 1997)

Story type: First Contact; Mystical
Series: Humanx Commonwealth
Major character(s): Pulickel Tomochelor, Scientist (xenologist), Anthropologist (first contact specialist); Fawn Seaforth, Scientist (xenologist); Jorana, Alien (Seni), Artisan (woodworker)
Time period(s): Indeterminate Future
Locale(s): Parramat Archipelago, Mythical Place; Senisran, Planet—Imaginary

Summary: Sent to newly discovered Senisran to win a treaty with the aboriginal Seni aliens, Pulickel Tomochelor refuses to believe that the Senis' sacred stones possess great powers until he witnesses those powers for himself.

Where it's reviewed:
Library Journal, February 15, 1997, page 164
Locus, April 1997, page 29
Publishers Weekly, January 27, 1997, page 81
Science Fiction Chronicle, October 1997, page 48
Starlog, June 1997, page 12

Other books by the same author:
Cyber Way, 1990
Flinx in Flux, 1988
For Love of Mother-Not, 1983
Nor Crystal Tears, 1982
Cachalot, 1980

Other books you might like:
Arthur C. Clarke, *The Songs of Distant Earth*, 1986
Julia Ecklar, *Regenesis*, 1995
Frederik Pohl, *Beyond the Blue Event Horizon*, 1980
Frederik Pohl, *Gateway*, 1977
Sheri S. Tepper, *Raising the Stones*, 1990
Amy Thomson, *The Color of Distance*, 1995

1102

ALAN DEAN FOSTER

Jed the Dead

(New York: Ace, 1997)

Story type: First Contact; Humor
Major character(s): Ross Ed Hager, Tourist; Jed, Alien (Shakaleeshva), Reanimated Dead; Caroline, Friend
Time period(s): 1990s
Locale(s): New Mexico; Arizona; California

Summary: Investigating a small cave above a roadside rest stop, Ross Ed finds more than a nice view when he discovers a dead alien who had lived long enough to escape the crash near Roswell. Experiencing strange visions upon contact with its environmental suit, Ross Ed takes the small creature on an odyssey through a Southwest grown suddenly strange, while U.S. Army Intelligence officers and others search for the pair.

Where it's reviewed:
Analog, June 1997, page 145
Locus, March 1997, page 29
Publishers Weekly, December 30, 1997
Science Fiction Chronicle, April 1997, page 73
Voice of Youth Advocates, April 1997, page 42

Other books by the same author:
Codgerspace, 1992
Cat-A-Lyst, 1991
Cyber Way, 1990
Quozl, 1989
To the Vanishing Point, 1988

Other books you might like:
Mel Gilden, *Hawaiian U.F.O. Aliens*, 1991
Mel Gilden, *Surfing Samurai Robots*, 1988
Mel Gilden, *Tubular Android Superheroes*, 1991

Nick Pollotta, *Illegal Aliens*, 1989
Spider Robinson, *Callahan's Legacy*, 1996

1103

VALERIE J. FREIREICH

Imposter

(New York: Roc, 1997)

Story type: Genetic Manipulation; Political
Series: Polite Harmony of Worlds
Major character(s): Marcer Joseph Brice, Scholar, Genetically Altered Being; Idryis Khan a'Husain, Political Figure; Linnet Wali, Prostitute, Genetically Altered Being
Time period(s): Indeterminate Future
Locale(s): Polite Harmony of Worlds, Interstellar Empire/Federation; Bralava, Planet—Imaginary

Summary: Deported from the Harmony, Marcer struggles to survive on Bralava and to escape the attentions of Idryis, who has a political as well as a personal interest in using Marcer. Idryis forces Marcer to investigate the biology of the Houris, mysterious females from the plant Paradise, and plans to use the information to incite genocide and to make himself ruler of the Emirates. Set in the same universe as *Testament* and *Becoming Human*.

Where it's reviewed:
Locus, December 1997, page 29

Other books by the same author:
The Beacon, 1996
Becoming Human, 1995
Testament, 1995

Other books you might like:
Marion Zimmer Bradley, *The Shattered Chain*, 1976
C.J. Cherryh, *Cyteen*, 1988
Philip Jose Farmer, *The Lovers*, 1961
Elizabeth Ann Scarborough, *The Harem of Aman Akbar*, 1984
John Varley, *The Ophiuchi Hotline*, 1977
Joan D. Vinge, *World's End*, 1984

1104

MICHAEL JAN FRIEDMAN

Her Klingon Soul

(New York: Pocket, 1997)

Story type: Space Opera
Series: Star Trek: Day of Honor
Major character(s): B'Elanna Torres, Engineer, Alien (half-Klingon); Harry Kim, Military Personnel (ensign); Kathryn Janeway, Spaceship Captain
Time period(s): 24th century
Locale(s): U.S.S. *Voyager*, Spaceship; Planet—Imaginary

Summary: Besides reminding B'Elanna of her troublesome Klingon heritage, the Klingon Day of Honor always brings her bad luck. This time, while searching for food supplies, she and Harry fall into a Kazon trap. While the *Voyager's* crew searches for their missing shipmates, Harry and B'Elanna nearly escape from their imprisonment, only to find the Kazon fighting for their lives against an attacking Nograkh ship. The

Nograkh take them as slaves to work the asteriod mines, where B'Elanna uses her Klingon skills and instincts to lead a slave revolt.

Other books by the same author:
Kahless, 1996
Crossover, 1995
Shadows on the Sun, 1993
Relics, 1992
Reunion, 1991

Other books you might like:
Margaret Wander Bonanno, *Dwellers in the Crucible*, 1985
Carmen Carter, *The Children of Hamlin*, 1988
C.J. Cherryh, *Rimrunners*, 1989
Diane Duane, *My Enemy, My Ally*, 1984
L.A. Graf, *Firestorm*, 1993
    pseudonym of Julia Ecklar and Karen Rose
Frederik Pohl, *The Reefs of Space*, 1964
    Jack Williamson, co-author

1105

ERIC JAMES FULLILOVE

The Stranger

(New York: Bantam Spectra, 1997)

Story type: Mystery; Theological
Series: Jenny Sixa
Major character(s): Jenny Sixa, Telepath, Detective—Amateur; Didi "Deeds" Myers, Robot, Researcher; Derrick Trent, Detective—Police
Time period(s): 2050s
Locale(s): Los Angeles, California

Summary: When, bored by her newly wealthy lifestyle, Jenny agrees to help Derrick identify a young murder victim, even her telepathic skills cannot reach the victim's last memories. Forensic tests show that an overdose of the illegal drug Zombie caused his death, while DNA tests prove him the son of a woman who denies ever having children. As thoughts broadcast by a sexual predator invade Jenny's dreams and a religious cult seeks to kill her, the police find another murdered teenager.

Where it's reviewed:
Publishers Weekly, October 6, 1997, page 81

Other books by the same author:
Circle of One, 1996

Other books you might like:
Isaac Asimov, *The Caves of Steel*, 1953
Alfred Bester, *The Demolished Man*, 1953
Philip K. Dick, *The Three Stigmata of Palmer Eldritch*, 1965
Lynn S. Hightower, *Alien Heat*, 1994
Colleen McCollough, *A Creed for the Third Millennium*, 1985
Amy Thomson, *Virtual Girl*, 1993

1106

DIANA G. GALLAGHER
MARTIN R. BURKE, Co-Author

The Chance Factor

(New York: Pocket, 1997)

Story type: Adventure; Young Adult
Series: Star Trek Voyager: Starfleet Academy
Major character(s): Kathryn Janeway, Student (Starfleet Academy), Leader
Time period(s): 24th century
Locale(s): Diehr IV, Planet—Imaginary; United Federation of Planets, Interstellar Empire/Federation

Summary: As a last opportunity to save her career, Starfleet Academy Cadet Kathryn Janeway leads a field study on a wilderness planet. The mission becomes more dangerous when they cannot leave the planet as expected.

Other books by the same author:
Honor Bound, 1997
The Alien Dark, 1990

Other books you might like:
Patricia Barnes-Svarney, *Quarantine*, 1997
Peter David, *Worf's First Adventure*, 1993
Alexei Panshin, *Rite of Passage*, 1968
Brad Strickland, *Crisis on Vulcan*, 1996
Brad Strickland, *The Star Ghost*, 1994
    Barbara Strickland, co-author
Bobbie J.G. Weiss, *Lifeline*, 1997
    David Cody Weiss, co-author

1107

R. GARCIA Y ROBERTSON

Atlantis Found

(New York: AvoNova, 1997)

Story type: Time Travel; Adventure
Series: Virgin and the Dinosaur
Major character(s): Jake Bento, Time Traveller, Guide; Sauromanta, Time Traveller, Warrior (Amazon); Hercules, Hero (demi-god)
Time period(s): Indeterminate Past; 27th century (2600s)
Locale(s): *Argo*, in the Air (airship); *Thetis*, Submarine

Summary: Jake leads a mission to the Bronze Age to rescue the three Special Temporal Operations teams lost trying to locate Atlantis. Jake and his team soon realize that future time travelers infiltrated their organization, stole the STOP equipment, and now attempt to block Jake's time from the portal. With the help of Hercules, Jake must rescue his team, take back his equipment and return to the future before Thera explodes, destroying Atlantis.

Other books by the same author:
The Virgin and the Dinosaur, 1996
The Spiral Dance, 1991

Other books you might like:
Poul Anderson, *Guardians of Time*, 1960

David Drake, *Arc Riders*, 1995
    Janet Morris, co-author
Fritz Leiber, *The Big Time*, 1961
Julian May, *The Many-Colored Land*, 1981
Andre Norton, *The Crossroads of Time*, 1956
S.D. Perry, *Timecop*, 1994

1108

JAMES ALAN GARDNER

Expendable

(New York: AvoNova, 1997)

Story type: Political; First Contact
Major character(s): Festina Ramos, Space Explorer, Military Personnel; Oar, Genetically Altered Being (glass woman); Yarrun Derigha, Space Explorer, Military Personnel
Time period(s): 25th century (2450s)
Locale(s): New Earth, Planet—Imaginary; *Jacaranda*, Spaceship; Melaquin, Planet—Imaginary

Summary: Since the Admiralty High Council noticed that the loss of ugly, unpopular crew members proves less disruptive to spaceship operations, all intelligent, physically flawed, but able children serve in the Explorer Corps. The League of Peoples prevents non-sapients, including anyone who would send a person to his death, from leaving his world. Festina and Yarrun must accompany the banished Admiral Chee to earthlike Melaquin, a planet from which no explorer has ever returned. On Melaquin, Festina discovers the High Council's ugly secret. First novel.

Where it's reviewed:
Locus, June 1997, page 29
Publishers Weekly, May 5, 1997, page 205

Other books you might like:
C.J. Cherryh, *Forty Thousand in Gehenna*, 1983
L. Warren Douglas, *Stepwater*, 1995
Anne McCaffrey, *The Ship Who Sang*, 1969
Elizabeth Moon, *Remnant Population*, 1996
Robert J. Sawyer, *Starplex*, 1996
Jack Vance, *Alastor*, 1995

1109

DAVID GARNETT, Editor

New Worlds

(Clarkston, Georgia: White Wolf, 1997)

Story type: Anthology

Summary: Contains an eight-page introduction, eight pages of authors' biographies, and 14 original stories by British authors or authors with strong ties to Great Britain, including one collaboration, "The White Stuff," by Peter F. Hamilton and Graham Joyce. From downbeat to ironic or humorous in tone, the stories explore diverse themes such as artificial reality, the future of death, rural life, technological innovation, relationships, and sports. Other authors include Brian W. Aldiss, Pat Cadigan, William Gibson, Garry Kilworth, Michael Moorcock, Kim Newman, Howard Waldrop, and Ian Watson.

Where it's reviewed:
Locus, October 1997, page 27

Other books you might like:
Kim Mohan, *Amazing Stories: The Anthology*, 1995
  editor
Michael Moorcock, *New Worlds 5*, 1974
  editor
Michael Moorcock, *New Worlds Quarterly Number 1-4*, 1971-1972
  editor
David Pringle, *The Best of Interzone*, 1997
  editor
Kristine Kathryn Rusch, *The Best of Pulphouse: The Hardback Magazine*, 1991
  editor

1110

DAVID GEMMELL

Wolf in Shadow
(New York: Ballantine Del Rey, 1997)

Story type: Post-Holocaust; Science Fantasy
Series: Stones of Power
Major character(s): Jon Shannow, Traveller, Warrior; Batik, Religious (satanist), Fugitive; Abaddon, Immortal, Ruler
Time period(s): Indeterminate Future
Locale(s): Rivervale, Fictional City; New Babylon, Fictional City

Summary: Centuries after civilization falls to natural catastrophe, humanity reestablishes itself. A wanderer in search of lost Jerusalem, Jon Shannow falls in with a band of pioneers looking for new land in a once-radioactive waste. Instead, they find a satanic empire and the beginnings of a new armageddon. First published in the United States as *The Jerusalem Man* (1987).

Where it's reviewed:
Kliatt, July 1997, page 14

Other books by the same author:
Ghost King, 1996
Knights of Dark Renown, 1993
Morningstar, 1993
Lion of Macedon, 1992
The King Beyond the Gate, 1988

Other books you might like:
Orson Scott Card, *Seventh Son*, 1987
Glen Cook, *The Black Company*, 1984
David Drake, *Old Nathan*, 1991
Stephen King, *The Dark Tower: The Gunslinger*, 1982
George R.R. Martin, *Fevre Dream*, 1982

1111

MOLLY GLOSS

The Dazzle of Day
(New York: Tor, 1997)

Story type: Generation Starship; Theological

Major character(s): Dolores Negrete, Settler; Juko Ohasi, Spacewoman; Cejo Indergard, Settler
Time period(s): 2050s; 23rd century (2250s)
Locale(s): Southwest; *Dusty Miller*, Spaceship; Planet—Imaginary

Summary: Dolores Negrete leaves the land her people farmed for 240 years when the Quakers buy a failed space station and emigrate to another solar system. Her descendant, Juko, lives with a curved sky in a Quaker society in which the small gene pool and radiation effects of sail work may damage offspring. Arriving at their destination proves stressful and requires immediate decisions that must take into account the high suicide rate.

Where it's reviewed:
Kirkus Reviews, April 15, 1997, page 597
Library Journal, May 15, 1997, page 106
New York Times Book Review, June 22, 1997, page 24
Science Fiction Chronicle, October 1997, page 48
Voice of Youth Advocates, October 1997, page 252

Other books you might like:
Brian W. Aldiss, *Starship*, 1959
Samuel R. Delany, *They Fly at Ciron*, 1993
Simon Hawke, *The Whims of Creation*, 1995
Joan Slonczewski, *Still Forms on Foxfield*, 1980
Sheri S. Tepper, *The Family Tree*, 1997
Sage Walker, *Whiteout*, 1996
Gene Wolfe, *Nightside the Long Sun*, 1993

1112

KATHLEEN ANN GOONAN

Mississippi Blue
(New York: Tor, 1997)

Story type: Genetic Manipulation; Arts
Major character(s): Verity, Clone, Genetically Altered Being; Blaze, Genetically Altered Being, Musician; Lightnin' Lil, Scientist (genetic engineer)
Time period(s): Indeterminate Future
Locale(s): Cincinnati, Ohio; *American Queen*, Mississippi River

Summary: Unwilling to fulfill her destiny as the queen of Queen City (Cincinnati), Verity infects the entire city with the Norleans Plague, which compels inhabitants to follow, via riverboat and raft, the fictional path of Tom Sawyer and Huckleberry Finn down the Mississippi River. En route, Verity and her charges encounter a wide variety of characters, including a woman infected to act as Mark Twain, some of whom know more about the Norleans Plague than they let on. Sequel to *Queen City Jazz*.

Where it's reviewed:
Kirkus Reviews, October 15, 1997, page 1560
Library Journal, November 15, 1997, page 79
Locus, January 1998, page 19
Publishers Weekly, November 24, 1997, page 56

Other books by the same author:
The Bones of Time, 1996
Queen City Jazz, 1994

Other books you might like:
Valerie J. Freireich, *Becoming Human*, 1995
Nicola Griffith, *Slow River*, 1995
Nancy Kress, *Beggars and Choosers*, 1994
Shariann Lewitt, *Interface Masque*, 1997
Linda Nagata, *The Bohr Maker*, 1995
Linda Nagata, *Deception Well*, 1997
Caroline Stevermer, *River Rats*, 1992
Tricia Sullivan, *Lethe*, 1995

1113

L.A. GRAF (Pseudonym of Julia Ecklar and Karen Rose Cercone)

Armageddon Sky

(New York: Pocket, 1997)

Story type: Space Opera; Disaster
Series: Star Trek: Day of Honor
Major character(s): Benjamin Sisko, Spaceship Captain, Military Personnel; Worf, Alien (Klingon), Military Personnel (commander); Julian Bashir, Doctor, Military Personnel
Time period(s): 24th century
Locale(s): Armageddon, Planet—Imaginary; U.S.S. *Defiant*, Spaceship; United Federation of Planets, Interstellar Empire/Federation

Summary: On a mission to rescue a shipload of scientists, Sisko and his crew have little trouble deflecting the cometary debris that bombards the planet. But they also must avoid betraying their presence to a Klingon ship and a Cardassian ship, in order to avert interstellar war. On the inhospitable planet, the Away Team discovers three groups of exiled Klingons, one of which holds the scientists and the key to a deadly secret.

Other books by the same author:
Time's Enemy, 1996
Caretaker, 1995
Extreme Prejudice, 1995
Death Count, 1992
Traitor Winds, 1990

Other books you might like:
C.J. Cherryh, *Downbelow Station*, 1981
Greg Cox, *Devil in the Sky*, 1995
 John Gregory Betancourt, co-author
Diane Duane, *My Enemy, My Ally*, 1984
Brad Ferguson, *A Flag Full of Stars*, 1991
Larry Niven, *Lucifer's Hammer*, 1977
 Jerry Pournelle, co-author
H. Beam Piper, *Little Fuzzy*, 1962
Howard Weinstein, *Deep Domain*, 1987

1114

SIMON R. GREEN

Deathstalker War

(New York: Roc, 1997)

Story type: Space Opera
Series: Life and Times of Owen Deathstalker

Major character(s): Owen Deathstalker, Revolutionary, Nobleman (deposed); Jenny Psycho, Revolutionary, Psychic; Frost, Military Personnel (investigator)
Time period(s): Indeterminate Future
Locale(s): Mistworld, Planet—Imaginary; Summerland, Planet—Imaginary

Summary: The rebellion comes to an end as Owen Deathstalker and his allies close in on Golgotha, capitol of the empire. However, the empress has many allies, while the threat of traitors and other hidden enemies remains.

Where it's reviewed:
Locus, September 1997, page 27
Starlog, August 1997, page 69

Other books by the same author:
Twilight of the Empire, 1997
Deathstalker Rebellion, 1996
Deathstalker, 1995
Blood and Honor, 1993
Hawk & Fisher, 1990

Other books you might like:
Iain M. Banks, *Consider Phlebas*, 1988
Allan Cole, *Sten*, 1984
 Chris Bunch, co-author
Frank Herbert, *Dune*, 1965
Sherwood Smith, *The Phoenix in Flight*, 1993
 Dave Trowbridge, co-author
David Weber, *On Basilisk Station*, 1993

1115

SIMON R. GREEN

Twilight of the Empire

(New York: Roc, 1997)

Story type: Space Opera; Collection
Series: Life and Times of Owen Deathstalker
Major character(s): Typhoid Mary, Psychic, Mentally Ill Person; John Silence, Military Personnel; Hunter, Pioneer
Time period(s): Indeterminate Future
Locale(s): Mistworld, Planet—Imaginary; Wolf IV, Planet—Imaginary

Summary: In the first of three short novels set just before the events of the Deathstalker Trilogy, Typhoid Mary pursues a strange mission on a planet of psychics. In the second, Silence investigates an abandoned mining colony, while in the third, a suicide planetary colonization team discovers an improbable paradise.

Where it's reviewed:
Starlog, September 1997, page 81

Other books by the same author:
Deathstalker War, 1997
Deathstalker Rebellion, 1996
Deathstalker, 1995
Shadow's Fall, 1994
Hawk & Fisher, 1990

Other books you might like:
Iain M. Banks, *The Player of Games*, 1989
Glen Cook, *The Dragon Never Sleeps*, 1988

Debra Doyle, *The Price of the Stars*, 1992
    John D. Macdonald, co-author
H. Beam Piper, *Space Viking*, 1963
Vernor Vinge, *A Fire upon the Deep*, 1992

1116

TERRENCE M. GREEN

Blue Limbo

(New York: Tor, 1997)

Story type: Cyberpunk; Political
Major character(s): Mitch Helwig, Police Officer; Sam Karoulis, Police Officer (Captain); Barbie Helwig, Child
Time period(s): 2000s
Locale(s): Toronto, Ontario, Canada

Summary: No longer able to stand by while corrupt police officers participate in criminal activity, Mitch gets fired for bombing their illegal drug operation. He buys illegal, state of the art weapons and goes slightly crazy when his wife proves to have a lover. Mitch must rescue his father and daughter, who have been kidnapped by criminals hirelings. Meanwhile, revival using Blue Limbo extends the life of Sam's brain for about a month, enabling him to clear Mitch.

Where it's reviewed:
Analog, July/August 1997, page 272
Fantasy & Science Fiction, April 1997, page 25
Kirkus Reviews, November 15, 1996, page 1639
Locus, January 1997, page 21
Starlog, June 1997, page 12

Other books by the same author:
Barking Dogs, 1988

Other books you might like:
Philip K. Dick, *Bladerunner*, 1982
Alan Dean Foster, *Montezuma Strip*, 1995
Katharine Kerr, *Polar City Blues*, 1990
Ian McDonald, *Terminal Cafe*, 1994
Neal Stephenson, *The Diamond Age*, 1995

1117

MARTIN H. GREENBERG, Editor

The New Hugo Winners, Volume IV

(New York: Baen, 1997)

Story type: Anthology; Science Fiction
Series: Hugo Winners

Summary: Contains brief individual introductions by Gregory Benford to nine stories given Science Fiction Achievement Awards, known as ''Hugo Awards,'' by voting members of World Science Fiction Conventions 1992-1994. Authors include Isaac Asimov, Janet Kagan, Nancy Kress, Charles Sheffield, Harry Turtledove and Connie Willis.

Other books by the same author:
Future Net, 1996 (Larry Segriff, co-editor)
After the King: Stories in Honor of J.R.R. Tolkien, 1992
The Super Hugos, 1992
Foundation's Friends, 1989

Amazing Science Fiction Stories: The Wild Years 1946-1955, 1987

Other books you might like:
Isaac Asimov, *The Hugo Winners 1-5*, 1962-1986
    editor
Isaac Asimov, *Isaac Asimov Presents the Great SF Stories: 1-25*, 1979-1992
    Martin H. Greenberg, co-editor
Isaac Asimov, *The New Hugo Winners*, 1989
    editor
James Morrow, *Nebula Awards 26-28*, 1992-1994
    editor
Connie Willis, *The New Hugo Winners, Volume III*, 1994
    Martin H. Greenberg, co-editor

1118

GAYLE GREENO

Mind Snare

(New York: DAW, 1997)

Story type: Arts; Family Saga
Major character(s): Glynn Webster Stanislaus, Actor, Teenager; Jerelynn Stanislaus, Actress; Vitarosa, Murderer, Religious
Time period(s): 22nd century (2158)
Locale(s): PabNeruda, Space Station; Texas Republic, Fictional Country (NetwArk and Houston); North America

Summary: Upon giving his ultimate performance in the Stanislaus Troupe, Glynn feels unprepared to relinquish his acting career, as required of males by troupe custom when they turn 15. When assassins almost kill his mother, the Great Jerelynn, Glynn preserves her mind in a forbidden brain box and takes over her roles while attempting to track down the would-be assassins.

Where it's reviewed:
Starlog, April 1988, page 14
Voice of Youth Advocates, December 1997, page 325

Other books by the same author:
Exiles' Return, 1995
Mind Speakers' Call, 1994
Finders-Seekers, 1993

Other books you might like:
Orson Scott Card, *The Worthing Saga*, 1991
Robert A. Heinlein, *Double Star*, 1956
Frederik Pohl, *Outnumbering the Dead*, 1992
Sheri S. Tepper, *Sideshow*, 1992
Jack Vance, *Showboat World*, 1975
Katie Waitman, *The Merro Tree*, 1997

1119

JOE HALDEMAN

Forever Peace

(New York: Ace, 1997)

Story type: Military; Political

Science Fiction

Major character(s): Julian Class, Military Personnel, Scientist; Amelia "Blaze" Harding, Scientist, Professor; Marty Larrin, Scientist
Time period(s): 2040s
Locale(s): Portobello, Mexico; Houston, Texas

Summary: In the Ngumi War, Julian, a platoon sergeant, maintains constant communication with his men and women, five of each, as part of his link to his remote-controlled soldierboy, a humanform robot. They maintain the link for ten days while in their pods at Portobello and then have 20 days off. Julian returns to Houston to teach and run physics experiments relating to the giant accelerator around Jupiter. Marty, an old friend of Blaze, invented the link and understands Blaze's desire to connect with Julian. The war troubles Julian because nanoforge technology produces everything. including nuclear weapons, although the war would by unnecessary if all could be trusted to use the technology fairly and responsibly.

Where it's reviewed:
Book World, October 26, 1997, page 8
Booklist, September 15, 1997, page 216
Kirkus Reviews, Septmeber 1, 1997, page 1344
Library Journal, October 15, 1997, page 97
Locus, October 1997, page 21

Other books by the same author:
None So Blind, 1996
Worlds Enough and Time, 1992
Worlds, 1981
All My Sins Remembered, 1977
The Forever War, 1975

Other books you might like:
Pat Cadigan, *Synners*, 1991
Michael Flynn, *In the Country of the Blind*, 1990
Robert J. Sawyer, *The Terminal Experiment*, 1995
Neal Stephenson, *Snow Crash*, 1992
G. Harry Stine, *Warbots*, 1988
Sage Walker, *Whiteout*, 1996

1120

PETER F. HAMILTON

Emergence

(New York: Warner Aspect, 1997)

Story type: Science Fiction; Political
Major character(s): Joshua Calvert, Businessman, Spaceman; Quinn Dexter, Religious
Time period(s): 26th century
Locale(s): Human Confederation, Interstellar Empire/Federation; Lalonde, Planet—Imaginary

Summary: Conflict arises between two fundamentally different starfaring cultures, the Edenists, genetically altered telepathic humans with sentient biological spaceships, and the Adamists, wizards of nanotechnology and computer science. First half of UK edition, *The Reality Dysfunction*, continued in *Expansion*.

Where it's reviewed:
Voice of Youth Advocates, February 1998, page 383

Other books by the same author:
Consolidation, 1998
The Nano Flower, 1998
Expansion, 1997
A Quantum Murder, 1997
Mindstar Rising, 1996

Other books you might like:
Roger MacBride Allen, *The Ring of Charon*, 1990
Cheryl J. Franklin, *Fire Crossing*, 1991
Cheryl J. Franklin, *Fire Get*, 1987
Cheryl J. Franklin, *Fire Lord*, 1989
Frank Herbert, *Dune*, 1965
Vernor Vinge, *A Fire upon the Deep*, 1992

1121

PETER F. HAMILTON

Expansion

(New York: Warner, 1997)

Story type: Space Opera
Series: The Reality Dysfunction
Major character(s): Graeme Nicholson, Reporter; Jenny Harris, Spacewoman; Joshua Calvert, Spaceman
Time period(s): 27th century
Locale(s): Outer Space

Summary: Humanity struggles to defeat the horrifying invasion that began in *Emergence* as it leapfrogs from one inhabited planet to the next across the galaxy. The invaders are truly nightmarish, a horde of the undead, with superpowers that fly in the face of both human science and religion.

Other books by the same author:
Emergence, 1997 (The Reality Dysfunction, Part 1)
A Quantum Murder, 1997
Mindstar Rising, 1996

Other books you might like:
Iain M. Banks, *Excession*, 1997
Greg Bear, *Eternity*, 1988
Victor Koman, *The Jehovah Contract*, 1987
Dan Simmons, *Endymion*, 1996
Dan Simmons, *The Rise of Endymion*, 1997
Vernor Vinge, *A Fire upon the Deep*, 1992

1122

PETER F. HAMILTON

A Quantum Murder

(New York: Tor, 1997)

Story type: Psychic Powers; Mystery
Series: Greg Mandel
Major character(s): Greg Mandel, Psychic, Detective; Edward Kitchener, Scientist; Eleanor Mandel, Spouse, Detective
Time period(s): 21st century
Locale(s): England

Summary: Ex-military psychic Greg Mandel tries to make an honest living, following the fall of the Marxist government in England. Then Event Horizon, the corporation that employed him in the past, calls him in to investigate the death of a

double Nobel laureate. There are too many leads, and some of them point to Mandel's uncomfortable past. Second in series, following *Mindstar Rising* and preceding *The Nano Flower*.

Where it's reviewed:
Booklist, October 1, 1997, page 312
Kirkus Reviews, September 15, 1997, page 1421
Library Journal, October 15, 1997, page 97
Publishers Weekly, September 22, 1997, page 73

Other books by the same author:
Emergence, 1997
Expansion, 1997
The Nano Flower, 1995
Mindstar Rising, 1993

Other books you might like:
Isaac Asimov, *The Caves of Steel*, 1954
Alfred Bester, *The Demolished Man*, 1996
Pat Cadigan, *Fools*, 1992
Larry Niven, *The Long ARM of Gil Hamilton*, 1976
Richard Paul Russo, *Destroying Angel*, 1992

`1123`

ELIZABETH HAND

Glimmering
(New York: HarperPrism, 1997)

Story type: Disaster; Future Shock
Major character(s): Jack Finnegan, Publisher, Recluse (AIDS survivor); Leonard Thorpe, Filmmaker; Trip Marlowe, Musician
Time period(s): 1990s (1999)
Locale(s): Yonkers, New York

Summary: The Millennium waits under a cloud of greenhouse gasses that turns the sky into a glowing sheet of color, while a dying publisher, a rock star obsessed by virtual reality, and the ''Hyacinth Girl'' wait in a dilapidated mansion for the end times. Then an enigmatic social observer arrives with a mystery, a cure, and the threat of the new.

Where it's reviewed:
Kirkus Reviews, January 15, 1997, page 104
Library Journal, March 15, 1997, page 93
Locus, March 1997, page 17
Publishers Weekly, February 3, 1997, page 99
Science Fiction Chronicle, November 1997, page 40

Other books by the same author:
12 Monkeys, 1995
Waking the Moon, 1995
Icarus Descending, 1993
AEstival Tide, 1992
Winterlong, 1990

Other books you might like:
J.G. Ballard, *The Drought*, 1976
Pat Cadigan, *Synners*, 1991
Stuart Gordon, *Smile on the Void*, 1981
Jonathan Lethem, *Amnesia Moon*, 1995
Michaela Roessner, *Vanishing Point*, 1993

`1124`

JACQUELINE HARPMAN

I Who Have Never Known Men
(New York: Seven Stories Press, 1997)

Story type: Post-Holocaust; Literary
Major character(s): I, Writer, Explorer; Anthea, Explorer; Greta, Explorer
Time period(s): Indeterminate Future
Locale(s): Earth

Summary: After civilization breaks down, men hold women captive in subterranean cages. By chance, at one prison the guards have just unlocked the women's door when an evacuation signal draws away all the guards. The 40 women escape, but must develop a new society, scavenging supplies from abandoned prisons and exploring the environment as time whittles away at their numbers. Winner of the 1996 Prix Medicis and translated from the 1995 French publication by Ros Schwartz. First novel published in English.

Where it's reviewed:
Asimov's Science Fiction, December 1997, page 148
New York Times Book Review, September 14, 1997, page 26

Other books you might like:
Richard Brautigan, *In Watermelon Sugar*, 1968
Marlen Haushofer, *The Wall*, 1991
Jean Hegland, *Into the Forest*, 1997
David R. Palmer, *Emergence*, 1984

`1125`

M. JOHN HARRISON

Signs of Life
(New York: St. Martin's, 1997)

Story type: Contemporary Realism; Genetic Manipulation
Major character(s): Mick ''China'' Rose, Truck Driver, Businessman; Isobel Avens, Genetically Altered Being; Choe Ashton, Truck Driver, Rebel
Time period(s): 1990s
Locale(s): London, England; Budapest, Hungary

Summary: The middle-aged and weary owner of a biological and medical delivery service, Mick Rose, relates how Isobel came into his life and left again. Mourning his loss, Mick struggles to understand why Isobel's dreams of flying led her to participate in dangerous and illegal molecular biology experiments.

Where it's reviewed:
Asimov's Science Fiction, March 1998, page 142
Kirkus Reviews, August 1, 1997, page 1136
Locus, June 1997, page 21
New York Times Book Review, November 2, 1997, page 36
Starlog, February 1998, page 36

Other books by the same author:
The Course of the Heart, 1992
Viriconium, 1988
The Ice Monkey and Other Stories, 1983
A Storm of Wings, 1980

Science Fiction

The Committed Men, 1971

Other books you might like:
J.G. Ballard, *Concrete Island*, 1974
J.G. Ballard, *Crash*, 1973
Nancy Kress, *Beggars and Choosers*, 1994
Christopher Priest, *The Perfect Lover*, 1977
S. Andrew Swann, *Specters of the Dawn*, 1994
H.G. Wells, *The Island of Dr. Moreau*, 1896

1126

WILLIAM HARTMANN

Mars Underground

(New York: Tor, 1997)

Story type: Political; Adventure
Major character(s): Alwyn Bryan Stafford, Explorer, Scientist (biology); Carter Jahns, Engineer, Administrator; Annie Pohaku, Journalist
Time period(s): 2030s (2032)
Locale(s): Hilo, Hawaii; Mars; Phobos, Mars ((moon of Mars))

Summary: On Mars longer than anyone else, Stafford disappears while on one of his semi-legal solo excursions, hoping the clues he left for Carter prove useful. Refusing to believe Stafford died when his oxygen ran out, Carter continues the search with Annie, who promises not to file her story without his permission when they uncover a conspiracy. First novel.

Where it's reviewed:
Booklist, June 1 & 15, 1997, page 1669
Kirkus Reviews, May 15, 1997, page 765
Library Journal, June 15, 1997, page 101
Locus, October 1997, page 27
Publishers Weekly, May 12, 1997, page 62

Other books you might like:
Greg Bear, *Moving Mars*, 1993
Ben Bova, *Mars*, 1992
William C. Dietz, *Mars Prime*, 1992
Robert A. Heinlein, *Red Planet*, 1949
Kim Stanley Robinson, *Red Mars*, 1993
S.C. Sykes, *Red Genesis*, 1991

1127

DAVID G. HARTWELL, Editor

The Science Fiction Century

(New York: Tor, 1997)

Story type: Anthology; Science Fiction

Summary: Contains a four-page introduction plus individual introductions to 45 stories, novellas and novelettes which investigate the truth of the human condition in this century as it relates to science and technology. From somber to upbeat in tone, the stories reflect diverse themes from well known authors including Poul Anderson, James Blish, Algis Budrys, Hal Clement, John Crowley, Harlan Ellison, Philip Jose Farmer, William Gibson, Frank Herbert, Rudyard Kipling, Nancy Kress, Philip Latham, Jack London, Frank Belknap Long, Richard A. Lupoff, James Morrow, Chad Oliver, Mar-

garet St. Clair, Michael Shaara, Robert Silverberg, Cordwainer Smith, Bruce Sterling, Michael Swanwick, William Tenn, George Turner, A.E. van Vogt, Jack Vance, Connie Willis, John Wyndham and Roger Zelazny.

Where it's reviewed:
Booklist, May 15, 1997, page 1567
Library Journal, June 15, 1997, page 100
Publishers Weekly, May 19, 1997 page 71

Other books by the same author:
Visions of Wonder: The Science Fiction Research Association Anthology, 1996 (Milton T. Wolf, co-editor)
Northern Stars: The Anthology of Canadian Science Fiction, 1994 (Glenn Grant, co-editor)
Masterpieces of Fantasy and Wonder, 1994
The Ascent of Wonder: The Evolution of Hard SF, 1994 (Kathryn Kramer, co-editor)
The World Treasury of Science Fiction, 1989

Other books you might like:
Mike Ashley, *The Random House Book of Science Fiction Stories*, 1997
editor
Isaac Asimov, *Isaac Asimov Presents the Great SF Stories: 1-25*, 1979-1992
Martin H. Greenberg, co-editor
Gardner Dozois, *Modern Classics of Science Fiction*, 1992
editor
Gardner Dozois, *The Year's Best Science Fiction Series*, 1984-1997
editor
Ursula K. Le Guin, *The Norton Book of Science Fiction: North American Science Fiction, 1960-1990*, 1993
Brian Attebery, co-editor
Tom Shippey, *The Oxford Book of Science Fiction Stories*, 1992
editor

1128

DAVID G. HARTWELL, Editor

Year's Best SF 2

(New York: HarperPrism, 1997)

Story type: Anthology; Science Fiction
Series: Year's Best SF

Summary: Contains a three-page introduction and individual introductions to 20 stories published in periodicals and anthologies in 1996. From humorous to somber in tone, the stories reflect diverse themes and genres such as hard science fiction, virtual reality, robots, modern society, space colonization, alternate universes, and evolution. Authors include Stephen Baxter, Gregory Benford, Terry Bisson, John Brunner, Kathleen Ann Goonan, Gwyneth Jones, James Patrick Kelly, Damon Knight, Robert Reed, Joanna Russ, Brian Stableford, Allen Steele, Bruce Sterling, Kate Wilhelm, Connie Willis, and Gene Wolfe.

Where it's reviewed:
Locus, June 1997, page 17

Other books by the same author:
Year's Best SF, 1996 (editor)

Visions of Wonder: The Science Fiction Research Association Anthology, 1996 (Milton T. Wolf, co-editor)
The Ascent of Wonder: The Evolution of Hard SF, 1994 (Kathryn Cramer, co-editor)
Northern Stars: The Anthology of Canadian Science Fiction, 1994 (Glenn Grant, co-editor)
The World Treasury of Science Fiction, 1989 (editor)

Other books you might like:
Isaac Asimov, *Isaac Asimov Presents the Great SF Stories: 1-25*, 1979-1992
    Martin H. Greenberg, co-editor
Greg Bear, *New Legends*, 1995
    Martin H. Greenberg, co-editor
Gardner Dozois, *The Year's Best Science Fiction Series*, 1984-
    editor
Jennifer Hershey, *Full Spectrum 5*, 1995
    Tom Dupree and Janna Silverstein, co-editors
Pamela Sargent, *Nebula Awards 31*, 1997
    editor

1129

RICHARD HATCH
CHRISTOPHER GOLDEN, Co-Author

Armageddon

(New York: Pocket, 1997)

Story type: Military
Series: Battlestar Galactica
Major character(s): Apollo, Warrior, Spaceman; Starbuck, Warrior, Spaceman
Time period(s): Indeterminate Future
Locale(s): Battlestar *Galactica*, Outer Space

Summary: With the succession of leadership in question and continuing threat from the Cylons, Apollo leaves Battlestar *Galactica* in search of Starbuck, presumed killed by Cylon raiders.

Other books you might like:
Roger MacBride Allen, *The Ring of Charon*, 1990
Christopher Golden, *Of Saints and Shadows*, 1994
Glen A. Larson, *Battlestar Galactica*, 1978
    Robert Thurston, co-author
Glen A. Larson, *The Cylon Death Machine*, 1979
    Robert Thurston, co-author
Glen A. Larson, *The Living Legend*, 1982
    Nicholas Yermakov, co-author
Glen A. Larson, *The Long Patrol*, 1984
    Ron Goulart, co-author

1130

JEAN HEGLAND

Into the Forest

(New York: Bantam, 1997)

Story type: Disaster
Major character(s): Eva, Teenager; Nell, Teenager, Writer
Time period(s): 1990s

Locale(s): California

Summary: Overseas warfare interrupts Eva's plans for a dance career and Nell's plans to attend Harvard. When civil strife causes electrical and telephone service to cease, Eva and Nell, now orphaned, must stretch their dwindling resources and learn to survive using the riches of the forest around their isolated home. First novel. Reissue of the 1996 Calyx Books edition.

Where it's reviewed:
Booklist, July 1996, page 1802
Library Journal, June 15, 1996, page 90
Publishers Weekly, May 13, 1996, page 71

Other books you might like:
Richard Brautigan, *In Watermelon Sugar*, 1968
David Brin, *The Postman*, 1985
Marlen Haushofer, *The Wall*, 1991
Sterling E. Lanier, *Hiero's Journey*, 1973
David R. Palmer, *Emergence*, 1984

1131

HOWARD V. HENDRIX

Lightpaths

(New York: Ace, 1997)

Story type: Space Colony; Utopia
Major character(s): Roger Cortland, Scientist, Researcher; Marissa Correa, Researcher, Student; Jhana Meniskos, Scientist, Researcher
Time period(s): 2040s
Locale(s): Orbital Biodiversity Preserve, Space Station (Orbital Park); High Orbital Mfg. Env., Space Station (Home)

Summary: On his way back to his laboratory on Orbital Park, Roger meets his new lab assistant, there to do research and study social systems with his mother, one of the founders of the Biodiversity Preserve. Also on the shuttle, Jhana, still troubled by the death of her ex-lover, shares Roger's line of study. Sent by one of the Earth-based investors of Orbital Park, Jhana must send back information about Diamond Thunderbolt, perhaps a weapon to be used against Earth. Meanwhile, the computer which controls the habitat seems more helpful lately.

Where it's reviewed:
Locus, October 1997, page 27

Other books by the same author:
The Vertical Fruit of the Horizontal Tree, 1994

Other books you might like:
Michael Flynn, *Firestar*, 1996
Melissa Scott, *Dreaming Metal*, 1997
Allen Steele, *Clarke County, Space*, 1990
Bruce Sterling, *Schismatrix Plus*, 1996
Harlan Thompson, *Silent Running*, 1972
John Varley, *Steel Beach*, 1992

Science Fiction

1132

JAMES P. HOGAN

Bug Park

(New York: Baen, 1997)

Story type: Adventure; Techno-Thriller
Major character(s): Kevin Heber, Teenager, Technician; Taki, Teenager, Technician; Vanessa Heber, Step-Parent, Scientist (neurophysiologist)
Time period(s): 1900s
Locale(s): Tacoma, Washington

Summary: Kevin thinks of his mini robots as toys to play with in Bug Park, a testing area in his back yard, but Vanessa's friends use them to kill people. When Kevin discovers that his father may become the next victim, he enlists Taki's help insinuating his robots into his father's car, his step-mother's car and her lover's boat. Caught by Vanessa, Kevin must find a way to escape and save his father's life.

Where it's reviewed:
Booklist, February 1, 1997, page 929
Kirkus Reviews, February 15, 1997, page 261
Library Journal, March 15, 1997, page 93
Publishers Weekly, March 24, 1997, page 63
Science Fiction Chronicle, October 1997, page 46

Other books by the same author:
Paths to Otherwhere, 1996
The Multiplex Man, 1992
The Proteus Operation, 1985
Code of the Lifemaker, 1983
The Gentle Giants of Ganymede, 1978

Other books you might like:
Stephen Bury, *Interface*, 1994
   pseudonyn of Neal Stephenson and George F. Jewsbury
Pat Cadigan, *Synners*, 1991
Wil McCarthy, *Murder in the Solid State*, 1996
Laura J. Mixon, *Glass Houses*, 1992
Sage Walker, *Whiteout*, 1996

1133

TERRY JONES

Douglas Adams's Starship Titanic

(New York: Harmony, 1997)

Story type: Humor; Adventure
Major character(s): Dan, Space Explorer, Traveller; Nettie, Space Explorer, Traveller; Lucy, Space Explorer, Traveller
Time period(s): Indeterminate Future
Locale(s): *Starship Titanic*, Spaceship; Outer Space

Summary: On the eve of the launch of his greatest achievement, designer Leovinus discovers unfinished and flawed construction on *Starship Titanic*, but cannot prevent its launch and immediate loss. Under autopilot, the ship lands on Earth and picks up Dan, Nettie and Lucy, who must explore the massive ship and help effect repairs, if they hope to see Earth again. Based on a CD-ROM adventure.

Where it's reviewed:
Booklist, September 15, 1997, page 180
Kirkus Reviews, September 1, 1997, page 1344
Publishers Weekly, September 22, 1997, page 73

Other books by the same author:
The Goblin Companion, 1996 (Brian Froud, Co-author)
Strange Stains and Mysterious Smells, 1996 (Brian Froud, Co-author)
Lady Cottington's Pressed Fairy Book, 1994 (Brian Froud, Co-author)
Nicobinus, 1987
The Saga of Eric the Viking, 1983

Other books you might like:
Douglas Adams, *The Hitchhiker's Guide to the Galaxy*, 1980
Douglas Adams, *The Restaurant at the End of the Universe*, 1982
Alan Dean Foster, *Dark Star*, 1974
Henry Kuttner, *Robots Have No Tails*, 1952
Ken Rolston, *Extreme Paranoia: Nobody Knows the Trouble I've Shot*, 1991
Charles Sheffield, *One Man's Universe*, 1993

1134

MICHAEL KANALY

Thoughts of God

(New York: Ace, 1997)

Story type: Theological; Science Fantasy
Major character(s): Dennison York, Mercenary, Hero; Yvonne Stafford, Abuse Victim; Arnie Watts, Serial Killer
Time period(s): 2000s
Locale(s): New York, New York; Lancaster, Pennsylvania

Summary: The experiment to further the development of immortal spirits by putting them into bodies may not succeed. Observation continues. On Earth, Arnie Watts escapes from Dennison York and his crew, kidnapping one of York's employees. York may go bankrupt, but cannot abandon the search for the serial killer despite his guilt at the death of his son's killers. First novel.

Where it's reviewed:
Kirkus Reviews, May 15, 1997, page 766
Library Journal, August 1997, page 141
New York Times Book Review, November 2, 1997, page 36
Voice of Youth Advocates, December 1997, page 36

Other books you might like:
David Brin, *Brightness Reef*, 1995
Orson Scott Card, *Lost Boys*, 1992
Parke Godwin, *Waiting for the Galactic Bus*, 1988
Ben Okri, *The Famished Road*, 1992
Susan Palwick, *Flying in Place*, 1992
Dan Simmons, *The Hollow Man*, 1992

1135

JAMES PATRICK KELLY

Think Like a Dinosaur and Other Stories

(Collinsville, Illinois: Golden Gryphon Press, 1997)

Story type: Collection

Summary: Contains a six-page introduction by John Kessel, the Hugo Award winning title story and 13 other stories from periodicals and anthologies 1984-1997. Varying in tone from downbeat to satirical, the stories feature diverse themes, such as heroism, dystopian futures, relationships, virtual reality, law and order, hallucinations and life in outer space.

Where it's reviewed:
Booklist, August 1997, page 1887
Kirkus Reviews, July 1, 1997, page 991
Locus, August 1997, page 17
Publishers Weekly, July 14, 1997, page 69
Science Fiction Chronicle, November 1997, page 40

Other books by the same author:
Wildlife, 1994
Look into the Sun, 1989
Planet of Whispers, 1984

Other books you might like:
Greg Bear, *The Wind From a Burning Woman*, 1983
John Kessel, *Freedom Beach*, 1985
    James Patrick Kelly, co-author
John Kessel, *Meeting in Infinity*, 1992
Nancy Kress, *The Aliens of Earth*, 1993
Lucius Shepard, *The Ends of the Earth*, 1991
James Tiptree Jr., *Her Smoke Rose Up Forever*, 1990

1136

KAY KENYON

The Seeds of Time

(New York: Bantam Spectra, 1997)

Story type: Time Travel; Dystopian
Major character(s): Clio Finn, Time Traveller, Pilot (Biotime Corp); Harper Teeg, Time Traveller, Traitor; Timothy Ashe, Time Traveller, Spy
Time period(s): Indeterminate Future; Indeterminate Past
Locale(s): *Starhawk*, Spaceship; *Galactique*, Spaceship; Niang, Planet—Imaginary

Summary: To revitalize Earth's biota, Biotime Corp time travelers explore the past of distant planets, searching for plants which could survive Earth's degraded environment. Illegally diverting forward in time on a mission, Clio Finn discovers the death of humanity in Earth's immediate future, then finds a possible miraculous solution to Earth's problems in Niang's past. When Harper Teeg attempts a mutiny which would force the team to stay on Niang, Clio's actions trigger cataclysmic changes which could provide humanity's survival, but with potentially disastrous consequences for all non-human life in the galaxy. First novel.

Where it's reviewed:
Locus, June 1997, page 29

Publishers Weekly, April 21, 1997, page 68
Other books you might like:
Greg Bear, *Eon*, 1985
Octavia E. Butler, *Dawn*, 1987
J.R. Dunn, *Days of Cain*, 1997
Fritz Leiber, *The Big Time*, 1961
Mike Resnick, *Prophet*, 1993
Joan Slonczewski, *A Door into Ocean*, 1986
John Varley, *Millennium*, 1983

1137

JOHN KESSEL

Corrupting Dr. Nice

(New York: Tor, 1997)

Story type: Time Travel; Theological
Major character(s): Owen Vannice, Scientist (palentologist), Time Traveller; Genevieva Faison, Con Artist, Time Traveller; Simon, Religious, Time Traveller
Time period(s): 1st century (AD 40); 21st century
Locale(s): Jerusalem, Middle East; Thornberry, Connecticut

Summary: Stranded in ancient Jerusalem with a rapidly growing baby dinosaur, Dr. Owen Vannice falls in love with Genevieve Faison, a time-traveling con artist. However, he must choose sides when Simon, a former disciple of Christ, leads a revolt against the time travelers who have turned Jerusalem into a tourist trap.

Where it's reviewed:
Booklist, January 1 & 15, 1997, page 826
Kirkus Reviews, November 15, 1997, page 1640
Library Journal, December 1996, page 152
Locus, January 1997, page 17
New York Times Book Review, January 26, 1997, page 22

Other books by the same author:
Intersections: The Sycamore Hill Anthology, 1996 (Mark L. Van Name, Richard Butner, co-editors)
Meeting in Infinity, 1992
Good News From Outer Space, 1989
Freedom Beach, 1985 (James Patrick Kelly, co-author)

Other books you might like:
Poul Anderson, *Guardians of Time*, 1981
Orson Scott Card, *Pastwatch: The Redemption of Christopher Columbus*, 1996
Bradley Denton, *Buddy Holly Is Alive and Well on Ganymede*, 1991
Parke Godwin, *Waiting for the Galactic Bus*, 1988
Connie Willis, *Remake*, 1995

1138

JOHN KESSEL

The Pure Product

(New York: Tor, 1997)

Story type: Collection

Summary: Contains a brief author's note plus two original and 17 stories from periodicals and anthologies 1980-1996. Vary-

ing in tone from serious to satirical, the stories explore themes such as time travel, alternate histories and popular literture, with three stories set in the milieu of *Corrupting Dr. Nice*.

Where it's reviewed:
Booklist, November 15, 1997, page 548
Kirkus Reviews, October 1, 1997, page 1494
Library Journal, October 15, 1997, page 97
Locus, November 1997, page 15
Publishers Weekly, October 27, 1997, page 56

Other books by the same author:
Corrupting Dr. Nice, 1997
Intersections: The Sycamore Hill Anthology, 1996 (Mark L. Van Name, Richard Butner, co-editors)
Meeting in Infinity, 1992
Good News From Outer Space, 1989
Freedom Beach, 1985 (James Patrick Kelly, co-cuthor)

Other books you might like:
Michael Flynn, *The Nanotech Chronicles*, 1991
Jonathan Lethem, *The Wall of the Sky, the Wall of the Eye*, 1996
Mary Rosenblum, *Synthesis & Other Virtual Realities*, 1996
Marc Stiegler, *The Gentle Seduction*, 1990
John Varley, *The Persistence of Vision*, 1978

1139

C.M. KORNBLUTH

His Share of Glory: The Complete Short Science Fiction of C.M. Kornbluth

(Framingham, Massachusetts: NESFA, 1997)

Story type: Collection

Summary: Contains a four-page introduction, ''Cyril,'' by Frederik Pohl, a two-page introduction by the editor, Timothy P. Szczesuil, and all 56 stories written by Kornbluth, best known for his collaborations with Judith Merril and Frederik Pohl. This volume includes his witty, acerbic and insightful stories, all first published before his death in 1958. The many classics include ''The Little Black Bag,'' ''The Mindworm,'' ''The Luckiest Man in Denv,'' ''The Silly Season,'' ''The Marching Morons'' and ''That Share of Glory.''

Where it's reviewed:
Booklist, April 1, 1997, page 1283
Library Journal, March 15, 1997, page 93
Locus, January 1998, page 15
Publishers Weekly, March 31, 1997, page 69
Science Fiction Chronicle, October 1997, page 48

Other books by the same author:
A Mile Beyond the Moon, 1958
Not This August, 1955
The Explorers, 1954
The Syndic, 1953
Takeoff, 1952

Other books you might like:
Alfred Bester, *Virtual Unrealities: The Short Fiction of Alfred Bester*, 1997
Henry Kuttner, *The Best of Henry Kuttner*, 1975
Fritz Leiber, *The Leiber Chronicles*, 1990

C.L. Moore, *The Best of C.L. Moore*, 1975
Theodore Sturgeon, *Thunder and Roses*, 1997

1140

NANCY KRESS

Dancing on Air

(San Francisco, California: Tachyon Publications, 1997)

Story type: Genetic Manipulation; Arts
Major character(s): Angel, Animal (dog); Caroline Olson, Dancer; Susan Matthews, Journalist, Parent
Time period(s): 21st century
Locale(s): New York, New York; Paris, France

Summary: The murder of genetically enhanced New York City Ballet Company dancers leads the director to lease Angel for Caroline's protection. Assigned to write a story on the ballet company, Susan, whose daughter studies with the company and hopes to dance with them professionally, becomes obsessed with genetic enhancement, which is illegal in the United States. Susan's investigation leads her to a professional conference on genetic enhancement and some horrifying possibilities. Contains a seven-page afterword by James Patrick Kelly.

Other books by the same author:
Beggar's Ride, 1996
Beggars and Choosers, 1994
Beggars in Spain, 1993
Brain Rose, 1990
An Alien Light, 1988

Other books you might like:
Peter S. Beagle, *The Rhinoceros Who Quoted Nietzsche and Other Odd Acquaintances*, 1997
Clifford D. Simak, *City*, 1952
Cordwainer Smith, *Norstrilia*, 1995
Cordwainer Smith, *The Rediscovery of Man*, 1993
Cherry Wilder, *Dealers in the Light and Darkness*, 1995

1141

FRITZ LEIBER

The Dealings of Daniel Kesserich

(New York: Tor, 1997)

Story type: Science Fiction
Major character(s): George Kramer, Writer; John Ellis, Doctor; Daniel Kesserich, Scientist
Time period(s): 1930s
Locale(s): Smithville, California

Summary: Subtitled ''A Study of the Mass-Insanity at Smithville,'' this short novel, written in the 1930s and lost for decades, relates the adventures of George Kramer, who comes to visit his good friends John Ellis and Daniel Kesserich following the death of Ellis's wife, and finds that the town is in the grip of the strange belief that she was buried prematurely. Seemingly supernatural materializations, disappearances and reappearances persuade Kramer that something extraordinary is going on, the explanation for which is rooted

in scientific research that Kesserich was involved in back in their college days.

Where it's reviewed:
Book World, February 2, 1997, page 11
Kirkus, January 1, 1997, page 28
Locus, April 1997, page 25
Necrofile #25, Summer 1997, page 10
Publishers Weekly, February 24, 1997, page 68

Other books by the same author:
Our Lady of Darkness, 1977
The Sinful Ones, 1953
Conjure Wife, 1953

Other books you might like:
L. Ron Hubbard, *Fear*, 1951
William Sloane, *To Walk the Night*, 1937
William Sloane, *The Edge of Running Water*, 1939

1142

JONATHAN LETHEM

As She Climbed Across the Table

(New York: Doubleday, 1997)

Story type: Satire
Major character(s): Alice Coombs, Scientist (particle physics); Philip Estrand, Professor
Time period(s): 1990s
Locale(s): California

Summary: An experiment creates a discontinuity in the fabric of the universe, a nothingness which the researchers name ''Lack.'' Lack develops intelligence and personality, becoming the object of Alice's obsession. In love with Alice and despairing at his loss of Alice's affection, Philip finally decides to confront Lack on his own.

Where it's reviewed:
Fantasy & Science Fiction, August 1997, page 21
Kirkus Reviews, January 15, 1997, page 83

Other books by the same author:
Girl in Landscape, 1998
The Wall of the Sky, the Wall of the Eye, 1996
Amnesia Moon, 1995
Gun, with Occasional Music, 1994

Other books you might like:
William Borden, *Superstoe*, 1968
Richard Brautigan, *The Hawkline Monster*, 1974
Alan Dean Foster, *To the Vanishing Point*, 1988
Christopher Priest, *The Prestige*, 1996
Kurt Vonnegut Jr., *Cat's Cradle*, 1963

1143

SHARIANN LEWITT

Interface Masque

(New York: Tor, 1997)

Story type: Arts; Political

Major character(s): Cecilie 8 Sept-Fortune, Apprentice, Computer Expert; David Gavrilli, Heir, Runaway; Lina, Apprentice, Singer
Time period(s): 21st century
Locale(s): Venice, Italy; Rome, Italy

Summary: Stunned that she must illegally hack into a computer system to pass her last apprentice test in the great Sept-Fortune computer guild, Cecilie learns about the Sept houses' attempts to control the net and restrict free thought, in part by prohibiting innovative forms of music such as jazz.

Where it's reviewed:
Booklist, April 1, 1997, page 1283
Kirkus Reviews, February 15, 1997, page 262
Library Journal, March 15, 1997, page 93
Locus, April 1997, page 27
Voice of Youth Advocates, October 1997, page 238

Other books by the same author:
Memento Mori, 1995
First and Final Rights, 1984

Other books you might like:
David Brin, *Glory Season*, 1993
Orson Scott Card, *Songmaster*, 1980
Nicola Griffith, *Slow River*, 1995
Katharine Kerr, *Palace*, 1996
    Mark Kreighbaum, co-author
S.N. Lewitt, *Blind Justice*, 1991
S.N. Lewitt, *Cyberstealth*, 1989
S.N. Lewitt, *Dancing Vac*, 1991
Linda Nagata, *The Bohr Maker*, 1995
Mary Rosenblum, *The Stone Garden*, 1995
Katie Waitman, *The Merro Tree*, 1997

1144

BRAD LINAWEAVER, Editor
EDWARD E. KRAMER, Co-Editor

Free Space

(New York: Tor, 1996)

Story type: Anthology

Summary: Contains a two-page introduction by Linaweaver plus individual introductions to two reprinted and 18 original stories, generally upbeat in tone, that explore Libertarian futures in space. Authors include Dafydd ab Hugh, Poul Anderson, Gregory Benford, Ray Bradbury, William F. Buckley, Jr., Arthur Byron Cover, Peter Crowther, John DeChancie, James P. Hogan, Victor Koman, Brad Linaweaver, Robert J. Sawyer, J. Neil Schulman, L. Neil Smith, Robert Anton Wilson, and William Wu.

Where it's reviewed:
Booklist, June 1 & 15, 1997, page 1669
Kirkus Reviews, May 1, 1997, page 686
Library Journal, August 1997, page 141
Locus, July 1997, page 17
Publishers Weekly, June 16, 1997, page 50

Other books by the same author:
Sliders: The Novel, 1996
Moon of Ice, 1988

Other books you might like:
Robert Adams, *Alternatives*, 1989
    Pamela Crippin Adams, co-author
Robert A. Heinlein, *The Moon Is a Harsh Mistress*, 1966
L. Neil Smith, *The Probability Broach*, 1980
F. Paul Wilson, *The LaNague Chronicles*, 1992

1145

HOLLY LISLE

Hunting the Corrigan's Blood

(New York: Baen, 1997)

Story type: Genetic Manipulation; Political
Major character(s): Cadence "Cady" Drake, Spaceship Captain; Strebban "Badger" Bede, Spaceman, Computer Expert; Peter Crane, Businessman (spaceship builder), Political Figure
Time period(s): Indeterminate Future
Locale(s): Cassamir Station, Space Station; *Hope's Reward*, Spaceship

Summary: Lifelong friends and companions since Cady ran away from her mother and the trouble she caused, Cady and Badger search for *Corrigan's Blood* stolen from Peter Crane. *Corrigan's Blood* uses a new drive which enables the spaceship to change course while in hyperdrive, making it very difficult to catch. It also seems that the thieves belong to a history cult whose members physically alter themselves to become super strong, but, unfortunately, can no longer survive without fresh human blood.

Where it's reviewed:
Kliatt, July 1997, page 18
Locus, May 1997, page 29
Science Fiction Chronicle, June 1997, page 41
Starlog, September 1997, page 81

Other books by the same author:
Mall, Mayhem and Magic, 1995 (Chris Guin, co-author)
Mind of the Magic, 1995
Minerva Wakes, 1994
Bones of the Past, 1993
Fire in the Mist, 1992

1146

H.P. LOVECRAFT

The Annotated H.P. Lovecraft

(New York: Dell, 1997)

Story type: Collection

Summary: Four stories by horror master H.P. Lovecraft, each annotated extensively with information on their composition, influences and historical lore. Included are "At the Mountains of Madness," a tale of horrors from beyond space and time that befall an expedition to the Anartic; "The Dunwich Horror," in which an extradimensional monster rampages through the New England countryside; and "The Colour out of Space," about a meteorite that unleashes an alien life form on a small farm. S.T. Joshi, the leading Lovecraft Scholar, contributes an introduction, an appendix outlining Love-

craft's philosophy of weird fiction, and a secondary bibliography.

Where it's reviewed:
Washington Post Book World, October 26, 1997, page 12

Other books by the same author:
The Shadow Over Insmouth, 1994
Dagon and Other Macabre Tales, 1986
The Dunwich Horror and Others, 1985
At the Mountains of Madness, 1985

Other books you might like:
Robert Bloch, *The Early Fears*, 1994
Frank Belknap Long, *The Hounds of Tindalos*, 1946
Clark Ashton Smith, *Out of Space and Time*, 1941
Donald Wandrei, *Don't Dream*, 1997

1147

H.P. LOVECRAFT

Tales of H.P. Lovecraft

(Hopewell, New Jersey: Ecco Press, 1997)

Story type: Collection

Summary: Joyce Carol Oates compiles and introduces a collection of ten of the best stories by H.P. Lovecraft, the writer whose tales of cosmic horror, published primarily in the pulp magazines of the early twentieth century, are credited with bringing the horror story out of the Gothic tradition and into the twentieth century. Included are "The Outsider," an homage to Poe; "The Shadow out of Time," about a man kidnapped by a cosmic race to write the history of the Earth; "The Shadow over Innsmouth," about a race of fish-like creatures who have taken over a New England seaside town; "The Music of Erich Zann," about a musician whose art opens the door to another dimension; and "The Call of Cthulhu," which maps the mythology of a race of extradimensional beings who embody the chaos of the universe.

Where it's reviewed:
Book World, October 26, 1997, page 12

Other books by the same author:
Don't Dream, 1997
Dagon and Other Macabre Tales, 1986
The Dunwich Horror and Others, 1985
At the Mountains of Madness, 1985

Other books you might like:
Robert Bloch, *The Early Fears*, 1994
Frank Belknap Long, *The Hounds of Tindalos*, 1946
Clark Ashton Smith, *Out of Space and Time*, 1941
Donald Wandrei, *Don't Dream*, 1997

1148

IAN R. MACLEOD

The Great Wheel

(New York: Harcourt Brace, 1997)

Story type: Theological; Medical
Major character(s): John "Skiddle" Alston, Religious (priest); Felipe, Religious (priest); Tim Purdoe, Doctor

Time period(s): Indeterminate Future

Locale(s): Hemhill, England; Endless City, Africa; Rome, Italy

Summary: As a child, John's brother explained how the Borderers worked the fields, as the Europeans could no longer stay out in the sun. Later, as a priest in the Endless City, John observes the suffering of the Borderers, trying to cure with medicine, but unable to give the modern medical implants which prevent disease. Unfortunately, John's immune system cannot protect him when he exposes himself to the Borderer environment. He acquires the acute myeloid anemia which seems to be spreading through the Endless City. First novel.

Where it's reviewed:

Asimov's Science Fiction, August, 1997, page 143
Fantasy & Science Fiction, October/November 1997, page 36
Kirkus Reviews, June 15, 1997, page 916
Publishers Weekly, June 30, 1997, page 64

Other books by the same author:
Voyages by Starlight, 1997

Other books you might like:
Patricia Anthony, *God's Fires*, 1997
James Blish, *A Case of Conscience*, 1958
Frank Herbert, *Dune*, 1965
Mary Doria Russell, *The Sparrow*, 1996
N. Lee Wood, *Faraday's Orphans*, 1997

1149

IAN R. MACLEOD

Voyages by Starlight

(Sauk City, Wisconsin: Arkham House, 1997)

Story type: Collection; Fantasy

Summary: Contains a four-page foreward by Michael Swanwick and 10 stories reprinted from periodicals 1990-1995. Frequently downbeat to horrifying in tone, the stories occasionally reflect more than genre and include diverse themes such as an industrialized fantasy world, growing up, events at a lonely Arctic weather station during World War II and a world like our own but with a three-sexed human race.

Where it's reviewed:

Locus, September 1997, page 29
Publishers Weekly, July 28, 1997, page 58
Science Fiction Chronicle, November 1997, page 40

Other books by the same author:
The Great Wheel, 1997

Other books you might like:
Alexander Jablokov, *The Breath of Suspension*, 1994
Nancy Kress, *The Aliens of Earth*, 1993
Mary Rosenblum, *Synthesis & Other Virtual Realities*, 1996
Michael Swanwick, *Gravity's Angels*, 1991
James Tiptree Jr., *Her Smoke Rose Up Forever*, 1990

1150

LOUISE MARLEY

Receive the Gift

(New York: Ace, 1997)

Story type: Lost Colony; Psychic Powers

Series: Sing the Light

Major character(s): Siri, Psychic (esper), Singer; Mreen, Psychic (esper), Child; Jakri, Psychic (esper), Singer

Time period(s): Indeterminate Future

Locale(s): Nevya, Planet—Imaginary

Summary: Only Singers trained at Conservatory generate enough heat to maintain a viable temperature during the years-long winters on Nevya, but fewer talented children have been discovered in recent years. Siri believes the sequestered life at Conservatory proves too difficult for many parents, so the talents go untrained. She starts her own school at Observatory for the talented children born there, since Conservatory refuses to recognize Observatory or send them the Singers they need to survive. Third in series.

Where it's reviewed:

Locus, November 1997, page 25

Other books by the same author:
Sing the Warmth, 1996
Sing the Light, 1995

Other books you might like:
Maya Kaathryn Bohnhoff, *The Meri*, 1992
Suzette Haden Elgin, *Earthsong*, 1994
Nina Kiriki Hoffman, *The Thread That Binds the Bones*, 1994
Rosemary Kirstein, *The Steerswoman*, 1989
Anne McCaffrey, *The Rowan*, 1990
Sheri S. Tepper, *Raising the Stones*, 1990

1151

SUSAN R. MATTHEWS

An Exchange of Hostages

(New York: AvoNova, 1997)

Story type: Medical; Political

Major character(s): Andrej Koscuisko, Physician, Student (inquisitor/torturer); Joslire Curran, Slave (bond-involuntary), Martial Arts Expert (student); Mergau Noycannir, Civil Servant (clerk of court), Student (inquisitor/torturer)

Time period(s): Indeterminate Future

Locale(s): Fleet Orientation Station Med., Space Station; Interstellar Empire/Federation

Summary: Bowing to family pressure, talented neurosurgeon Andrej Koscuisko submits to training in prolonging and intensifying pain, preparing for a career as inquisitor, one of the torturers necessary for maintaining control in an empire based on slavery. However, fellow student Mergau Noycannir intends to break the Fleet's monopoly on inquisitors by graduating as inquisitor without medical credentials. First novel.

Where it's reviewed:

Analog, October 1997, page 148
Locus, July 1997, page 25

Starlog, July 1997, page 67

Other books you might like:
Orson Scott Card, *Ender's Game*, 1985
Samuel R. Delany, *They Fly at Ciron*, 1993
Stephen R. Donaldson, *The Gap into Conflict: The Real Story*, 1991
Elizabeth A. Lynn, *The Sardonyx Net*, 1981
Gene Wolfe, *The Shadow of the Torturer*, 1980

1152

ANNE MCCAFFREY
MARGARET BALL, Co-Author

Acorna

(New York: HarperPrism, 1997)

Story type: First Contact; Political
Major character(s): Acorna, Alien, Foundling; Declan "Gill" Gioglie III, Spaceman, Miner; Judit Kendoro, Scientist (psycholinguistics), Heroine
Time period(s): Indeterminate Future
Locale(s): *Khedive*, Spaceship; Laboue, Planet—Imaginary; Maganos, Planet—Imaginary

Summary: Gill and the others on *Khedive*, a mining ship, rescue Acorna, an alien child. Acorna proves useful and intelligent, but the company they return to only wants to mutilate and abuse her. Judit helps Gill rescue Acorna, who soon uncovers a ring of child slavers led by a man known only as the Pied Piper.

Where it's reviewed:
Booklist, June 1 & 15, 1997, page 1669
Kirkus Reviews, May 1, 1997, page 684
Library Journal, June 15, 1997, page 101
Locus, May 1997, page 29
Voice of Youth Advocates, December 1997, page 326

Other books by the same author:
Freedom's Landing, 1995
Powers That Be, 1993 (Elizabeth Anne Scarborough, co-author)
Damia, 1992
Decision at Doona, 1969
Dragonflight, 1968

Other books you might like:
Margaret Ball, *Mathemagics*, 1996
Margaret Ball, *The Shadow Gate*, 1991
Orson Scott Card, *Wyrms*, 1987
Alan Dean Foster, *The Tar-Aiym Krang*, 1972
Sheri S. Tepper, *Grass*, 1989

1153

ANNE MCCAFFREY

Dragonseye

(New York: Ballantine, Del Rey, 1997)

Story type: Lost Colony; Political
Series: Pern
Major character(s): K'vin, Leader (Telgar Weyr); Chalkin, Leader (Bita Hold); Clisser, Musician, Professor
Time period(s): Indeterminate Future ((258 years after landing))
Locale(s): Pern, Planet—Imaginary; Telgar, Mythical Place; Fort Hold, Fictional City

Summary: Holder Chalkin refuses to prepare for Thread, endangering all Bitrians, as Thread, according to historical records, lasts 50 years and depletes available resources. Clisser encourages Jemmy to write the Duty ballad as a teaching tool for future generations. Fortunately music proves suitable for most subjects, overcoming the lack of material resources and failing Earth technology. British title is *Red Star Rising*, (published in 1996 in the U.K.). First novel in the second Chronicles of Pern series.

Where it's reviewed:
Booklist, December 15, 1996, page 692
Kirkus Reviews, December 15, 1996, page 1773
Library Journal, February 15, 1997, page 165
Locus, December 1996, page 33
School Library Journal, July 1997, page 116

Other books by the same author:
Freedom's Landing, 1995
The Crystal Singer, 1982
The Ship Who Sang, 1969
Decision at Doona, 1969
Dragonflight, 1969

Other books you might like:
David Brin, *Startide Rising*, 1995
L. Warren Douglas, *Cannon's Orb*, 1994
Janet Kagan, *Mirabile*, 1991
Ursula K. Le Guin, *The Word for World Is Forest*, 1976
Louise Marley, *Sing the Light*, 1996

1154

ANNE MCCAFFREY

Freedom's Choice

(New York: Ace/Putnam, 1997)

Story type: Adventure; First Contact
Series: Freedom's Landing
Major character(s): Kris Bjornson, Slave, Castaway; Zainal, Alien (Catteni), Castaway; Chuck Mitford, Military Personnel (sargeant), Castaway
Time period(s): 1990s
Locale(s): Botany, Planet—Imaginary

Summary: In the process of colonizing Botany, the castaways contact the aliens farming the planet, hoping to find an ally against the Catteni and the Eosi who use them. Zainal avoids a fate worse than death by remaining on Botany, while the Catteni, attempting to force his return, inadvertently antagonize the alien farmers.

Where it's reviewed:
Booklist, April 1, 1997, page 1269
Kirkus Reviews, April 1, 1997, page 509
Library Journal, May 15, 1997, page 106
Locus, March 1997, page 29
New York Times Book Review, June 22, 1997, page 24

Other books by the same author:
Dragonseye, 1997
Freedom's Landing, 1995
Decision at Doona, 1969
The Ship Who Sang, 1969
Dragonflight, 1968

Other books you might like:
David Brin, *Brightness Reef*, 1995
Rosemary Kirstein, *The Outskirter's Secret*, 1992
Amy Thomson, *The Color of Distance*, 1995
Vernor Vinge, *A Fire upon the Deep*, 1992
David Weber, *Mutineer's Moon*, 1991

1155

JACK MCDEVITT

Eternity Road

(New York: HarperPrism, 1997)

Story type: Post-Disaster; Quest
Major character(s): Chaka Milana, Hunter, Scholar; Flojian Endine, Businessman (ferry boat operator); Quait Esterhok, Military Personnel
Time period(s): Indeterminate Future
Locale(s): Mississippi River, North America; New England

Summary: Only one member of an expedition to find Abraham Polk's Haven returns, dying soon after. Nevertheless, chafing at restrictions on a woman's role in Illyria, Chaka Milana decides to mount a second expedition. When half their number die almost immediately, the three survivors continue, finding Haven different than they expect with an expanding civilization having more technology and further knowledge of the Roadmaker culture.

Where it's reviewed:
Booklist, May 15, 1997, page 1567
Kirkus Reviews, March 15, 1997, page 423
Library Journal, May 15, 1997, page 106
Locus, November 1997, page 21
Science Fiction Chronicle, June 1997, page 41

Other books by the same author:
Ancient Shores, 1996
Standard Candles: The Best Short Fiction of Jack McDevitt, 1996
The Engines of God, 1994
A Talent for War, 1989
The Hercules Text, 1986

Other books you might like:
Poul Anderson, *Orion Shall Rise*, 1983
Leigh Brackett, *The Long Tomorrow*, 1955
Kathleen Ann Goonan, *Queen City Jazz*, 1994
Sterling E. Lanier, *Hiero's Journey*, 1973
Andre North, *Daybreak. . .2250 A.D.*, 1954
Edgar Pangborn, *Davy*, 1964
Clifford D. Simak, *A Heritage of Stars*, 1977
Paul O. Williams, *The Song of the Axe*, 1984

1156

DONALD E. MCQUINN

With Full Honors

(New York: Ballantine Del Rey, 1997)

Story type: Political; Military
Major character(s): Casey, Royalty; Lannat, Military Personnel
Time period(s): Indeterminate Future
Locale(s): Interstellar Empire/Federation

Summary: As various forces scheme to overthrow the emperor and the rulers of the 12 planets, Prince Casey becomes the catalyst and rallying point for more than one faction. Torn between his personal devotion to Casey and his oath to the Empire, Lannat strives to save Casey's honor.

Other books by the same author:
Witch, 1994
Wanderer, 1993
Warrior, 1990

Other books you might like:
Gordon R. Dickson, *Dorsai!*, 1976
David Weber, *On Basilisk Station*, 1993
David Weber, *Path of the Fury*, 1992
M.K. Wren, *House of the Wolf*, 1981

1157

WALTER M. MILLER JR.

Saint Leibowitz and the Wild Horse Woman

(New York: Bantam, 1997)

Story type: Religious; Satire
Major character(s): Blacktooth "Nimmy" St. George, Religious (monk), Linguist; Elia Brownpony, Religious (cardinal), Leader (pope); Aedrea, Mutant, Femme Fatale
Time period(s): 33rd century
Locale(s): Great Plains, North America; Valana, Fictional City; Abbey of St. Leibowitz, Mythical Place

Summary: Learning to speak the Nomad tongue, Elia Cardinal Brownpony, Vicar Apostolic to the Three Hordes, spends his time and effort forging an alliance between the wild people of the Plains and the exiled papacy in its Rocky Mountain refuge at Valana. Obeying orders from his abbott while suffering a crisis of faith, and standing on the brink of expulsion from the Order of St. Leibowitz for his rebellion, Brother Blacktooth St. George accompanies Cardinal Brownpony as secretary and translator while Brownpony seeks to defeat the Emperor of Imperial Texark and reunite the church under one pope. Sequel to *A Canticle for Leibowitz*.

Where it's reviewed:
Booklist, September 1, 1997, page 7
Kirkus Reviews, August 15, 1997, page 1265
Library Journal, October 15, 1997, page 97
Locus, September 1997, page 17
Science Fiction Chronicle, November 1997, page 39

Other books by the same author:

Beyond Armaggedon: Twenty-One Sermons to the Dead, 1985 (Martin H. Greenberg, co-editor)
The Best of Walter M. Miller, Jr., 1980
The Science Fiction Stories of Walter M. Miller, Jr., 1978
The View From the Stars, 1965
A Canticle for Leibowitz, 1960

Other books you might like:

Neil Gaiman, *Good Omens: The Nice and Accurate Prophecies of Agnes Nutter, Witch,* 1990
   Terry Pratchett, co-author
Parke Godwin, *Waiting for the Galactic Bus,* 1988
Robert A. Heinlein, *Job: A Comedy of Justice,* 1984
James Morrow, *Bible Stories for Adults,* 1996
Anne Rice, *Memnoch the Devil,* 1995
Sheri S. Tepper, *Grass,* 1989
Paul O. Williams, *The Breaking of Northwall,* 1984

1158

L.E. MODESITT JR.

The Ecolitan Enigma

(New York: Tor, 1997)

Story type: Political; Space Opera
Series: Ecolitan Institute
Major character(s): Nathaniel Firstborne Whaler, Professor (economics), Agent (Ecolitan Institute); Sylvia Ferro-Maine, Professor (economics), Agent (Ecolitan Institute)
Time period(s): Indeterminate Future
Locale(s): Accord, Planet—Imaginary; Artos, Planet—Imaginary

Summary: Sent to the backwater colony planet Artos, ostensibly to perform an economic study, Nathaniel and his Ecolitan colleague Sylvia find themselves the targets of several sabotage and murder attempts. When they dig deeper and discover that two empires use Artos as the focal point of a brewing conflict, they employ every means at their disposal to avert an interstellar war.

Where it's reviewed:

Analog, November 1997, page 147
Booklist, June 1 & 15, 1997, page 1669
Kirkus Reviews, May 1, 1997, page 685
Library Journal, May 15, 1997, page 106
Publishers, Weekly, May 12, 1997, page 62

Other books by the same author:

Adiamante, 1996
The Parafaith War, 1996
The Ecologic Secession, 1990
The Ecolitan Operation, 1989
The Ecologic Envoy, 1986

Other books you might like:

Jane Emerson, *City of Diamond,* 1996
Valerie J. Freireich, *Becoming Human,* 1995
Frank Herbert, *Dune,* 1965
Kim Stanley Robinson, *Red Mars,* 1993
Sheri S. Tepper, *Grass,* 1989
Joan D. Vinge, *The Summer Queen,* 1991

Margaret Weis, *The Knights of Black Earth,* 1995
   Don Perrin, co-author

1159

STEPHEN MOLSTAD

Silent Zone

(New York: HarperPrism, 1997)

Story type: First Contact; UFO
Series: Independence Day
Major character(s): Albert Alexander Nimziki, Government Official (CIA); Brackish Okun, Genius, Researcher; Sam Dworkin, Researcher, Aged Person
Time period(s): 1970s (1972)
Locale(s): Area 51, Nevada; Washington, District of Columbia

Summary: Nimziki takes control of the project at Area 51, where a few aged scientists study the wrecked Roswell UFO and the three dead aliens. Recognizing the need for a new leader for the project, he finds the young Brackish Okun, about to graduate Cal Tech, and has him introduced on a five-year to life contract, during which time Brackish discovers how to work the power system and finds a functional, undiscovered UFO.

Other books you might like:

David Brin, *Earth,* 1990
A.C. Crispin, *V,* 1984
John DeChancie, *Living with Aliens,* 1995
Dean Devlin, *Independence Day,* 1996
   Roland Emmerich, Stephen Molstad, co-authors
Robert Doherty, *Area 51,* 1997
Anne McCaffrey, *Freedom's Landing,* 1995

1160

ELIZABETH MOON

Once a Hero

(New York: Baen, 1997)

Story type: Space Opera; Political
Major character(s): Esmay Suiza, Spacewoman, Military Personnel (lieutenant); Arhos Asperson, Criminal; Serrano, Military Personnel, Spacewoman
Time period(s): Indeterminate Future
Locale(s): *Harrier,* Spaceship; Altiplano, Planet—Imaginary; Koskiusko, Space Station

Summary: Having saved the planet Xavier from invasion after preventing the Captain from giving the ship to the *Bloodhorde,* Esmay stands trial for mutiny. Cleared by the Military Board for acting as captain and cleared by the court martial for mutiny, Esmay returns to Altiplano, there discovering the lies that had undermined her belief in herself. Now assigned to the *Koskiusko,* Esmay returns from leave, and she must prevent Arhos from giving it to the *Bloodhorde* for longevity drugs.

Where it's reviewed:

Booklist, February 1, 1997, page 929
Kirkus Reviews, January 1, 1997, page 28
Library Journal, March 15, 1997, page 93

Locus, January 1997, page 27
Science Fiction Age, March 1997, page 16

Other books by the same author:
Phases, 1997
Remnant Population, 1996
Hunting Party, 1993
Liar's Oath, 1992
Sheepfarmer's Daughter, 1988

Other books you might like:
Poul Anderson, *Ensign Flandry*, 1966
Lois McMaster Bujold, *Shards of Honor*, 1986
Alfred Coppel, *Glory's War*, 1995
David Feintuch, *Midshipman's Hope*, 1994
David Weber, *On Basilisk Station*, 1993

1161

ELIZABETH MOON

Phases

(New York: Baen, 1997)

Story type: Collection

Summary: Contains a brief introduction plus individual introductions to 15 stories published between 1986 and 1995, about half from *Lunar Activity* (1990) and half original to this volume. Themes include art, cloning, character, horses and humor.

Other books by the same author:
Once a Hero, 1997
Remnant Population, 1996
Hunting Party, 1993
Liar's Oath, 1992
Sheepfarmer's Daughter, 1988

Other books you might like:
Alfred Bester, *Virtual Unrealities: The Short Fiction of Alfred Bester*, 1997
Nancy Kress, *The Aliens of Earth*, 1993
Henry Kuttner, *The Best of Henry Kuttner*, 1975
Mary Rosenblum, *Synthesis & Other Virtual Realities*, 1996
Connie Willis, *Impossible Dreams*, 1994

1162

WARD MOORE

Bring the Jubilee

(New York: Ballantine Del Rey, 1997)

Story type: Time Travel; Alternate Universe
Major character(s): Hodgins ''Hodge'' Backmaker, Historian, Time Traveller; Rene Enfandin, Diplomat; Barbara Haggerwells, Inventor, Time Traveller
Time period(s): 1860s (1863); 20th century (1938-1952)
Locale(s): New York, New York; Pennsylvania; Alternate Earth

Summary: In an impoverished United States where the Confederacy won the Civil War, the War of Southern Independence, Hodge Backmaker goes to New York City and becomes involved with gangs. From Haven, a study institute in

Pennsylvania where Barbara Haggerwells invents time travel, Hodge travels to view the battle of Gettysburg and changes history to create our world. Contains a three-page introduction by Jeff Shaara. Reissue of the 1953 classic by Moore (1903-1978).

Where it's reviewed:
Realms of Fantasy, December 1997, page 18

Other books by the same author:
Lot and Lot's Daughter, 1996
Greener Than You Think, 1947
Breathe the Air Again, 1942

Other books you might like:
Terry Bisson, *Fire on the Mountain*, 1988
Andre Norton, *The Crossroads of Time*, 1956
Kevin Randle, *Remember Gettysburg*, 1988
   Robert J. Cornett, co-author
William Sanders, *The Wild Blue and the Gray*, 1991
Wilson Tucker, *The Lincoln Hunters*, 1958
Harry Turtledove, *The Guns of the South*, 1992
Connie Willis, *Lincoln's Dreams*, 1987

1163

MIKE MOSCOE

Second Fire

(New York: Ace, 1997)

Story type: Time Travel; Adventure
Series: Lost Millennium
Major character(s): Jack Walking Bear, Time Traveller, Military Personnel (captain); Launa O'Brian, Time Traveller, Military Personnel (lieutenant)
Time period(s): 40th century B.C.; 21st century
Locale(s): Europe

Summary: Sent back 6000 years to change the history of the world, Jack and Launa try to persuade the gentle hunter-gatherer tribes of Europe to resist the attacks of the fierce Horse Clans from the Dniepr River. They hope that the establishment of a Goddess-worshipping culture will turn the course of history away from the war and pollution that threaten their own century.

Where it's reviewed:
Locus, September 1997, page 70

Other books by the same author:
Lost Days, 1998
First Dawn, 1996

Other books you might like:
Poul Anderson, *Guardians of Time*, 1960
Jean M. Auel, *The Valley of Horses*, 1982
Stephen Baxter, *The Time Ships*, 1996
L. Sprague de Camp, *Lest Darkness Fall*, 1941
David Drake, *The Fourth Rome*, 1996
   Janet Morris, co-author
Barbara Hambly, *Ishmael*, 1985

Science Fiction

1164

BILL MYERS

Threshold

(Grand Rapids, Michigan: Zondervan, 1997)

Story type: Theological; Psychic Powers
Major character(s): Gertie Morrison, Psychic; Sarah Weintraub, Scientist (neurobiologist), Researcher; Helmut Reichner, Administrator, Scientist (physicist)
Time period(s): 1990s
Locale(s): Bethel Lake, Indiana; Katmandu, Nepal

Summary: Gertie prays and fasts to save the anointed one she sees in her dreams and thanks God for his approval. Still suffering from her abortion three years earlier, Sarah puts all her energy into her research into telekinesis. Meanwhile, Reichner travels to Nepal to meet his benefactor and discover the true purpose of his research institute.

Other books by the same author:
Blood of Heaven, 1996

Other books you might like:
Damien Broderick, *The White Abacus*, 1997
Tom Deitz, *Soulsmith*, 1991
Neil Gaiman, *Good Omens: The Nice and Accurate Prophecies of Agnes Nutter, Witch*, 1990
Terry Pratchett, co-author
Marc Laidlaw, *Neon Lotus*, 1988
Dan Simmons, *Endymion*, 1996

1165

LINDA NAGATA

Deception Well

(New York: Bantam Spectra, 1997)

Story type: Political; Alternate Intelligence
Major character(s): Lot Apolinario, Genetically Altered Being, Revolutionary; Urban, Revolutionary; Alta, Revolutionary
Time period(s): Indeterminate Future
Locale(s): Silk, Space Station (Orbital Colony); Deception Well, Planet—Imaginary

Summary: Ten years ago, Lot Apolinario's father led his devoted followers to their death as they attempted to reach Deception Well and enter the mysterious "Communion." Now a prisoner/ward of the orbiting city, Silk, Lot struggles with his inherited "charismata," an ability to affect others' emotions.

Where it's reviewed:
Kliatt, July 1997, page 18
Locus, January 1997, page 21
New York Times Book Review, February 23, 1997, page 20
Publishers Weekly, December 30, 1996, page 62

Other books by the same author:
Tech-Heaven, 1995
The Bohr Maker, 1995

Other books you might like:
Gregory Benford, *Great Sky River*, 1987

Arthur C. Clarke, *The City and the Stars*, 1956
Valerie J. Freireich, *Becoming Human*, 1995
Nancy Kress, *The Beggars in Spain Trilogy*, 1993-96
Tricia Sullivan, *Lethe*, 1995

1166

KIM NEWMAN
EUGENE BYRNE, Co-Author

Back in the USSA

(Shingletown, California: Mark V. Ziesing, 1997)

Story type: Alternate History; Political
Major character(s): Charles Hardin Holley, Musician, Revolutionary; Alphonse Capone, Political Figure (party chairman), Historical Figure; Issac Asimov, Television Personality (astrologer), Historical Figure
Time period(s): 1980s (1989); 1910s (1917)
Locale(s): Chicago, Illinois; New York, New York; Alternate Earth

Summary: In A.D. 1917 a revolution topples a corrupt regime and creates a state based, in theory, on the principles of Socialism, the United Socialiist States of America. When the revolutionary leadership of Eugene Debs passes to the iron regime of Al Capone, the dream self-destructs. Now, with the Socialist governments collapsing, the truth of those years can be told. Parts of the novel, in somewhat different form, appeared as stories in *Interzone* Magazine.

Where it's reviewed:
Publishers Weekly, October 13, 1997, page 57

Other books by the same author:
The Bloody Red Baron, 1995
Anno Dracula, 1993
Jago, 1993
Bad Dreams, 1991
The Night Mayor, 1990

Other books you might like:
Terry Bisson, *Voyage to the Red Planet*, 1990
Tim Powers, *Last Call*, 1992
Kim Stanley Robinson, *Red Mars*, 1993
Howard Waldrop, *Night of the Cooters*, 1990
Jack Womack, *Ambient*, 1987

1167

LARRY NIVEN

Destiny's Road

(New York: Tor, 1997)

Story type: Lost Colony; Political
Major character(s): Jemmy "Tim Hann" Bloocher, Fugitive, Cook; Loria Bednacort, Spouse; Damon ibn-Rushd, Businessman, Traveller (Caravan)
Time period(s): 28th century (2730s)
Locale(s): Destiny, Planet—Imaginary; Spiral Town, Fictional City

Summary: Without the speckles, people on Destiny lose their intelligence. In Spiral Town, the inhabitants trade with Caravans which carry speckles as money. After Jeremy kills a

merchant from the spring Caravan, he must leave Spiral Town to prevent his family's suffering from lack of speckles. He follows the road formed by the *Cavorite's* engines, joining the Caravan as a chef, while hoping to discover the fate of ship and crew.

Where it's reviewed:
Kirkus Reviews, Aril 15, 1997, page 597
Library Journal, June 15, 1997, page 100
Locus, June 1997, page 25
New York Times Book Review, August 31, 1997, page 22
Publishers Weekly, May 12, 1997, page 63

Other books by the same author:
The Ringworld Engineers, 1979
Tales of Known Space, 1975
Protector, 1973
Ringworld, 1970
Neutron Star, 1968

Other books you might like:
Helen Collins, *Mutagenesis*, 1993
L. Warren Douglas, *Cannon's Orb*, 1994
Marian Hughes, *Initiation*, 1995
Rosemary Kirstein, *The Steerswoman*, 1989
Elizabeth Moon, *Remnant Population*, 1996

1168

GARTH NIX

Shade's Children

(New York: HarperCollins, 1997)

Story type: Psychic Powers; Invasion of Earth
Major character(s): Robert ''Shade'' Ingman, Disembodied Personality; Ella, Psychic (esper), Teenager; Gold-eye, Child, Psychic (esper)
Time period(s): Indeterminate Future
Locale(s): Earth

Summary: In the 15 years since the Change, when the adults disappeared and the children under 14 years old were herded into Dormitories, Shade has rescued and trained many escaped children. The Change brought the Overlords, moved Shade from his body to a computer and gave many children psychic powers. The Overlords use the brains harvested from 14-year-olds in their fighting creatures. Ella, Gold-eye and their teammates work with the disintegrating Shade to vanquish the Overlords.

Where it's reviewed:
Booklist, October 1, 1997, page 320
The Horn Book Magazine, September/October 1997, page 576
Kirkus Reviews, August 15, 1997, page 1309
Locus, August 1997, page 29
School Library Journal, August 1997, page 158

Other books by the same author:
Sabriel, 1996
The Ragwitch, 1990

Other books you might like:
Jean Mark Gawron, *Dreams of Glass*, 1993
James P. Hogan, *The Multiplex Man*, 1992

Gwyneth Jones, *White Queen*, 1993
George R.R. Martin, *The Wild Cards Series*, 1987-1995
Sheri S. Tepper, *A Plague of Angels*, 1993

1169

LISANNE NORMAN

Razor's Edge

(New York: DAW, 1997)

Story type: Psychic Powers; Adventure
Series: Sholan Alliance
Major character(s): Carrie, Psychic; Kusac, Psychic, Alien (Sholan); Kaid, Military Personnel, Alien (Sholan)
Time period(s): Indeterminate Future
Locale(s): Shola, Planet—Imaginary; Jalna, Planet—Imaginary

Summary: As soon as she recovers from giving birth to her daughter, Carrie joins Kusac and Kaid in preparing to rescue the team of Sholans and Humans now trapped on Jalna. The three of them, like the other sets of Human-Sholan partners, struggle with the sexual and psychic strains of their new relationships, thus complicating the rescue attempt.

Where it's reviewed:
Locus, November 1997, page 62
Starlog, February 1998, page 60

Other books by the same author:
Fire Margins, 1996
Fortune's Wheel, 1995
Turning Point, 1993

Other books you might like:
C.J. Cherryh, *The Pride of Chanur*, 1982
Philip Jose Farmer, *Strange Relations*, 1960
Michael Jan Friedman, *Shadows on the Sun*, 1993
Mary Gentle, *Golden Witchbreed*, 1983
Robert A. Heinlein, *Stranger in a Strange Land*, 1991 revised
Anne McCaffrey, *The Rowan*, 1990
James H. Schmitz, *The Universe Against Her*, 1964

1170

ANDRE NORTON
SHERWOOD SMITH, Co-Author

Derelict for Trade

(New York: Tor, 1997)

Story type: Adventure
Series: Solar Queen
Major character(s): Dane Thorson, Spaceman, Trader; Rael Cofort, Spacewoman, Trader; Tooe, Alien (Rigellian)
Time period(s): Indeterminate Future
Locale(s): Harmony, Space Station

Summary: At the edge of human explored space, the crew of the *Solar Queen* find a derelict. Hoping to salvage it and turn a profit, the crew head for Harmony, run by humans and two alien races. Trying to stake their claim, they meet with interminable delays and several mysterious attacks, subsequently

discovering a hijacking scheme managed by a rogue Terran who controls all communications in and out of the Habitat.

Where it's reviewed:
Booklist, February 1, 1997, page 929
Kirkus Reviews, December 1, 1996, page 1707
Library Journal, December 1996, page 152
Publishers Weekly, January 27, 1997, page 82
Starlog, October 1997, page 12

Other books by the same author:
Brother to Shadows, 1993
Redline the Stars, 1993 (P.M. Griffin, co-author)
Voorloper, 1980
Postmarked the Stars, 1969
Sargasso of Space, 1955

Other books you might like:
Poul Anderson, *Trader to the Stars*, 1964
Robert Asprin, *Phule's Paradise*, 1992
Lois McMaster Bujold, *Ethan of Athos*, 1986
C.J. Cherryh, *Rimrunners*, 1989
Paula E. Downing, *Flare Star*, 1992
Debra Doyle, *Starpilot's Grave*, 1993
    James D. Macdonald, co-author
Sherwood Smith, *The Phoenix in Flight*, 1993
    Dave Trowbridge, co-author
S.M. Stirling, *The Ship Avenged*, 1997

1171

ANDRE NORTON
SHERWOOD SMITH, Co-Author

A Mind for Trade
(New York: Tor, 1997)

Story type: Adventure
Major character(s): Dane Thorson, Spaceman (Cargo Master); Tooe, Alien (Rigelian hybrid), Apprentice; Rip Shannon, Spaceman, Pilot
Time period(s): Indeterminate Future
Locale(s): *Solar Queen*, Spaceship; *North Star*, Spaceship

Summary: Aboard the *Solar Queen*'s new sister ship, the *North Star*, Dane Thorson and his fellow Free Traders travel to Hesprid IV, where a strange electromagnetic force kills stranded miners. Only Thorson's newly developed psi-link with his crewmates allows them to communicate with the Hesprid IV's inhabitants and avoid the planet's hidden dangers.

Where it's reviewed:
Booklist, October 1, 1997, page 312
Kirkus Reviews, August 15, 1997, page 1265
Library Journal, October 15, 1997, page 98
Publishers Weekly, September 29, 1997 page 71

Other books by the same author:
Derelict for Trade, 1997 (Sherwood Smith, co-author)
Redline the Stars, 1993 (P.M. Griffin, co-author)
Galactic Derelict, 1959
Plague Ship, 1956
Sargasso of Space, 1955

Other books you might like:
Anne Mason, *The Stolen Law*, 1986
Larry Segriff, *Spacer Dreams*, 1995
Charles Sheffield, *The Billion Dollar Boy*, 1997
Sherwood Smith, *The Phoenix in Flight*, 1993
    Dave Trowbridge, co-author
Sherwood Smith, *A Prison Unsought*, 1994
    Dave Trowbridge, co-author
Robyn Tallis, *Visions from the Sea*, 1989

1172

MEL ODOM

Headhunters
(New York: Roc, 1997)

Story type: Cyberpunk; Science Fantasy
Series: Shadowrun
Major character(s): Jack Skater, Mercenary, Cyborg; Archangel, Mythical Creature (elf), Computer Expert; Duran, Mythical Creature (orc), Mercenary
Time period(s): 2050s (2057)
Locale(s): Seattle, Washington

Summary: The trail of the plot leading to the dragon Dunkelzahn's assassination runs through a double agent, also conveniently dead. Jack Skater's team must steal the body out of the morgue. When they discover that a lot of powerful people want this corpse, they learn that keeping hold of a dead body may prove easier than staying alive.

Other books by the same author:
F.R.E.E. Lancers, 1995
Omega Score, 1994
Omega Blue, 1993
Stalker Analog, 1993
Lethal Interface, 1992

Other books you might like:
Pat Cadigan, *Fools*, 1992
Charles de Lint, *Svaha*, 1989
Eric James Fullilove, *Circle of One*, 1996
Ian McDonald, *Terminal Cafe*, 1994
Richard Paul Russo, *Destroying Angel*, 1992

1173

STEVE PERRY

The Digital Effect
(New York: Ace, 1997)

Story type: Space Colony; Mystery
Major character(s): Gil Sivart, Artist, Detective—Amateur; Patricia "Trish" Blackwell, Dancer; Ray El-Sayed, Detective—Police
Time period(s): 2090s
Locale(s): Robert E. Lee, Space Station

Summary: Certain that her significant other did not commit suicide, Trish asks Gil to check further. Behind schedule building the microscopic sea ships already commissioned, Gil starts to refuse but changes his mind after his ship gets bombed.

Where it's reviewed:
Science Fiction Chronicle, October 1997, page 48
Starlog, October 1997, page 12

Other books by the same author:
The Trinity Vector, 1996
Spindoc, 1994
Aliens: Earth Hive, 1992
The 97th Step, 1989
The Man Who Never Missed, 1985

Other books you might like:
J.M. Dillard, *Emissary*, 1993
Michael Flynn, *Firestar*, 1996
Howard V. Hendrix, *Lightpaths*, 1997
Katharine Kerr, *Polar City Blues*, 1990
Allen Steele, *Clarke County, Space*, 1990

1174

STEVE PERRY

Men in Black

(New York: Bantam, 1997)

Story type: Invasion of Earth; Humor
Major character(s): Kay, Government Official (Men in Black); James "Jay" Edwards, Government Official (Men in Black)
Time period(s): 1990s
Locale(s): New York, New York

Summary: Kay recruits James Edwards into the government's top secret bureau known as Men in Black, which keeps track of extraterrestrials operating covertly on Earth. Novelizes the film of the same name.

Other books by the same author:
The Trinity Vector, 1996
The 97th Step, 1989
The Machiavelli Interface, 1986
Matadora, 1986
The Man Who Never Missed, 1985

1175

STEVE PERRY

Target Earth

(New York: Warner Aspect, 1997)

Story type: First Contact; Invasion of Earth
Series: Leonard Nimoy's Primordials
Major character(s): Stewart Davies, Computer Expert, Student—Graduate; Zeerus, Alien (Avitaur), Criminal; Jake Holcroft, Child, Computer Expert
Time period(s): 2000s
Locale(s): Long Island, New York; Washington, District of Columbia; Outer Space

Summary: Zeerus' failed coup against the Primordials, who had rescued his species from Earth 65 million years ago, forces him to steal a spaceship to find allies. He heads for Earth where he knows an intelligent species has evolved, but Jake hacks his message from Stewart's SETI lab. The Feds hunt for Jake, who tries to run from his militia-involved father

and find his mother. Meanwhile, Stewart answers Zeerus' message. Includes a two-page foreword by Leonard Nimoy. Based on comic books.

Where it's reviewed:
Booklist, April 1, 1997, page 1283
Kirkus Reviews, March 1, 1997, page 341
Library Journal, March 15, 1997, page 93
Publishers Weekly, March 24, 1997, page 64
Voice of Youth Advocates, June 1997, page 120

Other books by the same author:
The Digital Effect, 1997
The Trinity Vector, 1996
Spindoc, 1994
Aliens: Earth Hive, 1992
The Man Who Never Missed, 1985

Other books you might like:
Juanita Coulson, *Tomorrow's Heritage*, 1981
Dean Devlin, *Independence Day*, 1996
    Roland Emmerich, Stephen Molstad, co-authors
Valerie J. Freireich, *The Beacon*, 1996
Larry Niven, *Footfall*, 1985
    Jerry Pournelle, co-author
David Weber, *Mutineer's Moon*, 1991

1176

FREDERIK POHL

The Siege of Eternity

(New York: Tor, 1997)

Story type: First Contact; Invasion of Earth
Series: Eschaton Sequence
Major character(s): Hilda Jeanne Morrisey, Government Official, Administrator; Jim Daniel "Dan" Dannerman, Spy, Clone; Patrice "Pat" Adcock, Scientist (astronomer), Clone
Time period(s): Indeterminate Future
Locale(s): Arlington, Virginia; Washington, District of Columbia

Summary: Having returned from Starlab with no knowledge of the objects implanted in their brains, Pat and Dan adamantly refuse to give permission for their removal. Rescued by the return of their clones, Pat and Dan work with Hilda to prevent the aliens from taking over Earth, if they have not already done so.

Where it's reviewed:
Analog, January 1998, page 146
Booklist, November 1, 1997, page 457
Kirkus Reviews, September 1, 1997, page 1345
Locus, January 1998, page 19
Publishers Weekly, September 22, 1997, page 73

Other books by the same author:
The Other End of Time, 1996
The Voices of Heaven, 1994
The Space Merchants, 1985 (C.M. Kornbluth, co-author, revised)
Gateway, 1977
Gladiator-at-Law, 1955 (C.M. Kornbluth, co-author)

Science Fiction

Other books you might like:
Patricia Anthony, *Brother Termite*, 1993
Wilhelmina Baird, *Chaos Come Again*, 1996
Stephen Baxter, *Timelike Infinity*, 1993
Greg Bear, *Eon*, 1985
Gregory Benford, *Furious Gulf*, 1994
Ursula K. Le Guin, *The Lathe of Heaven*, 1971

1177

NICK POLLOTTA

Shadowboxer

(New York: Roc, 1997)

Story type: Cyberpunk; Science Fantasy
Series: Shadowrun
Major character(s): Two Bears, Genetically Altered Being (dwarf); Silver, Computer Expert; Moonfeather, Wizard
Time period(s): 2050s
Locale(s): Seattle, Washington

Summary: Hired for an easy job, finding out what ''IronHell'' means, Two Bears quickly finds the easy job turns difficult, then lethal. Soon he and his team run through a maze of plots that have killed at least one runner team. Novelization based on a role-playing game.

Other books by the same author:
Doomsday Exam, 1992
Full Moonster, 1992
Bureau 13, 1991
Illegal Aliens, 1989 (Phil Foglio, co-author)

Other books you might like:
Steven Barnes, *Streetlethal*, 1983
Pat Cadigan, *Synners*, 1991
William Gibson, *Burning Chrome*, 1986
Richard Paul Russo, *Destroying Angel*, 1992
Walter Jon Williams, *Voice of the Whirlwind*, 1987

1178

PAUL PREUSS

Secret Passages

(New York: Tor, 1997)

Story type: Hard Science Fiction; Family Saga
Major character(s): Anne-Marie Brand, Photographer, Parent; Manolis Minakis, Scientist (physicist), Businessman; Peter Slater, Scientist (physicist), Professor
Time period(s): 1990s
Locale(s): Crete, Greece; Athens, Greece; Geneva, Switzerland

Summary: Desperate to win custody of her son from her ex-husband, Anne-Marie Brand agrees to spy on Manolis Minakis, a Greek business magnate and physicist who possesses rare and valuable Minoan artifacts. In turn, Minakis uses Anne-Marie to gain access to her new husband, Peter, whom Minakis hopes to recruit for his radical physics experiments.

Where it's reviewed:
Booklist, August 1997, page 1886

Kirkus Reviews, July 1, 1997, page 841
Library Journal, August 1997, page 140
Locus, December 1997, page 23
Publishers Weekly, July 14, 1997, page 69

Other books by the same author:
Starfire, 1988
Human Error, 1985
Broken Symmetries, 1983
Re-Entry, 1981
The Gates of Heaven, 1980

Other books you might like:
Greg Bear, *Eon*, 1985
Gregory Benford, *Timescape*, 1980
Arthur C. Clarke, *Richter 10*, 1996
    Mike McQuay, co-author
Greg Egan, *Quarantine*, 1995
Ursula K. Le Guin, *The Dispossessed*, 1974
Frederik Pohl, *The Singers of Time*, 1990
    Jack Williamson, co-author

1179

DAVID PRINGLE, Editor

The Best of Interzone

(New York: St. Martin's Press, 1997)

Story type: Anthology; Science Fiction

Summary: Published in conjunction with the 15th anniversary of the Hugo Award-winning British magazine *Interzone*, this volume contains a nine-page introduction outlining the magazine's origins and history, as well as 29 stories. Authors include Brian Aldiss, J.G. Ballard, Stephen Baxter, Chris Beckett, Eric Brown, Molly Brown, Eugene Byrne, Richard Calder, Paul De Filippo, Thomas M. Disch, David Garnett, Greg Egan, Timons Esaias, Peter F. Hamilton, Mary Gentle, Nicola Griffith, Ben Jeapes, Graham Joyce, Garry Kilworth, David Langford, Ian Lee, Ian R. MacLeod, Sean McMullen, John Meaney, Kim Newman, Paul Park, Geoff Ryman, Brian Stableford, Ian Watson and Cherry Wilder.

Where it's reviewed:
Locus, February 1997, page 15
Starlog, June 1997, page 11

Other books you might like:
Mike Ashley, *The Best of British SF*, 1977
    editor
John Clute, *Interzone: The 1st Anthology*, 1985
    David Pringle, Colin Greenland, co-editors
John Clute, *Interzone: The 4th Anthology*, 1989
    David Pringle, Simon Ounsley, co-editors
John Clute, *Interzone: The 2nd Anthology*, 1987
    David Pringle, Simon Ounsley, co-editors
John Clute, *Interzone: The 3rd Anthology*, 1988
    David Pringle, Simon Ounsley, co-editors
Paul Collins, *Metaworlds*, 1994
    editor
Gardner Dozois, *The Year's Best Science Fiction Series*, 1984-1997
    editor

David G. Hartwell, *Northern Stars: The Anthology of Canadian Science Fiction*, 1994
  Glenn Grant, co-editor
Kim Mohan, *Amazing Stories: The Anthology*, 1995
  editor
Pamela Sargent, *Nebula Awards 30*, 1996
  editor

1180

DANIEL QUINN

My Ishmael

(New York: Bantam, 1997)

Story type: Literary; Contemporary Realism
Major character(s): Julie Gerchak, Child, Student; Ishmael, Animal (gorilla), Telepath
Time period(s): 1990s
Locale(s): United States

Summary: When Ishmael again advertises for a student interested in saving the world, Julie answers, but must convince Ishmael that she can benefit from his tutelage. Julie's understanding of world events broadens with Ishmael as her mentor.

Where it's reviewed:
Booklist, September 15, 1997, page 181
Kirkus Reviews, September 1, 1997, page 1334
Publishers Weekly, September 22, 1997, pag 71

Other books by the same author:
Ishmael, 1992

Other books you might like:
Richard Bach, *Jonathan Livingston Seagull*, 1970
Antoine de Saint-Exupery, *The Little Prince*, 1943
Andrew Goldblatt, *The Bully Pulpit*, 1992
James Gurney, *Dinotopia*, 1992
C.S. Lewis, *That Hideous Strength*, 1946
Michael Tobias, *Voice of the Planet*, 1990

1181

ROBERT REED

Beneath the Gated Sky

(New York: Tor, 1997)

Story type: Space Opera; Family Saga
Major character(s): Porsche Neale, Alien (The Few), Fugitive; Cornell Novak, Fugitive; Trinidad, Alien (The Few), Traitor
Time period(s): 1990s
Locale(s): Texas; Jartee, Planet—Imaginary

Summary: On the run from the Cosmic Events Agency, an organization formed to investigate the mysterious Portal that replaced Earth's starry sky with a reflection of the planet, Porsche and Cornell try to prevent corrupt government officials from using alien technology to give the United States an unfair advantage over the rest of the world. Sequel to *Beyond the Veil of Stars*.

Where it's reviewed:
Booklist, September 15, 1997, page 216
Kirkus Reviews, August 1, 1997, page 1166
Locus, December 1997, page 70
Publishers Weekly, August 11, 1997, page 391

Other books by the same author:
An Exaltatation of Larks, 1995
Beyond the Veil of Stars, 1994
The Remarkables, 1992
Down the Bright Way, 1991
The Hormone Jungle, 1988

Other books you might like:
Greg Egan, *Quarantine*, 1995
Stephen Gould, *Wildside*, 1996
Zenna Henderson, *Ingathering: The Complete People Stories of Zenna Henderson*, 1995
Frederik Pohl, *The Other End of Time*, 1996
Michaela Roessner, *Vanishing Point*, 1993
John E. Stith, *Reunion on Neverend*, 1994

1182

MIKE RESNICK

The Widowmaker Reborn

(New York: Bantam Spectra, 1997)

Story type: Adventure; Genetic Manipulation
Series: Widowmaker
Major character(s): Jefferson ''Widowmaker'' Nighthawk, Clone, Mercenary; Ito Kinoshita, Martial Arts Expert; Ibn ben Khalid, Rebel
Time period(s): Indeterminate
Locale(s): Interstellar Empire/Federation

Summary: Created from the DNA of the famous Widowmaker, now a corpsicle waiting in cryostorage for a cure for his deadly disease, Jefferson Nighthawk has the experience as well as the body of the original Widowmaker, and the memories of the dead first clone. In order to pay for the continued care and hoped-for cure for the disease, he accepts an assignment to rescue the daughter of a corrupt politician and kill the rebel leader who holds her hostage. This time he will trust no one. Second in trilogy.

Where it's reviewed:
Analog, June 1997, page 147
Locus, October 1997, page 23
Starlog, October 1997, page 12

Other books by the same author:
The Widowmaker, 1996
Prophet, 1993
Oracle, 1992
Soothsayer, 1991
Second Contact, 1990

Other books you might like:
C.J. Cherryh, *Cyteen*, 1988
Gordon R. Dickson, *Dorsai!*, 1976
Ian Fleming, *You Only Live Twice*, 1964
Keith Laumer, *Retief at Large*, 1978
Rebecca Ore, *The Illegal Rebirth of Billy the Kid*, 1991
James H. Schmitz, *The Universe Against Her*, 1964

John Varley, *The Ophiuchi Hotline*, 1977

1183

SPIDER ROBINSON

Lifehouse

(New York: Baen, 1997)

Story type: Time Travel; Adventure
Major character(s): June Bellamy, Con Artist; Wallace "Wally" Kemp, Computer Expert (science fiction fan); Paul Donald Throtmanian, Con Artist
Time period(s): 1990s
Locale(s): Vancouver, British Columbia, Canada

Summary: Walking in the woods, June loses some memory, almost causing the end of the world, while Paul, pretending to come from the future, scams Wallace and Moira. June and Paul retire and decide to return the scam money, but the real time travelers destroy Paul's apartment and the money. The four new friends must find the time travelers to protect the present and get their money. Sequel to *Deathkiller*, a 1996 omnibus collecting *Mindkillers* and *Time Pressure*.

Where it's reviewed:
Starlog, July 1997, page 62

Other books by the same author:
Callahan's Legacy, 1996
Time Pressure, 1987
Callahan's Secret, 1986
Mindkiller, 1982
Telempath, 1976

Other books you might like:
Chester Anderson, *The Butterfly Kid*, 1967
John Barnes, *Patton's Spaceship*, 1997
Gordon R. Dickson, *Time Storm*, 1977
Larry Niven, *Fallen Angels*, 1991
    Jerry Pournelle, Michael Flynn, co-authors
Dan Simmons, *Hyperion*, 1989
Robert Charles Wilson, *A Bridge of Years*, 1991

1184

RUDY RUCKER

Freeware

(New York: Avon, 1997)

Story type: Alternate Intelligence; Cyberpunk
Series: Software
Major character(s): Monique, Robot (moldie); Tre Dietz, Artist, Inventor; Randy Karl Tucker, Kidnapper
Time period(s): 2050s
Locale(s): Santa Cruz, California; Luna, Montenegro; Bangalore, India

Summary: An artificial life form made of mold and plastic, Monique works for Tre Dietz as maid and bookkeeper at his wife's motel. Randy Karl, a fallen Heritagist, kidnaps Monique when she tries to insert a piece of herself as control in his brain. The Loonies download some programs from space which may lead to disaster for all. Sequel to *Software* and *Wetware*.

Where it's reviewed:
Asimov's Science Fiction, December 1997, page 150
Booklist, May 1, 1997, page 1483
Kirkus Reviews, March 15, 1997, page 423
Library Journal, May 15, 1997, page 105
Starlog, August 1997, page 68

Other books by the same author:
The Hacker and the Ants, 1994
Wetware, 1988
Master of Time and Space, 1984
Software, 1982
Spacetime Donuts, 1981

Other books you might like:
Tom Cool, *Infectress*, 1997
Jean Mark Gawron, *Dream of Glass*, 1993
Gwyneth Jones, *White Queen*, 1995
Ian McDonald, *Terminal Cafe*, 1994
Jeff Noon, *Vurt*, 1995

1185

MATT RUFF

Sewer, Gas & Electric

(New York: Atlantic Monthly Press, 1997)

Story type: Science Fiction; Humor
Major character(s): Joan Fine, Activist; Morris Kazenstein, Inventor, Activist; Sarah Emma "Kite" Edmonds, Aged Person (180 years old), Activist
Time period(s): 2030s (2023)
Locale(s): New York, New York; Atlanta, Georgia

Summary: Daughter of Catholic Women's Crusader Sister Ellen Fine and ex-wife of billionaire Harry Grant, Joan loses her job as a sewer worker after the rest of her crew becomes shark food. She accepts a job researching the possibility that an electric servant murdered its owner, an act considered impossible by all, but which provides the key to a deeper mystery endangering millions of lives.

Where it's reviewed:
Asimov's Science Fiction, December 1997, page 152
Kirkus Reviews, November 1, 1996, page 1560
Library Journal, November 15, 1996, page 152

Other books by the same author:
Fool on the Hill, 1988

Other books you might like:
David Brin, *Earth*, 1990
Laura J. Mixon, *Glass Houses*, 1992
Robert Shea, *The Illuminatus Trilogy*, 1988
    Robert Anton Wilson, co-author
Dan Simmons, *Hyperion*, 1989
Neal Stephenson, *The Diamond Age*, 1995
Jim Young, *Armed Memory*, 1995

1186

KRISTINE KATHRYN RUSCH

Alien Influences

(New York: Bantam Spectra, 1997)

Story type: First Contact; Political

Major character(s): Justin Schafer, Psychologist; Netta Goldin, Administrator; Latona Etanl, Activist (Extra-Species Alliance)

Time period(s): Indeterminate Future

Locale(s): Bountiful, Planet—Imaginary; Minor Base, Moon—Imaginary (of Bountiful)

Summary: Hired to express the situation between the colonists and nearly extinct native Dancers on Bountiful despite his previous disastrous error with the Minarans, Justin meets Netta on Bountiful. Netta explains the current situation: eight of the children have been brutally murdered using the same ritual the Dancers use to help their children into adulthood. The colonists want to blame the Dancers and want them removed, as the colonists no longer need the Dancers to produce the plants that go into the drug they export. Unfortunately, Justin finds the murderers to be other children. He cannot permit another alien species' destruction, despite the colonists' wishes. First published in England, 1994.

Where it's reviewed:
Analog, April 1998, page 146
Publishers Weekly, September 29, 1997, page 86
Starlog, February 1998, page 61

Other books by the same author:
The Changeling, 1996
The New Rebellion, 1996
The Sacrifice, 1996
Traitors, 1994
The White Mists of Power, 1991

Other books you might like:
C.J. Cherryh, *Foreigner*, 1994
L. Warren Douglas, *Cannon's Orb*, 1994
Alan Dean Foster, *The Tar-Aiym Krang*, 1972
James Gunn, *The Joy Machine*, 1996
  Theodore Sturgeon, co-author
Mary Doria Russell, *The Sparrow*, 1996
Sheri S. Tepper, *Grass*, 1989

1187

DOUGLAS RUSHKOFF

Ecstasy Club

(New York: HarperCollins, 1997)

Story type: Contemporary Realism; Mystical

Major character(s): George Thomas Duncan, Leader (guru), Revolutionary; Peter, Computer Expert, Technician; Zach, Teacher, Student

Time period(s): 1990s (1996)

Locale(s): Oakland, California

Summary: A group of young techno-idealists working with computers, mysticism, sex and drugs start a dance club as a base for their operations. When their theories prove a little too

sound and their experiments a little too successful, everyone from religious kooks to the police wants to get them. But, perhaps, what they have noticed has noticed them. First novel.

Other books you might like:
Lisa Goldstein, *The Dream Years*, 1985
Stuart Gordon, *Smile on the Void*, 1981
Richard Grant, *Tex and Molly in the Afterlife*, 1996
Stewart Home, *Come Before Christ and Murder Love*, 1997
Jeff Noon, *Vurt*, 1995

1188

RICHARD PAUL RUSSO

Carlucci's Heart

(New York: Ace, 1997)

Story type: Mystery; Medical

Major character(s): Francesco "Frank" Carlucci, Detective—Police; Ryland "Ry" Cage, Physician; Caroline Carlucci, Detective—Amateur

Time period(s): 21st century

Locale(s): San Francisco, California

Summary: When Caroline's terminally ill friend disappears from the hospice house, Caroline asks her father to help find him, passing on the name, "Cancer Cell," the only possible clue she has. Frank's investigation yields little, but soon expands as plague begins to engulf the city and federal troops move into the Tenderloin.

Where it's reviewed:
Analog, April 1998, page 146
Locus, December 1997, page 70

Other books by the same author:
Carlucci's Edge, 1995
Destroying Angel, 1992
Subterranean Gallery, 1989
Inner Eclipse, 1988

Other books you might like:
Greg Bear, *Blood Music*, 1985
Pat Cadigan, *Synners*, 1991
Mike Conner, *Archangel*, 1995
Philip K. Dick, *Bladerunner*, 1982
Frank Herbert, *The White Plague*, 1982
Katharine Kerr, *Polar City Blues*, 1990
David Alexander Smith, *In the Cube*, 1993

1189

FRED SABERHAGEN

Berserker Fury

(New York: Tor, 1997)

Story type: Military

Series: Berserker

Major character(s): Sebastian "Nifty" Gift, Spaceman, Military Personnel (spacer first class); Jory Yokusuka, Journalist

Time period(s): Indeterminate Future

Locale(s): Outer Space; Earth; Uhao, Planet—Imaginary

Summary: Now able to construct Berserker units which look like human-created androids, the Berserkers prepare a final attack on human-occupied space. Humanity's only hope lies in cracking the Berserker's cryptography and preparing against their battle plans.

Where it's reviewed:
Booklist, July, 1997, page 1806
Kirkus Reviews, June 1, 1997, page 842
Library Journal, August 1997, page 141
Publishers Weekly, July 28, 1997, page 58
Starlog, September 1997, page 80

Other books by the same author:
Berserker Kill, 1993
Berserker Lies, 1991
Berserker Blue Death, 1985
Berserker's Planet, 1975
Berserker, 1967

Other books you might like:
Roger MacBride Allen, *The Ring of Charon*, 1990
Roger MacBride Allen, *The Shattered Sphere*, 1994
Glen Cook, *The Dragon Never Sleeps*, 1988
Larry Niven, *Footfall*, 1985
    Jerry Pournelle, co-author
Vernor Vinge, *A Fire upon the Deep*, 1993

1190

PAMELA SARGENT, Editor

Nebula Awards 31

(New York: Harcourt Brace, 1997)

Story type: Anthology; Fantasy
Series: Nebula Awards

Summary: Subtitled "SFWA's Choices for the Best Science Fiction and Fantasy of the Year," this volume contains a six-page introduction by the editor, listing 1995 Nebula Award-finalists and winners; comments by six authors in "The Year in Science Fiction and Fantasy: A Symposium"; a 16-page article on fantastic films of 1995; memorials to John Brunner and Roger Zelazny; two poems by Rysling Award-winners David Lunde and Dan Raphael; 11 pages of appendixes including selected titles from the preliminary ballot and a list of previous winners; "Enchanted Village" by Grand Master Award-winner A.E. van Vogt; plus 10 other excerpts and stories by authors including Gregory Benford, Esther M. Friesner, Lisa Goldstein, Elizabeth Hand, James Patrick Kelly, Ursula K. Le Guin, Maureen F. McHugh and Robert J. Sawyer.

Where it's reviewed:
Booklist, March 15, 1997, page 1231
Kirkus Reviews, March 1, 1997, page 342
Kliatt, July 1997, page 18
Library Journal, April 15, 1997, page 124
Locus, May 1997, page 17

Other books by the same author:
Nebula Awards 29-30, 1995-1996
Women of Wonder, The Classic Years: Science Fiction by Women From the 1940s to the 1970s, 1995

Women of Wonder, The Contemporary Years: Science Fiction by Women From the 1970s to the 1990s, 1995
The New Women of Wonder: Science Fiction Novelettes by Women about Women, 1978
Bio-Futures: Science Fiction Stories about Biological Metamorphosis, 1976

Other books you might like:
Michael Bishop, *Nebula Awards 23-25*, 1989-1991
    editor
Jack Dann, *Nebula Awards 32*, 1998
    editor
Gardner Dozois, *The Year's Best Science Fiction Series*, 1984-1997
    editor
James Morrow, *Nebula Awards 26-28*, 1992-1994
    editor
George Zebrowski, *Nebula Awards 21-22*, 1987-1988
    editor

1191

AL SARRANTONIO

Personal Agendas

(New York: Dell, 1997)

Story type: Space Opera; Political
Series: Babylon 5
Major character(s): G'Kar, Alien (Narn), Prisoner; Londo Mollari, Alien (Centauri), Political Figure; Vir Cotto, Alien (Centauri), Political Figure
Time period(s): 23rd century (2261)
Locale(s): Centauri Prime, Planet—Imaginary; Babylon 5, Space Station

Summary: Determined to rescue former ambassador G'Kar from imprisonment on Centauri Prime, a group of Narn warriors threatens Londo Mollari's plans to use G'Kar as a diversion in his plot to kill the mad Emperor Cartagia. Meanwhile, Vir Cotto tries to disentangle himself from his fiancee's extravagant wedding preparations.

Other books by the same author:
Journey, 1997
Exile, 1996

Other books you might like:
Neal Barrett Jr., *The Touch of Your Shadow, the Whisper of Your Name*, 1996
Jeanne Cavelos, *The Shadow Within*, 1997
Kathryn M. Drennan, *To Dream in the City of Sorrows*, 1997
Jim Mortimore, *Clarke's Law*, 1996
S.M. Stirling, *Betrayals*, 1996
Lois Tilton, *Accusations*, 1995
John Vornholt, *Blood Oath*, 1995
John Vornholt, *Voices*, 1995

1192

RON SARTI

Legacy of the Ancients

(New York: AvoNova, 1997)

Story type: Political; Post-Holocaust
Series: Chronicles of Scar
Major character(s): Arn Brant, Royalty (prince), Military Personnel; Robert, Royalty, Handicapped; Sokol, Genetically Altered Being (Beastman), Diplomat
Time period(s): Indeterminate Future
Locale(s): Kenesee, Fictional Country; Arkan, Fictional Country; North America

Summary: In a future where civilization has collapsed and been resurrected, dinosaurs and prehistoric mammals wander the wilderness. Trying to keep his people safe, Prince Arn must travel 1,000 miles through allied and hostile countries to destroy a weapon that could destroy civilization again. Sequel to *The Chronicles of Scar*.

Other books by the same author:
The Chronicles of Scar, 1996

Other books you might like:
David Brin, *The Postman*, 1985
Octavia E. Butler, *Parable of the Sower*, 1993
Sterling E. Lanier, *Hiero's Journey*, 1973
Vonda N. McIntyre, *Dreamsnake*, 1978
Walter M. Miller Jr., *A Canticle for Leibowitz*, 1960
Jake Saunders, *The Texas-Israeli War: 1999*, 1974
    Howard Waldrop, co-author

1193

ROBERT J. SAWYER

Frameshift

(New York: Tor, 1997)

Story type: Genetic Manipulation; Hard Science Fiction
Major character(s): Pierre Tardivel, Researcher; Molly Bond, Psychologist, Psychic (esper); Ivan ''Burian Klimus'' Marchenko, Professor, Criminal
Time period(s): 1990s
Locale(s): Berkeley, California

Summary: When Pierre discovers his natural father suffers from Huntington's Chorea, he decides to win the Nobel Prize for finding the cure. Because he thinks in French, Molly can't read his mind and likes him instantly. They seem the perfect couple except that Molly wants a baby and someone wants Pierre dead. Burian volunteers to donate sperm for Molly, resulting in an abnormal baby.

Where it's reviewed:
Booklist, April 15, 1997, page 1387
Kirkus Reviews, March 15, 1997, page 424
Library Journal, May 15, 1997, page 196
Locus, August 1997, page 25
Science Fiction Chronicle, October 1997, page 49

Other books by the same author:
Starplex, 1996

The Terminal Experiment, 1995
Foreigner, 1994
Fossil Hunter, 1993
Far-Seer, 1992

Other books you might like:
Octavia E. Butler, *Parable of the Sower*, 1995
Frank Herbert, *The White Plague*, 1982
Elizabeth Moon, *Remnant Population*, 1996
Kathy Tyers, *Shivering World*, 1991
Jack Womack, *Heathern*, 1990

1194

ROBERT J. SAWYER

Illegal Alien

(New York: Ace, 1997)

Story type: First Contact; Mystery
Major character(s): Francis ''Frank'' Nobilio, Scientist, Government Official; Hask, Alien (Tosok); Dale Rice, Lawyer
Time period(s): 2010s
Locale(s): New York, New York (United Nations); Los Angeles, California (Valcour Hall, University of Southern California)

Summary: Seven aliens from Alpha Centauri arrive on Earth in need of help to repair their ship, having damaged it on the way. Frank and the rest of the contact team especially befriend Hask, the first alien to land. When all evidence in the murder of one of the humans on the team points to Hask, Frank hires Dale Rice, a prominent civil rights attorney, to defend him.

Where it's reviewed:
Analog, January 1998, page 145
Kirkus Reviews, November 1, 1997, page 1613
Publishers Weekly, November 10, 1997, page 59
Science Fiction Age, January 1998, page 12
Science Fiction Chronicle, November 1997, page 40

Other books by the same author:
Frameshift, 1997
Starplex, 1996
Fossil Hunter, 1993
Far-Seer, 1992
Golden Fleece, 1990

Other books you might like:
Pauline Ashwell, *Project Farcry*, 1995
Kathleen Ann Goonan, *Queen City Jazz*, 1994
Katharine Kerr, *Polar City Blues*, 1990
Ian McDonald, *Evolution's Shore*, 1995
Larry Niven, *Footfall*, 1985

1195

ROBERT J. SAWYER

Starplex

(New York: Ace, 1996)

Story type: First Contact; Time Travel

Major character(s): Gilbert ''Keith'' Lansing, Administrator, Immortal; Jag Kandaro em-Pelsh, Alien (Waldahud); Bottlenose, Animal (dolphin), Pilot (spaceship)

Time period(s): 2090s (2094)

Locale(s): Tau Ceti, Outer Space; Alpha Draconis, Outer Space

Summary: Jointly owned and operated by the four known intelligent species, *Starplex* uses the shortcut system, discovered ready to use, to explore new places. Through a newly opened shortcut, the *Starplex* crew discovers dark matter while Keith goes through later to emerge near an unknown, advanced ship carrying a clear, slightly aquamarine man from the future.

Where it's reviewed:
Booklist, October 15, 1996
Library Journal, August 1996, page 120

Other books by the same author:
The Terminal Experiment, 1995
End of an Era, 1994
Fossil Hunter, 1993
Far-Seer, 1992
Golden Fleece, 1990

Other books you might like:
Glen Cook, *The Dragon Never Sleeps*, 1988
John DeChancie, *Starrigger*, 1983
L. Warren Douglas, *Cannon's Orb*, 1994
Alan Dean Foster, *Design for Great-Day*, 1995
   Eric Frank Russell, co-author
Jack McDevitt, *The Engines of God*, 1994
Frederik Pohl, *The Other End of Time*, 1996
George Zebrowski, *Stranger Suns*, 1991

1196

JEFFERSON SCOTT

Terminal Logic

(Sisters, Oregon: Multnomah Publishers, 1997)

Story type: Techno-Thriller; Theological

Major character(s): Ethan Hamilton, Computer Expert; Jordan Hamilton, Child, Computer Expert; Yoseph, Artificial Intelligence

Time period(s): 2000s (2006)

Locale(s): Cyberspace; Tyler, Texas; Washington, District of Columbia

Summary: After vanquishing a homicidal hacker, Ethan builds a new home in rural Tyler, designed to completely repel a hacker attack. When Ethan finds stray AIs loose in the net he realizes he may have another battle to face. Unfortunately his home proves vulnerable to Yoseph, who targets Ethan as an enemy, not understanding the permanency of death for humans.

Other books by the same author:
Virtually Eliminated. 1996

Other books you might like:
Bruce Bethke, *Headcrash*, 1995
James Gunn, *The Joy Machine*, 1996
   Theodore Sturgon, co-author

Lisa Mason, *Arachne*, 1990
Mel Odom, *Lethal Interface*, 1992
Joan Slonczewski, *Daughter of Elysium*, 1993
Neal Stephenson, *Snow Crash*, 1992

1197

MELISSA SCOTT

Dreaming Metal

(New York: Tor, 1997)

Story type: Alternate Intelligence; Arts

Major character(s): Celinde ''Cissy'' Fortune, Magician (conjurer), Technician; Reverdy Jian, Pilot (spaceship); Fanning ''Fan'' Jones, Musician, Cousin

Time period(s): Indeterminate Future

Locale(s): Persephone, Planet—Imaginary; Landage, Fictional City

Summary: Fortune seeks a very sophisticated controller for her new trick, picking up two spaceship controllers and putting them together. It works amazingly well, and Fortune renames it ''Celeste.'' Part of Celeste comes from Reverdy who sells it because she no longer trusts Spelvin matrix technology after Manfred, another Spelvin matrix, almost killed her. To Reverdy, all Spelvins feel like potential artificial intelligences (AIs), while Persephone society still suffers from the riots resulting when Manfred, a Spelvin thought to be an AI, tried to kill its crew. Sequel to *Dreamships*.

Where it's reviewed:
Booklist, June 1 & 15, 1997, page 1669
Kirkus Reviews, May 1, 1997, page 685
Library Journal, May 15, 1997, page 106
Locus, October 1997, page 21
Publishers Weekly, June 16, 1997, page 50

Other books by the same author:
Night Sky Mine, 1996
Shadow Man, 1995
Trouble and Her Friends, 1994
Burning Bright, 1993
Dreamships, 1992

Other books you might like:
David Brin, *Earth*, 1990
Robert A. Heinlein, *The Moon Is a Harsh Mistress*, 1996
Steve Perry, *The Trinity Vector*, 1996
Alis A. Rasmussen, *Revolution's Shore*, 1990
John Varley, *Steel Beach*, 1992
Vernor Vinge, *A Fire upon the Deep*, 1992

1198

WILLIAM SHATNER

JUDITH REEVES-STEVENS, Co-Author
GARFIELD REEVES-STEVENS, Co-Author

Avenger

(New York: Pocket, 1997)

Story type: Mystery; Disaster

Series: Star Trek

Science Fiction

Major character(s): Jean-Luc Picard, Spaceship Captain; James T. Kirk, Spaceship Captain; Spock, Diplomat, Alien (Vulcan)

Time period(s): 24th century

Locale(s): Chal, Planet—Imaginary; Vulcan, Planet—Imaginary; United Federation of Planets, Interstellar Empire/Federation

Summary: Left in a Borg recycling center and restored to health, Kirk seeks his lost love on the planet Chal, suffering from the same ecological disaster that threatens life throughout the Federation. Meanwhile, Spock suspects that his father's death resulted from murder, not natural causes. Reunited, the two friends follow the clues to Tarsus IV where they learn the truth about the origins of the new plague with the help of the *Enterprise E.*

Where it's reviewed:
Library Journal, May 15, 1997, page 106
Publishers Weekly, April 12, 1997, page 64

Other books by the same author:
Man O'War, 1996
The Return, 1996 (Judith Reeves-Stevens, Garfield Reeves-Steven s, co-authors)
The Ashes of Eden, 1995 (Judith Reeves-Stevens, Garfield Reeves-Steven s, co-authors)
Tek Power, 1994
TekLords, 1991
TekWar, 1989

Other books you might like:
Michael Crichton, *The Andromeda Strain*, 1969
Michael Jan Friedman, *Reunion*, 1991
Lynn S. Hightower, *Alien Rites*, 1995
Jean Lorrah, *The IDIC Epidemic*, 1988
Jean Lorrah, *The Vulcan Academy Murders*, 1984
Judith Reeves-Stevens, *Prime Directive*, 1990
   Garfield Reeves-Stevens, co-author

`1199`
WILLIAM SHATNER
Delta Search
(New York: HarperPrism, 1997)

Story type: Adventure; Genetic Manipulation
Series: Quest for Tomorrow
Major character(s): Carl ''Carl Johnson'' Endicott, Fugitive; James ''Jimmy'' Endicott, Teenager, Genetically Altered Being; Catherine ''Cat'' Thibaudeaux, Spy
Time period(s): 23rd century (2280s)
Locale(s): San Francisco, California; Prima City, Fictional City; Wolfbane, Planet—Imaginary

Summary: Despite his father's disapproval, Jimmy sends his application to the Solis Space Academy, including his father's genotype. As soon as he discovers his son's actions, Carl abandons his home, taking his family with only what they can carry to a cabin in the woods. After an attack by people in space armor and being forced by his dying father to memorize a code, Jimmy realizes he must rescue his mother and discover who attacked his family and why. First in a series.

Where it's reviewed:
Booklist, January 1 & 15, 1997, page 780
Library Journal, February 15, 1997, page 165
Publishers Weekly, January 27, 1997, page 81

Other books by the same author:
In Alien Hands, 1997

Other books you might like:
Emily Devenport, *Shade*, 1991
David Feintuch, *Voices of Hope*, 1996
Alan Dean Foster, *The Tar-Aiym Krang*, 1972
Robert A. Heinlein, *Have Spacesuit—Will Travel*, 1958
Melissa Scott, *Night Sky Mine*, 1996
Joan D. Vinge, *Psion*, 1982

`1200`
WILLIAM SHATNER
Tek Net
(New York: Ace/Putnam, 1997)

Story type: Adventure
Series: Tek
Major character(s): Jake Cardigan, Detective—Private; Sid Gomez, Detective—Private
Time period(s): 22nd century
Locale(s): Earth

Summary: Shortly after Sid receives a request from his second ex-wife, currently working on a screenplay about an infamous TekLord thought dead, Sid and Jake's personal investigation receives official sanction when they learn a client places a premium on finding the TekLord alive.

Where it's reviewed:
Booklist, August 1997, page 1849
Library Journal, October 15, 1997, page 98
Publishers Weekly, September 8, 1997, page 63

Other books by the same author:
Tek Money, 1995
Tek Power, 1994
Tek Secret, 1993
Tek Vengeance, 1993
TekWar, 1989

Other books you might like:
Robert Cain, *Cybernarc*, 1991
Philip K. Dick, *A Scanner Darkly*, 1997
Lynn S. Hightower, *Alien Blues*, 1992
Ernest Hogan, *High Aztec*, 1992
Richard Paul Russo, *Carlucci's Heart*, 1997

`1201`
CHARLES SHEFFIELD
The Billion Dollar Boy
(New York: Tor, 1997)

Story type: Young Adult; Adventure
Major character(s): Shelby Cheever V, Teenager, Heir; Grace Trask, Spaceship Captain, Miner; Lana Trask, Spaceship Captain, Miner

Time period(s): Indeterminate Future
Locale(s): *Harvest Moon*, Spaceship; Messina Dust Cloud, Outer Space

Summary: Spoiled heir to one of Earth's largest private fortunes. Shelby Cheever takes an unauthorized trip through the interstellar node network, stranding himself in the Messina Dust Cloud. A group of transuranics miners takes Shelby in, teaching him that not wealth but only hard work and loyalty will earn their respect. Second in series.

Where it's reviewed:
Booklist, April1, 1997, page 1283
Library Journal, December 1996, page 152
Locus, February 1997, page 15
Publishers Weekly, March 31, 1997, page 68
Science Fiction Chronicle, October 1997, page 44

Other books by the same author:
Putting Up Roots, 1997
Higher Education, 1996 (Jerry Pournelle, co-author)
Georgia on My Mind and Other Places, 1995
The Ganymede Club, 1995
Proteus in the Underworld, 1995

Other books you might like:
Arthur C. Clarke, *Dolphin Island*, 1963
Stephen Gould, *Wildside*, 1996
Robert A. Heinlein, *Space Cadet*, 1948
Frederik Pohl, *Mining the Oort*, 1992
Jerry Pournelle, *West of Honor*, 1976
Larry Segriff, *Spacer Dreams*, 1995

1202

CHARLES SHEFFIELD

Convergence
(New York: Baen, 1997)

Story type: Space Opera; Science Fiction
Series: Heritage Universe
Major character(s): Darya Lang, Scientist, Adventurer; Atvar H'sial, Alien (Cecropian), Businesswoman; Louis Nenda, Adventurer
Time period(s): 63rd century
Locale(s): Genizee, Planet—Imaginary; *Indulgence*, Spaceship; Torvil Anfract, Outer Space

Summary: While escaping from Genizee, Louis Nenda and Atvar H'sial inadvertently capture a live Zardulu, worth millions back in the Benignity. Darya Lang must again go to space to refute a challenge to her theory of the origin of the Artifacts and the intent of the builders. Much to Darya's chagrin, the Artifacts continue to change, but some changes bring a lengthier future for human presence among the intelligent races of the Galaxy. Fourth in series.

Where it's reviewed:
Starlog, September 1997, page 80

Other books by the same author:
Proteus Combined, 1994
One Man's Universe, 1993
Transcendence, 1992
Divergence, 1991

Summertide, 1990

Other books you might like:
Greg Bear, *Eon*, 1985
David Brin, *Startide Rising*, 1983
Glen Cook, *The Dragon Never Sleeps*, 1988
Alis A. Rasmussen, *A Passage of Stars*, 1990
Robert J. Sawyer, *Starplex*, 1990
Dan Simmons, *Hyperion*, 1989

1203

CHARLES SHEFFIELD

Putting Up Roots
(New York: Tor, 1997)

Story type: First Contact; Young Adult
Major character(s): Joshua ''Josh'' Kerrigan, Hero, Outcast; Sapphire Karpov, Addict, Young Woman; Winnie Carlson, Technician, Spy
Time period(s): Indeterminate Future
Locale(s): Solferino, Planet—Imaginary

Summary: Sent with a party of throwaway teens to settle on Solferino, Joshua and his autistic cousin, Dawn, find no settlers waiting to greet them. Mysteriously shuttled around the planet with no off-world communications possible, Josh believes he has seen mining ships while his cousin says she has found intelligent aliens.

Where it's reviewed:
Booklist, August 1997, page 1887
Library Journal, August 1997, page 141
Publishers Weekly, August 11, 1997, page 391
Science Fiction Chronicle, October 1997, page 45

Other books by the same author:
The Billion Dollar Boy, 1997
Higher Education, 1996
The Ganymede Club, 1995
Godspeed, 1993
Cold as Ice, 1992

Other books you might like:
Gregory Benford, *The Jupiter Project*, 1975
Robert A. Heinlein, *Farmer in the Sky*, 1950
Colin Kapp, *The Survival Game*, 1976
Andre Norton, *The Stars Are Ours*, 1954
Frederik Pohl, *The Voices of Heaven*, 1994
Jerry Pournelle, *Birth of Fire*, 1976
Carol Severance, *Reefsong*, 1991
Joan D. Vinge, *Psion*, 1982

1204

CHARLES SHEFFIELD

Tomorrow and Tomorrow
(New York: Bantam Spectra, 1997)

Story type: Alternate Intelligence; Immortality
Major character(s): Walter Drake Merlin, Musician; Tom Lambert, Doctor; Anastasia ''Ana'' Merlin, Singer
Time period(s): 2000s; Indeterminate Future
Locale(s): Earth; Cyberspace

Summary: In love with his wife Ana from the first sound of her voice, Drake cannot accept her suddenly impending death from an extremely rare disease. He decides to have her cryogenically stored, develop himself as an expert to insure his revival and join her. The first time he wakes, Drake pretends the cure for his obsession with Ana worked, steals a spaceship and Ana's cryochamber, then heads out to Canopus. When, on his way back, he opens the casket, causing Ana permanent brain damage, Drake and Ana return to the chambers with instructions to revive Drake only if needed or if Ana can be cured.

Where it's reviewed:
Booklist, January 1 & 15, 1997, page 826
Kirkus Reviews, November 1, 1996, page 1570
Kliatt, May 1997, page 15
Library Journal, December 1996, page 152
Voice of Youth Advocates, August 1997, page 195

Other books by the same author:
Proteus Combined, 1994
Godspeed, 1993
Cold as Ice, 1992
My Brother's Keeper, 1982
Hidden Variables, 1981

Other books you might like:
John Brunner, *Age of Miracles*, 1973
Ken Grimwood, *Replay*, 1986
Joe Haldeman, *The Forever War*, 1997
   revised
Christopher Pike, *The Starlight Crystal*, 1996
Vernor Vinge, *A Fire upon the Deep*, 1992

1205

SHARON SHINN

Jovah's Angel
(New York: Ace, 1997)

Story type: Genetic Manipulation; Theological
Major character(s): Alleluia "Alleya" Wellin, Genetically Altered Being (angel), Leader (archangel); Caleb Augustus, Engineer, Scientist; Delilah "Lilah", Genetically Altered Being (angel), Singer
Time period(s): Indeterminate Future
Locale(s): Samaria, Planet—Imaginary; Luminaux, Fictional City; Eyrie, Mythical Place (angel stronghold)

Summary: Because Jovah no longer hears the Angels, the storms on Samaria continue to worsen. When Archangel Delilah breaks a wing, Alleluia, the only angel Jovah still hears, replaces her. While researching to fulfill her new position and find her partner for the Gloria, Alleluia inadvertently learns the language used by the Oracles to communicate with Jovah. Caleb works to repair Delilah's wing, after adding an external power source to fix the old music players. Sequel to *Archangel*.

Where it's reviewed:
Fantasy & Science Fiction, January 1998, page 29
Kirkus Reviews, April 1, 1997, page 530
Library Journal, May 15, 1997, page 106
Locus, April 1997, page 21

Starlog, November 1997, page 16

Other books by the same author:
Archangel, 1996
The Shape-Changer's Wife, 1995

Other books you might like:
Orson Scott Card, *The Memory of Earth*, 1992
Rosemary Kirstein, *The Outskirter's Secret*, 1992
Louise Marley, *Sing the Light*, 1995
Anne McCaffrey, *The Chronicles of Pern: First Fall*, 1993
Dan Simmons, *Endymion*, 1996

1206

SUSAN SHWARTZ

Vulcan's Forge
(New York: Pocket, 1997)

Story type: Adventure; Space Opera
Series: Star Trek
Major character(s): Spock, Spaceship Captain, Alien (Vulcan); David Rabin, Military Personnel (captain); Leonard McCoy, Doctor, Spaceman
Time period(s): 23rd century
Locale(s): U.S.S. *Intrepid II*, Spaceship; United Federation of Planets, Interstellar Empire/Federation

Summary: Assigned to a Federation outpost on the planet Obsidian, Captain Rabin tries to help the inhabitants improve their lives, but saboteurs destroy supplies and equipment. Captained by Spock, a boyhood friend with whom Rabin had once survived the desert known as Vulcan's Forge, the *Intrepid II* arrives in response to Rabin's request for help. With their shuttlecraft forced down in the desert, Dr. McCoy kidnapped and supplies running low, Rabin and Spock face another desert and a dangerous madman.

Where it's reviewed:
Publishers Weekly, May 19, 1997, page 70

Other books by the same author:
Shards of Empire, 1996
The Chaos Gate, 1994
The Grail of Hearts, 1992
Child of Faerie, Child of Earth, 1992
Byzantium's Crown, 1987

Other books you might like:
Margaret Wander Bonanno, *Dwellers in the Crucible*, 1985
C.J. Cherryh, *The Faded Sun: Kesrith*, 1978
J.M. Dillard, *The Lost Years*, 1989
Diane Duane, *Spock's World*, 1988
Diane Duane, *The Romulan Way*, 1987
   Peter Morwood, co-author
Michael Jan Friedman, *Crossover*, 1995
Frank Herbert, *Dune*, 1965
L.A. Taylor, *The Blossom of Erda*, 1986

1207

ROBERT SILVERBERG

Sorcerers of Majipoor

(New York: HarperPrism, 1997)

Story type: Political; Science Fantasy
Series: Majipoor
Major character(s): Korsibar, Royalty (prince); Prestimion, Royalty (prince); Thismet, Royalty (princess)
Time period(s): Indeterminate Future
Locale(s): Majipoor, Planet—Imaginary

Summary: Against all custom, Prince Korsibar becomes "coronal" of Majipoor, instead of the expected heir, Prince Prestimion. Resentful of this, Prestimion starts a rebellion, but must flee to Triggoin, a city of sorcerers, where he gains the wisdom to make a change of rulers meaningful before continuing his battle against Korsibar. Fifth in series.

Where it's reviewed:
Booklist, June 1 & 15, 1997, page 1620
Kirkus Reviews, June 1, 1997, page 842
Library Journal, June 15, 1997, page 101
Publishers Weekly, June 16, 1997, page 49
Science Fiction Age, September 1997, page 10

Other books by the same author:
Starborne, 1996
The New Springtime, 1990
Valentine Pontifex, 1983
The Majipoor Chronicles, 1982
Lord Valentine's Castle, 1980

Other books you might like:
Lois McMaster Bujold, *Barrayar*, 1991
Octavia E. Butler, *Patternmaster*, 1976
Orson Scott Card, *The Memory of Earth*, 1992
Katherine Kurtz, *The Bastard Prince*, 1994
Harry Turtledove, *The Stolen Throne*, 1995
Jack Vance, *Lyonesse*, 1983
Joan D. Vinge, *The Snow Queen*, 1980
Roger Zelazny, *Nine Princes in Amber*, 1970

1208

DAN SIMMONS

The Rise of Endymion

(New York: Bantam Spectra, 1997)

Story type: Theological; Alternate Intelligence
Series: Hyperion
Major character(s): Aenea, Genetically Altered Being, Religious (messiah); Raul Endymion, Hero, Prisoner; Martin Silenus, Writer (poet), Aged Person
Time period(s): 32nd century
Locale(s): Pacem, Planet—Imaginary; Hyperion, Planet—Imaginary; *Yggdrasill*, Spaceship (treeship)

Summary: While remaining in the Schroedinger Cat Box prison, Raul continues writing his remembrances of Aenea, the One Who Teaches, their developing relationship and their travels. Designed as a weapon to prevent the TechnoCore from completely enslaving or destroying human and alien

life, Aenea glimpses the future and sees her own death, permitting her to know how short a time remains to complete her task. A concluding fourth volume in the series is likely.

Where it's reviewed:
Booklist, August 1997, page 1887
Kirkus Reviews, June 15, 1997, page 917
Library Journal, September 15, 1997, page 106
Locus, September 1997, page 17
New York Times Book Review, August 31, 1997, page 22

Other books by the same author:
Endymion, 1996
The Hollow Man, 1992
The Fall of Hyperion, 1990
Hyperion, 1989
Phases of Gravity, 1989

Other books you might like:
Isaac Asimov, *Robots of Dawn*, 1983
David Brin, *Brightness Reef*, 1995
Frank Herbert, *Dune*, 1965
James P. Hogan, *The Immortality Option*, 1995
Larry Niven, *Protector*, 1973
Vernor Vinge, *A Fire upon the Deep*, 1992

1209

L. NEIL SMITH

Bretta Martyn

(New York: Tor, 1997)

Story type: Family Saga; Political
Series: Henry Martyn
Major character(s): Arran "Henry Martyn" Islay, Leader; Robretta "Bretta Martyn" Islay, Teenager; Lisa Woodgate, Ruler
Time period(s): 31st century (3020s)
Locale(s): Hanover, Planet—Imaginary; Monopolity of Hanover, Interstellar Empire/Federation; Skye, Planet—Imaginary

Summary: Lia, Ceo of Hanover, commissions Arran to destroy the slave trade which has claimed millions of people over the past millennium. Arran brings his wife and oldest daughter to Hanover and on the mission, with the story that they search for lost Earth. The slavers' spy rapes and attempts to kill Bretta, throwing her off the ship in a trash can where she should die from her wounds. With Earth inhabitable, the terraformed Moon flourishes with a free and independent population and many colonies throughout the spiral arm.

Where it's reviewed:
Booklist, July 1997, page 1806
Kirkus Reviews, June 15, 1997, page 917
Publishers Weekly, July 1997, page 1806

Other books by the same author:
The Lando Calrission Adventures, 1994
Henry Martyn, 1989
Tom Paine Maru, 1984
The Venus Belt, 1981
The Probability Broach, 1980

Other books you might like:
Lois McMaster Bujold, *Borders of Infinity*, 1989
F.M. Busby, *Rissa Kerguelen*, 1977
Orson Scott Card, *Wyrms*, 1987
Sheri S. Tepper, *Grass*, 1989
Jack Vance, *Madouc*, 1990

1210

CHRISTOPHER STASHEFF

A Wizard in Chaos

(New York: Tor, 1997)

Story type: Science Fantasy; Political
Series: Rogue Wizard
Major character(s): Magnus ''Gar Pike'' Gallowglass, Psychic, Troubleshooter; Dirk Dulaine, Sidekick, Military Personnel; Cort, Military Personnel (lieutenant)
Time period(s): Indeterminate Future
Locale(s): Durvie, Planet—Imaginary

Summary: Gar and Dirk arrive on Durvie, settled by idealistic anarchists, but now involved in constant war between rival strongholds. The only technology remains hidden in hollow hills regarded as fairy mounds by a superstitious peasantry. When Gar incurs the wrath of a villainous and wrathful steward, he and Dirk must get all factions working together to build some sort of governmental stability.

Where it's reviewed:
Booklist, November 1, 1997, page 457
Kirkus Reviews, October 15, 1997, page 1562
Library Journal, November 15, 1997, page 79
Publishers Weekly, November 10, 1997, page 60
Starlog, February 1998, page 60

Other books by the same author:
My Son, the Wizard, 1997
A Wizard in Peace, 1996
Quicksilver's Knight, 1995
A Company of Stars, 1991
The Warlock in Spite of Himself, 1969

Other books you might like:
Lloyd Biggle Jr., *The World Menders*, 1971
J.F. Bone, *Confederation Matador*, 1978
Colin Kapp, *The Wizard of Anharitte*, 1973
Lee Killough, *Liberty's World*, 1985
Barbara Paul, *Under the Canopy*, 1980
Mack Reynolds, *Planetary Agent X*, 1965
Arkady Strugatsky, *Hard to Be a God*, 1973
   Boris Strugatsky, co-author
Lawrence Watt-Evans, *Denner's Wreck*, 1988

1211

CHRISTOPHER STASHEFF

A Wizard in Peace

(New York: Tor, 1996)

Story type: Lost Colony; Political

Major character(s): Magnus ''Gar Pike'' Gallowglass, Psychic, Revolutionary; Dirk Dulaine, Sidekick, Adventurer; Orgoru, Fugitive, Imposter
Time period(s): 31st century
Locale(s): Planet—Imaginary

Summary: On a planet they think too individually repressive and puritanical, Magnus and Dirk organize revolutionaries to help loosen up the dictatorial rule.

Where it's reviewed:
Booklist, October 15, 1996, page 408
Kirkus Reviews, July 15, 1996, page 1014
Library Journal, September 15, 1996, page 101
Publishers Weekly, September 30, 1996, page 66

Other books by the same author:
A Wizard in Mind, 1995
A Wizard in War, 1995
A Company of Stars, 1991
A Wizard in Bedlam, 1979
The Warlock in Spite of Himself, 1969

Other books you might like:
Stephen Baxter, *Raft*, 1992
Orson Scott Card, *The Memory of Earth*, 1992
Rosemary Kirstein, *The Steerswoman*, 1989
Larry Niven, *The Integral Trees*, 1984
Joan Slonczewski, *A Door into Ocean*, 1986

1212

ALLEN STEELE

A King of Infinite Space

(New York: HarperPrism, 1997)

Story type: Alternate Intelligence; Space Colony
Series: Near Space Stories
Major character(s): William Alec Tucker III, Reanimated Dead, Cyborg; Pasquale Chicago, Businessman; Chip, Artificial Intelligence, Companion (Alec's)
Time period(s): 2090s (2099)
Locale(s): 4442 Garcia, Asteroid (1985 RB1); Clarke County, Space Station (Lagrange Five Colony)

Summary: Pasquale Chicago reanimates Alec from cryogenic suspension a century after his fatal accident, repairing his injuries and implanting Chip to aid his scrambled memories. Alec's feelings toward his role in the future and his benefactor change as he learns about Chicago's bold bid for power. When he discovers his girlfriend may also have survived the accident, Alec escapes Chicago's colony to find her.

Where it's reviewed:
Asimov's Science Fiction, January 1997, page 149
Locus, November 1997, page 62

Other books by the same author:
Rude Astronauts, 1993
Labyrinth of Night, 1992
Lunar Descent, 1991
Clarke County, Space, 1990
Orbital Decay, 1989

Other books you might like:
Ron Goulart, *When the Waker Sleeps*, 1975

Frederik Pohl, *The Age of the Pussyfoot*, 1969
Clifford D. Simak, *Why Call Them Back From Heaven?*, 1967
Ernest Tidyman, *Absolute Zero*, 1971
H.G. Wells, *When the Sleeper Wakes*, 1899
James White, *The Dream Millennium*, 1974

1213

S.M. STIRLING

The Ship Avenged

(New York: Baen, 1997)

Story type: Adventure; Space Colony
Series: Ship Who Sang
Major character(s): Joat Simeon-Hap, Spaceship Captain; Soamosa, Young Woman; Bro Sperin, Spy
Time period(s): Indeterminate Future
Locale(s): New Dentinies, Space Station; Kolnar, Space Station

Summary: Devastated by a designed virus, the Kolnari vow revenge, intending to drop a mind-destroying virus on the planet Bethel. When Joat Simeon-Hap needs to earn money quickly to pay a fine, she has to deal with the man who sold her into slavery and must meet with the Kolnari. Sequel to *The City Who Fought*.

Where it's reviewed:
Kirkus Reviews, December 15, 1996, page 1774
Publishers Weekly, January 27, 1997, page 82

Other books by the same author:
The Rose Sea, 1994 (Holly Lisle, co-author)
Saber & Shadow, 1992 (Sherley Meier, co-author)
Snowbrother, 1992
Under the Yoke, 1989
Marching through Georgia, 1988

Other books you might like:
Lois McMaster Bujold, *The Vor Game*, 1990
C.J. Cherryh, *Tripoint*, 1994
Alfred Coppel, *Glory*, 1993
Anne McCaffrey, *The City Who Fought*, 1993
  S.M. Stirling, co-author
Anne McCaffrey, *The Ship Who Sang*, 1969
Melissa Scott, *Five-Twelfths of Heaven*, 1985
John E. Stith, *Redshift Rendezvous*, 1990
Timothy Zahn, *Deadman Switch*, 1988

1214

JOHN E. STITH

Reckoning Infinity

(New York: Tor, 1997)

Story type: First Contact; Adventure
Major character(s): Alis Mary Nussem, Spacewoman, Pilot (spaceship); Karl Stanton, Spaceman, Pilot (spaceship)
Time period(s): Indeterminate Future
Locale(s): Tokyan Station, Space Station; *Ranger*, Spaceship; *Cantaloupe*, Spaceship

Summary: Karl accepts a position on *Ranger*, stationed near Pluto, hoping to escape the infamy he acquired when falsely blamed for an accident resulting from sabotage. Alis also hopes to escape her memories of the disaster when she sign on with *Ranger*, but meeting Karl there prohibits relief. Unwilling workmates, Alis and Karl together explore a fabulous alien vessel as it visits the Solar System.

Where it's reviewed:
Booklist, April 1, 1997, page 1283
Kirkus Reviews, February 1, 1997, page 177
Library Journal, March 15, 1997, page 93
Locus, July 1997, page 25
Science Fiction Chronicle, October 1997, page 46

Other books by the same author:
Manhattan Transfer, 1993
Redshift Rendezvous, 1990
Deep Quarry, 1989
Death Tolls, 1987
Memory Blank, 1986

Other books you might like:
Roger MacBride Allen, *The Ring of Charon*, 1990
Greg Bear, *Eon*, 1985
Vonda N. McIntyre, *Metaphase*, 1992
Larry Niven, *Ringworld*, 1970
John Varley, *Titan*, 1979

1215

L. ELIZABETH STORM

Angels Unaware

(New York: Boulevard, 1997)

Story type: Time Travel; Theological
Series: Quantum Leap
Major character(s): Sam Beckett, Time Traveller, Scientist; Teresa Bruckner, Student; Angelita Carmen Jiminez, Angel
Time period(s): 1990s (1995)
Locale(s): Boston, Massachusetts

Summary: Having met Sam as a child, Teresa believes in angels, but finds herself unable to accept the Hispanic flapper Angelita as an angel, even though she proves to have much information about Teresa that she shouldn't know. When Sam finds himself a local priest, he may be able to save Teresa from the drug dealers who want to kill her for stealing their drugs. Television tie-in.

Other books by the same author:
Pulitzer, 1995

Other books you might like:
Poul Anderson, *The Time Patrol*, 1991
Mona Clee, *Branch Point*, 1996
Carol Davies, *Obsessions*, 1997
S.D. Perry, *Timecop*, 1994
George Gaylord Simpson, *The Dechronization of Sam Magruder*, 1996

1216
THEODORE STURGEON

Killdozer!

(Berkeley, California: North Atlantic Books, 1996)

Story type: Collection; Science Fiction
Series: Complete Stories of Theodore Sturgeon

Summary: Contains a seven-page foreword by Robert Silverberg, a seven-page afterword by Robert A. Heinlein and 25 pages of story notes by the series editor, Paul Williams, including an unpublished alternate ending to ''Mewhu's Jet'' and the original ending of ''Killdozer!'' Varying in tone from light to downbeat, the 11 reprinted and four original stories all written 1941-1946, feature diverse themes including first contact, heavy construction equipment operation, human relationships, government folly, and space exploration. Third of the projected 10-volume series.

Where it's reviewed:
Science Fiction Age, January 1997, page 16

Other books by the same author:
Microcosmic God, 1995
The Ultimate Egoist, 1994
Godbody, 1986
Maturity, 1979
More than Human, 1953

Other books you might like:
Alfred Bester, *Star Light, Star Bright*, 1976
Philip K. Dick, *The Collected Stories of Philip K. Dick*, 1987
    five volumes
Clifford D. Simak, *Over the River & Through the Woods*, 1996
Cordwainer Smith, *The Rediscovery of Man*, 1993
John Varley, *Blue Champagne*, 1986

1217
THEODORE STURGEON

Thunder and Roses

(Berkeley, California: North Atlantic Books, 1997)

Story type: Collection; Science Fiction
Series: Complete Short Stories of Theodore Sturgeon

Summary: Contains a seven-page foreword by James Gunn, 18 pages of story notes by series editor Paul Williams, an appendix with the original second half of ''Maturity'' and 16 stories published 1946-1947, with one, ''Wham Bop!,'' previously not reprinted in book form. Themes include psychology, UFOs, politics, horror and the West. One of a ten-volume series.

Other books by the same author:
Killdozer!, 1996
Microcosmic God, 1995
The Ultimate Egoist, 1994
More than Human, 1953
The Dreaming Jewels, 1950

Other books you might like:
J.G. Ballard, *The Best Short Stories of J.G. Ballard*, 1978

Ray Bradbury, *Quicker than the Eye*, 1996
C.M. Kornbluth, *His Share of Glory: The Complete Short Science Fiction of C.M. Kornbluth*, 1997
Henry Kuttner, *The Best of Henry Kuttner*, 1975
Clifford D. Simak, *Over the River & Through the Woods*, 1996
John Varley, *The Persistence of Vision*, 1978

1218
TRICIA SULLIVAN

Someone to Watch over Me

(New York: Bantam Spectra, 1997)

Story type: Alternate Intelligence
Major character(s): Adrien Reyes, Experimental Subject, Slave; Sabina Lazarich, Musician, Composer; C, Disembodied Personality
Time period(s): Indeterminate Future
Locale(s): Earth

Summary: Adrien Reyes hopes to escape the slavery of life as a surrogate body, but the experimental brain implant may allow C to download itself permanently into Adrien's body.

Where it's reviewed:
Locus, September 1997, page 29

Other books by the same author:
Lethe, 1995

Other books you might like:
Stephen Bury, *Interface*, 1994
Raphael Carter, *The Fortunate Fall*, 1996
Peter R. Emshwiller, *The Host*, 1991
Sage Walker, *Whiteout*, 1996
David Weber, *Path of the Fury*, 1992

1219
MICHAEL SWANWICK

Jack Faust

(New York: Avon, 1997)

Story type: First Contact
Major character(s): Johannes ''Jack'' Faust, Scholar, Genius; Wagner, Student; Mephistopheles, Alien, Demon
Time period(s): 19th century; 20th century
Locale(s): Europe

Summary: Stopped by Wagner from completely burning his library, Faust demonstrates by debate that he needs more information. He realizes he will do anything for the truth when Mephistopheles tells him he will give Faust all the information he needs, but it will lead to the end of humanity.

Where it's reviewed:
Booklist, September 1, 1997, page 67
Kirkus Reviews, July 15, 1997 page 1073
Library Journal, September 1, 1997, page 221
Locus, September 1997, page 29
Science Fiction Age, November 1997, page 18

Other books by the same author:
The Iron Dragon's Daughter, 1994

Gravity's Angels, 1991
Stations of the Tide, 1991
Vacuum Flowers, 1987
In the Drift, 1985

Other books you might like:
Mary Gentle, *Ancient Light*, 1987
Jack McDevitt, *The Engines of God*, 1994
Christopher Pike, *The Eternal Enemy*, 1993
Mary Doria Russell, *The Sparrow*, 1996
Dan Simmons, *Hyperion*, 1989

1220

SHERI S. TEPPER

The Family Tree

(New York: Avon, 1997)

Story type: Genetic Manipulation; Time Travel
Major character(s): Dora Henry, Police Officer; Nassifeh "Opalears" Nazir, Time Traveller, Storyteller; Izakar "Izzy", Linguist, Time Traveller
Time period(s): 2000s; 51st century
Locale(s): United States

Summary: Defying her husband, Dora welcomes the weed. When she moves out, another finds her at her new home and seems to understand her. While the weed becomes a forest, Dora investigates the murder of a retired geneticist who, reportedly, created a talking pig. The environment no longer supports the range of wildlife needed to maintain itself due to overpopulation and construction, but the strange new trees change that with a little help from the future.

Where it's reviewed:
Kirkus Reviews, March 15, 1997, page 424
Library Journal, May 15, 1997, page 106
Locus, April 1997, page 21
Publishers Weekly, April 21, 1997, page 65
Science Fiction Age, July 1997, page 17

Other books by the same author:
Gibbon's Decline and Fall, 1996
A Plague of Angels, 1993
Raising the Stones, 1990
Grass, 1989
The Gate to Women's Country, 1988

Other books you might like:
David Brin, *Brightness Reef*, 1995
Paula E. Downing, *A Whisper of Time*, 1994
Thomas A. Easton, *Greenhouse*, 1991
Alan Dean Foster, *Quozl*, 1989
Kay Kenyon, *The Seeds of Time*, 1997
Megan Lindholm, *Alien Earth*, 1992
Catherine Wells, *The Earth is All That Lasts*, 1991

1221

DIANN THORNLEY

Dominion's Reach

(New York: Tor, 1997)

Story type: Family Saga; Military

Series: Saga of the Unified Worlds
Major character(s): Lujan Ansellic Serege, Military Personnel, Patient; Tristan Serege, Teenager, Military Personnel (volunteer); Darcie Dartmuth, Military Personnel (captain), Spouse
Time period(s): Indeterminate Future
Locale(s): Topawa, Planet—Imaginary; Issel, Planet—Imaginary; *Shadow*, Spaceship

Summary: Wounded during the signing of the Isselan Assistance Pact, Lujan recovers from a shattered vertebra and neurological damage suffered while saving the Isselan ambassador. Darcie helps him learn to communicate while he recovers and receives necessary neurological implants. The Isselan plot to take over the United Worlds from within provides military assistance to destroy the slavers. Third in series.

Where it's reviewed:
Kirkus Reviews, January 1, 1997, page 28
Library Journal, March 15, 1997, page 93
Publishers Weekly, February 24, 1997, page 69

Other books by the same author:
Echoes of Issel, 1996
Ganwold's Child, 1995

Other books you might like:
Lois McMaster Bujold, *Memory*, 1996
L. Warren Douglas, *Stepwater*, 1995
Scott G. Gier, *In the Shadow of the Moon*, 1996
Jerry Pournelle, *Falkenberg's Legion*, 1990
Jack Vance, *Alastor*, 1995

1222

DIANN THORNLEY

Echoes of Issel

(New York: Tor, 1996)

Story type: Political; Family Saga
Series: Unified Worlds
Major character(s): Lujan Ansellic Serege, Military Personnel (admiral), Parent; Tristan Serege, Teenager, Refugee; Libby Moses, Doctor, Military Personnel
Time period(s): Indeterminate Future
Locale(s): Saede, Planet—Imaginary; Issel II, Planet—Imaginary; Unified Worlds/Dominion, Interstellar Empire/Federation

Summary: Reunited, the Serege family stumbles toward mutual respect and understanding in this sequel to *Ganwold's Child*. Lujan works to gain Tristan's trust while helping his former enemies fight Masuki slavers. Tristan's knowledge of Issel II from his former imprisonment there permits the Unified Worlds military to attempt a rescue of Dominion soldiers in fortified Dominion strongholds controlled by alien Masuki.

Where it's reviewed:
Booklist, April 15, 1996, page 1425
Kirkus Reviews, January 15, 1996, page 106
Publishers Weekly, February 12, 1996, page 64

Other books by the same author:
Ganwold's Child, 1995

Other books you might like:
Eleanor Arnason, *Ring of Swords*, 1993
Lois McMaster Bujold, *Borders of Infinity*, 1989
F.M. Busby, *Rissa Kerguelen*, 1977
L. Warren Douglas, *A Plague of Change*, 1992
Alis A. Rasmussen, *The Price of Ransom*, 1990

1223

HARRY TURTLEDOVE

How Few Remain

(New York: Ballantine Del Rey, 1997)

Story type: Military; Political
Major character(s): Sam Clemens, Journalist, Historical Figure; Frederick Douglass, Journalist, Historical Figure (orator); George A. Custer, Military Personnel, Historical Figure
Time period(s): 1880s (1881-1882)
Locale(s): United States; North America (Confederate States of America); Alternate Earth

Summary: When the Confederacy moves to buy Sonora Chihuahua from the cash-strapped Mexican Empire, President James Blaine declares war. As the United Kingdom and France aid the Confederacy, the U.S.A. finds its shores blockaded and its cities bombarded. Realizing he cannot win, Blaine must develop other alliances.

Where it's reviewed:
Booklist, July 1997, page 1777
Kirkus Reviews, August 15, 1997, page 1265
Publishers Weekly, August 11, 1997, page 390
Realms of Fantasy, December 1997, page 10

Other books by the same author:
Worldwar: Striking the Balance, 1996
The Guns of the South, 1992
A World of Difference, 1990
A Different Flesh, 1988
Agent of Byzantium, 1987

Other books you might like:
Orson Scott Card, *Alvin Journeyman*, 1995
Richard Dreyfuss, *The Two Georges*, 1996
    Harry Turtledove, co-author
Alan Dean Foster, *Mad Amos*, 1996
Stephen King, *The Dark Tower: The Gunslinger*, 1982
Kirk Mitchell, *Never the Twain*, 1987
Kevin Randall, *Remember the Little Bighorn*, 1990
    Robert Cornett, co-author
Mike Resnick, *Bwana & Bully*, 1991
Mark Sumner, *Devil's Tower*, 1996

1224

JOHN UPDIKE

Toward the End of Time

(New York: Knopf, 1997)

Story type: Post-Disaster; Dystopian
Major character(s): Ben Turnbull, Aged Person
Time period(s): 2020s

Locale(s): Massachusetts

Summary: In a depopulated post-war America, Ben Turnbull retains some retirement amenities, despite social chaos. Ben becomes involved with the "many worlds" hypothesis derived from quantum theory as his identity follows the branches into the past and future, exploring various possibilities.

Where it's reviewed:
Kirkus Reviews, August 1, 1997, page 1149
Library Journal, September 15, 1997, page 103
Locus, October 1997, page 17
New York Times Book Review, October 12, 1997, page 9

Other books by the same author:
The Witches of Eastwick, 1984

Other books you might like:
Deborah Christian, *Mainline*, 1996
James P. Hogan, *Paths to Otherwhere*, 1996
Katharine Kerr, *Resurrection*, 1992
Nancy Kress, *Brain Rose*, 1990
Robert Reed, *Down the Bright Way*, 1991
Kurt Vonnegut Jr., *The Sirens of Titan*, 1959

1225

JACK VANCE

The Demon Princes: Volume One

(New York: Tor, 1997)

Story type: Adventure; Space Opera
Series: Demon Princes
Major character(s): Kirth Gersen, Journalist, Avenger; Viole Falushe, Kidnapper, Outlaw; Alusz Iphigenia, Companion, Fugitive
Time period(s): Indeterminate Future
Locale(s): Earth; Planet—Imaginary (the Rigel Concourse planetary system); Interstellar Empire/Federation

Summary: To avenge his parents' death in the Mount Pleasant massacre, Kirth Gersen must track down the five men involved, called Demon Princes, using any and all resources at his command. Omnibus edition of the first three books in the series, *The Star King* (1964), *The Killing Machine*(1964), and *The Palace of Love* (1967).

Where it's reviewed:
Kirkus Reviews, March 1, 1997, page 342
Library Journal, April 15, 1997, page 124
Science Fiction Chronicle, October 1997, page 47

Other books by the same author:
The Demon Princes: Volume Two, 1997
Night Lamp, 1996
Alastor, 1995
Planet of Adventure, 1993
Araminta Station, 1987
Galactic Effectuator, 1980

Other books you might like:
Ben Bova, *Orion*, 1984
Lois McMaster Bujold, *Memory*, 1996
Jack L. Chalker, *The Four Lords of the Diamond Series*, 1981-1983

Kate Elliott, *Jaran*, 1992
George R.R. Martin, *Dying of the Light*, 1977
Norman Spinrad, *The Void Captain's Tale*, 1983
Diann Thornley, *Ganwold's Child*, 1995
Vernor Vinge, *Tatja Grimm's World*, 1987

1226

JACK VANCE

The Demon Princes: Volume Two

(New Yor: Tor, 1997)

Story type: Adventure; Space Opera
Series: Demon Princes
Major character(s): Kirth Gersen, Avenger, Banker; Alice Wroke, Secretary, Spy; Lens Larque, Outlaw, Thief
Time period(s): Indeterminate Future
Locale(s): Dar Sai, Planet—Imaginary; Moudervelt, Planet—Imaginary; Interstellar Empire/Federation

Summary: As Kirth Gersen continues to seek the two remaining Demon Princes to avenge the death of his parents in the Mount Pleasant massacre, he discovers that even Lens Larque possesses some positive aspects. Contains the last two books in the series, *The Face* (1979) and *The Book of Dreams* (1981).

Where it's reviewed:
Kirkus Reviews, July 15, l997, page 1074
Library Journal, September 15, 1997, page 106

Other books by the same author:
The Demon Princes: Volume One, 1997
Ecce and Old Earth, 1991
Maske: Thaery, 1976
Showboat World, 1975
The Gray Prince, 1974
The Gray Prince, 1974
The Anome, 1973
The Anome, 1973

Other books you might like:
Lois McMaster Bujold, *The Vor Game*, 1990
Jack L. Chalker, *The Four Lords of the Diamond Series*, 1981-1983
Gordon R. Dickson, *Other*, 1994
George R.R. Martin, *Dying of the Light*, 1977
Andre Norton, *The Beast Master*, 1959
Mike Resnick, *Ivory: A Legend of Past and Future*, 1988
Allen Steele, *Clarke County, Space*, 1990
John E. Stith, *Reunion on Neverend*, 1994

1227

JULES VERNE

Paris in the Twentieth Century

(New York: Random House, 1996)

Story type: Dystopian; Satire
Major character(s): Michael Dufrenoy, Writer (poet), Orphan; Quinsonnas, Accountant, Musician
Time period(s): 1960s (1960-1961)
Locale(s): Paris, France

Summary: Denied artistic satisfaction at his bank job, Michael searches for higher meaning and love in a society which worships business and technology advance. Written, rejected by a publisher, and filed away, Verne's second novel remained lost for 125 years before its rediscovery by Verne's great-grandson and translation into English by Richard Howard. Includes a 17-page analytical introduction by Eugen Weber.

Where it's reviewed:
Book World, December 15, 1996, page 9
Kirkus Reviews, October 15, 1996, page 1492
Library Journal, November 15, 1996, page 90
Publishers Weekly, October 14, 1996, page 63

Other books by the same author:
The Mysterious Island, 1876
A Journey to the Center of the Earth, 1874
Around the World in 80 Days, 1873
20,000 Leagues under the Sea, 1873
Five Weeks in a Balloon, 1869

Other books you might like:
Edward Bellamy, *Looking Back 2000-1887*, 1888
Ray Bradbury, *Fahrenheit 451*, 1953
Aldous Huxley, *Brave New World*, 1932
George Orwell, *Nineteen Eighty-Four*, 1949
H.G. Wells, *When the Sleeper Wakes*, 1899

1228

KURT VONNEGUT JR.

Timequake

(New York: Putnam, 1997)

Story type: Time Travel; Contemporary Realism
Major character(s): Kurt ''Junior'' Vonnegut, Writer; Kilgore Trout, Writer
Time period(s): 2000s (2001)
Locale(s): Earth

Summary: Junior finds an old manuscript for *Timequake*, which he decides to incorporate, in part, in an updated version. He calls the older sections ''Timequake One'' and includes anecdotes from Kilgore Trout's life from 1935 to 2001. In 2001 a timequake forces everyone on Earth to relive 10 years with no means of changing anything or avoiding errors.

Where it's reviewed:
Booklist, August 1997, page 1849
Kirkus Reviews, August 1, 1997, page 1150
Library Journal, September 15, 1997, page 104
New York Times Book Review, September 28, 1997, page 14
Publishers Weekly, August 4, 1997, page 63

Other books by the same author:
Slaughterhouse Five, 1969
God Bless You, Mr. Rosewater, 1965
Cat's Cradle, 1963
The Sirens of Titan, 1959
Player Piano, 1952

Other books you might like:
Jack Finney, *From Time to Time*, 1995

Ken Grimwood, *Replay*, 1986
Pete Hautman, *Mr. Was*, 1996
Dan Simmons, *Hyperion*, 1989
Theodore Sturgeon, *The Ultimate Egoist*, 1994

1229

JOHN VORNHOLT

Mind Meld

(New York: Pocket, 1997)

Story type: Psychic Powers; Space Opera
Series: Star Trek
Major character(s): Spock, Alien (Vulcan), Chaperone; Teska, Alien (Vulcan), Telepath; James T. Kirk, Spaceship Captain
Time period(s): 23rd century
Locale(s): Rigel V, Planet—Imaginary; U.S.S. *Enterprise*, Spaceship; United Federation of Planets, Interstellar Empire/Federation

Summary: When Ambassador Sarek makes arrangements to promote unity between Romulans and Vulcans through the betrothal of a young Vulcan girl to a Romulan boy, Spock agrees to act as the ''uncle'' in the upcoming ceremonies. A stopover on Rigel en route to Vulcan turns deadly when Teska mindmelds with a dying man, learning the murderer's identity. She and Spock flee from a criminal network determined to silence Teska's evidence forever, while Kirk and his crew rescue the intended bridegroom from kidnappers.

Where it's reviewed:
Kliatt, July 1997, page 19

Other books by the same author:
Blood Oath, 1995
Voices, 1995
Antimatter, 1994
Contamination, 1991
Masks, 1989

Other books you might like:
C.J. Cherryh, *Angel with the Sword*, 1985
Michael Jan Friedman, *Crossover*, 1995
Eric James Fullilove, *Circle of One*, 1996
Lynn S. Hightower, *Alien Blues*, 1992
Jean Lorrah, *The Vulcan Academy Murders*, 1984
Jeri Taylor, *Unification*, 1991

1230

KATIE WAITMAN

The Merro Tree

(New York: Ballantine Del Rey, 1997)

Story type: Arts; Political
Major character(s): Mikk, Actor (Performance Master), Alien (Vyzanian); Thissizz, Alien (Droos), Singer; Huud Maroc, Actor (Performance Master), Alien (Vyzanian)
Time period(s): Indeterminate Future
Locale(s): Kekoi, Planet—Imaginary; Droos, Planet—Imaginary

Summary: The galaxy's most revered Performance Master, Mikk, stands trial for his life after performing the Somalite songdance in defiance of a galactic ban. First novel.

Where it's reviewed:
Publishers Weekly, August 18, 1997, page 89

Other books you might like:
Octavia E. Butler, *The Xenogenesis Trilogy*, 1987-1989
Orson Scott Card, *The Worthing Saga*, 1990
Robert A. Heinlein, *Double Star*, 1956
Anne Mason, *The Stolen Law*, 1986
Spider Robinson, *Stardance*, 1986
     Jeanne Robinson, co-author
Mary Rosenblum, *The Stone Garden*, 1995

1231

DAVID WEBER

In Enemy Hands

(New York, Baen, 1997)

Story type: Military; Space Opera
Series: Honor Harrington
Major character(s): Honor Harrington, Military Personnel, Noblewoman
Time period(s): Indeterminate Future
Locale(s): Star Kingdom of Manticore, Interstellar Empire/Federation; Outer Space

Summary: After a brief rest at home on Grayson, Honor accompanies a space convoy as guard, sacrificing her ship when the enemy springs a trap. Captured and tortured, Honor must escape or die.

Where it's reviewed:
Booklist, August 1997, page 1887
Kirkus Reviews, June 15, 1997, page 917
Library Journal, August 1997, page 141
Locus, Otober 1997, page 56
Publishers Weekly, August 25,1997, page 50

Other books by the same author:
Honor Among Enemies, 1996
Flag in Exile, 1995
Field of Dishonor, 1994
On Basilisk Station, 1993
Path of the Fury, 1992

1232

SCOTT WESTERFIELD

Polymorph

(New York: Roc, 1997)

Story type: Political; Science Fiction
Major character(s): Lee, Mythical Creature (shapeshifter); Freddie Smith, Computer Expert; Bonita, Mythical Creature (shapeshifter)
Time period(s): Indeterminate Future
Locale(s): New York, New York

Summary: Believing herself to be the only shapeshifter, Lee lives a solitary life, constantly changing and meeting new

Science Fiction

people as a stranger. Bonita not only has the gift, but also recognizes Lee as a threat to his/her plot to become the richest, most powerful person on the planet, forcing Lee to get involved. First novel.

Where it's reviewed:
Booklist, December 1, 1997, page 612

Other books you might like:
John W. Campbell, *Who Goes There? and Other Stories*, 1955
Stuart Hopen, *Warp Angel*, 1995
Nancy Kress, *Brain Rose*, 1990
Jennifer Roberson, *Shapechangers*, 1984

1233

JAMES WHITE

Final Diagnosis
(New York: Tor, 1997)

Story type: First Contact; Medical
Series: Sector General
Major character(s): Medalont, Alien (Melfan), Doctor; Hewlitt, Patient; Braithwaite, Psychologist (estraterrestrial)
Time period(s): Indeterminate Future
Locale(s): Sector General Hospital, Space Station; Outer Space

Summary: While in Sector General Hospital for many anomalous symptoms which began during his childhood, Patient Hewlitt cannot convince the doctors that his chidlhood experience on an alien planet may prove relevant. Constantly angry at not being believed, Hewlitt still manages to convince Braithwaite and Medalont that he retains his sanity, as well as perfect health, except for his occasional attacks of cardiac arrest. When his symptoms appear contagious, all on Sector General become alarmed.

Where it's reviewed:
Booklist, April 15, 1997, page 1387
Kirkus Reviews, March 15, 1997, page 424
Library Journal, May 15, 1997, page 105
Locus, April 1997, page 48
Science Fiction Chronicle, October 1997, page 48

Other books by the same author:
The Galactic Gourmet, 1996
The Genocidal Healer, 1992
Star Healer, 1985
Sector General, 1983
Ambulance Ship, 1979

Other books you might like:
David Brin, *Brightness Reef*, 1995
Murray Leinster, *The Med Series*, 1983
Jody Lynn Nye, *Taylor's Ark*, 1993
Alis A. Rasmussen, *A Passage of Stars*, 1990
Mary Rosenblum, *The Stone Garden*, 1995

1234

TAD WILLIAMS

City of Golden Shadow
(New York: DAW, 1997)

Story type: Cyberpunk; Political
Series: Otherland
Major character(s): Renie Sulaweyo, Teacher; !Xabbu, Traveller, Student; Orlando Teenager, Warrior
Time period(s): 1910s (1918); Indeterminate Future
Locale(s): Durban, South Africa; The Net, Cyberspace

Summary: In the near future, a worldwide network of virtual reality provides stores, entertainment, schools and nearly everything people need. When a mysterious disease begins to send children throughout the world into comas, a small group of people begin to realize that something strange lies behind the Net. First of a planned four-book series.

Where it's reviewed:
Booklist, October 1, 1996, page 292
Kirkus Reviews, October 1, 1996, page 1434
Library Journal, November 15, 1996, page 92
Locus, November 1996, page 62
Voice of Youth Advocates, June 1997, page 122

Other books by the same author:
To Green Angel Tower, 1993
Child of an Ancient City, 1992 (Nina Kiriki Hoffman, co-author)
Stone of Farewell, 1990
The Dragonbone Chair, 1988
Tailchaser's Song, 1985

Other books you might like:
Iain M. Banks, *Feersum Endjinn*, 1995
Pat Cadigan, *Mindplayers*, 1987
Nigel D. Findley, *No Limits*, 1996
Ian McDonald, *Terminal Cafe*, 1994
Brian Stableford, *The Werewolves of London*, 1990

1235

WALTER JON WILLIAMS

City on Fire
(New York: HarperPrism, 1997)

Story type: Political; Science Fantasy
Series: Metropolitan
Major character(s): Aiah, Political Figure, Police Officer; Constantine, Political Figure, Revolutionary; Ethemark, Police Officer, Genetically Altered Being
Time period(s): Indeterminate Future
Locale(s): Caraqui, Fictional City

Summary: Aiah flees her job one step ahead of the police, joining her partner in crime and sometimes lover, the once-Metropolitan Constantine, trying to build the city of his dreams. In this strange world, the sky shields, cities cover everything, and plasma provides the blood of civilization. Aiah and the revolutionaries must fight traitors, counterrevolutionaries, hostile neighbors, the criminal

underworld, and Constantine's dangerous ally, the ''hanged man,'' Taikon. Sequel to *Metropolitan*.

Where it's reviewed:
Kirkus Reviews, December 1, 1996, page 1708
Library Journal, December 1996, page 152
Locus, April 1997, page 23
New York Times Book Review, February 23, 1997, page 20
Publishers Weekly, December 30, 1996, page 59

Other books by the same author:
Metropolitan, 1995
Aristoi, 1992
The Crown Jewels, 1987
Voice of the Whirlwind, 1987
Hardwired, 1986

Other books you might like:
Alfred Bester, *The Demolished Man*, 1996
    revised
Glen Cook, *The Dragon Never Sleeps*, 1988
Frank Herbert, *Dune*, 1965
Cordwainer Smith, *Norstrilia*, 1975
Roger Zelazny, *Lord of Light*, 1967

1236

JACK WILLIAMSON

The Black Sun

(New York: Tor, 1997)

Story type: First Contact; Horror
Major character(s): Carlos Mondragon, Stowaway, Immigrant; Kip Virili, Child; Rima Virili, Scientist (biomedical officer)
Time period(s): Indeterminate Future
Locale(s): White Sands, New Mexico; Hellfrost, Planet—Imaginary

Summary: With no control over their destination, the passengers of Mission Starseed's 99th and last quantum-wave ship arrive at a frozen, dead planet in a black dwarf system. Their situation deteriorates further when mysterious black stones begin to possess and possibly even kill members of the crew.

Where it's reviewed:
Kirkus Reviews, December 15, 1996, page 1774
Library Journal, February 15, 1997, page 164
Locus, March 1997, page 25
New York Times Book Review, April 6, 1997, page 24
Voice of Youth Advocates, August 1997, page 197

Other books by the same author:
The Humanoids, 1996 (revised edition)
Demon Moon, 1994
Manseed, 1982
The Humanoids Touch, 1980
The Best of Jack Williamson, 1978

Other books you might like:
Arthur C. Clarke, *Childhood's End*, 1953
Michael Flynn, *Firestar*, 1996
Christopher Pike, *The Season of Passage*, 1992
Christopher Pike, *The Starlight Crystal*, 1996

Frederik Pohl, *The Singers of Time*, 1991
    Jack Williamson, co-author
Robert Silverberg, *Starborne*, 1996
A.E. Van Vogt, *The Voyage of the Space Beagle*, 1950
James White, *The Dream Millennium*, 1974

1237

CONNIE WILLIS

Bellwether

(New York: Bantam Spectra, 1996)

Story type: Contemporary Realism
Major character(s): Sandra ''Sandy'' Foster, Scientist, Researcher; Philippa J. ''Flip'' Orliotti, Clerk; Bennett ''Ben'' O'Reilly, Scientist, Researcher
Time period(s): 1990s
Locale(s): Boulder, Colorado

Summary: Getting nowhere with her research into a fad, bobbed hair, Sandy recognizes the incompetence of the support staffer, Flip. Redelivering a misdelivered package, Sandy meets Bennett whose research seems complementary. Bennett fascinates Sancy as he seems totally immune to fad and fashion.

Where it's reviewed:
Kirkus Reviews, February 1, 1996, page 183
Kliatt, July 1996, page 23
Locus, March 1996, page 17
Publishers Weekly, January 29, 1996, page 96
Voice of Youth Advocates, August 1996, page 173

Other books by the same author:
Uncharted Territory, 1994
Impossible Things, 1994
Remake, 1994
Doomsday Book, 1992
Lincoln's Dreams, 1987

Other books you might like:
John Brunner, *The Sheep Look Up*, 1972
Philip K. Dick, *A Scanner Darkly*, 1977
Suzette Haden Elgin, *Native Tongue*, 1984
Mark Leyner, *My Cousin, My Gastroenterologist*, 1990
Jack McDevitt, *Ancient Shores*, 1996
Tom Robbins, *Skinny Legs and All*, 1990

1238

CONNIE WILLIS
CYNTHIA FELICE, Co-Author

Promised Land

(New York: Ace, 1997)

Story type: Adventure; Science Fiction
Major character(s): Delanna Milleflores, Heiress, Spouse; Jay ''Mad Dog'' Madog, Businessman, Bachelor; Tarleton ''Sonny'' Tanner, Farmer, Spouse
Time period(s): Indeterminate Future
Locale(s): Grassedge, Fictional City; Keramos, Planet—Imaginary

Science Fiction

Summary: Sent off planet as a child by her mother, Delanna reluctantly returns to collect her inheritance and leave the planet her mother hated. Unfortunately, laws on Keramos prevent Delanna from selling or even keeping her land if she fails the residency requirement. Her surprise inherited marriage to Sonny also compromises her determination to leave.

Where it's reviewed:
Kirkus Reviews, January 1, 1997, page 28
Library Journal, February 15, 1997, page 165
Locus, April 1997, page 48
Publishers Weekly, January 27, 1997, page 82
Voice of Youth Advocates, June 1997, page 122

Other books by the same author:
Uncharted Territory, 1994
Doomsday Book, 1992
Waterwitch, 1982 (Cynthia Felice, co-author)

Other books you might like:
Eleanor Arnason, *A Woman of the Iron People*, 1991
F.M. Busby, *Rissa Kerguelen*, 1977
Elizabeth Moon, *Remnant Population*, 1996
James H. Schmitz, *The Demon Breed*, 1968
Joan D. Vinge, *Dreamfall*, 1996

1239

CONNIE WILLIS

To Say Nothing of the Dog

(New York: Bantam Spectra, 1998)

Story type: Time Travel; Humor
Series: Doomsday Book
Major character(s): Ned Henry, Historian, Time Traveller; Verity Kindle, Historian, Time Traveller; Lady Schrapnell, Wealthy (dowager)
Time period(s): 21st century; 19th century
Locale(s): Oxford, England; Coventry, England

Summary: Ned Henry is a 21st century historian working on a reconstruction of the hideously ugly Coventry Cathedral, which was destroyed during World War II. Dizzy and confused from a serious case of time lag, he is sent back to the Victorian era to correct a serious mistake made by another historian, who has accidentally brought a 19th century artifact back to the 21st century. This could alter history and destroy the entire space-time continuum. Unfortunately, Ned, half asleep on his feet, doesn't understand the assignment properly and things go hilariously astray.

Other books by the same author:
Bellwether, 1996
Remake, 1995
Uncharted Territory, 1994
Doomsday Book, 1992
Lincoln's Dreams, 1987
Firewatch, 1985

Other books you might like:
Peter Delacorte, *Time on My Hands*, 1997
J.R. Dunn, *Days of Cain*, 1997
Jerome K. Jerome, *Three Men in a Boat*,
John Kessel, *Corrupting Dr. Nice*, 1997

1240

DAVID NIALL WILSON

Chrysalis

(New York: Pocket, 1997)

Story type: First Contact
Series: Star Trek: Voyager
Major character(s): Kathryn Janeway, Spaceship Captain; Tom Paris, Pilot (spaceship), Military Personnel; Kes, Alien (Okampan), Telepath
Time period(s): 24th century
Locale(s): U.S.S. *Voyager*, Spaceship; Urrytha, Planet—Imaginary; United Federation of Planets, Interstellar Empire/Federation

Summary: Janeway and her crew stop to replenish their food supplies on a planet with abundant plant life, only to discover that the planet also harbors sentient life and an ancient civilization. When the seductively soothing effects of the vegetation send some of her crew into comas, the natives interpret this as a sign of the prophesied Awakening and interfere with efforts to find a cure.

Where it's reviewed:
Kliatt, July 1997, page 19

Other books by the same author:
The Fall of the House of Escher and Other Illusions, 1995

Other books you might like:
Carmen Carter, *Dreams of the Raven*, 1987
C.J. Cherryh, *Hestia*, 1979
Ursula K. Le Guin, *The Word for World Is Forest*, 1976
Rebecca Neason, *Guises of the Mind*, 1993
Dean Wesley Smith, *The Escape*, 1995
    Kristine Kathryn Rusch, co-author
John Varley, *Titan*, 1979
Joan D. Vinge, *The Snow Queen*, 1980

1241

DAVE WOLVERTON, Editor

L. Ron Hubbard Presents Writers of the Future, Vol. XII

(Los Angeles: Bridge Publications, 1996)

Story type: Anthology; Fantasy
Series: Writers of the Future

Summary: Contains a three-page introduction by Wolverton, three articles on writing and art by Doug Beason, L. Ron Hubbard and Paul Lehr plus 16 original stories with diverse themes and tones, written by emerging writers who recently won Writers of the Future contests. Concludes with 11 pages about the contest including contest rules and deadlines.

Other books by the same author:
The Golden Queen, 1994
L. Ron Hubbard Presents Writers of the Future, Volumes IX-XI, 1993-1995
Path of the Hero, 1993
Serpent Catch, 1991
On My Way to Paradise, 1989

Other books you might like:

Algis Budrys, *L. Ron Hubbard Presents Writers of the Future, Volumes I-VIII*, 1993-1992
editor

George R.R. Martin, *The John W. Campbell Awards, Volume 5*, 1984
editor

George R.R. Martin, *New Voices I-IV*, 1977-1981
editor

Victoria Schochet, *The Berkley Showcase: New Writings in Science Fiction and Fantasy, Volumes 1-4*, 1980-1981
John Silbersack, co-editor

Robin Scott Wilson, *Clarion I-III*, 1971-1973
editor

1242

N. LEE WOOD

Faraday's Orphans

(New York: Ace, 1997)

Story type: Post-Holocaust
Major character(s): Berkeley ''Berk'' Nielsen, Pilot (helicopter); ''Wy'' Wysaigh, Pilot (airplane); Leonard Cormack, Government Official (City Council), Pilot
Time period(s): 23rd century (2242)
Locale(s): Pittsburgh, North America

Summary: Having learned to love the freedom and open spaces outside the dome from his father, Berk continues to fly his helicopter for the city. The lack of support from Leonard or his wife only spurs Berk to crave exploration. Finally getting the exploratory run to Philadelphia, Berk lands, only to have his machine thrown off a 20 story building. Wounded and ill, Berk must learn enough about the society and environment to survive outside.

Where it's reviewed:
Booklist, May 15, 1997, page 1567
Kirkus Reviews, May 1, 1997, page 685
Library Journal, June 15, 1997, page 101
Locus, June 1997, page 17
Voice of Youth Advocates, October 1997, page 254

Other books by the same author:
Looking for the Mahdi, 1996

Other books you might like:
Octavia E. Butler, *Parable of the Sower*, 1993
Marjorie Bradley Kellogg, *Harmony*, 1991
Donald E. McQuinn, *Warrior*, 1990
Catherine Wells, *The Earth Is All That Lasts*, 1991
Paul O. Williams, *The Breaking of Northwall*, 1981

1243

JANINE ELLEN YOUNG

Cinderblock

(New York: Roc, 1997)

Story type: Cyberpunk; Post-Disaster

Major character(s): Alexander ''Sander'' Kitatimate, Prisoner, Computer Expert; Urban Myth, Computer Expert, Robot; Hawthorn ''D-base'', Artificial Intelligence
Time period(s): Indeterminate Future
Locale(s): Cyberspace

Summary: Imprisoned since birth by his uncle Hawthorne, Alexander meets Urban, who helps him escape with Cinderblock. Hawthorne works to corrupt young college students while Cinderblock and her crew of assistants attempt to destroy him. First novel.

Where it's reviewed:
Locus, February 1997, page 17
Starlog, July 1997, page 61

Other books you might like:
Tom Cool, *Infectress*, 1997
Neal Stephenson, *Snow Crash*, 1992
Sheri S. Tepper, *A Plague of Angels*, 1993
Michael D. Weaver, *A Second Infinity*, 1996
Walter Jon Williams, *Hardwired*, 1986

1244

ROGER ZELAZNY
JANE M. LINDSKOLD, Co-Author

Donnerjack

(New York: Avon, 1997)

Story type: Alternate Intelligence; Family Saga
Major character(s): Death, Artificial Intelligence, Mythical Creature; John D'Arcy Donnerjack, Computer Expert; Aryadyss, Artificial Intelligence, Mythical Creature (banshee)
Time period(s): 22nd century
Locale(s): Deep Field, Cyberspace; Virtu, Cyberspace; Eilean a'Tempull Dubh, Scotland (Verite)

Summary: When Death takes Aryadyss, John realizes his true love belonged in Virtu and could never have come to Verite. Despite this understanding he decides to visit Death to bargain for her return. Death promises to return her in Verite, a seemingly impossible feat, if John will build a castle and give Death his firstborn. Since children cannot result from such a liaison, John feels free to make the bargain. However, after moving to their newly constructed castle, one of the ghosts warns that the banshee howls to warn of death for her family, including the baby. In Virtu, the old gods invent a religion and plot to move into Verite.

Where it's reviewed:
Booklist, August 1997, page 1887
Kirkus Reviews, July 15, 1997, page 918
Locus, August 1997, page 57
New York Times Book Review, August 31, 1997, page 22
Publishers Weekly, June 30, 1997, page 70

Other books by the same author:
Doorways in the Sand, 1976
Nine Princes in Amber, 1970
Creatures of Light and Darkness, 1969
Lord of Light, 1967
This Immortal, 1967

Other books you might like:
James C. Bassett, *Living Real*, 1997
Raphael Carter, *The Fortunate Fall*, 1996
Jane M. Lindskold, *Marks of Our Brothers*, 1995
Neal Stephenson, *Snow Crash*, 1992
Janine Ellen Young, *Cinderblock*, 1997

1245

SARAH ZETTEL

Fool's War

(New York: Warner Aspect, 1997)

Story type: Alternate Intelligence; Space Opera
Major character(s): Katmer Al Shei, Businesswoman, Engineer; Evelyn Dobbs, Spacewoman, Psychologist (professional Fool)
Time period(s): Indeterminate Future
Locale(s): *Pasadena*, Spaceship; The Farther Kingdom, Planet—Imaginary; Guild Hall Station, Space Station ((Fool's Guild headquarters))

Summary: *Pasadena's* routine transportation and transfer of medical records data turns problematic when hospital officials accuse the crew of loosing an artificial intelligence into facil-ity computers. As *Pasadena's* crew attempt to reverse the damage and prevent further disaster, officials back home arrest Katmer Al Shei's husband, while events unmask the true nature of the Fool's Guild.

Where it's reviewed:
Analog, May 1997, page 145
Kliatt, July 1997, page 19
New York Times Book Review, April 6, 1997, page 24
Publishers Weekly, March 3, 1997, page 71
Voice of Youth Advocates, August 1997, page 198

Other books by the same author:
Reclamation, 1996

Other books you might like:
Roger MacBride Allen, *The Ring of Charon*, 1990
Raphael Carter, *The Fortunate Fall*, 1996
Glen Cook, *The Dragon Never Sleeps*, 1988
Katharine Kerr, *Palace*, 1996
    Mark Kreighbaum, co-author
Alis A. Rasmussen, *A Passage of Stars*, 1990
Neal Stephenson, *Snow Crash*, 1992
John Varley, *Steel Beach*, 1992
Vernor Vinge, *A Fire upon the Deep*, 1992
David Weber, *Path of the Fury*, 1992

Series Index

This index alphabetically lists series to which books featured in the entries belong. Beneath each series name, book titles are listed alphabetically with author names. Numbers refer to the entries that feature each title.

Time Period Index

This index chronologically lists the time settings in which the featured books take place. Main headings refer to a century; where no specific time is given, the headings INDETERMINATE PAST, INDETERMINATE FUTURE, and INDETERMINATE are used. The 18th through 21st centuries are broken down into decades when possible. (Note: 1800s, for example, refers to the first decade of the 19th century.) Featured titles are listed alphabetically beneath time headings, with author names and entry numbers also provided.

INDETERMINATE PAST

Meg - Steve Alten *h* 831
Murder in the Smokehouse - Amy Myers *m* 174
No Ordinary Princess - Pamela Morsi *r* 386
Prairie Rose - Susan Kirby *r* 349
Promise Me Tomorrow - Lori Wick *w* 631
Seeing a Large Cat - Elizabeth Peters *m* 186
Steel Ashes - Karen Rose Cercone *m* 34
Ticktock - Dean R. Koontz *h* 936
When Lilacs Bloom - Susan Kirby *r* 350
The Wolf's Cub - Richard Parry *w* 583

1910s

The Angel of Darkness - Caleb Carr *m* 33
Baby in a Basket - Gloria Rand *w* 588
Back in the USSA - Kim Newman *s* 1166
City of Golden Shadow - Tad Williams *s* 1234
The Fifth Element - Terry Bisson *s* 1053
Future Indefinite - Dave Duncan *f* 694
Lonesome Land - B.M. Bower *w* 467
The Royalscope Fe-As-Ko - Randall Beth
    Platt *w* 585
When Lilacs Bloom - Susan Kirby *r* 350
Writ in Blood - Chelsea Quinn Yarbro *h* 1031

1920s

Damsel in Distress - Carola Dunn *m* 70
Hunting a Detroit Tiger - Troy Soos *m* 216
A Letter of Mary - Laurie R. King *m* 141
Mask of the Night - Mary Ryan *h* 989
One Last Town - Matt Braun *w* 472
The Return - Walter de la Mare *h* 868

1930s

Black Gold - Frederic Bean *w* 450
A Blessing on the Moon - Joseph Skibell *f* 796
Children of the Dusk - Janet Berliner *f* 652
The Clark Gable and Carole Lombard Murder Case -
    George Baxt *m* 11
The Dealings of Daniel Kesserich - Fritz
    Leiber *s* 1141
Death of a Winter Shaker - Deborah
    Woodworth *m* 243
Time on My Hands - Peter Delacorte *s* 1077
To Be a Warrior - Robert Barlow Fox *w* 519

1940s

'48 - James Herbert *h* 914
A Blessing on the Moon - Joseph Skibell *f* 796
Days of Cain - J.R. Dunn *s* 1086
Five Past Midnight - James Thayer *m* 225
Los Alamos - Joseph Kanon *m* 137
Rose Cottage - Mary Stewart *m* 219
Stonekiller - J. Robert Janes *m* 131
Time on My Hands - Peter Delacorte *s* 1077
Time Station Paris - David Evans *s* 1093
Timeshare - Joshua Dann *s* 1074
To Be a Warrior - Robert Barlow Fox *w* 519

1950s

The Dog King - Christoph Ransmayr *f* 784
Dogland - Will Shetterly *f* 794
Root of All Evil - David A. Farrow *h* 881

1960s

Mask of the Night - Mary Ryan *h* 989
Paris in the Twentieth Century - Jules
    Verne *s* 1227
Secret Sins - Jasmine Cresswell *r* 290
Sharon's Hope - Nina Coyle *r* 289
Time Station Berlin - David Evans *s* 1092
Troubled Waters - Carolyn Wheat *m* 234

1970s

The Black Cat - Robert Poe *h* 978
Bonjour, Miss Seeton - Hamilton Crane *m* 47
I Know What You Did Last Summer - Lois
    Duncan *h* 875
Night of the Living Dead - John A. Russo *h* 987
Silent Zone - Stephen Molstad *s* 1159

1980s

Back in the USSA - Kim Newman *s* 1166
The Cellar - Richard Laymon *h* 942
Flying Saucers over Hennepin - Peter
    Gelman *f* 708
Key to Forever - Christina Skye *r* 425
Live Girls - Ray Garton *h* 888
The Psalm Killer - Chris Petit *m* 187
Return of the Living Dead - John A. Russo *h* 988
Risking Elizabeth - Walter McCloskey *m* 161
Voyager - Stephen Baxter *s* 1048
Wizard and Glass - Stephen King *h* 931

1990s

23 Shades of Black - K.j.a. Wishnia *m* 242
Accidental Roommates - Charlotte Maclay *r* 369
Agatha Raisin and the Terrible Tourist - M.C.
    Beaton *m* 12
AKA Jane - Maureen Tan *m* 222
All Emergencies, Ring Super - Ellen Emerson
    White *m* 235
All the Blood Relations - Deborah Adams *m* 1
Almost an Angel - Deb Stover *r* 430
Amber Beach - Elizabeth Lowell *r* 367
American Dreamer - Theresa Weir *r* 435
The Angel Tapes - David Kiely *m* 140
Angela and Diabola - Lynne Reid Banks *f* 646
Angels Unaware - L. Elizabeth Storm *s* 1215
Animal Appetite - Susan Conant *m* 41
Annie's Hero - Maggie Shayne *r* 418
Antibodies - Kevin J. Anderson *h* 832
Apparition Alley - Katherine V. Forrest *m* 85
The Arbitrary Placement of Walls - Martha
    Soukup *f* 797
Area 51 - Robert Doherty *s* 1080
The Art of Arrow Cutting - Stephen Dedman *f* 686
The Art of Breaking Glass - Matthew Hall *m* 107
As She Climbed Across the Table - Jonathan
    Lethem *s* 1142
Ask Mariah - Barbara Freethy *r* 308
Asylum - Patrick McGrath *h* 962
Backspin - Harlan Coben *m* 39
Bad Karma - Andrew Harper *h* 909
Bad Medicine - Aimee Thurlo *m* 226
The Barbed Coil - J.V. Jones *f* 730
Bellows Falls - Archer Mayor *m* 160
Bellwether - Connie Willis *s* 1237
Beneath the Gated Sky - Robert Reed *s* 1181
Beside a Dreamswept Sea - Victoria Barrett *r* 256
Between Floors - Thomas F. Monteleone *h* 967
Beyond the Promise - Barbara Bickmore *r* 262
Big Red Tequila - Rick Riordan *m* 199
Biggie and the Mangled Mortician - Nancy
    Bell *m* 15
The Bighead - Edward Lee *h* 943
Bird Dog - Philip Reed *m* 195
Black and Blue - Ian Rankin *m* 193
Black Diamond - Susan Holtzer *m* 124
The Blackstone Chronicles - John Saul *h* 990
Blood and Chocolate - Annette Curtis
    Klause *h* 932
Blood at the Root - Peter Robinson *m* 203
Blood Debt - Tanya Huff *h* 919
Bloody Shame - Carolina Garcia-Aguilera *m* 91
Blue Genes - Val McDermid *m* 162
Blues for the Buffalo - Manuel Ramos *m* 192
The Body in the Fjord - Katherine Hall
    Page *m* 180

The Bone Collector - Jeffery Deaver *m* 58
The Book of Night with Moon - Diane Duane *f* 692
Born in Twilight - Maggie Shayne *r* 419
Both Ends of the Night - Marcia Muller *m* 173
A Brace of Bloodhounds - Virginia Lanier *m* 143
Breakup - Dana Stabenow *m* 217
Bride of the Mist - Christina Skye *r* 424
Bright Shadow - Elizabeth Forrest *h* 883
Buddha Kiss - Peter Tasker *m* 223
Buffy the Vampire Slayer: The Harvest - Richie
    Tankersley Cusick *h* 863
The Bum's Rush - G.M. Ford *m* 84
The Burglar in the Library - Lawrence Block *m* 20
The Burning Plain - Michael Nava *m* 175
The Butter Did It - Phyllis Richman *m* 198
Cain - James Byron Huggins *h* 920
Camp Vamp - Elvira *h* 879
Cannibal Plateau - Joe Wise *w* 634
Captive - Brenda Joyce *r* 342
Carnivore - Leigh Clark *h* 859
Carried Away - Sue Civil-Brown *r* 281
The Case Has Altered - Martha Grimes *m* 102
*The Case of the Police Officer's Cock Ring and the
    Piano Player Who Had No Fingers* - Edward
    Lee *h* 944
Cat in a Flamingo Fedora - Carole Nelson
    Douglas *m* 67
Cats Raise the Dead - Shirley Rousseau
    Murphy *f* 769
Caught - Rachel Lee *r* 363
Celestial Dogs - J.S. Russell *h* 986
Charm City - Laura Lippman *m* 149
Chase the Moon - Dinah McCall *r* 375
Cimarron Rose - James Lee Burke *m* 29
Cleveland Local - Les Roberts *m* 201
Cold at Heart - Brian Hopkins *h* 917
Cold Case - Linda Barnes *m* 8
Cold Iron - Melisa Michaels *f* 762
Come Before Christ and Murder Love - Stewart
    Home *r* 725
Cop Out - Susan Dunlap *m* 69
Cosi Fan Tutti - Michael Dibdin *m* 62
Counting Coup - G.D. Gearino *m* 93
The Cowgirls of the Mariposa - Lana Dean
    James *w* 543
Crash Course - Kathy Hogan Trocheck *m* 228
A Cry for Self-Help - Jacqueline Girdner *m* 99
Cul-De-Sac - David Martin *h* 958
Curl Up and Die - Christine T. Jorgensen *m* 134
The Curse of Camp Cold Lake - R.L. Stine *h* 1007
Daddy by Accident - Paula Detmer Riggs *r* 412
The Dancing Floor - Barbara Michaels *m* 168
The Dark - Andrew Neiderman *h* 971
The Dark Canyon - Micah S. Hackler *m* 104
Daughter of Darkness - Steven Spruill *h* 1004
Dead Body Language - Penny Warner *m* 232
The Dead Horse Paint Company - Earl
    Emerson *m* 77
Dead Men Don't Dance - Margaret
    Chittenden *m* 37
Deadly Beloved - Jane Haddam *m* 105
A Deadly Vineyard Holiday - Philip R. Craig *m* 45
Deal on Ice - Les Standiford *m* 218
The Death and Life of Bobby Z - Don
    Winslow *m* 241
Death and the Language of Happiness - John
    Straley *m* 220
Death Dines Out - Claudia Bishop *m* 18
Death in a Mood Indigo - Francine
    Mathews *m* 157
Death in the Palazzo - Edward Sklepowich *m* 214
Death Is Now My Neighbor - Colin Dexter *m* 61
Death, Lies, and Apple Pies - Valerie S.
    Malmont *m* 151
Death of a Dentist - M.C. Beaton *m* 13
The Death of an Irish Tinker - Bartholomew
    Gill *m* 97
Death Takes Passage - Sue Henry *m* 118

21st CENTURY

2000s

2010s

2020s

2030s

2040s

2050s

2060s

2090s

22nd CENTURY

23rd CENTURY

24th CENTURY

25th CENTURY

26th CENTURY

27th CENTURY

Geographic Index

This index provides access to all featured books by geographic settings—such as countries, continents, oceans, and planets. States and provinces are indicated for the United States and Canada. Also interfiled are headings for fictional place names (Spaceships, Imaginary Planets, etc.). Sections are further broken down by city or the specific name of the imaginary locale. Book titles are listed alphabetically under headings, and author names and entry numbers are also provided.

AFRICA

The Book of Water - Marjorie Bradley Kellogg *f* 732
Evil Eye - Michael Slade *h* 996
Hope of Earth - Piers Anthony *s* 1036

Endless City
The Great Wheel - Ian R. MacLeod *s* 1148

Tripoli
Captive - Brenda Joyce *r* 342

ALTERNATE EARTH

Ancient Games - Scott Ciencin *f* 669
Back in the USSA - Kim Newman *s* 1166
Bring the Jubilee - Ward Moore *s* 1162
Changespell - Doranna Durgin *f* 695
Corum: The Coming of Chaos - Michael Moorcock *f* 766
The Dragon and the Gnarly King - Gordon R. Dickson *f* 688
Fabulous Harbors - Michael Moorcock *f* 767
How Few Remain - Harry Turtledove *s* 1223
Milton in America - Peter Ackroyd *f* 637
The Subtle Knife - Philip Pullman *f* 781
The War in the Waste - Felicity Savage *f* 790

Fasosi
The Duke of Sumava - Sara J. Wrench *f* 821

Nextdoor
Future Indefinite - Dave Duncan *f* 694

ALTERNATE UNIVERSE

The Hot-Wired Dodo - Jack L. Chalker *s* 1064
Magician's Ward - Patricia C. Wrede *f* 819
The War Amongst the Angels - Michael Moorcock *f* 768

AMERICAN COLONIES

Milton in America - Peter Ackroyd *f* 637
True Heart - Arnette Lamb *r* 358

Appalachian Mountains
Major Washington - Michael Kilian *w* 552

MASSACHUSETTS

Plymouth
The Rain From God - Mark Ammerman *w* 442

NEW YORK

New York
Remember the Morning - Thomas Fleming *w* 518

PENNSYLVANIA

Philadelphia
Major Washington - Michael Kilian *w* 552

RHODE ISLAND

Newport
The Secrets of Catie Hazard - Miranda Jarrett *r* 334

Providence
The Rain From God - Mark Ammerman *w* 442

SOUTH CAROLINA

Charleston
Jade - Betty Brooks *r* 269

VIRGINIA

Petals on the River - Kathleen Woodiwiss *r* 441

ANCIENT CIVILIZATION

Caesar's Bicycle - John Barnes *s* 1042
Hope of Earth - Piers Anthony *s* 1036
Thessalonica - Harry Turtledove *f* 805
Time Station Paris - David Evans *s* 1093

Rome
The House of the Vestals - Steven Saylor *m* 209
Time to Depart - Lindsey Davis *m* 55

Tyre
Iron Dawn - Matthew Woodring Stover *f* 802

ANTARCTICA

Carnivore - Leigh Clark *h* 859

ARCTIC

Ellesmere Island
Cold at Heart - Brian Hopkins *h* 917

ASIA MINOR

Cross and Crescent - Susan Shwartz *f* 795

ASTEROID

4442 Garcia
A King of Infinite Space - Allen Steele *s* 1212

Psyche
The White Abacus - Damien Broderick *s* 1056

AT SEA

Beast - Judith Ivory *r* 333
The Gift - Patrick O'Leary *f* 775
The Prince and the Prosecutor - Peter J. Heck *m* 117
Wizard of Bones - Robert N. Charrette *f* 665

Amistad
Amistad - Alexs Pate *w* 584

Charity
Mary's Land - Lucia St. Clair Robson *w* 598

AUSTRALIA

Sydney
Distress - Greg Egan *s* 1088

AUSTRIA

Styria
The Darker Passions: Carmilla - Amarantha Knight *h* 933

Vienna
Violin - Anne Rice *h* 983

BELGIUM

Brussels
The Colonel's Lady - Patricia Oliver *r* 392

BELIZE

Veritas - William Lashner   *m*   144

BRAZIL

Rio de Janeiro
Violin - Anne Rice   *h*   983

BYZANTINE EMPIRE

Constantinople
Cross and Crescent - Susan Shwartz   *f*   795

CANADA

Trader - Charles de Lint   *f*   685

Black Thunder
Howl - Christine Tanasiuk   *h*   1012

Cripple Camp
By Honor Bound - Alan Morris   *w*   574

Fort Whoop-Up
By Honor Bound - Alan Morris   *w*   574

ALBERTA

Calgary
The Art of Arrow Cutting - Stephen Dedman   *f*   686

Edmonton
The Night Watch - Sean Stewart   *f*   801

BRITISH COLUMBIA

New Westminster
Evil Eye - Michael Slade   *h*   996

Vancouver
Blood Debt - Tanya Huff   *h*   919
Lifehouse - Spider Robinson   *s*   1183
The Night Watch - Sean Stewart   *f*   801

ONTARIO

Toronto
Blue Limbo - Terrence M. Green   *s*   1116
Except the Dying - Maureen Jennings   *m*   132
Forever Knight: A Stirring of Dust - Susan
   Sizemore   *h*   995
Forever Knight: Intimations of Mortality - Susan M.
   Garrett   *h*   887
Free Reign - Rosemary Aubert   *m*   7
Keeper of the King - Nigel Bennett   *h*   838

YUKON TERRITORY

Dawson
Klondike Fever - Suzann Ledbetter   *w*   558
The Wolf's Cub - Richard Parry   *w*   583

CARIBBEAN

Paradise Island
The Paradise Man - Suzanne Simmons   *r*   421

San Carlos
Cleveland Local - Les Roberts   *m*   201

CHINA

Hong Kong
Nightmare Syndrome - William Marshall   *m*   153

CUBA

Havana
North of Havana - Randy Wayne White   *m*   236

CYBERSPACE

Cinderblock - Janine Ellen Young   *s*   1243
Exit to Reality - Edith Forbes   *s*   1098
Terminal Logic - Jefferson Scott   *s*   1196
Tomorrow and Tomorrow - Charles
   Sheffield   *s*   1204

Deep Field
Donnerjack - Roger Zelazny   *s*   1244

The Net
City of Golden Shadow - Tad Williams   *s*   1234

Network
Living Real - James C. Bassett   *s*   1046

Virtu
Donnerjack - Roger Zelazny   *s*   1244

Virtual Reality
Wyrm - Mark Fabi   *s*   1094

CYPRUS

Agatha Raisin and the Terrible Tourist - M.C.
   Beaton   *m*   12

CZECH REPUBLIC

Prague
The Fair Maid of Bohemia - Edward
   Marston   *m*   154

DENMARK

War of the Gods - Poul Anderson   *f*   641

EARTH

Acts of Conscience - William Barton   *s*   1044
Angela and Diabola - Lynne Reid Banks   *f*   646
Berserker Fury - Fred Saberhagen   *s*   1189
The Demon Princes: Volume One - Jack
   Vance   *s*   1225
The Earth Giant - Melvin Burgess   *s*   1058
A Game of Universe - Eric S. Nylund   *f*   774
I Who Have Never Known Men - Jacqueline
   Harpman   *s*   1124
''Repent, Harlequin!'' Said the Ticktockman - Harlan
   Ellison   *s*   1090
Ronin - D.A. Heeley   *f*   719
Shade's Children - Garth Nix   *s*   1168
Someone to Watch over Me - Tricia
   Sullivan   *s*   1218
Strange Deliverance - Mary Brown   *s*   1057
Tek Net - William Shatner   *s*   1200
Timequake - Kurt Vonnegut Jr.   *s*   1228
Tomorrow and Tomorrow - Charles
   Sheffield   *s*   1204
The White Abacus - Damien Broderick   *s*   1056

EGYPT

The Fifth Element - Terry Bisson   *s*   1053
The Right Hand of Amon - Lauren Haney   *m*   110

Cairo
As You Desire - Connie Brockway   *r*   268

Great Sand Sea
Hellboy: The Lost Army - Christopher
   Golden   *h*   897

Memphis
Eater of Souls - Lynda S. Robinson   *m*   202

Valley of the Kings
Seeing a Large Cat - Elizabeth Peters   *m*   186

ENGLAND

The Arrangement - Joan Wolf   *r*   439
Ashworth Hall - Anne Perry   *m*   184
Bride of the Mist - Christina Skye   *r*   424
Captive - Joan Johnston   *r*   338
The Case Has Altered - Martha Grimes   *m*   102
Cupid's Mistake - Karen Harbaugh   *r*   321
Damsel in Distress - Carola Dunn   *m*   70
The Dancing Floor - Barbara Michaels   *m*   168
Dangerous to Hold - Elizabeth Thornton   *r*   433
Dangerous to Love - Rexanne Becnel   *r*   258
The Deception - Marion Chesney   *r*   280
The Dragon and the Gnarly King - Gordon R.
   Dickson   *f*   688
Dream Lover - Virginia Henley   *r*   324
Enemy of God - Bernard Cornwell   *f*   678
Everything and the Moon - Julia Quinn   *r*   404
The Fair Maid of Bohemia - Edward
   Marston   *m*   154
Francesca's Rake - Lynn Kerstan   *r*   345
Freedom & Necessity - Steven Brust   *f*   660
Future Indefinite - Dave Duncan   *f*   694
A Garden Folly - Candice Hern   *r*   325
Gate of Ivory, Gate of Horn - Robert
   Holdstock   *f*   723
Gawain and Lady Green - Anne Eliot
   Crompton   *f*   679
God Save the Queen! - Dorothy Cannell   *m*   32
Gospel - Bill James   *m*   129
Grail - Stephen R. Lawhead   *f*   745
The Guardian - Joan Wolf   *r*   440
If You Love Me - Elaine Coffman   *r*   283
Indiscreet - Mary Balogh   *r*   252
Innocence Undone - Kat Martin   *r*   372
The Irish Rake - Emma Lange   *r*   361
Isabella's Rake - June Calvin   *r*   274
Knights - Linda Lael Miller   *r*   380
The Lady From Spain - Gail Eastwood   *r*   299
Lady Thorn - Catherine Archer   *r*   250
The Last Arrow - Marsha Canham   *r*   275
Lord of Danger - Anne Stuart   *r*   431
Lords of the Night - Monique Ellis   *r*   301
Mennyms Alive - Sylvia Waugh   *f*   811
Merlin - Jane Yolen   *f*   825
The Mermaid - Betina Krahn   *r*   352
My Steadfast Heart - Jo Goodman   *r*   318
The Notorious Abbess - Vera Chapman   *f*   664
The Offer - Catherine Coulter   *r*   288
Once upon a Rose - Judith O'Brien   *r*   390
One Perfect Rose - Mary Jo Putney   *r*   401
Pendragon's Banner - Helen Hollick   *r*   327
Pillow Talk - Kristine Rolofson   *r*   416
The Pride of Lions - Marsha Canham   *r*   276
A Prince Among Men - Kate Moore   *r*   384
The Prioress' Tale - Margaret Frazer   *m*   86
A Quantum Murder - Peter F. Hamilton   *s*   1122
Raven's Bride - Lynn Kerstan   *r*   346
Rejar - Dara Joy   *r*   341
Rose Cottage - Mary Stewart   *m*   219
Secrets in Satin - Haywood Smith   *r*   427
Shadow of the King - Helen Hollick   *f*   724
The Shattered Rose - Jo Beverley   *r*   260
The Silver Rose - Jane Feather   *r*   304
This Is All I Ask - Lynn Kurland   *r*   357
To Marry a British Lord - Judith O'Brien   *r*   391
To Shield the Queen - Fiona Buckley   *m*   28
Touch of Enchantment - Teresa Medeiros   *r*   377
A Valentine Bouquet - Paula Tanner Girard   *r*   316
Wonderful - Jill Barnett   *r*   255

Avalon
Lady of Avalon - Marion Zimmer Bradley   *f*   656

FICTIONAL COUNTRY

Great Irish Tales of Horror - Peter Haining h 904
Suffer Little Children - Peter Tremayne m 227
Wild Irish Skies - Nancy Richards-Akers r 410
A Wizard Abroad - Diane Duane f 693

Belfast
The Psalm Killer - Chris Petit m 187

Connacht
The Raid - Randy Lee Eickhoff f 697

Dublin
The Angel Tapes - David Kiely m 140
The Death of an Irish Tinker - Bartholomew
  Gill m 97
Maiden Voyage - Judith O'Brien r 389

Kilashane
Mask of the Night - Mary Ryan h 989

Ulster
The Raid - Randy Lee Eickhoff f 697

ISRAEL

Jerusalem
To Speak in Lifeless Tongues - David Niall
  Wilson h 1028

ITALY

Ghirlandaio's Daughter - John Spencer Hill m 122

Florence
Ghirlandaio's Daughter - John Spencer Hill m 122
Renaissance Moon - Linda Nevins f 770
The Stars Dispose - Michaela Roessner f 786

La Scala
The Devil in Music - Kate Ross m 204

Lake Como
The Devil in Music - Kate Ross m 204

Milan
The Devil in Music - Kate Ross m 204

Naples
Cosi Fan Tutti - Michael Dibdin m 62

Rome
Caesar's Bicycle - John Barnes s 1042
The Great Wheel - Ian R. MacLeod s 1148
Interface Masque - Shariann Lewitt s 1143

Venice
Death in the Palazzo - Edward Sklepowich m 214
Interface Masque - Shariann Lewitt s 1143
Mask of the Night - Mary Ryan h 989
Vaporetto 13 - Robert Girardi h 896

JAPAN

Nagasaki
The Way of the Traitor - Laura Joh
  Rowland m 205

Tokyo
Buddha Kiss - Peter Tasker m 223
Meeting the Minotaur - Carol Dawson f 684
The Salaryman's Wife - Sujata Massey m 155
The Toyotomi Blades - Dale Furutani m 88

JUPITER

Europa
3001: The Final Odyssey - Arthur C.
  Clarke s 1067

KOREA, SOUTH

Seoul
Slicky Boys - Martin Limon m 148

MADAGASCAR

Children of the Dusk - Janet Berliner f 652

MARS

The Fleet of Stars - Poul Anderson s 1034
Mars Underground - William Hartmann s 1126
The Martian Chronicles - Ray Bradbury s 1054
Voyager - Stephen Baxter s 1048

Phobos
Mars Underground - William Hartmann s 1126

MEXICO

Blues for the Buffalo - Manuel Ramos m 192
Hidden Agenda - Rochelle Alers r 246
Jacey's Reckless Heart - Cheryl Anne Porter r 398
The Promise of Jenny Jones - Maggie
  Osborne h 393
Senora Rodriguez and Other Worlds - Martha
  Cerda f 663

Aztlan
Aztec Autumn - Gary Jennings w 544

Casas Grandes
Spirits of the Ordinary - Kathleen Alcala f 638

Magdelena
While the Rivers Run - Wynema McGowan w 571

Mazatlan
Tropic of Orange - Karen Tei Yamashita f 823

Mexico City
Aztec Autumn - Gary Jennings w 544
In the Rogue Blood - James Carlos Blake w 460

Nogales
The Border Empire - Ralph Compton w 493

Portobello
Forever Peace - Joe Haldeman s 1119

Saltillo
Spirits of the Ordinary - Kathleen Alcala f 638

Toluca
The Border Empire - Ralph Compton w 493

MIDDLE EAST

A Diversity of Dragons - Anne McCaffrey f 757
The Djinn in the Nightingale's Eye - A.S.
  Byatt f 662
The Notorious Abbess - Vera Chapman f 664

Jerusalem
Corrupting Dr. Nice - John Kessel s 1137
Cross and Crescent - Susan Shwartz f 795

MONTENEGRO

The Fleet of Stars - Poul Anderson s 1034

Luna
Freeware - Rudy Rucker s 1184

MOON—IMAGINARY

Dark Man's Moon
Sky Trillium - Julian May f 756

Minor Base
Alien Influences - Kristine Kathryn Rusch s 1186

Ptero
Faun & Games - Piers Anthony f 642

MOROCCO

Marrakesh
The Broken Sword - Molly Cochran f 673

MYTHICAL PLACE

Forever Enchanted - Maggie Shayne r 420
Monet's Ghost - Chelsea Quinn Yarbro f 824
Ronin - D.A. Heeley f 719
Spires of Spirit - Gael Baudino f 649

Abbey of St. Leibowitz
Saint Leibowitz and the Wild Horse Woman - Walter
  M. Miller Jr. s 1157

Beast's Palace
Rose Daughter - Robin McKinley f 761

Blue Mountain
Captives of the Blue Mountain - Wendy Pini f 777

Costard's Superior Mine
The Mines of Behemoth - Michael Shea f 792

Danda-Vana Forest
The Iron Ring - Lloyd Alexander f 640

D'ni
The Book of D'ni - Rand Miller f 763

Drakmil
Kar Kalim - Deborah Christian f 668

Eyrie
Jovah's Angel - Sharon Shinn s 1205

Feyndala
Wrath of the Princes - Holly Lisle f 752

Inis Witrin
Lady of Avalon - Marion Zimmer Bradley f 656

Isle of Fincayra
The Seven Songs of Merlin - T.A. Barron f 648

Kingdoms of the West
Polgara the Sorceress - David Eddings f 696

M3 Center
Days of Cain - J.R. Dunn s 1086

Olympus
The Kronos Condition - Emily Devenport s 1078

Omphalos
/ - Greg Bear s 1049

The Otherworld
The Seven Songs of Merlin - T.A. Barron f 648

Parramat Archipelago
The Howling Stones - Alan Dean Foster s 1101

Pelagiris Forest
Owlflight - Mercedes Lackey f 743

The River
The Blackgod - J. Gregory Keyes f 737

Rose Cottage
Rose Daughter - Robin McKinley f 761

Rush
Forever Enchanted - Maggie Shayne r 420

Ryhope Wood
Gate of Ivory, Gate of Horn - Robert
  Holdstock f 723

Midkemia
Rage of a Demon King - Raymond E. Feist   *f*   703

Minbar
To Dream in the City of Sorrows - Kathryn M. Drennan   *s*   1084

Mistworld
Deathstalker War - Simon R. Green   *s*   1114
Twilight of the Empire - Simon R. Green   *s*   1115

Moudervelt
The Demon Princes: Volume Two - Jack Vance   *s*   1226

Nehwon
Return to Lankhmar - Fritz Leiber   *f*   748

Nevya
Receive the Gift - Louise Marley   *s*   1150

New Earth
Expendable - James Alan Gardner   *s*   1108

Niang
The Seeds of Time - Kay Kenyon   *s*   1136

Pacem
The Rise of Endymion - Dan Simmons   *s*   1208

Pell
Finity's End - C.J. Cherryh   *s*   1065

Pern
Dragonseye - Anne McCaffrey   *s*   1153

Persephone
Dreaming Metal - Melissa Scott   *s*   1197

Rigel V
Mind Meld - John Vornholt   *s*   1229

Saede
Echoes of Issel - Diann Thornley   *s*   1222

St. Helens
Zinnia - Jayne Castle   *r*   277

Samaria
Jovah's Angel - Sharon Shinn   *s*   1205

Senisran
The Howling Stones - Alan Dean Foster   *s*   1101

Shola
Razor's Edge - Lisanne Norman   *s*   1169

Skye
Bretta Martyn - L. Neil Smith   *s*   1209

Solferino
Putting Up Roots - Charles Sheffield   *s*   1203

Styreia
Kar Kalim - Deborah Christian   *f*   668

Summerland
Deathstalker War - Simon R. Green   *s*   1114

Tara
Blackmantle: A Triumph - Patricia Kennealy-Morrison   *f*   733

Thallon
End Game - Peter David   *s*   1075

Topawa
Dominion's Reach - Diann Thornley   *s*   1221

Trantor
Foundation's Fear - Gregory Benford   *s*   1050

Uhao
Berserker Fury - Fred Saberhagen   *s*   1189

Urrytha
Chrysalis - David Niall Wilson   *s*   1240

Vulcan
Avenger - William Shatner   *s*   1198

Wolf IV
Twilight of the Empire - Simon R. Green   *s*   1115

Wolfbane
Delta Search - William Shatner   *s*   1199

Z'Ha'dum
The Shadow Within - Jeanne Cavelos   *s*   1062

POLAND

A Blessing on the Moon - Joseph Skibell   *f*   796

Auschwitz
Days of Cain - J.R. Dunn   *s*   1086

PORTUGAL

Lisbon
God's Fires - Patricia Anthony   *s*   1035

Quintas
God's Fires - Patricia Anthony   *s*   1035

Sintra
The Club Dumas - Arturo Perez-Reverte   *m*   183

Vila do Mar
Impolite Society - Cynthia Smith   *m*   215

RUSSIA

Splendor - Brenda Joyce   *r*   343

Markovo
Siberian Light - Robin White   *m*   237

Moscow
Tarnished Icons - Stuart M. Kaminsky   *m*   136

St. Petersburg
Writ in Blood - Chelsea Quinn Yarbro   *h*   1031

SATURN

Saturn Rukh - Robert L. Forward   *s*   1100

Titan
Titan - Stephen Baxter   *s*   1047

SCOTLAND

Eyes of Love - Katherine Deauville   *r*   294
Holy Terror in the Hebrides - Jeanne M. Dams   *m*   53
Once a Warrior - Karyn Monk   *r*   383
One of These Nights - Susan Sizemore   *r*   423
The Pride of Lions - Marsha Canham   *r*   276
The Scottish Rose - Jill Jones   *r*   339
Season of Wishes - Christina Skye   *r*   426
True Heart - Arnette Lamb   *r*   358
A Well-Pleasured Lady - Christina Dodd   *r*   297

Aberdeen
Black and Blue - Ian Rankin   *m*   193

The Borderlands
The Raven's Moon - Susan King   *r*   348

Braikie
Death of a Dentist - M.C. Beaton   *m*   13

Creag Dhu
Son of the Morning - Linda Howard   *r*   330

Dumfries
A Surfeit of Guns - P.F. Chisholm   *m*   36

Edinburgh
Black and Blue - Ian Rankin   *m*   193
The Lover - Nicole Jordan   *r*   340

Eilean a'Tempull Dubh
Donnerjack - Roger Zelazny   *s*   1244

Highlands
Fairy Tale - Jillian Hunter   *r*   332
Starcatcher - Patricia Potter   *r*   400

Loch Ness
Testament of the Dragon - Margaret Weis   *f*   813

Lochdubh
Death of a Dentist - M.C. Beaton   *m*   13

SOLOMON ISLANDS

Guadalcanal
To Be a Warrior - Robert Barlow Fox   *w*   519

SOUTH AFRICA

Durban
City of Golden Shadow - Tad Williams   *s*   1234

SOUTH AMERICA

Hope of Earth - Piers Anthony   *s*   1036

SPACE STATION

Auriga
Alien Resurrection - A.C. Crispin   *s*   1071

Babylon 5
Personal Agendas - Al Sarrantonio   *s*   1191

Cassamir Station
Hunting the Corrigan's Blood - Holly Lisle   *s*   1145

Clarke County
A King of Infinite Space - Allen Steele   *s*   1212

Fleet Orientation Station Med.
An Exchange of Hostages - Susan R. Matthews   *s*   1151

Guild Hall Station
Fool's War - Sarah Zettel   *s*   1245

Harmony
Derelict for Trade - Andre Norton   *s*   1170

High Orbital Mfg. Env.
Lightpaths - Howard V. Hendrix   *s*   1131

Kolnar
The Ship Avenged - S.M. Stirling   *s*   1213

Koskiusko
Once a Hero - Elizabeth Moon   *s*   1160

New Dentinies
The Ship Avenged - S.M. Stirling   *s*   1213

Orbital Biodiversity Preserve
Lightpaths - Howard V. Hendrix   *s*   1131

PabNeruda
Mind Snare - Gayle Greeno   *s*   1118

Pell Station
Finity's End - C.J. Cherryh   *s*   1065

Robert E. Lee
The Digital Effect - Steve Perry   *s*   1173

Sector General Hospital
Final Diagnosis - James White   *s*   1233

Silk
Deception Well - Linda Nagata   *s*   1165

Diablo
Diablo - David Robbins   *w*   596

Fort Buchanan
Night of the Cougar - Frank Burleson   *w*   478

Globe
The Wagon Wars - James A. Ritchie   *w*   595

Grand Canyon
The Gaia Websters - Kim Antieau   *s*   1037

Payday
Flint's Gift - Richard S. Wheeler   *w*   628

Phoenix
I, Pearl Hart - Jane Candia Coleman   *w*   489
Only in the Ashes - Maxine O'Callaghan   *m*   176

Pima County
The Dansing Star - Kirby Jonas   *w*   548

San Carlos
Range Wars - Robert Vaughan   *w*   625

Tombstone
The Fourth Horseman - Randy Lee
   Eickhoff   *w*   514

Tucson
Apache Sundown - Hank Edwards   *w*   513

Whitecliff
Night of the Cougar - Frank Burleson   *w*   478

Window Rock
Tooth and Claw - Graham Masterton   *h*   960

Yuma Prison
I, Pearl Hart - Jane Candia Coleman   *w*   489

ARKANSAS

Arkansas River
The Long Hunters - Dodge Tyler   *w*   620

Camden
Ride, Rebels, Ride - Randal L. Greenwood   *w*   526

Covington Manor
Ride, Rebels, Ride - Randal L. Greenwood   *w*   526

Farberville
A Holly, Jolly Murder - Joan Hess   *m*   119

Fayetteville
Both Ends of the Night - Marcia Muller   *m*   173

Fort Destiny
The Long Hunters - Dodge Tyler   *w*   620

Fort Smith
Sunshine Rider - Ric Lynden Hardman   *w*   529

Maggody
The Maggody Militia - Joan Hess   *m*   120

Shakespeare
Shakespeare's Champion - Charlaine Harris   *m*   112

CALIFORNIA

As She Climbed Across the Table - Jonathan
   Lethem   *s*   1142
Blue Ride - Ken Wilkerson   *w*   632
The Death and Life of Bobby Z - Don
   Winslow   *m*   241
Heaven Loves a Hero - Nikki Holiday   *r*   326
Into the Forest - Jean Hegland   *s*   1130
Jed the Dead - Alan Dean Foster   *s*   1102
The Lost Coast: A Moses Wine Mystery - Roger L.
   Simon   *m*   213
The Promise of Jenny Jones - Maggie
   Osborne   *r*   393
Roughstock - Laura Crum   *m*   49

Son of Rosemary - Ira Levin   *h*   945
Timeshare - Joshua Dann   *s*   1074
Wyrm - Mark Fabi   *s*   1094

Beaver Hills
Camp Vamp - Elvira   *h*   879

Bellamy Park
Dead Men Don't Dance - Margaret
   Chittenden   *m*   37

Benecia
Sierra Baron - Tom W. Blackburn   *w*   459

Berkeley
Cop Out - Susan Dunlap   *m*   69
Frameshift - Robert J. Sawyer   *s*   1193
The Thirteenth Daughter of the Moon - Steven
   Nightingale   *f*   771

Bodie
The Refining Fire - W.E. Davis   *w*   506

Brea
The Ignored - Bentley Little   *h*   946

Carmel-by-the-Sea
The Bohemian Murders - Dianne Day   *m*   57

Catalina Island
Bad Karma - Andrew Harper   *h*   909

Emerald Isle
Seasons - Rebecca Forster   *r*   306

Encino
The Vampire's Beautiful Daughter - S.P.
   Somtow   *h*   1002

Flat Skunk
Dead Body Language - Penny Warner   *m*   232

Heavenly Valley
Dust Devils - Robert Laxalt   *w*   556

Hennington
Witchcraft - Bill Michaels   *h*   964

Hollywood
The Royalscope Fe-As-Ko - Randall Beth
   Platt   *w*   585
Time on My Hands - Peter Delacorte   *s*   1077

Huntington Beach
Winter Tides - James P. Blaylock   *h*   842

Irvines
Ticktock - Dean R. Koontz   *h*   936

Julian
Room 13 - Henry Garfield   *h*   886

Lake Tahoe
Obstruction of Justice - Perri O'Shaugnessy   *m*   178

Las Piernas
Hocus - Jan Burke   *m*   30

Los Angeles
Apparition Alley - Katherine V. Forrest   *m*   85
Bird Dog - Philip Reed   *m*   195
The Burning Plain - Michael Nava   *m*   175
Cain - James Byron Huggins   *h*   920
Celestial Dogs - J.S. Russell   *h*   986
The Clark Gable and Carole Lombard Murder Case -
   George Baxt   *m*   11
Cold Iron - Melisa Michaels   *f*   762
The Dark - Andrew Neiderman   *h*   971
Double Edge - Dennis Etchison   *h*   880
Earthquake Weather - Tim Powers   *f*   778
A Hard Light - Wendy Hornsby   *m*   125
Illegal Alien - Robert J. Sawyer   *s*   1194
Indigo Slam - Robert Crais   *m*   46
The Lost Coast: A Moses Wine Mystery - Roger L.
   Simon   *m*   213
Margin of Error - Edna Buchanan   *m*   27

The Night Crew - John Sandford   *m*   208
No Human Involved - Barbara Seranella   *m*   211
Omega - Patrick Lynch   *h*   953
Popcorn - Ben Elton   *h*   76
Ragged Angels - Della Van Hise   *h*   1017
Railroad Schemes - Cecilia Holland   *w*   539
Revision of Justice - John Morgan Wilson   *m*   240
Sole Survivor - Dean R. Koontz   *h*   935
The Stranger - Eric James Fullilove   *s*   1105
Survival of the Fittest - Jonathan Kellerman   *m*   138
The Toyotomi Blades - Dale Furutani   *m*   88
Tropic of Orange - Karen Tei Yamashita   *f*   823
Trunk Music - Michael Connelly   *m*   42

Malcasa Point
The Cellar - Richard Laymon   *h*   942

Marin County
A Cry for Self-Help - Jacqueline Girdner   *m*   99

Mariposa Ranch
The Cowgirls of the Mariposa - Lana Dean
   James   *w*   543

Mill Valley
Shadows - Jonathan Nasaw   *h*   970

Molena Point
Cats Raise the Dead - Shirley Rousseau
   Murphy   *f*   769

Monterey
Meg - Steve Alten   *h*   831
Sierra Baron - Tom W. Blackburn   *w*   459

Oakland
Ecstasy Club - Douglas Rushkoff   *s*   1187
Witness to Evil - Janet Dawson   *m*   56

Pacific Coast
The Long Walk - Amanda Cockrell   *w*   483

Pomo
A Wasteland of Strangers - Bill Pronzini   *m*   190

Rio Santo
The Seventh Heart - Marina Fitch   *f*   704

Sacramento
Blind Eagles - John S. McCord   *w*   568
Blood Will Tell - Terris McMahan Grimes   *m*   103
Lockhart's Nightmare - Wayne Barton   *w*   449
The MacKenzies: Luke - Ana Leigh   *r*   365

San Carmelita
Killer Calories - G.A. McKevett   *m*   165

San Diego
The Dollmaker's Daughters - Abigail
   Padgett   *m*   179
Meridian: A Novel of Kit Carson's West - Norman
   Zollinger   *w*   636
Ragged Angels - Della Van Hise   *h*   1017

San Francisco
Ask Mariah - Barbara Freethy   *r*   308
Both Ends of the Night - Marcia Muller   *m*   173
Carlucci's Heart - Richard Paul Russo   *s*   1188
Cold Iron - Melisa Michaels   *f*   762
Deadly Season - Tim Champlin   *w*   480
Delta Search - William Shatner   *s*   1199
Earthquake Weather - Tim Powers   *f*   778
A Hard Light - Wendy Hornsby   *m*   125
Illusions - Bill Pronzini   *m*   189
Jade - Ruth Langan   *r*   360
Millennium: Gehenna - Lewis Gannett   *h*   884
Past Tense - Stephen Greenleaf   *m*   100
The Rock Child - Win Blevins   *w*   462
Sixguns and Double Eagles - Ralph
   Compton   *w*   495
Starfleet Academy - Diane Carey   *s*   1061
Twice a Hero - Susan Krinard   *r*   355

Andersonville

Andersonville - Robert Vaughan   *w*   623

Atlanta

The Devil's Advocate - Gherbod Fleming   *h*   882
Down on Ponce - Fred Willard   *m*   239
Finding Laura - Kay Hooper   *r*   329
The Seraphim Rising - Elisabeth De Vos   *s*   1076
Sewer, Gas & Electric - Matt Ruff   *s*   1185
Strange Brew - Kathy Hogan Trocheck   *m*   229

Balsa City

A Brace of Bloodhounds - Virginia Lanier   *m*   143

Cedar Ridge

Valentine Delights - Meryl Sawyer   *r*   417

Cumberland Island National Sea

Endangered Species - Nevada Barr   *m*   9

Jeffersonville

Long Southern Nights - Heather MacAllister   *r*   368

Margrave

Killing Floor - Lee Child   *m*   35

Savannah

AKA Jane - Maureen Tan   *m*   222

GREAT PLAINS

Medicine Hat - Don Coldsmith   *w*   484
Tallgrass: A Novel of the Great Plains - Don
  Coldsmith   *w*   485

HAWAII

Hilo
Mars Underground - William Hartmann   *s*   1126

Maui
The Presence - John Saul   *h*   991

IDAHO

Moskow
/ - Greg Bear   *s*   1049

ILLINOIS

Fear of Frying - Jill Churchill   *m*   38
There Was a Season - T.V. Olsen   *w*   579
When Lilacs Bloom - Susan Kirby   *r*   350

Cave-in-Rock
Passage to Natchez - Cameron Judd   *w*   550

Chicago
Accidental Roommates - Charlotte Maclay   *r*   369
Back in the USSA - Kim Newman   *s*   1166
Eye of the Agency - Richard Moquist   *m*   170
Fever Rising - Maggie Ferguson   *r*   305
Flight Dreams - Michael Craft   *m*   44
Hard Bargain - Barbara D'Amato   *m*   52
Husband Needed - Cathie Linz   *r*   366
I, Pearl Hart - Jane Candia Coleman   *w*   489
Nobody's Baby but Mine - Susan Elizabeth
  Phillips   *r*   397
Testament of the Dragon - Margaret Weis   *f*   813

Hopewell
Running with the Demon - Terry Brooks   *f*   659

Thistle Down
Prairie Rose - Susan Kirby   *r*   349

INDIAN TERRITORY

Dark Trail to Dodge - Cotton Smith   *w*   605

INDIANA

Bethel Lake
Threshold - Bill Myers   *s*   1164

Pikeston
The Lieutenant's Lady - Rae Muir   *r*   387

IOWA

Ames
American Dreamer - Theresa Weir   *r*   435

Ames
The Soprano Sorceress - L.E. Modesitt Jr.   *f*   765

KANSAS

All God's Children - Tom Eidson   *w*   515
Cherished Love - Rosanne Bittner   *r*   263
The Courtship of Cade Kolby - Lori
  Copeland   *r*   287
Trail Drive - James Rice   *w*   593

Dodge City
Bumpo, Bill, and the Girls - Kent Conwell   *w*   499
Dark Trail to Dodge - Cotton Smith   *w*   605
The Killing Season - Ralph Compton   *w*   494
Sixguns and Double Eagles - Ralph
  Compton   *w*   495

Fort Gibson
Sunshine Rider - Ric Lynden Hardman   *w*   529

Fort Hays
Yesterday's Reveille - Robert Vaughan   *w*   626

Fort Leavenworth
Savage Plains - David William Ross   *w*   601

Hays
The Killing Season - Ralph Compton   *w*   494

Kansas River
Medicine Hat - Don Coldsmith   *w*   484
Tallgrass: A Novel of the Great Plains - Don
  Coldsmith   *w*   485

Lawrence
Blood on the Plains - Robert Vaughan   *w*   624

Liberty
Break the Young Land - T.V. Olsen   *w*   578

Pottawatomie
Cloudsplitter - Russell Banks   *w*   447

Topeka
Wizard and Glass - Stephen King   *h*   931

KENTUCKY

Wayward Angel - Patricia Rice   *r*   407

Boonesboro
Algonquin Massacre - Dodge Tyler   *w*   617
A River Run Red - Dodge Tyler   *w*   621

Delaplain
The Winds of Autumn - Jim R. Woolard   *w*   635

Kentucky Frontier
Just Once - Jill Marie Landis   *r*   359

New Zion
Chase the Moon - Dinah McCall   *r*   375

Ohio Valley
A River Run Red - Dodge Tyler   *w*   621

Tyler Plantation
The Winds of Autumn - Jim R. Woolard   *w*   635

LOUISIANA

Dayborn
Stone Angel - Carol O'Connell   *m*   177

Grand Isle
Rising Tides - Emilie Richards   *r*   408

Hardscrabble Plantation
No Remorse - James D. Brewer   *m*   26

New Orleans
A Dance with the Devil - Rexanne Becnel   *r*   257
Death Will Have Your Eyes: A Novel about Spies -
  James Sallis   *m*   207
Deep as the Rivers - Shirl Henke   *r*   323
The Fourth Horseman - Randy Lee
  Eickhoff   *w*   514
A Free Man of Color - Barbara Hambly   *m*   109
Gabriel Knight: Sins of the Fathers - Jane
  Jensen   *h*   924
The Gris-Gris Man - Don Davis   *h*   867
In the Rogue Blood - James Carlos Blake   *w*   460
Just Once - Jill Marie Landis   *r*   359
Risking Elizabeth - Walter McCloskey   *m*   161
Sixguns and Double Eagles - Ralph
  Compton   *w*   495
Sleeping with the Crawfish - D.J. Donaldson   *m*   65
Trick Question - Tony Dunbar   *m*   68
Violin - Anne Rice   *h*   983

MAINE

Beside a Dreamswept Sea - Victoria Barrett   *r*   256

Florence
Potshot - Gerry Boyle   *m*   25

Prosperity
Potshot - Gerry Boyle   *m*   25

Rufford
Blood Red Roses - Margaret Lawrence   *m*   146

MARYLAND

Baltimore
Booth - David Robertson   *w*   597
Charm City - Laura Lippman   *m*   149
Up Jumped the Devil - Blair S. Walker   *m*   230

Kent Fort Manor
Mary's Land - Lucia St. Clair Robson   *w*   598

Riverview
Blood and Chocolate - Annette Curtis
  Klause   *h*   932

MASSACHUSETTS

Toward the End of Time - John Updike   *s*   1224

Boston
Angels Unaware - L. Elizabeth Storm   *s*   1215
Cloudsplitter - Russell Banks   *w*   447
Cold Case - Linda Barnes   *m*   8
Coyote Summer - W. Michael Gear   *w*   523
The Garden Plot - J.S. Borthwick   *m*   22
Life Support - Tess Gerritsen   *h*   894
The MacGregor Brides - Nora Roberts   *r*   415
Sacred - Dennis Lehane   *m*   147
Small Vices - Robert B. Parker   *m*   182

Cambridge
Animal Appetite - Susan Conant   *m*   41
Renaissance Moon - Linda Nevins   *f*   770

Handley's Mill
The Healer's Road - J.L. Reasoner   *w*   590

Kingdom Head Island
The Stone Circle - Gary Goshgarian   *h*   898

Brady
The Hunted - James Reasoner *w* 591

Bronco
The Peacekeeper - Jeffrey Poston *w* 586

Cibolo Springs
Bumpo, Bill, and the Girls - Kent Conwell *w* 499

Cobb's Relay Station
Beyond the River - Wynema McGowan *w* 570

Dallas
Doc Holliday - Matt Braun *w* 470
Eden - Frederic Bean *w* 451
Meeting the Minotaur - Carol Dawson *f* 684

Davis Mountains
The Hunted - James Reasoner *w* 591

Deaf Smith
Cimarron Rose - James Lee Burke *m* 29

Dechman
I Rode with Jesse James - Charles
   Hackenberry *w* 527

Del Rio
Dust on the Wind - Bill Brooks *w* 474

El Paso
The Autumn of the Gun - Ralph Compton *w* 492
The Border Empire - Ralph Compton *w* 493

Fort Davis
The Courtship of Hannah and the Horseman - Johnny
   D. Boggs *w* 464

Fort Elliott
The Autumn of the Gun - Ralph Compton *w* 492

Fort Griffin
The Winchester Run - Ralph Compton *w* 496

Fort Worth
Hell's Half Acre - Frederic Bean *w* 452
Lockhart's Nightmare - Wayne Barton *w* 449

Franklin
Bandido Caballero - Jack Ballas *w* 445

Gonzales
Pure Justice - Suzann Ledbetter *w* 559

Guadalupe Mountains
This Man Colter - Johnny D. Boggs *w* 465

Hanging Tree
Jade - Ruth Langan *r* 360

Hell
Jezebel - Katherine Sutcliffe *w* 609

Hermosito
While the Rivers Run - Wynema McGowan *w* 571

Houston
Fall from Grace - Megan Chance *r* 278
Forever Peace - Joe Haldeman *s* 1119

Job's Crossing
Biggie and the Mangled Mortician - Nancy
   Bell *m* 15

Lampkin Springs
Silverthorne - Wayne Davis *w* 507

Laredo
In the Rogue Blood - James Carlos Blake *w* 460

Longview
Black Gold - Frederic Bean *w* 450

MFD Ranch
High Prairie - Hiram King *w* 553

Necesario
How the West Was Lost - Gene Shelton *w* 603

Odessa
Sunshine Rider - Ric Lynden Hardman *w* 529

Paint Rock
Journey to Shiloh - Will Henry *w* 533

Pecan Springs
Love Lies Bleeding - Susan Wittig Albert *m* 2

Red River
The Red River - Frederic Bean *w* 454

Richland Springs
The Hunted - James Reasoner *w* 591

Richmond
The Way Home - Megan Chance *r* 279

Rio Colorado
Across the Rio Colorado - Ralph Compton *w* 491

San Antonio
The Barons of Texas - Jory Sherman *w* 604
Big Red Tequila - Rick Riordan *m* 199
The Black Jacks - Jason Manning *w* 565
Blood of Texas - Will Camp *w* 479
Houston - Doug Bowman *w* 468

Singletree Ranch
How the West Was Lost - Gene Shelton *w* 603

Staked Plains
Beyond the River - Wynema McGowan *w* 570
The Black Jacks - Jason Manning *w* 565
Comanche Moon - Larry McMurtry *w* 572
Dark Trail to Dodge - Cotton Smith *w* 605
The Ghost Trail - Tracy Dunham *w* 510
Houston - Doug Bowman *w* 468
The Kiowa Verdict - Cynthia Haseloff *w* 531
The Long Trail Home - Tracy Dunham *w* 511

Stony Point
Ride, Rebels, Ride - Randal L. Greenwood *w* 526

Tubac
High Prairie - Hiram King *w* 553

Tyler
Terminal Logic - Jefferson Scott *s* 1196

Waxahachie
Einstein's Bridge - John Cramer *s* 1070

White Horse
The Way Home - Megan Chance *r* 279

UTAH

Ogden
To Be a Warrior - Robert Barlow Fox *w* 519

Uintah Mountains
Heartbreaker - Karen Robards *r* 414

Winona Basin
Mountains against the Sun - Perry Holmes *w* 541

VERMONT

Bellows Falls
Bellows Falls - Archer Mayor *m* 160

Brattleboro
Bellows Falls - Archer Mayor *m* 160

Fort Ticonderoga
Savage Wilderness - Harold Coyle *w* 502

VIRGINIA

War Woman - Robert J. Conley *w* 498

Arlington
The Siege of Eternity - Frederik Pohl *s* 1176

Cold Harbor
Andersonville - Robert Vaughan *w* 623

Crowley Creek
The Black Cat - Robert Poe *h* 978

Furnace
Furnace - Muriel Gray *h* 901

Harper's Ferry
Cloudsplitter - Russell Banks *w* 447

Lexington
Look Away - Harold Coyle *w* 501

Luntville
The Bighead - Edward Lee *h* 943
*The Case of the Police Officer's Cock Ring and the
   Piano Player Who Had No Fingers* - Edward
   Lee *h* 944

Mine Run
Until the End - Harold Coyle *w* 503

Richmond
Unnatural Exposure - Patricia Cornwell *m* 43
Until the End - Harold Coyle *w* 503
Wooing Wanda - Gwen Pemberton *r* 396

Spotsylvania
Play for a Kingdom - Tom Dyja *w* 512

Staunton
Remember the Time - Annette A. Reynolds *r* 406

Wilderness
Play for a Kingdom - Tom Dyja *w* 512

WASHINGTON

September Mourn - Mary Daheim *m* 50

Bellhaven
Out of Circulation - Jo Dereske *m* 60

Cascade Mountains
Out of Circulation - Jo Dereske *m* 60

Columbia River
Renegade River - Giff Cheshire *w* 481

LaConner
A Ritual Death - Father Brad Reynolds S.J. *m* 197

Lilian River Valley
Earthling - Tony Daniel *s* 1073

Mount Ranier
The Miser on the Mountain - Nancy Luenn *w* 563

Obstruction Bay
Just Before Midnight - Patricia Simpson *r* 422

San Juan Islands
Amber Beach - Elizabeth Lowell *r* 367

Seattle
/ - Greg Bear *s* 1049
The Bum's Rush - G.M. Ford *m* 84
Deception Pass - Earl Emerson *m* 78
Headhunters - Mel Odom *s* 1172
Just Before Midnight - Patricia Simpson *r* 422
Millennium: The Frenchman - Elizabeth
   Hand *h* 908
September Mourn - Mary Daheim *m* 50
Shadowboxer - Nick Pollotta *s* 1177
Three Brides, No Groom - Debbie Macomber *r* 371

Staircase
The Dead Horse Paint Company - Earl
   Emerson *m* 77

Tacoma
Bug Park - James P. Hogan *s* 1132
Out of Body - Thomas Baum *h* 836

Genre Index

This index lists the books featured as main entries in *What Do I Read Next?* by genre and story type within each genre. Beneath each of the six genres, the story types appear alphabetically, and titles appear alphabetically under story type headings. The name of the primary author and the book entry number also appear with each title. For definitions of the story types, see the "Key to Genre Terms" following the Introduction.

FANTASY

Adventure

Allamanda - Michael Williams *f* 817
Bijapur - Kara Dalkey *f* 680
The Book of Night with Moon - Diane Duane *f* 692
The Book of Water - Marjorie Bradley Kellogg *f* 732
Bridge of Valor - Anne Lesley Groell *f* 716
Captives of the Blue Mountain - Wendy Pini *f* 777
Cardmaster - Clayton Emery *f* 700
Children of Amarid - David B. Coe *f* 674
The Conjurer Princess - Vivian Vande Velde *f* 807
The Day of the Tempest - Jean Rabe *f* 782
A Dragon at World's End - Christopher Rowley *f* 787
Drum Calls - Jo Clayton *f* 671
Firewalk - Anne Logston *f* 753
The Gates of Vensunor - Carol Heller *f* 720
Hungry for Home: A Wolf Odyssey - 'Asta Bowen *f* 654
Kar Kalim - Deborah Christian *f* 668
Kindred Rites - Katharine Eliska Kimbriel *f* 738
King's Man and Thief - Christie Golden *f* 709
Landslayer's Law - Tom Deitz *f* 687
Legacy of the Darksword - Margaret Weis *f* 812
The Mines of Behemoth - Michael Shea *f* 792
Owlflight - Mercedes Lackey *f* 743
The Pearls of Lutra - Brian Jacques *f* 728
Planar Powers - J. Robert King *f* 739
Polgara the Sorceress - David Eddings *f* 696
Red Unicorn - Tanith Lee *f* 747
Song of the River - Sue Harrison *f* 717
The Still - David Feintuch *f* 702
Sword of Ice and Other Tales of Valdemar - Mercedes Lackey *f* 744
Talion: Revenant - Michael A. Stackpole *f* 799
Testament of the Dragon - Margaret Weis *f* 813
The Thief of Hermes - Ru Emerson *f* 699
Vinas Solamnus - J. Robert King *f* 740
The War in the Waste - Felicity Savage *f* 790
When the Gods Are Silent - Jane M. Lindskold *f* 750
Wizard of Bones - Robert N. Charrette *f* 665
Wrath of the Princes - Holly Lisle *f* 752

Alternate History

Milton in America - Peter Ackroyd *f* 637

Alternate Universe

The War in the Waste - Felicity Savage *f* 790

Alternate World

The Barbed Coil - J.V. Jones *f* 730
Changespell - Doranna Durgin *f* 695
The Dragon and the Gnarly King - Gordon R. Dickson *f* 688
Future Indefinite - Dave Duncan *f* 694
Gate of Ivory, Gate of Horn - Robert Holdstock *f* 723
God's Dice - S. Andrew Swann *f* 804
Landslayer's Law - Tom Deitz *f* 687
Monet's Ghost - Chelsea Quinn Yarbro *f* 824
My Son, the Wizard - Christopher Stasheff *f* 800
The Soprano Sorceress - L.E. Modesitt Jr. *f* 765
The Wiz Biz - Rick Cook *f* 677

Anthology

Bending the Landscape: Fantasy - Nicola Griffith *f* 715
Black Swan, White Raven - Ellen Datlow *f* 682
Elf Fantastic - Martin H. Greenberg *f* 713
The Horns of Elfland - Ellen Kushner *f* 741
The Mammoth Book of Fairy Tales - Mike Ashley *f* 643
Modern Classics of Fantasy - Gardner Dozois *f* 690
The Random House Book of Fantasy Stories - Mike Ashley *f* 644
Sword and Sorceress XIV - Marion Zimmer Bradley *f* 657
Sword of Ice and Other Tales of Valdemar - Mercedes Lackey *f* 744
Tarot Fantastic - Martin H. Greenberg *f* 714
Testament of the Dragon - Margaret Weis *f* 813
Treasures of Fantasy - Margaret Weis *f* 814

Collection

The Arbitrary Placement of Walls - Martha Soukup *f* 797
The Djinn in the Nightingale's Eye - A.S. Byatt *f* 662
Fabulous Harbors - Michael Moorcock *f* 767
Fractured Fairy Tales - A.J. Jacobs *f* 727
Giant Bones - Peter S. Beagle *f* 650
Kissing the Witch: Old Tales in New Skins - Emma Donoghue *f* 689
The Notorious Abbess - Vera Chapman *f* 664

Return to Lankhmar - Fritz Leiber *f* 748
The Rhinoceros Who Quoted Nietzsche and Other Odd Acquaintances - Peter S. Beagle *f* 651
Spires of Spirit - Gael Baudino *f* 649
Twelve Impossible Things Before Breakfast - Jane Yolen *f* 826
The World of Robert Jordan's The Wheel of Time - Robert Jordan *f* 731

Contemporary

The Art of Arrow Cutting - Stephen Dedman *f* 686
The Broken Sword - Molly Cochran *f* 673
Earthquake Weather - Tim Powers *f* 778
Hell on High - Holly Lisle *f* 751
In the Land of Winter - Richard Grant *f* 711
Mennyms Alive - Sylvia Waugh *f* 811
Neverwhere - Neil Gaiman *f* 707
Running with the Demon - Terry Brooks *f* 659
Trader - Charles de Lint *f* 685

Contemporary Realism

A Blessing on the Moon - Joseph Skibell *f* 796
Cats Raise the Dead - Shirley Rousseau Murphy *f* 769
Come Before Christ and Murder Love - Stewart Home *f* 725
Dogland - Will Shetterly *f* 794
Flying Saucers over Hennepin - Peter Gelman *f* 708
The Forgetting Room - Nick Bantock *f* 647
How Like a God - Brenda W. Clough *f* 672
Meeting the Minotaur - Carol Dawson *f* 684
Renaissance Moon - Linda Nevins *f* 770
The Seventh Heart - Marina Fitch *f* 704
The Thirteenth Daughter of the Moon - Steven Nightingale *f* 771

Historical

Bijapur - Kara Dalkey *f* 680
Children of the Dusk - Janet Berliner *f* 652
Devil's Engine - Mark Sumner *f* 803
The Dog King - Christoph Ransmayr *f* 784
The Duke of Sumava - Sara J. Wrench *f* 821
Freedom & Necessity - Steven Brust *f* 660
The Moon and the Sun - Vonda N. McIntyre *f* 759
Spirits of the Ordinary - Kathleen Alcala *f* 638
The Subtle Knife - Philip Pullman *f* 781
Thessalonica - Harry Turtledove *f* 805

HORROR

ROMANCE

SCIENCE FICTION

WESTERN

Character Name Index

This index alphabetically lists the major characters in each featured title. Each character name is followed by a description of the character. Citations also provide titles of the books featuring the character, listed alphabetically if there is more than one title; author names; and entry numbers.

A

Abaddon (Immortal; Ruler)
Wolf in Shadow - David Gemmell *s* 1110

Abivard (Military Personnel)
The Thousand Cities - Harry Turtledove *f* 806

Acorna (Alien; Foundling)
Acorna - Anne McCaffrey *s* 1152

Adams, John Quincy (Lawyer; Historical Figure)
Amistad - Alexs Pate *w* 584

Adams, Rex (Nobleman)
Indiscreet - Mary Balogh *r* 252

Adashek, David (Journalist)
Meg - Steve Alten *h* 831

Adcock, Patrice "Pat" (Scientist; Clone)
The Siege of Eternity - Frederik Pohl *s* 1176

Aditi (Sorcerer)
Bijapur - Kara Dalkey *f* 680

Adolphus, Max (Artist)
Prairie - Greg Tobin *w* 616

Aedrea (Mutant; Femme Fatale)
Saint Leibowitz and the Wild Horse Woman - Walter M. Miller Jr. *s* 1157

Aenea (Genetically Altered Being; Religious)
The Rise of Endymion - Dan Simmons *s* 1208

Agnes (Aged Person)
Well Wished - Franny Billingsley *f* 653

Agramonte, Maran (Noblewoman)
The Seer King - Chris Bunch *f* 661

a'Husain, Idryis Khan (Political Figure)
Imposter - Valerie J. Freireich *s* 1103

Aiah (Political Figure; Police Officer)
City on Fire - Walter Jon Williams *s* 1235

Aionwahta (Indian; Historical Figure)
Eagle Song - Joseph Bruchac *w* 476

Akhor (Mythical Creature; Royalty)
Song in the Silence - Elizabeth Kerner *f* 734

Akili (Genetically Altered Being)
Distress - Greg Egan *s* 1088

Al Shei, Katmer (Businesswoman; Engineer)
Fool's War - Sarah Zettel *s* 1245

Alain (Bastard Son; Military Personnel)
King's Dragon - Kate Elliott *f* 698

Alayna (Wizard)
Children of Amarid - David B. Coe *f* 674

Albain, Elandra (Ruler)
Realm of Light - Deborah Chester *f* 666
Shadow War - Deborah Chester *f* 667

Alcott, Tess (Thief; Con Artist)
Stolen Hearts - Michelle Martin *r* 373

Alec of Kerry (Apprentice; Spy)
Stalking Darkness - Lynn Flewelling *f* 705

Alena (Royalty)
Cossack Three Ponies - J.L. Reasoner *w* 589

Alexander (Religious)
The Bighead - Edward Lee *h* 943

Alexander of Trevigna (Royalty; Imposter)
A Prince Among Men - Kate Moore *r* 384

Alexander the Great (Historical Figure)
A Murder in Macedon - Anna Apostolou *m* 5

Algooth (Mythical Creature)
The Gates of Vensunor - Carol Heller *f* 720

Allard, Frank (Avenger; Rancher)
Mountains against the Sun - Perry Holmes *w* 541

Allika (Child; Thief)
King's Man and Thief - Christie Golden *f* 709

Allison, Clay (Gunfighter; Historical Figure)
Legend of a Badman: A Western Quintet - Ray Hogan *w* 537

Alston, John "Skiddle" (Religious)
The Great Wheel - Ian R. MacLeod *s* 1148

Alta (Revolutionary)
Deception Well - Linda Nagata *s* 1165

Alton, Marguerida "Margaret" (Heiress; Telepath)
The Shadow Matrix - Marion Zimmer Bradley *s* 1055

Alys of Summersedge (Noblewoman)
Lord of Danger - Anne Stuart *r* 431

Amaranth (Mythical Creature; Companion)
The Dragon's Touchstone - Irene Radford *f* 783

Amaro, Angelina (Young Woman)
Virgin Heat - Laurence Shames *m* 212

Ambras "Dog King" (Leader)
The Dog King - Christoph Ransmayr *f* 784

Ames, Celinda (Orphan; Teenager)
Passage to Natchez - Cameron Judd *w* 550

Amiss, Robert (Historian)
Murder in a Cathedral - Ruth Dudley Edwards *m* 72

Amnel, Kahlan (Magician; Leader)
Temple of the Winds - Terry Goodkind *f* 710

Ampelus (Mythical Creature)
Thessalonica - Harry Turtledove *f* 805

Amrey, Murl "Kar Kalim" (Magician; Warrior)
Kar Kalim - Deborah Christian *f* 668

Ananda (Musician; Lawyer)
The Thirteenth Daughter of the Moon - Steven Nightingale *f* 771

Anderson, Kristin (Rancher; Spinster)
Larkspur - Dorothy Garlock *r* 310

Anderson, Mali (Student; Police Officer)
If I Should Die - Grace Edwards *m* 71

Andrews, Pepper (Spouse; Saloon Hostess)
Stay Away From That City. . .They Call It Cheyenne - Stephen Bly *w* 463

Andrews, Tap (Lawman; Outlaw)
Stay Away From That City. . .They Call It Cheyenne - Stephen Bly *w* 463

Angel (Animal)
Dancing on Air - Nancy Kress *s* 1140

Angelica (Vampire)
Born in Twilight - Maggie Shayne *r* 419

Annalise (Companion; Slave)
Black Wine - Candas Jane Dorsey *s* 1082

Antar (Computer Expert)
The Calcutta Chromosome - Amitav Ghosh *h* 895

Anthea (Explorer)
I Who Have Never Known Men - Jacqueline Harpman *s* 1124

Anya (Dancer; Vampire)
Live Girls - Ray Garton *h* 888

ap Ieuan, Owain (Vampire)
The Devil's Advocate - Gherbod Fleming *h* 882

Apolinario, Lot (Genetically Altered Being; Revolutionary)
Deception Well - Linda Nagata *s* 1165

Apollo (Warrior; Spaceman)
Armageddon - Richard Hatch *s* 1129

Appenfell, Rudgar "Rudy" (Hero; Mountaineer)
War of the Three Waters - Douglas Niles *f* 772

Aqamdax (Indian)
Song of the River - Sue Harrison *f* 717

Arabella "Infectress" (Criminal; Revolutionary)
Infectress - Tom Cool *s* 1069

Arbati, Carlo (Detective—Police; Writer)
Ghirlandaio's Daughter - John Spencer Hill *m* 122

Arcangelo, Michael (Computer Expert)
Wyrm - Mark Fabi *s* 1094

Archangel (Mythical Creature; Computer Expert)
Headhunters - Mel Odom *s* 1172

Archangel (Writer; Activist)
Tropic of Orange - Karen Tei Yamashita *f* 823

Archer, Owen (Military Personnel; Spy)
The Riddle of St. Leonard's - Candace M.
Robb *m* 200

Archibald, Stephen (Nobleman; Gardener)
A Garden Folly - Candice Hern *r* 325

Arden, Nicholas (Nobleman; Guardian)
An Infamous Proposal - Joan Smith *r* 428

Ardis (Religious)
Four & Twenty Blackbirds - Mercedes
Lackey *f* 742

Arellano, Diane (Teenager)
The Cowgirls of the Mariposa - Lana Dean
James *w* 543

Arista, Tommaso (Apprentice)
The Stars Dispose - Michaela Roessner *f* 786

Arkendale, Charlotte (Investigator; Gentlewoman)
Affair - Amanda Quick *r* 402

Armon (Artist)
The Forgetting Room - Nick Bantock *f* 647

Armstrong, Kate Moran (Widow(er))
Remember the Time - Annette A. Reynolds *r* 406

Arthor (Bastard Son; Teenager)
The Eagle and the Sword - A.A. Attanasio *f* 645

Arthur (Royalty)
Enemy of God - Bernard Cornwell *f* 678
Grail - Stephen R. Lawhead *f* 745
Pendragon's Banner - Helen Hollick *r* 327
Shadow of the King - Helen Hollick *f* 724

Aryadyss (Artificial Intelligence; Mythical Creature)
Donnerjack - Roger Zelazny *s* 1244

Ashbrooke, Catherine Augustine (Bride)
The Pride of Lions - Marsha Canham *r* 276

Ashe, Timothy (Time Traveller; Spy)
The Seeds of Time - Kay Kenyon *s* 1136

Ashton, Celeste (Scientist)
The Mermaid - Betina Krahn *r* 352

Ashton, Choe (Truck Driver; Rebel)
Signs of Life - M. John Harrison *s* 1125

Ashton, Michael (Architect)
Ask Mariah - Barbara Freethy *r* 308

Asie (Indian; Musician)
The Rock Child - Win Blevins *w* 462

Asimov, Issac (Television Personality; Historical
Figure)
Back in the USSA - Kim Newman *s* 1166

Asperson, Arhos (Criminal)
Once a Hero - Elizabeth Moon *s* 1160

Atkinson, Henry (Military Personnel)
There Was a Season - T.V. Olsen *w* 579

Atrus (Writer; Magician)
The Book of D'ni - Rand Miller *f* 763

Augustus, Caleb (Engineer; Scientist)
Jovah's Angel - Sharon Shinn *s* 1205

Aurian (Wizard)
Dhiammara - Maggie Furey *f* 706

Austen, Jane (Writer; Historical Figure)
Jane and the Man of the Cloth - Stephanie
Barron *m* 10

Avelyn (Religious; Wizard)
The Demon Awakens - R.A. Salvatore *f* 789

Avens, Isobel (Genetically Altered Being)
Signs of Life - M. John Harrison *s* 1125

Avery, Rupert "Roo" (Businessman)
Rage of a Demon King - Raymond E. Feist *f* 703

Ayrlyn (Doctor)
The Chaos Balance - L.E. Modesitt Jr. *f* 764

B

Backmaker, Hodgins "Hodge" (Historian; Time
Traveller)
Bring the Jubilee - Ward Moore *s* 1162

Bailey, Deanie (Musician)
Once upon a Rose - Judith O'Brien *r* 390

Bailey, Geoffrey (Police Officer)
Without Consent - Frances Fyfield *m* 89

Baird, Lisbeth King (Widow(er))
Soaring Eagle - Stephanie Grace Whitson *r* 436

Bak (Military Personnel)
The Right Hand of Amon - Lauren Haney *m* 110

Baldridge, Masey (Gambler; Detective—Private)
No Remorse - James D. Brewer *m* 26

Baldwin, Roger (Lawyer)
Amistad - Alexs Pate *w* 584

Balthazar, Timothy (Businessman)
Wolf Moon - John R. Holt *h* 916

Bandelier, Cleve (Rancher)
Winchester Affidavit - G.G. Boyer *w* 469

Banks, Alan (Police Officer)
Blood at the Root - Peter Robinson *m* 203

Bannon, James (Military Personnel)
Look Away - Harold Coyle *w* 501
Until the End - Harold Coyle *w* 503

Bannon, Kevin (Military Personnel)
Look Away - Harold Coyle *w* 501
Until the End - Harold Coyle *w* 503

Bannon, Tyrel (Cowboy)
Dark Trail to Dodge - Cotton Smith *w* 605

Barbara (Young Woman)
Night of the Living Dead - John A. Russo *h* 987

Barbrossa, Edwin Amadeus (Scientist)
How Like a God - Brenda W. Clough *f* 672

Barclay, Richard (Journalist; Lover)
Blue Genes - Val McDermid *m* 162

Bard, Lily (Martial Arts Expert; Housekeeper)
Shakespeare's Champion - Charlaine Harris *m* 112

Bardell, Luke (Con Artist; Religious)
Ritual Sins - Anne Stuart *r* 432

Baretta, Jake (Twin; Imposter)
Chase the Moon - Dinah McCall *r* 375

Barku, Perkar Kar (Warrior; Hero)
The Blackgod - J. Gregory Keyes *f* 737

Barnett, Pierce (Businessman; Activist)
The Firebrand - Laurel Collins *r* 285

Baron, Martin (Rancher)
The Barons of Texas - Jory Sherman *w* 604

Barr, Temple (Public Relations)
Cat in a Flamingo Fedora - Carole Nelson
Douglas *m* 67

Barra (Warrior; Mercenary)
Iron Dawn - Matthew Woodring Stover *f* 802

Barringer, Billy (Teenager)
The Cowgirls of the Mariposa - Lana Dean
James *w* 543

Barrington, Clarissa (Spouse; Frontierswoman)
Night of the Cougar - Frank Burleson *w* 478

Barrington, Nathanial (Alcoholic; Drifter)
Devil Dance - Frank Burleson *w* 477

Barrington, Nathaniel (Rancher; Military Personnel)
Night of the Cougar - Frank Burleson *w* 478

Barrington, Zachary (Child)
Devil Dance - Frank Burleson *w* 477

Barron, Luke (Gunfighter)
Rattlesnake Mesa - Peter Dawson *w* 508

Bascomb, Ernie (Military Personnel)
Slicky Boys - Martin Limon *m* 148

Bashir, Julian (Doctor; Military Personnel)
Armageddon Sky - L.A. Graf *s* 1113

Bass, Titus (Mountain Man)
Crack in the Sky - Terry C. Johnston *w* 545

Bates, Verna (Publisher)
The Ladies of the Goldfield Stock Exchange - Sibyl
Downing *w* 509

Bateson, Morgan (Spaceship Captain)
Ship of the Line - Diane Carey *s* 1060

Batik (Religious; Fugitive)
Wolf in Shadow - David Gemmell *s* 1110

Bayles, China (Businesswoman; Lawyer)
Love Lies Bleeding - Susan Wittig Albert *m* 2

Baynes, Darnell (Mine Owner)
Nevada Tough - John S. McCord *w* 569

Baynes, Kit (Spouse)
Blind Eagles - John S. McCord *w* 568

Baynes, Ward (Rancher)
Blind Eagles - John S. McCord *w* 568

Bearpaw, Molly (Investigator; Indian)
The Spirit Caller - Jean Hager *m* 106

Beast (Animal)
Rose Daughter - Robin McKinley *f* 761

Beatrice (Handicapped; Psychic)
The Broken Sword - Molly Cochran *f* 673

Beaudry, Eliza (Farmer)
The Way Home - Megan Chance *r* 279

Beaumont, Dora (Adoptee; Religious)
Wayward Angel - Patricia Rice *r* 407

Beaumont, Gabe (Cowboy; Indian)
Tame the Wild Wind - Rosanne Bittner *w* 458

Beauty (Gardener)
Rose Daughter - Robin McKinley *f* 761

Becker, Triana (Musician)
Violin - Anne Rice *h* 983

Beckett, Sam (Time Traveller; Scientist)
Angels Unaware - L. Elizabeth Storm *s* 1215

Beckman, Tad (Journalist)
Counting Coup - G.D. Gearino *m* 93

Beckwourth, Jim (Mountain Man; Historical Figure)
Rendezvous - Richard S. Wheeler *w* 629

Bede, Strebban "Badger" (Spaceman; Computer
Expert)
Hunting the Corrigan's Blood - Holly Lisle *s* 1145

Bednacort, Loria (Spouse)
Destiny's Road - Larry Niven *s* 1167

Bee, Jane (Servant)
Death at Sandringham House - C.C. Benison *m* 16

C

Calef (Animal)
Hungry for Home: A Wolf Odyssey - 'Asta
   Bowen *f* 654

Calhoun, Mackenzie (Spaceship Captain)
End Game - Peter David *s* 1075

Calhoun, Princess (Heiress; Spinster)
No Ordinary Princess - Pamela Morsi *r* 386

Call, Woodrow (Lawman)
Comanche Moon - Larry McMurtry *w* 572

Callahan, Juanita "Nita" (Teenager; Wizard)
A Wizard Abroad - Diane Duane *f* 693

Callahan, King (Outlaw)
Railroad Schemes - Cecilia Holland *w* 539

Callahan, Rose (Religious)
Death of a Winter Shaker - Deborah
   Woodworth *m* 243

Callen, Kevin (Fugitive; Wizard)
Come Before Christ and Murder Love - Stewart
   Home *f* 725

Calling Crow (Indian; Chieftain)
Flight of the Crow - Paul Clayton *w* 482

Calloway, John (Rancher)
Houston - Doug Bowman *w* 468

Calvert, Joshua (Businessman; Spaceman)
Emergence - Peter F. Hamilton *s* 1120

Calvert, Joshua (Spaceman)
Expansion - Peter F. Hamilton *s* 1121

Camel, Teddy (Police Officer)
Cul-De-Sac - David Martin *h* 958

Cameron, Alexander (Imposter; Spy)
The Pride of Lions - Marsha Canham *r* 276

Cameron, Alexei (Nobleman; Artisan)
Key to Forever - Christina Skye *r* 425

Cameron, Andrew "Drew" (Nobleman; Cowboy)
The Scotsman Wore Spurs - Patricia Potter *r* 399

Cameron, Samantha (Teacher; Captive)
The Tin-Pan Man - P.A. Bechko *w* 456

Campbell, Amanda (Teacher; Suffragette)
With Love, Amanda - Shelly Ritthaler *r* 413

Campbell, Robert (Nobleman)
Everything and the Moon - Julia Quinn *r* 404

Campbell, Trey (Health Care Professional)
Bad Karma - Andrew Harper *h* 909

Camron (Nobleman; Warrior)
The Barbed Coil - J.V. Jones *f* 730

Canches, Alejandro (Doctor; Wanderer)
The Plague Tales - Ann Benson *s* 1051

Candace (Spirit)
The Seventh Heart - Marina Fitch *f* 704

Cannot Be Told (Chieftain)
The Long Walk - Amanda Cockrell *w* 483

Capehart, Emma (Widow(er))
An Infamous Proposal - Joan Smith *r* 428

Capone, Alphonse (Political Figure; Historical
   Figure)
Back in the USSA - Kim Newman *s* 1166

Caraval, Estela (Divorced Person)
Spirits of the Ordinary - Kathleen Alcala *f* 638

Caraval, Julio (Parent; Philosopher)
Spirits of the Ordinary - Kathleen Alcala *f* 638

Caraval, Zacarias (Prospector)
Spirits of the Ordinary - Kathleen Alcala *f* 638

Cardigan, Jake (Detective—Private)
Tek Net - William Shatner *s* 1200

Carew, Cappy (Orphan)
Goodbye, Buffalo Sky - John Loveday *w* 562

Carey (Courier)
Changespell - Doranna Durgin *f* 695

Carey, Robert (Nobleman; Historical Figure)
A Surfeit of Guns - P.F. Chisholm *m* 36

Carl (Actor)
The Arbitrary Placement of Walls - Martha
   Soukup *f* 797

Carl, Victor (Lawyer)
Veritas - William Lashner *m* 144

Carlisle, Desdemona (Orphan; Archaeologist)
As You Desire - Connie Brockway *r* 268

Carlson, Winnie (Technician; Spy)
Putting Up Roots - Charles Sheffield *s* 1203

Carlucci, Caroline (Detective—Amateur)
Carlucci's Heart - Richard Paul Russo *s* 1188

Carlucci, Francesco "Frank" (Detective—Police)
Carlucci's Heart - Richard Paul Russo *s* 1188

Carlyle, Carlotta (Detective—Private; Taxi Driver)
Cold Case - Linda Barnes *m* 8

Carmilla (Vampire)
The Darker Passions: Carmilla - Amarantha
   Knight *h* 933

Caroline (Friend)
Jed the Dead - Alan Dean Foster *s* 1102

Carpenter, Joe (Journalist)
Sole Survivor - Dean R. Koontz *h* 935

Carrie (Psychic)
Razor's Edge - Lisanne Norman *s* 1169

Carrington, Jade (Servant)
Jade - Betty Brooks *r* 269

Carson, Amelia (Mail Order Bride)
Texas Destiny - Lorraine Heath *r* 322

Carson, Kit (Mountain Man; Scout)
Meridian: A Novel of Kit Carson's West - Norman
   Zollinger *w* 636

Carter, Bushrod (Military Personnel)
The Black Flower - Howard Bahr *w* 444

Carter, John (Criminal)
Return of the Living Dead - John A. Russo *h* 988

Carthage, Lorenzo (Mine Owner)
Second Lives - Richard S. Wheeler *w* 630

Casey (Royalty)
With Full Honors - Donald E. McQuinn *s* 1156

Casey, Charles (Journalist)
Twice upon a Time - Emilie Richards *r* 409

Casey, Ed (Rancher)
Stay Away From That City...They Call It Cheyenne -
   Stephen Bly *w* 463

Casey, Fred (Police Officer)
Deadly Season - Tim Champlin *w* 480

Cassidy, Lily (Teenager; Spouse)
Texas Lily - Elizabeth Fackler *w* 517

Catcher, Selene (Scholar; Religious)
Renaissance Moon - Linda Nevins *f* 770

Catherine (Adventurer)
The Book of D'ni - Rand Miller *f* 763

Catlin, George (Artist)
A Portrait of Spotted Deer's Grandfather - Amy
   Littlesugar *w* 561

Cavish, Beka (Warrior; Teenager)
Stalking Darkness - Lynn Flewelling *f* 705

Cayne, Candy (Teenager; Fanatic)
Cold Iron - Melisa Michaels *f* 762

Celucci, Mike (Detective—Police)
Blood Debt - Tanya Huff *h* 919

Centaur, Cathryn (Mythical Creature; Guide)
Faun & Games - Piers Anthony *f* 642

Cerdic (Royalty; Warrior)
Shadow of the King - Helen Hollick *f* 724

Cerise (Adventurer)
Cardmaster - Clayton Emery *f* 700

Cha'dune, Hezhi Yehd (Royalty; Fugitive)
The Blackgod - J. Gregory Keyes *f* 737

Chakliux (Storyteller; Handicapped)
Song of the River - Sue Harrison *f* 717

Chalfont, Adrian (Nobleman)
My Wayward Lady - Evelyn Richardson *r* 411

Chalkin (Leader)
Dragonseye - Anne McCaffrey *s* 1153

Chalmers, Persia (Young Woman)
The Diary of Mattie Spenser - Sandra
   Dallas *w* 505

Chamberlain, Lucas (Lawman)
Pure Justice - Suzann Ledbetter *w* 559

Chambers, Christel (Relative)
The Misconceiver - Lucy Ferriss *s* 1095

Chambers, Phoebe (Criminal; Computer Expert)
The Misconceiver - Lucy Ferriss *s* 1095

Chance, Angela (Time Traveller; Student—
   Graduate)
Time Station Berlin - David Evans *s* 1092

Chandler, Zinc (Detective)
Evil Eye - Michael Slade *h* 996

Chandless, Jeff (Rancher)
Wild Water - Jeanne Williams *w* 633

Chapelo, Zant (Gunfighter)
Jacey's Reckless Heart - Cheryl Anne Porter *r* 398

Chapman, Merrick (Detective—Police)
Daughter of Darkness - Steven Spruill *h* 1004

Chapman, Zane (Vampire)
Daughter of Darkness - Steven Spruill *h* 1004

Charbonneau, Toussaint (Guide)
Sacagawea - Judith St. George *w* 608

Chastain, Adrienne (Captive)
The Kiowa Verdict - Cynthia Haseloff *w* 531

Chastain, Nick (Psychic; Businessman)
Zinnia - Jayne Castle *r* 277

Chauvin, Rene (Businessman)
The Gris-Gris Man - Don Davis *h* 867

Checker, John (Lawman; Rancher)
Dark Trail to Dodge - Cotton Smith *w* 605

Cheever, Shelby V (Teenager; Heir)
The Billion Dollar Boy - Charles Sheffield *s* 1201

Chen, Harry (Deity; Addict)
The Seraphim Rising - Elisabeth De Vos *s* 1076

Chestnut, Clutie Mae (Runaway; Teenager)
Leaving Missouri - Ellen Recknor *w* 592

Chet (Supernatural Being)
Thirsty - M.T. Anderson *h* 833

Chiara (Professor; Fugitive)
The Thirteenth Daughter of the Moon - Steven
   Nightingale *f* 771

Chicago, Pasquale (Businessman)
A King of Infinite Space - Allen Steele *s* 1212

Childe, Francesca (Noblewoman)
Francesca's Rake - Lynn Kerstan *r* 345

Chin, Lydia (Detective—Private)
No Colder Place - S.J. Rozan *m* 206

Chinnery, Thomas (Apothecary)
Bijapur - Kara Dalkey *f* 680

Chip (Artificial Intelligence; Companion)
A King of Infinite Space - Allen Steele s 1212

Chisolm, Casey (Religious)
Symphony - Charles L. Grant h 899

Chloe (Teenager)
Camp Vamp - Elvira h 879

Choate, Courtney (Nobleman; Bachelor)
Snowdrops and Scandalbroth - Barbara
  Metzger r 378

Choy, Mary (Police Officer)
/ - Greg Bear s 1049

Chris (Teenager; Vampire)
Thirsty - M.T. Anderson h 833

Christman, Barbara (Investigator)
Sole Survivor - Dean R. Koontz h 935

Christopher of Blackmour (Warrior; Handicapped)
This Is All I Ask - Lynn Kurland r 357

Church, Thomas (Religious)
The Gaia Websters - Kim Antieau s 1037

Churchill, Winston (Historical Figure)
Murder, Mrs. Hudson - Sydney Hosier m 126

Cimabue, Damastes a (Military Personnel; Prisoner)
The Seer King - Chris Bunch f 661

Cinque (Slave)
Amistad - Alexs Pate w 584

Cissie (Young woman)
'48 - James Herbert h 914

Clah, Ella (FBI Agent; Indian)
Bad Medicine - Aimee Thurlo m 226

Claire (Military Personnel; Governess)
The Night Watch - Sean Stewart f 801

Claire of Summersedge (Noblewoman)
Lord of Danger - Anne Stuart r 431

Clara (Slave)
Remember the Morning - Thomas Fleming w 518

Clark, William (Frontiersman; Explorer)
How We Crossed the West - Rosalyn
  Schanzer w 602

Class, Julian (Military Personnel; Scientist)
Forever Peace - Joe Haldeman s 1119

Clayborne, Adam (Scholar; Slave)
One Red Rose - Julie Garwood r 313

Clayborne, Douglas (Rancher)
One White Rose - Julie Garwood r 314

Clayborne, Travis (Hunter)
One Pink Rose - Julie Garwood r 312

Cleave, Peter (Doctor)
Asylum - Patrick McGrath h 962

Clemens, Sam (Journalist; Historical Figure)
How Few Remain - Harry Turtledove s 1223

Cleon, I (Ruler)
Foundation's Fear - Gregory Benford s 1050

Clio of Camrose (Noblewoman; Saloon Keeper/
  Owner)
Wonderful - Jill Barnett r 255

Clisser (Musician; Professor)
Dragonseye - Anne McCaffrey s 1153

Clough, Emma (Bartender)
Famine - Todd Komarnicki h 934

Coachman, Dosh (Prostitute)
Future Indefinite - Dave Duncan f 694

Coakley, Dana (Actress; Maintenance Worker)
All Emergencies, Ring Super - Ellen Emerson
  White m 235

Cobain, Maddie (Friend)
Three Brides, No Groom - Debbie Macomber r 371

Cobham, James (Writer; Wealthy)
Freedom & Necessity - Steven Brust f 660

Cobham, Richard (Writer; Wealthy)
Freedom & Necessity - Steven Brust f 660

Cochise (Indian; Chieftain)
Devil Dance - Frank Burleson w 477

Cochran, Sid (Vintner)
Earthquake Weather - Tim Powers f 778

Cochrane, Miles "David Gilman" (Scientist;
  Mentally Ill Person)
Alpha Centauri - William Barton s 1045

Cochrane, William (Government Official)
Rage of Spirits - Noel Hynd h 921

Cody, William (Scout; Historical Figure)
Devil's Engine - Mark Sumner f 803

Cofort, Rael (Spacewoman; Trader)
Derelict for Trade - Andre Norton s 1170

Cohen, Ghenghiz "Cohen the Barbarian" (Hero;
  Aged Person)
Interesting Times - Terry Pratchett f 779

Cohen, Julius (Scientist; Colonist)
Mother of Demons - Eric Flint s 1096

Colburne, Falcarrah "Falcon" (Gentlewoman;
  Heiress)
The Lady From Spain - Gail Eastwood r 299

Colby, Jake (Cowboy; Rancher)
Range Wars - Robert Vaughan w 625

Cole, Elvis (Detective—Private)
Indigo Slam - Robert Crais m 46

Cole, Marcus (Military Personnel)
To Dream in the City of Sorrows - Kathryn M.
  Drennan s 1084

Colin of Ravenshaw (Knight)
Touch of Enchantment - Teresa Medeiros r 377

Coll, Lorand (Wizard; Farmer)
Competition - Sharon Green f 712

Colloway, Stephen (Writer)
Shackled - Ray Garton h 889

Colt, Charlotte "Charley" (Avenger; Widow(er))
Matched Colts - Don Bendell w 457

Colt, Chris (Gunfighter; Scout)
Matched Colts - Don Bendell w 457

Colter, Raleigh (Guide)
This Man Colter - Johnny D. Boggs w 465

Connery, Rachel (Young Woman)
Ritual Sins - Anne Stuart r 432

Connolly, Fitzwilliam (Spirit)
Maiden Voyage - Judith O'Brien r 389

Connolly, Michael (Military Personnel)
Los Alamos - Joseph Kanon m 137

Constantine (Political Figure; Revolutionary)
City on Fire - Walter Jon Williams s 1235

Constantine, Miquel Kaliq (Vampire)
Ragged Angels - Della Van Hise h 1017

Cook, Jay (Archaeologist)
Time Blender - Michael Dorn s 1081

Cookie (Cowboy)
The Thirteenth Daughter of the Moon - Steven
  Nightingale f 771

Coombs, Alice (Scientist)
As She Climbed Across the Table - Jonathan
  Lethem s 1142

Cooper, Alexandra (Lawyer)
Likely To Die - Linda Fairstein m 81

Cooper, Harry (Businessman)
Night of the Living Dead - John A. Russo h 987

Cordell, Ashton (Nobleman; Recluse)
Raven's Bride - Lynn Kerstan r 346

Corio, Giovanna (Religious)
Renaissance Moon - Linda Nevins f 770

Cormack, Leonard (Government Official; Pilot)
Faraday's Orphans - N. Lee Wood s 1242

Cornelius, Vito (Religious)
The Fifth Element - Terry Bisson s 1053

Correa, Marissa (Researcher; Student)
Lightpaths - Howard V. Hendrix s 1131

Corso, Lucas (Detective—Amateur)
The Club Dumas - Arturo Perez-Reverte m 183

Cort (Military Personnel)
A Wizard in Chaos - Christopher Stasheff s 1210

Cortez, Hernan (Military Personnel)
Aztec Autumn - Gary Jennings w 544

Cortez, Rafaela (Housekeeper)
Tropic of Orange - Karen Tei Yamashita f 823

Cortland, Erin (Businesswoman)
Incognito - Francis Ray r 405

Cortland, Roger (Scientist; Researcher)
Lightpaths - Howard V. Hendrix s 1131

Cotto, Vir (Alien; Political Figure)
Personal Agendas - Al Sarrantonio s 1191

Coulton, Roger (Scientist)
Einstein's Bridge - John Cramer s 1070

Courtnay, Catherine (Spy; Writer)
Dangerous to Hold - Elizabeth Thornton r 433

Covington, Grace "Candi" (Social Worker)
Mama Stalks the Past - Nora DeLoach m 59

Covington, Simone (Lawyer)
Mama Stalks the Past - Nora DeLoach m 59

Coyote (Animal; Spirit)
Coyote and the Fire Stick - Barbara Diamond
  Goldin w 524

Crane, Abner (Farmer)
The Hunted - James Reasoner w 591

Crane, Peter (Businessman; Political Figure)
Hunting the Corrigan's Blood - Holly Lisle s 1145

Crane, Scott (Religious; Spirit)
Earthquake Weather - Tim Powers f 778

Craven, Nick (Detective)
Evil Eye - Michael Slade h 996

Cray, Jack (Military Personnel)
Five Past Midnight - James Thayer m 225

Creaghan, Michael (Military Personnel)
Hellboy: The Lost Army - Christopher
  Golden h 897

Creedath (Merchant; Psychic)
The Gates of Vensunor - Carol Heller f 720

Cricket (Indian; Sidekick)
Dust Devils - Robert Laxalt w 556

Croaker (Military Personnel; Doctor)
She Is the Darkness - Glen Cook f 676

Croaker, Fey (Police Officer)
Tequila Mockingbird - Paul Bishop m 19

Crockett, Davy (Frontiersman)
Blood Hunt - David Thompson w 611
Homecoming - David Thompson w 612
Mississippi Mayhem - David Thompson w 613
Sioux Slaughter - David Thompson w 614

Croft, Jessamyn (Actress)
The Ruby Tear - Rebecca Brand h 843

Cross (Police Officer)
The Psalm Killer - Chris Petit m 187

DeMarian, Demnor (Royalty; Teenager)
The Stone Prince - Fiona Patton *f* 776

DeMarian, Melesandra III (Royalty; Political Figure)
The Stone Prince - Fiona Patton *f* 776

Demarkian, Gregor (Detective—Private)
Deadly Beloved - Jane Haddam *m* 105

Demon (Demon)
Running with the Demon - Terry Brooks *f* 659

Denby, Kate (Doctor; Researcher)
Long After Midnight - Iris Johansen *r* 335

Derigha, Yarrun (Space Explorer; Military Personnel)
Expendable - James Alan Gardner *s* 1108

Detective, Nameless (Detective—Private)
Illusions - Bill Pronzini *m* 189

Devane, Kate (Journalist; Divorced Person)
Caught - Rachel Lee *r* 363

DeVere, Lilac (Debutante; Gentlewoman)
Rejar - Dara Joy *r* 341

Devereaux, Jason (Rake; Nobleman)
The Irish Rake - Emma Lange *r* 361

Devlin, Johnny (Rogue; Alcoholic)
Trader - Charles de Lint *f* 685

DeWitt, Katherine "Kate" Ariella (Prisoner)
Fortress on the Sun - Paul Cook *s* 1068

Dexter, Quinn (Religious)
Emergence - Peter F. Hamilton *s* 1120

di Sarc, Sira (Amnesiac; Alien)
A Thousand Words for Stranger - Julie E. Czerneda *s* 1072

Didier, Auguste (Cook)
Murder in the Smokehouse - Amy Myers *m* 174

Dietrich, Otto (Police Officer)
Five Past Midnight - James Thayer *m* 225

Dietz, Tre (Artist; Inventor)
Freeware - Rudy Rucker *s* 1184

di'Marano, Diora (Noblewoman; Widow(er))
The Broken Crown - Michelle West *f* 815

Dipper (Servant)
The Devil in Music - Kate Ross *m* 204

Distephano, Vincent (Military Personnel)
Alien Resurrection - A.C. Crispin *s* 1071

Djinn (Mythical Creature)
The Djinn in the Nightingale's Eye - A.S. Byatt *f* 662

D'Noch (Guide)
The Book of Water - Marjorie Bradley Kellogg *f* 732

Dobbs, Evelyn (Spacewoman; Psychologist)
Fool's War - Sarah Zettel *s* 1245

Dobbs, Jason (Military Personnel)
Battle Cry - Ken Englade *w* 516

Dr. Doom (Leader)
Between Floors - Thomas F. Monteleone *h* 967

Dodge, Harold (Civil Servant)
Bird Dog - Philip Reed *m* 195

Dog Brother (Supernatural Being)
Tooth and Claw - Graham Masterton *h* 960

Dogbrick (Thief; Philosopher)
The Dark Shore - Adam Lee *f* 746

Donahoe, Neal (Police Officer)
Fade to Black - Tony Gibbs *m* 96

Donaltsson, Marta (Magician; Midwife)
Kindred Rites - Katharine Eliska Kimbriel *f* 738

Donato, Rinio (Trader)
Vaporetto 13 - Robert Girardi *h* 896

Donner, Joshua (Mountain Man)
White Horse, Red Rider - Barry Brierley *w* 473

Donnerjack, John D'Arcy (Computer Expert)
Donnerjack - Roger Zelazny *s* 1244

Donovan, Honor (Businesswoman)
Amber Beach - Elizabeth Lowell *r* 367

Door (Gentlewoman; Fugitive)
Neverwhere - Neil Gaiman *f* 707

Dorman, Jeremy (Scientist)
Antibodies - Kevin J. Anderson *h* 832

Dorochenko, Viktor (Mercenary)
Cossack Three Ponies - J.L. Reasoner *w* 589

Doubletree, Nate (Military Personnel)
Beyond the River - Wynema McGowan *w* 570

Doubletree, Tom (Lawman)
While the Rivers Run - Wynema McGowan *w* 571

Douglas, Morric (Musician)
Blackmantle: A Triumph - Patricia Kennealy-Morrison *f* 733

Douglass, Frederick (Journalist; Historical Figure)
How Few Remain - Harry Turtledove *s* 1223

Dovero, Colinda (Adventurer)
Fabulous Harbors - Michael Moorcock *f* 767

Dowling, Samuel "White Fire" (Indian)
White Fire - Cassie Edwards *r* 300

Downes, Edgar (Lawyer)
A Christmas Bride - Mary Balogh *r* 251

Dracula (Vampire; Nobleman)
The Mammoth Book of Dracula - Stephen Jones *h* 927

Dragging Canoe (Indian; Renegade)
The Long Hunters - Dodge Tyler *w* 620

Drake, Cadence "Cady" (Spaceship Captain)
Hunting the Corrigan's Blood - Holly Lisle *s* 1145

Drakin, Seth (Mercenary)
Long After Midnight - Iris Johansen *r* 335

Drev (Ruler; Wizard)
The Dark Shore - Adam Lee *f* 746

Driskill, Frank (Rancher)
High Prairie - Hiram King *w* 553

Drumheller, Thorn (Companion; Wizard)
Shadow Dawn - Chris Claremont *f* 670

Drysdale, Lucy (Scholar; Chaperone)
Dangerous to Love - Rexanne Becnel *r* 258

du Cheyne, Gaetan (Spaceship Captain)
Acts of Conscience - William Barton *s* 1044

Du Pre, Gabriel (Inspector; Widow(er))
Notches - Peter Bowen *m* 24

DuBois, Cora (Settler; Mountain Woman)
Winter Woman - F.M. Parker *w* 582

Dubonnet, Tubby (Lawyer)
Trick Question - Tony Dunbar *m* 68

Ducas, Leo (Military Personnel)
Cross and Crescent - Susan Shwartz *f* 795

Dufrenoy, Michael (Writer; Orphan)
Paris in the Twentieth Century - Jules Verne *f* 1227

Dulaine, Dirk (Sidekick; Military Personnel)
A Wizard in Chaos - Christopher Stasheff *s* 1210

Dulaine, Dirk (Sidekick; Adventurer)
A Wizard in Peace - Christopher Stasheff *s* 1211

Dulcie (Animal)
Cats Raise the Dead - Shirley Rousseau Murphy *f* 769

Dumont, Claire (Time Traveller; Military Personnel)
Memories of You - Jane Goodgear *r* 317

Dun, Richard (Consultant; Vampire)
Keeper of the King - Nigel Bennett *h* 838

Duncan, George Thomas (Leader; Revolutionary)
Ecstasy Club - Douglas Rushkoff *s* 1187

Duncan, Sabrina (Spinster)
The Lover - Nicole Jordan *r* 340

dunMheric, Deymorin Rhomandi (Royalty)
Ring of Intrigue - Jane S. Fancher *f* 701

dunMheric, Mikhyel Rhomandi (Royalty; Handicapped)
Ring of Intrigue - Jane S. Fancher *f* 701

Duone, Kestrienne (Noblewoman; Wizard)
Emerald House Rising - Peg Kerr *f* 736

Duone, Morgan (Nobleman; Wizard)
Emerald House Rising - Peg Kerr *f* 736

Duran (Mythical Creature; Mercenary)
Headhunters - Mel Odom *s* 1172

Durant, Sebastian (Nobleman)
A Well-Pleasured Lady - Christina Dodd *r* 297

Duras, Andre (Military Personnel)
Taboo - Susan Johnson *r* 336

Durbin, Ashley (Journalist)
Hair of the Dog - Brett Davis *f* 683

Durmontov, Alexei (Royalty; Wizard)
Magician's Ward - Patricia C. Wrede *f* 819

Duzon (Nobleman; Warrior)
Touched by the Gods - Lawrence Watt-Evans *f* 810

Dvorak, Daniel (Doctor)
Life Support - Tess Gerritsen *h* 894

Dwayne (Teenager)
Fear Street: The Cat - R.L. Stine *h* 1008

Dworkin, Sam (Researcher; Aged Person)
Silent Zone - Stephen Molstad *s* 1159

Dyer, Mandy (Businesswoman)
Hung Up to Die - Dolores Johnson *m* 133

Dylan (Young Man)
Millennium: Gehenna - Lewis Gannett *h* 884

E

Ea (Linguist; Captive)
Black Wine - Candas Jane Dorsey *s* 1082

Eardley, Isabella (Debutante; Artist)
Isabella's Rake - June Calvin *r* 274

Earp, Wyatt (Lawman; Historical Figure)
Doc Holliday - Matt Braun *w* 470
The Fourth Horseman - Randy Lee Eickhoff *w* 514

Earth (Mythical Creature)
The Book of Water - Marjorie Bradley Kellogg *f* 732

Eckert, Angie (Noblewoman; Spouse)
The Dragon and the Gnarly King - Gordon R. Dickson *f* 688

Eckert, Jim (Nobleman; Magician)
The Dragon and the Gnarly King - Gordon R. Dickson *f* 688

Edain (Maiden; Witch)
Eyes of Love - Katherine Deauville *r* 294

Eddy, Pearl (Farmer; Widow(er))
All God's Children - Tom Eidson *w* 515

Edenderry, Rose (Prostitute)
Second Lives - Richard S. Wheeler *w* 630

Edgerton, Charlotte (Noblewoman; Ward)
Captive - Joan Johnston *r* 338

Fitzgerald, Kara (Publisher; Psychic)
Bride of the Mist - Christina Skye   r   424

Fitzgerald, Mike (Consultant; Architect)
Remember the Time - Annette A. Reynolds   r   406

fitzJulien, Magnus (Knight)
Eyes of Love - Katherine Deauville   r   294

Fitzroy, Henry (Writer; Vampire)
Blood Debt - Tanya Huff   h   919

Fitzwalter, Adrian (Nobleman; Rake)
The Dark Duke - Margaret Moore   r   385

Flanigan, Brianna (Rancher)
Warrior's Song - Janis Reams Hudson   r   331

Flattery, Erasmus (Apprentice; Adventurer)
Beneath the Vaulted Hills - Sean Russell   f   788

Flavius (Frontiersman; Sidekick)
Blood Hunt - David Thompson   w   611
Homecoming - David Thompson   w   612
Mississippi Mayhem - David Thompson   w   613
Sioux Slaughter - David Thompson   w   614

Fleetwood, Manley (Rancher)
Lonesome Land - B.M. Bower   w   467

Fletcher, Tristan (Rancher)
Winter Heart - Jane Bonander   r   265

Flint, Sam (Editor)
Flint's Gift - Richard S. Wheeler   w   628

Floyd, CJ (Bail Bondsman)
The Devil's Red Nickel - Robert Greer   m   101

Flynn, Judith McMonigle (Innkeeper)
September Mourn - Mary Daheim   m   50

Folger, Meredith (Police Officer)
Death in a Mood Indigo - Francine Mathews   m   157

Fontana, Mac (Fire Fighter)
The Dead Horse Paint Company - Earl Emerson   m   77

Ford (Scientist; Spy)
North of Havana - Randy Wayne White   m   236

Ford, Marcus (Doctor)
Omega - Patrick Lynch   h   953

Forester, David (Student)
Starfleet Academy - Diane Carey   s   1061

Forsythe, Catherine (Debutante; Fortune Hunter)
A Garden Folly - Candice Hern   r   325

Fortune, Celinde "Cissy" (Magician; Technician)
Dreaming Metal - Melissa Scott   s   1197

Foster, Sandra "Sandy" (Scientist; Researcher)
Bellwether - Connie Willis   s   1237

Fox, Jessica (Young Woman)
Innocence Undone - Kat Martin   r   372

Foxworth, Elizabeth (Social Worker)
Fragments - James F. David   h   866

Franklyn, Kit (Psychologist)
Sleeping with the Crawfish - D.J. Donaldson   m   65

Fraser, Duncan (Government Official)
The Scottish Rose - Jill Jones   r   339

Freeman, Alan (Scientist)
Extinct - Charles Wilson   h   1027

Freemark, Nest (Teenager)
Running with the Demon - Terry Brooks   f   659

Fremont, John Charles (Explorer; Military Personnel)
Meridian: A Novel of Kit Carson's West - Norman Zollinger   w   636

Freund, Solomon "Sol" (Psychic)
Children of the Dusk - Janet Berliner   f   652

Frevisse (Religious)
The Prioress' Tale - Margaret Frazer   m   86

Frewin, Mary (Child; Psychic)
The Red-Eared Ghosts - Vivian Alcock   f   639

Friar, Tuck (Foreman)
Stillwater Smith - Frank Roderus   w   600

Friedman, Kinky (Detective—Private)
Road Kill - Kinky Friedman   m   87

Friese, Adam "Iceberg" (Astronaut)
Ignition - Kevin J. Anderson   s   1033

Frost (Military Personnel)
Deathstalker War - Simon R. Green   s   1114

Frost, Melanie (Health Care Professional)
The Seventh Heart - Marina Fitch   f   704

Fuller, Gray (Doctor)
Angel Face and Amazing Grace - Lori Copeland   r   286

Fuller, Jack (Writer)
Cannibal Plateau - Joe Wise   w   634

Fuller, Samuel (Criminal)
Down on Ponce - Fred Willard   m   239

Furness, Carol (Friend)
Three Brides, No Groom - Debbie Macomber   r   371

Furness, Jack (Mountaineer)
Esau - Philip Kerr   m   139

G

Gable, Clark (Detective—Amateur; Historical Figure)
The Clark Gable and Carole Lombard Murder Case - George Baxt   m   11

Gable, Helen (Waiter/Waitress)
Symphony - Charles L. Grant   h   899

Gabrielle (Warrior; Storyteller)
The Thief of Hermes - Ru Emerson   f   699

Galeran of Heywood (Knight)
The Shattered Rose - Jo Beverley   r   260

Galingale, Cyrus "Cy" (Carpenter)
Waking Beauty - Paul Witcover   f   818

Gallow, Theresa (Civil Servant)
Blood Will Tell - Terris McMahan Grimes   m   103

Galloway, Elizabeth "Libby" Watson (Writer)
When Lilacs Bloom - Susan Kirby   r   350

Galloway, Ike (Farmer; Railroad Worker)
When Lilacs Bloom - Susan Kirby   r   350

Galloway, Isaac (Bachelor)
Prairie Rose - Susan Kirby   r   349

Gallowglass, Magnus "Gar Pike" (Psychic; Troubleshooter)
A Wizard in Chaos - Christopher Stasheff   s   1210

Gallowglass, Magnus "Gar Pike" (Psychic; Revolutionary)
A Wizard in Peace - Christopher Stasheff   s   1211

Galoran (Nobleman; Military Personnel)
Count Scar - C. Dale Brittain   f   658

Gandillon, Vivian (Teenager; Werewolf)
Blood and Chocolate - Annette Curtis Klause   h   932

Garner, Quinn (Journalist)
Shadow Walk - Jane Waterhouse   m   233

Garrett, Dobie (Outlaw; Lawman)
How the West Was Lost - Gene Shelton   w   603

Garrett, Edward (Nobleman; Military Personnel)
Secrets in Satin - Haywood Smith   r   427

Garrett, Lee (Lawman)
Black Gold - Frederic Bean   w   450

Garrity, Julia Callahan (Detective—Private; Businesswoman)
Strange Brew - Kathy Hogan Trocheck   m   229

Garuda (Mythical Creature; Adventurer)
The Iron Ring - Lloyd Alexander   f   640

Gaspar, James (Time Traveller)
Days of Cain - J.R. Dunn   s   1086

Gastner, William K. (Police Officer)
Privileged to Kill - Steven F. Havill   m   115

Gault, Jesse (Gunfighter)
Outlaw in Paradise - Patricia Gaffney   r   309

Gavin (Royalty)
Magelord: The Awakening - Thomas K. Martin   f   755

Gavrilli, David (Heir; Runaway)
Interface Masque - Shariann Lewitt   s   1143

Gawain (Knight)
Gawain and Lady Green - Anne Eliot Crompton   f   679

Gawen (Ruler; Religious)
Lady of Avalon - Marion Zimmer Bradley   f   656

Gay, Susan (Police Officer)
Blood at the Root - Peter Robinson   m   203

Gemcutter, Jena (Apprentice; Wizard)
Emerald House Rising - Peg Kerr   f   736

Genar-Hofoen, Byr (Diplomat)
Excession - Iain M. Banks   s   1041

Gennaro, Angela (Detective—Private)
Sacred - Dennis Lehane   m   147

Gennesko, Karl (Police Officer)
Black Diamond - Susan Holtzer   m   124

George (Artisan)
Thessalonica - Harry Turtledove   f   805

Gerchak, Julie (Child; Student)
My Ishmael - Daniel Quinn   s   1180

Germain (Criminal)
A Game of Universe - Eric S. Nylund   f   774

Geronimo (Indian; Warrior)
Night of the Cougar - Frank Burleson   w   478

Gerritsen, Aurore (Parent)
Rising Tides - Emilie Richards   r   408

Gerritsen, Dawn (Photographer)
Rising Tides - Emilie Richards   r   408

Gersen, Kirth (Journalist; Avenger)
The Demon Princes: Volume One - Jack Vance   s   1225

Gersen, Kirth (Avenger; Banker)
The Demon Princes: Volume Two - Jack Vance   s   1226

Gershon, Ralph (Astronaut)
Voyager - Stephen Baxter   s   1048

Ghidorah (Monster)
Godzilla 2000 - Marc Cerasini   s   1063

Giant (Alien; Child)
The Earth Giant - Melvin Burgess   s   1058

Gift, Sebastian "Nifty" (Spaceman; Military Personnel)
Berserker Fury - Fred Saberhagen   s   1189

Giles (Librarian)
Buffy the Vampire Slayer: The Harvest - Richie Tankersley Cusick   h   863

Gilgamesh (Deity; Immortal)
How Like a God - Brenda W. Clough   f   672

Gillian of Warewick (Noblewoman; Abuse Victim)
This Is All I Ask - Lynn Kurland   r   357

Gioglie, Declan "Gill" III (Spaceman; Miner)
Acorna - Anne McCaffrey   s   1152

Giovanni, Madeleine (Vampire)
The Road to Hell, Volume II - Robert
Weinberg *h* 1025

Gistere, Rurak (Knight)
The Day of the Tempest - Jean Rabe *f* 782

G'Kar (Alien; Prisoner)
Personal Agendas - Al Sarrantonio *s* 1191

Glendower, Toby (Archaeologist)
The Midas Murders - Margot Arnold *m* 6

Glibspet (Demon; Detective—Private)
Hell on High - Holly Lisle *f* 751

Godzilla (Monster)
Godzilla 2000 - Marc Cerasini *s* 1063

Gold-eye (Child; Psychic)
Shade's Children - Garth Nix *s* 1168

Goldin, Netta (Administrator)
Alien Influences - Kristine Kathryn Rusch *s* 1186

Gomez, Sid (Detective—Private)
Tek Net - William Shatner *s* 1200

Gomez, Simon (Landowner)
Hacienda - Albert R. Booky *w* 466

Gonzolos, Chapa (Outlaw)
The Killing Season - Ralph Compton *w* 494

Goodwin, Willie (Convict; Outlaw)
I Rode with Jesse James - Charles
Hackenberry *w* 527

Goosequill (Servant; Guide)
Milton in America - Peter Ackroyd *f* 637

Gordianus the Finder (Detective—Private)
The House of the Vestals - Steven Saylor *m* 209

Gourmet Detective (Investigator)
Spiced to Death - Peter King *m* 142

Graham, Charlotte (Actress)
Murder under the Palms - Stefanie
Matteson *m* 158

Grandby, Quentin (Director)
Heaven Loves a Hero - Nikki Holiday *r* 326

Grandville, Annabelle (Noblewoman; Widow(er))
The Guardian - Joan Wolf *r* 440

Grandville, Stephen (Nobleman; Guardian)
The Guardian - Joan Wolf *r* 440

Grange, Karen (Banker)
A Dry Spell - Susan Moloney *h* 965

Granger, Cole (Cowboy; Rancher)
High Prairie - Hiram King *w* 553

Granger, Cole (Bodyguard; Gunfighter)
Triumph of the Mountain Man - William W.
Johnstone *w* 547

Granny Weatherwax (Witch)
Maskerade - Terry Pratchett *f* 780

Grant, Isabel (Rancher)
One White Rose - Julie Garwood *r* 314

Gray, Virginia "Jenna" (Settler; Teacher)
Sweetwater - Dorothy Garlock *r* 311

Gray Wolf (Indian; Chieftain)
The Black Jacks - Jason Manning *w* 565

Green (Sorceress)
Gawain and Lady Green - Anne Eliot
Crompton *f* 679

Green, Annabelle (Prostitute; Teenager)
Hell's Half Acre - Frederic Bean *w* 452

Green, Margo (Anthropologist)
Reliquary - Douglas Preston *h* 979

Green, Sandra (Scientist; Spacewoman)
Saturn Rukh - Robert L. Forward *s* 1100

Greene, Cathy (Farmer)
The Taking - Donald Beman *h* 837

Greenstreet, Horace (Detective—Private)
Eye of the Agency - Richard Moquist *m* 170

Greenstreet, Sadie (Journalist)
Eye of the Agency - Richard Moquist *m* 170

Gregory, Alan (Psychologist)
Remote Control - Stephen White *m* 238

Greta (Explorer)
I Who Have Never Known Men - Jacqueline
Harpman *s* 1124

Grey, Joe (Animal)
Cats Raise the Dead - Shirley Rousseau
Murphy *f* 769

Grey, Lavinia (Religious)
Hasty Retreat - Kate Gallison *m* 90

Grey Mouser (Thief; Wizard)
Return to Lankhmar - Fritz Leiber *f* 748

Grier, Abigail (Rancher)
Heaven in West Texas - Susan Kay Law *r* 362

Griffin (Coach)
Fear Street: The Cat - R.L. Stine *h* 1008

Griffin, Beth (Health Care Professional)
Nazareth Hill - Ramsey Campbell *h* 851

Griffin, George (Scientist)
Einstein's Bridge - John Cramer *s* 1070

Griffin, Nic (Actor; Writer)
The Ruby Tear - Rebecca Brand *h* 843

Grove, Carson (Mountain Man; Sidekick)
Deadwood - Douglas Hirt *w* 535

Growler, Donald (Murderer)
Cul-De-Sac - David Martin *h* 958

Guardia, Lazaro (Political Figure)
The Grand Ones of San Ildefonso - Lauran
Paine *w* 580

Guiwenneth (Warrior)
Gate of Ivory, Gate of Horn - Robert
Holdstock *f* 723

Gunn, Marsali (Noblewoman)
Starcatcher - Patricia Potter *r* 400

Gunther, Joe (Police Officer)
Bellows Falls - Archer Mayor *m* 160

Guthrie, Anson (Cyborg)
The Fleet of Stars - Poul Anderson *s* 1034

Guthrie, Patterson Erskine (Secretary)
Against the Brotherhood - Quinn Fawcett *m* 82

Guthrie, Port (Laborer)
The Winchester Run - Ralph Compton *w* 496

Guzman, Henry (Detective—Private)
The Whipsaw Trail - Ray Hogan *w* 538

Gwalchavad (Knight; Nobleman)
Grail - Stephen R. Lawhead *f* 745

Gwenhwyfar (Royalty)
Pendragon's Banner - Helen Hollick *r* 327
Shadow of the King - Helen Hollick *f* 724

H

Haagen, Anneke (Computer Expert)
Black Diamond - Susan Holtzer *m* 124

Hadding (Ruler; Warrior)
War of the Gods - Poul Anderson *f* 641

Haden, Asa (Writer)
Separations - Oakley Hall *w* 528

Hafford, Jovvi (Wizard; Prostitute)
Competition - Sharon Green *f* 712

Hager, Ross Ed (Tourist)
Jed the Dead - Alan Dean Foster *s* 1102

Haggerwells, Barbara (Inventor; Time Traveller)
Bring the Jubilee - Ward Moore *s* 1162

Haines, Carolyn (Pilot)
Extinct - Charles Wilson *h* 1027

Hake, Denton (Construction Worker)
Out of Body - Thomas Baum *h* 836

Hake, Elliot (Insurance Investigator)
Out of Body - Thomas Baum *h* 836

Haley, Adam (Scientist)
Howl - Christine Tanasiuk *h* 1012

Halloran, Jack (Engineer)
Hell on High - Holly Lisle *f* 751

Halman (Artificial Intelligence)
3001: The Final Odyssey - Arthur C.
Clarke *s* 1067

Hamilton, Ethan (Computer Expert)
Terminal Logic - Jefferson Scott *s* 1196

Hamilton, Ira (Cowboy; Teenager)
Dust Devils - Robert Laxalt *w* 556

Hamilton, John D. (Rancher)
Dust Devils - Robert Laxalt *w* 556

Hamilton, Jordan (Child; Computer Expert)
Terminal Logic - Jefferson Scott *s* 1196

Hamilton, Richard (Mountain Man; Heir)
Coyote Summer - W. Michael Gear *w* 523

Hammer-Hand, Barnar (Adventurer)
The Mines of Behemoth - Michael Shea *f* 792

Handrar, Ser (Religious; Wizard)
Wizard of Bones - Robert N. Charrette *f* 665

Hanks, Arly (Police Officer)
The Maggody Militia - Joan Hess *m* 120

Hansen, Emily (Scientist)
Mother Nature - Sarah Andrews *m* 4

Haramis (Sorceress; Royalty)
Sky Trillium - Julian May *f* 756

Harcourt, Charles (Royalty; Handicapped)
Beast - Judith Ivory *r* 333

Hardgreip (Mythical Creature; Witch)
War of the Gods - Poul Anderson *f* 641

Hardin, John Wesley (Gunfighter; Murderer)
Pure Justice - Suzann Ledbetter *w* 559

Harding, Amelia "Blaze" (Scientist; Professor)
Forever Peace - Joe Haldeman *s* 1119

Harkta (Wizard)
The Conjurer Princess - Vivian Vande Velde *f* 807

Harlowe, Caroline (Activist)
The Firebrand - Laurel Collins *r* 285

Harpe, Micajah (Murderer; Historical Figure)
Passage to Natchez - Cameron Judd *w* 550

Harper, H. Albert (Lawyer)
Bumpo, Bill, and the Girls - Kent Conwell *w* 499

Harper, Marty (Teenager; Student—High School)
Fear Street: The Cat - R.L. Stine *h* 1008

Harper, Toby (Doctor)
Life Support - Tess Gerritsen *h* 894

Harpur, Colin (Police Officer)
Gospel - Bill James *m* 129

Harriman, Frank (Police Officer; Spouse)
Hocus - Jan Burke *m* 30

Harrington, Honor (Military Personnel;
Noblewoman)
In Enemy Hands - David Weber *s* 1231

Harris, Druce (Spouse)
Howl - Christine Tanasiuk   h   1012

Harris, Jenny (Spacewoman)
Expansion - Peter F. Hamilton   s   1121

Harris, Samantha (Scientist)
Howl - Christine Tanasiuk   h   1012

Harrowslough, Holly (Religious; Rebel)
Finder's Bane - Kate Novak   f   773

Hart, Frank (Gambler)
I, Pearl Hart - Jane Candia Coleman   w   489

Hart, Pearl (Outlaw; Abuse Victim)
I, Pearl Hart - Jane Candia Coleman   w   489

Hartman, Travis (Mountain Man)
Coyote Summer - W. Michael Gear   w   523

Hask (Alien)
Illegal Alien - Robert J. Sawyer   s   1194

Hassard, Dee (Con Artist; Murderer)
Dead Reckoning - Mike Blakely   w   461

Hastings, Philip (Nobleman)
To Marry a British Lord - Judith O'Brien   r   391

Hastings, Stanley (Detective—Private; Actor)
Scam - Parnell Hall   m   108

Hatcher, Agnes (Patient)
Bad Karma - Andrew Harper   h   909

Hathaway, Cassandra (Debutante)
Cupid's Mistake - Karen Harbaugh   r   321

Hatory, Anna (Journalist)
The Night Crew - John Sandford   m   208

Havers, Barbara (Police Officer)
Deception on His Mind - Elizabeth George   m   95

Hawk (Sidekick)
Small Vices - Robert B. Parker   m   182

Hawk-Hobby (Teenager)
Merlin - Jane Yolen   f   825

Hawken, Garrick (Heir)
Allamanda - Michael Williams   f   817

Hawkesmoor, Simon (Nobleman)
The Silver Rose - Jane Feather   r   304

Hawkins, Ben (Businessman; Cowboy)
The Wagon Wars - James A. Ritchie   w   595

Hawkins, Buck (Outlaw; Lawman)
How the West Was Lost - Gene Shelton   w   603

Hawkins, Ethorne (Worker)
Dogland - Will Shetterly   f   794

Hawthorn "D-base" (Artificial Intelligence)
Cinderblock - Janine Ellen Young   s   1243

Hay, Marsali (Young Woman)
Fairy Tale - Jillian Hunter   r   332

Hayes, Allison (Frontierswoman)
Diablo - David Robbins   w   596

Hayes, Donna (Travel Agent)
The Cellar - Richard Laymon   h   942

Hayes, Molly (Mother)
Love in a Small Town - Curtis Ann Matlock   r   374

Hayes, Roy (Criminal)
The Cellar - Richard Laymon   h   942

Hayes, Tommy Lee (Mechanic)
Love in a Small Town - Curtis Ann Matlock   r   374

Hays, Micah (Police Officer)
The Case of the Police Officer's Cock Ring and the Piano Player Who Had No Fingers - Edward Lee   h   944

Hazard, Catie Willman (Servant; Widow(er))
The Secrets of Catie Hazard - Miranda Jarrett   r   334

Hazelhof, Cornelia (Businesswoman; Genius)
Timeshare - Joshua Dann   s   1074

Hazelton, Jeremy (Nobleman; Military Personnel)
The Lady From Spain - Gail Eastwood   r   299

Heals Like the Willow (Indian)
Coyote Summer - W. Michael Gear   w   523

Heber, Kevin (Teenager; Technician)
Bug Park - James P. Hogan   s   1132

Heber, Vanessa (Step-Parent; Scientist)
Bug Park - James P. Hogan   s   1132

Heim, Walter (Agent)
Double Edge - Dennis Etchison   h   880

Helarion (Thief)
The Thief of Hermes - Ru Emerson   f   699

Hellboy (Supernatural Being)
Hellboy: The Lost Army - Christopher Golden   h   897

Helwig, Barbie (Child)
Blue Limbo - Terrence M. Green   s   1116

Helwig, Mitch (Police Officer)
Blue Limbo - Terrence M. Green   s   1116

Henderson, Bass (Trader)
Mountain Captive - John Legg   w   560

Henderson, Notch (Outlaw)
Battle Cry - Ken Englade   w   516

Hennison, Doc (Con Artist)
The Wolf's Cub - Richard Parry   w   583

Henriques, Tomas (Religious)
The Grand Ones of San Ildefonso - Lauran Paine   w   580

Henry, Dora (Police Officer)
The Family Tree - Sheri S. Tepper   s   1220

Henry, Ned (Historian; Time Traveller)
To Say Nothing of the Dog - Connie Willis   s   1239

Henry, Trey (Outlaw)
While the Rivers Run - Wynema McGowan   w   571

Henson, Rance (Lawman)
Lockhart's Nightmare - Wayne Barton   w   449

Herb (Animal)
The Arbitrary Placement of Walls - Martha Soukup   f   797

Herb-Woman (Healer; Parent)
Strange Deliverance - Mary Brown   s   1057

Herbert, Grisel (Young Woman)
The Return - Walter de la Mare   h   868

Hercules (Hero)
Atlantis Found - R. Garcia y Robertson   s   1107
The First Casualty - David L. Seidman   f   791

Hereford, Anna (Nurse)
The Black Flower - Howard Bahr   w   444

Herrick, Kate (Widow(er))
Rose Cottage - Mary Stewart   m   219

Hethercott, Regina (Noblewoman)
The Colonel's Lady - Patricia Oliver   r   392

Hewlitt (Patient)
Final Diagnosis - James White   s   1233

Hickok, Bill (Gunfighter; Lawman)
The Gamblers - Matt Braun   w   471

High Fox (Indian; Crime Suspect)
People of the Mist - Kathleen O'Neal Gear   w   522

Hill, Judy (Detective—Police)
Verdict Unsafe - Jill McGown   m   164

Hilliard, Danika (Teacher; Writer)
Carried Away - Sue Civil-Brown   r   281

Hilliard, Terrence (Telepath)
The Shadow Within - Jeanne Cavelos   s   1062

Hisvet (Mythical Creature)
Return to Lankhmar - Fritz Leiber   f   748

Hoare, Dido (Businesswoman)
Death's Autograph - Marianne Macdonald   m   150

Hodge, J. Benison (Vampire)
The Devil's Advocate - Gherbod Fleming   h   882

Hodierna (Religious; Adventurer)
The Notorious Abbess - Vera Chapman   f   664

Hoffman, Nick (Professor; Homosexual)
The Edith Wharton Murders - Lev Raphael   m   194

Hogan, Stan (Drifter)
Symphony - Charles L. Grant   h   899

Hoke (Pilot)
'48 - James Herbert   h   914

Holcroft, Jake (Child; Computer Expert)
Target Earth - Steve Perry   s   1175

Holiday, Raymond (Television Personality)
Mister Christmas - Linda Cajio   r   273

Holland, Billy Bob (Lawyer)
Cimarron Rose - James Lee Burke   m   29

Holland, R. Paul (Scientist)
Infinity's Child - Harry Stein   h   1005

Holley, Charles Hardin (Musician; Revolutionary)
Back in the USSA - Kim Newman   s   1166

Holliday, Doc (Gunfighter; Gambler)
Doc Holliday - Matt Braun   w   470
The Fourth Horseman - Randy Lee Eickhoff   w   514

Hollis, Adam (Reporter)
Algonquin Massacre - Dodge Tyler   w   617
Apache Revenge - Dodge Tyler   w   618
Death at Spanish Wells - Dodge Tyler   w   619
A River Run Red - Dodge Tyler   w   621

Hollister, Jake (Businessman)
The Paradise Man - Suzanne Simmons   r   421

Holloway, Percival (Veteran; Rancher)
Silverthorne - Wayne Davis   w   507

Holly (Mythical Creature)
Mister Christmas - Linda Cajio   r   273

Holmes, Harry (Detective—Police)
Root of All Evil - David A. Farrow   h   881

Holmes, Mycroft (Gentleman; Investigator)
Against the Brotherhood - Quinn Fawcett   m   82

Holmes, Sherlock (Detective—Private)
Deadly Season - Tim Champlin   w   480
A Letter of Mary - Laurie R. King   m   141

Honey Eater (Indian; Spouse)
Bloody Bones Canyon - Judd Cole   w   486
Renegade Siege - Judd Cole   w   487
River of Death - Judd Cole   w   488

Hong (Nobleman; Villain)
Interesting Times - Terry Pratchett   f   779

Hood, John Bell (Military Personnel)
The Black Flower - Howard Bahr   w   444
Nashville 1864 - Madison Jones   w   549

Hood, Virgil (Detective)
Noctet: Tales of Madonna-Moloch - Albert J. Manachino   h   955

The Hooded One (Wizard)
Lord of the Isles - David Drake   f   691

Hook, Rufus (Businessman)
Across the Rio Colorado - Ralph Compton   w   491

Hopkins, Marabelle (Farmer; Settler)
The Peacekeeper - Jeffrey Poston   w   586

Horan, Brent (Landowner)
American Blood - Jason Manning   w   564

M

McKinnon, Margery "Walks Fast" (Captive; Bride)
If You Love Me - Elaine Coffman   r   283

McLaren, Niall (Laird)
The Lover - Nicole Jordan   r   340

McMichaels, Scott (Computer Expert; Researcher)
Infectress - Tom Cool   s   1069

McMorrow, Jack (Journalist)
Potshot - Gerry Boyle   m   25

McNair, Shakespeare (Mountain Man; Sidekick)
Spanish Slaughter - David Thompson   w   615

McPherson, Ian (Revolutionary; Military Personnel)
Savage Wilderness - Harold Coyle   w   502

McPherson, Mary Beth (Southern Belle)
Look Away - Harold Coyle   w   501

McQuade, Chance (Wagonmaster; Frontiersman)
Across the Rio Colorado - Ralph Compton   w   491

McQuaid, Mike (Police Officer; Lover)
Love Lies Bleeding - Susan Wittig Albert   m   2

Medalont (Alien; Doctor)
Final Diagnosis - James White   s   1233

Melania (Noblewoman; Adventurer)
The Eagle and the Sword - A.A. Attanasio   f   645

Melchior (Religious; Wizard)
Count Scar - C. Dale Brittain   f   658

Melody (Alien)
Finity's End - C.J. Cherryh   s   1065

Melville, Raoul (Nobleman)
The Arrangement - Joan Wolf   r   439

Mende, Alice (Computer Expert)
Wyrm - Mark Fabi   s   1094

Meniskos, Jhana (Scientist; Researcher)
Lightpaths - Howard V. Hendrix   s   1131

Menlo, Anne (Psychologist)
Only in the Ashes - Maxine O'Callaghan   m   176

Mennym, Soobie (Mythical Creature)
Mennyms Alive - Sylvia Waugh   f   811

Mennym, Tulip (Mythical Creature)
Mennyms Alive - Sylvia Waugh   f   811

Mephistopheles (Alien; Demon)
Jack Faust - Michael Swanwick   s   1219

Mercerault, Peter (Gentleman)
The Offer - Catherine Coulter   r   288

Meren (Nobleman)
Eater of Souls - Lynda S. Robinson   m   202

Merkle, Carl (Outlaw)
Sunshine Rider - Ric Lynden Hardman   w   529

Merlin (Wizard; Leader)
The Eagle and the Sword - A.A. Attanasio   f   645

Merlin (Religious; Wizard)
Enemy of God - Bernard Cornwell   f   678

Merlin (Child; Orphan)
Merlin - Jane Yolen   f   825

Merlin, Anastasia "Ana" (Singer)
Tomorrow and Tomorrow - Charles
   Sheffield   s   1204

Merlin, Emrys (Child; Psychic)
The Seven Songs of Merlin - T.A. Barron   f   648

Merlin, Walter Drake (Musician)
Tomorrow and Tomorrow - Charles
   Sheffield   s   1204

Merlyn Britannicus, Caius (Leader; Writer)
The Eagles' Brood - Jack Whyte   f   816

Merrick, Ty (Detective—Police; Werewolf)
Opalite Moon - Denise Vitola   f   808

Merrill, Richard "Mairelon" (Magician)
Magician's Ward - Patricia C. Wrede   f   819

Merritt, Bill (Rancher)
Bumpo, Bill, and the Girls - Kent Conwell   w   499

Merritt, Linitta (Child)
Bumpo, Bill, and the Girls - Kent Conwell   w   499

Metcalf, Oliver (Editor)
The Blackstone Chronicles - John Saul   h   990

Miathan (Wizard)
Dhiammara - Maggie Furey   f   706

Midnight Louie (Animal)
Cat in a Flamingo Fedora - Carole Nelson
   Douglas   m   67

Mikal (Sorcerer)
Broken Blade - Ann Marston   f   754

Mikk (Actor; Alien)
The Merro Tree - Katie Waitman   s   1230

Milana, Chaka (Hunter; Scholar)
Eternity Road - Jack McDevitt   s   1155

Milleflores, Delanna (Heiress; Spouse)
Promised Land - Connie Willis   s   1238

Miller, Martin (Businessman)
The Darker Passions: Carmilla - Amarantha
   Knight   h   933

Miller, Pix (Housewife)
The Body in the Fjord - Katherine Hall
   Page   m   180

Miller, Tony (Archaeologist)
Time Blender - Michael Dorn   s   1081

Milligan, Turk (Criminal)
One Last Town - Matt Braun   w   472

Mills, Rosie (Orphan)
Prairie Rose - Catherine Palmer   w   581

Mills, Todd (Journalist; Homosexual)
Hostage - R.D. Zimmerman   m   244

Milton, Annie (Young Woman)
Cul-De-Sac - David Martin   h   958

Milton, John (Lawyer)
The Devil's Advocate - Andrew Neiderman   h   972

Milton, John (Writer; Leader)
Milton in America - Peter Ackroyd   f   637

Minakis, Manolis (Scientist; Businessman)
Secret Passages - Paul Preuss   s   1178

Minster, Joanne (Police Officer)
The World of Darkness: Watcher - Charles L.
   Grant   h   900

Miracle, Tori (Writer)
Death, Lies, and Apple Pies - Valerie S.
   Malmont   m   151

Mirri (Young Woman; Adventurer)
The Iron Ring - Lloyd Alexander   f   640

Mitchell, Richard (Businessman)
Buddha Kiss - Peter Tasker   m   223

Mitford, Chuck (Military Personnel; Castaway)
Freedom's Choice - Anne McCaffrey   s   1154

Mithra (Angel)
Ancient Games - Scott Ciencin   f   669

Moira (Witch)
The Wiz Biz - Rick Cook   f   677

Mollari, Londo (Alien; Political Figure)
Personal Agendas - Al Sarrantonio   s   1191

Mom (Artificial Intelligence)
Exit to Reality - Edith Forbes   s   1098

Monaghan, Tess (Detective—Private)
Charm City - Laura Lippman   m   149

Moncrief, Carrol (Religious; Outlaw)
Dead Reckoning - Mike Blakely   w   461

Mondragon, Carlos (Stowaway; Immigrant)
The Black Sun - Jack Williamson   s   1236

Monet, Claude (Spirit; Artist)
Monet's Ghost - Chelsea Quinn Yarbro   f   824

Monique (Robot)
Freeware - Rudy Rucker   s   1184

Monroe, Hannah (Captive)
The Long Trail Home - Tracy Dunham   w   511

Montague, Emerald (Gentlewoman)
Dream Lover - Virginia Henley   r   324

Montclaire, Thomas (Knight; Nobleman)
For My Lady's Kiss - Linda Needham   r   388

Montero, Britt (Journalist)
Margin of Error - Edna Buchanan   m   27

Montez, Luis (Lawyer)
Blues for the Buffalo - Manuel Ramos   m   192

Montoya, Anna (Captive)
Mountain Captive - John Legg   w   560

Montrovant (Vampire)
To Speak in Lifeless Tongues - David Niall
   Wilson   h   1028

Moon, Charlie (Police Officer; Indian)
The Shaman's Bones - James D. Doss   m   66

Moon, Gracie (Mountain Woman; Religious)
Chase the Moon - Dinah McCall   r   375

Mooney, Shawana (Single Parent; Traveller)
The Arbitrary Placement of Walls - Martha
   Soukup   f   797

Moonfeather (Wizard)
Shadowboxer - Nick Pollotta   s   1177

Moorcock, Margaret Rose (Revolutionary;
   Adventurer)
The War Amongst the Angels - Michael
   Moorcock   f   768

Moore, Steven (Child)
Nashville 1864 - Madison Jones   w   549

Moose Horn (Indian; Chieftain)
A Portrait of Spotted Deer's Grandfather - Amy
   Littlesugar   w   561

Morai (Criminal)
Talion: Revenant - Michael A. Stackpole   f   799

Morden (Linguist)
The Shadow Within - Jeanne Cavelos   s   1062

Moreau, Paul (Werewolf)
Hair of the Dog - Brett Davis   f   683

Morelli, Joe (Police Officer)
Three to Get Deadly - Janet Evanovich   m   80

Morgan, Cassandra "Cassie" (Captive)
So Wide the Sky - Elizabeth Grayson   r   320

Morgan, Grant (Drifter)
Giovanni's Gift - Bradford Morrow   m   171

Morgan, Jacob (Trapper; Mountain Man)
Winter Woman - F.M. Parker   w   582

Morgan, Jason (Spaceship Captain)
A Thousand Words for Stranger - Julie E.
   Czerneda   s   1072

Morgan, Lionel (Nobleman; Guardian)
Captive - Joan Johnston   r   338

Morgan, Patsy (Divorced Person)
A Family Wedding - Angela Benson   r   259

Morgan, Rod (Spaceship Captain)
Saturn Rukh - Robert L. Forward   s   1100

Morgian (Royalty; Sorceress)
Grail - Stephen R. Lawhead   f   745

Mori, Kazuo (Detective—Private)
Buddha Kiss - Peter Tasker   m   223

Morley, Thomas (Sea Captain)
Major Washington - Michael Kilian   *w*   552

Morris, Anne (Writer)
Winter Tides - James P. Blaylock   *h*   842

Morris, Dan (Military Personnel)
Blood on the Plains - Robert Vaughan   *w*   624

Morrisey, Hilda Jeanne (Government Official; Administrator)
The Siege of Eternity - Frederik Pohl   *s*   1176

Morrison, Gertie (Psychic)
Threshold - Bill Myers   *s*   1164

Morrison, Rebecca (Librarian)
The Blackstone Chronicles - John Saul   *h*   990

Morrow, Ethan (Farmer; Cowboy)
Sweeter than Wine - Stephanie Mittman   *r*   382

Morse (Police Officer)
Death Is Now My Neighbor - Colin Dexter   *m*   61

Mosala, Violet (Scientist)
Distress - Greg Egan   *s*   1088

Mosely (Detective—Police)
Gabriel Knight: Sins of the Fathers - Jane Jensen   *h*   924

Moses, Libby (Doctor; Military Personnel)
Echoes of Issel - Diann Thornley   *s*   1222

Mosiah (Wizard)
Legacy of the Darksword - Margaret Weis   *f*   812

Moss, Emmett (Rancher)
Texas Lily - Elizabeth Fackler   *w*   517

Motzin, Rebeka (Prisoner)
Days of Cain - J.R. Dunn   *s*   1086

Mreen (Psychic; Child)
Receive the Gift - Louise Marley   *s*   1150

Mulder, Fox (FBI Agent)
Antibodies - Kevin J. Anderson   *h*   832

Murchison, Joe (Military Personnel)
Yesterday's Reveille - Robert Vaughan   *w*   626

Murdoch, William (Detective—Police)
Except the Dying - Maureen Jennings   *m*   132

Murdock, Jacob (Rancher; Criminal)
Honor of the Mountain Man - William W. Johnstone   *w*   546

Murgen (Military Personnel; Psychic)
She Is the Darkness - Glen Cook   *f*   676

Murietta, Juaquin (Outlaw; Historical Figure)
Sierra Baron - Tom W. Blackburn   *w*   459

Murphy, James (Musician)
Landslayer's Law - Tom Deitz   *f*   687

Murphy, Mary Frances (Detective—Amateur; Religious)
Innocence - Suzanne Forster   *r*   307

Murphy, P.G. (Businessman)
The Wagon Wars - James A. Ritchie   *w*   595

Murray, Rowan (Laird)
One of These Nights - Susan Sizemore   *r*   423

Murugan, L. (Computer Expert)
The Calcutta Chromosome - Amitav Ghosh   *h*   895

Musgrave, Wycherly "Wych" (Alcoholic)
Gravelight - Marion Zimmer Bradley   *f*   655

Mussina, Isabella (Doctor)
Night of Broken Souls - Thomas F. Monteleone   *h*   968

Myers, Didi "Deeds" (Robot; Researcher)
The Stranger - Eric James Fullilove   *s*   1105

Myrilandel "Myri" (Healer)
The Dragon's Touchstone - Irene Radford   *f*   783

Myth, Urban (Computer Expert; Robot)
Cinderblock - Janine Ellen Young   *s*   1243

Mythmaker (Storyteller)
The Ghost Trail - Tracy Dunham   *w*   510

N

NaBlaine, Ruairi (Nobleman)
Bridge of Valor - Anne Lesley Groell   *f*   716

Nakimure, Grace (Worker)
Gabriel Knight: Sins of the Fathers - Jane Jensen   *h*   924

Nalls, Miller (Volunteer)
Journey to Shiloh - Will Henry   *w*   533

Navarre, Jackson "Tres" (Detective—Private)
Big Red Tequila - Rick Riordan   *m*   199

Nazir, Nassifeh "Opalears" (Time Traveller; Storyteller)
The Family Tree - Sheri S. Tepper   *s*   1220

Neale, Porsche (Alien; Fugitive)
Beneath the Gated Sky - Robert Reed   *s*   1181

Ned (Orphan; Genius)
Hope of Earth - Piers Anthony   *s*   1036

Negrete, Dolores (Settler)
The Dazzle of Day - Molly Gloss   *s*   1111

Neihart, Fletcher Robert (Orphan; Teenager)
Finity's End - C.J. Cherryh   *s*   1065

Nell (Teenager; Writer)
Into the Forest - Jean Hegland   *s*   1130

Nelson, Annie (Teacher)
Annie's Hero - Maggie Shayne   *r*   418

Nelson, Lynn (Television Personality)
Heartbreaker - Karen Robards   *r*   414

Nelson, Richard "Ren" (Truck Driver; Spirit)
Annie's Hero - Maggie Shayne   *r*   418

Nelson, Vicki (Detective—Private)
Blood Debt - Tanya Huff   *h*   919

Nelson, Willie (Musician)
Road Kill - Kinky Friedman   *m*   87

Nenda, Louis (Adventurer)
Convergence - Charles Sheffield   *s*   1202

Nest, Henrich Joseph (Vampire)
Buffy the Vampire Slayer: The Harvest - Richie Tankersley Cusick   *h*   863

Nettie (Space Explorer; Traveller)
Douglas Adams's Starship Titanic - Terry Jones   *s*   1133

Neville, Christopher "Kit" (Nobleman)
Once upon a Rose - Judith O'Brien   *r*   390

Nevyn (Counselor)
The Red Wyvern - Katharine Kerr   *f*   735

Newcastle, Damian (Architect)
Buttons and Beaus - Margaret Brownley   *r*   271

Nichols, Harford (Government Official)
Night of Broken Souls - Thomas F. Monteleone   *h*   968

Nichols, Jane (Spy; Writer)
AKA Jane - Maureen Tan   *m*   222

Nichols, Payson (Lawyer; Military Personnel)
Wayward Angel - Patricia Rice   *r*   407

Nicholson, Graeme (Reporter)
Expansion - Peter F. Hamilton   *s*   1121

Nielsen, Berkeley "Berk" (Pilot)
Faraday's Orphans - N. Lee Wood   *s*   1242

Nifft the Lean (Adventurer)
The Mines of Behemoth - Michael Shea   *f*   792

Night Hawk (Trader)
The Long Walk - Amanda Cockrell   *w*   483

Nighteyes (Animal; Telepath)
Assassin's Quest - Robin Hobb   *f*   722

Nighthawk, Craig (Rancher; Indian)
Nighthawk - Rachel Lee   *r*   364

Nighthawk, Jefferson "Widowmaker" (Clone; Mercenary)
The Widowmaker Reborn - Mike Resnick   *s*   1182

Nimbulan "Lan" (Magician; Warrior)
The Dragon's Touchstone - Irene Radford   *f*   783

Nimziki, Albert Alexander (Government Official)
Silent Zone - Stephen Molstad   *s*   1159

Nina (Mentally Ill Person; Military Personnel)
Planar Powers - J. Robert King   *f*   739

Nirobus (Wizard; Drug Dealer)
My Son, the Wizard - Christopher Stasheff   *f*   800

Nitt, Agnes (Singer)
Maskerade - Terry Pratchett   *f*   780

Nix, Chris (Child)
Dogland - Will Shetterly   *f*   794

Nix, Luke (Businessman)
Dogland - Will Shetterly   *f*   794

Nobilio, Francis "Frank" (Scientist; Government Official)
Illegal Alien - Robert J. Sawyer   *s*   1194

Noble, Bentley (Journalist)
Shackled - Ray Garton   *h*   889

Noir, Julie (Teenager)
The Black Cat - Robert Poe   *h*   978

Nolan, Ronan (Teenager; Wizard)
A Wizard Abroad - Diane Duane   *f*   693

Northrop, Silas (Writer; Military Personnel)
Carried Away - Sue Civil-Brown   *r*   281

Norton (Mythical Creature; Activist)
Steel Rose - Kara Dalkey   *f*   681

Novak, Cornell (Fugitive)
Beneath the Gated Sky - Robert Reed   *s*   1181

Nowek, Gregori (Government Official; Scientist)
Siberian Light - Robin White   *m*   237

Noycannir, Mergau (Civil Servant; Student)
An Exchange of Hostages - Susan R. Matthews   *s*   1151

Nukurren (Warrior; Alien)
Mother of Demons - Eric Flint   *s*   1096

Nuria (Child; Orphan)
Well Wished - Franny Billingsley   *f*   653

Nussem, Alis Mary (Spacewoman; Pilot)
Reckoning Infinity - John E. Stith   *s*   1214

Nygerski, Cyrus "Moondog" (Driver; Werewolf)
Room 13 - Henry Garfield   *h*   886

Nylan (Engineer)
The Chaos Balance - L.E. Modesitt Jr.   *f*   764

O

Oakenhurst, Sam (Adventurer)
The War Amongst the Angels - Michael Moorcock   *f*   768

Oakley, Annie (Entertainer; Historical Figure)
Shooting Star - Debbie Dadey   *w*   504

Oar (Genetically Altered Being)
Expendable - James Alan Gardner   *s*   1108

Q

R

Rawlins, Steve (Police Officer; Homosexual)
Hostage - R.D. Zimmerman   *m*   244

Reacher, Jack (Drifter; Veteran)
Killing Floor - Lee Child   *m*   35

Reagan, Ronald "Dutch" (Historical Figure; Actor)
Time on My Hands - Peter Delacorte   *s*   1077

Rebus, John (Police Officer)
Black and Blue - Ian Rankin   *m*   193

Red Knot (Crime Victim; Indian)
People of the Mist - Kathleen O'Neal Gear   *w*   522

Red Wolf (Indian; Warrior)
By Honor Bound - Alan Morris   *w*   574

Rede, Pippa (Single Parent)
In the Land of Winter - Richard Grant   *f*   711

Reed, Samuel (Military Personnel; Nobleman)
With This Ring - Carla Kelly   *r*   344

Reed, Sharon (Magician)
The Road to Hell, Volume I - Robert
    Weinberg   *h*   1024
The Road to Hell, Volume II - Robert
    Weinberg   *h*   1025

Reichner, Helmut (Administrator; Scientist)
Threshold - Bill Myers   *s*   1164

Reid, Savannah (Detective—Private)
Killer Calories - G.A. McKevett   *m*   165

Reilly, Nina (Lawyer; Single Parent)
Obstruction of Justice - Perri O'Shaugnessy   *m*   178

Reilly, Rosemary (Parent)
Son of Rosemary - Ira Levin   *h*   945

Rejar (Time Traveller; Spirit)
Rejar - Dara Joy   *r*   341

Relkin (Military Personnel)
A Dragon at World's End - Christopher
    Rowley   *f*   787

Renaud de Verdelay, Griffyn (Mercenary; Knight)
The Last Arrow - Marsha Canham   *r*   275

Reo, Sam (Businessman; Criminal)
The Eye of the Hawk - P.A. Bechko   *w*   455

Resnick, Charlie (Police Officer)
Still Waters - John Harvey   *m*   113

Reuven (Secretary)
Legacy of the Darksword - Margaret Weis   *f*   812

Reyes, Adrien (Experimental Subject; Slave)
Someone to Watch over Me - Tricia
    Sullivan   *s*   1218

Reyes-Guzman, Estelle (Detective—Police)
Privileged to Kill - Steven F. Havill   *m*   115

Reynolds, Alvin (Computer Expert)
The Road to Hell, Volume I - Robert
    Weinberg   *h*   1024
The Road to Hell, Volume II - Robert
    Weinberg   *h*   1025

Reynolds, Jane (Child-Care Giver)
The Ignored - Bentley Little   *h*   946

Reynolds, Kelly (Journalist)
Area 51 - Robert Doherty   *s*   1080

Rhea of Coos (Witch)
Wizard and Glass - Stephen King   *h*   931

Rhenford, Liam (Scholar; Detective—Amateur)
Beggar's Banquet - Daniel Hood   *f*   726

Rhiannon "Rhia" (Child; Psychic)
The Seven Songs of Merlin - T.A. Barron   *f*   648

Rhiow (Animal; Wizard)
The Book of Night with Moon - Diane Duane   *f*   692

Rhodenbarr, Bernie (Thief; Businessman)
The Burglar in the Library - Lawrence Block   *m*   20

Rhodes, Emma (Detective—Private)
Impolite Society - Cynthia Smith   *m*   215

Rhyme, Lincoln (Criminologist; Handicapped)
The Bone Collector - Jeffery Deaver   *m*   58

Ribalt, Jacques (Trapper; Mountain Man)
McKendree - Douglas Hirt   *w*   536

Rice, Dale (Lawyer)
Illegal Alien - Robert J. Sawyer   *s*   1194

Richards, Bryce (Lawyer; Single Parent)
Beside a Dreamswept Sea - Victoria Barrett   *r*   256

Richter, Marta (Lawyer)
Rough Justice - Lisa Scottoline   *m*   210

Rick (Editor)
God's Dice - S. Andrew Swann   *f*   804

Rickard, Robert (Maintenance Worker)
Room 13 - Henry Garfield   *h*   886

Riker, William (Military Personnel)
Ship of the Line - Diane Carey   *s*   1060

Riley, Jim (Gunfighter)
The Wolf's Cub - Richard Parry   *w*   583

Rille, Cailet Ambrai (Leader; Teacher)
The Mageborn Traitor - Melanie Rawn   *f*   785

Rincewind (Wizard)
Interesting Times - Terry Pratchett   *f*   779

Rios, Henry (Lawyer; Homosexual)
The Burning Plain - Michael Nava   *m*   175

Ripinsky, Hy (Lover)
Both Ends of the Night - Marcia Muller   *m*   173

Ripley (Clone; Hero)
Alien Resurrection - A.C. Crispin   *s*   1071

Rippen, Jack (Producer)
Celestial Dogs - J.S. Russell   *h*   986

Rivers, Neal (Professor; Vampire)
Keeper of the King - Nigel Bennett   *h*   838

Roanhorse, Carolyn (Doctor; Indian)
Bad Medicine - Aimee Thurlo   *m*   226

Robert (Royalty; Handicapped)
Legacy of the Ancients - Ron Sarti   *s*   1192

Rockman, John (Architect)
Wooing Wanda - Gwen Pemberton   *r*   396

Rockman, Wanda (Spouse)
Wooing Wanda - Gwen Pemberton   *r*   396

Rocky (Police Officer)
God's Dice - S. Andrew Swann   *f*   804

Rodrigo (Royalty; Heir—Dispossessed)
The Still - David Feintuch   *f*   702

Rodriguez (Spouse; Parent)
Senora Rodriguez and Other Worlds - Martha
    Cerda   *f*   663

Rohona (Indian; Slave)
Acoma: A Novel of Conquest - Lana M.
    Harrigan   *w*   530

Rohonar (Chieftain)
The Island Tribe - Charlotte Prentiss   *w*   587

Roland of Gilead (Gunfighter)
Wizard and Glass - Stephen King   *h*   931

Rolfson, Bjorn (Hunter; Wizard)
Magelord: The Awakening - Thomas K.
    Martin   *f*   755

Ronay, Kinna (Revolutionary)
The Fleet of Stars - Poul Anderson   *s*   1034

Roo, Luger (Farmer; Werewolf)
*The Case of the Police Officer's Cock Ring and the
    Piano Player Who Had No Fingers* - Edward
    Lee   *h*   944

Rook, Jim (Teacher)
Rook - Graham Masterton   *h*   959
Tooth and Claw - Graham Masterton   *h*   960

Rosato, Benedetta "Bennie" (Lawyer)
Rough Justice - Lisa Scottoline   *m*   210

Rose, Mick "China" (Truck Driver; Businessman)
Signs of Life - M. John Harrison   *s*   1125

Roselle (Animal)
Sunshine Rider - Ric Lynden Hardman   *w*   529

Rosenberg, Isaac (Scientist)
Titan - Stephen Baxter   *s*   1047

Ross, John (Psychic)
Running with the Demon - Terry Brooks   *f*   659

Rostnikov, Porfiry (Police Officer)
Tarnished Icons - Stuart M. Kaminsky   *m*   136

Rosvenir, Collan (Minstrel; Nobleman)
The Mageborn Traitor - Melanie Rawn   *f*   785

Rottenson, Mary (Noblewoman; Imposter)
A Well-Pleasured Lady - Christina Dodd   *r*   297

Rourke, Hannah (Businesswoman)
The Dansing Star - Kirby Jonas   *w*   548

Rowan, Daniel (Bartender)
Famine - Todd Komarnicki   *h*   934

Rowland, Althea (Actress)
Timeshare - Joshua Dann   *s*   1074

Roxanne (Child)
My Best Friend Is Invisible - R.L. Stine   *h*   1009

Rubra, Rose (Bride)
Waking Beauty - Paul Witcover   *f*   818

Rucker, Judgement (Hunter)
The Cellar - Richard Laymon   *h*   942

Rufin, Tal (Police Officer)
Four & Twenty Blackbirds - Mercedes
    Lackey   *f*   742

Rumer (Prostitute)
Waking Beauty - Paul Witcover   *f*   818

Russell, Joanna (Antiquarian)
Key to Forever - Christina Skye   *r*   425

Russell, Katrinka (Housewife)
Violin - Anne Rice   *h*   983

Russell, Mary (Detective—Private; Scholar)
A Letter of Mary - Laurie R. King   *m*   141

Russell, Reshelle "Flame" (Frontierswoman)
White Fire - Cassie Edwards   *r*   300

Rustin (Royalty)
The Still - David Feintuch   *f*   702

Rusty Red (Military Personnel)
To Be a Warrior - Robert Barlow Fox   *w*   519

Ruthven, Lucy (Actress)
Slave of My Thirst - Tom Holland   *h*   915

Rutledge, Andrew (Writer)
Root of All Evil - David A. Farrow   *h*   881

Ryan, Lacey (Teenager)
Shackled - Ray Garton   *h*   889

Ryan, Zach (Engineer)
Almost an Angel - Deb Stover   *r*   430

Ryder (Walkman), Kathleen (Fugitive; Single Parent)
Tallchief - Dinah McCall   *r*   376

Rylus (Entertainer)
When the Gods Are Silent - Jane M.
    Lindskold   *f*   750

Teppish, Vladimir X. III (Vampire; Parent)
The Vampire's Beautiful Daughter - S.P.
Somtow *h* 1002

Teska (Alien; Telepath)
Mind Meld - John Vornholt *s* 1229

Thalassa (Prostitute; Heroine)
The Forging of the Shadows - Oliver Johnson *f* 729

Thatcher, John Putnam (Banker)
A Shark Out of Water - Emma Lathen *m* 145

Theodoulos (Linguist; Mythical Creature)
Cross and Crescent - Susan Shwartz *f* 795

Thibaudeaux, Catherine "Cat" (Spy)
Delta Search - William Shatner *s* 1199

Thismet (Royalty)
Sorcerers of Majipoor - Robert Silverberg *s* 1207

Thissizz (Alien; Singer)
The Merro Tree - Katie Waitman *s* 1230

Thistledown, Tipperton "Tip" (Mythical Creature; Adventurer)
Into the Forge - Dennis L. McKiernan *f* 760

Thomas, Maggie (Businesswoman)
Flashpoint - Tracey Tillis *r* 434

Thomason, John "Jean Vitterand" (Policeman; Time Traveller)
Time Station Paris - David Evans *s* 1093

Thompson, Emily (Heir; Fugitive)
The Night Watch - Sean Stewart *f* 801

Thomson, Cort (Gunfighter; Criminal)
The Gamblers - Matt Braun *w* 471

Thoreau, Henry David (Writer)
Cloudsplitter - Russell Banks *w* 447

Thorn, Victoria (Noblewoman)
Lady Thorn - Catherine Archer *r* 250

Thorne, Colin (Orphan; Sea Captain)
My Steadfast Heart - Jo Goodman *r* 318

Thorne, Titus (Professor)
The Mermaid - Betina Krahn *r* 352

Thornton, Alexandra (Historian; Time Traveller)
Captive - Brenda Joyce *r* 342

Thornton, Gage (Businessman)
Petals on the River - Kathleen Woodiwiss *r* 441

Thornton, Ivan (Nobleman; Bastard Son)
Dangerous to Love - Rexanne Becnel *r* 258

Thorpe, Leonard (Filmmaker)
Glimmering - Elizabeth Hand *s* 1123

Thorson, Dane (Spaceman; Trader)
Derelict for Trade - Andre Norton *s* 1170

Thorson, Dane (Spaceman)
A Mind for Trade - Andre Norton *s* 1171

Three Elk (Indian; Warrior)
Broken Lance - Michele Sorensen *w* 607

Throtmanian, Paul Donald (Con Artist)
Lifehouse - Spider Robinson *s* 1183

Ticktockman (Government Official)
"Repent, Harlequin!" Said the Ticktockman - Harlan Ellison *s* 1090

Tighe, Epiphanius "Eppy" (Storyteller)
A Diversity of Dragons - Anne McCaffrey *f* 757

Tilghman, Bill (Lawman)
One Last Town - Matt Braun *w* 472

Tilghman, Zoe (Spouse)
One Last Town - Matt Braun *w* 472

Tim (Teenager; Adventurer)
The Gift - Patrick O'Leary *f* 775

Timpson, Freda (Teacher)
The Red-Eared Ghosts - Vivian Alcock *f* 639

Tirrell (Ruler)
Talion: Revenant - Michael A. Stackpole *f* 799

Toledo, Indira (Historian; Colonist)
Mother of Demons - Eric Flint *s* 1096

Tolivar (Nobility; Teenager)
Sky Trillium - Julian May *f* 756

Tomlinson (Writer; Genius)
North of Havana - Randy Wayne White *m* 236

Tommy T. (Streetperson; Child)
The Night Remembers - Kathleen Eagle *r* 298

Tomochelor, Pulickel (Scientist; Anthropologist)
The Howling Stones - Alan Dean Foster *s* 1101

Tooe (Alien)
Derelict for Trade - Andre Norton *s* 1170

Tooe (Alien; Apprentice)
A Mind for Trade - Andre Norton *s* 1171

Torregrossa, Ethan (Lawman; Gunfighter)
The Eye of the Hawk - P.A. Bechko *w* 455

Torres, B'Elanna (Engineer; Alien)
Her Klingon Soul - Michael Jan Friedman *s* 1104

Tortelli, Mia (Producer)
Heaven Loves a Hero - Nikki Holiday *r* 326

Touch the Sky (Indian; Shaman)
Bloody Bones Canyon - Judd Cole *w* 486
Renegade Siege - Judd Cole *w* 487
River of Death - Judd Cole *w* 488

Townsend, Ben (Journalist)
Rising Tides - Emilie Richards *r* 408

Townsend, Gabriel (Guide)
Just Before Midnight - Patricia Simpson *r* 422

Townsend, Mark (Religious)
A Ritual Death - Father Brad Reynolds S.J. *m* 197

Trader, Max (Artisan; Businessman)
Trader - Charles de Lint *f* 685

Tradescent, Heather (Young Woman; Gardener)
The Dancing Floor - Barbara Michaels *m* 168

Trampe, Fane (Wanderer)
Nevada Tough - John S. McCord *w* 569

Trampe, Micajah (Kidnapper)
Blind Eagles - John S. McCord *w* 568

Trask, Grace (Spaceship Captain; Miner)
The Billion Dollar Boy - Charles Sheffield *s* 1201

Trask, Lana (Spaceship Captain; Miner)
The Billion Dollar Boy - Charles Sheffield *s* 1201

Travis, Melanie (Animal Trainer; Teacher)
Hair of the Dog - Laurien Berenson *m* 17

Travis, William Barrett (Military Personnel)
Blood of Texas - Will Camp *w* 479

Tremayne, Emma (Artist; Gentlewoman)
The Passions of Emma - Penelope Williamson *r* 438

Tremayne, Wes (Bastard Son; Gunfighter)
The Autumn of the Gun - Ralph Compton *w* 492

Trent, Derrick (Detective—Police)
The Stranger - Eric James Fullilove *s* 1105

Trevor, Hannah (Healer)
Blood Red Roses - Margaret Lawrence *m* 146

Trimble, Horace (Military Personnel; Prisoner)
Andersonville - Robert Vaughan *w* 623

Trinidad (Alien; Traitor)
Beneath the Gated Sky - Robert Reed *s* 1181

Tristan of Shara (Royalty)
Forever Enchanted - Maggie Shayne *r* 420

Trout, Kilgore (Writer)
Timequake - Kurt Vonnegut Jr. *s* 1228

Troutbeck, "Jack" (Noblewoman)
Murder in a Cathedral - Ruth Dudley Edwards *m* 72

Troys, Taylor Thaddeus "Taytay" (Handicapped; Son)
Meeting the Minotaur - Carol Dawson *f* 684

True Dragon (Deity)
Testament of the Dragon - Margaret Weis *f* 813

Truitt, April (Feminist)
Angel Face and Amazing Grace - Lori Copeland *r* 286

Truitt, Charity (Businesswoman; Store Owner)
Deep Waters - Jayne Ann Krentz *r* 353

Tualha (Animal; Minstrel)
A Wizard Abroad - Diane Duane *f* 693

Tucker, Randy Karl (Kidnapper)
Freeware - Rudy Rucker *s* 1184

Tucker, Rose (Scientist)
Sole Survivor - Dean R. Koontz *h* 935

Tucker, William Alec III (Reanimated Dead; Cyborg)
A King of Infinite Space - Allen Steele *s* 1212

Tunstall, Mac (Wagonmaster)
The Winchester Run - Ralph Compton *w* 496

Turcotte, Mike (Military Personnel)
Area 51 - Robert Doherty *s* 1080

Turnbull, Ben (Aged Person)
Toward the End of Time - John Updike *s* 1224

Turpin, Richard (FBI Agent; Werewolf)
The World of Darkness: Watcher - Charles L. Grant *h* 900

Turtle Woman (Indian; Grandparent)
Shifting Stars: A Novel of the West - Page Lambert *w* 555

Tutankhamon (Historical Figure; Ruler)
Eater of Souls - Lynda S. Robinson *m* 202

Twain, Mark (Writer; Historical Figure)
The Prince and the Prosecutor - Peter J. Heck *m* 117
The Rock Child - Win Blevins *w* 462

Twilight (Indian; Young Woman)
The Bear Paw Horses - Will Henry *w* 532

Two Bears (Genetically Altered Being)
Shadowboxer - Nick Pollotta *s* 1177

Two Hats, Johnny (Indian; Warrior)
The Ghost Trail - Tracy Dunham *w* 510
The Long Trail Home - Tracy Dunham *w* 511

Two Songs (Indian; Widow(er))
Goodbye, Buffalo Sky - John Loveday *w* 562

Tyler, Blaine (Frontiersman)
The Winds of Autumn - Jim R. Woolard *w* 635

Tyler, Blake (Frontiersman)
The Winds of Autumn - Jim R. Woolard *w* 635

Tyler, Clardy (Wanderer; Frontiersman)
Passage to Natchez - Cameron Judd *w* 550

Tyner, Sally (Prostitute; Detective—Private)
No Remorse - James D. Brewer *m* 26

Typhoid Mary (Psychic; Mentally Ill Person)
Twilight of the Empire - Simon R. Green *s* 1115

Tywi (Orphan)
The Dark Shore - Adam Lee *f* 746

Tzikas (Military Personnel; Traitor)
The Thousand Cities - Harry Turtledove *f* 806

U

Ublaz Mad Eyes (Animal; Ruler)
The Pearls of Lutra - Brian Jacques   *f*   728

Ufgood, Torquil (Sorcerer)
Shadow Dawn - Chris Claremont   *f*   670

Uncas (Indian; Warrior)
The Rain From God - Mark Ammerman   *w*   442

Underbridge, Kin (Judge)
Wrath of the Princes - Holly Lisle   *f*   752

Urban (Revolutionary)
Deception Well - Linda Nagata   *s*   1165

Urmila (Journalist)
The Calcutta Chromosome - Amitav Ghosh   *h*   895

Uroh (Hunter)
The Island Tribe - Charlotte Prentiss   *w*   587

Urruah (Animal; Wizard)
The Book of Night with Moon - Diane Duane   *f*   692

Uther Pendragon (Warrior)
The Eagles' Brood - Jack Whyte   *f*   816

Uthred of Ravenspur (Religious; Wizard)
The Forging of the Shadows - Oliver Johnson   *f*   729

V

Vadeviya (Religious)
Touched by the Gods - Lawrence Watt-Evans   *f*   810

Valdoria kva Skolia, Kelricson Garlin (Nobleman; Psychic)
The Last Hawk - Catherine Asaro   *s*   1038

Valerian (Wizard)
Magelord: The Awakening - Thomas K. Martin   *f*   755

Van, Judyth (Mail Order Bride; Teacher)
Devil's Rim - Sam Brown   *w*   475

Van Vorst, Catalyntie (Captive; Trader)
Remember the Morning - Thomas Fleming   *w*   518

Van Zandt, Andy (Child)
The Stone Circle - Gary Goshgarian   *h*   898

Van Zandt, Peter (Archaeologist)
The Stone Circle - Gary Goshgarian   *h*   898

Vandermeer, Louise (Heiress)
Beast - Judith Ivory   *r*   333

Vandiver (Military Personnel)
Extinct - Charles Wilson   *h*   1027

Vannice, Owen (Scientist; Time Traveller)
Corrupting Dr. Nice - John Kessel   *s*   1137

Varden (Mythical Creature; Healer)
Spires of Spirit - Gael Baudino   *f*   649

Vaughan, Lucus (Religious)
Spiritride - Mark Shepherd   *f*   793

Vendramin, Caterina (Young Woman)
Vaporetto 13 - Robert Girardi   *h*   896

Vereskaya, Anna (Scientist)
Siberian Light - Robin White   *m*   237

Veriam, Tanaquil (Wanderer; Sorceress)
Red Unicorn - Tanith Lee   *f*   747

Verity (Clone; Genetically Altered Being)
Mississippi Blue - Kathleen Ann Goonan   *s*   1112

Veronica (Religious)
Cardmaster - Clayton Emery   *f*   700

Vetter, Tracy (Detective—Homicide)
Forever Knight: Intimations of Mortality - Susan M. Garrett   *h*   887

Vikstrom, Borg (Farmer; Immigrant)
Break the Young Land - T.V. Olsen   *w*   578

Villon, Herbert (Police Officer)
The Clark Gable and Carole Lombard Murder Case - George Baxt   *m*   11

Viner, Lily (Teenager; Orphan)
Railroad Schemes - Cecilia Holland   *w*   539

Viola (Animal; Adventurer)
The Pearls of Lutra - Brian Jacques   *f*   728

Virili, Kip (Child)
The Black Sun - Jack Williamson   *s*   1236

Virili, Rima (Scientist)
The Black Sun - Jack Williamson   *s*   1236

Vitarosa (Murderer; Religious)
Mind Snare - Gayle Greeno   *s*   1118

Vizuelos, Ramon (Friend; Criminal)
Meeting the Minotaur - Carol Dawson   *f*   684

Vladislov, Pete (Boarder; Alcoholic)
Klondike Fever - Suzann Ledbetter   *w*   558

Voerbeck, Grut (Landowner)
Winchester Affidavit - G.G. Boyer   *w*   469

Voight, Susan (Writer; Wealthy)
Freedom & Necessity - Steven Brust   *f*   660

von Cragga, Ivo (Vampire)
The Ruby Tear - Rebecca Brand   *h*   843

von Darkmoor, Erik (Military Personnel)
Rage of a Demon King - Raymond E. Feist   *f*   703

von Sacher, Ludwig (Genetically Altered Being; Historian)
Lives of the Monster Dogs - Kirsten Bakis   *s*   1040

von Wolgast, Klemens Manfred (Businessman)
Writ in Blood - Chelsea Quinn Yarbro   *h*   1031

Vonnegut, Kurt "Junior" (Writer)
Timequake - Kurt Vonnegut Jr.   *s*   1228

W

Wade, Cody (Cowboy; Lawman)
Hell's Half Acre - Frederic Bean   *w*   452

Wager, Gabe (Police Officer)
The Leaning Land - Rex Burns   *m*   31

Wagner (Student)
Jack Faust - Michael Swanwick   *s*   1219

Wahler, Jukes (Doctor)
Shade of Pale - Greg Kihn   *h*   929

Wali, Linnet (Prostitute; Genetically Altered Being)
Imposter - Valerie J. Freireich   *s*   1103

Walker, Amos (Detective—Private)
Never Street - Loren D. Estleman   *m*   79

Walker, Clay (Indian; Military Personnel)
To Be a Warrior - Robert Barlow Fox   *w*   519

Walker, Tom "Gerald Tarkington Crane" (Military Personnel; Fortune Hunter)
No Ordinary Princess - Pamela Morsi   *r*   386

Walking Bear, Jack (Time Traveller; Military Personnel)
Second Fire - Mike Moscoe   *s*   1163

Wallace, Aaron (Farmer)
The Way Home - Megan Chance   *r*   279

Wallace, Indra (Historian)
3001: The Final Odyssey - Arthur C. Clarke   *s*   1067

Wallace, Tess (Saloon Keeper/Owner)
The Ladies of the Goldfield Stock Exchange - Sibyl Downing   *w*   509

Wallenberg, Carl (Doctor)
Life Support - Tess Gerritsen   *h*   894

Walsh, Charity (Student)
The Bighead - Edward Lee   *h*   943

Walton, David (Writer)
Cannibal Plateau - Joe Wise   *w*   634

Warden (Police Officer)
The Tetherballs of Bougainville - Mark Leyner   *f*   749

Wardieu d'Amboise, Brenna (Noblewoman; Warrior)
The Last Arrow - Marsha Canham   *r*   275

Ware, Fortitude (Nobleman)
Something Wicked - Jo Beverley   *r*   261

Warner, Violet (Friend)
Murder, Mrs. Hudson - Sydney Hosier   *m*   126

Washington (Slave; Trapper)
Tallgrass: A Novel of the Great Plains - Don Coldsmith   *w*   485

Washington, George (Military Personnel; Surveyor)
Major Washington - Michael Kilian   *w*   552

Water (Mythical Creature)
The Book of Water - Marjorie Bradley Kellogg   *f*   732

Water Spider (Government Official)
The Night Watch - Sean Stewart   *f*   801

Waterman, Leo (Detective—Private)
The Bum's Rush - G.M. Ford   *m*   84

Watson, Libby (Writer; Store Owner)
Prairie Rose - Susan Kirby   *r*   349

Watson, Sam (Lawyer)
Pratt's Landing - Martha Kirkland   *r*   351

Watt, Peter (Spy)
Millennium: Gehenna - Lewis Gannett   *h*   884

Watts, Arnie (Serial Killer)
Thoughts of God - Michael Kanaly   *s*   1134

Weatherford, Biggie (Widow(er); Grandparent)
Biggie and the Mangled Mortician - Nancy Bell   *m*   15

Webb, Fiona (Doctor)
Website - Ray Garton   *h*   890

Weintraub, Sarah (Scientist; Researcher)
Threshold - Bill Myers   *s*   1164

Weiss, Selene (Witch)
Shadows - Jonathan Nasaw   *h*   970

Wellin, Alleluia "Alleya" (Genetically Altered Being; Leader)
Jovah's Angel - Sharon Shinn   *s*   1205

Wells, Joey (Rancher; Gunfighter)
Honor of the Mountain Man - William W. Johnstone   *w*   546

Weser, Erich "Erich Alois" (Leader; Animal Trainer)
Children of the Dusk - Janet Berliner   *f*   652

West, Helen (Lawyer)
Without Consent - Frances Fyfield   *m*   89

West, Joshua (Angel)
Heaven in West Texas - Susan Kay Law   *r*   362

Westcott, Archie (Journalist)
How the West Was Lost - Gene Shelton   *w*   603

Weston, Wade (Religious; Outlaw)
Jade - Ruth Langan   *r*   360

Westphal, Connor (Journalist; Handicapped)
Dead Body Language - Penny Warner   *m*   232

Wetzon, Leslie (Businesswoman)
The Groaning Board - Annette Meyers   *m*   167

Wexford, Reginald (Police Officer)
Road Rage - Ruth Rendell   *m*   196

Whaler, Nathaniel Firstborne (Professor; Agent)
The Ecolitan Enigma - L.E. Modesitt Jr.   s   1158

Whalley, Vida (Young Woman)
A Dry Spell - Susan Moloney   h   965

Wharton, Marcus (Nobleman; Handicapped)
After the Kiss - Joan Johnston   r   337

Wheatley, Chas (Journalist)
The Butter Did It - Phyllis Richman   m   198

Wheatley, Gillian (Linguist)
The Seventh Heart - Marina Fitch   f   704

Wheaton, Anna (Child)
Jumpers - R. Patrick Gates   h   891

Wheeler, Asa (Rancher)
Stillwater Smith - Frank Roderus   w   600

Whirlwind (Indian; Chieftain)
War Woman - Robert J. Conley   w   498

Whistler, Jamey (Vampire)
Shadows - Jonathan Nasaw   h   970

White, Ashley (Child)
Husband Needed - Cathie Linz   r   366

White, Kayla (Single Parent; Businesswoman)
Husband Needed - Cathie Linz   r   366

Whitefield, Jane (Guide; Indian)
Shadow Woman - Thomas Perry   m   185

Whittaker, Josephine (Traveller; Cook)
Forget Me Not - Stef Ann Holm   w   540

Wilder, Anne (Widow(er); Thief)
All through the Night - Connie Brockway   r   267

Wilkerson, Lilian (Traveller)
Promised Land - Jason Manning   w   566

Williams, Jonathan (Spaceship Captain)
The Martian Chronicles - Ray Bradbury   s   1054

Williams, Terry (Scholar; Divorced Person)
The Poison Tree - Tony Strong   m   221

Williamson, Luke (Sailor; Detective—Private)
No Remorse - James D. Brewer   m   26

Williamson, Olivia (Child-Care Giver)
The Marriage Bed - Stephanie Mittman   r   381

Williamson, Spencer (Farmer)
The Marriage Bed - Stephanie Mittman   r   381

Wilson, Collingsworth (Young Man)
I Know What You Did Last Summer - Lois
   Duncan   h   875

Wind in His Hair (Indian; Warrior)
Yesterday's Reveille - Robert Vaughan   w   626

Wine, Moses (Detective—Private)
The Lost Coast: A Moses Wine Mystery - Roger L.
   Simon   m   213

Wine, Simon (Activist)
The Lost Coast: A Moses Wine Mystery - Roger L.
   Simon   m   213

Wingate, Johanna (Teacher)
Ask Mariah - Barbara Freethy   r   308

Winnowill (Mythical Creature)
Captives of the Blue Mountain - Wendy Pini   f   777

Winter, Catty (Child; Handicapped)
Well Wished - Franny Billingsley   f   653

Winter, Holly (Journalist; Animal Trainer)
Animal Appetite - Susan Conant   m   41

Winterbelle (Child)
In the Land of Winter - Richard Grant   f   711

Winters, Catherine (Widow(er))
Indiscreet - Mary Balogh   r   252

Winters, Elias (Consultant; Store Owner)
Deep Waters - Jayne Ann Krentz   r   353

Winthrop, Peter (Principal)
Stray Hearts - Annie Kimberlin   r   347

Wirz, Henry (Military Personnel)
Andersonville - Robert Vaughan   w   623

Wise, Gretchen (Friend)
Three Brides, No Groom - Debbie Macomber   r   371

Wolde, David (Linguist)
My Soul to Keep - Tannarive Due   h   873

Wolde, Kira (Child)
My Soul to Keep - Tannarive Due   h   873

Wolf (Veteran; Shaman)
Spiritride - Mark Shepherd   f   793

Wolf (Indian; Drifter)
Warrior's Song - Janis Reams Hudson   r   331

Wolf Voice (Indian; Warrior)
Winter Woman - F.M. Parker   w   582

Wolf Who Hunts Smiling (Indian; Renegade)
Bloody Bones Canyon - Judd Cole   w   486
Renegade Siege - Judd Cole   w   487
River of Death - Judd Cole   w   488

Wolfe, Jackson (Lawman; Adventurer)
Warrior Heart - Jane Bonander   r   264

Wolverine (Indian; Chieftain)
Cossack Three Ponies - J.L. Reasoner   w   589

Woodbaine, Anna (Gentlewoman)
Nick of Time - Casey Claybourne   r   282

Woodgate, Lisa (Ruler)
Bretta Martyn - L. Neil Smith   s   1209

Woodhouse, Andy (Religious)
Son of Rosemary - Ira Levin   h   945

Woods, Roy (Lawman)
Black Gold - Frederic Bean   w   450

Woodville, William (Nobleman; Artist)
If You Love Me - Elaine Coffman   r   283

Wooten, Solomon (Outlaw; Veteran)
The Courtship of Hannah and the Horseman - Johnny
   D. Boggs   w   464

Worabex (Magician)
Red Unicorn - Tanith Lee   f   747

Worf (Alien; Military Personnel)
Armageddon Sky - L.A. Graf   s   1113

Worth, Andrew (Journalist; Filmmaker)
Distress - Greg Egan   s   1088

Worthen, Elise (Young Woman)
If Only - Debra Cowan   w   500

Wovoka (Shaman; Historical Figure)
The Ghost Trail - Tracy Dunham   w   510

Wray, Helen (Businesswoman)
Omega - Patrick Lynch   h   953

Wren, Mason (Doctor; Scientist)
Alien Resurrection - A.C. Crispin   s   1071

Wroke, Alice (Secretary; Spy)
The Demon Princes: Volume Two - Jack
   Vance   s   1226

Wu, Victor "Orf" (Robot; Scientist)
Earthling - Tony Daniel   s   1073

Wycombe, Charles (Nobleman)
Brighter than the Sun - Julia Quinn   r   403

Wylie, Eva (Sports Figure; Security Officer)
Musclebound - Liza Cody   m   40

Wyndon, Elbryan (Teenager; Adventurer)
The Demon Awakens - R.A. Salvatore   f   789

Wysaigh, "Wy" (Pilot)
Faraday's Orphans - N. Lee Wood   s   1242

X

!Xabbu (Traveller; Student)
City of Golden Shadow - Tad Williams   s   1234

Xena (Warrior; Royalty)
The Thief of Hermes - Ru Emerson   f   699

Y

Yellow Horse (Indian; Chieftain)
Death at Spanish Wells - Dodge Tyler   w   619

Yellow Legs (Indian; Warrior)
American Woman - R. Garcia y Robertson   w   521

Yokusuka, Jory (Journalist)
Berserker Fury - Fred Saberhagen   s   1189

York, Dennison (Mercenary; Hero)
Thoughts of God - Michael Kanaly   s   1134

York, Natalie (Scientist)
Voyager - Stephen Baxter   s   1048

York, Nathaniel (Spaceship Captain)
The Martian Chronicles - Ray Bradbury   s   1054

Yoseph (Artificial Intelligence)
Terminal Logic - Jefferson Scott   s   1196

Younger, Cecil (Detective—Private)
Death and the Language of Happiness - John
   Straley   m   220

Z

Zach (Teacher; Student)
Ecstasy Club - Douglas Rushkoff   s   1187

Zainal (Alien; Castaway)
Freedom's Choice - Anne McCaffrey   s   1154

Zalman (Religious)
A Blessing on the Moon - Joseph Skibell   f   796

Zeeman, Richard (Werewolf; Teacher)
The Killing Dance - Laurell K. Hamilton   h   907

Zeerus (Alien; Criminal)
Target Earth - Steve Perry   s   1175

Zen, Aurelio (Police Officer)
Cosi Fan Tutti - Michael Dibdin   m   62

Zerek, Cassandra (Religious)
Simply Love - Catherine Anderson   r   249

Zo'e'minira "Zoe" (Supernatural Being)
The Duke of Sumava - Sara J. Wrench   f   821

Zukas, Helma (Librarian)
Out of Circulation - Jo Dereske   m   60

Zumwalt, William Irving "Wiz" (Computer Expert;
   Wizard; Witch)
The Wiz Biz - Rick Cook   f   677

Zwakh, Ignatz (Revolutionary; Addict)
Dead Things - Richard Calder   s   1059

Character Description Index

This index alphabetically lists descriptions of the major characters in featured titles. The descriptions may be occupations (astronaut, lawyer, etc.) or may describe persona (amnesiac, runaway, teenager, etc.). For each description, character names are listed alphabetically. Also provided are book titles, author names, and entry numbers.

ABUSE VICTIM

Elizabeth, Countess of Ravenwold
Secrets in Satin - Haywood Smith   r   427

Eversleigh, Sabrina
The Offer - Catherine Coulter   r   288

Gillian of Warewick
This Is All I Ask - Lynn Kurland   r   357

Hart, Pearl
I, Pearl Hart - Jane Candia Coleman   w   489

Ormsby, Amy Kay
Beyond the River - Wynema McGowan   w   570

Patterson, Stacy
Daddy by Accident - Paula Detmer Riggs   r   412

Prescott, Angela
The Night Remembers - Kathleen Eagle   r   298

Sandoz, Mari
Mari - Jane Valentine Barker   w   448

Stafford, Yvonne
Thoughts of God - Michael Kanaly   s   1134

ACCIDENT VICTIM

Edwards, Gillian
The Irish Rake - Emma Lange   r   361

ACCOUNTANT

Quinsonnas
Paris in the Twentieth Century - Jules Verne   s   1227

ACTIVIST

Archangel
Tropic of Orange - Karen Tei Yamashita   f   823

Barnett, Pierce
The Firebrand - Laurel Collins   r   285

Edmonds, Sarah Emma "Kite"
Sewer, Gas & Electric - Matt Ruff   s   1185

Etanl, Latona
Alien Influences - Kristine Kathryn Rusch   s   1186

Fareham, Harriet
My Wayward Lady - Evelyn Richardson   r   411

Fine, Joan
Sewer, Gas & Electric - Matt Ruff   s   1185

Harlowe, Caroline
The Firebrand - Laurel Collins   r   285

Kazenstein, Morris
Sewer, Gas & Electric - Matt Ruff   s   1185

Marm, Everett C. "Harlequin"
"Repent, Harlequin!" Said the Ticktockman - Harlan Ellison   s   1090

Norton
Steel Rose - Kara Dalkey   f   681

Ralph
Steel Rose - Kara Dalkey   f   681

Sorby, Helen
Steel Ashes - Karen Rose Cercone   m   34

Wine, Simon
The Lost Coast: A Moses Wine Mystery - Roger L. Simon   m   213

ACTOR

Booth, John Wilkes
Booth - David Robertson   w   597

Bracewell, Nicholas
The Fair Maid of Bohemia - Edward Marston   m   154

Carl
The Arbitrary Placement of Walls - Martha Soukup   f   797

Griffin, Nic
The Ruby Tear - Rebecca Brand   h   843

Hastings, Stanley
Scam - Parnell Hall   m   108

Kenyon, Stephen
One Perfect Rose - Mary Jo Putney   r   401

Maroc, Huud
The Merro Tree - Katie Waitman   s   1230

Mikk
The Merro Tree - Katie Waitman   s   1230

Reagan, Ronald "Dutch"
Time on My Hands - Peter Delacorte   s   1077

Stanislaus, Glynn Webster
Mind Snare - Gayle Greeno   s   1118

ACTRESS

Coakley, Dana
All Emergencies, Ring Super - Ellen Emerson White   m   235

Croft, Jessamyn
The Ruby Tear - Rebecca Brand   h   843

Dellon, Melusine "Sinah"
Gravelight - Marion Zimmer Bradley   f   655

Graham, Charlotte
Murder under the Palms - Stefanie Matteson   m   158

Jordan, Rosalind
One Perfect Rose - Mary Jo Putney   r   401

Leckner, Elsie
The Royalscope Fe-As-Ko - Randall Beth Platt   w   585

Rowland, Althea
Timeshare - Joshua Dann   s   1074

Ruthven, Lucy
Slave of My Thirst - Tom Holland   h   915

Stanislaus, Jerelynn
Mind Snare - Gayle Greeno   s   1118

Taylor, Marian
Lockhart's Nightmare - Wayne Barton   w   449

ADDICT

Chen, Harry
The Seraphim Rising - Elisabeth De Vos   s   1076

Karpov, Sapphire
Putting Up Roots - Charles Sheffield   s   1203

Mancini, Munch
No Human Involved - Barbara Seranella   m   211

Zwakh, Ignatz
Dead Things - Richard Calder   s   1059

ADMINISTRATOR

Goldin, Netta
Alien Influences - Kristine Kathryn Rusch   s   1186

Hunter, Nicole "Panther"
Ignition - Kevin J. Anderson   s   1033

Jahns, Carter
Mars Underground - William Hartmann   s   1126

501

Nukurren
Mother of Demons - Eric Flint   *s*   1096

Soleta
End Game - Peter David   *s*   1075

Spock
Avenger - William Shatner   *s*   1198
Mind Meld - John Vornholt   *s*   1229
Vulcan's Forge - Susan Shwartz   *s*   1206

sud Sarc, Barac
A Thousand Words for Stranger - Julie E.
   Czerneda   *s*   1072

Teska
Mind Meld - John Vornholt   *s*   1229

Thissizz
The Merro Tree - Katie Waitman   *s*   1230

Tooe
Derelict for Trade - Andre Norton   *s*   1170
A Mind for Trade - Andre Norton   *s*   1171

Torres, B'Elanna
Her Klingon Soul - Michael Jan Friedman   *s*   1104

Trinidad
Beneath the Gated Sky - Robert Reed   *s*   1181

Worf
Armageddon Sky - L.A. Graf   *s*   1113

Zainal
Freedom's Choice - Anne McCaffrey   *s*   1154

Zeerus
Target Earth - Steve Perry   *s*   1175

AMNESIAC

di Sarc, Sira
A Thousand Words for Stranger - Julie E.
   Czerneda   *s*   1072

ANDROID

Data
Intellivore - Diane Duane   *s*   1085

Lipstick
Dead Things - Richard Calder   *s*   1059

ANGEL

Brown, Hilary
Almost an Angel - Deb Stover   *r*   430

Ezekiel "Zeke"
The Seraphim Rising - Elisabeth De Vos   *s*   1076

Jiminez, Angelita Carmen
Angels Unaware - L. Elizabeth Storm   *s*   1215

Mithra
Ancient Games - Scott Ciencin   *f*   669

Phaeton
Planar Powers - J. Robert King   *f*   739

West, Joshua
Heaven in West Texas - Susan Kay Law   *r*   362

ANIMAL

Angel
Dancing on Air - Nancy Kress   *s*   1140

Beast
Rose Daughter - Robin McKinley   *f*   761

Bottlenose
Starplex - Robert J. Sawyer   *s*   1195

Calef
Hungry for Home: A Wolf Odyssey - 'Asta
   Bowen   *f*   654

Coyote
Coyote and the Fire Stick - Barbara Diamond
   Goldin   *w*   524

Dulcie
Cats Raise the Dead - Shirley Rousseau
   Murphy   *f*   769

Elk
The Miser on the Mountain - Nancy Luenn   *w*   563

Grey, Joe
Cats Raise the Dead - Shirley Rousseau
   Murphy   *f*   769

Herb
The Arbitrary Placement of Walls - Martha
   Soukup   *f*   797

Imbri, Mare
Faun & Games - Piers Anthony   *f*   642

Ishmael
My Ishmael - Daniel Quinn   *s*   1180

Jess
Changespell - Doranna Durgin   *f*   695

Marta
Hungry for Home: A Wolf Odyssey - 'Asta
   Bowen   *f*   654

Midnight Louie
Cat in a Flamingo Fedora - Carole Nelson
   Douglas   *m*   67

Nighteyes
Assassin's Quest - Robin Hobb   *f*   722

Oldtooth
Hungry for Home: A Wolf Odyssey - 'Asta
   Bowen   *f*   654

Peeve
Red Unicorn - Tanith Lee   *f*   747

Rabbit
Coyote and the Fire Stick - Barbara Diamond
   Goldin   *w*   524

Rhiow
The Book of Night with Moon - Diane Duane   *f*   692

Roselle
Sunshine Rider - Ric Lynden Hardman   *w*   529

Saash
The Book of Night with Moon - Diane Duane   *f*   692

Tansy
The Pearls of Lutra - Brian Jacques   *f*   728

Tualha
A Wizard Abroad - Diane Duane   *f*   693

Ublaz Mad Eyes
The Pearls of Lutra - Brian Jacques   *f*   728

Urruah
The Book of Night with Moon - Diane Duane   *f*   692

Viola
The Pearls of Lutra - Brian Jacques   *f*   728

ANIMAL TRAINER

Siddon, Jo Beth
A Brace of Bloodhounds - Virginia Lanier   *m*   143

Travis, Melanie
Hair of the Dog - Laurien Berenson   *m*   17

Weser, Erich "Erich Alois"
Children of the Dusk - Janet Berliner   *f*   652

Winter, Holly
Animal Appetite - Susan Conant   *m*   41

ANTHROPOLOGIST

Green, Margo
Reliquary - Douglas Preston   *h*   979

Oliver, Gideon
Twenty Blue Devils - Aaron Elkins   *m*   74

Sheridan, Anna
The Shadow Within - Jeanne Cavelos   *s*   1062

Silver, Rob
The Presence - John Saul   *h*   991

Spring, Penny
The Midas Murders - Margot Arnold   *m*   6

Sundquist, Katherine
The Presence - John Saul   *h*   991

Tomochelor, Pulickel
The Howling Stones - Alan Dean Foster   *s*   1101

ANTIQUARIAN

Russell, Joanna
Key to Forever - Christina Skye   *r*   425

ANTIQUES DEALER

Maughan, Daisy
Mennyms Alive - Sylvia Waugh   *f*   811

APOTHECARY

Chinnery, Thomas
Bijapur - Kara Dalkey   *f*   680

APPRENTICE

Alec of Kerry
Stalking Darkness - Lynn Flewelling   *f*   705

Arista, Tommaso
The Stars Dispose - Michaela Roessner   *f*   786

Byron
Cardmaster - Clayton Emery   *f*   700

Darian
Owlflight - Mercedes Lackey   *f*   743

Delroy, Lylene
The Conjurer Princess - Vivian Vande Velde   *f*   807

Flattery, Erasmus
Beneath the Vaulted Hills - Sean Russell   *f*   788

Gemcutter, Jena
Emerald House Rising - Peg Kerr   *f*   736

Kim
Magician's Ward - Patricia C. Wrede   *f*   819

Lina
Interface Masque - Shariann Lewitt   *s*   1143

Sept-Fortune, Cecilie 8
Interface Masque - Shariann Lewitt   *s*   1143

Tooe
A Mind for Trade - Andre Norton   *s*   1171

ARCHAEOLOGIST

Branfield, Anastasia
Hellboy: The Lost Army - Christopher
   Golden   *h*   897

Carlisle, Desdemona
As You Desire - Connie Brockway   *r*   268

Cook, Jay
Time Blender - Michael Dorn   *s*   1081

Emerson, Amelia Peabody
Seeing a Large Cat - Elizabeth Peters   *m*   186

Emerson, Radcliffe
Seeing a Large Cat - Elizabeth Peters   *m*   186

Glendower, Toby
The Midas Murders - Margot Arnold   *m*   6

Miller, Tony
Time Blender - Michael Dorn   s   1081

Van Zandt, Peter
The Stone Circle - Gary Goshgarian   h   898

ARCHITECT

Ashton, Michael
Ask Mariah - Barbara Freethy   r   308

Fitzgerald, Mike
Remember the Time - Annette A. Reynolds   r   406

Newcastle, Damian
Buttons and Beaus - Margaret Brownley   r   271

Rockman, John
Wooing Wanda - Gwen Pemberton   r   396

ARTIFICIAL INTELLIGENCE

Aryadyss
Donnerjack - Roger Zelazny   s   1244

Bolt
The Last Hawk - Catherine Asaro   s   1038

Chip
A King of Infinite Space - Allen Steele   s   1212

Death
Donnerjack - Roger Zelazny   s   1244

Halman
3001: The Final Odyssey - Arthur C.
   Clarke   s   1067

Hawthorn "D-base"
Cinderblock - Janine Ellen Young   s   1243

Jill
/ - Greg Bear   s   1049

Mom
Exit to Reality - Edith Forbes   s   1098

Ratio
The White Abacus - Damien Broderick   s   1056

Setebos
A Game of Universe - Eric S. Nylund   f   774

Sleeper Service
Excession - Iain M. Banks   s   1041

Yoseph
Terminal Logic - Jefferson Scott   s   1196

ARTISAN

Cameron, Alexei
Key to Forever - Christina Skye   r   425

George
Thessalonica - Harry Turtledove   f   805

Jorana
The Howling Stones - Alan Dean Foster   s   1101

Malledd
Touched by the Gods - Lawrence Watt-Evans   f   810

Trader, Max
Trader - Charles de Lint   f   685

ARTIST

Adolphus, Max
Prairie - Greg Tobin   w   616

Armon
The Forgetting Room - Nick Bantock   f   647

Blervaque, Rose
Living Real - James C. Bassett   s   1046

Catlin, George
A Portrait of Spotted Deer's Grandfather - Amy
   Littlesugar   w   561

Curzon, Harrison
Isabella's Rake - June Calvin   r   274

Dietz, Tre
Freeware - Rudy Rucker   s   1184

Eardley, Isabella
Isabella's Rake - June Calvin   r   274

Jackson, Esther
Nighthawk - Rachel Lee   r   364

Jackson, Jocelyn
Water Rites - Guy N. Smith   h   1001

Kaminski, Tiffany Jeanine "T.J."
Steel Rose - Kara Dalkey   f   681

Katsuleris, Aubrey
The Broken Sword - Molly Cochran   f   673

Keeper, Tom
Ancient Games - Scott Ciencin   f   669

MacLeish, Elinor
Dream a Little Dream - Antoinette
   Stockenberg   r   429

Manning, Rowena Pearce
Writ in Blood - Chelsea Quinn Yarbro   h   1031

Monet, Claude
Monet's Ghost - Chelsea Quinn Yarbro   f   824

Preston, Selina
The Rakehell's Reform - Elisabeth Fairchild   r   302

Rafael
The Forgetting Room - Nick Bantock   f   647

Sivart, Gil
The Digital Effect - Steve Perry   s   1173

Stark, Edgar
Asylum - Patrick McGrath   h   962

Sterling, Justin
Testament of the Dragon - Margaret Weis   f   813

Sutherland, Laura
Finding Laura - Kay Hooper   r   329

Tallchief, Morgan
Tallchief - Dinah McCall   r   376

Tremayne, Emma
The Passions of Emma - Penelope
   Williamson   r   438

Woodville, William
If You Love Me - Elaine Coffman   r   283

ASSISTANT

Proctor, Jeremy
Person or Persons Unknown - Bruce
   Alexander   m   3

Taggert, Stevie
The Angel of Darkness - Caleb Carr   m   33

ASTRONAUT

Benacerraf, Paula
Titan - Stephen Baxter   s   1047

Friese, Adam "Iceberg"
Ignition - Kevin J. Anderson   s   1033

Gershon, Ralph
Voyager - Stephen Baxter   s   1048

Hunter, Nicole "Panther"
Ignition - Kevin J. Anderson   s   1033

Jiang Ling
Titan - Stephen Baxter   s   1047

Poole, Frank
3001: The Final Odyssey - Arthur C.
   Clarke   s   1067

AVENGER

Allard, Frank
Mountains against the Sun - Perry Holmes   w   541

Bodine, Rafe
Desperate - Millie Criswell   r   291

Brandt, Halley
Pure Justice - Suzann Ledbetter   w   559

Burke, Andrew
Across the Rio Colorado - Ralph Compton   w   491

Colt, Charlotte "Charley"
Matched Colts - Don Bendell   w   457

de Bastitas, Rafael
Jezebel - Katherine Sutcliffe   w   609

Fane, Nessa
While the Rivers Run - Wynema McGowan   w   571

Gersen, Kirth
The Demon Princes: Volume One - Jack
   Vance   s   1225
The Demon Princes: Volume Two - Jack
   Vance   s   1226

K'os
Song of the River - Sue Harrison   f   717

Porter, Holly
The River at Sundown - Earl Murray   w   576

Stone, Nathan
The Autumn of the Gun - Ralph Compton   w   492
The Killing Season - Ralph Compton   w   494

Stone, Wes
The Border Empire - Ralph Compton   w   493

BACHELOR

Burfield
The Deception - Marion Chesney   r   280

Choate, Courtney
Snowdrops and Scandalbroth - Barbara
   Metzger   r   378

Galloway, Isaac
Prairie Rose - Susan Kirby   r   349

Madog, Jay "Mad Dog"
Promised Land - Connie Willis   s   1238

BAIL BONDSMAN

Floyd, CJ
The Devil's Red Nickel - Robert Greer   m   101

BAKER

Phan, Gi Minh
Ticktock - Dean R. Koontz   h   936

BANDIT

Fallon, Tom
Bandido Caballero - Jack Ballas   w   445

BANKER

Gersen, Kirth
The Demon Princes: Volume Two - Jack
   Vance   s   1226

Grange, Karen
A Dry Spell - Susan Moloney   h   965

Thatcher, John Putnam
A Shark Out of Water - Emma Lathen   m   145

BARTENDER

Big John "BJ"
When Wolves Cry - Chris N. Africa *h* 830

Clough, Emma
Famine - Todd Komarnicki *h* 934

Rowan, Daniel
Famine - Todd Komarnicki *h* 934

BASTARD DAUGHTER

Kaeler, Lanen
Song in the Silence - Elizabeth Kerner *f* 734

BASTARD SON

Alain
King's Dragon - Kate Elliott *f* 698

Arthor
The Eagle and the Sword - A.A. Attanasio *f* 645

Blaylock, Nathan
The Wolf's Cub - Richard Parry *w* 583

Farseer, FitzChivalry "Tom"
Assassin's Quest - Robin Hobb *f* 722

Thornton, Ivan
Dangerous to Love - Rexanne Becnel *r* 258

Tremayne, Wes
The Autumn of the Gun - Ralph Compton *w* 492

BOARDER

Vladislov, Pete
Klondike Fever - Suzann Ledbetter *w* 558

BODYGUARD

Bering
The Dog King - Christoph Ransmayr *f* 784

Granger, Cole
Triumph of the Mountain Man - William W. Johnstone *w* 547

Hunter, Jake
Incognito - Francis Ray *r* 405

Keylan, Brynda al
Broken Blade - Ann Marston *f* 754

McCall, Ian
Season of Wishes - Christina Skye *r* 426

Strang, Mark
Patton's Spaceship - John Barnes *s* 1043

BOUNTY HUNTER

Horn, Tom
Range Wars - Robert Vaughan *w* 625

Kolby, Cade
The Courtship of Cade Kolby - Lori Copeland *r* 287

McCannon, Quint
Dust on the Wind - Bill Brooks *w* 474

Plum, Stephanie
Three to Get Deadly - Janet Evanovich *m* 80

BRIDE

Ashbrooke, Catherine Augustine
The Pride of Lions - Marsha Canham *r* 276

McKinnon, Margery "Walks Fast"
If You Love Me - Elaine Coffman *r* 283

Rubra, Rose
Waking Beauty - Paul Witcover *f* 818

Saunders St. Gregory, Megan
Knights - Linda Lael Miller *r* 380

BUSINESSMAN

Avery, Rupert "Roo"
Rage of a Demon King - Raymond E. Feist *f* 703

Balthazar, Timothy
Wolf Moon - John R. Holt *h* 916

Barnett, Pierce
The Firebrand - Laurel Collins *r* 285

Bell, John
The Bell Witch - Brent Monahan *h* 966

Binder, Columbus
Flying Saucers over Hennepin - Peter Gelman *f* 708

Calvert, Joshua
Emergence - Peter F. Hamilton *s* 1120

Chastain, Nick
Zinnia - Jayne Castle *r* 277

Chauvin, Rene
The Gris-Gris Man - Don Davis *h* 867

Chicago, Pasquale
A King of Infinite Space - Allen Steele *s* 1212

Cooper, Harry
Night of the Living Dead - John A. Russo *h* 987

Crane, Peter
Hunting the Corrigan's Blood - Holly Lisle *s* 1145

Dalton, Edmund
Winter Tides - James P. Blaylock *h* 842

Endine, Flojian
Eternity Road - Jack McDevitt *s* 1155

Hawkins, Ben
The Wagon Wars - James A. Ritchie *w* 595

Hollister, Jake
The Paradise Man - Suzanne Simmons *r* 421

Hook, Rufus
Across the Rio Colorado - Ralph Compton *w* 491

ibn-Rushd, Damon
Destiny's Road - Larry Niven *s* 1167

Jameson, Charles
Between Floors - Thomas F. Monteleone *h* 967

Kilbourne, Daniel
Finding Laura - Kay Hooper *r* 329

LaVine, Martin
When Shadows Fall - Brian Scott Smith *h* 998

Lockhart, James
Lockhart's Nightmare - Wayne Barton *w* 449

London, Stefan
Ragged Angels - Della Van Hise *h* 1017

Madog, Jay "Mad Dog"
Promised Land - Connie Willis *s* 1238

Mallory, Jake
Amber Beach - Elizabeth Lowell *r* 367

Marino, Max
Seasons - Rebecca Forster *r* 306

Markley, Alan
Between Floors - Thomas F. Monteleone *h* 967

Marris, Steve
This Matter of Marriage - Debbie Macomber *r* 370

Mayhew, Richard
Neverwhere - Neil Gaiman *f* 707

McCandles, Chase
Promise Me Tomorrow - Lori Wick *w* 631

Miller, Martin
The Darker Passions: Carmilla - Amarantha Knight *h* 933

Minakis, Manolis
Secret Passages - Paul Preuss *s* 1178

Mitchell, Richard
Buddha Kiss - Peter Tasker *m* 223

Murphy, P.G.
The Wagon Wars - James A. Ritchie *w* 595

Nix, Luke
Dogland - Will Shetterly *f* 794

Quinn, Dave
Winter Tides - James P. Blaylock *h* 842

Reo, Sam
The Eye of the Hawk - P.A. Bechko *w* 455

Rhodenbarr, Bernie
The Burglar in the Library - Lawrence Block *m* 20

Rose, Mick "China"
Signs of Life - M. John Harrison *s* 1125

Satterlee, Clifton
Triumph of the Mountain Man - William W. Johnstone *w* 547

Smith, Joseph
To Marry a British Lord - Judith O'Brien *r* 391

Stuart, Kyle
Long Southern Nights - Heather MacAllister *r* 368

Taggart, Luke
Simply Love - Catherine Anderson *r* 249

Thornton, Gage
Petals on the River - Kathleen Woodiwiss *r* 441

Trader, Max
Trader - Charles de Lint *f* 685

von Wolgast, Klemens Manfred
Writ in Blood - Chelsea Quinn Yarbro *h* 1031

BUSINESSWOMAN

Al Shei, Katmer
Fool's War - Sarah Zettel *s* 1245

Bayles, China
Love Lies Bleeding - Susan Wittig Albert *m* 2

Bradshaw, Zoe
The Courtship of Cade Kolby - Lori Copeland *r* 287

Brennan, Sarah
Jonathan's Wife - Dee Holmes *r* 328

Burr, Rona
The Eye of the Hawk - P.A. Bechko *w* 455

Cortland, Erin
Incognito - Francis Ray *r* 405

Donovan, Honor
Amber Beach - Elizabeth Lowell *r* 367

Dyer, Mandy
Hung Up to Die - Dolores Johnson *m* 133

Garrity, Julia Callahan
Strange Brew - Kathy Hogan Trocheck *m* 229

Hazelhof, Cornelia
Timeshare - Joshua Dann *s* 1074

Hoare, Dido
Death's Autograph - Marianne Macdonald *m* 150

H'sial, Atvar
Convergence - Charles Sheffield *s* 1202

Jasper, Kate
A Cry for Self-Help - Jacqueline Girdner *m* 99

Jones, Caroline Fremont
The Bohemian Murders - Dianne Day *m* 57

507

Faison, Genevieva
Corrupting Dr. Nice - John Kessel   s   1137

Hassard, Dee
Dead Reckoning - Mike Blakely   w   461

Hennison, Doc
The Wolf's Cub - Richard Parry   w   583

Jackson, Wylie
Sunshine Rider - Ric Lynden Hardman   w   529

Taylor, Marian
Lockhart's Nightmare - Wayne Barton   w   449

Throtmanian, Paul Donald
Lifehouse - Spider Robinson   s   1183

CONSTRUCTION WORKER

Hake, Denton
Out of Body - Thomas Baum   h   836

CONSULTANT

Bois, Jules
The Dark - Andrew Neiderman   h   971

Dun, Richard
Keeper of the King - Nigel Bennett   h   838

Fitzgerald, Mike
Remember the Time - Annette A. Reynolds   r   406

Jefferson, Maggie
Long Southern Nights - Heather MacAllister   r   368

Winters, Elias
Deep Waters - Jayne Ann Krentz   r   353

CONTRACTOR

Deal, John
Deal on Ice - Les Standiford   m   218

Martin, Sam
Pillow Talk - Kristine Rolofson   r   416

McGuire, Bill
The Blackstone Chronicles - John Saul   h   990

CONVICT

Goodwin, Willie
I Rode with Jesse James - Charles
   Hackenberry   w   527

Kearney, Tim
The Death and Life of Bobby Z - Don
   Winslow   m   241

O'Byrne, Rian
Wild Irish Skies - Nancy Richards-Akers   r   410

COOK

Bloocher, Jemmy "Tim Hann"
Destiny's Road - Larry Niven   s   1167

Didier, Auguste
Murder in the Smokehouse - Amy Myers   m   174

Lee, Heaven
A Stiff Risotto - Lou Jane Temple   m   224

Quilliam, Meg
Death Dines Out - Claudia Bishop   m   18

Whittaker, Josephine
Forget Me Not - Stef Ann Holm   w   540

COUNSELOR

Nevyn
The Red Wyvern - Katharine Kerr   f   735

COURIER

Carey
Changespell - Doranna Durgin   f   695

Liath
King's Dragon - Kate Elliott   f   698

COUSIN

Jones, Fanning "Fan"
Dreaming Metal - Melissa Scott   s   1197

COWBOY

Bannon, Tyrel
Dark Trail to Dodge - Cotton Smith   w   605

Beaumont, Gabe
Tame the Wild Wind - Rosanne Bittner   w   458

Belissari, Pete
The Courtship of Hannah and the Horseman - Johnny
   D. Boggs   w   464

Cameron, Andrew "Drew"
The Scotsman Wore Spurs - Patricia Potter   r   399

Colby, Jake
Range Wars - Robert Vaughan   w   625

Cookie
The Thirteenth Daughter of the Moon - Steven
   Nightingale   f   771

Granger, Cole
High Prairie - Hiram King   w   553

Hamilton, Ira
Dust Devils - Robert Laxalt   w   556

Hawkins, Ben
The Wagon Wars - James A. Ritchie   w   595

Leigh, Houston
Texas Destiny - Lorraine Heath   r   322

Morrow, Ethan
Sweeter than Wine - Stephanie Mittman   r   382

Parker, Maris Gabrielle "Gabe"
The Scotsman Wore Spurs - Patricia Potter   r   399

Sanders, Ty
The Promise of Jenny Jones - Maggie
   Osborne   r   393

Smith, Concho
Devil's Rim - Sam Brown   w   475

Sommers, Henry
Wild Rose of Ruby Canyon - John D.
   Nesbitt   w   577

Wade, Cody
Hell's Half Acre - Frederic Bean   w   452

CRIME SUSPECT

High Fox
People of the Mist - Kathleen O'Neal Gear   w   522

CRIME VICTIM

Red Knot
People of the Mist - Kathleen O'Neal Gear   w   522

CRIMINAL

Arabella "Infectress"
Infectress - Tom Cool   s   1069

Asperson, Arhos
Once a Hero - Elizabeth Moon   s   1160

Booth, John Wilkes
Booth - David Robertson   w   597

Calderon, Webb
Innocence - Suzanne Forster   r   307

Carter, John
Return of the Living Dead - John A. Russo   h   988

Chambers, Phoebe
The Misconceiver - Lucy Ferriss   s   1095

Faracon, George
Time Station Paris - David Evans   s   1093

Fuller, Samuel
Down on Ponce - Fred Willard   m   239

Germain
A Game of Universe - Eric S. Nylund   f   774

Hayes, Roy
The Cellar - Richard Laymon   h   942

Ingalls, Sam
Rattlesnake Mesa - Peter Dawson   w   508

Kearney, Tim
The Death and Life of Bobby Z - Don
   Winslow   m   241

Long John Silver
Celestial Dogs - J.S. Russell   h   986

Marchenko, Ivan "Burian Klimus"
Frameshift - Robert J. Sawyer   s   1193

Max, Ziggy
Virgin Heat - Laurence Shames   m   212

Milligan, Turk
One Last Town - Matt Braun   w   472

Morai
Talion: Revenant - Michael A. Stackpole   f   799

Murdock, Jacob
Honor of the Mountain Man - William W.
   Johnstone   w   546

Orogastus
Sky Trillium - Julian May   f   756

Quilp
A Game of Universe - Eric S. Nylund   f   774

Rahl, Drefan
Temple of the Winds - Terry Goodkind   f   710

Reo, Sam
The Eye of the Hawk - P.A. Bechko   w   455

Satterlee, Clifton
Triumph of the Mountain Man - William W.
   Johnstone   w   547

Surratt, John
Booth - David Robertson   w   597

Thomson, Cort
The Gamblers - Matt Braun   w   471

Vizuelos, Ramon
Meeting the Minotaur - Carol Dawson   f   684

Zeerus
Target Earth - Steve Perry   s   1175

CRIMINOLOGIST

Rhyme, Lincoln
The Bone Collector - Jeffery Deaver   m   58

CRITIC

Malory, Sheila
Mrs. Malory and the Only Good Lawyer - Hazel
   Holt   m   123

CYBORG

Guthrie, Anson
The Fleet of Stars - Poul Anderson   s   1034

Friedman, Kinky
Road Kill - Kinky Friedman m 87

Garrity, Julia Callahan
Strange Brew - Kathy Hogan Trocheck m 229

Gennaro, Angela
Sacred - Dennis Lehane m 147

Glibspet
Hell on High - Holly Lisle f 751

Gomez, Sid
Tek Net - William Shatner s 1200

Gordianus the Finder
The House of the Vestals - Steven Saylor m 209

Greenstreet, Horace
Eye of the Agency - Richard Moquist m 170

Guzman, Henry
The Whipsaw Trail - Ray Hogan w 538

Hastings, Stanley
Scam - Parnell Hall m 108

Holmes, Sherlock
Deadly Season - Tim Champlin w 480
A Letter of Mary - Laurie R. King m 141

Howard, Jeri
Witness to Evil - Janet Dawson m 56

Jacovich, Milan
Cleveland Local - Les Roberts m 201

Kenzie, Patrick
Sacred - Dennis Lehane m 147

Lavine, Rosalynd "Rosie"
Cold Iron - Melisa Michaels f 762

Massey, Phillip
The Ivory Duchess - Delia Parr r 395

McCone, Sharon
Both Ends of the Night - Marcia Muller m 173

McGraw, Jay
Deadly Season - Tim Champlin w 480

Monaghan, Tess
Charm City - Laura Lippman m 149

Mori, Kazuo
Buddha Kiss - Peter Tasker m 223

Navarre, Jackson "Tres"
Big Red Tequila - Rick Riordan m 199

Nelson, Vicki
Blood Debt - Tanya Huff h 919

Reid, Savannah
Killer Calories - G.A. McKevett m 165

Rhodes, Emma
Impolite Society - Cynthia Smith m 215

Russell, Mary
A Letter of Mary - Laurie R. King m 141

Scudder, Matthew
Even the Wicked - Lawrence Block m 21

Shapiro, Desiree
Murder Can Wreck Your Reunion - Selma Eichler m 73

Shugak, Kate
Breakup - Dana Stabenow m 217

Smith, Bill
No Colder Place - S.J. Rozan m 206

Solano, Lupe
Bloody Shame - Carolina Garcia-Aguilera m 91

Spenser
Small Vices - Robert B. Parker m 182

Tanner, John Marshall
Past Tense - Stephen Greenleaf m 100

Taylor, Holland
Practice to Deceive - David Housewright m 127

Tyner, Sally
No Remorse - James D. Brewer m 26

Walker, Amos
Never Street - Loren D. Estleman m 79

Waterman, Leo
The Bum's Rush - G.M. Ford m 84

Williamson, Luke
No Remorse - James D. Brewer m 26

Wine, Moses
The Lost Coast: A Moses Wine Mystery - Roger L. Simon m 213

Younger, Cecil
Death and the Language of Happiness - John Straley m 220

DIPLOMAT

Enfandin, Rene
Bring the Jubilee - Ward Moore s 1162

Genar-Hofoen, Byr
Excession - Iain M. Banks s 1041

Sokol
Legacy of the Ancients - Ron Sarti s 1192

Spock
Avenger - William Shatner s 1198

Sverayov, Nicholas
Splendor - Brenda Joyce r 343

DIRECTOR

Delamitri, Bruce
Popcorn - Ben Elton m 76

Grandby, Quentin
Heaven Loves a Hero - Nikki Holiday r 326

DISEMBODIED PERSONALITY

Brand, Matthew Tyler
The Hot-Wired Dodo - Jack L. Chalker s 1064

C
Someone to Watch over Me - Tricia Sullivan s 1218

Ingman, Robert "Shade"
Shade's Children - Garth Nix s 1168

DIVORCED PERSON

Caraval, Estela
Spirits of the Ordinary - Kathleen Alcala f 638

Devane, Kate
Caught - Rachel Lee r 363

Marris, Steve
This Matter of Marriage - Debbie Macomber r 370

Morgan, Patsy
A Family Wedding - Angela Benson r 259

Potter, Sharon
Sharon's Hope - Nina Coyle r 289

Tate, Caline "Cally"
Beside a Dreamswept Sea - Victoria Barrett r 256

Williams, Terry
The Poison Tree - Tony Strong m 221

DOCTOR

Ayrlyn
The Chaos Balance - L.E. Modesitt Jr. f 764

Bashir, Julian
Armageddon Sky - L.A. Graf s 1113

Black, Sara
The Healer's Road - J.L. Reasoner w 590

Black, Thomas
The Healer's Road - J.L. Reasoner w 590

Blade, Gwendolyn
The MacGregor Brides - Nora Roberts r 415

Bladestone, Hugh
Fortress on the Sun - Paul Cook s 1068

Blaine, Grant
The Dark - Andrew Neiderman h 971

Broussard, Andy
Sleeping with the Crawfish - D.J. Donaldson m 65

Burrows
The Hill of Dreams - Arthur Machen h 954

Burtonall, Clare
Different Women Dancing - Jonathan Gash m 92

Canches, Alejandro
The Plague Tales - Ann Benson s 1051

Cleave, Peter
Asylum - Patrick McGrath h 962

Croaker
She Is the Darkness - Glen Cook f 676

Cross, Jonathan
Lorena - Frederic Bean w 453

Crowe, Janie
The Plague Tales - Ann Benson s 1051

Crusher, Beverly
Intellivore - Diane Duane s 1085

Denby, Kate
Long After Midnight - Iris Johansen r 335

Dvorak, Daniel
Life Support - Tess Gerritsen h 894

Elaira
Fugitive Prince - Janny Wurts f 822

Eliot, John
Slave of My Thirst - Tom Holland h 915

Ellis, John
The Dealings of Daniel Kesserich - Fritz Leiber s 1141

Ford, Marcus
Omega - Patrick Lynch h 953

Fuller, Gray
Angel Face and Amazing Grace - Lori Copeland r 286

Harper, Toby
Life Support - Tess Gerritsen h 894

Hrluska, Jenn
Daughter of Darkness - Steven Spruill h 1004

Jackson, Wylie
Sunshine Rider - Ric Lynden Hardman w 529

Keating, Michael
Night of Broken Souls - Thomas F. Monteleone h 968

Knight, Jeffrey
Fever Rising - Maggie Ferguson r 305

Kreizler, Laszlo
The Angel of Darkness - Caleb Carr m 33

Lambert, Natalie
Forever Knight: A Stirring of Dust - Susan Sizemore h 995
Forever Knight: Intimations of Mortality - Susan M. Garrett h 887

Lambert, Tom
Tomorrow and Tomorrow - Charles Sheffield s 1204

MacAuley, Boyd
Daddy by Accident - Paula Detmer Riggs r 412

DRIFTER

MacKenzie, Alex
The Garden Plot - J.S. Borthwick   *m*   22

McCoy, Leonard
Vulcan's Forge - Susan Shwartz   *s*   1206

Medalont
Final Diagnosis - James White   *s*   1233

Moses, Libby
Echoes of Issel - Diann Thornley   *s*   1222

Mussina, Isabella
Night of Broken Souls - Thomas F.
Monteleone   *h*   968

Patou, Lucy
Omega - Patrick Lynch   *h*   953

Purdoe, Tim
The Great Wheel - Ian R. MacLeod   *s*   1148

Roanhorse, Carolyn
Bad Medicine - Aimee Thurlo   *m*   226

Scarpetta, Kay
Unnatural Exposure - Patricia Cornwell   *m*   43

Silverthorne, Tal
Silverthorne - Wayne Davis   *w*   507

Wahler, Jukes
Shade of Pale - Greg Kihn   *h*   929

Wallenberg, Carl
Life Support - Tess Gerritsen   *h*   894

Webb, Fiona
Website - Ray Garton   *h*   890

Wren, Mason
Alien Resurrection - A.C. Crispin   *s*   1071

DRIFTER

Barrington, Nathanial
Devil Dance - Frank Burleson   *w*   477

Faith, John
A Wasteland of Strangers - Bill Pronzini   *m*   190

Hogan, Stan
Symphony - Charles L. Grant   *h*   899

Morgan, Grant
Giovanni's Gift - Bradford Morrow   *m*   171

Reacher, Jack
Killing Floor - Lee Child   *m*   35

Wolf
Warrior's Song - Janis Reams Hudson   *r*   331

DRIVER

Nygerski, Cyrus "Moondog"
Room 13 - Henry Garfield   *h*   886

DRUG DEALER

Nirobus
My Son, the Wizard - Christopher Stasheff   *f*   800

EDITOR

Flint, Sam
Flint's Gift - Richard S. Wheeler   *w*   628

Larsen, Alexandra
The Gris-Gris Man - Don Davis   *h*   867

Metcalf, Oliver
The Blackstone Chronicles - John Saul   *h*   990

Owen, Davey
Live Girls - Ray Garton   *h*   888

Rick
God's Dice - S. Andrew Swann   *f*   804

Sinclair, Hal
Snowflake Wishes - Lydia Browne   *r*   270

ENGINEER

Al Shei, Katmer
Fool's War - Sarah Zettel   *s*   1245

Augustus, Caleb
Jovah's Angel - Sharon Shinn   *s*   1205

Daniels, Casey
Cripple Creek - Douglas Hirt   *w*   534

Halloran, Jack
Hell on High - Holly Lisle   *f*   751

Jahns, Carter
Mars Underground - William Hartmann   *s*   1126

kai Ortega, Maeru "Kai"
Alpha Centauri - William Barton   *s*   1045

McCullogh, Maddie
One of These Nights - Susan Sizemore   *r*   423

Nylan
The Chaos Balance - L.E. Modesitt Jr.   *f*   764

Ryan, Zach
Almost an Angel - Deb Stover   *r*   430

Torres, B'Elanna
Her Klingon Soul - Michael Jan Friedman   *s*   1104

ENTERTAINER

Blackfoot Bill
I Rode with Jesse James - Charles
Hackenberry   *w*   527

Kateralbin, Crispin
The War in the Waste - Felicity Savage   *f*   790

Kayrlis
Ancient Games - Scott Ciencin   *f*   669

Oakley, Annie
Shooting Star - Debbie Dadey   *w*   504

Rylus
When the Gods Are Silent - Jane M.
Lindskold   *f*   750

EQUESTRIAN

Brinsby, Ophelia
A Prince Among Men - Kate Moore   *r*   384

Saunders, Gail
The Arrangement - Joan Wolf   *r*   439

EXPERIMENTAL SUBJECT

Matalon, Cynthia
The Hot-Wired Dodo - Jack L. Chalker   *s*   1064

Reyes, Adrien
Someone to Watch over Me - Tricia
Sullivan   *s*   1218

EXPLORER

Anthea
I Who Have Never Known Men - Jacqueline
Harpman   *s*   1124

Burton, Richard
The Rock Child - Win Blevins   *w*   462

Clark, William
How We Crossed the West - Rosalyn
Schanzer   *w*   602

Fremont, John Charles
Meridian: A Novel of Kit Carson's West - Norman
Zollinger   *w*   636

Greta
I Who Have Never Known Men - Jacqueline
Harpman   *s*   1124

I
I Who Have Never Known Men - Jacqueline
Harpman   *s*   1124

Lewis, Meriwether
How We Crossed the West - Rosalyn
Schanzer   *w*   602
Sacagawea - Judith St. George   *w*   608

Stafford, Alwyn Bryan
Mars Underground - William Hartmann   *s*   1126

FANATIC

Cayne, Candy
Cold Iron - Melisa Michaels   *f*   762

FARMER

Beaudry, Eliza
The Way Home - Megan Chance   *r*   279

Bjorklund, Haakan
A Land to Call Home - Lauraine Snelling   *w*   606

Brown, John
Cloudsplitter - Russell Banks   *w*   447

Coll, Lorand
Competition - Sharon Green   *f*   712

Crane, Abner
The Hunted - James Reasoner   *w*   591

Eddy, Pearl
All God's Children - Tom Eidson   *w*   515

Galloway, Ike
When Lilacs Bloom - Susan Kirby   *r*   350

Greene, Cathy
The Taking - Donald Beman   *h*   837

Hopkins, Marabelle
The Peacekeeper - Jeffrey Poston   *w*   586

Hulhe
When the Gods Are Silent - Jane M.
Lindskold   *f*   750

Morrow, Ethan
Sweeter than Wine - Stephanie Mittman   *r*   382

Roo, Luger
*The Case of the Police Officer's Cock Ring and the
Piano Player Who Had No Fingers* - Edward
Lee   *h*   944

Sadler, Cole
Savage Plains - David William Ross   *w*   601

Sadler, Dennis
Savage Plains - David William Ross   *w*   601

Senatra, Nathan
American Dreamer - Theresa Weir   *r*   435

Tanner, Tarleton "Sonny"
Promised Land - Connie Willis   *s*   1238

Vikstrom, Borg
Break the Young Land - T.V. Olsen   *w*   578

Wallace, Aaron
The Way Home - Megan Chance   *r*   279

Williamson, Spencer
The Marriage Bed - Stephanie Mittman   *r*   381

FBI AGENT

Black, Frank
Millennium: Gehenna - Lewis Gannett   *h*   884
Millennium: The Frenchman - Elizabeth
Hand   *h*   908

Clah, Ella
Bad Medicine - Aimee Thurlo   m   226

Jamison, Diane
Infectress - Tom Cool   s   1069

McGruder, Jim
Bright Shadow - Elizabeth Forrest   h   883

Mulder, Fox
Antibodies - Kevin J. Anderson   h   832

Scully, Dana
Antibodies - Kevin J. Anderson   h   832

Turpin, Richard
The World of Darkness: Watcher - Charles L.
   Grant   h   900

FEMINIST

Truitt, April
Angel Face and Amazing Grace - Lori
   Copeland   r   286

FEMME FATALE

Aedrea
Saint Leibowitz and the Wild Horse Woman - Walter
   M. Miller Jr.   s   1157

FIANCE(E)

Cunningham, Cameron
True Heart - Arnette Lamb   r   358

Hotchkiss, Velma
Back to Malachi - Robert J. Conley   w   497

FILMMAKER

MacGowen, Maggie
A Hard Light - Wendy Hornsby   m   125

Thorpe, Leonard
Glimmering - Elizabeth Hand   s   1123

Worth, Andrew
Distress - Greg Egan   s   1088

FIRE FIGHTER

Elliott, Jack
Husband Needed - Cathie Linz   r   366

Fontana, Mac
The Dead Horse Paint Company - Earl
   Emerson   m   77

FOREMAN

Brothers, TJ
The Deer Mouse - Ken Grant   w   525

Friar, Tuck
Stillwater Smith - Frank Roderus   w   600

Lenning, Buck
Larkspur - Dorothy Garlock   r   310

Ransom, Lord
Winchester Affidavit - G.G. Boyer   w   469

FORTUNE HUNTER

Forsythe, Catherine
A Garden Folly - Candice Hern   r   325

Walker, Tom "Gerald Tarkington Crane"
No Ordinary Princess - Pamela Morsi   r   386

FOSTER PARENT

Bradshaw, Zoe
The Courtship of Cade Kolby - Lori
   Copeland   r   287

St. John, Clancy
Apache Sundown - Hank Edwards   w   513

Scott, Hannah
The Courtship of Hannah and the Horseman - Johnny
   D. Boggs   w   464

FOUNDLING

Acorna
Acorna - Anne McCaffrey   s   1152

FRIEND

Caroline
Jed the Dead - Alan Dean Foster   s   1102

Cobain, Maddie
Three Brides, No Groom - Debbie Macomber   r   371

Furness, Carol
Three Brides, No Groom - Debbie Macomber   r   371

Vizuelos, Ramon
Meeting the Minotaur - Carol Dawson   f   684

Warner, Violet
Murder, Mrs. Hudson - Sydney Hosier   m   126

Wise, Gretchen
Three Brides, No Groom - Debbie Macomber   r   371

FRONTIERSMAN

Boone, Dan'l
Algonquin Massacre - Dodge Tyler   w   617
Apache Revenge - Dodge Tyler   w   618
Death at Spanish Wells - Dodge Tyler   w   619
The Long Hunters - Dodge Tyler   w   620
A River Run Red - Dodge Tyler   w   621
Winter Kill - Dodge Tyler   w   622

Boone, Hunter Sinclair
Just Once - Jill Marie Landis   r   359

Clark, William
How We Crossed the West - Rosalyn
   Schanzer   w   602

Crockett, Davy
Blood Hunt - David Thompson   w   611
Homecoming - David Thompson   w   612
Mississippi Mayhem - David Thompson   w   613
Sioux Slaughter - David Thompson   w   614

Finley, Webster
The Long Hunters - Dodge Tyler   w   620

Flavius
Blood Hunt - David Thompson   w   611
Homecoming - David Thompson   w   612
Mississippi Mayhem - David Thompson   w   613
Sioux Slaughter - David Thompson   w   614

Hunter, Matt
Jade - Betty Brooks   r   269

Lewis, Meriwether
How We Crossed the West - Rosalyn
   Schanzer   w   602
Sacagawea - Judith St. George   w   608

McQuade, Chance
Across the Rio Colorado - Ralph Compton   w   491

Portillo, Rubio
Blood of Texas - Will Camp   w   479

Spenser, Luke
The Diary of Mattie Spenser - Sandra
   Dallas   w   505

Tyler, Blaine
The Winds of Autumn - Jim R. Woolard   w   635

Tyler, Blake
The Winds of Autumn - Jim R. Woolard   w   635

Tyler, Clardy
Passage to Natchez - Cameron Judd   w   550

FRONTIERSWOMAN

Barrington, Clarissa
Night of the Cougar - Frank Burleson   w   478

Calder, Mary
Blood of Texas - Will Camp   w   479

Evans, Wannie
Warrior's Prize - Georgina Gentry   r   315

Ferrenden, Hannah
The Winds of Autumn - Jim R. Woolard   w   635

Hayes, Allison
Diablo - David Robbins   w   596

Jones, Jenny
The Promise of Jenny Jones - Maggie
   Osborne   r   393

MacDonald, Skye
Shifting Stars: A Novel of the West - Page
   Lambert   w   555

Pryor, Jenny Sanders
Desperate Crossing: The Jenny Sanders Pryor Story -
   Barbara Riefe   w   594

Russell, Reshelle "Flame"
White Fire - Cassie Edwards   r   300

Spenser, Mattie
The Diary of Mattie Spenser - Sandra
   Dallas   w   505

FUGITIVE

Batik
Wolf in Shadow - David Gemmell   s   1110

Belacqua, Lyra
The Subtle Knife - Philip Pullman   f   781

Bloocher, Jemmy "Tim Hann"
Destiny's Road - Larry Niven   s   1167

Brown, Joe Bob
The Hard Land - Jack Ballas   w   446

Callen, Kevin
Come Before Christ and Murder Love - Stewart
   Home   f   725

Cha'dune, Hezhi Yehd
The Blackgod - J. Gregory Keyes   f   737

Chiara
The Thirteenth Daughter of the Moon - Steven
   Nightingale   f   771

Danaher, Kate
The Ivory Duchess - Delia Parr   r   395

Door
Neverwhere - Neil Gaiman   f   707

Endicott, Carl "Carl Johnson"
Delta Search - William Shatner   s   1199

Iphigenia, Alusz
The Demon Princes: Volume One - Jack
   Vance   s   1225

Magpie
Tallgrass: A Novel of the Great Plains - Don
   Coldsmith   w   485

Neale, Porsche
Beneath the Gated Sky - Robert Reed   s   1181

Novak, Cornell
Beneath the Gated Sky - Robert Reed   s   1181

O'Byrne, Rian
Wild Irish Skies - Nancy Richards-Akers *r* 410

Orgoru
A Wizard in Peace - Christopher Stasheff *s* 1211

Ormsby, Amy Kay
Beyond the River - Wynema McGowan *w* 570

Parry, William "Will"
The Subtle Knife - Philip Pullman *f* 781

Picot, Annora
Wild Irish Skies - Nancy Richards-Akers *r* 410

Pridgeon, Rachel
Snowflake Wishes - Lydia Browne *r* 270

Prophet
All God's Children - Tom Eidson *w* 515

Ryder (Walkman), Kathleen
Tallchief - Dinah McCall *r* 376

Sanford, Jess
The Hard Land - Jack Ballas *w* 446

Sloan, Philip
Come Before Christ and Murder Love - Stewart Home *f* 725

Thompson, Emily
The Night Watch - Sean Stewart *f* 801

GAMBLER

Baldridge, Masey
No Remorse - James D. Brewer *m* 26

Bell, Lucas
The Ghost of Major Pryor - Donald Honig *w* 542

Crow, Joe
Ring Game - Pete Hautman *m* 114

Hart, Frank
I, Pearl Hart - Jane Candia Coleman *w* 489

Holliday, Doc
Doc Holliday - Matt Braun *w* 470
The Fourth Horseman - Randy Lee Eickhoff *w* 514

Karaquazian, Jack
Fabulous Harbors - Michael Moorcock *f* 767
The War Amongst the Angels - Michael Moorcock *f* 768

McGann, Mike
Sierra Baron - Tom W. Blackburn *w* 459

Pike, Mississippi
The Tin-Pan Man - P.A. Bechko *w* 456

Radieu, Dianna
Colorado Reverie - Suzann Ledbetter *w* 557

Silks, Mattie
The Gamblers - Matt Braun *w* 471

GARDENER

Archibald, Stephen
A Garden Folly - Candice Hern *r* 325

Beauty
Rose Daughter - Robin McKinley *f* 761

Faun, Forrest
Faun & Games - Piers Anthony *f* 642

Tradescent, Heather
The Dancing Floor - Barbara Michaels *m* 168

GENETICALLY ALTERED BEING

Aenea
The Rise of Endymion - Dan Simmons *s* 1208

Akili
Distress - Greg Egan *s* 1088

Apolinario, Lot
Deception Well - Linda Nagata *s* 1165

Avens, Isobel
Signs of Life - M. John Harrison *s* 1125

Blaze
Mississippi Blue - Kathleen Ann Goonan *s* 1112

Brice, Marcer Joseph
Imposter - Valerie J. Freireich *s* 1103

Delilah "Lilah"
Jovah's Angel - Sharon Shinn *s* 1205

Endicott, James "Jimmy"
Delta Search - William Shatner *s* 1199

Ethemark
City on Fire - Walter Jon Williams *s* 1235

Fairfax, Aaron Lee
Rewind - Terry England *s* 1091

Lutz, Klaue
Lives of the Monster Dogs - Kirsten Bakis *s* 1040

Oar
Expendable - James Alan Gardner *s* 1108

Sokol
Legacy of the Ancients - Ron Sarti *s* 1192

Two Bears
Shadowboxer - Nick Pollotta *s* 1177

Verity
Mississippi Blue - Kathleen Ann Goonan *s* 1112

von Sacher, Ludwig
Lives of the Monster Dogs - Kirsten Bakis *s* 1040

Wali, Linnet
Imposter - Valerie J. Freireich *s* 1103

Wellin, Alleluia "Alleya"
Jovah's Angel - Sharon Shinn *s* 1205

GENIUS

Faust, Johannes "Jack"
Jack Faust - Michael Swanwick *s* 1219

Hazelhof, Cornelia
Timeshare - Joshua Dann *s* 1074

Ned
Hope of Earth - Piers Anthony *s* 1036

Okun, Brackish
Silent Zone - Stephen Molstad *s* 1159

Quilp
A Game of Universe - Eric S. Nylund *f* 774

Tomlinson
North of Havana - Randy Wayne White *m* 236

GENTLEMAN

Holmes, Mycroft
Against the Brotherhood - Quinn Fawcett *m* 82

Kestrel, Julian
The Devil in Music - Kate Ross *m* 204

Mardimil, Rion
Competition - Sharon Green *f* 712

Mercerault, Peter
The Offer - Catherine Coulter *r* 288

St. Ives, Baxter
Affair - Amanda Quick *r* 402

GENTLEWOMAN

Arkendale, Charlotte
Affair - Amanda Quick *r* 402

Brent, Margaret
Mary's Land - Lucia St. Clair Robson *w* 598

Browne, Carolyn
Splendor - Brenda Joyce *r* 343

Colburne, Falcarrah "Falcon"
The Lady From Spain - Gail Eastwood *r* 299

DeVere, Lilac
Rejar - Dara Joy *r* 341

Door
Neverwhere - Neil Gaiman *f* 707

Eversleigh, Sabrina
The Offer - Catherine Coulter *r* 288

Matalon, Cynthia
The Hot-Wired Dodo - Jack L. Chalker *s* 1064

Montague, Emerald
Dream Lover - Virginia Henley *r* 324

O'Hearn, Shemaine
Petals on the River - Kathleen Woodiwiss *r* 441

Partland, Kathlyn
Snowdrops and Scandalbroth - Barbara Metzger *r* 378

Perkins, Lydia
With This Ring - Carla Kelly *r* 344

Phillips, Sterling
Sweeter than Wine - Stephanie Mittman *r* 382

St. Joseph, Emmaline
Desperate - Millie Criswell *r* 291

Stapleton, Helena
A Christmas Bride - Mary Balogh *r* 251

Tremayne, Emma
The Passions of Emma - Penelope Williamson *r* 438

Woodbaine, Anna
Nick of Time - Casey Claybourne *r* 282

GLADIATOR

E'non, Caelan
Realm of Light - Deborah Chester *f* 666

GOVERNESS

Claire
The Night Watch - Sean Stewart *f* 801

Lloyd, Constance
To Marry a British Lord - Judith O'Brien *r* 391

Lyndon, Victoria
Everything and the Moon - Julia Quinn *r* 404

Sherringham, Eliza
After the Kiss - Joan Johnston *r* 337

GOVERNMENT OFFICIAL

Byrd, Tom
Living Real - James C. Bassett *s* 1046

Cochrane, William
Rage of Spirits - Noel Hynd *h* 921

Cormack, Leonard
Faraday's Orphans - N. Lee Wood *s* 1242

Dahl, Deha
The Last Hawk - Catherine Asaro *s* 1038

Edwards, James "Jay"
Men in Black - Steve Perry *s* 1174

Everett, Radmilla
Rewind - Terry England *s* 1091

Feldman, Jess
Heartbreaker - Karen Robards *r* 414

Fraser, Duncan
The Scottish Rose - Jill Jones *r* 339

GRANDPARENT

GUARDIAN

GUIDE

GUNFIGHTER

HANDICAPPED

HEALER

Delaney, Raven
Fever Rising - Maggie Ferguson   r   305

Edlyn
A Knight to Remember - Christina Dodd   r   296

Herb-Woman
Strange Deliverance - Mary Brown   s   1057

Macrae, Mihairi
The Raven's Moon - Susan King   r   348

Myrilandel "Myri"
The Dragon's Touchstone - Irene Radford   f   783

Pinheiro, Berenice
God's Fires - Patricia Anthony   s   1035

Stone, Gloria
The Gaia Websters - Kim Antieau   s   1037

Tay-bodal
Witch of the Palo Duro - Mardi Oakley
  Medawar   m   166

Trevor, Hannah
Blood Red Roses - Margaret Lawrence   m   146

Varden
Spires of Spirit - Gael Baudino   f   649

HEALTH CARE PROFESSIONAL

Campbell, Trey
Bad Karma - Andrew Harper   h   909

Frost, Melanie
The Seventh Heart - Marina Fitch   f   704

Griffin, Beth
Nazareth Hill - Ramsey Campbell   h   851

Jaye, Evaline
Just Before Midnight - Patricia Simpson   r   422

HEIR

Cheever, Shelby V
The Billion Dollar Boy - Charles Sheffield   s   1201

Gavrilli, David
Interface Masque - Shariann Lewitt   s   1143

Hamilton, Richard
Coyote Summer - W. Michael Gear   w   523

Hawken, Garrick
Allamanda - Michael Williams   f   817

King, Matthew
Eden - Frederic Bean   w   451

Radon
Firewalk - Anne Logston   f   753

Thompson, Emily
The Night Watch - Sean Stewart   f   801

HEIR—DISPOSSESSED

Rodrigo
The Still - David Feintuch   f   702

Telmah, Lord Cima
The White Abacus - Damien Broderick   s   1056

HEIRESS

Alton, Marguerida "Margaret"
The Shadow Matrix - Marion Zimmer
  Bradley   s   1055

Bennett, Jane
The Paradise Man - Suzanne Simmons   r   421

Calhoun, Princess
No Ordinary Princess - Pamela Morsi   r   386

Colburne, Falcarrah "Falcon"
The Lady From Spain - Gail Eastwood   r   299

Finnegan, Maura
Maiden Voyage - Judith O'Brien   r   389

Howell, Rachel
Silverthorne - Wayne Davis   w   507

Knight, Jamee
Season of Wishes - Christina Skye   r   426

Milleflores, Delanna
Promised Land - Connie Willis   s   1238

O'Hurley, Jemma
Just Once - Jill Marie Landis   r   359

Picot, Annora
Wild Irish Skies - Nancy Richards-Akers   r   410

Priscian
Beggar's Banquet - Daniel Hood   f   726

Sanders, Graciela
The Promise of Jenny Jones - Maggie
  Osborne   r   393

Vandermeer, Louise
Beast - Judith Ivory   r   333

HERBALIST

Pinheiro, Berenice
God's Fires - Patricia Anthony   s   1035

HERO

Appenfell, Rudgar "Rudy"
War of the Three Waters - Douglas Niles   f   772

Barku, Perkar Kar
The Blackgod - J. Gregory Keyes   f   737

Cohen, Ghenghiz "Cohen the Barbarian"
Interesting Times - Terry Pratchett   f   779

Endymion, Raul
The Rise of Endymion - Dan Simmons   s   1208

Hercules
Atlantis Found - R. Garcia y Robertson   s   1107
The First Casualty - David L. Seidman   f   791

Jayal
The Forging of the Shadows - Oliver Johnson   f   729

Kerrigan, Joshua "Josh"
Putting Up Roots - Charles Sheffield   s   1203

Maddox, Cory "Cori Kassemi"
The Hot-Wired Dodo - Jack L. Chalker   s   1064

Malledd
Touched by the Gods - Lawrence Watt-Evans   f   810

Ripley
Alien Resurrection - A.C. Crispin   s   1071

York, Dennison
Thoughts of God - Michael Kanaly   s   1134

HEROINE

Kaeler, Lanen
Song in the Silence - Elizabeth Kerner   f   734

Kendoro, Judit
Acorna - Anne McCaffrey   s   1152

Thalassa
The Forging of the Shadows - Oliver Johnson   f   729

HISTORIAN

Amiss, Robert
Murder in a Cathedral - Ruth Dudley
  Edwards   m   72

Backmaker, Hodgins "Hodge"
Bring the Jubilee - Ward Moore   s   1162

Henry, Ned
To Say Nothing of the Dog - Connie Willis   s   1239

Kindle, Verity
To Say Nothing of the Dog - Connie Willis   s   1239

Thornton, Alexandra
Captive - Brenda Joyce   r   342

Toledo, Indira
Mother of Demons - Eric Flint   s   1096

von Sacher, Ludwig
Lives of the Monster Dogs - Kirsten Bakis   s   1040

Wallace, Indra
3001: The Final Odyssey - Arthur C.
  Clarke   s   1067

HISTORICAL FIGURE

Adams, John Quincy
Amistad - Alexs Pate   w   584

Aionwahta
Eagle Song - Joseph Bruchac   w   476

Alexander the Great
A Murder in Macedon - Anna Apostolou   m   5

Allison, Clay
Legend of a Badman: A Western Quintet - Ray
  Hogan   w   537

Asimov, Issac
Back in the USSA - Kim Newman   s   1166

Austen, Jane
Jane and the Man of the Cloth - Stephanie
  Barron   m   10

Beckwourth, Jim
Rendezvous - Richard S. Wheeler   w   629

Bragg, Braxton
Journey to Shiloh - Will Henry   w   533

Bridger, Jim
Rendezvous - Richard S. Wheeler   w   629

Caesar, Julius
Caesar's Bicycle - John Barnes   s   1042

Capone, Alphonse
Back in the USSA - Kim Newman   s   1166

Carey, Robert
A Surfeit of Guns - P.F. Chisholm   m   36

Churchill, Winston
Murder, Mrs. Hudson - Sydney Hosier   m   126

Clemens, Sam
How Few Remain - Harry Turtledove   s   1223

Cody, William
Devil's Engine - Mark Sumner   f   803

Custer, George A.
American Woman - R. Garcia y Robertson   w   521
Deadwood - Douglas Hirt   w   535
How Few Remain - Harry Turtledove   s   1223
Yesterday's Reveille - Robert Vaughan   w   626

de Medici, Caterina
The Stars Dispose - Michaela Roessner   f   786

Douglass, Frederick
How Few Remain - Harry Turtledove   s   1223

Earp, Wyatt
Doc Holliday - Matt Braun   w   470
The Fourth Horseman - Randy Lee
  Eickhoff   w   514

Fielding, John
Person or Persons Unknown - Bruce
  Alexander   m   3

Kazenstein, Morris
Sewer, Gas & Electric - Matt Ruff   s   1185

INVESTIGATOR

Arkendale, Charlotte
Affair - Amanda Quick   r   402

Bearpaw, Molly
The Spirit Caller - Jean Hager   m   106

Bradley, Barbara Joan "Bo"
The Dollmaker's Daughters - Abigail
Padgett   m   179

Christman, Barbara
Sole Survivor - Dean R. Koontz   h   935

Gourmet Detective
Spiced to Death - Peter King   m   142

Holmes, Mycroft
Against the Brotherhood - Quinn Fawcett   m   82

Maxwell, Lauren
Killer Whale - Elizabeth Quinn   m   191

JEWELER

Massey, Phillip
The Ivory Duchess - Delia Parr   r   395

JOURNALIST

Adashek, David
Meg - Steve Alten   h   831

Barclay, Richard
Blue Genes - Val McDermid   m   162

Beckman, Tad
Counting Coup - G.D. Gearino   m   93

Benedek, Walter
Live Girls - Ray Garton   h   888

Benedict, Sally
Infinity's Child - Harry Stein   h   1005

Billups, Darryl
Up Jumped the Devil - Blair S. Walker   m   230

Carpenter, Joe
Sole Survivor - Dean R. Koontz   h   935

Casey, Charles
Twice upon a Time - Emilie Richards   r   409

Clemens, Sam
How Few Remain - Harry Turtledove   s   1223

Dalrymple, Daisy
Damsel in Distress - Carola Dunn   m   70

Deacon, Michael
The Echo - Minette Walters   m   231

Devane, Kate
Caught - Rachel Lee   r   363

Douglass, Frederick
How Few Remain - Harry Turtledove   s   1223

Durbin, Ashley
Hair of the Dog - Brett Davis   f   683

Garner, Quinn
Shadow Walk - Jane Waterhouse   m   233

Gersen, Kirth
The Demon Princes: Volume One - Jack
Vance   s   1225

Greenstreet, Sadie
Eye of the Agency - Richard Moquist   m   170

Hatory, Anna
The Night Crew - John Sandford   m   208

Hudson, Robin
Revenge of the Cootie Girls - Sparkle
Hayter   m   116

Jacobs-Wolde, Jessica
My Soul to Keep - Tananarive Due   h   873

Jones, Nathaniel
Deadwood - Douglas Hirt   w   535

Justice, Benjamin
Revision of Justice - John Morgan Wilson   m   240

Kelly, Irene
Hocus - Jan Burke   m   30

Lang, Alice "Lancaster"
Einstein's Bridge - John Cramer   s   1070

Manning, Mark
Flight Dreams - Michael Craft   m   44

Marsala, Cat
Hard Bargain - Barbara D'Amato   m   52

Matthews, Susan
Dancing on Air - Nancy Kress   s   1140

McMorrow, Jack
Potshot - Gerry Boyle   m   25

Mills, Todd
Hostage - R.D. Zimmerman   m   244

Montero, Britt
Margin of Error - Edna Buchanan   m   27

Noble, Bentley
Shackled - Ray Garton   h   889

Perry, Jerrica
The Bighead - Edward Lee   h   943

Poe, John Charles
The Black Cat - Robert Poe   h   978

Pohaku, Annie
Mars Underground - William Hartmann   s   1126

Reynolds, Kelly
Area 51 - Robert Doherty   s   1080

Smith, Jane
Curl Up and Die - Christine T. Jorgensen   m   134

Smithback, Bill
Reliquary - Douglas Preston   h   979

Sorby, Helen
Steel Ashes - Karen Rose Cercone   m   34

Templeton, Alexandra
Revision of Justice - John Morgan Wilson   m   240

Townsend, Ben
Rising Tides - Emilie Richards   r   408

Urmila
The Calcutta Chromosome - Amitav Ghosh   h   895

Westcott, Archie
How the West Was Lost - Gene Shelton   w   603

Westphal, Connor
Dead Body Language - Penny Warner   m   232

Wheatley, Chas
The Butter Did It - Phyllis Richman   m   198

Winter, Holly
Animal Appetite - Susan Conant   m   41

Worth, Andrew
Distress - Greg Egan   s   1088

Yokusuka, Jory
Berserker Fury - Fred Saberhagen   s   1189

JUDGE

Fielding, John
Person or Persons Unknown - Bruce
Alexander   m   3

Knott, Deborah
Killer Market - Margaret Maron   m   152

Underbridge, Kin
Wrath of the Princes - Holly Lisle   f   752

KIDNAPPER

de Clifford, Robert
The Dragon and the Gnarly King - Gordon R.
Dickson   f   688

Falushe, Viole
The Demon Princes: Volume One - Jack
Vance   s   1225

Trampe, Micajah
Blind Eagles - John S. McCord   w   568

Tucker, Randy Karl
Freeware - Rudy Rucker   s   1184

KNIGHT

Bright
Gawain and Lady Green - Anne Eliot
Crompton   f   679

Colin of Ravenshaw
Touch of Enchantment - Teresa Medeiros   r   377

de Beaucourt, Merrick
Wonderful - Jill Barnett   r   255

fitzJulien, Magnus
Eyes of Love - Katherine Deauville   r   294

Galeran of Heywood
The Shattered Rose - Jo Beverley   r   260

Gawain
Gawain and Lady Green - Anne Eliot
Crompton   f   679

Gistere, Rurak
The Day of the Tempest - Jean Rabe   f   782

Gwalchavad
Grail - Stephen R. Lawhead   f   745

Montclaire, Thomas
For My Lady's Kiss - Linda Needham   r   388

Renaud de Verdelay, Griffyn
The Last Arrow - Marsha Canham   r   275

Savage, Gilbert
A Tournament of Murders - P.C. Doherty   m   64

LABORER

Guthrie, Port
The Winchester Run - Ralph Compton   w   496

LAIRD

MacElgin, Duncan "Black Duncan"
Fairy Tale - Jillian Hunter   r   332

MacFane, Malcolm
Once a Warrior - Karyn Monk   r   383

McLaren, Niall
The Lover - Nicole Jordan   r   340

Murray, Rowan
One of These Nights - Susan Sizemore   r   423

LANDOWNER

Gomez, Simon
Hacienda - Albert R. Booky   w   466

Horan, Brent
American Blood - Jason Manning   w   564

Kemp, Allister
Diablo - David Robbins   w   596

K'vin
Dragonseye - Anne McCaffrey   s   1153

Lenifee, Ben
Mountains against the Sun - Perry Holmes   w   541

Marta
Hungry for Home: A Wolf Odyssey - 'Asta
   Bowen   f   654

Merlin
The Eagle and the Sword - A.A. Attanasio   f   645

Merlyn Britannicus, Caius
The Eagles' Brood - Jack Whyte   f   816

Milton, John
Milton in America - Peter Ackroyd   f   637

Ratio
The White Abacus - Damien Broderick   s   1056

Rille, Cailet Ambrai
The Mageborn Traitor - Melanie Rawn   f   785

Wellin, Alleluia "Alleya"
Jovah's Angel - Sharon Shinn   s   1205

Weser, Erich "Erich Alois"
Children of the Dusk - Janet Berliner   f   652

LESBIAN

Delafield, Kate
Apparition Alley - Katherine V. Forrest   m   85

Lauri
Spires of Spirit - Gael Baudino   f   649

LIBRARIAN

Giles
Buffy the Vampire Slayer: The Harvest - Richie
   Tankersley Cusick   h   863

Morrison, Rebecca
The Blackstone Chronicles - John Saul   h   990

Zukas, Helma
Out of Circulation - Jo Dereske   m   60

LINGUIST

Ea
Black Wine - Candas Jane Dorsey   s   1082

Izakar "Izzy"
The Family Tree - Sheri S. Tepper   s   1220

Morden
The Shadow Within - Jeanne Cavelos   s   1062

St. George, Blacktooth "Nimmy"
Saint Leibowitz and the Wild Horse Woman - Walter
   M. Miller Jr.   s   1157

Theodoulos
Cross and Crescent - Susan Shwartz   f   795

Wheatley, Gillian
The Seventh Heart - Marina Fitch   f   704

Wolde, David
My Soul to Keep - Tananarive Due   h   873

LOVER

Barclay, Richard
Blue Genes - Val McDermid   m   162

Justina, Helena
Time to Depart - Lindsey Davis   m   55

Lloyd
Verdict Unsafe - Jill McGown   m   164

McQuaid, Mike
Love Lies Bleeding - Susan Wittig Albert   m   2

Ripinsky, Hy
Both Ends of the Night - Marcia Muller   m   173

MADAM

Jewel, Jade
Jade - Ruth Langan   r   360

Silks, Mattie
The Gamblers - Matt Braun   w   471

MAGICIAN

Amnel, Kahlan
Temple of the Winds - Terry Goodkind   f   710

Amrey, Murl "Kar Kalim"
Kar Kalim - Deborah Christian   f   668

Atrus
The Book of D'ni - Rand Miller   f   763

Donaltsson, Marta
Kindred Rites - Katharine Eliska Kimbriel   f   738

Eckert, Jim
The Dragon and the Gnarly King - Gordon R.
   Dickson   f   688

Elora Danan
Shadow Dawn - Chris Claremont   f   670

Fortune, Celinde "Cissy"
Dreaming Metal - Melissa Scott   s   1197

Jaad
Ronin - D.A. Heeley   f   719

Kayli
Firewalk - Anne Logston   f   753

Keatley, Thompson
A Dry Spell - Susan Moloney   h   965

Kheperu
Iron Dawn - Matthew Woodring Stover   f   802

Kim
Magician's Ward - Patricia C. Wrede   f   819

Merrill, Richard "Mairelon"
Magician's Ward - Patricia C. Wrede   f   819

Nimbulan "Lan"
The Dragon's Touchstone - Irene Radford   f   783

Rand
Four & Twenty Blackbirds - Mercedes
   Lackey   f   742

Reed, Sharon
The Road to Hell, Volume I - Robert
   Weinberg   h   1024
The Road to Hell, Volume II - Robert
   Weinberg   h   1025

Sorensson, Alfreda "Alli"
Kindred Rites - Katharine Eliska Kimbriel   f   738

Worabex
Red Unicorn - Tanith Lee   f   747

MAIDEN

Edain
Eyes of Love - Katherine Deauville   r   294

MAIL ORDER BRIDE

Behr, Honey
The MacKenzies: Luke - Ana Leigh   r   365

Carson, Amelia
Texas Destiny - Lorraine Heath   r   322

Finnegan, Emily
One Pink Rose - Julie Garwood   r   312

Peyson, Valeria
Lonesome Land - B.M. Bower   w   467

Van, Judyth
Devil's Rim - Sam Brown   w   475

MAINTENANCE WORKER

Coakley, Dana
All Emergencies, Ring Super - Ellen Emerson
   White   m   235

Rickard, Robert
Room 13 - Henry Garfield   h   886

MARTIAL ARTS EXPERT

Bard, Lily
Shakespeare's Champion - Charlaine Harris   m   112

Curran, Joslire
An Exchange of Hostages - Susan R.
   Matthews   s   1151

Kinoshita, Ito
The Widowmaker Reborn - Mike Resnick   s   1182

Lescevre, Thibault
Bridge of Valor - Anne Lesley Groell   f   716

Radineaux, Jenifleur
Bridge of Valor - Anne Lesley Groell   f   716

Shadrack
Ronin - D.A. Heeley   f   719

MECHANIC

Damen, Clyde
Cats Raise the Dead - Shirley Rousseau
   Murphy   f   769

Hayes, Tommy Lee
Love in a Small Town - Curtis Ann Matlock   r   374

Kateralbin, Crispin
The War in the Waste - Felicity Savage   f   790

Mancini, Munch
No Human Involved - Barbara Seranella   m   211

Spenser, Vernon
Bright Shadow - Elizabeth Forrest   h   883

MENTALLY ILL PERSON

Bradley, Barbara Joan "Bo"
The Dollmaker's Daughters - Abigail
   Padgett   m   179

Cochrane, Miles "David Gilman"
Alpha Centauri - William Barton   s   1045

Nina
Planar Powers - J. Robert King   f   739

Plumtree, Janis
Earthquake Weather - Tim Powers   f   778

Portal, Ellis
Free Reign - Rosemary Aubert   m   7

Sloan, Philip
Come Before Christ and Murder Love - Stewart
   Home   f   725

Soul Catcher
She Is the Darkness - Glen Cook   f   676

Ted
The Kronos Condition - Emily Devenport   s   1078

Typhoid Mary
Twilight of the Empire - Simon R. Green   s   1115

King, Nathaniel
Spanish Slaughter - David Thompson   w   615

MacDonald, Gregory
Shifting Stars: A Novel of the West - Page Lambert   w   555

McKendree, Josiah
McKendree - Douglas Hirt   w   536

McNair, Shakespeare
Spanish Slaughter - David Thompson   w   615

Morgan, Jacob
Winter Woman - F.M. Parker   w   582

Ribalt, Jacques
McKendree - Douglas Hirt   w   536

Skye, Barnaby
Rendezvous - Richard S. Wheeler   w   629

Sterling, Jedediah
Tallgrass: A Novel of the Great Plains - Don Coldsmith   w   485

MOUNTAIN WOMAN

DuBois, Cora
Winter Woman - F.M. Parker   w   582

King, Winona
Spanish Slaughter - David Thompson   w   615

Moon, Gracie
Chase the Moon - Dinah McCall   r   375

MOUNTAINEER

Appenfell, Rudgar "Rudy"
War of the Three Waters - Douglas Niles   f   772

Furness, Jack
Esau - Philip Kerr   m   139

MURDERER

Growler, Donald
Cul-De-Sac - David Martin   h   958

Hardin, John Wesley
Pure Justice - Suzann Ledbetter   w   559

Harpe, Micajah
Passage to Natchez - Cameron Judd   w   550

Hassard, Dee
Dead Reckoning - Mike Blakely   w   461

Kimbo Luke
Dust on the Wind - Bill Brooks   w   474

Vitarosa
Mind Snare - Gayle Greeno   s   1118

MUSICIAN

Ananda
The Thirteenth Daughter of the Moon - Steven Nightingale   f   771

Asie
The Rock Child - Win Blevins   w   462

Bailey, Deanie
Once upon a Rose - Judith O'Brien   r   390

Becker, Triana
Violin - Anne Rice   h   983

Blaze
Mississippi Blue - Kathleen Ann Goonan   s   1112

Clisser
Dragonseye - Anne McCaffrey   s   1153

Daffyd
The Soprano Sorceress - L.E. Modesitt Jr.   f   765

Danaher, Kate
The Ivory Duchess - Delia Parr   r   395

Douglas, Morric
Blackmantle: A Triumph - Patricia Kennealy-Morrison   f   733

Holley, Charles Hardin
Back in the USSA - Kim Newman   s   1166

Horne, Evan
The Sound of the Trumpet - Bill Moody   m   169

January, Benjamin
A Free Man of Color - Barbara Hambly   m   109

Joel
Finder's Bane - Kate Novak   f   773

Jones, Fanning "Fan"
Dreaming Metal - Melissa Scott   s   1197

Jorandel "Jorie"
Cold Iron - Melisa Michaels   f   762

Lazarich, Sabina
Someone to Watch over Me - Tricia Sullivan   s   1218

Marlowe, Trip
Glimmering - Elizabeth Hand   s   1123

Merlin, Walter Drake
Tomorrow and Tomorrow - Charles Sheffield   s   1204

Murphy, James
Landslayer's Law - Tom Deitz   f   687

Nelson, Willie
Road Kill - Kinky Friedman   m   87

Quinsonnas
Paris in the Twentieth Century - Jules Verne   s   1227

s'Ffalenn, Arithon
Fugitive Prince - Janny Wurts   f   822

Stefanovsky, Stephan
Violin - Anne Rice   h   983

MUTANT

Aedrea
Saint Leibowitz and the Wild Horse Woman - Walter M. Miller Jr.   s   1157

MYTHICAL CREATURE

Akhor
Song in the Silence - Elizabeth Kerner   f   734

Algooth
The Gates of Vensunor - Carol Heller   f   720

Amaranth
The Dragon's Touchstone - Irene Radford   f   783

Ampelus
Thessalonica - Harry Turtledove   f   805

Archangel
Headhunters - Mel Odom   s   1172

Aryadyss
Donnerjack - Roger Zelazny   s   1244

Binah
Cross and Crescent - Susan Shwartz   f   795

Bonita
Polymorph - Scott Westerfeld   s   1232

Bridin of Rush
Forever Enchanted - Maggie Shayne   r   420

Broketail, Bazil
A Dragon at World's End - Christopher Rowley   f   787

Centaur, Cathryn
Faun & Games - Piers Anthony   f   642

Cutter
Captives of the Blue Mountain - Wendy Pini   f   777

Death
Donnerjack - Roger Zelazny   s   1244
Maskerade - Terry Pratchett   f   780

Djinn
The Djinn in the Nightingale's Eye - A.S. Byatt   f   662

Duran
Headhunters - Mel Odom   s   1172

Earth
The Book of Water - Marjorie Bradley Kellogg   f   732

Eros
Cupid's Mistake - Karen Harbaugh   r   321

Fanuilh
Beggar's Banquet - Daniel Hood   f   726

Faun, Forrest
Faun & Games - Piers Anthony   f   642

Garuda
The Iron Ring - Lloyd Alexander   f   640

Hardgreip
War of the Gods - Poul Anderson   f   641

Hisvet
Return to Lankhmar - Fritz Leiber   f   748

Holly
Mister Christmas - Linda Cajio   r   273

Jasmine "Jas"
Finder's Bane - Kate Novak   f   773

Jorandel "Jorie"
Cold Iron - Melisa Michaels   f   762

Lakshmi
My Son, the Wizard - Christopher Stasheff   f   800

Lauri
Spires of Spirit - Gael Baudino   f   649

Lee
Polymorph - Scott Westerfeld   s   1232

Leetah
Captives of the Blue Mountain - Wendy Pini   f   777

Lesseth
Kar Kalim - Deborah Christian   f   668

Luccia
Vinas Solamnus - J. Robert King   f   740

Lugh
Landslayer's Law - Tom Deitz   f   687

Makepeace, Sebastian
The Last Wizard - Simon Hawke   f   718

Malystryx the Red
The Day of the Tempest - Jean Rabe   f   782

Mennym, Soobie
Mennyms Alive - Sylvia Waugh   f   811

Mennym, Tulip
Mennyms Alive - Sylvia Waugh   f   811

Norton
Steel Rose - Kara Dalkey   f   681

Petrus
Spiritride - Mark Shepherd   f   793

Rabble
When the Gods Are Silent - Jane M. Lindskold   f   750

Ralph
Steel Rose - Kara Dalkey   f   681

Sianna
Lady of Avalon - Marion Zimmer Bradley   *f*   656

Theodoulos
Cross and Crescent - Susan Shwartz   *f*   795

Thistledown, Tipperton "Tip"
Into the Forge - Dennis L. McKiernan   *f*   760

Varden
Spires of Spirit - Gael Baudino   *f*   649

Water
The Book of Water - Marjorie Bradley
Kellogg   *f*   732

Winnowill
Captives of the Blue Mountain - Wendy Pini   *f*   777

NEIGHBOR

Byrne, Donal
Maiden Voyage - Judith O'Brien   *r*   389

NOBILITY

Tolivar
Sky Trillium - Julian May   *f*   756

NOBLEMAN

Adams, Rex
Indiscreet - Mary Balogh   *r*   252

Archibald, Stephen
A Garden Folly - Candice Hern   *r*   325

Arden, Nicholas
An Infamous Proposal - Joan Smith   *r*   428

Braddock, William
Dream a Little Dream - Antoinette
Stockenberg   *r*   429

Bright
Gawain and Lady Green - Anne Eliot
Crompton   *f*   679

Burfield
The Deception - Marion Chesney   *r*   280

Burke-Jones, Prometheus
Leaving Missouri - Ellen Recknor   *w*   592

Cameron, Alexei
Key to Forever - Christina Skye   *r*   425

Cameron, Andrew "Drew"
The Scotsman Wore Spurs - Patricia Potter   *r*   399

Campbell, Robert
Everything and the Moon - Julia Quinn   *r*   404

Camron
The Barbed Coil - J.V. Jones   *f*   730

Carey, Robert
A Surfeit of Guns - P.F. Chisholm   *m*   36

Chalfont, Adrian
My Wayward Lady - Evelyn Richardson   *r*   411

Choate, Courtney
Snowdrops and Scandalbroth - Barbara
Metzger   *r*   378

Cordell, Ashton
Raven's Bride - Lynn Kerstan   *r*   346

dav Aidan, Kenzie "Catfoot"
Broken Blade - Ann Marston   *f*   754

de Barenton, Lucien
The Moon and the Sun - Vonda N. McIntyre   *f*   759

de Carabas
Neverwhere - Neil Gaiman   *f*   707

de Clifford, Robert
The Dragon and the Gnarly King - Gordon R.
Dickson   *f*   688

Deathstalker, Owen
Deathstalker War - Simon R. Green   *s*   1114

Devereaux, Jason
The Irish Rake - Emma Lange   *r*   361

Dracula
The Mammoth Book of Dracula - Stephen
Jones   *h*   927

Duone, Morgan
Emerald House Rising - Peg Kerr   *f*   736

Durant, Sebastian
A Well-Pleasured Lady - Christina Dodd   *r*   297

Duzon
Touched by the Gods - Lawrence Watt-Evans   *f*   810

Eckert, Jim
The Dragon and the Gnarly King - Gordon R.
Dickson   *f*   688

Fitzwalter, Adrian
The Dark Duke - Margaret Moore   *r*   385

Galoran
Count Scar - C. Dale Brittain   *f*   658

Garrett, Edward
Secrets in Satin - Haywood Smith   *r*   427

Grandville, Stephen
The Guardian - Joan Wolf   *r*   440

Gwalchavad
Grail - Stephen R. Lawhead   *f*   745

Hastings, Philip
To Marry a British Lord - Judith O'Brien   *r*   391

Hawkesmoor, Simon
The Silver Rose - Jane Feather   *r*   304

Hazelton, Jeremy
The Lady From Spain - Gail Eastwood   *r*   299

Hong
Interesting Times - Terry Pratchett   *f*   779

Jayal
The Forging of the Shadows - Oliver Johnson   *f*   729

Kenyon, Stephen
One Perfect Rose - Mary Jo Putney   *r*   401

Kierston, Leo
The Diamond Slipper - Jane Feather   *r*   303

Lanart-Hastur, Mikhail
The Shadow Matrix - Marion Zimmer
Bradley   *s*   1055

Larath, Deveren
King's Man and Thief - Christie Golden   *f*   709

Lytton, Marcus
Dangerous to Hold - Elizabeth Thornton   *r*   433

MacKinnon, Duncan
Bride of the Mist - Christina Skye   *r*   424

Marquess of Blythland
Cupid's Mistake - Karen Harbaugh   *r*   321

McCall, Ian
Season of Wishes - Christina Skye   *r*   426

Melville, Raoul
The Arrangement - Joan Wolf   *r*   439

Meren
Eater of Souls - Lynda S. Robinson   *m*   202

Montclaire, Thomas
For My Lady's Kiss - Linda Needham   *r*   388

Morgan, Lionel
Captive - Joan Johnston   *r*   338

NaBlaine, Ruairi
Bridge of Valor - Anne Lesley Groell   *f*   716

Neville, Christopher "Kit"
Once upon a Rose - Judith O'Brien   *r*   390

O'Toole, Sean
Dream Lover - Virginia Henley   *r*   324

Ottokar
The Duke of Sumava - Sara J. Wrench   *f*   821

Pender, Galen
Francesca's Rake - Lynn Kerstan   *r*   345

Penderyn, Geraint
Truly - Mary Balogh   *r*   253

Ramsay, Jack "Rakehell"
The Rakehell's Reform - Elisabeth Fairchild   *r*   302

Ravis
The Barbed Coil - J.V. Jones   *f*   730

Reed, Samuel
With This Ring - Carla Kelly   *r*   344

Rosvenir, Collan
The Mageborn Traitor - Melanie Rawn   *f*   785

St. Gregory, Dane
Knights - Linda Lael Miller   *r*   380

Seaton, Matthew
Innocence Undone - Kat Martin   *r*   372

Swinburn, Richard
The Colonel's Lady - Patricia Oliver   *r*   392

Tenamaxtli
Aztec Autumn - Gary Jennings   *w*   544

Thornton, Ivan
Dangerous to Love - Rexanne Becnel   *r*   258

Valdoria kva Skolia, Kelricson Garlin
The Last Hawk - Catherine Asaro   *s*   1038

Ware, Fortitude
Something Wicked - Jo Beverley   *r*   261

Wharton, Marcus
After the Kiss - Joan Johnston   *r*   337

Woodville, William
If You Love Me - Elaine Coffman   *r*   283

Wycombe, Charles
Brighter than the Sun - Julia Quinn   *r*   403

NOBLEWOMAN

Agramonte, Maran
The Seer King - Chris Bunch   *f*   661

Alys of Summersedge
Lord of Danger - Anne Stuart   *r*   431

Brandenburg, Cordelia
The Diamond Slipper - Jane Feather   *r*   303

Brinsby, Ophelia
A Prince Among Men - Kate Moore   *r*   384

Childe, Francesca
Francesca's Rake - Lynn Kerstan   *r*   345

Claire of Summersedge
Lord of Danger - Anne Stuart   *r*   431

Clio of Camrose
Wonderful - Jill Barnett   *r*   255

dar Dero, Halleyne
Wrath of the Princes - Holly Lisle   *f*   752

de la Crois, Marie-Josephe
The Moon and the Sun - Vonda N. McIntyre   *f*   759

di'Marano, Diora
The Broken Crown - Michelle West   *f*   815

Duone, Kestrienne
Emerald House Rising - Peg Kerr   *f*   736

Eckert, Angie
The Dragon and the Gnarly King - Gordon R.
Dickson   *f*   688

Edgerton, Charlotte
Captive - Joan Johnston   *r*   338

Stone, Jasper
Texas Lily - Elizabeth Fackler   *w*   517

Stubbs, Harry
The Hunted - James Reasoner   *w*   591

Weston, Wade
Jade - Ruth Langan   *r*   360

Wooten, Solomon
The Courtship of Hannah and the Horseman - Johnny D. Boggs   *w*   464

PARANORMAL INVESTIGATOR

Jourdemayne, Truth
Gravelight - Marion Zimmer Bradley   *f*   655

PARENT

Brand, Anne-Marie
Secret Passages - Paul Preuss   *s*   1178

Caraval, Julio
Spirits of the Ordinary - Kathleen Alcala   *f*   638

Cuthberton-Jones
Angela and Diabola - Lynne Reid Banks   *f*   646

Deeds, A.J.
Meeting the Minotaur - Carol Dawson   *f*   684

Gerritsen, Aurore
Rising Tides - Emilie Richards   *r*   408

Herb-Woman
Strange Deliverance - Mary Brown   *s*   1057

Lawford, Arthur
The Return - Walter de la Mare   *h*   868

MacDonald, Gregory
Shifting Stars: A Novel of the West - Page Lambert   *w*   555

Matthews, Susan
Dancing on Air - Nancy Kress   *s*   1140

Reilly, Rosemary
Son of Rosemary - Ira Levin   *h*   945

Rodriguez
Senora Rodriguez and Other Worlds - Martha Cerda   *f*   663

Serege, Lujan Ansellic
Echoes of Issel - Diann Thornley   *s*   1222

Teppish, Vladimir X. III
The Vampire's Beautiful Daughter - S.P. Somtow   *h*   1002

PAROLE OFFICER

Ortega, Felix
Out of Body - Thomas Baum   *h*   836

PATIENT

Hatcher, Agnes
Bad Karma - Andrew Harper   *h*   909

Hewlitt
Final Diagnosis - James White   *s*   1233

Serege, Lujan Ansellic
Dominion's Reach - Diann Thornley   *s*   1221

PEDDLER

Kane, Zachariah
The Tin-Pan Man - P.A. Bechko   *w*   456

PHILOSOPHER

Caraval, Julio
Spirits of the Ordinary - Kathleen Alcala   *f*   638

Dogbrick
The Dark Shore - Adam Lee   *f*   746

PHOTOGRAPHER

Brand, Anne-Marie
Secret Passages - Paul Preuss   *s*   1178

Burke, Peter
Cold at Heart - Brian Hopkins   *h*   917

Gerritsen, Dawn
Rising Tides - Emilie Richards   *r*   408

Magistrale, Michelangelo "Mage"
The Art of Arrow Cutting - Stephen Dedman   *f*   686

Marlow, Lee
Double Edge - Dennis Etchison   *h*   880

McCarthy, Gwen
This Man Colter - Johnny D. Boggs   *w*   465

Quinn, Connor
Caught - Rachel Lee   *r*   363

PHYSICIAN

Cage, Ryland "Ry"
Carlucci's Heart - Richard Paul Russo   *s*   1188

Koscuisko, Andrej
An Exchange of Hostages - Susan R. Matthews   *s*   1151

PILOT

Blaze, Chastity
Saturn Rukh - Robert L. Forward   *s*   1100

Bottlenose
Starplex - Robert J. Sawyer   *s*   1195

Cormack, Leonard
Faraday's Orphans - N. Lee Wood   *s*   1242

Finn, Clio
The Seeds of Time - Kay Kenyon   *s*   1136

Haines, Carolyn
Extinct - Charles Wilson   *h*   1027

Hoke
'48 - James Herbert   *h*   914

Jasmine "Jas"
Finder's Bane - Kate Novak   *f*   773

Jian, Reverdy
Dreaming Metal - Melissa Scott   *s*   1197

Nielsen, Berkeley "Berk"
Faraday's Orphans - N. Lee Wood   *s*   1242

Nussem, Alis Mary
Reckoning Infinity - John E. Stith   *s*   1214

Paris, Tom
Chrysalis - David Niall Wilson   *s*   1240

Sakai, Catherine
To Dream in the City of Sorrows - Kathryn M. Drennan   *s*   1084

Scoresby, Lee
The Subtle Knife - Philip Pullman   *f*   781

Shannon, Rip
A Mind for Trade - Andre Norton   *s*   1171

Stanton, Karl
Reckoning Infinity - John E. Stith   *s*   1214

Stern
'48 - James Herbert   *h*   914

Wysaigh, "Wy"
Faraday's Orphans - N. Lee Wood   *s*   1242

PIONEER

Hunter
Twilight of the Empire - Simon R. Green   *s*   1115

PIRATE

Engor
Engor's Sword Arm - David C. Smith   *h*   999

PLANTATION OWNER

Lawrence, Emma
Pratt's Landing - Martha Kirkland   *r*   351

POLICE OFFICER

Aiah
City on Fire - Walter Jon Williams   *s*   1235

Anderson, Mali
If I Should Die - Grace Edwards   *m*   71

Bailey, Geoffrey
Without Consent - Frances Fyfield   *m*   89

Banks, Alan
Blood at the Root - Peter Robinson   *m*   203

Benton, Dvid
Return of the Living Dead - John A. Russo   *h*   988

Brady, Joanna
Skeleton Canyon - J.A. Jance   *m*   130

Buscarsela, Filomena
23 Shades of Black - K.j.a. Wishnia   *m*   242

Camel, Teddy
Cul-De-Sac - David Martin   *h*   958

Casey, Fred
Deadly Season - Tim Champlin   *w*   480

Choy, Mary
/ - Greg Bear   *s*   1049

Croaker, Fey
Tequila Mockingbird - Paul Bishop   *m*   19

Cross
The Psalm Killer - Chris Petit   *m*   187

D'Agosta, Vincent
Reliquary - Douglas Preston   *h*   979

Delafield, Kate
Apparition Alley - Katherine V. Forrest   *m*   85

Dietrich, Otto
Five Past Midnight - James Thayer   *m*   225

Donahoe, Neal
Fade to Black - Tony Gibbs   *m*   96

Ethemark
City on Fire - Walter Jon Williams   *s*   1235

Evans, Evan
Evans Above - J. Rhys Bowen   *m*   23

Feiffer, Harry
Nightmare Syndrome - William Marshall   *m*   153

Fenn
The Fleet of Stars - Poul Anderson   *s*   1034

Fine, Mike
A Hard Light - Wendy Hornsby   *m*   125

Folger, Meredith
Death in a Mood Indigo - Francine Mathews   *m*   157

Gastner, William K.
Privileged to Kill - Steven F. Havill   *m*   115

Endymion, Raul
The Rise of Endymion - Dan Simmons   *s*   1208

G'Kar
Personal Agendas - Al Sarrantonio   *s*   1191

Kitatimate, Alexander "Sander"
Cinderblock - Janine Ellen Young   *s*   1243

Lewin, Alma Marie
Days of Cain - J.R. Dunn   *s*   1086

Motzin, Rebeka
Days of Cain - J.R. Dunn   *s*   1086

Seventeen
The Road to Hell, Volume I - Robert
   Weinberg   *h*   1024

Trimble, Horace
Andersonville - Robert Vaughan   *w*   623

PRODUCER

Kincaid, Taylor
The Scottish Rose - Jill Jones   *r*   339

Rippen, Jack
Celestial Dogs - J.S. Russell   *h*   986

Tortelli, Mia
Heaven Loves a Hero - Nikki Holiday   *r*   326

PROFESSOR

Brandon, Richard
God's Dice - S. Andrew Swann   *f*   804

Chiara
The Thirteenth Daughter of the Moon - Steven
   Nightingale   *f*   771

Clisser
Dragonseye - Anne McCaffrey   *s*   1153

Darlington, Jane
Nobody's Baby but Mine - Susan Elizabeth
   Phillips   *r*   397

Deane, Sarah
The Garden Plot - J.S. Borthwick   *m*   22

Estrand, Philip
As She Climbed Across the Table - Jonathan
   Lethem   *s*   1142

Ferro-Maine, Sylvia
The Ecolitan Enigma - L.E. Modesitt Jr.   *s*   1158

Harding, Amelia "Blaze"
Forever Peace - Joe Haldeman   *s*   1119

Hoffman, Nick
The Edith Wharton Murders - Lev Raphael   *m*   194

Jennings, Patricia
The Taking - Donald Beman   *h*   837

Marchenko, Ivan "Burian Klimus"
Frameshift - Robert J. Sawyer   *s*   1193

Pelletier, Karen
Quieter than Sleep - Joanne Dobson   *m*   63

Plant, Melrose
The Case Has Altered - Martha Grimes   *m*   102

Rivers, Neal
Keeper of the King - Nigel Bennett   *h*   838

Skena, Harry
Patton's Spaceship - John Barnes   *s*   1043

Slater, Peter
Secret Passages - Paul Preuss   *s*   1178

Thorne, Titus
The Mermaid - Betina Krahn   *r*   352

Whaler, Nathaniel Firstborne
The Ecolitan Enigma - L.E. Modesitt Jr.   *s*   1158

PROSPECTOR

Caraval, Zacarias
Spirits of the Ordinary - Kathleen Alcala   *f*   638

PROSTITUTE

Bonn
Different Women Dancing - Jonathan Gash   *m*   92

Brown, Molly
Black Gold - Frederic Bean   *w*   450

Brown, Sugar
Dust on the Wind - Bill Brooks   *w*   474

Coachman, Dosh
Future Indefinite - Dave Duncan   *f*   694

Edenderry, Rose
Second Lives - Richard S. Wheeler   *w*   630

Elder, Kate
Doc Holliday - Matt Braun   *w*   470
The Fourth Horseman - Randy Lee
   Eickhoff   *w*   514

Green, Annabelle
Hell's Half Acre - Frederic Bean   *w*   452

Hafford, Jovvi
Competition - Sharon Green   *f*   712

Lake, Ramona
Double Dead - Gary Hardwick   *m*   111

Place, Laura
Range Wars - Robert Vaughan   *w*   625

Rumer
Waking Beauty - Paul Witcover   *f*   818

Thalassa
The Forging of the Shadows - Oliver Johnson   *f*   729

Tyner, Sally
No Remorse - James D. Brewer   *m*   26

Wali, Linnet
Imposter - Valerie J. Freireich   *s*   1103

PSYCHIC

Beatrice
The Broken Sword - Molly Cochran   *f*   673

Bond, Molly
Frameshift - Robert J. Sawyer   *s*   1193

Carrie
Razor's Edge - Lisanne Norman   *s*   1169

Chastain, Nick
Zinnia - Jayne Castle   *r*   277

Creedath
The Gates of Vensunor - Carol Heller   *f*   720

Cuthberton-Jones, Angelica
Angela and Diabola - Lynne Reid Banks   *f*   646

Cuthberton-Jones, Diabola
Angela and Diabola - Lynne Reid Banks   *f*   646

Ella
Shade's Children - Garth Nix   *s*   1168

E'non, Caelan
Realm of Light - Deborah Chester   *f*   666
Shadow War - Deborah Chester   *f*   667

Farseer, FitzChivalry "Tom"
Assassin's Quest - Robin Hobb   *f*   722

Fitzgerald, Kara
Bride of the Mist - Christina Skye   *r*   424

Freund, Solomon "Sol"
Children of the Dusk - Janet Berliner   *f*   652

Frewin, Mary
The Red-Eared Ghosts - Vivian Alcock   *f*   639

Gallowglass, Magnus "Gar Pike"
A Wizard in Chaos - Christopher Stasheff   *s*   1210
A Wizard in Peace - Christopher Stasheff   *s*   1211

Gold-eye
Shade's Children - Garth Nix   *s*   1168

Jakri
Receive the Gift - Louise Marley   *s*   1150

Kusac
Razor's Edge - Lisanne Norman   *s*   1169

Lillorigga "Lilli"
The Red Wyvern - Katharine Kerr   *f*   735

Mandel, Greg
A Quantum Murder - Peter F. Hamilton   *s*   1122

Masters, Gil
Fragments - James F. David   *h*   866

Merlin, Emrys
The Seven Songs of Merlin - T.A. Barron   *f*   648

Morrison, Gertie
Threshold - Bill Myers   *s*   1164

Mreen
Receive the Gift - Louise Marley   *s*   1150

Murgen
She Is the Darkness - Glen Cook   *f*   676

Proteus
Exit to Reality - Edith Forbes   *s*   1098

Psycho, Jenny
Deathstalker War - Simon R. Green   *s*   1114

Rhiannon "Rhia"
The Seven Songs of Merlin - T.A. Barron   *f*   648

Ross, John
Running with the Demon - Terry Brooks   *f*   659

Sally
The Kronos Condition - Emily Devenport   *s*   1078

Shunlar
The Gates of Vensunor - Carol Heller   *f*   720

Siri
Receive the Gift - Louise Marley   *s*   1150

Spring, Zinnia
Zinnia - Jayne Castle   *r*   277

Ted
The Kronos Condition - Emily Devenport   *s*   1078

Typhoid Mary
Twilight of the Empire - Simon R. Green   *s*   1115

Valdoria kva Skolia, Kelricson Garlin
The Last Hawk - Catherine Asaro   *s*   1038

PSYCHOLOGIST

Bond, Molly
Frameshift - Robert J. Sawyer   *s*   1193

Braithwaite
Final Diagnosis - James White   *s*   1233

Brandon, Richard
God's Dice - S. Andrew Swann   *f*   804

Burke, Martin
/ - Greg Bear   *s*   1049

Delaware, Alex
Survival of the Fittest - Jonathan Kellerman   *m*   138

Dobbs, Evelyn
Fool's War - Sarah Zettel   *s*   1245

Franklyn, Kit
Sleeping with the Crawfish - D.J. Donaldson   *m*   65

Gregory, Alan
Remote Control - Stephen White   *m*   238

Martin, Wes
Fragments - James F. David   *h*   866

REFUGEE

Sam
Hope of Earth - Piers Anthony   s   1036

Serege, Tristan
Echoes of Issel - Diann Thornley   s   1222

REINCARNATED PERSON

daCosta, Nick
Nick of Time - Casey Claybourne   r   282

Fiona
Ronin - D.A. Heeley   f   719

Jaad
Ronin - D.A. Heeley   f   719

McKenzie, Mary Kate
Twice upon a Time - Emilie Richards   r   409

Shadrack
Ronin - D.A. Heeley   f   719

RELATIVE

Chambers, Christel
The Misconceiver - Lucy Ferriss   s   1095

Lee, Amy
The Earth Giant - Melvin Burgess   s   1058

Lee, Peter
The Earth Giant - Melvin Burgess   s   1058

Mallard
An Embarrassment of Corpses - Alan
  Beechey   m   14

RELIGIOUS

Aenea
The Rise of Endymion - Dan Simmons   s   1208

Alexander
The Bighead - Edward Lee   h   943

Alston, John "Skiddle"
The Great Wheel - Ian R. MacLeod   s   1148

Ardis
Four & Twenty Blackbirds - Mercedes
  Lackey   f   742

Avelyn
The Demon Awakens - R.A. Salvatore   f   789

Bardell, Luke
Ritual Sins - Anne Stuart   r   432

Batik
Wolf in Shadow - David Gemmell   s   1110

Beaumont, Dora
Wayward Angel - Patricia Rice   r   407

Black Robe
Prairie - Greg Tobin   w   616

Bolivar
The Red River - Frederic Bean   w   454

Brownpony, Elia
Saint Leibowitz and the Wild Horse Woman - Walter
  M. Miller Jr.   s   1157

Caillean
Lady of Avalon - Marion Zimmer Bradley   f   656

Callahan, Rose
Death of a Winter Shaker - Deborah
  Woodworth   m   243

Catcher, Selene
Renaissance Moon - Linda Nevins   f   770

Chisolm, Casey
Symphony - Charles L. Grant   h   899

Church, Thomas
The Gaia Websters - Kim Antieau   s   1037

Corio, Giovanna
Renaissance Moon - Linda Nevins   f   770

Cornelius, Vito
The Fifth Element - Terry Bisson   s   1053

Crane, Scott
Earthquake Weather - Tim Powers   f   778

Dexter, Quinn
Emergence - Peter F. Hamilton   s   1120

Evans, Marged
Truly - Mary Balogh   r   253

Felipe
The Great Wheel - Ian R. MacLeod   s   1148

Fidelma
Suffer Little Children - Peter Tremayne   m   227

Frevisse
The Prioress' Tale - Margaret Frazer   m   86

Gawen
Lady of Avalon - Marion Zimmer Bradley   f   656

Grey, Lavinia
Hasty Retreat - Kate Gallison   m   90

Handrar, Ser
Wizard of Bones - Robert N. Charrette   f   665

Harrowslough, Holly
Finder's Bane - Kate Novak   f   773

Henriques, Tomas
The Grand Ones of San Ildefonso - Lauran
  Paine   w   580

Hodierna
The Notorious Abbess - Vera Chapman   f   664

Joel
Finder's Bane - Kate Novak   f   773

Keeper, Tom
Ancient Games - Scott Ciencin   f   669

Kilroy, Sarah
American Woman - R. Garcia y Robertson   w   521

Luke
Thessalonica - Harry Turtledove   f   805

Mara
Time Blender - Michael Dorn   s   1081

McKenzie, Mary Kate
Twice upon a Time - Emilie Richards   r   409

Melchior
Count Scar - C. Dale Brittain   f   658

Merlin
Enemy of God - Bernard Cornwell   f   678

Moncrief, Carrol
Dead Reckoning - Mike Blakely   w   461

Moon, Gracie
Chase the Moon - Dinah McCall   r   375

Murphy, Mary Frances
Innocence - Suzanne Forster   r   307

O'Donnell, Reena
By Honor Bound - Alan Morris   w   574

Owen
Beguiled - Alice Borchardt   r   266

Pessoa, Manoel
God's Fires - Patricia Anthony   s   1035

St. George, Blacktooth "Nimmy"
Saint Leibowitz and the Wild Horse Woman - Walter
  M. Miller Jr.   s   1157

Sanchez, Damion
The Grand Ones of San Ildefonso - Lauran
  Paine   w   580

Sien
Shadow War - Deborah Chester   f   667

Simon
Corrupting Dr. Nice - John Kessel   s   1137

Solamnus, Vinas
Vinas Solamnus - J. Robert King   f   740

Soothslayer
Soothslayer: A Magical Fantasy - D.J.
  Conway   f   675

Townsend, Mark
A Ritual Death - Father Brad Reynolds S.J.   m   197

Uthred of Ravenspur
The Forging of the Shadows - Oliver Johnson   f   729

Vadeviya
Touched by the Gods - Lawrence Watt-Evans   f   810

Vaughan, Lucus
Spiritride - Mark Shepherd   f   793

Veronica
Cardmaster - Clayton Emery   f   700

Vitarosa
Mind Snare - Gayle Greeno   s   1118

Weston, Wade
Jade - Ruth Langan   r   360

Woodhouse, Andy
Son of Rosemary - Ira Levin   h   945

Zalman
A Blessing on the Moon - Joseph Skibell   f   796

Zerek, Cassandra
Simply Love - Catherine Anderson   r   249

RENEGADE

Dragging Canoe
The Long Hunters - Dodge Tyler   w   620

One Eye
Apache Revenge - Dodge Tyler   w   618

O'Toole, Sean
Dream Lover - Virginia Henley   r   324

Wolf Who Hunts Smiling
Bloody Bones Canyon - Judd Cole   w   486
Renegade Siege - Judd Cole   w   487
River of Death - Judd Cole   w   488

REPORTER

Hollis, Adam
Algonquin Massacre - Dodge Tyler   w   617
Apache Revenge - Dodge Tyler   w   618
Death at Spanish Wells - Dodge Tyler   w   619
A River Run Red - Dodge Tyler   w   621

Nicholson, Graeme
Expansion - Peter F. Hamilton   s   1121

RESEARCHER

Correa, Marissa
Lightpaths - Howard V. Hendrix   s   1131

Cortland, Roger
Lightpaths - Howard V. Hendrix   s   1131

Denby, Kate
Long After Midnight - Iris Johansen   r   335

Dworkin, Sam
Silent Zone - Stephen Molstad   s   1159

Foster, Sandra "Sandy"
Bellwether - Connie Willis   s   1237

Leopold, Lark
American Dreamer - Theresa Weir   r   435

Drev
The Dark Shore - Adam Lee *f* 746

Gawen
Lady of Avalon - Marion Zimmer Bradley *f* 656

Hadding
War of the Gods - Poul Anderson *f* 641

Lephi the White
The Chaos Balance - L.E. Modesitt Jr. *f* 764

Orwen, Feng
The White Abacus - Damien Broderick *s* 1056

Rahl, Richard "the Seeker"
Temple of the Winds - Terry Goodkind *f* 710

Sharbaraz
The Thousand Cities - Harry Turtledove *f* 806

Tirrell
Talion: Revenant - Michael A. Stackpole *f* 799

Tutankhamon
Eater of Souls - Lynda S. Robinson *m* 202

Ublaz Mad Eyes
The Pearls of Lutra - Brian Jacques *f* 728

Woodgate, Lisa
Bretta Martyn - L. Neil Smith *s* 1209

RUNAWAY

Chestnut, Clutie Mae
Leaving Missouri - Ellen Recknor *w* 592

Gavrilli, David
Interface Masque - Shariann Lewitt *s* 1143

O'Dell, Dinah
Winter Heart - Jane Bonander *r* 265

O'Hurley, Jemma
Just Once - Jill Marie Landis *r* 359

SAILOR

Skinner, Martin
Mary's Land - Lucia St. Clair Robson *w* 598

Skye, Barnaby
Rendezvous - Richard S. Wheeler *w* 629

Williamson, Luke
No Remorse - James D. Brewer *m* 26

SALESMAN

Salmoneus
The First Casualty - David L. Seidman *f* 791

SALOON HOSTESS

Andrews, Pepper
Stay Away From That City. . .They Call It Cheyenne - Stephen Bly *w* 463

SALOON KEEPER/OWNER

Bell, Lucas
The Ghost of Major Pryor - Donald Honig *w* 542

Clio of Camrose
Wonderful - Jill Barnett *r* 255

McGill, Cady
Outlaw in Paradise - Patricia Gaffney *r* 309

Wallace, Tess
The Ladies of the Goldfield Stock Exchange - Sibyl Downing *w* 509

SCHOLAR

Brice, Marcer Joseph
Imposter - Valerie J. Freireich *s* 1103

Catcher, Selene
Renaissance Moon - Linda Nevins *f* 770

Clayborne, Adam
One Red Rose - Julie Garwood *r* 313

Drysdale, Lucy
Dangerous to Love - Rexanne Becnel *r* 258

Faust, Johannes "Jack"
Jack Faust - Michael Swanwick *s* 1219

Hulhe
When the Gods Are Silent - Jane M. Lindskold *f* 750

McClellan, Victoria
Dreaming of the Bones - Deborah Crombie *m* 48

Milana, Chaka
Eternity Road - Jack McDevitt *s* 1155

Perholt, Gillian
The Djinn in the Nightingale's Eye - A.S. Byatt *f* 662

Rhenford, Liam
Beggar's Banquet - Daniel Hood *f* 726

Russell, Mary
A Letter of Mary - Laurie R. King *m* 141

St. John, Grace
Son of the Morning - Linda Howard *r* 330

Saryon
Legacy of the Darksword - Margaret Weis *f* 812

Williams, Terry
The Poison Tree - Tony Strong *m* 221

SCIENTIST

Adcock, Patrice "Pat"
The Siege of Eternity - Frederik Pohl *s* 1176

Ashton, Celeste
The Mermaid - Betina Krahn *r* 352

Augustus, Caleb
Jovah's Angel - Sharon Shinn *s* 1205

Barbrossa, Edwin Amadeus
How Like a God - Brenda W. Clough *f* 672

Beckett, Sam
Angels Unaware - L. Elizabeth Storm *s* 1215

Brand, Matthew Tyler
The Hot-Wired Dodo - Jack L. Chalker *s* 1064

Class, Julian
Forever Peace - Joe Haldeman *s* 1119

Cochrane, Miles "David Gilman"
Alpha Centauri - William Barton *s* 1045

Cohen, Julius
Mother of Demons - Eric Flint *s* 1096

Coombs, Alice
As She Climbed Across the Table - Jonathan Lethem *s* 1142

Cortland, Roger
Lightpaths - Howard V. Hendrix *s* 1131

Coulton, Roger
Einstein's Bridge - John Cramer *s* 1070

Dana, Gregory
Voyager - Stephen Baxter *s* 1048

Darlington, Jane
Nobody's Baby but Mine - Susan Elizabeth Phillips *r* 397

Darrow, Troy
Carnivore - Leigh Clark *h* 859

Dorman, Jeremy
Antibodies - Kevin J. Anderson *h* 832

Einhorn, Carl
Rage of Spirits - Noel Hynd *h* 921

Ford
North of Havana - Randy Wayne White *m* 236

Foster, Sandra "Sandy"
Bellwether - Connie Willis *s* 1237

Freeman, Alan
Extinct - Charles Wilson *h* 1027

Green, Sandra
Saturn Rukh - Robert L. Forward *s* 1100

Griffin, George
Einstein's Bridge - John Cramer *s* 1070

Haley, Adam
Howl - Christine Tanasiuk *h* 1012

Hansen, Emily
Mother Nature - Sarah Andrews *m* 4

Harding, Amelia "Blaze"
Forever Peace - Joe Haldeman *s* 1119

Harris, Samantha
Howl - Christine Tanasiuk *h* 1012

Heber, Vanessa
Bug Park - James P. Hogan *s* 1132

Holland, R. Paul
Infinity's Child - Harry Stein *h* 1005

Hutchings, Ian McFarland
Fortress on the Sun - Paul Cook *s* 1068

Hutton, Andrew
Earthling - Tony Daniel *s* 1073

Kastle
Devil's Engine - Mark Sumner *f* 803

Kendoro, Judit
Acorna - Anne McCaffrey *s* 1152

Kesserich, Daniel
The Dealings of Daniel Kesserich - Fritz Leiber *s* 1141

Kitchener, Edward
A Quantum Murder - Peter F. Hamilton *s* 1122

Lang, Darya
Convergence - Charles Sheffield *s* 1202

Larrin, Marty
Forever Peace - Joe Haldeman *s* 1119

Lightnin' Lil
Mississippi Blue - Kathleen Ann Goonan *s* 1112

Lynch, Raymond
Infinity's Child - Harry Stein *h* 1005

Maggie
Cain - James Byron Huggins *h* 920
Fear Street: The Cat - R.L. Stine *h* 1008

Meniskos, Jhana
Lightpaths - Howard V. Hendrix *s* 1131

Minakis, Manolis
Secret Passages - Paul Preuss *s* 1178

Mosala, Violet
Distress - Greg Egan *s* 1088

Nobilio, Francis "Frank"
Illegal Alien - Robert J. Sawyer *s* 1194

Nowek, Gregori
Siberian Light - Robin White *m* 237

O'Reilly, Bennett "Ben"
Bellwether - Connie Willis *s* 1237

Reichner, Helmut
Threshold - Bill Myers *s* 1164

Rosenberg, Isaac
Titan - Stephen Baxter *s* 1047

Sandoz, Jules
Mari - Jane Valentine Barker   *w*   448

Sawyer, Kelly
Carnivore - Leigh Clark   *h*   859

Seaforth, Fawn
The Howling Stones - Alan Dean Foster   *s*   1101

Seldon, Hari
Foundation's Fear - Gregory Benford   *s*   1050

Sena, Miranda
Rewind - Terry England   *s*   1091

Slater, Peter
Secret Passages - Paul Preuss   *s*   1178

Snow, David
Cold at Heart - Brian Hopkins   *h*   917

Soleta
End Game - Peter David   *s*   1075

Stafford, Alwyn Bryan
Mars Underground - William Hartmann   *s*   1126

Swift, Stella
Esau - Philip Kerr   *m*   139

Tanaka, Terry
Meg - Steve Alten   *h*   831

Tarosh, Valentine
Carnivore - Leigh Clark   *h*   859

Taylor, Jonas
Meg - Steve Alten   *h*   831

Tomochelor, Pulickel
The Howling Stones - Alan Dean Foster   *s*   1101

Tucker, Rose
Sole Survivor - Dean R. Koontz   *h*   935

Vannice, Owen
Corrupting Dr. Nice - John Kessel   *s*   1137

Vereskaya, Anna
Siberian Light - Robin White   *m*   237

Virili, Rima
The Black Sun - Jack Williamson   *s*   1236

Weintraub, Sarah
Threshold - Bill Myers   *s*   1164

Wren, Mason
Alien Resurrection - A.C. Crispin   *s*   1071

Wu, Victor "Orf"
Earthling - Tony Daniel   *s*   1073

York, Natalie
Voyager - Stephen Baxter   *s*   1048

SCOUT

Blackfoot Bill
I Rode with Jesse James - Charles
Hackenberry   *w*   527

Carson, Kit
Meridian: A Novel of Kit Carson's West - Norman
Zollinger   *w*   636

Cody, William
Devil's Engine - Mark Sumner   *f*   803

Colt, Chris
Matched Colts - Don Bendell   *w*   457

Horn, Tom
Range Wars - Robert Vaughan   *w*   625

Jalbert, Lone Hunter
So Wide the Sky - Elizabeth Grayson   *r*   320

St. John, Clancy
Apache Sundown - Hank Edwards   *w*   513

SEA CAPTAIN

Blackwell, Xavier
Captive - Brenda Joyce   *r*   342

Morley, Thomas
Major Washington - Michael Kilian   *w*   552

Thorne, Colin
My Steadfast Heart - Jo Goodman   *r*   318

SECRETARY

Blaine, Dee Dee
Jumpers - R. Patrick Gates   *h*   891

Cabot, Wentworth
The Prince and the Prosecutor - Peter J.
Heck   *m*   117

Guthrie, Patterson Erskine
Against the Brotherhood - Quinn Fawcett   *m*   82

Jervis, Katherine
Milton in America - Peter Ackroyd   *f*   637

Kharyat, Judy
Son of Rosemary - Ira Levin   *h*   945

Reuven
Legacy of the Darksword - Margaret Weis   *f*   812

St. Ives, Baxter
Affair - Amanda Quick   *r*   402

Wroke, Alice
The Demon Princes: Volume Two - Jack
Vance   *s*   1226

SECURITY OFFICER

Surrey, John
Timeshare - Joshua Dann   *s*   1074

Wylie, Eva
Musclebound - Liza Cody   *m*   40

SERIAL KILLER

Watts, Arnie
Thoughts of God - Michael Kanaly   *s*   1134

SERVANT

Bee, Jane
Death at Sandringham House - C.C. Benison   *m*   16

Carrington, Jade
Jade - Betty Brooks   *r*   269

Dipper
The Devil in Music - Kate Ross   *m*   204

Goosequill
Milton in America - Peter Ackroyd   *f*   637

Hazard, Catie Willman
The Secrets of Catie Hazard - Miranda
Jarrett   *r*   334

Ranira "Renra"
Shadows over Lyra - Patricia C. Wrede   *f*   820

Sparrow, Anicah
Mary's Land - Lucia St. Clair Robson   *w*   598

SETTLER

Bjorklund, Haakan
A Land to Call Home - Lauraine Snelling   *w*   606

Bjorklund, Ingeborg
A Land to Call Home - Lauraine Snelling   *w*   606

Burke, Andrew
Across the Rio Colorado - Ralph Compton   *w*   491

DuBois, Cora
Winter Woman - F.M. Parker   *w*   582

Gray, Virginia "Jenna"
Sweetwater - Dorothy Garlock   *r*   311

Hopkins, Marabelle
The Peacekeeper - Jeffrey Poston   *w*   586

Hunter, Seth
Prairie Rose - Catherine Palmer   *w*   581

Indergard, Cejo
The Dazzle of Day - Molly Gloss   *s*   1111

Knutson, Kaaren
A Land to Call Home - Lauraine Snelling   *w*   606

McCraken, Callie
Broken Lance - Michele Sorensen   *w*   607

McCraken, Silas
Broken Lance - Michele Sorensen   *w*   607

Negrete, Dolores
The Dazzle of Day - Molly Gloss   *s*   1111

Pryor, John
Desperate Crossing: The Jenny Sanders Pryor Story -
Barbara Riefe   *w*   594

Sommers, Henry
Wild Rose of Ruby Canyon - John D.
Nesbitt   *w*   577

Spenser, Luke
The Diary of Mattie Spenser - Sandra
Dallas   *w*   505

Spenser, Mattie
The Diary of Mattie Spenser - Sandra
Dallas   *w*   505

Stapleton, Malcolm
Remember the Morning - Thomas Fleming   *w*   518

Stone, Hunter
By Honor Bound - Alan Morris   *w*   574

SHAMAN

Crowfoot
The Bear Paw Horses - Will Henry   *w*   532

Others' Child
The Long Walk - Amanda Cockrell   *w*   483

Panther
People of the Mist - Kathleen O'Neal Gear   *w*   522

Perika, Daisy
The Shaman's Bones - James D. Doss   *m*   66

Pipe Bearer
Medicine Hat - Don Coldsmith   *w*   484

Slocum, Frances
The Red Heart - James Alexander Thom   *w*   610

Touch the Sky
Bloody Bones Canyon - Judd Cole   *w*   486
Renegade Siege - Judd Cole   *w*   487
River of Death - Judd Cole   *w*   488

Wolf
Spiritride - Mark Shepherd   *f*   793

Wovoka
The Ghost Trail - Tracy Dunham   *w*   510

SHIPOWNER

McBride, Jedediah
Lady Thorn - Catherine Archer   *r*   250

SIDEKICK

Cricket
Dust Devils - Robert Laxalt   *w*   556

Crutchfield, Jeff
This Man Colter - Johnny D. Boggs   *w*   465

de Marigny, Henri Laurent
Titus Crow, Volume One - Brian Lumley   *h*   949
Titus Crow, Volume Three - Brian Lumley   *h*   950
Titus Crow, Volume Two - Brian Lumley   *h*   951

Dulaine, Dirk
A Wizard in Chaos - Christopher Stasheff   *s*   1210
A Wizard in Peace - Christopher Stasheff   *s*   1211

Flavius
Blood Hunt - David Thompson   *w*   611
Homecoming - David Thompson   *w*   612
Mississippi Mayhem - David Thompson   *w*   613
Sioux Slaughter - David Thompson   *w*   614

Grove, Carson
Deadwood - Douglas Hirt   *w*   535

Hawk
Small Vices - Robert B. Parker   *m*   182

Man Killer
Matched Colts - Don Bendell   *w*   457

McNair, Shakespeare
Spanish Slaughter - David Thompson   *w*   615

Pike, Joe
Indigo Slam - Robert Crais   *m*   46

Salmoneus
The First Casualty - David L. Seidman   *f*   791

SINGER

Brill
The Soprano Sorceress - L.E. Modesitt Jr.   *f*   765

Delilah "Lilah"
Jovah's Angel - Sharon Shinn   *s*   1205

Jakri
Receive the Gift - Louise Marley   *s*   1150

Lina
Interface Masque - Shariann Lewitt   *s*   1143

Marshall, Anna
The Soprano Sorceress - L.E. Modesitt Jr.   *f*   765

Merlin, Anastasia "Ana"
Tomorrow and Tomorrow - Charles
   Sheffield   *s*   1204

Nitt, Agnes
Maskerade - Terry Pratchett   *f*   780

Perry, Genevieve
One Red Rose - Julie Garwood   *r*   313

Siri
Receive the Gift - Louise Marley   *s*   1150

Thissizz
The Merro Tree - Katie Waitman   *s*   1230

SINGLE PARENT

Fine, Mike
A Hard Light - Wendy Hornsby   *m*   125

Jeffrey, Jane
Fear of Frying - Jill Churchill   *m*   38

MacGowen, Maggie
A Hard Light - Wendy Hornsby   *m*   125

Mooney, Shawana
The Arbitrary Placement of Walls - Martha
   Soukup   *f*   797

Rede, Pippa
In the Land of Winter - Richard Grant   *f*   711

Reilly, Nina
Obstruction of Justice - Perri O'Shaugnessy   *m*   178

Richards, Bryce
Beside a Dreamswept Sea - Victoria Barrett   *r*   256

Ryder (Walkman), Kathleen
Tallchief - Dinah McCall   *r*   376

Sanders, Kenny
A Family Wedding - Angela Benson   *r*   259

White, Kayla
Husband Needed - Cathie Linz   *r*   366

SLAVE

Annalise
Black Wine - Candas Jane Dorsey   *s*   1082

Bjornson, Kris
Freedom's Choice - Anne McCaffrey   *s*   1154

Breith
Drum Calls - Jo Clayton   *f*   671

Brown, Joe Bob
The Hard Land - Jack Ballas   *w*   446

Cinque
Amistad - Alexs Pate   *w*   584

Clara
Remember the Morning - Thomas Fleming   *w*   518

Clayborne, Adam
One Red Rose - Julie Garwood   *r*   313

Curran, Joslire
An Exchange of Hostages - Susan R.
   Matthews   *s*   1151

Essa
Black Wine - Candas Jane Dorsey   *s*   1082

MacKenzie, Virginia
True Heart - Arnette Lamb   *r*   358

Reyes, Adrien
Someone to Watch over Me - Tricia
   Sullivan   *s*   1218

Rohona
Acoma: A Novel of Conquest - Lana M.
   Harrigan   *w*   530

Washington
Tallgrass: A Novel of the Great Plains - Don
   Coldsmith   *w*   485

SOCIAL WORKER

Covington, Grace "Candi"
Mama Stalks the Past - Nora DeLoach   *m*   59

Foxworth, Elizabeth
Fragments - James F. David   *h*   866

SON

Troys, Taylor Thaddeus "Taytay"
Meeting the Minotaur - Carol Dawson   *f*   684

SORCERER

Aditi
Bijapur - Kara Dalkey   *f*   680

Bilitu
Engor's Sword Arm - David C. Smith   *h*   999

Farblood, Corri
Soothslayer: A Magical Fantasy - D.J.
   Conway   *f*   675

Jones, Umber
Rook - Graham Masterton   *h*   959

liMarchborg, Tradain
The White Tribunal - Paula Volsky   *f*   809

Mikal
Broken Blade - Ann Marston   *f*   754

Orogastus
Sky Trillium - Julian May   *f*   756

Silverhair, Imandoff
Soothslayer: A Magical Fantasy - D.J.
   Conway   *f*   675

Soothslayer
Soothslayer: A Magical Fantasy - D.J.
   Conway   *f*   675

Ufgood, Torquil
Shadow Dawn - Chris Claremont   *f*   670

SORCERESS

Brill
The Soprano Sorceress - L.E. Modesitt Jr.   *f*   765

dar Dero, Halleyne
Wrath of the Princes - Holly Lisle   *f*   752

Green
Gawain and Lady Green - Anne Eliot
   Crompton   *f*   679

Haramis
Sky Trillium - Julian May   *f*   756

Inya
Kar Kalim - Deborah Christian   *f*   668

Leather-woman
Spires of Spirit - Gael Baudino   *f*   649

Marshall, Anna
The Soprano Sorceress - L.E. Modesitt Jr.   *f*   765

Morgian
Grail - Stephen R. Lawhead   *f*   745

Polgara
Polgara the Sorceress - David Eddings   *f*   696

Shiara
The Wiz Biz - Rick Cook   *f*   677

Veriam, Tanaquil
Red Unicorn - Tanith Lee   *f*   747

SOUTHERN BELLE

Lloyd, Constance
To Marry a British Lord - Judith O'Brien   *r*   391

McPherson, Mary Beth
Look Away - Harold Coyle   *w*   501

SPACE EXPLORER

Dan
Douglas Adams's Starship Titanic - Terry
   Jones   *s*   1133

Derigha, Yarrun
Expendable - James Alan Gardner   *s*   1108

Lucy
Douglas Adams's Starship Titanic - Terry
   Jones   *s*   1133

Nettie
Douglas Adams's Starship Titanic - Terry
   Jones   *s*   1133

Ramos, Festina
Expendable - James Alan Gardner   *s*   1108

SPACEMAN

Apollo
Armageddon - Richard Hatch   *s*   1129

Bede, Strebban "Badger"
Hunting the Corrigan's Blood - Holly Lisle   *s*   1145

Calvert, Joshua
Emergence - Peter F. Hamilton   *s*   1120
Expansion - Peter F. Hamilton   *s*   1121

Spy (column 1)

Leckner, E.M.
The Royalscope Fe-As-Ko - Randall Beth Platt w 585

MacKenzie, Alex
The Garden Plot - J.S. Borthwick m 22

MacMillan, Elizabeth
Seasons - Rebecca Forster r 306

Mandel, Eleanor
A Quantum Murder - Peter F. Hamilton s 1122

McGann, Beatriz
Sierra Baron - Tom W. Blackburn w 459

Milleflores, Delanna
Promised Land - Connie Willis s 1238

Others' Child
The Long Walk - Amanda Cockrell w 483

Otter
Medicine Hat - Don Coldsmith w 484

Page, Sarah
The Refining Fire - W.E. Davis w 506

Pitt, Charlotte
Ashworth Hall - Anne Perry m 184

Place, Laura
Range Wars - Robert Vaughan w 625

Pryor, John
Desperate Crossing: The Jenny Sanders Pryor Story - Barbara Riefe w 594

Radon
Firewalk - Anne Logston f 753

Rathenau, Miriam "Miriam Alois"
Children of the Dusk - Janet Berliner f 652

Rockman, Wanda
Wooing Wanda - Gwen Pemberton r 396

Rodriguez
Senora Rodriguez and Other Worlds - Martha Cerda f 663

St. Gregory, Dane
Knights - Linda Lael Miller r 380

Stratton, Dan
Secret Sins - Jasmine Cresswell r 290

Tanner, Tarleton "Sonny"
Promised Land - Connie Willis s 1238

Tilghman, Zoe
One Last Town - Matt Braun w 472

SPY

Alec of Kerry
Stalking Darkness - Lynn Flewelling f 705

Archer, Owen
The Riddle of St. Leonard's - Candace M. Robb m 200

Ashe, Timothy
The Seeds of Time - Kay Kenyon s 1136

Blaire, Lorena
Lorena - Frederic Bean w 453

Boniol, Joan
Bandido Caballero - Jack Ballas w 445

Brooks, Clara
Lorena - Frederic Bean w 453

Brown, Greeley
The Phantom Legion - Cameron Judd w 551

Cameron, Alexander
The Pride of Lions - Marsha Canham r 276

Carlson, Winnie
Putting Up Roots - Charles Sheffield s 1203

Courtnay, Catherine
Dangerous to Hold - Elizabeth Thornton r 433

Dannerman, Jim Daniel "Dan"
The Siege of Eternity - Frederik Pohl s 1176

"David"
Death Will Have Your Eyes: A Novel about Spies - James Sallis m 207

Deacon, Amy
The Phantom Legion - Cameron Judd w 551

Fallon, Tom
Bandido Caballero - Jack Ballas w 445

Ford
North of Havana - Randy Wayne White m 236

MacKenzie, Alana
Rebel - Heather Graham r 319

Nichols, Jane
AKA Jane - Maureen Tan m 222

Pollifax, Emily
Mrs. Pollifax, Innocent Tourist - Dorothy Gilman m 98

Radieu, Dianna
Colorado Reverie - Suzann Ledbetter w 557

Seregil
Stalking Darkness - Lynn Flewelling f 705

Shelby, Samuel Sheridan
Deep as the Rivers - Shirl Henke r 323

Sperin, Bro
The Ship Avenged - S.M. Stirling s 1213

Stride, Elizabeth
Haven - John R. Maxim m 159

Thibaudeaux, Catherine "Cat"
Delta Search - William Shatner s 1199

Watt, Peter
Millennium: Gehenna - Lewis Gannett h 884

Wroke, Alice
The Demon Princes: Volume Two - Jack Vance s 1226

STEP-PARENT

Heber, Vanessa
Bug Park - James P. Hogan s 1132

STORE OWNER

Truitt, Charity
Deep Waters - Jayne Ann Krentz r 353

Watson, Libby
Prairie Rose - Susan Kirby r 349

Winters, Elias
Deep Waters - Jayne Ann Krentz r 353

STORYTELLER

Chakliux
Song of the River - Sue Harrison f 717

Gabrielle
The Thief of Hermes - Ru Emerson f 699

McCaffrey, Anne
A Diversity of Dragons - Anne McCaffrey f 757

Mythmaker
The Ghost Trail - Tracy Dunham w 510

Nazir, Nassifeh "Opalears"
The Family Tree - Sheri S. Tepper s 1220

Teller
The Gift - Patrick O'Leary f 775

Tighe, Epiphanius "Eppy"
A Diversity of Dragons - Anne McCaffrey f 757

STOWAWAY

Mondragon, Carlos
The Black Sun - Jack Williamson s 1236

STREETPERSON

Brown Wolf, Jesse
The Night Remembers - Kathleen Eagle r 298

Portal, Ellis
Free Reign - Rosemary Aubert m 7

Tommy T.
The Night Remembers - Kathleen Eagle r 298

STUDENT

Anderson, Mali
If I Should Die - Grace Edwards m 71

Bruckner, Teresa
Angels Unaware - L. Elizabeth Storm s 1215

Correa, Marissa
Lightpaths - Howard V. Hendrix s 1131

Crowe, Janie
The Plague Tales - Ann Benson s 1051

Cymel
Drum Calls - Jo Clayton f 671

Evans, Sean
A Diversity of Dragons - Anne McCaffrey f 757

Forester, David
Starfleet Academy - Diane Carey s 1061

Gerchak, Julie
My Ishmael - Daniel Quinn s 1180

Janeway, Kathryn
The Chance Factor - Diana G. Gallagher s 1106

Johnson, Duffy
Wolf Moon - John R. Holt h 916

Kendall, Meg
The Ladies of the Goldfield Stock Exchange - Sibyl Downing w 509

Koscuisko, Andrej
An Exchange of Hostages - Susan R. Matthews s 1151

Lescevre, Thibault
Bridge of Valor - Anne Lesley Groell f 716

Noycannir, Mergau
An Exchange of Hostages - Susan R. Matthews s 1151

Pira, Cleo
Lives of the Monster Dogs - Kirsten Bakis s 1040

St. Claire, Nicole
Wolf Moon - John R. Holt h 916

Wagner
Jack Faust - Michael Swanwick s 1219

Walsh, Charity
The Bighead - Edward Lee h 943

!Xabbu
City of Golden Shadow - Tad Williams s 1234

Zach
Ecstasy Club - Douglas Rushkoff s 1187

STUDENT—COLLEGE

Kaminski, Tiffany Jeanine "T.J."
Steel Rose - Kara Dalkey f 681

Heber, Kevin
Bug Park - James P. Hogan   s   1132

Howe, Geena
Monet's Ghost - Chelsea Quinn Yarbro   f   824

Islay, Robretta "Bretta Martyn"
Bretta Martyn - L. Neil Smith   s   1209

James, Julie
I Know What You Did Last Summer - Lois
Duncan   h   875

Jilseponie "Pony"
The Demon Awakens - R.A. Salvatore   f   789

Jones, T.J.
Rook - Graham Masterton   h   959

Kayrlis
Ancient Games - Scott Ciencin   f   669

Larson, Sugar
The Cowgirls of the Mariposa - Lana Dean
James   w   543

Leyner, Mark
The Tetherballs of Bougainville - Mark
Leyner   f   749

MacDonald, Skye
Shifting Stars: A Novel of the West - Page
Lambert   w   555

MacFarlane, Griffin
Furnace - Muriel Gray   h   901

Neihart, Fletcher Robert
Finity's End - C.J. Cherryh   s   1065

Nell
Into the Forest - Jean Hegland   s   1130

Noir, Julie
The Black Cat - Robert Poe   h   978

Nolan, Ronan
A Wizard Abroad - Diane Duane   f   693

O'Malley, Barlow David
Klondike Fever - Suzann Ledbetter   w   558

Prettiance "Pretty"
Strange Deliverance - Mary Brown   s   1057

Priestley, Amy
Nazareth Hill - Ramsey Campbell   h   851

Raitt, Johnny
The Vampire's Beautiful Daughter - S.P.
Somtow   h   1002

Ryan, Lacey
Shackled - Ray Garton   h   889

Serege, Tristan
Dominion's Reach - Diann Thornley   s   1221
Echoes of Issel - Diann Thornley   s   1222

Stanislaus, Glynn Webster
Mind Snare - Gayle Greeno   s   1118

Summers, Buffy
Buffy the Vampire Slayer: The Harvest - Richie
Tankersley Cusick   h   863

Sundquist, Michael
The Presence - John Saul   h   991

Taki
Bug Park - James P. Hogan   s   1132

Tamerlane "Tam"
Strange Deliverance - Mary Brown   s   1057

Teague, Aiden
Blood and Chocolate - Annette Curtis
Klause   h   932

Teppish, Rebecca
The Vampire's Beautiful Daughter - S.P.
Somtow   h   1002

Tim
The Gift - Patrick O'Leary   f   775

Tolivar
Sky Trillium - Julian May   f   756

Viner, Lily
Railroad Schemes - Cecilia Holland   w   539

Wyndon, Elbryan
The Demon Awakens - R.A. Salvatore   f   789

TELEPATH

Alton, Marguerida "Margaret"
The Shadow Matrix - Marion Zimmer
Bradley   s   1055

Dellon, Melusine "Sinah"
Gravelight - Marion Zimmer Bradley   f   655

Ezekiel "Zeke"
The Seraphim Rising - Elisabeth De Vos   s   1076

Hilliard, Terrence
The Shadow Within - Jeanne Cavelos   s   1062

Ishmael
My Ishmael - Daniel Quinn   s   1180

Kes
Chrysalis - David Niall Wilson   s   1240

Lanart-Hastur, Mikhail
The Shadow Matrix - Marion Zimmer
Bradley   s   1055

Lewis, Rob
How Like a God - Brenda W. Clough   f   672

Nighteyes
Assassin's Quest - Robin Hobb   f   722

Silberhutte, Hank
Titus Crow, Volume Three - Brian Lumley   h   950
Titus Crow, Volume Two - Brian Lumley   h   951

Sixa, Jenny
The Stranger - Eric James Fullilove   s   1105

Teska
Mind Meld - John Vornholt   s   1229

TELEVISION PERSONALITY

Asimov, Issac
Back in the USSA - Kim Newman   s   1166

Holiday, Raymond
Mister Christmas - Linda Cajio   r   273

Nelson, Lynn
Heartbreaker - Karen Robards   r   414

TERRORIST

O'Connor, Padraic
Shade of Pale - Greg Kihn   h   929

Philipe
The Ignored - Bentley Little   h   946

THIEF

Alcott, Tess
Stolen Hearts - Michelle Martin   r   373

Allika
King's Man and Thief - Christie Golden   f   709

Dogbrick
The Dark Shore - Adam Lee   f   746

Fafhrd
Return to Lankhmar - Fritz Leiber   f   748

Grey Mouser
Return to Lankhmar - Fritz Leiber   f   748

Helarion
The Thief of Hermes - Ru Emerson   f   699

Larath, Deveren
King's Man and Thief - Christie Golden   f   709

Larque, Lens
The Demon Princes: Volume Two - Jack
Vance   s   1226

Marrika
King's Man and Thief - Christie Golden   f   709

Rhodenbarr, Bernie
The Burglar in the Library - Lawrence Block   m   20

Scott, Rowan
The Raven's Moon - Susan King   r   348

Seregil
Stalking Darkness - Lynn Flewelling   f   705

Shea, Glenys
Raven's Bride - Lynn Kerstan   r   346

Wilder, Anne
All through the Night - Connie Brockway   r   267

TIME TRAVELLER

Ashe, Timothy
The Seeds of Time - Kay Kenyon   s   1136

Backmaker, Hodgins "Hodge"
Bring the Jubilee - Ward Moore   s   1162

Beckett, Sam
Angels Unaware - L. Elizabeth Storm   s   1215

Bento, Jake
Atlantis Found - R. Garcia y Robertson   s   1107

Brennan, Coleman
Memories of You - Jane Goodgear   r   317

Chance, Angela
Time Station Berlin - David Evans   s   1092

Dumont, Claire
Memories of You - Jane Goodgear   r   317

Faison, Genevieva
Corrupting Dr. Nice - John Kessel   s   1137

Faracon, George
Time Station Paris - David Evans   s   1093

Finn, Clio
The Seeds of Time - Kay Kenyon   s   1136

Gaspar, James
Days of Cain - J.R. Dunn   s   1086

Haggerwells, Barbara
Bring the Jubilee - Ward Moore   s   1162

Henry, Ned
To Say Nothing of the Dog - Connie Willis   s   1239

Izakar "Izzy"
The Family Tree - Sheri S. Tepper   s   1220

ja N'Wook, Chrysamen "Chrys"
Caesar's Bicycle - John Barnes   s   1042

Kindle, Verity
To Say Nothing of the Dog - Connie Willis   s   1239

Lennox, Tabitha
Touch of Enchantment - Teresa Medeiros   r   377

Lewin, Alma Marie
Days of Cain - J.R. Dunn   s   1086

McCullogh, Maddie
One of These Nights - Susan Sizemore   r   423

Nazir, Nassifeh "Opalears"
The Family Tree - Sheri S. Tepper   s   1220

O'Brian, Launa
Second Fire - Mike Moscoe   s   1163

Prince, Gabriel
Time on My Hands - Peter Delacorte   s   1077

Rejar
Rejar - Dara Joy   r   341

Rivers, Neal
Keeper of the King - Nigel Bennett   *h*   838

Sabra
Keeper of the King - Nigel Bennett   *h*   838

Sainte Germain
Writ in Blood - Chelsea Quinn Yarbro   *h*   1031

Santos
To Speak in Lifeless Tongues - David Niall
   Wilson   *h*   1028

Striescu, Aldo
Shadows - Jonathan Nasaw   *h*   970

Tch'muchgar
Thirsty - M.T. Anderson   *h*   833

Teppish, Rebecca
The Vampire's Beautiful Daughter - S.P.
   Somtow   *h*   1002

Teppish, Vladimir X. III
The Vampire's Beautiful Daughter - S.P.
   Somtow   *h*   1002

von Cragga, Ivo
The Ruby Tear - Rebecca Brand   *h*   843

Whistler, Jamey
Shadows - Jonathan Nasaw   *h*   970

VAMPIRE HUNTER

Blake, Anita
The Killing Dance - Laurell K. Hamilton   *h*   907

Summers, Buffy
Buffy the Vampire Slayer: The Harvest - Richie
   Tankersley Cusick   *h*   863

VETERAN

Holloway, Percival
Silverthorne - Wayne Davis   *w*   507

Kensington, Jared
If Only - Debra Cowan   *w*   500

Littleton, Evan
The Hunted - James Reasoner   *w*   591

Lucier, Kevin
Jumpers - R. Patrick Gates   *h*   891

McKenzie, Kenneth
Sharon's Hope - Nina Coyle   *r*   289

Pike, Joe
Indigo Slam - Robert Crais   *m*   46

Reacher, Jack
Killing Floor - Lee Child   *m*   35

Smith, Stillwater
Stillwater Smith - Frank Roderus   *w*   600

Wolf
Spiritride - Mark Shepherd   *f*   793

Wooten, Solomon
The Courtship of Hannah and the Horseman - Johnny
   D. Boggs   *w*   464

VETERINARIAN

Cully, Lawrence
The Black Cat - Robert Poe   *h*   978

Lacey, James
Agatha Raisin and the Terrible Tourist - M.C.
   Beaton   *m*   12

Lucks, JoLayne
Lucky You - Carl Hiaasen   *m*   121

March, Melissa
Stray Hearts - Annie Kimberlin   *r*   347

McCarthy, Gail
Roughstock - Laura Crum   *m*   49

VILLAIN

Hong
Interesting Times - Terry Pratchett   *f*   779

VINTNER

Cochran, Sid
Earthquake Weather - Tim Powers   *f*   778

VOLUNTEER

Burnet, Buck
Journey to Shiloh - Will Henry   *w*   533

Nalls, Miller
Journey to Shiloh - Will Henry   *w*   533

WAGONMASTER

McQuade, Chance
Across the Rio Colorado - Ralph Compton   *w*   491

Tunstall, Mac
The Winchester Run - Ralph Compton   *w*   496

WAITER/WAITRESS

Gable, Helen
Symphony - Charles L. Grant   *h*   899

Lacerda, Zefty
Trader - Charles de Lint   *f*   685

Lawrence, Emma
Pratt's Landing - Martha Kirkland   *r*   351

Payne, Deliverance "Del"
Ticktock - Dean R. Koontz   *h*   936

WANDERER

Canches, Alejandro
The Plague Tales - Ann Benson   *s*   1051

Essa
Black Wine - Candas Jane Dorsey   *s*   1082

Little, Edward
In the Rogue Blood - James Carlos Blake   *w*   460

Little, John
In the Rogue Blood - James Carlos Blake   *w*   460

Peares, Jay
The Peacekeeper - Jeffrey Poston   *w*   586

Sanford, Jess
The Hard Land - Jack Ballas   *w*   446

Scurlock, Lee
Diablo - David Robbins   *w*   596

Sterling, Jedediah
Tallgrass: A Novel of the Great Plains - Don
   Coldsmith   *w*   485

Trampe, Fane
Nevada Tough - John S. McCord   *w*   569

Tyler, Clardy
Passage to Natchez - Cameron Judd   *w*   550

Veriam, Tanaquil
Red Unicorn - Tanith Lee   *f*   747

WARD

Edgerton, Charlotte
Captive - Joan Johnston   *r*   338

Proctor, Jeremy
Person or Persons Unknown - Bruce
   Alexander   *m*   3

WARRIOR

Amrey, Murl "Kar Kalim"
Kar Kalim - Deborah Christian   *f*   668

Apollo
Armageddon - Richard Hatch   *s*   1129

Barku, Perkar Kar
The Blackgod - J. Gregory Keyes   *f*   737

Barra
Iron Dawn - Matthew Woodring Stover   *f*   802

Big Tree
The Kiowa Verdict - Cynthia Haseloff   *w*   531

Black Niall
Son of the Morning - Linda Howard   *r*   330

Black Snake
Prairie - Greg Tobin   *w*   616

Cadarn, Derfel
Enemy of God - Bernard Cornwell   *f*   678

Camron
The Barbed Coil - J.V. Jones   *f*   730

Cavish, Beka
Stalking Darkness - Lynn Flewelling   *f*   705

Cerdic
Shadow of the King - Helen Hollick   *f*   724

Christopher of Blackmour
This Is All I Ask - Lynn Kurland   *r*   357

Cuchlainn
The Raid - Randy Lee Eickhoff   *f*   697

de Florisoun, Hugh
A Knight to Remember - Christina Dodd   *r*   296

Duzon
Touched by the Gods - Lawrence Watt-Evans   *f*   810

Fafhrd
Return to Lankhmar - Fritz Leiber   *f*   748

Gabrielle
The Thief of Hermes - Ru Emerson   *f*   699

Geronimo
Night of the Cougar - Frank Burleson   *w*   478

Guiwenneth
Gate of Ivory, Gate of Horn - Robert
   Holdstock   *f*   723

Hadding
War of the Gods - Poul Anderson   *f*   641

Horse Hate
The Dansing Star - Kirby Jonas   *w*   548

Ichiro, Sano
The Way of the Traitor - Laura Joh
   Rowland   *m*   205

ja N'Wook, Chrysamen "Chrys"
Caesar's Bicycle - John Barnes   *s*   1042

Kane
Fire Hawk - Justine Dare   *r*   293

Katanaquat
The Rain From God - Mark Ammerman   *w*   442

Kelahnus
The Stone Prince - Fiona Patton   *f*   776

Leucas
Iron Dawn - Matthew Woodring Stover   *f*   802

MacFane, Malcolm
Once a Warrior - Karyn Monk   *r*   383

Nimbulan "Lan"
The Dragon's Touchstone - Irene Radford   *f*   783

Jones, Bob
The Ignored - Bentley Little   *h*   946

Knight, Gabriel
Gabriel Knight: Sins of the Fathers - Jane
Jensen   *h*   924

Kramer, George
The Dealings of Daniel Kesserich - Fritz
Leiber   *s*   1141

Lang, Alice "Lancaster"
Einstein's Bridge - John Cramer   *s*   1070

Leyner, Mark
The Tetherballs of Bougainville - Mark
Leyner   *f*   749

MacDonald, Sean
The Taking - Donald Beman   *h*   837

Marlow, Jenny
Double Edge - Dennis Etchison   *h*   880

McCaffrey, Anne
A Diversity of Dragons - Anne McCaffrey   *f*   757

Merlyn Britannicus, Caius
The Eagles' Brood - Jack Whyte   *f*   816

Milton, John
Milton in America - Peter Ackroyd   *f*   637

Miracle, Tori
Death, Lies, and Apple Pies - Valerie S.
Malmont   *m*   151

Morris, Anne
Winter Tides - James P. Blaylock   *h*   842

Nell
Into the Forest - Jean Hegland   *s*   1130

Nichols, Jane
AKA Jane - Maureen Tan   *m*   222

Northrop, Silas
Carried Away - Sue Civil-Brown   *r*   281

O'Brien, Anne
I Met a Man Who Wasn't There - Mary R.
Callaghan   *h*   849

Olson, Zenobia
Flying Saucers over Hennepin - Peter
Gelman   *f*   708

Phan, Tommy
Ticktock - Dean R. Koontz   *h*   936

Prince, Gabriel
Time on My Hands - Peter Delacorte   *s*   1077

Raine of the Three Waters
War of the Three Waters - Douglas Niles   *f*   772

Rutledge, Andrew
Root of All Evil - David A. Farrow   *h*   881

Sandoz, Mari
Mari - Jane Valentine Barker   *w*   448

Selway, Ellen
A Face at the Window - Dennis McFarland   *h*   961

Silenus, Martin
The Rise of Endymion - Dan Simmons   *s*   1208

Stoker, Bram
Slave of My Thirst - Tom Holland   *h*   915

Swithin, Oliver
An Embarrassment of Corpses - Alan
Beechey   *m*   14

Taylor, Lucian
The Hill of Dreams - Arthur Machen   *h*   954

Thoreau, Henry David
Cloudsplitter - Russell Banks   *w*   447

Tomlinson
North of Havana - Randy Wayne White   *m*   236

Trout, Kilgore
Timequake - Kurt Vonnegut Jr.   *s*   1228

Twain, Mark
The Prince and the Prosecutor - Peter J.
Heck   *m*   117
The Rock Child - Win Blevins   *w*   462

Voight, Susan
Freedom & Necessity - Steven Brust   *f*   660

Vonnegut, Kurt "Junior"
Timequake - Kurt Vonnegut Jr.   *s*   1228

Walton, David
Cannibal Plateau - Joe Wise   *w*   634

Watson, Libby
Prairie Rose - Susan Kirby   *r*   349

YOUNG MAN

Dallaugher, Danny
When Shadows Fall - Brian Scott Smith   *h*   998

Dylan
Millennium: Gehenna - Lewis Gannett   *h*   884

Smith, Eugene
Nice Guys Finish Last - Gary Jonas   *h*   925

Wilson, Collingsworth
I Know What You Did Last Summer - Lois
Duncan   *h*   875

YOUNG WOMAN

Amaro, Angelina
Virgin Heat - Laurence Shames   *m*   212

Barbara
Night of the Living Dead - John A. Russo   *h*   987

Chalmers, Persia
The Diary of Mattie Spenser - Sandra
Dallas   *w*   505

Cissie
'48 - James Herbert   *h*   914

Connery, Rachel
Ritual Sins - Anne Stuart   *r*   432

Deacon, Jane
The Hill of Dreams - Arthur Machen   *h*   954

Elvira
Camp Vamp - Elvira   *h*   879

Fawn
Crack in the Sky - Terry C. Johnston   *w*   545

Fox, Jessica
Innocence Undone - Kat Martin   *r*   372

Hay, Marsali
Fairy Tale - Jillian Hunter   *r*   332

Herbert, Grisel
The Return - Walter de la Mare   *h*   868

Hutchins, Flora
God Save the Queen! - Dorothy Cannell   *m*   32

Jess
Changespell - Doranna Durgin   *f*   695

Karpov, Sapphire
Putting Up Roots - Charles Sheffield   *s*   1203

Kori
The Island Tribe - Charlotte Prentiss   *w*   587

Kyla
Engor's Sword Arm - David C. Smith   *h*   999

Laura
The Darker Passions: Carmilla - Amarantha
Knight   *h*   933

Lawford, Sheila
The Return - Walter de la Mare   *h*   868

Lenifee, Joyce
Mountains against the Sun - Perry Holmes   *w*   541

MacIntyre, Matilda "Tildy"
The Lieutenant's Lady - Rae Muir   *r*   387

Milton, Annie
Cul-De-Sac - David Martin   *h*   958

Mirri
The Iron Ring - Lloyd Alexander   *f*   640

Pretty Water
Crack in the Sky - Terry C. Johnston   *w*   545

Rakoczy, Merry-Grace
Flint's Gift - Richard S. Wheeler   *w*   628

Salazar-Montoya, Elena
The Purgatory River - Frank Roderus   *w*   599

Silvermoon
The Rain From God - Mark Ammerman   *w*   442

Snow, Julie
Cold at Heart - Brian Hopkins   *h*   917

Soamosa
The Ship Avenged - S.M. Stirling   *s*   1213

Stephenson, Jenny
Mask of the Night - Mary Ryan   *h*   989

Tradescent, Heather
The Dancing Floor - Barbara Michaels   *m*   168

Twilight
The Bear Paw Horses - Will Henry   *w*   532

Vendramin, Caterina
Vaporetto 13 - Robert Girardi   *h*   896

Whalley, Vida
A Dry Spell - Susan Moloney   *h*   965

Worthen, Elise
If Only - Debra Cowan   *w*   500

Author Index

This index is an alphabetical listing of the authors of books featured in entries and those listed within entris under the rubrics "Other books by the author" and "Other books you might like." For each author, the titles of books described or listed in this edition and their entry numbers appear. Bold numbers indicate a featured main entry; light-face numbers refer to books recommended for further reading.

Wild Magnolia 269

Brooks, Bill
Buscadero 474
Dust on the Wind **474**, 508, 586
The Last Law There Was 468, 474

Brooks, Janice Young
Fear of Frying 38

Brooks, Terry
The Black Unicorn 659
Hook 659
Magic Kingdom for Sale-Sold! 659
Running with the Demon **659**
The Sword of Shannara 659, 754, 815
Wizard at Large 659

Broomall, Robert W.
California Kingdoms 459

Brouwer, S.W.
Moon Basket 463, 506

Brown, Irene Bennett
The Plainswoman 505, 515

Brown, J.P.S.
The Forests of the Night 580

Brown, Mary
Master of Many Treasures 1057
Pigs Don't Fly 1057
Strange Deliverance **1057**
The Unlikely Ones 728, 1057

Brown, Micki
Once a Rebel 319

Brown, Rita Mae
The Sneaky Pie Series 67

Brown, Sam
The Big Lonely 475
The Crime of Coy Bell 475, 525
Devil's Rim **475**, 631
The Long Drift 475
Ross Henry 475
The Trail to Honk Ballard's Bones 475

Brown, Sandra
Breath of Scandal 434
French Silk 353, 367, 434

Browne, Lydia
Heart Strings 270, 360
Snowflake Wishes **270**, 351, 387, 395
Spring Dreams 270

Browner, Jesse
Conglomeros 708

Brownley, Margaret
Buttons and Beaus **271**
Chocolate Kisses 247, **272**, 417
Ribbons in the Wind 271

Brownworth, Victoria
Night Bites: Vampire Stories by Women 877

Bruce, Leo
The Carolus Deene Series 14

Bruchac, Joseph
Dawn Land 476, 587
Eagle Song **476**
Flying with the Eagle, Racing the Great Bear 476
The Girl Who Married the Moon 567
The Great Ball Game 476, 563
Long River 476, 483

Brunner, John
Age of Miracles 1204
The Sheep Look Up 1237
The Shockwave Rider 1088

Times Without Number 1092, 1093

Brust, Steven
Agyar 843
Freedom & Necessity **660**
The Gypsy 660
Jhereg 658, 660, 688, 700, 716, 719, 726, 748, 773, 785, 789, 820
The Phoenix Guards 660, 696
The Reign in Hell 660
The Sun, the Moon and the Stars 660

Bryant, Ed
Aqua Sancta 944
Fetish 925

Buchanan, Edna
Act of Betrayal 27
The Britt Montero Series 91
Contents under Pressure 27
Margin of Error **27**
Miami, It's Murder 27
Suitable for Framing 27

Buchanan, Ken
This House Is Made of Mud 593

Buck, Carole
Love Goddesses 366, 369

Buck, Gayle
Full Moon Magic 354

Buckland, Raymond
The Committee 836, 921

Buckley, Fiona
The Robsart Affair 36
To Shield the Queen **28**

Budrys, Algis
L. Ron Hubbard Presents Writers of the Future, Volumes I-VIII 1089, 1241

Bujold, Lois McMaster
Barrayar 1207
Borders of Infinity 1209, 1222
Dreamweaver's Dilemma 1099
Ethan of Athos 1170
Memory 1221, 1225
Shards of Honor 1160, 1231
The Spirit Ring 705, 736, 753, 807, 820
The Vor Game 1213, 1226
The Warrior's Apprentice 1065, 1066

Bull, Emma
Bone Dance 660, 1037, 1057
Double Feature 1099
Finder 660, 807
Freedom & Necessity **660**
The Princess and the Lord of Night 660
War for the Oaks 660, 681, 741, 762, 765, 793

Bunch, Chris
The Darkness of God 661
The Demon King 661
Hunt the Heavens 661
The Seer King **661**, 676
The Wind After Time 661

Burgess, Melvin
An Angel for May 1058
The Baby and Fly Pie 1058
Burning Issy 1058
The Earth Giant 639, **1058**

Burke, James Lee
Black Cherry Blues 24, 171
Burning Angel 29
Cadillac Jukebox 29
Cimarron Rose **29**
The Dave Robicheaux Series 21, 42, 65, 177, 181
Dixie City Jam 29

Heaven's Prisoners 93
In the Electric Mist with Confederate Dead 29, 109
The Neon Rain 161
A Stained White Radiance 29

Burke, Jan
Dear Irene 30
Goodnight, Irene 30
Hocus **30**
The Irene Kelly Series 27, 52, 125, 149, 208, 233
Remember Me, Irene 30
Sweet Dreams, Irene 30

Burke, John
The Hammer Horror Omnibus 858
Ladygrove 837
The Second Hammer Horror Film Omnibus 858

Burke, Martin R.
The Chance Factor **1106**

Burkhardt, Mary
Highland Ecstasy 276, 424, 426

Burks, Arthur J.
Black Medicine 855, 1021

Burks, Brian
Runs with Horses 561

Burleson, Frank
Desert Hawks 477, 478
Devil Dance **477**, 478, 487, 548, 618
Night of the Cougar **478**
Savage Frontier 477, 478
War Eagles 477, 478
White Apache 477, 478, 619

Burnell, Mark
Glittering Savages 1004

Burns, Cliff
Genuinely Inspired Primitive 846
The Reality Machine **846**, 974, 1022
Sex and Other Acts of the Imagination 846

Burns, Rex
Bloodline 31
Endangered Species 31
The Gabe Wager Series 192
Ground Money 31
The Killing Zone 31
The Leaning Land **31**
Strip Search 31

Burns, Ron
Enslaved 109
The Livinius Severus Series 5, 55, 209
The Mysterious Death of Meriwether Lewis 146, 166

Burrage, A.M.
Between the Minute and the Hour 847
Intruders 847
The Occult Files of Francis Chard: Some Ghost Stories 841, 847
Seeker to the Dead 847
Some Ghost Stories 864, 957
Someone in the Room: Strange Tales Old and New **847**, 1019

Burroughs, Edgar Rice
At the Earth's Core 897

Burroughs, William S.
Ghost of Chance 637
Interzone 846, 1022
Nova Express 749

Bury, Stephen
Interface 1049, 1132, 1218

Busby, F.M.
Rissa Kerguelen 1209, 1222, 1238

Butler, Octavia E.
Dawn 1044, 1059, 1068, 1136
Imago 1072
Mind of My Mind 1055, 1078
Parable of the Sower 823, 1192, 1193, 1242
Patternmaster 1207
The Xenogenesis Trilogy 1230

Byatt, A.S.
Angels and Insects 662
The Djinn in the Nightingale's Eye **662**, 682, 826
Possession: A Romance 662

Byers, Cordia
Lady Fortune 283

Byers, Richard Lee
The Ebon Mask 1024, 1025
Netherworld 900
The Vampire's Apprentice 1017

Byrne, Eugene
Back in the USSA **1166**

C

Cacek, P.D.
Leavings **848**

Cadigan, Pat
Fools 1122, 1172
Mindplayers 1098, 1234
Synners 1046, 1088, 1119, 1123, 1132, 1177, 1188

Cadnum, Michael
Skyscape 962, 971

Cady, Jack
The Off Season 655, 707, 771, 778, 794, 961
The Sons of Noah and Other Stories 797
The Well 966

Caidin, Martin
A Life in the Future 1067

Cail, Carol
The Maxey Burnell Series 133, 134

Caille, Julie
A Mother's Heart 263
A Valentine's Day Fancy 321

Cain, Robert
Cybernarc 1200

Cajio, Linda
Bossman 273
Mister Christmas **273**, 356

Calder, Richard
Dead Boys 1059
Dead Girls 1059
Dead Things **1059**

Callaghan, Mary R.
I Met a Man Who Wasn't There **849**
Mothers 849

Calvin, June
Isabella's Rake **274**

Calvino, Italo
The Castle of Crossed Destinies 714, 850
Fantastic Tales: Visionary and Everyday **850**
If on a Winter's Night a Traveller 850
Italian Folktales 850

L

N

Nabb, Magdalen
The Marshal Guarnaccia Series 62, 122, 214

Nagata, Linda
The Bohr Maker 1112, 1143, 1165
Deception Well 1112, **1165**
Tech-Heaven 1165

Nasaw, Jonathan
Shadows 970
The World on Blood 970

Nassim, Liza
Musclebound **40**

Nava, Michael
The Burning Plain **175**
The Death of Friends 175
Goldenboy 175
The Henry Rios Series 192, 240, 244
The Hidden Law 175
How Town 175
The Little Death 175

Neason, Rebecca
Guises of the Mind 1240

Needham, Linda
For My Lady's Kiss **388**

Neel, Janet
The John McLeish and Francesca Wilson Series 164

Neely, Barbara
Blanche on the Lam 59
The Blanche White Series 71, 103, 112

Neiderman, Andrew
After Life 971, 972
The Dark **971**, 972
The Devil's Advocate 971, **972**
Duplicates 971, 972
The Immortal 971, 972
The Need 971, 972

Nesbitt, John D.
One-Eyed Cowboy Wild 446, 577
One Foot in the Stirrup 577
Twin Rivers 577, 596
Wild Rose of Ruby Canyon 475, 489, **577**

Neugenboren, Jay
Poli 466, 588

Nevins, Linda
Renaissance Moon **770**

Newcomb, Kerry
Ride the Panther 503, 601

Newman, Christopher
The Joe Dante Series 19

Newman, Kim
Anno Dracula 915, 1031, 1166
Back in the USSA 637, **1166**
Bad Dreams 843, 1166
The Bloody Red Baron 915, 1031, 1166
Jago 1166
The Night Mayor 1166
The Original Dr. Shade and Other Stories 1010
The Quorum 972

Newman, Sharan
Death Comes as Epiphany 86, 227

Neyers, Maan
The High Constable 146

Nightingale, Steven
The Lost Coast 771
The Thirteenth Daughter of the Moon **771**

Niles, Douglas
A Breach in the Watershed 729, 737, 772, 789
The Coral Kingdom 772
Darkenheight 772
The Druid Queen 772
The Kagonesti 772
War of the Three Waters 772

Niswander, Adam
The Charm 960

Niven, Larry
Destiny's Road **1167**
Fallen Angels 1183
Footfall 1071, 1175, 1189, 1194
The Integral Trees 1100, 1211
The Long ARM of Gil Hamilton 1122
Lucifer's Hammer 1113
The Mote in God's Eye 1095
Neutron Star 1167
Protector 1167, 1208
Ringworld 1167, 1214
The Ringworld Engineers 1167
The Smoke Ring 1100
Tales of Known Space 1052, 1167
A World out of Time 1067

Nix, Garth
The Ragwitch 1168
Sabriel 640, 721, 1168
Shade's Children **1168**

Nixon, Joan Lowery
Don't Scream 1008
The Stalker 879

Nofziger, Lyn
Tackett and the Teacher 603

Nolan, Ted
Hell on High **751**

Noon, Jeff
Vurt 1184, 1187

Norfolk, Lawrence
The Pope's Rhinoceros 183

Norman, Lisanne
Fire Margins 1169
Fortune's Wheel 1169
Razor's Edge **1169**
Turning Point 1169

North, Andre
Daybreak. . .2250 A.D. 1155

Northcote, Amyas
In Ghostly Company **973**

Norton, Andre
The Beast Master 1226
Breed to Come 769
Brother to Shadows 1170
Catseye 692
The Crossroads of Time 1107, 1162
Derelict for Trade **1170**, 1171
Dread Companion 642
Elvenbane 720
Elvenblood 720, 732, 734, 757, 789
Galactic Derelict 1171
Golden Trillium 756
Imperial Lady 795
A Mind for Trade **1171**
Plague Ship 1171
Postmarked the Stars 1170
Redline the Stars 1170, 1171
Sargasso of Space 1170, 1171
The Stars Are Ours 1203
Voorloper 1170

Witch World 1038

Novak, Kate
Azure Bonds 773
Finder's Bane **773**
Masquerades 773
Song of the Saurials 773
The Wyvern's Spur 773

Nutman, Phil
Wetwork 987, 988

Nye, Jody Lynn
Mythology Abroad 693
Taylor's Ark 1233

Nylund, Eric S.
Dry Water 672, 774, 817
A Game of Universe **774**
Pawn's Dream 774

O

Oates, Joyce Carol
American Gothic Tales 1014
Haunted: Tales of the Grotesque 923, 1003

Oboler, Arch
The Obler Omnibus 858

O'Brien, Elaine F.
Anita of Rancho del Mar 466

O'Brien, Fitz-James
The Supernatural Tales of Fitz-James O'Brien 912

O'Brien, Judith
Ashton's Bride 317, 389, 390, 391
Maiden Voyage **389**, 391
Once upon a Rose 389, **390**, 391
Rhapsody in Time 389, 390, 391
To Marry a British Lord **391**

O'Callaghan, Maxine
Only in the Ashes **176**
Shadow of a Child 176

O'Connell, Carol
The Kathleen Mallory Series 211
Killing Critics 177
Mallory's Oracle 42, 177
The Man Who Cast Two Shadows 177
Stone Angel 35, **177**, 190

O'Connell, Jack
Box Nine 181

O'Dell, Scott
The King's Fifth 530
Thunder Rolling in the Mountains 519, 608

Odom, Mel
F.R.E.E. Lancers 1172
Headhunters **1172**
Lethal Interface 1172, 1196
Omega Blue 1172
Omega Score 1172
Stalker Analog 1172

O'Donnell, Lillian
The Norah Mulcahney Series 69

O'Donnell, Peter
The Modesty Blaise Series 222

O'Kane, Leslie
The Molly Masters Series 38, 99, 133

Oke, Janette
Another Homecoming 350
Drums of Change 574
Love Comes Softly 436
The Matchmakers 349

The Tender Years: A Prairie Legacy 349

O'Keefe, Claudia
Ghost Tide 984

Okri, Ben
The Famished Road 685, 1134

Olcott, Anthony
Murder at the Red October 136, 237

O'Leary, Patrick
Door Number Three 775
The Gift **775**

Oleksiw, Susan
The Joe Silva Series 160

Oliver, Chad
Broken Eagle 521
The Wolf Is My Brother 565

Oliver, Patricia
The Colonel's Lady **392**
Lord Gresham's Lady 392
Lord Harry's Angel 392
Miss Drayton's Downfall 392
The Runaway Duchess 392

Olsen, T.V.
Break the Young Land **578**
The Burning Sky 578, 579
The Golden Chance 578, 579, 630
A Killer Is Waiting 578, 579
Red Is the River 578, 579
There Was a Season 579, 597
Under the Gun 578, 579

Olson, Paul F.
Post-Mortem: New Tales of Ghostly Horror 984, 1023

O'Marie, Carol Anne
Death Goes on Retreat 90, 243

Ore, Rebecca
Alien Bootlegger and Other Stories 1079, 1087
The Illegal Rebirth of Billy the Kid 1182

O'Rourke, Michael
The Undine 929

Orwell, George
1984 1090
Nineteen Eighty-Four 1227

Osborn, Karen
Between Earth and Sky 576

Osborne, Carey
Iroshi 686

Osborne, Maggie
The Brides of Bowie Stone 310, 399
The Brides of Prairie Gold 291, 393
Family Secrets 393
The Promise of Jenny Jones 311, **393**
The Seduction of Samantha Kincade 278, 309, 393, 399
To Love a Thief 393
The Wives of Bowie Stone 311, 393

O'Shaugnessy, Mary
Obstruction of Justice **178**

O'Shaugnessy, Pamela
Obstruction of Justice **178**

O'Shaugnessy, Perri
Invasion of Privacy 178
Motion to Suppress 178
The Nina Reilly Series 128
Obstruction of Justice **178**

Osier, Jeffrey
Driftglider and Other Stories 974

Author Index

Author Index

Title Index

This index alphabetically lists all titles featured in entries and those listed within entries under "Other books by the author" and "Other books you might like." Each title is followed by the author's name and the number of the entry where the book is described or listed. Bold numbers indicate featured main entries; light-face numbers refer to books recommended for further reading.

G

I

The Music Room
McFarland, Dennis   961

Musical Chairs
Friedman, Kinky   87

Mutagenesis
Collins, Helen   1167

Mutineer's Moon
Weber, David   1045, 1047, 1080, 1154, 1175

My Best Friend Is Invisible
Stine, R.L.   1007, **1009**

My Brother's Keeper
Sheffield, Charles   1204

My Cousin Jane
Barbour, Anne   280

My Cousin, My Gastroenterologist
Leyner, Mark   708, 749, 1237

My Enemy, My Ally
Duane, Diane   1085, 1104, 1113

My First Duchess
Sizemore, Susan   261, 304, 423, 433

My Foot's in the Stirrup. . .My Pony Won't Stand
Bly, Stephen   463, 600

My Ishmael
Quinn, Daniel   **1180**

My Lady Notorious
Beverley, Jo   260, 261, 297, 304, 324, 352, 433

My Lucky Lady
Claybourne, Casey   282

My Only Love
Sutcliffe, Katherine   250

My Own True Love
Sizemore, Susan   423

My Sister, the Moon
Harrison, Sue   717

My Son, the Wizard
Stasheff, Christopher   **800**, 1210

My Soul to Keep
Due, Tananarive   **873**

My Soul to Take
Spruill, Steven   1004

My Steadfast Heart
Goodman, Jo   250, **318**

My Teacher Is an Alien
Coville, Bruce   1007, 1009, 1058

My Warrior's Heart
Krahn, Betina   352

My Wayward Lady
Richardson, Evelyn   274, 344, **411**

The Myron Bolitar Series
Coben, Harlan   182

Mysteries of the World
Wiater, Stanley   948, 982

The Mysteries of the Worm
Bloch, Robert   854

The Mysterious Death of Meriwether Lewis
Burns, Ron   146, 166

The Mysterious Island
Verne, Jules   1227

The Mysterious West
Hillerman, Tony   634

Mysterium
Wilson, Robert Charles   1064

Mystique
Quick, Amanda   296, 402, 410

Mythago Wood
Holdstock, Robert   685, 723, 743, 778, 817

Mythology Abroad
Nye, Jody Lynn   693

N

The Nabob's Ward
Richardson, Evelyn   411

Naked in Death
Robb, J.D.   277

The Name of the Rose
Eco, Umberto   64

The Name of the Sun
Clough, Brenda W.   672

Nameless
Campbell, Ramsey   964

The Nameless Detective Series
Pronzini, Bill   21, 79, 100

Nameless Sins
Collins, Nancy A.   940, 941, 1010

The Nan Robinson Series
Cannon, Taffy   30

The Nano Flower
Hamilton, Peter F.   1120, 1122

The Nanotech Chronicles
Flynn, Michael   1097, 1138

The Nantucket Diet Murders
Rich, Virginia   165

Nantucket Slayrides
Shepard, Lucius   977

Narrow Houses
Crowther, Peter   862

Nashville 1864
Jones, Madison   444, 453, 501, 512, **549**, 590

Nasty Breaks
Elkins, Charlotte   **75**

The Natalie Gold Series
Jaffe, Jody   49

The Nate Heller Series
Collins, Max Allan   11

Native Tongue
Elgin, Suzette Haden   1082, 1095, 1237

Native Tongue
Hiaasen, Carl   114, 121, 212, 241

Nazareth Hill
Campbell, Ramsey   **851**

The Neal Rafferty Series
Wiltz, Chris   68, 161

Nebula Awards 21-22
Zebrowski, George   1190

Nebula Awards 23-25
Bishop, Michael   1190

Nebula Awards 26-28
Morrow, James   1117, 1190

Nebula Awards 29-30
Sargent, Pamela   1190

Nebula Awards 30
Sargent, Pamela   1179

Nebula Awards 31
Sargent, Pamela   1128, **1190**

Nebula Awards 32
Dann, Jack   1083, 1190

The Necronancers
Benson, R.H.   839

The Necronomicon
Price, Robert M.   **980**, 981

Necroscope
Lumley, Brian   1000

Necroscope Series
Lumley, Brian   949, 950, 951

The Need
Neiderman, Andrew   971, 972

Needful Things
King, Stephen   972

Needles and Sins
Arnzen, Michael A.   976

The Neil Hockaday Series
Adcock, Thomas   21

Nekomah Creek
Crew, Linda   476

The Nell Bray Series
Linscott, Gillian   34

The Nell Fury Series
Pincus, Elizabeth   85

The Nemesis of Evil
Carter, Lin   854

Neon Lotus
Laidlaw, Marc   704, 718, 1164

The Neon Rain
Burke, James Lee   161

Netherworld
Byers, Richard Lee   900

Neutron Star
Niven, Larry   1167

Nevada Dawn
Gentry, Georgina   315

Nevada Tough
McCord, John S.   **569**, 596

Never Land
Harper, Andrew   909

Never Street
Estleman, Loren D.   **79**

Never the Twain
Mitchell, Kirk   1223

Nevermore
Hjortsberg, William   978

Nevernever
Shetterly, Will   683, 794

Neverwhere
Gaiman, Neil   **707**

A New Day Rising
Snelling, Lauraine   578, 606

New England Ghosts
McSherry, Frank D. Jr.   992

New Eves: Science Fiction about the Extraordinary Women of Today and Tomorrow
Frank, Janrae   1032

The New Hugo Winners
Asimov, Isaac   1117

The New Hugo Winners, Volume III
Willis, Connie   1117

The New Hugo Winners, Volume IV
Greenberg, Martin H.   **1117**

New Legends
Bear, Greg   1128

The New Lovecraft Circle
Price, Robert M.   834, 980

The New Neighbor
Garton, Ray   888, 889

New Noir
Shirley, John   913

New Orleans Legacy
Ripley, Alexandra   323

New Orleans Requiem
Donaldson, D.J.   65

The New Rebellion
Rusch, Kristine Kathryn   1186

The New Springtime
Silverberg, Robert   1207

New Terrors
Clark, Ramsey   1029

New Voices I-IV
Martin, George R.R.   1241

The New Women of Wonder: Science Fiction Novelettes by Women about Women
Sargent, Pamela   1190

New Worlds
Garnett, David   **1109**

New Worlds 5
Moorcock, Michael   1109

New Worlds Quarterly Number 1-4
Moorcock, Michael   1109

The New York Detective
Marshall, William   33

The New York Trilogy
Auster, Paul   934

The Next Man in Texas
Rolofson, Kristine   416

Nice Girls Finish Last
Hayter, Sparkle   116

Nice Guys Finish Last
Jonas, Gary   885, **925**

Nice Little Stories Jam-Packed with Depraved Sex and Violence
Hemmingson, Michael   913

A Nice Murder for Mom
Yaffe, James   59

Title Index